D0934269

TORTS: THE CIVIL LAW OF REPARATION FOR HARM DONE BY WRONGFUL ACT

LEXISNEXIS LAW SCHOOL ADVISORY BOARD

Lenni B. Benson
Professor of Law &
Associate Dean for Professional Development
New York Law School

Raj Bhala
Rice Distinguished Professor
University of Kansas, School of Law

Charles P. Craver
Freda H. Alverson Professor of Law
The George Washington University Law School

Richard D. Freer
Robert Howell Hall Professor of Law
Emory University School of Law

Craig Joyce
Andrews Kurth Professor of Law &
Co-Director, Institute for Intellectual Property and Information Law
University of Houston Law Center

Ellen S. Podgor
Professor of Law &
Associate Dean of Faculty Development and Electronic Education
Stetson University College of Law

Paul F. Rothstein
Professor of Law
Georgetown University Law Center

Robin Wellford Slocum
Professor of Law & Director,
Legal Research and Writing Program
Chapman University School of Law

David I. C. Thomson
LP Professor & Director, Lawyering Process Program
University of Denver, Sturm College of Law

TORTS: THE CIVIL LAW OF REPARATION FOR HARM DONE BY WRONGFUL ACT

Third Edition

Joseph W. Little
Emeritus Professor of Law
University of Florida
Levin College of Law

Lyrissa B. Lidsky
Stephen C. O'Connell Chair and Professor of Law
University of Florida
Levin College of Law

Robert H. Lande
Venable Professor of Law
University of Baltimore
School of Law

Library of Congress Card Number: 2009934626

ISBN: 978-1-4224-7353-5

This publication is designed to provide accurate and authoritative information in regard to the subject matter covered. It is sold with the understanding that the publisher is not engaged in rendering legal, accounting, or other professional services. If legal advice or other expert assistance is required, the services of a competent professional should be sought.

LexisNexis and the Knowledge Burst logo are registered trademarks and Michie is a trademark of Reed Elsevier Properties Inc., used under license. Matthew Bender and the Matthew Bender Flame Design are registered trademarks of Matthew Bender Properties Inc.

Copyright © 2009 Matthew Bender & Company, Inc., a member of the LexisNexis Group.
All Rights Reserved.

No copyright is claimed in the text of statutes, regulations, and excerpts from court opinions quoted within this work. Permission to copy material exceeding fair use, 17 U.S.C. § 107, may be licensed for a fee of 25¢ per page per copy from the Copyright Clearance Center, 222 Rosewood Drive, Danvers, Mass. 01923, telephone (978) 750-8400.

NOTE TO USERS
To ensure that you are using the latest materials available in this area, please be sure to periodically check the LexisNexis Law School website for downloadable updates and supplements at www.lexisnexis.com/lawschool.

Editorial Offices
121 Chanlon Rd., New Providence, NJ 07974 (908) 464-6800
201 Mission St., San Francisco, CA 94105-1831 (415) 908-3200
www.lexisnexis.com

MATTHEW◊BENDER

(2009–Pub.742)

Preface

This edition of this book retains the basic structure of the original text and first revision up through Chapter 15 (Tortious Damage to Interests in Property). Because of the widespread reduction in the number of credits assigned to required torts courses, former individual Chapters 16, 17, and 18 have been condensed into one, Chapter 16. Here the elements of workers' compensation, automobile no-fault laws, 42 USC Sec. 1983, and a few other statutory fields are highlighted but not developed in detail. New Chapter 17 covers defamation and privacy torts with more emphasis on defamation.

The text is thoroughly up-to-date in regard to both statutory and judicial developments within the torts field. In particular, it has been enriched with law and economics analyses and commentary at key places throughout.

The structure of the book still builds upon the realities that most torts actions are filed as negligence cases and most ancillary torts principles (i.e., causation, proximate causation, damages, and multiple defendant factors) have been developed in negligence actions. Negligence also provides a rich environment for learning and testing the various modes of legal reasoning and doctrinal development. Once the law of negligence is understood, learning and assimilating other theories of tort liability readily follow with less effort and time.

For these reasons and others this book begins with the law of negligence and develops it fully in the first eleven chapters. Thereafter, the text develops alternative theories of tort liability (and statutory remedies) in individual chapters. These chapters include all the primary non-negligence theories of liability ranging from intentional torts and strict liability to defamation, invasion of privacy and constitutional torts.

We believe this structure provides the optimal approach for teaching and learning torts. For teachers who teach in curriculums that devote five or six hours to torts, the entire book provides a text for teaching a comprehensive torts course. For teachers who teach in curriculums that have trimmed the number of hours assigned to first year courses, the first 11 chapters provide an excellent text for a basic course centered on negligence, and the remainder of the book provides an equally good text for adding additional materials or teaching an advanced course.

We would be pleased to receive notice of errors and suggestions for improvements from law students, law teachers and other uses of this book.

Joseph W. Little
Lyrissa B. Lidsky
Gainseville, Florida
Robert H. Lande
Baltimore, Maryland

Table of Contents

Table of Contents

Table of Contents

Table of Contents

Table of Contents

Table of Contents

Table of Contents

Table of Contents

Table of Contents

Table of Contents

Table of Contents

Table of Contents

Chapter 1

AN INTRODUCTION TO THE BACKGROUND AND THEORY OF TORT LAW

This is a law student's book for learning what lawyers need to know in practicing in the field of torts. Rather than being a mere study of doctrines, rules and stratagems, the book attempts to convey a pervasive sense of the general function of the law in the specific field of tortious wrongs.

Although the hearty individualism of the common law of torts hardly admits of it, the authors contend that all of the law represents society's institutional system for regulating human behavior. Viewed in this way, the law of torts can be seen to have various regulatory goals. One is to discourage unwanted behavior. In general, this is activity that causes harm to someone other than the actor. Another goal is to encourage desirable modes of behavior. As far as the law of torts is concerned, these are activities that minimize the risk of harm. Still another goal is to make reparations to persons who suffer loss as a consequence of tortious wrongs.

Making wrongdoers pay for harm done is clearly one way of discouraging unwanted behavior. Although making reparations is now generally recognized as a legitimate social goal, in the common law reparations did not seem as important as individual accountability. Thus, the law left many injuries uncompensated. Furthermore, although some common law tort theories do discourage wrongful behavior to the extent that forced reparations can do it, they are nevertheless imperfect and hardly allow for the degree of reparations and loss prevention that enlightened humanity requires. Modern society demands relief for wrongfully broken bodies and lives, and the impulse to assist victims of disaster, no matter whose fault, has recently matured. Society itself suffers when injuries occur. As shall be seen, however, the humanitarian impulse is more strongly directed to the consequences of physical and mental injury and death rather than to mere economic losses. It is best expressed by workers' compensation and no-fault automobile reparations statutes laws — that build upon but are not true parts of the law of torts.

A final goal of the law of torts is to perform what is essentially a neutral refereeing function in transferring the economic consequences of civil wrongs between disputing parties. Central to this is the job of repairing the harm done by wrongful acts. Because there is no good way to restore damages done by tort in specie, especially in cases of personal injury, the common law developed a substitute exchange medium that is employed up to this day. That medium is money. Hence, the harm-causing actor must give the injured victim money to compensate for the harm done. The function of transferring the consequences of torts from victims to wrongdoers also includes, for example, deciding how to allocate losses in situations where all the involved parties are essentially innocent. If two automobiles collide and neither driver is at fault, who must pay? Moreover, tort law must also prescribe rules for sharing the blame when more than one actor has contributed to the harm caused a third person. Which of the multiple wrongdoers must pay, and how much each? And, it must also handle situations wherein someone other than the wrongdoer has made reparation and thereafter seeks to redeem what has been paid. If a health insurance company pays the medical bills of an injured victim of the wrongful act of another person, can it reclaim from the wrongdoer what was paid? The law's tools for achieving these goals are examined in this book.

To understand the present state of the law, the student must know something about its origins and development. This poses something of a dilemma because, if not done with extreme care, examining the historical development of the law while simultaneously attempting to analyze its present status can be misleading. The greatest danger lies in confusing what has been with what is. This book attempts to avoid confusion by providing a thumbnail overview of the evolution of the law in these few pages and then examining in detail the development of various torts theories and doctrines in a sequence that generally follows the development in the overview. Chapters 2 and 3 examine in more depth certain major evolutionary points in the law of torts. Chapter 4 provides a concise overview of the law of negligence. Chapters 5 through 10 examine negligence doctrines in detail. And the remainder of the text examines many additional tort doctrines and theories.

In the view of these authors, the status of the modern American law of torts, as exemplified by the law of personal injury and property damage, seems to have been shaped by the tensions between two basic social policies that are somewhat at war with each other. One is the strong belief in self-responsibility of each person as an individual that underpins the historical common law. The other is a growing acknowledgment of institutional responsibility of artificial entities exemplified by corporations, governments and their agencies. In a crowded world of complex mechanisms, innocent people are constantly exposed to risk from institutional and mechanical malfunctions. It matters not whether these risks are created by bloodless machines, such as blast furnaces and automobiles, or by giant systems of human involvement, such as busy highway and air traffic systems. Inevitably human error or something else will cause them to fail, hurting innocent people almost at random.

Modern law is challenged to merge new attitudes of institutional responsibility and old ideas of individual responsibility into a modern legal system that adequately meets agreed goals without undercutting any deeply held cultural tenets. The emerging law will almost certainly hold institutions accountable for risks that they would not have been responsible for under the early common law, and injured victims will now be less frequently left without a remedy because of some shortcoming in their own behavior. While it can be argued that this new beneficence will dampen self-responsibility, there is no strong evidence that economic responsibility alone augments the personal disincentives posed by fear of harm, concern for others, and, to a lesser extent, sanctions of the criminal law and general social disapprobation. Neither is there much evidence that they do not. While this subject will occupy countless hours of argumentation among social theorists, proof of the argument is not likely to affect the present thrust of the law. For that reason, the subject will not be considered further as an independent topic, but may make for lively debate in class discussion of developing theories.

Some legal scholars believe that the very early common law was once set on a course of absolute responsibility. That is, if a person were to put into motion forces that hurt someone else, then the actor would always be held responsible to compensate the injured person for the injury suffered. On first blush the theory of absolute liability seems sound. Weakness appears, however, where the agent that caused the harm is innocent of wrongdoing and the injured victim is not. Suppose, for example, that a teamster were carefully driving a wagon and team of horses and that a drunk pedestrian lurched into the street and fell under the wagon wheels. It could not be denied that the driver's wagon caused the injury in the sense that the wheels broke the flesh and not vice versa. Neither could it be denied that the driver was innocent of wrongdoing, and the injured person was not. Acknowledging the unfairness of imposing absolute liability in such a case (and, implicitly recognizing that the goal of discouraging unwanted behavior would not be served), later common law courts rejected absolute liability in favor of the doctrine of fault. Under this doctrine at-fault persons who cause harm must compensate innocent injured victims. (The authors of this text doubt that courts ever imposed absolute liability as the ordinary rule of liability.) These courts also thought that if both persons were at fault, the goal of discouraging unwanted behavior could not be served by shifting the economic losses. So the common law provided no remedy and left the losses where they lay. The same rationale prevailed where both parties were innocent of fault. Since neither party's behavior was to be discouraged, the law merely left the losses on the shoulders of the injured person.

At that point in the evolution of the law various institutions had not attained the prominence that they enjoy today. Life was relatively simple. Perhaps it was because of this that making reparations did not emerge as a strong independent goal in the early days. Few, if any, institutions were capable of shifting losses from injured persons to a larger, better risk-bearing population. But with the onset of the industrial revolution, a good risk-spreading institution emerged. The evolution of capitalism and mechanized industry not only introduced machines and systems that caused industrial injuries, but also created the wherewithal to shift the economic consequences of industrial injuries from the workers and their families to a larger population. The aggregated cost could be defrayed by augmenting the price of the industrial product by an increment small enough to be borne by everyone without unduly burdening anyone. The common law ignored this potentiality, but as shall be seen herein, legislatures did not.

In retrospect, common law judges can be criticized for single-minded devotion to the noble idea of self-responsibility in the face of the emerging, inevitable institutional risks of the industrial revolution. As iron machines came, failed, and broke frail bodies, the judges asked, "Who was to blame?" rather than, "What was to blame?" As seen through the tunnel vision of self-responsibility, the injured worker had often erred; or a lowly fellow servant had; or no fault at all could be assigned in the failure of a mere machine. As a consequence, the common law compensated relatively few industrial injuries, because no responsible person had wielded the instrument of harm in a wrongful manner. Millions of broken workers were discarded and replaced by the countless waiting, all to the benefit of the burgeoning industrial plant. History sorrowfully recounts that many of the sacrificed were children. The industrial institution stood blameless and bore little of the human burdens of its failures.

Many 19th century observers deemed this system to be inherently unfair and socially irresponsible. They noted that industrial institutions bore the cost of worn out and broken down capital stock and wondered why human flesh and blood were wholly expendable. They decried the lack of a general reparation plan and also decried a lack of incentive to force industry to provide workers a safe place to toil. Because worker injuries were not charged to industry while the costs of safety measures were, economic prudence dictated that safety be minimized or ignored. Too often industry responded by adopting the economically prudent approach and ignored the safety and well being of employees. When the times called loudly for an ethic of institutional responsibility, the individualistic notions of the common law did not permit the courts to develop an adequate response.

Ultimately, pressures external to the captainship of industry forced the adoption of remedial measures. The need for reparations and safety, decent hours of work, humane treatment of women and children, and security for retired workers were among the first issues to induce collective action among industrial employees. First on the European continent, then in England, and always somewhat later in the United States, change came. As to industrial injuries, workers' compensation laws guaranteed injured workers the right of medical care and some economic benefits during periods of disability, without regard to who, if anyone, was at fault. The costs of reparation were borne by the industrial employer whether or not the employer individually had done a wrongful act. In enacting workers' compensation laws, legislatures broke with the past and clearly acknowledged the prevalence of institutional risks and the inevitability of human and mechanical fallability in the operation of complex systems. Making reparations for the consequences of the failures without regard to individual fault was finally acknowledged as a legitimate social goal. Thus institutional responsibility emerged in our law, albeit by statute and not court decree.

Although the common law judges were never able to make the full transition between individual responsibility based on fault and institutional responsibility without consideration of fault, the 19th century common law did develop a restricted theory of liability without fault as to certain activities that were deemed to be unusually hazardous. This is examined in Chapter 13. Twentieth century judges have extended this theory to apply to defective products, as examined in Chapter 14, but the earlier judges were too dedicated to *stare decisis* to do more than soften the impact of institutional risks with a few palliative doctrines of limited application. It was left to politics and legislation to create institutional liability in the workers' compensation laws. By the early 1960s every state in the United States had adopted such a law. These are briefly examined in Chapter 16.

Placing reparations responsibility upon industrial institutions encouraged them to minimize risks. Fulfilling reformist expectations, American industry became more safety conscious with a steady falling off in numbers of industrial accidents. Nevertheless, an economic system that balances costs of reparations against costs of prevention will tend toward an equilibrium that accepts some preventable injuries if the costs of avoidance are more than the costs of compensation. Recognizing that the American industrial system may have reached this state, Congress enacted the Occupational Safety and Health Act (OSHA) in 1970 and thereby imposed a new safety regime throughout the nation. OSHA takes the humanitarian goals of workers' compensation laws a step further. Not only must industry compensate injuries without regard to fault, but OSHA also mandates preventive measures that are more costly than compensating the prevented injuries. Blood is now dearer than money. OSHA is prophylactic. When injuries occur anyway, tort law and workers' compensation continue to apply.

Perhaps the modem highway transportation network is the only system comparable to industry in complexity and inevitability of risk of human and mechanical fallability. The automobile age came relatively late in the development of the common law of torts and might have been expected to evolve a no-fault reparations component somewhat along the lines of workers' compensation. It did not, perhaps for the following reasons. First, workers' compensation was invented by legislatures, not judges. Being jealous of their prerogatives, judges typically do not acknowledge legislative modifications of judge-made law except in precise detail of the modification. In judicial jargon, "Laws passed in derogation of the common law are to be strictly construed." Following this doctrine, judges would quite naturally conclude that workers' compensation theory, which was a product of legislation, pertained only to industrial injuries. Second, automobile crashes may have been so few in number in the earliest days that the inevitability of crashes was not foreseen. By the time it was perceived, the common law was locked in by stare decisis. Third, individual human error, rather than institutional risk, was often seen as an immediate cause of crashes. In the mind of the common law, assigning full responsibility to the immediate cause was consistent with the tenets of individual responsibility. Whatever the reasons, the old common law was imported into the automobile age and the judiciary thereafter lost the ability to do anything about it.

Despite what is said above, history records that a veritable blood bath of human losses began as soon as motor vehicles appeared in great numbers. Pressure mounted to find a general loss shifting mechanism, such as workers' compensation, but the highway transportation system had no commodity akin to the product of industry whose price could bear the blood of the victims. Human error, and not the automobile itself, was seen as the cause of the losses.

As a substitute for commodity price, insurance schemes sprang up to shift crash losses to the entire population of insured drivers. In retrospect, the true goal of liability insurance, the most common of these insurance schemes, is singularly unflattering. The purpose was not to help victims but to guard negligent drivers against the economic risks of hurting someone else. Moreover, liability insurance was merely grafted onto the common law of torts. An injured victim receives an insurance recovery only if two conditions were satisfied; first, the victim was free of fault and, second, an insured defendant negligently caused the injury. It cannot be denied that a multitude of injured victims have benefitted from liability insurance, but the real goal remains to protect the economic status of the insured people. Other insurance schemes emerged to augment liability insurance, including uninsured motorist and medical payments coverages, but even these refinements left many automobile crash victims with inadequate reparations or even none at all. And often compensation was paid only after long and costly court battles about fault.

By the 1930s highway losses had mounted high enough to stimulate reform measures. The first no-fault plan emerged from Columbia University in this decade but at the wrong time. Shortly after the Columbia plan appeared, the onset of World War II drastically eased the highway mayhem, and reform was ignored for the duration of the conflict. But highway slaughter came back with a vengeance in the 1950s and still occurs. In the meantime the legal environment changed. The federal government moved firmly into the automobile crash and injury prevention field by enacting the National Highway Safety and the Traffic and Motor Vehicle Safety Acts of 1966. Still, the matter of reparations continued to be handled by the common law fault system. Hence, insofar as highway losses are concerned, money is still dearer than blood.

In fairness, it must be reported that some judges invented doctrines to blunt the harshness of the common law. These applied more generously to highway injuries than to industrial injuries, which may account for the longer endurance of the contributory negligence defense rule system in the highway loss context. Most courts moderated the common law contributory negligence rule with a doctrine known as "last clear chance," and some states partially offset it with comparative negligence. These doctrines are examined in later chapters. But it was not until the 1960s that institutional no-fault reparations were incorporated into the highway loss system. Spurred mainly by the leadership of Judge Robert Keeton, then a Harvard professor, and Professor Jeffrey O'Connell, then of Illinois, a no-fault reform movement swelled in the late 1960s and culminated in the 1970 enactment of a no-fault automobile reparations law in Massachusetts. Florida followed suit in 1971, and by the mid-1970s no fewer than 23 states had enacted a no-fault law. After that, however, the movement seemed to lose most of its momentum. These laws are briefly examined in Chapter 16, *infra*.

In the highway risk field, *Larsen v. General Motors* and its progeny are the vanguard of the law as it tends toward institutionalizing risks. Under the theory of *Larsen*, automobile manufacturers are responsible both for defects that *cause* crashes and also for design defects that *exacerbate* injuries after crashes have occurred; even crashes not caused by defects in the motor vehicle. Under this theory, a manufacturer must use reasonable care to make a vehicle interior safe for a foreseeable human impact even though the manufacturer was not responsible for the cause of the crash. The "crash-worthiness" doctrine was rejected by another line of cases headed by *Evans v. General Motors*, but has more recently predominated over that view.

No description of the law's movement from individual to institutional responsibility would be complete without mention of the fast developing law of product liability. In the late 1800s common law judges were well aware that some defective products, such as mislabeled drugs and poorly made firearms, were inherently dangerous to users and consumers. They were also aware that consumers were defenseless against the risks of concealed defects and could seldom prove that any responsible person had been at fault. Hence, to apply the common law in its full rigor would again sacrifice blood on the altar of institutional freedom from risk. Some common law judges, unable to stomach this outcome, cut away various common law defenses in defective product actions. First, privity defenses were shunted aside where injury was caused by an inherently dangerous instrumentality, and, then, the famous New York Court of Appeal case of *McPherson v. Buick Motor Company* extended liability wherever harm was caused by an unreasonably dangerous defect in virtually any product, whether inherently dangerous or not. Then, in recognition that industry ought to be made to warrant that products are carefully made, *Baxter v. Ford Motor Company*, *Henningsen v. Bloomfield Motors, Inc.* and a multitude of other cases imposed liability upon manufacturers without a showing of fault. As shall be seen, however, even warranty theories retained doctrinal defenses that stood in the way of full institutional responsibility. *Greenman v. Yuba Power Products* summarily cut most of them away to impose strict liability upon sellers whenever a dangerous defective product injures an innocent user. The *Greenman* theory has been refined and adopted by the American Law Institute as Restatement, Torts, Second § 402 A. It is now accepted in most states.

In the product liability field the *Sindell v. Abbott Laboratories* theory of market share liability has pressed institutional liability to its furthest reach. Under special circumstances, the plaintiff need not prove that a particular defendant produced the particular product (usually a drug) that caused harm; the plaintiff must only prove that the defendant had a measured share of the sales in the market where the defective product was sold.

All of these products liability theories and remaining defenses, as well as the cases cited above, are examined in detail in Chapter 14, *infra. Sindell* is set out in § 7.04, *infra.*

The foregoing overview traces the evolution of the list of civil wrongs in rough outline. The law of torts as it applies to ownership of real property and to the use of speech also changed rapidly after the 1940s. In every instance, except in the law of defamation, the trend is toward more generous reparation and the institutionalization of risks. Only in defamation, where the countervailing goal of free and unimpeded speech is dominant, has there been an important countertrend.

Despite the nature of this introduction, it would be wrong to leave an impression that plaintiffs' lawyers spend most of their time suing institutions rather than individuals. Automobile crashes continue to generate more tort litigation than any other kind of wrong. The majority of states do not have a no-fault law; some may not recognize crashworthiness; and a few have not yet adopted comparative negligence. The common law of torts is bent but not broken. The emerging law of reparation supplements but does not supplant. In sum, common law fault and individual responsibility remain as cornerstones in the law, and beside them a foundation is being prepared for a new cornerstone of universal reparation. The following materials examine the totality of the emerging system that rises above these bases.

Chapter 2

PRELIMINARY CONCEPTS

"Historical explanations lead one to rational explanations, in the sense that there was a time when the rule in question was a sane and intelligent adjustment of means to an end."[1]

F.H. Lawson

§ 2.01 INTRODUCTION

Most legal work does not entail the preparation and execution of trials so dramatically portrayed in the media's depictions of lawyers. The law of torts is an exception. The entire body of law is designed with an eye to resolution of disputes by trial. This is important to the torts student for several reasons.

First, the torts student must learn how to distinguish sets of facts that give a basis for bringing a lawsuit from those that do not. These bases are referred to as "substantive law." When all the substantive elements of a tort are present, lawyers say that the plaintiff has a cause of action.

Second, the torts student must learn how a case is presented in court. The "how to" is known as "procedural law." No matter how sound the substantive law supporting a plaintiff's cause of action, a plaintiff cannot win if the case is not presented correctly.

Third, the torts student must learn how substance and procedure relate to and influence each other. Often, whether a litigant possesses a legitimate cause of action can be tested by prescribed procedural maneuvers prior to trial. Thus, the plaintiff's lawyer must know how and when the substantive cause of action will be tested, while the defendant's lawyer must know how and when to raise and pursue the appropriate procedural challenges.

All this will become understandable in the course of time. Nevertheless, because a lawsuit is an adversarial encounter, it can be roughly illustrated at the outset by reference to similar, more familiar, encounters. Take football for example. The methods of scoring are somewhat analogous to substantive law. A team either gets a touchdown, a field goal, an extra point, a safety, or it gets no points. No matter how many yards the offense piles up, how many first downs, how many passes are completed and so on, unless the team scores points, it cannot win the football game. By analogy, a plaintiff who cannot prove each and every substantive element of a cause of action cannot win a lawsuit, no matter what else may be going in the plaintiff's favor.

---

[1] Lawson, The Rational Strength of English Law at 12.

Similarly, a ball team comprised of superior athletes could never win a football game if none of the team members knew the procedures they were supposed to follow. To use an extreme illustration, a team would never score if it always punted whenever it got the ball. The same can be said of lawsuits. A lawyer who does not know how to move a suit along, no matter how substantively meritorious it may be, cannot win the case for a client.

The third point, that of testing substance through procedural maneuvers, is harder to illustrate with football. A rough analogy is presented when the team that wins the coin toss elects to kick off to start the game rather than to receive the kick. This permits the kicking team to test the strength of its opponent's offense (*i.e.*, its "substantive case") at the outset of the match.

§ 2.02   COMMON LAW HERITAGE — CAUSES OF ACTION

The law of torts is largely comprised of judicial opinions. This distinguishes it from statutory law prescribed by legislatures. Legislatures make laws in more or less complete packages, attempting to specify a comprehensive set of guidelines covering various areas of human behavior. By contrast, judges make law in little bits as cases come before them. The precise holding of each case constitutes a brick in the body of what is referred to as the "corpus juris." Each succeeding case builds on those preceding it to lay down a more and more complete system of law. For this reason, lawyers must know how to find past cases and how to equate them to or distinguish them from the particular case to be decided.

This backward-looking aspect of the common law influenced the historic development of tort law in two distinct ways, both of which had the conservative effect of working against novelty. First, common law judges were loath to acknowledge a cause of action in circumstances under which actions had never been recognized in the past. The fact that the law had never given a remedy under similar circumstances was good and often compelling reason to believe that the law provided none. Consequently, courts have long held that not every harmful episode gives rise to legal redress; some losses are *damnum absque injuria*. The reader will see this attitude at work especially in the older cases in this book. It is more reflective of the conservatism of nineteenth-century English courts than of modern American courts. The latter are more likely to evaluate novel situations in terms of competing policies, such as the capacity of the courts to decide matters of the particular sort, the availability of other remedies, prevailing notions of justice, and sometimes even upon economic analysis of which of the parties is better able to spread the loss or avoid the risk of harm. This policy-oriented approach will be seen in many of the modern cases in the book.

The second backward-looking characteristic of the common law is the doctrine of *stare decisis*, or precedence. This doctrine rests on the mythical premise that judges do not make law, but instead "discover" it piece by piece through the process of adjudication. Once discovered, if the law is thereafter to be changed, it must be done by the lawmaking body — the legislature — and not by the courts. Under this view, once a particular legal decision is assimilated into the body of the common law of a particular jurisdiction, it must thereafter be adhered to by all the courts within that jurisdiction. Each American state has an appellate court of last resort, most often called the supreme court, which is the ultimate precedent-making court of the state.

Despite the myth that courts only discover law, American appellate courts sometimes, but not often, reverse or modify earlier precedential holdings, thereby deviating from *stare decisis*. English courts are much more reluctant to do this. It was only in 1966 that the House of Lords, the highest English appellate court, announced that it would not thereafter be invariably bound by its own precedents.

In early English law, lawsuits were begun in common law courts by obtaining a document from the court called a writ. This writ was then served by the sheriff upon the defendant, thereby establishing a basis for the court to issue legally binding orders and judgments upon the parties.

Under the writ system, the law afforded remedies only for a limited number of rather specifically described circumstances. A plaintiff could obtain a writ from a court only if a complaint fit one of the recognized forms of action. Each "form of action" was available to a plaintiff whose factual allegations fit neatly into a pattern that the law had already recognized as giving rise to a legal remedy. Students of the law will find these terms employed routinely in old opinions but rarely in modern ones. Nevertheless, the old forms of action are important to modern common law, because the substance of this early system has evolved into modern causes of action. The two conservative forces described above have preserved vestiges of the old forms in some jurisdictions, especially in England where doctrine continues to have a firmer hold than in the United States. But in most American jurisdictions the more fluid operation of policy consideration has erased most remnants of the old forms, except for blurry shadows.

Among the more important forms of action were the antecedents of the modern law of contracts — referred to as *assumpsit* — and the modern law of torts — referred to as *trespass*. Now, as then, a contract action depends primarily upon a promise made and broken, while a tort action depends upon a damaging intrusion upon the plaintiff's person or property. Also now, as then, it is sometimes difficult on a given set of facts to specify whether the correct action is one of contract or of tort. This lack of precision made the practice of law intellectually stimulating and also risky. A plaintiff who started with the wrong form under the writ system would lose and be given no second chance. Modern procedure is much more tolerant of early mistakes in pleading, but it still takes a knowledgeable lawyer to move cases along successfully.

The original trespass forms of action appeared to require a direct physical invasion of a legally protected interest resulting in a specific kind of harm. Several particular subspecies were recognized, each possessing a descriptive Latin title. *Trespass vi et armis* required physical intrusion onto the plaintiff's person or property with "force and arms." It bespeaks violence. *Trespass quare clausum fregit* required an unlawful entry upon the plaintiff's lands. It bespeaks an infringement on the plaintiff's right to possess and enjoy home and lands free of the interference of other people. *Trespass de bonis asportatis* required that the defendant seize property belonging to the plaintiff and unlawfully make away with it. It bespeaks a dispossessing and carrying away of the plaintiff's personal property.

All the foregoing trespass forms of action presupposed some sort of direct action by the defendant culminating in immediate harm. Often, however, a plaintiff's harm would not fit into any recognized form of action. For example, a passing cattle herder might drive cattle onto the pasture of another to permit them to graze for a short time. This would be a *trespass quare clausum fregit* because it resulted from a direct invasion of the plaintiff's land and immediately damaged it. Suppose later the pasture was rendered useless by an overgrowth of noxious weeds that entered the field from droppings left by the trespassing cattle? The resulting harm would not be *trespass quare clausum fregit*, because it lacked the direct, immediate consequence that was inherent to all the trespass writs.

In the early common law, plaintiffs whose allegations did not fit a recognized "form of action" were denied relief in the common law courts, but often found a remedy in competing courts of equity. At least partially because of the "competition" among courts, even the old writ system could not remain so hidebound as to refuse remedies for indirect and consequential wrongs such as this. Instead, a more flexible form of action called *trespass on the similar case*, commonly, "trespass on the case" or simply "case," was invented. Elaboration of this more general form eventually produced the modern law of negligence. By the same token, elaboration of the older, more rigid trespass forms produced most of the remainder of the modern law of torts, especially those torts now referred to as intentional torts. Just as it was sometimes difficult to distinguish *assumpsit* from *trespass*, it was sometimes difficult to distinguish *case* from *trespass*. This is exemplified by *Fowler v. Lanning* which appears later in this chapter.

This narrative briefly traces how the law of torts came to be separate from the law of contract and how negligent torts came to be separated from intentional torts. It is no more than a descriptive summary. The precise course of evolution is shrouded and much of it lost in poorly reported or unrecorded history. Furthermore, many of the known nuances and peculiarities of the writ system and forms of action are simply beyond the scope of this book.

So far as the common law of torts is concerned, only the doctrine of strict liability has yet to be mentioned. Strict liability connotes wrongs that tort law will remedy despite the absence of any intention to do harm (*i.e., trespass*) or negligence (*i.e., case*). The mere doing of the act that causes harm creates a cause of action.

Modern strict liability torts fall into two distinct categories, both of which are examined in detail in later chapters. One has to do with harms caused when a property owner makes use of land in a novel-way and damages a neighbor. *Rylands v. Fletcher* (Ch. 13, *infra*). An 1868 decision of the English House of Lords is the intellectual footing of this cause of action. The second category involves harm caused by dangerous defects in goods produced by commercial enterprises. Its intellectual footing is *Greenman v. Yuba Power Products, Inc.* (§ 14.03, *infra*), a 1962 decision of the California Supreme Court. Although this latter cause of action has been adopted by virtually all United States jurisdictions, it remained foreign to English law, until the Parliament enacted a product strict liability statute in 1988 to conform to a directive of the European Economic Community.

In addition to the foregoing, which might be referred to as *pure* tort causes of action, certain actions have a quasi-tort, quasi-contract character. Primarily, these are tort actions that rest upon a breach of a warranty, which is an attribute of contract law. These are treated as tort actions when the warranty is implied by law rather than actually agreed to by the parties. As shall be seen, the importance of this theory has been diminished but not eliminated by the rapid and wide acceptance of enterprise strict liability.

Even modern causes of action do not provide a remedy every time one person harms another. What happens then? What does the outcome of *Stanley v. Powell* suggest?

STANLEY v. POWELL
[1891] 1 Q.B. 86[2]

Nov. 3. DENMAN, J. This case was tried before me and a special jury at the last Maid-stone Summer Assizes.

In the statement of claim the plaintiff alleged that the defendant had *negligently and wrongfully and unskilfully* fired his gun and wounded the plaintiff in his eye, and that the plaintiff, in consequence, had lost his sight and suffered other damage. The defendant denied the negligence alleged. After the evidence on both sides, which was conflicting, had been heard, I left the three following questions to the jury: 1. Was the plaintiff injured by a shot from defendant's gun? 2. Was the defendant guilty of negligence in firing the charge to which that shot belonged as he did? 3. Damages.

The undisputed facts were, that on November 29, 1888, the defendant and several others were pheasant shooting in a party, some being inside and some outside of a wood which the beaters were beating. The right of shooting was in one Greenwood, who was of the party. The plaintiff was employed by Greenwood to carry cartridges and the game which might be shot. Several beaters were driving the game along a plantation of saplings towards an open drive. The plaintiff stood just outside a gate which led into a field outside the plantation, at the end of the drive. The defendant was walking along in that field a few yards from the hedge which bounded the plantation. As he was walking along, a pheasant rose inside the plantation; the defendant fired one barrel at this bird, and, according to the evidence for the defendant, struck it with his first shot. There was a considerable conflict of evidence as to details; but the jury must, I think, be taken to have adopted the version of the facts sworn by the defendant's witnesses. They swore that the bird, when struck by the first shot, began to lower and turn back towards the beaters, whereupon the defendant fired his second barrel and killed the bird, but that a shot, glancing from the bough of an oak which was in or close to the hedge, and, striking the plaintiff, must have caused the injury complained of. The oak in question, according to the defendant's evidence, was partly between the defendant and the bird when the second barrel was fired, but it was not in a line with the plaintiff, but, on the contrary, so much out of that line, that the shot must have been diverted to a considerable extent from the direction in which the gun must have been pointed in order to hit the plaintiff. The distance between the plaintiff and the defendant, in a direct line, when the second barrel was fired, was about thirty yards. The case for the plaintiff was entirely different; but I think it must be held that the jury took the defendant's account of the matter, for they found the second question left to them in the negative.

Before summing up the case to the jury, I called the attention of the parties to the doctrine which seemed to have been laid down in some old cases — that, even in the absence of negligence, an action of trespass might lie; and it was agreed that I should leave the question of negligence to the jury, but that, if necessary, the

---

[2] [Ed. — Queen's Bench Law Reports of the principal English trial court, appeals there-from, and certain criminal appeals; decision of a trial court.]

pleadings were deemed to have been amended so as to raise any case or defense open upon the facts with liberty to the Court to draw inferences of fact, and that the damages should be assessed contingently. The jury assessed them at 100 pounds. I left either party to move the Court for judgment; but it was afterwards agreed that the case should be argued before myself on further consideration, and that I should give judgment, . . .

Having heard the arguments, I am of opinion that, by no amendment that could be made consistently with the finding of the jury could I properly give judgment for the plaintiff. It was contended on his behalf that this was a case in which an action of trespass would have lain before the Judicature Acts; and this contention was mainly founded on certain dicta which, until considered with reference to those cases in which they are uttered, seem to support that contention; but no decision was quoted, nor do I think that any can be found which goes so far as to hold, that if A. is injured by a shot from a gun fired at a bird by B., an action of trespass will necessarily lie, even though B. is proved to have fired the gun without negligence and without intending to injure the plaintiff or to shoot in his direction.

The jury having found that there was no negligence on the part of the defendant, the most favourable way in which it is now possible to put the case for the plaintiff is to consider the action as brought for a trespass, and to consider that the defendant has put upon the record a defense denying negligence and specifically alleging the facts, sworn to by his witnesses, which the jury must be considered to have found proved, and then to consider whether those facts, coupled with the absence of negligence established by the jury, amount to an excuse in law. . . .

The case of *Underwood v. Hewson*, decided in 1724, was relied on for the plaintiff. The report is very short. "The defendant was uncocking a gun, and the plaintiff standing to see it, it went off and wounded him; and at the trial it was held that the plaintiff might maintain trespass — Strange pro defendente." The marginal note in Nolan's edition of 1795, not necessarily Stranger's own composition, is this — "Trespass lies for an accidental hurt;" and in that edition there is a reference to Buller's N. P., p. 16. On referring to Buller, p. 16, where he is dealing with *Weaver v. Ward*, I find he writes as follows. "So (it is no battery) if one soldier hurt another in exercise; but if he plead it he must set forth the circumstances, so as to make it appear to the Court that it was inevitable, and that he committed no negligence to give occasion to the hurt, for it is not enough to say that he did it casualiter, et per infortunium, et contra voluntatem suam; for no man shall be excused of a trespass, unless it be justified entirely without his default: *Weaver v. Ward*; and, therefore, it has been holden that an action lay where the plaintiff standing by to see the defendant uncock his gun was accidentally wounded: *Underwood v. Hewson*." On referring back to *Weaver v. Ward*, I can find nothing in the report to show that the Court held, that in order to constitute a defense in the case of a trespass it is necessary to shew that the act was *inevitable*. If *inevitable*, it would seem that there was a defense under the general issue; but a distinction is drawn between an act which is inevitable and an act which is excusable, and what *Weaver v. Ward* really lays down is that "no man shall be excused of a trespass except it may be judged utterly without his fault."

Day v. Edwards merely decides that where a man negligently *drives* a cart against the plaintiff's carriage, the injury being committed by the *immediate* act complained of, the remedy must be trespass and not case.

But the case upon which most reliance was placed by the plaintiff's counsel was *Leame v. Bray*. That was an action of trespass in which the plaintiff complained that the defendant with force and arms drove and struck a chaise which he was driving on the highway against the plaintiff's curricle, which the plaintiff's servant was driving, by means whereof the servant was thrown out, and the horses ran away, and the plaintiff, who jumped out to save his life, was injured. The facts stated in the report include a statement that "the accident happened in a dark night, owing to the defendant driving his carriage on the wrong side of the road, and the parties not being able to see each other; and that if the defendant had kept his right side there was ample room for the carriages to have passed without injury." The report goes on to state: "But it did not appear that blame was imputable to the defendant in any *other* respect as to the manner of his driving. It was therefore objected for the defendant, that the injury *having happened from negligence* and not willfully, the proper remedy was by an action on the case, and not of trespass vi et armis; and the plaintiff was thereupon nonsuited." On the argument of the rule to set aside the verdict the whole discussion turned upon the question whether the injury was, as put by Lawrence, J., at p. 596 of the report, immediate from the defendant's act, or consequential only from it, and in the result the nonsuit was set aside. But it clearly appears from the report that there was evidence upon which the jury might have found negligence, and indeed the defendant's counsel assumed it in the very objection which prevailed with Lord Ellenborough when he nonsuited the plaintiff. There is nothing in any of the judgments to show that if in that case a plea had been pleaded denying any negligence, and the jury had found that the defendant was not guilty of any negligence, but (for instance) that the accident happened wholly through the darkness of the night making it impossible to distinguish one side of the road from the other and without negligence on either side, the Court would have held that the defendant would have been liable either in trespass or in case.

All the cases to which I have referred were before the Court of Exchequer in 1875, in the case of *Holmes v. Mather* and Bramwell, B., in giving judgment in that case, dealt with them thus: "as to the cases cited, most of them are really decisions on the form of action, whether case or trespass. The result of them is this, and it is intelligible enough: if the act that does an injury is an act of direct force vi et armis, trespass is the proper remedy (if there is any remedy), where the act is wrongful either as being willful or as being the result of negligence. Where the act is not wrongful for either of these reasons, no action is maintainable, though trespass would be the proper form of action if it were wrongful. That is the effect of the decisions."

This view of the older authorities is in accordance with a passage cited by Mr. Dickens from Bacon's Abridgment, Trespass, I., p. 706, with a marginal reference to *Weaver v. Ward*. In Bacon the word "inevitable" does not find a place. "If the circumstance which is specially pleaded in an action of trespass do not make the act complained of lawful" (by which I understand justifiable even if purposely done to the extent of purposely inflicting the injury, as for instance, in a case of self-defense) "and only make it excusable, it is proper to plead this circumstance in excuse; and it is in this case necessary for the defendant to shew not only that the act complained of was accidental" (by which I understand, "that the injury was unintentional,") "but likewise that it was not owing to neglect or want of due caution."

In the present case the plaintiff sued in respect of an injury owing to the defendant's negligence, — there was no pretence for saying that it was intentional so far as any injury to the plaintiff was concerned, — and the jury negatived such negligence. It was argued that nevertheless, inasmuch as the plaintiff was injured by a shot from the defendant's gun, that was an injury owing to an act of force committed by the defendant, and therefore an action would lie. I am of opinion that this is not so, and that against any statement of claim which the plaintiff could suggest the defendant must succeed if he were to plead the facts sworn to by the witnesses for the defendant in this case, and the jury believing those facts, as they must now be taken by me to have done, found the verdict which they have found as regards negligence. In other words, I am of opinion that if the case is regarded as an action on the case for an injury by negligence the plaintiff has failed to establish that which is the very gist of such an action; if, on the other hand, it is turned into an action for trespass, and the defendant (as he must be) supposed to have pleaded a plea denying negligence and establishing that the injury was accidental in the sense above explained, the verdict of the jury is equally fatal to the action. I am, therefore, of opinion that I am bound to give judgment for the defendant. As to costs, they must follow unless the defendant foregoes his right.

Judgment for the defendant.

NOTES AND QUESTIONS

(1)   The court system of England is presently composed of two sorts of trial courts and two levels of appellate courts. The County Courts are trial courts of local and limited jurisdiction. More important cases are tried in the High Court which is divided into three divisions. The Queen's Bench division (known as King's Bench when a male is the sovereign) tries both criminal and civil cases that would have been tried in the old Common Law courts; the Chancery Division tries equity matters and others assigned it by law; the Probate, Divorce and Admiralty Division tries cases described by the name. Most important tort actions would now be tried before the Queen's Bench.

Appeals from these primary trial courts are to the Court of Appeal. From that court further appeal may be had to the judicial committee of the House of Lords, but only upon leave either of the Court of Appeal or the House of Lords.[3]

In reading old English cases, you will find decisions from antiquated courts whose jurisdictions have been merged into the modern system. The Court of the Exchequer first had jurisdiction over tax matters and later branched out into debtor-creditor matters. The Court of Common Pleas heard cases between common subjects. The Court of King's Bench heard important cases, especially those involving the sovereign. London was the seat of all the Royal Courts, but judges from the various branches periodically ventured to localities away from London to hear cases. Rather than apply local law, the assizes, as these extra-London sessions were called, applied the law that would be applied in the courts sitting in Westminster. It was the assizes that made the law "common" throughout England, thus deriving the term "Common Law."

---

[3] The Judicial Appellate Committee of the House of Lords ceased to exist on September 30, 2009. Most of its final appellate review jurisdiction was transferred to a Supreme Court of the United Kingdom established by the Constitutional Reform Act 2005.

The Court of Chancery found ways to circumvent the rigidities of the various common law courts that clung assiduously to the forms of action. Thus, the concept of equity evolved to afford a just result when the strict common law provided no remedy. Hence, Chancery was a foil to the common law. Later, the common law courts invented the more flexible *trespass on the case* writ to keep Chancery from usurping too great a part of their work.

In addition, the Court of Admiralty dealt with admiralty matters, Ecclesiastical Courts dealt with wills and matrimony, and the local courts applied local laws to matters of all sorts until they were gradually squeezed out by the assizes.

(2) *Stanley v. Powell* clearly distinguishes between *allegations* and *fact*. Allegations are made in the document that starts the lawsuit, be it the writ in the old forms of action, the "statement of claim" of *Stanley*, or the complaint or petition for relief used in modern United States courts. An allegation is something a party says occurred; a fact is something that has been determined to be legally true based upon evidence presented to the court. Did Stanley's case fail because his allegations were inadequate or because he failed to prove them?

(3) *Stanley v. Powell* illustrates how judges look back to old cases to determine what the law is. It also illustrates the distinction between the actual grounds or *holding* of a decision, sometimes referred to as the *ratio decidendi* by English courts, and a judicial statement that is not the actual ground of the decision, or *dictum.* What is the holding of *Stanley*? Are examples of dicta to be found there?

(4) Why does Denman, J. insist upon assuming that the jury believed the defendant's version of what happened?

(5) Suppose the plaintiff's view of the law in *Stanley v. Powell* had been accepted. How would that have affected freedom of action in everyday activities within our culture? In that regard, what meaning did the plaintiff attempt to ascribe to the term "inevitable" as used in *Weaver v. Ward?* An American court had earlier rejected any extreme connotation in the use of that term, saying, "To make an accident or casualty, or as the law sometimes states it, inevitable accident, it must be such an accident as the defendant could not have avoided by the use of the kind and degree of care necessary to the exigency, and in the circumstances in which he was placed." *Brown v. Kendall*, 60 Mass. 292, 296 (1850).

FOWLER v. LANNING
[1959] 1 Q.B. 426[4]

DIPLOCK J. read the following judgment.

"The distinction between actions of trespass on the case and trespass vi et armis should be most carefully and precisely observed. Otherwise we shall introduce much confusion and uncertainty." So said de Grey C.J. in 1773 in *Scott v. Shepherd.* It must gratify the ghosts of generations of special pleaders that today, nearly a century after the passing of the Judicature Act, 1875, I would be invited to decide whether such a distinction still exists where an unintentional injury to the person of the plaintiff arises directly from an act of the defendant, and should be invited to decide this point upon what is the modern equivalent of demurrer.

---

[4] [Ed. — Queen's Bench Law Reports of the principal English trial court, appeals there-from and certain criminal appeals; decision of a trial court.]

The writ in this case claims damages for trespass to the person committed by the defendant at Corfe Castle, in the county of Dorset, on November 19, 1957. The statement of claim alleges laconically that at that place and on that date "the defendant shot the plaintiff," and that by reason thereof the plaintiff sustained personal injuries and has suffered loss and damage. By his defense the defendant, in addition to traversing the allegations of fact, raises the objection "that the statement of claim is bad in law and discloses no cause of action against him on the ground that the plaintiff does not allege that the said shooting was either intentional or negligent." An order has been made that this point of law be disposed of before the trial of the issues of fact in the action. That order is binding upon me, and, in disposing of it, I can look no further than the pleadings. I must confess that at first glance at the pleadings I felt some anxiety lest I was being invited to decide a point which has long puzzled the professors (see the article by Professors Goodhart and Winfield, 1933 Law Quarterly Review, vol. 49, p. 359; Pollock on Torts, 15th ed., p. 128; Salmond on Torts, 12th ed., p. 311; Winfield on Torts, 5th ed., p. 213), only to learn ultimately that, just as in *Donoghue v. Stevenson*, there was in fact no snail in the ginger-beer bottle,[5] so in this case there was in fact no pellet in the defendant's gun.

The point of law is not, however, a mere academic one even at the present stage of the action. The alleged injuries were, I am told, sustained at a shooting party; it is not suggested that the shooting was intentional. The practical issue is whether, if the plaintiff was in fact injured by a shot from a gun fired by the defendant, the onus lies upon the plaintiff to prove that the defendant was negligent, in which case, under the modern system of pleading, he must so plead and give particulars of negligence (see R.S.C., Ord. 19, r. 4), or whether it lies upon the defendant to prove that the plaintiff's injuries were not caused by the defendant's negligence, in which case the plaintiff's statement of claim is sufficient and discloses a cause of action (see R.S.C., Ord. 19, r. 25). The issue is thus a neat one of onus of proof.

I am much indebted to counsel on both sides for their diligence and erudition in tracing the history of the distinction between trespass vi et armis and trespass on the case before the passing of the Judicature Acts, 1873 and 1875.

. . .

What by 1852 was the essential difference between the two alternative remedies based on identical facts? It is fashionable today to regard trespass to the person as representing the historic principle that every man acts at his peril and is liable for all the consequences of his acts; negligence as representing the more modern view that a man's freedom of action is subject only to the obligation not to infringe any duty of care which he owes to others: see *per* Lord Macmillan in *Read v. J. Lyons & Co. Ltd.* But however true this may have been of trespass in medieval times — and I respectfully doubt whether it ever was — the strict principle that every man acts at his peril was not applied in the case of trespass to the person even as long ago as 1617. It is true that in that year, in the much-cited case of *Weaver v. Ward*, which arose out of a shooting accident during an exercise of trained bands, the Court of King's Bench held that a plea that "the defendant casualiter et per infortuniam et contra voluntatem suam, in discharging of his piece did hurt and wound the plaintiff" was demurrable. But it would seem that this was because the plea, which was a special plea, was insufficient because, although it denied

---

[5] [Examined in § 4.02, *infra.*]

intention, it did not negative negligence on the part of the defendant. It is clear from the report that the court was of opinion that the action of trespass to the person would fail if it should appear that the accident was "inevitable and that the defendant had committed no negligence to give occasion to the hurt."

This phrase is repeated in many of the later cases. Where it appears, however, it must be read in its historical context and not as if it were being used by judges to whom modern concepts of negligence, contributory negligence and causation were familiar. An examination of the cases up to 1842 in which this or a similar phrase was adopted shows, I think, that the word "inevitable" was superfluous, and that the phrase meant no more than that the accident could not have been avoided by the exercise of reasonable care on the part of the defendant.

Apart from the question of onus of proof, which I must now examine, there does not appear by 1852 to have been any difference between the substantive law applicable whether the action were framed in trespass on the case or trespass to the person. Differences as regards pleading were, of course, in those days, vital, but are not relevant for the purposes of the present case in 1959, except in so far as they throw any light upon where the onus of proof lay.

In trespass on the case the onus of proof of the defendant's negligence undoubtedly lay upon the plaintiff. Where it lay in trespass is much more difficult to determine. The defense that the accident "was inevitable and that the defendant had commited no negligence to give occasion to the hurt" was available to the defendant upon a plea to the general issue by the end of the seventeenth century: see *Gibbons v. Pepper*, and this appears to have been accepted by the Court of Common Pleas as late as 1823: see *Wakeman v. Robinson* — a case still cited as authority in the third edition of Bullen & Leake in 1868. Since the plea to the general issue [*i.e.*, in modern terms, a general denial of liability. Ed.] merely denied the existence of the necessary ingredients of the tort, this would suggest that in the case of trespass to the person the onus lay upon the plaintiff to show that the defendant's act was either intentional or negligent. Lord Ellenborough, on the other hand, sitting at nisi prius in 1810, had already decided in *Knapp v. Salsbury* that such a defense must be specially pleaded [*i.e.*, in modern terms, a specific denial that the defendant had committed a wrongful act. — Ed.], and the Court of King's Bench in 1842 in *Hall v. Fearnley* appears to have come down on the pleading point on the side of Lord Ellenborough, although the differences between the two reports of this case make it difficult to elicit the ratio decidendi. But although the two last-cited cases destroy the force of any inference as to onus of proof which might be drawn from *Gibbons v. Pepper*, they do not themselves give rise to the contrary inference. With the growth of special pleading, and in particular after the "general rules" of Hil. Term. 1834, there were many matters the onus of proof of which if disputed lay upon the plaintiff, which were not regarded as traversed [*i.e.*, "denied." — Ed.] by a plea to the general issue: see Bullen & Leake, 3rd ed., pp. 699–704.

I do not find the pre-Common Law Procedure Act, 1852, cases conclusive or, indeed, helpful as to where the onus of proof of the defendant's negligence or absence of negligence lay where the action was founded upon trespass to the person and not on trespass on the case. The reported cases turn upon points of pleading, a science upon which the legal mind was then wonderfully concentrated, and when, in any particular case, that science had achieved its object in arriving at an issue of fact for the jury in an action of trespass to the person, it could only be very rarely that the question of onus of proof was crucial. Since trespass to the person only lay where the injury to the plaintiff was the direct consequence of the personal act of the defendant, proof that the defendant did the act and that the plaintiff was thereby injured would normally be prima facie evidence of the defendant's negligence sufficient also to sustain an action on the case in accordance with the common-sense view applied at nisi prius long before Pollock C.B. in *Byrne v. Boadle* translated it into Latin as res ipsa loquitur. At the time the case came before the jury, therefore, there can have been little practical difference between trespass and case, even if in the former the onus of negativing negligence did lie upon the defendant, while in the latter the onus of proving negligence lay upon the plaintiff. But whatever the reason, I can find no trace in the reports that the possibility that the onus of proof might be different in the two classes of cases was a question which ever occurred to the judges of those days, or that their charge to the jury differed according to whether the action were framed in trespass or in case.

. . .

Little assistance is to be obtained from any later cases. Since *Stanlev v. Powell*, and perhaps as a result of that decision, there appears to be no case in the reports where \ill\ trespass to the person has been relied upon as distinct from negligence, despite the encouragement of the learned authors of the article on Trespass and Negligence in the Law Quarterly Review in 1933 (45 Law Quarterly Review 359), and the continued appearance in successive editions of Bullen & Leake of a precedent of a pleading in trespass to the person in which neither intention nor negligence is alleged. No doubt in many cases it is the master who is sued for the act of his servant, and here trespass as opposed to case would never lie; but in the 68 years which have passed since *Stanley v. Powell* there must have been many cases where the injury to the plaintiff was the direct consequence of the act of the defendant himself. But no practitioner seems to have thought, and certainly no court has decided, that to do so would affect the onus of proof.

I think that what appears to have been the practice of the profession during the present century is sound in law. I can summarise the law as I understand it from my examination of the cases as follows:

(1) Trespass to the person does not lie if the injury to the plaintiff, although the direct consequences of the act of the defendant, was caused unintentionally and without negligence on the defendant's part.

. . .

(3) If it were right to say with Blackburn in 1866 that negligence is a necessary ingredient of unintentional trespass only where the circumstances are such as to show that the plaintiff had taken upon himself the risk of inevitable injury (*i.e.*, injury which is the result of neither intention nor carelessness on the part of the defendant), the plaintiff must today in this crowded world be considered as taking upon himself the risk of inevitable injury from any acts of his neighbour which, in the absence of damage to the plaintiff, would not in themselves be unlawful — of which discharging a gun at a shooting party in 1957 or a trained band exercise in 1617 are obvious examples. For . . . a man's freedom of action is subject only to the obligation not to infringe any duty of care which he owes to others.

(4) The onus of proving negligence, where the trespass is not intentional, lies upon the plaintiff, whether the action be framed in trespass or in negligence. This has been unquestioned law in highway cases ever since *Holmes v. Mather*, and there is no reason in principle, nor any suggestion in the decided authorities, why it should be any different in other cases. It is, indeed, but an illustration of the rule that he who affirms must prove, which lies at the root of our law of evidence.

. . .

I hold that the statement of claim in its present form discloses no cause of action.

Leave to make immediate amendments to statement of claim granted.

NOTES AND QUESTIONS

(1)   The notion of "onus of proof," which is more commonly referred to as "burden of proof" by United States courts, prevents deadlocks in litigation. A football game can end in a tie score, in which event both teams go home being neither winner nor loser. This does not happen in litigation. Either the plaintiff is able to prove the cause of action and win the case, or cannot and loses. The parties can compromise, of course, but unlike the rules of football, the rules of litigation will necessarily produce a winning side if the dispute is permitted to go completely through a trial.

This is the function of the burden of proof. To prevail, the plaintiff must prove each and every element of the cause of action upon which the plaintiff's case is based. In some instances, the evidence of a particular point may be so closely balanced that the factfinder cannot determine whether it has been proved or not. On those occasions the party assigned the burden of proof necessarily loses.

Burden of proof is not substantive law but is a convention of litigation. Who makes the assignment of the burden? What factors influence which party is to be assigned it?

(2)   In *Fowler v. Lanning*, Diplock, J. was sitting as a trial court judge. Thus, the *Fowler* opinion reported his view as expressed during the trial of the case. This is a common practice in the English High Courts and in United States federal district courts but is unusual in the United States state courts. Most reported written opinions from state courts are issued by appellate courts in deciding whether or not the trial court judge made some error in the trial proceedings.

(3)   What is the substantive outcome of *Fowler v. Lanning*? Assume the plaintiff is permitted to replead. Draft a revised complaint that would survive the defendant's demurrer (motion to dismiss). May a lawyer file such a complaint in the total absence of evidence to prove it? Why did the plaintiff's lawyer initially draft the complaint so "laconically?"

(4)   Why is the decision in *Stanley v. Powell* of greater substantive importance than that in *Fowler v. Lanning?*

(5)   In omitted portions of the judgment, Diplock rejected the argument that the burden of proof of negligence was different for highway crashes than for any other class of case. Although this distinction is not accepted in England and the United States, at least one common law jurisdiction does accept it. See *Venning v.*

Chin, (1974) 10 S.A.S.R. 299 (F.C. South Australia). Furthermore, the modern law in Canada appears to adopt the precise rule the plaintiff contended for in *Fowler v. Lanning*. As stated in *Larin v. Goshen*, 56 D.L.R. (3d) 719, 722, "The law in Canada at present is this: In an action for damages in trespass where the plaintiff proves that he has been injured by the direct act of the defendant, the onus falls upon the defendant to prove that his act was both *unintentional and without negligence* on his part, in order for him to be entitled to a dismissal of the action."

(6)   As to the proposition that at some point in history the law would hold a person absolutely liable for consequences of action even in the absence of negligence or intentional fault, Diplock expressed "doubt that it ever was." After examining the same historical predicates, Oliver Wendell Holmes, Jr., had reached the same conclusion of doubt much earlier. Holmes, The Common Law (Harvard Presses, 1963), pp. 72, 73.

(7)   What was the significance of the defendant's plea *"casusaliter, et per infortunium, et contra voluntatem suam"* in *Weaver v. Ward*?

§ 2.03   THE LITIGATION PROCESS

The litigation process may be divided into three stages: the pleadings, the evidentiary trial, and the appeal. The purposes of the pleadings are to make allegations and to isolate the points that are genuinely in dispute. Done well, the pleadings will narrow the issues in dispute only to those that must be resolved in order to dispose of the litigation.

The purpose of the evidentiary trial is to resolve the issues that remain in dispute. Usually these disputes are about facts. For example, in a shooting case like *Fowler v. Lanning*, disputed facts might be: Did the defendant fire his gun? Did the defendant's shot hit the plaintiff? What damages were caused the plaintiff by the shooting? Each party would testify, call other witnesses and present non-testimonial evidence to prove or disprove the points. Once the facts are ascertained, their legal consequences must be stated. The judge is the source of the law and often can instruct the jury as to the exact outcome upon the various findings of fact open to it.

Sometimes, however, factual and legal issues are confused in what is sometimes called a mixed question of law and fact. In the United States, the parties are constitutionally entitled to have a jury decide both facts and mixed questions of fact and law in many classes of actions. See, e.g., *Seals v. Hickey*, 186 Conn. 337, 441 A.2d 604 (1982). In England, however, the use of juries in most civil litigation was eliminated by *Ward v. James*, (1965) 1 Q.B. 273, and the legislation construed therein. To guide the jury in deciding mixed questions of fact and law, the United States judge instructs the jury as to what the law is on the disputed point. For example, the judge might tell the jury, "The law is that one man may not intentionally shoot another. If you find that the defendant intentionally shot the plaintiff, then you must render a judgment for the plaintiff." This is an instruction. How many outcomes on facts and mixed questions of fact and law are possible under that instruction?

The purpose of appeals is to correct errors made by the trial judge during the pleading and trial stages of the proceedings. In the United States the only information available to the appellate judges is the record of the trial proceedings, the written briefs of the parties, and the arguments made by the advocates. An appeal affords no opportunity to present new evidence or make new arguments. English appellate courts will occasionally accept new evidence. Ordinarily, an appeal must allege that the trial judge made an error of law. Complaints that a mistake was made in findings of fact are usually unavailing, because the appellate judges deem the jurors and trial judges who saw and heard the witnesses to be able to evaluate the credibility and weight of the evidence better than they can from a mere reading of the record. Thus, trial decisions are only infrequently reversed on grounds that the findings of fact were erroneous.

Various procedural devices help the parties narrow the issues and test the adequacy of allegations and proof. A plaintiff files a *complaint* to begin a lawsuit. The complaint must allege facts that give rise to a valid cause of action. The defendant responds with an *answer* which may deny the plaintiff's allegations and also allege defenses that would defeat the plaintiff's cause of action. At the appropriate time, either party may make a motion as follows: "For the sake of argument, I agree with all the facts the plaintiff (defendant) has alleged, but I maintain that those facts do not establish a cause of action (affirmative defense)." At common law such a pleading was called a *demurrer*; whereas under modern rules it is more often called a *motion to dismiss*. This motion may have the valuable effect of removing issues with no legal consequence from the ensuing trial and of permitting some cases to be disposed of without trial.

Thus, if the defendant demurs to the complaint and the demurrer is sustained, the plaintiff has lost without trial unless the underlying facts permit an amendment to the complaint to make it withstand a subsequent demurrer. This is what Diplock, J. gave the plaintiff leave to attempt in *Fowler v. Lanning*. On the other hand, if the defendant's demurrer is overruled, then the trial will give the plaintiff an opportunity to prove the allegations of the complaint. At that stage the defendant's admission for the sake of argument in the demurrer becomes of no effect. The plaintiff's allegations must be proven with evidence.

Similar devices operate at other stages of the process to further limit the issues to be tried. The *motion for summary judgment* is a pre-trial device for testing the sufficiency of the evidence the parties *might* be able to adduce if the trial is permitted to take place. The *motion for directed verdict* is a device used during the course of a trial for testing the sufficiency of the evidence actually submitted. For example, a plaintiff ordinarily must produce all the evidence available to prove the *prima facie* case before the defendant presents any defensive evidence. After the plaintiff has no more evidence to introduce, the defendant might move for a directed verdict. The effect of this motion is to assert, "The defendant does not need to present evidence because the plaintiff's evidence fails to prove the allegations." Motions for directed verdict can also be made by either party after all the evidence is presented and before the jury retires to deliberate its decision.

In ruling on motions for summary judgment or directed verdict, trial court judges view the evidence (or statements about evidence in summary judgments) most favorably to the position of the "non-moving" party (that is, the party who did not make the motion). What is the purpose of this convention? If the judge finds that the party bearing the burden of proof on a claim (or affirmative defense) has failed to present evidence from which a jury could find that what must be proved has been proved, the court will grant the motion for summary judgment or directed verdict and dismiss the claim (or defense). If the court finds some evidence has been presented to prove the claim or defense, the court will deny the motion.

If all motions for directed verdict are denied, the advocates are permitted to make closing arguments to the jury and, finally, the judge instructs the jury about the law. Ordinarily, the parties are permitted to propose *jury instructions* written as they believe they should be given. The judge will accept some, refuse others, and may prepare still others not proposed by either side. As the last step in the trial before the jury retires to deliberate and return a verdict, the judge instructs the jury as to the law it is to apply.

Although trial judges only infrequently modify jury verdicts, certain motions may nevertheless be made to challenge a jury's decision. The motion for judgment *nonobstante veredicto* (called N.O.V.) requests the judge to render a judgment notwithstanding the jury's verdict against the moving party. The gravamen of the motion is that the jury's verdict is not sustainable under any possible interpretation of the evidence. Less drastic motions available in tort cases are for *remittitur* or *additur*. The former would be made by a defendant on grounds that the amount of the jury's verdict is too high and ought to be reduced; the latter would be made by a plaintiff for opposite purposes.

Each time a trial court rules on any motion, one party or the other is disadvantaged by the outcome and may allege that an error of law has been made. Such allegations of error are the grist of the job of appeals courts, and appellate opinions disposing of the allegations of error form the body of the common law.

QUESTIONS

At what stage of the litigation process did the issue discussed in *Fowler v. Lanning* arise? What procedural device was used to raise the issue? What conventions were employed by Diplock, J.?

Chapter 3

THE SEPARATION OF NEGLIGENCE AND INTENTIONAL TORTS

Two major divisions in the law of torts are between those causes of action that require an element of wrongdoing and those that do not and, as to those that require wrongdoing, between those that require proof of intentional wrong and those that require proof of negligence. The strict liability torts that require no proof of wrongdoing are examined mainly in Chapters 13 and 14, *infra*. The present chapter gives a historical glimpse of how negligent torts and intentional torts emerged as distinct and independent causes of action. Chapters 4 through 9 elaborate the law of negligence, and Chapter 12 concentrates upon intentional torts.

In reading these cases the student is reading history. But the structure and divisions of the modem law of torts derive from that history and many terms of art that continue to appear in modern judicial opinions would seem to be artificial contrivances if divorced from their historical origins.

WILLIAMS v. HOLLAND
(H.L. 1833) 10 Bing. 112, 131 Eng. Rep. 848*

TINDALL C.J. This was an action on the case, in which the declaration states that the Plaintiff was possessed of a cart, and horse drawing the same, in which cart were the Plaintiff's son and daughter, and that Defendant was possessed of a gig, and horse drawing the same, "which gig and horse were then under the care, &c. of Defendant, who was driving the same in and along the highway:" nevertheless Defendant "so carelessly, unskillfully, and improperly drove, &c. his said gig and horse," that through the carelessness of the Defendant the said gig and horse of Defendant ran and struck with great violence upon and against the horse and cart of Plaintiff, and thereby broke to pieces the same, and the son and daughter of Plaintiff were greatly hurt, &c. The Defendant pleaded the general issue [*i.e.*, denied liability. — Ed.]; and on the trial the question left to the jury was, whether the injury was occasioned by the negligence and carelessness of the Defendant; which question the jury found in the affirmative, and gave their verdict for the Plaintiff, with 12 pounds. damages. After the trial, the present rule [*i.e.*, judgment notwithstanding the verdict. — Ed.] was obtained for setting aside the verdict and entering a nonsuit, under leave given for that purpose, upon the ground that the injury having been occasioned by the immediate act of the Defendant himself, the action ought to have been trespass, and that the case was not maintainable; and amongst other cases cited by the Defendant's counsel in support of this objection,

---

* [Ed. — English Reports, general reporter of older English cases; decision of House of Lords; Bingham's reports.]

25

that of *Leame v. Bray* (3 East, 593)was principally relied upon as an authority in point.

The declaration, in this case, states the grounds of action to be an injury occasioned by the carelessness and negligence of the Defendant in driving his own gig. That such carelessness and negligence is, strictly and properly in itself, the subject of an action on the case, would appear, if any authority were wanting, from Com. Dig. tit. "Action upon the Case for Negligence." And the jury have found in the very terms of the declaration, that the injury was so occasioned. Under such a form of action, therefore, and with such a finding by the jury, the present objection ought not to prevail, unless some positive and inflexible rule of law, or some authority too strong to be overcome, is brought forward in its support. If such are to be found, they must, undoubtedly, be adhered to; for settled forms of action, adapted to different grievances, contribute much to the certain administration of justice.

But upon examining the cases cited in argument, both in support of, and in answer to, the objection, we cannot find one in which it is distinctively held, that the present form of action [*i.e.*, trespass on the case. — Ed.] is not maintainable under the circumstances of this case.

For as to *Leame v. Bray*, on which the principal reliance is placed by the Defendant, in which the form of action was trespass, and the circumstances very nearly the same as those in the case now under consideration, the only rule established is, that an action of trespass might be maintained, not that an action on the case could not. The case of *Saignac v. Roome*, in which the Court held that case would not lie where the defendant's servant willfully drove against the plaintiff's carriage, was founded on the principle, that no action would lie against the master for the willful act of his servant; and in that of *Day v. Edwards*, in which it was ruled that trespass was the proper remedy, and not case, it should be observed that the question arose upon a special demurrer to the declaration; and that the declaration stated that the defendant "so furiously, negligently, and improperly drove his cart and horse, that through the furious, negligent, and improper conduct of the defendant, the cart and horse were driven and struck with great force and violence upon and against the carriage of the plaintiff;" the question therefore arising upon a special demurrer, where the Court could look to nothing but the legal construction of the declaration, is very differently circumstanced from this, where the jury have found that negligence was the ground of the injury. On the other hand, the cases of *Rogers v. Imbleton*, and *Ogle v. Barnes and Others*, are simply in favour of the proposition, that the present form of action, is, under the circumstances, maintainable.

We hold it, however, to be unnecessary, to examine very minutely the grounds of the various decisions; for the late case of *Moreton v. Hardern and Others* appears to us to go the full length of deciding, that where the injury is occasioned by the carelessness and negligence of the Defendant, although it be occasioned by his immediate act, the plaintiff may, if he thinks proper, make the negligence of the Defendant the ground of his action, and declare in case. It has been urged, indeed, in answer to that case, that it was decided on the ground, that the action was brought against one of the proprietors who was driving, and against his co-proprietors who were absent, but whose servant was on the box at the time; and that as trespass would not have been maintainable against the co-proprietors who were absent, so case was held maintainable in order that all the proprietors might be included. But it is manifest that the Court did not rest their opinion upon so narrow a ground; nor indeed would it have been a solid foundation for the judgment, that the master, who was present, should be made liable to a different form of action than he otherwise would have been if the servant of the other proprietors had not been there.

We think the case last above referred to has laid down a plain and intelligible rule, that where the injury is occasioned by the carelessness and negligence of the Defendant, the Plaintiff is at liberty to bring an action on the case, notwithstanding the act is immediate, so long as it is not a willful act; and, upon the authority of that case, we think the present form of action maintainable to recover damages for the injury.

Rule discharged [*i.e.*, the trial court's order that granted the defendant's motion JNOV and dismissed the action was overruled and the jury verdict for the plaintiff reinstated.] — Ed.].

QUESTIONS

(1)   What procedural devices were employed by the parties in *Williams v. Holland* and the cases discussed therein? Do these devices help clarify the substantive law?

(2)   What appears to be the substantive law conclusion of the case? Does it reflect rigidification or liberalization of the forms of action?

(3)   Notice the argument pertaining to the different basis of actions against a co-proprietor who was driving a negligently operated coach and an action against another absent co-proprietor whose servants were present. The common law long ago accepted some theories of vicarious liability; that is a doctrine for holding a non-negligent person liable for the negligence of another. The most common of these doctrines is *respondeat superior* under which a master (employer) is vicariously liable for the negligence of a servant (employee) as to job related injuries. Nevertheless, the common law also held that *respondeat superior* actions must be pleaded as trespass in the case; never in simple trespass. This, then was the background of the defendant's argument that prior actions against actively negligent co-proprietor had been permitted in case rather than trespass; according to the defendant such a pleading was necessary to avoid an absurd result. Does an argument reductio ad absurdum receive a friendlier reception in the next case?

(4)   The inquiring student is likely to wonder just how actions in trespass differed from those in trespass on the case. These cases show that nineteenth century judges were puzzled by that question when the difference continued to be of operative importance, so it is too much to us to figure it out now when the importance is no more. Nevertheless, a comparison of the old decisions demonstrates how lawyers and judges distinguish small but vital details between two cases to reach opposite results that to a lay observer appear contradictory. For example, Lord Kenyon's entire recorded judgment in *Day v. Edwards*, 101 Eng. Rep. 361 (1794) states:

> The distinction between the actions of trespass vi et armis and on the case is perfectly clear. If the injury be committed by the immediate act complained of, the action must be trespass; if the injury be merely consequential upon that act, an action upon the case is the proper remedy.

In 1 Str. 636, it is said, "If a man throw a log into the highway, and in that act it hits me, I may maintain trespass, because it is an immediate wrong: but if, as it lies there, I tumble over it, and receive an injury, I must bring an action upon the case." In the present case the plaintiff complains of the immediate act, and therefore he should have brought trespass.

Day v. Edwards was decided on a demurrer to a complaint and *Williams v. Holland* on a motion JNOV. Is the difference in the litigation setting an adequate basis for applying a different decisional rule?

LETANG v. COOPER
(C.A. 1965) 1 Q.B. 232*

Lord Denning M.R. read the following judgment: On July 10, 1957, the plaintiff was on holiday in Cornwall. She was staying at a hotel and thought she would sunbathe on a piece of grass where cars were parked. While she was lying there the defendant came into the car park driving his Jaguar motor car. He did not see her. The car went over her legs and she was injured.

On February 2, 1961, more than three years after the accident, the plaintiff brought this action against the defendant for damages for loss and injury caused by (1) the negligence of the defendant in driving a motor car and (2) the commission by the defendant of a trespass to the person.

The sole question is whether the action is statute-barred. The plaintiff admits that the action for negligence is barred after three years, but she claims that the action for trespass to the person is not barred until six years have elapsed. The judge has so held and awarded her 575 pounds damages for trespass to the person.

Under the Limitation Act, 1939, the period of limitation was six years in all actions founded "on tort"; but, in 1954, Parliament reduced it to three years in actions for damages for personal injuries, provided that the actions come within these words of section 2(1) of the Law Reform (Limitation of Actions, etc.) Act, 1954: "actions for damages for negligence, nuisance or breach of duty (whether the duty exists by virtue of a contract or of provision made by or under a statute or independently of any contract or any such provision) where the damages claimed by the plaintiff for the negligence, nuisance or breach of duty consist of or include damages in respect of personal injuries to any person."

The plaintiff says that these words do not cover an action for trespass to the person and that therefore the time bar is not the new period of three years, but the old period of six years.

The argument, as it was developed before us, became a direct invitation to this court to go back to the old forms of action and to decide this case by reference to them. The statute bars an action on the case, it is said, after three years, whereas trespass to the person is not barred for six years. The argument was supported by reference to text-writers, such as Salmond on Torts, 13th ed. (1961), p. 790. I must say that if we are, at this distance of time, to revive the distinction between trespass and case, we should get into the most utter confusion. The old common lawyers tied themselves in knots over it, and we should do the same. Let me tell

---

* [Ed. — Queen's Bench Law Reports of the principal English trial court, appeals there-from and certain criminal appeals; decision of the Court of Appeal.]

you some of their contortions. Under the old law, whenever one man injured another by the direct and immediate application of force, the plaintiff could sue the defendant in trespass to the person, without alleging negligence (see *Leame v. Bray*), whereas if the injury was only consequential, he had to sue in case. You will remember the illustration given by Fortescue J. in *Reynolds v. Clarke*: "If a man throws a log into the highway, and in that act it hits me, I may maintain trespass because it is an immediate wrong; but if as it lies there I tumble over it, and receive an injury, I must bring an action upon the case; because it is only prejudicial in consequence." Nowadays, if a man carelessly throws a piece of wood from a house into a roadway, then whether it hits the plaintiff or he tumbles over it the next moment, the action would not be trespass or case, but simply negligence. Another distinction the old lawyers drew was this: if the driver of a horse and gig negligently ran down a passer-by, the plaintiff could sue the driver either in trespass or in case (see *Williams v. Holland*), but if the driver was a servant, the plaintiff could not sue the master in trespass, but only in case: see *Sharrod v. London and North Western Railway Co.* In either case today the action would not be trespass or case, but only negligence.

If we were to bring back these subtleties into the law of limitation, we should produce the most absurd anomalies and all the more so when you bear in mind that under the Fatal Accidents Act the period of limitation is three years from the death. The decision of Elwes J. if correct would produce these results: it would mean that if a motorist ran down two people, killing one and injuring another, the widow would have to bring her action within three years, but the injured person would have six years. [Note: actions arising out of deaths must be brought under a "wrongful death statute", which in England has a three-year limitations. — Ed.] It would mean also that if a lorry driver was in collision at a cross-roads with an owner-driver, an injured passenger would have to bring his action against the employer of the lorry driver within three years, but he would have six years in which to sue the owner-driver. Not least of all the absurdities is a case like the present. It would mean that the plaintiff could get out of the three-year limitation by suing in trespass instead of in negligence.

I must decline, therefore, to go back to the old forms of action in order to construe this statute. I know that in the last century Maitland said "the forms of action we have buried, but they still rule us from their graves" (see Maitland, Forms of Action (1909), p. 296), but we have in this century shaken off their trammels. These forms of action have served their day. They did at one time form a guide to substantive rights; but they do so no longer. Lord Atkin, in *United Australia Ltd. v. Barclays Bank Ltd.*, told us what to do about them: "When these ghosts of the past stand in the path of justice clanking their mediaeval chains the proper course for the judge is to pass through them undeterred."

The truth is that the distinction between trespass and case is obsolete. We have a different sub-division altogether. Instead of dividing actions for personal injuries into trespass (direct damage) or case (consequential damage), we divide the causes of action now according as the defendant did the injury intentionally or unintentionally. If one man intentionally applies force directly to another, the plaintiff has a cause of action in assault and battery, or, if you so please to describe it, in trespass to the person. "The least touching of another in anger is a battery," *per* Holt C.J. in *Cole v. Turner*. If he does not inflict injury intentionally, but only unintentionally, the plaintiff has no cause of action today in trespass. His only cause of action is in negligence, and then only on proof of want of reasonable care. If the plaintiff cannot prove want of reasonable care, he may have no cause of action at all. Thus, it is not enough nowadays for the plaintiff to plead that "the defendant shot the plaintiff." He must also allege that he did it intentionally or negligently. If intentional, it is the tort of assault and battery. If negligent and causing damage, it is the tort of negligence.

The modern law on this subject was well expounded by Diplock J. in *Fowler v. Lanning*, with which I fully agree. But I would go this one step further: when the injury is not inflicted intentionally, but negligently, I would say that the only cause of action is negligence and not trespass. If it were trespass, it would be actionable without proof of damage; and that is not the law today.

In my judgment, therefore, the only cause of action in the present case, where the injury was unintentional, is negligence and is barred by reason of the express provision of the statute. . . .

I come, therefore, to the clear conclusion that the plaintiff's cause of action here is barred by the Statute of Limitations. Her only cause of action here, in my judgment, where the damage was unintentional, was negligence and not trespass to the person. It is therefore barred by the word "negligence" in the statute . . .

DANCKWERTS, L.J. [Agrees with Lord Denning.]

DIPLOCK L.J. read the following judgment: A cause of action is simply a factual situation the existence of which entitles one person to obtain from the court a remedy against another person. Historically, the means by which the remedy was obtained varied with the nature of the factual situation and causes of action were divided into categories according to the "form of action" by which the remedy was obtained in the particular kind of factual situation which constituted the cause of action. But that is legal history, not current law. If A., by failing to exercise reasonable care, inflicts direct personal injury upon B., those facts constitute a cause of action on the part of B. against A. for damages in respect of such personal injuries. The remedy for this cause of action could, before 1873, have been obtained by alternative forms of action, namely, originally either trespass vi et armis or trespass on the case, later either trespass to the person or negligence: (see Bullen & Leake, Precedents of Pleading, 3rd ed. (1868)). Certain procedural consequences, the importance of which diminished considerably after the Common Law Procedure Act, 1852, flowed from the plaintiff's pleader's choice of the form of action used. The Judicature Act, 1873, abolished forms of action. It did not affect causes of action; so it was convenient for lawyers and legislators to continue to use, to describe the various categories of factual situations which entitled one person to obtain from the court a remedy against another, the names of the various "forms of action" by which formerly the remedy appropriate to the particular category of factual situation was obtained. But it is essential to realize that when, since 1873, the name of a form of action is used to identify a cause of action, it is used as a convenient and succinct description of a particular category of factual situation which entitles one person to obtain from the court a remedy against another person. To forget this will indeed encourage the old forms of action to rule us from their graves.

If A., by failing to exercise reasonable care, inflicts direct personal injuries upon B., it is permissible today to describe this factual situation indifferently, either as a cause of action in negligence or as a cause of action in trespass, and the action brought to obtain a remedy for this factual situation as an action for negligence or an action for trespass to the person — though I agree with Lord Denning M.R. that today "negligence" is the expression to be preferred. But no procedural consequences flow from the choice of description by the pleader: see *Fowler v. Lanning*. They are simply alternative ways of describing the same factual situation.

In the judgment under appeal, Elwes J. has held that the Law Reform (Limitation of Actions, etc.) Act, 1954, has by section 2(1) created an important difference in the remedy to which B. is entitled in the factual situation postulated according to whether he chooses to describe it as negligence or as trespass to the person. If he selects the former description, the limitation period is three years; if he selects the latter, the limitation period is six years. The terms of the subsection have already been cited, and I need not repeat them.

. . .

It is not, I think, necessary to consider whether there is today any respect in which a cause of action for unintentional as distinct from intentional trespass to the person is not equally aptly described as a cause of action for negligence. The difference stressed by Elwes J. that actual damage caused by failure to exercise reasonable care forms an essential element in the cause of action for negligence, but does not in the cause of action in trespass to the person, is, I think, more apparent than real when the trespass is unintentional; for, since the duty of care, whether in negligence or in unintentional trespass to the person, is to take reasonable care to avoid causing actual damage to one's neighbour, there is no breach of the duty unless actual damage is caused. Actual damage is thus a necessary ingredient in unintentional as distinct from intentional trespass to the person. But whether this be so or not, the subsection which falls to be construed is concerned only with actions in which actual damage in the form of personal injuries has in fact been sustained by the plaintiff. Where this factor is present, every factual situation which falls within the description "trespass to the person" is, where the trespass is unintentional, equally aptly described as negligence. I am therefore of opinion that the facts pleaded in the present action make it an action "for negligence" . . . where the damages claimed by the plaintiff for the negligence . . . consist of or "include damages in respect of personal injuries to" the plaintiff, within the meaning of the subsection, and that the limitation period was three years.

. . .

The Act is a limitation Act; it relates only to procedure. It does not divest any person of rights recognized by law; it limits the period within which a person can obtain a remedy from the courts for infringement of them. The mischief against which all limitation Acts are directed is delay in commencing legal proceedings; for delay may lead to injustice, particularly where the ascertainment of the relevant facts depends upon oral testimony. This mischief, the only mischief against which the section is directed, is the same in all actions in which damages are claimed in respect of personal injuries. It is independent of any category into which the cause of action which gives rise to such a claim falls. I see no reason for approaching the construction of an enactment of this character with any other presumption than that Parliament used the words it selected in their ordinary meaning and meant what it chose to say.

NOTES AND QUESTIONS

(1)   The majority view of *Letang v. Cooper* clearly separates the law of negligent torts from the law of intentional torts, thus defining the bases for two major branches of the law of torts. Nowadays, except in a few jurisdictions referred to in Note 4, *infra*, mere negligent behavior causing personal injury does not give rise to a cause of action in trespass or its modern equivalent — intentional tort. The only action would be in negligence. As both *Williams v. Holland* and *Letang v. Cooper* demonstrate, however, the separate torts emerged shakily from the confused doctrines of trespass and trespass on the case.

(2)   Under what circumstances would Diplock's view permit a plaintiff to maintain a cause of action that would not be sustainable under the view of Lord Denning? Is it conceivable that a victim of an unintentional trespass to the person would be entitled to a remedy at law in the absence of "personal injuries to any person?"

(3)   *Letang v. Cooper* introduces the crucial role statutes of limitation may play in tort litigation. What effect do these statutes have on common law causes of actions? Why do they exist? What discretion is available to judges in applying them? How did the operation of the statute help clarify the substantive law of torts in England? What is the substantive point of the case?

Statutes of limitation are enacted by legislatures. Because of diverse views of different legislatures, the specific period of limitation that applies to each cause of action may vary from jurisdiction to jurisdiction. At this point it would be instructive for you to examine the structure of the statute(s) of limitation of your own, or one particular, jurisdiction.

(4)   American state court judges are frequently influenced by common law decisions from other courts but are not bound to follow them. At one time, American courts commonly looked to English decisions for guidance and vice versa, but this probably occurs less frequently now. It remains very common, however, for common law courts of the British Commonwealth of Nations to be influenced by English decisions and, to some extent, vice versa. For example, in an omitted portion of his *Letang v. Cooper* judgment, Diplock, L.J. referred approvingly to a judgment from the supreme court of the state of Victoria in Australia.

Cross-fertilization enriches the law and helps it progress with considerable uniformity among jurisdictions. Nevertheless, the discretion possessed by each independent court to accept or reject the views of other independent courts also virtually assures diversity in the common law among the jurisdictions. For example, the plaintiff in *Letang v. Cooper* would probably have prevailed in South Australia, because South Australian law seems to permit a plaintiff to proceed either in negligence or in trespass on facts such as these. See, for example, *Venning v. Chin*, (1974) 10 S.A.S.R. 299 (F.C.). In the same vein, Canada still permits actions in the form of trespass when the nature of the act is negligent and not willful. See *Eisner v. Maxwell*, (1951) 1 D.L.R. 816. In the United States, at least Alabama also permits such an action. See *Honeycutt v. Louis Pizitz Dry Goods Co.*, 180 So. 91 (Ala. 1938), reaffirmed, *McDonald v. Royal Globe Ins. Co.*, 413 So.2d 1046 (Ala. 1982).

(5) The reading of opinions may familiarize you with the style, if not the character, of particular judges. Lord Denning, writer of the principal judgment in *Letang v. Cooper*, is surely one of the most notable English jurists of the twentieth century. He was remarkably less bound to the rigidities of *stare decisis* than were most English judges. Denning sat on the Court of Appeal, then in the House of Lords, and later again on the Court of Appeal as Master of the Rolls, a position with both administrative and judicial functions.

Perhaps the most important torts judgment issued by an English jurist in the twentieth century was that of Lord Atkin in *Donoghue v. Stevenson*, § 4.02, *infra.* It fairly dominates the development of the English law of negligence since 1932.

In the United States, Benjamin N. Cardozo influenced the law of torts more than any other twentieth-century judge. His influence was mainly manifested in well-known opinions he wrote as a member of the New York Court of Appeals. See, e.g., *Palsgraf v. Long Island Railroad*, (see § 4.02, *infra*), and *MacPherson v. Buick Motor Company* (see § 14.01, *infra*). To a lesser extent, his influence continued during his subsequent tenure on the United States Supreme Court. In the late nineteenth and early twentieth centuries, Oliver Wendell Holmes, Jr. exercised great influence on the law while sitting on the Supreme Judicial Court of Massachusetts and later as a member of the United States Supreme Court. During their state court tenures, Holmes was the conservative and Cardozo the liberal, as far as tort issues were concerned. Cardozo replaced Holmes on the Supreme Court upon the latter's resignation in 1932 and served until his own death in 1938. There, both were social liberals within the thought of their times.

In the middle portion of the twentieth century, Judge Robert Traynor of the California Supreme Court probably influenced the American law of torts more than any other judge. His most notable achievement was advocacy of enterprise liability in *Greenman v. Yuba Power Products, Inc.* (see § 14.03, *infra*) and other cases.

(6) The judgments in *Letang v. Cooper* demonstrate how English opinions are rendered. Rather than have an opinion of the court and dissenting opinions, the system calls for each judge either to write an individual judgment or to join in the judgment of another. The rule of the case, and ultimately the status of the law, is derived by compiling the individual positions of the judges on each point. It takes a majority to prevail on a point. For the purposes of this book, some judgments are omitted. Unless otherwise noted, however, the outcome of all cases was consistent with the judgments presented.

Fortunately for American law students, most American opinions are rendered *per curiam*; that is, by the court. Points of disagreement are highlighted by dissenting and concurring opinions.

(7) The clarifying rule of *Letang v. Cooper* has not been adopted everywhere. For example, Alabama courts continue to distinguish between actions in trespass and actions on the case based upon the dichotomy between direct and indirect consequences of negligent acts. See, *e.g., Archie v. Enterprise Hospital and Nursing Home*, 508 So. 2d 693, 695 (Ala. 1987).

Chapter 4

NEGLIGENCE OVERVIEW

§ 4.01 INTRODUCTION

In strict legal analysis, negligence means more than heedless or careless conduct, whether in omission or commission: it properly connotes the complex concept of duty, breach and damages thereby suffered by the person to whom the duty was owing: on all this the liability depends. . . .

Lockgelly Iron & Coal Co. v. McMullan, (1934) A.C. 1, 25 (H.L.), per Lord Wright.

Lord Wright's statement illustrates that the law of negligence ultimately escaped the confines of the forms of action, even as relaxed by trespass on the case, and evolved into a modern more fluid cause of action. Lord Wright identified duty, breach and damages as elements of the negligence cause of action. To that may be added causation, including its two confusing aspects, cause-in-fact and proximate causation. In sum, the elements of a prima facie case of negligence are duty, breach, causation, and damages. If the complaint does not state facts sufficient to allege the existence of each and every element of the cause of action, the plaintiff has failed to make a prima facie case and a demurrer (or motion to dismiss for failure to state a cause of action) by the defendant will be sustained. If the complaint is sufficient but the plaintiff thereafter is unable to prove each and every element of a properly alleged cause of action, the action will fail at trial.

This chapter presents materials to introduce the broad and essential meaning of these elements. Succeeding chapters examine each of them in more detail.

§ 4.02 DUTY

"Negligence [represents] the more modern view that a man's freedom of action is subject only to the obligation not to infringe any duty of care which he owes to others."

Diplock, J.[1]

PROBLEM A

The plaintiff filed the following complaint:

> The plaintiff, who is a fishwife and who was about eight months pregnant, was a passenger on a tramway car which was proceeding in the direction of Colinton along the Colinton Road, which was taken as a southwesterly direction, and which stopped at a stopping place at a short distance before Colinton Road is joined at right angles by Glenlockhart Road from the southeast, that is, on the near side of the tramcar. The

---

[1] Fowler v. Lanning, [1959] 1 Q.B. 426.

plaintiff alighted and went round the near side and front of the tramcar, in order to lift her fish-basket from the off-side of the driver's platform. Meantime, the motorcyclist, travelling in the same direction as the tramcar, had come up and, as the plaintiff was getting her basket, he passed on the near side of the tramcar and, when mostly across the opening of Glenlockhart Road, his cycle collided with a motor car, which had been travelling in the opposite direction, but had turned across the path of the cycle in order to enter Glenlockhart Road. The cyclist, who was travelling at an excessive speed, was thrown on to the street and sustained injuries from which he died. Upon hearing the crash, plaintiff ran back around the tram to its near side to a point where she saw the wreckage about forty or fifty feet distance. She then ran over to the wreckage where she came upon the motorcyclist's dead body that was mutilated and covered with gore. Plaintiff was shocked and revulsed by the sight. She immediately became emotionally distraught and took to her bed. The next day her unborn child miscarried and was born dead. Plaintiff has suffered emotional and mental pain and anguish and has been deprived of her capacity to sell fish and to make a home for her husband. Wherefore, plaintiff demands relief in the amount of £75.

The defendant, who is the executor of the deceased motorcyclist's estate, filed this motion:

Wherefore plaintiff's complaint alleges no fact that imposed a duty upon the defendant to exercise care for the sake of the plaintiff, the defendant demurs to said complaint and moves the honorable court to dismiss said action.

(a) You are the trial court judge. The cases which follow are brought to your attention by the advocates. Write a brief opinion sustaining or overruling the demurrer.

(b) Assume that the demurrer was sustained. Redraft the complaint in words that would withstand a demurrer. When in the litigation process will the critical issue be raised? Does delaying the timing bestow any advantage upon the plaintiff?

HEAVEN v. PENDER
[1883] 11 Q.B.D. 503 (C.A.)[2]

BRETT, M.R. [This case was tried and judgment entered for the plaintiff on a jury verdict. An intermediate appellate court reversed and dismissed the action. The plaintiff then brought this appeal.] In this case the plaintiff was a workman in the employ of Gray, a ship painter. Gray entered into a contract with a shipowner whose ship was in the defendant's dock to paint the outside of his ship. The defendant, the dock owner, supplied, under a contract with the shipowner, an ordinary stage to be slung in the ordinary way outside the ship for the purpose of painting her. It must have been known to the defendant's servants, if they had considered the matter at all, that the stage would be put to immediate use, that it would not be used by the shipowner, but that it would be used by such a person as the plaintiff, a working ship painter. The ropes by which the stage was slung, and

---

[2] [Ed. — Queens Bench Division Law Reports of the principal English trial court and certain crown cases; decision of the Court of Appeal.]

which were supplied as a part of the instrument by the defendant, had been scorched and were unfit for use and were supplied without a reasonably careful attention to their condition. When the plaintiff began to use the stage the ropes broke, the stage fell, and the plaintiff was injured. The Divisional Court held that the plaintiff could not recover against the defendant. The plaintiff appealed. The action is in form and substance an action for negligence. That the stage was, through want of attention of the defendant's servants, supplied in a state unsafe for use is not denied. But want of attention amounting to a want of ordinary care is not a good cause of action, although injury ensue from such want, unless the person charged with such want of ordinary care had a duty to the person complaining to use ordinary care in respect of the matter called in question. Actionable negligence consists in the neglect of the use of ordinary care or skill towards a person to whom the defendant owes the duty of observing ordinary care and skill, by which neglect the plaintiff, without contributory negligence on his part, has suffered injury to his person or property. The question in this case is whether the defendant owed such a duty to the plaintiff.

If a person contracts with another to use ordinary care or skill towards him or his property the obligation need not be considered in the light of a duty; it is an obligation of contract. It is undoubted, however, that there may be the obligation of such a duty from one person to another although there is no contract between them with regard to such duty. Two drivers meeting have no contract with each other, but under certain circumstances they have a reciprocal duty towards each other. So two ships navigating the sea. So a railway company which has contracted with one person to carry another has no contract with the person carried but has a duty towards that person. So the owner or occupier of house or land who permits a person or persons to come to his house or land has no contract with such person or persons, but has a duty towards him or them. . . .

We have not in this case to consider the question of a fraudulent misrepresentation express or implied, which is a well recognised head of law. The questions which we have to solve in this case are — what is the proper definition of the relation between two persons other than the relation established by contract, or fraud, which imposes on the one of them a duty towards the other to observe, with regard to the person or property of such other, such ordinary care or skill as may be necessary to prevent injury to his person or property; and whether the present case falls within such definition. When two drivers or two ships are approaching each other, such a relation arises between them when they are approaching each other in such a manner that, unless they use ordinary care and skill to avoid it, there will be danger of an injurious collision between them. This relation is established in such circumstances between them, not only if it be proved that they actually know and think of this danger, but whether such proof be made or not.

. . .

In the case of a railway company carrying a passenger with whom it has not entered into the contract of carriage the law implies the duty, because it must be obvious that unless ordinary care and skill be used the personal safety of the passenger must be endangered. With regard to the condition in which an owner or occupier leaves his house or property, other phraseology has been used, which it is necessary to consider. If a man opens his shop or warehouse to customers it is said that he invites them to enter, and that this invitation raises the relation between them which imposes on the inviter the duty of using reasonable care so to keep his house or warehouse that it may not endanger the person or property of the person invited. This is in a sense an accurate phrase, and as applied to the circumstances a sufficiently accurate phrase. Yet it is not accurate if the word "invitation" be used in its ordinary sense. By opening a shop you do not really invite, you do not ask A. B. to come in to buy; you intimate to him that if it pleases him to come in he will find things which you are willing to sell. So, in the case of shop, warehouse, road, or premises, the phrase has been used that if you permit a person to enter them you impose on yourself a duty not to lay a trap for him. This, again, is in a sense a true statement of the duty arising from the relation constituted by the permission to enter. It is not a statement of what causes the relation which raises the duty. What causes the relation is the permission to enter and the entry. But it is not a strictly accurate statement of the duty. To lay a trap means in ordinary language to do something with an intention. Yet it is clear that the duty extends to a danger the result of negligence without intention. And with regard to both these phrases, though each covers the circumstances to which it is particularly applied, yet it does not cover the other set of circumstances from which an exactly similar legal liability is inferred. It follows, as it seems to me, that there must be some larger proposition which involves and covers both sets of circumstances.

The logic of inductive reasoning requires that where two major propositions lead to exactly similar minor premises there must be a more remote and larger premises which embraces both of the major propositions. That, in the present consideration, is, as it seems to me, the same proposition which will cover the similar legal liability inferred in the cases of collision and carriage. The proposition which these recognised cases suggest, and which is, therefore, to be deduced from them, is that whenever one person is by circumstances placed in such a position with regard to another that every one of ordinary sense who did think would at once recognize that if he did not use ordinary care and skill in his own conduct with regard to those circumstances he would cause danger of injury to the person or property of the other, a duty arises to use ordinary care and skill to avoid such danger. Without displacing the other propositions to which allusion has been made as applicable to the particular circumstances in respect of which they have been enunciated, this proposition includes, I think, all the recognised cases of liability. It is the only proposition which covers them all. It may, therefore, safely be affirmed to be a true proposition, unless some obvious case can be stated in which the liability must be admitted to exist, and which yet is not within this proposition. There is no such case. . . .

I cannot conceive that if the facts were proved which would make out the proposition I have enunciated, the law can be that there would be no liability. Unless that be true, the proposition must be true. If it be the rule the present case is clearly within it. This case is also, I agree, within that which seems to me to be a minor proposition — namely, the proposition which has been often acted upon, that there was in a sense, an invitation of the plaintiff by the defendant, to use the stage. The appeal must, in my opinion, be allowed, and judgment must be entered for the plaintiff.

COTTON, L.J. Bowen, L.J., concurs in the judgment I am about to read.

In this case the defendant was the owner of a dock for the repair of ships, and provided for use in the dock the stages necessary to enable the outside of the ship to be painted while in the dock, and the stages which were to be used only in the dock were appliances provided by the dock owner as appurtenant to the dock and its use. After the stage was handed over to the shipowner it no longer remained under the control of the dock owner. But when ships were received into the dock for repair and provided with stages for the work on the ships which was to be executed there, all those who came to the vessels for the purpose of painting and otherwise repairing them were there for business in which the dock owner was interested, and they, in my opinion, must be considered as invited by the dock owner to use the dock and all appliances provided by the dock owner as incident to the use of the dock. To these persons, in my opinion, the dock owner was under an obligation to take reasonable care that at the time the appliances provided for immediate use in the dock were provided by him they were in a fit state to be used — that is, in such a state as not to expose those who might use them for the repair of the ship to any danger or risk not necessarily incident to the service in which they are employed. . . .

For any neglect of those having control of the ship and the appliances he would not be liable, and to establish his liability it must be proved that the defect which caused the accident existed at the time when the article was supplied by the dock-owner. . . .

This decides this appeal in favor of the plaintiff, and I am unwilling to concur with the Master of the Rolls in laying down unnecessarily the larger principle which he entertains, inasmuch as there are many cases in which the principle was impliedly negatived. . . .

. . . .

For the reasons stated I agree that the plaintiff is entitled to judgment, though I do not entirely concur with the reasoning of the Master of the Rolls.

NOTES

(1)   Given the judgment of Cotton and Bowen, what is the basis for the decision of *Heaven v. Pender*? Brett plainly states one of his "minor propositions" in the last paragraph of his judgment. What are the others? Why do Cotton and Bowen reject Brett's "larger proposition," if they do?

(2)   Brett's opinion explicitly portrays the inductive process that is the central evolutionary force in the advance of the common law. This process was elaborated by Lord Diplock in *Home Office v. Dorset Yacht Co. Ltd.*, [1970] App. Cas. 1004 [H.L.], this section.

DONOGHUE v. STEVENSON
[1932] A.C. 562 (House of Lords)[3]

APPEAL against an interlocutor of the Second Division of the Court of Session in Scotland recalling an interlocutor of the Lord Ordinary (Lord Moncrieff). [In modern American practice a Scottish "interlocutor" would be referred to as an "order" of the court. — Ed.]

---

[3] [Ed. — Appeal Cases Law Reports, decision of House of Lords.]
[4] [Reserved]

By an action brought in the Court of Session the appellant, who was a shop assistant, sought to recover damages from the respondent, who was a manufacturer of aerated waters, for injuries she suffered as a result of consuming part of the contents of a bottle of ginger-beer which had been manufactured by the respondent, and which contained the decomposed remains of a snail. The appellant by her condescendence [i.e., her complaint. — Ed.] averred that the bottle of ginger-beer was purchased for the appellant by a friend in a café at Paisley, which was occupied by one Minchella; that the bottle was made of dark opaque glass and that the appellant had no reason to suspect that it contained anything but pure ginger-beer; that the said Minchella poured some of the ginger-beer out into a tumbler, and that the appellant drank some of the contents of the tumbler; that her friend was then proceeding to pour the remainder of the contents of the bottle into the tumbler when a snail, which was in a state of decomposition, floated out of the bottle; that as a result of the nauseating sight of the snail in such circumstances, and in consequence of the impurities in the ginger-beer which she had already consumed, the appellant suffered from shock and severe gastro-enteritis. The appellant further averred that the ginger-beer was manufactured by the respondent to be sold as a drink to the public (including the appellant); that it was bottled by the respondent and labeled by him with a label bearing his name; and that the bottles were thereafter sealed with a metal cap by the respondent. She further averred that it was the duty of the respondent to provide a system of working his business which would not allow snails to get into his ginger-beer bottles, and that it was also his duty to provide an efficient system of inspection of the bottles before the ginger-beer was filled into them, and that he had failed in both these duties and had so caused the accident.

The respondent objected that these averments were irrelevant and insufficient to support the conclusions of the summons.

The Lord Ordinary held that the averments disclosed a good cause of action and allowed a proof.

The Second Division by a majority (the Lord Justice-Clerk, Lord Ormidale, and Lord Anderson; Lord Hunter dissenting) recalled the interlocutor of the Lord Ordinary and dismissed the action.

LORD BUCKMASTER. [The following portion of Buckmaster's judgment makes a valuable statement about sources of legal authority.]

Before examining the merits two comments are desirable: (1.) That the appellant's case rests solely on the ground of a tort based not on fraud but on negligence; and (2.) that throughout the appeal the case has been argued on the basis, undisputed by the Second Division and never questioned by counsel for the appellant or by any of your Lordships, that the English and the Scots law on the subject are identical. It is therefore upon the English law alone that I have considered the matter, and in my opinion it is on the English law alone that in the circumstances we ought to proceed.

The law applicable is the common law, and, though its principles are capable of application to meet new conditions not contemplated when the law was laid down, these principles cannot be changed nor can additions be made to them because any particular meritorious case seems outside their ambit.

Now the common law must be sought in law books by writers of authority and in judgments of the judges entrusted with its administration. The law books give no assistance [in this case], because the work of living authors, however deservedly eminent, cannot be used as authority, though the opinions they express may demand attention; and the ancient books do not assist. I turn, therefore, to the decided cases to see if they can be construed so as to support the appellant's case. One of the earliest is the case of Langridge v. Levy. It is a case often quoted and variously explained. There a man sold a gun which he knew was dangerous for the use of the purchaser's son. The gun exploded in the son's hands, and he was held to have a right of action in tort against the gunmaker. How far it is from the present case can be seen from the judgment of Parke B., who, in delivering the judgment of the Court, used these words: "We should pause before we made a precedent by our decision which would be an authority for an action against the vendors, even of such instruments and articles (as are dangerous in themselves,) at the suit of any person whomsoever into whose hands they might happen to pass, and who should be injured thereby"; and in Longmeid v. Holliday the same eminent judge points out that the earlier case was based on a fraudulent misstatement, and he expressly repudiates the view that it has any wider application. The case of Langridge v. Levy, therefore, can be dismissed from consideration with the comment that it is rather surprising it has so often been cited for a proposition it cannot support.

[Buckmaster voted to dismiss the appeal.]

Lord Atkin. My Lords, the sole question for determination in this case is legal: Do the averments made by the pursuer in her pleading, if true, disclose a cause of action? I need not restate the particular facts. The question is whether the manufacturer of an article of drink sold by him to a distributor, in circumstances which prevent the distributor or the ultimate purchaser or consumer from discovering by inspection any defect, is under any legal duty to the ultimate purchaser or consumer to take reasonable care that the article is free from defect likely to cause injury to health. I do not think a more important problem has occupied your Lordships in your judicial capacity: important both because of its bearing on public health and because of the practical test which it applies to the system under which it arises

In the present case we are not concerned with the breach of the duty; if a duty exists, that would be a question of fact which is sufficiently averred and for present purposes must be assumed. We are solely concerned with the question whether, as a matter of law in the circumstances alleged, the defender owed any duty to the pursuer to take care.

It is remarkable how difficult it is to find in the English authorities statements of general application defining the relations between parties that give rise to the duty. The Courts are concerned with the particular relations which come before them in actual litigation, and it is sufficient to say whether the duty exists in those circumstances. The result is that the Courts have been engaged upon an elaborate classification of duties as they exist in respect of property, whether real or personal, with further divisions as to ownership, occupation or control, and distinctions based on the particular relations of the one side or the other, whether manufacturer, salesman or landlord, customer, tenant, stranger, and so on. In this way it can be ascertained at any time whether the law recognizes a duty, but only where the case can be referred to some particular species which has been examined and classified. And yet the duty which is common to all the cases where liability is established must logically be based upon some element common to the cases where it is found to exist. To seek a complete logical definition of the general principle is probably to go beyond the function of the judge, for the more general the definition the more likely it is to omit essentials or to introduce non-essentials. The attempt was made by Brett M.R. in Heaven v. Pender, in a definition to which I will later refer. As framed, it was demonstrably too wide, though it appears to me, if properly limited, to be capable of affording a valuable practical guide.

At present I content myself with pointing out that in English law there must be, and is, some general conception of relations giving rise to a duty of care, of which the particular cases found in the books are but instances. The liability for negligence, whether you style it such or treat it as in other systems as a species of "culpa," is no doubt based upon a general public sentiment of moral wrongdoing for which the offender must pay. But acts or omissions which any moral code would censure cannot in a practical world be treated so as to give a right to every person injured by them to demand relief. In this way rules of law arise which limit the range of complainants and the extent of their remedy.

The rule that you are to love your neighbour becomes in law, you must not injure your neighbour; and the lawyer's question, Who is my neighbour? receives a restricted reply. You must take reasonable care to avoid acts or omissions which you can reasonably foresee would be likely to injure your neighbour. Who, then, in law is my neighbour? The answer seems to be — persons who are so closely and directly affected by my act that I ought reasonably to have them in contemplation as being so affected when I am directing my mind to the acts or omissions which are called in question. This appears to me to be the doctrine of Heaven v. Pender as laid down by Lord Esher (then Brett M.R.) when it is limited by the notion of proximity introduced by Lord Esher himself and A. L. Smith L.J. in Le Lievre v. Gould. Lord Esher says: "That case established that, under certain circumstances, one man may owe a duty to another, even though there is no contract between them. If one man is near to another, or is near to the property of another, a duty lies upon him not to do that which may cause a personal injury to that other, or may injure his property." So A. L. Smith L.J.: "The decision of Heaven v. Pender was founded upon the principle, that a duty to take due care did arise when the person or property of one was in such proximity to the person or property of another that, if due care was not taken, damage might be done by the one to the other." I think that this sufficiently states the truth if proximity be not confined to mere physical proximity, but be used, as I think it was intended, to extend to such close and direct relations that the act complained of directly affects a person whom the person alleged to be bound to take care would know would be directly affected by his careless act.

That this is the sense in which nearness of "proximity" was intended by Lord Esher is obvious from his own illustration in Heaven v. Pender of the application of his doctrine to the sale of goods. "This" (i.e., the rule he has just formulated) "includes the case of goods, etc., supplied to be used immediately by a particular person or persons, or one of a class of persons, where it would be obvious to the person supplying, if he thought, that the goods would in all probability be used at once by such persons before a reasonable opportunity for discovering any defect which might exist, and where the thing supplied would be of such a nature that a neglect of ordinary care or skill as to its condition or the manner supplying it would probably cause danger to the person or property of the person for whose use it was supplied, and who was about to use it. It would exclude a case in which the goods are supplied under circumstances in which it would be a chance by whom they would be used or whether they would be used or not, or whether they would be used before there would probably be means of observing any defect, or where the goods would be of such a nature that a want of care or skill as to their condition or the manner of supplying them would not probably produce danger of injury to person or property."

I draw particular attention to the fact that Lord Esher emphasizes the necessity of goods having to be "used immediately" and "used at once before a reasonable opportunity of inspection." This is obviously to exclude the possibility of goods having their condition altered by lapse of time, and to call attention to the proximate relationship, which may be too remote where inspection even of the person using, certainly of an intermediate person, may reasonably be interposed.

With this necessary qualification of proximate relationship as explained in Le Lievre v. Gould, I think the judgment of Lord Esher expresses the law of England; without the qualification, I think the majority of the Court in Heaven v. Pender were justified in thinking the principle was expressed in too general terms. There will no doubt arise cases where it will be difficult to determine whether the contemplated relationship is so close that the duty arises. But in the class of case now before the Court I cannot conceive any difficulty to arise.

NOTE

In *Donoghue* the plaintiff's appeal was approved; consequently, the plaintiff was permitted to take the case to trial on various other issues including whether the defendant had breached the duty and whether in fact there was a snail in the ginger beer. As it so often happens after a point of law is resolved on interlocutory appeal, the case was ultimately disposed of without trial.

PALSGRAF v. LONG ISLAND RAILROAD CO.
New York Court of Appeals
248 N.Y. 339, 162 N.E. 99 (1928)

[Action by Helen Palsgraf against the Long Island Railroad Company. Judgment entered on the verdict of a jury in favor of the plaintiff was affirmed by the Appellate Division by a divided court (222 App. Div. 166, 225 N.Y.S. 412), and defendant appeals.]

CARDOZO, C. J.

Plaintiff was standing on a platform of defendant's railroad after buying a ticket to go to Rockaway Beach. A train stopped at the station, bound for another place. Two men ran forward to catch it. One of the men reached the platform of the car without mishap, though the train was already moving. The other man, carrying a package, jumped aboard the car, but seemed unsteady as if about to fall. A guard on the car, who had held the door open, reached forward to help him in, and another guard on the platform pushed him from behind. In this act, the package was dislodged, and fell upon the rails. It was a package of small size, about fifteen inches long, and was covered by a newspaper. In fact it contained fireworks, but there was nothing in its appearance to give notice of its contents. The fireworks when they fell exploded. The shock of the explosion threw down some scales at the other end of the platform many feet away. The scales struck the plaintiff, causing injuries for which she sues.

The conduct of the defendant's guard, if a wrong in its relation to the holder of the package, was not a wrong in its relation to the plaintiff, standing far away. Relatively to her it was not negligence at all. Nothing in the situation gave notice that the falling package had in it the potency of peril to persons thus removed. Negligence is not actionable unless it involves the invasion of a legally protected interest, the violation of a right. "Proof of negligence in the air, so to speak, will not do." Pollock, Torts (11th Ed.) p. 455 . . . The plaintiff, as she stood upon the platform of the station, might claim to be protected against intentional invasion of her bodily security. Such invasion is not charged. She might claim to be protected against unintentional invasion by conduct involving in the thought of reasonable men an unreasonable hazard that such invasion would ensue. These, from the point of view of the law, were the bounds of her immunity, with perhaps some rare exceptions, survivals for the most part of ancient forms of liability, where conduct is held to be at the peril of the actor. Sullivan v. Dunham, 161 N.Y. 290, 55 N. E. 923, 76 Am. St. Rep. 274, 47 L. R. A. 715. If no hazard was apparent to the eye of ordinary vigilance, an act innocent and harmless, at least to outward seeming, with reference to her, did not take to itself the quality of a tort because it happened to be a wrong, though apparently not one involving the risk of bodily insecurity, with reference to some one else. "In every instance, before negligence can be predicated of a given act, back of the act must be sought and found a duty to the individual complaining, the observance of which would have averted or avoided the injury." McSherry, C. J., in West Virginia Central & P. R. Co. v. State, 96 Md. 652, 666, 54 A. 669, 671 (61 L. R. A. 574). "The ideas of negligence and duty are strictly correlative." Bowen, L. J., in Thomas v. Quartermaine, 18 Q. B. D. 685, 694. The plaintiff sues in her own right for a wrong personal to her, and not as the vicarious beneficiary of a breach of duty to another.

A different conclusion will involve us, and swiftly too, in a maze of contradictions. A guard stumbles over a package which has been left upon a platform. It seems to be a bundle of newspapers. It turns out to be a can of dynamite. To the eye of ordinary vigilance, the bundle is abandoned waste, which may be kicked or trod on with impunity. Is a passenger at the other end of the platform protected by the law against the unsuspected hazard concealed beneath the waste? If not, is the result to be any different, so far as the distant passenger is concerned, when the guard stumbles over a valise which a truckman or a porter has left upon the walk? The passenger far away, if the victim of a wrong at all, has a cause of action, not derivative, but original and primary. His claim to be protected against invasion of his bodily security is neither greater nor less because the act resulting in the invasion is a wrong to another far removed.

In this case, the rights that are said to have been violated, the interests said to have been invaded, are not even of the same order. The man was not injured in his person nor even put in danger. The purpose of the act, as well as its effect, was to make his person safe. If there was a wrong to him at all, which may very well be doubted, it was a wrong to a property interest only, the safety of his package. Out of this wrong to property, which threatened an injury to nothing else, there has passed, we are told, to the plaintiff by derivation or succession a right of action for the invasion of an interest of another order, the right to bodily security. The diversity of interests emphasizes the futility of the effort to build the plaintiff's right upon the basis of a wrong to some one else. The gain is one of emphasis, for a like result would follow if the interests were the same. Even then, the orbit of the danger as disclosed to the eye of reasonable vigilance would be the orbit of the duty. One who jostles one's neighbor in a crowd does not invade the rights of others standing at the outer fringe when the unintended contact casts a bomb upon the ground. The wrongdoer as to them is the man who carries the bomb, not the one who explodes it without suspicion of the danger. Life will have to be made over, and human nature transformed, before prevision so extravagant can be accepted as the norm of conduct, the customary standard to which behavior must conform.

The argument for the plaintiff is built upon the shifting meanings of such words as "wrong" and "wrongful," and shares their instability. What the plaintiff must show is "a wrong" to herself; i.e., a violation of her own right, and not merely a wrong to some one else, nor conduct "wrongful" because unsocial, but not "a wrong" to any one. We are told that one who drives at reckless speed through a crowded city street is guilty of a negligent act and therefore of a wrongful one, irrespective of the consequences. Negligent the act is, and wrongful in the sense that it is unsocial, but wrongful and unsocial in relation to other travelers, only because the eye of vigilance perceives the risk of damage. If the same act were to be committed on a speedway or a race course, it would lose its wrongful quality.

The risk reasonably to be perceived defines the duty to be obeyed, and risk imports relation; it is risk to another or to others within the range of apprehension. Seavey, Negligence, Subjective or Objective, 41 H. L. Rv. 6; Boronkay v. Robinson & Carpenter, 247 N.Y. 365, 160 N.E. 400. This does not mean, of course, that one who launches a destructive force is always relieved of liability, if the force, though known to be destructive, pursues an unexpected path. "It was not necessary that the defendant should have had notice of the particular method in which an accident would occur, if the possibility of an accident was clear to the ordinarily prudent eye." Munsey v. Webb, 231 U.S. 150, 156, 34 S. Ct. 44, 45 (58 L. Ed. 162); Condran v. Park & Tilford, 213 N.Y. 341, 345, 107 N.E. 565; Robert v. United States Shipping Board Emergency Fleet Corp., 240 N.Y. 474, 477, 148 N.E. 650. Some acts, such as shooting, are so imminently dangerous to any one who may come within reach of the missile however unexpectedly, as to impose a duty of prevision not far from that of an insurer. Even today, and much oftener in earlier stages of the law, one acts sometimes at one's peril.

Jeremiah Smith, Tort and Absolute Liability, 30 H. L. Rv. 328; Street, Foundations of Legal Liability, vol. 1, pp. 77, 78. Under this head, it may be, fall certain cases of what is known as transferred intent, an act willfully dangerous to A resulting by misadventure in injury to B. Talmage v. Smith, 101 Mich. 370, 374, 59 N.W. 656, 45 Am. St. Rep. 414. These cases aside, wrong is defined in terms of the natural or probable, at least when unintentional. Parrot v. Wells-Fargo Co. (The Nitro-Glycerine Case) 15 Wall. 524, 21 L. Ed. 206. The range of reasonable apprehension is at times a question for the court, and at times, if varying inferences are possible, a question for the jury. Here, by concession, there was nothing in the situation to suggest to the most cautious mind that the parcel wrapped in newspaper would spread wreckage through the station. If the guard had thrown it down knowingly and willfully, he would not have threatened the plaintiff's safety, so far as appearances could warn him. His conduct would not have involved, even then, an unreasonable probability of invasion of her bodily security. Liability can be no greater where the act is inadvertent.

Negligence, like risk, is thus a term of relation. Negligence in the abstract, apart from things related, is surely not a tort, if indeed it is understandable at all. Bowen, L.J., in Thomas v. Quartermaine, 18 Q. B. D. 685, 694. Negligence is not a tort unless it results in the commission of a wrong, and the commission of a wrong imports the violation of a right, in this case, we are told, the right to be protected against interference with one's bodily security. But bodily security is protected, not against all forms of interference or aggression, but only against some. One who seeks redress at law does not make out a cause of action by showing without more that there has been damage to his person. If the harm was not willful, he must show that the act as to him had possibilities of danger so many and apparent as to entitle him to be protected against the doing of it though the harm was unintended. Affront to personality is still the keynote of the wrong. Confirmation of this view will be found in the history and development of the action on the case.

Negligence as a basis of civil liability was unknown to mediaeval law. 8 Holdsworth, History of English Law, p. 449; Street, Foundations of Legal Liability, vol. 1, pp. 189, 190. For damage to the person, the sole remedy was trespass, and trespass did not lie in the absence of aggression, and that direct and personal. Holdsworth, op. cit. p. 453; Street, op. cit. vol. 3, pp. 258, 260, vol. 1, pp. 71, 74. Liability for other damage, as where a servant without orders from the master does or omits something to the damage of another, is a plant of later growth. Holdsworth, op. cit. 450, 457; Wigmore, Responsibility for Tortious Acts, vol. 3, Essays in Anglo-American Legal History, 520, 523, 526, 533. When it emerged out of the legal soil, it was thought of as a variant of trespass, an offshoot of the parent stock. This appears in the form of action, which was known as trespass on the case. Holdsworth, op. cit. p. 449; Cf. Scott v. Shepard, 2 Wm. Black, 892; Green, Rationale of Proximate Cause, p. 19. The victim does not sue derivatively, or by right of subrogation, to vindicate an interest invaded in the person of another. Thus to view his cause of action is to ignore the fundamental difference between tort and crime. Holland, Jurisprudence (12th Ed.) p. 328. He sues for breach of a duty owing to himself.

The law of causation, remote or proximate, is thus foreign to the case before us. The question of liability is always anterior to the question of the measure of the consequences that go with liability. If there is no tort to be redressed, there is no occasion to consider what damage might be recovered if there were a finding of a tort. We may assume, without deciding, that negligence, not at large or in the abstract, but in relation to the plaintiff, would entail liability for any and all consequences, however novel or extraordinary. There is room for argument that a distinction is to be drawn according to the diversity of interests invaded by the act, as where conduct negligent in that it threatens an insignificant invasion of an interest in property results in an unforeseeable invasion of an interest of another order, as, e.g., one of bodily security. Perhaps other distinctions may be necessary. We do not go into the question now. The consequences to be followed must first be rooted in a wrong.

The judgment of the Appellate Division and that of the Trial Term should be reversed, and the complaint dismissed, with costs in all courts.

ANDREWS, J. (dissenting).

. . . .

But we are told that "there is no negligence unless there is in the particular case a legal duty to take care, and this duty must be one which is owed to the plaintiff himself and not merely to others." Salmond Torts (6th Ed.) 24. This I think too narrow a conception. Where there is the unreasonable act, and some right that may be affected there is negligence whether damage does or does not result. That is immaterial. Should we drive down Broadway at a reckless speed, we are negligent whether we strike an approaching car or miss it by an inch. The act itself is wrongful. It is wrong not only to those who happen to be within the radius of danger, but to all who might have been there — a wrong to the public at large. Such is the language of the street. Such is the language of the courts when speaking of contributory negligence. Such again and again their language in speaking of the duty of some defendant and discussing proximate cause in cases where such a discussion is wholly irrelevant on any other theory. Perry v. Rochester Line Co., 219 N.Y. 60, 113 N.E. 529, L. R. A. 1917B, 1058. As was said by Mr. Justice Holmes many years ago:

> The measure of the defendant's duty in determining whether a wrong has been committed is one thing, the measure of liability when a wrong has been committed is another.

Spade v. Lynn & Co., 172 Mass. 488, 491, 52 N.E. 747, 748 (70 Am. St. Rep. 298, 43 L. R. A. 832).

Due care is a duty imposed on each one of us to protect society from unnecessary danger, not to protect A, B, or C alone.

. . . .

The proposition is this: Every one owes to the world at large the duty of refraining from those acts that may unreasonably threaten the safety of others. Such an act occurs. Not only is he wronged to whom harm might reasonably be expected to result, but he also who is in fact injured, even if he be outside what would generally be thought the danger zone. There needs be duty due the one complaining, but this is not a duty to a particular individual because as to him harm might be expected. Harm to some one being the natural result of the act, not only that one alone, but all those in fact injured may complain. We have never, I think, held otherwise. Indeed in the Di Caprio Case we said that a breach of a general ordinance defining the degree of care to be exercised in one's calling is evidence of negligence as to every one. We did not limit this statement to those who might be expected to be exposed to danger. Unreasonable risk being taken, its consequences are not confined to those who might probably be hurt.

———————

NOTES AND QUESTIONS

(1) *Palsgraf* is perhaps the most famous American torts decision. Its fame derives from the Cardozo-Andrews debate as to whether the particular facts raise an issue of duty or an issue of proximate causation. Cardozo's opinion is placed at this point, because its conception of the meaning of duty has been almost universally adopted by common law courts. But see, *Schuster v. Alternberg*, 424 N.W. 2d 159 (Wis. 1988), which adopts Andrew's more expansive view of duty. Even Wisconsin limits the reach of Andrew's conception of duty with judge- applied "public policy" factors. *Smaxwell v. Bayard*, 682 N.W.2d 923, 936 (Wi. 2006). Judge Andrews's

conception of proximate causation is also notable. For that reason, it is printed in full in § 8.02, infra, examining proximate causation more particularly. In *Palsgraf* itself, three judges voted with Cardozo in the majority and two with Andrews in his dissent.

(2)   Why does it matter whether the issue is treated as one of proximate causation or duty? Can your answer be inferred from the final order of the Court of Appeals in *Palsgraf*?

(3)   In *Letang v. Cooper* [1965] 1 Q.B. 247 [see Chapter 3, *supra*], Lord Diplock deals with the plaintiff's assertion that the term "breach of duty" used in the Limitations Act had reference to negligence but not to trespass in the form of unintentional, but direct, injury. Does Diplock's statement below support the view of Cardozo or of Andrews?

> Counsel for the plaintiff has, however, submitted that an action for trespass to the person is not an action for "breach of duty" at all. It is, he contends, an action for the infringement by the defendant of a general right of the plaintiff; there is no concomitant duty upon the defendant to avoid infringing the plaintiff's general right. This argument or something like it, for I do not find it easy to formulate, found favour with Elwes J. He drew a distinction between what he described as a "particular duty" owed by a particular defendant to a particular plaintiff which he said . . . was an essential element in the cause of action in negligence, and a "general duty" not to inflict on anyone; but to describe the latter, which is merely the obverse of the plaintiff's cause of action in trespass to the person, as a "duty" was, he thought, not to use the language of precision as known to the law.
>
> I would observe in passing that a duty not to inflict direct injury to the person of anyone is by its very nature owed only to those who are within range — a narrower circle of Atkinsonian neighbours than in the tort of negligence. But in any event this distinction between a duty which is "particular" because it is owed to a particular plaintiff and a duty which is "general" because the duty owed to the plaintiff is similar to that owed to everyone else is fallacious in relation to civil actions. A. has a cause of action against B. for any infringement by B. of a right of A. which is recognised by law. Ubi jus, ibi remedium. B. has a corresponding duty owed to A. not to infringe any right of A. which is recognised by law. A. has no cause of action against B. for an infringement by B. of a right of C. which is recognised by law. B. has no duty owed to A. not to infringe a right of C., although he has a duty owed to C. not to do so. The number of other people to whom B. owes a similar duty cannot affect the nature of the duty which he owes to A. which is simply a duty not to infringe any of A.'s rights. In the context of civil actions a duty is merely the obverse of a right recognised by law. The fact that in the earlier cases the emphasis tended to be upon the right and in more modern cases the emphasis tends to be upon the duty merely reflects changing fashions in approach to juristic as to other social problems, and must not be allowed to disguise the fact that right and duty are but two sides of a single medal.

What does *ubi jus, ibi remedium* mean?

(4)   In 2005 the American Law Institute adopted Restatement (Third) of Torts: Liability for Physical Harm § 7 that appears to have adopted Justice Andrews' view in *Palsgraf*. That provision states:

§ 7(a) An actor ordinarily has a duty to exercise reasonable care when the actor's conduct creates a risk of physical harm.

(b) In exceptional cases, when an articulated countervailing principle or policy warrants denying or limiting liability in a particular class of cases, a court may decide that the defendant has no duty or that the ordinary duty of reasonable care requires modification.

As of 2009 few courts have examined whether or not § 7 should modify existing duty analyses. Over a dissenting opinion that would have eliminated foreseeability from the duty equation, *Satterfield v. Breeding Insulation*, 266 S.W. 3d 347 (Tenn. 2008) continued to "rely heavily on foreseeability when determining the scope and existence of duty." *Satterfield* held that the employer of an employee who worked in an asbestos-contaminated workplace owed a duty to warn a family member who washed the asbestos-contaminated work clothes of the risk of mesothelioma from handling the contaminating clothing over a long period of time. Is such an employee unforeseeable under Justice Cardozo's analysis? Is this case within the scope of *Donoghue v. Stevenson*?

Gipson v. Kasey, 150 P.3d 228 (Ariz. 2007), purports to eliminate "foreseeability" as an element of the duty analysis in part on the ground that doing so "recognizes the jury's role of factfinder and requires courts to articulate clearly" other reasons "that might support duty or no-duty determinations." *Id.*, at 150 P.3d 231. Just as in Wisconsin, in Arizona these other reasons include "public policy." The facts in *Gipson* are that A, having received an intoxicating pharmaceutical drug legally, gave it to B for "recreational" use, knowing that B was likely to give it to C for "recreational" use. C died from the use. Was the risk to C foreseeable to A under Justice Cardozo's analysis? In any event, whether other courts will abandon the traditional view, expressed as follows, seems doubtful: "The most important of these considerations in establishing duty is foreseeability." *Tarasoff v. Regents of University of California*, 551 P.2d 334, 342 (Cal. 1976). See also, *Wofford v. Eastern State Hosp.*, 795 P.2d 516, 519 (Okla.1990) ("Of such considerations the most important in establishing duty is foreseeability.")

(5)   Tort law has three principal economic goals. The first is compensating those who are victims of torts. The second is optimally modifying the behavior of tortfeasors. The prospect of tort liability gives both individuals and businesses a powerful incentive not to engage in unreasonably dangerous behavior. The third is providing the legal system relatively clear, simple, and predictable rules. Only then can people structure their activities to avoid both tort litigation and tort liability.

These economic goals do not always manifest themselves equally. Consider again the opinions of Justices Cardozo and Andrews. Which is more concerned with these economic goals? Which goals?

DALLAS v. GRANITE CITY STEEL COMPANY
Illinois Appellate Court
211 N.E.2d 907 (1965)

GOLDENHERSH, JUSTICE.

Defendant, Granite City Steel Company, appeals from the judgment of the Circuit Court of Madison County, entered upon a jury verdict in the amount of $115,000.00.

Plaintiff's amended complaint alleges that on January 13, 1961, defendant was the owner of certain real estate known as 1816 Omaha Avenue, in Granite City, that defendant permitted the unoccupied house there situated to remain in a state of disrepair, permitted trash, rubbish and miscellaneous junk to remain on the premises, that plaintiff, then 4 years of age, was playing in a concrete block enclosure on said premises, which enclosure contained trash, rubbish and other junk, that defendant was aware that children residing in the immediate area were attracted by the abandoned house and premises and often played there, that as a direct and proximate result of defendant's negligence plaintiff was attracted to the premises and while playing there was struck in the face by trash, and suffered serious and permanent injuries.

The evidence shows that defendant operates a large steel plant in Granite City, part of which lies adjacent to Omaha Avenue. It had received a number of complaints from residents of the neighborhood because its operations caused smoke and vibration. Because of this problem, in 1958, it commenced a program of buying the property comprising several city blocks, which lay across Omaha Avenue from its plant. At that time the area it sought to acquire was primarily residential. At the time of plaintiff's injury, defendant had acquired 180 parcels of land, and at the time of trial, had effected the purchase of an additional 66 parcels, for a total of 246, of approximately 280 such parcels in the area. Most of the property was improved with small residences, and on many of the lots there were garages, sheds or other outbuildings.

Several witnesses called by plaintiff testified that prior to defendant's purchases in the area the homes and premises were well kept, that when defendant purchased the various parcels, it permitted junk and debris to accumulate in yards and ash pits, permitted the buildings to deteriorate, shingles to fall off roofs, porches to fall away from houses and in general described a condition of extensive dilapidation. Photographs offered and received in evidence corroborate this testimony.

Defendant's assistant treasurer, called by plaintiff and examined under Section 60 of the Practice Act, and called again by defendant in the presentation of its case, testified that defendant had boarded up the residences, at times ranging from shortly after acquisition of a property, to several months after obtaining possession, that its plant guards patrolled the area several times daily, that its employees, on several occasions had cut the grass and weeds in the yards of the parcels it owned, that it had investigated the possibility of fencing the area, but had abandoned the idea because to do so would cost $165,000.00, that the cost of razing the buildings on all the property purchased to the time of trial was estimated at $55,000.00, approximately $200.00 per parcel. He stated that defendant had no intention of using the houses or sheds in any way. He testified that defendant was aware that children resided in the area, that despite the patrolling of the area by defendant's plant guards, children played in the yards, sheds and garages. After boarding up the houses, defendant had done nothing about the sheds, garages or ash pits. Defendant knew of the presence of junk and trash in the various yards and ash pits, and was informed that children were playing with these things.

On January 13, 1961, plaintiff was 4 years and 7 months old. He lived with his parents and two older brothers, Billy and Joey, aged respectively 10 and 9, at 1810 Omaha Avenue. At the time of plaintiff's injury, plaintiff's place of residence was surrounded on three sides by vacant property owned by defendant, and was directly across Omaha Avenue from defendant's steel plant. The houses located at 1812, 1814, and 1816 Omaha Avenue had all been purchased by defendant some time between March and June of 1958. These houses had been boarded up. There were sheds or garages behind the boarded up houses, and behind the house known as 1816 Omaha Avenue, there was an ash pit, constructed of concrete blocks, approximately 4 to 5 feet square and 4½ feet high. The ash pit was approximately 75 or 80 feet from plaintiff's home.

Plaintiff and a playmate, Allyn Greer, then aged 4 years and 11 months, went to the premises at 1816 Omaha. They placed an old chair alongside the ash pit and climbed up into the pit. While playing in the ash pit, plaintiff tugged at a saw protruding from the ashes in the pit, and immediately thereafter began to cry. Plaintiff's older brothers, Billy and Joey, and a playmate of Billy's, Larry Mangiaracino, aged 10, were on the roof of a shed near the ash pit when they heard plaintiff cry out. They testified that they were pulling nails out of the roof, and intended to use the nails in the construction of a club-house located in the yard in back of a vacant house several houses down the street. They had thrown some rocks and pieces of glass off the roof, but thought they had thrown them toward the alley, not toward the ash pit. They thought several minutes had elapsed between the time that they had last thrown a rock or piece of glass, and the time when they heard plaintiff cry out.

When the older boys heard plaintiff crying, they came down off the shed, Billy lifted plaintiff out of the ash pit and carried him home. He was bleeding from the eye. He was taken to the office of a pediatrician who referred plaintiff's parents to an eye doctor, and plaintiff was taken to McMillan hospital in St. Louis.

It is plaintiff's theory that when plaintiff pulled or tugged on the saw, which was partially buried in the ash pit, he succeeded in pulling it loose, and when the saw was pulled up and out of the ashes, it struck plaintiff in the eye.

. . .

A saw was identified as having been found near the ash pit some time after January 13, 1961, and was offered and admitted into evidence.

Defendant argues that the verdict and judgment are based upon speculation and conjecture, that plaintiff failed to prove the injury was caused by a known defective structure, or dangerous instrumentality or agency on defendant's premises, the judgment should be reversed and judgment entered for defendant. Plaintiff contends that the evidence shows that defendant should have foreseen the probability of harm to the plaintiff by reason of the conditions which existed on defendant's property, that the verdict is supported by evidence of facts and circumstances from which the jury drew reasonable inferences, and the judgment should be affirmed.

In Kahn v. James Burton Co., 5 Ill. 2d 614, 126 N.E.2d 836, our Supreme Court enunciated the modern version of the doctrine which had its origin in the "turntable" or "attractive nuisance" cases. This doctrine is a clearly defined exception to the general rule that infants have no greater right than adults to go upon the land of others, and that their minority, of itself, imposes no burden on the occupier of land to expect them, or to prepare for their safety. In its opinion, at page 625, 126 N.E.2d at page 842, the Court said: "It is recognized, however, that an exception exists where the owner or person in possession knows, or should know, that young children habitually frequent the vicinity of a defective structure or dangerous agency existing on the land, which is likely to cause injury to them because they, by reason of their immaturity, are incapable of appreciating the risk involved, and where the expense or inconvenience of remedying the condition is slight compared to the risk to the children. In such cases there is a duty upon the owner or other person in possession and control of the premises to exercise due care to remedy the condition or otherwise protect the children from injury resulting from it. Wagner v. Kepler, 411 Ill. 368, 104 N.E.2d 231. The element of attraction is significant only in so far as it indicates that the trespass should be anticipated, the true basis of liability being the foreseeability of harm to the child." . . . .

There was sufficient evidence for the jury to draw the inference that the saw embedded in the trash pit was the instrument that caused plaintiff's injury, and the verdict will not be set aside merely because the jury could have drawn different inferences from the evidence. Lindroth v. Walgreen Co., 407 Ill. 121, 94 N.E.2d 847.

Defendant contends further that the evidence fails to prove, as required by Kahn v. Burton, that the expense of remedying the condition is slight compared to the risk to the children. The evidence shows that the cost of razing the buildings and cleaning up the yards of all the properties acquired by defendant would be $55,000.00, or somewhat over $200.00 per parcel. The testimony shows that defendant had no plans to use the buildings and intended ultimately to raze them. The evidence supports the conclusion that the expense or inconvenience of remedying the condition is slight compared to the risk to the children. In view of the evidence and the above authorities, the court properly refused to direct a verdict for defendant and properly refused to enter judgment for defendant notwithstanding the verdict.

NOTES AND QUESTIONS

(1)   The question of whether harm was "foreseeable" was referred to in *Dallas*. Does the mere fact that an injury does not seem unusual, after the fact, necessarily mean that a duty was owed, before the fact, to prevent the injury?

In *Lance v. Senior*, 36 Ill. 2d 516, 224 N.E.2d 231, 233 (1967), a nine-year-old hemophiliac sustained serious injury when he swallowed a needle while he was an overnight guest at the defendant's home. "The amended complaint alleged that at the time of his injury, the plaintiff was a nine-year-old boy who suffered from hemophilia, which the defendants knew; that he was an overnight guest in the defendants' home and that on the morning of August 15, 1964, the defendants 'negligently and carelessly permitted and allowed' the plaintiff to play with a needle 'which was caused to and did get into the throat of the plaintiff and was thereafter sucked into the inner part of the plaintiff's lung,' causing the injuries for which the plaintiff sought to recover in the sum of $50,000." *Id.*, 224 N.E. 2d at 232. The trial judge dismissed the action, but it was reinstated by an intermediate appellate court. The second ruling was reversed by the Illinois Supreme Court, saying:

> After the event, hindsight makes every occurrence foreseeable, but whether the law imposes a duty does not depend upon foreseeability alone. The likelihood of injury, the magnitude of the burden of guarding against it and the consequences of placing that burden upon the defendant, must also be taken into account. In the present case the risk that a nine-year-old boy would swallow or otherwise ingest a needle is minimal. The allegation that the defendants knew that the plaintiff was a hemophiliac does not justify the imposition of this duty, for it suggests that the plaintiff, who was not alleged to be mentally defective, would have been taught to guard against the special hazards to which his condition made him particularly vulnerable. The burden sought to be imposed upon the defendants is a heavy one, which would require intimate and constant surveillance. The existence of such a legal obligation, if generally known, would discourage persons in the position of the defendants from affording opportunities for children like the plaintiff to mingle with others, and would tend to isolate those children in their own homes. For these reasons, we hold that the complaint was properly dismissed because it does not allege facts upon which a recovery may be made.

> The judgment of the appellate court is reversed.

(2) Is the economic capability of the defendant a new factor in the ascertainment of duty, or is it implicit in the analyses of the preceding cases? Is it, for example, within the ambit of "general public sentiment of moral wrongdoing" as stated by Lord Atkin in *Donoghue v. Stevenson*?

Economic considerations have influenced the law of torts for decades, but academic pressure to enhance their importance increased during the second half of the twentieth century. Some writers argue that questions such as which of the parties can better bear the loss by diffusing it over a wider group of people through insurance or otherwise, and which of them is in a better position to avoid risks are more appropriate determinants of duty than traditional factors. These arguments emerge in various contexts throughout this text. When economic considerations are integrated into a general consideration of the humanity of the situation, as in *Herrington* (Note 3, infra) and *Granite City Steel Company*, courts have been more prone to give them credence than they are when the economic analyses are presented as the reason for a position.

For example, in *Caltex Oil (Australia) Pty., Ltd. v. The Dredge "Willemsted,"* 136 C.L.R. 529 (1976), the High Court of Australia was asked to adopt a particular ruling on the strength of economic analyses. The response of Stephen, J. reflects what may be a typical traditional view:

> . . . I wish to make some concluding remarks on the topic of economic loss. In any reference to the writings on this topic, and articles abound in the law journals of the last fifteen years in the common law countries, frequent mention will be found of the important role to be played by insurance and of the significance which judicial policy considerations should

accord to it and to what has come to be known as "loss spreading." If due weight be given to these two factors they will, it is sometimes said, point to the conclusion that liability in negligence should not be further extended and that, however logically unsatisfying may be the suggested (exclusory rule), the correct pragmatic solution is to deny recovery. . . .

I have myself avoided reference to either of these two factors and I should explain my reasons for doing so. If loss-inflicting consequences of an act are reasonably foreseeable and the necessary proximity is shown to exist, the present state of the law of torts, unreformed by any fundamental departure from fault liability, suggests no reason why the tortfeasor should not bear the consequences of his conduct. The task of the courts remains that of loss fixing rather than loss spreading and if this is to be altered it is, in my view, a matter for direct legislative action rather than for the courts. It should be undertaken, if at all, openly and after adequate public inquiry and parliamentary debate and not worked towards covertly, in the course of judicial decision, by the adoption of policy factors which assume its desirability as a goal and operate to further its attainment.

Accordingly I have adopted the perhaps unsophisticated concept that it is just and fair that a negligent tortfeasor, able reasonably to foresee that his conduct will occasion loss to another in a situation of proximity to that conduct, should be found liable to compensate the sufferer of the loss rather than that the victim should bear it himself. An opposing view, that loss should, in the case of involuntary torts, lie where it falls, there to be spread by recourse to the relatively efficient device of loss insurance (more efficient, for various reasons, than liability insurance) may have much to be said for it. Particularly is this so in areas in which insurance of one sort or another in fact becomes universal, whether or not as a result of governmental intervention. But there is, I think, no justification for the courts, when deciding actions in tort between private litigants, to make use of such views as policy determinants in the absence of any independent opportunity to test their soundness and without parliamentary sanction for the departure from pre-existing goals of the law of torts which their espousal involves.

Accord, *Lubin v. Iowa City*, 131 N.W.2d 765, 771 (Iowa 1964), where the court said "we cannot accept such a basis [e.g., loss bearing analysis] for determining liability in most cases." In fact, the *Lubin* case was one of the exceptions; it being a case in which the court used economic analysis to impose the standard of strict liability, which is examined in later chapters.

(3) What additional factor does the following excerpt from Lord Reid's judgment in *British Railways Board v. Herrington*, [1972] App. Cas. 877 (H.L.), add to the foregoing analyses? In *British Railways* an action was brought by a six-year-old child who trespassed through a broken and dilapidated fence onto railroad premises where he was badly injured on an electrified rail. At that time English case law imposed no duty on land owners to take care as to the condition of premises as to trespassers, adults or children. Contrary to the earlier cases the trial judge and the Court of Appeal had permitted the trespassing child to recover. The defendant appealed, claiming that the law recognized no duty of care owing to a trespasser. Lord Reid said:

. . . it appears to me that an occupier's duty to trespassers must vary according to his knowledge, ability and resources. It has often been said that trespassers must take the land as they find it. I would rather say that they must take the occupier as they find him.

So the question whether an occupier is liable in respect of an accident to a trespasser on his land would depend on whether a conscientious human man with his knowledge, skill and resources could reasonably have been expected to have done or refrained from doing before the accident something which would have avoided it. If he knew before the accident that there was a substantial probability that trespassers would come, I think that most people would regard as culpable failure to give any thought to their safety. He might often reasonably think, weighing the seriousness of the danger and the degree of likelihood of trespassers coming against the burden he would have to incur in preventing their entry or making his premises safe, or curtailing his own activities on his land, that he could not fairly be expected to do anything. But if he could at small trouble and expense take some effective action, again I think that most people would think it inhumane and culpable not to do that. If some such principle is adopted, there will no longer be any need to strive to imply a fictitious licence.

It would follow that an impecunious occupier with little assistances at hand would often be excused from doing something which a large organisation with ample staff would be expected to do.

It is always easy to be wise after the event and in judging what ought to have been done one would have to put out of one's mind the fact that an accident had occurred and visualise the position of the occupier before it had happened. Quite probably this would not be the only point on his land where trespass was likely. One would have to look at his problem as a whole and ask whether if he had thought about the matter it would have been humane or decent of him to do nothing. That may sound a low standard but in fact I believe that an occupier's failure to take any preventive steps is more often caused by thoughtlessness than by any shirking of his moral responsibility. I think that current conceptions of social duty do require occupiers to give reasonable attention to their responsibilities as occupiers, and I see nothing in legal principles to prevent the law from requiring them to do that.

If I apply that test to the present case, I think that the appellants must be held responsible for this accident. They brought onto their land in the live rail a lethal and to a young child a concealed danger. It would have been very easy for them to have and enforce a reasonable system of inspection and repair of their boundary fence. They know that children were entitled and accustomed to play on the other side of the fence and must have known, had any of their officers given the matter a thought, that a young child might easily cross a defective fence and run into grave danger. Yet they did nothing. I do not think that a large organisation is acting with due regard to humane consideration if its officers do not pay more attention to safety. I would not single out the station master for blame. The trouble appears to have been general slackness in the organisation. For that the appellants are responsible and I think in the circumstances, culpable. I would therefore hold them liable to the respondent and dismiss this appeal.

The House of Lords permitted the plaintiff to recover not because the defendant owed the plaintiff a duty of care but because it owed him a duty of "common humanity." This is novel nomenclature and may introduce an unsatisfactory anomaly into the English law of negligence to the extent it applies to one set of circumstances and not generally. The opinion reflects a new, if somewhat uncertain, balance between the countervailing forces of the justice of permitting a recovery on the one hand and the fear of extending liability too far on the other. The point discussed by Lord Reid in the foregoing short extract is but one of many discussed by the judges. What new element does it add? To what extent is the *Herrington* decision merely a particular expression of this sentiment: "More care must be exercised toward children than toward persons of mature years"? *Roberson v. Ahl,* 214 S.E. 119, 123 (S.C. 1975).

(4)   The wealth of the defendant is not supposed to factor into a court's decision as to whether defendant owes a duty to plaintiff or, if it does, in the court's decision as to how this duty should be carried out. (The sole exception is in the area of punitive damages. Since the goal of punitive damages is to modify the behavior of the tortfeasor, it is permissible for courts to consider the wealth of the defendant when they set the level of punitive damages.) Is this logical? Should the wealthy owe the same duty as the poor? Should courts be more likely to impose a duty to prevent an accident if the defendant (such as the defendant in *British Railways Board*) is likely to be wealthy? To answer this question, focus on the all three of the economic goals of the tort system; compensation of victims, optimal behavior modification, and the needs of the legal system for clear, simple and predictable rules.

ROBERSON v. ALLIED FOUNDRY & MACHINERY CO.
Alabama Supreme Court
447 So. 2d 720 (1984)

FAULKNER, JUSTICE.

This is an appeal from a summary judgment granted by the Circuit Court of Escambia County to Allied Foundry and Machinery Company (Allied), Brewton, Alabama, in a negligence action. We affirm.

In 1981, Robert L. Watts and Milton C. Doss were inmates at the Fountain Correctional Facility, Atmore, Alabama. Prior to and on November 10-11, 1981, Watts and Doss were engaged in the prison's "work release program," through which they were employed by Allied. Watts and Doss were working the third shift at Allied on November 10-11, 1981, and were scheduled to be on duty from 11:00 p.m. on November 10, 1981, to 7:00 a.m. on November 11, 1981.

Betty Lou Roberson is the manager of the Delta Mart, a convenience store in Brewton located approximately 100 yards from the Allied plant. It can be seen from the plant both day and night. On the night of November 10-11, 1981, Mrs. Roberson was working as the cashier at Delta Mart. She came to work at 2:00 a.m. and was the only employee at the store during her shift.

Watts and Doss left the Allied premises and walked over to the Delta Mart three times during the night of November 10-11, 1981. On the first trip, shortly after 2:00 a.m., Watts and Doss merely bought a cup of coffee and left the premises. About twenty-five minutes later, Watts and Doss returned to the Delta Mart, bought some wine and left again. On their third trip, about thirty minutes after their second trip, Watts and Doss entered the store, robbed Mrs. Roberson, assaulted her, causing serious physical injuries, and attempted to rape her.

Watts and Doss fled from the store when two customers arrived and attempted to stop the attack. The customers called the police, and Watts and Doss were apprehended at the Allied plant shortly after the incident.

There is evidence that several officials at Allied, including the supervisors of Watts and Doss, knew, or were highly suspicious, that Watts and Doss were drinking intoxicants on the night of the incident. Also, there is evidence that Allied officials had reason to believe that Watts and Doss had, on previous occasions, drunk intoxicants while on the job. It is also shown that Allied officials allowed work release inmates, including Watts and Doss, to leave the Allied premises during break time, in keeping with company policy for all employees.

On January 19, 1982, Mrs. Roberson filed a four-count complaint against Watts, Doss, and Allied. This appeal concerns only Count Three, which alleges a cause of action against Allied for negligent supervision of the work release employees.

On April 7, 1982, Allied filed a motion to dismiss, or, in the alternative, a motion for summary judgment as to Count Three. The relevant part of Allied's motion states (1) that the torts of Watts and Doss were not foreseeable by Allied; (2) that Allied owed no special duty to Mrs. Roberson because Watts and Doss were work release inmates; (3) that the acts of Watts and Doss were intervening, independent, and efficient causes of Mrs. Roberson's injuries; (4) that no employer-employee relationship existed between Watts and Doss and Allied; and (5) that, as a matter of law, Allied had no duty, right, or privilege to restrain Watts and Doss for the purpose of protecting the general public.

Mrs. Roberson filed a response to Allied's motion, stating (1) that Allied had failed to establish the absence of any triable issue of material fact, (2) that the evidence before the court showed there was an issue of material fact as to whether Allied was negligent, and (3) that Allied was not entitled to summary dismissal or judgment since there was a triable issue of material fact. Mrs. Roberson submitted evidence to the court in support of her position, including depositions, an affidavit, answers to interrogatories and various other documents.

A hearing was held on Allied's motions, and on March 10, 1983, the trial court granted summary judgment in Allied's favor. The judgment provided that there was no genuine issue of material fact as to Count Three, as last amended, and that Allied was entitled to a judgment as a matter of law. Mrs. Roberson is before this court, on appeal, arguing that the trial court erred in granting Allied's motion for summary judgment. Mrs. Roberson asserts that Allied had a duty to supervise its employees who were state inmates so as to protect her from the criminal actions of those employees. She argues that Allied breached this duty and is liable for the injuries received by her as a result thereof.

This is a case of first impression in Alabama and, so far as our research reveals, has never been addressed in the United States.[5]

The threshold question is whether an employer owes a duty to protect third persons from the criminal acts of state work release employees.

Mrs. Roberson argues that a special relationship exists between an employer and his work release employees by virtue of the fact that they are state inmates, with criminal propensities; she argues that as such inmates they require special supervision by the employer. Mrs. Roberson would have the court adopt a rule of "special duty" on the part of employers who employ work release inmates to supervise and control those employees outside the scope of their employment. This we are not prepared to do.

Work release inmates are certified to the employer by the State Board of Corrections to be "non-dangerous." Also, employers are instructed by the Board to treat work release employees in the same manner as other employees and to apply the same policies with them as with other employees. Except with regard to a few restrictions imposed by the Board on employers and work release employees, those employees stand in the same relationship with their employers as non-inmate employees. We cannot justify a finding of a special relationship in this case on the bare fact that work release employees are state inmates.

There is no authority in Alabama addressing the specific question at hand. However, our decision seems to be in keeping with recent decisions in Alabama, following the general rule that one has no duty to protect another from criminal attack by a third party. See Berdeaux v. City National Bank, 424 So. 2d 594 (Ala. 1982 (bank owes no duty to protect customer from injury during armed robbery); Gaskin v. Republic Steel Corporation, 420 So. 2d 37 (Ala. 1982) (employer owes no duty to protect employee from attack by third party on employer's premises); Parham v. Taylor, 402 So. 2d 884 (Ala. 1981) (employer owes no duty to protect employee from criminal acts of third parties on employer's premises).

We are sympathetic with Mrs. Roberson and understand that she has suffered severe injury. We cannot agree, however, that she should be compensated by rewriting the law of torts. Finding no authority or justification for the premise that a special relationship exists between Allied and its work release employees sufficient to impose a duty on Allied to supervise these employees outside the scope of their employment, we hold that no such duty exists in this case. The trial court's

---

[5] A very few cases have dealt with the issue of the employer's duty to control the actions of his employee outside the scope of employment. See Fletcher v. Baltimore and Potomac R.R. Co., 168 U.S. 135, 18 S. Ct. 35, 42 L. Ed. 411 (1897) (employer railroad company who knows employees are throwing objects off its trains has duty to restrain employees to protect general public from injury); International Distrib. Corp. v. American Dist. Tel., 569 F.2d 136 (D.C.Cir. 1977) (employer has duty to supervise conduct of its employees who are privileged, because of their employment, to enter property of another); S. Birch & Sons v. Martin, 244 F.2d 556 (9th Cir. 1957) (highway construction company had no duty to protect passing motorists from injury by its employees celebrating end of construction); Trammell v. Ramey, 231 Ark. 260, 329 S.W.2d 153 (1959) (employer has no duty to control drunk employee on his own mission, even though employer knew of and helped employee with treatment of his drinking problem); Hogle v. H.H. Franklin Mfg. Co., 199 N.Y. 388, 92 N.E. 794 (1910) (employer who knows employees are throwing missiles out factory window has duty to restrain employees to protect passers-by from injury). We have found no case that deals with an employer's duty to control the actions of a work release employee in particular outside the scope of his employment.

decision granting summary judgment to Allied was therefore not in error, and is, thus, affirmed.

Affirmed.

QUESTIONS

(1)   As a general matter, does the law impose a duty of care upon one person to prevent another independent person of unimpaired physical and mental faculties from causing harm to third persons? What differentiates *Roberson* from the cases cited by the court in footnote 1? What additional facts would have created a duty in *Roberson*?

(2)   What evidence was considered by the court in *Roberson*? What was the most important fact in the decision? Was that fact in dispute?

(3)   A number of courts have acknowledged the general rule that "no person owes duty to another to anticipate that crime will be committed, and to act upon that belief." *O'Conner v. Corbett Lumber Company*, 352 S.E. 2d 267 (N.C. 1987) (facts and result indistinquishable from *Roberson*) and *Gray v. Scott*, 565 P.2d 76, 77 N.C. App. (Utah 1977) (in the complete absence of prior shooting occurrences proprietors of a private lodge had no duty to anticipate criminal shooting at a private party.)

(4)   *K.M. ex rel. D.M. v. Publix Super Markets, Inc.*, 895 So. 2d 1114 (Fla. 4th DCA 2005) also denied recovery in a sympathy involving the sexual abuse of a child. *K.M.* applied Restatement (Second) of Torts, Section 315 and numerous cases that have considered it. That provision states:

> § 315 General Principle
>
> There is no duty so to control the conduct of a third person as to prevent him from causing physical harm to another unless
>
> (a) a special relation exists between the actor and the third person which imposes a duty upon the actor to control the third person's conduct, or
>
> (b) a special relation exists between the actor and the other which gives to the other a right to protection.

HOME OFFICE v. DORSET YACHT CO., LTD.
[1970] App. Cas. 1004 [H.L.][6]

[Evolution of the law of duty necessarily requires bridging the gap between cases where a duty has been acknowledged (as in the cases cited in footnote 1 of Roberson) and those where no duty exists (e.g., Roberson itself). The theory has perhaps been expounded with no more clarity than in Lord Diplock's exposition in this case. The question was whether the government (the Home Office) ought to be liable for damages done to a private yacht by borstal (reformatory) boys who took flight from a minimum security encampment on an island. Prior decisions had recognized a duty of care upon a person (e.g., the Home Office) who had a right to control the movements of both the independent wrongdoer (e.g., the borstal boys) and the injured third party (e.g., a fellow borstal boy), but no duty had been

---

[6] [Ed. — Appeal Cases Law Reports, decision of House of Lords.]

recognized where the movements of the injured third party (e.g., the yacht owner) were not subject to the control of the defendant. In this action the trial judge denied the defendant's motion to dismiss (or the English equivalent). The Court of Appeal affirmed and review was obtained in the House of Lords.]

LORD DIPLOCK

. . .

The justification of the courts' role in giving the effect of law to the judges' conception of the public interest in the field of negligence is based upon the cumulative experience of the judiciary of the actual consequences of lack of care in particular instances. And the judicial development of the law of negligence rightly proceeds by seeking first to identify the relevant characteristics that are common to the kinds of conduct and relationship between the parties which are involved in the case for decision and the kinds of conduct and relationships which have been held in previous decisions of the courts to give rise to a duty of care.

The method adopted at this stage of the process is analytical and inductive. It starts with an analysis of the characteristics of the conduct and relationship involved in each of the decided cases. But the analyst must know what he is looking for, and this involves his approaching his analysis with some general conception of conduct and relationships which ought to give rise to a duty of care. This analysis leads to a proposition which can be stated in the form:

In all the decisions that have been analysed a duty of care has been held to exist wherever the conduct and the relationship possessed each of the characteristics A,B,C,D, etc., and has not so far been found to exist when any of these characteristics were absent.

For the second stage, which is deductive and analytical, that proposition is converted to: "In all cases where the conduct and relationship possess each of the characteristics A,B,C,D, etc., a duty of care arises." The conduct and relationship involved in the case for decision is then analysed to ascertain whether they possess each of these characteristics. If they do, the conclusion follows that a duty of care does arise in the case for decision.

But since ex hypothesi the kind of case which we are now considering offers a choice whether or not to extend the kinds of conduct or relationships which give rise to a duty of care, the conduct or relationship which is involved in it will lack at least one of the characteristics A,B,C, or D, etc. And the choice is exercised by making a policy decision as to whether or not a duty of care ought to exist if the characteristic which is lacking were absent or redefined in terms broad enough to include the case under consideration. The policy decision will be influenced by the same general conception of what ought to give rise to a duty of care as was used in approaching the analysis. The choice to extend is given effect by redefining the characteristics in more general terms so as to exclude the necessity to conform to limitations imposed by the former definition which are considered to be inessential.

. . . .

Inherent in this methodology, however, is a practical limitation which is imposed by the sheer volume of reported cases. The initial selection of previous cases to be analysed will itself eliminate from the analysis those in which the conduct or relationship involved possessed characteristics which are obviously absent in the case for decision. The proposition used in the deductive stage is not a true universal. It needs to be qualified so as to read:

In all cases where the conduct and relationship possess each of the characteristics A,B,C and D, etc. but do not possess any of the characteristics Z, Y or X etc. which were present in the cases eliminated from the analysis, a duty of care arises.

But this qualification, being irrelevant to the decision of the particular case, is generally left unexpressed.

This was the reason for the warning by Lord Atkin in Donoghue v. Stevenson [1932] A.C.562, itself when he said, at pp.583-584:

. . . in the branch of the law which deals with civil wrongs, dependent in England at any rate entirely upon the application by judges of general principles also formulated by judges, it is of particular importance to guard against the danger of stating propositions of law in wider terms than is necessary, lest essential factors be omitted in the wider survey and the inherent adaptability of English law be unduly restricted. For this reason it is very necessary in considering reported cases in the law of torts that the actual decision alone should carry authority, proper weight, of course, being given to the dicta of the judges.

The plaintiff's argument in the present appeal disregards this warning. It seeks to treat as a universal not the specific proposition of law in Donoghue v. Stevenson which was about a manufacturer's liability for damage caused by his dangerous products but the well-known aphorism used by Lord Atkin to describe a "general conception of relations giving rise to a duty of care" [Lord Atkin's "good neighbour" principle omitted].

Used as a guide to characteristics which will be found to exist in conduct and relationships which give rise to a legal duty of care this aphorism marks a milestone in the modern development of the law of negligence. But misused as a universal, it is manifestly false.

[Upon consideration of prior cases, Diplock concluded.]

I should therefore hold that any duty of a Borstal officer to use reasonable care to prevent a Borstal trainee from escaping from his custody was owed only to persons whom he could reasonably foresee had property situated in the vicinity of the place of detention of the detainee which the detainee was likely to steal or to appropriate and damage in the course of eluding immediate pursuit and recapture. Whether or not any person fell within this category would depend upon the facts of the particular case including the previous criminal and escaping record of the individual trainee concerned and the nature of the place from which he escaped.

So to hold would be a rational extension of the relationship between the custodian and the person sustaining the damage which was accepted in Ellis v. Home Office [1953] 2 All E.R. 149 and D'Arcy v. Prison Commissioners, "The Times," November 17, 1955, as giving rise to a duty of care on the part of the custodian to exercise reasonable care in controlling his detainee. In those two cases the custodian had a legal right to control the physical proximity of the person or property sustaining the damage to the detainee who caused it. The extended relationship substitutes for the right to control the knowledge which the custodian possessed or ought to have possessed that physical proximity in fact existed.

In the present appeal the place from which the trainees escaped was an island from which the only means of escape would presumably be a boat accessible from the shore of the island. There is thus material fit for consideration at the trial for holding that the plaintiff, as the owner of a boat moored off the island, fell within the category of persons to whom a duty of care to prevent the escape of the trainees was owed by the officers responsible for their custody.

If, therefore, it can be established at the trial of this action that it was reasonably foreseeable by the officers that if these particular trainees did escape they would be likely to appropriate a boat moored in the vicinity of Brownsea Island for the purpose of eluding immediate pursuit and to cause damage to it, the Borstal officers would be in breach of a duty of care owed to the plaintiff and the plaintiff would, in my view, have a cause of action against the Home Office as vicariously liable for the "negligence" of the Borstal officers.

[The appeal was denied.]

NOTES

(1)   To test Lord Diplock's approach in *Home Office v. Dorset Yacht Co., Ltd.* ask yourself how he would have decided *Roberson v. Allied Foundry & Machinery Co.* How would the Alabama court have decided *Home Office*? See also, *Ancell v. McDermott*, [1993] 4 All Eng. Rep. 355, which suggests that *Dorset Yacht* would have been decided differently if the boat had been merely a passing yacht in navigable waters rather than one of a small number of moored yachts the defendant knew about.

(2)   Note that most of the cases in this section have referred to "policy" as a factor to be considered in determining the duty question. How strong is that factor? Consider this excerpt from *Hooks SuperX, Inc. v. McLaughlin*, 642 N.E.2d 514 (Ind. 1994), in which the survivors of a suicide victim sued a pharmacist for having filled the decedent's prescription more frequently than ordered by the prescribing physician. The complaint alleged that an overdose of the prescribed drug caused derangement and suicide. Is the policy factor any more or less weighty than in the preceding cases? Than the other ingredients of duty?

. . . .

Where a pharmacy customer is having a prescription for a dangerous drug refilled at an unreasonably faster rate than the rate prescribed, the pharmacist has a duty to cease refilling the prescription pending direct and explicit directions from the prescribing physician.

. . . .

It is axiomatic that without a duty, there can be no recovery in negligence. Webb v. Jarvis (1991), Ind., 575 N.E.2d 992, 995; Miller v. Griesel (1974), 261 Ind. 604, 611, 308 N.E.2d 701, 706. Whether the law recognizes any obligation on the part of a particular defendant to conform his conduct to a certain standard for the benefit of the plaintiff is a question of law exclusively for the court. Gariup Constr. Co. v. Foster (1988), Ind., 519 N.E.2d 1224, 1227. In Webb v. Jarvis, this Court utilized a three-part analysis to be applied when deciding whether a duty exists. Likewise, we will consider (1) the relationship between the parties; (2) the foreseeability of the harm; and (3) public policy issues. 575 N.E.2d at 995.

1. Relationship. It has long been established that the existence of a duty upon one to act with respect to another arises out of the relation between them. Gariup, 519 N.E.2d at 1227-28. That the law recognizes a relationship between pharmacist and customer as one that gives rise to a duty in other circumstances is well-established. See, e.g., Forbes v. Walgreen Co. (1991), Ind. App., 566 N.E.2d 90, 91 (pharmacist liable for dispensing wrong medicine); Ingram v. Hooks Drugs, Inc. (1985), Ind.App., 476 N.E.2d 881, 883 (pharmacist required to inform patient of warnings included in the prescription). Ingram and Forbes recognize a duty on the part of the pharmacist to follow the physician's instructions contained in the prescription. Here, we must determine whether the pharmacist has a duty under certain circumstances to refrain from dispensing the prescription as written.

The relationship between pharmacist and customer is a direct one based upon contract and is independent of the relationship between physician and patient. Our law is replete with instances where privity of contract is a relationship sufficient to form the basis for tort liability. . . . It is a matter of common expectation as well as statute that pharmacists possess expertise regarding the dispensing of prescription drugs.

It is a matter of common understanding that customers rely upon pharmacists for that expertise. Upon this basis, we conclude that the relationship between pharmacist and customer is sufficiently close to justify imposing a duty. [Note: is the court holding that the duty arose out of the actual sale contract of the drugs sold, or out of the relationship that gave rise to the sales? — Ed.]

2. Foreseeability. Turning to the next factor to be considered, we note that it is well-established that a duty is imposed only where a reasonably foreseeable victim is injured by reasonably foreseeable harm. . . . It is not disputed here that one who consumes sufficient quantities of addictive substances may become addicted to them, and that such an addiction carries with it certain reasonably foreseeable consequences. But cf. Webb, 575 N.E.2d at 997 (causal connection between the use of steroids and violent behavior not well-established; not reasonably foreseeable that physician's prescribing medication would put patient in such a state that patient would use a weapon to cause harm to another). Thus, we are satisfied that, for purposes of determining whether a duty exists, the risk of McLaughlin's addiction was foreseeable from the series of events that took place.

3. Public Policy. The third factor to be considered is that of public policy. "What the public policy of a state is must be determined from a consideration of its Constitution, its statutes, the practice of its officers in the course of administration, and the decisions of its court of last resort." Hogston v. Bell (1916), 185 Ind. 536, 545, 112 N.E. 883, 886. We perceive three policy considerations at stake here: preventing intentional and unintentional drug abuse, not jeopardizing the physician/patient relationship, and avoiding

unnecessary health care costs. There are several explanations for why a pharmacy customer might have a prescription for a dangerous drug refilled at a rate unreasonably faster than that prescribed. Among them are that the customer may have developed an addiction to the drug or that the customer is improperly disposing of the drug. Both of these explanations give rise to the strong public policy interest in preventing intentional and unintentional drug abuse.

Our legislature has expressed this policy interest in many enactments. [The court rejected the defendants' countervailing contentions that to acknowledge a pharmacist-customer duty would intrude upon the physician-patient relationship between the prescribing physician and patient and would add unjustifiably to the cost of medicines. Are these insignificant "public policies"? Does an appellate court have the basis for deciding among the competing policies in tort litigation? — Ed.]

Consideration of the three pertinent factors — the relationship between the parties, foreseeability of the harm, and public policy concerns — convince us that a duty should be recognized here. Clearly, society has an interest in preventing the overuse and misuse of prescription drugs. Recognizing that pharmacists have a duty in this regard helps further that goal. The duty imposed is simply a practical recognition of the relationship between pharmacist and customer.

(3) Should courts use "public policy" to enlarge or restrict the scope of duty determined upon application of standard analyses?

COMMENTARY: A LAW AND ECONOMICS APPROACH TO DUTY

The foregoing cases and commentary examine the approach common law courts have taken to decide the duty issue ever since negligence began to evolve as a discrete tort cause of action. In the latter decades of the twentieth century economics minded legal scholars, including some judges, have undertaken to reexamine the issue under the general proposition that duty ought to be assigned to the person who could most efficiently prevent or compensate the injury. An introductory examination of this approach is provided below.

(1) The "Least Cost" Approach to Assigning Duty

The "least cost" principle for assigning duty would have the court place the duty of avoiding or preventing the accident on whichever party could avoid or prevent the accident at the lowest cost.

As the cases throughout this book demonstrate, courts have no simple tool to assign duty when novel cases emerge. As *Heaven v. Pender* shows, courts start with the presumption of no duty and then sometimes impose a duty based upon factors such as foreseeability, knowledge, reliance, morality, and contracts.[7] *Heaven v. Pender* also illustrates that these factors are often difficult to apply. For example, couldn't several of the parties claim to have relied upon another party to inspect the ropes for defects? Couldn't each claim it did not inspect the ropes because it assumed another party would do it?

---

[7] For example, there is no general duty to rescue people. However, if someone signs a contract to be a lifeguard, they then have a duty in Tort law to make a reasonable attempt to rescue a drowning person.

An economics approach provides a different analytical tool to assigning duty. A Law and Economics judge would ask: "Who can best inspect the ropes?" The judge would then put the duty on whichever party would best inspect them or could have avoided the accident for the lowest cost.[8] It probably would be wasteful in *Heaven v. Pender* for every party to inspect the ropes for safety. But suppose the defective item was a soft drink bottle that might possibly explode? Should a court impose the duty to inspect it on everyone who had any contract pertaining to the soft drink bottle, even the retailer? Similarly, suppose a car's wheels might collapse? Should a court require retailers to inspect the wheels of every car they sell? Because inspections are expensive and inspection costs are likely to be passed on to consumers, wouldn't it be better to figure out which party (i.e., the manufacturer, the retailer, or the consumer) could best perform the inspection needed to prevent the accident,[9] and put the duty of inspection on this party alone?

We can illustrate the Law & Economics approach to assigning duty by paring Heaven v. Pender down to two parties: 1. An Owner, who owns the ship, the dock, and the ropes, and a boat to be painted; 2. A Painter. Also assume there is nothing explicit in the painting contract about who should inspect the ropes for safety; that there is no relevant industry custom or statute; and, that no one else could readily inspect the ropes. Consider two contracts.

Contract #1. If the court assigns Painter the duty of inspecting the ropes, Painter will add the expected cost of this inspection (assume $100) onto the price of the paint job which otherwise would cost $1,000. This would raise the total cost of painting the boat to $1,100.

Contract #2. If the court imposes the duty of rope inspection on Owner (remember, Owner can inspect the ropes relatively inexpensively), Owner will perform the inspection and accrue the cost of inspecting the ropes (say, $10). Painter does the rest of the work for $1,000. The total cost to Owner of getting the boat painted is therefore $1,010.

These contrasting contracts demonstrate that a court would actually do Owner a favor to assign it the duty of rope inspection, because Owner is better at inspecting ropes than Painter. If Owner does the inspection, it gets the ship painted for $90 less than if the duty had been placed on Painter.

The key to deciding who should be assigned the duty is to ascertain, predictably and in advance, which party could best perform the inspection and thereby prevent the accident.[10] No matter which party is assigned this duty, however, Owner would pay its expected future cost as a part of the cost of getting the ship painted. Because Owner would prefer to have the ship painted for $1,010 rather than $1,100, the "least cost" rule for assigning duty is beneficial. Painter is also benefited because

---

[8] For simplicity we usually call this the "least cost" approach to assigning duty. In reality, however, there sometimes can be quality issue; perhaps one party could do a better job of preventing the accident than another party. Of course quality of accident prevention counts, and we focus exclusively upon cost only to simplify the analysis.

[9] A very different question is whether the accident should have been prevented at all. Some accidents are, unfortunately, too expensive or difficult to prevent. This issue will be discussed throughout the Breach section of this book.

[10] A major drawback to using the least cost approach to assigning duty is that often there is no way to predictably determine in advance which party could have prevented the accident best. In these cases the least cost principle cannot be used.

Painter, on average, will get more painting business at $1,010 per ship than at $1,100 per ship.[11]

Suppose, however, the court ignores the least cost approach to determining duty. Instead of determining "who can best prevent the accident," the court puts the duty of prevention on Painter. Will Painter actually carry out the inspection? Maybe not, for reasons that can be explained by the Coase Theorem.

(2) The Coase Theorem

Although the Coase Theorem can be articulated in many different ways,[12] the following definition can help courts assign duty:

If there are no significant transaction costs, the lowest cost method of preventing an accident will arise regardless which party is assigned the duty of preventing the accident.

An alternative way of expressing the Coase Theorem in this context is:

Unless the costs of contracting around any relevant court decisions are too high, the lowest cost solution will arise no matter which party originally is assigned the duty. Since there are almost always costs of contracting around a court decision, the Coase Theorem prescribes that courts should assign the duty to whichever party can best prevent the accident. Doing this will result in the lowest cost of preventing the accident and save any extra costs of arriving at this result.

To illustrate the "least cost" approach to assigning duty consider again the version of *Heaven v. Pender* that has been pared down to two parties, Owner and Painter. Also assume the court has ignored the "least cost principle" and assigned the duty to Painter, even though Owner could inspect the ropes and prevent the accident with less cost (for $10 instead of $100). Although assigning the duty to Painter adds $90 to the costs, the parties might be able to transact around the judge's decision if the costs of doing this are not too high. (For example legal costs.) Let's assume two different costs of transacting around the court's decision.[13] First, assume a low amount of $50, and then a high amount of $200.

If the costs of contracting around the court's decision are only $50, the parties should do it. They would spend $50 to save $90 ($100 - $10). The final cost of painting the boat would be $1060 and the contract would have saved them $40.

By contrast, if the cost of contracting around the court's decision were $200, the parties would not spend the money. The potential $90 savings is less than the $200 costs of gaining the savings. The lowest cost solution would never be achieved.

---

[11] Suppose the plaintiff was a mere worker who had no role in inspecting the ropes but only in working where and when he was told, as was probably the actual case in *Heaven v. Pender*. Should the least-cost argument between Owner and Painter have any effect on his rights against either?

[12] *See* Ronald H. Coase, *The Problem of Social Cost*, 3 J. Law & Econ. 1 (1960). A very general articulation of the Coase Theorem is: "Absent transaction costs, the most efficient outcome will arise regardless which party is assigned the initial property right or obligation." In the circumstance under discussion, the duty to prevent an accident can be thought of as a property obligation.

[13] The costs of transacting around the court's decision could fall in the long run, as the parties learn to utilize standard form contracts.

In theory there could be no costs to transacting around a court's decision. In the real world, however, these situations are highly unusual.

Instead Painter would perform the rope inspection and the painting job would cost $1100.

In summary, if the transaction costs of contracting around the court's decision are lower than $90, the lowest cost solution would arise no matter which party the court assigns the duty of preventing the accident. But in a case with high ($200) transaction costs, the lowest cost solution will never arise. In either case, would the parties have been better off if the court had used the "least cost" approach and directly assigned the duty to the party that could have prevented the accident for the lowest cost?

(3) Tort issues could be considered to be implied Contract issues

Has economic analysis implicitly turned a Torts issue into a Contracts issue? In effect, it asks: "What contract would the parties have entered into if they had thought about the relevant issue in advance?" The Coase Theorem concludes that the parties probably would have agreed upon the least costly option. Accordingly, the law may impose a contract calling for the least costly option on the parties afterwards, except that we call it "Tort law" rather than "Contract law".

Under this analysis, would the parties in *Heaven v. Pender* have assigned the duty to inspect the ropes to the lowest cost party if they had thought it in advance?[14] Since the expected future costs of painting the ship would be incurred by the ship's owner, Owner would have wanted the lowest cost contract. The lowest cost contract would benefit Painter as well because this would, on average, provide more painting business. If they forgot to include this term in their contract, should the court do it for them? Should the court, in effect, write the "least cost" contract for the parties post hoc and call it Tort law rather than Contract law? The Coase Theorem says that the parties will arrive at the least cost solution anyway unless the transaction costs of getting there are too high. Should the court therefore save the parties the cost of getting to the best solution on their own by imposing the duty to inspect on the party that could prevent the accident at the lowest cost?

If every tort case may be thought of as an implied contract case, what happens when a driver negligently hits another car? Courts conventionally call this a "tort" case and impose damages on the driver that is deemed to be negligent. Could we just as easily think of this as an implied contract situation? What contract would the parties have agreed to in advance if they had thought about the crucial issue? Wouldn't most drivers have agreed that all drivers should drive reasonably? Shouldn't courts then impose this contract on both parties after the fact — except calling it "tort" law, not "contract" law?

Throughout this book, we may always ask: What contract would the parties have entered into if they had thought about the issue in advance? Sometimes the Coase Theorem will help reach an answer by reminding us that the parties probably would have preferred the lowest cost solution. If the parties could have determined the lowest cost solution in advance, should the Tort system impose this contract on the parties afterwards?

---

[14] This assumes there is no contrary contact between the parties, industry custom, or statute, and that no one else reasonably could prevent the accident.

§ 4.03 BREACH

PROBLEM B

Mary Jones, a sixty-nine-year-old widow, was badly injured when a baseball hit her as she walked along a sidewalk toward her home on Elm Street. The ball had been hit by Tom Damon, an eighteen-year-old high school baseball player, while taking his turn at bat in a high school baseball game. Tom Damon regularly hit long balls by local standards, but the longest he had ever before hit was caught forty feet short of the fence measured from a point near where Mary was struck. Special care had been taken to mark the spot, because none of the participants on that day had ever seen such a long ball hit by a local player.

It was 403 feet from home plate where Damon struck the ball to the point where Mary Jones was hit, which happened to be the point on the sidewalk closest to home plate. There was a three-foot fence between the playing field and the sidewalk and the field sloped gradually upward so that the sidewalk at the point of impact was two feet in elevation above home plate.

The baseball field was owned by the County School Board and was used regularly for high school, sand lot and local league games. It had been used for baseball continuously for 75 years. None of the present participants or school authorities ever heard of anyone's having ever before hit a ball onto the sidewalk. Two old timers in the neighborhood recollect, however, that two players who had played in the 1960s had cleared the fence "once or twice" each.

One of them played in the major leagues during the late 1970s and throughout the 1980s but was killed in the Iraq War. The other was lost sight of and is also believed to be dead.

Elm Street is a residential street and is lightly used except by occupants of adjacent houses and the morning and afternoon rush of school children. Mary Jones had regularly strolled on the street several times a day for almost fifty years.

Mary Jones brings an action in negligence against the School Board and Tom Damon. The defendants deny the allegations of negligence and make a motion for summary judgment. The lawyers present affidavits to the judge outlining the evidence that may be adduced to support all the allegations of fact described above and no others.

(1) Draft a complaint that would be adequate to state Mary Jones's cause of action in this case.

(2) Draft an answer that admits any allegations that the defendants have no interest in disputing and that denies the allegations that should properly be denied to raise the central issue.

(3) Draft a short opinion granting or denying each defendant's motion for summary judgment and clearly explaining the reasons for the court's action.

VAUGHAN v. MENLOVE
3 Bing. (N.C.) 467 132 E.R. 490 (1837)[15]

[Two cottages owned by the plaintiffs were destroyed when a hayrick owned and maintained by the defendant on his land burst into flames as a result of spontaneous combustion and burned across the intervening fields to the cottages. The plaintiffs won a verdict in the trial court. The defendant made a motion (or sought a "rule") for a new trial.]

At the trial it appeared that the rick in question had been made by the Defendant near the boundary of his own premises; that the hay was in such a state when put together, as to give rise to discussions on the probability of fire: that though there were conflicting opinions on the subject, yet during a period of five weeks, the Defendant was repeatedly warned of his peril; that his stock was insured; and that upon one occasion, being advised to take the rick down to avoid all danger, he said "he would chance it." He made an aperture or chimney through the rick; but in spite, or perhaps in consequence of this precaution, the rick at length burst into flames from the spontaneous heating of its materials; the flames communicated to the Defendant's barns and stables, and thence to the Plaintiff's cottages, which were entirely destroyed.

Patteson J. before whom the cause was tried, told the jury that the question for them to consider, was, whether the fire had been occasioned by gross negligence on the part of the Defendant; adding, that he was bound to proceed with such reasonable caution as a prudent man would have exercised under such circumstances.

A verdict having been found for the Plaintiff, a rule nisi for a new trial was obtained, on the ground that the jury should have been directed to consider, not, whether the Defendant had been guilty of gross negligence with reference to the standard of ordinary prudence, a standard too uncertain to afford any criterion; but whether he had acted bona fide to the best of his judgment; if he had, he ought not to be responsible for the misfortune of not possessing the highest order of intelligence. The action under such circumstances, was of the first impression.

TINDAL C.J. I agree that this is a case primae impressionis; but I feel no difficulty in applying to it the principles of law as laid down in other cases of a similar kind. Undoubtedly this is not a case of contract, such as a bailment or the like where the bailee is responsible in consequence of the remuneration he is to receive: but there is a rule of law which says you must so enjoy your own property as not to injure that of another; and according to that rule the Defendant is liable for the consequence of his own neglect: and though the Defendant did not himself light the fire, yet mediately, he is as much the cause of it as if he had himself put a candle to the rick: for it is well known that hay will ferment and take fire if it be not carefully stacked. It has been decided that if an occupier burns weeds so near the boundary of his own land that damage ensues to the property of his neighbour, he is liable to an action for the amount of injury done, unless the accident were occasioned by a sudden blast which he could not forsee: Turbervill v. Stamp (1 Salk. 13). But put the case of a chemist making experiments with ingredients, singly innocent, but when combined, liable to ignite; if he leaves them together, and

[15] [Ed — English Reports, general reporter of older English cases; decision of House of Lords; Bingham's reports, new cases.]

injury is thereby occasioned to the property of his neighbour, can any one doubt that an action on the case would lie?

It is contended, however, that the learned Judge was wrong in leaving this to the jury as a case of gross negligence, and that the question of negligence was so mixed up with reference to what would be the conduct of a man of ordinary prudence that the jury might have thought the latter the rule by which they were to decide; that such a rule would be too uncertain to act upon; and that the question ought to have been whether the Defendant had acted honestly and bona fide to the best of his own judgment. That, however, would leave so vague a line as to afford no rule at all, the degree of judgment belonging to each individual being infinitely various: and though it has been urged that the care which a prudent man would take, is not an intelligible proposition as a rule of law, yet such has always been the rule adopted in cases of bailment, as laid down in Coggs v. Bernard (2 Ld. Raym. 909). Though in some cases a greater degree of care is exacted than in others, yet in "the second sort of bailment, viz. commodatum or lending gratis, the borrower is bound to the strictest care and diligence to keep the goods so as to restore them back again to the lender; because the bailee has a benefit by the use of them, so as if the bailee be guilty of the least neglect he will be answerable; as if a man should lend another a horse to go westward, or for a month; if the bailee put this horse in his stable, and he were stolen from thence, the bailee shall not be answerable for him: but if he or his servant leave the house or stable doors open and the thieves take the opportunity of that, and steal the horse, he will be chargeable, because the neglect gave the thieves the occasion to steal the horse." The care taken by a prudent man has always been the rule laid down; and as to the supposed difficulty of applying it, a jury has always been able to say, whether, taking that rule as their guide, there has been negligence on the occasion in question.

Instead, therefore, of saying that the liability for negligence should be co-extensive with the judgment of each individual, which would be as variable as the length of the foot of each individual, we ought rather to adhere to the rule which requires in all cases a regard to caution such as a man of ordinary prudence would observe. That was in substance the criterion presented to the jury in this case, and therefore the present rule must be discharged.

PARK J. I entirely concur in what has fallen from his Lordship.

As to the direction of the learned Judge, it was perfectly correct. Under the circumstances of the case it was proper to leave it to the jury whether with reference to the caution which would have been observed by a man of ordinary prudence, the Defendant had not been guilty of gross negligence. After he had been warned repeatedly during five weeks as to the consequences likely to happen, there is no colour for altering the verdict, unless it were to increase the damages.

GASELEE J. concurred in discharging the rule.

VAUGHAN J. The principle on which this action proceeds, is by no means new. It has been urged that the Defendant in such a case takes no duty on himself; but I do not agree in that position: every one takes upon himself the duty of so dealing with his own property as not to injure the property of others. It was, if any thing, too favourable to the Defendant to leave it to the jury whether he had been guilty of gross negligence: for when the Defendant upon being warned as to the consequences likely to ensue from the condition of the rick, said, "he would chance it," it was manifest he adverted to his interest in the insurance office. The conduct of a prudent man has always been the criterion for the jury in such cases: but it is by no means confined to them. In insurance cases, where a captain has sold his vessel after damage too extensive for repairs, the question has always been, whether he had pursued the course which a prudent man would have pursued under the same circumstance. Here, there was not a single witness whose testimony did not go to establish gross negligence in the Defendant. He had repeated warnings of what was likely to occur, and the whole calamity was occasioned by his procrastination.

Rule discharged.

QUESTION

What particularly does the next case add to *Vaughan v. Menlove*?

BROWN v. KENDALL
Massachusetts Supreme Judicial Court
60 Mass. 292 (1850)

[Trying to break up a fight between two dogs, the defendant, Kendall, inadvertently struck the plaintiff with a stick. While simultaneously backing up and flailing at the dogs, the defendant struck the plaintiff's eye on a backstroke. The trial court refused to give the jury certain instructions requested by the defendant and gave others requested by the plaintiff over the objection of the defendant. The jury rendered a verdict for the plaintiff and the defendant appealed.]

SHAW, C.J. [A portion of the opinion treating the distinction between trespass vi et armis and trespass on the case is omitted.]

We think, as the result of all the authorities, the rule is correctly stated by Mr. Greenleaf, that the plaintiff must come prepared with evidence to show either that the intention was unlawful, or that the defendant was in fault; for if the injury was unavoidable, and the conduct of the defendant was free from blame, he will not be liable. 2 Greenl. Ev. §§ 85 to 92; Wakeman v. Robinson, 1 Bing. 213. If, in the prosecution of a lawful act, a casualty purely accidental arises, no action can be supported for an injury arising there-from. Davis v. Saunders, 2 Chit. R. 639; Com. Dig. Battery, A. (Day's Ed.) and notes; Vincent v. Stinehou 69 r, 7 Verm. In applying these rules to the present case, we can perceive no reason why the instructions asked for by the defendant ought not to have been given; to this effect, that if both plaintiff and defendant at the time of the blow were using ordinary care, or if at that time the defendant was using ordinary care, and the plaintiff was not, or if at that time, both the plaintiff and defendant were not using ordinary care, then the plaintiff could not recover.

In using this term, ordinary care, it may be proper to state, that what constitutes ordinary care will vary with the circumstances of cases. In general, it means that kind and degree of care, which prudent and cautious men would use, such as is required by the exigency of the case, and such as is necessary to guard against probable danger. A man who should have occasion to discharge a gun, on an open and extensive marsh, or in a forest, would be required to use less circumspection and care, than if he were to do the same thing in an inhabited town, village, or city. To make an accident, or casualty, or as the law sometimes states it, inevitable accident, it must be such an accident as the defendant could not have avoided by the use of the kind and degree of care necessary to the exigency, and in the circumstances in which he was placed.

We are not aware of any circumstances in this case, requiring a distinction between acts which it was lawful and proper to do, and acts of legal duty. There are cases, undoubtedly, in which officers are bound to act under process, for the legality of which they are not responsible, and perhaps some others in which this distinction would be important. We can have no doubt that the act of the defendant in attempting to part the fighting dogs, one of which was his own, and for the injurious acts of which he might be responsible, was a lawful and proper act, which he might do by proper and safe means. If, then, in doing this act, using due care and all proper precautions necessary to the exigency of the case, to avoid hurt to others, in raising his stick for that purpose, he accidentally hit the plaintiff in his eye, and wounded him, this was the result of pure accident, or was involuntary and unavoidable, and therefore the action would not lie. Or if the defendant was chargeable with some negligence, and if the plaintiff was also chargeable with negligence, we think the plaintiff cannot recover without showing that the damage was caused wholly by the act of the defendant, and that the plaintiff's own negligence did not contribute as an efficient cause to produce it.

The court instructed the jury, that if it was not a necessary act, and the defendant was not in duty bound to part the dogs, but might with propriety interfere or not as he chose, the defendant was responsible for the consequences of the blow, unless it appeared that he was in the exercise of extraordinary care, so that the accident was inevitable, using the word not in a strict but a popular sense.[16]

This is to be taken in connection with the charge afterwards given, that if the jury believed, that the act of interference in the fight was unnecessary, (that is, as before explained, not a duty incumbent on the defendant,) then the burden of proving extraordinary care on the part of the defendant, or want of ordinary care on the part of plaintiff, was on the defendant.

The court are of opinion that these directions were not conformable to law. If the act of hitting the plaintiff was unintentional, on the part of the defendant, and done in the doing of a lawful act, then the defendant was not liable, unless it was done in the want of exercise of due care, adapted to the exigency of the case, and therefore such want of due care became part of the plaintiff's case, and the burden of proof was on the plaintiff to establish it. 2 Greenl. Ev. § 85; Powers v. Russell, 13 Pick. 69, 76; Tourtellot v. Rosebrook, 11 Met. 460.

Perhaps the learned judge, by the use of the term extraordinary care, in the above charge, explained as it is by the context, may have intended nothing more than that increased degree of care and diligence, which the exigency of particular circumstances might require, and which men of ordinary care and prudence would use under like circumstances, to guard against danger. If such was the meaning of

---

[16] [Ed — The jury was also instructed that if the act was a necessary one, or one the defendant was under a duty to do, then he was not responsible provided he used ordinary care.]

this part of the charge, then it does not differ from our views, as above explained.

But we are of opinion, that the other part of the charge, that the burden of proof was on the defendant, was incorrect. Those facts which are essential to enable the plaintiff to recover, he takes the burden of proving. The evidence may be offered by the plaintiff or by the defendant; the question of due care, or want of care, may be essentially connected with the main facts, and arise from the same proof; but the effect of the rule, as to the burden of proof, is this, that when the proof is all in, and before the jury, from whatever side it comes, and whether directly proved, or inferred from circumstances, if it appears that the defendant was doing a lawful act, and unintentionally hit and hurt the plaintiff, then unless it also appears to the satisfaction of the jury, that the defendant is chargeable with some fault, negligence, carelessness, or want of prudence, the plaintiff fails to sustain the burden of proof, and is not entitled to recover.

New trial ordered.

NOTE AND QUESTIONS

Does the standard of care in negligence as it is clarified in *Brown v. Kendall* differ importantly from the standard in *Vaughan v. Menlove*? *Brown v. Kendall* also draws the plaintiff's own behavior into the consideration of whether the defendant is to be liable for the damages done. How is plaintiff's behavior taken into account, and what effect does it have on the right to recover? These matters are developed more fully in § 4.07 and in Chapter 9.

LESTER v. SAYLES
Supreme Court of Missouri
850 S.W.2d 858 (Mo. 1993)

LIMBAUGH, JUDGE.

This is an appeal from jury verdicts entered in favor of Latonya Lester and her mother, Wanda Thompson, following an accident in which Latonya, then age four years and nine months, was struck by a truck and severely injured. The Court of Appeals, Eastern District, transferred the case to this Court after opinion. Because one of the issues involves the validity of a statute, this Court has jurisdiction of the entire case. Art. V, § 3, Mo. Const. The judgment in favor of Latonya Lester is reversed and remanded for a new trial. The judgment in favor of Wanda Thompson is affirmed.

BACKGROUND

Latonya sustained injuries on the afternoon of Monday, June 20, 1988, just after 2:00 p.m., when she was hit by a one-ton flat-bed truck owned by defendant McHenry Truck Equipment Inc. and operated by defendant-employee Mark Sayles.

Plaintiffs, Wanda Thompson and her daughter Latonya Lester, lived with their family in an apartment on the south side of St. Louis Avenue near the intersection of St. Louis Avenue and Elliot Street in the City of St. Louis. St. Louis Avenue is a four-lane through street with parking on each side. A fire hydrant is located on the southwest corner of the intersection, approximately 45 feet east of the doorway entrance to the apartment. Earlier in the afternoon, someone had opened this hydrant, apparently seeking respite from the afternoon heat.

A powerful flow of water, surrounded by spray and mist, gushed from the hydrant to a distance nearly half way across St. Louis Avenue. The water then spilled over into the westbound lane of traffic and meandered to the far side of the avenue where a clogged storm drain along the curb was converted to a temporary wading pool. About 2:00 p.m., Wanda crossed the street with her two-year-old nephew so that he could play in the makeshift pool, but she left her daughter, Latonya, at the doorway playing with their dog.

A few moments later, defendant Sayles, who had just made a delivery and was returning to the company offices, was traveling west on the inside westbound lane of St. Louis Avenue approaching the intersection at Elliot Street. He testified that he observed the spray of water from the hydrant as well as a number of children and adults on the sidewalk nearby, and at that point, he slowed the truck considerably. Latonya had apparently been crossing the street as the truck went through the intersection and the wet pavement. She was hit broadside, swept underneath, and run over. Sayles testified that he never saw Latonya and that he stopped the truck only because he heard a "thud" and realized he had hit something. At trial, the testimony regarding the speed of the vehicle at the time of the accident was grossly inconsistent. Some of the several witnesses stated that the truck had slowed down to as little as 5 m.p.h.; others testified that the truck was traveling at as fast as 30 to 35 m.p.h.

Latonya now suffers from substantial and irreparable injuries. She is a spastic quadriplegic; she cannot walk, crawl or reach out; she will be committed to a wheelchair for the rest of her life and will require lifelong physical care. In addition, brain damage has left her with the mental capabilities of a two-year-old. She will never be able to function independently, much less support herself by working. Her mother, Wanda, is her full-time caretaker.

The jury returned a verdict in favor of Latonya and against Sayles and McHenry Truck Equipment in the amount of $19,817,000. Wanda Thompson's damages on her claims for medical expenses and for loss of Latonya's "services, society and companionship" were assessed at $1,860,000. . . .

ISSUES PRESENTED

The defendants pose the following points of error: [(1) and (2) and (4) through (8) omitted.]

. . . .

(3) The trial court erred in denying defendants leave to amend their answer to allege the comparative fault [contributory negligence] of Latonya Lester and also erred in refusing to submit a comparative fault [contributory negligence] instruction on that issue.

. . . .

We rule issues (1) and (3) in favor of defendants and against plaintiff Latonya Lester. Both the damages and the liability components of her verdict were the result of reversible error; therefore, her claims are remanded for new trial.

There was no reversible error, however, in the proceedings brought by Wanda Thompson, and her judgment is affirmed.

Because issues (1) and (3) are dispositive of the appeal of Latonya's judgment, we will address them first. . . .

COMPARATIVE FAULT [CONTRIBUTORY NEGLIGENCE] OF LATONYA LESTER

Defendants next raise two interrelated allegations of prejudicial error: 1) the refusal of the trial court to allow defendants to amend their pleadings to allege Latonya Lester's comparative fault [contributory negligence] and 2) the refusal of the court to submit an instruction that would allow the jury to assess fault against Latonya. Procedurally, the defendants sought leave to file amended answers on the day of trial in order to include the comparative fault [contributory negligence] of Latonya Lester as a defense. Later, during the instruction conference, defendants sought to have the jury instructed on this same issue. The trial court ruled against defendants in both instances.

These claims of error cannot be addressed until we resolve the underlying issue-whether the fault of Latonya Lester is a question of fact for the jury, or whether Latonya, a child of tender years, is incapable of fault as a matter of law. Only if we resolve this issue in favor of defendants and against Latonya, do we address the particular points raised by defendants.

Furthermore, defendants' allegations have been perfected only as they pertain to the claims of Latonya Lester. The point of error on these issues does refer to the amendments and instructions proposed by defendants, however, in violation of Rule 84.04(d), defendants fail to state why the action of the trial court was erroneous as to Wanda Thompson's claims, and fail to offer citations of authority on the matter. The assessment and application of Latonya's comparative fault [contributory negligence] to reduce the recovery of co-plaintiff, Wanda Thompson, is an issue that is not only problematic but also separate and distinct from the focus of the point of error-whether fault can be assessed against a child of tender years. Defendants have neither identified nor briefed this separate issue. Under these circumstances, we decline to review the point of error as it purports to apply to Wanda's claim.

A. Various courses have been charted on the issue of contributory negligence, and now, the issue of comparative fault,[17] and their application to children of tender years. In this area, courts must necessarily balance an appropriate concern that children cannot be expected to conform their conduct to adult standards with a countervailing concern that the general public should not shoulder all liability created by the avoidable carelessness of children.

---

[17] [Footnote 2 in reported opinion.] Although most of the cases and authorities cited herein address the issue with reference to a child's contributory negligence, they apply equally well with reference to a child's comparative fault. Under the system of contributory negligence or under the system of comparative fault, the jury must decide the same question: whether plaintiff's conduct was in any measure negligent. *See Gustafson v. Benda*, 661 S.W.2d 11 (Mo. banc 1983).

A large number of states resolve this difficulty under the "tender years doctrine," which calls for the establishment of a fixed age below which a child will be conclusively presumed incapable of negligence (or fault). See, e.g., Yarborough v. Berner, 467 S.W.2d 188, 190 (Tex.1971) (below age five); Swindell v. Hellkamp, 242 So. 2d 708, 710 (Fla.1970) (below age six).[18] The most severe line drawing, however, occurs under the so-called "Illinois Rule," recognized in several states. See, e.g., Mort v. Walter, 98 Ill. 2d 391, 75 Ill. Dec. 228, 457 N.E.2d 18 (1983); Pino v. Szuch, 185 W. Va. 476, 408 S.E.2d 55, 57 (1991). Derived from biblical and criminal common law antecedents, this rule places an almost mystical importance on the age seven and multiples thereof.[19] It is applied so that a child under seven is incapable of negligence as a matter of law. Children between seven and fourteen are presumed incapable of negligence. Only at age fourteen is a child presumed to possess sufficient mental capability to comprehend and avoid danger. Pino, 408 S.E.2d at 58.

In stark contrast to the (Illinois Rule(is the modern trend which rejects fixed and arbitrarily drawn age limits. See, e.g., Honeycutt by and through Phillips v. City of Wichita, 247 Kan. 250, 796 P.2d 549, 552 (1990); Peterson v. Taylor, 316 N.W.2d 869 (Ia.1982); Toetschinger v. Ihnot, 312 Minn. 59, 250 N.W.2d 204 (1977). These jurisdictions hold that the question of contributory negligence of young children is ordinarily a question of fact for the jury to decide. Honeycutt, 796 P.2d at 552. A minor's incapacity for negligence may be determined as a matter of law only if the child is so young, or the evidence of incapacity so overwhelming, that reasonable minds could not differ on the matter. *Id.* at 551, citing Quillian v. Mathews, 86 Nev. 200, 467 P.2d 111-13 (1970).

Although this approach is not without its critics,[20] it has been cited with favor in Prosser and Keeton on the Law of Torts:

Most courts have attempted to fix a minimum age, below which the child is held to be incapable of all negligence. . . . Other courts have rejected any such fixed and arbitrary rules of delimitation, and have held that children well under the age of seven can be capable of some negligent conduct. Undoubtedly there is an irreducible minimum, probably in the neighborhood of four years of age, but it arguably ought not to be fixed by rules laid down in advance without regard to the particular case. As the age decreases, there are simply fewer possibilities of negligence, until finally, at some indeterminate point, there is none at all. Prosser and Keeton at 180.

In a series of cases near the turn of the century, this Court adopted in essence what we have described here as the modern trend. Holmes v. Missouri Pac. Ry. Co., 190 Mo. 98, 88 S.W. 623 (banc 1905); Spillane v. Missouri Pac. Ry. Co., 135 Mo.

---

[18] [Footnote 3 in reported opinion.] W. Page Keeton, et al., Prosser and Keeton on the Law of Torts § 31, at 179-82 (5th ed. 1984); F. Harper, et al., The Law of Torts § 16.8, at 438-60 (2d ed. 1986). Other jurisdictions, while not adopting a specific age, hold that at some undetermined age a child is incapable of negligence as a matter of law. Above this age, the issue is reserved for the jury as a question of fact. *See, e.g., Christian v. Goodwin*, 188 Cal. App. 2d 650, 10 Cal. Rptr. 507 (1961) (between age four and five); *Taylor v. Armiger*, 277 Md. 638, 358 A.2d 883, 889 (1976) (probably below age five).

[19] [Footnote 4 in reported opinion.] *Prosser and Keeton*, § 32, at 180.

[20] [Footnote 6 in reported opinion.] *See, e.g., Clark v. Circus-Circus, Inc.*, 525 F.2d 1328, 1331-33 (9th Cir.1975) (Hill, J., dissenting); *Pino v. Szuch*, 408 S.E.2d at 58 (the Restatement standard set forth in Section 283A is "too vague to assist a jury."); *see generally* F. Harper, et al., The Law of Torts § 16.8 at 438-60; O. Gray, The Standard of Care for Children Revisited, 45 Mo. L. Rev. 597 (1980).

414, 37 S.W. 198 (1896); Burger v. Missouri Pac. Ry. Co., 112 Mo. 238, 20 S.W. 439 (1892); accord Berry v. St. Louis M. & S.E.R. Co., 214 Mo. 593, 114 S.W. 27 (1908). In Holmes, the Court stated that "the question of whether a child is old enough to be held responsible for his conduct, as for contributory negligence, is always a question of fact. . . . " Holmes, 88 S.W. at 624-25 (citations omitted)[21] The only exception to this rule is where a child is exceedingly young or where there is otherwise no doubt as to the child's capacity, in which case the trial court will decide the issue as a matter of law. *Id.* When evaluating responsibility for conduct, "no higher degree of care will be expected of [a child] than is usually exercised by persons of similar age, judgment, and experience." *Id.*

Subsequent appellate decisions, however, began to erode the holdings of the Holmes era cases. For example, in Quirk v. Metropolitan Street Ry. Co., 200 Mo. App. 585, 210 S.W. 103 (1919), it was held that a seven-year-old child who had jumped from a streetcar could not be contributorily negligent, in part, because of his tender years. Quirk, 210 S.W. at 105-06. In Volz v. City of St. Louis, 326 Mo. 362, 32 S.W.2d 72 (1930), this Court stated in dicta that "we deem it advisable to say that it is the general rule that a boy six years of age cannot be guilty of contributory negligence." *Id.* 32 S.W.2d at 74. Similarly, this Court noted, again through dicta, in Schmidt v. Allen, 303 S.W.2d 652, 658 (Mo.1957), that a four-year-old child, struck by a car while attempting to cross a major thoroughfare in St. Louis, could not be contributorily negligent. Because of these and other similar cases, the viability and validity of Holmes is called into question.[22]

We believe, however, that the "modern trend," espoused in Holmes and adopted early on by this Court, is more sound and more likely to ensure just results. Although jurisdictions which have adopted either the "Illinois Rule" or other arbitrary age distinctions have the advantage of consistency and ease of application, that is also the principal shortcoming of their approach. Positing a predetermined age at which negligence or fault can occur has little basis in reason or logic; one day's difference in age should not serve as the dividing line as to whether or not a child is capable of negligence or fault. See Toetschinger, 250 N.W.2d at 211. We prefer a rule that allows for a degree of flexibility in the handling of each case so that a child's negligence or fault is determined in relation to the expectations held for other children in same or similar circumstances.

To summarize, we reaffirm the holding of Holmes. The fault of a child should be determined by the fact-finder in each case, based upon that degree of care exercised by children of the same or similar age, judgment, and experience. Only if the child is so young or the evidence of incapacity so overwhelming that reasonable minds could not differ on the issue, should trial courts rule as a matter of law, usually pursuant to a motion for directed verdict, that the child cannot be capable of fault.

---

[21] [Footnote 7 in reported opinion.] The Holmes Court reversed the judgment of the trial court which had found an eight-year-old boy contributorily negligent as a matter of law. This situation is the "flipside" of a tender years case where a child could not, as a matter of law, be contributorily negligent. The Holmes analysis applies equally well in both instances.

[22] [Footnote 8 in reported opinion.] Missouri courts continued to follow Holmes and its progeny in those cases involving older children. *See, e.g.*, *Carter v. Boys' Club of Greater Kansas City*, 552 S.W.2d 327, 332-33 (Mo. App.1977) (age 12); *Wilson v. White*, 272 S.W.2d 1, 6-7 (Mo. App.1954) (age 13). Only in cases involving children of tender years and then only in dicta did this Court depart from the rule established near the turn of the century.

CONCLUSION

The judgment in favor of Latonya Lester is reversed and remanded for new trial. The judgment in favor of Wanda Thompson is affirmed.

NOTES AND QUESTIONS

(1)   Does *Lester* depart from the objective standard of *Vaughan v. Menlove*? In The Common Law, pp. 108, 109, Holmes addressed the question of the child's standard of care as follows:

> The standards of the law are standards of general application. The law takes no account of the infinite varieties of temperament, intellect, and education which make the internal character of a given act so different in different men. It does not attempt to see men as God sees them, for more than one sufficient reason. In the first place, the impossibility of nicely measuring a man's powers and limitations is far clearer than that of ascertaining his knowledge of law, which has been thought to account for what is called the presumption that every man knows the law. But a more satisfactory explanation is, that, when men live in society, a certain average of conduct, a sacrifice of individual peculiarities going beyond a certain point, is necessary to the general welfare. If, for instance, a man is born hasty and awkward, is always having accidents and hurting himself or his neighbours, no doubt his congenital defects will be allowed for in the courts of Heaven, but his slips are no less troublesome to his neighbours than if they sprang from guilty neglect. His neighbours accordingly require-him, at his proper peril, to come up to their standard, and the courts which they establish decline to take his personal equation into account . . .

> There are exceptions to the principle that every man is presumed to possess ordinary capacity to avoid harm to his neighbours, which illustrate the rule, and also the moral basis of liability in general. When a man has a distinct defect of such a nature that all can recognize it as making certain precautions impossible, he will not be held answerable for not taking them. A blind man is not required to see at his peril; and although he is, no doubt, bound to consider his infirmity in regulating his actions, yet if he properly finds himself in a certain situation, the neglect of precautions requiring eyesight would not prevent his recovering for an injury to himself, and, it may be presumed, would not make him liable for injuring another. So it is held that, in cases where he is the plaintiff, an infant of very tender years is only bound to take the precautions of which an infant is capable; the same principle may be cautiously applied where he is defendant.

Quoted by Owen, J., in *McHale v. Watson*, [1966] 115 C.L.R. 199 (High Court, Australia).

(2)   *Camberlinck v. Thomas*, 312 N.W. 2d 260 (Neb. 1981), reviewed most of the variations of the child's standard applied in various courts. Among those is the "Illinois rule," alluded to in *Lester*, which is often referred to as the "rule of sevens." See, e.g., *Dickeson v. Baltimore & Ohio Chicago Terminal RR. Co.*, 245 N. E. 2d 762 (Ill. 1969). This rule is that children under the age of 7 years are conclusively presumed to be incapable of negligence; from years 7 to 14 a rebuttable presumption of capacity for negligence exists; and, children over age 14 are held to the adult

standard of care absent evidence rebutting capacity. Even under this rule a court may occasionally find the evidence so clear that a holding of negligence (or not) may be entered as a matter of law. See, e.g., *Smith v. Diamond*, 421 N. E. 1172 (Ind. App. 1981) (holding 12 year old boy to have contributorily negligent as a matter of law in entering a street without looking). Others follow what me called the "Massachusetts rule," i.e., a child of tender age is conclusively presumed to be incapable of negligence, but older children are judged in light of their age, experience, and intelligence. See. e.g., *Toetschinger v. Ihnot*, 250 N.W.2d 204 (Minn. 1977). Still others apply a rebuttable presumption of incapacity for children of tender age. See, e.g., *Bush v. New Jersey & New York Transit Co., Inc.* 153 A.2d 28 (N. J. 1959) (child of less than seven years is rebuttably presumed to be incapable of negligence, and issue of capacity may not be submitted to jury in the absence of evidence of child's training and experience from which jury could infer existence of capacity to avoid the danger in question). Some early American authority purported to apply no child standard See, *Williams v. Hay*, 38 N.E. 449, 143 N.Y. 442 (1894).

(3)   Most courts that have considered the matter hold that the same rule applies to a child's primary negligence as applies to contributory negligence. *Standard v. Shine*, 295 S.E.2d 786 (S.C.1982), involved an action against a six year old child charging that the child had negligently started a fire that destroyed the plaintiff's property. The court overruled its prior application of the Illinois rule and applied the standard that "a minor's conduct should be judged by the standard of behavior to be expected of a child of like age, intelligence, and experience under the circumstances" for both primary and contributory negligence. 295 S.E.2d at 787. Do you agree that the standard for negligence as applied to children of tender years in Camerlinck and Standard is more fitting than the common law Illinois rule? A most thorough examination of this entire subject was given by the various judges on the High Court of Australia in *McHale v. Watson*, [1966] 115 C.L.R. 199 (High Court, Australia).

On the point as to whether negligence and contributory negligence are measured by different standards of care, American jurisdictions would agree with the following statement from *Ellis v. D'Anglo*, 253 P.2d 675, 678 (Cal. App. 1953):

> We may take it as settled in the case of infants that "no different measure [of negligence] is to be applied to their primary than to their contributory faults." In a case involving the question of the liability of an infant for his negligent conduct the court in Hoyt v. Rosenberg, 80 Cal.App.2d 500 at pages 506, 507, 182 P.2d 234, at page 238, 173 A.L.R. 883, said: "While the question as to whether a minor has been negligent in certain circumstances is ordinarily one of fact for the jury, an affirmative finding thereon must conform to and be in accordance with the established rule that a minor is expected to use, not the quantum of care expected of an adult, but only that degree or amount of care which is ordinarily used by children of the same age under similar circumstances." This is the same test applied in determining a child's contributory negligence.

(4)   As do some other states, South Carolina has a "Parental Responsibility Act," which in that state reads:

> When any unmarried minor under the age of seventeen years and living with his parent shall maliciously and intentionally destroy, damage or steal property, real, personal or mixed, the owner of such property shall be

entitled to recover from such parent of such minor actual damages in a civil action in an amount not exceeding one thousand dollars . . .

Standard v. Shine, 295 S. E.2d at 787. Do you think it appropriate for the court in Standard to abrogate the Illinois rule in a case in which the "Parental Responsibility Act" also had potential application?

(5)   Should the activity the minor was engaged in affect his entitlement to a special instruction on the minor's duty of care? Suppose, for example, the minor was accused of negligence in the operation of a bicycle? A motor vehicle? See, e.g., *Terre Haute First National Bank v. Stewart*, 455 N.E.2d 362 (Ind. App. 1983) (13-year-old on moped); *Davis v. Wateman*, 420 So. 2d 1063 (Miss. 1982) (13-year-old, motor bike); and *Robinson v. Lindsey*, 20 Wash. 2d 410, 596 P.2d 392, 393, 394 (Wash. 1979) ((We believe a better rationale is that when the activity a child engages in is inherently dangerous, as in the operation of a powerful mechanized vehicle [an 11 year old driving a snowmobile], the child should be held to an adult standard of care.")

(6)   What other conditions or statuses personal to a particular person should entitle him to be held to a standard of care either higher or lower than the general standard? Why? As to the standard of care of mentally deficient people, see *Vaughn v. Menlove*, supra., § 6.05 infra., and *Gould v. American Family Mutual Insurance Co.*, 543 N.W. 282 (Wis. 1996). To the assertion that acknowledging a child's standard of care would inappropriately defer to the "the idiosyncrasies of the particular person," Australian judge Windeyer retorted, "Childhood is not an idiosyncrasy!" *McHale v. Watson, supra.* Does that statement provide a legitimate basis for distinguishing between children and mentally deficient adults?

(7)   *Lester* brings out again the notion of contributory negligence that surfaced in *Brown v. Kendall*. Is this a matter of defense to be raised and proved by the defendant, or is negating its presence a job for the plaintiff? Why? The issue of contributory negligence is examined further in §§ 4.07 and 9.01, infra.

(8)   *Lester* applied the standard of a child of "like age, judgment and experience." Although a number of other courts apply that standard in some content, a large number applied the standard of a "like child of the same age, intelligence, and experience." See *Camberlinck v. Thomas, supra.* Is the difference semantic or substantive? In either case, who makes the determination?

(9)   How many children of 4 years and 9 months possess the capacity to exercise care for their safety. How may possess the capacity to do an intentional act?

GLASCOW CORPORATION v. MUIR
[1943] A.C. 448 (House of Lords)[23]

[An action was brought against the proprietor of a public tea room on behalf of several small children who were scalded when two men bringing a tea urn through a narrow passageway permitted the urn to fall and dump its contents. No evidence was submitted as to why the urn fell. The two men were bringing the tea for consumption by picnickers who were on the premises with the permission of the proprietor. The urn and the tea were not the property of the proprietor and the men were not in the proprietor's employment. The evidence suggested that the

---

[23] [Ed. — Appeal Cases, Law Reports, decision of House of Lords.]

passageway would admit the passage of the men with the urn. The man entered the premises with the urn without notifying the proprietor that they had arrived.

The action alleged that the proprietor ought to have cleared the room before admitting the men with the urn. After the case was tried, the trial judge dismissed the action on grounds that the evidence did not establish negligence. The appellate court reinstated the action. The parties agreed to the amount of damages and the case came to the House of Lords for review of the issue of liability.]

LORD MACMILLAN.

My Lords, the degree of care for the safety of others which the law requires human beings to observe in the conduct of their affairs varies according to the circumstances. There is no absolute standard, but it may be said generally that the degree of care required varies directly with the risk involved. Those who engage in operations inherently dangerous must take precautions which are not required of persons engaged in the ordinary routine of daily life. It is, no doubt, true that in every act which an individual performs there is present a potentiality of injury to others. All things are possible, and, indeed, it has become proverbial that the unexpected always happens, but, while the precept alterum non laedere requires us to abstain from intentionally injuring others, it does not impose liability for every injury which our conduct may occasion. In Scotland, at any rate, it has never been a maxim of the law that a man acts at his peril. Legal liability is limited to those consequences of our acts which a reasonable man of ordinary intelligence and experience so acting would have in contemplation. "The duty to take care," as I essayed to formulate it in Bourhill v. Young (I), "is the duty to avoid doing or omitting to do anything the doing or omitting to do which may have as its reasonable and probable consequence injury to others, and the duty is owed to those to whom injury may reasonably and probably be anticipated if the duty is not observed." This, in my opinion, expresses the law of Scotland and I apprehend that it is also the law of England. The standard of foresight of the reasonable man is, in one sense, an impersonal test. It eliminates the personal equation and is independent of the idiosyncrasies of the particular person whose conduct is in question. Some persons are by nature unduly timorous and imagine every path beset with lions. Others, of more robust temperament, fail to foresee or nonchalantly disregard even the most obvious dangers. The reasonable man is presumed to be free both from over-apprehension and from over-confidence, but there is a sense in which the standard of care of the reasonable man involves in its application a subjective element. It is still left to the judge to decide what, in the circumstances of the particular case, the reasonable man would have had in contemplation, and what, accordingly, the party sought to be made liable ought to have foreseen. Here there is room for diversity of view, as, indeed, is well illustrated in the present case. What to one judge may seem far-fetched may seem to another both natural and probable.

With these considerations in mind I turn to the facts of the occurrence on which your Lordships have to adjudicate. Up to a point the facts have been sufficiently ascertained. . . .

The question, as I see it, is whether Mrs. Alexander, when she was asked to allow a tea urn to be brought into the premises under her charge, ought to have had in mind that it would require to be carried through a narrow passage in which there were a number of children and that there would be a risk of the contents of the urn being spilt and scalding some of the children. If, as a reasonable person, she ought to have had these considerations in mind, was it her duty to require that she should be informed of the arrival of the urn, and, before allowing it to be carried through the narrow passage, to clear all the children out of it in case they might be splashed with scalding water?

The urn was an ordinary medium-sized cylindrical vessel of about fifteen inches diameter and about sixteen inches in height made of light sheet metal with a fitting lid, which was closed. It had a handle at each side. Its capacity was about nine gallons, but it was only a third or a half full. It was not in itself an inherently dangerous thing and could be carried quite safely and easily by two persons exercising ordinary care. A caterer called as a witness on behalf of the pursuers, who had large experience of the use of such urns, said that he had never had a mishap with an urn while it was being carried. The urn was in charge of two responsible persons, McDonald, the church officer, and the lad, Taylor, who carried it between them. When they entered the passage way they called out to the children there congregated to keep out of the way and the children drew back to let them pass. Taylor, who held the front handle, had safely passed the children, when, for some unexplained reason, McDonald loosened hold of the other handle, the urn tilted over, and some of its contents were spilt, scalding several of the children who were standing by. The urn was not upset, but came to the ground on its base.

In my opinion, Mrs. Alexander had no reason to anticipate that such an event would happen as a consequence of granting permission for a tea urn to be carried through the passage way where the children were congregated, and, consequently, there was no duty incumbent on her to take precautions against the occurrence of such an event. I think that she was entitled to assume that the urn would be in charge of responsible persons (as it was) who would have regard for the safety of the children in the passage (as they did have regard), and that the urn would be carried with ordinary care, in which case its transit would occasion no danger to bystanders.

The pursuers have left quite unexplained the actual cause of the accident. The immediate cause was not the carrying of the urn through the passage, but McDonald's losing grip of his handle. How he came to do so is entirely a matter of speculation. He may have stumbled or he may have suffered a temporary muscular failure. We do not know, and the pursuers have not chosen to enlighten us by calling McDonald as a witness. Yet it is argued that Mrs. Alexander ought to have foreseen the possibility, nay, the reasonable probability of an occurrence the nature of which is unascertained. Suppose that McDonald let go his handle through carelessness. Was Mrs. Alexander bound to foresee this as reasonably probable and to take precautions against the possible consequences? I do not think so. The only ground on which the view of the majority of the learned judges of the First Division can be justified is that Mrs. Alexander ought to have foreseen that some accidental injury might happen to the children in the passage if she allowed an urn containing hot tea to be carried through the passage, and ought, therefore, to have cleared out the children entirely during its transit, which Lord Moncrieff describes as "the only effective step." With all respect, I think that this would impose on Mrs. Alexander a degree of care higher than the law exacts.

There is a passage in Mrs. Alexander's evidence on which reliance is placed as tantamount to an admission on her part of a failure of duty, but the answers which she gave with creditable candour to the leading questions of cross-examining counsel are, in my opinion, quite natural expressions on her part of wisdom after the distressing event. She says that, if she had been told of the arrival of the men with the urn, as she expected she would be, she "certainly would have got them [the children] away from the entrance at the doorway." That is just what McDonald and Taylor evidently did. I do not think that Mrs. Alexander's evidence amounts to an admission of negligence on her part, and, in any case, it is not an admission binding on the defenders. No special point arises from the circumstance that the injured children were invitees on the defenders' premises. They were entitled to rely on not being exposed while on the premises to any risk occasioned by the negligence of the defenders or their servants. As, in my opinion, no negligence has been established, I agree with what I understand to be the view of all your Lordships that the appeal should be allowed and the judgment [i.e., liability not proved] of the Lord Ordinary restored.

[The appeal was granted and judgment ordered for the defendant.]

NOTES AND QUESTIONS

(1) The issue of whether a duty of care has been breached requires a two-step analysis. The first is to define as specifically as possible the parameters of the standard. How would you articulate the standard as defined by the foregoing cases? It has been said, "In English jurisprudence [the prudent and reasonable man] has been traditionally described as 'the man on the Clapham omnibus' . . . " Luntz et al. Torts: Cases and Commentary (1980), at 152. See also, *Hall v. Brooklands Auto Racing Club*, [1933] 1 K.B. 205, 224. Does that help?

You may assume that courts and juries have always accounted for the "reasonable Woman" under the rubric "reasonable man under the same or similar circumstances." Nevertheless, A.P. Herbert, the common lawspoofster, once noted: "In all the mass of authorities which bear upon this branch of the law there is no single mention of a reasonable woman." Herbert, Misleading Cases in the Common Law, 12-16, quoted in *Bell Cab Company v. Vasquez*, 434 S.W. 2d 714, 722 (Tex. App. 1968) (dissenting opinion). Despite Herbert's statement, several American courts have explicitly alluded to the "reasonable woman" in negligence cases, see. e.g., *Broussard v. American Indemnity Company*, 125 So. 2d 499, 501 (La. App. 1961), *Struthers Wells-Gulfport v. Bradford*, 304 So. 2d 645, 647 (Miss. 1974), *Hainlin v. Budge*, 47 So. 825 (Fla. 1908), and *Weitz v. Baurot*, 406 A.2d 1138, 1141 (Pa. Super. 1979), and the "reasonable woman" appears to be the standard in sexual harassment cases. See, e.g. *Lehmann v. Toys' R Us, Inc.*, 626 A 2d 445, 457 (N.J. 1993).

The second step in the breach analysis is to weigh the various circumstances that would influence the behavior of the man on the Clapham omnibus. What kinds of factors seem to be at work in the foregoing cases? Which of these are permissible to consider: foresight, practicality, cost, gravity of risk, probability of risk, social utility of the defendant's behavior, the ability of the defendant to pay the judgment, the need of the plaintiff for a recovery? One judge stated, "as a general proposition, a defendant's wealth is an unreliable indicator of fault, and should play no part, at least consciously, in the legal analysis of the problem." Richardson, J. (dissenting), *Sindell v. Abbott Laboratories*, 607 P.2d 924, 941 (Cal. 1980). Can you conceive of exceptions to that proposition?

Identifying appropriate factors is one matter, and there surely is no inclusive or exclusive list to which all courts would agree — the process seems too fluid. A matter of even less agreement and structure is mixing and weighing the various factors to decide whether the duty of care was breached. In *United States v. Carroll Towing Co.*, 159 F.2d 169 (2d Cir. 1947), Learned Hand, a famous federal appellate judge, tried to quantify the standard as stated below. The particular issue was whether a barge company had been negligent in permitting the bargee (the barge tender) to go ashore on the particular occasion upon which the barge happened to break loose. The evidence proved, among other things, that the bargee had initially lied about why he had been away from the barge for so long.

> It appears from the foregoing review that there is no general rule to determine when the absence of a bargee or other attendant will make the owner of the barge liable for injuries to other vessels if she breaks away from her moorings.
>
> . . .
>
> It becomes apparent why there can be no such general rule, when we consider the grounds for such a liability. Since there are occasions when every vessel will break from her moorings, and since, if she does, she becomes a menace to those about her; the owner's duty, as in other similar situations, to provide against resulting injuries is a function of three variables: (1) The probability that she will break away; (2) the gravity of the resulting injury, if she does; (3) the burden of adequate precautions. Possibly it serves to bring this notion into relief to state it in algebraic terms: if the probability be called P; the injury, L; and the burden, B; liability depends upon whether B is less than L multiplied by P: i.e., whether $B < PL$. Applied to the situation at bar, the likelihood that a barge will break from her fasts and the damage she will do, vary with the place and time; for example, if a storm threatens, the danger is greater; so it is, if she is in a crowded harbor where moored barges are constantly being shifted about. On the other hand, the barge must not be the bargee's prison, even though he lives aboard; he must go ashore at times. We need not say whether, even in such crowded waters as New York Harbor a bargee must be aboard at night at all; it may be that the custom is otherwise, as Ward, J., supposed in The Kathryn B. Guinan, . . . and that, if so, the situation is one where custom should control. We leave that question open; but we hold that it is not in all cases a sufficient answer to a bargee's absence without excuse, during working hours, that he has properly made fast his barge to a pier, when he leaves her. In the case at bar the bargee left at five o'clock in the afternoon of January 3rd, and the flotilla broke away at about two o'clock in the afternoon of the following day, twenty-one hours afterwards. The bargee had been away all the time, and we hold that his fabricated story was affirmative evidence that he had no excuse for his absence. In such circumstances [busy harbor, wartime activities] . . . it was a fair requirement that [there] should have been a bargee aboard (unless he had some excuse for his absence), during the working hours of daylight.

United States v. Carroll Towing Co., 159 F.2d 169, 173, 174. To Hand's list of factors, some courts add a fourth, "the social utility of the defendant's conduct."

Meche v. Gulf States Utilities Co., 436 So. 2d 538, 542 (La. 1983), Blanche, J., dissenting.

Does Hand's attempt to quantify the judgment help you? Apparently, judges deem it to be of little help either to themselves or to juries because Hand's formulation is seldom alluded to in appellate opinions. Does it suggest that the question of moral blameworthiness is commonly viewed in terms of dollars?

(2) The following excerpts are descriptive of the less formalized manner in which most courts evaluate negligence. Note also that these statements address themselves to the delicate question of when a judge should not permit a fact question to be decided by a jury. What fears lurk in the minds of the judges, especially as exemplified by the second statement?

In *Metropolitan Railroad Co. v. Jackson*, [1877] App. Cas. 193, the plaintiff was hurt while moving through a railcar when a passageway door slammed shut as the train lurched. In a negligence action the jury returned a verdict for the plaintiff. The defendant appealed, alleging that the issue of negligence should not have been permitted to go to the jury. Lord Cairns said, at 197, 198:

> The case as to negligence having been left to the jury, the jury found a verdict for the Respondent with . . . damages. There was not, at your Lordships' bar, any serious controversy as to the principles applicable to the case of this description. The Judge has a certain duty to discharge, and the jurors have another and a different duty. The Judge has to say whether any facts have been established by evidence from which negligence may be reasonably inferred; the jurors have to say whether, from those facts, when submitted to them, negligence ought to be inferred. It is, in my opinion, of the greatest importance in the administration of justice that these separate functions should be maintained, and should be maintained distinct. It would be a serious inroad on the province of the jury, if, in a case where there are facts from which negligence may reasonably be inferred, the Judge were to withdraw the case from the jury upon the ground that, in his opinion, negligence may reasonably be inferred; and it would, on the other hand, place in the hands of the jurors a power which might be exercised in the most arbitrary manner, if they were at liberty to hold that negligence might be inferred from any state of facts whatever. To take the instance of actions against railway companies: a company might be unpopular, unpunctual, and irregular in its service; badly equipped as to its staff; unaccommodating to the public; notorious, perhaps, for accidents occurring on the line; and when an action was brought for the consequences of an accident, jurors, if left to themselves, might, upon evidence of general carelessness, find a verdict against the company in a case where the company was really blameless. It may be said that this would be set right by an application to the Court in banc, on the ground that the verdict was against evidence; but it is to be observed that such an application, even if successful, would only result in a new trial; and on a second trial, and even on subsequent trials, the same thing might happen again.
>
> In the present case I am bound to say that I do not find any evidence from which, in my opinion, negligence could reasonably be inferred. The negligence must in some way connect itself, or be connected by evidence, with the accident. It must be, if I might invent an expression founded upon

a phrase in the civil law, incuria dans locum injuriae. In the present case there was no doubt negligence in the company's servants, in allowing more passengers than the proper number to get on at the Gower Street Station; and it may also have been negligence if they saw these supernumerary passengers, or if they ought to have seen them, at Portland Road, not to have then removed them; but there is nothing, in my opinion, in this negligence which connects itself with the accident that took place. If, when the train was leaving Portland Road, the overcrowding had any effect on the movements of the Respondent; if it had any effect on the particular portion of the carriage where he was sitting, if it made him less a master of his actions when he stood up or when he fell forward, this ought to have been made matter of evidence; but no evidence of the kind was given. [The court reversed the judgment for the plaintiff and ordered the lower court to nonsuit the plaintiff.]

In *Railroad Company v. Stout*, 84 U.S. 657, 663, 664 (1873), Justice Hunt said:

It is true, in many cases, that where the facts are undisputed the effect of them is for the judgment of the court, and not for the decision of the jury. This is true in that class of cases where the existence of such facts come in question rather than where deductions or inferences are to be made from the facts. If a deed be given in evidence, a contract proven, or its breach testified to, the existence of such deed, contract, or breach, there being nothing in derogation of the evidence, is no doubt to be ruled as a question of law. In some cases, too, the necessary inferences from the proof are so certain that it may be ruled as a question of law. If a sane man voluntarily throws himself in contact with a passing engine, there being nothing to counteract the effect of this action, it may be ruled as a matter of law that the injury to him resulted from his own fault, and that no action can be sustained by him or his representatives. So if a coachdriver intentionally drives within a few inches of a precipice, and an accident happens, negligence may be ruled as a question of law. On the other hand, if he had placed a suitable distance between his coach and the precipice, but by the breaking of a rein or an axle, which could not have been anticipated, an injury occurred, it might be ruled as a question of law that there was no negligence and no liability.

But these are extreme cases. The range between them is almost infinite in variety and extent. It is in relation to these intermediate cases that the opposite rule prevails. Upon the facts proven in such cases, it is a matter of judgment and discretion, of sound inference, what is the deduction to be drawn from the undisputed facts. Certain facts we may suppose to be clearly established from which one sensible, impartial man would infer that proper care had not been used, and that negligence existed; another man equally sensible and equally impartial would infer that proper care had been used, and that there was no negligence. It is this class of cases and those akin to it that the law commits to the decision of a jury. Twelve men of the average of the community, comprising men of education and men of little education, men of learning and men whose learning consists only in what they have themselves seen and heard, the merchant, the mechanic, the farmer, the laborer; these sit together, consult, apply their separate experience of the affairs of life to the facts proven, and draw a unanimous conclusion. This average judgment thus given it is the great effort of the law to obtain. It is assumed that twelve men know more of the common affairs of life than does one man, that they can draw wiser and safer conclusions from admitted facts thus occurring than can a single judge.

In no class of cases can this practical experience be more wisely applied than in that which we are considering. We find, accordingly, although not uniform or harmonious, that the authorities justify us in holding in the case before us, that although the facts are undisputed it is for the jury and not for the judge to determine whether proper care was given, or whether they establish negligence.

Is the *Metropolitan* outcome inconsistent with the approach in *Stout*? Nowadays, of course, the jury would play no role in the English case. This accounts for Lord MacMillan's statement in *Glascow* that certain questions that appear to be issues of fact are "Still left to the judge to decide." In United States courts, the statement in the same context would be that those factors are "still left to the jury to decide."

(3) The *Stout* and *Metropolitan Railway Co.* cases help differentiate the job of the judge from that of the jury. The judge prescribes law; the jury decides facts and applies the law to the facts to determine the outcome of the case. The job of application is sometimes referred to as a mixed question of fact and law. It is also sometimes referred to as a determination of ultimate fact. For example, a railroad might be charged with negligence on grounds that the train was being driven fast on an occasion that called for slow speed. Whether the train in fact was traveling "fast" is an evidentiary fact peculiarly in the province of the jury. Whether the fact of traveling fast was negligence is an ultimate fact. Deciding that question requires an understanding of what negligence is in law. It is the job of the judge to give proper instructions about the law to the jury so as to enable it to make determination of ultimate fact. Fear of "runaway" juries caused some courts to lay down rather rigid rules of liability. See, e.g., Malone, The Formative Era of Contributory Negligence, 41 Ill. L. Rev. 151 (1941).

(4) Reviewing all the opinions from *Vaughan v. Menlove* to this point, would you say that the negligence standard of care is objective or subjective? That is, do the attributes of a particular person count for anything in deciding whether what that person satisfied or breached the standard?

COMMENTARY: THE ROLE OF COST/BENEFIT ANALYSIS IN TORT LAW

(1) Life is priceless, far beyond value. Even though we do value life infinitely in the abstract, this truism is almost useless from a public policy perspective. Suppose someone asked, "How much money would you require to give up your life; $1 million? $10 million?" Many people would reply "Not only am I not interested in discussing your offer but I am also offended you would even ask such a horrible question." Unfortunately, a society with limited resources cannot behave as if human life or safety were infinitely valuable.

For example, we would all prefer to drive an extremely safe car, but we also would not want to pay too much for it. Could you purchase a safer car than the one you drive if you spent $50,000 or more? If so, why don't you purchase it? For most of us the answers are, "I can't afford it." Or, "I prefer to spend the money on something else (such as on legal education)." Someone might also ask, "Should society ban every car but the safest from the highways?" Or, is it "negligent" or "contributorily negligent" to drive any car other than the safest car, no matter the cost? Cost/benefit analysis provides a "no" answer to each of them. With limited resources safety must be balanced against costs, and safety is a matter of degree, not an all-or nothing. Because of these cost/benefit considerations, it took years for the United States government to require automobile manufacturers to install seat belts in motor vehicles and more years to install air bags (at greater cost and less benefit). Most other commercial decisions trade off economic benefits against increased risks of harm. Tall buildings have economic benefits but are more risky to occupants than low ones. Who should bear the losses resulting from the added risks? Coal mining and building bridges are necessary in our culture but impose inherent risks of harm to the workers involved. Who should bear the losses when work injuries and deaths do occur? In short, "Who should absorb the damages when the inherent risks manifest themselves in harm?" Should these victims be without recourse? Or, should the employers be held liable for work injuries under a negligence system, a strict liability system, or a workers' compensation system?[24]

(2)   The Tort system sometimes employs a cost/benefit analysis to help make these decisions. When a court determines that a defendant breached the duty of care, it has decided that the defendant's conduct was not reasonable under the circumstances. One way to determine "reasonableness" is to balance the cost or burden of preventing a harm against the probability the harm will occur and gravity of the harm when it does occur. This is cost/benefit analysis. Hence, the Tort system must consider when cost/benefit analysis is relevant, its proper role in a particular case, and how to balance a cost/benefit analysis against relevant non-economic factors, such as fairness and morality.

Sometimes a cost/benefit analysis will compare dollars to dollars. For example, suppose were decided that any automobile manufacturer that fails to install seatbelts is negligent. Suppose, also, that two different types of seatbelts work equally well but one is less expensive than the other. A cost/benefit analysis would choose the cheaper of the two. On the other hand, suppose the balance is a tradeoff between dollars spent and lives lost (or injuries suffered). Then, a cost/benefit analysis could clarify the tradeoff, (i.e., placing a value on a life at $1 million or at $100 million) but it could not ultimately direct us what to do.

United States v. Carroll Towing, referred to in the notes after *Glascow Corporation v. Muir*, pioneered the use of cost/benefit analyses in Tort law by defining breach in a negligence case in cost/benefit terms. Judge Learned Hand proposed a formula employing three interacting factors, B, P, and L, to determine whether an actor was negligent in a particular case:

B is the burden or cost of preventing the harm.

P is the probability of the harm would occur.

L is the gravity or amount of the loss the harm would cause at would arise if the accident occurred.

Judge Hand posited that a defendant would be deemed to be negligent if, and

---

[24] Moreover, what would happen if society decided not to mine coal because coal mining is dangerous and people can be injured or die mining coal? How would we keep warm during the winter without coal? By using nuclear power? This would give rise to other safety issues. So would importing more foreign oil.

only if, $B < P \times L$. This has become known as the Learned Hand formula. It is often called the economic definition of negligence and has become a fundamental factor in the economic analysis of Tort law.

To illustrate this approach, suppose a defendant's expenditure of $100 would have prevented an injury that occurred 10% of the time and resulted in a loss of $50,000 when it did occur. The expectation of harm ($P \times L$) was 10% x $50,000 = $5,000. The burden to prevent the loss (B) was $100. Thus the defendant could have prevented an expected loss of $5,000 for only $100. A cost/benefit analysis would deem a defendant who failed to spend the $100 to avoid this potential harm to have been negligent, and if the accident did occur the defendant should be made to pay all of the damages. On the other hand, suppose the burden of preventing the harm was $10,000. Then, the cost to prevent harm would exceed the $5,000 expectation of loss and a cost/benefit analysis would conclude the defendant was not negligent.

(3) To employ a cost/benefit analysis to decide how much to spend to prevent harm in advance of taking a particular action requires a defendant to quantify B, P, and L, at least to a reasonable degree. In *Carroll Towing* itself, the calculation would have been unreliable because no reasonable defendant could have placed even approximate values on the three factors in advance. What information would a reasonable defendant need to quantify B, P, and L to make that calculation? Indeed, rarely, would a defendant be able to quantify B, P, and L in advance in ad hoc cases such as *Carroll Towing*. Consequently, the Learned Hand formula is most useful in two discrete situations. First, consider a manufacturer that produces, say, 1,000,000 automobiles or 1,000,000,000 bottles of soft drinks. Based upon statistical records, such a manufacturer might be able to quantify the necessary probabilities, costs and expected losses with a reasonable degree of accuracy in advance. The cost/benefit approach could work.

Second, consider cases in which an implicit, numberless form of the B v. P x L formula could be useful. Not all risky behavior should be treated the same — some modes lead to severe consequences and implicitly call for defendants to make heavy expenditures to avoid them, while others cause only minor harm. In some cases of this sort, an implicit understanding that one or more factors in the calculation is so dramatically high — or low — would permit a decisionmaker to apply the formula without quantifying the factors. Can you think of situations where the formula could be applied implicitly even though a reasonable decisionmaker could not quantify precise numbers? Was *Carroll Towing* one of these?

(4) As we have seen, the "least cost" principle assigns the duty to prevent a harm to the party who can prevent it at least cost. In *Carroll Towing* no other party could have prevented the loss, so the duty question was easy. In other cases, however, two or more parties might have prevented the harm. When this occurs, a Law & Economics judge would combine the Learned Hand formula and the least-cost principle in a two step process. First, the judge would use the formula (i.e., is $B < P \times L$) to determine whether the harm should have been prevented. If "yes," then the judge would ask, "Which party could have prevented the harm for the least cost?" This two-step approach would assign duty and liability to the least-cost party.

(5) The B v. P x L formula may also be used to assess the validity of defenses. For example, in *Carroll Towing* Judge Hand noted that the barge attendant "had no excuse for his absence." Suppose, however, that the barge attendant left the

barge for only 10 minutes to rescue a child who would have drowned without the assistance of the barge attendant? Would the 10 minutes have been better spent on the barge or rescuing the drowning child? A cost/benefit analysis surely would conclude that the expected value (P x L) of the time would have yielded a higher figure if the attendant rescued the drowning child. If so, the court should accept the defense that the defendant was not negligent to leave the barge for 10 minutes to rescue the child. By contrast, if the barge attendant had left the barge unattended to get drunk, a cost/benefit analysis would reject the defense.

(6) The Learned Hand formula is a neutral approach to determining negligence. It does not favor plaintiffs or defendants, barge owners or potential victims. Its goals are to avoid unnecessary costs and maximize the total wealth of society. It sometimes will conclude that preventing a particular harm was too expensive and, therefore, a defendant that declined to expend the money required to prevent the accident was not negligent. Suppose this had been the outcome in *Carroll Towing*? Would the owner of a nearby ship that had been damaged by the unmoored barge be satisfied that a "neutral" formula had defeated their Tort claim? Or would the injured party prefer a Tort rule that imposed strict liability on the owner of the barge that caused the harm? In other words, when B > P x L (and the defendant, therefore, was not negligent), should a court still impose liability on the owner of the barge? Such an outcome would declare, in effect: "This accident was too expensive to prevent, but, we nevertheless have decided to impose strict liability on the defendant. We intend that the future expected costs of these injuries be passed on to those who purchase the services of the barge (for example, shippers). We also believe it is more desirable for every purchaser of barge services to pay more for these services than it is for a victim of harm to absorb the losses." This would be strict liability, which in effect bundles an insurance policy into the cost of the activity in question (for example, barge transportation services). Some believe that most people are risk averse,[25] and assert that the Tort system should sometimes impose strict liability and bundle the cost of liability insurance into the prices of many products. Other people believe this function should be performed by permitting risk averse people to buy insurance separately. This point of view denies that the Tort system should be used to force people to pay for insurance which has, in effect, been embedded in the price of products they buy. Where do you stand on this issue?

(7) A party who receives all the gains and also absorbs all the losses from a particular activity must balance the costs against benefits to chose a course of action to maximize overall economic well-being. If the cost of preventing harm is less than the expectation of harm, a prudent person makes the expenditure. If the cost exceeds the expectation of harm, the prudent person declines to do so. For example, suppose a merchant owns $100,000 worth of frozen food and is at risk of a 1/1000 chance of a power failure that would render it worthless.[26] Assuming risk

---

[25] Most cost/benefit analysis assumes risk neutrality. To illustrate the effects of risk, suppose an activity poses a 1/1000 probability of causing $20,000 harm. The B v. P x L calculation produces a $20 expectation of harm. Hence, a reasonable person would spend $20 to avoid it. However, suppose $20,000 is your total worth and you face a 1/1,000 risk of losing all of it. Would you pay $25 to purchase insurance against this loss (this would include a $5 risk premium)? Risk avoiders would purchase the insurance and pay the $5 risk premium to avoid losing everything. Risk seekers would prefer to take the risk.

[26] This example is adapted from Richard A. Posner, Economic Analysis of Law 167 (Sixth edition 2003).

neutrality, the expectation of harm from a power failure is $100.[27] Suppose an $80 emergency power generator would prevent the loss? Cost/benefit analysis calls for this expenditure, but would not call for an expenditure exceeding $100. Is purchasing the generator merely another method of buying insurance?

Without the Tort system, a cost/benefit analysis would not work well when the party that is the beneficiary of the gains might not have to pay all the potential losses. Suppose a driver wants to assess whether it would be economically advantageous to drive no faster than 65 mph. Driving 100 mph would save time but would also increase the risk of endangering someone else.[28] Only if the driver's cost/benefit analysis were implemented through the Tort system would the driver be forced to balance all the expected harms from the risk of the added speed against the benefit accrued from it. The Tort system[29] will impose liability for the harm caused to others upon a driver that drives faster than was reasonable under the circumstance. Thus, from an economic perspective the Tort system forces people to account for the expected harms to others caused by their activities as well as the benefits. The Tort system helps force people to internalize the true total social costs of their activities rather than transfer those costs onto others who are external to the activity.

§ 4.04   CAUSE-IN-FACT

PROBLEM C

A bottling company truck broke down in the northbound lane of a two-lane highway on a wet overcast day. The driver left the truck to seek help and did not put out red flags, which were available in the truck and which company policy required to be put out 100 feet from a disabled vehicle to warn approaching drivers.

Two vehicles travelling in the same direction as the heading of the disabled truck soon approached. When about 400 feet from the truck, X, driving a passenger car, began to pass Y, driving a slow-moving heavy truck. At about 100 feet from the stopped truck X realized the truck ahead was stopped and that he would not be able to pass Y in time for Y to veer aside or stop short. Accordingly, X ran off on the opposite shoulder and turned over, injuring himself. Y attempted to avoid the stopped truck but failed. Y was injured in the crash.

X and Y sue the bottling company and the driver. The evidence proves that the bottling truck broke down because of non-negligent reasons. X testified that had a red flag or flare been set out 100 feet from the disabled truck, he "believes" he could have gotten out of Y's way in time to avoid the crashes. Y testified that if the flag or flare had been put out, he "believes" that he would have been able to stop in time. The bottling truck driver testified that the visibility was so poor that a flag "could not have been seen for more than fifteen or twenty feet." Both X and Y testified that they had been driving about "50 to 55 miles per hour" immediately prior to the episode.

The defendants move for directed verdicts. Should they be given?

---

[27] This assumes no chance of a tort or contract recovery against the power company.

[28] This also could endanger the driver and lead to traffic fines but presumably the driver will take these potential harms into account when they decide whether to drive at 100 mph.

[29] The criminal law system also provides an incentive to drive at no more than the posted speed limits.

JEFFERS v. AMOCO PRODUCTION CO.
Louisiana Court of Appeals
405 So. 2d 1227 (1981)

[This was an action brought by workmen who were injured in an oil field fire. Among the many defendants was Cameron Iron Works, Inc., manufacturer of a device called a "blow-out preventer" which was intended to avoid explosions. Plaintiffs alleged that the preventer was defective and thus failed to prevent the fire. Cameron defended on the grounds that the preventer could not have been in use at the time of the explosion because of the presence in the hole of a device called "the Kelly" when the explosion occurred. The plaintiff is appealing a summary judgment that dismissed the action.]

WATKINS, JUDGE.

. . .

The fire or blow-out occurred at approximately 8:30 a.m. on July 7, 1979. All of the injuries sued upon resulted from this fire. Approximately an hour and a half later, an explosion occurred which totally destroyed the rig. No further personal injuries were sustained in the second fire or explosion.

Cameron's motion for summary judgment was supported by a deposition of Matthews Cormier, who was drilling foreman for Amoco. The well was being drilled by a drilling contractor, Power Rig, for Amoco. Plaintiffs' basis for possible liability on the part of Cameron was that Cameron manufactured a blow-out preventer which had been installed on the well but which failed to function, thus contributing to the flash fire and injuries sued upon.

Cormier's clear and unequivocal testimony is that Cameron's blow-out preventer was never activated. The Kelly was at that time in the hole, according to Cormier's testimony, and the Cameron blow-out preventer could not be activated when the Kelly was in the hole.

Plaintiff Quelle (whose brief as stated is the only plaintiff's brief filed) contends that counsel for plaintiffs attempted to introduce the depositions of Emile Durr, Jr. and Stephen Barnard, which would have shown that the Kelly was not in the hole. Hence, the inference is that, if standard oil field procedure had been followed, the Cameron blow-out preventer would have been activated at the time of the flash fire. The trial court, according to Quelle's brief, improperly refused to admit the depositions of Durr and Barnard.

After taking the matter under advisement, the trial court granted summary judgment, as we have indicated.

If the blow-out preventer had not been activated before the flash fire occurred, as Cormier's testimony unequivocally states, clearly Cameron could not be liable, as the sole basis of contended liability on the part of Cameron was the alleged malfunction of the Cameron blow-out preventer. Although plaintiff Quelle contends the depositions of Durr and Barnard were improperly ruled inadmissible, plaintiff did not make an effort to proffer the excluded, depositions. There is thus no genuine issue as to a material fact, as the sole testimony available in the record before this court indicates that the Cameron blow-out preventer was not activated before the flash fire occurred.

. . .

Thus, under the record before us, summary judgment was proper.

Hence, the judgment of the trial court is affirmed, at appellants' cost.

Affirmed.

NOTES AND QUESTIONS

(1) Why did the plaintiff lose the action? Can you articulate a test to encapsulate the legal principle that disposed of the case? See, e.g., *Dixie Drive It Yourself System v. American Beverage Co.*, 137 So. 2d 298 (La. 1962).

(2) Do you think the blow-out preventer actually was in the hole? If so, how can the decision be justified?

(3) In *Chester v. Afshar*, [2004] UKHL 41, a surgeon neglected to inform a patient of a 1-2% chance of suffering a severe neurological side effect of an operation even in the absence of negligence. The surgery was completed without negligence but the unlikely injury occurred. The patient testified that she would have refused to undergo the operation at the time it was performed if she had been informed of the risk but she could not swear that she would never have taken the risk upon reflection. Was the surgeon's negligence the cause in fact of the harm? What result does the but-for test produce? The majority affirmed a judgment in the plaintiff's favor, holding that the special circumstances — i.e., the surgeon's negligence plainly denied the plaintiff her autonomy to make an informed decision -required a modification of the standard but-for test of causation. The dissenters held that the defendant had not increased the risk of harm because undergoing the operation at a future time would still have exposed the plaintiffs to the identical 1-2% chance of the injury.

(4) The judgments in *Fairchild v. Glenhaven Funeral Services Ltd and Others*, [2003] 1 A.C. 32 [H.L.] provide an extensive examination of the use and limits of the but-for test of causation.

(5) D1 negligently produced a small fire, F1, that by itself would not have caused any damage to P's house. D2 independently produced a small fire, F2, that by itself also would not have caused any damage to P's house. F1 and F2 merged to produce a great fire that destroyed P's house. Who is liable for the destruction? Suppose before they merged F1 and F2 would each have independently destroyed P's house? The merged fire destroyed the house. Does that change the outcome?

(6) Both Maryland tomatoes and Virginia tomatoes were selling in Washington, D.C. for one-dollar per pound. P regularly bought tomatoes from brokers and resold them at a Washington farmer's market. P was partial to Virginia tomatoes and would not purchase or sell Maryland tomatoes. P bought 1000 pounds of Virginia tomatoes from D at 75 cents per pound. D also sold Maryland tomatoes at 75 cents per pound. D negligently provided P Maryland tomatoes and P accepted them. (Virginia and Maryland tomatoes cannot be distinguished by sight.) By the time P got the tomatoes to market in Washington the market price on all tomatoes had declined and both Maryland and Virginia tomatoes were selling for 50 cents per pound. P lost $250 plus expected profit of $250. Is D liable for the loss? See *Moore*

v. PaineWebber, Inc., 189 F.3d 165 (2d Cir. 1999), Calabresi, concurring.

TICE v. TICE
Alabama Supreme Court
361 So. 2d 1051 (1978)

SHORES, JUSTICE.

Margaret Tice served as a babysitter for her son's children during the days while her son and daughter-in-law worked. For this, she was paid between $100 and $150 each month. On February 18, 1976, while carrying groceries into the house with her grandson, Aaron, she slipped and fell in the front yard. Mrs. Tice filed suit against her son and his wife, Cabell and Debra Tice, alleging that her injury resulted from their negligence in permitting the premises to exist in an unreasonable and dangerous condition. The defendants, by answer, denied liability and asserted contributory negligence on Mrs. Tice's part. They also filed a motion for summary judgment maintaining that Mrs. Tice had failed to produce sufficient evidence to create a jury question as to negligence on the part of the defendants.

The only evidence before the trial court on motion for summary judgment was the depositions of Margaret, Cabell and Aaron Tice, and an affidavit of Margaret Tice. There were no eyewitnesses to the fall. The evidence showed that Mrs. Tice was walking up an incline on a sidewalk leading to the front of her son's home when she either stepped onto the grass where she slipped and fell or slipped from the sidewalk onto the grass where she fell. There was also evidence that toys were generally present throughout the yard, that there were several small holes in the ground, and that the ground was covered with a layer of leaves. Mrs. Tice could not state the cause of her fall, only that she believed it must have been caused by stepping on one of the toys. Based upon this evidence, the court granted summary judgment in favor of defendants. Mrs. Tice filed a motion to vacate the summary judgment which was denied. She then appealed from the summary judgment. We affirm.

The plaintiff claims the status of a business invitee on her son's property. Assuming that she is an invitee, the duty owed to her by the defendants is the exercise of ordinary and reasonable care to keep the premises in a reasonably safe condition. Winn-Dixie v. Godwin, 349 So. 2d 37 (Ala. 1977); May-Bilt, Inc. v. Deese, 281 Ala. 579, 206 So. 2d 590 (1967). The owner of a premises in such cases is not an insurer of the safety of his invitees, and the principle of res ipsa loquitur is not applicable. There is no presumption of negligence which arises from the mere fact of an injury to an invitee. Delchamps, Inc. v. Stewart, 47 Ala. App. 406, 255

So.2d 586 (1971); cert. denied, 287 Ala. 729, 255 So. 2d 592 (1971); Great Atlantic and Pacific Tea Co. v. Bennett, 267 Ala. 538, 103 So. 2d 177 (1958). Furthermore, the owner of premises has no duty to warn an invitee of open and obvious defects in the premises which the invitee is aware of or should be aware of in the exercise of reasonable care. Hand v. Butts, 289 Ala. 653, 270 So.2d 789 (1972); Crawford Johnson & Co. v. Duffner, 279 Ala. 678, 189 So.2d 474 (1966). In the instant case, the plaintiff must prove, in order to recover, that her fall resulted from a defect or instrumentality located on the premises as a result of the defendants' negligence and of which the defendants had or should have had notice at the time of the accident. See, Wynn, Slip and Fall Cases in Alabama, 27 Ala. Law. 419 (1966), and authorities cited therein. The plaintiff has not presented any evidence tending to show that the defendants breached any duty owed to her. She asserts only that her fall may have been caused by toys, leaves or holes in the yard. It is her opinion that she tripped on a child's toy, many of which were frequently in the yard.

She contends that this establishes a question of fact for the jury under *Folmar v. Montgomery Fair Company, Inc.*, 293 Ala. 686, 309 So.2d 818 (1975). In that case, the plaintiff tripped and fell in defendant's department store while walking in an aisle between two tables holding merchandise. No instrumentality or defect was discovered which could have caused her fall other than a table leg which protruded beyond the top of the table. By affidavit, the plaintiff asserted that this could have been the only cause of her fall. Under these facts, we held that summary judgment was improper. *Folmar, supra,* is distinguishable from the case at hand, however.

In that case, the plaintiff produced evidence from which a jury could find that Montgomery Fair breached a duty owed to the plaintiff by obstructing aisles intended for walkways by customers. The plaintiff here has not done that. She shows only that there were things in the yard over which she might have tripped. All of these are things which are normally in yards of persons with small children; and the plaintiff's knowledge of them was equal or superior to that of the defendants. The plaintiff has simply failed to produce any evidence from which a jury could conclude that the defendants have breached any duty owed to her. There was, therefore, no error in granting summary judgment in defendants' favor.

Affirmed.

NOTES AND QUESTIONS

(1)   Why did Mrs. Tice lose her case? Was it that she failed to prove that her son owed her a duty of care? Or that she failed to prove that he breached the duty? Or, that she failed to prove that his breach caused her harm? Does the Alabama court unequivocally answer the question?

(2)   Did Mrs. Tice satisfy the definition of "cause" prescribed in *Coray v. Southern Pacific Co.*, 185 P.2d 963, 968 (Utah 1947), as follows:

> The "cause" must, of course, be the legal cause, in order to be the basis of recovery. To show merely that the injury would not have occurred had there been no violation of the act is not the equivalent of showing that the violation was the cause thereof.

> In order to be the legal cause of another's harm, it is not enough that the harm would not have occurred had the actor not been negligent . . . The negligence must also be a substantial factor as well as an actual factor in bringing about the plaintiff's harm. The word "substantial" is used to denote the fact that the defendant's conduct has such an effect in producing the harm as to lead reasonable men to regard it as a cause, using that word in the popular sense in which there always lurks the idea of responsibility, rather than in the so-called "philosophic sense," which includes every one of the great number of events without which any happening would not have occurred. Each of these events is a cause in the so-called "philosophic sense," yet the effect of many of them is so insignificant that no ordinary mind would think of them as causes.'

Restatement of the Law of Torts, § 431, Comment (a). See also *Room v. Caribe Hilton Hotel*, 659 F.2d 5 (1st Cir. 1981).

(3)   Suppose two fires, one set by A and one set by B, merge to burn down P's house. Under what circumstances would the law hold that A or B did not cause the damage? Suppose A was an "act of God" (e.g., lightning) and B was a sparking locomotive? See, e.g., *Anderson v. Minneapolis, St. Paul & S.S.M. Railway*, 179 N.W. 45 (Minn. 1920).

§ 4.05   PROXIMATE CAUSATION

PROBLEM D

In September 1984 a collision occurred between two vehicles, one of which was driven by the appellant Chapman and the other by one Emery, who is not a party to these proceedings. The collision occurred at a point where Balcombe Avenue joins Tapley's Hill Road on the eastern side. Both vehicles were travelling along Tapley's Hill Road towards the north and that which Emery was driving was the leading car. Approaching the Balcombe Avenue junction, Emery slowed down and indicated by a signal that he was about to turn to the right. As Emery was turning Chapman's car struck the near-side corner of Emery's car with the result that it overturned in the mouth of Balcombe Avenue. Apparently the door of Chapman's car swung open, and he was deposited on the road while the car itself veered off to the left and came to rest on an adjacent golf course after breaking through a fence. After being thrown from his car Chapman remained unconscious on the roadway lying lengthwise along the road and about three feet to the west of the center line. At the time of or almost immediately after the accident, Dr. Cherry drove his car from the nearby golf course entrance. He stopped his vehicle and went to Chapman's assistance. At about the same time two other vehicles arrived at the scene of the accident from the north. The drivers of these cars, Simmons and Nolte, each saw Chapman lying on the road and stopped their cars a little further on. They both commenced to go to Chapman's assistance but they observed that another person, Dr. Cherry, had reached him first and then, hearing cries from the overturned car, they went to it and helped to extricate some of the occupants. Within a few minutes of the time when Dr. Cherry reached Chapman, another car came along the road from the south and the driver of this vehicle, the respondent Hearse, failed to see either Dr. Cherry or the injured man until it was too late to avoid them. In the result his vehicle struck Dr. Cherry and caused him injuries as the result of which he died. It was dark and it was raining at the time, and there seems little doubt that visibility was poor.

Dr. Cherry's survivors sued Hearse and Chapman. Each defended on the ground that his negligence, if any, was not a proximate cause of Dr. Cherry's death. Hearse settled the claim brought by Dr. Cherry's survivors and sought contribution from Chapman. Should the contribution action prevail?

WING v. MORSE
Maine Supreme Judicial Court
300 A.2d 491 (1973)

[Defendant Wing made an illegal U turn from the northbound to the southbound lane of a limited access highway. In doing so he was struck by a fast moving passenger vehicle towing a trailer. Wing's car came to rest in the middle of the highway, causing a jam up of traffic. The car and trailer continued without stopping and were not identified.

About ten minutes later, plaintiff Morse approached the situs driving a trailer truck. He braked his truck too late to stop short of the traffic jam and crashed, causing injuries to himself. Morse sued Wing. The case was tried, the jury returned a verdict for the plaintiff and judgment was entered against Wing. On appeal, Wing asserts that the claim of proximate causation between his negligence and Morse's injury had been severed.]

Very few words commonly employed in the law of torts have occasioned as much case law and confusion as the term "proximate cause."

The word "proximate" is a legacy of Lord Chancellor Bacon. Bacon, Maxims of the Law, Reg. 1.

When the word "proximate" was first taken up by the courts, it had connotations of proximity of both time and space. These connotations have long since disappeared. It is a confusing and therefore an unfortunate word because it improperly places emphasis on the physical or mechanical closeness of the cause under investigation and the happening of the event in issue. Of this, most modern authorities are in agreement. See for example, Edgerton, Legal Cause, 72 U. Pa. L. Rev. 211 (1924); Morris, On the Teaching of Legal Cause, 39 Column. L. Rev. 1087 (1931).

There are other situations in which a "cause" is clearly near in both point of time and distance, but yet, because of legal policy considerations working in the framework of the particular facts, such cause is not held to be a "legal cause." In such cases there is the intervention of an unrelated cause, (unrelated in the sense of not being within the policy considerations) not reasonably foreseeable, which intervening cause is itself an efficient cause. See, for example: Curtis v. Jacobson, 142 Me. 351, 54 A.2d 520 (1947).

It is for this reason our Court has defined proximate cause to mean:

> . . . that cause which, in natural and continuous sequence, unbroken by an efficient intervening cause, produces the injury, and without which the result would not have occurred.

Johnson v. Dubois, Me., 256 A.2d 733, 734 (1969).

In Marsh v. Great Northern Paper Company, 101 Me. 489, 502, 64 A. 844, 850 (1906), it was said:

> Another important rule which must be taken into consideration, and which is very generally agreed to, is that time or distance is not a decisive test of proximity of cause. The expression means closeness of causal relation, not nearness in time or distance, although it is undoubtedly true

that time and distance, in some cases, may have an important bearing upon the question of causal relation.

A complete and thorough discussion of the whole question of proximate cause as applied to a situation not substantially unlike that here before us is to be found in an opinion by Chief Judge Magruder in Marshall v. Nugent and Socony-Vacuum Oil Company, 222 F.2d 604, 610-612 (1st Cir. 1955). See also Apanovich v. Wright, 226 F.2d 656 (1st Cir. 1955).

In approaching any problem of proximate cause one must start with the premises that the act or conduct, to be negligent toward another, must involve an unreasonable risk of

> (1) causing harm to a class of persons of which the other is a member, and

> (2) subjecting the other to a hazard from which the harm results.

Cause, in the philosophic sense, includes each of the substantial number of events without which any happening would not have occurred. Each of the events is a cause in that sense. The effect of many of them, however, is so insignificant that no reasonable mind would ordinarily think of them as causes.

A negligent act, i.e., a violation of the duty to use reasonable care toward another, is a legal cause of harm to such other person if

> (a) the actor's conduct is a substantial factor in bringing about the harm, and

> (b) there is no rule of law relieving the actor from liability because of the manner in which his negligence has resulted in the harm.

Here, in the case before us, it is clear that as a matter of law this defendant owed a duty to all travelers on the highway to exercise reasonable care toward all such travelers whom he ought reasonably to have had in contemplation as a traveler to be affected by the doing of his negligent act at the time he did such act. There was certainly no rule of law relieving him from liability.

His failure to deport himself in accordance with the standard of care by which he was bound, was most certainly a substantial factor, though clearly not the only factor, in bringing about this plaintiff's misfortune.

It is also clear the defendant's negligence in attempting to negotiate the U-turn from the northbound lane into the southbound lane caused the collision with the unidentified motor vehicle to which the house trailer was attached. This the defendant concedes in his brief.

The accident in which the plaintiff received injuries, although happening ten minutes or more after the first collision, occurred at a time the highway was partially clogged by traffic and before the southbound lane had become cleared. The risks created by the defendant's departure from the standard of care required of all travelers on the highway were still viable.

The question whether the defendant's violation of the law prohibiting the U-turn, which admittedly brought about the collision with the unidentified vehicle, was a "proximate cause" or "legal cause" of the plaintiff's injuries was for the jury. Johnson v. Dubois, supra; Marsh v. Great Northern Paper Company, supra.

The jury found it was such legal cause.

We cannot say as a matter of law it was not.

. . .

NOTES AND QUESTIONS

(1)   In *Bell v. Campbell*, 434 S.W. 2d 117 (Tex. 1968), a case with similar facts, the Texas Supreme Court held as a matter of law that the original defendant's negligence was not the proximate cause of the harm done to bystanders who were helping clean up the wreckage when a third party negligently drove into them. Would the Maine court agree? If not, which is the better approach?

(2)   *Haber v. Walker*, 1963 Vict. S. Ct. 339 (Full Court, Supreme Court of Victoria), involved a wrongful death action arising out of a suicide that allegedly resulted from mental imbalance caused by a physical injury negligently inflicted by the defendant. The plaintiff won in the trial court, and the defendant appealed, claiming no legal cause. On appeal, the Australian court stated:

> The legal principles governing questions of causation are in some respects unsettled. It is, of course, clearly established that the ideas of causation with which the law is concerned when attributing responsibility for harm suffered are not those of the philosophers or the scientists but are those of the plain man, guided by common-sense considerations . . . But the statements to this effect that are to be found in the cases are not uncommonly accompanied by observations suggesting that common-sense considerations do not provide clear principles for the solution of problems of causation . . . The number of causation problems, however, to which this view is today applicable has been much reduced by the detailed analysis of the subject of causation that has taken place in recent years. The concepts relating to causation that are latent in ordinary thought and speech have been closely examined, together with the decisions of the courts giving effect to them. And I venture to think that, at least in its main principles, the legal doctrine of causation based on common-sense considerations has now been made reasonably clear. Moreover, it has now become plain, I consider, that the fears which have sometimes been entertained that reliance upon such considerations might lead to an undue extension of responsibility for harms were not well founded.

> Confining attention to what is relevant to the present case, the main principles, I consider, are these. In the first place a wrongful act or omission cannot ordinarily be held to have been a cause of subsequent harm unless that harm would not have occurred without the act or rendered it wrongful. Exceptions to this first principle are narrowly confined. Secondly, where the requirements of this first principle are satisfied, the act or omission is to be regarded as a cause of the harm unless there intervenes between the act or omission and the harm an occurrence which is necessary for the production of the harm and is sufficient in law to sever the causal connexion. And, finally, the intervening occurrence, if it is to be sufficient to sever the connexion, must ordinarily be either —

> (a) human action that is properly to be regarded as voluntary, or

(b) a causally independent event the conjunction of which with the wrongful act or omission is by ordinary standards so extremely unlikely as to be termed a coincidence. . . .

What then is the result when these principles are applied to the question whether here the death of the deceased by suicide was a consequence of the defendant's negligence? The evidence at the trial clearly showed that the requirements of the first principle were satisfied. Furthermore, there was no real question of the causal connexion having been severed by the occurrence of a coincidence. We are not concerned here with a physical event as distinct from human action, nor with an act of a third person: compare Hart and Honore, op. cit., Ch. VI, esp. at pp. 164-5 and 168-9. And here the proof that the requirements of the first principle were satisfied involved that the deceased's conduct which led to his death was not independent of the defendant's negligence. Accordingly, the critical question of causation which arose at the trial was whether the deceased's conduct which led to his death was properly to be regarded as a voluntary act.

In some contexts expressions such as "voluntary act" and "act of volition" are construed so widely as to cover any act which cannot be said to have been reflex or done without understanding of its nature and quality or due to irresistible impulse. In relation, however, to the principle of causation now in question, the word "voluntary" does not carry this wide meaning; and for an act to be regarded as voluntary it is necessary that the actor should have exercised a free choice. This, of course, is a conception involving question of degree. But if his choice has been made under substantial pressure created by the wrongful act, his conduct should not ordinarily be regarded as voluntary. . . .

Accordingly, the deceased's act in hanging himself was not, for the purposes of the relevant principle of causation, a "voluntary" act, if the deceased, in consequence of the defendant's negligence, was acting under the pressure of a mental disorder such as was described in the evidence at the trial and he was thereby prevented from exercising a free choice

. . .

A different view of such matters has been taken in the United States of America. There, even if a deceased person's act of suicide has been done under the pressure of a mental disorder caused by the defendant's negligence, the death is not considered to be a consequence of the negligence, except perhaps where the deceased did not know what he was doing or was subjected to an irresistible impulse: see Scheffer v. Washington City, etc., Railroad Co., (1882), 105 U.S. 249; Prosser, Law of Torts, at pp. 273-274. But the view of the matter that I have already put is supported not only by the English cases last cited but also by a long line of cases upon the analogous question of the effect of suicide upon a chain of causation under the workers compensation legislation in the United Kingdom. [Judgment for the plaintiff affirmed.]

(3)   Despite the statement in *Haber v. Walker*, according to Prosser and Keeton on Torts (5th ed. 1984) at 310-11:

It is the prevailing view that when insanity prevents the decedent from realizing the nature of his act or controlling his conduct, the suicide is to be regarded as a direct result, and no intervening force at all, or else as a normal incident of the consequences inflicted, for which the defendant will be liable.

(4) See also *Chapman v. Hearse*, (1961) 106 C.L.R. 112 (High Court, Aust.)

§ 4.06 DAMAGES

One vital distinction between the common law actions of trespass vi et armis and trespass on the case is that actual harm to the plaintiff or the plaintiff's property is a necessary element of the latter but not the former. This distinction was noted in the speech of Lord Denning, in *Letang v. Cooper*, Chapter 3, supra, and, as noted in the speech of Lord Wright set out at the beginning of this chapter, the existence of damages is now deemed to be an essential element of a negligence action. This imposes a disquieting air of unpredictability upon the law of negligence. Perhaps Oliver Wendell Holmes, Jr. best captured this attribute of negligence actions when he said:

> The business of the law of torts is to fix the dividing lines between those cases in which a man is liable for harm which he has done, and those which he is not. But it cannot enable him to predict with certainty whether a given act under given circumstances will make him liable, because an act will rarely have that effect unless followed by damage, and for the most part, if not always, the consequences of an act are not known, but only guessed at as more or less probable. All the rules that the law can lay down beforehand are rules for determining the conduct which will be followed by liability if it is followed by harm, — that is, the conduct which a man pursues at his peril. The only guide for the future to be drawn from a decision against a defendant in an action of tort is that similar acts, under circumstances which cannot be distinguished except by the result from those of the defendant, are done at the peril of the actor; that if he escapes liability, it is simply because by good fortune no harm comes of his conduct in the particular event.

Therefore, in negligence actions two questions must be asked. First, was any legally cognizable harm done the plaintiff? Second, how is it to be quantified? The existence of harm was amply established in the next two cases. They are presented to demonstrate the general reparation goal of the law of negligence and two specific legal doctrines that might deprive a plaintiff of full recovery.

LIVINGSTONE v. THE RAWYARDS COAL COMPANY
5 App. Cas. 25 (H.L. 1880)[30]

[Appellant, Livingstone, owned an acre and a half of coal-bearing lands that had some miners' cottages upon them. Unknown to him, he owned the mineral rights as well as the surface rights. Respondents, thinking they owned the mineral rights, mined out the coal on appellant's land while mining coal on abutting land. The appellant sued for damages, including the value of the coal extracted from the land

---

[30] [Ed. — Appeal Cases Law Reports, decision of House of Lords.]

and damage done to the houses by subsidence.

In a trial before the Lord Ordinary, evidence was presented to establish the following:

The Lord Ordinary [i.e., trial court. — Ed.] awarded damages in the amount of £515. 12s. Id. The First Division of the Court of Session, an appellate court, modified the judgment and awarded £171. 7s. 6d. plus a further sum that would indemnify the plaintiff for damage done to the houses, which was without objection accepted as £200. From that judgment, the plaintiff-appellant appeals, seeking to restore the judgment of Lord Ordinary.]

EARL CAIRNS, L.C.: —

. . .

Now, my Lords, under these circumstances the question arises, what is the measure of damage to which the Appellant is entitled?

Of course the value of the coal taken must be the value to the person from whom it was taken, because I do not understand that there is any rule in this country, or in Scotland, that you have a right to follow the article which is taken away, the coal which is severed from the inheritance, into whatever place it may be carried or under whatever circumstances it may come to be disposed of, and to fasten upon any increment of value which from exceptional circumstances may be found to attach to that coal. The question is, what may fairly be said to have been the value of the coal to the person from whose property it was taken at the time it was taken.

[The Court discussed the evidence supporting the values stated above. A witness for the plaintiff testified that he would not have advised the appellant to sell for £100 but would have advised to sell for the same royalty that the abutting landowners were receiving. That would amount to £171 7s. 6d. plus damages to the houses.]

Upon that evidence the Court of Session say,

We are of opinion that the value to this Appellant of this coal was the money that would have been produced if he had sold the coal, and the money that he would have got if he had sold the coal would have been £171 7s. 6d.; but that would have been accompanied and guarded by a further payment which would have indemnified him for the damage done to the houses upon the surface in getting the coal, and that further sum he must have, in addition to the £171 7s. 6d.

My Lords, I own that under the very peculiar circumstances of this case, there being only the element to consider to which I have referred, namely, the element of value to the Appellant, I think he has received in the judgment of the Court of Session that which is the proper value, and I see no reason for differing from the judgment of the learned Judges. I therefore advise your Lordships, and move your Lordships, that the appeal be dismissed with costs.

LORD BLACKBURN: —

I also think that the judgment of the Court below should be affirmed, and that consequently the appeal should be dismissed with costs.

The point may be reduced to a small compass when you come to look at it. I do not think there is any difference of opinion as to its being a general rule that, where any injury is to be compensated by damages, in settling the sum of money to be given for reparation of damages you should as nearly as possible get at that sum of money which will put the party who has been injured, or who has suffered, in the same position as he would have been in if he had not sustained the wrong for which he is now getting his compensation or reparation. That must be qualified by a great many things which may arise — such, for instance, as by the consideration whether the damage has been maliciously done, or whether it has been done with full knowledge that the person doing it was doing wrong. There could be no doubt that there you would say that everything would be taken into view that would go most against the willful wrongdoer — many things which you would properly allow in favour of an innocent mistaken trespasser would be disallowed as against a willful and intentional trespasser on the ground that he must not qualify his own wrong, and various things of that sort. But in such a case as the present, where it is agreed that the Defenders, without any fault whatever on their part, have innocently, and, being ignorant, with as little negligence or carelessness as possible, taken this coal, believing it to be their own, when in fact it belonged to the Pursuer, then comes the question, — how are we to get at the sum of money which will compensate them?

Now, my Lords, there was a technical rule in the English Courts in these matters. When something that was part of the realty (we are talking of coal in this particular case) is severed from the realty and converted into a chattel, then instantly on its becoming a chattel, it becomes the property of the person who had been the owner of the fee in the land whilst it remained a portion of the land; and then in estimating the damages against a person who had carried away the chattel, it was considered and decided that the owners of the fee was to be paid the value of the chattel at the time when it was converted, and it would in fact have been improper, as qualifying his own wrong, to allow the wrongdoer anything for that mischief which he had done, or for that expense which he had incurred in converting the piece of rock into a chattel, which he had no business to do.

Such was the rule of the Common Law. Whether or not that was a judicious rule at any time I do not take upon myself to say; but a long while ago (and when I say a long while I mean twenty-five years ago) Mr. Baron Parke put this qualification on it, as far as I am aware for the first time. He said, If however the wrongdoer has taken it perfectly innocently and ignorantly, without any negligence and so forth, and if the jury, in estimating the damages, are convinced of that, then you should consider the mischief that has been really done to the Plaintiff who lost it whilst it was part of the rock, and therefore you should not consider its value when it had been turned into a piece of coal after it had been severed from the rock, but you should treat it at what would have been a fair price if the wrongdoer had bought it whilst it was yet a portion of the land as you would buy a coal-field. That was the rule to be applied where it was an innocent person that did the wrong; that rule was followed in the case of Jegon v. Vivian, which has been so much mentioned; it was followed in the Court of Chancery, and, so far as I know, it has never been questioned since, that where there is an innocent wrongdoing the point that is to be made out for the damages is, as was expressed in the minutes of the decree: — "The Defendants to be charged with the fair value of such coal and other minerals at the same rate as if the mines had been purchased by the Defendants at the fair market value of the district;" that I understand to mean as if the mines had been purchased while the minerals were yet part of the soil. That, I apprehend, is what is to be done here, and that is what both the Lord Ordinary and the First Division of the Court of Session have endeavoured to do. They have come to different pecuniary results, and the question really comes to be which is correct.

Upon that the Lord Ordinary, as I understand, has gone upon this position. He said,

I have taken evidence, and the result of that is, that it is agreed on all hands that this coal, when it was brought to the surface, actually did sell for £1768 5s. 10d. I look at the evidence, and I take the evidence to be that the actual amount expended by the Defendants (there is contradictory evidence on such points as might have been expected, and it is not all very clear), was 4s. 3d. per ton and, deducting that from the £1768 5s. 10d., he makes it £515 12s. 1d., which is what he says is the sum that the Pursuer ought to recover taking off all the expenses that the Defenders have incurred.

. . .

But then the Lord Ordinary himself observes that, taking that way of getting it, and giving the Pursuer £515 12s. 1d.,

The truth of the matter is, that the removal of the Pursuer's coal by the Defenders, in place of being a misfortune, has been to the Pursuer a singular stroke of luck. The size of his feu is less than an acre and a half, and the coal which it contained could not have been wrought to profit by itself. The expense of sinking a pit and providing machinery would many times over have exceeded the value of the minerals. Possibly, no doubt, the Pursuer might have endeavoured to make with the Defenders terms upon which his coal might have been raised along with the coal of which they were the tenants. But the return which would have been rendered to him under such an arrangement must have fallen far short of what has been awarded by the Lord Ordinary. The lordship, in the circumstances, could not be expected to be higher than that paid by the Defenders for the adjoining portions of the seam; and this, upon the quantity taken out, even if increased by reasonable damages for injury through subsidence to the houses on the surface, would certainly have fallen considerably short of £500.

Now, when you find that the Lord Ordinary himself, who is professing to ascertain what is the money value of the damage that the Pursuer has received, says: "I have got at it in this particular way, but that money value is very considerably above the damage that you have received: it has been a singular stroke of good luck to you that you should get it," it occurs to one at once, prima facie, that there must have been something wrong in the way in which that money value was got at, and I think that there was an error in it, and that error was that the Lord Ordinary thought he was bound by decisions (which I do not think he was) to take that mode, and that mode only, of getting at the value of the coal in situ, namely, the price which the coal fetched when it was sold, deducting from that the cost of hewing and drawing and so forth, and so to ignore totally the fact this was an isolated small patch of land from which the Pursuer, as he himself admits, could not possibly have got coal by any practical means whatever, except by bargaining with the Defenders. I think there the Lord Ordinary was under a mistake.

[Lord Blackburn concluded that the Court of Session measured damages correctly.]

My Lords, I only wish to say one word to guard against any misapprehension on a point which I at first a little misapprehended. I do not think that this decision of the Court of Session is that the royalty is the measure of the damages. It is only that it is evidence of the value which is the measure of the damages.

. . .

Interlocutor appealed against affirmed; and appeal dismissed with costs.

NOTES AND QUESTIONS

(1)   Suppose the plaintiff had owned a 1000 acre parcel of coal-bearing land and the defendant negligently mined out the coal from under one and a half of them? Would the damages have been the same?

(2)   Suppose the defendant had intentionally mined out the coal, hoping to get by with it. Would the damages have been the same? See *Stearnes & Culver Lumber Co., v. Cawthon*, 56 So. 555 (Fla. 1911).

CARBONARO v. JOHNS-MANVILLE CORP.
United States District Court, Eastern District of Pennsylvania
526 F. Supp. 260 (1981)

GILES, DISTRICT JUDGE.

In this asbestos suit, defendant Owens-Corning Fiberglas moves for summary judgment against plaintiff on the ground of res judicata. The motion will be granted.

In 1979, plaintiffs initiated suit in Pennsylvania state court for asbestos-related injuries. See Carbonaro v. Johns-Manville Corp., Jan. Term 1979, No. 4052 (Case No. 27) (Pa. C.P.). They alleged that defendants' misdeeds and negligence caused plaintiffs:

> to contract diseases and injuries to their body systems, lungs, respiratory systems, heart and damage to various organs of their bodies including injury to tissue and bone, the full extent of which has not been determined, and including, but not limited to asbestosis, scarred lungs, respiratory disorders, and the risk of mesothelioma and other cancers, some or all of which may be permanent and/or fatal.

Amended Complaint. In January, 1981, defendant Johns-Manville moved for summary judgment on the ground that the action was barred by the statute of limitations. A similar motion was filed by Keene Corporation on behalf of all other defendants. Instead of opposing those motions, plaintiffs brought this action in federal court against the identical defendants, alleging:

> diseases and injuries to [their] . . . body systems, lungs, respiratory systems, heart and damage to various organs of their bodies including injury to tissue and bone, the full extent of which has not been determined, and including, Adenocarcinoma of the transverse colon and the risk of mesothelioma and other cancers some or all of which may be permanent and/or fatal.

Complaint, 23. On May 21, 1981, Judge Takiff entered judgment in the state-court action in favor of all defendants and against plaintiff. Defendants now seek judgment in their favor in the federal action because Judge Takiff's orders are res judicata.

Plaintiffs oppose the motion, arguing that the Common Pleas' decision does not foreclose the issue in this court. They advance two reasons in support of their argument. First, they contend that because they allege admiralty jurisdiction, laches, rather than limitations, controls this action. Second, they say that the cancer which is the focus of the federal suit neither was discoverable at the time the state suit was started, nor was it a ground for Judge Takiff's order.[31]

For these two reasons, plaintiffs argue that the federal suit presents issues not controlled by the state judgment.

If the question before me were one of issue preclusion, plaintiffs might prevail. Res judicata, however, is a doctrine of claim preclusion. Because plaintiffs have confused these doctrines, and because courts sometimes use confusing language in discussing the preclusive effect of prior judgments, a brief sketch of their principles is in order.

To preserve the finality of judgments from collateral relitigation, the common law has developed two major preclusive doctrines: issue preclusion, often called collateral estoppel, and claim preclusion, also called "merger and bar," "res judicata," or "the rule against splitting a cause of action." Issue preclusion makes a prior final judgment conclusive when an issue was actually litigated, and was essential to the outcome of the prior judgment. E.g., Restatement (2d), supra note 3, § 68 (T.D. No. 4, 1977). In addition, a final judgment also extinguishes the claim, barring another action by plaintiff on the same claim. E.g., id. § 48 (T.D. No. 1, 1973). Claim preclusion bars a later suit ever, though it raises new grounds, new theories, or asks for new remedies or increased damages. E.g., id. § 61.1 & Comment c (T.D. No. 5, 1978). Claim preclusion also operates to bar relitigation of issues not raised in the prior suit. E.g., Cromwell v. County of Sac, 94 U.S. 351, 352-53, 24 L. Ed 195 (1877); see note 2 supra. Because defendant's motion is grounded on claim preclusion, plaintiffs' argument that the issues are different is irrelevant. The question before me is whether the federal suit raises the same "claim."

Although a variety of tests have been suggested for determining the scope of a claim, see, e.g., 1B Moore's Federal Practice 0.410[1], at 1157 (1980), the modern approach is transactional; the prior judgment extinguishes "all rights of the plaintiff to remedies against the defendant with respect to all or any part of the transaction, or series of connected transactions, out of which the action arose." Restatement (2d), supra note 3, § 61(1) (T.D. No. 5, 1978). The prior state complaint relates to exactly the same transactions — defendants' alleged negligence, strict liability, fraud, etc., and the same period of exposure to asbestos — as the complaint before me. Thus, at first glance, this claim is barred.

One of plaintiffs' contentions, however, might serve to narrow the scope of the first claim. They argue that (1) the cancer alleged in the current action was not

---

[31] Plaintiffs argue that judgment was entered in the state suit because of their early discovery of asbestos-induced lung diseases, whereas in the federal suit, they complain of adenocarcinoma of the transverse colon-a cancer of the large intestine.

discoverable until after the first suit was brought, and (2) that a cause of action for cancer accrued after the first suit was brought. Therefore, one might conclude that judgment on the first suit cannot bar an action for cancer which was then undiscoverable. Because the first proposition is a disputed material fact, I shall take it as true for purposes of this motion. The second argument is questionable. But, even assuming arguendo its correctness, the proposed conclusion does not follow.

The most important reason for rejecting the conclusion is that the prior complaint embraces the injury alleged in the subsequent suit. The state complaint includes all types of then-existing and future bodily injuries caused by asbestos exposure. Both complaints specifically allege "risk of mesothelomia and other cancers." The only relevant difference between the pleadings is that the second complaint mentions "[a]denocarcinoma of the transverse colon." In this respect, the injuries alleged in the second complaint are not different; they are merely more specific. Had plaintiffs prevailed in the state court action, they would have been entitled to recover for all cancers in that action, and a subsequent action would have been prevented by the claim-preclusion rule of "merger."

. . .

In fact, the cancer which plaintiffs focus on here might well have caused Judge Takiff to rule the other way, if only plaintiffs had brought that information to his attention. The plaintiffs knew of the newly discovered injury no later than August, 1980, at least four months prior to the first motion for summary judgment on the statute of limitations. Likewise, plaintiffs' counsel were aware of the diagnosis at least as early as the filing of the federal complaint, which occurred two months prior to Judge Takiff's decision. Thus, the failure to present this evidence in the prior action results from a deliberate bypass of available state process.

Plaintiff suffers from cancer allegedly caused by defendants. He cuts a sympathetic figure. It is difficult to tell someone in his position that he lacks a remedy at law. It is my duty, however, to decide cases without sympathy, by reference to the appropriate legal principles. Under those principles, the current claim is within the scope of the prior claim. None of the exceptions to the rules of merger and bar applies. See generally Restatement (2d), supra note 3, § 61.2 (T.D. No. 5, 1978). Defendants therefore are entitled to judgment on the ground that this action is barred by a prior final judgment on the same claim.

NOTES AND QUESTIONS

(1) "Fiat Justitia ruat coelum." — "Let right be done, though the heavens should fall." This maxim is attributed to Lord Mansfield, a famous late eighteenth century jurist. Does the last paragraph of Judge Gile's decision involve this principle?

(2) Doctrines of res judicata and collateral estoppel are examined in detail in courses in civil procedure. These doctrines are employed by courts to avoid redundant and repetitive litigation, thereby conserving judicial resources and preventing unfairness to the parties. Res judicata means essentially that the matter has already been adjudged as between the parties. It prevents a disappointed loser from merely trying again to win the case he has already lost. Collateral estoppel means essentially that the legal point in issue has been decided as between the parties in collateral judicial proceedings. For example, a tort action might turn on

this issue: "Was the plaintiff the defendant's employee or an independent contractor at the time of the injury?" If that precise question had been litigated between the two at an earlier time concerning, say, payment for services, then the resolution of the relationship (i.e., employee or independent contractor) in the first litigation would be binding on that issue and only that issue in the subsequent litigation.

(3) The judgment rules applied in *Carbonaro* make a trial for damages, including damages that are expected to manifest themselves in the future, a once and for all event. In a personal injury action, for example, future medical expenses, future wage loss, and future pain and suffering must ordinarily all be sought in the initial trial or be lost, as *Carbonaro* indicates. Why? What effect does this have on trial strategy?

Whereas questions of this sort are now commonly considered in terms of collateral estoppel and res judicata, earlier cases sometimes treated them as an element of the law of damages. See, e.g., *Mims v. Reid*, 98 So. 2d 498 (Fla. 1957). The following excerpts from the judgment of Lord Fitzgerald in *The Darley Main Colliery Company v. Mitchell*, 11 App. Cas. 127 (H.L., 1886), is illustrative of what has been referred to as the "once and for all" rule.

Darley Main mined coal in such a manner as to cause subsidence in 1868 of the land occupied by Mitchell's houses. Damages were paid, and Darley Main mined no more. In 1882 further subsidence took place, causing further injury. Mitchell sued again seeking a remedy for further damages. Darley Main moved to dismiss on the ground of the "once and for all" rule. Lord Fitzgerald said:

> . . . I think that we may deduce from the authorities some propositions as now settled in law, and applicable to the circumstances of the appeal now before your Lordships' House, and to similar cases: — I proceed to state those propositions . . .

> That the owner of the surface has a natural and legal right to the undisturbed enjoyment of that surface in the absence of any binding agreement to the contrary.

> That the owner of the subjacent minerals may excavate and remove them to the utmost extent, but should exercise that right so as not to disturb the lawful enjoyment of the owner of the surface.

> But that, when, in consequence of not leaving or providing sufficient supports, a disturbance of the surface takes place, that disturbance is an invasion of the right of the owner of the surface, and constitutes his cause of action.

> The foundation of the plaintiff's action then seems to be that although the excavations of the minerals were acts by the defendants in the lawful enjoyment of their own property, yet when subsequently damage arose there-from to the plaintiff in the enjoyment of his property, the defendants become responsible.

> For although the law encourages a man to the free use of his own property, yet, if in doing a lawful thing in the enjoyment of that property he occasions damage to his neighbour which might have been avoided, he will be answerable for that damage whenever it occurs.

In 1882 a fresh and distinct subsidence took place, causing special damage to the plaintiff.

It was admitted before your Lordships, rather later in the argument, but for the purpose of better enabling your Lordships to come to a conclusion: — "That after the partial subsidence in 1868 the strata remained practically quiescent until the working of the coal in the next adjoining land by the owner thereof in the year 1881, which working caused a creep and a further subsidence." And further: — "That if the owner of the adjoining land had not worked his coal there would have been no further subsidence, and that if the coal under the respondent's (plaintiff's) land had not been taken out, or if the appellants (defendants) had left sufficient support under the respondent's (plaintiff's) land, then the working of the adjoining owner would have done no harm."

It will be observed on these admissions that the partial subsidence of 1868 had practically ceased, and that a fresh creep and subsidence took place in 1882, which would not have taken place if the defendants had left sufficient natural support under the plaintiff's land, or, we may add, had substituted adequate artificial support.

There can be no doubt that though there has been no act of commission by the defendants since the completion of the excavation of 1868, yet if there had been no subsidence causing damage to the plaintiff prior to that of 1882, the present action could be maintained; but it is alleged that as the plaintiff had a complete cause of action in 1868, arising from the prior excavation and the subsidence of 1868, the Statute of Limitations then commenced to operate, and has barred the present action. It was further argued that in 1868 the plaintiff could and ought to have insisted on recovering once and for all any damage that might arise prospectively from the excavation of 1868, according to the rule of law which, in order to prevent a multiplicity of actions, provides that damages resulting from one and the same cause of action must be assessed and recovered once and for all.

We have to consider what was the cause of action in 1868, and whether the cause of action of 1882 (the creep and subsidence of 1882), is one and the same cause of action as that of 1868. If it is so, then the defendants are entitled to succeed on the defense of the Statute of Limitations.

This appeal represents a class of cases peculiar and exceptional, to meet which and to avoid grave inconvenience, if not injustice, our flexible common law has somewhat moulded itself.

[Lord Fitzgerald quotes, as follows, from judgments in *Buckhouse v. Bonomi*, 9 H.L.C. 503.]

Lord Westbury, says, "I think it is abundantly clear, both on 'rinciple and authority, that when the enjoyment of the house is interfered with by the actual occurrence of the mischief, the cause of action then arises, and the action may then be maintained." And Lord Cranworth, adds: — "It has been supposed that the right of the party whose land is interfered with is a right to what is called the pillars or the support. In truth, his right is to the ordinary enjoyment of his land, and until that ordinary enjoyment is interfered with he has nothing of which to complain. That seems the principle on which the case ought to be disposed of."

It seems to me that Buckhouse v. Bonomi did decide that the removal of the subjacent strata was an act (I will not say an innocent act) done in the legitimate exercise of ordinary ownership, which, per se, gave no right of action to the owner of the surface, and that the latter had no right of action until his enjoyment of the surface was actually disturbed. The disturbance then constituted his right of action.

There was a complete cause of action in 1868, in respect of which compensation was given, but there was a liability to further disturbance. The defendants permitted the state of things to continue without taking any steps to prevent the occurrence of any future disturbance of the plaintiff's enjoyment, which gave him a new and distinct cause of action.

If this view is correct, then it follows that the cause of action now insisted on by the plaintiff is not the same cause of action as that of 1868, but is in point of law, as it is physically, a new and independent cause of action arising in 1882, and to which the defence of the Statute of Limitations is not applicable. . . .

What was the ground of the judgment in *Darley Main Colliery*? Did the "once and for all rule" not apply, or was this an exception to it?

(4)   For a decision that appears to be directly contradictory to *Carbonaro*, see *Wilson v. Johns-Manville Sales Corporation*, 684 F.2d 111 (D.C. Cir. 1982).

§ 4.07   DEFENSES AND PARTIES

BUTTERFIELD v. FORRESTER
11 East. 59, 103 E.R. 926 (K.B. (C.A.) 1809)[32]

BAYLEY, J.

The plaintiff was proved to be riding as fast as his horse could go, and this was through the streets of Derby. If he had used ordinary care, he must have seen the obstruction; so that the accident appeared to happen entirely from his own fault.

LORD ELLENBOROUGH, C.J.

A party is not to cast himself upon an obstruction which has been made by the fault of another, and avail himself of it, if he do not himself use common and ordinary caution to be in the right. In cases of persons riding upon what is considered to be the wrong side of the road, that would not authorize another purposely to ride up against them. One person being in fault will not dispense with another's using ordinary care for himself. Two things must concur to support this action, an obstruction in the road by the fault of the defendant, and no want of ordinary care to avoid it on the part of the plaintiff.

---

[32] [Ed. — English Reporter, general reporter of older English cases, King's Bench Court of Appeals decision; East's reports.]

Per Curiam. Rule refused.

NOTE

(1) *Butterfield* is the most widely cited progenitor of the doctrine of contributory negligence. There, the plaintiff was hurt when he drove his horse into an obstruction created in the road by the defendant who was making some repairs to his house. After being instructed that the plaintiff must lose if he was "riding along the street extremely hard, and without ordinary care," the jury issued a verdict for the defendant. Plaintiff's appeal against the instruction received the succinct replies set out above.

In a real sense the notion that a plaintiff cannot recover if his own wrong was a contributing factor, even slight, in the cause of his harm is attributable to a somewhat pious common law view that a court would not come to the aid of a wrongdoer. Courts of equity would express the same sentiment by demanding that the recipient of an equitable remedy come to the court with clean hands. The following case demonstrates another manifestation of importance to the law of torts.

(2) *Brown v. Kendall*, 60 Mass. 292 (1850), § 4.03, supra, placed the burden of proof of contributory negligence upon the defendant, which is the generally accepted practice. Nevertheless, there is some early common law authority that the plaintiff bears the burden of proving himself faultless. See, for example, *Dressler v. Davis*, 7 Wis. 49, 452 (1858), wherein it is said, "We . . . think it was necessary for the plaintiff, in order to make out a prima facie case in the first instance, to prove, not only that the injury in question arose from the carelessness or negligence of the defendants, but also that his own carelessness or negligence did not contribute to it."

(3) Negligence defenses are examined in detail in Chapter 9, *infra*.

MERRYWEATHER v. NIXAN
8 T.R. 186, 101 E.R. 1337 (1799)[33]

One Starkey brought an action on the case against the present plaintiff and defendant for an injury done by them to his reversionary estate [i.e., an ownership interest] in a mill, in which was included a count in trover, for the machinery belonging to the mill; and having recovered 840 pounds, he levied the whole on the present plaintiff, who thereupon brought this action against the defendant for a contribution of a moiety, as for so much money paid to his use.

At the trial, before Mr. Baron Thomson, at the last York Assizes, the plaintiff was nonsuited, the learned Judge being of opinion that no contribution could by law be claimed as between joint wrong-doers; and, consequently, this action, upon an implied assumpsit, could not be maintained on the mere ground that the plaintiff had alone paid the money which had been recovered against him and the other defendant in that action.

---

[33] [Ed. — English Reporter, general reporter of older English cases; decision of King's Bench division.]

Chambre now moved to set aside the nonsuit; contending, that as the former plaintiff had recovered against both these parties, both of them ought to contribute to pay the damages; but

Lord Kenyon, Ch.J. said, there could be no doubt but that the nonsuit was proper: that he had never before heard of such an action having been brought, where the former recovery was for a tort: that the distinction was clear between this case and that of a joint judgment against several defendants in an action of assumpsit: and that this decision would not affect cases of indemnity, where one man employed another to do acts, not unlawful in themselves, for the purpose of asserting a right.

Rule refused.

NOTES AND QUESTIONS

(1) *Merryweather v. Nixan* was a tort action but was not based on the law of negligence. Indeed, the law of negligence was in embryonic form at that early date. Application of the no-contribution rule in *Merryweather* shows that it is not limited to any particular cause of action but pertains generally to the exercise of the courts' remedial powers. Accordingly, later courts readily applied the rule in negligence cases without concern about the precise causes of action in earlier decisions.

(2) *Merryweather v. Nixan* also exemplifies several other rules pertaining to the jurisdiction of the court. When two or more wrongdoers collaborated to cause harm to a plaintiff and, later, when two or more wrongdoers independently harmed the plaintiff, producing a merged injury that could not be divided and allocated to each of them, the wrongdoers were known as joint tortfeasors. A plaintiff could join the two in a single action and obtain a judgment against the two that was known as a joint and several judgment. "Several" meant that each joint tortfeasor was individually (severally) liable for the entire judgment. "Joint" meant that no tortfeasor was released from liability until the entire judgment was satisfied.

The rule of *Merryweather v. Nixan* gave a plaintiff an option to execute a judgment any way the plaintiff saw fit: all from one joint tortfeasor, some from all or any combination. The only limit was not to exceed full satisfaction of the judgment. Joint tortfeasors, on the other hand, were without options. Their only hope was that the plaintiff would execute against someone else.

As in most instances when rigid rules reach results seen as unjust, lawyers and judges find ways to circumvent them. These take the form of exceptions, alternative doctrines and manipulation of facts which, as they affect this topic, are examined in later sections.

(3) Joint and several liability comes in many varieties. For example, if A and B conspire to defraud C and succeed, then the single indivisible wrongful act is their joint product. A and B are joint tortfeasors in the strictest sense. Nevertheless, even if A and B were total strangers, the law under some circumstances might still deem them to be jointly and severally liable to the plaintiff. For example, suppose A drives a car negligently toward the east and B drives a car negligently toward the west, and the two collide causing a collision that injures C, a pedestrian. Although in strict terms A and B would be concurrent rather than joint tortfeasors, modern law would hold them jointly and severally liable, unless C's injuries could be separated and wholly allocated to the fault of one or the other of the tortfeasors.

See, e.g., *Matthews v. Delaware, etc.*, R. R. Co., 56 N.J.L. 34, 27 A. 919 (1893).

By contrast, suppose A and B and C all are hunting alone in the woods, when A negligently fires a gun and hits C in the leg. About the same time B negligently fires a gun and hits C in the arm. Then, A and B would not be joint tortfeasors; each would be individually responsible for the specific injury each caused and no more.

(4)   A third variety of joint and several liability imputes the wrong of one person who actually perpetrated it to another who is actually blameless but is deemed by the law to be responsible for the wrongs of the other. For example, if M is the employer (or master, to use old common law terminology) of S (the employee or servant), then M is jointly and severally liable with S as to wrongs negligently perpetrated by S in the course of employment to M, even though M and S are not strictly joint tortfeasors. The last clause of Lord Kenyon's judgment in *Merryweather v. Nixan* indicates that the no-contribution rule does bar an action by M against S to be indemnified (i.e., to get all the money reimbursed) when the plaintiff has collected the entire judgment from M. In such a situation M may bring what is called an indemnification action against S to obtain reimbursement of the full amount M paid to P. By contrast, if M had been personally negligent, as in carelessly choosing S as an employee, then M and S would be true joint tortfeasors. See, e.g., *McNamara v. Chapman*, 81 N.H. 169, 123 A. 229 (1923). The legal effect, however, is the same, as far as the interests of the plaintiff is concerned.

Imputed legal responsibility is generally referred to as vicarious liability. The law imputes liability sparingly, usually requiring some special relationship between the wrongdoer and the imputed wrongdoer. For example, the doctrine of imputing the liability of a servant to a master is known as respondeat superior (let the superior respond). One of the fundamental attributes of the master-servant relationship is that the master has the legal right of control over the servant, not only of what he does in the course of employment but also how he does it. Thus, it follows that the servant's actions are under the legal control of the master, and the latter ought to be responsible when things go wrong. Therefore, S's negligence is imputed to M, making them joint tortfeasors. The injured party could get a joint and several judgment against both and execute it against M.

Other relationships justify vicarious liability for different reasons. Which of these is appropriate of itself: spouse-to-spouse; child-to-parent; parent-to-child; business partner-to-business partner; motor vehicle driver-to-owner of motor vehicle; law student-to-law teacher, law student-to-law student; client-to-lawyer; lawyer-to-client? Contrast, *Lester v. Magic Chef, Inc.*, 230 Kan. 643, 641 P.2d 353 (1982) (parent and two-year-old child), and *Carver v. Carver*, 314 S.E.2d 739 (N.C. 1984) (spouse and spouse).

(5)   The subject of parties to tort actions is examined in more detail in Chapter 11, *infra*.

Chapter 5

DUTY

In the decision of whether or not there is a duty, many factors interplay: the hand of history, our ideals of morals and justice, the convenience of administration of the rule, and our social ideas as to where the loss should fall. In the end the court will decide whether there is a duty on the basis of the mores of the community "always keeping in mind the fact that we endeavor to make a rule in each case that will be practical and in keeping with the general understanding of mankind."[1]

§ 5.01 INTRODUCTION

This chapter puts meat on the bones of the skeletal analysis of duty presented in Chapter 4. Section 5.02 includes two cases in which the courts grapple with the question of whether duty ought to be acknowledged in the context of novel facts. Although the style of the opinions is not as formal as that of Lord Diplock in *Home Office v. Dorset Yacht Co. Ltd.*, *supra*, the inductive approach clearly is at work in them.

The succeeding sections undertake a different task. For various reasons, the common law threw up what may be called no-duty rules that were applied to classes of factual situations. Thus, if a plaintiff's complaint was within the ambit of such a rule, then the defendant was entitled to prevail as a matter of law. These rules serve to economize judicial resources, but they are heavily weighted for the defendant in appropriate cases. Each section below presents cases that reveal (1) the scope of various no-duty rules and some of the reasons for their existence, and (2) how the no-duty rule may have been modified in recent times and why.

The status of these rules, however, varies greatly among the jurisdictions. To determine the current status of the law in a particular jurisdiction, it is necessary to carefully research that jurisdiction's body of case law.

---

[1] Trusiani v. Cumberland and York Distributors, Inc., 538 A.2d 258, 261 (Me. 1988), quoting Prosser, *Palsgraf Revisited*, 52 Mich. L. Rev. 1, 15 (1953).

§ 5.02   GENERAL PRINCIPLES

MICKLE v. BLACKMON
South Carolina Supreme Court
166 S.E.2d 173 (1969)

BRAILSFORD, JUSTICE.

On May 29, 1962, in the City of Rock Hill, seventeen-year-old Janet Mickle was a passenger in a 1949 Ford automobile, driven by Kenneth Hill. At the intersection of Jones Avenue and Black Street, this vehicle was in collision with an automobile driven by Larry Blackmon.

Janet was impaled on the gearshift lever, which entered her body behind the left armpit, penetrated to her spine, damaged the spinal cord at about breast level and caused complete and permanent paralysis of her body below the point of injury. She sued (1) Larry Blackmon, alleging negligence in the operation of his automobile, (2) Cherokee, Inc., a construction company which was engaged in widening Black Street, alleging negligence with respect to the removal of stop signs at the intersection and the failure to take proper precautions thereafter, and (3) Ford Motor Company, alleging negligence in the design and composition of the gearshift lever and of the knob or ball affixed thereto.

The trial resulted in an apportioned verdict for plaintiff against Cherokee, Inc., for $468,000.00 actual damages and against Ford Motor Company for $312,000.00 actual damages. The jury found no damages against Blackmon, and he is not a party to the appeal.

Cherokee moved unsuccessfully for judgment notwithstanding the verdict, for a new trial and for a new trial on after-discovered evidence and has appealed from the denial of these motions.

The circuit judge granted the motion of Ford Motor Company for judgment notwithstanding the verdict, and plaintiff has appealed. The court found no merit in Ford's alternative motion for a new trial, and Ford has filed a contingent and alternative appeal by which it seeks to preserve for review the grounds of this motion.

. . .

Plaintiff's case against Ford rests upon the claim that Ford was negligent in the design and placement of the gearshift lever, which, without an adequate protective ball or knob, created an unreasonable risk of injury to a passenger upon the happening of a collision; and that this risk was realized when the protective knob shattered on the impact of plaintiff's body and she was impaled on the spear-like lever. Ford, while defending the suitability of its gearshift lever assembly at the time of the production and initial sale of the car, disclaims any duty to manufacture an automobile in which it is safe to have a collision, or to exercise care to minimize the collision connected hazards presented to occupants by the design of the passenger compartment. Ford urges that its only duty in this respect is to manufacture a product which is free of latent defects and reasonably fit for its intended use, and that such use does not include colliding with other vehicles or objects.

McPherson v. Buick Motor Co., 217 N.Y. 382, 111 N.E. 1050, L.R.A. 1916F, 696 (1916), has resulted in general agreement upon the rule that a manufacturer is liable, under ordinary negligence principles, for a dangerously defective product which, while being put to an intended use, causes an accident and resulting injury to its user or to some third party. Ford concedes this principle, which we adopted in *Salladin v. Tellis*, 247 S.C. 267, 146 S.E.2d 875, and which has nigh universal support. Prosser on Torts, 661 (3d ed.).

On the other hand, there is scant authority on the specific issue which Ford tenders, *i.e.*, whether the manufacturer of automobile owes a duty in the design and composition of his product to avoid creating unreasonable risks of injury to passengers in a collision of the automobile with another object. Stated differently, does the manufacturer owe a duty of care to reasonably minimize the risk of death or serious injury to collision victims who, quite predictably, will upon impact be forcefully thrown against the interior of the car or outside of it?

Whether Ford owed such a duty is a question of law. If not, plaintiff has no case against Ford. If so, whether Ford breached this duty to plaintiff's injury is a question of fact, unless, of course the evidence is susceptible of only one reasonable inference.

It is a matter of common knowledge that a high incidence of injury-producing motor vehicle collisions is a dread concomitant of travel upon our streets and highways, and that a significant proportion of all automobiles produced are involved in such smashups at sometime during their use. Thus, an automobile manufacturer knows with certainty that many users of his product will be involved in collisions, and that the incidence and extent of injury to them will frequently be determined by the placement, design and construction of such interior components as shafts, levers, knobs, handles and others. By ordinary negligence standards, a known risk of harm raises a duty of commensurate care. We perceive no reason in logic or law why an automobile manufacturer should be exempt from this duty.

The only two appellate court decisions in which this issue has been agitated and decided, which have come to our attention, reached opposed conclusions. Ford relies upon *Evans v. General Motors Corp.*, 359 F.2d 822 (7th Cir. 1966), in which plaintiff sued for the death of her intestate on the theory that the defendant was negligent in using an X frame in a 1961 Chevrolet station wagon, instead of the perimeter frame in general use, because, foreseeing the possibility of broadside collisions, the defendant owed a duty to provide side rails as reasonable protection against death or serious injury from such impacts. A divided court concluded that the complaint failed to state a cause of action. The rationale of the majority is fairly disclosed by the following excerpts from the opinion:

> A manufacturer is not under a duty to make his automobile accident-proof or fool-proof; nor must he render the vehicle "more" safe where the danger to be avoided is obvious to all. (Citing *Campo v. Scofield*, 1950, 301 N.Y. 468, 95 N.E. 2d 802, 804.) . . .

> . . .

> The intended purpose of an automobile does not include its participation in collisions with other objects, despite the manufacturer's ability to foresee the possibility that such collisions may occur. . . .

Defendant had a duty to test its frame only to ensure that it was reasonably fit for its intended purpose.

359 F.2d at 824 & 825.

It is apparent that the majority gave controlling weight to the concept of safety for the intended use or purpose as the limit of the defendant's obligation to exercise care. On the other hand, the dissent, applying elementary principles of the law of negligence, soundly, we think, found a duty to exercise care to furnish reasonable protection to collision victims in the statistical certainty that there would be such victims among the users of the cars produced and in the clear foreseeability of harm to such victims if care were not exercised.

In *Larsen v. General Motors Corp.*, 391 F.2d 495 (8th Cir.), decided March 11, 1968, a unanimous court adopted the view of the dissenting judge in *Evans*. The plaintiff, driver of a 1963 Chevrolet Corvair, was injured in a head-on collision by a rearward thrust of the steering shaft. The complaint alleged that plaintiff's injury was caused or aggravated by the defendant's negligence in extending the steering shaft to a point in front of the forward surface of the front tires, thus greatly increasing the rearward thrust of the shaft upon impact. General Motors again disavowed any "duty of care in the design of an automobile to make it more safe to occupy in the event of a collision." Relying upon the *Evans* decision and upon several intervening district court cases which had followed the *Evans* line, the district court sustained this position and granted summary judgment. In a well-reasoned and documented opinion, which analyzes the decisions relied upon by General Motors and other decisions tending to support the view adopted by it, the court of appeals reversed. We are convinced of the soundness of the following excerpt from the opinion, which demonstrates Ford's duty of reasonable care to avoid unreasonable risk of injury to collision victims:

We think the "intended use" construction urged by General Motors is much too narrow and unrealistic. Where the manufacturer's negligence in design causes an unreasonable risk to be imposed upon the user of its products, the manufacturer should be liable for the injury caused by its failure to exercise reasonable care in the design. These injuries are readily foreseeable as an incident to the normal and expected use of an automobile. While automobiles are not made for the purpose of colliding with each other, a frequent and inevitable contingency of normal automobile use will result in collisions and injury-producing impacts. No rational basis exists for limiting recovery to situations where the defect in design or manufacture was the causative factor of the accident, as the accident and the resulting injury, usually caused by the so-called "second collision" of the passenger with the interior part of the automobile, all are foreseeable. Where the injuries or enhanced injuries are due to the manufacturer's failure to use reasonable care to avoid subjecting the user of its products to an unreasonable risk of injury, general negligence principles should be applicable. . . .

Larsen v. General Motors Corp., 391 F.2d at 502.

We shall not rehash the other decisions, pro and con, which are reviewed in *Evans* and *Larsen*. None of them is on strictly analogous facts. However, we cannot omit reference to the persuasive opinion by Judge J. Spencer Bell in *Spruill v. Boyle-Midway, Inc.*, 308 F.2d 79 (4th Cir. 1962.) Although the product involved was poisonous furniture polish, which was ingested by an infant while his mother was temporarily out of the room, the cogent grounds of the court's rejection of the claim that the manufacturer was not liable because the product was not intended to be consumed are, in part, fully applicable here, quoting:

> We agree with the general principle but the application the defendants would have us make of it here is much too narrow. *"Intended use" is but a convenient adaptation of the basic test of "reasonable foreseeability"* framed to more specifically fit the factual situations out of which arise questions of a manufacturer's liability for negligence. "Intended use" is not an inflexible formula to be apodictically applied to every case. Normally a seller or manufacturer is entitled to anticipate that the product he deals in will be used only for the purposes for which it is manufactured and sold; thus he is expected to reasonably foresee only injuries arising in the course of such use.
>
> *However, he must also be expected to anticipate the environment which is normal for the use of his product* and where, as here, that environment is the home, he must anticipate the reasonably foreseeable risks of the use of his product in such an environment. These are risks which are inherent in the proper use for which his product is manufactured. . . .

(Emphasis added.) 308 F.2d at 83–84.

We can add nothing to the force of Judge Bell's logic and will not attempt to do so. It is notable that the above quotation may be shaped to our facts by simply substituting the word "highway" for the word "home" in the first sentence of the second paragraph.

[Thus, the court resolved the duty question in favor of the plaintiff]

NOTES AND QUESTIONS

(1) At one time *Larsen* and *Evans* stood at the head of two distinct lines of authority on the point of this case. *Blankenship v. General Motors Corp.*, 406 S.E.2d 781 (W. Va. 1991), adopted the *Larsen* view and stated that all courts now follow it.

(2) *Mickle v. Blackmon* discussed *Spruill v. Boyle-Midway, Inc.*, a controversial decision. Whether the *Spruill* decision is sound depends in large part on which issues or policy considerations are most important to the decisionmaker.

If the court emphasizes "foreseeability," liability in *Spruill* probably follows because it is foreseeable that a number of purchasers of furniture polish will leave lids off polish cans, thus enabling small children to ingest the poisonous polish.

Suppose instead the court asks the standard Law & Economics question: "Who could have best prevented this accident?" and places the duty on the party that could have prevented the accident at the lowest cost? The choice would be between the parents of the infant child and the polish manufacturer. A Law & Economics judge might well place the duty on the parents because it would be less costly for them to put the polish away or secure the top than for the manufacturer to produce an edible polish. Doing this would give the parents a greater incentive to prevent the injury. This would also be consistent with the view that individuals should take responsibility for their own actions rather than rely on others to protect them.

On the other hand, the "least cost" decision might leave many victims without compensation, as when parents are not wealthy enough to provide compensation.

Which issue should factor most heavily into the outcome of a case like *Spruill*: foreseeability, behavior modification, individual responsibility, or compensation?

OLSON v. VILLAGE OF OAK LAWN
Illinois Appellate Court
432 N.E.2d 1120 (1982)

GOLDBERG, JUSTICE:

Summary judgment was entered in favor of the Village of Oak Lawn (defendant) and against Charles E. Olson (plaintiff), a minor who appears by Janet E. Olson, his mother and next friend. Plaintiff has appealed.

Plaintiff was seriously injured on February 24, 1977, by a fall while riding a skateboard on a public sidewalk running north and south on the west side of Laramie Street in defendant village. Plaintiff's second amended complaint charged defendant with negligence in that one slab of the sidewalk was dropped and displaced with a resulting disparity apparent at the joinder of the two slabs. In Count II of his complaint plaintiff joined Wieboldt's Stores, Inc., which had allegedly sold plaintiff a device known as a skateboard. Counts III and IV of the complaint were against Santa Monica Research, Inc., a corporation, allegedly the manufacturer of the skateboard which was described as unreasonably dangerous. This appeal involves only the summary judgment entered on Count I.

Defendant's motion for summary judgment includes a copy of the second amended complaint; answer of defendant thereto; the deposition of the plaintiff; photographs of the site of the occurrence; a written memorandum filed by defendant; an answering memorandum filed by plaintiff; and a reply memorandum filed by defendant.

On the date of the occurrence, plaintiff was 13 years old. Plaintiff lived at 10720 South Laramie in the defendant village. The mishap occurred some six houses south of plaintiff's home on the sidewalk on the west side of Laramie Street. Plaintiff had previously ridden the skateboard on the walk but this was the first time he had used it at the point of the accident. Plaintiff had walked over that portion of the sidewalk without the skateboard several times a week for some years without any problem.

Plaintiff testified he was going south at the time and did not see the disparity between the two sidewalk slabs. When the skateboard passed over the drop, plaintiff was "sling-shotted" forward and fell upon his hands and knees. He did not know the dimension of the disparity but he stated one slab was higher than the other. He generally proceeded on the skateboard without looking at the sidewalk as he went. On this particular occasion he did not see the sidewalk disparity.

Pursuant to the pertinent statute (Ill. Rev.Stat.1979, ch. 110, par. 57(3)), summary judgment is properly granted when the record reveals " 'no genuine issue as to any material fact' " and also that the moving party is entitled to summary judgment " 'as a matter of law.' " See *Smith v. Metropolitan Sanitary District of Greater Chicago* (1979), 77 Ill. 2d 390, 33 Ill. Dec. 135, 396 N.E.2d 524, quoting from *Econo Lease, Inc. v. Noffsinger* (1976), 63 Ill. 2d 390, 393, 349 N.E.2d 1.

In the instant case there is no dispute as to any material fact. The problem arises in determining whether defendant is entitled to a judgment as a matter of law. " 'It is fundamental that there can be no recovery in tort for negligence unless the defendant has breached a duty owed to the plaintiff.' " (*Pippin v. Chicago Housing Authority* (1979), 78 Ill. 2d 204, 208, 35 Ill. Dec. 530, 399 N.E.2d 596, quoting from *Boyd v. Racine Currency Exchange, Inc.* (1973), 56 Ill. 2d 95, 97, 306 N.E.2d 39.) The question of existence of a duty which is defined as "the legal obligation imposed upon one for the benefit of another, is a question of law to be determined by the court. . . . " *Fancil v. Q.S.E. Fords, Inc.* (1975), 60 Ill. 2d 552, 555, 328 N.E.2d 538; see also *Bence v. Crawford Savings & Loan Association* (1980), 80 Ill. App. 3d 491, 492, 35 Ill. Dec. 902, 400 N.E.2d 39.

It is a definitely accepted principle of law that a municipality owes the general public a duty of taking the necessary steps to maintain its sidewalks in a reasonably safe condition. Where the defect is such that " 'a reasonably prudent man should anticipate some danger to persons walking' " upon the sidewalk, a factual issue as to the existence of negligence by the municipality is presented. (*Baker v. City of Granite City* (1979), 75 Ill. App. 3d 157, 160, 31 Ill. Dec. 117, 394 N.E.2d 33, *leave to appeal denied*, 79 Ill. 2d 619, quoting from *Arvidson v. City of Elmhurst* (1957), 11 Ill. 2d 601, 605, 145 N.E.2d 105.) However, this principle has be en evolved by the courts in connection with the rights of pedestrians. In the case at bar, we are concerned with a minor riding a skateboard upon a municipal sidewalk. This requires initially an examination of the skateboard and its operation.

The skateboard is described in the record. Basically, it is a board mounted on two wheels in the front and two in the back. It has no brakes, no motor and no steering device. The operator places one foot on the board and pushes the skateboard until it gains speed. He is then able to place both feet upon the board and to proceed at a goodly pace. The machine is propelled entirely by the rider. It has no vertical handle at the front end. The operator can change its direction only by shifting his weight. Able counsel for plaintiff makes the point "skateboards have attained wide popularity and the trial court in its opinion recognized and took notice of their wide use."

We find no authority in Illinois bearing directly upon the pertinent legal issue here. However, the following authorities are of value:

In *Cygielman v. City of New York* (1978), 93 Misc. 2d 232, 402 N.Y.S.2d 539, a 14-year-old operator of a skateboard was injured because of a break in the sidewalk. The court formulated the duty of the municipality as that of reasonable care in maintaining a reasonably safe condition for "ordinary, customary and usual modes of use." (402 N.Y.S.2D 539, 540.) The court cited precedents involving means of transportation such as a sled and a bicycle. The court stated that the nature of the skateboard was such that it was the use of this device which brought about the injury. The court also noted (402 N.Y.S.2D 539, 542):

> That this accident happened; that others will continue to happen, can be predicted with almost awesome certainty. It is beyond peradventure that without proper equipment, including helmet, knee and elbow pads and a mastery of the technique, skateboarding is inherently dangerous. Possessing no braking system, once a rider has lost control or has fallen off, the skateboard will, by inertia, continue on its own, menacing unwitting

pedestrians. This alone is sufficient to refuse to expand the City's liability. The answer is, of course, in the establishment of skateboard parks designed specifically to accommodate the novice as well as the expert. The young people of this country have often petitioned for such facilities. It would be anything but foolhardy, however, to believe that they will abstain from skateboarding until their pleas are acted upon. Until such time, the pursuit of this sport will continue to resolve itself into a matter of flesh and concrete. Neither empathy nor sympathy however, is the basis for liability where none exists.

The New York court entered judgment in favor of defendant, dismissing the complaint.

In *Errante v. City of New York* (1979), 98 Misc. 2d 896, 414 N.Y.S.2d 603, the court held there was a municipal duty to maintain the sidewalks in proper condition for the use of persons traveling on roller skates. The court cited *Cygielman* and expressly differentiated the use of roller skates as a contrast to a "skateboard, sled, bicycle or other such user-propelled coasting device. . . . " The New York court then used this language (414 N.Y.S.2d 603, 604):

> As the aforementioned cases illustrate, municipalities have consistently been found free from liability in negligence for injuries sustained as a result of sidewalks which are not customary. In all of these cases, it was the skateboard, sled, bicycle or other such user-propelled coasting device of the injured party which removed the case from what the city was expected to contemplate as the ordinary usage of its sidewalks. The extra degree of speed which can be attained by such devices and the limited amount of control which can be exercised in their use makes them inherently dangerous in and of themselves. It was for this reason that the City did not owe a duty to make its sidewalks safe for their use.

In *Bartell v. Palos Verdes Peninsula School District* (1978), 83 Cal. App. 3d 492, 147 Cal. Rptr. 898, plaintiffs' son suffered fatal injuries in playing a game involving the use of a skateboard upon a school playground. The California court held there was no duty and hence no liability upon the school authority. The court pointed out that the injuries "were the direct result of the dangerous conduct of plaintiffs' son and his companion and not of any defective or dangerous condition of the property." 147 Cal. Rptr. 898, 900.

The basic nature of the skateboard necessarily renders virtually any sidewalk variation dangerous to its operator. Therefore, to impose a duty on municipalities to insure that sidewalks are safe for skateboard riders, would drastically expand the current duty to maintain sidewalks. (See *e.g. Arvidson*, 11 Ill. 2d 601, 604, 145 N.E.2d 105, holding minor defects are unactionable as a matter of law.) We believe such an expansion of this duty would result in devastating public expense without affording appreciably greater safety for skateboard riders.

We conclude a municipality owes no duty regarding sidewalk conditions when injuries result from riding a skateboard upon the sidewalk. The order for summary judgment in favor of defendant is accordingly affirmed.

Judgment affirmed.

NOTES AND QUESTIONS

(1)   Compare *Larson v. City of Chicago*, 491 N.E.2d 165 (Ill. App. 1st Dist. 1986), holding a duty of care is owed to roller skaters and *McCann v. City of Boston*, 575 N.E.2d 87 (Mass. App. 1991), holding the contrary. What factual differences could justify the opposite results? *See also Rosner v. Chicago*, 502 N.E.2d 357 (Ill. App. 1980) (No duty owed to pedestrian crossing street except those in a crosswalk).

(2)   The final portion of the *Olsen v. Village of Oak Lawn* case referred to a balance between expense and risk as a factor in the determination of duty. As is more fully developed in Chapter 6 herein, a modern law and economic analysis movement has sought to introduce more conscious economic balancing into tort liability questions, particularly in determining the breach of duty issue. Nevertheless, many courts incorporate the so-called risk-benefit balance in deciding the duty question. *Sharpe v. Moore, Inc.*, 796 P.2d 506, 509, 510 (Idaho 1990), discussed this idea in connection with foreseeability of harm as follows:

Foreseeability is a flexible concept which varies with the circumstances of each case. Where the degree of result or harm is great, but preventing it is not difficult, a relatively low degree of foreseeability is required. Conversely, where the threatened injury is minor but the burden of preventing such injury is high, a higher degree of foreseeability may be required. See *U.S. v. Carroll Towing Co.*, 159 F.2d 169, 173 (2d Cir.1947) (Judge Learned Hand); *Isaacs v. Huntington Memorial Hosp.*, 38 Cal. 3d 112, 211 Cal. Rptr. 356, 695 P.2d 653, 658 (1985). Thus, foreseeability is not to be measured by just what is more probable than not, but also include whatever result is likely enough in the setting of modern life that a reasonably prudent person would take such into account in guiding reasonable conduct.

§ 5.03   EMOTIONAL HARM — NOT CAUSED BY PHYSICAL CONTACT

The reason why an independent action for such damages cannot and ought not be sustained, is found in the remoteness of such damages- . . . . Vague and shadowy, there is no possible standard by which such an injury can be justly compensated, or even approximately measured. Easily simulated and impossible to disprove, it falls within all of the objections to speculative damages, which are universally excluded because of their uncertain character. That damages so imaginary, so metaphysical, so sentimental, shall be ascertained and assessed by a jury, with justness, not by way of punishment to the defendant, but as mere compensation to the plaintiff, is not to be expected.

Lurton, J., (dissenting) *Wadsworth v. Western Union Tel. Co.*, 8 S.W. 574 (Tenn. 1888).

MITCHELL v. ROCHESTER RAILWAY CO.
New York Court of Appeals
151 N.Y. 107, 45 N.E. 354 (1896)

Martin, J.

[The trial court non-suited the plaintiff after trial on the grounds that no cause exists for negligent infaction of fright above even though physical injury results from the fright. The appellate division reversed and ordered a new trial. Plaintiff then filed a motion for new trial on the ground that the court erred to take the case from the jury. The trial court held that the non-suit had been erroneously granted and granted the motion for new trial. The defendant appealed this order.]

The facts in this case are few and may be briefly stated. On the first day of April, 1891, the plaintiff was standing upon a crosswalk on Main street in the city of Rochester, awaiting an opportunity to board one of the defendant's cars which had stopped upon the street at that place. While standing there, and just as she was about to step upon the car, a horse car of the defendant came down the street. As the team attached to the car drew near, it turned to the right and came so close to the plaintiff that she stood between the horses' heads when they were stopped.

She testified that from fright and excitement caused by the approach and proximity of the team she became unconscious, and also that the result was a miscarriage and consequent illness. Medical testimony was given to the effect that the mental shock which she then received was sufficient to produce that result.

Assuming that the evidence tended to show that the defendant's servant was negligent in the management of the car and horses, and that the plaintiff was free from contributory negligence, the single question presented is whether the plaintiff is entitled to recover for the defendant's negligence which occasioned her fright and alarm, and resulted in the injuries already mentioned. While the authorities are not harmonious upon this question, we think the most reliable and better considered cases, as well as public policy, fully justify us in holding that the plaintiff cannot recover for injuries occasioned by fright, as there was no immediate personal injury. The learned counsel for the respondent in his brief very properly stated that, "The consensus of opinion would seem to be that no recovery can be had for mere fright,". . . .

If it be admitted that no recovery can be had for fright occasioned by the negligence of another, it is somewhat difficult to understand how a defendant would be liable for its consequences. Assuming that fright cannot form the basis of an action, it is obvious that no recovery can be had for injuries resulting there from. That the result may be nervous disease, blindness, insanity, or even a miscarriage, in no way changes the principle. These results merely show the degree of fright or the extent of the damages. The right of action must still depend upon the question whether a recovery may be had for fright. If it can, then an action may be maintained, however slight the injury. If not, then there can be no recovery, no matter how grave or serious the consequences. Therefore, the logical result of the respondent's concession would seem to be, not only that no recovery can be had for mere fright, but also that none can be had for injuries which are the direct consequences of it.

If the right of recovery in this class of cases should be once established, it would naturally result in a flood of litigation in cases where the injury complained of may be easily feigned without detection, and where the damages must rest upon mere conjecture or speculation. The difficulty which often exists in cases of alleged physical injury, in determining whether they exist, and if so, whether they were caused by the negligent act of the defendant, would not only be greatly increased, but a wide field would be opened for fictitious or speculative claims. To establish such a doctrine would be contrary to principles of public policy.

Moreover, it cannot be properly said that the plaintiff's miscarriage was the proximate result of the defendant's negligence. Proximate damages are such as are the ordinary and natural results of the negligence charged, and those that are usual and may, therefore, be expected. It is quite obvious that the plaintiff's injuries do not fall within the rule as to proximate damages. The injuries to the plaintiff were plainly the result of an accidental or unusual combination of circumstances, which could not have been reasonably anticipated, and over which the defendant had no control, and, hence, her damages were too remote to justify a recovery in this action.

These considerations lead to the conclusion that no recovery can be had for injuries sustained by fright occasioned by the negligence of another, where there is no immediate personal injury.

The orders of the General and Special Terms should be reversed, and the order of the Trial Term granting a nonsuit affirmed, with costs.

All concur, except HAIGHT, J., not sitting, and VANN, J., not voting.

Ordered accordingly.

NOTES AND QUESTIONS

(1) *Mitchell* relied upon *Commissioners v. Coultas*, 13 A.C. 222, an English case which may be the progenitor of the no-impact, no-duty rule for emotional injury. A number of early American decisions declined to apply the rule in all circumstances. *See, e.g., Jones v. Roach*, 54 S.W. 240 (Tex. 1899) (permitting recovery for mental suffering arising out of negligent failure to deliver a telegram summoning a husband to attend to his dying wife.) Contra., *Norton v. Western Union Tel. Co.*, 41 N.E. 689 (Ohio 1895) (the court affirmed judgment denying recovery for a plaintiff who did not receive a telegraph stating: "Come immediately Mother dying." The Ohio court said, "the judgment rests upon the elementary principle that mere mental pain or anxiety are too vague for legal redress where no injury is done to person, property, health or reputation.").

(2) *Mitchell* was expressly overruled by *Battalia v. State*, 176 N.E.2d 729 (N.Y. 1961), and *Coultas* was overruled by *McLoughlin v. O'Brian, infra*, but the no-impact no-duty rule still prevails in some jurisdictions. For example, in *Gilliam v. Stewart*, 291 So. 2d 593 (Fla. 1974), the Florida Supreme Court declined to recede from it as a general proposition but did later apply a relaxed rule in so-called "bystander" cases. *Champion v. Gray*, 487 So. 2d 17 (Fla. 1985). The rule has been modified in many jurisdictions. See 1 Minzer, et al., Damages in Tort Actions, Chapter 5, *Negligent Infliction of Emotional Distress* (Matthew Bender & Co.), for

an extensive discussion of this entire subject. The next two cases and notes show some of the forms the revisions have taken.

———

WAUBE v. WARRINGTON
Wisconsin Supreme Court
258 N.W. 497 (1935)

WICKHEM, JUSTICE.

In the statement of facts in both briefs it is said that deceased was looking out the window of her house watching her child cross the highway, and witnessed the negligent killing of the child by defendant. While upon a demurrer the sole question is whether the facts alleged in the complaint state a cause of action, we consider that the statement of facts concurred in by plaintiff and defendant constitutes an informal amendment to the complaint by stipulation, and will determine the questions presented as though the complaint were amended to conform to the statement of facts.

The question presented is whether under the Wisconsin equivalent of Lord Campbell's Act, decedent's husband may recover for her death under such circumstances. Under the provisions of section 331.03, Stats., in order that he may recover for her death, the circumstances must have been such as to have entitled Susie Waube, had she lived, to maintain an action for her injuries. *Koehler v. Waukesha Milk Co.*, 190 Wis. 52, 208 N.W. 901. Thus the question presented is whether the mother of a child who, although not put in peril or fear of physical impact, sustains the shock of witnessing the negligent killing of her child, may recover for physical injuries caused by such fright or shock.

The problem must be approached at the outset from the viewpoint of the duty of defendant and the right of plaintiff, and not from the viewpoint of proximate cause. The right of the mother to recover must be based, first, upon the establishment of a duty on the part of defendant so to conduct herself with respect to the child as not to subject the mother to an unreasonable risk of shock or fright, and, second, upon the recognition of a legally protected right or interest on the part of the mother to be free from shock or fright occasioned by the peril of her child. It is not enough to find a breach of duty to the child, follow the consequences of such breach as far as the law of proximate cause will permit them to go, and then sustain a recovery for the mother if a physical injury to her by reason of shock or fright is held not too remote.

. . .

The only case squarely dealing with this problem is *Hambrook v. Stokes Bros.*, [1925] 1 K. B. 141. In this case a servant of defendants was in charge of a motortruck belonging to defendants and parked it at the top of a hill on Dover street in Folkestone, leaving it unattended, with the motor running, and without taking proper precautions to prevent it from moving. During his absence the truck started to run down the hill. The street was narrow, being not more than six feet wide in some places, and there was a curve at the lower end of it. The truck eventually came to a standstill by reason of running against the side of a house at a point below the curve. On the day in question Mrs. Hambrook, whose house was at the bottom of Dover Street, accompanied her three children, a girl and two boys, part of the distance on their way to school.

She walked with them to a point a little below the curve in Dover street, and then left them. Shortly afterwards she saw the truck coming rapidly around the curve in her direction. She was not in any personal danger, as the truck stopped some distance short of where she was standing, and in any case she would have had ample opportunity to step into a position of safety. She immediately became fearful for the safety of her children. A crowd collected and there were rumors of an accident. She inquired who had been injured, and a friend stated that it was a little girl with glasses. It appeared that her little girl wore glasses. She went to the hospital and found that her daughter had been injured. She sustained a severe shock and consequent physical injuries from which she died.

The trial court directed the jury that if the nervous shock was caused by fear of her child's safety, as distinguished from her own, plaintiff could not recover. From a verdict in favor of defendants, plaintiff appealed. The judgment was set aside and a new trial granted for misdirection. The court reviewed the state of the English law with respect to this subject, pointing out that the *Coultas* Case, *supra*, had been modified, and recognizing also that the *Dulieu* Case, *supra*, had limited the recovery in fright cases to situations where the fright was occasioned by the peril of the person affrighted. Viewing the matter from the standpoint of proximate cause rather than duty, the court held that there should be no distinction between shock sustained by a mother as a result of fear for her own safety, and that sustained by reason of peril to her child.

The court considered that defendant ought to have anticipated that if the unattended truck ran down this narrow street it might terrify some woman to such an extent, through fear of some immediate bodily injury to herself, that she would receive a mental shock with resultant physical injuries, and that defendant ought also to have anticipated that such a shock might result from the peril to the child of such a woman.

While the majority, mistakenly, as it seems to us, approach this problem from the standpoint of proximate cause, the dissenting opinion of Sargant, L. J., approaches it from the standpoint of duty. The dissenting opinion concedes that since it was defendant's duty to exercise due care in the management of his vehicle so as to avoid physical injury to those on or near the highway, this duty cannot be limited to physical injuries caused by actual physical impact. The dissenting opinion, however, states that the matter is quite different where the shock to plaintiff is due, not to immediate fear of personal impact, but to the sight or apprehension of impact upon a third person. Reference is made to the unreported case of *Smith v. Johnson & Co.*, referred to by Wright, J., in his judgment in *Wilkinson v. Downton*, [1897] 2 Q. B. 61. There the plaintiff became ill from the shock of seeing another killed, the death being due to the negligence of the defendant. It was held that the plaintiff could not recover, not on the ground that the harm was too remote, "but on (what is often practically equivalent) a consideration of the extent of the duty of the defendant towards the plaintiff and others on and near the highway." The dissenting opinion then states that "it would be a considerable and unwarranted extension of the duty of owners of vehicles towards others in or near the highway, if it were held to include an obligation not to do anything to render them liable to harm through nervous shock caused by the sight or apprehension of damage to third persons." The dissenting opinion concludes that there is no sound reason for erecting an exception in favor of the mother of a child, and points out that once the defendant's duty is held to extend to those outside the field of physical peril, a doctrine is stated to which no rational boundaries can be erected.

The American Law Institute, in its Restatement of Torts, thus states the law:

§ 313. Emotional Distress Unintended.

If the actor unintentionally causes emotional distress to another, he is liable to the other for illness or bodily harm of which the distress is a legal cause if the actor

    (a) should have realized that his conduct involved an unreasonable risk of causing the distress, otherwise than by knowledge of the injury or peril of a third person, and

    (b) from facts known to him should have realized that the distress, if it were caused, might result in illness or bodily harm.

It is thus recognized that as the law exists, there is no liability for fright, negligently occasioned, where that fright or shock is the result of knowledge of the injury or peril of a third person. The Institute, however, adds a caveat as follows: "The Institute expresses no opinion as to whether an actor whose conduct is negligent as involving an unreasonable risk of causing bodily harm to a child or spouse is liable for an illness or other bodily harm caused to the parent or spouse who witnesses the peril or harm of the child or spouse and thereby suffers anxiety or shock which is the legal cause of the parent's or spouse's illness or bodily harm."

Whether this caveat was added because of a difference of opinion, a dearth of authority, or a consideration of the English case is immaterial. At any rate, there is no authority except the English case, and possibly the Alabama case, for extending the duty of the defendant as contended for by plaintiff in this case, nor do we think that sound principle calls for such an extension.

With due deference to the learned judges who concurred in the decision, we cannot escape the conclusion that the determination in the *Hambrook* Case is incorrect, both in its initial approach and in its conclusion, and that the doctrine contended for by plaintiff, and there approved, would constitute an unwarranted enlargement of the duties of users of the highway. Fundamentally, defendant's duty was to use ordinary care to avoid physical injury to those who would be put in physical peril, as that term is commonly understood, by conduct on his part falling short of that standard. It is one thing to say that as to those put in peril of physical impact, impact is immaterial if physical injury is caused by shock arising from the peril. It is the foundation of cases holding to this liberal ruling that the person affrighted or sustaining shock was actually put in peril of physical impact, and under these conditions it was considered immaterial that the physical impact did not materialize. It is quite another thing to say that those who are out of the field of physical danger through impact shall have a legally protected right to be free from emotional distress occasioned by the peril of others, when that distress results in physical impairment. The answer to this question cannot be reached solely by logic, nor is it clear that it can be entirely disposed of by a consideration of what the defendant ought reasonably to have anticipated as a consequence of his wrong. The answer must be reached by balancing the social interests involved in order to ascertain how far defendant's duty and plaintiff's right may justly and expediently be extended. It is our conclusion that they can neither justly nor expediently be extended to any recovery for physical injuries sustained by one out of the range of ordinary physical peril as a result of the shock of witnessing another's danger. Such consequences are so unusual and extraordinary, viewed after the event, that a user of the highway may be said not to subject others to an unreasonable risk of them by the careless management of his vehicle. Furthermore, the liability imposed by such a doctrine is wholly out of proportion to the culpability of the negligent tort-feasor, would put an unreasonable burden upon users of the highway, open the way to fraudulent claims, and enter a field that has no sensible or just stopping point.

It was recognized by the court in the *Hambrook* Case that had the mother there merely been told of the injury to her child, instead of having been virtually a witness to the transaction, there would have been no liability. The court thus selected at least one arbitrary boundary for the extension. While there is no suggestion in the caveat attached to section 188B, Restatement, Torts, as to what the proper rule should be, it is implied that any possible extension of the rule as stated would be limited (1) to the relationship of parent and child or husband and wife, and (2) to persons sustaining the shock as a result of witnessing the peril. It was suggested in the dissenting opinion in the *Hambrook* Case that if the mother may recover, why not a child whose shock was occasioned by the peril of the mother? It is not necessary to multiply these illustrations. They can be made as numerous as the varying degrees of human relationship, and they shade into each other in such a way as to leave no definite or clear-cut stopping place for the suggested doctrine, short of a. recovery for every person who has sustained physical injuries as a result of shock or emotional distress by reason of seeing or hearing of the peril or injury of another. No court has gone this far, and we think no court should go this far.

It is our view that fairness and justice, as well as expediency, require the defendant's duty to be defined as heretofore stated, in accordance with the weight of liberal authority and the general statement of the rule by the American Law Institute. Human wrongdoing is seldom limited in its injurious effects to the immediate actors in a particular event. More frequently than not, a chain of results is set up that visits evil consequences far and wide. While from the standpoint of good morals and good citizenship the wrongdoer may be said to violate a duty to those who suffer from the wrong, the law finds it necessary, for reasons heretofore considered, to attach practical and just limits to the legal consequences of the wrongful act. As was said by the New York court, speaking through Judge Cardozo, in *Palsgraf v. Long Island R. R. Co., supra*:

> "Negligence is not a tort unless it results in the commission of a wrong, and the commission of a wrong imports the violation of a right, in this case, we are told, the right to be protected against interference with one's bodily security. But bodily security is protected, not against all forms of interference or aggression, but only against some. One who seeks redress at law does not make out a cause of action by showing without more that there has been damage to his person. If the harm was not willful, he must show that the act as to him had possibilities of danger so many and apparent as to entitle him to be protected against the doing of it though the harm was unintended. Affront to personality is still the keynote of the wrong."

The allegations in plaintiff's complaint do not bring the interest of Susie Waube within the field of legally protected rights.

Order reversed, and cause remanded, with directions to sustain the demurrer.

NOTES AND QUESTIONS

(1)   Many courts adopted the "zone of danger" rule to replace or to supplant the "impact" or "physical injury rule." For example, in *Consolidated Rail Corporation v. Gottshall*, 512 U.S. 532, 114 S. Ct. 2396, 129 L. Ed 2d 427 (1994), the Supreme Court held that negligent infliction of emotional distress is a cognizable cause of action under the zone-of-danger test in actions governed by the Federal Employers Liability Act (FELA). Many courts have also supplanted former impact rule or zone-of-danger rule decisions with more flexible tests explified by *McLouglin v. O'Brian* that follows these notes, but other have not. *See, e.g., Leo v. Hillman*, 665 A.2d 572 (Vt. 1995).

(2)   A few courts have been called upon to decide whether the fear experienced by a person in the zone of danger must be for the person's own safety or whether fear for the safety of another is sufficient. Some hold that the fear must be for the plaintiff's own safety, *see e.g., Lawson v. Salt Lake Trappers, Inc.*, 901 P.2d 1013, 1016 (Utah 1995) (plaintiff must fear physical injury or peril to self and must experience either "physical or mental symptoms."), whereas others require only that the plaintiff be in the zone of danger. *See, e.g., Kraszewski v. Baptist Medical Center of Oklahoma, Inc.*, 916 P.2d 247 (Ok. 1996) (plaintiff must be a "direct victim" and not a mere bystander to recover for emotional distress of seeing another person (his spouse) injured.) *See also Keck v. Jackson*, 593 P.2d 668 (Ariz. 1979) (impact plus fear for another's safety is sufficient.)

(3)   Whether a person in the zone of danger must actually suffer a physical injury from the shock caused by fear for personal safety to recover for emotional distress was considered in *Ballinger v. Palm Springs Aerial Tramway*, 269 Cal. Rptr. 583 (Cal. App. 1990). The court held that the zone of danger plaintiff who witnessed the death of another could recover for emotional distress caused by fear for safety of self in the absence of physical injury. The question seems to have

seldom arisen.   (4)   The Wisconsin Supreme Court abrogated the zone of danger rule of *Waube* in *Bowen Lumbermens Mutual Causalty Company*, 517 N.W. 2d 432 (Wis. 1994). It now applies a version of the rule applied in the following case, limited by public policy considerations. As to the application of public policy considerations, the court said:

> The application of public policy considerations is a function solely of the court. While it is generally better procedure to submit negligence and cause-in-fact issues to the jury before addressing legal cause, that is, public policy issues, *Padilla v. Bydalek*, 56 Wis.2d 772, 779-80, 203 N.W.2d 15 (1973), *Pfeifer v. Standard Gateway Theater, Inc.*, 262 Wis. 229, 240, 55 N.W.2d 29 (1952), the circuit court or this court may grant summary judgment on public policy grounds before a trial or a court may bar liability on public policy considerations after trial. When the pleadings present a question of public policy, the court may make its determination on public policy grounds before trial.FN26 In contrast, when the issues are complex or the factual connections attenuated, it may be desirable for a full trial to precede the court's determination.

Id., 517 N.W. 2d at 654, 655. Applicable public policy limitations include:

(1) The injury is too remote from the negligence; or (2) the injury is too wholly out of proportion to the culpability of the negligent tort-feasor; or (3) in retrospect it appears too highly extraordinary that the negligence should have brought about the harm; or (4) because allowance of recovery would place too unreasonable a burden on the negligent tort-feasor; or (5) because allowance of recovery would be too likely to open the way for fraudulent claims; or (6) allowance of recovery would enter a field that has no sensible or just stopping point.

Sussex Tool & Supply, Inc. v. Mainline Sewer and Water, Inc., 605 N.W.2d 620 (Wis. App. 1999).

Is this rule more or less inclusive than that applied in the next case? Other courts continue to apply a zone of danger test. See, *e.g.*, *State Farm Mut. Auto. Ins. Co. v. Connolly ex rel. Connolly*, 132 P.3d 1197 (Ariz. App. 2006).

McLOUGHLIN v. O'BRIAN & OTHERS
[1982] 2 All E.R. 298 (H.L)[2]

Lord Wilberforce:

My Lords,

[Plaintiff's husband and three of her children were involved in a serious car crash caused by the defendants. Plaintiff heard of the crash and rushed to the hospital where she found two of her children and her husband, covered with blood and grime, being treated for severe wounds. There she learned that her youngest child was killed in the crash.

Plaintiff suffered nervous shock and resulting physical injury. The trial court dismissed the action for damages for her own injuries on grounds of no duty of care. The court of appeal upheld the dismissal.]

The appellant now appeals to this House. The critical question to be decided is whether a person in the position of the appellant, *i.e.*, one who was not present at the scene of grievous injuries to her family but who comes upon those injuries at an interval of time and space, can recover damages for nervous shock.

[Discussion of evolution of the law omitted.]

To argue from one factual situation to another and to decide by analogy is a natural tendency of the human and the legal mind. But the lawyer still has to enquire whether, in so doing, he has crossed some critical line behind which he ought to stop. That is said to be the present case. The reasoning by which the Lords Justices decided not to grant relief to the plaintiff is instructive. Both Stephenson L.J. and Griffiths L.J. accepted that the "shock" to the plaintiff was foreseeable; but from this, at least in presentation, they diverge. Stephenson L.J. considered that the defendants owed a duty of care to the plaintiff, but that for reasons of policy the law should stop short of giving her damages: it should limit relief to those on or near the highway at or near the time of the accident caused by the defendants' negligence. He was influenced by the fact that the courts of this country, and of other common law jurisdictions, had stopped at this point: it was

---

[2] [Ed. — The All England Law Reports, decision of House of Lords.]

indicated by the barrier of commercial sense and practical convenience. Griffiths L.J. took the view that although the injury to the plaintiff was foreseeable, there was not duty of care. The duty of care of drivers of motor vehicles was, according to decided cases, limited to persons and owners of property on the road or near to it who might be directly affected. The line should be drawn at this point. It was not even in the interest of those suffering from shock as a class to extend the state of the defendants' liability. To do so would quite likely delay their recovery by immersing them in the anxiety of litigation.

I am deeply impressed by both of these arguments, which I have only briefly summarised. Though differing in expression, in the end, in my opinion, the two presentations rest upon a common principle, namely that, at the margin, the boundaries of a man's responsibility for acts of negligence have to be fixed as a matter of policy. Whatever is the correct jurisprudential analysis, it does not make any essential difference whether one says, with Stephenson L.J., that there is a duty but, as a matter of policy, the consequences of breach of it ought to be limited at a certain point, or whether, with Griffiths L.J., one says that the fact that consequences may be foreseeable does not automatically impose a duty of care, does not do so in fact where policy indicates the contrary. This is an approach which one can see very clearly from the way in which Lord Atkin stated the neighbor principle in *Donoghue v. Stevenson* [1932] AC 2, 580.

. . .

This is saying that foreseeability must be accompanied and limited by the law's judgment as to persons who ought, according to its standards of value or justice, to have been in contemplation. Foreseeability, which involves a hypothetical person, looking with hindsight at an event which has occurred, is a formula adopted by English law, not merely for defining, but also for limiting the persons to whom duty may be owed, and the consequences for which an actor may be held responsible. It is not merely an issue of fact to be left to be found as such. When it is said to result in a duty of care being owed to a person or a class, the statement that there is a "duty of care" denotes a conclusion into the forming of which considerations of policy have entered. That foreseeability does not of itself, and automatically, lead to a duty of care is, I think, clear. I gave some examples in *Anna v. Merton London Borough* [1978] AC 728, 752, [1977] 2 All ER 492. Anns itself being one. I may add what Lord Reid said in *McKew v. Holland & Hannen & Cubitts*. "A defender is not liable for a consequence of a kind which is not foreseeable. But it does not follow that he is liable for every consequence which a reasonable man could foresee." [1969] 3 All ER 1621, 1623.

We must then consider the policy arguments. In doing so we must bear in mind that cases of "nervous shock" and the possibility of claiming damages for it, are not necessarily confined to those arising out of accidents in public roads. To state, therefore, a rule that recoverable damages must be confined to persons on or near the highway is to state not a principle in itself, but only an example of a more general rule that recoverable damages must be confined to those within sight and sound of an event caused by negligence or, at least, to those in close, or very close, proximity to such a situation.

The policy arguments against a wider extension can be stated under four heads.

First, it may be said that such extension may lead to a proliferation of claims, and possibly fraudulent claims, to the establishment of an industry of lawyers and psychiatrists who will formulate a claim for nervous shock damages, including what in America is called the customary miscarriage, for all, or many, road accidents and industrial accidents.

Secondly, it may be claimed that an extension of liability would be unfair to defendants, as imposing damages out of proportion to the negligent conduct complained of. In so far as such defendants are insured, a large additional burden will be placed on insurers, and ultimately upon the class of persons insured — road users or employers.

Thirdly, to extend liability beyond the most direct and plain cases would greatly increase evidentiary difficulties and tend to lengthen litigation.

Fourthly, it may be said — and the Court of Appeal agreed with this — that an extension of the scope of liability ought only to be made by the legislature, after careful research. This is the course which has been taken in New South Wales and the Australian Capital Territory.

The whole argument has been well summed up by Dean Prosser:

"The reluctance of courts to enter this zone even where the mental injury is clearly foreseeable, and the frequent mention of the difficulties of proof, the facility of fraud and the problem of finding a place to stop and draw the line, suggest that here it is the nature of the interest invaded and the type of damages which is the real obstacle" (Prosser, Law of Torts, 4th Ed. p. 256).

Since he wrote, the type of damage has, in this country at least, become more familiar and less deterrent to recovery. And some of the arguments are susceptible of answer. Fraudulent claims can be contained by the courts, who, also, can cope with evidentiary difficulties. The scarcity of cases which have occurred in the past, and the modest sums recovered, give some indication that years of a flood of litigation may be exaggerated — experience in other fields suggests that such fears usually are. If some increase does occur, that may only reveal the existence of a genuine social need: that legislation has been found necessary in Australia may indicate the same thing.

But these discounts accepted, there remains, in my opinion, just because "shock" in its nature is capable of affecting so wide a range of people, a real need for the law to place some limitation upon the extent of admissible claims. It is necessary to consider three elements inherent in any claim: The class of persons whose claims should be recognised; the proximity of such persons to the accident; and the means by which the shock is caused. As regards the class of persons, the possible range is between the closest of family ties — of parent and child, or husband and wife, and the ordinary bystander. Existing law recognises the claims of the first: it denies that of the second, either on the basis that such persons must be assumed to be possessed of fortitude sufficient to enable them to endure the calamities of modern life, or that defendants cannot be expected to compensate the world at large. In my opinion, these positions are justifiable, and since the present case falls within the first class, it is strictly unnecessary to say more. I think, however, that it should follow that other cases involving less close relationships must be very carefully scrutinised. I cannot say that they should never be admitted. The closer the tie (not merely in relationship, but in care) the greater the claim for consideration. The claim, in any case, has to be judged in the light of the other factors, such as proximity to the scene in time and place, and the nature of the accident.

As regards proximity to the accident, it is obvious that this must be close in both time and space. It is, after all, the fact and consequence of the defendant's negligence that must be proved to have caused the "nervous shock." Experience has shown that to insist on direct and immediate sight or hearing would be impractical and unjust and that under what may be called the "aftermath" doctrine, one who, from close proximity comes very soon upon the scene, should not be excluded. In my opinion, the result in *Benson v. Lee* was correct and indeed inescapable. It was based, soundly, upon "direct perception of some of the events which go "to make up the accident as an entire event, and this includes . . . the immediate aftermath". The High Court's majority decision in *Chester v. Waverley Council* (1939) 62 CLR 1, where a child's body was found floating in a trench after a prolonged search, may perhaps be placed on the other side of a recognisable line (Evatt J. in a powerful dissent placed it on the same side), but in addition, I find the conclusion of Lush J. to reflect developments in the law.

Finally, and by way of reinforcement of "aftermath" cases, I would accept, by analogy with "rescue" situations, that a person of whom it could be said that one could expect nothing else than that he or she would come immediately to the scene — normally a parent or a spouse, could be regarded as being within the scope of foresight and duty. Where there is not immediate presence, account must be taken of the possibility of alterations in the circumstances, for which the defendant should not be responsible.

Subject only to these qualifications, I think that a strict test of proximity by sight or hearing should be applied by the courts.

My Lords, I believe that these indications, imperfectly sketched, and certainly to be applied with common sense to individual situations in their entirety, represent either the existing law, or the existing law with only such circumstantial extension as the common law process may legitimately make. They do not introduce a new principle. Nor do I see any reason why the law should retreat behind the lines already drawn. I find on this appeal that the appellant's case falls within the boundaries of the law so drawn. I would allow her appeal.

Lastly, as regards communication, there is no case in which the law has compensated shock brought about by communication by a third party. In *Hambrook v. Stokes* indeed, it was said that liability would not arise in such a case and this is surely right. It was so decided in *Abramzik v. Brenner* (1967) 65 DLR (2d) 651. The shock must come through sight or hearing of the event or of its immediate aftermath. Whether some equivalent of sight or hearing, *e.g.*, through simultaneous television, would suffice may have to be considered.

Lord Edmund-Davies: (Agreed with speech of Wilberforce)

Lord Russell of Killowen:

My Lords,

. . .

. . . If the effect of this wife and mother of the results of the negligence is considered to have been reasonably foreseeable, I do not see the justification for not finding the defendants liable in damages therefor. I would not shrink from regarding in an appropriate case policy as something which may feature in a judicial decision. But in this case what policy should inhibit a decision in favour of liability to the plaintiff? Negligent driving on the highway is only one form of negligence which may cause wounding or death and thus induce a relevant mental trauma in a person such as the plaintiff. There seems to be no policy requirement that the damage to the plaintiff should be on or adjacent to the highway. In the last analysis any policy consideration seems to be rooted in a fear of floodgates opening — the tacit question "What next?". I am not impressed by that fear — certainly not sufficiently to deprive this plaintiff of just compensation for the reasonably foreseeable damage done to her. I do not consider that such deprivation is justified by trying to answer in advance the question posed "What next?" by a consideration of relationships of plaintiff to the sufferers or deceased, or other circumstances: to attempt in advance solutions, or even guidelines, in hypothetical cases may well, it seems to me, in this field, do more harm than good.

I also would allow this appeal.

LORD SCARMAN:

My Lords,

I have had the advantage of reading in draft the speech of my noble and learned friend, Lord Bridge of Harwich. It cannot be strengthened or improved by any words of mine. . . .

LORD BRIDGE of Harwich:

. . .

The question, then, for your Lordships' decision is whether the law, as a matter of policy, draws a line which exempts from liability a defendant whose negligent act or omission was actually and foreseeably the cause of the plaintiff's psychiatric illness and, if so, where that line is to be drawn. In thus formulating the question, I do not, of course, use the word "negligent" as prejudging the question whether the defendant owes the plaintiff a duty, but I do use the word "foreseeably" as connoting the normally accepted criterion of such a duty.

. . .

In approaching the question whether the law should, as a matter of policy, define the criterion of liability in negligence for causing psychiatric illness by reference to some test other than that of reasonable foreseeability it is well to remember that we are concerned only with the question of liability of a defendant who is, ex hypothesi, guilty of fault in causing the death, injury or danger which has in turn triggered the psychiatric illness. A policy which is to be relied on to narrow the scope of the negligent tortfeasor's duty must be justified by cogent and readily intelligible considerations, and must be capable of defining the appropriate limits of liability by reference to factors which are not purely arbitrary. A number of policy considerations which have been suggested as satisfying these requirements appear to me, with respect, to be wholly insufficient. I can see no ground whatever for suggesting that to make the defendant liable for reasonably foreseeable psychiatric illness caused by his negligence, would be to impose a crushing burden on him out of proportion to his moral responsibility. However liberally the criterion of reasonable foreseeability is interpreted, both the number of successful claims in this field and the quantum of damages they will attract are likely to be moderate. I cannot accept as relevant the well-known phenomenon that litigation may delay recovery from a psychiatric illness. If this were a valid policy consideration, it would lead to the conclusion that psychiatric illness should be excluded altogether from the heads of damage which the law will recognise. It cannot justify limiting the cases in which damages will be awarded for psychiatric illness by reference to the circumstances of its causation.

To attempt to draw a line at the furtherest point which any of the decided cases happen to have reached, and to say that it is for the legislature, not the courts, to extend the limits of liability any further, would be, to my mind, an unwarranted abdication of the court's function of developing and adapting principles of the common law to changing conditions, in a particular corner of the common law which exemplifies, par excellence, the important and indeed necessary part which that function has to play. In the end I believe that the policy question depends on weighing against each other two conflicting considerations. On the one hand, if the criterion of liability is to be reasonable foreseeability simpliciter, this must, precisely because questions of causation in psychiatric medicine give rise to difficulty and uncertainty, introduce an element of uncertainty into the law and open the way to a number of arguable claims which a more precisely fixed criterion of liability would exclude. I accept that the element of uncertainty is an important factor. I believe that the "floodgates" argument, however, is, as it always has been, greatly exaggerated. On the other hand, it seems to me inescapable that any attempt to define the limit of liability by requiring, in addition to reasonable foreseeability, that the plaintiff claiming damages for psychiatric illness should have witnessed the relevant accident, should have been present at or near the place where it happened, should have come upon its aftermath and thus have some direct perception of it, as opposed to merely learning of it after the event, should be related in some particular degree to the accident victim — to draw a line by reference to any of these criteria must impose a largely arbitrary limit of liability. I accept, of course, the importance of the factors indicated in the guidelines suggested by Tobriner J. in *Dillon v. Legg* as bearing upon the degree of foreseeability of the plaintiff's psychiatric illness. . . .

. . .

My Lords, I have no doubt that this is an area of the law of negligence where we should resist the temptation to try yet once more to freeze the law in a rigid posture which would deny justice to some who, in the application of the classic principles of negligence derived from *Donoghue v. Stevenson* [1932] AC 562, ought to succeed, in the interests of certainty, where the very subject-matter is uncertain and continuously developing, or in the interest of saving defendants and their insurers from the burden of having sometimes to resist doubtful claims. I find myself in complete agreement with Tobriner J. that the defendant's duty must depend on reasonable foreseeability and "must necessarily be adjudicated only upon a case-by-case basis. We cannot now pre-determine defendant's obligation in every situation by a fixed category; no immutable rule can establish the extent of that obligation for every circumstance of the future". To put the matter in another way, if asked where the thing is to stop, I should answer, in an adaptation of the language of Lord Wright and Stephenson L.J., "Where in the particular case the good sense of the judge, enlightened by progressive awareness of mental illness, decides."

. . .

My Lords, I would accordingly allow the appeal.

DISPOSITION:

Appeal allowed.

NOTES AND QUESTIONS

(1)   The California Supreme Court's opinion in *Dillon v. Legg*, 68 Cal. 2d 728, 69 Cal. Rptr. 72, 441 P.2d 912 (1968), cited extensively by the *McLoughlin* judgments, has been the most influential American decision eroding the no-duty-for-emotional harm rule. The liberalized rule of *Dillon* was formulated as follows:

> Since the chief element in determining whether defendant owes a duty or an obligation to plaintiff is the foreseeability of the risk, that factor will be of prime concern in every case. Because it is inherently intertwined with foreseeability, such duty or obligation must necessarily be adjudicated only upon a case-by-case basis. We cannot now predetermine defendant's obligation in every situation by a fixed category; no immutable rule can establish the extent of that obligation for every circumstance of the future. We can, however, define guidelines which will aid in the resolution of such an issue as the instant one.

> We note, first, that we deal here with a case in which plaintiff suffered a shock which resulted in physical injury and we confine our ruling to that case. In determining, in such a case, whether defendant should reasonably foresee the injury to plaintiff, or, in other terminology, whether defendant owes plaintiff a duty of due care, the courts will take into account such factors as the following: (1) Whether plaintiff was located near the scene of the accident as contrasted with one who was a distance away from it. (2) Whether the shock resulted from a direct emotional impact upon plaintiff from the sensory and contemporaneous observance of the accident, as contrasted with learning of the accident from others after its occurrence. (3) Whether plaintiff and the victim were closely related, as contrasted with an absence of any relationship or the presence of only a distant relationship.

> The evaluation of these factors will indicate the *degree* of the defendant's foreseeability: obviously defendant is more likely to foresee that a mother who observes an accident affecting her child will suffer harm than to foretell that a stranger witness will do so. Similarly, the degree of foreseeability of the third person's injury is far greater in the case of his contemporaneous observance of the accident than that in which he subsequently learns of it. The defendant is more likely to foresee that shock to the nearby, witnessing mother will cause physical harm than to anticipate that someone distant from the accident will suffer more than a temporary emotional reaction. All these elements, of course, shade into each other; the fixing of obligation, intimately tied into the facts, depends upon each case.

> In light of these factors the court will determine whether the accident and harm was *reasonably* foreseeable. Such reasonable foreseeability does not turn on whether the particular defendant as an individual would have

in actuality foreseen the exact accident and loss; it contemplates that courts, on a case-to-case basis, analyzing all the circumstances, will decide what the ordinary man under such circumstances should reasonably have foreseen. The courts thus mark out the areas of liability, excluding the remote and unexpected.

. . .

441 P.2d at 921.

In dissenting, Justice Burke argued:

The majority, obviously recognizing that they are now embarking upon a first excursion into the "fantastic realm of infinite liability" (*Amaya*, at p. 315 of 59 Cal. 2d, 29 (Cal. Rptr. 33, 379 P.2d 513)), undertake to provide so-called "guidelines" for the future. But notwithstanding the limitations which these "guidelines" purport to impose, it is only reasonable to expect pressure upon our trial courts to make their future rulings conform to the spirit of the new elasticity proclaimed by the majority.

Moreover, the majority's "guidelines" (ante, 69 Cal. Rptr. pp. 80, 81) are simply a restatement of those suggested earlier by Professor Prosser (Prosser, Torts, 2d ed., 1955, p. 184); they have already been discussed and expressly rejected by this court in *Amaya* (pp. 312–313, 29 Cal. Rptr. 33, 379 P.2d 513). Upon analysis, their seeming certainty evaporates into arbitrariness, as inexplicable distinctions appear. As we asked in *Amaya*: What if the plaintiff was honestly *mistaken* in believing the third person to be in danger or to be seriously injured? What if the third person had assumed the risk involved? How "close" must the relationship be between the plaintiff and the third person? *I.e.*, what if the third person was the plaintiff's beloved niece or nephew, grandparent, fiance, or lifelong friend, more dear to the plaintiff than her immediate family? Next, how "near" must the plaintiff have been to the scene of the accident, and how "soon" must shock have been felt? Indeed, what is the magic in the plaintiff's being actually present? Is the shock any less real if the mother does not know of the accident until her injured child is brought into her home? On the other hand, is it any less real if the mother is physically present at the scene but is nevertheless unaware of the danger or injury to her child until after the accident has occurred? No answers to these questions are to be found in today's majority opinion. Our trial courts, however, will not so easily escape the burden of distinguishing between litigants on the basis of such artificial and unpredictable distinctions.

441 P.2d at 926.

Is *Dillon* a more or less liberal rule than *McLaughlini*?

Page v. Smith, [1996] A.C. 155 (H.L.) concerned slightly different issues. There, the court held that a "primary victim" of emotional injury, *i.e.*, one to whom physical injury was foreseeable, would be permitted to recover provable psychiatric damages; whereas, a "secondary victim," *i.e.*, one not in the zone of danger, would be required to satisfy the *McLoughlin* requirements. *Alcock v. Chief Constable of South Yorkshire Police* [1992] 1 AC 310; [H.L.], held that viewing a disaster on TV did not satisfy the *McLoughlin* proximity requirement, and that the mere fact of a particular family relationship alone was not enough; instead, the proof of existence of actual "ties of love and affection" was required as to the close relationship requirement. The California Supreme Court has also narrowly construed the reach of *Dillon v. Legg*. See, *e.g., Bird v. Saenz*, 51 P.3d 324, 332 (Cal. 2002) reconfirming that to recover a plaintiff must have been "present at the scene of the injury-producing event" at the time it occurred and must have been "then aware" that it was "causing injury to the victim."

(2) *Dillon* has been followed by a large number of cases. *See* 1 Minzer, et al., Damages in Tort Actions, § 5.20, "Plaintiff as Bystander" (Matthew Bender & Co.), for a thorough discussion of *Dillon* and related case-law developments.

Most of these decisions impose limiting conditions such as these stated in *Dillon* and discussed by Lord Wilberforce in *McLoughlin*. See discussion in *Clohessy v. Bachelo*, 675 A.2d 852 (Conn. 1996), and *James v. Lieb*, 375 N.W.2d 109 (Neb. 1985). The California supreme court has tightened up the *Dillon* requirements by requiring that the emotional distress plaintiff actually "observe" the "negligently inflicted injury of a third person" within the limits otherwise fixed by *Dillon.; Thing v. LaChusa*, 771 P.2d 814 (Cal. 1989). Another court has suggested that while direct contemporaneous observation of the injury to another may not be required, the facts of *McLaughlin* are at the outer limit of the nearness in time and space required to obtain recovery. *Champion v. Gray*, 487 So. 2d 17 (Fla. 1985). *Shultz v. Barberton Glass Co.*, 447 N.E.2d 109 (Ohio 1983), permitted recovery for a plaintiff who suffered severe emotional shock upon directly observing the gruesome injuries of a person who was unrelated to the plaintiff.

(3) A few American courts have abandoned all concrete conditions and adopted the "general negligence" approach espoused by Lord Bridge of Harwick in *McLoughlin*. See, e.g., *Camper v. Minor*, 915 S.W.2d 437 (Tenn. 1996). Even these courts have imposed some limits. As stated by *Camper* at 915 S.W.2d 446:

After considering the strengths and weaknesses of the options used in other jurisdictions, we conclude that these cases should be analyzed under the general negligence approach discussed above. In other words, the plaintiff must present material evidence as to each of the five elements of general negligence — duty, breach of duty, injury or loss, causation in fact, and proximate, or legal, cause, . . . in order to avoid summary judgment. Furthermore, we agree that in order to guard against trivial or fraudulent actions, the law ought to provide a recovery only for "serious" or "severe" emotional injury . . . A "serious" or "severe" emotional injury occurs "where a reasonable person, normally constituted, would be unable to adequately cope with the mental stress engendered by the circumstances of the case." . . . Finally, we conclude that the claimed injury or impairment must be supported by expert medical or scientific proof. See *Leong v. Takasaki*, 55 Haw. 398, 520 P.2d 758, 766–67 (1974) ("the plaintiff should be permitted to prove medically the damages occasioned by his mental responses to defendant's negligent act").

(4) Mary, complaining of a urinary tract disorder, called upon Dr. X. Dr. X negligently and incorrectly diagnosed syphilis. Wrongly believing herself to have been infected by her husband, Steve, Mary charged him with infidelity and sued for divorce. Steve was extremely upset by what he knew to be false charges and the divorce. Later, Mary learned that the syphilis diagnosis was wrong, but had in the meantime remarried. Steve sues Dr. X for loss of consortium and emotional harm. Will he recover under any of the foregoing tests? See *Molien v. Kaiser Foundation*

Hospital, 167 Cal. Rptr. 831, 616 P.2d 813 (Cal. 1980).

(5)   Mary K. gave birth to a child, Jane K., in Mercy Hospital. Soon after birth, the infant was abducted from a temporarily unattended nursery, but was returned to her parents four months later. Mary K. and her spouse sue the hospital for emotional distress suffered during the four-month absence. Should the cause of action survive a motion to dismiss? *See Johnson v. Jamaica Hospital,* 62 N.Y.2d 523, 467 N.E.2d 502 (1984).

(6)   The Restatement (Third) of Torts: Liability for Physical Harm (Tentative Drafts) has proposed these restatements:

§ 46. Negligent Conduct Directly Inflicting Emotional Disturbance On Another (Tentative Draft No. 5)

An actor whose negligent conduct causes serious emotional disturbance to another is subject to liability to the other if the conduct:

(a) places the other in immediate danger of bodily harm and the emotional disturbance results from the danger; or

(b) occurs in the course of specified categories of activities, undertakings, or relationships in which negligent conduct is especially likely to cause serious emotional disturbance.

§ 47. Negligent Infliction Of Emotional Disturbance Resulting From Bodily Harm To A Third Person (Tentative Draft No. 5)

An actor who negligently causes serious bodily injury to a third person is subject to liability for serious emotional disturbance thereby caused to a person who:

(a) perceives the event contemporaneously, and

(b) is a close family member of the person suffering the bodily injury.

Which, if any, of the foregoing decisions support these tentative restatements?

§ 5.04   OWNERS AND OCCUPIERS OF LAND

T]he home of every one is to him as his castle and fortress as well for his defense against injury and violence, as well as for repose.[3]

Sir Edward Coke, *Semayne's Case* (1604) 5 Co. L. Rep. 919.

---

[3]   More dramatically, the William Pitt, Earl of Chatham is said to have declared:

The poorest man may in his cottage bid defiance to all the forces of the Crown. It may be frail — its roof may shake — the wind may blow through it — the storm may enter — the rain may enter — but the King of England cannot enter — all his force dares not cross the threshold of the ruined tenement.

Chic Fashions (West Wales) Ltd. v. Jones, [1968] 2 Q.B. 299, 308 (C.A.)

[A] General

This particular facet of tort law well illustrates how the common law has been modified to meet the requirements of social change. The following quotation and case indicate the status of the law as it was. The remaining sections illustrate some changes.

> In feudal England the emphasis was all on the side of the proprietors of landed estates. It was to be expected that in an age in which feudal lords were practical sovereigns they would not ordinarily be subject to liability for harm to persons on the land. Surely, if even the king could not enter without permission, there was some basis for the rule that the possessor of land had no duty to anticipate trespassing or guard against harm to trespassers. . . . Consequently the general rule was that there was no liability whatever upon the possessor for harm caused to infant or adult trespassers, or to trespassing animals, for harm received by them upon the land. Indeed, except for dogs, the owners of trespassing animals were absolutely liable to the landowner for harm caused to the land.

Eldredge, *Tort Liability to Trespassers*, 12 Temple L.Q. 32, 33 (1937–38).[4]

Reflecting the importance of the ownership and possession of land in England and America, the law of negligence developed special rules of duty as it pertains to injuries caused to a person upon the land of another by the condition of premises and by acts of the possessor of the land. As the following excerpt reveals, the extent of the duty varied according to the status of the injured person on the land.

ROBERT ADDIE & SONS (COLLIERIES) v. DUMBRECK
[1929] App. Cas. 358 (H.L.)[5]

LORD HAILSHAM:

My Lords, this is an appeal from an interlocutor of the first Division of the Court of Session, pronounced on appeal from a decision of the Sheriff-Substitute of Lanarakshire, whereby the appellants were ordered to pay to the respondent 100 [pounds] damages in respect of the death of the pupil son of the respondent, who received fatal injuries at the wheel pit of the haylage apparatus on the appellants' premises at View Park Colliery, Uddingston, on April 21, 1926.

The first and in my opinion the only question which arises for determination is the capacity in which the deceased child was in the field and at the wheel on the occasion of the accident. There are three categories in which persons visiting premises belonging to another person may go

(1) By the invitation, express or implied, of the occupier;

(2) With the leave and licence of the occupier, and

(3) As trespassers.

---

[4] Reprinted with permission of Temple Law Quarterly. Copyright 1937 by Temple Law Quarterly.

[5] [Ed. — Appeal Cases Law Reports, decision of House of Lords.]

It was suggested in argument that there was a fourth category of persons who were not on the premises with the leave or licence of the occupier, but who were not pure trespassers. I cannot find any foundation for this suggestion either in English or Scotch law, and I do not think that the category exists.

The duty which rests upon the occupier of premises towards the persons who come on such premises differs according to the category into which the visitor falls. The highest duty exists towards those persons who fall into the first category, and who are present by the invitation of the occupier. Towards such persons the occupier has the duty of taking reasonable care that the premises are safe.

In the case of persons who are not there by invitation, but who are there by leave and licence, express or implied, the duty is much less stringent — the occupier has no duty to ensure that the premises are safe, but he is bound not to create a trap or to allow a concealed danger to exist upon the said premises, which is not apparent to the visitor, but which is known — or ought to be known — to the occupier.

Towards the trespasser the occupier has no duty to take reasonable care for his protection or even to protect him from concealed danger. The trespasser comes on to the premises at his own risk. An occupier is in such a case liable only where the injury is due to some wilful act involving something more than the absence of reasonable care. There must be some act done with the deliberate intention of doing harm to the trespasser, or at least some act done with reckless disregard of the presence of the trespasser. . . .

The only question, therefore, that remains for decision in this case is whether, upon the findings of fact of the Court of Session (which are not open to review), the respondent's son may properly be regarded as having been at the wheel at the time of the accident with the leave and licence of the appellants. If this had been proved. I should have been prepared to hold that the wheel which was at time stationary and which was started without any warning, and which was, in the words of the Court of Session, "dangerous and attractive to children and insufficiently protected at the time of the accident," amounted to a trap, and that the respondent would therefore have been entitled to recover. But in my opinion, the findings of fact effectually negative that. It is found that the appellants warned children out of the field and reproved adults who came there, and all that can be said is that these warnings were frequently neglected and that there was a gap in the hedge through which it was easy to pass on to the field. I cannot regard the fact that the appellants did not effectively fence the field or the fact that their warnings were frequently disregarded as sufficient to justify an inference that they permitted the children to be on the field, and, in the absence of such a permission, it is clear that the respondent's child was merely a trespasser. The sympathy which one cannot help feeling for the unhappy father must not be allowed to alter one's view of the law, and I have no doubt that in law the respondent's son was a mere trespasser, and that as such the appellants owed him no duty to protect him from injury. On these grounds I am of opinion that this appeal succeeds and must be allowed with costs, and I move you Lordships accordingly: [The child trespasser lost his case.]

NOTE

The law as stated in *Addie's* case was incorporated virtually lock, stock and barrel in all American states. The harshness of the rules, however, resulted in a proliferation of exceptions and outright manipulation of facts to avoid, in many circumstances, what seemed to be untenable results. (For example, what would have been the result in *Addie's* case if the child had been considered a licensee?) A few courts, even at early dates, flatly refused to adopt every element of the hierarchy. For example, in *Railroad v. Fain*, 80 Tenn. 34, 14 L.R.A. 43 (1883), the court said, " . . . the fact that the injured party is a trespasser [does not] deprive him of the right of action. He is still entitled to recover for injuries negligently inflicted by another which might have been averted by ordinary and proper prudence on the part of the latter." How does that differ from Lord Hailsham's statement?

The following cases and notes elaborate some of the myriad specialties of the law of negligence as it pertains to owners and occupiers of land.

PRESTON v. SLEZIAK
Michigan Supreme Court
175 N.W.2d 759 (1970)

T. M. KAVANAGH, JUSTICE.

Plaintiffs, both adults, were spending the weekend as social guests at defendants' hilltop cottage overlooking the State Park at Grand Haven, Michigan. Access to the cottage was by either a 113-step stairway or a lift consisting of a car which was raised or lowered along railed tracks by means of cables and electric winch. The lift was of the home made variety, but the defendant husband repeatedly assured plaintiffs that it was safe. The parties entered the lift, and as the car was descending a shaft broke causing the car to crash to the bottom, injuring plaintiffs.

Plaintiffs filed an action alleging defendants were negligent in constructing, maintaining and operating the lift. The jury returned a verdict of no cause of action. Upon appeal, the Court of Appeals held that the trial judge did not properly instruct the jury as to the duty of a host to his guests, and reversed and remanded the cause for a new trial. 16 Mich. App. 18, 167 N.W.2d 477.

Defendants, here on leave granted (382 Mich. 755), state as the sole question on appeal:

Is the duty owing by a host to an adult social guest the same as that owing to a business invitee?

The trial judge charged the jury in part as follows:

> Now, in this particular case there is an unusual relationship between the plaintiffs and the defendants. It is clear that the plaintiffs were the guests of the defendants in the defendants' home. This brings us to what is their status and how can we consider this. It has sometimes been said that a

guest in a home such as this is a gratuitous invitee and that the host's only duty is not to injure by active or affirmative negligence a guest whose presence is known, not to set a trap or pitfall for the guest, to warn against or remove any defects which the host knows are likely to cause harm to the guest and which he has reasonable grounds to believe the guest is not likely to discover for himself, and generally not to cause injury by gross negligence, recklessness or wanton and willful misconduct.

I should, therefore, inform you at this very point that there is no evidence in my opinion of any gross negligence, recklessness or wanton and willful misconduct, so that if you find liability you will have to find it on one of the other grounds, and I will discuss that more carefully with you.

I should further inform you that a gratuitous invitee, which is the status of Mr. and Mrs. Preston, who goes upon his host's land, the host has the duty to advise — excuse me; strike That — that the host must exercise reasonable care to disclose to the guest the dangerous defects which were known to him and were likely to be undiscovered by the guest.

I should further inform you that with regard to this status that a social guest injured by a defect in the premises cannot recover against his host in the absence of evidence establishing something more than ordinary negligence in the maintenance of the premises.

More specifically, it has been held that a guest can recover only where his injury is the result of active and affirmative negligence of the host while the guest was known to be on the premises, or of the failure of the host to remove or warn against defects amounting to a trap or pitfall known by the host to present a danger to the guest, and which he also knows the guest will not, in the exercise of reasonable care, discover and avoid for himself.

There is no duty on the part of the host to reconstruct or improve the premises for the purpose of making his. house more convenient or more safe for those accepting his hospitality, gratuitously extended. The guest assumes the ordinary risks which attach to the premises.

Now, the reason for this rule is that a host merely offers his premises for enjoyment by his guests with the same security that the host and the members of his family who reside with him have in that particular home.

The Court of Appeals acknowledged that the rule in a majority of jurisdictions is as stated by the trial judge. See 25 A.L.R.2d 598. The Court, however, relying upon the case of *Genese Merchants Bank & Trust Company v. Payne* (1967), 6 Mich. App. 204, at 208, 148 N.W.2d 503, as a specific rejection of the general rule indicated that the Michigan cases have uniformly cited with approval Cooley on Torts, p. 605:

> "One is under no obligation to keep his premises in safe condition for the visits of trespassers. On the other hand, when he expressly or by implication invites others to come upon his premises, whether for business, *or for any other purpose*, it is his duty to be reasonably sure that he is not inviting them into danger, and to that end he must exercise ordinary care and prudence to render the premises reasonably safe for the visit." . . . (Emphasis supplied.)

It, therefore, reversed and remanded for a new trial on the grounds that Michigan law classifies the social guest as an invitee. Such construction erroneously departs from the well-established rule of law in this State respecting social guests.

It is true that Cooley's oft-quoted statement on torts accurately expressed the law in this State. But a careful reading of Cooley's work indisputably discloses that the enunciated rule applies solely to invitees. Every authority cited and illustration given concern a business invitee or general public invitee. To seize upon the words "or for any other purpose" as justification for equating an invited social guest and a legally defined "invitee" is unwarranted. It should be noted that Justice Cooley, expressing this rule in *Samuelson v. Cleveland Iron Mining Company* (1882), 49 Mich. 164, at 170, 13 N.W. 499, himself deleted this overly broad phraseology. Furthermore, to attribute a legally synonymous meaning to social guest and invitee discordantly blurs the distinction so carefully preserved by the author at pp. 193, 194:

> An invitation may be inferred when there is a common interest or mutual advantage, a license when the object is the mere pleasure or benefit of the person using it.

> To come under an implied invitation, as distinguished from a mere license, the visitor must come for a purpose connected with the business with which the occupant of the premises is engaged, or which he permits to be carried on there. There must be some mutuality of interest in the subject to which the visitor's business relates, although the particular business which is the object of the visit may not be for the benefit of the occupant.

> The distinction between a visitor who is a mere licensee and one who is on the premises by invitation turns largely on the nature of the business that brings him there, rather than on the words or acts of the owner which precede his coming. Permission involves leave and license, but it gives no right.

3 Cooley on Torts, § 440 (4th Ed.).

Consonant with the above distinction and more in keeping with the factual circumstances surrounding the case of a social guest is the statement found at p. 198:

> The owner or occupant of premises is not under any legal duty to keep them free or safe from the danger of obstructions, pitfalls, excavations, trapdoors or openings in floors for persons who go upon, into, or through the premises, *not by his invitation, express or implied, but for their own pleasure or convenience, though by his acquiescence or permission, and who, therefore, are mere licensees. Such a visitor enjoys the license subject to the attendant risk.*

(Emphasis supplied.)

The Restatement of Torts (2d), § 332, p. 176, defines "invitee" as follows:

> (1) An invitee **is** either a public invitee or a business visitor.

> (2) A public invitee is a person who is invited to enter or remain on land as a member of the public for a purpose for which the land is held open to the public.

(3) A business visitor is a person who is invited to enter or remain on land for a purpose directly or indirectly connected with business dealings with the possessor of the land.

The comment under Reporter's Notes following section 332 reads in part:

a. *Invitee.* "Invitee" is a word of art, with a special meaning in the law. This meaning is more limited than that of "invitation" in the popular sense, and not all of those who are invited to enter upon lands are invitees. A social guest may be cordially invited, and strongly urged to come, but he is not an invitee.

This definition fairly represents the law of this State pertaining to what constitutes the legal status of an invitee. *Samuelson v. Cleveland Iron Mining Company, supra; Blakely v. White Star Line* (1908), 154 Mich. 635, 118 N.W. 482; *Torma v. Montgomery Ward & Company* (1953), 336 Mich. 468, 58 N.W.2d 149; *Kroll v. Katz* (1965), 374 Mich. 364, 132 N.W.2d 27.

As one commentator pointed out, however, the social guest holds the paradoxical position of being "an invitee who is not an invitee." 2 Harper & James, Torts, § 27.11, p. 1477; see, also Prosser, Business Visitors and Invitees (1942), 26 Minn. L.Rev. 573, 578, 603–605. The usual basis upon which the distinction between the social guest *vis-a-vis* the invitee is drawn is well stated in Restatement of Torts (2d), § 330, comment h.. . . 3., p. 175:

Social guests. Some confusion has resulted from the fact that, although a social guest normally is invited, and even urged to come, he is not an "invitee," within the legal meaning of that term, as stated in § 332. He does not come as a member of the public upon premises held open to the public for that purpose, and he does not enter for a purpose directly or indirectly connected with business dealings with the possessor. The use of the premises is extended to him merely as a personal favor to him. The explanation usually given by the courts for the classification of social guests as licensees is that there is a common understanding that the guest is expected to take the premises as the possessor himself uses them, and does not expect and is not entitled to expect that they will be prepared for his reception, or that precautions will be taken for his safety, in any manner in which the possessor does not prepare or take precautions for his own safety, or that of the members of his family. This has not gone without criticism, and an undercurrent of dissent, based upon the contention that it is not in accord with modern social custom and understanding when a guest is invited; but the decisions thus far have been all but unanimous to the effect that the social guest is no more than a licensee.

The controlling Michigan case in this area of adult social guests is *Miller v. Miller* (1964), 373 Mich. 519, 129 N.W.2d 885. In *Miller* the plaintiff had gone to her son's home for a social visit and as she attempted to leave discovered the screen porch door was stuck. Upon the advice of her son to "give it a kick, it sticks sometimes," plaintiff kicked the door, which opened suddenly, hurling plaintiff down the porch steps.

Although two opinions were filed in *Miller*, the Court unanimously considered the social guest as a licensee.

[In *Miller* the court held that the defendants owed the plaintiff only the exercise of reasonable care to warn of dangers the defendants knew about and that were unlikely to be discovered by the plaintiff.]

Thus we conclude under either opinion filed in *Miller, supra,* that in this jurisdiction the adult social guest is to be viewed as a licensee.

. . .

For the above reasons, we reverse the Court of Appeals and affirm the judgment of the trial court.

T. G. KAVANAGH, JUSTICE (For Affirmance).

However handy labels may be for identification purposes, we must avoid the temptation to substitute labels for reason.

Whether an individual may properly be labelled an "invitee" or not should not determine whether he should recover for injuries suffered as the result of someone's negligence.

In every suit for damages for injuries suffered as a result of asserted negligence, the proper inquiry determines three things: 1) Was the defendant negligent? 2) Did that negligence proximately cause the plaintiff's injury? 3) What was plaintiff's damage?

The standard for judging conduct is *always* "What would a reasonably prudent man have done under the same or similar circumstances?" The test for determining negligence is "Did defendant measure up to this standard?"

If a person "invites" another onto his premises for the economic benefit of one or the other the person invited is said to be a business invitee. This circumstance is *one* of the considerations a jury may take into account when determining what a reasonably prudent man would have done.

Likewise the circumstance that a person comes on another's premises as a social guest — the invitee who is not an invitee — should also be taken into consideration by the jury in determining what a reasonably prudent man would have done.

Unless we are to make negligence a matter of law by saying the equivalent of "No social invitee has a right to expect the host to make the premises reasonably safe for the purpose of the visit" or "A host is never under obligation to make the premises reasonably safe for the purpose of the visit unless there is some monetary benefit to be derived from the visit," the jury should be free to determine the issue of negligence in every case.

In the case before us, the trial court's instruction, couched in the traditional verbiage of obfuscatory labelling in my view diverted the attention of the jury from their special task of determining whether the defendant under all the circumstances accorded the plaintiff the treatment and consideration he owed as a reasonably prudent man.

The rule applied by the court of appeals is the better rule, and if it has not always been the rule it now is because it should be.

I would affirm with costs to appellee.

NOTES AND QUESTIONS

(1) As do many courts, Michigan continues to adhere to the common law categories and duties. As stated in *Stitt v. Holland Abundant Life Fellowship*, 614 N.W.2d 88 (Mi.,2000) (holding that a visitor to a church is a licensee and not invitee):

> Thus, we hold that the owner's reason for inviting persons onto the premises is the primary consideration when determining the visitor's status: In order to establish invitee status, a plaintiff must show that the

premises were held open for a commercial purpose. *Id.*, 614 N.W. 2d at 604. Stitt explicitly rejected the suggestion in *Preston v. Sleziak* that a "public invitee" was to be owned the duty of care owed to a business invitee. In *Leveque v. Leveque*, 199 N.W.2d 675 (Mich. 1972), the Michigan Supreme Court, despite *Preston*, held that it was erroneous to grant a summary judgment against the plaintiff when the facts could be construed to involve more than a social visit. In *Leveque* the plaintiff was dropping off the home owner's child whom the plaintiff had driven home from school. The court quoted the following excerpts approvingly.

> Where a person enters upon the premises of another for a purpose connected with the business there conducted, or the visit may reasonably be said to confer or anticipate a business, commercial, monetary or other tangible benefit to the occupant, the visitor is held to be an invitee.

Wilson v. Bogert, 347 P.2d 341, 347 (Idaho 1959).

> Nevertheless, a member of a family or household group or group of acquaintances rendering friendly help in household routine or common-place tasks to another member of the group does not cease to be a licensee or social visitor unless the character or circumstances of the assistance make it clearly the dominant aspect of the relationship rather than a routine incident of social or group activities.

Pandiscio v. Bowen, 173 N.E.2d 634, 636 (Mass. 1961).

> While acknowledging that many courts hold that occupiers of land owe no higher standard of care to child social guests than is owed to adults, a later Michigan decision held that occupiers of land owe a duty to "a child social guest to exercise reasonable or ordinary care to prevent injury to the child."

Klimek v. Drzewicki, 352 N.W.2d 361, 264 (Mich. App. 1984).

(2) In *Carter v. Kinney*, 896 S.W.2d 926 (Mo. En banc 1995), a member of a bible study group slipped and fell on the premises of the host of the group on the occasion. The plaintiff sought to claim status of an invitee because of the "invitation" he had to attend the bible study session. In response, the court stated:

> In feudal England the emphasis was all on the side of the proprietors of landed estates. It was to be expected that in an age in which feudal lords were practical sovereigns they would not ordinarily be subject to liability for harm to persons on the land. Surely, if even the king could not enter without permission, there was some basis for the rule that the possessor of land had no duty to anticipate trespassing or guard against harm to trespassers. . . . Consequently the general rule was that there was no liability whatever upon the possessor for harm caused to infant or adult

trespassers, or to trespassing animals, for harm received by them upon the land. Indeed, except for dogs, the owners of trespassing animals were absolutely liable to the landowner for harm caused to the land.

A social guest is a person who has received a social invitation . . . Though the parties seem to believe otherwise, Missouri does not recognize social guests as a fourth class of entrant . . . In Missouri, social guests are but a subclass of licensees. The fact that an invitation underlies a visit does not render the visitor an invitee for purposes of premises liability law. This is because "[t]he invitation was not tendered with any material benefit motive" . . . and "[t]he invitation was not extended to the public generally or to some undefined portion of the public from which invitation, . . . entrants might reasonably expect precautions have been taken, in the exercise of ordinary care, to protect them from danger." Thus, this Court held that there "is no reason for concluding it is unjust to the parties . . . to put a social guest in the legal category of licensee." . . . It does not follow from this that a person invited for purposes not strictly social is perforce an invitee. . . . [a]n entrant becomes an invitee when the possessor invites with the expectation of a material benefit from the visit or extends an invitation to the public generally. *See also* Restatement (Second) of Torts, § 332 (defining an invitee for business purposes) and 65 C.J.S. Negligence, § 63(41) (a person is an invitee "if the premises are thrown open to the public and [the person] enters pursuant to the purposes for which they are thrown open."). Absent the sort of invitation from the possessor that lifts a licensee to invitee status, the visitor remains a licensee as a matter of law.

The record shows beyond cavil that Mr. Carter did not enter the Kinneys' land to afford the Kinneys any material benefit. He is therefore not an invitee under the definition of invitee contained in Section 332 of the Restatement. The record also demonstrates that the Kinneys did not "throw open" their premises to the public in such a way as would imply a warranty of safety. The Kinneys took no steps to encourage general attendance by some undefined portion of the public; the invited only church members who signed up at church. They did nothing more that give permission to a limited class of persons — church members — to enter their property.

. . .

The trial court concluded as a matter of law that Mr. Carter was a licensee, that the Kinneys had no duty to protect him from unknown dangerous conditions, and that the defendants were entitled to summary judgment as a matter of law. In that conclusion, the trial court was eminently correct.

Compare Nagaragadde v. Pandurangi, 216 S.W.3d 241 (Mo.App. 2007). There, a social guest's clothing caught fire when it accidently came into contact with the flame of a Hindu prayer lamp that the homeowner left burning. Although bound by the rule that the social guest was owed no duty as to the premises except to be warned of traps, the court permitted a recovery for the licensee, saying: "we similarly conclude that Raghu's failure to extinguish an oil lamp cannot be considered a defective condition of the property itself. The pleadings and the evidence at trial established an affirmative act of negligence that was unrelated to the passive condition of the home in which it occurred." *Id.*, 216 S.W.3rd at 245. The Hindu prayer lamp was regularly extinguished upon completion of prayers, but suppose it had been customary to keep the lamp lit continuously. Should the outcome of the case have been different?

(3) Many cases state in dicta that the only duty owed a trespasser is to avoid willful and wanton injury, meaning that there is no liability for defective premises, no matter how dangerous. A licensee was better off only to the extent that the occupier had the duty to warn of "traps." Although the pristine common law may prevail in some jurisdictions, the great weight of authority and better reasoning impose a duty of ordinary care as to affirmative actions of the landowners, as distinguished from the condition of the premises, to all persons on the premises that the owner knows about. See, *e.g., Hix v. Billen*, 284 So. 2d 269 (Fla. 1973); *Potts v. Amis*, 384 P.2d 825 (Wash. App. 1963); and *Cullmann v. Mumper*, 228 N.E.2d 276 (III. App. 1967). Should this duty be extended to trespassers and licensees whose presence is anticipable?

(4) Under the common law as traditionally and still applied in many jurisdictions, the so-called "public invitee" defined in Restatement, Torts, Second § 332, quoted in *Preston*, would be treated as a mere licensee as far as the owner's duties are concerned. Visitors to patients in hospitals, to churches, to memorials open to the public and the like would fall into this category. Some cases, however, have followed the Restatement lead and reclassified these persons as "public invitees." How does that change the duty owed by the landowner? See *Post v. Lunney*, 261 So. 2d 146 (Fla. 1972). Many courts have not deviated from the common law rule that a person present in a public place by mere license, and without a business or economic purpose related to the landowner, is owed only the duties available to a licensee. *See, e.g., Edwards v. City of Birmingham*, 447 So. 2d 704 (Ala. 1984).

(5) What is the status of fire fighters and police officers when in the line of duty they come upon private premises to answer emergency calls? If injured by a defect in the premises, is such a person an invitee, a licensee or a mere trespasser? What arguments can be made on each side of the issue? For differing views on the so-called "fireman's rule," *see Christensen v. Murphy*, 678 P.2d 1210 (Ore. 1984), and *Krauth v. Geller*, 157 A.2d 129 (N.J. 1983). *Hack v. Gillespie*, 658 N.E.2d 1046 (Oh. 1996), and *Carson v. Headrick*, 900 S.W.2d 685 (Tenn. 1995), reaffirmed the typical rule that fire fighters and police officers who enter premises on emergency calls are owed no duty by the occupiers except those owed to licensees in the common law. Some courts hold, however, that once on the premises, these officers are owed an ordinary duty of care as to subsequent acts that are independent of those that called them to the premises, *Neighbarger v. Irwin Industries, Inc.*, 882 P.2d 347 (Cal. en banc 1994) and *Heck v. Robey*, 659 N.E.2d 498 (Ind. 1995). Florida and Oregon have abrogated the fireman's rule by statutes, Sec. 112.182 Fla. Stat., and Minn. Stat. § 604.06, and, in a case of first impression in North Carolina, *Newton v. New Hanover Count Board of Education*, 467 S.E.2d 58, 63 (N.C. 1996), rejected the fireman's rule and accorded invitee status to police officers on emergency calls ("the officer's invitation to enter the premises should be implied in law."). *See also Charstensen v. Murphy*, 678 P.2d 1210 (Minn. 1984).

ROWLAND v. CHRISTIAN
California Supreme Court
69 Cal. 2d 108, 70 Cal. Rptr. 97, 443 P.2d 561 (1968)

PETERS, JUSTICE.

Plaintiff appeals from a summary judgment for defendant Nancy Christian in this personal injury action.

In his complaint plaintiff alleged that about November 1, 1963, Miss Christian told the lessors of her apartment that the knob of the cold water faucet on the bathroom basin was cracked and should be replaced; that on November 30, 1963, plaintiff entered the apartment at the invitation of Miss Christian; that he was injured while using the bathroom fixtures, suffering severed tendons and nerves of his right hand; and that he has incurred medical and hospital expenses. He further alleged that the bathroom fixtures were dangerous, that Miss Christian was aware of the dangerous condition, and that his injuries were proximately caused by the negligence of Miss Christian. Plaintiff sought recovery of his medical and hospital expenses, loss of wages, damage to his clothing, and $100,000 general damages. It does not appear from the complaint whether the crack in the faucet handle was obvious to an ordinary inspection or was concealed.

Miss Christian filed an answer containing a general denial except that she alleged that plaintiff was a social guest and admitted the allegations that she had told the lessors that the faucet was defective and that it should be replaced. Miss Christian also alleged contributory negligence and assumption of the risk. In connection with the defenses, she alleged that plaintiff had failed to use his "eyesight" and knew of the condition of the premises. Apart from these allegations, Miss Christian did not allege whether the crack in the faucet handle was obvious or concealed.

Miss Christian's affidavit in support of the motion for summary judgment alleged facts showing that plaintiff was a social guest in her apartment when, as he was using the bathroom, the porcelain handle of one of the water faucets broke in his hand causing injuries to his hand and that plaintiff had used the bathroom on a prior occasion. In opposition to the motion for summary judgment, plaintiff filed an affidavit stating that immediately prior to the accident he told Miss Christian that he was going to use the bathroom facilities, that she had known for two weeks prior to the accident that the faucet handle that caused injury was cracked, that she warned the manager of the building of the condition, that nothing was done to repair the condition of the handle, that she did not say anything to plaintiff as to the condition of the handle, and that when plaintiff turned off the faucet the handle broke in his hands severing the tendons and medial nerve in his right hand.

[In opposing to the defendant's motion for summary judgment, the plaintiff had submitted that the defect in the faucet was known to the defendant, and thus a "trap." Why the trial court properly rejected this arguments was stated by the California appellate division, as follows:

> The application of any theory of defendant's argument thus depends upon whether or not the condition which injured him was concealed or otherwise imperceptible. In turn, the answer to the question before us-whether his counteraffidavit states facts sufficient to present a triable

issue of fact-therefore depends upon whether or not he showed this essential fact in opposition to the motion for summary judgment. He did not. Neither the counteraffidavit nor any other source in the record contains any allegation, factual or conclusionary, which describes the faucet, its appearance, its location, the lighting, the bathroom, or which states any other fact which would support the conclusion that plaintiff was injured by a concealed danger. Consequently, we need not decide whether any of his theories of triable fact should apply because none can: and, since he neither alleged nor suggested the essential underlying fact, no triable issue of fact exists on any theory.

Rowland v. Christian, 63 Cal Rptr. 98, 104 (Cal. App. 1967).]

. . .

Although the invitor owes the invitee a duty to exercise ordinary care to avoid injuring him (*Oettinger v. Stewart, supra,* 24 Cal. 2d 133, 137, 148 P.2d 19, 156 A.L.R. 1221; *Hinds v. Wheadon,* 19 Cal. 2d 458, 460–461, 121 P.2d 724), the general rule is that a trespasser and licensee or social guest are obliged to take the premises as they find them insofar as any alleged defective condition thereon may exist, and that the possessor of the land owes them only the duty of refraining from wanton or willful injury. (*Palmquist v. Mercer,* 43 Cal. 2d 92, 102, 272 P.2d 26; see *Oetinger v. Stewart, supra, 24* Cal. 2d 133, 137 et seq., 148 P.2d 19, 156 A.L.R. 1221.) The ordinary justification for the general rule severely restricting the occupier's liability to social guests is based on the theory that the guest should not expect special precautions to be made on his account and that if the host does not inspect and maintain his property the guest should not expect this to be done on his account. See 2 Harper and James, The Law of Torts, *supra,* p. 1477.)

An increasing regard for human safety has led to a retreat from this position, and an exception to the general rule limiting liability has been made as to active operations where an obligation to exercise reasonable care for the protection of the licensee has been imposed on the occupier of land. (*Oettinger v. Stewart, supra,* 24 Cal. 2d 133, 138–139, 148 P.2d 19, 156 A.L.R. 1221 [disapproving contrary cases]; see Rest.2d Torts, § 341; Prosser on Torts, *supra,* pp. 388–389.) In an apparent attempt to avoid the general rule limiting liability, courts have broadly defined active operations, sometimes giving the term a strained construction in cases involving dangers known to the occupier.

[Omitted is a discussion of cases wherein the court mislabeled a trespasser as a licensee or invitee in order to permit recovery, and cases that permitted a recovery when a licensee fell into what is known in the law as a trap; that is, a concealed danger that the owner knows about and that is not discoverable by ordinary observation of the licensee.]

Without attempting to labor all of the rules relating to the possessor's liability, it is apparent that the classifications of trespasser, licensee, and invitee, the immunities from liability predicated upon those classifications, and the exceptions to those immunities, often do not reflect the major factors which should determine whether immunity should be conferred upon the possessor of land. Some of those factors, including the closeness of the connection between the injury and the defendant's conduct, the moral blame attached to the defendant's conduct, the policy of preventing future harm, and the prevalence and availability of insurance, bear little, if any, relationship to the classifications of trespasser, licensee and invitee and the existing rules conferring immunity.

Although in general there may be a relationship between the remaining factors and the classifications of trespasser, licensee, and invitee, there are many cases in which no such relationship may exist. Thus, although the foreseeability of harm to an invitee would ordinarily seem greater than the foreseeability of harm to a trespasser, in a particular case the opposite may be true. The same may be said of the issue of certainty of injury. The burden to the defendant and consequences to the community of imposing a duty to exercise care with resulting liability for breach may often be greater with respect to trespassers than with respect to invitees, but it by no means follows that this is true in every case. In many situations, the burden will be the same, *i.e.*, the conduct necessary upon the defendant's part to meet the burden of exercising due care as to invitees will also meet his burden with respect to licensees and trespassers. The last of the major factors, the cost of insurance, will, of course, vary depending upon the rules of liability adopted, but there is no persuasive evidence that applying ordinary principles of negligence law to the land occupier's liability will materially reduce the prevalence of insurance due to increased cost or even substantially increase the cost.

Considerations such as these have led some courts in particular situations to reject the rigid common law classifications and to approach the issue of the duty of the occupier on the basis of ordinary principles of negligence.

A man's life or limb does not become less worthy of protection by the law nor a loss less worthy of compensation under the law because he has come upon the land of another without permission or with permission but without a business purpose. Reasonable people do not ordinarily vary their conduct depending upon such matters, and to focus upon the status of the injured party as a trespasser, licensee, or invitee in order to determine the question whether the landowner has a duty of care, is contrary to our modern social mores and humanitarian values. The common law rules obscure rather than illuminate the proper considerations which should govern determination of the question of duty.

It bears repetition that the basic policy of this state set forth by the Legislature in section 1714 of the Civil Code is that everyone is responsible for an injury caused to another by his want of ordinary care or skill in the management of his property. The factors which may in particular cases warrant departure from this fundamental principle do not warrant the wholesale immunities resulting from the common law classifications, and we are satisfied that continued adherence to the common law distinctions can only lead to injustice or, if we are to avoid injustice, further fictions with the resulting complexity and confusion. We decline to follow and perpetuate such rigid classifications. The proper test to be applied to the liability of the possessor of land in accordance with section 1714 of the Civil Code is whether in the management of his property he has acted as a reasonable man in view of the probability of injury to others, and, although the plaintiff's status as a trespasser, licensee, or invitee may in the light of the facts giving rise to such status have some bearing on the question of liability, the status is not determinative.

Once the ancient concepts as to the liability of the occupier of land are stripped away, the status of the plaintiff relegated to its proper place in determining such liability, and ordinary principles of negligence applied, the result in the instant case presents no substantial difficulties.

As we have seen, when we view the matters presented on the motion for summary judgment as we must, we must assume defendant Miss Christian was aware that the faucet handle was defective and dangerous, that the defect was not obvious, and that plaintiff was about to come in contact with the defective condition, and under the undisputed facts she neither remedied the condition nor warned plaintiff of it. Where the occupier of land is aware of a concealed condition involving in the absence of precautions an unreasonable risk of harm to those coming in contact with it and is aware that a person on the premises is about to come in contact with it, the trier of fact can reasonably conclude that a failure to warn or to repair the condition constitutes negligence. Whether or not a guest has a right to expect that his host will remedy dangerous conditions on his account, he should reasonably be entitled to rely upon a warning of the dangerous condition so that he, like the host, will be in a position to take special precautions when he comes in contact with it.

. . .

The judgment is reversed.

TRAYNOR, C. J., and TOBRINER, MOSK and SULLIVAN, JJ., concur.

BURKE, JUSTICE (dissenting).

I dissent. In determining the liability of the occupier or owner of land for injuries, the distinctions between trespassers, licensees and invitees have been developed and applied by the courts over a period of many years. They supply a reasonable and workable approach to the problems involved, and one which provides the degree of stability and predictability so highly prized in the law. The unfortunate alternative, it appears to me, is the route taken by the majority in their opinion in this case; that such issues are to be decided on a case by case basis under the application of the basic law of negligence, bereft of the guiding principles and precedent which the law has heretofore attached by virtue of the relationship of the parties to one another.

Liability for negligence turns upon whether a duty of care is owed, and if so, the extent thereof. Who can doubt that the corner grocery, the large department store, or the financial institutionowes a greater duty of care to one whom it has invited to enter its premises as a prospective customer of its wares or services than it owes to a trespasser seeking to enter after the close of business hours and for a nonbusiness or even an antagonistic purpose? I do not think it unreasonable or unfair that a social guest (classified by the law as a licensee, as was plaintiff here) should be obliged to take the premises in the same condition as his host finds them or permits them to be. Surely a homeowner should not be obliged to hover over his guests with warnings of possible dangers to be found in the condition of the home (*e.g.*, waxed floors, slipping rugs, toys in unexpected places, etc., etc.). Yet today's decision appears to open the door to potentially unlimited liability despite the purpose and circumstances motivating the plaintiff in entering the premises of another, and despite the caveat of the majority that the status of the parties may "have some bearing on the question of liability . . . ," whatever the future may show that language to mean.

In my view, it is not a proper function of this court to overturn the learning, wisdom and experience of the past in this field. Sweeping modifications of tort liability law fall more suitably within the domain of the Legislature, before which all affected interests can be heard and which can enact statutes providing uniform standards and guidelines for the future.

I would affirm the judgment for defendant.

McCOMB, J., concurs.

NOTES AND QUESTIONS

(1) Are you satisfied of the wisdom of the revision of California law made by *Rowland v. Christian*? Or do you still believe that a person's home is a "castle and fortress" that the law should not be permitted too lightly to assail? How important was the civil code to the California decision? In *O'Leary v. Coenen*, 251 N.W.2d 746, 749–50 (N.D. 1977), the North Dakota Supreme Court canvassed reasons for making a change, as follows:

Reasons cited for abandoning the common law categories include: (1) that the policy considerations that led to the judicial creation of invitee, licensee, and trespasser immunities no longer retain their viability under modern conditions because such categories bear no logical relationship to the exercise of reasonable care for the safety of others, because, in today's society, human safety is of greater importance than is a land occupier's unrestricted freedom, and because public opinion today favors assigning enterprise liability or distributing losses over a greater segment of society through insurance in lieu of forcing the entrant to suffer such burden; (2) that it is becoming increasingly difficult to categorize the circumstances of modern life into the rigid common law classifications of invitee, licensee, and trespasser . . . (3) that the use of common law classifications prevents a jury from applying changing community standards to the duty owed by an occupier of premises to entrants thereon . . . (4) that jury confusion sometimes results over the inclusion of social guests, no matter how formally invited, in the licensee category and not the invitee category; and (5) that the many exceptions and distinctions make the use of the common law categories complex, confusing, inequitable, and, paradoxically, nonuniform . . .

(2) At least ten other states[6] have followed the lead of *Rowland v. Christian* and eliminated the hard and fast role of status in owner and occupier cases. In those states the issue is one of reasonable care under the circumstances. Nevertheless, after it initial impetus this trend faltered and even reversed itself. The Colorado legislature restored the categories by statute, see, *Lakeview Associates, Ltd. v. Maes*, 907 P.2d 580 (Colo. En Banc 1995) (holding that the duty owed by a landowner to a tenant was also owed to the tenant's guest); and *Tantimonico v.*

---

[6] *Moloso v. State*, 644 P.2d 205 (Alaska 1982); *Mile High Fence Co. v. Radovich*, 489 P.2d 300 (Col. 1971); *Pickard v. City & County of Honolulu*, 452 P.2d 445 (Haw. 1969) (duty of reasonable care to persons reasonably anticipated); *Shelton v. Aetna Casualty & Surety Company*, 334 So. 2d 406 (La. 1976) (status may have bearing but is not determinative); *Ouellette v. Blanchard*, 364 A.2d 631 (N.H. 1976) (duty is of reasonable care under the circumstances even as to a trespasser); *Basso v. Miller*, 352 N.E.2d 868 (N.Y. 1976) (rigid classifications dispensed with but status is a factor); *Mariorenze v. Joseph DiPonte, Inc.*, 333 A.2d 127 (R.I. 1975) (assigns trichotomy to past; duty is of reasonable care); *Moody v. Manny's Auto Repair*, 871 P.2d 935 (Nev. 1994); Ill. Premises Liability Act, Complied Stat. Ann. 1300/2 (1994); and *Hoffer v. Meyer*, 295 N.W.2d 333 (S.D. 1980) (under S.D. civil code, status no longer determinative but has a bearing).

Allendale Mut. Ins. Co., 637 A.2d 1056, 1062 (R.I. 1994) (restored the common law trespasser category).

In addition, at least twelve states,[7] the District of Columbia,[8] and the maritime jurisdiction[9] of the United States have eliminated any legal distinction between the duty owed invitees and the duty owed licensees; the duty owed to an invitee applies to both. These jurisdictions have declined to modify the duty owed to trespassers.

A few states[10] have taken the more conservative approach of reclassifying certain traditional licensees to be public invitees as suggested by Restatement, Torts, Second § 332. Florida has extended this by also reclassifying social guests to be invitees, leaving a much smaller licensee class.[11]

Also, a few states[12] have held that a known licensee is entitled to due care as to an occupier's activities as distinguished from the condition of the premises.

Despite this apparent flurry of activity, however, most states that have reconsidered the issue have declined to abrogate the common law status distinctions.[13]

---

[7] *Peterson v. Balach*, 199 N.W.2d 639 (Minn. 1977). (declines to rule on trespassers); *Armstrong v. Mailand*, 285 N.W.2d 343 (Minn. 1979) (firemen owed duty of reasonable care); *O'Leary v. Coenen*, 251 N.W.2d 746 (N.D. 1977) (equates licensees and invitees but declines to change rule as to trespassers); *Antoniowicz v. Roscynski*, 236 N.W.2d 1 (Wis. 1975) (invitee-licensee distinction abolished, but not trespasser rule); *Hudson v. Gaitan*, 675 S.W.2d 699 (Tenn. 1984) (common law classifications of invitee and licensee are no longer determinative); *Jones v. Hanson*, 867 P.2d 303 (Kan. 1994); *Poulin v. Colby College*, 402 A.2d 846 (Me. 1979); *Mounsey v. Ellard*, 297 N.E.2d 43 (Mass. 1973); *Heins v. Webster County*, 552 N.W.2d 51 (Neb. 1996); *Ford v. Board of County Commissioners*, 879 P.2d 766 (N.M. 1994); *Clark v. Beckwith*, 858 P.2d 293 (Wyo. 1993); *Rhodes v. Illinois Central Gulf Railroad*, 665 N.E.2d 1260 (Ill. 1996) (invitee-licensee distinction abrogated by statute); and *Tantimonico v. Allendale Mut. Ins. Co.*, 637 A.2d 1056 (R.I. 1994).)

[8] *Blumenthal v. Cairo Hotel Corp.*, 256 A.2d 400 (D.C. Ct. App. 1969); *Washington Metropolitan Area Transit Authority v. Ward*, 433 A.2d 1072 (D.C. Ct. App. 1981) (concurring judge urges status be abolished as to trespasser).

[9] Kermarec v. Campaignie Generale Transatlantique, 358 U.S. 625, 79 S. Ct. 406, 3 L. Ed. 2d 550 (1959) (maritime torts).

[10] *Post v. Lunney*, 261 So. 2d 146 (Fla. 1972); and *McKinnon v. Washington Federal Savings & Loan Assn.*, 414 P.2d 773 (Wash. 1966).

[11] *Wood v. Camp*, 284 So. 2d 691 (Fla. 1973).

[12] *Hix v. Billen*, 284 So. 2d 209 (Fla. 1973); *Scheibel v. Hillis*, 531 S.W.2d 285 (Mo. 1976) (significance of status largely disappears, at least as to active negligence, once presence is known); and *Hardin v. Harris*, 507 S.W.2d 172 (Ky. 1974) (same duty of care owed known licensee as owed invitee as to farm activities).

[13] *Benham v. King*, 700 N.W.2d 314 (Ia. 2005), summed up the status as follows: In total, twenty-six courts have abrogated the common-law distinctions between invitees and licensees. Thirteen of these jurisdictions have abandoned the common-law distinctions between invitees, licensees, and trespassers. See *Kermarec v. Compagnie Generale Transatlantique*, 358 U.S. 625, 631-32, 79 S.Ct. 406, 410, 3 L.Ed.2d 550, 555 (1959) (abolishing the distinction as it applied to admiralty law); *Smith v. Arbaugh's Rest., Inc.*, 469 F.2d 97, 107 (D.C.Cir.1972); *Webb v. City & Borough of Sitka*, 561 P.2d 731, 734 (Alaska 1977), abrogated in part by statute as stated in *Univ. of Alaska v. Shanti*, 835 P.2d 1225, 1228 n. 5 (Alaska 1992); *Rowland v. Christian*, 69 Cal.2d 108, 70 Cal.Rptr. 97, 443 P.2d 561, 568 (1968); *Mile High Fence Co. v. Radovich*, 175 Colo. 537, 489 P.2d 308, 314-15 (1971); *Pickard v. City & County of Honolulu*, 51 Haw. 134, 452 P.2d 445, 446 (1969); *Cope v. Doe*, 102 Ill.2d 278, 80 Ill.Dec. 40, 464 N.E.2d 1023, 1028 (1984) (abolishing only with respect to child entrants); *Cates v. Beauregard Elec. Coop., Inc.*, 328 So.2d 367, 370-71 (La.1976); *Limberhand v. Big Ditch Co.*, 218 Mont. 132, 706 P.2d 491, 496 (1985); *Moody v. Manny's Auto Repair*, 110 Nev. 320, 871 P.2d 935, 942 (1994); *Ouellette v. Blanchard*, 116 N.H. 552, 364 A.2d 631, 634 (1976); *Basso v. Miller*, 40 N.Y.2d 233, 386 N.Y.S.2d 564, 352 N.E.2d 868, 871-73 (1976); *Mariorenzi v. Joseph DiPonte, Inc.*, 114 R.I. 294, 333 A.2d 127, 133 (1975). But see Colo.Rev.Stat. §

This is exemplified by the following statement of the Florida Supreme Court:[14]

> We decline to recognize the purportedly innocuous rule . . . that a jury should merely be instructed that the duty of care of the landowner is "whether the landowner's actions were reasonable in light of all the factual circumstances in the case." This is too vague and unreasonable a test to apply to a landowner because of the remaining, inherent distinctions in relationships involved between persons who come upon an owner's property; neither does it sufficiently afford a reasonable standard which can be applied as a measure by the jury.
>
> In sum, there has been no revolutionary assignment of the common law status structure to the pages of history. Consequently, the torts lawyer must not only understand the common law, but be prepared to discover and apply local departures from it.

(3) In England, The Occupiers' Liability Act, 1957 (5 & 6 Eliz. 2 ch 31) abolished the distinction between licensees and invitees. The Judicial Committee of the House of Lords later acknowledged a duty of care even as to trespassers under carefully constrained circumstances.

(4) To claim the limited duties acknowledged in the common law hierarchy, the defendant must be an owner or occupier of land with a possessory interest sufficient to exclude the plaintiff from the premises. Otherwise ordinary negligence standards will apply to determine whether a duty is owed. *See, e.g., Munsh v. H.D. Electric Cooperative, Inc.*, 460 N.W.2d 149 (S.D. 1990) (even though plaintiff may have been a trespasser as to the owner of the land, he was not a trespasser as to electric company to whom the landowner had granted a mere license to erect a power line, which did not include the power to exclude others from the property.)

(5) In general, land owners and occupiers owe no duty of care to a person on abutting properties (*e.g.* sidewalks) or on the property itself as to risks inherent to

---

13-21-115(3) (1996) (restoring the distinctions); *Tantimonico v. Allendale Mut. Ins. Co.*, 637 A.2d 1056, 1057 (R.I.1994) (restoring status category of trespasser). Thirteen jurisdictions have limited the abrogation to the common-law distinctions between invitees and licensees. See *Wood v. Camp*, 284 So.2d 691, 695 (Fla.1973); *Jones v. Hansen*, 254 Kan. 499, 867 P.2d 303, 310 (1994); *Poulin v. Colby Coll.*, 402 A.2d 846, 851 (Me.1979); *Mounsey v. Ellard*, 363 Mass. 693, 297 N.E.2d 43, 51-52, n. 7 (1973); *Peterson v. Balach*, 294 Minn. 161, 199 N.W.2d 639, 642 (1972); *Heins v. Webster County*, 250 Neb. 750, 552 N.W.2d 51, 57 (1996); *Ford v. Bd. of County Comm'rs*, 118 N.M. 134, 879 P.2d 766, 770 (1994); *Nelson v. Freeland*, 349 N.C. 615, 507 S.E.2d 882, 892 (1998); *O'Leary v. Coenen*, 251 N.W.2d 746, 751 (N.D.1977); *Hudson v. Gaitan*, 675 S.W.2d 699, 703 (Tenn.1984), overruled in part on other grounds by *McIntyre v. Balentine*, 833 S.W.2d 52, 57 (Tenn.1992); *Mallet v. Pickens*, 206 W.Va. 145, 522 S.E.2d 436, 446 (1999); *Antoniewicz v. Reszcynski*, 70 Wis.2d 836, 236 N.W.2d 1, 11 (1975); *Clarke v. Beckwith*, 858 P.2d 293, 296 (Wyo.1993). Justices or judges in at least six states that have retained the distinctions have published dissenting or concurring opinions arguing for change. *Shaw v. Petersen*, 169 Ariz. 559, 821 P.2d 220, 224-28 (Ct.App.1991) (Fidel, J., concurring specially); *Alexander*, 646 N.W.2d at 80-87 (Lavorato, C.J., concurring specially) (Streit, J., concurring specially); *Sheets*, 581 N.W.2d at 603-07 (plurality opinion); *Kirschner v. Louisville Gas & Elec. Co.*, 743 S.W.2d 840, 845-49 (Ky.1988) (Liebson, J., dissenting); *Little ex rel. Little v. Bell*, 719 So.2d 757, 764-68 (Miss.1998) (McRae, J., dissenting); *Vega ex rel. Muniz v. Piedilato*, 154 N.J. 496, 713 A.2d 442, 449-60 (1998) (Handler, J., concurring); *Musch v. H-D Elec. Coop.*, 460 N.W.2d 149, 156-57 (S.D.1990) (Miller, J., concurring). The Restatement (Third) of Torts: Liability for Physical Harm (Proposed Final Draft No. 1, April 6, 2005) appears to abrogate the common-law distinctions between invitees and licensees. *Id.* §§ 40(a), 40(b)(3). *Id.* 700 N.W. 2d at 322, n.4. In addition, *Pinnell v. Bates*, 838 So.2d 198 (Miss. 2002) declined to eliminate the common law distinction between licensees and invitees.

[14] *Wood v. Camp*, 284 So. 2d 691, 695 (Fla. 1973).

natural conditions on the land (*e.g.*, naturally occurring vegetation and wild animals). *Deberjeous v. Schneider*, 604 A.2d 210 (N.J. Super. 1991). By contrast, possessors do owe a duty of care to those outside the land as to dangers posed by artificial conditions that the landowner creates or permits to remain on the land. *Id.* and *Hutchins v. 1001 Fourth Avenue Associate*, 802 P.2d 1360 (Wash. En Banc 1991). Some courts impose no duty as to the natural growth of planted vegetation. *See, e.g., Sullivan v. Silver Palm Properties, Inc.*, 558 So. 2d 409 (Fla. 1990). *British Railways Board v. Herrington*, [1973] App. Cas. 877 (H.L.). *Williams v. Davis*, 974 So. 2d 1052 (Fla. 2007) held that a landowner owes users of abutting highways no duty as to growth of foliage that remains wholly on the landowner's property, but also stated: "We do recognize, however, that all property owners owe a duty. . . . not to permit the growth of foliage on their property to extend outside the bounds of the property and into the public right-of-way so as to interfere with a motorist's ability to safely travel on the adjacent roadway."

MERRILL v. JANSMA
Supreme Court of Wyoming
86 P.3d 270 (2004)

KITE, Justice.

Sue A. Merrill appeals from a summary judgment dismissing her claims for personal injury resulting from a fall on rental property belonging to Alvina Jansma. She claims the district court erred in ruling that, as a matter of law, Ms. Jansma owed no duty to Ms. Merrill under the Residential Rental Property Act, Wyo. Stat. Ann. § 1-21-1202 (LexisNexis 2001) and no genuine issue of material fact existed under the common law as set forth in Restatement (Second) of Torts § 326 (1965). We reverse and hold the Residential Rental Property Act imposes a duty on landlords to maintain leased premises in a fit and habitable condition. We further hold that this duty establishes the standard of care applicable generally to personal injuries occurring on leased premises-a standard of reasonable care under the circumstances. Finally, we hold that the statutory duty and the standard arising from it replace the common law rule of landlord immunity and its exceptions.

. . .

FACTS

The facts, viewed in the light most favorable to the party opposing the summary judgment motion, are that on February 19, 2000, Ms. Merrill injured her right shoulder when she fell as she was ascending the front steps leading to the porch and front door of the mobile home her daughter, Sherri Pritchard, rented from Ms. Jansma. The step became loose during the time Ms. Pritchard rented the home. Prior to the fall, Ms. Pritchard attempted to repair the step by securing it with nails. When that failed, she informed the manager of the property that the step was loose. The manager suggested Ms. Pritchard try using screws to secure the step. Ms. Pritchard told the manager she did not have a screw gun. The manager had one and said she would screw the step into place. Subsequently, and without Ms. Pritchard's knowledge, the manager attempted to repair the step. Apparently, that effort was unsuccessful and Ms. Merrill fell when the step separated from the porch as she stepped on it.

Ms. Merrill filed a negligence claim against Ms. Jansma as the owner of the property alleging she knew or reasonably should have known the step was dangerous and failed to exercise reasonable care to alleviate the danger. She further alleged Ms. Jansma owed a duty of care to her as a visitor to the rental property. She sought damages for the injuries she sustained in the fall from the step, including medical expenses, lost earnings and damages for emotional distress and pain and suffering. Ms. Jansma answered the complaint and then filed a motion for summary judgment, claiming she owed no legal duty to Ms. Merrill. The district court granted Ms. Jansma's motion for summary judgment, holding that, as a matter of law, she had no legal duty to Ms. Merrill under either the Residential Rental Property Act or the common law as set forth in § 362 of the Restatement.

. . .

DISCUSSION

1. Residential Rental Property Act

a. Historical Development

For centuries, landlord immunity was the rule in landlord-tenant law.

Since 16th century feudal England a lease has been considered a conveyance of an interest in land, carrying with it the doctrine of *caveat emptor*.

The lessor impliedly covenanted that he had the legal right to transfer possession and that he would leave the tenant in "quiet enjoyment of the leasehold," but he did not impliedly warrant as to the habitability or fitness of the premises for any particular use.

As a lessee of real property a 16th century tenant in England was expected to inspect the premises prior to the "sale," and in the absence of express covenants to the contrary, he took possession with whatever defects existed at the time of the lease. Nor did the landlord have an implied responsibility to maintain the leasehold in a reasonable state of repair during the term of the lease. . . .

It was in this setting that the principle of tort immunity for the landlord developed . . . as part and parcel of the concept that a lease is primarily a conveyance of real estate. The landlord was not liable to the tenant or third persons for personal injury or personal property damage caused by a defect present at the transfer of possession or by defects arising during the term of the leasehold.

Old Town Development Company v. Langford, 349 N.E.2d 744, 753-54 (Ind.App.1976) (footnotes omitted).

With the transition from a mostly rural to a more urban society, however, the rule of landlord immunity gave way slightly to some judicially recognized exceptions.

During and following the Industrial Revolution, the population migration from rural to urban areas accentuated the importance of the structural improvements on the premises, and a corresponding decrease in the significance of the land itself.

Leases often developed into complex transactions. The typical lease began to look more like a contract than a conveyance of real estate, often containing numerous express covenants alien to common law transfers of nonfreehold estates.

Accompanying this migration was an ever-increasing distaste for the continued application of caveat emptor, or caveat lessee, to urban leases of both commercial and residential property. Modern and more complex buildings brought added maintenance costs. At the same time tenants were less able to cope with the machinery and sophisticated systems in dwellings and commercial structures, which they had neither the expertise nor the funds to repair. But caveat lessee did not change, and remained firmly entrenched in both English and American common law protecting the lessor from liability for personal injury or personal property damage arising out of defective conditions on the leased premises.

While the cloak of immunity remained draped over the landlord as social and economic conditions changed, certain judicial exceptions were gradually, and grudgingly, carved-out "when such action could be harmonized with the rules governing the liability of a vendor of real property, or when the characterization of a lease as a conveyance was so contrary to social and economic realities that justice required the creation of an exception to the general rule." Love, Landlord's Liability for Defective Premises: Caveat Lessee, Negligence or Strict Liability?, 1975 Wis.L.Rev. 19, 50 (1975). Id. at 754-55. Five exceptions to the rule of landlord immunity emerged.

A landlord could be held liable in tort for (1) defects in premises leased for admission of the public; (2) a breach of a covenant to repair; (3) negligent repairs; (4) defects in "common areas" under the landlord's control; and more recently (5) defects constituting a violation of a provision of the applicable building or housing code.

. . .

Despite, or perhaps in part because of the exceptions, there was by the 1960s increasing "discontent with the appearance of unfairness in the landlord's general immunity from tort liability, and with the artificiality and increasing complexity of the various exceptions to this seemingly archaic rule of nonliability." W.L. Prosser & W.P. Keeton, Prosser & Keeton on Torts, 446 (5th ed.1984). As a result, some courts began to re-examine landlord tenant law.[15] One of the first of these was the Wisconsin Supreme Court, which in Pines v. Perssion, 14 Wis.2d 590, 111 N.W.2d 409 (1961), adopted a rule that residential leases between landlord and tenant carried with them an implied warranty of habitability and fitness-that is, a promise that the premises would be fit for human habitation. In reaching this result, the court said:

> [T]he frame of reference in which the old common-law rule operated has changed.
>
> Legislation and administrative rules, such as the safeplace statute, building codes, and health regulations, all impose certain duties on a property owner with respect to the condition of his premises. Thus, the

---

[15] [Fn 2 in opinion.] Actually, at least one state rejected the common law rule much earlier. In 1895, the Georgia legislature enacted a statute imposing a duty of reasonable care on landlords and providing a remedy in the form of damages for injuries resulting from a landlord's failure to keep the premises in repair. O.C.G.A. § 44-7-14.

legislature has made a policy judgment-that it is socially (and politically) desirable to impose these duties on a property owner-which has rendered the old common-law rule obsolete.

Id. at 595, 111 N.W.2d 409. Pines was followed by Lemle v. Breeden, 51 Haw. 426, 462 P.2d 470 (1969) and Javins v. First National Realty Corporation, 428 F.2d 1071 (D.C.Cir.1970). . . .Like the court in Old Town, the courts in Lemle and Javins recognized that an implied warranty of habitability applied to rental property. Since then a number of other courts have followed the lead of Pines and its progeny.[16]

In addition to the courts that rejected the common law in favor of recognition of an implied warranty of habitability, other courts cast aside landlord immunity on the basis of general negligence principles. In Sargent v. Ross, 113 N.H. 388, 308 A.2d 528, 530 (1973), the court said: . . .

> [h]enceforth, landlords as other persons must exercise reasonable care not to subject others to an unreasonable risk of harm. A landlord must act as a reasonable person under all of the circumstances including the likelihood of injury to others, the probable seriousness of such injuries, and the burden of reducing or avoiding the risk. We think this basic principle of responsibility for landlords as for others "best expresses the principles of justice and reasonableness upon which our law of torts is founded." The questions of control, hidden defects and common or public use, which formerly had to be established as a prerequisite to even considering the negligence of a landlord, will now be relevant only inasmuch as they bear on the basic tort issues such as the foreseeability and unreasonableness of the particular risk of harm.

Id. at 534. . . .

As mentioned in *Sargent*, the re-evaluation of landlord-tenant law has not been confined to the judiciary. In the past thirty years, legislatures in nearly every state have enacted statutes imposing new duties on landlords. The Uniform Residential Landlord and Tenant Act (URLTA) likely played a role in this development and served as a model for similar legislation, with varying degrees of amendment, in many states. 7B Uniform Laws Annotated (West Group 2000), Uniform Residential Landlord and Tenant Act, 527 (1972); . . . Although the URLTA differs in many respects from Wyoming's Residential Rental Property Act, both acts contain provisions requiring landlords to maintain the premises in a fit, safe and habitable condition. Both acts are also illustrative of the overwhelming movement nationwide away from landlord immunity and toward landlord responsibility for known dangers and those which ought to be known with the exercise of reasonable care. For that reason, we briefly discuss the URLTA.

The purposes of the URLTA as stated in § 1.102 are generally to modernize the law and the rights and obligations of landlords and tenants, encourage both lessor and lessee to maintain rental premises, and make uniform the laws among those

---

[16] [Fn. 3 in opinion.] Other courts which have recognized an implied warranty of habitability in the context of rental property include: Marini v. Ireland, 56 N.J. 130, 265 A.2d 526 (1970); Kline v. Burns 111 N.H. 87, 276 A.2d 248 (1971); Jack Spring, Inc. v. Little, 50 Ill.2d 351, 280 N.E.2d 208 (1972); Mease v. Fox, 200 N.W.2d 791 (Iowa 1972); Boston Housing Authority v. Hemingway, 363 Mass. 184, 293 N.E.2d 831 (1973); Green v. Superior Court of San Francisco, 10 Cal.3d 616, 111 Cal.Rptr. 704, 517 P.2d 1168 (1974); Steele v. Latimer, 214 Kan. 329, 521 P.2d 304 (1974); Detling v. Edelbrock, 671 S.W.2d 265 (Mo.1984).

states that adopt it. Uniform Laws Annotated, supra, at 534. Among other things, the URLTA provides:

§ 2.104. [Landlord to Maintain Premises].

(a) A landlord shall

* * *

(2) make all repairs and do whatever is necessary to put and keep the premises in a fit and habitable condition;

* * *

(4) maintain in good and safe working order and condition all electrical, plumbing, sanitary, heating, ventilating, air-conditioning, and other facilities and appliances . . . supplied or required to be supplied by him[.]

* * *

Id. at 566. Section 4.101(a) of the URLTA authorizes the tenant to provide written notice to a landlord who is not in noncompliance with the preceding section that the lease will terminate if the condition is not corrected. Id. at 609. Section 4.101(b) allows the tenant to recover actual damages for the landlord's noncompliance in addition to the remedies available under § 4.101(a). Section 1.105 also provides for the recovery of appropriate damages by the aggrieved party and the right to bring an action to enforce the rights and obligations declared by the act. Id. at 537. As of 2001, fifteen states had adopted the URLTA in whole or in part.[17]

Altogether, over forty states have discarded the common law rule of landlord immunity and recognize a duty in some form, either through legislation, judicial declaration, or both.[18] Among the states with legislation addressing the landlord-tenant relationship, the statutory language varies considerably, with some following the example of the URLTA quite closely and others adopting their own version of landlord tenant statutory law. Just as the statutory language varies, the approaches taken by the courts differ in deciding whether the statute creates a duty and, if so, what the legal basis for the duty is and what remedies are available for breach of the duty. As noted, although there is considerable variation from state to state in the statutory language employed and judicial interpretation of that language, nearly every court is in agreement that landlords in the modern era have duties they did not have at common law.

In *Thompson v. Crownover*, 259 Ga. 126, 381 S.E.2d 283, 284-85 (1989), for example, after noting the Georgia legislature's early rejection of the common law in favor of a duty of reasonable care, the court said:

---

[17] [Fn. 4 in opinion.] Alaska, Arizona, Florida, Hawaii, Iowa, Kansas, Kentucky, Montana, Nebraska, New Mexico, Oregon, Rhode Island, South Carolina, Tennessee and Virginia. Uniform Laws Annotated, 2003 Supp., at 78.

[18] [Fn. 5 in opinion.] The following states have recognized a duty in some form by legislation, judicial declaration, or both: Alaska, Arizona, California, Colorado, Connecticut, Delaware, Florida, Georgia, Hawaii, Idaho, Indiana, Iowa, Kansas, Kentucky, Maine, Maryland, Massachusetts, Michigan, Minnesota, Missouri, Montana, Nebraska, Nevada, New Hampshire, New Jersey, New Mexico, New York, North Carolina, North Dakota, Ohio, Oklahoma, Oregon, Rhode Island, South Carolina, South Dakota, Tennessee, Texas, Utah, Vermont, Virginia, Washington, West Virginia, and Wisconsin.

The public policy of this state supports the position advanced by The Restatement of Law 2d, Property, § 17.6:

A landlord should be subject to liability for physical harm caused to the tenant and others upon the leased property with the consent of the tenant or his subtenants by a dangerous condition existing before or arising after the tenant has taken possession, if he has failed to exercise reasonable care to repair the condition and the existence of the condition is in violation of:

(1) an implied warranty of habitability; or

(2) a duty created by statute or administrative regulation.

. . .

Even in states sometimes cited as having neither a statute nor court decision imposing liability on landlords,[19] the law has evolved away from landlord immunity. In Colorado, for example, where there is no legislation similar to the URLTA or Wyoming's Residential Rental Property Act, the courts have allowed recovery by injured persons for a landlord's failure to use reasonable care on the basis of the landowner liability statutes. C.R.S. § 13-21-115 (1993 Cum.Supp.); Maes v. Lakeview Associates, 892 P.2d 375 (Colo.App.1994).

In contrast to the forty-plus states that have done away with landlord immunity, a few states have retained the common law except as explicitly provided in their particular landlord-tenant act. Nebraska, for example, enacted the URLTA but has since substantially modified it, including adding a provision that states: "The obligations imposed by this section are not intended to change existing tort law in the state." Neb.Rev.Stat. § 76-1419 (1974). The Nebraska Supreme Court has interpreted this provision to mean that the act does not change the common law, thus a landlord owes no duty to a tenant to repair leased premises absent a contractual provision to that effect or retention of control of the area where an injury occurs. Tighe v. Cedar Lawn, Inc., 11 Neb.App. 250, 649 N.W.2d 520 (2002). It bears repeating, however, that Nebraska is one of only a very few states that adheres strictly to the common law "no duty" rule.

Unlike Nebraska, other states that continue to apply the common law allow personal injury claims against a landlord on the basis of various legal theories. In Ohio, for example, despite the courts' continued adherence to the common-law rule, a landlord may be liable in tort for failing to maintain leased premises in a fit and habitable condition as required under Ohio's Landlords and Tenants Act. Ohio Rev.Code Ann. 5321.04 (1974); Shump, 644 N.E.2d at 296. The Ohio statute is viewed as an exception to a landlord's common-law immunity and as expanding the duties a landlord owes to those using rental property. *Id.*. . .

As this discussion illustrates, landlord-tenant law has evolved considerably from the days when the common law rule was established. Today, the vast majority of states recognize that a landlord has a duty to maintain rental property in a safe, habitable condition. With this overview in mind, we turn to a discussion of the law in Wyoming.

---

[19] [Fn. 7 in opinion.] . . . Alabama, Arkansas, Colorado, Indiana, Mississippi, South Carolina and Utah. Our research reveals that of these states, at least four allow recovery either by statute or judicial decision by individuals injured as a result of a landlord's failure to maintain rental premises-Colorado, Indiana, South Carolina and Utah.

b. The law in Wyoming

Despite the overwhelming movement in other states to replace the rule of landlord immunity, Wyoming up to now has continued to apply the common law rule-absent a contractual provision to repair, a landlord generally owes no duty to a tenant or a tenant's guests for dangerous or defective conditions of the premises. Hefferin v. Scott Realty Co., 71 Wyo. 114, 254 P.2d 194, 197 (1953). The only exceptions we have recognized to this general rule are where:

1. Hidden or latently dangerous conditions known to the landlord and unknown to the tenant cause an injury.

2. The premises are leased for public use and a member of the public is injured.

3. An injury occurs on a part of the premises retained under the control of the landlord but open to the tenant's use.

4. The landlord contracts to repair the premises.

5. The landlord negligently makes repairs.

Ortega v. Flaim, 902 P.2d 199, 202 (Wyo.1995). In all but the five limited circumstances listed above, we have held to the common law rule that a landlord owes no duty to a tenant and have declined on several occasions to join the majority of states by judicially adopting landlord liability. *Id., Pavuk v. Rogers*, 2001 WY 75, 30 P.3d 19 (Wyo.2001). Such a change in the common law, we have said, is best left to the legislature. *Id.* Most notably, in *Ortega*, we said:

In order for social guest Ortega to succeed in imposing landlord liability in this case, Wyoming's adherence to the common law rule must be abandoned. . . . Other states have construed statutes, contracts, or an implied warranty of habitability as imposing tort liability upon landlords. Since the 1970s, this legal trend has resulted in the majority of states abrogating the common law rule of landlord nonliability under various legal theories. Presently, Wyoming has no legal basis for landlord tort liability as it has not enacted legislation on this issue, has not judicially recognized an implied warranty of habitability for rental premises and has not judicially altered the common law rule. . . .

. . .

Presumably with Ortega in mind, the legislature in short order took up the matter of landlord-tenant law. . . .[d]uring the 1999 legislative session, it was modified, reintroduced, amended, and passed into law as the Wyoming Residential Rental Property Act, § 1-21-1201, et seq.

[Detailed statement of the Act omitted. Its essential elements are those in §2.104 of the URLTA quoted above.]

The act does . . . clearly and expressly impose a duty on landlords not previously recognized in Wyoming law. Section 1-21-1202(a) requires landlords to maintain rental units in a safe, sanitary and habitable condition. . . . We hold that the Residential Rental Property Act imposed a duty on landlords to provide and maintain premises in a safe and sanitary condition fit for human habitation. We further hold that this legislatively created duty establishes a new standard of conduct for purposes of personal injuries occurring on rental property. . . . We turn to the question whether Ms. Merrill's claim is precluded because she failed to give written notice of the broken step as required in the act.

As set forth above, § 1-21-1203(b) requires a tenant who has a reasonable belief supported by evidence that the premises are not safe, sanitary and fit for habitation to advise the landlord in writing of the defective condition and the corrective action he wants the landlord to take. Section 1-21-1206(b) further provides that if the landlord does not respond to the first notice, the tenant may serve a second notice. If the landlord again fails to respond or disputes the claim, the tenant then may file a civil action in county or justice of the peace court under § 1-21-1206(c). Upon showing the landlord unreasonably refused or failed to use diligence to correct an unsafe condition, the tenant may recover costs, damages, including rental payments, and affirmative relief which may include termination of the lease or an order directing the landlord to make reasonable repairs.

As set forth above, § 1-21-1203(b) requires a tenant who has a reasonable belief supported by evidence that the premises are not safe, sanitary and fit for habitation to advise the landlord in writing of the defective condition and the corrective action he wants the landlord to take. Section 1-21-1206(b) further provides that if the landlord does not respond to the first notice, the tenant may serve a second notice. If the landlord again fails to respond or disputes the claim, the tenant then may file a civil action in county or justice of the peace court under § 1-21-1206(c). Upon showing the landlord unreasonably refused or failed to use diligence to correct an unsafe condition, the tenant may recover costs, damages, including rental payments, and affirmative relief which may include termination of the lease or an order directing the landlord to make reasonable repairs.

[The defendant argued that this provision barred an action for personal injury that had not been preceded by notice and demand to repair.] Pursuant to the clear language of the act, there is no question the tenant is required to provide written notice to the landlord before he is entitled to the relief available under § 1-21-1206. . . .Therefore, for purposes of the remedies available under the Residential Rental Property Act [ed., repairs or return of rental], Ms. Pritchard was required to advise Ms. Jansma in writing of the condition of the step. Her failure to provide the notice required precludes any claim Ms. Merrill may have had to the relief available under the act.

Ms. Merrill, however, did not seek the relief available under the act. . . . Instead, Ms. Merrill sought personal injury damages, including medical expenses exceeding $25,000, pain and suffering, loss of enjoyment of life and lost earnings-damages clearly not contemplated by the Residential Rental Property Act and, in the case of her claims for emotional damages, expressly precluded by § 1-21-1203(e) of the act.

[T]he remedies provided in [the Act] are cumulative. . . .For example, the remedy of depositing rental payments with the clerk of court is grossly inadequate to compensate tenants for the types of [personal] injuries sustained in the present case. . . . An alternative remedy of termination of the lease is also not an adequate or viable option for many tenants when there is a lack of availability of other apartments and considering the costs involved in relocating. Thus, the new remedies given tenants in [the Act] are intended to be preventive and supplemental to other remedial measures. . . . [it] would be inconsistent with the duty to maintain imposed by the act to exempt from tort liability a landlord who fails in this duty. Our legislature by adopting the act has manifested acceptance of the policy reasons behind the URLTA and other statutes and judicial decisions imposing a duty on landlords. Maintaining the common law rule and its exceptions in personal injury cases, while imposing a new duty only in cases seeking repair, return of rent or termination of the lease, cannot be squared with that policy. It simply makes no sense to permit a tenant to withhold rent or terminate a lease because of a broken step while denying him a remedy for personal injuries sustained as a result of it. . . . We hold that the remedies provision of the act is exclusive to cases in which corrective action is sought and does not apply in personal injury actions. Therefore, Ms. Pritchard's failure to provide written notice of the broken step as required under § 1-21-1203(b) does not preclude Ms. Merrill's claim.

. . .

Reversed and remanded for further proceedings.

NOTES AND QUESTIONS

(1) The obligation of a landlord to tenants in residence on leased premises and other people there in the right of tenants was also tightly circumscribed in the common law. In general, the only duty was to warn of "traps," as previously defined. Although a current newcomer to the law might view this as an ideal place to apply the invitee status because of the economic benefit of the tenancy to the landlord, the common law rule derived from notions of property. Among the strongest held of these in the common law, and even today in many settings, was *caveat emptor* — let the buyer beware. Implicit in it is the assumption of an arms-length transaction between parties of equal bargaining power. The lessee could inspect before leasing and took the risk of defects that the landlord knew about and that a reasonable inspection would disclose.

As to common areas retained under the control of the landlord, such as parking lots and elevators, tenants and those present in their right are treated as invitees as to the landlord. Other people take on the status that is appropriate to the circumstances.

As *Dwyer* suggests, some courts now impose substantially heavier burdens upon landlords, even as to demised premises. Illustrative is *Mansur v. Eubanks*, 401 So. 2d 1328 (Fla. 1981), wherein the court imposed duties upon a landlord of residential property to make a reasonable inspection before leasing property, do necessary repairs to make the property reasonably safe and, further, make repairs after possession is turned over to the tenant once a dangerous defect is brought to the attention of the landlord. Other decisions imposing a duty of ordinary care upon landlords as to tenants include *Corrigan v. Janney*, 626 P.2d 841 (Mont. 1981), and *Trentacost v. Brussel*, 412 A.2d 447 (N.J. 1982). Change in this area often is brought about by a court's acknowledgment of a warranty of habitability. *See, e.g., Kline v. Burns*, 276 A.2d 248 (N.H. 1971). The status of the law varies widely between the common law and warranty extremes, requiring careful research in each jurisdiction of interest.

For a short time, California held that a residential landlord is strictly liable to a tenant as to defective conditions upon leased premises. *Becker v. IRM Corporation*, 698 P.2d 116 (Cal. 1985). This imposed a greater duty than *Dwyer* does because strict liability makes a landlord responsible for any defect, even those that a reasonable inspection would not discover. *Becker* was overruled by *Peterson v. Superior Court*, 899 P.2d 905 (Cal. En Banc 1995), leaving theories of negligence and implied warranty of habitability in place in that state. *See* 698 P.2d at 120.

At common law, the seller owed no duty to the buyer of real property in respect of the condition of the premises except to warn of traps. In some jurisdictions the law in this area is also in a state of transition much as described above. For example, *Smith v. Old Warson Development Company*, 479 S.W.2d 795 (Mo. Bank 1972), and *Gable v. Silver*, 264 So. 2d 418 (Fla. 1972), both held that builder-vendors of new homes owe first purchasers a warranty of habitability as to latent defects. *See also Lane v. Tenholm Building Co.*, 229 S.E.2d 728 (S.C. 1985) (providing warranty to first purchasers as to property losses.)

(2) Not every court, however, has been willing to abrogate the common law rules of *caveat emptor*. Consider the following excerpt from *Miles v. Shauntee*, 664 S.W.2d 512, 517–18 (Ky. 1984):

At early common law, a lease was considered a conveyance of an estate in land and was equivalent to a sale of the premises to the lessee for the term of the demise. The lessee, as a purchaser of the estate of land, was subjected to a strict common law property rule of caveat emptor. The lessee had the duty to inspect the property for defects and took the land as he S.W.2d 65 (Mo. App. 1973). There was no implied warranty by the lessor that the demised premises were habitable or fit for the purpose leased. A lessee wishing to protect himself as to the fitness of the premises had to exact an express covenant from the landlord for that purpose. *King, supra*, at 69.

Kentucky courts have followed other common law jurisdictions in applying the strict property rule of caveat emptor to leaseholds. As is often the case with strict rules, however, exceptions to concept of caveat emptor were created. In *Holzhauer v. Sheeny*, 127 Ky. 28, 104 S.W. 1034 (1907), the then Court of Appeals of Kentucky stated:

The rule of caveat emptor applies to a contract of letting. The tenant must take the premises as he may find them. There is no implied covenant on the part of the landlord that they are fit for the purpose for which they are rented, or that they are in particular condition; but there is extension of the rule: If the landlord knows that the premises are defective or dangerous, and such defect is not discoverable by the tenant by ordinary care and the landlord conceals or fails to disclose the dangerous condition, he is liable to the tenant, his family and servants, or even his guests, for injuries sustained therefrom. *Holzhauer v. Sheeny*, 104 S.W. at 1035.

This extension was carefully limited in application to cases where actual knowledge was brought home to the landlord. *Franklin v. Tracy*, 117 Ky. 267, 77 S.W. 1113 (1904).

Kentucky courts have also recognized exceptions to this general rule of law where a portion of the demised premises was retained by the lessor for the common use and benefit of a number of tenants, and where actions by the landlord constitutes a constructive eviction.

. . .

The general rule in effect in Kentucky is that a tenant takes premises as he finds them. *Whitehouse v. Lorch*, Ky., 347 S.W.2d 512 (1961). In the absence of a special agreement to do so, made when the contract is entered into, there is no obligation upon the landlord to repair the leased premises. *Horstman v. Newman*, Ky., 291 S.W.2d 567 (1956); *Mahan-Jellico Coal Company v. Dulling*, 282 Ky. 698, 139 S.W.2d 749 (1940).

Appellants argue that an implied warranty of habitability should arise from local housing or health codes absent an express provision in the contract of lease and absent such a provision in the ordinance or regulation in question. Absent an expression to the contrary such provisions do not create an implied warranty of habitability, or create a cause of action in the tenants. The remedies for violations are found within the codes, ordinances or regulations themselves. It is for the legislature to create rights and duties nonexistent under the common law.

Miller v. Cundiff, 245 S.W.3d 786 (Ky. App. 2007), distinguished *Merrill v. Jansma* and declined to hold that the Kentucky version of the URLTA created any remedies for personal injury beyond the specific remedies prescribed by the act. The Kentucky act authorized local ordinances, one of which was at issue, and did not apply URLTA provisions state wide. Should this make a difference?

See also Brooks v. *Colony Ltd.*, 1993 W.L. 339301 (Tenn. App. 1993), *Scott v. Missouri Investment Trust*, 753 S.W.2d 73 (Mo. App. 1988), *Richwind Joint Venture 4 v. Brunson*, 645 A.2d 1147 (Md. 1994), and *Young v. Morrisy*, 329 S.E.2d 426 (S.C. 1985), declining to apply warranties of habitability in residential tenancies.

[B]   Children

What, then, is it fair to require of an owner as against strangers? If they enter without his license, they are trespassers, however incompetent and wanting in judgment they may be. What then must he do to diminish his rights? Clearly, it is not enough that he puts something on his land which may attempt to allure a child or a fool . . . It must be something which by a general standard of understanding gives leave to enter.

Oliver Wendell Holmes, J., *Chenery v. Fitchburg Railroad*, 35 N.E. 554, 555 (Mass. 1893).

UNITED ZINC & CHEMICAL CO. v. BRITT
United States Supreme Court
258 U.S. 268, 42 S. Ct. 299, 66 L. Ed. 615 (1921)

MR. JUSTICE HOLMES delivered the opinion of the Court.

This is a suit brought by the respondents against the petitioner to recover for the death of two children, sons of the respondents. The facts that for the purposes of decision we shall assume to have been proved are these. The petitioner owned a tract of about twenty acres in the outskirts of the town of Iola, Kansas. Formerly it had there a plant for the making of sulphuric acid and zinc spelter. In 1910 it tore the buildings down but left a basement and cellar, in which in July, 1916, water was accumulated, clear in appearance but in fact dangerously poisoned by sulphuric acid and zinc sulphate that had come in one way or another from the petitioner's works, as the petitioner knew. The respondents had been travelling and encamped at some distance from this place. A travelled way passed within 120 or 100 feet of it. On July 27, 1916, the children, who were eight and eleven years old, came upon the petitioner's land, went into the water, were poisoned and died. The petitioner saved the question whether it could be held. At the trial the Judge instructed the jury that if the water looked clear but in fact was poisonous and thus the children were allured to it the petitioner was liable. The respondents got a verdict and judgment, which was affirmed by the Circuit Court of Appeals. 264 Fed. 785.

Union Pacific Ry. Co. v. McDonald, 152 U. S. 262, 14 Sup. Ct. 619, 38 L. Ed. 434, and kindred cases were relied upon as leading to the result, and perhaps there is language in that and in *Sioux City & Pacific Ry. Co. v. Stout*, 17 Wall. 657, 21 L. Ed. 745, that might seem to justify it; but the doctrine needs very careful statement not to make an unjust and impracticable requirement. If the children had been adults they would have had no case. They would have been trespassers and the owner of the land would have owed no duty to remove even hidden danger; it would have been entitled to assume that they would obey the law and not trespass. The liability for spring guns and mantraps arises from the fact that the defendant has not rested on that assumption, but on the contrary has expected the trespasser and prepared an injury that is no more justified than if he had held the gun and fired it. *Chenery v. Fitchburg R. R. Co.*, 160 Mass. 211, 213, 35 N. E. 554, 22 L. R. A. 575.

Infants have no greater right to go upon other people's land than adults, and the mere fact that they are infants imposes no duty upon landowners to expect them and to prepare for their safety. On the other hand the duty of one who invites another upon his land not to lead him into a trap is well settled, and while it is very plain that temptation is not invitation, it may be held that knowingly to establish and expose, unfenced, to children of an age when they follow a bait as mechanically as a fish, something that is certain to attract them, has the legal effect of an invitation to them although not to an adult. But the principle if accepted must be very cautiously applied.

In *Railroad Co. v. Stout*, 21 L. Ed. 745, 17 Wall. 657, the well-known case of a boy injured on a turntable, it appeared that children had played there before to the knowledge of employees of the railroad, and in view of that fact and the situation of the turntable near a road without visible separation, it seems to have been assumed without much discussion that the railroad owed a duty to the boy. Perhaps this was as strong a case as would be likely to occur of maintaining a known temptation, where temptation takes the place of invitation. A license was implied and liability for a danger not manifest to a child was declared in the very similar case of *Cooke v. Midland Great Western Ry. of Ireland* [1909], A. C. 229.

In the case at bar it is. at least doubtful whether the water could be seen from any place where the children lawfully were and there is no evidence that it was what led them to enter the land. But that is necessary to start the supposed duty. There can be no general duty on the part of the landowner to keep his land safe for children, or even free from hidden dangers, if he has not directly or by implication invited or licensed them to come there. The difficulties in the way of implying a license are adverted to in *Chenery v. Fitchburg R. R. Co.*, 160 Mass. 211, 212, 35 N. E. 554, 22 L. R. A. 575, but need not be considered here. It does not appear that children were in the habit of going to the place; so that foundation also fails.

Union Pacific Ry. Co. v. McDonald, 152 U.S. 262, 14 Sup. Ct. 619, 38 L. Ed. 434, is less in point. There a boy was burned by falling into burning coal slack close by the side of a path on which he was running homeward from other boys who had frightened him. It hardly appears that he was a trespasser and the path suggests an invitation; at all events boys habitually resorted to the place where he was. Also the defendant was under a statutory duty to fence the place sufficiently to keep out cattle. The decision is very far from establishing that the petitioner is liable for poisoned water not bordering a road, not shown to have been the inducement that led the children to trespass, if in any event the law would deem it sufficient to excuse their going there, and not shown to have been the indirect inducement because known to the children to be frequented by others. It is suggested that the roads across the place were invitations. A road is not an invitation to leave it elsewhere than at its end.

Judgment reversed.

Mr. Justice Clarke, dissenting.

The courts of our country have sharply divided as to the principles of law applicable to "attractive nuisance" cases, of which this one is typical.

At the head of one group, from 1873 until the decision of to-day, has stood the Supreme Court of the United States, applying what has been designated as the "humane" doctrine. Quite distinctly the courts of Massachusetts have stood at the head of the other group, applying what has been designated as a "hard doctrine" — the "Draconian doctrine." Thompson on Negligence, vol. 1, §§ 1027 to 1054, inclusive, especially sections 1027, 1047 and 1048. Cooley on Torts (3d Ed.) p. 1269 et seq.

In 1873, in *Railroad Co. v. Stout*, 21 L. Ed. 745, 17 Wall. 657, this court, in a turntable case, in a unanimous decision, strongly approved the doctrine that he who places upon his land, where chidren of tender years are likely to go, a construction or agency, in its nature attractive, and therefore a temptation, to such children, is culpably negligent if he does not take reasonable care to keep them away, or to see that such dangerous thing is so guarded that they will not be injured by it when following the instincts and impulses of childhood, of which all mankind has notice. The court also held that where the facts are such that different minds may honestly draw different conclusions from them, the case should go to the jury.

. . .

This pool is indefinitely located within a tract of land about 1,000 feet wide by 1,200 feet long, about which there had not been any fence whatever for many years, and there was no sign or warning of any kind indicating the dangerous character of the water in the pool. There were several paths across the lot, a highway ran within 100 to 120 feet of the pool, and a railway track was not far away. The land was immediately adjacent to a city of about 10,000 inhabitants, with dwelling houses not far distant from it. The testimony shows that not only the two boys who perished had been attracted to the pool at the time, but that there were two or three other children with them, whose cries attracted men who were passing near by, who, by getting into the water, succeeded in recovering the dead body of one child and in rescuing the other in such condition that, after lingering for a day or two, he died. The evidence shows that the water in the pool was highly impregnated with sulphuric acid and zinc sulphate, which certainly caused the death of the children, and that the men who rescued the boys suffered seriously, one of them for as much as two weeks, from the effects of the poisoned water.

The case was given to the jury in a clear and comprehensive charge, and the judgment of the District Court upon the verdict was affirmed by the Circuit Court of Appeals. The court charged the jury that if the water in the pool was not poisonous and if the boys were simply drowned there could be no recovery, but that if it was found, that the defendant knew or in the exercise of ordinary care should have known that the water was impregnated with poison, that children were likely to go to its vicinity, that it was in appearance clear and pure and attractive to young children as a place for bathing, and that the death of the children was caused by its alluring appearance and by its poisonous character, and because no protection or warning was given against it, the case came within the principle of the "attractive nuisance" or "turntable" cases and recovery would be allowed.

This was as favorable a view of the federal law, as it has been until today, as the petitioner deserved. The Supreme Court of Illinois, on the authority of the *Stout* Case, held a city liable for the death of a child drowned in a similar pool of water not poisoned. *City of Pekin v. McMahon*, 154 Ill. 141, 39 N. E. 484, 45 Am. St. Rep. 114, 27 L. R. A. 206.

The facts, as stated, make it very clear that in the view most unfavorable to the plaintiffs below there might be a difference of opinion between candid men as to whether the pool was so located that the owners of the land should have anticipated that children might frequent its vicinity, whether its appearance and character rendered it attractive to childish instincts so as to make it a temptation to children of tender years, and whether, therefore, it was culpable negligence to maintain it in that location, unprotected and without warning as to its poisonous condition. This being true, the case would seem to be one clearly for a jury, under the ruling in the *Stout* Case, *supra*.

Believing as I do that the doctrine of the *Stout* and *McDonald* Cases, giving weight to, and making allowance, as they do, for, the instincts and habitual conduct of children of tender years, is a sound doctrine, calculated to make men more reasonably considerate of the safety of the children of their neighbors, than will the harsh rule which makes trespassers of little children which the court is now substituting for it, I cannot share in setting aside the verdict of the jury in this case, approved by the judgments of two courts, upon what is plainly a disputed question of fact and in thereby overruling two decisions which have been accepted as leading authorities for half a century, and I therefore dissent from the judgment and opinion of the court.

The CHIEF JUSTICE and MR. JUSTICE DAY concur in this opinion.

————————

Restatement, Torts, Second[20]

§ 339 Artificial Conditions Highly Dangerous to Trespassing Children

A possessor of land is subject to liability for physical harm to children trespassing thereon caused by an artificial condition upon the land if

(a) the place where the condition exists is one upon which the possessor knows or has reason to know that children are likely to trespass, and

(b) the condition is one of which the possessor knows or has reason to know and which he realizes or should realize will involve an unreasonable risk of death or serious bodily harm to such children, and

————————

[20] Copyright 1965 by The American Law Institute. Reprinted with the permission of The American Law Institute.

(c) the children because of their youth do not discover the condition or realize the risk involved in intermeddling with it or in coming within the area made dangerous by it, and

(d) the utility to the possessor of maintaining the condition and the burden of eliminating the danger are slight as compared with the risk to children involved, and

(e) the possessor fails to exercise reasonable care to eliminate the danger or otherwise to protect the children.

Caveat:

The Institute expresses no opinion as to whether the rule stated in this Section may not apply to natural conditions of the land.

Comment:

a. This Section is concerned only with conditions on the land, and not with activities of the possessor. As to liability to children for such activities, see §§ 333, 334, and 336. A "condition," however, includes controllable forces already in operation, as in the case of machinery in motion. (Cf. § 338.)

b. The rule stated in this Section is now accepted by the great majority of the American courts. It is still rejected in seven or eight jurisdictions, in all of which, however, liability to the trespassing child may be found under various special circumstances. The rule originated in 1873 in *Sioux City & Pacific R. Co. v. Stout*, 84 U.S. (17 Wall.) 657, 21 L. Ed. 745 (1873), where a child was injured while playing with a railroad turntable. From that case, and others like it, the rule acquired the name of the "turntable doctrine." An early Minnesota decision, *Keffe v. Milwaukee & St. Paul R. Co.*, 21 Minn. 207, 18 Am. Rep 393 (1875), supplied the theory that the child had been allured or enticed onto the premises by the condition created by the defendant, so that the defendant was himself responsible for the trespass, and could not set it up against the child. From this theory the rule also acquired the misnomer of "attractive nuisance," by which it is still known in many courts.

c. Children. In the great majority of the cases in which the rule here stated has been applied, the plaintiff has been a child of not more than twelve years of age. . . .

A few courts have attempted to state arbitrary age limits, setting a maximum age of fourteen for the possible application of the rule. . . .

d. Conditions upon the land. The rule stated in this Section is limited to structures or other artificial conditions upon the land. . . .

NOTES AND QUESTIONS

(1)   As the Comments to Restatement, Torts, Second, § 339 *supra*, state, the *Britt* case stands for a slight liberalization of the so-called "draconian rule" applied to child trespassers in *Chenery* and other cases. How great is the liberalization?

(2)　Although most American courts now follow § 339, some still adhere to some version of this "attractive nuisance" doctrine, and at least one American jurisdiction adheres in form to the "draconian rule" of *Chenery*. *See Macke Laundry Service Co. v. Weber*, 298 A.2d 27 (Md. 1972). Even in *Weber*, however, a child trespasser, in fact, was permitted to recover by the sleight-of-hand of labeling him an invitee for the purposes of the litigation. Among the many opinions that apply § 339 are *Rosenair v. City of Estherville*, 199 N.W.2d 125 (Iowa 1972), and *Thunder Hawk v. Union Pacific Railroad Company*, 844 P.2d 1045 (Wyo. 1992).

(3)　Suppose a child were to attempt to use the "attractive nuisance" doctrine as a shield rather than as a sword? In *Insurance Company of North America v. Cuevas*, 199 N.W.2d 681 (Mich. 1972), a child trespasser caused substantial damage to the owner's property. When sued, the child sought to defend on grounds that the fault was that of the owner himself because the child had been attracted onto the property. To that the Michigan Supreme Court replied, at 684:

> We hold that the doctrine of attractive nuisance will excuse young children for trespassing on the land that contains the attractive nuisance, but will not excuse their negligence.

(4)　Of the courts that have liberalized the child trespasser rule without adopting § 339, some require that the child be attracted onto the defendant's property by the thing of danger and others do not. *Cf. Johnson v. Bathey*, 376 So. 2d 848 (Fla. 1979), and *Moore v. Tuscon Electric Power Company*, 761 P.2d 1091 (Ariz. App. 1988), for the first point, and *Rosario v. City of Lansing*, 268 N.W.2d 230 (Mich. 1978), for the second.

(5)　The Judicial Committee of the House of Lords took a child trespasser case as a vehicle to recede from the view that no duty of care is owed trespassers. Still, the standard is not ordinary care, as in *Rowland v. Christian*, but is more limited as indicated by these excerpts from Lord Diplock's judgment in *British Railways Board v. Herrington*, [1973] App. Cas. 877 (H.L.):

> **First:** The duty does not arise until the occupier has actual knowledge either of the presence of the trespasser upon his land or of facts which make it likely that the trespasser will come on to his land; and has also actual knowledge of facts as to the condition of his land or of activities carried out upon it which are likely to cause personal injury to a trespasser who is unaware of the danger. He is under no duty to the trespasser to make any inquiry or inspection to ascertain whether or not such facts do exist. His liability does not arise until he actually knows of them.

> **Secondly:** Once the occupier has actual knowledge of such facts, his own failure to appreciate the likelihood of the trespasser's presence or the risk to him involved, does not absolve the occupier from his duty to the trespasser if a reasonable man possessed of the actual knowledge of the occupier would recognise that likelihood and that risk.

> **Thirdly:** The duty when it arises is limited to taking reasonable steps to enable the trespasser to avoid the danger. Where the likely trespasser is a child too young to understand or heed a written or a previous oral warning, this may involve providing reasonable physical obstacles to keep the child away from the danger.

Fourthly: The relevant likelihood to be considered is of the trespasser's presence at the actual time and place of danger to him. The degree of likelihood needed to give rise to the duty cannot, I think, be more closely defined than as being such as would impel a man of ordinary humane feelings to take some steps to mitigate the risk of injury to the trespasser to which the particular danger exposes him. It will thus depend on all the circumstances of the case: the permanent or intermittent character of the danger; the severity of the injuries which it is likely to cause; in the case of children, the attractiveness to them of that which constitutes the dangerous object or condition of the land; the expense involved in giving effective warning of it to the kind of trespasser likely to be injured, in relation to the occupier's resources in money or in labour.

---

§ 5.05   ECONOMIC HARM

[A]   Negligent Misrepresentation

ULTRAMARES v. TOUCHE, NIVEN & CO.
New York Court of Appeals
255 N.Y. 170, 174 N.E. 441 (1931)

CARDOZO, C. J.

The action is in tort for damages suffered through the misrepresentations of accountants, the first cause of action being for misrepresentations that were merely negligent, and the second for misrepresentations charged to have been fraudulent.

In January, 1924, the defendants, a firm of public accountants, were employed by Fred Stern & Co. Inc., to prepare and certify a balance sheet exhibiting the condition of its business as of December 31, 1923. They had been employed at the end of each of the three years preceding to render a like service. Fred Stern & Co., Inc., which was in substance Stern himself, was engaged in the importation and sale of rubber. To finance its operations, it required extensive credit and borrowed large sums of money from banks and other lenders. All this was known to the defendants. The defendants knew also that in the usual course of business the balance sheet when certified would be exhibited by the Stern Company to banks, creditors, stockholders, purchasers, or sellers, according to the needs of the occasion, as the basis of financial dealings. Accordingly, when the balance sheet was made up, the defendants supplied the Stern Company with thirty-two copies certified with serial numbers as counterpart originals. Nothing was said to the persons to whom these counterparts would be shown or the extent or number of the transactions in which they would be used. In particular there was no mention of the plaintiff, a corporation doing business chiefly as a factor, which till then had never made advances to the Stern Company, though it had sold merchandise in small amounts. The range of the transactions in which a certificate of audit might be expected to play a part was as indefinite and wide as the possibilities of the business that was mirrored in the summary.

By February 26, 1924, the audit was finished and the balance sheet made up. It stated assets in the sum of $2,550,671.88 and liabilities other than capital and surplus in the sum of $1,479,956.62, thus showing a net worth of $1,070,715.26. Attached to the balance sheet was a certificate as follows:

"Touche, Niven & Co.

"Public Accountants

"Eighty Maiden Lane

"New York

"February 26, 1924.

"Certificate of Auditors

"We have examined the accounts of Fred Stern & Co., Inc., for the year ending December 31, 1923, and hereby certify that the annexed balance sheet is in accordance therewith and with the information and explanations given us. We further certify that, subject to provision for federal taxes on income, the said statement, in our opinion, presents a true and correct view of the financial condition of Fred Stern & Co., Inc., as at December 31, 1923.

"Touche, Niven & Co.,

"Public Accountants."

Capital and surplus were intact if the balance sheet was accurate. In reality both had been wiped out, and the corporation was insolvent. The books had been falsified by those in charge of the business so as to set forth accounts receivable and other assets which turned out to be fictitious. The plaintiff maintains that the certificate of audit was erroneous in both its branches.

The first branch, the asserted correspondence between the accounts and the balance sheet, is onepurporting to be made as of the knowledge of the auditors. The second branch, which certifies to a belief that the condition reflected in the balance sheet presents a true and correct picture of the resources of the business, is stated as a matter of opinion. In the view of the plaintiff, both branches of the certificate are either fraudulent or negligent. As to one class of assets, the item of accounts receivable, if not also as to others, there was no real correspondence, we are told, between balance sheet and books, or so the triers of the facts might find. If correspondence, however, be assumed, a closer examination of supporting invoices and records, or a fuller inquiry directed to the persons appearing on the books as creditors or debtors, would have exhibited the truth.

The plaintiff, a corporation engaged in business as a factor, was approached by Stern in March, 1924, with a request for loans of money to finance the sales of rubber. Up to that time the dealings between the two houses were on a cash basis and trifling in amount. As a condition of any loans the plaintiff insisted that it receive a balance sheet certified by public accountants, and in response to that demand it was given one of the certificates signed by the defendants and then in Stern's possession. On the faith of that certificate the plaintiff made a loan which was followed by many others. The course of business was for Stern to deliver to the plaintiff documents described as trust receipts which in effect were executory assignments of the moneys payable by purchasers for goods thereafter to be sold.

When the purchase price was due, the plaintiff received the payment, reimbursing itself therefrom for its advances and commissions. Some of these transactions were effected without loss. Nearly a year later, in December, 1924, the house of cards collapsed. In that month, plaintiff made three loans to the Stern Company, one of $100,000, a second of $25,000, and a third of $40,000. For some of these loans no security was received. For some of the earlier loans the security was inadequate. On January 2, 1925, the Stern Company was declared a bankrupt.

This action, brought against the accountants in November, 1926, to recover the loss suffered by the plaintiff in reliance upon the audit, was in its inception one for negligence. On the trial there was added a second cause of action asserting fraud also. The trial judge dismissed the second cause of action without submitting it to the jury. As to the first cause of action, he reserved his decision on the defendants' motion to dismiss, and took the jury's verdict. They were told that the defendants might be held liable if with knowledge that the results of the audit would be communicated to creditors they did the work negligently, and that negligence was the omission to use reasonable and ordinary care. The verdict was in favor of the plaintiff for $187,576.32. On the coming in of the verdict, the judge granted the reserved motion. The Appellate Division (229 App. Div. 581, 243 N.Y.S. 179) affirmed the dismissal of the cause of action for fraud, but reversed the dismissal of the cause of action for negligence, and reinstated the verdict. The case is here on cross-appeals.

The two causes of action will be considered in succession, first the one for negligence and second that for fraud.

1. We think the evidence supports a finding that the audit was negligently made, though in so saying we put aside for the moment the question whether negligence, even if it existed, was a wrong to the plaintiff. To explain fully or adequately how the defendants were at fault would carry this opinion beyond reasonable bounds. A sketch, however, there must be, at least in respect of some features of the audit, for the nature of fault, when understood, is helpful in defining the ambit of the duty.

We begin with the item of accounts receivable. . . .

[Reviewing the evidence, Cardozo concluded that "a mere glance" by the auditor would have revealed some of the discrepancies in the accounts.]

If the defendants owed a duty to the plaintiff to act with the same care that would have been due under a contract of employment, a jury was at liberty to find a verdict of negligence upon a showing of a scrutiny so imperfect and perfunctory. No doubt the extent to which inquiry must be pressed beyond appearances is a question of judgment, as to which opinions will often differ.

No doubt the wisdom that is born after the event will engender suspicion and distrust when old acquaintance and good repute may have silenced doubt at the beginning. All this is to be weighed by a jury in applying its standard of behavior, the state of mind, and conduct of the reasonable man. Even so, the adverse verdict, when rendered, imports an alignment of the weights in their proper places in the balance and a reckoning thereafter. The reckoning was not wrong upon the evidence before us, if duty be assumed.

We are brought to the question of duty, its origin and measure.

The defendants owed to their employer a duty imposed by law to make their certificate without fraud, and a duty growing out of contract to make it with the care and caution proper to their calling. Fraud includes the pretense of knowledge when knowledge there is none. To creditors and investors to whom the employer exhibited the certificate, the defendants owed a like duty to make it without fraud, since there was notice in the circumstances of its making that the employer did not intend to keep it to himself. *Eaton, Cole & Burnham Co. v. Avery*, 83 N. Y. 31, 38 Am. Rep. 389; *Tindle v. Birkett*, 171 N. Y. 520, 64 N. E. 210, 89 Am. St. Rep. 822. A different question develops when we ask whether they owed a duty to these to make it without negligence. If liability for negligence exists, a thoughtless slip or blunder, the failure to detect a theft or forgery beneath the cover of deceptive entries, may expose accountants to a liability in an indeterminate amount for an indeterminate time to an indeterminate class. The hazards of a business conducted on these terms are so extreme as to enkindle doubt whether a flaw may not exist in the implication of a duty that exposes to these consequences. . . .

. . .

Three cases in this court are said by the plaintiff to have committed us to the doctrine that words, written or oral, if negligently published with the expectation that the reader or listener will transmit them to another, will lay a basis for liability though privity be lacking. These are *Glanzer v. Shepard*, 233 N. Y. 236, 238, 135 N. E. 275, 23 A. L. R. 1425; *International Products Co. v. Erie R. R. Co.*, 244 N. Y. 331, 155 N. E. 662, 56 A. L. R. 1377, and *Doyle v. Chatham & Phenix Nat. Bank*, 253 N. Y. 369, 171 N. E. 574.

In *Glanzer v. Shepard*, the seller of beans requested the defendants, public weighers, to make return of the weight and furnish the buyer with a copy. This the defendants did. Their return, which was made out in duplicate, one copy to the seller and the other to the buyer, recites that it was made by order of the former for the use of the latter. The buyer paid the seller on the faith of the certificate which turned out to be erroneous. We held that the weighers were liable at the suit of the buyer for the moneys overpaid. Here was something more than the rendition of a service in the expectation that the one who ordered the certificate would use it thereafter in the operations of his business as occasion might require. Here was a case where the transmission of the certificate to another was not merely one possibility among many, but the "end and aim of the transaction," as certain and immediate and deliberately willed as if a husband were to order a gown to be delivered to his wife, or a telegraph company, contracting with the sender of a message, were to telegraph it wrongly to the damage of the person expected to receive it. . . . The bond was so close as to approach that of privity, if not completely one with it.

Not so in the case at hand. No one would be likely to urge that there was a contractual relation, or even one approaching it, at the root of any duty that was owing from the defendants now before us to the indeterminate class of persons who, presently or in the future, might deal with the Stern Company in reliance on the audit. In a word, the service rendered by the defendant in *Glanzer v. Shepard* was primarily for the information of a third person, in effect, if not in name, a party to the contract, and only incidentally for that of the formal promisee. In the case at hand, the service was primarily for the benefit of the Stern Company, a convenient instrumentality for use in the development of the business, and only incidentally or collaterally for the use of those to whom Stern and his associates might exhibit it thereafter. Foresight of these possibilities may charge with liability for fraud. The conclusion does not follow that it will charge with liability for negligence.

In the next of the three cases (*International Products Co. v. Erie R. R. Co., supra*) the plaintiff, an importer, had an agreement with the defendant, a railroad company, that the latter would act as bailee of goods arriving from abroad. The importer, to protect the goods by suitable insurance, made inquiry of the bailee as to the location of the storage. The warehouse was incorrectly named, and the policy did not attach. Here was a determinate relation, that of bailor and bailee, either present or prospective, with peculiar opportunity for knowledge on the part of the bailee as to the subject-matter of the statement and with a continuing duty to correct it if erroneous. Even the narrowest holdings as to liability for unintentional misstatement concede that a representation in such circumstances may be equivalent to a warranty. . . .

In one respect the decision in *International Products Co. v. Erie R. R. Co.* is in advance of anything decided in *Glanzer v. Shepard.* The latter case suggests that the liability there enforced was not one for the mere utterance of words without due consideration, but for a negligent service, the act of weighing, which happened to find in the words of the certificate its culmination and its summary. This was said in the endeavor to emphasize the character of the certificate as a business transaction, an act in the law, and not a mere casual response to a request for information.

The ruling in the case of the Erie Railroad shows that the rendition of a service is at most a mere circumstance and not an indispensable condition. The Erie was not held for negligence in the rendition of a service. It was held for words and nothing more. So in the case at hand. If liability for the consequences of a negligent certificate may be enforced by any member of an indeterminate class of creditors, present and prospective, known and unknown, the existence or non-existence of a preliminary act of service will not affect the cause of action. The service may have been rendered as carefully as you please, and its quality will count for nothing if there was negligence thereafter in distributing the summary.

Doyle v. Chatham & Phenix Nat. Bank, supra, the third of the cases cited, is even more plainly indecisive. A trust company was a trustee under a deed of trust to secure an issue of bonds. It was held liable to a subscriber for the bonds when it certified them falsely. A representation by a trustee intended to sway action had been addressed to a person who by the act of subscription was to become a party to the deed and a cestui que trust.

The antidote to these decisions and to the overuse of the doctrine of liability for negligent misstatement may be found in *Jaillet v. Cashman*, 235 N. Y. 511, 139 N. E. 714, and *Courteen Seed Co. v. Hong Kong & Shanghai Banking Corporation*, 245 N. Y. 377, 381, 157 N. E. 272, 273, 56 A.L.R. 1186. In the first of these cases the defendant supplying ticker service to brokers was held not liable in damages to one of the broker's customers for the consequences of reliance upon a report negligently published on the ticker. If liability had been upheld, the step would have been a short one to the declaration of a like liability on the part of proprietors of newspapers. In the second the principle was clearly stated by Pound, J., that "negligent words are not actionable unless they are uttered directly, with knowledge or notice that they will be acted on, to one to whom the speaker is bound by some relation of duty, arising out of public calling, contract or otherwise, to act with care if he acts at all."

From the foregoing analysis the conclusion is, we think, inevitable that nothing in our previous decisions commits us to a holding of liability for negligence in the circumstances of the case at hand, and that such liability, if recognized, will be an extension of the principle of those decisions to different conditions, even if more or less analogous. The question then is whether such an extension shall be made.

The extension, if made, will so expand the field of liability for negligent speech as to make it nearly, if not quite, coterminous with that of liability for fraud. Again and again, in decisions of this court, the bounds of this latter liability have been set up, with futility the fate of every endeavor to dislodge them. Scienter has been declared to be an indispensable element, except where the representation has been put forward as true of one's own knowledge (*Hadcock v. Osmer*, 153 N. Y. 604, 47 N. E. 923), or in circumstances where the expression of opinion was a dishonorable pretense. Even an opinion, especially an opinion by an expert, may be found to be fraudulent if the grounds supporting it are so flimsy as to lead to the conclusion that there was no genuine belief back of it. Further than that this court has never gone.
. . .

If this action is well conceived, all these principles and distinctions, so nicely wrought and formulated, have been a waste of time and effort. They have even been a snare, entrapping litigants and lawyers into an abandonment of the true remedy lying ready to the call. The suitors thrown out of court because they proved negligence, and nothing else, in an action for deceit, might have ridden to triumphant victory if they had proved the self-same facts, but had given the wrong another label, and all this in a state where forms of action have been abolished. So to hold is near to saying that we have been paltering with justice. A word of caution or suggestion would have set the erring suitor right. Many pages of opinion were written by judges the most eminent, yet the word was never spoken. We may not speak it now. A change so revolutionary, if expedient, must be wrought by legislation. *Landell v. Lybrand*, 264 Pa. 406, 107 A. 783, 8 A.L.R. 461.

We have said that the duty to refrain from negligent representation would become coincident or nearly so with the duty to refrain from fraud if this action could be maintained. A representation, even though knowingly false, does not constitute ground for an action of deceit unless made with the intent to be communicated to the persons or class of persons who act upon it to their prejudice. *Eaton, Cole & Burnham Co. v. Avery, supra.* Affirmance of this judgment would require us to hold that all or nearly all the persons so situated would suffer an impairment of an interest legally protected if the representation had been negligent. We speak of all "or nearly all," for cases can be imagined where a casual response, made in circumstances insufficient to indicate that care should be expected, would permit recovery for fraud if willfully deceitful. Cases of fraud between persons so circumstanced are, however, too infrequent and exceptional to make the radii greatly different if the fields of liability for negligence and deceit be figured as concentric circles. The like may be said of the possibility that the negligence of the injured party, contributing to the result, may avail to overcome the one remedy, though unavailing to defeat the other. Neither of these possibilities is noted by the plaintiff in its answer to the suggestion that the two fields would be coincident. Its answer has been merely this, first, that the duty to speak with care does not arise unless the words are the culmination of a service, and, second, that it does not arise unless the service is rendered in the pursuit of an independent calling, characterized as public. As to the first of these suggestions, we have already had occasion to observe that given a relation making diligence a duty, speech as well as conduct must conform to that exacting standard. *International Products Co. v. Erie R. R. Co., supra.* As to the second of the two suggestions, public accountants are public only in the sense that their services are offered to any one who chooses to employ them. This is far from saying that those who do not employ them are in the same position as those who do.

Liability for negligence if adjudged in this case will extend to many callings other than an auditor's. Lawyers who certify their opinion as to the validity of municipal or corporate bonds, with knowledge that the opinion will be brought to the notice of the public, will become liable to the investors, if they have overlooked a statute or a decision, to the same extent as if the controversy were one between client and adviser. Title companies insuring titles to a tract of land, with knowledge that at an approaching auction the fact that they have insured will be stated to the bidders, will become liable to purchasers who may wish the benefit of a policy without payment of a premium. These illustrations may seem to be extreme, but they go little, if any, farther than we are invited to go now. Negligence, moreover, will have one standard when viewed in relation to the employer, and another and at times a stricter standard when viewed in relation to the public. Explanations that might seem plausible, omissions that might be reasonable, if the duty is confined to the employer, conducting a business that presumably at least is not a fraud upon his creditors, might wear another aspect if an independent duty to be suspicious even of one's principal is owing to investors. "Every one making a promise having the quality of a contract will be under a duty to the promisee by virtue of the promise, but under another duty, apart from contract, to an indefinite number of potential beneficiaries when performance has begun. The assumption of one relation will mean the involuntary assumption of a series of new relations, inescapably hooked together" *Moch Co. v. Rensselaer Water Co., supra,* at page 168 of 247 N. Y., 159 N. E. 896, 899. "The law does not spread its protection so far" *Robins Dry Dock & Repair Co. v. Flint, supra,* at page 309 of 275 U. S., 48 S. Ct. 134, 135.

Our holding does not emancipate accountants from the consequences of fraud. It does not relieve them if their audit has been so negligent as to justify a finding that they had no genuine belief in its adequacy, for this again is fraud. It does no more than say that, if less than this is proved, if there has been neither reckless misstatement nor insincere profession of an opinion, but only honest blunder, the ensuing liability for negligence is one that is bounded by the contract, and is to be enforced between the parties by whom the contract has been made. We doubt whether the average business man receiving a certificate without paying for it, and receiving it merely as one among a multitude of possible investors, would look for anything more.

. . .

[The court of appeals reversed the appellate division's decision on the negligence action, thus reinstating the trial court's order that granted the defendant's motion for directed verdict and dismissal of that count. Hence, the plaintiff's claim for negligent misrepresentation failed. The court of appeal also held that the trial court and appellate division erred to dismiss the plaintiff's action based upon a theory of intentional misrepresentation and reversed for a new trial on that count. This issue is examined in Chapter 12 of this text.]

Judgment accordingly.

NOTES AND QUESTIONS

(1)   The no-duty rule for negligent misrepresentation is usually attributed to *Derry v. Peek*, [L.R.] 14 A.C. 337, but as noted by Lord Hodson in his speech in *Hedley Bryne & Co. v. Heller & Co.*, note 3, *infra*, to read *Derry v. Peek* for that proposition is an exaggeration. What *Derry v. Peek* actually did was to expand the meaning of fraud beyond occasions when the defendant knew he was lying to encompass also occasions when the defendant knew that he did not know whether he was lying or telling the truth. It is perhaps perverse that a case that actually expanded the scope of liability for false words became a precedent for totally forbidding actions for mere negligence, but that was the effect given it by the courts, both in England and in the United States. Judge Cardozo found plenty of policy reasons to stick with the rule in *Ultramares*.

(2)   In *Ultramares* Judge Cardozo also canvassed the few exceptions that had been acknowledged up to the time it was decided. What were they? He also recounted the "absurd" consequences that would flow from extending the duty of care owed by providers of professional services, such as accountants, appraisers, architects, engineers, lawyers, surveyors, title examiners and the like, to their clients (*i.e.*, those in privity of contract with them), such as the plaintiff in *Ultramares*. When should such a duty be created?

A very large numbers of cases have grappled with this issue in a myriad of settings and most of them refer to *Ultramares* and the no-duty to duty spectrum created by the factual distinctions stretching between *Ultramares* on the no-duty end and *Glanzer v. Sheppard* on the duty end. *See, e.g., Leyba v. Whitley*, 907 P.2d 172 (N.M. 1995) (lawyer owed duty to potential beneficiary of wrongful death suit); *St. Paul Fire & Marine Insurance Company v. Touche Ross Company*, 507 N.W.2d 275 (Neb. 1993) (accountant owned duty to third party to whom it personally delivered a negligently prepared statement as to the financial status of its client); *Barrier v. V.P. Exterminators, Inc.*, 625 So. 2d 1007 (La. 1993) (termite inspector hired by seller of home to conduct pre-sale termite inspection of house owned duty of care to purchaser who relied upon it); *Bily v. Arthur Young & Company*, 834 P.2d 745 (Cal. En Bank 1992) (independent auditor of corporation that made public offering of stock owed no duty of care to general public investors in preparing audit); *Bethelehem Steel Corporation v. Ernst & Whinney*, 822 S.W.2d 592 (Tenn. 1991) (adopts principles of Restatement of Torts Second, section 552 to govern liability of accountants to third parties); *Boykin v. Arthur Andersen & Company*, 639 So. 2d 504 (Ala. 1994) (same); and *A.R. Moyer v. Graham*, 285 So. 2d 397 (Fla. 1973) (supervising architect hired by owner of building under construction owes duty of care to general contractor who wins bid to construct the building).

The *Ultramares* rule as applied in New York is frequently referred to as a "near privity approach."

By contrast, the approach specified in Restatement of Torts Second, section 552, as follows, is referred to as an intermediate approach:

> (1) One who, in the course of his business, profession or employment, or in any other transaction in which he has a pecuniary interest, supplies false information for the guidance of others in their business transactions, is

subject to liability for pecuniary loss caused to them by their justifiable reliance upon the information, if he fails to exercise reasonable care or competence in obtaining or communicating the information.

(2) Except as stated in Subsection (3), the liability stated in Subsection (1) is limited to loss suffered

(a) by the person or one of a limited group of persons for whose benefit and guidance he intends to supply the information or knows that the recipient intends to supply it; and

(b) through reliance upon it in a transaction that he intends the information to influence or knows that the recipient so intends or in a substantially similar transaction.

(3) The liability of one who is under a public duty to give the information extends to loss suffered by any of the class of persons whose benefit the duty is created, in any of the transactions in which it is intended to protect them.

Quoted, *First National Bank of Bluefield v. Crawford*, 386 S.E.2d 310, 313 (W.Va. 1989) (for application to accountants). How different from *Ultramares* is this rule? *Gilcrest Timber Company v. ITT Rayonier, Inc.*, 696 So.2d 334 (Fla. 1997) explicitly adopted R552 as the rule of the decision and also applied contributory negligence as a defense.

The most liberal rule of duty in this field is the rule of general foreseeability adopted in *Citizen State Bank v. Timm, Schmidt & Co.*, 335 N.W.2d 361, 366 (Wis. 1983)as follows:

We conclude that accountants' liability to third parties should be determined under the accepted principles of Wisconsin negligence law. According to these principles, a finding of non-liability will be made only if there is a strong public policy requiring such a finding.

Very few courts have adopted the Wisconsin approach, *see, e.g., Touche Ross & Co. v. Commercial Union Ins. Co.*, 514 So. 2d 315 (Miss. 1987), and *H. Rosenbaum, Inc. v. Adler*, 461 A.2d 138 (N.J. 1983), and Wisconsin itself rejects it as applied to the duty owed by lawyers to non-clients. As stated in *Hap's Aerial Enterprises, Inc. v. General Aviation Corporation*, 496 N.W.2d 680, 683, n.6 (Wis. 1992):

The fundamental principle of Wisconsin negligence law does not apply to the liability of attorneys to non-clients. An attorney is not liable to a non-client plaintiff for mere negligence. *Green Spring Farms v. Kersten*, 136 Wis. 2d 304, 307, 401 N.W.2d 816, 817 (1987). An exception-to-the-exception exists. The attorney who draws a will is liable to the intended beneficiary who received nothing by reason of the attorney's negligence. *Auric v. Continental Casualty Co.*, 111 Wis. 2d 507, 509, 331 N.W.2d 325, 327 (1983).

What policies justify holding lawyers to a lesser scope of duty to third parties than the duty other professional service providers must satisfy?

(3)   *Hedley Bryne & Co. v. Heller & Co.*, [1941] App. Cas. 465 [H.L.], which is the English counterpart to *Ultramares*, is perhaps the most well-known English torts case since *Donoghue v. Stevenson*. First, the facts are stated by Lord Hodson.

Then, a portion of Lord Pearce's judgment is presented:

LORD HODSON.

My Lords, the appellants, who are advertising agents, claim damages for loss which they allege they have suffered through the negligence of the respondents, who are merchant bankers. The negligence attributed to the respondents consists of their failure to act with reasonable skill and care in giving references as to the credit-worthiness of a company called Easipower Ltd. which went into liquidation after the references had been given so that the appellants were unable to recover the bulk of the costs of advertising orders which Easipower Ltd. had placed with them. The learned judge at the trial found that the respondent bankers had been negligent in the advice which they gave in the form of bankers' references, the appellants being a company which acted in reliance on the references and suffered financial loss accordingly, but that he must enter judgment for the respondents since there was no duty imposed by law to exercise care in giving these references, the duty being only to act honestly in so doing. [Note: The actual inquiry was made by the plaintiffs' bank on their behalf. Hence, the actual communication was bank to bank.]

The respondents have at all times maintained that they were in no sense negligent and further that no damage flowed from the giving of references, but first they took the point that whether or not they were careless and whether or not the appellants suffered damages as a result of their carelessness, they must succeed on the footing that no duty was owed by them. This point has been taken throughout as being, if the respondents are right, decisive of the whole matter, I will deal with this first, although the underlying question is whether the respondent bankers who at all time disclaimed responsibility ever assumed any duty at all.

The appellants depend on the existence of a duty said to be assumed by or imposed on the respondents when they gave a reference as to the credit-worthiness of Easipower Ltd. knowing that it would or might be relied upon by the appellants or some other third party in like situation.

    . . .

LORD PEARCE:

How wide the sphere of the duty of care in negligence is to be laid depends ultimately upon the courts' assessment of the demands of society for protection from the carelessness of others. Economic protection has lagged behind protection in physical matters where there is injury to person and property. It may be that the size and the width of the range of possible claims has acted as a deterrent to extension of economic protection.

[Omitted is discussion of several cases including *Glanzer v. Shepard* and *Ultramares* and two English cases: (1) *Shiells v. Blackburn*, a case in which a gratuitous bailee becomes liable for harm done to the bailment of the bailor, and (2) another in which a surgeon became liable in negligence to a child with whom he had no direct contract of treatment. As to the latter two cases, Pearce continued:]

In those cases there was no dichotomy between negligence in act and in word, nor between physical and economic loss. The basis underlying them is that if persons holding themselves out in a calling or situation or profession take on a task within that calling or profession, they have a duty of skill and care. In terms of proximity one might say that they are in particularly close proximity to those who, as they know, are relying on their skill and care although the proximity is not contractual. . . .

Was there such a special relationship in the present case as to impose on the defendants a duty of care to the plaintiffs as the undisclosed principals for whom the National Provincial Bank was making the inquiry? The answer to that question depends on the circumstances of the transaction. If, for instance, they disclosed a casual social approach to the inquiry, no such special relationship or duty of care would be assumed. To import such a duty the representation must normally, I think, concern a business or professional transaction whose nature makes clear the gravity of the inquiry and the importance and influence attached to the answer . . . [b]ut the facts in that case were wholly different from those in the present case. A most important circumstance is the form of the inquiry and of the answer. Both were here plainly stated to be without liability. Mr. Gardiner argues that those words are not sufficiently precise to exclude liability for negligence. Nothing, however, except negligence could, in the facts of this case, create a liability (apart from fraud, to which they cannot have been intended to refer and against which the words would be no protection, since they would be part of the fraud). I do not, therefore, accept that even if the parties were already in contractual or other special relationship the words would give no immunity to a negligent answer. But in any event they clearly prevent a special relationship from arising. They are part of the material from which one deduces whether a duty of care and a liability for negligence was assumed. If both parties say expressly (in a case where neither is deliberately taking advantage of the other) that there shall be no liability, I do not find it possible to say that a liability was assumed.

In *Robinson v. National Bank of Scotland Ltd.*, also the correspondence expressly excluded responsibility. Possibly that factor weighed with Lord Haldane when he said: "But when a mere inquiry is made by one banker of another, who stands in no special relation to him, then, I the absence of special circumstances from which a contract to be careful can be inferred, I think there is no duty excepting the duty of common honesty to which I have referred." I appreciate Mr. Gardiner's emphasis on the general importance to the business world of bankers' references and the desirability that in an integrated banking system there should be a duty of care with regard to them, but on the facts before us it is in my opinion not possible to hold that there was a special duty of care and a liability for negligence.

I would therefore dismiss the appeal.

Appeal dismissed.

(4)   How would *Hedley Bryne* have been decided in New York and how would *Ultramares* have been decided in England? Suppose the bank's statement had been made in writing. Would the result change? *See Berkline Corp. v. Bank of Mississippi*, 453 So. 2d 699 (Miss. 1984).

[B]   Economic Injury in the Absence of Personal Injury or Property Damage

Ultramarers and *Hedley Bryna* examined liability for negligent misrepresentation. The next two cases examine liability for negligent acts that cause economic loss but no property damage or personal injury. In the common law, no duty was owed as to mere economic damages in isolation. This rule stems from *Cattle v. Stockton Waterworks Co.*, L.R. 10 Q.B. 453 (1875), a case in which a defendant's negligent act put a road contractor to considerable extra expense in completing a construction project. As a result, the plaintiff lost money in fulfilling his contract with a third party. The court denied recovery because pure economic injury was not the "proximate and direct consequences of the wrongful acts," and, therefore, was too remote to be actionable. Instead of limiting *Cattle* to its particular facts, both English and American courts deemed it to be precedent for the rule that no duty is owed for mere economic consequences of negligent acts that cause no personal injury or property damage.

PPG INDUSTRIES, INC. v. BEAN DREDGING COMPANY
Louisiana Supreme Court
447 So. 2d 1058 (1984)

LEMMON, JUSTICE.

The issue in this case is whether a dredging contractor who negligently damaged a natural gas pipeline may be held liable for the economic losses incurred by the pipeline owner's contract customer who was required to seek and obtain gas from another source during the period of repair. Thus, this case brings into focus the broad question of recovery of an indirect economic loss incurred by a party who had a contractual relationship with the owner of property negligently damaged by a tortfeasor.[21]

We conclude that while the situation giving rise to the question in this case falls literally within the expansive terms of La. C.C.Art. 2315, in that the dredging contractor's "act . . . cause[d] damage to another", the customer cannot recover his indirect economic loss.[22]

For the policy reasons hereinafter stated in a duty-risk analysis, we hold that the damages to the economic interest of the contract purchaser of natural gas, caused by a dredging contractor's negligent injury to property which prevents the pipeline owner's performance of the contract to supply natural gas to the

---

[21] Recovery of economic losses for *negligent* interference with contractual relations is almost uniformly denied in other jurisdictions. See Restatement (Second) of Torts § 766 C comment a (1977). On the other hand, recovery for *intentional* interference with contractual relations has been permitted in every jurisdiction in this country except Louisiana. Malone, *The Work of the Louisiana Appellate Courts for the 1963–1964 Term* 25 La.L.Rev. 341 (1965). See also W. Prosser, Law of Torts § 129 at 930 (4th ed. 1971) There is considerable sentiment for permitting recovery in Louisiana for intentional interference with contracts, such as by the deliberate inducing of breach of contract.

However, that issue is not presented in this case.

[22] La. C.C.Art. 2315 provides in pertinent part:

> Every act whatever of man that causes damage to another obliges him by whose fault it happened to repair it.

[23] [Reserved]

purchaser, do not fall within the scope of the protection intended by the law's imposition of a duty on dredging contractors not to damage pipelines negligently.

Bean Dredging Company's dredging operations in the Calcasieu River caused damage to Texaco's natural gas pipeline. As a result, Texaco was unable to fulfill its contract to supply natural gas to PPG Industries for operation of its manufacturing plant, and PPG had to obtain fuel from another source at an increased cost. PPG filed this suit against Bean, seeking to recover the increased cost of obtaining natural gas. Bean filed an exception of no cause of action, contending that Louisiana has never recognized the right of recovery for negligent interference with contractual relations.

The trial court sustained Bean's exception of no cause of action. The court of appeal affirmed. We granted certiorari.

When the question of recovery of indirect economic losses caused by a negligent injury to property that interferes with contractual relations has been presented in previous cases, the courts of this state have generally denied recovery without analyzing the problem, taking a mechanical approach to the unreasoned conclusion that the petition fails to state a cause of action for which relief can be granted. Most cases have cited *Robins Dry Dock & Repair Co. v. Flint*, 275 U.S. 303, 48 S. Ct. 34, 72 L. Ed. 290 (1927), and *Forcum-James Co. v. Duke Transportation Co.* [93 So. 2d 228 (La. 1957)], which were relied on by the court of appeal in the present case.

In *Robins*, an admiralty case, the charterer of a vessel sought recovery of damages for its loss of use while the vessel was out of service after the dry dock operator negligently damaged its propeller. The Supreme Court denied recovery on the basis that the negligent repairer, who acted unintentionally while unaware of the contract of charter, cannot be held liable unless the party seeking damages had a proprietary interest in the damaged property. [Note: the charterer did not own the vessel.]

Although knowledge does not seem to be a relevant factor to the determination of the defendant's liability to the charterer, the case has been cited countless times for the proposition that recovery is generally denied for negligent interference with contractual relations.[23]

The Supreme Court of Louisiana relied on *Robins* in deciding the *Forcum-James* case. The plaintiff in *Forcum-James* was a contractor who was required by a contract with the Department of Highways to repair a state-owned bridge that had been damaged by the tortfeasor. Plaintiff sued the tortfeasor to recover the cost of the repairs. The court held that the state, as owner, was the proper party to sue for the damage to the bridge and maintained an exception of no *right* of action as to plaintiff's suit against the tortfeasor. As to plaintiff's damages sustained by reason of having to repair the bridge, the court, relying on *Robins*, stated that "where a third person suffers damage by reason of a contractual obligation to the injured party, such damage is too remote and indirect to become the subject of a direct action ex delicto, in the absence of subrogation". 93 So. 2d at 230.

The obvious purpose of the *Forcum-James* decision was to prevent the tortfeasor from having to pay twice for the same damage, and the court in effect required that suit for the damage to the bridge be filed by either the owner of the bridge or a party subrogated to the rights of the owner. Because evidence of subrogation had been excluded in the trial court, the court remanded for introduction of such evidence. The instant case presents a different, but related, problem. In *Forcum-James*, the cost of repairing the bridge was a loss to be recovered by either one party or the other, but not both. Here, only one party was entitled to recover the cost of repairing the pipeline, but both Texaco and PPG (and perhaps other

A better reasoned explanation for the *Robins* decision was suggested in F. Harper & F. James, The Law of Torts § 6.10 (1956), as follows:

> It is the reluctance of the Court to hold the tort-feasor liable, in addition to the physical damage to the vessel, for the value of *two* bargains. Under the contract with the owners, the charterers were excused from paying rent while the ship was laid up for repairs. This loss was included in the settlement between the defendants and the owners. Having made good one bargain, the tort-feasor is now asked to make good the still better bargain of the charterer. This, conceivably, *could go on and on. The Court drew the line after the first.* The *multiplicity of actions* and the *unforeseeable extension of liability* may well have influenced the Court in denying the charterer's claim, as a *matter of policy.*

(Emphasis supplied.)

Similar policy considerations lead to our decision in the present case. Under the alleged facts, there appears to be no question that Bean is liable to Texaco for the costs of repairing the pipeline and for the direct economic losses sustained by Texaco during the period of repair. However, the rule of law which prohibits negligent damage to property does not necessarily require that a party who negligently causes injury to property must be held legally responsible to *all* persons for *all* damages flowing in a "but for" sequence from the negligent conduct.

Rules of conduct are designed to protect *some* persons under *some* circumstances against *some* risks. Malone, *Ruminations on Cause-in-Fact, 9* Stan.L.Rev. 60 (1956). Policy considerations determine the reach of the rule, and there must be an ease of association between the rule of conduct, the risk of injury, and the loss sought to be recovered. A judge, when determining whether the interest of the party seeking recovery of damages is one that falls within the intended protection of the rule of law whose violation gave rise to the damages, should consider the particular case in the terms of the moral, social and economic values involved, as well with a view toward the ideal of justice.

There is clearly an ease of association in the present case between the rule of law which imposes a duty not to negligently damage property belonging to another and the risk of injury sustained by Texaco because of the damage to its property. As noted, however, a rule of law is seldom intended to protect *every* person against *every* risk. It is much more difficult to associate the same rule of law, in terms of the moral, social and economic values involved, with the risk of injury and the economic loss sustained by the person whose only interest in the pipeline damaged by the tortfeasor's negligence arose from a contract to purchase gas from the pipeline owner. It is highly unlikely that the moral, social and economic considerations underlying the imposition of a duty not to negligently injure property encompass the risk that a third party who has contracted with the owner of the injured property will thereby suffer an economic loss.

Moreover, imposition of responsibility on the tortfeasor for such damages could create liability "in an indeterminate amount for an indeterminate time to an indeterminate class". *Ultramares Corp. v. Touche,* 255 N.Y. 170, 179, 174 N.E. 441, 444 (1931). If any of PPG's employees were laid off while PPG sought to obtain

---

parties) incurred economic losses during the period of repair that would not have been incurred *but for* the tortfeasor's negligence.

another source of fuel for its plant, they arguably sustained damages which in all likelihood would not have occurred *but for* defendant's negligence.

If any of PPG's customers had contracted to purchase products that PPG could not produce and deliver because of the accident, perhaps they sustained damages which in all likelihood would not have occurred *but for* defendant's negligence. Because the list of possible victims and the extent of economic damages might be expanded indefinitely, the court necessarily makes a policy decision on the limitation of recovery of damages.

We conclude that the duty allegedly violated in the present case did not encompass the particular risk of injury sustained by PPG and did not intend protection from the particular loss for which recovery is sought in PPG's petition.

Accordingly, the judgments of the lower courts are affirmed.

CALOGERO, JUSTICE, dissenting.

I applaud the majority's applying a duty risk analysis in the consideration of tort recovery for negligent interference with contractual relations, and its abandoning the per se exclusion of such damages which our courts have heretofore adopted on the heels of *Robins* and *Forcum-James.*

Where I disagree, is in the majority's determination that PPG's economic loss, from added fuel cost, is not a risk encompassed within the duty not to negligently injure Texaco's pipelines.

PPG's loss of profits; PPG's employees' loss of jobs and income; PPG's customers' losses, because PPG could not produce and deliver; are all economic losses which might properly be determined to fall outside the scope of the protection intended by the law's imposing a duty on dredging contractors not to damage pipelines negligently. The same cannot be said for PPG's added fuel cost.

Bean was dredging the waterway that ran right along the side of PPG's plant. There were signs along the waterway warning of the existence of the gas pipeline and cautioning against dredging in the area. There were also maps of the water bottom showing the pipelines. At the time Bean negligently dredged through the waterway, there could have been no doubt to anyone that the pipeline in question was providing PPG with its fuel to run its plant. The damages suffered by PPG were *not unforeseen*, at least as far as the added fuel costs go.

If PPG is to be denied its added fuel cost I can perceive no instance in which a non-owner of negligently damaged property may recover from a tortfeasor. In light of the result here it would probably have been better if the majority had simply affirmed the jurisprudential rule established in *Robins* and *Forcum-James* which has prevailed so long.

NOTES AND QUESTIONS

(1)   On remarkably similar facts *Caltex Oil (Australia) Pty., Ltd. v. The Dredge "Willemstad,"* 136 C.L.R. 529 (1 Aus. 1976), acknowledged a duty of care to Caltex, who was the user of the severed pipeline. In a narrowly drawn judgment, Stephan, J. opined:

> As the body of precedent accumulates some general area of demarcation
> between what is and is not a sufficient degree of proximity in any particular

class of case of economic loss will no doubt emerge; but its emergence
neither can be, nor should it be, other than as a reflection of the piecemeal
conclusions arrived at in precedent cases. The present case contains a
number of salient features which will no doubt ultimately be recognized as
characteristic of one particular class of case among the generality of cases
involving economic loss. This will be typical of the development of the
common law in which, in the words of Barwick C.J. in *Mutual Life &
Citizens' Assurance Co. Ltd. v. Evatt* (19), the elements of the relationships
out of which a duty of care is imposed by law "will be elucidated in the
course of time as particular facts are submitted for consideration in cases
coming forward for decision." The existence of these features leaves no
doubt in my mind that there exists in this case sufficient proximity to entitle
the plaintiff to recover its reasonably foreseeable economic loss.

These features comprise the following:

(1) the defendant's knowledge that the property damaged, a set of
pipelines, was of a kind inherently likely, when damaged, to be productive of consequential economic loss to those who rely directly upon its
use. To damage an item of productive equipment or an item used in
conveying goods or services, such as power or water, is inherently likely
to cause to its users economic loss quite apart from the physical injury
to the article itself. Moreover the nature of a pipeline, used in conveying
refined products from a refinery to another's terminal, is such as to
indicate very clearly the existence of something akin to Lord Roche's
common adventure, the person to whom the petroleum products are
being delivered through it having a very real interest in its continued
operation as a means of conveyance, whether or not possessing a
proprietary or possessory interest in the pipes themselves;

(2) the defendant's knowledge or means of knowledge, from certain
charts then in use on the dredge, that the pipelines extended across
Botany Bay from the A.O.R. refinery to the plaintiff's Banks- meadow
terminal, leading to the quite obvious inference that their use was to
convey refined products from refinery to terminal, the plaintiff being in
this sense a user of the pipeline.

These two factors lead to the conclusion that Caltex was within the
reasonable contemplation of the defendants as a person likely to suffer
economic loss if the pipelines were cut. Now, because the facts referred
to in (1) and (2) above were within the reasonable contemplation of the
defendants, it should have been apparent to them that more than one
party was likely to be exposed to loss should the pipelines be severed by
the defendants' negligence; accordingly the tortious infliction of property damage on any one of these parties becomes relevant; hence the
significance of the following factor:

(3) the infliction of damage by the defendant to the property of a third
party, A.O.R., as a result of conduct in breach of a duty of care owed to
that third party.

There are two other relevant factors:

(4) the nature of the detriment suffered by the plaintiff; that is to say its loss of use, in the above sense, of the pipeline;

(5) the nature of the damages claimed, which reflect that loss of use, representing not some loss of profits arising because collateral commercial arrangements are adversely affected but the quite direct consequence, of the detriment suffered, namely the expense directly incurred in employing alternative modes of transport.

These factors demonstrate a close degree of proximity between the defendant's conduct in severing the pipelines and the economic loss which Caltex suffered when its chosen means of supplying its terminal with products was interrupted by the injury to the pipelines. The acknowledgement that a duty of care was owed to A.O.R.; the fact that Caltex was not less proximately concerned than was A.O.R. in the continued integrity of the pipeline; the very nature of the pipeline, a major mode of conveyance of products to an identifiable recipient, whose use of its terminal was for the receipt of such products; the nature of the economic loss, direct and inevitably flowing from the severing of the pipeline and not in any sense a matter for speculation only; all these characteristics of the present case combine to constitute a relationship of sufficient proximity to give rise to a duty of care owed to Caltex for breach of which it may recover its purely economic loss.

(2)   Does factor number 3 re-open the debate between Cardozo and Andrews in *Palsgraf?*

(3)   Suppose Caltex had been forced to cut back on oil production while the pipeline was under repair. Could it recover the profits lost because of the sales that were not made?

(4)   Suppose a defendant negligently severed a high power electrical cable that supplied a nearby manufacturing plant. The cable was not owned by the manufacturing plant and was not on its property. Nevertheless, cutting off the electricity stopped the manufacturing machinery during the course of operations. Some of the machines were full of liquified raw materials that hardened in the stopped machines and damaged them. *SCM (United Kingdom) v. W.J. Whittall & Son, Ltd.*, [1970] 2 All Eng. Rep. 417 (Q.B. Div.), held that a duty was owed as to the damage done to the machines and economic losses stemming therefrom.

PETITION OF KINSMAN TRANSIT COMPANY
United States Court of Appeals, Second Circuit
388 F.2d 821 (1968)

IRVING R. KAUFMAN, CIRCUIT JUDGE:

The difficult question presented by this appeal is whether certain expenses incurred by claimant-appellants Cargill, Inc. (Cargill) and Cargo Carriers, Inc. (Cargo Carriers), as a result of an unusual concatenation of events on the Buffalo River during the night of January 21, 1959, are recoverable as a matter of law.

The misadventures leading to the catastrophe on the river that fateful evening were set forth when this litigation was previously before this court, 338 F.2d 708 (1964). For our purposes it is sufficient to state that as a result of the negligence of the Kinsman Transit Company and the Continental Grain Company the S.S. MacGilvray Shiras broke loose from her moorings and careened stern first down the narrow, S-shaped river channel. She struck the S.S. Michael K. Tewksbury, which in turn broke loose from her moorings and drifted downstream — followed by the Shiras — until she crashed into the Michigan Avenue Bridge. The bridge collapsed and its wreckage, together with the Tewksbury and the Shiras, formed a dam which caused extensive flooding and an ice jam reaching almost 3 miles upstream. As a result of this disaster, transportation on the river was disrupted until approximately March 13, 1959 — a period of about 2 months. Subsequent to our previous adjudication of the negligence issues, Judge Burke appointed a Commissioner to determine the damages of the various claimants.

At the time of the accident, Cargill had some 336,000 bushels of wheat stored aboard the S.S. Donald B. Gillies berthed in the Buffalo harbor below the Michigan Avenue Bridge. (It is apparently not an uncommon practice for companies to "winter storage" wheat in this manner.) Cargill, it appears, was under contract to deliver 124,000 bushels of the Gillies' wheat during the period from January through March 1959. Because of the accident the vessel could not be moved to Cargill's grain elevators located above the collapsed bridge so that it could be unloaded. In order to comply with its contractual obligations, Cargill was required to secure replacement wheat in the Midwest. The Commissioner allowed Cargill $30,231.38 for its extra transportation costs and $8,232 for increased "storage costs."[24]

Cargo Carriers' claim is somewhat different. When the calamity occurred it was in the process of unloading a cargo of corn from the S.S. Merton E. Farr at elevators located above the Michigan Avenue Bridge. Apparently the Farr was struck by one of the two free-drifting ships. Its cargo was undamaged but it broke loose from the dock at which it was moored. The by-product of this was that an ice jam formed between the Farr and the dock and normal unloading became impossible; the city fireboat and the harbor towing tugs which ordinarily would have broken up the ice jam were below the bridge wreckage and thus could not be of any assistance. The consequence of all this was that Cargo Carriers, which was under contract to transfer 10,322 bushels of the Farr's corn, was required to continue the ship's unloading with the aid of specially rented equipment. The Commissioner awarded it $1,590.40 for these incurred expenses.

Judge Burke refused to confirm either the Gillies or the Farr awards made by the Commissioner. He reasoned that the evidence established that the damages to Cargill and Cargo Carriers were caused by negligent interference with their contractual relations. In the absence of proof that the interference was intentional or with knowledge of the existence of the contracts, he concluded recovery could not be grounded in tort. We too deny recovery to the claimants, but on other grounds.

We do not encounter difficulty with Judge Burke's analysis because it lacks some support in the case law; instead, we hesitate to accept the "negligent interference with contract" doctrine in the absence of satisfactory reasons for differentiating contractual rights from other interests which the law protects. The

---

[24] The wheat abroad the Gillies had been financed and the "storage costs" represented the accumulated interest for the period during which the wheat could not be utilized. In addition, in an award not contested on this appeal, Cargill recovered $9,790 for flood damage to its upriver installations.

argument, frequently heard, that to allow recovery in such instances would impose a penalty far out of proportion to the defendant's fault or open the field to collusive claims and increased litigation, see Prosser, The Law of Torts, 964 (3d ed. 1964), which are the spectres commonly raised whenever the law extends its protection. Here, as elsewhere, the answer must be that courts have some expertise in performing their almost daily task of distinguishing the honest from the collusive or fraudulent claim. And, "[i]f the result is out of all proportion to the defendant's fault, it can be no less out of proportion to the plaintiff's entire innocence." *Id.* at 296. Moreover, several cases often cited as illustrations of the application of the "negligent interference with contract" doctrine have been convincingly explained in terms of other, more common tort principles. See 1 Harper and James, The Law of Torts, 505–10 (1956). Indeed, Professors Harper and James suggest that the application of the doctrine is wholly artificial in most instances. *Id.* at 501. We therefore prefer to leave the rock-strewn path of "negligent interference with contract" for more familiar tort terrain. Cargill and Cargo Carriers argue broadly that they suffered damage as a result of defendants' negligence and we will deal with their claims in these terms instead of on the more esoteric "negligent interference" ground.

Having determined our course, we nevertheless conclude that recovery was properly denied on the facts of this case because the injuries to Cargill and Cargo Carriers were too "remote" or "indirect" a consequence of defendants' negligence.

Numerous principles have been suggested to determine the point at which a defendant should no longer be held legally responsible for damage caused "in fact" by his negligence. See Prosser, supra, 282–329; 2 Harper and James, supra, 1132–61; Hart and Honoré, Causation in the Law, chs. VI and IX (1959). Such limiting principles must exist in any system of jurisprudence for cause and effect succeed one another with the same certainty that night follows day and the consequences of the simplest act may be traced over an ever-widening canvas with the passage of time. In Anglo-American law, as Edgerton has noted, "[e]xcept only the defendant's intention to produce a given result, no other consideration so affects our feeling that it is or is not just to hold him for the result so much as its foreseeability" *Legal Cause*, 72 U.Pa.L.Rev. 211, 352 (1924). *E.g., Brady v. Southern Railway Co.*, 320 U.S. 476, 483, 64 S. Ct. 232, 88 L. Ed. 239 (1946).

When the instant case was last here, we held — although without discussion of the Cargill and Cargo Carriers claims — that it was a foreseeable consequence of the negligence of the City of Buffalo and Kinsman Transit Company that the river would be dammed. It would seem to follow from this that it was foreseeable that transportation on the river would be disrupted and that some would incur expenses because of the need to find alternative routes of transportation or substitutes for goods delayed by the disaster. It may be that the specific manner was not foreseeable in which the damages to Cargill and Cargo Carriers would be incurred but such strict foreseeability — which in practice would rarely exist except in hindsight — has not been required. Hart and Honoré, *supra* at 233.[25]

---

[25] We previously held that "all the claimants here met the *Palsgraf [v. Long Island R. R.*, 248 N.Y. 339, 162 N.E. 99, 59 A.L.R. 1253 (1928),] requirement of being persons to whom the actor owed a 'duty of care.'" 338 F.2d at 722. This passage is certainly applicable to Cargill's claim for flood damage to its upstream property. See fn. 3, *supra.*

On the previous appeal we stated aptly: "somewhere a point will be reached when courts will agree that the link has become too tenuous — that what is claimed to be consequence is only fortuity." 338 F.2d at 725. We believe that this point has been reached with the Cargill and Cargo Carriers claims. Neither the Gillies nor the Farr suffered any direct or immediate damage for which recovery is sought. The instant claims occurred only because the downed bridge made it impossible to move traffic along the river.[26]

Under all the circumstances of this case, we hold that the connection between the defendants' negligence and the claimants' damages is too tenuous and remote to permit recovery. "The law does not spread its protection so far." Holmes, J., in *Robins Dry Dock, supra,* 275 U.S. at 309, 48 S. Ct. at 135.[27]

We need not decide which, if any, defendants owed Cargill a duty of care with respect to its unrelated claims based on the Gillies' immobility, since even if *Palsgraf is* satisfied, compensation may be precluded where — as here — the relationship between the negligence and the injury becomes too tenuous. See *infra.* We recognize that frequently identical questions are involved whether we speak in terms of "duty" or some other standard for determining where recovery should be denied. Prosser, *supra* at 283.

In the final analysis, the circumlocution whether posed in terms of "foreseeability," "duty," "proximate cause," "remoteness," etc. seems unavoidable. As we have previously noted, 338 F.2d at 725, we return to Judge Andrews' frequently quoted statement in *Palsgraf v. Long Island R. R.,* 248 N.Y. 339, 354–355, 162 N.E. 99, 104, 59 A.L.R. 1253 (1928) (dissenting opinion):

> "It is all a question of expediency . . . of fair judgment, always keeping in mind the fact that we endeavor to make a rule in each case that will be practical and in keeping with the general understanding of mankind."

Affirmed.

NOTES AND QUESTIONS

(1)   If one were to apply the *Caltex* analysis to the *Kinsman* facts, and vice versa, would one reach the same conclusions as to liability as reached by the courts?

(2)   Which case provided the greater liberalization of recovery under the law? The proximate causation approach *of Kinsman* has not gathered a large following.

---

[26] The claim of Cargo Carriers is the more troublesome of the two because the Farr was struck by either the Shiras or the Tewksbury and where there is physical damage to a vessel the owner can recover for the loss of its use until repairs are completed. *The Aurora,* 64 F. Supp. 502 (E.D. La.), aff'd, 5 Cir., 153 F.2d 224 (1945); 1 Harper and James, *supra* at 503, n. 4. But apparently Cargo Carriers has not sought recovery for physical damage to the Farr. And, as we understand the facts, the Farr could have been unloaded without additional expense were it not for the fact that the tugs which ordinarily are used to break up ice jams were caught below the Michigan Avenue Bridge.

[27] Although to reason by example is often merely to restate the problem, the following illustration may be an aid in explaining our result. To anyone familiar with N. Y. traffic there can be no doubt that a foreseeable result of an accident in the Brooklyn Battery Tunnel during rush hour is that thousands of people will be delayed. A driver who negligently caused such an accident would certainly be held accountable to those physically injured in the crash. But we doubt that damages would be recoverable against the negligent driver in favor of truckers or contract carriers who suffered provable losses because of the delay or to the wage earner who was forced to "clock in" an hour late. And yet it was surely foreseeable that among the many who would be delayed would be truckers and wage earners.

See, e.g., Nebraska Innkeepers, Inc. v. Pittsburgh-Des Moines Corporation, 345 N.W.2d 124 (Ia. 1984) (bridge closing case: "we conclude that plaintiffs cannot maintain a claim for purely economic damages arising out of defendant's alleged negligence because it lacks a legal foundation to support it."). In fact, *Barber Lines A/S v. M/V Donau Maru*, 764 F.2d 50 (1st Cir. 1985) denied that *Kinsman* was decided on proximate cause grounds. Barber Lines opined:

> Appellants argue that Kinsman II raises a factual issue of "foreseeability." We read Kinsman II, however, not as saying that the injury, as a matter of fact, was unforeseeable but, rather, as drawing a legal line, based on considerations of policy, cf. Sinram, supra, that forbids compensation for certain types of foreseeable, negligently caused, financial injury. The details of the Kinsman II accident were unusual, but the precise details of many, or most, accidents cannot be foreseen in advance. Rather, foreseeability is a matter of a class, or type, of harm. And, in terms of perfectly traditional, reasonably specific, commonsense classes, the Kinsman II blockade, delay, and extra cost were foreseeable. Still more so are the extra costs involved in the analogous Kinsman II example, the extra trucking costs arising from tunnel accident delays. Viewing the legal implications of Kinsman II in this way, we cannot distinguish a barrier created by an oil spill from a barrier created by a careening ship, each of which increases unloading costs by requiring other ships to go elsewhere. It is still more difficult for us to distinguish this case from delays created by, say, tunnel accidents, which are likely to mean extra cost for truckers, shippers and merchants, all of which are foreseeable.

Id., 764 F.2d at 52. Do you agree with this assessment of *Kinsman*? *Barber Lines* applied the rule of *Robins Dry Dock & Repair Co. v. Flint*, 275 U.S. 303, 48 S.Ct. 134, 72 L.Ed. 290 (1927), to deny recovery as a matter of law for added costs of unloading a cargo from a ship that was kept away from its intended dock by an oil spill.

(3)   Closely related to the no duty rule for pure economic losses in negligence law is a more expansive doctrine often referred to as the "economic loss rule" that is applied to strict liability and warranty as well as negligence actions. The essential thrust of the doctrine is economic; that is, a contracting party such as the seller of a product makes a bargain as to the condition and specifications of the product in contract negotiations and, in the absence of property damage or personal injury caused by some defect, should not be liable for economic losses arising out of defects in the product except under the contract. As stated by Justice Traynor in *Seely v. White Motor Company*, 403 P.2d 145, 155 (Cal. 1965):

> The distinction that the law has drawn between tort recovery for physical injuries and warranty recovery for economic loss is not arbitrary and does not rest on the "luck" of one plaintiff in having an accident causing physical injury. The distinction rests, rather, on an understanding of the nature of the responsibility a manufacturer must undertake in distributing his products. He can appropriately be held liable for physical injuries caused by defects by requiring his goods to match a standard of safety defined in terms of conditions that create unreasonable risks of harm. He can not be held for the level of performance of his products in the consumer's business unless he agrees that the product was designed to meet the consumer's demands. A consumer should not be charged at the

will of the manufacturer with bearing the risk of physical injury when he buys a product on the market. He can, however, be fairly charged with the risk that the product will not match his economic expectations unless the manufacturer agrees that it will.

Hence, a buyer of a product who is disappointed that the product fails to meet specifications is limited to contract remedies unless the failure of the product damages some item of property other than the product itself or causes personal injury. Thus, if a buyer purchases a defective boat motor that catches on fire and destroys itself plus the yacht the buyer installs in it, the buyer may be able to sue in tort for loss of the yacht but the economic loss rule would limit the action for loss of the motor to contract remedies. *See Florida Power & Light Co. v. Westinghouse Elec. Corp.*, 510 So. 2d 899 (Fla. 1987).

The rule has been extended to pure economic losses suffered by non purchasers (*i.e.*, beyond those in privity with the seller). For example, in *Casa Clara Condominium Assn., Inc. v. Charley Toppino & Sons, Inc.*, 620 So. 2d 1244 (Fla. 1993), a condominium developer purchased defective concrete from the defendant and used it to construct condominiums that it sold to the plaintiffs. Sometime after the condominiums were transferred to the plaintiffs, the consequences of the defective concrete imposed major repair expenses upon the condominium owners. The owners' attempt to sue the concrete supplier in tort was defeated by the economic loss rule. *Morris v. Osmose Wood Preserving*, 667 A.2d 624, 628 (Md. 1995), applied the rule on similar facts but acknowledged an exception for conditions "presenting a clear danger of death or personal injuries."

Students should be aware that some courts have been enticed to apply the "economic loss rule" in contexts beyond its proper boundaries. It should not, for example, be applied to bar independent intentional torts, such as deceit in inducement and intentional interference with economic interests.

If applied thoughtlessly, the economic loss rule would prevent negligence malpractice actions on behalf of persons who have purchased professional services from physicians, lawyers, accountants and the like. Although the court acknowledged that "in most instances, a negligence action will not lie when parties are in privity of contract," *Tommy Griffin Plumbing & Heating v. Jordan, Jones & Gauling, Inc.*, 463 S.E.2d 85, 87 (S.C. 1995), properly held, "When . . . there is a special relationship between the alleged tortfeasor and the injured party not arising in contract, the breath of the duty of care will support a tort action." The court held that a professional engineer had such a special relationship to a client. It also acknowledged that lawyers and accountants may also incur special relationships creating duty. Why did the court not mention physicians and patients? *See also, Congregation of the Passion, Holy Cross Province v. Touche Ross & Company*, 636 N.E.2d 503 (Ill. 1994), *cert. denied* 115 S. Ct. 358 (1994) (economic loss rule does not bar negligence malpractice action against an accountant) and *McAlvain v. General Ins. Co.*, 554 P.2d 955 (Idaho 1977), applying the "special relationship" exception to the economic loss rule.

§ 5.06   RESCUERS

HORSLEY v. MACLAREN
11 D.L.R. 3d 277 (Ont. 1970), *app. dism'd*, [1972] S.C.R. 441[28]

A passenger on a motorboat fell overboard through no fault of the operator, defendant MacLaren. In attempting to rescue him, MacLaren reversed the engines and approached the passenger stern first instead of approaching bow on. Because the man overboard appeared to have lost consciousness and because the boat, when stopped, kept drifting away, the rescue attempt was unsuccessful. After 3 or 4 minutes, Horsley, a second passenger, removed his trousers and dived in the water where he died of shock as a result of the sudden immersion in the extremely cold temperature. This was a wrongful death action by Horsley's survivors. The trial court awarded damages against the operator of the boat for the death of Horsley.

[The defendant appealed to the Ontario Court of Appeals.]

Judgment of SCHROEDER, J.A., concurred in by MCGILLIVRAY, J.A., omitted here, but set out in § 6.06, *infra*.

JESSUP, J.A.

This unique case, the facts of which might have been contrived for a bar examination, raises several questions of first instance.

. . .

On an evening in early May the defendant MacLaren, operating a 30-foot six inch, twin- engined, twin screwed cabin cruiser, and while impaired in judgment by the consumption of drink, embarked on a voyage on the icy cold waters of Lake Ontario accompanied by six guests. Since the entire company had been partying most of the afternoon, it is perhaps not surprising that one of them, Matthews, fell overboard. However, there is no evidence as to what caused the mishap except that it occurred without any fault of MacLaren.

The uncontradicted evidence of two marine experts was that the emergent situation of "man overboard" is a common one which a competent and prudent seaman would instantly cope with by turning his boat about, approaching bow on with the boat under control of propeller and rudder, and coming alongside the victim so that he could then be reached by a pikepole and hauled in by passengers or crew. Instead of implementing that drill, and although the boat was then 40 to 50 feet beyond Matthews, MacLaren backed towards him. Because the height of the rear transom obscured his vision and for fear of fouling Matthews in the propellers, MacLaren had to put the engines in neutral and halt the progress of his boat when it was too distant for Matthews to be reached by a pikepole being manned by one of the passengers. The boat being without control by engines or rudder then drifted still further away. At least once more MacLaren attempted to approach nearer to Matthews by backing the boat, but with the same frustrating result.

---

[28] [Ed. — Dominion Law Reports, a reporter of Canadian decisions, decision of Ontario Court of Appeal; Canada Supreme Court Reports.]

Matthews was meanwhile head up in the water but obviously unconscious. He made no effort to grasp a life-jacket thrown immediately in front of him by one of the passengers. In this situation of increasing desperateness Horsley, one of the passengers, dived overboard to the rescue. Almost immediately following Horsley, Matthews's body having toppled face forward into the water, Mrs. Jones, another of the passengers, also leaped to the rescue but Matthews sank and disappeared under the boat.

Upon seeing his wife in the water, Mr. Jones, also a passenger, took over the controls of the boat from MacLaren and, approaching her with the boat bow on, her rescue was effected without event. MacLaren then resumed control of the boat but this time adopted the bow on procedure and Horsley's body was recovered.

The evidence is that Horsley must have died from shock almost immediately upon his immersion in the intensely cold water. It is therefore of no causal effect that he failed to attach a line to himself or to don a life-jacket. He had removed his trousers but there is no evidence they would have prolonged his life.

Against just the situation with which he had to cope, MacLaren had practised the proper rescue procedure. He did not attempt to justify his abortive method of attempted rescue but claimed an error in judgment. While he was able to operate the simple controls of a power boat, there was ample evidence to support the trial Judge's finding that he was so affected by drink as to be impaired in judgment; accordingly, it was especially dangerous for him to be the master of a ship responsible for the safety of passengers in the emergencies inseparable from boating on navigable waters. In my view the finding of the trial Judge that MacLaren failed to exercise the reasonable care of an ordinary, prudent, reasonable power boat operator was fully warranted by the evidence as was his finding that MacLaren's failure of judgment did not excuse his negligence since his judgment was self-impaired.

The probabilities are that Matthews also died instantly on his immersion in the water and the learned trial Judge therefore dismissed the action by Matthews' dependents because the negligence in effecting his rescue was not causative of his death. However, he held that MacLaren was under a legal duty to rescue Matthews and that the action of Horsley was within the ambit of risk created by MacLaren's negligence so that he gave judgment for Horsley's dependents.

Fundamental of course to MacLaren's liability to Horsley's dependents is his duty to Matthews. Conceived in the forms of action and nurtured by the individualistic philosophies of past centuries, no principle is more deeply rooted in the common law than that there is no duty to take positive action in aid of another no matter how helpless or perilous his position is. In this area the civil law has shown more regard for morality. It is a principle which is not reached by the doctrine of *M'Alister (or Donoghue) v. Stevenson*, [1932] A.C. 562, since that case leaves open only the categories of neighbours to whom there is owed a duty not to cause harm; its *ratio* has not yet been extended to enlarge the class to whom there is owed a duty to confer a benefit. So, despite the moral outrage of the text writers, it appears presently the law that one can, with immunity, smoke a cigarette on the beach while one's neighbour drowns and, without a word of warning, watch a child or blind person walk into certain danger; and so, more than half a century ago, the Appellate Division in *VanValkenburg v. Northern Navigation Co.* (1913), 30 O.L.R. 142, 19 D.L.R. 649, there being no precedent save a single American decision, could equably hold that the defendant had no duty to attempt the rescue of a seaman who had fallen from its ship by reason of his own negligence. Even the Legislature of our collectivist society, while readily assuming for the State the care of the individual, have not moved often to burden him with the care of his neighbour. . . .

The learned trial Judge in giving judgment for Horsley's dependents against MacLaren . . . concluded that at common law there is a legal duty, implicit in the universal custom of the sea and demanded by the social ethic of today, of the master of a ship to aid his passenger who has fallen overboard. I agree with that conclusion. The trial Judge noted that in several American jurisdictions the common law reluctance to penalize non-feasance has yielded to a duty of affirmative care in situations of special relationship between the plaintiff and the defendant as employer and employee, carrier and passenger and occupier and his lawful visitor. A passenger on a ship is in the position of total dependence on the master and I think that peculiar relationship must now be recognized as invoking a duty of the master, incident to the duty to use due care in the carriage by sea of a passenger, of aid against the perils of the sea. Falling overboard is such a peril and in that situation I do not think the common law can do otherwise than to adopt the statutory duty to render assistance. I have already expressed the view that there is a duty to avoid frustrating rescue by negligence in rendering assistance.

If MacLaren had a duty to render assistance to Matthews and to use reasonable care in so doing, there remains the question of whether Horsley's rescue attempt with consequent injury to him was within the ambit of risk resulting from MacLaren's negligence. *Haynes v. Harwood*,[1935] 1 K.B. 146; *Baker v. T. E. Hopkins & Son Ltd.*, [1959] 1 W.L.R. 966, and *Videan v.British Transport Commission*, [1963] 2 Q.B. 650, [1963] 2 All E.R. 860, establish the principle that where one creates a situation of peril through negligence it is a foreseeable consequence that a rescuer will go to the aid of a person in danger from the peril with resulting liability to the rescuer, for any injury sustained by him, of the person responsible for the peril. Here, of course, MacLaren did not create the peril of drowning but, for all that was apparent to the actors in the drama, his negligence prolonged Matthews' exposure to it permitting a potential risk of death to actualize and I consider that the principle of the cases cited logically and properly extends to such a situation. However, while MacLaren reasonably should have foreseen the intervention of a rescue attempt by one of his passengers as a consequence of his own negligently mishandled effort, the evidence is he had earlier warned Horsley to remain in the cockpit or cabin because he was unaware if Horsley had any experience with boating. By that command I think MacLaren, as effectively as he could, insulated Horsley from such perils of the voyage as were eventually encountered and put it beyond his reasonable contemplation that Horsley in particular would engage in the intervention he in fact undertook. On that narrow ground I would allow the appeal.

As an alternative basis for liability the learned trial Judge held that MacLaren, having undertaken a rescue operation, was liable for his negligence in performing it even if he was not under a legal duty to commence the undertaking, and Lacourciere, J., relied on a passage from Prosser on Torts (1941), pp. 194–5, where the learned author cites American precedents to that effect. I think it is an unfortunate development in the law which leaves the Good Samaritan liable to be mulcted in damages, and apparently in the United States it is one that has produced a marked reluctance of doctors to aid accident victims. . . .

I concur in Schroeder, J.A.'s disposition of the appeal.

Appeal allowed.

NOTES AND QUESTIONS

(1)   Common law courts uniformly apply the no duty to rescue rule in proper context. As stated in *Rhodes v. Illinois Central Gulf Railroad*, 665 N.E.2d 1260 (Ill. 1996) (holding that railroad company had no duty to come to the rescue of a trespasser who sought shelter on the railroad's premises after having been injured elsewhere):

> Our common law generally imposes no duty to rescue an injured stranger upon one who did not cause the injury in the first instance. . . . See also Restatement (Second) of Torts § 314 (1965) (the general rule is that the mere fact that an actor realizes or should realize that his action is necessary for the aid of another, while perhaps imposing a moral duty to act, does not in itself impose a legal duty to act).

Courts may acknowledge a duty of care when a sufficient "special relationship" exists between the victim and the person who fails to give aid. *See Rhodes and Jackson v. Mercy Health Center, Inc.*, 864 P.2d 839 (Okla. 1993) (hospital did not have a special relationship with spouse of hospital patient).

The next case, *Tarasoff v. Regents*, examines the special relationship doctrine in depth.

(2)   What is the narrowest ground of a common law duty to rescue acknowledged in the speech of Jessup, J.A.? *Horsley v. MacLaren* was affirmed on appeal to the Canada Supreme Court, but on the duty issue the Court stated *per curiam:*

> There was a duty on the part of [MacLaren] in his capacity as host and as the owner and operator of the cabin cruiser to do the best he could to effect the rescue of M.

Horsley v. MacLaren, [1972] S.C.R. 441, 442.

(3)   Suppose it could be shown that defendant's attempted rescue of Matthews kept a nearby helicopter from coming to the rescue. Assume the helicopter pilot testified that he could have picked up Matthews within one or two minutes of his having fallen into the water. How does this affect the case of Matthews' survivors against the operator of the boat? *See, e.g., DeLong v. County of Erie*, 60 N.Y.2d 296, 469 N.Y.S.2d 611 (1983). May an action be maintained against the helicopter pilot?

(4)   The no duty to rescue rule is often confused with the so called "rescuer doctrine," which is in fact its opposite. As confirmed in *Heck v. Robey*, 659 N.E.2d 498, 501 (Ind. 1995), the rescuer doctrine imposes a duty of care upon "one who has, through his negligence, endangered the safety of another" such that the one who negligently created the danger "may be held liable for injuries sustained by a third person in attempting to save [the endangered] person from injury." The duty owed by one who negligently creates the need for rescue was cemented in the common law by Judge Cardozo's opinion in *Wagner v. International Rg. Co.*, 133 N.E. 437 (N.Y. 1921) (a case involving the death of a passenger who disembarked from a stopped train to help search for the body of his cousin who had fallen from the train), as follows:

Danger invites rescue. The cry of distress is the summons to relief. The law does not ignore these reactions of the mind in tracing conduct to its consequences. It recognizes them as normal. It places their effects within the range of the natural and the probable. The wrong that imperils life is a wrong to the imperiled victim; it is a wrong also to his rescuer.

Reeves v. North Broward Hosp. Dist., 821 So.2d 319, 321 (Fla. 4th DCA 2002), stated: "For the rescue doctrine to come into play the defendant must have been negligent, the person (or property) to be rescued must have been in imminent peril, and the rescuer must have acted reasonably."

Most courts hold that the rescuer doctrine does not create an open ended duty but expires after the spontaneous excitement to rescue has passed. *See, e.g., Bryant v. Glasletter*, 38 Cal. Rptr. 2d 291, 298 (Cal. App. 1995), declining to apply the rescuer doctrine in an action brought by a professional emergency care provider who the court deemed "was performing the job he had been hired to do." The court repeated this oft-quoted statement: "The rescue doctrine contemplates a voluntary act by one who, in an emergency and prompted by spontaneous human motive to save human life, attempts a rescue he had no duty to attempt by virtue of a legal obligation or duty fastened on him by his employment. (57 Am.Jur. 2d, Negligence, S 696 . . .)."

(5) In *Horsley*, Jessup, J.A. referred to the fear that victims who were not saved by a rescue attempt would mulct Good Samaritans in damages for negligence in having been unsuccessful in the rescue. While it is true that voluntary rescuers undertake a duty not to worsen the plight of the victim either by causing a new injury or by interfering with what would otherwise have been a successful rescue attempt by someone else, in the absence of such a worsening courts regularly hold that a rescuer's abandonment of a rescue attempt, *see, e.g., Miller v. Arnal Corporation*, 632 P.2d 987 (Ariz. App. 1981) (ski resort planned and then abandoned attempt to rescue hiker who was stranded in a snow storm), or failure to commence a promised rescue, *see, e.g., Parker v. Mineral County*, 729 P.2d 491 (Nev. 1986) (sheriff never undertook to investigate a passerby's report that decedent was lying helpless on the roadside in inclement weather), gives no rise to a duty of care to complete the rescue.

Despite the almost uniform lack of success of actions brought by victims against rescuers, apprehension of being sued if a rescue attempt goes wrong is commonly believed to deter would-be rescuers from rendering assistance to persons needing medical assistance in emergencies. This perceived risk is believed to be particularly inhibiting to rescues by physicans and other medically trained people. To relieve this apprehension, many legislatures have enacted so-called Good Samaritan statutes to grant immunities or to lower the standard of care in specified emergency situations. How effective is the following statute in serving that goal?

(a) Everyone is responsible, not only for the result of his willful acts, but also for an injury occasioned to another by his want of ordinary care or skill in the management of his property or person, except so far as the latter has, willfully or by want of ordinary care, brought the injury upon himself, and except as hereinafter provided: (1) Where no prior contractual relationship exists, any person licensed to practice any method of treatment of human ailments, disease, pain, injury, deformity, mental or physical condition, or licensed to render services ancillary thereto, including licensed registered and practical nurses, who, under emergency circumstances that suggest the giving of aid is the only alternative to probable death or serious bodily injury, in good faith, voluntarily and without compensation, renders or attempts to render emergency care to an injured person or any person who is in need of immediate medical aid, wherever required, shall not be liable for damages as a result of any acts or omissions except for committing gross negligence or willful or wanton wrongs in rendering the emergency care.

76 Oka. Stat. 1991 § 5. *See Jackson v. Mercy Health Center, Inc.*, 864 P.2d 839 (OK. 1993).

(6)   Suppose in *Horslev v. MacLaren* another passenger, X, who was a stranger to Matthews, was standing nearby when Matthews fell overboard. X could easily have saved Matthews' life by immediately tossing him a life ring readily at hand but declined to do so. X was a stranger to Matthews and had nothing to do with his being on the motorboat or falling overboard. Did X breach a duty owed to Matthews? Suppose Y were standing there, too. Y knew Matthews very well, hated him and was not unhappy to see him drown, but had nothing to do with his being on the motorboat or falling overboard. Did Y breach a duty owed to Matthews?

TARASOFF v. REGENTS OF UNIVERSITY OF CALIFORNIA
California Supreme Court
17 Cal. 3d 425, 131 Cal. Rptr. 14, 551 P.2d 334 (1976)

TOBRINER, JUSTICE.

On October 27, 1969, Prosenjit Poddar killed Tatiana Tarasoff. Plaintiffs, Tatiana's parents, allege that two months earlier Poddar confided his intention to kill Tatiana to Dr. Lawrence Moore, a psychologist employed by the Cowell Memorial Hospital at the University of California at Berkeley. They allege that on Moore's request, the campus police briefly detained Poddar, but released him when he appeared rational. They further claim that Dr. Harvey Powelson, Moore's superior, then directed that no further action be taken to detain Poddar. No one warned plaintiffs of Tatiana's peril.

Concluding that these facts set forth causes of action against neither therapists and policemen involved, nor against the Regents of the University of California as their employer, the superior court sustained defendants' demurrers to plaintiffs' second amended complaints without leave to amend. This appeal ensued.

Plaintiffs' complaints predicate liability on two grounds: defendants' failure to warn plaintiffs of the impending danger and their failure to bring about Poddar's confinement pursuant to the Lanterman-Petris-Short Act (Welf. & Inst. Code, § 5000ff.) Defendants, in turn, assert that they owed no duty of reasonable care to Tatiana and that they are immune from suit under the California Tort Claims Act of 1963 (Gov. Code, § 810ff.).

. . .

Plaintiffs can state a cause of action against defendant therapists for negligent failure to protect Tatiana.

The second cause of action can be amended to allege that Tatiana's death proximately resulted from defendants' negligent failure to warn Tatiana or others likely to apprise her of her danger. Plaintiffs contend that as amended, such allegations of negligence and proximate causation, with resulting damages, establish a cause of action. Defendants, however, contend that in the circumstances of the present case they owed no duty of care to Tatiana or her parents and that, in the absence of such duty, they were free to act in careless disregard of Tatiana's life and safety.

In analyzing this issue, we bear in mind that legal duties are not discoverable facts of nature, but merely conclusory expressions that, in cases of a particular type, liability should be imposed for damage done. As stated in *Dillon v. Legg* (1968) 68 Cal. 2d 728, 734, 69 Cal. Rptr. 72, 76, 441 P.2d 912, 916: "The assertion that liability must . . . be denied because defendant bears no 'duty' to plaintiff 'begs the essential question — whether the plaintiff's interests are entitled to legal protection against the defendant's conduct . . . [Duty] is not sacrosanct in itself, but only an expression of the sum total of those considerations of policy which lead the law to say that the particular plaintiff is entitled to protection.' (Prosser, Law of Torts [3d ed. 1964] at pp. 332–333.)"

In the landmark case *of Rowland v. Christian* (1968) 69 Cal. 2d 108, 70 Cal. Rptr. 97, 443 P.2d 561, Justice Peters recognized that liability should be imposed "for an injury occasioned to another by his want of ordinary care or skill" as expressed in section 1714 of the Civil Code. Thus, Justice Peters, quoting from *Heaven v. Pender* (1883) 11 Q.B.D. 503, 509 stated: " 'whenever one person is by circumstances placed in such a position with regard to another . . . that if he did not use ordinary care and skill in his own conduct . . . he would cause danger of injury to the person or property of the other, a duty arises to use ordinary care and skill to avoid such danger.' "

We depart from "this fundamental principle" only upon the "balancing of a number of considerations"; major ones "are the foreseeability of harm to the plaintiff, the degree of certainty that the plaintiff suffered injury, the closeness of the connection between the defendant's conduct and the injury suffered, the moral blame attached to the defendant's conduct, the policy of preventing future harm, the extent of the burden to the defendant and consequences to the community of imposing a duty to exercise care with resulting liability for breach, and the availability, cost and prevalence of insurance for the risk involved.

The most important of these considerations in establishing duty is foreseeability. As a general principle, a "defendant owes a duty of care to all persons who are foreseeably endangered by his conduct, with respect to all risks which make the conduct unreasonably dangerous." As we shall explain, however, when the avoidance of foreseeable harm requires a defendant to control the conduct of another person, or to warn of such conduct, the common law has traditionally imposed liability only if the defendant bears some relationship to the dangerous person or to the potential victim. Since the relationship between a therapist and his patient satisfies this requirement, we need not here decide whether foreseeability alone is sufficient to create a duty to exercise reasonable care to protect a potential victim of another's conduct.

. . . Applying this exception to the present case, we note that a relationship of defendant therapists to either Tatiana or Poddar will suffice to establish a duty of care; as explained in section 315 of the Restatement Second of Torts, a duty of care may arise from either "(a) a special relation . . . between the actor and the third person which imposes a duty upon the actor to control the third person's conduct, or (b) a special relation . . . between the actor and the other which gives to the other a right of protection."

Although plaintiffs' pleadings assert no special relation between Tatiana and defendant therapists, they establish as between Poddar and defendant therapists the special relation that arises between a patient and his doctor or psychotherapist. Such a relationship may support affirmative duties for the benefit of third persons. Thus, for example, a hospital must exercise reasonable care to control the behavior of a patient which may endanger other persons. A doctor must also warn a patient if the patient's condition or medication renders certain conduct, such as driving a car, dangerous to others.

Although the California decisions that recognize this duty have involved cases in which the defendant stood in a special relationship *both* to the victim and to the person whose conduct created the danger, we do not think that the duty should logically be constricted to such situations. Decisions of other jurisdictions hold that the single relationship of a doctor to his patient is sufficient to support the duty to exercise reasonable care to protect others against dangers emanating from the patient's illness. The courts hold that a doctor is liable to persons infected by his patient if he negligently fails to diagnose a contagious disease (*Hofmann v. Blackmon* (Fla. App.1970) 241 So. 2d 752), or, having diagnosed the illness, fails to warn members of the patient's family.

. . .

[Because] predictions of violence are often erroneous, amicus concludes, the courts should not render rulings that predicate the liability of therapists upon the validity of such predictions.

The role of the psychiatrist, who is indeed a practitioner of medicine, and that of the psychologist who performs an allied function, are like that of the physician who must conform to the standards of the profession and who must often make diagnoses and predictions based upon such evaluations. Thus the judgment of the therapist in diagnosing emotional disorders and in predicting whether a patient presents a serious danger of violence is comparable to the judgment which doctors and professionals must regularly render under accepted rules of responsibility.

Amicus contends, however, that even when a therapist does in fact predict that a patient poses a serious danger of violence to others, the therapist should be absolved of any responsibility for failing to act to protect the potential victim. In our view, however, once a therapist does in fact determine, or under applicable professional standards reasonably should have determined, that a patient poses a serious danger of violence to others, he bears a duty to exercise reasonable care to protect the foreseeable victim of that danger. While the discharge of this duty of due care will necessarily vary with the facts of each case, in each instance the adequacy of the therapist's conduct must be measured against the traditional negligence standard of the rendition of reasonable care under the circumstances. (Accord *Cobbs v. Grant* (1972) 8 Cal. 3d 229, 243, 104 Cal. Rptr. 505, 502 P.2d 1.) As explained in Fleming and Maximov, *The Patient or His Victim: The Therapist's Dilemma* (1974) 62 Cal.L.Rev. 1025, 1067: " . . . the ultimate question of resolving the tension between the conflicting interests of patient and potential victim is one of social policy, not professional expertise. . . . In sum, the therapist owes a legal duty not only to his patient, but also to his patient's would-be victim and is subject in both respects to scrutiny by judge and jury."

Contrary to the assertion of amicus, this conclusion is not inconsistent with our recent decision in *People v. Burnick, supra,* 14 Cal. 3d 306, 121 Cal. Rptr. 488, 535 P.2d 352. Taking note of the uncertain character of therapeutic prediction, we held in *Burnick* that a person cannot be committed as a mentally disordered sex offender unless found to be such by proof beyond a reasonable doubt. (14 Cal. 3d at p. 328, 121 Cal. Rptr. 488, 535 P.2d 352.) The issue in the present context, however, is not whether the patient should be incarcerated, but whether the therapist should take any steps at all to protect the threatened victim; some of the alternatives open to the therapist, such as warning the victim, will not result in the drastic consequences of depriving the patient of his liberty. Weighing the uncertain and conjectural character of the alleged damage done the patient by such a warning against the peril to the victim's life, we conclude that professional inaccuracy in predicting violence cannot negate the therapist's duty to protect the threatened victim.

The risk that unnecessary warnings may be given is a reasonable price to pay for the lives of possible victims that may be saved. We would hesitate to hold that the therapist who is aware that his patient expects to attempt to assassinate the President of the United States would not be obligated to warn the authorities because the therapist cannot predict with accuracy that his patient will commit the crime.

Defendants further argue that free and open communication is essential to psychotherapy (see *In re Lifschutz* (1970) 2 Cal. 3d 415, 431–434, 85 Cal. Rptr. 829, 467 P.2d 557); that "Unless a patient . . . is assured that . . . information [revealed by him] can and will be held in utmost confidence, he will be reluctant to make the full disclosure upon which diagnosis and treatment . . . depends." (Sen.Com. on Judiciary, comment on Evid. Code, § 1014.) The giving of a warning, defendants contend, constitutes a breach of trust which entails the revelation of confidential communications.

We recognize the public interest in supporting effective treatment of mental illness and in protecting the rights of patients to privacy (see *In re Lifschutz, supra, 2* Cal. 3d at p. 432, 85 Cal. Rptr. 829, 467 P.2d 557), and the consequent public importance of safeguarding the confidential character of psychotherapeutic communication. Against this interest, however, we must weigh the public interest in safety from violent assault. The Legislature has undertaken the difficult task of balancing the countervailing concerns. In Evidence Code section 1014, it established a broad rule of privilege to protect confidential communications between patient and psychotherapist. In Evidence Code section 1024, the Legislature created a specific and limited exception to the psychotherapist-patient privilege: "There is no privilege . . . if the psychotherapist has reasonable cause to believe that the patient is in such mental or emotional condition as to be dangerous to himself or to the person or property of another and that disclosure of the communication is necessary to prevent the threatened danger."

We realize that the open and confidential character of psychotherapeutic dialogue encourages patients to express threats of violence, few of which are ever executed. Certainly a therapist should not be encouraged routinely to reveal such threats; such disclosures could seriously disrupt the patient's relationship with his therapist and with the persons threatened. To the contrary, the therapist's obligations to his patient require that he not disclose a confidence unless such disclosure is necessary to avert danger to others, and even then that he do so discreetly, and in a fashion that would preserve the privacy of his patient to the fullest extent compatible with the prevention of the threatened danger. (See Fleming & Maximov, *The Patient or His Victim: The Therapist's Dilemma* (1974) 62 Cal.L.Rev. 1025, 1065–1066.)

The revelation of a communication under the above circumstances is not a breach of trust or a violation of professional ethics; as stated in the Principles of Medical Ethics of the American Medical Association (1957), section 9: "A physician may not reveal the confidence entrusted to him in the course of medical attendance . . . *unless he is required to do so by law or unless it becomes necessary in order to protect the welfare of the individual or of the community."* (Emphasis added.) We conclude that the public policy favoring protection of the confidential character of patient-psychotherapist communications must yield to the extent to which disclosure is essential to avert danger to others. The protective privilege ends where the public peril begins.

Our current crowded and computerized society compels the interdependence of its members. In this risk-infested society we can hardly tolerate the further exposure to danger that would result from a concealed knowledge of the therapist that his patient was lethal. If the exercise of reasonable care to protect the threatened victim requires the therapist to warn the endangered party or those who can reasonably be expected to notify him, we see no sufficient societal interest that would protect and justify concealment. The containment of such risks lies in the public interest. For the foregoing reasons, we find that plaintiffs' complaints can be amended to state a cause of action against defendants Moore, Powelson, Gold, and Yandell and against the Regents as their employer, for breach of duty to exercise reasonable care to protect Tatiana.

. . .

Turning now to the police defendants, we conclude that they do not have any such special relationship to either Tatiana or to Poddar sufficient to impose upon such defendants a duty to warn respecting Poddar's violent intentions. Plaintiffs suggest no theory, and plead no facts that give rise to any duty to warn on the part of the police defendants absent such a special relationship. They have thus failed to demonstrate that the trial court erred in denying leave to amend as to the police defendants.

. . .

MOSK, JUSTICE (concurring and dissenting).

I concur in the result in this instance only because the complaints allege that defendant therapists did in fact predict that Poddar would kill and were therefore negligent in failing to warn of that danger. Thus the issue here is very narrow: we are not concerned with whether the therapist, pursuant to the standards of their profession, "should have" predicted potential violence; they allegedly did so in actuality. Under these limited circumstances I agree that a cause of action can be stated.

Whether plaintiffs can ultimately prevail is problematical at best. As the complaints admit, the therapists *did* notify the police that Poddar was planning to kill a girl identifiable as Tatiana.

While I doubt that more should be *required*, this issue may be raised in defense and its determination is a question of fact.

I cannot concur, however, in the majority's rule that a therapist may be held liable for failing to predict his patient's tendency to violence if other practitioners, pursuant to the "standards of the profession," would have done so. The question is, what standards? Defendants and a responsible amicus curiae, supported by an impressive body of literature discussed at length in our recent opinion in *People v. Burnick* (1975) 14 Cal. 3d 306, 121 Cal. Rptr. 488, 535 P.2d 352, demonstrate that psychiatric predictions of violence are inherently unreliable.

. . .

CLARK, JUSTICE (dissenting).

Until today's majority opinion, both legal and medical authorities have agreed that confidentiality is essential to effectively treat the mentally ill, and that imposing a duty on doctors to disclose patient threats to potential victims would greatly impair treatment. Further, recognizing that effective treatment and society's safety are necessarily intertwined, the Legislature has already decided effective and confidential treatment is preferred over imposition of a duty to warn.

The issue whether effective treatment for the mentally ill should be sacrificed to a system of warnings is, in my opinion, properly one for the Legislature, and we are bound by its judgment. Moreover, even in the absence of clear legislative direction, we must reach the same conclusion because imposing the majority's new duty is certain to result in a net increase in violence.

COMMON LAW ANALYSIS

Entirely apart from the statutory provisions, the same result must be reached upon considering both general tort principles and the public policies favoring effective treatment, reduction of violence, and justified commitment.

Generally, a person owes no duty to control the conduct of another. Exceptions are recognized only in limited situations where (1) a special relationship exists between the defendant and injured party, or (2) a special relationship exists between defendant and the active wrongdoer, imposing a duty on defendant to control the wrongdoer's conduct. The majority does not contend the first exception is appropriate to this case.

Policy generally determines duty. Principal policy considerations include foreseeability of harm, certainty of the plaintiff's injury, proximity of the defendant's conduct to the plaintiff's injury, moral blame attributable to defendant's conduct, prevention of future harm, burden on the defendant, and consequences to the community.

Overwhelming policy considerations weigh against imposing a duty on psychotherapists to warn a potential victim against harm. While offering virtually no benefit to society, such a duty will frustrate psychiatric treatment, invade fundamental patient rights and increase violence.

NOTES AND QUESTIONS

(1) Is *Tarasoff an* exception to the no duty to rescue rule? Can the same result be justified by applying the approach of Lord Diplock in *Home Office v. Dorset Yacht Co, Ltd.?*

(2) A large number of decisions have considered *Tarasoff in* similar contexts. Most that follow it require a "special relationship" between the defendant and the plaintiff-victim with the minimum requirement being that the plaintiff was a "readily identifiable" potential victim. *See Fraser v. United States*, 674 A.2d 811 (Conn. 1996) (declining to find a duty owed to a plaintiff who was neither a readily identified victim nor the member of a foreseeable class of victims), for a discussion of cases, and *Eiseman v. State*, 511 N.E.2d 1128 (N.Y. 1987) (no duty owed to community at large.). *Boyton v. Burglass*, 590 So. 2d 446 (Fla. App. 1991), rejected *Tarasoff* on its own terms.

The *Tarasoff court* itself has reconfirmed the "readily identifiable victim" nature of the special relationship, *Thompson v. County of Alemeda*, 614 P.2d 728 (Cal. En Banc 1980) (no duty owed to unknown five year old child who was murdered by released inmate known to have violent and dangerous tendencies), and has also declined to extend the *Tarasoff duty* theory beyond professional experts *(i.e.,* the *Tarasoff* psychiatrist) to unpaid lay counselors. *Nally v. Grace Community Church of the Valley*, 763 P.2d 948 (Cal. En Banc 1988), *cert. denied*, 490 U.S. 1007, 109 S. Ct. 1644, 104 L. Ed. 2d 159 (1989) (nontherapist pastor-counselor owed no duty to refer suicidal counselee to professional therapist).

(3) A few courts have extended the *Tarasoff* duty rationale to plaintiffs who were neither specifically identifiable nor members of an at-risk class under circumstances in which it might be said that "danger at large" was foreseeable. *See, e.g., Bradley Center Inc. v Wessner*, 296 S.E.2d 69 (Ga. 1982), *Peterson v. State*, 671 P.2d 230 (Wash. 1983), *Davis v. Puryear*, 673 So. 2d 1298 (La. App. 1996); *Nova University, Inc. v. Wagner*, 491 So. 2d 1116 (Fla. 1986), and *Lipari v. Sears, Roebuck & Co.*, 497 F. Supp. 185 (D. Neb. 1980). Does this approach sever all connection with the no duty to rescue doctrine? Does it violate the central premise of *Palsgraf v. Long Island Railroad Co.?*

(4) *A*, a drug addict, consults *D*, a physician for medical help to cure the addiction. *D* prescribes drug therapy that requires *A* to be injected in the doctor's office. *D* informs *A* that he will be disoriented by the drug and warns him not to drive before the passage of eight hours. *A* drives away from the doctor's office immediately after receiving his first injection, becomes disoriented and crashes into a car driven by *C. A*, *C* and *B*, who was *A's* spouse and a passenger in his car, were all killed. Which estate may sustain a wrongful death action against *D?*

(5) Same as 3, except *D* prescribes a drug that, because of the disorientation it causes, is to be taken immediately before *A* goes to bed. *D* informs *A* of this and also warns him not to drive under any circumstances within eight hours of taking the drug. *A* takes the drug before retiring, but then decides to go out for a beer. *A* and *C*, driver of a car *A* crashes into, are injured. Which, if any, of them may sustain an action against *D? See, e.g., Forlaw v. Fitzer*, 456 So. 2d 432, (Fla. 1984); *Gooden v. Tips*, 651 S.W.2d 364 (Tex. App. 1983); and *Myers v. Quesenberry*, 193 Cal. Rptr. 733 (Cal. App. 1983).

§ 5.07   HARM TO UNBORN CHILDREN

. . . no case so far as we know has ever decided that if the infant survived, it could maintain an action for injuries received by it while in its mother's womb. Yet that is the test of the principle relied on by the plaintiff who can hardly avoid contending that a pretty large field of litigation has been unexplored until the present moment.

Holmes, J., *Dietrich v. North Hampton*, 138 Mass. 14, 52 Am. Rep. 242, 243 (1884).

BONBREST v. KOTZ
United States District Court, D. C. District
65 F. Supp. 138 (1946)

MCGUIRE, JUSTICE.

The question raised by the motion is whether an infant through its father and next friend has a right of action springing from the alleged fact it was taken from its mother's womb through professional malpractice, with resultant consequences of a detrimental character.

It is a novel one in this jurisdiction, and judicial opinion, in those where it has been met, has held that at common law, in the absence of statute, prenatal injury affords no basis for an action in tort, in favor either of the child or its personal representative.

This conclusion is predicated, it appears, on the assumption that a child en ventre sa mere has no juridical existence, and is so intimately united with its mother as to be a "part" of her and as a consequence is not to be regarded as a separate, distinct, and individual entity.

This rather anomalous doctrine was announced by Mr. Justice Holmes in the leading case of *Dietrich v. Inhabitants of Northampton*, which apparently has been relied upon as dispositive and controlling ever since, except in those few cases where recovery was barred on the theory of no contract and, therefore, no duty.

The Court, in the opinion referred to, disposes of the analogy drawn from the common law of property and crimes and then adds significantly:

Taking all the foregoing considerations into account, and further, that, as the unborn child was a part of the mother at the time of the injury, *any damage to it which was not too remote* (italics supplied) to be recovered for at all was recoverable by her. . . .

But on the assumed facts here we have not, as in the *Dietrich* case, "an injury transmitted from the actor to a person through his own organic substance, or through his mother, before he became a person" standing "on the same footing as an injury transmitted to an existing person through other intervening substances outside him, . . . " but a direct injury to a *viable* child — the distinction is an important one — by the defendants in their professional capacities.

This seems to me to be the solid factual ground on which the two cases stand distinguished.

It is further to be noted that the Court, alluding to what it termed the difficulty of remoteness in predicating a right of action for injury transmitted to a person through what it calls " . . . other *intervening* (italics supplied) substances outside him," has this to say:

If these general difficulties could be got over, and if we should assume, irrespective of precedent, that a man might owe a civil duty and incur a conditional prospective liability in tort to one not yet in being, and if we should assume also that causing an infant to be born prematurely stands on the same footing as wounding or poisoning, we should then be confronted by the question raised by the defendant, whether an infant *dying before it was able to live separated from its mother* (italics supplied) could be said to have become a person recognized by the law as capable of having a locus standi in court. . . .

Here, however, we have a viable child — one capable of living outside the womb — and which has demonstrated its capacity to survive by *surviving* — are we to say *now* it has no locus standi in court or elsewhere?

As to a viable child being "part" of its mother — this argument seems to me to be a contradiction in terms. True, it is in the womb, but it is capable now of extrauterine life — and while dependent for its continued development on sustenance derived from its peculiar relationship to its mother, it is not a "part" of the mother in the sense of a constituent element — as that term is generally understood. Modern medicine is replete with cases of living children being taken from dead mothers. Indeed, apart from viability, a non-viable foetus is not a part of its mother.

From the viewpoint of the civil law and the law of property, a child en ventre sa mere is not only regarded as human being, but as such from the moment of conception — which it is in fact.

Why a "part" of the mother under the law of negligence and a separate entity and person in that of property and crime?

Why a human being, under the civil law, and a non-entity under the Common Law?

It has, if viable, its own bodily form and members, manifests all of the anatomical characteristics of individuality, possesses its own circulatory, vascular and excretory systems and is capable *now* of being ushered into the visible world.

The Supreme Court of Canada, in permitting recovery in a case of this character — although the negligence alleged was in the operation of a tram — had this to say:[29]

The wrongful act which constitutes the crime may constitute also a tort, and if the law recognizes the separate existence of the unborn child sufficiently to punish the crime, it is difficult to see why it should not also recognize its separate existence for the purpose of redressing the tort.

Further it cogently — and more pertinently — observes:

---

[29] Montreal Tramways v. Leveille, 1933, 4 Dom.L.R. 337. In this case a woman seven months pregnant was descending from a tram, when, as a result of the negligence of the operator, she was thrown, or fell to the street. Two months later she gave birth to a child with club feet. The company defended on the ground (1) a child en ventre sa mere is not an existing person in rerum natura, but *only a part of its mother* (italics supplied); (2) the company's liability was founded on contract express or implied and there had been no contract with the child. Citing Walker v. Great Nor. Ry. of Ireland, *supra.* See also: 22 B.U.L.R., 1942, p. 621 et seq.; 26 H.L.R., 1912–13, p. 638.

If a child *after birth* (italics supplied) has no right of action for prenatal injuries, we have a wrong inflicted for which there is no remedy, for, although the father may be entitled to compensation for the loss he has incurred and the mother for what she has suffered, yet there is a residuum of injury for which compensation cannot be had save at the suit of the child. If a right of action be denied to the child it will be compelled, without any fault on its part, to go through life carrying the seal of another's fault and bearing a very heavy burden of infirmity and inconvenience without any compensation therefor. To my mind it is but natural justice that a child, if born alive and *viable* (italics supplied) should be allowed to maintain an action in the courts for injuries wrongfully committed upon its person while in the womb of its mother.

The logic of this position, it seems to me, is unassailable.

But Mr. Justice Holmes has said "the life of the law has been *not logic*: it has been *experience*" (italics supplied) and here we find a willingness to face the facts of life rather than a myopic and specious resort to precedent to avoid attachment of responsibility where it ought to *attach* and to permit idiocy, imbecility, paralysis, loss of function, and like residuals of another's negligence to be locked in the limbo of uncompensable wrong, because of a legal fiction, long outmoded.

The common law is not an arid and sterile thing, and it is anything but static and inert.

Indeed as Chief Justice Stone has so well said:

If, with discerning eye, we see differences as well as resemblances in the facts and experiences of the present when compared with those recorded in the precedents, we take the decisive step toward the achievement of a progressive science of law. If our appraisals are mechanical and superficial, the law which they generate will likewise be mechanical and superficial, to become at last but a dry and sterile formalism.

It is just here, within the limited area where the judge has freedom of choice of the rule which he is to adopt, and in his comparison of the experiences of the past with those of the present, that occurs the most critical and delicate operation in the process of judicial lawmaking.

Strictly speaking, he is often engaged not so much in extracting a rule of law from the precedents, as we were once accustomed to believe, as in making an appraisal and comparison of social values, the result of which may be decisive weight in determining what rule he is to apply. . . . The skill, resourcefulness and insight with which judges and lawyers weigh competing demands of social advantage, not unmindful that continuity and symmetry of the law are themselves such advantages, and with which they make choice among them in determining whether precedents shall be extended or restricted, chiefly give the measure of the vitality of the common-law system and its capacity for growth.

The absence of precedent should afford no refuge to those who by their wrongful act, if such be proved, have invaded the right of an individual — employed as the defendants were in this case to attend, in their professional capacities, both the mother and child. And what right is more inherent, and more sacrosanct, than that of the individual in his possession and enjoyment of his life, his limbs and his body?

In the recent case of *Daily v. Parker*, in which no precedent could be found to recognize a cause of action by children against a woman who caused their father to leave them, the Court had this to say, in holding against the proposition that there is no remedy because there is no precedent:

. . . the common law has been and is sufficiently elastic to meet changing conditions. We quote from Dean Pound's book, 'The Spirit of the Common Law,' p. 183:

Anglo-American law is fortunate indeed in entering upon a new period of growth with a well-established doctrine of law-making by judicial decision. . . . Undoubtedly . . . judicial empiricism was proceeding over-cautiously at the end of the last century. . . . If the last century insisted over-much upon predetermined premises, and a fixed technique, it did not lose to our law the method of applying the judicial experience of the past to the judicial questions of the present.

That a right of action in cases of this character would lead to others brought in bad faith and might present insuperable difficulties of proof — a premise with which I do not agree — is no argument. The law is presumed to keep pace with the sciences and medical science certainly has made progress since 1884. We are concerned here only with the right and not its implementation.

The motion for summary judgment is denied and counsel will prepare order.

NOTES AND QUESTIONS

(1)　After *Bonbrest v. Kotz* was decided, American courts abandoned en masse the firm no-duty rule as to liability to unborn children. Somewhat ironically, however, *Bonbrest's* reference to a *viable* unborn child had the effect of creating a secondary no-duty rule of its own; that is, no duty is owed to an unborn child that is not *viable* at the time of the incident allegedly causing the injury. What, according to *Bonbrest*, is the test of viability? Is it the same as "quickness"?

Despite the no-duty to unborn children history, the drafters of the Restatement, Torts, Second, asserted that the true issue is one of causation, and proposed the rule that "one who tortiously causes harm to an unborn child is subject to liability to the child for such harm if it is born alive." § 869, Tentative Draft No. 16. Many courts have now adopted this more expansive view, believing that modern medical science can help the courts weed out "false or fraudulent claims." *See, e.g., Day v. Nationwide Mutual Insurance Co.*, 328 So. 2d 560 (Fla. App. 1976) ("We hold that a child born alive, having suffered pre-natal injuries at any time after its conception, has a course of action against the alleged tortfeasor.") and *Womack v. Buckhorn*, 187 N.W.2d 218 (Mich. 1971). (cataloging and classifying numerous decisions.)

Curiously, very little litigation on this point appeared in England and the Commonwealth countries until late in the twentieth century. The most well known case is *Watt v. Rama*, [1972] Vict.R. 353 (F.C.), of the supreme court of the Australian state of Victoria, which applied general negligence principles rather than the no-duty rule. Much later, *Burton v. Islingtom Health Authority*, [1993] QB 204 (CA), acknowledged that an infant in vitro may be owed a duty of care in tort. The judgment of Dillon, L.J., adverted to many American and other common law authorities but also noted that many English decisions "have adopted as part of English law the maxim of the civil law that an unborn child shall be deemed to be born whenever its interests require it."

(2)   As the next section shows, the common law provided no cause of action for the death of any person, much less an unborn child. Therefore, all tort actions arising out of deaths are statutory; whether or not recovery can be had for the death of an unborn child depends upon the wording and interpretation of the statute. In most instances this comes down to deciding whether an unborn child is a "person" as that word is employed in the statute. In interpreting statutes the central job of a court is to determine what the legislature intended by using a particular term or word. Following that guideline, some courts have decided that an unborn child is a "person" for purposes of the wrongful death act and others have decided that it is not. For examples of the former, *see Fowler, Administrator, v. Woodward*, 138 S.E.2d 42 (S.C. 1964); and *Wiersma v. Maple Leaf Farms*, 543 N.W.2d 787 (S.D. 1996), and for the latter, *see Stern v. Miller*, 348 So. 2d 303 (Fla. 1977); and *Miller v. Kirk*, 905 P.2d 194 (N.M. 1995).

GROVER et al. v. ELI LILLY AND COMPANY et al.

No. 90-1030 Supreme Court of Ohio
Submitted Feb. 11, 1992
Decided June 10, 1992

WRIGHT, JUSTICE.

The United States District Court for the Northern District of Ohio has certified the following question to us: "Does Ohio recognize a cause of action on behalf of a child born prematurely, and with severe birth defects, if it can be established that such injuries were proximately caused by defects in the child's mother's reproductive system, those defects in turn being proximately caused by the child's grandmother ingesting a defective drug (DES) during her pregnancy with the child's mother?"

For purposes of this question, we are required to assume that Charles Grover can prove that his injuries were proximately caused by his mother's exposure to DES.We are not evaluating the facts of this case, but determining, as a matter of law, whether Charles Grover has a legally cognizable cause of action.

DES was prescribed to pregnant women during the 1940s, 1950s and 1960s to prevent miscarriage. The FDA banned its use by pregnant women in 1971 after medical studies discovered that female children exposed to the drug in utero had a high incidence of a rare type of vaginal cancer. See 36 Fed.Reg. 21,537 (1971). Candy Grover was exposed to DES as a fetus. Her son, Charles Grover, claims that his mother's DES-induced injuries were the cause of his premature birth and resulting injuries.

Because the mother and the child whose injury results from her injury are uniquely interrelated, and because it is possible that the mother may not discover the extent of her own injury until she experiences difficulties during pregnancy, the facts of this case pose a novel issue. Courts and commentators refer to the child's potential cause of action in such cases as a "preconception tort." See, *e.g.*, Note, *Preconception Torts: Foreseeing the Unconceived* (1977), 48 U.Colo.L.Rev. 621. The terminology stems from the fact that a child is pursuing liability against a party for a second injury that flows from an initial injury to the mother that occurred before the child was conceived.

Only a handful of courts have addressed whether a child has a cause of action for a preconception tort. One recurring issue is whether a child has a cause of action if a physician negligently performs a surgical procedure on the mother, such as an abortion or a Caesarean section, and the negligently performed procedure causes complications during childbirth several years later that injure the infant. See *Albala v. New York* (1981), 54 N.Y.2d 269, 445 N.Y.S.2d 108, 429 N.E.2d 786 (child has no cause of action for doctor's negligence during abortion performed four years prior to his conception); *Bergstreser v. Mitchell* (C.A.8, 1978), 577 F.2d 22 (construing Missouri law) (child has a cause of action against a doctor based on the doctor's negligence during a Caesarean section performed two years prior to the child's conception). In another malpractice suit, the Illinois Supreme Court recognized that a child had a cause of action against a hospital that negligently transfused her mother with Rh-positive blood eight years prior to the child's conception. *Renslow* v. *Mennonite Hospital* (1977), 67 Ill. 2d 348, 10 Ill. Dec. 484, 367 N.E.2d 1250. As a result, the mother's body produced antibodies to the Rh-positive blood that later injured her fetus during pregnancy. See, also, *Monusko v. Postle* (1989), 175 Mich. App. 269, 437 N.W.2d 367 (allowing cause of action by child against her mother's physicians for failure to inoculate the mother with rubella vaccine prior to the child's conception).

In *McAuley v. Wills* (1983), 251 Ga. 3, 303 S.E.2d 258, the Supreme Court of Georgia evaluated a wrongful death action brought on behalf of an infant who died during childbirth due to the mother's paralysis. The suit was brought against the driver who had originally caused the mother's paralysis in an automobile accident. The court held that a person may owe a duty of care to a child conceived in the future, but also held that the injury in that case was too remote as a matter of law to support recovery. *Id.* at 6–7, 303 S.E.2d at 260–261. The driver could not reasonably foresee, as a matter of law, that his lack of care in driving a motor vehicle would result in complications during the delivery of a child who was not yet conceived at the time of the accident. *Id.*[30]

This court declines to adopt an absolute rule at this time, but addresses an alleged cause of action that is far more tenuous than that raised in *Albala v. New York*. See, also, *Bergstreser v. Mitchell* (C.A.8, 1978), 577 F.2d 22 (for a fact pattern similar to the facts *of Albala v. New York*). At least arguably, a doctor should comprehend, at the time that he or she performs an abortion or a Caesarean section, that a negligently performed procedure could cause the woman's uterus to rupture during a subsequent pregnancy. It is more difficult to imagine that a pharmaceutical company, during the 1940s to the 1960s, could have foreseen the effect that a drug would have not only on a patient's unborn child, but also on that child's children.

The facts of these cases are significantly different from those of the case before us. The cause of action certified to us involves the scope of liability for the manufacture of a prescription drug that allegedly had devastating side effects on the original patient's female fetus. However, this case is not about the devastating side effects of DES on the women who were exposed to it, which have indeed been

---

[30] The Supreme Court of Georgia limited its holding to the facts of the case before it. The Court of Appeals for New York has taken the opposite approach and held that a plaintiff does not have a cause of action for any preconception tort, regardless of the facts alleged. See *Albala v. New York* (1981), 54 N.Y.2d 269, 445 N.Y.S.2d 108, 429 N.E.2d 786. It is this absolute rule that Prosser has criticized as a "blanket no-duty rule." See Prosser & Keeton, Law of Torts (5 Ed.1984) 369, Section 55.

well documented in medical studies and court opinions. See authorities cited infra at 701–702 (Resnick, J., dissenting) and the discussion of the state of medical research at 702–703 (Resnick, J., dissenting). This case is concerned with the rippling effects of that exposure on yet another generation, when that female child reaches sexual maturity and bears a child. Because a plaintiff in Charles Grover's position cannot be injured until the original patient's child bears children, the second injury will typically have occurred more than sixteen years after the ingestion of the drug. Several courts have addressed a fact pattern virtually identical to the facts of the case currently before this court. The New York Court of Appeals held that a child does not have a cause of action, in negligence or strict liability, against a prescription drug company based on the manufacture of DES if the child was never exposed to the drug in utero. *Enright v. Eli Lilly & Co.* (1991), 77 N.Y.2d 377, 568 N.Y.S.2d 550, 570 N.E.2d 198, certiorari denied (1991), 502 U.S. — , 112 S. Ct. 197, 116 L.Ed.2d 157. The court relied in part on its earlier opinion in *Albala v. New York, supra.* In both cases, the court was concerned with the "staggering implications of any proposition which would honor claims assuming the breach of an identifiable duty for less than a perfect birth and by what standard and the difficulty in establishing a standard or definition of perfection. . . . " *Id.*, 54 N.Y.2d at 273, 445 N.Y.S.2d at 109, 429 N.E.2d at 788. See *Enright v. Eli Lilly & Co., supra,* 77 N.Y.2d at 384, 568 N.Y.S.2d at 553, 570 N.E.2d at 201. The court was troubled by the possibility that doctors would forgo certain treatments of great benefit to persons already in existence out of fear of possible effects on future children. *Albala, supra,* 54 N.Y.2d at 274, 445 N.Y.S.2d at 110, 429 N.E.2d at 788–789. In *Enright,* the court noted that "the cause of action plaintiffs ask us to recognize here could not be confined without the drawing of artificial and arbitrary boundaries. For all we know, the rippling effects of DES exposure may extend for generations. It is our duty to confine liability within manageable limits. . . . Limiting liability to those who ingested the drug or were exposed to it in utero serves this purpose." *Id., 77* N.Y.2d at 387, 568 N.Y.S.2d at 555, 570 N.E.2d at 203. See, also, *Loerch v. Eli Lilly & Co.* (Minn.1989), 445 N.W.2d 560 (the evenly divided Supreme Court of Minnesota affirmed, without opinion, a lower court's decision that a child who was not exposed to DES has no cause of action).

One court has held that a plaintiff situated similarly to Charles Grover has a cause of action. The United States Court of Appeals for the Seventh District reversed a lower court's directed verdict on the issue of a pharmaceutical company's liability to a child for injuries caused by a premature birth. *McMahon v. Eli Lilly & Co. (C.A.7,* 1985), 774 F.2d 830. The court concluded that under Illinois law the company could be liable for failing to warn of the dangerous propensities of the drug, and need not have anticipated a particular side effect. *Id.* at 834–835.

We find the reasoning applied by the New York Court of Appeals persuasive on the issue currently before us. As an initial matter, we note that the pharmaceutical companies' conduct must be evaluated based on whether they knew or should have known of a particular risk through the exercise of ordinary care. The marketing of prescription drugs differs significantly from other consumer goods. Each drug is tested and approved for use by the Food and Drug Administration and is selected for use by a physician, who then prescribes the drug to the ultimate user. As a result, the drug manufacturer's primary responsibility is to provide adequate warnings to the physician. Prosser & Keeton, Law of Torts (5 Ed. 1984) 688, Section 96. The manufacturer does not breach its duty to warn — in negligence . . . — until the company knew or should have known of a particular risk through the exercise of ordinary care. *Id.; Crislip v. TCH Liquidating Co.* (1990), 52 Ohio St. 3d 251, 257, 556 N.E.2d 1177, 1182–1183, fn. 1.

It is on this point that Ohio law differs from Illinois law as construed in *McMahon v. Eli Lilly & Co., supra,* 774 F.2d at 834–835. The Seventh Circuit held that knowledge of the general dangerous propensities of the drug was sufficient to subject the company to liability for failure to warn. This court has stated that "[i]n a products liability case where a claimant seeks recovery for failure to warn or warn adequately, it must be proven that the manufacturer knew, or should have known, in the exercise of ordinary care, of the risk or hazard about which it failed to warn." (Footnote omitted.) *Crislip v. TCH Liquidating Co., supra,* 52 Ohio St. 3d at 257, 556 N.E.2d at 1182–1183. Even if knowledge of the drug's "dangerous propensities" is sufficient to create liability to the women exposed to the drug in utero, this same knowledge does not automatically justify the extension of liability to those women's children. It is one thing to say that knowledge of a propensity to harm the reproductive organs is sufficient to impose liability for a variety of different injuries to the reproductive organs. It is yet another thing to say that this generalized knowledge is sufficient to impose liability for injuries to a third party that occur twenty-eight years later.[31]

Knowledge of a risk to one class of plaintiffs does not necessarily extend an actor's liability to every potential plaintiff. While we must assume that DES was the proximate cause of Charles Grover's injuries, an actor is not liable for every harm that may result from his actions.

". . . The plaintiff sues in her own right for a wrong personal to her, and not as the vicarious beneficiary of a breach of duty to another." *Palsgraf v. Long Island RR. Co.* (1928), 248 N.Y. 339, 342, 162 N.E. 99, 100. An actor does not have a duty to a particular plaintiff unless the risk to that plaintiff is within the actor's "range of apprehension." *Id.* at 344, 162 N.E. at 100. ". . . If the actor's conduct creates such a recognizable risk of harm only to a particular class of persons, the fact that it in fact causes harm to a person of a different class, to whom the actor could not reasonably have anticipated injury, does not make the actor liable to the persons so injured." 2 Restatement of the Law 2d, Torts (1965), Section 281, Comment c; *Jeffers v. Olexo* (1989), 43 Ohio St. 3d 140, 142–143, 539 N.E.2d 614, 616–617. The existence of a legal duty is a question for the court, unless alternate inferences are feasible based on the facts. *Palsgraf, supra,* 248 N.Y. at 345, 162 N.E. at 101.

When a pharmaceutical company prescribes drugs to a woman, the company, under ordinary circumstances, does not have a duty to her daughter's infant who will be conceived twenty-eight years later. Charles Grover's injuries are not the result of his own exposure to the drug, but are allegedly caused by his mother's injuries from her in utero exposure to the drug. Because of the remoteness in time and causation, we hold that Charles Grover does not have an independent cause of action, and answer the district court's question in the negative. A pharmaceutical

---

[31] It is on this same point of law that the dissent confuses the issue by characterizing the question as whether the pharmaceutical companies should have known that DES could cause reproductive abnormalities in a developing fetus. The issue is not whether the pharmaceutical companies knew of some dangers from the use of this drug. To the contrary, the question is whether the drug companies should have known, at the time that it was prescribed, that DES could cause a birth defect that would result in the delivery of a premature child twenty or thirty years later. Modern studies may provide us with twenty-twenty hindsight, but the only medical studies relevant to this issue are those that occurred before DES was banned in 1971.

company's liability for the distribution or manufacture of a defective prescription drug does not extend to persons who were never exposed to the drug, either directly or in utero. Judgment accordingly.

ALICE ROBIE RESNICK, J, dissenting.

I dissent from the result reached in this case, but more importantly from the superficial treatment of the issue which was certified to this court, in light of its complexity. It is critical that we consider the exact issue which the federal court certified to this court: "Does Ohio recognize a cause of action on behalf of a child born prematurely, and with severe birth defects, if it can be established that such injuries were proximately caused by defects in the child's mother's reproductive system, those defects in turn being proximately caused by the child's grandmother ingesting a defective drug (DES) during her pregnancy with the child's mother?" . . .

I discern no sound basis, in law or public policy, for holding that there is no duty owed to persons in Charles Grover's position. We are dealing with a drug which was widely prescribed for many years to virtually millions of pregnant women. It was a drug which had FDA approval but, perhaps, was not adequately tested in view of a considerable body of scientific and medical literature that raised serious questions concerning the safety of DES to the developing fetus and its efficacy for treatment of pregnancy complications. Petitioners aver that, despite warnings from independent researchers dating back to the 1930s that DES caused reproductive tract abnormalities and cancer in exposed animal offspring, that drug companies, including Eli Lilly, performed no tests as to the effects of DES on the developing fetus, either in animals or humans. Petitioners also assert that by 1947 there were twenty-one studies which supported these findings; that recent medical studies have established a significant link between DES exposure and various uterine and cervical abnormalities in DES daughters; and that these studies have demonstrated that mature DES daughters have a significantly higher risk of miscarriage, infertility and premature deliveries.

. . .

DES continues to create difficult legal and social problems nationwide. The majority has failed to consider the uniqueness of DES. Instead, it has simply applied an arbitrary "blanket no-duty rule." Today's holding will have profound and devastating effects. To hold under these circumstances that Charles Grover's injuries were not foreseeable is to ignore an entire body of scientific information which was available or could have easily become available with a measure of care concerning the effects of DES on subsequent generations.

Having reviewed and considered the competing public policy concerns, the case law recognizing preconception torts, respected legal commentary and the available scientific studies, I would conclude that individuals such as Charles Grover properly have a cause of action for their injuries. This in no way opens the floodgates because litigation can easily be concluded with Charles Grover's generation. Moreover, the majority completely disregards the fact that the petitioners still bear the burden of proving proximate cause. I strenuously dissent.

NOTES AND QUESTIONS

(1)   *Bergstreser v. Mitchell,* referred to in *Grover,* relied in part on the legal maxim "where there is a right there is a remedy" to acknowledge a preconception duty. When a court does this it clearly is departing from the staid common law precedential and doctrinal approach and inching further toward the sweeping view of Brett, M.R. in *Heaven v. Pender.* Or is this approach even broader?

Bergstreser held that a duty of care was owed to the plaintiff who was injured while *in utero* because of weakness in his mother's uterus that had been negligently caused during delivery of a child by Caesarean section several years before. Several courts have followed *Bergstreser* in its own or similar contexts. See *Lough v. Rolla Women's Clinics, Inc.*, 866 S.W.2d 851 (Mo. En Banc. 1993) (duty was owed to child *in utero* as to damaging Rh factor in the mother's blood as a result of medical procedures the mother was subjected to before the plaintiff was conceived.) *Torres v. Sarasota County Public Hospital*, 961 So.2d 961 (Fla. 2nd DCA 2007) held that preconception duty was owed to a later born child, as did *Grover.*

Is the additional intervening generation, as in *Grover,* sufficient of itself to justify a firm no duty rule? *Lough* criticized *Grover* with this statement:

> The reason for not adopting a rule that would absolutely bar claims for preconception torts is demonstrated by the following hypothetical: Assume a balcony is negligently constructed. Two years later, a mother and her one-year-old child step onto the balcony and it gives way, causing serious injuries to both the mother and the child. It would be ludicrous to suggest that only the mother would have a cause of action against the builder but, because the infant was not conceived at the time of the negligent conduct, no duty of care existed toward the child. It is unjust and arbitrary to deny recovery to [a plaintiff] simply because he had not been conceived at the time of [the defendant's] negligence.

866 S.W.2d at 853. Are you persuaded?

(2)   The constitutions of many states include a provision to the effect, "The courts shall be open to every person for the redress of any injury and justice shall be administered without sale, denial or delay." Most courts deem that to be protective in the sense that all people have access to the courts of law for whatever protection the law provides. There is a tendency in some courts, however, to render it a substantive meaning, which sometimes helps them acknowledge duty where the common law never did.

§ 5.08   WRONGFUL DEATH AND SURVIVAL

BAKER v. BOLTON
1 Camp. 237, .170 Eng. Rep. 1033 (1808)[32]

This was an action against the defendants as proprietors of a stage-coach, on the top of which the plaintiff and his late wife were travelling from Portsmouth to London, when it was overturned; whereby the plaintiff himself was much bruised,

---

[32] [Ed. — English Reports, general reporter of older English cases; Nisi Prius decision; Campbell's reports.]

and his wife was so severely hurt, that she died about a month after in an hospital. The declaration besides other special damage, stated, that "by means of the premises, the plaintiff had wholly lost, and been deprived of the comfort, fellowship, and assistance of his said wife, and had from thence hitherto suffered and undergone great grief, vexation, and anguish of mind."

It appeared that the plaintiff was much attached to his deceased wife and that, being a publican, she had been of great use to him in conducting his business.

But Lord Ellenborough said, the jury could only take into consideration the bruises which the plaintiff had himself sustained, and the loss of his wife's society, and the distress of mind he had suffered on her account, from the time of the accident till the moment of her dissolution.

In a civil Court, the death of a human being could not be complained of as an injury; and in this case the damages, as to the plaintiff's wife, must stop with the period of her existence.

Verdict for the plaintiff, with £100 damages.

NOTES AND QUESTIONS

(1) *Baker v. Bolton* crystalized what is now the accepted common law rule; namely, there can be no civil cause of action brought by the survivors or the estate of a killed person in respect of the wrongful act that killed him. Although the origins of this rule are shrouded in history, Professor Malone has pulled together a revealing thesis in his article, *The Genesis of Wrongful Death*, 17 Stan. L. Rev. 1043 (1965).

Whereas other no-duty rules have been modified, if at all, mainly by court decisions, the no-action for death rule has been universally abrogated by statutes, commonly referred to in United States jurisdictions as wrongful death acts. It is these statutes, not the common law, that provide whatever remedies may be available in a particular jurisdiction. (May a court add remedies to those prescribed by statute?) The progenitor and, at one time, virtual universal model for these statutes was the English Fatal Accidents Act, 1846 (9 & 10 Vict. c. 93), commonly known as Lord Campbell's Act. The operative provisions of Lord Campbell's Act are:

> 1. When death is caused by negligence an action shall be maintainable. — Whensoever the death of a person shall be caused by wrongful act, neglect, or default, and the act, neglect, or default is such as would (if death had not ensued) have entitled the party injured to maintain an action and recover damages in respect thereof, then and in every such case the person who would have been liable if death had not ensued shall be liable to an action for damages, notwithstanding the death of the person injured, and although the death shall have been caused under such circumstances as amount in law to felony.

> 2. Action to be for the benefit of certain relations, and brought by executor or administrator of deceased. — Every such action shall be for the benefit of the wife, husband, parent, and child of the person whose death shall have been so caused, and shall be brought by and in the name of the executor or administrator of the person deceased; and in every such action

the jury may give such damages as they think proportioned to the injury resulting from such death to the parties respectively for whom and for whose benefit such action shall be brought; and the amount so recovered, after deducting the costs not recovered from the defendant, shall be divided amongst the before-mentioned parties in such shares as the jury by their verdict shall find and direct.

(12 Halsbury's Complete Laws of England.)

(2)   A second common law rule was that no personal cause of action survives the death either of the plaintiff or the defendant. Thus, if *A* negligently hurt *B*, and *B* died of natural causes before his cause of action for the injury was legally satisfied, the cause of action expired. Similarly, if *A*, the tortfeasor, died before *B's* cause of action was satisfied, *B's* cause of action expired. In sum, in the pristine common law personal causes of action expired with the death of either the tortfeasor or the victim. Survival, also, has been addressed by statute.

See 3 Minzer, et al., Damages in Tort Actions, Chaps. 20–23 (Matthew Bender & Co.), for in-depth discussions and analyses of wrongful death and survival actions. The next two cases examine some of the issues that arise in application of survival and wrongful death statutes.

(3)   As noted earlier, Tort law has three principal goals; first, to compensate Tort victims; second, to prevent dangerous behavior, and, third, to provide relatively clear, simple, and predictable Tort rules.

How well does the common law wrongful death rule perform these functions? As to deterrence, could any rule be worse? As to compensation, does the rule give tortfeasors an incentive to kill rather than maim victims? As to clear simple and predictable rules, what could be better? How did the common law wrongful death rule affect the length of Tort litigation?

JACKSONVILLE STREET RAILWAY v. CHAPPELL ADM'X
Florida Supreme Court
1 So. 10 (1886)

RANEY, J.

[Decedent was killed in a railroad accident. Decedent's administratrix sued for, among other things, medical expenses accrued between the date of injury and date of death and loss of time (i.e., wage equivalent) during the same period. The plaintiff recovered at judgment in the trial court.] At the common law the death of either party to an action abated it; and, says Blackstone, (marginal page 302, book 3, vol. 2,) "in actions merely personal, arising *ex delicto*, for wrongs actually done or committed by the defendant, as trespass, battery, and slander, the rule is that *actio personalis moritur cum persona;* and it never shall be revived either by or against the executors or other representatives. For," says he, neither the executors of the plaintiff have received, nor those of the defendant have committed, in their own personal capacity, any manner of wrong or injury; but in actions arising *ex contractu*, by breach of promise and the like, . . . the suits . . . may be revived against or by the executors; being, indeed, rather actions against the property than the person, in which the executors have now the same interest that their testator had before.

Chitty (pages 77, 78, vol. 1) on Pleading, after remarking that actions for the breach of a *contract* survive, states:

But in case of torts, when the action must be in form *ex delicto*, for the recovery of damages, and the plea not guilty, the rule at common law was otherwise; . . . but if the action can be framed in form *ex contractu*, this rule does not apply. . . . In the case of injuries to the person, whether by assault, battery, false imprisonment, slander, or otherwise, if either the party who received or committed the injury die, no action can be supported either by or against the executors or personal representatives, for the statute of 4 Edw. III. *c.* 7, has made no change in this respect. . . . At common law, in cases of injury to *personal property*, if either party died, in general no action could be supported by or against the personal representative where the action must have been in form *ex delicto*, and the plea not guilty; but if any *contract* could be implied, as if the wrong-doer converted the property into money, or if the goods remained *in specie* in the hands of the executor of the wrong-doer, *assumpsit* might be supported at common law by or against the executors in the former case, and trover against the executors in the latter. The statute of Edward provided for a survival of the action to the executor of the testator whose personal property was carried away or injured and rendered less valuable; and 3 & 4 Wm. IV. *c.* 42, § 3, gives executors and administrators rights of action for torts to real or personal estate injured, but not for mere injuries to the person.

Stephens, J., in *Newsom v. Jackson, 29* Ga. 62, speaking as to what is included under the head of *"Actio Personalis,"* says, the most satisfactory explanation is that given by Judge Tucker, in his commentaries, which is: "If the cause of action *can* be maintained in form *ex contractu*, it survives; but, if it is necessarily in form *ex delicto*, it dies with the death of either party;" and, an action of deceit, being necessarily in form *ex delicto*, was held to die with the defendant.

It was observed in *Knights v. Quarles*, 2 Brod. & B. 102, that if a man contracted for a safe conveyance by a coach, and sustained an injury by a fall by which his means of improving his personal estate were destroyed, and that property in consequence injured, though it was clear he, in his life-time, might, at his election, sue the coach proprietor in contract or in tort, it could not be doubted that his executor might sue in *assumpsit* for the consequences of the coach proprietor's breach of contract. *Raymond v. Fitch, 2* Cromp. M. & R. 588.

It may be regarded as settled that, under the common law, a common carrier can be sued for an injury done to a passenger through its negligence, either in an action of tort (trespass on the case) for a breach of its duty as a public carrier, — such action against a carrier in this case being founded "upon the custom of the realm, which was but another name for the common law," — or in an action *ex contractu (assumpsit)* upon the passenger's contract with the carrier. Hutch. Carr. §§ 738–740; *Pennsylvania R. Co. v. Peoples*, 31 Ohio St. 537. There are certain characteristics distinguishing these two actions, but the only one material here is that the former action does not survive to the personal representative of the passenger, or against those of the defendant, in case the death of such plaintiff or defendant; but the latter does survive. Hutch. Carr. § 743.

In *Huff v. Watkins*, 20 S. C. 477, where a plaintiff sued in form *ex delicto*, and the defendant died before judgment, and it was held that the action could not be revived against the personal representatives of the deceased, it was said that, accepting the propositions made by the plaintiff's counsel to be true, "it might be enough to say that this action, now proposed to be revived against the executor of Watkins, was brought against the testator in his life-time, — not *assumpsit* on any supposed promise, express or implied, but clearly *ex delicto* for a wrong done. The action has *already taken form, and we have no authority to change its whole nature in order to revive it* against the executor. Upon the *face of the record itself,* the cause of action arose *ex delicto*, and, as it seems to us, was buried with the offender."

If the action presented by the declaration and record before us is an action of tort for the breach of duty as a common carrier, it, at the common law, and independent of our statute declaring what actions shall die with the person, does not survive to the administratrix, the appellee in this court. On the other hand, if it is, in effect, an action *of assumpsit* upon the carrier's contract with the intestate, it, barring the effect of the statute, does survive to the administratrix.

In the declaration before us there is no averment of any promise to carry, or of any such promise for a consideration, nor of any breach of the promise, — no statement of any contract or agreement, even, as an inducement to the averment of the common-law duty. It merely states the facts out of which the duty as a common carrier to carry the intestate as a passenger arose, and the negligent performance or breach of such duty, and the injury and expense and damage resulting therefrom. It seems to have been copied from Chitty's precedent of a declaration in tort for injury to a passenger. 2 Chit. 492. It is true, it states as damages expenses and loss of time, which naturally create a diminution of the intestate's personal estate. This, however, is no statement of a contract, and a breach thereof as a cause of action, but only of damage sought to be recovered for in the action. I frankly confess that at one time it seemed to me that the first count in the declaration might be construed as laid upon a contract, but a further consideration of the subject, after calling it to the attention of counsel, convinces me that I was in error, and we are all of the opinion that it, and the whole declaration, can only be treated as one in case for a breach of duty by the defendant as a common carrier, and that at common law the action died with the intestate. Of course, if there was one count in *assumpsit* or upon contract, it would not, under our system of pleading, be impaired by the fact that the other counts were in tort.

This makes it necessary to pass upon our statute as to the abatement of actions by death of parties. It provides as follows: "Hereafter all actions for personal injuries shall die with the person, to-wit, assault and batteries, slander, false imprisonment, and malicious prosecution. All other actions shall and may be maintained in the name of the representative of the deceased." McClellan, Dig. § 77, p. 830.

Statutes are to be construed according to their intent and meaning, and a good rule is this intent and meaning are to be derived from the language used as applied to the subject-matter of the enactment. We have in this statute a plain declaration that hereafter all actions for personal injuries shall die with the person, and then, after a word, ("to wit") which would properly introduce or precede an enumeration of all recognized actions for personal injuries, or all wrongs resulting in personal injury, and for which an action was maintainable, we find an enumeration of only some of the personal wrongs or injuries for which actions dying with the person were maintainable at common law. After this follows the declaration, not that all other actions for personal injuries, but that all other actions, shall and may be maintained in the name of the representatives of the deceased.

. . .

It seems to us clear that the purpose of the legislature, to be seen from a view of the entire act, was that all actions for personal injuries should die with the person. To say that the enumeration of a few personal wrongs or injuries after a *videlicet* changes the plain meaning of the simple but strong and broad language preceding, so as to limit it to the particular cases covered by the enumeration, is to give the statute an effect both unnatural and at war with the plain sense of all other expressions in it. It is to expound the act neither according to its letter nor its evident meaning. A thing which is within the object, spirit, and meaning of a statute is as much within the statute as if it were within the letter of it. *Id.* 179. An action based on a personal wrong or injury other than one of those enumerated is as much within the meaning, and even the letter, of this act, looking at its context, as one based on a false imprisonment, or other enumerated wrong.

We are of the opinion that at least any action for a personal injury, which did not survive at common law, does not survive under the statute, and consequently that the action set up by the declaration died with the intestate. Whether, under the statute, the action, if framed as upon a contract, would, under the circumstances of this case, have died with the intestate, we do not decide, as the declaration is not so framed.

Judgment reversed.

NOTE

Does your state have a survival statute similar to the one construed in *Jacksonville Street Railway?* Does the court's construction of the statute seem unnecessarily rigid?

FLORIDA EAST COAST RAILWAY v. McROBERTS
Florida Supreme Court
149 So. 631 (1933)

DAVIS, CHIEF JUSTICE.

In an action for wrongful death brought under the Florida statute, W. C. McRoberts, plaintiff below, for the alleged wrongful death of his wife, recovered a judgment against the defendant, Florida East Coast Railway Company, in the sum of $22,500. Writ of error brings the case to this court.

[The lower court held for the plaintiff and awarded compensation and exemplary damages.]

. . . [T]he sole question presented to us by this writ of error is whether or not under the Florida wrongful death statute (sections 4960, 4961, R. G. S., sections 7047, 7048, C. G. L.) exemplary or punitive damages are recoverable where the facts of the case before the jury would warrant the recovery of such exemplary or punitive damages, had no death ensued from the negligence proved. In this connection it is appropriate to state at this point that for the purposes of this writ of error, it is conceded by counsel for the railway company that a sufficient factual basis for the recovery of exemplary damages was laid by plaintiff in his evidence, provided it should be determined that, in an action for wrongful death, such damages are recoverable as a matter of law.

The Florida statute (section 7047) on the subject of recovery for wrongful death reads as follows:

[Omitted is the virtually verbatim version of Lord Campbell's Act as it pertained to this case.]

The common law afforded no remedy for death by wrongful act. Hence the right and the remedy are purely statutory. *Florida Cent. & P. R. Co. v. Foxworth*, 41 Fla. 1, 25 So. 338, 79 Am. St. Rep. 149; *Flanders v. Georgia Southern & F. R. Co.*, 68 Fla. 479, 67 So. 68. In order to supply the want of a remedy in those cases where negligent acts resulted in the death of the injured party, there was enacted in England, in the year 1846, an act of Parliament known as Lord Campbell's Act. This law for the time provided a right of action for death by wrongful act. Since that time, Lord Campbell's Act, in various forms, has been substantially enacted in every state in the United States except one. In Louisiana a remedy of equivalent import is provided according to the course of the civil law which prevails in that state.

. . .

So it may be said to have been well established, both in England and the United States, as a principle of the common law, that in all actions for torts the jury may be authorized to inflict what are called punitive or exemplary damages, having in view the enormity of the offense which has occasioned the injury, rather than the measure of compensation to be awarded to the plaintiff therefor.

In cases of injury to the person, in addition to the right of action of the party receiving the physical injury to recover compensatory, or even punitive damages therefor, causes of action sometimes accrued to persons who stood to the injured party in the relation of master, parent, or husband, for the recovery by the latter of damages for loss of services or society. The maxim, "actio personalis moritur cum persona," had no application to damages recoverable by persons of the latter description for the loss of services or society which took place before death; that is, during the period of time intervening a fatal injury and actual dissolution. Such was the holding of the leading English cases that antedated the passage of Lord Campbell's Act in 1846.

Consequently we find that the English common-law rule originating in the early case of *Higgins v. Butcher*, 1 Yelverton, 89, decided in 1606, and reaffirmed by Lord Ellenborough in the case *of Baker v. Bolton*, 1 Camp. 493, decided in 1808, was definitely to the effect that, in an action for negligence brought against one for so severely injuring plaintiff's wife that she died within a comparatively short time thereafter, the only recovery permissible in the action was the loss of the wife's society to the plaintiff, and his distress of mind on her account, from the time of the accident to the moment of the wife's dissolution. Where the negligent death was instantaneous, no recovery at all could be had, since the rule "actio personalis moritur" applied to the deceased, and no right, under the circumstances, for damages otherwise, could accrue to the surviving husband.

Whatever may have been the wisdom or justice of the common-law rule, as it had been early declared in *Higgins v. Butcher, supra*, and later restated without serious challenge of its correctness, in *Baker v. Bolton, supra*, the fact remains that the rule of the common law as it was finally epitomized in *Baker v. Bolton*, by Lord Ellenborough, became and was recognized in this state as a part of the common law of Florida, and was so regarded by our Legislature when it undertook to change that rule by the enactment of chapter 3429, Acts of 1883, which subsequently became section 7047, C. G. L., section 4960, R. G. S., our death by wrongful act statute.

While it has been observed by many jurists and text-writers that Lord Ellenborough's statement of the common-law rule just referred to in *Baker v. Bolton, supra*, was made by him without any attempt to support it by giving his reasons, nor the citation by him of any authority purporting to justify the existence of any such common-law rule as was then declared by him, nevertheless his statement that such was the applicable law of that case has been accepted since then in nearly all subsequent cases in England as well as in this country. Consequently it is now generally acknowledged to be a final and authoritative declaration of the common-law rule on the subject of what, if any, recovery of damages may be had by a husband, in case of the death of his wife alleged to have been brought about by another's wrongful act. And, as conculusive of what should be declared to be the common-law rule in this state, this court feels impelled to accept Lord Ellenborough's summarization in *Baker v. Bolton, supra*, as a correct statement of the common law of Florida, absent any statute providing for a right to sue for recovery of damages sustained in suits for damages alleged to have been suffered by a death by wrongful act.

. . .

Having seen that this conclusion is irrefutable, that the statutes grant a new right of action for death by wrongful act, and not merely a continuation of the old one by way of a substituted form of action in favor of the deceased's representatives, for recovery of the particular damages the deceased himself might have recovered by reason of the wrongful infliction of the injuries from which he died, it would seem to be clear on principle, if there were no authority on the subject, that exemplary, punitive, or vindictive damages cannot be recovered by those whom the statute vests with authority to bring suit, nor for recovery of the damages the deceased himself might have become entitled to recover, but for recovery by the statutory plaintiffs of compensation for the death of the person injured by the wrongful act or default of another.

. . .

In this case, the plaintiff's right to recover damages was expressly admitted by the defendant below at the trial. And indeed the same admission was made at the bar of this court during the course of the oral argument. We therefore consider that, while this is an appropriate case wherein a new trial should be awarded, such new trial should be awarded only as to the amount of damages to be allowed plaintiff, and that all other issues should be deemed settled by the judgment appealed from conclusively in favor of defendant in error.

The verdict of the jury is accordingly set aside and a new trial awarded on the question of damages, with directions to exclude from the jury, on a subsequent trial of that issue all evidence and instructions to the jury to the effect that plaintiff has any right to recover exemplary or punitive damages as an element of his recovery. In all other respects the plaintiff's judgment against the defendant, and all the issues adjudicated thereby except the amount of plaintiff's damages, is affirmed, and the cause remanded for further proceedings to be had according to law.

New trial awarded as to damages, and cause remanded for further proceedings, with directions.

On Petition for Rehearing.

PER CURIAM.

At common law the principle was well settled that an action for personal injuries dies with the injured party. Assuming that under the common law a willfully or wantonly inflicted personal injury necessarily carried with the right to recover compensatory damages the further or incidental right to recover punitive damages as well, and assuming that punitive damages were thus permitted to be recovered against the wrongdoer, because of the law's desire to protect society, the same rule of the common law which caused the principal right of action to die with the injured party also caused to die with the action the incidental right to punitive damages. The common-law right to recover punitive damages having accrued as an incident to the right of the injured party to recover from the tortious injury inflicted in this case, the death of such injured party caused both the right of action and the incidents to it to die at the same time. And having once died, our holding is that the language of the statute creating a new statutory action for wrongful death, affirmatively negatives the idea that punitive damages are to be considered as an incident to the damages allowed for the new statutory cause of action.

Rehearing denied.

NOTES AND QUESTIONS

(1) This case strikingly demonstrates the absorption of the common law of England into the common law of an American state. Does this seem peculiar in a state like Florida which was not in existence as a state until well after the American revolution and which has an early history of Spanish rule? What explains this acceptance of the common law of England?

(2) How an issue such as the one in *McRoberts* is resolved is ordinarily dependent upon the specific provisions of the wrongful death statute in question. How should the issue be resolved under the statute enacted in your state?

The precise holding *of McRoberts*, that punitive damages are not available under the Florida Wrongful Death Act, was receded from after the Florida statute was later modified. *See Atlas Properties, Inc. v. Didick*, 226 So. 2d 684 (Fla. 1969), wherein the court said, "It is difficult to accept reasoning that envisions that a person can be punished only for his malicious and reckless actions when they maim another but not for those same despicable actions when they kill the victim." Should that statement be material in the construction of a statute? See also *Martin v. United Security Services*, 314 So. 2d 765 (Fla. 1975).

In a novel decision that affirms a more general common judicial law power to craft wrongful death recoveries, *Gaudett v. Webb*, 284 N.E.2d 223, 228 (Mass. 1972), held: ". . . we are convinced that the law in this Commonwealth has evolved to the point where it may now be held that the right to recovery for wrongful death is of common law origin, and we so hold. . . . Consequently, our wrongful death statutes will no longer be regarded as 'creating the right' to recovery for wrongful death."

Herbert v. Herbert, 415 A.2d 679, 681 (N.H. 1980), rejected the "common law origin" holding *of Gaudett* as not persuasive.

(3) Suppose a pregnant woman is negligently injured in an automobile crash. As a result, the fetus is spontaneously aborted. What determines whether the prospective parents may maintain a wrongful death action for the death of the fetus? *Cf. Wiersma v. Maple Leaf Farms*, 543 N.W.2d 787 (S.D. 1996) (holding that the wrongful death act provides a cause of action for the death of a nonviable unborn child), with *Chatelain v. Kelley*, 910 S.W.2d 215 (Ark. 1995) (holding an unborn fetus is not a person under the Arkansas wrongful death act.)

Suppose a nonviable fetus is injured *in utero*, is miscarried because of the injury, lives a short time after birth, and then dies? May a wrongful death action be maintained? *Cf. Farley v. Sartin*, 466 S.E.2d 522 (W. Va. 1995) (the wrongful death act provides a cause of action), with *Miller v. Kirk*, 905 P.2d 194 (N.M. 1995) (wrongful death act does not provide a cause of action.).

(4) Suppose X is badly injured by the negligent act of Y. X brings an action against Y and receives and executes a judgment. X then dies of his injuries. May X's survivors maintain a wrongful death action against Y? *Cf. Alfone v. Sarno*, 87 N.J. 99, 432 A.2d 857 (1981), and *Variety Children's Hosp. v. Perkins*, 445 So. 2d 1010 (Fla. 1983).

(5) Contrary to the common law rule, "an action does lie under general maritime law for death caused by violation of maritime duties." *Moragne v. States Marine Lines, Inc.*, 398 U.S. 417, 90 S. Ct. 1772, 1792 (1970).

(6) Excerpts from the Model Survival and Death Act are presented below. How do they differ from Lord Campbell's Act? From the Wrongful Death Statute in your jurisdiction?

MODEL SURVIVAL AND DEATH ACT[33]

§ 1 [Definitions]

As used in this Act:

(1) "Actionable conduct" means an act or omission that causes the death of a person for which the person could have brought and maintained a personal injury action if he had not died; the term includes an act or omission for which the law imposes strict liability or liability for breach of warranty.

(2) "Survivors of a decedent" means:

(i) the surviving spouse, ascendants and descendants of the decedent, and

(ii) individuals who were wholly or partially dependent upon the decedent for support and were members of the decedent's household or related to the decedent by blood or marriage.

(3) "Closely-related survivors" means the surviving spouse and ascendants and descendants of the decedent.

---

[33] Copyright 1979 by National Conference of Commisioners on Uniform State Laws. Reprinted with permission.

§ 2 [Survival Actions]

(a) An action or a [claim for relief] [cause of action]:

(1) does not abate by reason of the death of a person to or against whom it accrued, unless by its terms it was limited to the person's lifetime;

(2) may be maintained by or against the personal representative of a decedent; and

(3) is subject to all defenses to which it was subject during the decedent's lifetime.

(b) Damages recoverable in behalf of a decedent under this section for an injury causing his death are limited to those that accrued to him before his death, plus reasonable burial expenses paid or payable from his estate. Damages so recovered become a part of the decedent's estate and are distributable in the same manner as other assets of the estate. This section does not affect the measure of damages allowable under the law for any other damages recoverable under any other [claim for relief] [cause of action].

§ 3 [Death Actions]

(a) With respect to any death caused by actionable conduct, the decedent's personal representative, acting in a fiduciary capacity on behalf of the survivors of the decedent, may bring and maintain a death action against any person or the estate of any person legally responsible for the damages, including an insurer providing applicable uninsured or underinsured motorist coverage. The death action is subject to all defenses that might have been asserted against the decedent had he survived.

(b) If no personal representative is appointed [within six months after decedent's death] the death action may be brought and maintained by a closely-related survivor acting in a fiduciary capacity.

(c) Any survivor having a potential conflict of interest with other survivors may be represented independently in the death action.

(d) In the death action, damages awarded to survivors of a decedent are limited to the following elements:

(1) Medical expenses incident to the injury resulting in death and reasonable burial expenses, paid or payable by the survivors, to the extent that the decedent's estate could have recovered under Section 2 had the payments been made by the decedent or his estate; [and]

(2) The [present] monetary value of support, services, and financial contributions they would have received from the decedent had death not ensued[.] [; and]

(3) For closely-related survivors, [reasonable compensation for decedent's pain and suffering before death if not separately recoverable under Section 2, and reasonable compensation for mental anguish and loss of companionship [not exceeding the sum of $ —].

(e) Punitive or exemplary damages [are not recoverable] [are recoverable only if they would have been recoverable by the decedent had death not ensued].

(f) The trier of fact shall make separate awards to each of the survivors entitled to damages. Conduct of a survivor which contributed to the death is a defense to the survivor's recovery to the same extent as in other actions.

(g) The decedent's personal representative or a closely-related survivor qualifying under subsection (b) may compromise any claim arising under this section, before or after an action is brought, subject to confirmation by a judge of the court [in which the action is or could have been brought] [appointing the personal representative]. The personal representative or closely-related survivor shall apply to the court for confirmation by [petition], stating the terms of the compromise, the reasons therefor, and the names of all survivors having an interest in the distribution of the proceeds. The court, upon notice, shall hold a hearing which all survivors and their legal representatives may attend, and shall confirm or disapprove the settlement. If the settlement is confirmed and any of the survivors or their representatives disagree with the distribution prescribed by it, the judge shall order any distribution a trier of fact may make under subsection (f).

§ 4 [Joinder of Actions]

Actions under Sections 2 and 3 are separate actions but shall be joined for trial if they are based upon the same actionable conduct. Separate verdicts and awards shall be rendered in each action.

§ 5.09 WRONGFUL BIRTH AND WRONGFUL LIFE

BOONE v. MULLENDORE
Alabama Supreme Court
416 So. 2d 718 (1982)

TURBERT, CHIEF JUSTICE.

This is a medical malpractice case wherein the trial court granted summary judgment in favor of the defendant on the ground that plaintiff, Repsie Rhea Boone, is limited in her recovery of damages to the amount of the settlement with the hospital measured in terms of her actual medical expenses incurred in giving birth. Mrs. Boone appeals and we reverse.

In 1976, Repsie Rhea Boone visited Dr. M. M. Mullendore, complaining of cramps and bloating in her abdomen. On July 6, 1976, Mrs. Boone was admitted to Colbert County Hospital for exploratory surgery. During the surgery, Dr. Mullendore discovered and removed cysts in Mrs. Boone's Fallopian tubes and ovaries. After the surgery, Dr. Mullendore dictated an operative summary and procedure that stated that "the left and right [Fallopian] tubes were removed." Additionally, the plaintiff also alleges that Dr. Mullendore informed her that her Fallopian tubes had been removed and that she was sterile. As a result of this representation, Mrs. Boone did not use contraceptive methods. She became pregnant, however, and in April 1978 delivered a healthy child.

The Boones brought suit against Colbert County Hospital and Dr. Mullendore for negligently representing that her Fallopian tubes had been removed and that she was sterile, or, in the alternative, for negligent failure to remove the Fallopian tubes. Mrs. Boone sought compensatory damages for medical expenses and costs reasonably incurred in the rearing of the child. At the pretrial hearing, Mr. Boone withdrew as a party plaintiff and following the pre-trial hearing, Mrs. Boone reached a pro tanto settlement with the hospital for $1,500.00, which was conceded to be the amount of her medical expenses. Subsequently, Dr. Mullendore moved for, and the trial court granted, a summary judgment on the ground that, as a matter of law, Mrs. Boone could not recover more that the settlement amount for actual medical expenses incurred in giving birth. This appeal followed.

The issue on appeal is what damages may be recovered by a parent as a result of the negligent treatment, or the negligent misrepresentation of a doctor that the parent is incapable of having children. For the reasons set forth below, we hold that the trial court erred in limiting damages to out-of-pocket medical expenses.

Mrs. Boone contends that a health care provider should be subject to liability in damages for negligence that results in the wrongful birth of a child. At this point, it will be helpful to make distinctions in the terminology used by the parties. A claim for "wrongful birth" is one brought against a physician who "failed to inform parents of the increased possibility that the mother would give birth to a child suffering from birth defects . . . [thereby providing] an informed decision about whether to have a child." *Phillips v. United States*, 508 F. Supp. 544, 545 n.1 (D.S.C.1981) (quoting Comment, 8 Hofstra L.Rev. 257, 257–58 (1979)). A claim for "wrongful life" is one by which a child seeks recovery for being born with infirmities. See, *Elliot v. Brown*, 361 So. 2d 546 (Ala. 1978), wherein this Court refused to recognize a cause of action for "wrongful life." This case is, instead, more suited to a traditional medical malpractice, negligence action. In the court below, the plaintiff alleged that Dr. Mullendore was negligent in failing to remove her Fallopian tubes or, in the alternative that her Fallopian tubes had been removed and that she was sterile. Some jurisdictions have defined actions of this type as an action for "wrongful pregnancy."

    . . .

Among the difficult issues in an action of this type is the measure of damages to be ascertained. Several theories have been proposed by other courts and by the parties to this action. Dr. Mullendore urges this Court to find that, as a matter of law, the benefits accruing to the parents of a healthy child outweigh the economic and emotional detriment of having an unwanted, unanticipated child. *See, e.g., Terrell v. Garcia*, 496 S.W.2d 124 (Tex. Civ. App.1973), *cert. denied*, 415 U.S. 927, 94 S. Ct. 1434, 39 L. Ed. 2d 484 (1974); *Rieck v. Medical Protective Co.*, 64 Wis. 2d 514, 219 N.W.2d 242 (1974). Under this theory the holding of the trial court would have to be affirmed.

In California, it has been held that all costs and expenses of rearing such a child, and also emotional distress, are recoverable. *Custodio v. Bauer*, 251 Cal. App. 2d 303, 59 Cal. Rptr. 463 (1967). A third view of damages is that the parents may recover only damages for pregnancy- related costs and expenses, and damages for pain and suffering. *Wilbur v. Kerr*, Ark., 628 S.W.2d 568 (1982); *Coleman v. Garrison*, 349 A.2d 8 (Del.1975).

The fourth view of damages, which is urged by the appellant, is known as the "benefit" rule of damages. Under the "benefit" rule, parents may recover for damages proximately caused by the physician's negligence, including pregnancy-related expenses and the economic damages to the family resulting from the birth and rearing of the additional child. These damages may be offset, however, by the benefits accruing to the family as a result of the child's birth. *Sherlock v. Stillwater Clinic*, 260 N.W.2d 169 (Minn. 1977). See also, Restatement (Second) of Torts, § 920 (1977). Mrs. Boone contends that the losses and benefits resulting from a wrongful pregnancy are relatively tangible and are measurable factors for the jury to consider separately. We cannot agree.

Today, we adopt as the measure of damages in an action of this type essentially the standard set out in *Coleman v. Garrison*, 327 A.2d 757 (Del. Super. Ct. 1974), *aff'd*, 349 A.2d 8 (Del. 1975). This Court believes that damages should be limited to the actual expenses and the injury attending the unexpected pregnancy. Thus, the damages recoverable would include: (1) The physical pain and suffering, and mental anguish of the mother as a result of her pregnancy; (2) the loss to the husband of the comfort, companionship, services, and consortium of the wife during her pregnancy and immediately after the birth; and (3) the medical expenses incurred by the parents as a result of the pregnancy. Any additional damages would tend to be extremely speculative in nature, and awarding such damages could have a significant impact on the stability of the family unit and the subject child.

As indicated, numerous courts have addressed these issues in recent years and have come to various conclusions. A large number, however, have held that for public policy and other reasons the expenses of rearing a child to the age of majority should be denied. *Wilbur v. Kerr*, Ark., 628 S.W.2d 568 (1982); *Coleman v. Garrison*, 327 A.2d 757 (Del. Super. Ct.1974), *aff'd*, 349 A.2d 8 (Del.1975); *Wilczynski v. Goodman*, 73 Ill. App. 3d 51, 29 Ill. Dec. 216, 391 N.E.2d 479 (1979); *Stewart v. Long Island College Hospital*, 35 A.D.2d 531, 313 N.Y.S.2d 502 (1970), *aff'd*, 30 N.Y.2d 695, 332 N.Y.S.2d 640, 283 N.E.2d 616 (1972); *Hays v. Hall*, 477 S.W.2d 402 (Tex. Civ. App.1972); *Rieck v. Medical Protective Co.*, 64 Wis. 2d 514, 219 N.W.2d 242 (1974). The cornerstone of this denial is the idea that a normal healthy life should *not* be the basis for a compensable wrong. "The existence of a normal, healthy life is an esteemed right under our laws, rather than a compensable wrong." *Wilczynski v. Goodman*, *29* Ill. Dec. at 224, 391 N.E.2d at 487. As one court has stated:

> To permit the parents to keep their child and shift the entire cost of its upbringing to a physician who failed to determine or inform them of the fact of pregnancy would be to create a new category of surrogate parent. Every child's smile, every bond of love and affection, every reason for parental pride in a child's achievements, every contribution by the child to the welfare and well-being of the family and parents, is to remain with the mother and father. For the most part, these are intangible benefits, but they are nonetheless real. . . . We hold that such result would be wholly out of proportion to the culpability involved, and that the allowance of recovery would place too unreasonable a burden upon physicians, under the facts and circumstances here alleged.

Rieck v. Medical Protective Co., 219 N.W.2d at 244–45.

The birth of a healthy child, and the joy and pride in rearing that child, are benefits on which no price tag can be placed. This joy far outweighs any economic loss that might be suffered by the parents

. . . To allow damages under the "benefit rule" as urged by Mrs. Boone, would only invite speculative and ethically questionable assessments of damages that in the long run would cause a great emotional impact on the child, its siblings, and the parents.

Another problem is the possible harm that can be caused to the unwanted child who will one day learn that he not only was not wanted by his or her parents, but was reared by funds supplied by another person. Some authors have referred to such a child as an "emotional bastard" in a realistic, but harsh, attempt to describe the stigma that will attach to him once he learns the true circumstances of his upbringing. 50 Cin.L.Rev. 65 (1981); *Wilbur v. Kerr*, Ark., 628 S.W.2d 568 (1982). Mrs. Boone, however, contends that such damages are not for the child, but are, as stated by the Illinois Court of Appeals in *Doerr v. Villate*, 74 Ill. App. 2d 332, 220 N.E.2d 767 (Ill. Ct. App.1966), "to replenish the family exchequer so that a new arrival will not deprive other members of the family of what was planned as their just share of family income." We cannot agree. If the "benefit rule" is adopted, it will place the parent in the win-lose situation that if they admit that the child is a welcome addition and that they will love the child and rear it properly, they may get no damages at all. It would thus be to their advantage, at least monetarily so, to deny any affection for the child and to emphasize all of the economic problems the child will cause, thus increasing damages and the possibility of emotional trauma in the child at the time he or she learns of the earlier proceedings.

This dilemma leads to several more problems in the assessment of damages. First, in Alabama one seeking to hold another liable for damages is required to use reasonable efforts to avoid or mitigate his or her damages. *Bates. v. General Steel Tank Co.*, 36 Ala. App. 261, 55 So. 2d 213, *cert. dismissed*, 256 Ala. 466, 55 So. 2d 218 (1951). Yet courts recognizing this cause of action have rejected the argument that parents should choose the various methods of mitigation — adoption, abortion, etc. — seeing the moral issues begin to make inroads into an already emotional and speculative process of determining damages. The issue is one "which meddles with the concept of life and the stability of the family unit." *Wilbur v. Kerr*, 628 S.W.2d at 571.

Another problem arises in regard to the damages that may be awarded — namely, what to do with the money recovered. If damages are awarded for the care and maintenance of the child, should the money go directly to the family to use as the parents see fit, should the money be placed in a special trust fund for the child, or should a guardian ad litem be appointed for the benefit of the child to insure that the money recovered actually goes to the rearing of the child?

As stated by the Supreme Court of Arkansas in *Wilbur v. Kerr:*

> It is a question which meddles with the concept of life and the stability of the family unit. Litigation cannot answer every question; every question cannot be answered in terms of dollars and cents. We are also convinced that the damage to the child will be significant; that being an unwanted or "emotional bastard," who will some day learn that its parents did not want it and, in fact, went to court to force someone else to pay for its raising, will be harmful to that child. It will undermine society's need for a strong and healthy family relationship. We have not become so sophisticated a society to dismiss that emotional trauma as nonsense. 628 S.W.2d at 571.

We must emphasize that our holding is in the restricted context of a healthy, though unplanned and unexpected, child. Nothing in this opinion should be construed as addressing, or commenting upon, the measure of damages attendant with a right of action, if any, in favor of the parents of a child, in an action of this type, when the child is born and afflicted with *predetermined or readily foreseeable genetic or hereditary defects.*

In conclusion, this Court holds that there is no viable reason for exempting a physician from liability when his negligence proximately and wrongfully causes a patient to become pregnant. Because the issues of negligence and proximate cause are generally questions of fact for the jury, and because we hold that the trial court erred in limiting the amount of damages recoverable to the out of pocket expenses of delivering, the holding of the trial court is reversed and the cause remanded. If, at trial, liability is established, the damages recoverable by the plaintiffs include: (1) compensation for the physical pain and suffering, and mental anguish of the mother as a result of the pregnancy; (2) the loss to the husband of the comfort, companionship, services, and consortium of the wife during her pregnancy and immediately after the birth; and (3) the medical expenses incurred as a result of the pregnancy.

Reversed and remanded.

FAULKNER, JUSTICE (concurring specially).

My difference with the majority is simply that I would hold that damages here should be assessed under the "benefit" rule.

. . .

Under the "benefit" rule, parents may recover for damages proximately caused by the physician's negligence, including pregnancy-related expenses and the economic damages to the family of the birth and rearing of an additional child. These damages may be offset, however, by the benefits accruing to the family on the birth of the child. Section 920 of the Restatement (Second) of Torts (1979), states:

Where the defendant's tortious conduct has caused harm to the plaintiff or to his property and in so doing has conferred upon the plaintiff a special benefit to the interest which was harmed, the value of the benefit conferred is considered in mitigation of damages, *where this is equitable.* [Emphasis added.]

This rule permits the factfinder flexibility in determining the extent of benefits accruing to the parents in different circumstances. As the court in *Troppi v. Scarf,* 31 Mich. App. at 256–57, 187 N.W.2d at 518–19, points out, the trier of fact must have the power to evaluate the benefit according to all the facts and circumstances in a particular case. "Family size, family income, age of the parents, and marital status are some, but not all of the factors" which the trier of fact may consider in awarding damages. *Id.*

The major difficulty in applying the "benefit rule" is that comment 6 to Section 920 of the *Restatement* indicates that benefits to one type of interest may not offset damages to another type of interest. Nevertheless, the benefit rule is rooted in the equitable principle of unjust enrichment. See *Sherlock v. Stillwater Clinic,* 260 N.W.2d at 176. In a cause of action for "wrongful pregnancy," it would be unfair and would result in unjust enrichment to strictly apply the "same interest" limitation. Since the economic burden and emotional distress of rearing an unexpected child are inextricably related to each other, I would hold that the reasonable costs of rearing a child may be offset by the value of the economic and emotional benefits conferred on the parents by a child. See *Troppi v. Scarf,* 31 Mich. App. at 258, 187

N.W.2d at 518. *Accord, Sherlock v. Stillwater Clinic*, 260 N.W.2d at 176. In the case of a normal, healthy child, these expenses usually do not extend beyond the age of majority when the parents are no longer under an obligation of support. *Id.* These damages may be offset by the value of the child's aid, comfort and society. *Id.*

The majority also asserts that such a measure of damages is unascertainable and entirely speculative. Nonetheless, the pregnancy-related expenses, medical and hospital bills, lost wages and so forth are readily ascertainable. Likewise, the cost of rearing a child is an expense routinely computed by juries. Mrs. Boone's damages for pain and suffering are ascertainable, as this court recently recognized in *Taylor v. Baptist Medical Center*, 400 So. 2d 369 (Ala. 1981). The only uncertainty arises from the application of the "benefits" rule. While the exact dollar value of the benefits accruing to the parents is difficult to determine, it is enough that the plaintiff shows the extent of damages as a matter of reasonable and justifiable inference. *Story Parchment Co. v. Paterson Parchment Co.*, 282 U.S. 555, 51 S. Ct. 248, 75 L. Ed. 544 (1931); *American LifeInsurance Co. v. Shell*, 265 Ala. 306, 90 So. 2d 719 (1956). The rule in Alabama is that when damages are not capable of being precisely measured, the amount of damages to be granted rests largely within the discretion of the jury. *Summerlin* v. *Robinson*, 42 Ala. App. 116, 154 So. 2d685 (1963). The most fundamental principle of tort law is that a party should recover for injuries caused by the wrongdoing of others. A party who is wronged should have an opportunity to present to the jury the question of what are reasonable and proper damages. This Court and courts of other jurisdictions have permitted the question of damages to be submitted to a jury in analogous situations. See, *e.g.*, *Smith v. Richardson*, 277 Ala. 389, 171 So. 2d 96 (1965) (recovery of parents for permanently injured child). *Sellman v. Fahey*, Minn. 375, 233 N.W.2d 563 (1975) (recovery for wrongful death). Juries have been able to comprehend and determine the amount of damages in similar situations, and are capable of determining fair and reasonable damages in an action for wrongful pregnancy.

An action for wrongful pregnancy, in which damages are measurable, may be distinguished from an action for "wrongful life," in which damages are said to be incalculable. It should be recalled that in an action for wrongful life, an action is brought on behalf of a child for negligently permitting the child to be born. See *Elliott v. Brown*, 361 So. 2d 546 (Ala. 1978). Several courts have denied actions for wrongful life, based on the rationale that we cannot measure "the value of life with impairments against the nonexistence of life itself." *Id.* at 547 (quoting *Gleitman v. Cosgrove*, 49 N.J. 22, 227 A.2d 687 (1967)); *Dumer v. St. Michael's Hospital*, 69 Wis.2d 766, 233 N.W.2d 372 (1975). Justice Almon, speaking for this Court, has noted that there is no legal right not to be born. *Elliott* v. *Brown*, 361 So. 2d at 548. Nevertheless, several courts which have refused to recognize an action for wrongful life have recognized an action for wrongful pregnancy. See *Phillips v. United States*, 508 F. Supp. 544 (D.S.C.1981); *Phillips v. United States*, 508 F. Supp. 537 (D.S.C.1980); *Sherlock v. Stillwater Clinic*, 260 N.W.2d 169 (Minn. 1977); *Berman v. Allan*, 80 N.J. 421, 404 A.2d 8 (N.J. 1979); *Speck v. Finegold*, 268 Pa. Super. 342, 408 A.2d 496 (1979). These cases distinguish wrongful life actions in two ways. First, the courts state that whether it is better to be born with defects, or not at all, is beyond our current ability to understand or calculate. Second, and more important, is that a cause of action is not cognizable at law for the right not to be born. These courts have permitted recovery for wrongful pregnancy. A parent has the right not to have a child. Thus, a legal right has been damaged. Furthermore, damages for rearing a child are similar to damages already committed to the power and domain of the jury.

The appellee also contends that Mrs. Boone may not recover for wrongful pregnancy because she failed to mitigate damages by aborting the child or giving it up for adoption. The Michigan appellate court addressed this question in *Troppi v. Scarf*, 31 Mich. App. 240, 187 N.W.2d 511 (1971). The court eloquently stated this conclusion:

However, to impose such a duty upon the injured plaintiff is to ignore the very real difference which our law recognizes between the avoidance of conception and the disposition of the human organism after conception. . . . At the moment of conception, an entirely different set of legal obligations is imposed upon the parents. A living child almost universally gives rise to emotional and spiritual bonds which few parents can bring themselves to break.

Once a child is born he obviously should be treated with love regardless of whether he was wanted when he was conceived. Many, perhaps most, persons living today are conceptional accidents in the sense that their parents did not desire that a child result from the particular intercourse in which the person was conceived. Nevertheless, when the child is born, most parents accept him with love. That the plaintiffs accepted their eighth child does not change the fact that the birth of another child, seven years younger than the youngest of their previously born children, unbalanced their life style and was not desired by them.

JONES and SHORES, JUSTICES (Concurring specially).

We are in complete agreement with the majority opinion, both as to the issue of liability and as to the measure of damages recoverable in such cases. We concur specially in order to amplify the rationale for rejection of the "benefit" rule and to clarify the mental anguish element set forth in the opinion as a portion of item 1 of the recoverable elements of damages.

While we agree that Plaintiff has suffered damages beyond the medical expenses incurred in the prenatal care and birth of her child, we further agree that legal damages may not be extended to cover the economic burden or rearing the child to the age of majority.

To adopt such a measure of damages would reduce the value of the parent/child relationship to a mathematical formula, subject to being diminished only by incalculable future events. But, more than this, it would equate the right of the mother to elect, in the first instance, not to conceive with a presupposed subsequent attitude of "not wanting" the child born of her "wrongful pregnancy." A woman's personal right to exercise the option not to become pregnant does not necessarily mean that a child conceived as a result of the breach of that initial right is an "unwanted" child. To the contrary, it is more accurately an "unexpected" or "unanticipated" child.

. . .

On the other hand, the law should recognize that an alleged wrong, if legally established, results in denial of Plaintiff's lawful right to exercise the option not to become pregnant. The wrong is directly and exclusively related to her personal right not to become pregnant. In reliance on the Defendant doctor's representation, she says, she proceeded on the assumption that her choice not to become pregnant had been assured, and thus did not exercise other methods of contraception.

Consequently, assuming liability as alleged, Mrs. Boone is entitled to recover, if proved, those elements of damages enumerated in the Court's opinion, including any mental anguish suffered by her for the violation of her personal right not to conceive a child.

NOTES AND QUESTIONS

(1)   The *Boone* opinion drew a distinction between wrongful birth in which parents seek to recover certain damages pertaining to the rearing of a defective child, and wrongful life in which a deformed or otherwise congenitally defective child seeks to recover general damages for having been permitted to be born. Usually, the latter cases involve failed abortions or the failure of a physician to warn parents of the probability of a congenital defect. The next case is of this variety. Can a rational distinction be drawn between these cases? Should any damages be permitted to the parents in wrongful life actions? For in-depth analyses of wrongful birth and wrongful life causes of action, see 3 Minzer, et al., Damages in Tort Actions, Chapter 18, "Prenatal Injuries — Wrongful Birth and Life" (Matthew Bender & Co.).

(2)   Many decisions have held that a wrongful birth cause of action is cognizable. As *Boone* indicates, the primary disagreement among jurisdictions comes in determining how to fashion a damage remedy. *Greco v. United States*, 893 P.2d 345 (Nev. 1995), permitted the plaintiff mother to recover "extraordinary medical and custodial expenses associated with caring for [the child] for whatever period of time it is established that [the child] will be dependent upon her to provide such care." *Id.*, at 349. The basis for extending the mother's recovery beyond the age of majority was "that Nevada law requires the parents of a handicapped child to support that child beyond the age of majority if the child cannot support itself." *Id.* If the law were otherwise, should the mother's economic damages terminate when the child attains majority age? *Id.*, 893 P.2d at 349, n. 8. *Greco* also permitted the mother to recover for emotional damages, but not for loss of the child's services and companionship. Is the distinction justifiable?

(3)   Suppose adoptive parents adopt a child that appears to be healthy but turns out to inflicted with a debilitating congenital illness that imposes extraordinary medical and rearing costs upon the adoptive parents. Should a cause of action of wrongful adoption be permitted against an adoption agency that negligently withheld the medical status of the child from the adoptive parents? *See Mohr v. Commonwealth*, 653 N.E.2d 1104 (Mass. 1995). Is this a more or less deserving action than wrongful birth? Wrongful life?

(4)   *Boone* discussed four possible approaches to awarding damages in wrongful pregnancy cases. Evaluate each in terms of all three of the economic goals of the Tort system: victim compensation, deterrence of harmful behavior, and providing clear, simple and predictable rules. Which of the four approaches is best or worst for compensation? For deterrence? For providing clear, simple and predicable legal rules?

HARBESON v. PARKE-DAVIS, INC.
Washington Supreme Court
98 Wash. 2d 460, 656 P.2d 483 (1983)

PEARSON, JUSTICE.

[As a result of having been prescribed Dilantin, Mrs. Harbeson conceived and delivered two deformed babies. Mr. and Mrs. Harbeson brought an action for wrongful birth and the children brought an action for wrongful life. The wrongful birth action was permitted with an award of damages in an amount that is "in excess of the cost of the birth and rearing of two normal children."]

WRONGFUL LIFE

In a wrongful life claim, [t]he child does not allege that the physician's negligence caused the child's deformity. Rather, the claim is that the physician's negligence — his failure to adequately inform the parents of the risk — has caused the *birth* of the deformed child. The child argues that *but for* the inadequate advice, it would not have been born to experience the pain and suffering attributable to the deformity.

Comments, *"Wrongful Life": The Right Not To Be Born*, 54 Tul.L.Rev. 480, 485 (1980).

To this definition we would add that the physician's negligence need not be limited to failure to adequately inform the parents of the risk. It may also include negligent performance of a procedure intended to prevent the birth of a defective child: sterilization or abortion.

Wrongful life is the child's equivalent of the parents' wrongful birth action. However, whereas wrongful birth actions have apparently been accepted by all jurisdictions to have considered the issue, wrongful life actions have been received with little favor. There is an excellent discussion of the law relating to recognition of an action for wrongful life in *Curlender v. Bio-Science Labs*, 106 Cal. App. 3d 811, 165 Cal. Rptr. 477 (1980). The action has been rejected in Alabama, *Elliott v. Brown*, 361 So. 2d 546 (Ala.1978); New Jersey, *Berman v. Allan*, 80 N.J. 421, 404 A.2d 8 (1979); New York, *e.g., Becker v. Schwartz*, 46 N.Y.2d 401, 413 N.Y.S.2d 895, 386 N.E.2d 807 (1978); South Carolina, *Phillips v. United States*, 508 F. Supp. 537 (D.S.C. 1980); Texas, *Jacobs v. Theimer*, 519 S.W.2d 846 (Tex. 1975); and Wisconsin, *Dumer v. St. Michael's Hosp.*, 69 Wis. 2d 766, 233 N.W.2d 372 (1975).

Two other jurisdictions have come closer to embracing the cause of action. In Pennsylvania, a trial court decision that the action was not legally cognizable was affirmed only as a result of the even division of the Supreme Court. *Speck v. Finegold*, 497 Pa. 77, 439 A.2d 110 (1981). The Supreme Court of California rejected the claim of a child for general damages, but allowed the recovery of extraordinary medical expenses occasioned by the child's defect. *Turpin v. Sortini*, 31 Cal. 3d 220, 182 Cal. Rptr. 337, 348, 643 P.2d 954, 965 (1982). The court acknowledges that "it would be illogical and anomalous to permit only parents, and not the child, to recover for the cost of the child's own medical care." We agree. The child's need for medical care and other special costs attributable to his defect will not miraculously disappear when the child attains his majority. In many cases, the burden of those expenses will fall on the child's parents or the state. Rather than allowing this to occur by refusing to recognize the cause of action, we prefer to place the burden of those costs on the party whose negligence was in fact a proximate cause of the child's continuing need for such special medical care and training.

We hold, accordingly, that a child may maintain an action for wrongful life in order to recover the extraordinary expenses to be incurred during the child's lifetime, as a result of the child's congenital defect. Of course, the costs of such care for the child's minority may be recovered only once. *Wooldridge v. Woolett*, 96 Wash. 2d 659, 666, 638 P.2d 566 (1981). If the parents recover such costs for the child's minority in a wrongful birth action, the child will be limited to the costs to be incurred during his majority.

The analysis whereby we arrived at our holding is similar to that which we used in considering the parents' wrongful birth action. It is convenient therefore to consider wrongful life according to the four traditional tort concepts of duty, breach, injury, and proximate cause.

We begin with duty. The first potential difficulty with this element of a wrongful life action is that in every case the alleged negligent act will occur before the birth of the child, and in many cases (including the one before us) before the child is conceived. Prenatal injuries to a fetus have been recognized as actionable in this state for 20 years. *Seattle-First Nat'l Bank v. Rankin*, 59 Wash. 2d 288, 367 P.2d 835 (1962). We have not previously considered whether a duty could exist prior to conception. Other courts have recognized such a preconception duty. *e.g., Turpin v. Sortini, supra*, and authorities cited therein. We now hold that a duty may extend to persons not yet conceived at the time of a negligent act or omission. Such a duty is limited, like any other duty, by the element of foreseeability. *Hunsley v. Giard*, 87 Wash.2d 424, 435–36, 553 P.2d 1096 (1976). A provider of health care, or anyone else, will be liable only to those persons foreseeably endangered by his conduct. In most wrongful life cases, it should not be difficult to establish foreseeability. In the case before us, for example, the parents informed the defendant physicians of their intention to have further children. Such future children were therefore foreseeably endangered by defendants' failure to take reasonable steps to determine the danger of prescribing Dilantin for their mother.

One reason for the reluctance of other jurisdictions to recognize a duty to the child appears to be the attitude that to do so would represent a disavowal of the sanctity of a less-than-perfect human life. *Berman v. Allan*, 80 N.J. at 430, 404 A.2d 8. This reasoning was rejected in *Turpin v. Sortini*, at 233, 182 Cal. Rptr. 337, 643 P.2d 954.

[I]t is hard to see how an award of damages to a severely handicapped or suffering child would "disavow" the value of life or in any way suggest that the child is not entitled to the full measure of legal and nonlegal rights and privileges accorded to all members of society.

We agree.

Furthermore, the policies which persuaded us (along with several other jurisdictions) to recognize parents' claims of wrongful birth apply equally to recognition of claims of wrongful life. Imposition of a corresponding duty to the child will similarly foster the societal objectives of genetic counseling and prenatal testing, and will discourage malpractice. In a footnote, the court in *Turpin v.*

Sortini wrote at 349 n. 15, 182 Cal. Rptr. 337, 643 P.2d 954:

Permitting recovery of these extraordinary out-of-pocket expenses whether the cost is to be borne by the parents or the child should also help ensure that the available tort remedies in this area provide a comprehensive and consistent deterrent to negligent conduct.

In addition to providing a comprehensive and consistent deterrent to malpractice, recognition of the duty will provide more comprehensive and consistent compensation for those injured by such malpractice (at least for extrordinary out-of-pocket expenses) than would be available were the duty confined to the parents. In order to achieve these ends, therefore, we recognize the existence of a duty to the unborn or unconceived child.

This duty will be breached by failure to observe the appropriate standard of care. *See* Rogers at 332–33.

The most controversial element of the analysis in other jurisdictions has been injury and the extent of damages. The New Jersey Supreme Court gave two reasons for rejecting a child's wrongful life claim in *Berman v. Allan.* First, the quantum of damages in such an action would be impossible to compute because the trier of fact would be required to "measure the difference in value between life in an impaired condition and the 'utter void of nonexistence.'" 80 N.J. at 427, 404 A.2d 8. Second, to recognize life itself as an actionable injury would be inimical to deeply held beliefs that life is more precious than non-life.

We agree with the New Jersey court that measuring the value of an impaired life as compared to nonexistence is a task that is beyond mortals, whether judges or jurors. However, we do not agree that the impossibility of valuing life and nonexistence precludes the action altogether. General damages are certainly beyond computation. They are therefore incapable of satisfying the requirement of Washington law that damages be established with "reasonable certainty." *Dyal v. Fire Companies Adj. Bur., Inc.,* 23 Wash. 2d 515, 521, 161 P.2d 321 (1945). But one of the consequences of the birth of the child who claims wrongful life is the incurring of extraordinary expenses for medical care and special training. These expenses are calculable. Thus, although general damages are impossible to establish with reasonable certainty, such special damages can be proved. In respect of special damages, therefore, the objection advanced in *Berman v. Allan* is not persuasive.

The second objection advanced by the New Jersey court in *Berman v. Allan* we have already discussed. Suffice it to say here that we do not agree that requiring a negligent party to provide the costs of health care of a congenitally deformed child does not appear to us to be a disavowal of the sanctity of human life.

The final element which requires consideration is proximate cause.

The causation issue in a wrongful life claim is whether "[b]ut for the physician's negligence, the parents would have avoided conception, or aborted the pregnancy, and the child would not have existed." Comments, 54 Tul.L.Rev. at 491. Some early cases advanced a proximate cause argument based on the fact that the negligence of the physician did not cause the defect from which the plaintiff suffered; rather, the negligence was in failing to disclose the existence of the defect. *e.g., Gleitman v. Cosgrove,* 49 N.J. 22, 27–28, 227 A.2d 689 (1967). This argument does not convince us. It is clear in the case before us that, were it not for the negligence of the physicians, the minor plaintiffs would not have been born, and would consequently not have suffered fetal hydantoin syndrome. More particularly, the plaintiffs would not have incurred the extraordinary expenses resulting from that condition. There appears to be no reason a finder of fact could not find that the physicians' negligence was a proximate cause of the plaintiffs' injuries.

For these reasons, we hold that a claim for wrongful life may be maintained in this state. We therefore answer the District Court's questions 3 and 4, as follows.

Elizabeth and Christine Harbeson may maintain a wrongful life action. We have held that the physicians' duty to inform the parents of the risks associated with Dilantin extends to the unconceived children. The District Court held that this standard was breached by the Madigan physicians in failing to conduct a literature search. The minor plaintiffs suffer an actionable injury to the extent that they require special medical treatment and training beyond that required by children not afflicted with fetal hydantoin syndrome. They may recover damages to the extent of the cost of such treatment and training. The standard appropriate to the conduct of the physicians is the standard of the "average practitioner." RCW 4.24.290 does not apply to the Harbesons' claim.

NOTES AND QUESTIONS

(1) A Michigan appellate court rejected even the limited wrongful life recovery permitted by *Harbeson v. Parke-Davis, Inc.*, and *Turpin v. Sontini* cited therein. According to the Michigan court:

Plaintiff's damages, general and special, consist of the difference between his present life with defects and no life at all. Plaintiff's economic liabilities, like the daily pain and suffering he must endure, are a part and parcel of his life with birth defects. Therefore, this Court cannot view those economic losses apart from the incalculable benefit of life conferred upon plaintiff by the events antecedent to his birth. Consequently, we conclude that plaintiff's special damages are as incognizable as any general damages for pain and suffering.

Strohmaier v. Associates in Obstetrics & Gynecology, 332 N.W.2d 432, 435 (Mich. App. 1982). Do you agree with the legal reasoning? The outcome? Does the character of the antecedent events matter?

(2) Courts in numerous jurisdictions have considered the so-called wrongful life cause of action but only a small number has recognized it as a basis of obtaining legal relief for the child. *Greco v. United States*, 893 P.2d 345 (Nev. 1995). Recovery, if at all, ordinarily must be obtained in a parent's wrongful birth action. The wrongful life action was rejected in England in *McKay v. Essex Area Health Authority*, [1982] Q.B. 1166 (C.A.), on the ground that it would be against public policy to permit a cause of action that violated the sanctity of human life. The English court noted that the thread of American authority opposed the action.

(3) In *Saunders v. United States*, 64 F.3d 482 (9th Cir. 1995), applying Mississippi law, a plaintiff child sued for damages arising from being born with severe permanent injuries stemming from premature birth caused by a correctable defect in his mother's uterus. The child's complaint was that had his mother's uterus been properly repaired *before* his conception he would have been born without the injuries. The court distinguished *Saunders* from the wrongful life cases, in which only the birth but not the defect could have been prevented, and permitted the

plaintiff to recover *inter alia* loss of earning capacity based upon normal life expectancy.

(4)   *Hickman v. Group Health Plan, Inc.*, 396 N.W.2d 10, 11 (Minn. 1986), upheld the following statue against constitutional challenge:

145.424 PROHIBITION OF TORT ACTIONS.

Subdivision 1. Wrongful life action prohibited. No person shall maintain a cause of action or receive an award of damages on behalf of himself based on the claim that but for the negligent conduct of another, he would have been aborted.

Subd. 2. Wrongful birth action prohibited. No person shall maintain a cause of action or receive an award of damages on the claim that but for the negligent conduct of another, a child would have been aborted.

Subd. 3. Failure or refusal to prevent a live birth. Nothing in this section shall be construed to preclude a cause of action for intentional or negligent malpractice or any other action arising in tort based on the failure of a contraceptive method or sterilization procedure or on a claim that, but for the negligent conduct of another, tests or treatment would have been provided or would have been provided properly which would have made possible the prevention, cure, or amelioration of any disease, defect, deficiency, or handicap; provided, however, that abortion shall not have been deemed to prevent, cure, or ameliorate any disease, defect, deficiency, or handicap. The failure or refusal of any person to perform or have an abortion shall not be a defense in any action, nor shall that failure or refusal be considered in awarding damages or in imposing a penalty in any action.

Minn. Stat. § 145.424 (1984). *See also Shelton v. St. Anthony's Med. Ctr.*, 781 S.W.2d 48 (Mo. 1989), applying Missouri statute that prohibits a cause of action that but for the negligence of another, the plaintiff would not have been born.

Molloy v. Meier, 679 N.W.2d 711 (Minn. 2004), acknowledged that the foregoing statute abrogates wrongful birth and wrongful life causes of action, but held that it does not abrogate "wrongful conception." Hence, parents who suffered birth of one genetically defective child and were not told of the genetic risks to any child conceived by the union could state a cognizable cause of action against physicians who allegedly failed to inform them of the risks as to future children. *Taylor v. Kurapati*, 600 N.W. 2nd 679 (Mich. App. 199) abolished the "wrongful birth" cause of action in Michigan. Thereafter the Michigan legislature enacted this statute:

Sec. 2971. (1) A person shall not bring a civil action on a wrongful birth claim that, but for an act or omission of the defendant, a child or children would not or should not have been born.

(2) A person shall not bring a civil action for damages on a wrongful life claim that, but for the negligent act or omission of the defendant, the person bringing the action would not or should not have been born.

(3) A person shall not bring a civil action for damages for daily living, medical, educational, or other expenses necessary to raise a child to the age of majority, on a wrongful pregnancy or wrongful conception claim that, but for an act or omission of the defendant, the child would not or should not have been conceived.

(4) The prohibition stated in subsection (1), (2), or (3) applies regardless of whether the child is born healthy or with a birth defect or other adverse medical condition. The prohibition stated in subsection (1), (2), or (3) does not apply to a civil action for damages for an intentional or grossly negligent act or omission, including, but not limited to, an act or omission that violates the Michigan penal code, 1931 PA 328, MCL 750.1 to 750.568.

M.C.L.A. 600.2971

(5)   In *McFarlane v Tayside Health Board* [2000] 2 A.C. 59, the House of Lords rejected parents' claim to recover as damages the cost of bringing up a healthy and normal child which was conceived as a consequence of a botched vasectomy on the husband. *Rees v. Darlington Memorial Hospital NHS Trust,* [2004] P.I.Q.R. P14 (HL), examined whether the same rule should apply to a handicapped woman who wished to avoid conception because of her physical inability to care for a child. Although the House of Lords held that *McFarlane* was sound, a divided House permitted the recovery of a "conventional sum" of £15,000 in *Rees.*

Chapter 6

BREACH

§ 6.01 GENERAL PRINCIPLES

There is no fixed standard in the law by which a court is enabled to arbitrarily say in every case what conduct shall be considered reasonable and prudent, and what shall constitute ordinary care, under any and all circumstances. . . .

The policy of the law has relegated the determination of such questions to the jury, under proper instructions from the court. . . .

It is only where the facts are such that all reasonable men must draw the same conclusion from them that the question of negligence is ever considered as one of law for the court. . . .

Lamar, J., *Grand Trunk Railway Co. v. Ives*, 144 U.S. 408, 417 (1892).

PROBLEM A

A worker was injured when a bulldozer caught fire while being repaired. The machine had broken down and was being repaired by defendant, an independent repair company. The worker was asked to remain on the machine to operate certain levers during the repair, which entailed welding. Sparks from the weld ignited traces of grease and the resulting flames spread to the gasoline system. Evidence was presented to establish that the repairs could have been made without requiring the operator to remain on the machine. Against the defendant's objection, the following instruction was given: "You may find the Defendant liable to the Plaintiff if you find there was a safer method to repair the bulldozer; and, if the safer method had been used, Plaintiff would not have been injured." A verdict was returned for the plaintiff.

Write an appellate opinion, affirming or reversing the verdict.

GRIFFIN v. WATKINS
North Carolina Supreme Court
153 S.E. 356 (1967)

Plaintiff sues for personal injuries and property damages resulting from a collision between plaintiff's 1965 Pontiac automobile and a 1960 John Deere tractor owned by the corporate defendant (Dickerson) and operated by its agent, defendant Watkins. Defendants deny plaintiff's allegations of negligence, plead plaintiff's contributory negligence, and defendant Watkins counterclaims for personal injuries. The collision occurred in a 55 MPH speed zone on August 19, 1965, on U. S. Highway No. 601 about two miles north of Monroe and three-tenths of a mile south of a rural paved road, known as Ridge Road. At this point the pavement, unlined black asphalt newly laid, was 24 feet wide. The west shoulder was 9 feet in width; the east shoulder, 15 feet.

Plaintiff alleged and offered evidence tending to show: At about 7:25 p.m., plaintiff was traveling south on Highway 601 at a speed of 30 MPH. The weather was cloudy, and it was dark at the time. (Plaintiff alleged that the accident occurred at about 7:25 p.m.; he testified that he "figured it was 7:45.") All the cars which he met had their headlights burning; his were on low beam. He met and passed a truck with blinding headlights. As soon as the truck passed, plaintiff saw Dickerson's tractor, stopped 40–50 feet ahead in his lane of travel without lights of any kind on it. There were no flags, flares, or flambeaux to give warning of the tractors' presence. Plaintiff applied his brakes and skidded 37 feet, but he was unable to avoid a collision with the rear end of the tractor. Plaintiff, 71 years old, was seriously and permanently injured, and his automobile was damaged in the sum of $2,350.00. The force of the impact knocked the right rear wheel from the tractor. The tractor came to rest about 81 feet from a pool of oil, which apparently came from its axle, broken in the collision.

Defendants alleged and offered evidence tending to show: Defendant Watkins, operating Dickerson's tractor, which was equipped with a front rotary-sweeper broom, ran out of gasoline in the south-bound lane of Highway 601 about 7:00 p. m. He was able to get only the right wheels (18 inches wide and about 5 feet high) off the pavement. The total weight of the tractor and sweeper was 4,300 pounds; its total width, 5 feet 10 inches. The rear of the tractor was equipped with a large, elevated sign saying CAUTION. This sign was approximately 3 feet above the rear wheels of the tractor. On each side of it, at the top, was a yellow light, which blinked when turned on. The tractor was also equipped with headlights and a tail lamp. Leaving all the lights burning on the tractor, Watkins boarded the truck of another employee of Dickerson and went for gasoline. They returned in 15–20 minutes, put the gasoline in the tractor, and Watkins was attempting to start its engine when plaintiff, traveling at a speed of 60–65 MPH, crashed into the rear of the tractor. Defendant Watkins was thrown to the shoulder of the road and his back was injured. At the time of the collision, all the lights on the tractor were burning, and the two yellow lights were blinking. It was, however, not yet dark; sunset was at 7:06 p.m. Neither plaintiff nor operators of other vehicles on the highway had then turned on their headlights.

Issues were submitted to the jury and answered as follows:

"1. Was the plaintiff injured and his automobile damaged by the negligence of the defendants, as alleged in the complaint? ANSWER: Yes.

"2. If so, did the plaintiff by his own negligence contribute to his injuries and damages, as alleged in the answer? ANSWER: No.

"3.What amount, if anything, is the plaintiff entitled to recover of the defendants?

"(a) For damages to his automobile: ANSWER: $ None.

"(b) For personal injuries: ANSWER: $40,000.

"4. Was the defendant, LeRoy Thomas Watkins, injured by the negligence of the plaintiff as alleged in the answer? ANSWER: _____

"5. What amount, if anything, is the defendant entitled to recover of the plaintiff? ANSWER: $_____ "

From the judgment entered upon the verdict, defendants appeal.

SHARP, JUSTICE.

In specifying the acts of omission and commission which they contend constituted negligence and contributory negligence on the part of plaintiff, defendants allege that he failed to operate his automobile at a speed which would permit him to stop within the range of his headlights.

. . .

Defendants also assigned as error the following portion of his Honor's instruction to the jury:

[I]f plaintiff has satisfied you from the evidence and by its greater weight that the defendants were negligent in any one or more of the following respects, *i.e.: that they failed to exercise due care*; that they failed to have the lights on as provided by statute if it was thirty minutes after sunset or the visibility was less than two hundred feet; or [that] they parked on the highway when it was practical or reasonably practical to park off the highway as provided by section 20–161 of the General Statutes; and . . . [that] the negligence in any one or more of those respects was a proximate cause of the collision and the injury and damage resulting to the plaintiff, then it would be your duty to answer the first issue YES in favor of the plaintiff. (Emphasis added.)

Failure to exercise due care is the failure to perform some specific duty required by law. To say that one has failed to use due care or that one has been negligent, without more, is to state a mere unsupported conclusion. "[N]egligence is not a fact in itself, but is the legal result of certain facts." *Shives v. Sample*, 238 N.C. 724, 726, 79 S.E.2d 193, 195. In his charge, the trial judge must tell the jury what specific acts or omissions, under the pleadings and evidence, constitute negligence, that is, the failure to use due care. Defendants justly complain that this instruction gave the jury *carte blanche* to find them *generally* careless or negligent for any reason which the evidence might suggest to them.

For the errors indicated, there must be a new trial. We do not consider defendants' other assignments of error; the questions presented may not arise in the next trial.

New Trial.

PARKER, CHIEF JUSTICE (concurring in part and dissenting in part).

I agree with the majority opinion that the defendants are entitled to a new trial for failure of the court in its charge to apply the provisions of G.S. § 20-141(e) to defendants' evidence tending to show that plaintiff was guilty of contributory negligence, as set forth in the second issue. I do not agree with this statement in the majority opinion: "To say that one has failed to use due care . . . is to state a mere unsupported conclusion," and that "[d]efendants justly complain that this instruction gave the jury *carte blanche* to find them *generally* careless or negligent for any reason which the evidence might suggest to them."

Sir A. P. Herbert wittily and happily said in the Uncommon Law, p. 1: "The Common Law of England has been laboriously built about a mythical figure — the figure of 'The Reasonable Man.' " To this may be added: The law of negligence has been laboriously built about the figure of "The Reasonable Man's" failure to use due care. "Due care" is a duty lying at the root of the social compact. In the dawn of the history of the human race, the Lord said unto Cain: "Where is Abel thy brother? And he, said, I know not: Am I my brother's keeper?" Genesis, Ch. 4, v. 9 (King James Version). An old, old question but yet new with all. Whatever doubt may have arisen in the mind of the unhappy man who first asked it, no doubt exists in the law on the right answer, then and now. The law hedges around the lives and persons of men with much more care than it employs when guarding their property, so that, in this particular, it makes, in a way, everyone his brother's keeper. Negligence is the failure to exercise that degree of care for others' safety which a reasonably prudent man, under like circumstances, would exercise. It has also been defined as the failure to exercise proper care in the performance of some legal duty which defendant owes the injured party under the circumstances in which they are placed. Of course, failure to exercise due care for another's safety to be actionable must be the proximate cause of injury, and foreseeability is an element of proximate cause. 3 Strong's N.C. Index, Negligence, § 1.

Winborne, J., in *Hawes v. Atlantic Refining Co.*, 236 N.C. 643, 74 S.E.2d 17, said: "And it is a general rule of law, even in the absence of statutory requirement, that the operator of a motor vehicle must exercise ordinary care, that is, that degree of care which an ordinarily prudent person would exercise under similar circumstances."

Bobbitt, J., said in *Henderson v. Henderson*, 239 N.C. 487, 80 S.E.2d 383: "Apart from safety statutes prescribing specific rules governing the operation of motor vehicles, a person operating a motor vehicle must exercise proper care in the way and manner of its operation, proper care being that degree of care that an ordinarily prudent person would exercise under the same or similar circumstances and when charged with like duty. Thus, he must exercise due care as to keeping a proper lookout, as to keeping his car under proper control, and generally so as to avoid collision with persons or other vehicles on the highway."

"It may be assumed that the jury will understand that a want of 'due care,' 'ordinary care,' or 'reasonable care' given in special charges is equal to negligence, and if the plaintiff deems such charges misleading, he should request an explanatory charge." 38 Am. Jur., Negligence, § 364, p. 1078. In my opinion, the failure to use due care is not a mere unsupported conclusion, but is a fact and is generally used and understood as such in the language of the ordinary man, although speaking most technically it may be considered by some as a mere conclusion.

NOTES AND QUESTIONS

(1)   Draft a set of instructions to satisfy the criteria of this case. Examine those set out in the next case as models.

(2)   The following statement is the approved standard negligence jury instruction in another state. Is the implicit point of view different from that evinced in *Griffin v. Watkins*? See also *Richard v. Dravo Corp.*, 375 A.2d 750 (Pa. Super. 1977).

Negligence is the failure to use reasonable care. Reasonable care is that degree of care which a reasonably careful person would use under like circumstances. Negligence may consist either in doing something that a reasonably careful person would not do under like circumstances or in failing to do something that a reasonably careful person would do under like circumstances.

DOUGLAS v. GREAT ATLANTIC & PACIFIC TEA CO.
Mississippi Supreme Court
405 So. 2d 107 (1981)

PATTERSON, CHIEF JUSTICE, for the Court:

In the Circuit Court of the First Judicial District of Harrison County, the jury returned a verdict for A & P grocery store, the defendant, in a slip and fall negligence action brought by appellant, Mary Douglas, for damages.

Douglas appeals from the verdict, assigning several errors, combined herein as two.

I. The trial court erroneously refused plaintiff's Instructions 1, 2, 3, 7, 9, and 13.

II. The jury verdict was not supported by the evidence, being against the overwhelming weight of the credible evidence, evincing bias, passion, and prejudice on the part of the jury; and the trial court erred in overruling Douglas' motion for judgment notwithstanding the verdict, or, in the alternative, a new trial.

On July 3, 1979, Mary Douglas went to the A & P in Gulfport to buy two weeks supply of groceries. It being a holiday eve, the store was quite crowded. She had one more aisle to go and was standing near the frozen food case with a basket full of groceries when she slipped and fell on something wet. When she attempted to get up, she experienced a sharp, burning pain.

Curtis Fairley, the manager of the A & P, saw Douglas at about 1:00 p.m. immediately after the accident and observed about a gallon or so of water on the floor adjacent to the frozen food case. He did not know how long the water had been there, but was sure it came from the frozen food case. He prepared an accident report on July 3, describing the defective condition as water on the floor caused by the "frozen food case leaking water on the floor." To Fairley's personal knowledge, the floor had last been cleaned six or seven hours before the accident.

Fairley further testified he walks the aisles about fifteen or twenty times each day, and on the morning of the accident, he walked through the store about 6 to 8 times. He walked aisle nine, site of the accident, about five times and did not notice any water in the aisle. He last walked aisle nine at 11:30 a. m., an hour and a half before Douglas slipped and fell. Prior to July 3, the frozen food case had not leaked.

The porter of the A & P, Bill Hickman, whose duties include sweeping and scrubbing the aisles on the night shift testified he spent six to eight hours on the night of July 2 and the early hours of July 3 sweeping and scrubbing the floors. He observed no water pooling in aisle nine while working and had never seen any in the past. He also testified that water occasionally comes off the frozen food case and collects on the floor, but that it is wiped dry as soon as observed. He also stated the floor should ideally be swept every three hours. Hickman and Fairley both admitted no sweeper's log was kept because of laziness or indifference.

Bobby Beeson, in charge of stocking the frozen food case, testified the case was stocked from 6:30 a. m. to 12:30 p. m. on July 3. The last time he went down aisle nine was 12:10 p. m. Beeson noticed no water pooling in the aisle nor was there a problem with leakage from the frozen food case.

The evidence on damages, not the primary issue on appeal showed Mary Douglas sustained back injuries from her fall in the A & P which required medical care, hospitalization, and absenteeism from work.

This brings us to appellant's assignment of error that Instructions P-1 and P-2, peremptory instructions, were erroneously refused by the trial court. We think, the trial court properly refused these based on the conflicting evidence of negligence. See *Butler v. Chrestman*, 264 So. 2d 812 (Miss. 1972). Also much of the evidence is circumstantial and such a case should rarely be taken from the jury. *Davis v. Flippen*, 260 So. 2d 847 (Miss. 1972).

We are also of the opinion Instructions P-3, P-7, P-9, and P-13 were correctly refused. These instructions are quoted herein:

JURY INSTRUCTION NO. P-3

The Court instructs the Jury that if you believe by a preponderance of the evidence in this case that the wet floor in the aisle of the A & P on July 3, 1979, created a hazardous condition, and that this condition was created by the Defendant, The Great Atlantic and Pacific Tea Company, or under its authority and if you further believe by a preponderance of the evidence that said condition was the proximate cause of the injuries and damages sustained by the Plaintiff, then you must return a verdict for the Plaintiff, Mary Douglas.

JURY INSTRUCTION NO. P-7

The Court instructs the Jury that if you believe from a preponderance of the evidence in this case that the Defendant, by and through its employees, negligently allowed water to accumulate in the aisle where the Plaintiff was shopping and negligently failed to remove the same from the aisle, and if you further find from a preponderance of the evidence that the water as it was situated in the aisle constituted a hazard to persons using the aisle when shopping and that the Defendant negligently failed to use reasonable care in keeping the aisle dry so that a person exercising reasonable care therein could avoid injury to themselves, and if you further believe from a preponderance of the evidence that the negligence, if any, of the Defendant approximately caused or contributed to the injuries of the Plaintiff, Mary Douglas, then it is the sworn duty of the Jury to return a verdict for the Plaintiff.

JURY INSTRUCTION NO. P-9 [omitted]

JURY INSTRUCTION NO. P-13 [omitted]

The primary reason these jury instructions were refused, and properly so, in our opinion, was the failure to require plaintiff to prove the proprietor had actual or constructive notice of the wet condition. The applicable rules concerning proof of notice are stated in *Winn Dixie v. Hughes*, 247 Miss. 575, 584, 156, So. 2d 734, 736 (1963) as follows:

With respect to the necessity of evidence concerning notice of the dangerous floor condition, "there are two rules of fundamental significance. The first of these is that where the floor condition is one which is traceable to the proprietor's own act — that is, a condition created by him or under his authority — or is a condition in connection with which the proprietor is shown to have taken action, no proof of notice is necessary.

"Thus, it has been said that matters as to notice, including questions as to the length of time the dangerous condition existed are eliminated where it appears that the condition was created by defendant or persons for whose conduct he is responsible." Anno., 61 A.L.R.2d at 24.

The second rule, in contrast with that applicable to a floor condition resulting from the act of the proprietor, is this: " . . . where it appears that a floor in a store or similar place of business has been made dangerous by litter or debris present thereon, and that the presence of the litter or debris is traceable to persons for whom the proprietor is not responsible, proof that the proprietor was negligent in relation to the floor condition requires a showing that he had actual notice thereof, or that the condition existed for such a length of time that, in the exercise of reasonable care, he should have known of it." Anno., 61 A.L.R.2d at 26; 2 A.L.I., Rest. of Torts, § 343; 38 Am. Jur. Negligence, § 136; 65 C.J.S. Negligence §§ 45, 51.

Here there was not a scintilla of evidence a third party created the wet hazardous condition; moreover, there was no proof the proprietor created the wet condition. Thus it was the plaintiff's burden to prove either actual or constructive notice on the part of the proprietor of the dangerous wet condition of the floor in front of the frozen food case. In *Helveston v. Gibson Products Company of Hattiesburg, Inc.*, 192 So. 2d 389 (Miss. 1966), we affirmed a jury verdict for defendant wherein plaintiff slipped and fell on a puddle of liquid in Gibson's. There we held proof of actual or constructive notice is required where there is no proof the dangerous condition is the result of an affirmative act of the store proprietor or any of his employees. Here, appellant also failed to prove the wet hazardous condition was a result of an affirmative act of the proprietor or his employees so plaintiff had the burden of proving notice; thus the jury must be properly instructed as to notice.

It is possible to reasonably infer from circumstantial evidence presented at trial that the water originated from the adjacent frozen food case; however, even if this be so, proof of the water's presence on the floor for a sufficient amount of time to give reasonable notice to the proprietor is required. This the appellant did not prove. A similar case to the present is *Hill v. Allied Supermarkets, Inc.*, 42 N.C. App. 442, 257 S.E.2d 68 (1979)where plaintiff slipped and fell on some water next to a vegetable bin in a supermarket. There was no evidence to indicate the source of the water or how long the water had been there, and plaintiff's testimony that she guessed the water came from the vegetable bin was viewed by the North Carolina Court as speculation and conjecture. In affirming the directed verdict for the proprietor, that court reasoned as follows:

Moreover, even if the speculations of the plaintiff and her witness identifying the bin as the source of the water should turn out to be correct, there is no evidence as to how long the water had been there nor was there any evidence to show that the defendant knew or in the exercise of reasonable inspection should have known of its presence in time to have removed it before plaintiff stepped into it and fell. There was no evidence that the freezing components of the vegetable bin were malfunctioning in any way or that, if they were, defendant knew or in the exercise of reasonable inspection should have known that this was the case. The testimony of plaintiff's niece that the water "maybe dripped" and that "[w]hen something is defrosting, the more it defrosts or runs the more water," obviously represents no more than speculation on her part. Such conjectures as to possibilities furnish no adequate basis for a jury finding that water in fact did drip from the vegetable bin as result of defrosting and that the dripping water did accumulate on the floor over a long enough period of time to give defendant notice of its presence. Upon all of the evidence, the jury could do no more than speculate about the water's source and about the length of time it had been on the floor. 257 S.E.2d at 71. Turning to appellant's assertion the jury verdict is against the weight of the credible evidence so as to evince passion and prejudice, we again are of the opinion this is without merit. We exercise with the utmost care the power to set aside a jury verdict and grant a new trial. *Williams v. Hood*, 237 Miss. 355, 114 So. 2d 854 (1959). Here the appellant failed to sustain her burden of proving actual or constructive notice so the jury verdict, we find, is in accord with the evidence.

Affirmed.

NOTES AND QUESTIONS

(1) Why, precisely, was it proper for the trial court not to give requested instructions P-3 and P-7? In the context of the evidence, would it be possible to make either of them acceptable by modification?

(2) Does it not appear that instruction P-3, if given, narrows the scope of discretion of the jury in determining negligence? Compare this rule stated in *Winn-Dixie Stores, Inc. v. Marcotte*, 553 So. 2d 213, 215 (Fla. App. 1989):

> Where . . . there is no evidence the premises possessor had actual knowledge of the dangerous condition prior to the injury, and there is no evidence as to the length of time the dangerous condition existed prior to the injury, the premises possessor is entitled to a judgment as a matter of law and a jury is not authorized to speculate or arbitrarily impose strict liability on the mere contention that the premises possessor "should have known" of the dangerous condition.

In *Owens v. Publix Supermarkets*, 802 So. 2d 315 (Fla. 2001) the Florida Supreme Court dramatically abrogated the constructive notice requirement in cases in which a business falls on a transitory foreign substance on the floor of a commercial establishment and held:

> . . . . once the plaintiff establishes that he or she fell as a result of a transitory foreign substance, a rebuttable presumption of negligence arises. At that point, the burden shifts to the defendant to show by the greater weight of evidence that it exercised reasonable care in the maintenance of the premises under the circumstances.

Id. 802 So. 2d at 331. With lightning speed, the Florida legislature enacted this statute:

> (1) The person or entity in possession or control of business premises owes a duty of reasonable care to maintain the premises in a reasonably

safe condition for the safety of business invitees on the premises, which includes reasonable efforts to keep the premises free from transitory foreign objects or substances that might foreseeably give rise to loss, injury, or damage.

(2) In any civil action for negligence involving loss, injury, or damage to a business invitee as a result of a transitory foreign object or substance on business premises, the claimant shall have the burden of proving that:

(a) The person or entity in possession or control of the business premises owed a duty to the claimant;

(b) The person or entity in possession or control of the business premises acted negligently by failing to exercise reasonable care in the maintenance, inspection, repair, warning, or mode of operation of the business premises. Actual or constructive notice of the transitory foreign object or substance is not a required element of proof to this claim. However, evidence of notice or lack of notice offered by any party may be considered together with all of the evidence; and

(c) The failure to exercise reasonable care was a legal cause of the loss, injury, or damage.

F.S.A. § 768.0710. Where does this leave the state of the law?

(3) At one point in time, under the tutelage of Justice Holmes, courts tended to favor concrete rules of negligence for various circumstances, leaving to the jury only the job of deciding whether the criteria for application of the rule are satisfied. The most famous case was *Baltimore & Ohio R.R. v. Goodman*, 275 U.S. 66, 48 S.Ct. 24, 72 L.Ed. 167 (1927), wherein the Court decided that a motorist was negligent as a matter of law if he did not *stop, look* and *listen* upon approaching obstructed rail crossings. Although the Supreme Court retreated from the *Goodman* rule in *Pokara v. Wabash Ry.*, 292 U.S. 98, 54 S.Ct. 580, 78 L.Ed. 1149 (1934), other such rules survive here and there in the law, as exemplified by instruction P-3.

Professor Morris examines this subject in Morris on Torts (2d), 58–61. You should weigh the following caveat.

> Just how far courts have used and will use Holmes' preferred technique is a difficult question. But Holmes' ideal (that the technique should be used at an accelerated pace until exact standards are developed by judges for all important types of cases) has not guided courts in the last half century. Lawyers preparing cases do their job well only when they have searched the precedents carefully for applicable judicially announced concrete standards, but they still will find few of them.

Id. at 60.

MICKLE v. BLACKMON
South Carolina Supreme Court
166 S.E.2d 173 (1969)

[See fact statement set out at § 5.02, *supra*]

Having resolved the legal question of Ford's duty to exercise care in plaintiff's favor, we now examine the sufficiency of the evidence to support the jury's factual finding that there was a breach of that duty. Of course, the evidence and all inferences to be drawn there-from must be viewed in the light most favorable to plaintiff.

The 1949 Ford was equipped with a manual transmission. The gearshift lever was mounted on the right of the steering shaft below the wheel. It was a slender, cylindrical, steel rod about 12 inches in length, with a slight taper to a diameter of 5/16 of an inch at the end on which a plastic knob or ball was mounted. This rod protruded some two inches beyond the rim of the wheel and was pointed generally in the direction of a passenger on the right side of the front seat. In high or third gear the lever was pointed downward toward the seat. Without an adequate protective knob, the lever was quite capable of piercing the body of any person who might be thrown upon it, and the jury could reasonably have concluded that the rod presented an unreasonable risk of injury unless effectively guarded.

The end of the gearshift lever was covered by a knob or ball of a plastic material manufactured by Tennessee Eastman Company of Kingsport, Tennessee, labeled tennite butyrate, also referred to in the record as acetate butyrate. The ball was moulded by Ford in two hollow sections, the bottom section with a hole slightly smaller in diameter than the end of the lever. The two sections were glued together and the slightly heated ball was force-fitted over a series of annular grooves around the end of the rod. This resulted in a firm, permanent attachment. The knob could not be removed without rupturing it.

The plastic material was available in a wide range of colors, including black. Ford chose to use white tennite butyrate for the knobs in its 1949 model. Exposure to the ultraviolet rays of sunlight caused this material to deteriorate. Carbon, which is the coloring agent used to produce black tennite butyrate, is highly resistant to ultraviolet rays. Ford switched to black butyrate for the knobs in its 1950 model. After exposure to sunlight for an undetermined length of time, the greater the exposure the more rapid the deterioration, the white knobs became crazed. Hairline cracks which developed on the surface in this process destroyed the force distributing quality of the plastic knob and caused it to shatter easily on impact. After developing these cracks, a 1949 white ball was of no value as a protective guard but remained serviceable as a knob. The presence of the hairline cracks was apparent on visual inspection. However, their deteriorating effect would not necessarily be comprehended by a person of ordinary reason. The black 1950 balls never developed these cracks. Rigidly attached to the gearshift lever, they were not subject to wear, as are moving parts of machinery, and there is no evidence that the black knobs deteriorated with age or normal use.

When questioned about the expected life of the material furnished to Ford for the 1949 knobs, an Eastman expert testified: "That is a hard question to answer because it is dependent on the type of exposure, but, generally speaking, I think it would be expected to last six or eight years without any question. More if it had less exposure to ultraviolet."

. . . Without regard to the reason for affixing the ball, however, counsel argues that the burden was on plaintiff to prove that the assembly was "unreasonably dangerous at the time this automobile was first sold." Counsel urges that the absence of evidence "that this knob would have shattered if this impact had occurred in 1949, 1950 or subsequent thereto during the normal life expectancy of this plastic material," results in a failure of proof.

It is implicit in the verdict that the gearshift lever presented an unreasonable risk of injury if not adequately guarded. At the time of plaintiff's injury the knob on the Hill car continuedto serve its functional purpose as a handhold, but it had become useless as a protective guard. It is inferable that the condition of the knob did not arise from ordinary wear and tear, but from an inherent weakness in the material of which Ford was aware when the selection was made. In the light of the insidious effect on this material of exposure to sunlight in the normal use of an automobile, it could reasonably be concluded that Ford should have foreseen that many thousands of the one million vehicles produced by it in 1949 would, in the course of time, be operated millions of miles with gearshift lever balls which, while yet serving adequately as handholds, would furnish no protection to an occupant who might be thrown against the gearshift lever. The jury could reasonably conclude that Ford's conduct, in manufacturing a needed safety device of a material which could not tolerate a frequently encountered aspect of the environment in which it would be employed, exposed many users of its product to unreasonably great risk of harm.

In a products liability case against the manufacturer, plaintiff does, of course, have the burden of establishing that the defect complained of existed at the time the product was sold by the defendant. "There is no duty on a manufacturer to furnish a machine that will not wear out." *Auld v. Sears, Roebuck & Co.*, 261 App. Div. 918, 25 N.Y.S.2d 491, aff'd, 288 N.Y. 515, 41 N.E. 2d 927. We subscribe to the following statement of the law which is applicable to the facts of this case:

> If the chattel is in good condition when it is sold, the seller is not responsible when it undergoes subsequent changes, or wears out. The mere lapse of time since the sale by the defendant, during which there had been continued safe use of the products, is always relevant, as indicating that the seller was not responsible for the defect. There have been occasional cases in which, upon the particular facts, it has been held to be conclusive. It is, however, quite certain that *neither long continued lapse of time nor changes in ownership will be sufficient in themselves to defeat recovery when there is clear evidence of an original defect in the thing sold.* (Emphasis added.)

Prosser on Torts, 667 (3d ed. 1964).

Lynch v. International Harvester Co. of America, 60 F.2d 223, 224 (10th Cir.), involving five years' continuous use of a threshing machine, was one of the cases holding that protracted safe use of a product was conclusive against liability of the manufacturer. Some years later, this case was overruled by the court which decided it. See *Pryor v. Lee C. Moore, Corp.*, 262 F.2d 673 (10th Cir. 1958), in which the mast or derrick of a drilling rig collapsed under ordinary strain after fifteen years of satisfactory service. The mishap was caused by the failure of a weld at the foot of one leg of the derrick, which, according to expert testimony, indicated that the weld had not been properly fused at the point of failure. The court, after reviewing a number of decisions refusing to foreclose liability as a matter of law after prolonged safe use of a product, stated:

> The proposition that prolonged safe use bars any inference of negligent manufacture has not gained wide acceptance in the application of the

MacPherson doctrine. . . . Certainly no firmly established body of tort law has grown up around it. A reappraisal of the problem in the light of subsequent decisions persuades us to recede from the rule in *Lynch*, and to hold that prolonged use of a manufactured article is but one factor, albeit an important one, in the determination of the factual issue whether the negligent manufacture proximately caused the harm.

262 F.2d at 675. There was no evidence in *Pryor* that the weld could not withstand the strain of the drilling operation when the rig was first sold by the manufacturer. The contrary plainly appears from fifteen years' safe use. However, this did not bar submission of the issue of liability to the jury when there was other evidence tending to establish that the ultimate collapse was caused by the manufacturer's failure to properly fuse the weld.

In *Darling v. Caterpillar Tractor Co.*, 171 Cal. App. 2d 713, 341 P.2d 23, plaintiff was injured when the hinge on the inspection plate in the deck of a bulldozer, because of a defective weld, broke off under his weight. The bulldozer had been in hard use for about three years. Inferentially, the inspection cover had been stepped upon many times by various operators. There was undisputed expert testimony that the weld was defective, that it did not fail suddenly, but that "it failed gradually over a considerable period of time." In response to the manufacturer's claim of immunity from liability by proof of protracted safe use, the court said in part:

> The hinge in question was not a moving part that was subject to wear and strain while the machine was in operation. It was not a hinge that had been properly and efficiently welded to the deck plate and the inspection cover which gave way as a result of long continued use; it was a part that was defective in construction and which gave way as a result of use which would not have caused it to fail if it had been properly and efficiently constructed. 341 P.2d at 29.

In *Fredericks v. Farrington*, 227 F.2d 450 (2d Cir. 1955), an iron support under a skid used in unloading vessels broke after two and one-half years of safe use and "normally rough handling." In this suit against the fabricator of the iron there was expert testimony that a faulty design created a "stress raiser" or "localizer," because of which the metal eventually cracked and ruptured. In dealing with the protracted safe use objection to recovery, the court said:

> The mere passage of time confers no immunity upon a negligent wrongdoer; but it has relevance to the likelihood, depending upon the circumstances of a particular case, that deterioration due to use, perhaps accelerated by misuse, will be mistaken by a jury for a defect due to negligent manufacture or fabrication. On the evidence before us in this case, we cannot say the jury went beyond permissible and rational inference in attributing the accident to Farrington's negligent fabrication of the skid iron, which cracked and came apart, despite at least two and one-half years of apparently safe use and normally rough handling. . . . 227 F.2d at 452.

The above excerpt from *Fredericks* was quoted with approval in *Carney v. Sears, Roebuck & Co.*, 309 F.2d 300, 305 (4th Cir.), in which plaintiff was injured by the collapse of a ladder after fifteen months' use, and there was evidence that a defective rivet gave way under continued strain to cause the collapse.

Here, as in the cases just referred to, there was evidence of an original weakness in the gearshift assembly which caused the collapse of the protective knob. The deterioration of the product and its consequent failure was the very risk created by the negligent choice of material, or the jury could so find. The rule relied upon, that a manufacturer is not liable for the failure of a product due to deterioration from ordinary wear and tear or misuse, simply does not fit these facts.

We readily concede that the passage of thirteen years between the marketing of a product and its injury-producing failure is a formidable obstacle to fastening liability upon the manufacturer. However, it may reasonably be inferred in this case that the advanced age of the ball was coincidental with its failure rather than the cause of it, and that the knob would have shattered upon a comparable impact had it occurred much earlier in the life of the car. The important inquiry is not how long the knob lasted but what caused its failure. Mere passage of time should not excuse Ford if its negligence was the cause. Since this conclusion finds support in the evidence, the issue was for the jury.

. . .

Therefore, the court erred in granting Ford's motion for judgment notwithstanding the verdict.

[Court's discussion of issues raised in Ford's appeal omitted]

WATSON v. STATE FARM FIRE AND CASUALTY INSURANCE CO.

Supreme Court of Louisiana
469 So. 2d 967 (1985)

CALOGERO, JUSTICE.

A lawsuit was brought by Ora Watson, individually and as tutrix of her minor child, and six major Watson children, against Earl Creel and his insurer, State Farm Fire and Casualty Insurance Co., for the wrongful death of Ora's husband and the children's father, Doyle Watson. The claim arose out of a hunting accident in which Earl Creel's minor son, Shane, shot and killed the fifty-three year old Watson with a high-powered rifle. A trial jury rendered a verdict in favor of defendants, finding decedent Watson 100% at fault in connection with the accident. The First Circuit Court of Appeal, 459 So. 2d 1235, affirmed.

We granted writs in this essentially factual dispute because we perceived the Court of Appeal to have applied an inappropriate standard of review. The Court of Appeal found that the jury's verdict was "based upon a reasonable evaluation of credibility," an applied review standard which seemed quite similar to the "reasonable basis for [a trial court's] finding" test which this Court found insufficient in *Arceneaux v. Domingue*, 365 So. 2d 1330, 1333 (La.1978). In fact the appropriate standard is that a finding of fact by the trial court should be upheld "unless it is clearly wrong," or manifestly erroneous. Furthermore, it just seemed so clearly wrong for the lower courts to have determined that the victim of this accidental shooting by a deer hunter was the only party at fault; especially inasmuch as comparative fault, rather than the bar of contributory negligence, prevailed in the law when the shooting took place.

The accident occurred on the Watson farm in Mt. Hermon, a community located in Washington Parish, in the early evening hours of December 29, 1981. [The court recounts in detail how the shooting occurred. In sum, the inexperienced 12 year old Shane had been left alone with a high powered rifle on a tree stand. When the decedent Watson approached along a dim tree shaded lane in the forest, Shane mistook him for a deer and killed him with a single rifle shot to the head. Watson was not wearing an orange garment despite a statute that provides:

> Any person hunting deer shall display on his head or chest, and/or back a total of not less than four hundred square inches of material of daylight fluorescent orange color known as "Hunter orange". . . . Whoever violates the provision of this section shall be fined not more than $100 or imprisoned for not more than ninety days, or both.]

Plaintiffs' attorney sought to establish the negligence of Earl Creel, Shane's father, on several bases: (1) giving his son Shane a high-powered rifle on the child's twelfth birthday; (2) not properly instructing Shane in the use of that weapon; (3) not adequately supervising Shane at the time of the accident, particularly in failing to show him how to sight game with the rifle's scope. On the other hand, plaintiffs' counsel attempted in his opening statement to the jury to minimize Shane's fault, which he described as "very slight, if any." Counsel for the defense countered that the accident would not have occurred had Mr. Watson worn the "Hunter orange" vest, or signified his presence when he walked in the area which he had personally designated for hunting.

We agree with the lower courts to this extent. Watson was not without fault in this accidental shooting. However, the concept of comparative negligence, written into La. Civ. Code Ann. art. 2323,[1] permits a plaintiff such as Mr. Watson (or his wife and children) to recover damages, notwithstanding his own negligence.

A pure comparative fault system was adopted in Louisiana in 1979. . . . It was specifically designed to ameliorate the harshness of the contributory negligence doctrine by apportioning losses between the plaintiff and defendant when both are negligent. This allocation of shares of negligence, however, is not an easy task for the factfinder, and the Louisiana statute does not describe with particularity how it should be accomplished.[2]

Clearly, however, the concept of comparative negligence is not applicable when the victim alone is the party at fault. In this case, the jury in response to interrogatories found that Earl Creel was not at fault in causing the accident, that Shane Creel was not at fault in causing the accident, and that Doyle Watson was at

---

[1] La. Civ. Code Ann. art. 2323 provides: When contributory negligence is applicable to a claim for damages, its effect shall be as follows: If a person suffers injury, death or loss as the result partly of his own negligence and partly as a result of the fault of another person or persons, the claim for damages shall not thereby be defeated, but the amount of damages recoverable shall be reduced in proportion to the degree or percentage of negligence attributable to the person suffering the injury, death or loss.

[2] A "fault line" has been suggested as a method of conceptualizing the share of negligence attributable to each party. One end, designated with a value of zero, would indicate the absence of fault; at the other end. a value of ten would indicate deliberate wrongdoing. The factfinder can then designate on the line where the conduct of each party falls. From the scale, the various allocations of fault can be converted to percentages. R. Pearson. *Apportionment of Losses Under Comparative Fault Laws*, 40 La. L. Rev. at 348–49.

fault. Expressed in terms of a percent, the jury answered that Watson's degree of fault was "100%."

Upon appellate review Louisiana courts have jurisdiction with regard to both law and facts. La. Const. art. V, § 10(B). However, we have held that when there is evidence before the trier of fact which, upon its reasonable evaluation of credibility, furnishes a reasonable factual basis for the trial court's finding, on review the appellate court should not disturb this factual finding in the absence of manifest error. Stated another way, the reviewing court must give great weight to factual conclusions of the trier of fact; where there is conflict in the testimony reasonable evaluations of credibility and reasonable inferences of fact should not be disturbed upon review, even though the appellate court may feel that its own evaluations and inferences are as reasonable. . . .

This standard of appellate review was not intended to be applied so as to require upholding the ruling of a trial court simply, "when the evidence before the trier of fact furnishes a reasonable basis for its finding." *Arceneaux v. Domingue*, 365 So. 2d 1330, 1333 (La. 1978). Instead, a finding of fact by a trial court should be upheld "unless it is clearly wrong." And "appellate review of facts is not completed by reading so much of the record as will reveal a reasonable factual basis for the finding in the trial court." *Id.* Proper review requires that the appeal court determine from the record that the trial court finding is not clearly wrong or manifestly erroneous. Here, the jury was clearly wrong, considering all the evidence, in deciding that Earl Creel and his twelve year old son Shane were each without fault in the accidental death of Doyle Watson. It is incomprehensible that no negligence was involved in Earl Creel's arming an untrained twelve year old boy with a high-powered rifle, from which the boy had had occasion to fire previously only two shells, and leaving him alone in the woods to hunt a species of animal which he had never seen. So too, it is incomprehensible that the boy did not share some fault in this tragic accident, for it surely constitutes negligence to fire a rifle at a moving object without ascertaining with certainty that it is not a human being.

The Court of Appeal stated that they were required to uphold the finding of a jury when "based upon a reasonable evaluation of credibility." Shane's testimony about sighting a deer and firing at it after properly identifying his target, the Court of Appeal considered quite positive testimony. And they held that the jury could reasonably have concluded that Shane had exercised reasonable care and had in fact identified a deer before firing. As noted at the outset of this opinion, the Court of Appeal's upholding the jury verdict upon finding it "based upon a reasonable evaluation of credibility" is the application of a standard of review quite similar to the test rejected in *Arceneaux, supra.* It is not enough to sustain the determination of the district court when "there is some reasonable evidence to support the finding." Rather, the appropriate question is, was that finding clearly wrong or manifestly erroneous. Our answer to this question is that it was clearly wrong. Shane's testimony regarding the sighting of the deer was quite equivocal. Even his statement quoted by the Court of Appeal clearly progresses, with the benefit of leading questions, from an expression of doubt, to assurance concerning the object sighted. Shane initially responded that "I thought I saw something," explained that "[t]o the best of my knowledge, I saw a deer," and finally asserted in answer to a direct question that there was no doubt in his mind that he was looking at a deer when he fired. And, since it is highly unlikely that a deer would have been meandering across a field, drinking water in close proximity to a man walking in the open along a nearby field road, it is much more likely, if not entirely certain, that there was no deer, and that Shane was following the movements of Doyle Watson as he was walking along a rutted road, partially obscured by a knoll in the center of the field and grass about two feet high.

Although the accident might have been avoided had Mr. Watson worn the "Hunter orange" vest or called out to Shane on entering the field, it seems equally likely that an experienced hunter, such as Earl Creel, would have correctly interpreted the moving object as a man rather than a deer. We believe that Earl Creel's negligence in either failing to provide his young son with a supervised experience in sighting large game through a scope and firing this high-powered rifle, or closely supervising him on this occasion was a cause in fact of Mr. Watson's accidental death. We also believe that causation for the accident must be attributed to Shane as well as to his father. The twelve year old must share some responsibility for this death in view of his own negligence in firing a dangerous weapon at a man he presumed to be a deer.

Having determined that the jury's allocation of 100% fault to the plaintiff was against the weight of the evidence, and was clearly wrong, we are empowered by La. Code Civ. Pro. Ann. art. 2164 to "render any judgment which is just, legal, and proper upon the record on appeal." We recognize that a standard for determining percentages of fault has not been provided by the Legislature, and we are therefore presented with an opportunity to offer guidelines as we apportion fault in this instance. In so doing we have looked to the Uniform Comparative Fault Act, 2(b) and Comment (as revised in 1979),[3] which incorporates direction for the trier of fact. Section 2(b) provides:

In determining the percentages of fault, the trier of fact shall consider both the nature of the conduct of each party at fault and the extent of the causal relation between the conduct and the damages claimed. In assessing the nature of the conduct of the parties, various factors may influence the degree of fault assigned, including: (1) whether the conduct resulted from inadvertence or involved an awareness of the danger, (2) how great a risk was created by the conduct, (3) the significance of what was sought by the conduct, (4) the capacities of the actor, whether superior or inferior, and (5) any extenuating circumstances which might require the actor to proceed in haste, without proper thought. And, of course, as evidenced by concepts such as last clear chance, the relationship between the fault/negligent conduct and the harm to the plaintiff are considerations in determining the relative fault of the parties.

Our consideration of these factors suggest that the majority of the fault must rest with the Creels. The causal relation between negligently firing a dangerous weapon and/or negligently failing to instruct or supervise a minor child in the use of the weapon, and plaintiff's death, is a direct one. On the other hand, plaintiff's failure to wear Hunter orange or signify his presence may have contributed to the youth's fatal error in identifying his target. But it was not as directly related to the

---

[3] Uniform Acts are drafted by the National Conference of Commissioners on Uniform State Laws, composed of representatives, termed Commissioners, from within the legal profession of each of the fifty states as well as the District of Columbia and Puerto Rico. In order "to promote uniformity in state law on all subjects where uniformity is deemed desirable and practical," the Conference recommends acts for general adoption throughout the jurisdiction of the United States.

. . . .

plaintiff's demise as was the conduct of the Creels.

Furthermore, the factors suggested in evaluating the conduct of the parties indicate that a lesser degree of fault should be attributed to plaintiff. His conduct, at least in walking along the field road within the boy's rifle range, was inadvertent. His failure to don the bright hunting vest, however, was a conscious action which necessarily involved adverting to, or consciously considering the risk, or possible danger. Nevertheless, plaintiff's omissions at worse had only an indirect causative impact on the accident. In contrast, none of the actions of Shane or his father Earl Creel can be considered inadvertent. They were aware that the high-powered rifle was deadly and that it was imperative to discern a target with certainty before firing. In a similar vein, the risk of firing or failing to train and supervise the firing of such a weapon had a direct potential for fatal consequences. And, in considering possible mitigating factors, the Creels had no higher motive than sport when their acts of negligence occurred, and their actions were not dictated by any emergency or other circumstance which could lessen the fault attributed to this poor judgment. Finally, with regard to capacity, the age and experience of Watson and Earl Creel would require a greater imposition of fault on them for their negligent conduct, in comparison to that of the twelve year old youth, Shane. After weighing the factors discussed hereinabove, we apportion the fault as follows. To plaintiff, we assign 20% of the fault in this fatal accident. We find further that Earl Creel and his son, Shane Creel, were each also at fault, and the degree or percentage of negligence attributable to them was 40% each. There remain in this lawsuit issues concerning quantum which are still to be resolved and which we determine should appropriately be decided by the Court of Appeal. This includes the assessment of damages for each of the plaintiffs, as well as reduction thereof by virtue of 1) Doyle Watson's percentage of contributing fault, and 2) the possible reduction attendant to plaintiffs' having settled prior to trial with Farm Bureau Insurance Company.

DECREE

The judgments of the district court and the Court of Appeal are therefore reversed; the case is remanded to the Court of Appeal for further consideration and for entry of judgment consistent with law and with the views expressed herein.

NOTES AND QUESTIONS

(1)   To what extent does *Watson* propose a formulation of "breach of duty," *i.e.*, negligence, for use by a jury that is different from the standard "reasonable care of a person of ordinary prudence in the same or similar circumstances"? Does it retreat from the core teaching of *Vaughan v. Menlove?*

(2)   Because of the inviolability of the jury's deliberation, we have little reliable information about how juries reach their decisions. Do you believe the *Watson* appellate court's assessment and weighing of the evidence comports with the typical jury process? Do you agree that the jury's decision should have been overturned?

(3)   Courts are loathe to overturn jury verdicts as to purely factual determinations, especially those involving so-called "ultimate" facts such as whether a party was guilty of negligence. What standard of review does the Louisiana court apply? Is that the same as the standard applied in your own jurisdiction? Note that state constitutional provisions pertaining to the right of trial by jury might be an

important factor in this regard. Because Louisiana is a civil law jurisdiction, its legal heritage and constitution may be less solicitous of jury sanctity than those in a more typical common law jurisdiction.

(4) *Watson* provides an initial glimpse at the concept of "comparative fault" that is developed in detail in Chapter 9, *supra.* Note that the Louisiana system required the jury to determine which of the parties was at fault and to assign a proportion of fault to each at-fault party with a sum of 100%. Why do you suppose the jury assigned 100% fault to the decedent? Is that not the same as finding that the defendant was not negligent? The power of the Louisiana appellate courts to reassess fault without remanding the issue for retrial by a jury may be novel in the United States.

(5) *Watson* involved behavior of a character that represents the myriad of typical actions each of us takes each day. In *Watson* the wrongful behavior was the permitting of the 12 year old child to be possessed of a rifle in a hunting party without supervision. Some kinds of behavior permit more of a deliberate assessment of whether to engage in it on the basis of costs versus risks. The next case is of that variety. Although we may assume that juries have always taken into account costs and risks in making fault determinations, in the past few decades a determined academic and to some extent judicial movement has expressed itself in terms of "risk/benefit" or "risk/utility" analyses. The next case, also from Louisiana, exemplifies this tendency.

WASHINGTON v. LOUISIANA POWER AND LIGHT COMPANY
Supreme Court of Louisiana
555 So. 2d 1350 (1990)

DENNIS, JUSTICE.

We granted certiorari in this power line accident case to review the Court of Appeal's judgment setting aside a jury award to the adult children of a man who was electrocuted when he accidentally allowed a citizens band radio antenna to come into contact with an uninsulated 8000 volt electrical wire that spanned the backyard of his residence. . . . We affirm.

The jury verdict for the plaintiffs was manifestly erroneous. Although the gravity of the injury in a powerline accident is usually severe, under the circumstances of this case the magnitude of the risk was not great because the possibility that the radio antenna would have been brought into contact with the powerline was very slight: five years before his fatal accident the deceased narrowly escaped death or serious injury in a similar mishap; he expressed concern for his life and afterwards exercised great caution and avoided moving the antenna near the powerline; inspections by the power company would have shown only that the antenna was stationed securely at a safe distance from the power line right-of-way; on the occasion of his fatal accident, however, the deceased deliberately and for no apparent good reason raised the antenna from a position lying on the ground a safe distance from the powerline and walked with it in an erect attitude to within a dangerous proximity of the uninsulated wire, where he was electrocuted.

Because it was clearly unlikely that the deceased had forgotten about the hot wire, a warning by the power company would not have averted the accident.

Consequently, the only safety measures the company might have taken to avoid the accident were to insulate the line, place it underground or raise it to an abnormal height. We conclude that the burden of taking any of these precautions in a case such as this clearly outweighs the magnitude of the risk.

This is not a situation in which there was a significant possibility of an accident due to ignorance or inadvertence. If the power company were to be required to redesign or relocate its line here, then it would be forced to do so immediately, and thereafter continually, in the hundreds, perhaps thousands, of locations along its high voltage line rights-of-way at which tall television or radio antennas are safely installed.

The deceased, John Washington, Sr., lived in a subdivision in Mirror, Louisiana with a back yard 118 feet wide. LP & L had a five foot right-of-way across the decedent's backyard, over which it had strung an uninsulated eight thousand (8000) volt electrical distribution line, approximately 21 and 1/2 feet above the ground and 23 feet inside the rear property line and fence. LP & L's right of way and power line ran through many lots adjacent to and beyond Mr. Washington's property in both directions. The line was clearly visible.

. . .

[The court recounts that Mr. Washington was aware of the danger of the power line and that he had placed his antenna at a place that he thought minimized the risk. The Court also recounts how Mr. Washington had had a "narrow escape" in 1980 when he inadvertently touched his antenna to the defendant's power line and how in 1985 his dead body was found electrocuted in his back yard beside the antenna. The evidence permitted a finding that Washington had inadvertently touched the antenna against the power line, causing his death.]

After a trial on the merits, a jury found LP & L at fault in the accident and awarded plaintiffs $500,000 for pain and suffering and the loss of life of the decedent and $75,000 for each plaintiff's loss of love, affection and support. LP & L appealed suspensively. The Court of Appeal, noting that the decedent had five years earlier received an electrical shock when he touched the antenna to the same line, and had since that time been extremely careful to never move the antenna alone or towards the line until the day of the fatal accident, reversed, concluding that LP & L did not breach any duty owed to the decedent. *Washington v. LP & L*, 532 So. 2d 798 (La. App. 4th 1988). When the evidence is clear, as in the present case, that the power company either knew or should have known of the possibility of an accident that materialized in the decedent's electrocution, the remaining negligence issue is whether the possibility of such injury or loss constituted an unreasonable risk of harm. . . . Such a case invites "a sharp focus upon the essential balancing process that lies at the heart of negligence." Malone, *Work of Appellate Courts*, 29 La. L. Rev. 212, 212 (1969). . . . In this regard, we recently held that the power company's duty to provide against resulting injuries, as in similar situations, is a function of three variables: (1) the possibility that the electricity will escape; (2) the gravity of the resulting injury, if it does; (3) the burden of taking adequate precautions that would avert the accident. When the product of the possibility of escape multiplied times the gravity of the harm, if it happens, exceeds the burden of precautions, the risk is unreasonable and the failure to take those precautions is negligence . . . see L. Hand, J., in . . . *United States v. Carroll Towing Co.*, 159 F.2d 169, 173 (2nd Cir.1947). . . .

Applying the negligence balancing process, we conclude that although there was a cognizable risk that the antenna stationed in the corner of Mr. Washington's backyard could be lowered and moved to within a dangerous proximity of the power line, that possibility could not be characterized as an unreasonable risk and the power company's failure to take additional precautions against it was not negligence. Under the circumstances, there was not a significant possibility before the accident that Mr. Washington or anyone acting for him would detach the antenna and attempt to carry it under or dangerously near the power line. Standing alone, Mr. Washington's 1980 accident might have caused an objective observer to increase his estimate of the chances that this particular antenna might be handled carelessly. The other surrounding circumstances, however, overwhelmingly erase any pre-accident enlargement of the risk at that site. Except for the single occasion of the 1980 accident, the antenna was stationed safely in the corner of the backyard for many years, one to three years before the 1980 mishap and five years afterwards. Most of that time it was maintained safely in the pipe receptacle which, by Mr. Washington's design, allowed it to be lowered only in a safe direction. Between his close call in 1980 and his fatal accident in 1985, Mr. Washington had never been known to handle the antenna carelessly. Indeed, after he and his son narrowly escaped death or serious injury in 1980, his remarks to friends and relatives indicated that the experience had convinced him to keep the antenna far away from the power line. That he continued to be aware of the danger and take exemplary precautions to avoid it until his fatal accident was further illustrated by the care that he and his friend took when they lowered and laid it next to the fence several days before the accident. The likelihood that the antenna in this case would be brought into contact with the power line was not as great as the chances of an electrical accident in situations creating significant potential for injuries to victims who may contact or come into dangerous proximity with the powerline due to their unawareness of or inadvertence to the charged wire.

Prior to the accident, the anticipated gravity of the loss if the risk were to take effect was, of course, of a very high degree. The deaths and serious injuries in this and other electrical accidents verify that the weight of the loss threatened by a power line accident is not trivial. While some accidents, such as Mr. Washington's 1980 mishap, do not lead to dire consequences, a consideration of all losses resulting from this type of risk indicates that the gravity of the loss if it occurs is usually extreme. Yet when this high degree of gravity of loss is multiplied by the very small possibility of the accident occurring in this case, we think it is clear that the product does not outweigh the burdens or costs of the precautions of relocating or insulating the power line. This does not mean, of course, that it would not have been worth what it would have cost to place the line underground or to insulate it in order to save the decedent's life if it had been known that the accident would happen or even if the chance of it occurring had been greater. Nor does it mean, on the other hand, that we stop with a consideration of only the burden of an effective precaution in this single case. Common knowledge indicates that within any power company's territory there probably are a great number of situations involving antennas that have been safely installed, but which conceivably could be detached and carelessly moved about dangerously near a power line. In fairness, in this case, in which the coexistence of the powerline and the safely installed antenna was no riskier than countless other similar coexistences not considered to involve negligence, the burden to the company of taking precautions against all such slight possibilities of harm should be balanced against the total magnitude of all these risks, including the relatively few losses resulting from the total of all those insignificant risks. Just as single case applications of the Hand formula can understate the benefits of accident prevention by overlooking all other accidents that could be avoided by the same safety expenditures, . . . the burdens of taking precautions in all similar cases may be depreciated by single case consideration here.

The foregoing, of course, is merely a shorthand expression of the mental processes involved in such considerations. We cannot mathematically or mechanically quantify, multiply or weigh risks, losses and burdens of precautions. As many scholars have noted, the formula is primarily helpful in keeping in mind the relationship of the factors involved and in centering attention upon which of them may be determinative in any given situation. See . . . Epstein, *A Theory of Strict Liability*, 2 The Jour. of Legal Studies 151, 157 (1973).[4]

Nevertheless, the formula would seem to be of greater assistance in cases of the present type, in which the power company's ability to perceive risks is superior and its duty is utmost . . . than other notions, such as "reasonable man," "duty" or "foreseeability," for example, which must be little more than labels to be applied after some sort of balancing or weighing that the formula attempts to describe. In the present case, the balancing process focuses our attention on the fact that the possibility of an accident appeared to be slight beforehand and on the reality that precautions against such slight risks would be costly and burdensome because they exist in great number and have not usually been considered unreasonable or intolerable.

. . .

For the reasons assigned, the judgment of the court of appeal is affirmed.

NOTES AND QUESTIONS

(1) To what extent is the "risk/benefit" balancing test helpful in determining whether a party was guilty of the "blameworthiness" that is at the core of tort fault based liability, as expressed by Lord Atkin in *Donoghue v. Stevenson*? Does its utility differ in determination of the duty issue as distinguished from the determination of the breach issue? If so, why? Are you satisfied with the appellate courts' determinations that the jury verdict must be reversed?

(2) Note that the *Washington* decision referred to Judge Learned Hand's "expectation of harm" test that he first espoused in the *Carroll Towing Company* case. Judge Hand's expectation of harm is merely the product of the probability that a particular harmful event will ensue as a consequence of a particular act multiplied by the gravity of the damage caused should the harmful event occur. Presumably, a prudent person would not engage in a particular behavior if the

---

[4] As Professor Epstein has observed, Judge Hand himself stated it well only two years after *Carroll Towing* was decided: "But of these factors care [or precaution] is the only one ever susceptible of quantitative estimate, and often that is not. The injuries are always a variable within limits, which do not admit of even approximate ascertainment; and, although probability might theoretically be estimated, if any statistics were available, they never are; and, besides, probability varies with the severity of the injuries. It follows that all such attempts are illusory, and, if serviceable at all, are so only to center attention upon which one of the factors may be determinative in any given situation." *Moisan v. Loftus*, 178 F.2d 148, 149 (2d Cir.1949).

expectation of harm is greater than the cost of modifying the behavior. For example, if Mr. Washington's life were assessed to have a value of $1,000,000 and the probability that he would be killed if the power line were kept in place were assessed at 1 in 1000, then the expectation of harm would be $1000. Hence, the defendant would be negligent if the cost of moving the power line were less than $1000. Do you agree?

The *Washington* court actually used a non-quantitative version of the Hand formula. It deemed L to be very high and P extremely low. It also found the cost of preventing the harm (insulating the power line, placing it underground, or raising it higher) to be extremely high. The court did not need numbers to make the cost/benefit analysis but concluded *a priori* "when this high degree of gravity of loss is multiplied by the very small probability of the accident occurring in this case, we think it is clear that the product does not outweigh the burdens or costs of the precautions or costs of the precautions of relocating or insulating the power line." Accordingly, the court found no negligence. Are you persuaded?

Suppose the court had employed the "least cost" analysis to assign duty. Would it have needed to reach the breach question? Or to compare B to P × L?

(3) Does Judge Hand's formula provide a coherent means to determine fault? Is it practical?

A few decisions have discussed these matters in some detail. Does the following decision, written by Judge Posner, a leading proponent of so-call "economic analysis" of law persuade you of the utility of the approach?

(4) Facts are often decisive. Cf. *Levi v. Slemco*, 542 So. 2d 1081 (La. 1989), in which the same court held that an electric company did breach the duty of care it owed the operator of a truck-boom in the placement of its power line.

(5) Does *Washington*'s focus on the specific facts of the case to render its risk analysis differ from the focus of the South Carolina court in *Mickle v. Blackmon?* Do you suppose a plaintiff could gather evidence that a reasonable electric company should know that some careless person would be put at risk by a company wide policy of installing 8000 volt power lines in the back yards of residential users?

UNITED STATES FIDELITY & GUARANTY COMPANY v. PLOVIDBA

United States Court of Appeals, Seventh Circuit683 F.2d 1022 (7th Cir. 1982)

[This was an appeal from a judgment of the United States District Court in which a jury exonerated the shipowner defendant from negligence in connection with the claim of survivors of a longshoreman ("Huck") who fell to his death through an open hatch in a dark hold of a ship after stevedoring operations had ceased for the day. The decedent was the employee of a stevedoring company that had been hired by the shipowner to load and unload the ship. The appellants argued that the district court should have entered a judgment of liability against the shipowner as a matter of law notwithstanding the jury verdict to the contrary. Judge Posner first endorsed a general statement of the meaning of breach of duty as it had been applied in maritime cases and then demonstrated how judges might employ Judge Hand's famous mathematical formula for measuring negligence in tort cases.]

Posner, J.

[It is true that] if the shipowner "fails to exercise due care to avoid exposing longshoremen to harm from hazards they may encounter in areas, or from equipment, under the active control of the vessel during the stevedoring operation," he is liable under the negligence standard of [applicable maritime law] . . ., [but] we find nothing . . . inconsistent with the negligence formula . . . which requires "balancing the usefulness to the ship of the dangerous condition and the burden involved in curing it against the probability and severity of the harm it poses." This formula echoes that of Judge Learned Hand in *United States v. Carroll Towing Co.*, 159 F.2d 169, 173 (2d Cir. 1947), also a maritime negligence case. . . . Judge Hand, designating by "B" the burden of the precautions necessary to avert an accident, by "L" the magnitude of the loss if the accident occurred, and by "P" the probability that if the precautions were not taken the accident would occur, reasoned that a shipowner or other alleged tortfeasor was negligent if B < PL, that is, if the burden of precautions was less than the harm if the accident occurred discounted (*i.e.*, multiplied) by the probability that it would occur. The higher P and L are, and the lower B is, the likelier is a finding of negligence.

Though mathematical in form, the Hand formula does not yield mathematically precise results in practice; that would require that B, P, and L all be quantified, which so far as we know has never been done in an actual lawsuit. Nevertheless, the formula is a valuable aid to clear thinking about the factors that are relevant to a judgment of negligence and about the relationship among those factors. It gives federal district courts in maritime cases, where the liability standard is a matter of federal rather than state law, a useful framework for evaluating proposed jury instructions, for deciding motions for directed verdict and for judgment notwithstanding the verdict, and, in nonjury cases. . . . We do not want to force the district courts into a straitjacket, so we do not hold that they must use the Hand formula in all maritime negligence cases. We merely commend it to them as a useful tool — one we have found helpful in this case in evaluating the plaintiff's challenge to the jury instructions and its contention that negligence was shown as a matter of law.

Three jury instructions are challenged. The first reads: "A shipowner's duty to provide longshoremen with a reasonably safe place to work is confined to those areas of the vessel where longshoremen may reasonably be expected to go." This instruction is consistent with the Hand formula. Of course it is possible that a longshoreman will stray into a part of the ship where he has no business, but the probability (P in the Hand formula) seems too low to warrant the shipowner's taking precautions against an accident to him. If Huck had wandered into the captain's stateroom and slipped on a throw rug there, it would be unreasonable to impose liability on the shipowner even if the cost of doing without the throw rug would have been slight. Hold number 1 was not so remote from Huck's work area as the captain's stateroom would be, but all the challenged instruction did was ask the jury to decide whether it was a place where the shipowner should have expected Huck to be when the accident occurred, and this was proper.

The next challenged instruction reads: "The responsibility for the safety of the longshoremen in areas where long-shoring work is being conducted rests with the (stevedore), and if you find the (stevedore) to be negligent, the shipowner is not to be held liable for the (stevedore's) negligence." The first clause in the instruction can be criticized in the abstract as an overgeneralization. . . . The stevedore has the primary but not exclusive responsibility for the safety of the longshoremen. If Huck had been injured as a result of a defect that was due to the shipowner's negligence and was neither known nor reasonably knowable to the stevedore, the shipowner would be liable even if the accident had occurred in an area where long-shoring operations were being conducted. But since the accident occurred in an area where long-shoring operations were not being conducted, we do not see how the plaintiff could have been prejudiced by this instruction; if anything, the instruction implies, helpfully to the plaintiff, that responsibility for the safety of longshoremen in areas where long-shoring operations are not being conducted, such as hold number 1 when the accident occurred, is the shipowner's. If there was error, it was harmless. . . .

The third challenged instruction is unexceptionable and, again, harmless. It reads: "After stevedoring operations begin, the shipowner has no duty to superintend the operations of the stevedore or its employees." This could be a paraphrase of the . . . shipowner's duty to inspect. The Court made clear that the shipowner does not have a duty to look over the stevedore's shoulder, as it were, to make sure that he is conducting the stevedoring operations with due regard for the safety of his employees. . . . In the terms of the Hand formula the probability of an accident, given that the stevedore rather than the shipowner is actually conducting the stevedoring operations, is too slight to warrant making the shipowner take his own backup precautions to prevent the accident. In any event Huck could not be hurt by this instruction, for his theory was not that the shipowner had failed adequately to superintend the stevedore's operations but that the shipowner had created a hidden danger to any longshoreman who strayed from the area where those operations were in progress.

. . .

The plaintiff also contends that even if the instructions were satisfactory, the undisputed facts showed negligence by the shipowner as a matter of law. We again use the Hand formula to frame this issue. L, the loss if the accident occurred, was large. There was a 25 foot drop from the upper'tween deck of hold number 1 to the bottom of the hold, and a fall from that height was very likely to cause serious injury or, as in this case, death. As to B, the burden of precautions, there were various ways the shipowner could have prevented the accident. He could have lit the hold, locked the hatchway leading to it from the weather deck of hold number 2, roped off the open hatch, or placed a sign at the hatchway (though the effectiveness of this last precaution may be doubted). Probably the cheapest way of avoiding the accident, however, would have been for the ship's crew not to open the hatches until all the longshoremen had left the ship. This would have meant either the crew's working after normal working hours, or, if the opening of the hatches was postponed till the following morning, delay in beginning stevedoring operations at the next port of call. We doubt that either alternative would be very costly so we judge B in this case to have been, at most, moderate, and possibly small. If P, the probability of an accident if the precautions that would avert it were not taken, was high, then it would appear, in light of our discussion of L and B, that the shipowner was negligent in failing to take one of the precautions that we have mentioned. But probably P was low. There was no reason for a longshoreman to reenter a hold after he had completed his work there and moved on to another part of the ship. The plaintiff speculates that Huck may have left a piece of clothing in hold number 1 and gone back to retrieve it. It does not seem very likely that anyone would enter a pitch-black hold to retrieve a glove or a sock or a jacket, when he could easily ask for light. It is far more likely that Huck entered for an illicit purpose. This would not defeat a recovery if the shipowner were negligent; neither assumption of risk nor contributory negligence is a defense to liability in a negligence action under section 905(b). See S.Rep.No.1125, *supra*, at 12; 1A Benedict on Admiralty §§ 116-17 (7th ed. 1981). But Huck's motive in entering hold number 1 bears on the probability of the accident and hence on the cost-justified level of precautions by the shipowner. . . . Unless it is common for longshoremen to try to pilfer from darkened holds — and it was the plaintiff's burden to show that it is — the shipowner would have no reason to think it so likely that a longshoreman would be in a darkened hold as to require precautions against his falling through an open hatch.

Moreover, the relevant probability, so far as the Hand formula is concerned, is not the probability that a longshoreman would enter a darkened hold but the probability that he would fall into an open hatch in such a hold. The probability was small. The darkness was as effective a warning of danger as a sign would have been. Any longshoreman would know that there was a hatch on the floor and he could not rationally assume that it was closed. Only a reckless person would walk about in the hold in these circumstances, especially if he had no flashlight; Huck had none. There are reckless people as there are dishonest people; but the plaintiff did not try to prove that there are so many reckless dishonest longshoremen as to require the precautions that the defendant in this case would have had to take to avert injury to them. We do not know whether Huck was aware of the custom of opening the hatches after the longshoremen left the hold, and for the reasons just suggested it is not critical whether he was or not. But probably he was. His body was found well forward of where he would have fallen had he walked straight into the hold. No doubt he was trying to skirt what he knew to be an open hatch. The shipowner was not required to anticipate that a longshoreman knowing of the open shaft would not be able to avoid it; this was possible — it happened — but the probability was too remote to warrant precautions beyond the implicit warning of darkness itself. Another factor bearing on the probability of an accident is that Huck was under the general supervision of the stevedore company that employed him. Even if the defendant should have regarded Huck as no better than a sheep wandering about the ship with no rational concern for his own safety, it was entitled to regard the stevedore as his principal shepherd. The stevedore had a work rule forbidding longshoremen to be anywhere on the ship except where stevedoring operations were actually in progress. The shipowner was entitled to rely on the stevedore to enforce this rule, if not 100 percent at least enough to make it highly improbable, in light of the other circumstances that we have discussed, that one of the longshoremen would stray away from the rest and fall into a darkened hold.

The fact that the practice of leaving the hatches open in darkened holds was customary (or so the jury could find) and not just an idiosyncrasy of this Yugoslavian ship or shipowner has additional relevance to this case. Although custom is not a defense to a charge of negligence, *The T. J. Hooper*, 60 F.2d 737, 740 (2d Cir. 1932), it is a material consideration in evaluating the charge, especially where the victim and the alleged tortfeasor are linked, even if indirectly, in a voluntary relationship, as they were here. If a shipowner were to follow a practice that flunked the Hand formula — that in other words was not cost-justified, because the expected accident costs associated with the practice exceeded the costs of abandoning the practice and so preventing any accident from happening — then he would have to pay his stevedores higher rates, to compensate them for the additional risk to their employees, the longshoremen, whom the stevedores must compensate under 33 U.S.C. § 904, regardless of fault, for any injury the longshoremen sustain in the course of their employment. And since by hypothesis the cost to the stevedores of the additional compensation — the expected accident cost, in other words — would exceed the cost of abandoning the practice (for otherwise the practice would be cost-justified), it would pay the shipowner to abandon it. *Cf.* Coase, *The Problem of Social Cost*, 3 J.L. & Econ. 1 (1961). Hence if the shipowner persists in a dangerous practice — if the whole trade persists in the practice — that is some evidence, though not conclusive, that the practice is cost-justified, and not negligent.

But all this is not to say that the defendant's conduct in this case was, in fact, nonnegligent. We are not the triers of fact. The jury found the defendant nonnegligent and our job is just to decide whether a reasonable jury could have so found. Obviously we think the jury's finding was reasonable. . . .

[The judgment exonerating the shipowner was affirmed.]

NOTES AND QUESTIONS

(1)   Do you understand why the actual use of Judge Hand's formula in instructing juries would be unlikely to be useful? Do you agree that the Hand concept is helpful to judges in deciding whether or not particular instructions are to be given? To appellate judges in deciding whether error was made in connection with instructions given and not given by a trial judge?

(2)   Without regard to the actual holding on appeal, do you find Judge Posner's discussion of what may have been Huck's unknown reason for being in the darkened hold to be within the scope of an appellate court's review of a case in which a jury has rendered a verdict? Why did Judge Posner make no comment as to whose duty it was to present evidence pertaining to Huck's reasons?

(3)   Do you follow Judge Posner's argument in the next to last paragraph in the portion of the opinion printed above? Does it go this way? A reasonable ship owner would leave hatches open if that were cheaper than closing them even though it resulted in injuries that closing them would avoid; this ship owner left the hatches open. We may therefore assume that leaving the hatches open and paying for resulting injuries one way or the other is cheaper than closing the hatches. This ship owner left the hatches open; ergo, the ship owner was not negligent. Does this violate the principle of *Vaughan v. Menlove*? Huck was killed. Does tort law deem killing a few people to save money to be reasonable behavior?

§ 6.02   RES IPSA LOQUITUR

BYRNE v. BOADLE
2 H. & C. 722 (Ex. 1866)[5]

Declaration. For that the defendant, by his servants, so negligently and unskilfully managed and lowered certain barrels of flour by means of a certain jugger-hoist and machinery attached to the shop of the defendant, situated in a certain highway, along which the plaintiff was then passing, that by and through the negligence of the defendant, by his said servants, one of the said barrels of flour fell upon and struck against the plaintiff, whereby the plaintiff was thrown down, wounded, lamed, and permanently injured, and was prevented from attending to his business for a long time, to wit, thence hitherto, and incurred great expense for medical attendance, and suffered great pain and anguish, and was otherwise damnified.

Plea. Not guilty.

At the trial before the learned Assessor of the Court of Passage at Liverpool, the evidence adduced on the part of the plaintiff was as follows: — A witness named Critchley said: "On the 18th July, I was in Scotland Road, on the right side going north, defendant's shop is on that side. When I was opposite to his shop, a barrel of flour fell from a window above in defendant's house and shop, and knocked the plaintiff down. He was carried into an adjoining shop. A horse and cart came opposite the defendant's door. Barrels of flour were in the cart. I do not think the barrel was being lowered by a rope. I cannot say: I did not see the barrel until it struck the plaintiff. It was not swinging when it struck the plaintiff. It struck him on the shoulder and knocked him towards the shop. No one called out until after the accident." The plaintiff said: "On approaching Scotland Place and defendant's shop, I lost all recollection. I felt no blow. I saw nothing to warn me of danger. I was taken home in a cab. I was helpless for a fortnight." (He then described his sufferings.) "I saw the path clear. I did not see any cart opposite defendant's shop." Another witness said: "I saw a barrel falling. I don't know how, but from defendant's." The only other witness was a surgeon, who described the injury which the plaintiff had received. It was admitted that the defendant was a dealer in flour.

It was submitted, on the part of the defendant, that there was no evidence of negligence for the jury. The learned Assessor was of that opinion, and nonsuited the plaintiff, reserving leave to him to move the Court of Exchequer to enter the verdict for him with 50 pounds damages, the amount assessed by the jury.

Littler, in the present term, obtained a rule nisi to enter the verdict for the plaintiff on the ground of misdirection of the learned Assessor in ruling that there was no evidence of negligence on the part of the defendant; against which

Charles Russell now shewed cause.

POLLOCK, C. B. We are all of opinion that the rule must be absolute to enter the verdict for the plaintiff. The learned counsel was quite right in saying that there are many accidents from which no presumption of negligence can arise, but I think it would be wrong to lay down as a rule that in no case can presumption of

---

[5] [Ed. — Hurlston and Coltman's Exchequer Reports, decision of Court of Appeal.]

negligence arise from the fact of an accident. Suppose in this case the barrel had rolled out of the warehouse and fallen on the plaintiff, how could he possibly ascertain from what cause it occurred? It is the duty of persons who keep barrels in a warehouse to take care that they do not roll out, and I think that such a case would, beyond all doubt, afford prima facie evidence of negligence. A barrel could not roll out of a warehouse without some negligence, and to say that a plaintiff who is injured by it must call witnesses from the warehouse to prove negligence seems to me preposterous. So in the building or repairing a house, or putting pots on the chimneys, if a person passing along the road is injured by something falling upon him, I think the accident alone would be prima facie evidence of negligence. Or if an article calculated to cause damage is put in a wrong place and does mischief, I think that those whose duty it was to put it in the right place are prima facie responsible, and if there is any state of facts to rebut the presumption of negligence, they must prove them. The present case upon the evidence comes to this, a man is passing in front of the premises of a dealer in flour and there falls down upon him a barrel of flour. I think it apparent that the barrel was in the custody of the defendant who occupied the premises, and who is responsible for the acts of his servants who had the control of it; and in my opinion the fact of its falling is prima facie evidence of negligence, and the plaintiff who was injured by it is not bound to shew that it could not fall without negligence, but if there are any facts inconsistent with negligence it is for the defendant to prove them.

BRAMWELL, B. I am of the same opinion.

CHANNELL, B. I am of the same opinion. The first part of the rules assumes the existence of negligence, but takes this shape, that there was no evidence to connect the defendant with the negligence. The barrel of flour fell from a warehouse over a shop which the defendant occupied, and therefore prima facie he is responsible. Then the question is whether there was any evidence of negligence, not a mere scintilla, but such as in the absence of any evidence in answer would entitle the plaintiff to a verdict. I am of opinion that there was. I think that a person who has a warehouse by the side of a public highway, and assumes to himself the right to lower from it a barrel of flour into a cart, has a duty cast upon him to take care that persons passing along the highway are not injured by it. I agree that it is not every accident which will warrant the inference of negligence. On the other hand, I dissent from the doctrine that there is no accident which will in itself raise a presumption of negligence. In this case I think that there was evidence for the jury, and that the rule ought to be absolute to enter the verdict for the plaintiff.

PIGOTT, B. I am of the same opinion.

Rule absolute.

QUESTION

To what extent did the evidence alluded to by the judges in *Byrne v. Boadle* support the allegations?

ESCOLA v. COCA COLA BOTTLING COMPANY
California Supreme Court
24 Cal.2d 453, 150 P.2d 436 (1944)

GIBSON, CHIEF JUSTICE.

Plaintiff, a waitress in a restaurant, was injured when a bottle of Coca Cola broke in her hand. She alleged that defendant company, which had bottled and delivered the alleged defective bottle to her employer, was negligent in selling "bottles containing said beverage which on account of excessive pressure of gas or by reason of some defect in the bottle was dangerous . . . and likely to explode." This appeal is from a judgment upon a jury verdict in favor of plaintiff.

Defendant's driver delivered several cases of Coca Cola to the restaurant, placing them on the floor, one on top of the other, under and behind the counter, where they remained at least thirty-six hours. Immediately before the accident, plaintiff picked up the top case and set it upon a near-by ice cream cabinet in front of and about three feet from the refrigerator. She then proceeded to take the bottles from the case with her right hand, one at a time, and put them into the refrigerator. Plaintiff testified that after she had placed three bottles in the refrigerator and had moved the fourth bottle about 18 inches from the case "it exploded in my hand." The bottle broke into two jagged pieces and inflicted a deep five-inch cut, severing blood vessels, nerves and muscles of the thumb and palm of the hand. Plaintiff further testified that when the bottle exploded, "It made a sound similar to an electric light bulb that would have dropped. It made a loud pop." Plaintiff's employer testified, "I was about twenty feet from where it actually happened and I heard the explosion." A fellow employee, on the opposite side of the counter, testified that plaintiff "had the bottle, I should judge, waist high, and I know that it didn't bang either the case or the door or another bottle . . . when it popped. It sounded just like a fruit jar would blow up . . . " The witness further testified that the contents of the bottle "flew all over herself and myself and the walls and one thing and another."

The top portion of the bottle, with the cap, remained in plaintiff's hand, and the lower portion fell to the floor but did not break. The broken bottle was not produced at the trial, the pieces having been thrown-away by an employee of the restaurant shortly after the accident.

Plaintiff, however, described the broken pieces and a diagram of the bottle was made showing the location of the "fracture line" where the bottle broke in two.

One of defendant's drivers, called as a witness by plaintiff, testified that he had seen other bottles of Coca Cola in the past explode and had found broken bottles in the warehouse when he took the cases out, but that he did not know what made them blow up.

Plaintiff then rested her case, having announced to the court that being unable to show any specific acts of negligence she relied completely on the doctrine of res ipsa loquitur.

Defendant contends that the doctrine of res ipsa loquitur does not apply in this case, and that the evidence is insufficient to support the judgment.

Many jurisdictions have applied the doctrine in cases involving exploding bottles of carbonated beverages. It would serve no useful purpose to discuss the reasoning of the foregoing cases in detail, since the problem is whether under the facts shown in the instant case the conditions warranting application of the doctrine have been satisfied.

Res ipsa loquitur does not apply unless (1) defendant had exclusive control of the thing causing the injury and (2) the accident is of such a nature that it ordinarily would not occur in the absence of negligence by the defendant. *Honea v. City Dairy, Inc.*, 22 Cal.2d 614, 616, 617, 140 P.2d 369, and authorities there cited; cf. *Hinds v. Wheadon*, 19 Cal.2d 458, 461, 121 P.2d 721; Prosser on Torts [1911], 293–301.

Many authorities state that the happening of the accident does not speak for itself where it took place some time after defendant had relinquished control of the instrumentality causing the injury. Under the more logical view, however, the doctrine may be applied upon the theory that defendant had control at the time of the alleged negligent act, although not at the time of the accident, *provided* plaintiff first proves that the condition of the instrumentality had not been changed after it left the defendant's possession. See cases collected in *Honea v. City Dairy, Inc.*, 22 Cal.2d 614, 617, 618, 140 P.2d 369. As said in *Dunn v. Hoffman Beverage Co.*, 126 N.J.I. 556, 20 A.2d 352, 354, "defendant is not charged with the duty of showing affirmatively that something happened to the bottle after it left its control or management; . . . to get to the jury the plaintiff must show that there was due care during that period." Plaintiff must also prove that she handled the bottle carefully. The reason for this prerequisite is set forth in Prosser on Torts, *supra*, at page 300, where the author states: "Allied to the condition of exclusive control in the defendant is that of absence of any action on the part of the plaintiff contributing to the accident. Its purpose, of course, is to eliminate the possibility that it was the plaintiff who was responsible. If the boiler of a locomotive explodes while the plaintiff engineer is operating it, the inference of his own negligence is at least as great as that of the defendant, and res ipsa loquitur will not apply until he has accounted for his own conduct." See, also, *Olson v. Whitthorne & Swan*, 203 Cal. 206, 208, 209, 263 P. 518, 58 A.L.R. 129. It is not necessary, of course, that plaintiff eliminate every remote possiblity of injury to the bottle after defendant lost control, and the requirement is satisfied if there is evidence permitting a reasonable inference that it was not accessible to extraneous harmful forces and that it was carefully handled by plaintiff or any third person who may have moved or touched it. Cf. Prosser, *supra*, p. 300. If such evidence is presented, the question becomes one for the trier of fact (see, *e.g.*, *MacPherson v. Canada Dry Ginger Ale, Inc.*, 129 N.J.L. 365, 29 A.2d 868, 869), and, accordingly, the issue should be submitted to the jury under proper instructions.

In the present case no instructions were requested or given on this phase of the case, although general instructions upon res ipsa loquitur were given. Defendant, however, has made no claim of error with reference thereto on this appeal.

Upon an examination of the record, the evidence appears sufficient to support a reasonable inference that the bottle here involved was not damaged by any extraneous force after delivery to the restaurant by defendant. It follows, therefore, that the bottle was in some manner defective at the time defendant relinquished control, because sound and properly prepared bottles of carbonated liquids do not ordinarily explode when carefully handled.

The next question, then, is whether plaintiff may rely upon the doctrine of res ipsa loquitur to supply an inference that defendant's negligence was responsible for the defective condition of the bottle at the time it was delivered to the restaurant. Under the general rules pertaining to the doctrine, as set forth above it must appear that bottles of carbonated liquid are not ordinarily defective without negligence by the bottling company. In 1 Shearman and Redfield on Negligence (Rev. Ed. 1941), page 153, it is stated that: "The doctrine . . . requires evidence which shows at least the probability that a particular accident could not have occurred without legal wrong by the defendant."

An explosion such as took place here might have been caused by an excessive internal pressure in a sound bottle, by a defect in the glass of a bottle containing a safe pressure, or by a combination of these two possible causes. The question is whether under the evidence there was a probability that defendant was negligent in any of these respects. If so, the doctrine of res ipsa loquitur applies.

The bottle was admittedly charged with gas under pressure, and the charging of the bottle was within the exclusive control of defendant. As it is a matter of common knowledge that an over-charge would not ordinarily result without negligence, it follows under the doctrine of res ipsa loquitur that if the bottle was in fact excessively charged an inference of defendant's negligence would arise. If the explosion resulted from a defective bottle containing a safe pressure, the defendant would be liable if it negligently failed to discover such flaw. If the defect were visible, an inference of negligence would arise from the failure of defendant to discover it. Where defects are discoverable, it may be assumed that they will not ordinarily escape detection if a reasonable inspection is made, and if such a defect is overlooked an inference arises that a proper inspection was not made. A difficult problem is presented where the defect is unknown and consequently might have been one not discoverable by a reasonable, practicable inspection. In the *Honea* case we refused to take judicial notice of the technical practices and information available to the bottling industry for finding defects which cannot be seen. In the present case, however, we are supplied with evidence of the standard methods used for testing bottles.

A chemical engineer for the Owens-Illinois Glass Company and its Pacific Coast subsidiary, maker of Coca Cola bottles, explained how glass is manufactured and the methods used in testing and inspecting bottles. He testified that his company is the largest manufacturer of glass containers in the United States, and that it uses the standard methods for testing bottles recommended by the glass containers association. A pressure test is made by taking a sample from each mold every three hours — approximately one out of every 600 bottles — and subjecting the sample to an internal pressure of 450 pounds per square inch, which is sustained for one minute. (The normal pressure in Coca Cola bottles is less than 50 pounds per square inch.) The sample bottles are also subjected to the standard thermal shock test. The witness stated that these tests are "pretty near" infallible.

It thus appears that there is available to the industry a commonly-used method of testing bottles for defects not apparent to the eye, which is almost infallible. Since Coca Cola bottles are subjected to these tests by the manufacturer, it is not likely that they contain defects when delivered to the bottler which are not discoverable by visual inspection. Both new and used bottles are filled and distributed by defendant. The used bottles are not again subjected to the tests referred to above, and it may be inferred that defects not discoverable by visual inspection do not develop in bottles after they are manufactured. Obviously, if such defects do occur in used bottles there is a duty upon the bottler to make appropriate tests before they are refilled, and if such tests are not commercially practicable the bottles should not be re-used. This would seem to be particularly true where a charged liquid is placed in the bottle. It follows that a defect which would make the bottle unsound could be discovered by reasonable and practicable tests.

Although it is not clear in this case whether the explosion was caused by an excessive charge or a defect in the glass there is a sufficient showing that neither cause would ordinarily have been present if due care had been used. Further, defendant had exclusive control over both the charging and inspection of the bottles. Accordingly, all the requirements necessary to entitle plaintiff to rely on the doctrine of res ipsa loquitur to supply an inference of negligence are present.

It is true that defendant presented evidence tending to show that it exercised considerable precaution by carefully regulating and checking the pressure in the bottles and by making visual inspections for defects in the glass at several stages during the bottling process. It is well settled, however, that when a defendant produces evidence to rebut the inference of negligence which arises upon application of the doctrine of res ipsa loquitur, it is ordinarily a question of fact for the jury to determine whether the inference has been dispelled. *Druzanich v. Criley*, 19 Cal.2d 439, 444, 122 P.2d 53; *Michener v. Hutton*, 203 Cal. 604, 610, 265 P. 238, 59 A.L.R. 480.

The judgment is affirmed.

SHENK, CURTIS, CARTER, and SCHAUER, JJ., concurred.

TRAYNOR, JUSTICE.

I concur in the judgment, but I believe the manufacturer's negligence should no longer be singled out as the basis of a plaintiff's right to recover in cases like the present one. In my opinion it should now be recognized that a manufacturer incurs an absolute liability when an article that he has placed on the market, knowing that it is to be used without inspection, proves to have a defect that causes injury to human beings.

. . .

This court and many others have extended protection according to such a standard to consumers of food products, taking the view that the right of a consumer injured by unwholesome food does not depend "upon the intricacies of the law of sales" and that the warranty of the manufacturer to the consumer in absence of privity of contract rests on public policy. . . . Dangers to life and health inhere in other consumers' goods that are defective and there is no reason to differentiate them from the dangers of defective food products. See Bohlen, Studies in Torts, Basis of Affirmative Obligations, American Cases Upon The Liability of Manufacturers and Vendors of Personal Property, 109, 135; Llewellyn, *On Warranty of Quality and Society*, 36 Col. L. Rev. 699, 704, note 14: Prosser, Torts, p. 692.

. . .

QUESTIONS

What was the main dispute in *Escola*: Excluding the plaintiff's negligence or establishing the defendant's exclusive control? Does the reasoning of the next case eliminate the difficulty, or something else?

DAYTON TIRE AND RUBBER CO. v. DAVIS
Florida District Court of Appeal
348 So. 2d 575 (1977)

[Ronnie Davis, a minor, was killed when the car in which he was a passenger crashed. The wrongful death plaintiffs alleged that the cause of death was a blow-out of a tire that had been manufactured by Dayton and retailed by John Mott Sunoco Service, Inc. The evidence established that the tire was six months old and had been driven 4000 miles and that there was a defect in cords of the tire that could have been caused by overheating during manufacture. The jury returned a verdict against Dayton. Dayton appeals on grounds that it was improper to have given the jury a *res ipsa loquitur* instruction.]

BOYER, CHIEF JUDGE:

. . . What caused the tire to blow out. Obviously, if the blowout resulted solely from actions or omissions on the part of Davis then there can be no right of recovery. It was determined at trial, and we have affirmed, that Mott was not responsible. It follows then that in order for Davis to recover against Dayton on the theory of negligence some action or omission which caused the blowout must be visited upon Dayton. On that issue there was evidence both pro and con. As already recited, the witnesses called by Dayton testified that the blowout was not caused by any act or omission on the part of Dayton. However, one of the witnesses called by the plaintiff clearly and unequivocally testified that the cause of the blowout was tire failure; that the tire failure was caused by weakened cords inside the tire; that the cords were weakened as a result of being burned and that the burn occurred prior to the exterior rubber being applied to the tire which, by application of common logic and deductive reasoning, means during the manufacturing process. The witness could not, of course, testify as to what caused the burn.

It was at that stage that the plaintiff sought to have applied the doctrine of res ipsa loquitur, urging that the situation speaks for itself and that if indeed the tire failed because of burned cords as the witness had testified and if those cords were burned while the tire was in the exclusive control of Dayton, viz: during the process of manufacture, as the last above mentioned witness' testimony suggested, then a fortiori the defect could only have resulted from negligence on the part of Dayton's employees either in burning the cords or in failing to properly inspect before application of the rubber to the cords.

As already stated, a party is not precluded from a requested instruction simply because his adversary has adduced evidence which, if believed by a jury, would render the instruction inapplicable. On the contrary, if credible evidence has been adduced based upon which, and if believed by a jury, the jury may properly apply the law sought to have charged via the requested instruction then that instruction should be given. It is for the jury, not the judge, (trial or appellate) to determine which evidence is true and the jury is entitled to be charged upon the law applicable to such evidence as it finds to be true.

Although the evidence was conflicting and if weighted by numbers of witnesses preponderated in favor of Dayton, nevertheless there was substantial competent evidence from whence reasonable jurors could have found that (a) Ronnie Davis died as a result of an automobile accident which (b) was caused by a blow-out which (c) resulted from a defect in the tire manufactured by Dayton which (d) was defectively manufactured by reason of (e) incorporation of burned cords which (f) were burned in Dayton's plant prior to being incorporated in the tire and that (g) the thing speaks for itself, viz: But for negligence either in burning the cords or in failing to inspect the cords or in failing to detect upon inspection the defect would not have occurred.

The fact that there was contradictory evidence from whence the jury could have found res ipsa loquitur inapplicable did not obviate the right of the jury to have the instruction.

Under the peculiar evidence of this particular case we find that the challenged instruction was properly given.

. . .

Affirmed in part and reversed in part and remanded for further proceedings consistent herewith.

MILLS, J., concurs and SMITH J., concurring and dissenting.

SMITH, JUSTICE, concurring and dissenting:

I concur in the court's disposition of all issues except the propriety of a *res ipsa loquitur* charge supporting plaintiff's claim against Dayton. On that issue I dissent. The *res ipsa* charge should be reserved for those exceptional cases in which the very character of the accident, unaided by plaintiff's evidence tending to isolate the cause as defendant's negligence, may properly be considered by the jury as creating an inference of negligence. In this case the inference of negligence did not arise from the blowout, speaking for itself, but from plaintiff's other circumstantial evidence tending to show decedent did not under-inflate or otherwise abuse the tire, the tire was not exposed to other extraordinary use or damaging impact, and the failure was due to fibers weakened by the manufacturing process. Dayton's evidence was to the contrary in every important respect.

Entirely apart from whether a *res ipsa* charge was made inappropriate by Dayton's conflicting proof of under-inflation by decedent, no inference of negligence can arise from the failure, considered alone, of a tire driven 4,000 miles. Common sense does not suggest negligence, let alone manufacturer's negligence, as the probable cause of such an accident. In such a case, a *res ipsa* charge is but a finishing stroke, administered by the charging judge, in a plaintiff's case which is built step by step until the last on ordinary circumstantial evidence that defendant was negligent and plaintiff's decedent was not. There the charge is sheer judicial argument for a plaintiff's verdict and is inappropriate.

. . .

Although the decisions foreclosing a *res ipsa loquitur* instruction in these circumstances are variously reasoned — some suggesting the opportunity for intervening damage was too great, others simply noting the time interval without elucidation — I am persuaded those decisions rest primarily on a clear perception that such an accident does not, without aid of plaintiff's evidence tending to isolate the cause as defendant's negligence, "speak for itself" as in *Byrne v. Boadle*, 2 H. & C. 722, 159 Eng. Rep. 299 (Ex. 1863).

In *Byrne, res ipsa* was an unaffected and intelligible appeal to the most basic reasoning powers of judges and juries: it is untrue that negligence can *never* be "inferred from the mere happening of an accident alone", because *some* accidents by their nature suggest negligence and point to the responsible party even when evidence is unavailable. The thing speaks for itself. Thus Baron Pollock refuted the doctrinaire "never" as simply as Dr. Johnson, by kicking a boulder, is said to refuted Berkeley's theory of the nonexistence of matter. The *Byrne* decision was heavily influenced by plaintiff's inability to extract an explanation from defendant.[6]

But today, more than a hundred years after Boadle's flour barrel fell on Byrne from a second story window, the adverse witness rule, modern discovery methods and the resourcefulness of expert testimony have penetrated many mysteries of that era and have made rare the cases "where direct proof is wanting." And *res ipsa*, far from withering by the removal of its original cause, has become an expanding and complex doctrine, unruly in application. Its recent history in Florida is strewn with the wreckage of reversed judgments — hardly a favorable commentary on our understanding and consistent application of a simple idea concerning the accident that "speaks for itself."

The disarray of *res ipsa loquitur* may be attributed to "the strong general trend towards strict liability and social insurance — a trend which is corroding a system of liability nominally based on fault" and, as in this case, to confusion stemming from plaintiff's reliance both on *res ipsa* and on sophisticated and specific evidence of negligence. Our Supreme Court stated in *West Coast Hospital, supra* n.7, that "one may not avail himself of the doctrine if he proves specific negligence," 52 So. 2d at 804, and expressed the same thought in *Roth v. Dade County*, 71 So. 2d 169, 170 (Fla. 1954), but silently retracted those statements in *McKinney Supply Co. v. Orovitz*, 96 So. 2d 209 (Fla. 1957). The Court later held the *West Coast Hospital* and *Roth* statements were obiter dicta and, by discharging certiorari let stand the conflicting decision in *South Florida Hosp. Corp. v. McCrea*, 112 So. 2d 393 (Fla.3d DCA 1959), cert. dism., 118 So. 2d 25 (Fla. 1960). Reliance on both *res ipsa* and specific proof of negligence has since become commonplace. *National Airlines, Inc. v. Fleming*, 141 So. 2d 343 (Fla. 1st DCA 1962); *Kulczynski v. Harrington*, 207 So. 2d 505 (Fla.3d DCA 1968); *Cortez Roofing Co., Inc. v. Barolo*, 323 So. 2d 45 (Fla.2d DCA 1975).

In any putative *res ipsa* case, it is necessary for the court to consider "the circumstances" in determining whether the jury could find the accident "speaks for itself" concerning negligence. There are no pure tire blowout cases; rather, there are cases in which a new tire exploded while being mounted on the rim, and cases in which a tire failed after 4,000 miles of driving. The accident that "spoke for itself" in *Byrne v. Boadle* was not simply a barrel falling, but a barrel falling "from

---

[6] Baron Bramwell stated: "Looking at the matter in a reasonable way it comes to this — an injury is done to the plaintiff, who has no means of knowing whether it was the result of negligence; *the defendant, who knows how it was caused, does not think fit to tell the jury.*" Lawyer Russell responded: "The plaintiff cannot, by a defective proof on his case, compel the defendant to give evidence in explanation." 159 Eng. Rep. at 301 (emphasis added).

a window above in defendant's house and shop," at the door of which stood a horse-drawn cart ladened with barrels of flour. The abstract problem of identifying the circumstances which do or do not "speak for themselves" is compounded when, by plaintiff's specific proof, all antecedent circumstances are arrayed to show defendant's negligence and to negate other possible causes. Here, for example, the majority do not regard this case as involving an exploding tire, or a tire driven 4,000 miles; to them, for *res ipsa* purposes, this case involves a properly-inflated tire that failed after 4,000 miles of ordinary driving and revealed burned fiber characteristic of a manufacturing mishap. To them, therefore, the thing "speaks for itself," or at least the jury may think so if it accepts plaintiff's rather than defendant's circumstantial evidence and "theory of the case." It is in the majority's unrestrained resort to plaintiff's circumstantial evidence of antecedent events that I part with them in determining the propriety of a *res ipsa* charge. Their reasoning blends plaintiff's circumstantial evidence case for *res ipsa* with his circumstantial evidence case isolating the cause as Dayton's manufacturing negligence.

Harper and James spoke worlds when they wrote "the happening of an accident *and a description of some of the facts surrounding it* may permit an inference of defendant's negligence without any direct testimony as to his conduct at the very time that such negligence occurred." If the *res ipsa* net is cast wide enough in search of "the facts surrounding" the accident, any circumstantial evidence case sufficient for the jury on the issue of proven negligence may be transformed into one suitable for *res ipsa*.[7]

But while any jury will likely infer negligence when a driver runs down a pedestrian, it is hardly thought necessary or appropriate — at least, not yet — that the trial judge should incite such a finding on a jury issue by a *res ipsa* charge.[8]

. . .

I recognize that urging a restricted view of the circumstances constituting "the accident itself" — *i.e.*, that this was a tire blowout after 4,000 miles, not a blowout after 4,000 miles of a properly maintained tire made of burned fibre — does not entirely relieve the embarrassing difficulty of stating criteria, useful in other factual contexts, for identifying the circumstances relevant to the *res ipsa* issue. While the restricted view still must have a boundary, which one judge and another may draw differently in a case for which there is no factual precedent, one would expect the area of potential disagreement to contract with the circumference of

---

[7] The influence of plaintiff's specific proof of negligence on the *res ipsa* issue may be hidden in a narrow but questionable formulation of the circumstances which are said to justify a *res ipsa* charge. In *Springer v. Reimers*, 4 Cal. App.3d 325, 333–34, 84 Cal. Rptr. 486, 490 (1970), the court applying *res ipsa* found "reasonable support for the inference of negligence from the happening of the accident alone because a man standing on top of a truck trailer does not ordinarily fall there from unless someone has been negligent." That dubious assertion would likely not have been made if the evidence was that plaintiff had a history of fainting spells or was startled by a thunderclap. In fact, defendant's vehicle on which plaintiff was standing suddenly jerked.

[8] In *McGinley v. Chancey*, 70 So. 2d 357 (Fla. 1957), the Supreme Court made the point which I wish to establish here: that *res ipsa* cannot take the place of specific proof of negligence when a guest passenger is injured by defendant's crashing an automobile into a light pole. The accident was held not to "speak for itself" because it was theoretically possible "defendant had blacked out, become paralyzed, or was trying to avoid hitting a child . . . " Hence *res ipsa* has been held "unavailable in cases of automobile negligence." *Abrams v. Nolan Brown Cad. Co.*, 228 So. 2d 131, 132 (Fla.3d DCA 1969), cert. den., 237 So. 2d 536 (Fla. 1970); *Burgin v. Merritt, supra* n. 1, 311 So. 2d at 691. There are contrary decisions. 1 Frumer and Friedman, Products Liability 292 (1976).

"the accident itself." That would promote predictability in trial court rulings and appellate review on *res ipsa* — a laudable purpose in itself.

Moreover, a restricted examination of "the accident itself" would tend to disregard collateral circumstances which often are disputed by the evidence, or which often support conflicting inferences, *e.g.*, the presence or absence of abnormal tread-wear on a failing tire. After surviving such a test, a *res ipsa* charge is less likely to be misunderstood as inviting the jury uncritically to infer negligence from inferences which are themselves disputed. If the failure or malfunction of an instrument which passed beyond defendant's absolute control is found not to imply probable negligence, no concern need be given the frequently contested secondary criterion for *res ipsa*, that in the interval the instrument was not *in fact* subjected to harm. *E.g., Goodyear Tire & Rubber Co. v. Hughes Supply Inc., supra* n.1. Plaintiff may rely on his direct or circumstantial (and disputed) evidence negating harm to the instrument since it left defendant's control, but neither that evidence nor plaintiff's specific evidence of negligence should be considered in the threshold determination whether the accident was of a sort that ordinarily does not occur in the absence of someone's negligence.

Florida courts have special reasons to avoid jury charges on *res ipsa loquitur* when common experience or expert testimony[9] does not show the accident was of a sort that ordinarily cannot occur in the absence of negligence. Although the charge merely permits and does not require the jury to infer that defendant was negligent, it can hardly be doubted that the charge in its most innocuous form is a judicial suggestion that the jurors find negligence where otherwise they might not. The charge has no other purpose. The impact of Florida's standard instruction on *res ipsa*, is only modestly neutralized by the qualifying. . . .

If you find that the circumstances of the occurrence were such that, in the ordinary course of events, it would not have happened in the absence of negligence, that the instrumentality causing an injury was in the exclusive control of the defendant at the time the negligent act or omission, if any, must have occurred and that the instrumentality, after leaving the defendant's control, was not improperly used or handled by others or subjected to harmful forces or conditions, you may infer that the defendant was negligent . . . ,

. . . unless, taking into consideration all of the evidence in the case, you conclude that the occurrence was not due to any negligence on the part of the defendant.

It does not seem entirely speculative to say that a Florida jury is more likely than a jury elsewhere to accept the judicial hint, pass over the troublesome questions, and go home. Florida's standard jury instructions seek to "express the applicable issues and guiding legal principles briefly and in simple, understandable language,

---

[9] Expert testimony if otherwise admissible may establish for *res ipsa* purposes, when common experience cannot, that an accident of a particular sort ordinarily cannot happen without negligence. But such testimony, absent in the case before us, should not be confused with expert testimony analyzing antecedent events and collateral circumstances and tending thereby to isolate the cause as defendant's negligence. There was abundant expert testimony of the latter type in this case. See also *Baker v. B. F. Goodrich Co.*, 115 Cal. App.2d 221, 252 P.2d 24 (1953), which Frumer and Friedman discuss without distinguishing between what I have called the threshold issue and the secondary issue of whether the probable negligence was probably the defendant's. 1 Products Liability 300–303 (1976).

without argument, without unnecessary repetition and without reliance on negative charges." Florida juries no longer are charged that negligence is not to be "inferred from the mere happening of an accident alone" — the simplistic truism which provoked Baron Pollock in the first instance — nor that circumstantial evidence is different from direct evidence, nor that there are such things as unavoidable accidents, that one is presumed to exercise reasonable care for his own safety, that one may assume others will do so, that one has a duty to inspect and maintain his vehicle in safe condition. Florida's commitment is that juries, assisted by counsel's argument, are capable of drawing appropriate inferences from the evidence and deductions from the law generally stated. Jury charges in other states are often longer and more detailed. In Florida, where *res ipsa* is the stark exception to brief jury instructions containing no hint of judicial commentary on circumstantial evidence and inferences, it may be assumed that a *res ipsa* charge carries more impact than if it were lost in a lengthy dissertation on all the ramifications of negligence and its proof. That alone is reason enough to take seriously the taming of *res ipsa loquitur*, to remove unwarranted judicial argument from the charge, and to expand liability, where that is thought desirable, by more appropriate substantive doctrines.

NOTES AND QUESTIONS

(1)   In *Goodyear Tire & Rubber v. Hughes Supply, Inc.*, 358 So. 2d 1339 (Fla. 1978), the Florida Supreme Court reversed *Dayton Tire* on the res ipsa loquitur instruction. Said the court at 1342, 43:

> Plainly, the threshold inquiry is whether that which occurred is a phenomenon which does not ordinarily happen except in the absence of due care. The initial burden is on the plaintiff to establish that the circumstances attendant to the injury are such that, in the light of past experience, negligence is the probable cause and the defendant is the probable actor. An injury standing alone, of course, ordinarily does not indicate negligence. The doctrine of res ipsa loquitur simply recognizes that in rare instances an injury may permit an inference of negligence if coupled with a sufficient showing of its immediate, precipitating cause.

> . . .

> Not only was the use of the negligence inference inappropriate in these cases because the facts surrounding the incident were discoverable and provable, and because they were not of a nature typically suggestive of negligence by the defendants, but the inference was inappropriate because the plaintiffs in these cases failed to allege and prove the essential element of defendant's exclusive control over the injury-causing instrumentality. In *Schott v. Pancoast Properties*, 57 So. 2d 431 (Fla. 1952), we held:

> The doctrine may not be invoked unless it appear [sic] that the thing causing the injury was so completely in the control of the defendant that, in the ordinary course of events, the mishap could not have occurred had there been proper care on the defendant's part.

> In the two cases before us, the evidence presented to establish the tire companies' sole control was wholly insufficient. Given the time of plaintiffs' control over the tires and the extent of their usage, it is impossible to assert

that the tire companies had "exclusive control" at the time of the injuries.

We recognize that there are exceptions to the exclusive control requirement in Florida. Each is supported, however, by a justifiable basis for inferring that the cause of injury was probably the defendant's negligence. It is untenable to suggest that anything inherent in the product warrants creating an exception for automobile or truck tires once they have left the manufacturer's possession and have been put to the intended use.

More generally, the court agreed with Judge Smith "that the doctrine of res ipsa loquitur has developed a judicial gloss which was never intended." *Id.*, at 1341. But see, *Marrero v. Goldsmith*, 486 So. 2d 530 (Fla. 1986), which holds, despite *Goodyear*, that the introduction of some direct proof of negligence does not deprive a plaintiff of a res ipsa loquitur instruction.

(2) To what extent are *Escola* and Judge Smith's opinion irreconcilable on the basis of pure res ipsa doctrine? Can *Escola* be justified as an exception?

(3) *Giles v. City of New Haven*, 636 A.2d 1335 (Conn. 1994), involved an action by a passenger who was injured when an elevator fell because the chain suspending it broke. Why it broke was not proven. The passenger sued the contracting company hired by the elevator's owner to maintain and repair it and sought to invoke res ipsa loquitur. The defendant opposed it for lack of exclusive control. The court permitted the res ipsa instruction saying, in part, at 636 A.2d 1339, 1340:

> The growing trend in res ipsa loquitur jurisprudence is not to apply the "control" condition in such a way that renders it a fixed, mechanical and rigid rule. " 'Control,' if it is not to be pernicious and misleading, must be a very flexible term. It may be enough that the defendant has the right or power of control, and the opportunity to exercise it. . . . It is enough that the defendant is under a duty which he cannot delegate to another. . . . There is now quite general agreement that the fact that the plaintiff is . . . using an appliance, which the defendant has manufactured or maintained, will not prevent the application of res ipsa loquitur when the evidence reasonably eliminates other explanations than the defendant's negligence." W. Prosser & W. Keeton, *supra*, § 39, p. 250. . . .

> In many jurisdictions, courts now deemphasize the role of exclusive control as a condition of res ipsa loquitur, even though their earlier decisions included such a requirement. . . . Thus, the inference may be drawn jointly against the owner of an elevator and the elevator company which maintains the same. . . . If the jury could reasonably find that the defendant's control was sufficient to warrant an inference that the defendant was more likely responsible for the incident than someone else, even in the absence of proof of absolute exclusivity and control over the instrumentality by the defendant, the trial court must allow the jury to draw that inference. . . .

>> "[T]here is no necessity for a plaintiff to eliminate all other possible causes of the accident. All that is required is that the plaintiff produce sufficient evidence from which a reasonable [person] could say that, on the whole, it was more likely than not that there was negligence on the part of the defendant. . . . [T]he possibility of other causes does not have to be eliminated completely, but their likelihood must be so reduced that

the jury can reasonably find that the negligence, if any, lies at the defendant's door."

Parrillo v. Giroux Co., 426 A.2d 1313, 1319 (R.I.1981). . . .

We agree with the Appellate Court that the evidence established an evidentiary basis from which the jury could find that the plaintiff's injuries resulted from the defendant's negligence.

Would Judge Smith approve of the use of res ipsa loquitur in *Giles*? Are the cases distinguishable on their facts?

(4)   Precisely what inference, if any, is a jury required to draw from the res ipsa instruction quoted in Judge Smith's opinion? On that point, does the instruction appear in line with the usual view that the finder of fact is permitted but not required to infer that the incident of itself proves that the defendant was negligent? See, *e.g., United States v. Chesapeake & Delaware Shipyard*, 369 F. Supp. 744 (D. Md. 1971). Apparently, some courts hold the view that res ipsa loquitur "has the effect of shifting the burden of proof to the defendant to show an absence of negligence on his part." *Sheppard v. Travelers Insurance Co.*, 333 So. 2d 342 (La. App. 1976). See note 6, below.

(5)   Would it be proper to grant the res ipsa loquitur instruction where a plaintiff has alleged specific acts of negligence and has adduced some evidence to prove them? Judge Smith alludes to the confusion on this point, and the courts are divided on it. See, Annot. 2 A.L.R. 3d 1335 (1965). What are the arguments for and against res ipsa loquitur under these circumstances? Should merely alleging specific acts of negligence eliminate the charge? Re-read *Bryne v. Boadle*, § 6.02, *supra*.

(6)   What is the legal effect of a *res ipsa loquitur* instruction? Does it assure that the plaintiff will prevail? One view is:

> The legal effect of meeting the three criteria of *res ipsa loquitur* is that the fact finder is warranted in inferring that the defendant was negligent. In the oft-quoted language of the Supreme Court . . . res ipsa loquitur means that the facts of the occurrence warrant the inference of negligence, not that they compel such an inference; that they furnish circumstantial evidence of negligence where direct evidence of it may be lacking, but it is evidence to be weighed, not necessarily to be accepted as sufficient. . . . (*Sweeney v. Erving*, 228 U.S. 233, 240, 33 S.Ct. 416, 418, 57 L.Ed. 815 (1913).

Jesionowski v. Boston & Maine Railroad Co., 329 U.S. 452, 67 S.Ct. 401, 404, 91 L.Ed. 416 (1947); *Johnson v. United States, supra* at 48 of 333 U.S. 68 S.Ct. 391. If the trier of the facts draws an inference of negligence, *procedural* implications arise. *Johnson v. United States, supra* at 49–50, 68 S.Ct. 391; *Blumenthal v. United States*, 189 F. Supp. 439, 445 (D.C. Pa. 1960). Although the burden of proof by a preponderance of the evidence still rests upon the plaintiff, once an inference of negligence is drawn after a weighing of the facts, the plaintiff has established a *prima facie* case of negligence. *Sweeney v. Erving, supra* at 239 of 228 U.S. 33 S.Ct. 416; *Smith v. Pennsylvania Central Airlines Corp.*, 76 F.Supp. 940, 943 (D.D.C. 1948). Consequently, the burden of going forward with the evidence shifts to the defendant, and it is for him to produce for rebuttal evidence or run the risk of non-persuasion:

. . . they [the facts] call for explanation or rebuttal, not necessarily that they require it; that they make a case to be decided by the jury, not that they forestall the verdict. [*Sweeney v. Erving, supra* at 240, of 228 U.S., at 418 of 33 S.Ct.].

United States v. Chesapeake & Delaware Shipyard, 369 F. Supp. 711 (D. Md. 1971).

Some courts give res ipsa loquitur different weight. For example, *Ray v. Ameri-Care Hospital*, 400 So. 2d 1127 (La. App. 1980) states: "Once it is determined that the doctrine is applicable the burden of proof is shifted to the defendant to show an absence of negligence."

(7)   Is there any reason to be especially cautious in the use of res ipsa loquitur in medical malpractice cases? One court has said:

In medical malpractice actions the rule may be invoked only where a layman is able to say as a matter of common knowledge and observation that the consequences of the professional treatment were not such as ordinarily would have followed if due care had been exercised. The rule, however, may not be applied where expert medical evidence is required to show not only what was done, but how and why it occurred since the question is then outside the realm of the layman's experience. See Annot., 162 A.L.R. 1265, 1269 (1946). Last, the fact that the treatment was unsuccessful or terminated with poor or unfortunate results does not of itself raise an inference of negligence nor is it sufficient to invoke the doctrine of res ipsa loquitur. *Trotter v. Hewett*, Fla. App. 1964, 163 So. 2d 510.

Anderson v. Gordon, 334 So. 2d 107 (Fla. App. 1976). But see also *Perin v. Hayne*, 210 N.W.2d 609 (Iowa 1973), § 6.07, *infra.*

---

§ 6.03   BREACH OF STATUTE

PROBLEM B

Jeff and Molly, his girlfriend, were spooning in Jeff's car which he had parked on the edge of a little-used, unpaved county road that threaded itself in and out of the trees in a state owned forestry preserve. Shortly after nightfall, Jeff started his car to return home and suddenly remembered that his lights did not work. He decided to make his way slowly to the highway, which was about a mile distant, and attempt to hale a ride into town. The car had traveled about a quarter mile when a shot was fired, sending a bullet through the windshield of the automobile and into Molly's chest. She suffered grievous wounds which resulted in this lawsuit.

It happened that Tom Hunter fired the shot. He was hunting in the preserve when he dimly saw the form of the vehicle creeping in the gloom about 400 yards away. "Being as big as it was, I was sure it was a stag deer or maybe a bear," Tom explained to the police who investigated the shooting, "So I took aim and let fire."

Molly brought actions in negligence against Jeff and Tom as joint tortfeasors and sought to introduce the following two statutes into evidence.

Statute 113.5 *Lights on Motor Vehicles*

It shall be unlawful for any person to drive a motor vehicle on this state on any public road, highway or lane or on any public property between the period 30 minutes prior to sunset on any day and thirty minutes after sunset on the next succeeding day unless said vehicle is equipped with headlights and taillights conforming to the requirements of the motor vehicle equipment law of this state and unless said lights are lighted.

Statute 492.7 *Discharging Firearms in State Game Preserve*

It shall be unlawful for any person to discharge a firearm in any game preserve of this state.

Should the statutes be admitted? For what purpose? What weight should be assigned their violation?

MELERINE v. AVONDALE SHIPYARDS, INC.
United States Court of Appeals, Fifth Circuit
659 F.2d 706 (1981)

ALVIN B. RUBIN, Circuit Judge:

In a negligence action, regulations promulgated under the Occupational Safety and Health Act of 1970, 29 U.S.C. §§ 651, 678(1976) ("OSHA"), provide evidence of the standard of care exacted of employers, but they neither create an implied cause of action nor establish negligence per se. While they are evidence of a general standard of care due employees, they establish no standard of care due third persons. Therefore, in this negligence action, we reject the argument that the failure of a third party that was not the plaintiff's employer to follow OSHA regulations establishes that third party's negligence. Because we accept the trial judge's conclusions based on the other claims of negligence and because there are no other factual disputes, we affirm the judgment denying recovery.

The trial judge found these facts. Mission Viking ("MV") owned a cargo ship. It contracted with Avondale Shipyards to do part of the work necessary to convert the ship so that it could be used in drilling oil wells. It engaged other contractors to do other parts of the necessary work. Thus, it contracted directly with Technical Sea Services to outfit the vessel.

The ship's equipment included pedestal cranes. As part of its service to MV, Avondale furnished a qualified crane operator to make lifts for all work crews participating in the conversion whether employed by Avondale or by one of the other contractors that had contracted directly with MV. The established procedure was for the contractor who needed a lift to provide workers to hook the load and to direct its movement by signaling the crane operator.

Anthony Melerine, Jr., was employed by Technical as a welder and fitter. As part of Technical's work, it was necessary to move a heavy mooring bitt from one side of the ship to the other. Melerine's foreman, Ronald Macalusa, directed him to help Macalusa in moving the bitt. Macalusa asked the Avondale crane operator, Louis Easter, to lift and move the bitt with the crane. From Easter's station as crane operator, he could not see the bitt, so Melerine acted as signalman.

After Easter raised the crane boom, Melerine and Macalusa hooked the lifting line to the bitt, and Easter took up the slack on the line. Melerine and Macalusa then realized that, as the lifting line traveled across the ship while carrying the bitt, it would approach a scaffold that had been erected on the deck. Melerine then signaled Easter, the crane operator, to stop the lift, and Easter complied. On Macalusa's instructions, Melerine climbed the scaffold to guide the line away from it, if necessary, after the lift was resumed. Melerine then took a position in clear view of Easter, almost directly in front of him. Easter then, on Melerine's signal, began the lift.

Once the load was raised off the deck, Easter had a full view of it, except for a short time when it passed behind some boards. While the load was passing behind these boards, it caught on something. Melerine again signaled Easter to stop, and Easter did. Still standing on the scaffold, Melerine grasped the line and tried to pull the load free. When he succeeded in doing so, the line quivered and struck the scaffold, causing Melerine to fall backward and injure his back. Melerine sued Avondale for negligence.

Because Melerine was not a seaman but a ship repairman, 33 U.S.C. § 905(b), and because Avondale was neither the shipowner nor the employer of Melerine, the action is grounded on general maritime law; and the duty owed by Avondale to Melerine is the usual negligence duty of reasonable care under the circumstances. *See* 1 M. Norris, The Law of Martitime Personal Injuries § 2, at 4 5 (3d ed. 1975); *id.* § 63 at 117 18.

Melerine contends that Avondale, through its employee, Easter, was negligent both in law and in fact. He bases his negligence in law argument on Easter's alleged violation of the following: (1) an OSHA regulation requiring that a tag line[10] be used in moving a load likely to require guidance, 29 C.F.R. § 1915.66(c) (1980);[11] (2) an OSHA regulation requiring the use of a qualified signalman in moving a load when the hoist operator cannot see the load, *id.* § 1915.66(k);[12] and (3) a professional organization's standard for crane operations, American National Standards Institute ("ANSI") Safety Standards for Cranes, Derricks, Hoists, Hooks, Jacks, and Slings (Standard B30.4) § 5.31(d) (1973).[13]

He argues that Easter's alleged violation of these OSHA regulations and the ANSI standard constituted negligence per se.

Melerine bases his negligence in fact argument on two grounds. The first is that Easter was negligent in failing to use his "knowledge, authority, and

---

[10] A tag line is a line attached to a load that can be used to direct the load's movement. The use of a tag line enables a person to stand on the deck and at a safe distance from the load while helping the crane operator in moving it. It thus minimizes the danger that the load will strike the person directing its movement.

[11] Section 1915.66(c) provides: "Tag lines shall be provided on loads likely to swing or to need guidance.

[12] Section 1915.66(k) provides: An individual who is familiar with the signal code in use shall be assigned to act as a signalman when the hoist operator cannot see the load being handled. Communications shall be made by means of clear and distinct visual or auditory signals except that verbal signals shall be permitted.

[13] Section 5 3.1.3(d) of ANSI standard B30.4 provides: The [crane] operator shall be responsible for those operations under his direct control. Whenever there is any doubt as to safety, the operator shall have the authority to stop and refuse to handle loads until safety has been assured.

responsibility" to prevent or prohibit what Melerine contends was an "inherently unsafe" lifting operation. The second, related to but more specific than the first, is that Easter's alleged violation of the OSHA regulations and ANSI standard, even if insufficient to establish that Easter was negligent per se, nevertheless is evidence that Easter was negligent.

The trial judge did not evaluate these contentions separately. However, in that part of his judgment labeled "Conclusions of Law," he found: "[a]t all pertinent times [Easter] acted in a prudent and reasonable manner"; "[t]here was no negligence on the part of any Avondale employee or any other person for whom Avondale can be held legally responsible"; and "[t]he sole proximate cause of the accident was the action of the foreman, Macalusa, in directing Melerine to guide the crane line around the platform by using his hands, instead of using a tagline." We first discuss Melerine's contention that the trial judge was in error because Easter violated the OSHA regulations and ANSI standard and that this alleged violation constituted negligence per se.

OSHA was adopted "to assure . . . safe and healthful working conditions." 29 U.S.C. § 65(b). The Secretary of Labor enforces its requirements by citations for violations of the safety and health standards promulgated by him under the Act's authority and by assessing fines for these violations. The Occupational Safety and Health Review Commission ("OSHRC") reviews challenges to these enforcement actions. The Act was designed to achieve compliance through these prescribed compliance procedures. *B & B Insulation, Inc. v. OSHRC*, 583 F.2d 1364, 1371 (5th Cir. 1978). It provides, therefore, that it neither enlarges nor diminishes "common law or statutory rights, duties, or liabilities." 29 U.S.C. § 653(b) (4). This means that neither its express provisions nor the regulations adopted pursuant to its authority create a civil cause of action against either a plaintiff's employer or a third party who is not the plaintiff's employer.

Melerine does not, therefore, contend that the OSHA regulations create a civil cause of action against Avondale. He urges instead that their violation establishes Avondale's negligence per se in a cause of action given him by general maritime law. See *Lowe v. General Motors Corp.*, 624 F.2d 1373, 1379 81 (5th Cir. 1980). To establish that a defendant's violation of a statute or regulation is negligence per se, a plaintiff must prove "th[e] violation of a statute which is intended to protect the class of persons to which the plaintiff belongs against the risk of the type of harm which has in fact occurred." *Marshall v. Isthmian Lines, Inc.*, 334 F.2d 131, 134 (5th Cir. 1964). If the plaintiff thus establishes the defendant's negligence, he must then prove that the violation of the statute or regulation was the proximate cause of his harm. The threshold issue, therefore, is whether Melerine was a member of the class that the OSHA regulations were intended to protect: To resolve this issue we must look at the basis for these regulations.

. . .

Whether OSHA regulates only the obligation of the employer to provide safe work conditions for his employees or also states a standard of care due third persons has been the subject of "complex dispute." Some courts have held that, given the language of OSHA's clauses on the duties of employers, OSHA's broad statement of purpose, and OSHA's generally broad language, OSHA regulations protect not only an employer's own employees, but *all* employees who may be harmed by the employer's violation of the regulations. This court, however, along with others, has held that OSHA regulations protect only an employer's own employees.

. . .

In this circuit, therefore, the class protected by OSHA regulations comprises only employers' own employees. Furthermore, this interpretation of the scope of coverage of OSHA regulations also accords with the scope of coverage explicitly given to the specific OSHA regulations at issue in this case. The regulation that gives OSHA accreditation to these and other LHWCA regulations states: "Each employer shall protect the employment and places of employment of each of *his* employees engaged in ship repair or a related employment, by complying with the appropriate standards prescribed by [29 C.F.R. §§ 1915.1 to.111]." 29 C.F.R. § 1910.13(a) (italics added.)

The OSHA tag line regulation does not, therefore, define the duty owed by Avondale and Easter, its employee, to Melerine, the employee of another company. The trial judge correctly refused to use it to establish negligence per se. Instead he found that, although a person exercising due care would have directed Melerine to use a tag line, Technical's foreman, Macalusa, was the person responsible for failing to require Melerine to do so. Macalusa and Melerine selected the load, attached the crane's line to it, signaled Easter, and directed him where to place the load. Even if, as Melerine asserts in his brief, Macalusa and Melerine were unaware of the danger of their conduct, and Easter "was the only person participating in the lifting operation who had knowledge of the risk and danger involved," the responsibility under OSHA for this danger and its consequences nevertheless remained with Technical. . . .

The regulation that requires the use of a qualified signalman is also an OSHA regulation, and does not define the duty owed by Avondale to other employers' employees. Moreover, as Melerine's expert witness acknowledged, Melerine's injury was caused by neither an improper signal nor miscomprehension of a signal. Even if this regulation were applicable, it would be useless to Melerine in his attempt to establish Avondale's negligence per se; for its violation was patently not the cause in fact nor, a fortiori, the proximate cause of Melerine's injury. *See* pp. 709, 710 *supra.*

Finally, Melerine relies on an alleged violation of the ANSI standard that makes the crane operator responsible for operations under his direct control. Unlike many other ANSI standards, this one was never adopted as part of any OSHA regulation on ship repairing. See 29 C.F.R. § 1915.5. Thus it is not a "legislative enactment," W. Prosser, *supra* note 9, § 36, at 192, so it could not establish Avondale's negligence per se.

NOTES AND QUESTIONS

(1)   Which specific element of his cause of action did the plaintiff hope to prove by the introduction of the proffered OSHA regulation?

(2)   *Kress v. Truck Trailer Equipment Co.*, 501 P.2d 285 (Wash. 1972), is among numbers of cases that have expanded the criteria that must be satisfied before a statute might be given the weight sought for it in *Melerine. Kress* explicitly adopted

the rule stated by Restatement, Torts, Second § 286 (1965) as follows:

> In determining whether or not the trial court erred in refusing plaintiff's request for an instruction of negligence per se, this court will consider the rules stated by the Restatement (Second) of Torts § 286 (1965):
>
> The court may adopt as the standard of conduct of a reasonable man the requirements of a legislative enactment or an administrative regulation whose purpose is found to be exclusively or in part
>
> (a) to protect a class of persons which includes the one whose interest is invaded, and
>
> (b) to protect the particular interest which is invaded, and
>
> (c) to protect that interest against the kind of harm which has resulted, and
>
> (d) to protect that interest against the particular hazard from which the harm results.[14]

501 P.2d at 289

(3) What criterion did the *Melerine* statute fail to satisfy? See *Kelly v. Koppers Company, Inc.*, 293 So. 2d 763 (Fla. App. 1974), to illustrate a statute that pertained to a different hazard than the one that caused death. See also *Brown v. Shyne*, 151 N.E. 176 (N.Y. 1926), to illustrate a statute that was merely regulatory and thus did not serve to particularize a standard of care for any purpose.

(4) *Melerine* addresses the question as to when a statute should be admitted to particularize the standard of care. This raises two further questions, one fundamental to the dignity of the jury system and the other practical. The fundamental question is whether the use of a statute to particularize a standard of care is an impermissible intrusion into the province of the jury. What are the arguments pro and con? What weight is to be given the violation of a statute?

In *Melerine*, the plaintiff wanted an instruction that if the jury found the regulation to have been violated, it then must find that the violation was negligence in itself. That is, if the regulation were violated, the jury would be prohibited from weighing all the evidence and making an independent finding of no negligence. That clearly limits the jury's discretion. Despite this clear intrusion into the jury's function, negligence per se is the weight courts typically give the violation of a legislative enactment whose purpose was to promote the safety of a particular protected class of persons. Some courts hold that the violation creates a rebuttable presumption of negligence. See, *e.g.*, *Barnum v. Williams*, 504 P.2d 122 (Ore. 1972). Others permit the jury to use its discretion in deciding what weight should be given to the violation. See, *e.g.*, *Murray v. Alabama Power Co.*, 413 So. 2d 1109 (Ala. 1982).

Which of these standards is most favorable to a plaintiff? One court has gone so far as to hold that if a statute designed to protect a particular class of people against a risk the members of the class are incapable of protecting themselves against, then not only is the violation proof of negligence but it also precludes the defense of

---

[14] Copyright 1965 by The American Law Institute. Reprinted with the permission of The American Law Institute.

contributory negligence and also proves causation. *de Jesus v. Seaboard Coast Line Railroad*, 281 So. 2d 198 (Fla. 1973), and *Sloan v. Coit International, Inc.*, 292 So. 2d 15 (Fla. 1974). Are those extensions justifiable?

(5) There is some authority for the proposition that even if a statute does not satisfy the admission criteria necessary for the negligence per se rule it still might be admitted to be considered by the jury as some evidence as to what the standard of care ought to be. See *Disabitino Brothers, Inc. v. Baio*, 366 A.2d 508 (Del. 1976). Does this practice seem unduly prejudicial to the party opposing the introduction of the statute?

(6) The discussion by the court in *Melerine* proceeds as if the OSHA regulation in question had equal dignity to a statute, even though it was promulgated administratively. This is justifiable under OSHA, which is a federal statute that provides a detailed regulation-making process and explicitly states that the regulations shall have the force of law. *Sammons v. Ridgeway*, 293 A.2d 547 (Del. 1972), permitted a regulation prescribed by a state agency under a state law to take on the evidentiary weight of a statute. Many other cases hold, however, that a mere regulation may be considered by a jury only as some evidence of what the standard of due care requires and not as setting the standard definitively.

In recent years, however, many states have formalized the regulation-making process that must be followed by state agencies, thereby giving credence to the position that the ensuing regulations ought to be given equal weight to statutes. One judge has strongly protested this, however, on grounds that legislators have to answer to the electorate through the ballot box whereas administrative regulators do not. *Jackson v. Harsco Corp.*, 364 So. 2d 808 (Fla. App. 1978), Barkdull, J. concurring.

Courts are prone not to give the weight of negligence per se to violations of laws made by lawmakers of mere political subdivisions of state, such as county or municipal governments. More often the jury will be instructed to treat the violation only as evidence of negligence. Cf. *Waverly & Ogden, Inc.*, 165 N.E.2d 181 (N.Y. 1980), and *Douglas v. Edgewater Park Co.*, 119 N.W.2d 567 (Mich. 1963).

(7) Does it occur to you that on some occasions it is extremely unjust to require a jury to find that a defendant was negligent per se without being permitted to weigh other evidence in mitigation? Suppose, for example, that a defendant was driving in excess of the speed limit while rushing a badly injured person to a hospital? With a police escort? Treating violations as negligence per se prohibits consideration of factors such as this. Seeing the injustice in an invariable rule, some courts have permitted a jury to excuse, in effect, the violation as negligence per se and to make a decision on the basis of all the evidence. A mere "good excuse" may not be enough, however; one leading case requires it to be shown that it was safer to violate the statute than to conform to it. See *Tedla v. Ellman*, 19 N.E.2d 987 (N.Y. 1939). See also *Chase v. Tingle Bros.*, 149 N.W. 654 (Minn. 1914) (vehicle was thrown across the center line due to no fault of the driver; statute forbidding crossing of center line would not be admitted to establish negligence), and *Cameron v. Stewart*, 134 A.2d 474 (Me. 1957) (jury permitted to consider plaintiff's testimony that it was safer to violate statute and walk with traffic rather than facing it). See also *Beaumaster v. Crandall*, 576 P.2d 988, 991 (Alaska 1978), holding that a traffic law that forbids stopping in a driving lane would not be applied to establish negligence when the defendant stopped to aid occupants of an overturned car,

pulled off the road as far as was possible, and activated emergency blinking lights.

Along the lines of excuse is some authority that violation of a statute creates a presumption of negligence only when the record is devoid of other evidence. Thus, when actual evidence of what happens is available, a jury would be permitted to find no negligence despite the statutory violation. See, *e.g.*, *Noonan v. Valek*, 224 N.W. 657 (Mich. 1924).

(8)   What restraint should be imposed upon a jury's discretion to find breach of duty when the defendant fully complied with administrative safety standards promulgated by a government agency? See, *e.g.*, *Blueflame Gas, Inc. v. Van Hoose*, 679 P.2d 579 (Colo. 1984); *Dorsey v. Honda Motor Co.*, 655 F.2d 650 (5th Cir. 1981); *Seaboard Coastline Railroad Company v. Louallen*, 479 S.2d 781 (Fla. App. 1985) (jury permitted to find defendant negligent even though safety standards were complied with); and *Nobriga v. Raybestos-Manhattan, Inc.*, 683 P.2d 389 (Hawaii 1984).

(9)   Should a lawyer's violation of disciplinary rule of the Code of Professional Responsibility be deemed to be negligence per se? The courts apparently uniformly hold that the code does not set a standard of care as far as tort liability is concerned but only provides a basis for lawyer discipline. See, *e.g.*, *Davis v. Findley*, 422 S.E.2d 859 (Ga. 1992). Is this consistent with the general theory of this section?

(10)   Review the *Watson* case in section 6.01 *supra*. What weight did the court give to the decedent's failure to wear Hunter's orange in the determination of negligence?

§ 6.04   CUSTOM

MAYHEW v. SULLIVAN MINING CO.
Maine Supreme Judicial Court
76 Me. 100 (1884)

Barrows, J.

The plaintiff claimed to recover damages of the defendants on the ground that, prior to the 3d day of December, 1881, he had entered into a written contract with them to break down the rock and ore for a certain distance so as to disclose the vein in a certain drift in their mine leading northerly from the main shaft at a distance of two hundred and seventy feet from the surface, at an agreed price for each horizontal foot of rock and ore so broken down, he to furnish his own powder and oil and the men to run the machine (who were to be paid by him), the company to furnish the steam drill and keep the drift clear of rock as he broke it down, — that long prior to that date the company had constructed a substantial platform in their shaft at the 270 foot level and at the entrance of the drift in which the plaintiff and his men were performing their labor under that contract, which platform until that day entirely filled the shaft at that point excepting a hole in one corner known as the bucket-hole, — that it was provided in the contract that the plaintiff and his men were to have the use of the platform and of the bucket to go up and down while performing the contract, — that defendants were bound to keep said platform in a suitable and safe condition for the use of all persons properly upon and using the same, and up to that time it had been used by the plaintiff and others employed in that drift in the ordinary course of their labors daily, — that on that day the defendants carelessly and negligently caused a hole three feet in length by twenty-six inches in breadth to be cut for a ladder-hole in that platform near the centre of it directly back of the bucket-hole and twenty inches distant there-from, without placing any rail or barrier about it, or any light or other warning there, and without giving the plaintiff notice that any such dangerous change had been made in the platform, — and that without any knowledge of its existence or fault on his part, the plaintiff, in the ordinary course of his business having occasion to go upon the platform fell through this new hole a distance of thirty-five feet, and received serious bodily injury.

[Plaintiff prevailed at trial and defendant took exceptions to several rulings of the trial court, including the following.]

5. The defendants complain because they were not allowed to ask Stanley (who made this hole in the platform, under the direction of the defendants' superintendent, and who testified that he was a miner of twenty-five years experience, that he had worked in several different mines and had constructed other ladder-holes, and noticed many more,) the following questions:

"Have you ever known ladder-holes at a lower level to be railed or fenced round?"

"As a miner, is it feasible, in your opinion, to use a ladder-hole with a railing round it?"

"Have you ever seen a ladder-hole in a mine, below the surface, with a railing round it?"

Also that they were not allowed to ask one Dugan (who gave similar testimony as to the length of his experience as a miner, and that he had worked in many different mines and observed the ladder-holes in them,) this question: "From your experience as a miner, whether or not this ladder-hole, as Mr. Stanley left it, was constructed in the usual and ordinary manner of ladder-holes in mines, and in a proper way?"

Defendants' counsel claim that the favorable answers to these questions which they had a right to expect would have tended to show that there was no want of "average ordinary care" on the part of the defendants. We think the questions were properly excluded. The nature of the act in which the defendants' negligence was asserted to consist, with all the circumstances of time and place, whether of commission or omission, and its connection with the plaintiff's injury, presented a case as to which the jury were as well qualified to judge as any expert could be. It was not a case where the opinion of experts could be necessary or useful. See for analogous instances: *Cannell v. Ins. Co.* 59 Maine, 582, 591; *State v. Watson*, 65 Maine, 76, 77, and cases there cited. See also, Lord Mansfield's opinon in *Carter v. Boehm*, 3 Burr. 1905, and note to S.C. Smith's Leading Cases, 6th Am. Ed. Vol. 1, part 2, p. 769. If the defendants had proved that in every mining establishment that has existed since the days of Tubal-Cain, it has been the practice to cut ladder-holes in their platforms, situated as this was while in daily use for mining operations, without guarding or lighting them, and without notice to contractors or workmen, it would have no tendency to show that the act was consistent with ordinary prudence, or a due regard for the safety of those who were using their premises by their invitation. The gross carelessness of the act appears conclusively upon its recital. Defendants' counsel argue that "if it should appear that they rarely had railings, then it tends to show no want of ordinary care in that respect," that "if one conforms to custom he is so far exercising average ordinary care." The argument proceeds upon an erroneous idea of what constitutes ordinary care. "Custom" and "average" have no proper place in its definition.

It would be no excuse for a want of ordinary care that carelessness was universal about the matter involved, or at the place of the accident, or in the business generally. Ordinary care is the care which persons of ordinary prudence — not careless persons — would take under all the circumstances. See definition approved in *Topsham v. Lisbon*, 65 Maine, 455. "Reasonable care is perhaps as good a term and conveys as correct an idea of the care required." It was held not sufficient to relieve the defendant from the imputation of negligence, to show that the elevator way "was constructed in the manner usual in the defendants' business." *Indermauer v. Dames* (in the Exchequer Chamber), 2 L.R.C.P. 310.

The remark in *Low v. G.T. Ry Co.* 72 Maine, 320, that "in fitting up a place for business purposes, one is at liberty to consult his own convenience and profit, but not without a reasonable regard for the safety of those whom his operations bring upon his premises upon lawful business errands; in particular, everything which may operate as a trap or pitfall . . . is to be avoided, if reasonable care will accomplish security to life and limb in that respect," is applicable here.

The tendency of part of the questions to raise collateral issues is obvious.

. . .

One substantial ground for excluding evidence of collateral facts, is that it is seldom that such identity in all essentials, is found, that a legitimate inference respecting the one case can be drawn from the other, and a host of collateral issues are brought in to distract the attention of the jury from the real point. The fear of this has sometimes, perhaps, produced decisions excluding evidence, which might throw light upon the issue; but the present case well illustrates the absurdity that would attend an indiscriminate admission of it. It is not probable that the defendants could show a single instance where, while a mine was in active operation, a ladder-hole so dangerously located as this, was cut and left without railing or light, or notice to the workmen; and the naked fact (whatever it may have been) as to the existence of railings about such holes in other mines, could not have even the semblance of a bearing upon the contention here, without proof that they were cut under like circumstances.

Here, there was no pretence of any notice to the plaintiff of the existence of the chasm into which he fell.

There is no motion to set aside the verdict as against evidence in any particular, nor any complaint that the damages are excessive.

We find no error in the conduct of the trial, or in the instructions to the jury, which requires correction in order that justice may be done.

Exceptions overruled.

———

NOTES AND QUESTIONS

(1) Precisely why was the defendant seeking to gain answers to the questions that were asked in *Mayhew*? Had the evidence been admitted, what element of the case would it have tended to prove or disprove? Does it occur to you that permitting testimony about custom of a trade has the effect of invading the province of the jury? Is this any more or less justified than in permitting the existence of a criminal statute to be introduced?

(2) According to Morris on Torts (2d ed. 1980), at 99, proof of custom has two "permissible uses." One is to "point up the onus of the plaintiff's burden of proof." The other is, "Lack of opportunities to learn of safeguards from other members of defendant's craft is one of the circumstances to be taken into account in judging whether or not defendant was excusably ignorant of a feasible safeguard." If so, why wasn't the defendant permitted to adduce the evidence in *Mayhew*?

The most noted case on this point is *The T.J. Hooper*, 60 F.2d 737 (2nd Cir. 1932), wherein a tug operator was not permitted to rely on the failure of most tugboats to use a radio to receive weather forecasts to justify his own failure to use one. Said Judge Learned Hand, "Indeed, in most cases reasonable prudence is in fact common prudence; but strictly speaking it is never its measure; a whole calling may have unduly lagged in the adoption of new and available devices." This same thought had been expressed much earlier in this form: "No degree of antiquity can give sanction to a usage bad in itself." *Leach v. Three of the King's Messengers*, 19 How. St. Trials 1027 (1765), cited in *Gleason v. Title Guarantee Company*, 300 F.2d 813, 814 (5th Cir. 1962).

Would a prudent owner of the T. J. Hooper have purchased a radio if it had used a cost/benefit analysis? Assume a radio cost $100, the tug was worth $50,000, and the risk of sinking was 1 in 1000. The owner would have calculated an expectation of loss of $50 (PxL) and would not have spent $100 to avoid it. Hence, Judge Hand would conclude the owner was not negligent. But has the owner considered all the risks? Suppose the risk of drowning the tug's operater was also one in 1000 and the value of a life was $1 million? Then, the expectation of loss would rise to $1050 and a prudent owner would have spent $50 to avoid it. In short, correct application of Judge Hand's formula would require the owner to include all expected losses and not only those pertaining to the owner's personal interests.

A more modern, and perhaps surprising, case is *Helling v. Carey*, 519 P.2d 981 (Wash. 1974). The plaintiff alleged that her eye doctor had been negligent in not testing for glaucoma upon making a routine examination of her eyes when she was age 32. The defendant sought to prove that it was the custom of ophthalmologists not to administer glaucoma tests as a part of routine eye examinations to persons under 40 years of age on grounds that the incidence of the disease was no more than 1 in 25,000 in that population. The Washington court held as a matter of law that it was negligence not to administer the test. The court seemed to be persuaded by the evidence that the test was "simple" and "harmless" and, presumably, cheap. Are these appropriate factors for the court to consider? Should the standard of a so-called learned profession carry more weight with the court than that of a mere industrial association?

Helling v. Carey illustrates how a cost/benefit analysis helps ration scarce resources. Because glaucoma is usually an age-related disease, younger people are not normally tested for it. Suppose a test cost $30 (B) and the risk of occurrence (P) in the below-40 population is one in 25,000? Suppose we do not have a reliable number for expectation of loss (PxL)? What would that figure have to be to justify paying $30 each to test the under-40 population? Because B = PxL, B is $30, and P is 1/25,000, doing the math produces an expectation of loss of $750,000. Do you agree with the calculation? If that should prove to be the correct number, should a court require the $30 expenditure to avoid the losses?

(3)   Should a customary practice that violates the law be admissible to particularize the standard of care for the benefit of the defendant? See *Smith v. Bradford*, 512 So. 2d 50 (Ala. 1987) (custom of instructing state troopers to "catch up" with speeders before activating lights and sirens could not be admitted to excuse or justify operation of police vehicles in excess of speed limit as state statute required).

(4)   Is *Mayhew* in conflict with some aspect of Judge Posner's opinion in Plovidba, § 6.01 *supra*?

(5)   When were the "days of Tubal-Cain?" What significance does that have to the issue in *Mayhew?*

ST. LOUIS-SAN FRANCISCO RAILWAY CO. v. WHITE
Florida District Court of Appeal
369 So. 2d 1007 (1979), *cert. denied*, 378 So. 2d 349 (Fla. 1979)

[The car driven by the wrongful death act plaintiff's decedent was struck at a railroad crossing on a remote country road. At the trial the judge admitted into evidence a railroad industry standard requiring that railroad cross buck signs be placed at all rail crossings to warn motorists of the hazard of train traffic. None were in place at the fatal crossing. The jury returned a verdict for the plaintiff. Among the defendant's grounds of appeal was that the judge should not have given the following instruction (No. 4.9) to the jury:]

. . . violation of a standard prescribed by an industry is evidence of negligence. It is not, however, conclusive evidence of negligence. If you find that the railroad violated such standards, you may consider that fact together with the other facts and circumstances in determining whether such person was negligent.

MELVIN, JUDGE: [After quoting the foregoing instruction.].

As stated earlier, there was no railroad-supplied, crossing protection equipment at the site of this fatal accident, the sole warning to the public of this crossing being the yellow D.O.T. advance warning signs. The industry standard referred to in the court's instruction recommended as mandatory the placement of railroad-highway crossing signs (cross-buck) at all crossings.

In our earlier opinion in *St. Louis-San Francisco Railway Company v. Burlison*, 262 So. 2d 280 (Fla. App. 1972), *cert. den.* 266 So. 2d 350 (Fla. 1972), this Court considered and rejected the railroad's argument regarding the admissibility of industry standards, stating:

The evidence adduced concerning recommended signalization and defendant's failure to provide the recommended signalization is, standing alone, sufficient evidence upon which the jury's finding of negligence can rest. We do not hold that failure to conform one's own practices with those generally recognized by an industry safety council or committee is negligence per se. We hold merely that evidence of noncompliance can be considered by the jury which may, but need not, find negligence as a result of the failure to follow a generally recognized safety rule.

. . .

We can assume that in promulgating the safety rule in question, the American Association of Railroads consulted with leading experts in the field of railroad highways crossings and garnered from their facts and recommendations an acceptable standard of conduct tending to preserve the safety of the highway using public, evolving standards with which an operating railroad could conform without unduly restricting its operational or fiscal capacities.

(262 So. 2d at 281)

In *Florida Freight Terminals, Inc. v. Cabanas, supra*, the District Court of Appeal, Third District, held it reversible error for the trial court to refuse to instruct that violation of an applicable Federal Aviation Administration (FAA) regulation was negligence per se. The particular regulation made the pilot in command responsible for the tying-down of all cargo to eliminate the possibility of its shifting. Evidence presented at trial indicated that the plane's load of Christmas trees had shifted to the rear, upon takeoff, causing the plane to crash. Florida Freight requested that the jury be instructed that violation of the FAA regulation was negligence per se; however, the court denied the request and, instead, instructed that violation of the regulation was non-conclusive evidence of negligence. Extending the rationale *of deJesus v. Seaboard Coast Line Railroad Company, supra*, and *Sloan v. Coit International, Inc.*, 292 So. 2d 15 (Fla. 1974), that it is negligence per se to violate a statute designed to protect a particular class of persons from their inability to protect themselves or to violate a statute which establishes a duty to take precautions to protect a particular class of persons from a particular type of injury, the District Court held that the jury should not have been at liberty to decide that violation of the regulation was *not* negligence and reversed because the trial court refused to give the *per se* instruction.

We need not go as far as *Florida Freight*. The requirement to place cross-bucks is established by statute and by industry standard. We have already held that the court may instruct that a violation of the statute (Section 351.03) is negligence per se. We have also held that violation of an industry standard is admissible as *evidence* of negligence. *St. Louis-San Francisco Railway Company v. Burlison, supra*. We see no detriment to the appellant by the trial court instructing that violation of an industry standard is *evidence* of negligence. Conversely, it would appear proper to instruct that compliance with a standard is non-conclusive evidence of freedom of liability. Accordingly, we hold that it was not error to instruct that a violation of an industry safety standard is non-conclusive evidence of negligence.

. . .

Affirmed.

ROBERT P. SMITH, ACTING CHIEF JUDGE, specially concurring:

I concur in the judgment of affirmance and in the Court's disposition of all issues except the propriety of charging the trial jury that any violation by the railroad of an "industry standard" is "evidence of negligence." Such a charge is an argumentative comment on the evidence, which in Florida is the function of trial counsel, not that of the trial judge. Although I cannot regard the charge as harmful in the particular circumstances of this case, it was error nonetheless; and I deplore our reversion to the discredited and abandoned practice of bestowing judicial favor on certain evidence by charges to the jury. For the same reason I disagree with the majority opinion's decision that:

Conversely, it would appear proper to instruct that compliance with a standard is non-conclusive evidence of freedom of liability.

This is not to say that violation of an industry standard is not evidence of negligence. Of course it is: *St. Louis-San Francisco Railway Co. v. Burlison*, 262 So. 2d 280 (Fla. 1st DCA 1972), *cert. den.*, 266 So. 2d 350 (Fla. 1972). But that is no reason for the trial judge to sing a duet with claimant's lawyer. Nor, if there is evidence that the railroad complied with an industry safety standard, is that an occasion for the trial judge to give an "on the other hand" charge distinguishing that evidence from all the evidence from which the jury is to infer negligence or the lack of it. Evidence of an industry standard is simply evidence, and it neither requires nor justifies judicial comment. As the railroad's counsel said in objecting to the charge given in this case,

Jumping off a roof is evidence of negligence on the part of the jumper, too, but the Court wouldn't give any instructions [on] that fact. This is nothing more than common known [sic; comment on] evidence.

[In the next passage Judge Smith refers to Florida Standard Jury Instruction 4.11, informing juries that violation of a traffic regulation may be considered as evidence of negligence.]

. . . And as I wrote in an analogous case,

But while any jury will likely infer negligence when a driver runs down a pedestrian, it is hardly thought necessary or appropriate — at least, not yet — that the trial judge should incite such a finding on a jury issue by a *res ipsa* charge.

Dayton Tire and Rubber Co. v. Davis, 348 So. 2d 575, 589–90 (Fla. 1st DCA 1977) (dissenting opinion), *reversed*, 358 So. 2d 1339 (Fla. 1978).

For decades our Supreme Court has disapproved judicial comment on the evidence.

In my opinion the chief value of charge 4.11, when employed to explain the effect of a statute or ordinance, or the effect of a regulation, lies in its advice that the standard, of which the jury must be advised, is not conclusive. To the extent that the charge suggests that such a standard is more important than "reasonable care under the circumstances," I regard it as an unfortunate, if unavoidable, intrusion on the function of counsel and the jury.

Therein lies my aversion to the court's extended application, in this case, of charge 4.11. The trial judge does not read industry standards to the jury, nor does the judge read back other evidence submitted for the jury's consideration. Therefore there is no need to cancel or qualify the seemingly authoritative effect of the judge's reading of a statute. If standards prescribed by traffic statutes or ordinances are thought to occupy some middle ground of importance, greater than those standards which are suggested by the evidence and argument but lesser than standards to which charge 4.9 applies, there is no reason, in my opinion, to assign "industry standards" to that favored middle ground. To the extent that "industry standards" are prescribed by government, charges 4.9 and 4.11 permit judicial comment because the charging judge is, for the jury, the source of applicable law. But standards prescribed by voluntary industrial organizations are not law, and endorsement of them should not be found in the mouth of a trial judge. A charge such as this has none of the justifications of 4.11 but has all of its disadvantages.

In extending charge 4.11 to cover "industry standards," I fear the majority are misled by the discrete written form in which the railroad cross-buck standard was evidenced in this particular case. *Ante* p. 1010 fn. 1. Certainly the industry's cross-buck standard is not made equivalent to a statute or ordinance by the fact that it is written. Particular customs or standards of reasonable care in organized commercial activity, be it railroading, manufacturing, medical practice, or some other, are not always proved by so handy a document as Bulletin No. 7 of the Association of American Railroads. Standards are subject also to proof by expert witnesses. . . .

I think it no more justifiable for a trial judge to comment favorably on a vocational standard evidenced in writing than to comment on a standard shown by opinion testimony or other competent evidence. If it is the Court's purpose to restrict the charge to standards of associations "composed of and directed by the very operators that are to be guided by the standards," *ante* p. 1011 fn. 2, justification of the charge becomes even more attenuated, suggesting as it does that judicial comment is appropriate where there is an asserted admission against interest, but not otherwise. We do not ordinarily single out admissions against interest for comment in the charge.

Claimants' counsel need not celebrate today's decision. The availability of a jury charge commenting favorably on the vocational standard suggested by claimant's evidence inevitably makes available, as the majority have today foretold, a countervailing charge that compliance with a vocational standard is evidence of due care. That is the phenomenon of judicial evenhandedness. Thus do self-serving vocational standards become more important as straw men in the defense of tort actions. . . .

There can be no more telling climax to a strategy of trial to the jury, whether by claimant or defendant, than a charge by the trial judge which seems to endorse one's theory of claim or defense. Though I am persuaded that the subject charge was error, and that the Court's approval of it and a countervailing charge bodes ill for jury trials in Florida, I cannot conclude on the record that the judgment should be reversed. In the light of the evidence on liability and the court's proper charge that violation of the cross-buck statute was negligence, I consider it extravagant but harmless that the court added that violation of an industry cross-buck standard is "evidence of negligence."

I therefore concur in the judgment on this point and in the court's opinion on all others.

NOTES AND QUESTIONS

(1)   How does the use of custom in this case differ from its intended use in *Mayhew* and the *T.J. Hooper*? According to Judge Smith, how is the jury to make use of custom, once proved, and how is it to find out about the proper use? How does the majority differ on the latter point?

(2)   Suppose the plaintiff proves a custom and that the defendant departed from the custom in the episode that caused harm. Would it necessarily follow that the jury must thereafter find that the defendant had been negligent? For example, suppose most bridge contractors use motorized cranes in moving certain heavy structures but a particular contractor does not, choosing to do the job by the use of hand labor. Would it be proper to permit a jury to find that the defendant was negligent when no other evidence about the mishap was presented? See *Cunningham v. Ft. Pitt Bridge Works*, 47 A. 846 (1901).

(3)   In an omitted portion of the majority opinion in *White*, the court permitted the introduction of evidence of the railroad's *own* speed limit and of the fact that it was exceeded. What, specifically, does this go to prove? Should it have the same weight and effect as the proof of an industry standard and violation of it? What different treatment, if any, was given the two in *White*? See also *Fisher v. Walters*, 428 So. 2d 431 (La. 1983) and *Babcock v. Cheasapeake & Ohio Ry. Co.*, 404 N.E. 2d 931 (Ill. App. 1980). *Pulsifer v. Berry*, 32 A. 986 (Me. 1895) refused to admit evidence of how a defendant personally and ordinarily does a thing for the purpose of setting the standard of care. Courts regularly apply this rule. Does it conform to the teaching of *Vaughan v. Menlove?* Is an attempt to use personal habit to set the standard of care different from an attempt to use personal habit as evidence that a person conformed to the habit on a particular occasion? Should habit have been admissible for the latter purpose? See *Haider v. Finken*, 239 N.W.2d 508 (N.D. 1976).

(4)   Proof of custom is not always as easy as it was in *White* where the industry had memorialized its custom in a published standard. More often custom must be proved either by the aggregation of evidence from many sources or by permitting a qualified expert to testify as to what his perception of the custom is, given his presumed reliable knowledge of what most of the operators in the field in fact do. Are custom and habit different things? Would it be permissible to permit an expert to reply to the question, "How did the defendant customarily do this procedure?," if the purpose is to prove custom? See *Sea Board Air Line Ry. v. Watson*, 94 Fla. 571, 113 So. 716 (1927).

(5)   Should courts be suspicious of industry customs? Economic analysis may help us ascertain the economic incentives of each industry and thus heighten or defuse our suspicions.

In *The T. J. Hooper* and *Mayhew v. Sullivan Mining Co.*, the industries had an incentive to scrimp on safety. Unless the Tort system forces them to pay for harm done, they would not invest in safety optimally, but would save themselves money by not buying radios or installing railings.

Are the incentives different in *Helling v. Carey*? There, the patients (or their insurance companies) must pay the costs of the glaucoma testing. No doubt the ophthalmologists made a profit on each test, thus, if anything, creating an incentive to test too many people. *Helling v. Carey* may have set too low an age cutoff for glaucoma testing, not too high. (Could ophthalmologists profit more by testing children who have only a miniscule probability of getting glaucoma?) Accordingly, the *Helling v. Carey* decision to hold the ophthalmologist negligent "as a matter of law" for failing to test a 32 year old is controversial. (To stem the over-testing temptation the insurance industry frequently refuses to pay for "unnecessary" medical tests.)

---

§ 6.05   MODIFIED STANDARD — LOWER CAPACITY

[See *Lester v. Sayles*, 850 S.W. 2d 858 (Mo. 1993), § 4.03, *supra.*]

NOTES AND QUESTIONS

(1)   Review *Camerlinck v. Thomas* to ascertain the various positions taken by American courts for the proper standard of care to measure a child's performance against. Is to hold a child to the standard of an ordinary child of the same age the same as holding him to the standard of a child of the same age, experience and intelligence? If not, which of the two is more defensable in light of the general proposition that the standard of care ought to be objective?

(2)   Are there any circumstances under which a child should not be entitled to a special standard of care? See, *e.g., Daniels v. Evans*, 224 A.2d 63 (N.H. 1966), and *Gunnels v. Dethlage*, 366 So. 2d 1104 (Ala. 1977).

RAMEY v. KNORR
Washington Appellate Division
130 Wash.App. 1003 (2005)

Cox, C.J.

. . . .

This personal injury action arises from a head-on automobile collision on I-405. While in a delusional state, Knorr turned her car around towards oncoming traffic, removed her seatbelt, and drove head-on into Ramey's car. At the time of the incident, Knorr believed she was the object of a conspiracy to attack her. She was trying to commit suicide. Ramey suffered substantial injuries from the collision. She sued Knorr for negligence. Knorr raised the defense of sudden mental incapacity.

Pre-trial, the trial court denied Knorr's motion for summary judgment. At the close of all the evidence at trial, both Knorr and Ramey moved for directed verdicts. The trial court granted a directed verdict for Ramey, ruling that as a matter of law, Knorr's sudden mental incapacity defense could not be sustained on the basis of the evidence. The jury returned a verdict for Ramey in the amount of $497,578.00. The trial court denied Knorr's post-trial motion for judgment as a matter of law or, alternatively, a new trial. Following entry of judgment on the jury verdict, Knorr appealed.

. . . .

Knorr argues that the trial court erred in denying her motions for a judgment as a matter of law and in granting Ramey's motion for a directed verdict. We disagree.

. . . .

Insanity and Other Mental Deficiencies as Defenses

Both for historical and other reasons, insanity or other mental deficiencies generally are not recognized as defenses to negligence. Washington, along with the majority of states, holds the mentally ill to the standard of a reasonable person under like circumstances.[15] Traditionally, courts have relied on several rationales to hold the mentally ill to an objective standard of liability for negligence. The most common justification is that innocent victims should be compensated for their injuries. Another common reason is that the existence and degree of one's mental illness can be difficult to measure and is a major obstacle for applying a mental deficiency defense. Other rationales include the belief that liability of the mentally ill will encourage caretakers to look after them and the difficulty of drawing a line between mental illness and variations of temperaments, intellect, and emotional balance.

Knorr expressly disclaims an insanity defense or an argument that mental illness alone is a defense to negligence. Instead, she maintains that "a driver who suffers an acute psychotic episode, which incapacitates the driver, is not chargeable with negligence." While noting that Washington has not addressed this issue, Knorr primarily relies on authority from the state of Wisconsin, *Breunig v. American Family Ins. Co.*[16] Accordingly, we consider whether that case is applicable to the matter before us.

"Sudden Mental Incapacity" Defense

In *Breunig*, the defendant, Erma Veith was driving her car when she believed that God was taking control of the steering wheel and directing her car. Believing she could fly "because Batman can," Mrs. Veith stepped on the gas and collided with an oncoming truck. At trial, a psychiatrist testified that Mrs. Veith was unable to operate the vehicle with her conscious mind. A jury returned a verdict in the plaintiff's favor.

The Wisconsin Supreme Court in Breunig recognized an exception for sudden mental incapacity and adopted a two part test stating,

> [the] disorder must be such as to [1(a)] affect the person's ability to understand and appreciate the duty which rests upon him to drive his car with ordinary care, or [1(b)] if the insanity does not affect such under-standing and appreciation, it must affect his ability to control his car in an ordinarily prudent manner. And . . . [2] there must be an absence of notice or forewarning to the person that he may be suddenly subject to such a type of insanity or mental illness.

---

[15] [Fn. 10 in the opinion.] Restatement (Second) of Torts § 283B; See Criez v. Sunset Motor Co., 123 Wash. 604, 608, 213 P. 7 (1923); J.A. Bryant, Jr., Liability of Insane Person For His Own Negligence, 49 A.L.R.3d 189 (1973).

[16] [Fn. 14 in the opinion.] 45 Wis.2d at 536.

The *Breunig* test was further explained by the same court in *Jankee v. Clark County*. Sudden mental incapacity is a "rare exception [and] applies only when two conditions are met: (1) the person has no prior notice or forewarning of his or her potential for becoming disabled, and (2) the disability renders the person incapable of conforming to the standards of ordinary care."[17]

The *Breunig* court upheld the jury's verdict, finding Mrs. Veith did have knowledge or forewarning that her hallucinations could affect her driving. Mrs. Veith had previously experienced delusional visions and should have known she posed a risk to others if she drove. The Wisconsin Supreme Court later limited the Breunig rule stating, " '[a]ll we hold is that a sudden mental incapacity equivalent in its effect to such physical causes as a sudden heart attack, epileptic seizure, stroke, or fainting should be treated alike and not under the general rule of insanity.' "[18]

Absence of Notice or Forewarning

Whether Knorr had notice or forewarning that her paranoia could affect her driving is the more difficult question presented. In order to meet the first prong of sudden mental incapacity, the defendant must have "no prior notice or forewarning of his or her potential for becoming disabled."

The standard of whether a defendant had notice or forewarning of the mental incapacity depends on whether the defendant had any forewarning or knowledge of a prior mental disability or disorder that incapacitates him from conforming his conduct to the standard of care. The driver must have been incapable of knowing that a mental incapacity could occur while driving, preventing the driver from avoiding a collision.

Whether a person has knowledge or forewarning of their condition is based on an objective standard. When the occurrence of an illness or loss of consciousness should have been reasonably foreseen by a person of ordinary intelligence and prudence, the driver of a motor vehicle is negligent as a matter of law. "The negligence is not in the manner of driving but rather in driving at all, if the person should reasonably have foreseen that the illness or lack of consciousness might occur and affect the person's manner of driving."[19]

The Wisconsin cases provide several examples defining notice and forewarning. In *Jankee*, the court declared that forewarning exists when a person is under the treatment of medication.[20] The court discussed *Stuyvesant Assoc. v. John Doe*[21] to illustrate when forewarning is satisfied with regard to taking medication. In *Stuyvesant Assoc.*, a schizophrenic man was receiving injections every other week for his illness and knew if he missed an injection, deterioration would result. The defendant also knew of the risks he posed if he fell into a psychotic state. The defendant missed an appointment for his medication and committed vandalism while in a psychotic state. "The court held the defendant to an objective standard

---

[17] [Fn. 20 in the opinion.] *Jankee*, 235 Wis.2d at 735 (citing *Breunig*, 45 Wis.2d at 541, 543).

[18] [Fn. 23 in the opinion.] *Jankee*, 235 Wis.2d at 735 (quoting *Breunig*, 45 Wis.2d at 544).

[19] [Fn. 29 in the opinion.] *Krause v. General Casualty Co.*, 192 Wis.2d 763, *6, 532 N.W.3d 469 (1995).

[20] [Fn. 30 in the opinion.] *Jankee*, 235 Wis.2d at 736, n. 12 ("This level of forewarning is acutely apparent for persons who are under the treatment of medication. For instance, epileptics and diabetics are negligent if a foreseeable seizure or incapacitation leads them to cause an accident.").

[21] [Fn. 31 in the opinion.] 221 N.J.Super. 340, 534 A.2d 448 (1987).

of care and found him liable, reasoning that the patient was cognizant of his condition and the risks posed by refraining from the medication. . . . "[22]

In *Johnson v. Lambotte*, the defendant was being treated for "chronic schizophrenic state of paranoid type" when she left the hospital and having little or no apparent control of her vehicle, collided with another car.[23] In *Breunig*, the court stated that "*Johnson is* not a case of sudden mental seizure with no forewarning [because the] defendant knew she was being treated for a mental disorder and hence would not have come under the nonliability rule herein stated." 1[24]

In addition, symptoms of a mental disability provide adequate notice and forewarning. In *Breunig*, Mrs. Veith was found to have had notice and forewarning of her mental condition because she had previously experienced delusional visions. The issue of forewarning went to the jury in *Breunig* because there was not substantial evidence whether Mrs. Veith had knowledge or forewarning. Mrs. Veith was not previously treated for a mental disorder and her friends testified that she was normal for some months prior to the accident.

In the case at hand, Knorr does not meet the test of sudden mental incapacity because the evidence clearly establishes she had notice and forewarning of her mental condition. The testimony at trial showed that in 1994, Knorr had a mental breakdown and was hospitalized for ten days. During that period, Knorr believed the person she worked for was conspiring to steal her and her husband's assets, was going to kill them, and was poisoning her. She also had concerns about her brother being a murderer. The delusions escalated to a point where she believed the neighbors were part of this scheme of "taking them out." Knorr was diagnosed with possible delusional disorder, was put on medication, and was advised to see a psychiatrist.

When Knorr was released from the hospital she was given Lithium along with other medication, which helped end her delusional thoughts. The hospital directed Knorr to see a psychiatrist and she saw Dr. McConnaughy. After three months, Knorr quit seeing Dr. McConnaughy and quit taking her medication. Knorr testified at trial that in July of 1994, she "started to get real anxious again" and had to go back to the hospital. At the admittance office, Knorr "started snapping out of it" and decided to go back home and see how she felt. When Knorr returned home she felt fine and no longer had anxiety or other symptoms until 2001.

The testimony at trial further showed that beginning in March 2001, Knorr's delusional thoughts about her brother being a murderer came back. Knorr and her family testified that by November 2001, her thoughts escalated and Mr. Knorr tried to get her to agree to go to the hospital. Knorr wanted to wait until after the holidays to go to the hospital and had an appointment scheduled for two days after the accident.

The day before the accident Knorr believed intruders were coming to her house and were going to kidnap her and her husband and rape them. The morning of the accident a friend offered to take Knorr to the hospital, but she refused to go. At trial, Dr. Young testified that people with delusional beliefs almost never believe something is wrong with them. He further testified that on the day of the accident,

---

[22] Quoting, *Jankee*, 235 Wis.2d at 736.

[23] [Fn. 36 in the opinion.] *Johnson v. Lambotte*, 147 Colo. 203, 204, 363 P.2d 165 (1961).

[24] [Fn. 37 in the opinion.] *Breunig*, 45 Wis.2d at 543.

Knorr's delusional beliefs caused her to panic, and "it's at that point that erratic or dangerous behavior can occur." Dr. Young testified that Knorr's delusional beliefs that caused her to panic were "relatively sudden."

The trial court concluded that under *Breunig* and Johnson, Knorr had forewarning because she knew she had been treated for a mental condition in 1994 and chose not to continue with the medication, and therefore did not fall within the sudden mental incapacity exception. We agree. We note further that the episodes continued and existed in this case as recently as the day preceding the auto collision. The record shows that Knorr was forewarned of the condition that again arose on the day of the accident.

Knorr heavily relies on the expert testimony of Dr. Young, which she describes as "unrebutted." However, the question before the court at the time of the motions was whether there was a legally sufficient evidentiary basis to allow the defense. The court was neither required to only consider the evidence of the expert nor to believe that evidence.

More importantly, when one views the testimony by Dr. Young and the other witnesses in the light most favorable to Knorr, there is substantial evidence to conclude that Knorr had knowledge and forewarning of her mental disorder. Knorr was treated for delusional beliefs in 1994, decided to stop that treatment, including taking her medication, began experiencing delusions again almost a year prior to the accident, and had ample opportunity to go to the hospital and seek help. Knorr also agreed to go to the hospital, which further supports her knowledge of her mental disorder. Therefore, the trial court properly granted a directed verdict in favor of Ramey.

Although Knorr had no history of being dangerous or violent, or any problems with her driving, that is not required under *Breunig*. Knorr experienced delusional beliefs for several months prior to the accident and believed the night before the accident that intruders were going to come into her family's home and rape and kill them. Under an objective standard, a reasonable person would have foreseen that Knorr's mental condition could affect her driving. Therefore, Knorr's mental incapacity while driving was foreseeable.

Incapable of Conforming to Standards of Ordinary Care

Addressing the other prong of sudden mental incapacity, the *Breunig* court stated:

> [the] disorder must be such as to affect the person's ability to understand and appreciate the duty which rests upon him to drive his car with ordinary care, or if the insanity does not affect such understanding and appreciation, it must affect his ability to control his car in an ordinarily prudent manner.1[25]

The court in *Jankee* later clarified the rule from Breunig and stated "the disability [must] render[ ] the person incapable of conforming to the standards of ordinary care."[26]

---

[25] [Fn. 40 in the opinion.] *Breunig*, 45 Wis.2d at 541.

[26] [Fn. 41 in the opinion.]

Jankee, 235 Wis.2d at 735 (citing *Breunig*, 45 Wis.2d at 541, 543).

Ramey argues that because Knorr did not lose physical control of her vehicle, she does not meet the second prong of Breunig. However, lack of ordinary care does not only require loss of physical capacity. Lack of ordinary care occurs when there is either an inability to understand and appreciate the duty to drive with ordinary care, or an inability to control the vehicle with ordinary care. Although Knorr was in physical control of her vehicle, her delusional beliefs prevented her from understanding and appreciating her duty to drive with ordinary care. Because Knorr was mentally incapable of conforming to the standards of ordinary care while driving, she meets the second prong of *Breunig.*

Knorr relies, in part, on Washington authority that holds that, "[a] driver who becomes suddenly stricken by an unforeseen loss of consciousness, and is unable to control the vehicle, is not chargeable with negligence."[27] In *Kaiser v. Suburban Transp. Sys.*, the doctor did not warn the driver of a bus of the side effects of drowsiness or lassitude, and the court held the driver could not be liable for negligence unless he had "knowledge of the pill's harmful qualities." The general rule from *Kaiser* applies only to a sudden physical incapacity or loss consciousness that is unforeseeable, and has never applied to a mental incapacity with no loss of consciousness. *Kaiser* is not applicable to the case before us because Knorr remained in physical control of her vehicle and never lost consciousness.

. . . .

JURY INSTRUCTIONS

Lastly, Knorr argues the trial court committed reversible error in failing to instruct the jury on the sudden mental incapacity defense and in giving certain jury instructions. Knorr bases this argument on the trial court's alleged error in granting a directed verdict for Ramey and preventing Knorr from arguing her theory of the case to the jury.

A party is entitled to have the jury instructed on his or her theory of the case as long as there is evidence to support the theory. The trial court has discretion whether to give a particular instruction to the jury and the "trial court's refusal to give a requested instruction is reviewed only for abuse of discretion." Where there is substantial evidence to support a theory, a trial court must instruct the jury on that theory. [Nevertheless]. . . . Sudden mental incapacity generally is not accepted as a defense to negligence and there is substantial evidence that Knorr does not meet the sudden mental incapacity exception. Because it was not error for the trial court to grant a directed verdict for Ramey, the trial court did not abuse its discretion in failing to instruct the jury on the sudden mental incapacity defense. The proposed jury instructions on sudden mental incapacity were properly withheld and the instructions without the defense were properly given.

. . . .

We affirm the trial court rulings in all respects.

NOTES AND QUESTIONS

(1)   Is the rule that insanity is no defense merely an application of the objective standard of *Vaughan v. Menlove?*

---

[27] [Fn. 43 in the opinion.] *Kaiser v. Suburban Transp. Sys.*, 65 Wn.2d 461, 466, 398 P.2d 14 (1965).

(2) In *Gould v. American Family Mutual Insurance Company*, 543 N.W. 2d 282 (Wis. 1996), the Wisconsin court declined to recede from the established common law rule pertaining to the liability of insane people, but did acknowledge a limited exception in a case in which the defendant, who suffered dementia caused by Alzheimer's disease, injured a member of the staff in the hospital. Holding the demented defendant to be incapable of negligence in the particular case, the Court said, 543 N.W. 2d at 287:

> In sum, we agree with the Goulds that ordinarily a mentally disabled person is responsible for his or her torts. However, we conclude that this rule does not apply in this case because the circumstances totally negate the rationale behind the rule and would place an unreasonable burden on the negligent institutionalized mentally disabled. When a mentally disabled person injures an employed caretaker, the injured party can reasonably foresee the danger and is not "innocent" of the risk involved. By placing a mentally disabled person in an institution or similar restrictive setting, "those interested in the estate" of that person are not likely to be in need of an inducement for greater restraint. It is incredible to assert that a tortfeasor would "simulate or pretend insanity" over a prolonged period of time and even be institutionalized in order to avoid being held liable for damages for some future civil act. Therefore, we hold that a person institutionalized, as here, with a mental disability, and who does not have the capacity to control or appreciate his or her conduct cannot be liable for injuries caused to caretakers who are employed for financial compensation.

See also, *Anicet v. Gant*, 580 So. 2d 273 (Fla. App. 1991), cert. denied, 591 So. 2d 181 (Fla. 1991) (an insane person who is placed in a mental institution is not capable of negligence as to the members of the staff of the institution who are charged with caring for the person.). *Creasy v. Rusk*, 730 N.E.2d 659 (Ind.2000) and *Berberian v. Lynn*, 845 A.2d 122 (N.J. 2004) applied the same rule.

(3) A Law and Economics Tort analysis of harm caused by a defendant suffering the mental defect described in *Ramey* would apply the three standard criteria: optimal deterrence of injuries, compensation of victims, and the need for clear, predictable, and simple Tort rules. From a deterrence perspective, should the Tort system afford the actor (or guardian) an incentive to control the dangerous behavior? Without forewarning of the risk could anyone modify behavior? Do you agree that without forewarning a reasonable person would not have thought it necessary to control the behavior to avoid harm and would not be negligent not to do so?

From the compensation perspective, do you agree that both defendant and victim are relatively innocent of wrongdoing? Should the Tort system nevertheless deem a forewarned defendant to be "less innocent" and impose liability?

From the perspective of clear, predictable, and simple rules, should the Tort system permit defendants to avoid liability upon a claim of mental illness? Whether legitimate or not, would these claims be costly to litigate? Would a mental illness defense also introduce uncertainties as to the standard of behavior that may be expected from other people and thus make planning more difficult? Remember *Vaughan v. Menlove*? Do you agree that these considerations justify making it difficult for insane people to escape Tort responsibility? Does the *Ramey* opinion provide an adequate exception to this general rule?

§ 6.06   MODIFIED STANDARD — EMERGENCY

HORSLEY v. MACLAREN
11 D.L.R. 3d 277 (1970), *appeal dismissed*, [1972] S.C.R. 441[28]

[See § 5.06 *et seq.*, *supra*, for other judgments in this case. Plaintiff's decedent, Mathews, fell off defendant's boat into Lake Ontario and died quickly either of exposure to the cold or by drowning. The body was never recovered. The facts show that defendant was not at fault in causing Matthews to fall overboard. Liability, if at all, rests upon fault in the attempted rescue. Defendant attempted to back down to pick up the deceased, which plaintiff alleges as negligence in view of testimony as to correct procedure.]

SCHROEDER, J.A.

. . .

Matthews, as were the others, was a gratuitous passenger, but it is well settled that the owner or master of a vessel is nevertheless under a duty to carry such passengers with due care. It becomes a question as to whether this duty extends to and embraces a duty to effect a rescue of a passenger who, from whatever cause, is cast into the water, and to use due care in effecting his rescue, a breach of which duty may afford a basis for establishing liability in tort. Whatever may have been the more primitive notion of the duty of a master or owner of a pleasure craft towards his passengers in such circumstances, the proposition formulated by Lord Atkin which is familiar to us as "the neighbour principle", is relevant for consideration. That dictum, while not affording ground for disregarding existing categories of liability, makes it plain that these categories are never closed, and is authority for opening up new categories. The classic statement to which I refer appears in Lord Atkin's judgment in *M'Alister (or Donoghue) v. Stevenson*, [1932] A.C. 562 at p. 580, from which I quote: —

[See Lord Atkin's "Who is my Neighbor" speech in *Donoghue v. Stevenson*, § 4.01, *supra.*]

That declaration, which was hailed as a new point of departure in our law of tort, is not to be given too broad an interpretation or application, and jurists should not treat it as an open invitation to them to depart from their traditional function as expounders and interpreters of the law and to assume the function of legislators. Nevertheless, the law must ever continue to be a living force to achieve its true ends, and Judges have not shrunk from the task of moulding the law to keep pace with changing mores as civilization progresses. Here the defendant was not at fault for the plight in which Matthews found himself, but by every social and moral standard the relationship between him and his passengers was one which would impose upon him an obligation at least to make a reasonable effort to rescue him. It is immaterial in the present case whether or not it be treated as a legal duty since MacLaren recognized that obligation and took the steps above outlined, but it is contended that he did not act in the emergency as a reasonable and prudent master would have acted.

---

[28] [Ed. — Dominion Law Reports, a reporter of Canadian decisions, decision of Ontario Court of Appeal.]

To establish a breach of duty on the defendant's part the plaintiff relied on the evidence of two expert witnesses, Captain Livingstone and Captain Mumford. They testified as to the proper rescue procedures to be followed in case a man fell overboard. They both agreed that the procedure of reversing the engines and backing toward the man in the water should never be adopted except in a confined area where the boat could not be turned around. They stated that this procedure should be automatic and ought to be known to every person who undertakes the operation of a boat such as the "Ogopogo"; that the man in the water should be approached "bow on", and that to bear down upon him stern first was evidence of incompetence. The defendant MacLaren admitted that this was recognized by him as the correct procedure, but maintained that on the spur of the moment and in the emergency which presented itself he had done what he thought would be most conducive to an early rescue.

Captain Mumford would not state that there was no reasonable chance of picking up a person in the water by backing the boat, but stated that there was a better chance of doing it by the method which he proposed, adding that it was a matter for the master to decide. Captain Livingstone stated that it was inadvisable for a person to remove his clothing before entering very cold water. In fact, he disapproved of anyone jumping into the water in the course of a rescue operation since one would be "compounding the situation by having two persons in the water instead of one".

In my respectful opinion the evidence of the two experts spells out a standard of text-book perfection given at a time when all the evidence had been sifted and all the facts ascertained in the calm and deliberate atmosphere of a judicial investigation. It is ever so easy to be wise after the event and to state *ex post facto* that the conduct of the appellant, who had to rely upon the co-operation of the other passengers in effecting the rescue of Matthews, fell short of the standard of reasonableness. He is surely entitled to be judged in the light of the situation as it appeared to him at the time and in the context of immediate and pressing emergency, even if a duty of using reasonable care in effecting the rescue of Matthews was properly cast upon him. The learned trial Judge excused the conduct of Horsley [a rescuer who jumped into the icy water and drowned] in the light of the emergency but failed to apply the same test to the appellant whose problems and responsibilities were much greater and more complex. The excitement created by the cry "Roly's overboard", the fact that the appellant had to act immediately, the confusion attendant upon the suddenness of the tragic occurrence, the lack of time and opportunity for mature consideration, all these circumstances must be taken into account in approaching a determination of whether the appellant was guilty of negligence in backing the vessel towards Matthews instead of proceeding towards him "bow on", assuming that the standard contended for is applicable.

KLEPPER v. BRESLIN
Florida Supreme Court
83 So. 2d 587 (1955)

THORNAL, JUSTICE.

The appellant, Raphael Klepper, as plaintiff in the trial court, sued the appellees for damages resulting from the fatal injury of his four-year old son, Scott Robert

Klepper, allegedly caused by the negligent operation of the automobile of the appellee, George W. Breslin, by his wife, Alma Conway Breslin. The jury rendered a verdict for the defendants and after denial of a motion for new trial, the plaintiff appeals.

The parties all lived in a strictly residential area known as Ridgewood in Duval County. The defendants resided some five hundred feet or more north of the plaintiff and his family on the opposite side of the street. It was generally known that there were numerous small children living in the community. Signs warning "Children — Slow" were posted around the area. Immediately prior to the accident, Mrs. Breslin backed out of her driveway and proceeded along Peachtree Circle East in a southerly direction. There is a conflict as to the speed at which she was driving.

At a distance of four to five hundred feet from the accident Mrs. Breslin saw three small children and a dog playing in the park area on the east side of the street immediately contiguous to the paved roadway. As she approached the scene, two of the children were standing several feet off of the road. One was a little girl about five years old and the other was Robert's little brother Russell, aged two years. The little girl appeared to be holding him back from the road. Scott Robert Klepper, age four, was standing by a fence with his arm around a fence rail which was shown to be some 18 feet east of the east edge of the paved road, which was also 18 feet wide. There was no sidewalk. Mrs. Breslin had noticed the small dog running after the boy toward the fence away from the road. At this point the dog evidently turned because it ran across the road in front of the Breslin automobile. Mrs. Breslin veered to the right to miss the dog and after learning from her maid, who was sitting on the front seat by her, that she had missed the dog, she again glanced to her right, then straightened up, as she testified, "to pay attention to my driving". The maid held Mrs. Breslin's baby on her lap and there were two larger children on the back seat of her car. It appears from the record that she assumed the children were safely off the road where she had last seen them. Thereupon, she noticed the Klepper child running across the road and he seemed to stumble and fall directly in front of her automobile. She stated that the running of the dog, the veering of the car, her "straightening up" and the running of the boy all happened in a matter of "four or five seconds". The car struck the child and Mrs. Breslin stated that she did not apply the brakes of her car immediately in an effort to avoid actually passing over the little boy but without the application of her brakes her car came to a stop approximately 40 feet from the point of contact with the child. There were marks along the pavement described as "scuff marks" for a distance of approximately 40 feet back of the automobile up to the point where the child's body was found. The little boy was pronounced dead upon arrival at the hospital shortly after the accident. The deceased child's mother was in her home preparing the evening meal at the time of the tragedy. The Klepper home was almost directly across the street from the area where the children were playing by the fence mentioned above. The Kleppers had previously fenced in their back yard as a playing area for the little boy but for several months prior to the accident, his mother had permitted him to play in the front yard. The plaintiff-father knew of this practice. The mother had never known him to run across the road unattended. He had been taught safety precautions in kindergarten. She stated that she checked on him about every five minutes glancing out of her kitchen window. She testified further that she had noticed the children in her own front yard about five minutes prior to the unfortunate occurrence.

One witness testified that she saw the Breslin car some distance prior to the accident and that in her judgment it was traveling 30 to 35 miles per hour. Mrs. Breslin testified that actually she was traveling 15 to 18 miles per hour just before the accident; that immediately prior to the contact with the child, she had stepped on her brakes to avoid the dog, and that at the time of contact she had just moved her foot from the brakes and was in the act of stepping on the accelerator to get her car under way again.

The case was tried on the defenses of a general denial and the alleged contributory negligence of the mother of the deceased on the theory that she had failed to maintain adequate supervision and control over the small child. The Court among other instructions charged the jury, at the request of the defendants, on the doctrine of "sudden emergency," "unavoidable accident," "darting out," and contributory negligence by the mother as being chargeable against the plaintiff-father. The plaintiff appeals alleging that these charges constitute errors and in addition he contends that the trial judge should have directed a verdict for the plaintiff on the alleged negligence of the defendants.

By assignment of errors numbered 6, 8 and 9, the appellant-father contends that the trial judge committed reversible error by instructing the jury, at the request of the appellees, as follows:

Where the operator of an automobile by a sudden emergency, not due to her own negligence, is placed in a position of imminent danger and has insufficient time to determine with certainty the best course to pursue, she is not held to the same accuracy of judgment as is required under ordinary circumstances, and if she pursues a course of action to avoid an accident such as a person of ordinary prudence placed in a like position might choose, she is not guilty of negligence, even though she did not adopt the wisest choice.

If you find from the evidence that the plaintiff's decedent, Scott Robert Klepper, darted or ran suddenly onto the highway in front of the defendant's automobile, provided there was no negligence on the part of the defendant, Mrs. Breslin, such automobile was too close for her to avoid hitting him in the exercise of ordinary care, as defined in these instructions, the collision by the defendants' automobile and said Scott Robert Klepper would be an unavoidable accident, and you should find the defendants not guilty.

Where a child is in a place of safety on a sidewalk or elsewhere and exhibits no intention to cross the street or makes any movement showing such a purpose until the car is so near that it cannot be stopped, and the child suddenly darts in front of it and is injured, the owner of the car is not chargeable with negligence because of the failure of the driver to stop the car.

It is the contention of the appellant that if a "sudden emergency" existed it resulted from the negligence of the driver of the automobile and further that the accident could not have been "unavoidable" for the reason that in the view of the appellant the driver of the automobile had ample opportunity to see the dangerous situation long before the accident occurred and by the exercise of reasonable care and caution under all of the circumstances therein obtaining, particularly including the presence of small children in the area, could have avoided striking the little boy.

While on the surface the position of the appellant might appear to have merit, it should be noted that the instructions to which he offers objection were cautiously framed on the condition that the driver of the automobile would have to be without negligence on her own part. It is clear from this record that the trial judge adopted the view that under all of the evidence the question of negligence, contributory negligence, and the related issues as to whether the driver of the automobile exercised due care appropriate to the particular circumstances, should be submitted to the jury as involving a factual conflict which could not otherwise be resolved as a matter of law.

It should further be noted that at the request of the appellant, the trial judge had carefully instructed the jury on the unpredictable nature of small children and the fact that their movements are erratic and that they cannot be relied upon to exercise the degree of care for their own safety in the manner to be demanded of adults. The trial judge appropriately instructed the jury as to the responsibility of the driver of motor vehicles in regard to anticipating these unpredictable movements of young children and, by his instructions, he imposed upon the motorist the duty to keep a vigilant lookout where such motorist observes children of tender years playing along the side of the road. He told them it was a matter of common knowledge that often times children under these circumstances strayed upon the road and that the motorist was required to govern himself accordingly.

. . .

It appears to this Court that the trial judge very completely and properly advised the jury as to the law applicable under all of the circumstances and then with propriety deposited with the jury the problem of resolving the factual conflicts in the light of the law as pronounced by the Court.

Affirmed.

THOMAS, HOBSON and SEBRING JJ., concur.

DREW, CHIEF JUSTICE (dissenting).

I am unable to agree with the opinion of Mr. Justice Thornal for two major reasons.

I think the instruction of the lower court with reference to an unavoidable accident under the facts in this case was clearly erroneous. Briefly and succinctly I am of the view that the negligence of the driver of the car created the situation which resulted in the death of the child and that the doctrine of sudden emergency is wholly inapplicable. What was said in the case of *Seitner v. Clevenger*, Fla. 1953; 68 So. 2d 396, 397, viz: "To recognize the right of a defendant to escape liability under such circumstances would be to reward one for his own negligence," is clearly applicable here.

NOTES AND QUESTIONS

(1) Are you persuaded by either *Horsley v. MacLaren* or *Klepper v. Breslin* that defendants ought to be entitled to have the judge instruct the jury about emergency circumstances? If appropriate evidence is presented to the jury, would not the jurors on their own accord give proper weight to the exigencies of the

situation in evaluating what a reasonable person would have done "under the circumstances?"

(2)   Does the instruction given in *Klepper* permit the jury to find that a genuine emergency existed, that it was not caused by the defendant, and, notwithstanding, that the defendant was negligent? See, *e.g., Whicher v. Phinney*, 124 F.2d 929 (1st Cir. 1942).

(3)   At one time it was commonplace for courts to give particularized instructions, such as the "sudden emergency" and "darting art" instructions referred to in *Klepper*. For example, *Shields v. L. W. Easterling*, 676 So. 2d 293 (Miss. 1996), approved the use of this "unavoidable accident" instruction:

> The Court instructs the Jury that in the course of human events, and the progress of civilization, unavoidable accidents occur, and it is recognized by law that unavoidable accidents do indeed occur and as a result of which people are injured when there is no negligence, and in this case, if the Jury believes that the accident in question and the resulting injuries, if any, were the result of an unavoidable accident and not of negligence on the part of Defendant, C.W. Easterling, then it shall be your sworn duty to return your verdict for the Defendant.

Do instructions of this sort unduly prejudice the position of one party or the other before the jury? Some courts hold them in disfavor. *Lyons v. Midnight Sun Transp. Services, Inc.*, 928 P.2d 1202, 1205 (Alaska,1996) opined, "The sudden emergency doctrine arose as a method of ameliorating the, sometimes harsh, 'all or nothing' rule in contributory negligence systems." Although the court deemed the doctrine to be compatible with a comparative fault scheme, it nevertheless "discouraged its use" . . . "given the redundancy of the instruction and its potential for sowing confusion." *Id.*, 928 P2d at 206. See also *George v. Guerette*, 306 A.2d 138 (Me. 1973). *Vasquez v. Wal-Mart Stores, Inc.*, 913 P.2d 441, 442 (Wyo. 1996) declined to rule on whether an "unavoidable accident" instruction is prejudicial but found that this instruction, which it deemed not to be of that variety, was not: "The fact that damages or injury occurred is not, in itself, sufficient to show that either party was negligent." Do you agree the instruction is not of the "unavoidable accident" character? Or with the conclusion that it favors neither side?

§ 6.07   MALPRACTICE

PERIN v. HAYNE
Iowa Supreme Court
210 N.W.2d 609 (1983)

McCormick, Justice.

This is an appeal from a directed verdict for a doctor in a malpractice action. We affirm.

The claim arose from an anterior approach cervical fusion performed on plaintiff Ilene Perin by defendant Robert A. Hayne, a Des Moines neurosurgeon, on November 26, 1968. The fusion was successful in eliminating pain, weakness and numbness in plaintiff's back, neck, right arm and hand caused by two protruded cervical discs, but plaintiff alleged she suffered paralysis of a vocal chord because of injury to the right recurrent laryngeal nerve during surgery. The paralyzed vocal chord impaired plaintiff's voice which had been normal before surgery. The injury reduced her voice to a hoarse whisper.

She sought damages on four theories: specific negligence, res ipsa loquitur, breach of express warranty and battery or trespass. After both parties had rested, trial court sustained defendant's motion for directed verdict, holding the evidence insufficient to support jury consideration of the case on any of the pleaded theories. Plaintiff assigns this ruling as error. We must review each of the pleaded bases for recovery in the light of applicable law and the evidence.

I. *Specific negligence.* Plaintiff alleges there was sufficient evidence to support jury submission of her charge defendant negligently cut or injured the recurrent laryngeal nerve. Plaintiff had protruded discs at the level of the fifth and sixth cervical interspaces. The purpose of surgery was to remove the protruded discs and fuse the vertebrae with bone dowels from her hip. Removal of a disc ends the pinching of the nerve in the spinal column which causes the patient's pain. The bone supplants the disc.

The procedure involves an incision in the front of the neck at one side of the midline at a level slightly below the "adam's apple." Four columns run through the neck. The vertebrae and spinal chord are in the axial or bone column at the rear. In order to get to the axial column the surgeon must retract the visceral column which lies in front of it. The visceral column, like the vascular column on each side of it, is covered with a protective fibrous sheath, called fascia. It contains the esophagus and trachea. The recurrent laryngeal nerve, which supplies sensitivity to the muscles that move the vocal chords, is located between the esophagus and trachea.

The surgeon does not enter the visceral column during the cervical fusion procedure. The same pliancy which enables the neck to be turned enables the visceral column to be retracted to one side to permit access to the axial column. The retraction is accomplished by using a gauze-padded retractor specifically designed for retraction of the visceral column during this surgery.

. . .

Dr. Walter Eidbo, a Des Moines surgeon, testified for plaintiff. He is not a neurosurgeon but has assisted neurosurgeons including defendant in anterior approach cervical fusion surgery. Dr. Eidbo confirmed that the visceral column is not entered in such surgery. He contrasted it with thyroid surgery in which the thyroid gland is entered and there is a risk the laryngeal nerve, which runs through it, may be cut. He said it is usually possible to avoid injury to the nerve during the cervical fusion procedure. "It would not be usual" to encounter the nerve. He did not express an opinion as to the precise nature of the injury or its cause in this case. He did speculate it might be possible to stretch the nerve too far in retracting the visceral column. He also said, "If you should happen to hit it as you were pulling it or if your retractor would touch on it, it might be just enough to do it. I don't know." Dr. Eidbo also testified the injury could occur despite the exercise of all proper skill and care.

We recognize three possible means to establish specific negligence of a physician. One is through expert testimony, the second through evidence showing the physician's lack of care is so obvious as to be within comprehension of a layman, and the third (actually an extension of the second) through evidence that the physician injured a part of the body not involved in the treatment. The first means is the rule and the others are exceptions to it. *Sinkey v. Surgical Associates,* 186 N.W.2d 658, 660 (Iowa 1971).

In this case plaintiff asserts a jury question was generated by the first and third means. We do not agree.

Plaintiff alleges the laryngeal nerve was negligently cut or injured. The record is devoid of any evidence the nerve was severed during surgery. At most the expert testimony from Dr. Eidbo and defendant would support a finding of negligence if the nerve had been cut, but there is no evidence it was. The evidence from both experts tended to show injury to the nerve would occur from retraction of the visceral column in a small percentage of cases in spite of all possible care.

The doctors agree the technique employed by defendant was proper. The sole basis for suggesting the expert testimony would support a finding of specific negligence is that the nerve was injured during retraction. Where an injury may occur despite due care, a finding of negligence cannot be predicated solely on the fact it did occur. Prosser on Torts, § 39 at 228 (Fourth Ed. 1971); see *Hair v. Sorensen,* 215 Iowa 1229, 247 N.W. 651 (1933); *Siverson v. Weber,* 57 Cal.2d 834, 22 Cal. Rptr. 337, 339, 372 P.2d 97, 99 (1962) ("The fact that a particular injury suffered by a patient as the result of an operation is something that rarely occurs does not in itself prove that the injury was probably caused by the negligence of those in charge of the operation.")

Plaintiff also maintains there is evidence of negligence from the fact this is a case of injury to a part of the body not involved in the treatment. However, that is not so. The surgical procedure did include retraction of the visceral column. It was very much in the surgical field.

We have been unable to locate any other case involving a claim based on vocal chord paralysis as a result of anterior approach cervical fusion surgery. Several such claims have been litigated after thyroidectomies. Plaintiff relies on two cases where vocal chord paralysis occurred following thyroidectomies, *Patrick v. Sedwick,* 391 P.2d 453 (Alaska 1964) and *McPhee v. Bay City Samaritan Hospital,* 10 Mich. App. 567, 159 N.W.2d 880 (1968). Neither case is apposite. In *Patrick* the nerve was severed and there was expert testimony surgical destruction of the nerve was consistent with due care only in circumstances which the jury could find absent in that case. In *McPhee* there was expert testimony the nerve could and should have been avoided in the surgery involved. The testimony in the present case is the converse of that in *Patrick* and *McPhee.* For cases finding insufficient evidence of negligence in alleged surgical injury to the laryngeal nerve during thyroidectomies see *Watson v. Clutts,* 262 N.C. 153, 136 S.E.2d 617 (1964); [etc.]

Trial court did not err in directing a verdict for defendant on the issue of specific negligence in this case.

II. *Res ipsa loquitur.* Plaintiff also alleges the applicability of the doctrine of res ipsa loquitur. Our most recent statement of the doctrine appears in *Fischer, Inc. v. Standard Brands, Inc.,* 204 N.W.2d 579, 583 (Iowa 1973):

Under the doctrine of res ipsa loquitur, where (1) injury or damage is caused by an instrumentality under the exclusive control of defendant and (2) the occurrence is such as in the ordinary course of things would not happen if reasonable care had been used, the happening of the injury permits, but does not compel, an inference defendant was negligent.

The contest in this case concerns presence of the second foundation fact.

Plaintiff points to evidence which supports two inferences, one (not disputed) that her laryngeal nerve was injured during the surgery, and the other that such injury is extremely rare in such surgery. This evidence is primarily in the expert testimony of Dr. Eidbo and defendant. Defendant argues the second foundation fact for res ipsa loquitur is absent because it does not lie in the common knowledge of laymen to say injury to the laryngeal nerve does not occur if due care is exercised in anterior approach cervical fusion surgery.

We must initially decide what has previously been an open question in this jurisdiction: may the common experience to establish the second foundation fact for res ipsa loquitur be shown by expert testimony? See Loth, *Res Ipsa Loquitur in Iowa*, 18 Drake L. Rev. 1, 18 (1968).

In asserting such common experience must be a matter of common knowledge in the lay community, defendant cites *Fehrman v. Smirl*, 20 Wis.2d 1, 121 N.W.2d 255, 122 N.W.2d 439 (1963). However, that case does not support defendant's position. The Wisconsin court held the foundation for res ipsa loquitur may rest either in the common knowledge of laymen or in expert testimony. In the facts of that case the court held there was insufficient basis in common knowledge but there was sufficient basis in expert testimony. *Id.*, 121 N.W.2d at 268. . . . See also Prosser on Torts, § 39 at 217 (Fourth Ed. 1971) ("Even where . . . a basis of common knowledge is lacking, . . . expert testimony may provide a sufficient foundation. . . "); 2 Harper and James, The Law of Torts, § 19.6 at 1083 (1956) ("Expert evidence along this line is clearly admissible"). We see no reason to say the common experience required to establish the second foundation fact for res ipsa loquitur may not include the common experience of experts. . . .

In this case however, even considering the expert testimony, the record at best only supports an inference plaintiff suffered an extremely rare injury in anterior approach cervical fusion surgery which may occur even when due care is exercised. Rarity of the occurrence is not a sufficient predicate for application of res ipsa loquitur. "Where risks are inherent in an operation and an injury of a type which is rare does occur, the doctrine should not be applicable unless it can be said that, in the light of past experience, such an occurrence is more likely the result of negligence than some cause for which the defendant is not responsible." *Siverson v. Weber*, 57 Cal.2d 834, 22 Cal. Rptr. 337, 339–340, 372 P.2d 97, 99–100 (1962); see also 1 Louisell and Williams, Medical Malpractice, § 14.04 at 426–427 (1970). There is no basis in the present case, in expert testimony or otherwise, for saying plaintiff's injury is more likely the result of negligence than some cause for which the defendant is not responsible.

. . .

III. *Express warranty.* Plaintiff alleges there was a jury issue on her theory defendant expressly warranted she would be able to live a normal life after the surgery. She asserts the impairment of her voice breached such warranty.

We have long held a physician does not by undertaking treatment impliedly warrant a cure or guarantee the best possible result. See *Whetstine v. Moravec*, 228 Iowa 352, 369, 291 N.W. 425, 433 (1940), and citations. As a neurosurgeon, defendant impliedly warranted he possessed and would apply that degree of skill, care and learning ordinarily possessed and exercised by other neurosurgeons in similar circumstances

. . .

Nevertheless, it is generally held that a physician may bind himself in a given situation to perform a cure or obtain specific results by treatment or an operation. . . .

[Discussion of facts omitted.]

We recognize that what a physician may view as therapeutic reassurance may in some cases be taken by his patient as something more. There comes a point when a question of fact may be generated as to whether the doctor has warranted a cure or a specific result. See, *e.g.*, *Guilmet v. Campbell*, 385 Mich. 57, 188 N.W.2d 601 (1971). However, in the present case the evidence does not rise to that level. We do not believe the evidence would support a jury finding that defendant promised or warranted the surgery would be either successful or free from complications. Plaintiff candidly admits defendant's assurances were qualified and expressed only in terms of experience of most other patients. What he said was factual and was neither given nor received as a risk-free guarantee. The surgery was of course successful except for the unfortunate collateral result.

Trial court was right in refusing to submit the issue of express warranty to the jury.

IV. *Battery or trespass.* Plaintiff contends there was also sufficient evidence to submit the case to the jury on the theory of battery or trespass. In effect she alleges she consented to fusion of two vertebrae (removal of only one protruded disc) thinking there would be a separate operation if additional vertebrae had to be fused. She asserts the fact four vertebrae were fused combined with defendant's assurances and failure to warn her of specific hazards vitiated her consent and makes the paralyzed vocal chord the result of battery or trespass for which defendant is liable even without negligence. There was no evidence or contention by her in the trial court nor is there any assertion here that she would not have consented to the surgery had she known those things she says were withheld from her prior to surgery.

Defendant testified plaintiff was fully advised as to the nature of her problem and the scope of corrective surgery. He acknowledges he did not advise her of the hazard of vocal chord paralysis. He believed the possiblity of such occurrence was negligible and outweighed by the danger of undue apprehension if warning of the risk was given.

We discussed the concept of informed consent in *Grosjean v. Spencer*, 258 Iowa 685, 140 N.W.2d 139 (1966). That case involved a claim of negligence based on alleged inadequate disclosure of information by a physician to the wife of his patient. It did not involve a claim of battery or trespass. The contention here is based on battery or trespass rather than negligence.

The distinction between these theories is explained in *Cobbs v. Grant*, 8 Cal.3d 229, 104 Cal. Rptr. 505, 502 P.2d 1 (1972). We approve and adopt the following discussion from that case:

Where a doctor obtains consent of the patient to perform one type of treatment and subsequently performs a substantially different treatment for which consent was not obtained, there is a clear case of battery. (*Berkey v. Anderson* (1969) *supra*, 1 Cal. App.3d 790, 82 Cal. Rptr. 67 (allegation of consent to permit doctor to perform a procedure no more complicated than the electromyograms plaintiff had previously undergone, when the actual procedure was a myelogram involving a spinal puncture); *Bang v. Charles T. Miller Hosp.* (1958) 251 Minn. 427, 88 N.W.2d 186 (plaintiff consented to a prostate resection when uninformed that this procedure involved tying off his sperm ducts); *Corn v. French* (1955) 71 Nev. 280, 289 P.2d 173 (patient consented to exploratory surgery; doctor performed a mastectomy); *Zoterell v. Repp* (1915) 187 Mich. 319, 153 N.W. 692 (consent given for a hernia operation during which doctor also removed both ovaries).

However, when an undisclosed potential complication results, the occurrence of which was not an integral part of the treatment procedure but merely a known risk, the courts are divided on the issue of whether this should be deemed to be a battery or negligence. . . .

Dean Prosser surveyed the decisions in this area and concluded, "The earliest cases treated this as a matter of vitiating the consent, so that there was liability for battery. Beginning with a decision in Kansas in 1960 [*Natanson v. Kline* (1960) *supra*, 187 Kan. 186 [354 P.2d 670]], it began to be recognized that this was really a matter of the standard of professional conduct. . . . [T]he prevailing view now is that the action. . . . is in reality one for negligence in failing to conform to the proper standard. . . . "(Fns. omitted; Prosser on Torts (4th Ed. 1971) pp. 165–166.)

Although this is a close question, either prong of which is supportable by authority, the trend appears to be towards categorizing failure to obtain informed consent as negligence. That this result now appears with growing frequency is of more than academic interest; it reflects an appreciation of the several significant consequences of favoring negligence over a battery theory. . . . [M]ost jurisdictions have permitted a doctor in an informed consent action to interpose a defense that the disclosure he omitted to make was not required within his medical community. However, expert opinion as to community standard is not required in a battery count, in which the patient must merely prove failure to give informed consent and a mere touching absent consent. Moreover a doctor could be held liable for punitive damages under a battery count . . . (Comment, *Informed Consent in Medical Malpractice* (1967) 55 Cal. L. Rev. 1396). Additionally, in some jurisdictions the patient has a longer statute of limitations if he sues in negligence.

We agree with the majority trend. The battery theory should be reserved for those circumstances when a doctor performs an operation to which the patient has not consented. When the patient gives permission to perform one type of treatment and the doctor performs another, the requisite element of deliberate intent to deviate from the consent given is present. However, when the patient consents to certain treatment and the doctor performs that treatment but an undisclosed inherent complication with a low probability occurs, no intentional deviation from the consent given appears; rather, the doctor in obtaining consent may have failed to meet his due care duty to disclose pertinent information. In that situation the action should be pleaded in negligence.

Id. 104 Cal. Rptr. at 511, 502 P.2d at 7–8.

From our approval of this analysis it should be clear we believe the battery or trespass theory pleaded by plaintiff in this case is limited in its applicability to surgery to which the patient has not consented. There must be a substantial difference between the surgery consented to and the surgery which is done. Plaintiff asserts she consented to only one fusion rather than two. Assuming this is true, the most that could be argued is the second fusion was a battery or trespass. But she does not claim damages for a second fusion. She asks damages because of injury to the laryngeal nerve during surgery. The evidence is undisputed that whether one or two fusions were to be done the path to the axial column had to be cleared by retraction of the visceral column. Hence, any injury caused by such retraction occurred during a procedure to which consent had been given. Retraction of the visceral column during the surgery was not a battery or trespass.

We have no occasion to reach the question whether failure to advise plaintiff of the risk of laryngeal nerve injury would in the circumstances of this case have generated a jury issue on negligence, but we do point out that recovery on such basis is precluded unless a plaintiff also establishes he would not have submitted to the procedure if he had been advised of the risk

. . . .

There is no evidence plaintiff would have withheld her consent in this case.

Trial court did not err in refusing to submit the case on plaintiff's theory of battery or trespass.

Since there was insufficient evidence to support submission of the case on any of the four pleaded theories, trial court correctly sustained defendant's motion for directed verdict. The case is affirmed.

Affirmed.

NOTES AND QUESTIONS

(1) *Perin v. Hayne* discusses two distinct causes of action that might be available to a plaintiff in a medical malpractice case. The theory of battery is of an intentional wrong rather than a negligent wrong. The intentional torts are examined in detail in later sections of the book. Some American courts, but not all, agree that negligence actions supplant intentional tort actions in virtually all medical malpractice cases. See, *e.g.*, *Miller v. Kennedy*, 522 P.2d 852 (Wash. 1974). See *Karl J. Pizzalloto, M.D., Ltd., v. Wilson*, 437 So. 2d 859 (La. 1983), treating malpractice as a battery. In England, the intentional tort theory is not commonly accepted. See also *Chatterton v. Gerson*, [1981] Q.B. 432.

(2) What precisely did the plaintiff allege as the basis of the battery action? How might physicians protect themselves against unfounded claims of this nature?

(3) What is informed consent? In *ZeBarth v. Swedish Hospital Medical Center*, 81 Wash.2d 12, 499 P.2d 1 (1972), the court said:

The duty of a medical doctor to inform his patient of the risks of harm reasonably to be expected from a proposed course of treatment does not place upon the physician a duty to elucidate upon all of the possible risks, but only those of a serious nature. Nor does it contemplate that the patient or those in whose charge he may be are completely ignorant of medical matters. A patient is obliged to exercise the intelligence and act on the knowledge which an ordinary person would bring to the doctors' office. The law does not contemplate that a doctor need conduct a short course in anatomy, medicine, surgery, and therapeutics nor that he do anything which in reasonable standards for practice of medicine in the community might be inimical to the patient's best interests. *The doctrine of informed consent does not require the doctor to risk frightening the patient out of a course of treatment which sound medical judgment dictates the patient should undertake, nor does the rule assume that the patient possesses less knowledge of medical matters than a person of ordinary understanding could reasonably be expected to have or by law should be charged with having.* Nor should the rule declaring a duty to inform be so stated or applied that a physician, in the interest of protecting himself from an overburden of law suits and the attendant costs upon his time and purse, will always follow the most conservative therapy — which, while of doubtful benefit to the patient exposes the patient to no affirmative medical hazards and the doctor to no risks of litigation. Thus, the information required of the doctor by the general rule is that information which a reasonable physician or medical specialist of that medical community should or would know to be essential to enable a patient of ordinary understanding to intelligently decide whether to incur the risk by accepting the proposed treatment or avoid that risk by foregoing it (emphasis supplied).

Would the consent of an insane person be informed consent? See *Aponte v. United States*, 582 F. Supp. 65 (D.P.R. 1984).

(4)   According to *Ritz v. Florida Patient's Compensation Fund*, 436 So. 2d 987 (Fla. App. 1983), most courts require plaintiffs to produce evidence that the appropriate standard of medical care required the physician to inform the patient of the particular risk. In *Chatterton v. Gerson, supra*, the English judge opined: "The duty of the doctor is to explain what he intends to do, and its implications, in the way a careful and responsible doctor in similar circumstances would have done." How does a jury determine whether the duty was breached? *Keel v. St. Elizabeth Medical Center*, 842 S.W.2d 860 (Ky. 1992), is illustrative of cases that hold that no expert testimony is required where the failure to inform is so apparent that lay people would easily recognize it from evidence within the realm of common knowledge. By contrast, other courts apply what is known as the "patient's needs" standard. *Carr v. Strode*, 904 P.2d 489, 500 (Haw. 1995) explained this standard, as follows:

The dispositive inquiry regarding the physician's duty to disclose in an informed consent case, therefore, is not what the physician believes his or her patient needs to hear in order for the patient to make an informed and intelligent decision; the focus should be on what a reasonable person objectively needs to hear from his or her physician to allow the patient to make an informed and intelligent decision regarding proposed medical treatment.

See also *Hudson v. Parvin*, 582 So. 2d 403 (Miss. 1991).

(5) *Phelps v. Dempsey*, 656 So. 2d 377 (Ala.1995) summed up the usual elements of medical malpractice torts, as follows:

> The elements of a cause of action against a physician for failure to obtain informed consent are: (1) the physician's failure to inform the plaintiff of all material risks associated with the procedure, and (2) a showing that a reasonably prudent patient, with all the characteristics of the plaintiff and in the position of the plaintiff, would have declined the procedure had the patient been properly informed by the physician.

Id. 656 So. 2d at 380.

PEDERSON v. DUMOUCHEL
Washington Supreme Court
431 P.2d 973 (1967)

WEAVER, JUDGE.

Plaintiff, as guardian ad litem of Larry C. Neal, a minor, appeals from a judgment, entered after a jury verdict for defendants, dismissing this action with prejudice. We refer to the minor as plaintiff; he reached his majority before trial.

This is an action for damages allegedly arising from medical malpractice. It is against M. L. Dumouchel, a medical doctor; Walter D. Heikel, a dentist; and St. Joseph Hospital, a corporation, in Aberdeen, Washington.

Plaintiff was injured in an automobile accident in the early morning of June 6, 1961. He was placed in St. Joseph Hospital under the care of Dr. M. L. Dumouchel, who first saw him at 8 a.m. After treatment of minor injuries, it was determined that plaintiff had a fractured jaw. Dr. Dumouchel associated Dr. Heikel, a dentist, to reduce plaintiff's fractured jaw under general anesthetic in surgery at the hospital. Dr. Dumouchel, who examined plaintiff prior to surgery, testified, in his opinion, plaintiff did not have any "gross or even minor brain injury."

The operation commenced at 10:20 a.m. the next day, June 7, 1961, and was concluded at noon. Anesthetic was administered by a nurse employed by the hospital. Dr. Heikel, the dentist, testified that he had no working knowledge of the use or administration of a general anesthetic and had left the responsibility and control of the anesthetic to the nurse. Neither Dr. Dumouchel nor any other medical doctor was present in the surgery. Dr. Heikel testified that on 11 prior occasions, when he had reduced a fractured jaw under a general anesthetic in the hospital, a medical doctor had been present; that on only one prior occasion a medical doctor had not been present.

Dr. Dumouchel left the hospital before surgery commenced. Shortly after noon and while in the recovery room, plaintiff suffered convulsive seizures. Dr. Dumouchel could not be located; it was his "afternoon off." No medical doctor was available in the hospital at the time.

About 1:30 p.m. a nurse from the surgical floor located Dr. John D. Fletcher, a surgeon, who was then visiting his patients in the hospital. He examined plaintiff, found him unconscious and experiencing convulsive seizures. Dr. Fletcher performed a spinal tap "to determine the inter-spinal pressure and to determine whether there is any gross blood in the spinal fluid." The spinal tap was essentially normal.

Concluding that plaintiff was suffering "some type of brain injury," Dr. Fletcher consulted Dr. Lawrence Knopp, a neurosurgeon at St. Frances Cabrini Hospital in Seattle. They decided that plaintiff should be removed to Seattle at once.

As plaintiff was being taken to the ambulance about 4:30 p.m., Dr. Dumouchel returned to the hospital and learned for the first time that plaintiff was still unconscious and having seizures.

Dr. Knopp and Dr. William Sata, a neurologist of Seattle, treated plaintiff in the Seattle hospital during the period of nearly a month that he was unconscious following surgery.

The nurse anesthetist testified that she had been a narcotic user from 1958 or 1959 until the month before the surgery. To replace narcotics, she commenced drinking alcohol. August 4, 1961, she was committed to Western State Hospital where she was a patient for 7 months. At the trial she had a bare minimum of independent recollection and relied almost entirely on the anesthesia chart to describe what had transpired in surgery on June 7, 1961. The nurse was hired and paid by the hospital; the hospital billed the patient for her services.

For the purpose of this opinion, it is sufficient to state that the record contains competent, expert, medical testimony, if believed by a jury, to support the conclusion that plaintiff suffered severe and permanent brain damage from cerebral anoxia or hypoxia (complete or partial deprivation of oxygen to the brain) while he was anesthetized during surgery, and that cerebral anoxia or hypoxia was due to inadequate ventilation of the patient during the anesthesia or post-operative period.

Plaintiff's 14 assignments of error present 4 major questions of law:

1. The correctness of the instructions of the trial court concerning the standard of care applicable to doctors, dentists, and hospitals.

2. The failure of the trial court to give a requested instruction on the doctrine of res ipsa loquitur.

3. The correctness of hypothetical questions asked.

4. Alleged improper argument of defense counsel.

Instructions on Standard of Care

As To Doctors and Dentists

Plaintiff's first 7 assignments of error are directed to instructions given; they relate to the standard of care that doctors, dentists, and hospitals must meet. The eighth assignment is directed to the court's refusal to give requested instruction No. 7, which embodies plaintiff's theory of the standard of care that should have been applied.

It would unduly extend this opinion to set forth all the questioned instructions verbatim; however, the nub of the problem is expressed in instruction No. 7, wherein the following language is used:

The standard, I remind you, was set by the learning, skill, care and diligence ordinarily possessed and practiced by others in the same profession in good standing, engaged in like practice, *in the same locality or in similar localities*, and under similar circumstances and at the same time. (Italics ours.)

The same thought (italicized above) is threaded through each of the standard-of-care instructions as they apply to doctors, dentists, and hospitals.

We find some conflicting language in Washington cases concerning the scope or area qualifications of the standard of care applicable to medical doctors. Cases in the first group refer to the standard "in the same community" or "in the locality where he practices." Cases in the second group refer to the standard of care "in the same or similar communities."

Each line of decisions appears to have overlooked the other; although as early as 1913 this court said in a malpractice case:

The instruction is faulty in that it makes the standard of treatment that of the locality alone in which the appellant was practicing; whereas, the true standard is that of all similar localities. *Craneford v. O'Shea*, 75 Wash. 33, 134 P. 486 (1913).

The original reason for the "locality rule" is apparent. When there was little inter-community travel, courts required experts who testified to the standard of care that should have been used to have a personal knowledge of the practice of physicians in that particular community where the patient was treated. It was the accepted theory that a doctor in a small community did not have the same opportunities and resources as did a doctor practicing in a large city to keep abreast of advances in his profession; hence, he should not be held to the same standard of care and skill as that employed by doctors in other communities or in larger cities. Parenthetically, we note that the law of this jurisdiction has never recognized a difference in the professional competency of a lawyer in a small community from that of the professional competency required of a lawyer in a large city.

The "locality rule" had two practical difficulties: first, the scarcity of professional men in the community who were qualified or willing to testify about the local standard of care; and second, the possibility of a small group, who, by their laxness or carelessness, could establish a local standard of care that was below that which the law requires. The fact that several careless practitioners might settle in the same place cannot affect the standard of diligence and skill which local patients have a right to expect. Negligence cannot be excused on the ground that others in the same locality practice the same kind of negligence. No degree of antiquity can give sanction to usage bad in itself.

Broadening the rule to include "similar localities" or "similar communities" alleviated, to a certain extent, the first practical difficulty of the "locality rule" — additional witnesses might be available; but it did little to remove the deficiencies springing from the second.

In *Teig v. St. John's Hospital*, 63 Wash. 2d 369, 387 P.2d 527 (1963), this court approached modifying the "similar locality" rule, for it upheld the admission of expert testimony by a Portland, Oregon doctor in a malpractice action arising in Longview, Washington. The court took judicial notice that Longview and Portland are approximately 50 miles apart. We take further judicial notice that they are not "similar localities or similar communities." It was not necessary for the court to examine the rule, however, for the Portland doctor testified he was familiar with the standards of general practitioners in the vicinity of Portland *and Longview.*

Now there is no lack of opportunity for a physician or surgeon to keep abreast of the advances made in his profession and to be familiar with the latest methods and practices adopted.

The comprehensive coverage of the Journal of the American Medical Association, the availability of numerous other journals, the ubiquitous "detail men" of the drug companies, closed circuit television presentations of medical subjects, special radio networks for physicians, tape recorded digests of medical literature, and hundreds of widely available postgraduate courses all serve to keep physicians informed and increasingly to establish nationwide standards. Medicine realizes this, so it is inevitable that the law will do likewise. Louisell and Williams, The Parenchyma of Law (Professional Medical Publications, Rochester, N.Y. 1960) p. 183.

We have found no better statement of existing conditions. The "locality rule" has no present day vitality except that it may be considered as *one* of the elements to determine the degree of care and skill which is to be expected of the average practitioner of the class to which he belongs. The degree of care which must be observed is, of course, that of an average, competent practitioner acting in the same or similar circumstances. In other words, local practice within geographic proximity is one, but not the only factor to be considered. No longer is it proper to limit the definition of the standard of care which a medical doctor or dentist must meet solely to the practice or custom of a particular locality, a similar locality, or a geographic area.

The "locality rule" has never been suggested in any English case. (Nathan, Medical Negligence (Butterworth & Co., Ltd. 1957), p. 21.) In England, the same standard is applicable throughout the country. The extent of our country is such, however, that we hestitate to fix a definite geographic limit upon the standard of care — be it statewide or expanded to the Pacific Northwest, as suggested by plaintiff's requested instruction.

A qualified medical or dental practitioner should be subject to liability, in an action for negligence, if he fails to exercise that degree of care and skill which is expected of the average practitioner in the class to which he belongs, acting in the same or similar circumstances. This standard of care is that established in an area coextensive with the medical and professional means available in those centers that are readily accessible for appropriate treatment of the patient. The instant case is a good example: plaintiff was taken almost immediately from Aberdeen to Seattle, a distance of 110 miles.

We conclude, therefore, that plaintiff's assignments of error to the instructions given are well-taken, and plainitff is granted a new trial against Dr. Dumouchel and Dr. Heikel. . . .

Instructions on Standard

of Care as to Hospitals

Much that we have said also applies to the jury instructions given concerning hospitals. They, too, are members of national organizations and subject to accreditation. We appreciate, however, that in addition to administrative supervision, they are also governed by physical facilities that influence their accreditation.

Whether a hospital is accredited or not (and defendant hospital is accredited), we conclude that it is negligence as a matter of law for a hospital to permit a surgical operation upon a patient under general anesthetic without the presence and supervision of a medical doctor in the operating room, in the absence of extraordinary and emergent circumstances.

Our conclusion is fortified by the fact that the hospital permitted the breach of one of its own rules.

Patients requiring dental service may be co-admitted by a member of the medical staff and a local dentist who is qualified, legally, professionally and ethically to practice here. The former shall perform an adequate medical examination prior to dental surgery, and be responsible for the patient's medical care. Rule and Regulation No. 5 of St. Joseph Hospital, p. 16.

Dr. Dumouchel did not assume the responsibility "for the patient's medical care" while in surgery.

The judgment dismissing this action against the hospital is reversed, and the case is remanded for a new trial limited to a determination of whether the hospital's negligence was a proximate cause of plaintiff's injury, if any, and if so, the amount of damages.

AETNA INSURANCE CO. v. HELLMUTH, OBATA & KASSABAUM, INC.

United States Court of Appeals, Eighth Circuit
392 F.2d 472 (1968)

GIBSON, Circuit Judge.

This case concerns the alleged negligence of an architect in supervising the construction of a project. The appellant Aetna Insurance Company, a Corporation, (Aetna) sued Hellmuth, Obata & Kassabaum, Inc., hereafter referred to as "Architect," for damages occasioned by the alleged negligent failure of the Architect in supervising the construction of a Terminal Plaza at Lambert-St. Louis Airport.

The jury awarded Aetna damages of $15,000 but the District Court (E.D. Mo.) sustained the Architect's Motion for Judgment in Accordance with its Motion for a Directed Verdict (n.o.v.) and alternatively awarded a new trial on all issues. Aetna appeals from the judgment entered n.o.v. and asks a remand for a new trial. The alternative new trial was awarded on the basis of inadequacies and errors in the instructions and these issues are not presented on this appeal. We reverse and remand for a new trial. . . .

We think an architect whose contractual duties include supervision of a construction project has the duty to supervise the project with reasonable diligence and care. An architect is not a guarantor or an insurer but as a member of a learned and skilled profession he is under the duty to exercise the ordinary, reasonable technical skill, ability and competence that is required of an architect in a similar situation; and if by reason of a failure to use due care under the circumstances, a foreseeable injury results, liability accrues. Whether the required standard of care was exercised presents a jury question. *Miller v. DeWitt*, 59 Ill.

App. 2d 38, 208 N.E.2d 249, 284 (1965), aff'd in relevant part, 37 Ill.2d 273, 226 N.E.2d 630 (Ill. 1967).

This question was also considered by Judge Donovan in the Minnesota case *of Peerless, supra,* who aptly noted at pp. 953, 954 of 199 F.Supp.:

". . . the standards of reasonable care, which apply to the conduct of architects, are the same as those applying to lawyers, doctors, engineers, and like professional men engaged in furnishing skilled services for compensation . . . "; and that general negligence principles apply — ". . . reasonable care, which is such care as a person of ordinary prudence would have exercised under the same or similar circumstances. . . " is imposed on an architect as related to the skill, ability and professional competence ordinarily required of a person licensed to practice that profession. Also see, *Fidelity & Casualty Company of New York v. J. A. Jones Construction Company,* 325 F.2d 605 (8 Cir. 1963) (recognizing architect's liability to third parties for negligent supervision of a construction project).

Appellee Architect also contends that Aetna failed to establish the standard of care owed by a supervising architect, failed to show a breach of any standard, failed to show any damages proximately resulting from the alleged negligence, and, therefore, failed to make a submissible case. Since this case will be re-tried no purpose would be served in elaborating on the evidence. The standard of care applicable is that of ordinary reasonable care required of a professional skilled architect under the same or similar circumstances in carrying out his technical duties in relation to the services undertaken by his agreement. This includes the knowledge and experience ordinarily required of a member of that profession and includes the performing of skills necessary in adequately coping with engineering and construction problems, which skills are ordinarily not possessed by laymen. The words in the architect's contract requiring "supervision of construction" or words of similar import are not words of art and should be accorded their ordinary and usual denotation. This should be true in the absence of evidence showing a different or more restrictive connotation. There is, however, evidence in the record of what an architect would ordinarily be required to do under the circumstances presented. While this evidence is not as extensive as might be desirable, it was sufficient to make a submissible case on negligence and damages.

The Architect asserts that the word "supervision" is a word of art and that evidence must be presented of what constituted due care in the exercise of professional supervision. We do not think the common term "supervision" is used as, or understood to be, a word of art in the construction contract. If it is a word of art, the general rule requiring expert testimony to establish the standard of care applied to professions requiring knowledge, competency and technical skill would be applicable. *Morgan v. Rosenberg,* 370 S.W.2d 685 (St. L. Ct. App. 1963), clearly held expert medical testimony is essential to establish the standard of proper skill and care required of a physician, as laymen have insufficient knowledge to pass upon that issue. The requirement of expert testimony on the standard of care was applied to architects in *Paxton v. Alameda County,* 119 Cal.App.2d 393, 259 P.2d 934, 938 (1953); and in *Pittman Construction Company v. City of New Orleans,* 178 So. 2d 312, 321 (Ct. App., La. 1965).

Most of the cases stating the general rule on expert testimony to establish the standard of professional care required deal with physicians and surgeons, but the sample principle is applicable to attorneys, architects and engineers and other professional men. As Prosser, Law of Torts (3rd Ed.) points out at 164:

Professional men in general, and those who undertake any work calling for special skill, are required not only to exercise reasonable care in what they do, but also to possess a standard minimum of special knowledge and ability.

Prosser notes that expert testimony is necessary to establish the standard of care required of those engaged in practicing medicine, as laymen are normally incompetent to pass judgment on questions of medical science or technique, but that

Where the matter is regarded as within the common knowledge of laymen, as where the surgeon saws off the wrong leg, or there is injury to a part of the body not within the operative field, it has been held that the jury may infer negligence without the aid of any expert. *Id.* p. 167.

It is a matter of common knowledge that it is often difficult to secure the services of a professional man to testify in a case involving a claim of dereliction of duty by a fellow member in the profession. This undoubtedly holds true in architectural circles as well as others. There is some evidence in the case at bar regarding the duties of an architect in supervising a construction project and in carrying out his contract duties. This evidence is not as extensive as is desired but was sufficient to make a submissible case. It does appear that there are certain duties patently required of the architect that are within the common knowledge and experience of laymen serving as jurors. It requires no particular technical knowledge on the part of the jury to pass upon the failure to supervise the back-filling of the sewer ditch when specifically required under the contract, the failure to correct misaligned forms utilized in retaining and supporting a poured concrete wall, or the significance of a sewer pipe that is misaligned and crooked. The jury is competent to pass on these issues without knowledge of the professional skills and competency required of architects in the ordinary performance of their skilled duties. Questions relating to stress and strain and weight-bearing capacities of structural elements are beyond the ordinary comprehension of most laymen and the court and jury require expert enlightenment on issues of this type. It, therefore, appears that the general rule requiring expert testimony to establish a reasonable standard of professional care is necessary when issues are presented that are beyond the ordinary competency of laymen jurors, but is not necessary in passing on commonplace factual situations that the ordinary jury layman can readily grasp and understand.

We think that sufficient evidence is in the record to justify the submission of the issue of the Architect's negligence and that upon a re-trial more consideration can be given to any technical questions involved in the submission.

Reversed and remanded for proceedings not inconsistent with this opinion.

NOTES AND QUESTIONS

(1) How does the standard of care for architects differ from that for medical doctors? *Aetna Insurance Co. v. Hellmuth el al.* is in apparent accord with the consensus view. See, *e.g., Loyland v. Stone & Webster Engineering Corp.*, 514 P.2d 184 (Wash. App. 1973).

(2)   As to lawyers, it is said in "rendering legal services, an attorney must perform in such manner as lawyers of ordinary skill and capacity possess and exercise." *Heyer* v. *Flaig*, 449 P.2d 161 (Cal. 1969). See also *Hughes v. Klein*, 427 A.2d 353 (Vt. 1981) ("customary skill and knowledge").

(3)   It would be erroneous to assume that all courts have retreated from the locality rule as to medical doctors or to assume that it does not apply to other professions. For example, in *Dean v. Conn.* 419 So. 2d 148, 150 (Miss. 1982), the court said:

Generally, the same standards of professional conduct are applicable to the attorney and physician alike, namely:

(1) Both are required to use that degree of care, skill and diligence which is commonly possessed and exercised by attorneys/physicians in that locality.

(2) Neither is an insurer or guarantor of results which will be attained.

(3) Unsuccessful results do not give rise to a presumption of negligence.

(4) Both are liable only for negligent failure to use the requisite care and skill.

And, in *Hodge v. Carter*, 80 S.E. 114 (N.C., 1954), the same or similar locality rule was applied to lawyers.

(4)   Is there a class of cases in which a jury should not be permitted to find a medical doctor negligent in the absence of expert testimony? Explain. Is there a class of cases in which expert testimony of due care might be ignored by a jury? See, *e.g.*, *Atkins v. Hume*, 110 So. 2d 663 (Fla. 1959), and *Boyce v. Brown*, 77 P.2d 455 (Ariz. 1955). See also *Willage v. Law Offices of Wallace & Breslow*, 415 So. 2d 767 (Fla. App. 1982).

(5)   Because of a surge of medical malpractice cases and recoveries, some states have passed statutes interposing mediation, arbitration or other forms of dispute resolution prior to trial. See Chapter 18, *infra*, for elaboration. One mediation statute was invalidated on grounds that it capriciously denied due process under the state constitution. *Aldana v. Holub*, 381 So. 2d 231 (Fla. 1980).

§ 6.08   MODIFIED STANDARD — COMMON CARRIERS & HAZARDOUS ACTIVITIES

BLUEFLAME GAS, INC. v. VAN HOOSE
Colorado Supreme Court
679 P.2d 579 (1984)

QUINN, JUSTICE.

We granted and consolidated these three separate petitions for certiorari, filed by the petitioner-defendants, to review the court of appeals' decision in *Van Hoose v. Blueflame Gas, Inc.*, 642 P.2d 36 (Colo. App. 1981). The respondent-plaintiffs, James and Louisa Van Hoose, had sued the petitioner-defendants, Phillips Oil Company (Phillips), Diamond Shamrock Corporation (Diamond Shamrock), and

Blueflame Gas, Inc. (Blueflame), for damages resulting from a propane gas explosion in their home. The court of appeals reversed a judgment for the defendants and ordered a new trial because, in its view, the trial court erroneously instructed the jury on the standard of care applicable to suppliers of propane gas. . . . We affirm the judgment of the court of appeals.

I.

James and Louisa Van Hoose filed suit against Phillips, Diamond Shamrock, and Blueflame for damages as the result of injuries sustained by James in a gas explosion at their home in Pueblo County, Colorado, on July 23, 1972. The complaint included separate claims in negligence and strict liability in tort. The claim in negligence alleged that the defendants failed to properly odorize the propane gas with ethyl mercaptan, as required by an administrative regulation promulgated by the State Inspector of Oils, failed to test for appropriate odorization prior to the sale of the propane to the Van Hooses, and failed to warn them of the inadequate odorization.

. . .

[Plaintiffs used propane in their household. An explosion occurred causing the complained of damages. The evidence supported findings that a cause was the accumulation of propane gas in the basement of the dwelling. The gas in its natural state is odorless. The negligent claim alleged that the defendants had negligently failed to odorize the gas, thereby denying plaintiffs an opportunity to detect the accumulating gas.]

At the conclusion of the evidence the plaintiffs tendered an instruction that, in addition to noting that "[t]he degree of care must be equal to the degree of danger involved", stated that "one who has in his possession, or under his control, an exceptionally dangerous instrumentality is bound to take exceptional precautions to prevent an injury being done by the instrumentality." The trial court refused this instruction and, after defining negligence as the failure to use reasonable care, gave Instruction No. 12 which stated that "[r]easonable care is that degree of care which a reasonably prudent person would use under the same or similar circumstances." Plaintiffs' counsel objected to Instruction No. 12 on the ground that his tendered instruction set forth the appropriate standard of care applicable to the negligence claim.

. . .

The jury returned verdicts in favor of the defendants on all claims. The plaintiffs thereafter appealed to the court of appeals which reversed the judgment and ordered a new trial. With regard to the negligence claim the court of appeals held that the plaintiffs, having properly objected to the instruction (Instruction No. 12) given by the court on the standard of care, were entitled to an instruction on an enhanced standard of care applicable to suppliers of propane gas.

. . .

II.

Before we examine the trial court's instructions on the standard of care applicable to a propane supplier and on the plaintiffs' burden of proof on their strict liablity claim under § 402A of the Restatement (Second) of Torts, we must consider as a threshold matter whether the plaintiffs' objections to the challenged instructions were adequate to preserve the issue of their correctness for appellate review. The defendants claim that appellate review of the propriety of these instructions was foreclosed by reason of the general nature of the objections. In our view the plaintiffs' objection to the instruction on the standard of care applicable to a propane supplier (Instruction No. 12) was adequate to preserve this issue for appellate review.

. . .

C.R.C.P. 51 states, in pertinent part, that "[a]ll instructions shall be submitted to the parties, who shall make all objections thereto before they are given to the jury," and that "[o]nly the grounds so specified shall be considered on motion for a new trial or on appeal or certiorari." The purpose of this requirement is to "enable trial judges to clarify or correct misleading or erroneous instructions before they are given to the jury, and thereby prevent costs of retrials necessitated by obvious and prejudicial error." *Scheer v. Cromwell*, 158 Colo. 427, 429, 407 P.2d 344, 345 (1965). A general objection that states no ground of error is the equivalent of no objection at all because it deprives the trial court of any meaningful opportunity to correct its own error . . . Where, however, the objection sufficiently directs the court's attention to the asserted error, the purpose of C.R.C.P. 51 has been satisfied. See *Lewis v. La Nier*, 84 Colo. 376, 270 P. 656 (1928).

In objecting to Instruction No. 12, which delineated the standard of care applicable to the plaintiffs' negligence claim, plaintiffs' counsel stated that the correct standard of care had been set out in his tendered instruction on this point of controversy. The tendered instruction referred to by plaintiffs' counsel stated basically that the degree of care must be commensurate with the danger and that one in possession of "an exceptionally dangerous instrumentality" must take "exceptional precautions" to prevent injury to others. The objection to Instruction No. 12 was sufficient to direct the court's attention to the legal question relating to the standard of care and provided the court with an opportunity to correct any error in the challenged instruction.

. . .

III.

The trial court, in Instruction No. 12, defined the standard of care applicable to the plaintiffs' negligence claim as "that degree of care which a reasonably prudent person would use under the same or similar circumstances." The court of appeals, in reversing the judgment and ordering a new trial, held that the trial court erred in giving Instruction No. 12. We agree with the court of appeals that the trial court erred in instructing on reasonable care, rather than a higher degree of care, in connection with the plaintiffs' negligence claim.

It is axiomatic in the law of negligence that the greater the risk, the greater the amount of care required to avoid injury to others. . . . Thus, greater care may be required of one who dispenses a product in the stream of commerce when the product itself, by virtue of its inherent character, poses a high risk of injury to others. . . .

Electricity is an example of an instrumentality requiring an enhanced degree of care by those supplying it to others for domestic and commercial use. In *Denver Consolidated Electric Co. v. Simpson*, 21 Colo. 371, 376–77, 41 P. 499, 501 (1895), the court held that an electric utility company must be held to the "highest degree of care which skill and foresight can attain consistent with the practical conduct of its business under the known methods and the present state of the particular art." *Accord Federal Insurance Co. v. Public Service Co.*, 194 Colo. 107, 570 P.2d 239 (1977);[29]

Blankette v. Public Service Co, 90 Colo. 456, 10 P.2d 327 (1932). There are other substances that, due to the gravity of the risk created by them, require an emhanced measure of care on the part of distributors. See, *e.g., Ambriz v. Petrolane, Ltd.*, 49 Cal.2d 470, 319 P.2d 1 (1957) (high degree of care required of those handling butane gas); *Crane v. Adams*, 226 Miss. 436, 84 So. 2d 530 (1956) (gasoline is a "dangerous agency" requiring highest degree of care); *Hammond v. Nebraska Natural Gas Co.*, 204 Neb. 80, 281 N.W.2d 520 (1979) (distributor of natural gas, a dangerous commodity, was required to exercise a high degree of care to prevent injury to public from escaped gas); *Herman v. Midland Ag Service*, 200 Neb. 356, 264 N.W.2d 161 (1978) (explosive potential of anhydrous ammonia fertilizer calls for highest degree of care by supplier). Applying the maxim that a dangerous substance requires a degree of care commensurate with the gravity of the risk, other courts have required suppliers of propane to exercise an enhanced degree of care to prevent injury to others from its escape. . . .

Although this court has made no express statement on the amount of care required of propane suppliers, we have recognized that it is a "dangerous substance" to be "handled with the care and caution commensurate with its dangerous character." *Grange Mutual Fire Insurance Co. v. Golden Gas Co.*, 133 Colo. at 543, 298 P.2d at 953; *accord Ward v. Aero-Spray, Inc.*, 170 Colo. 26, 458 P.2d 744 (1969). In view of the gravity of the risk posed by vaporized propane, the presence of which is undetectable without the addition of an appropriate odorizer, those involved in its distribution should take special precautions to provide warning to persons that escaping gas is in their midst. We therefore hold that suppliers of propane must exercise the highest degree of care, consistent with the practical conduct of their business under the present state of the art, in making certain that the propane is sufficiently odorized so that those persons who use this substance as a source of energy for heaters, stoves and other appliances will be alerted to the presence of escaping gas.

The trial court erred in defining the defendants' duty as one of reasonable care only. Instead, the court should have informed the jury by appropriate instruction that, because of its dangerous character, the defendants were obliged to exercise the highest degree of care with respect to the odorization of the propane sold to the plaintiffs. An instruction formulated in terms of the highest degree of care is nothing more than a plain statement to the jury that the inordinate risk posed by escaping propane requires an amount of care commensurate with that risk.

---

[29] In *Federal Insurance*, the court observed that compelling reasons continue to exist to warrant the highest degree of care on the part of electrical utility companies because "(1) electrical energey possesses inherently dangerous properties, (2) electric utilities possess expertise in dealing with electric phenomena and in operating facilities for delivery of electricity, and (3) the general public is not able to recognize and guard against the dangerous potential of certain situations." 194 Colo. at 112, 570 P.2d at 242.

NOTE

That common carriers owe their patrons a standard of care higher than ordinary negligence is rooted deep in the common law and is probably accepted in some form by all jurisdictions. Still, as *Vaughn v. New Orleans Public Service, Inc.*, 314 So. 2d 545 (La. App. 1975), demonstrates, the standard is not strict liability. Some courts also elevate various other activities to a higher (or highest) standard of care. For example, as noted in *Van Hoose*, many hold suppliers of electricity to an elevated standard in connection with the electrical system. See, *e.g., City of Starkville v. Delta Utility Co.*, 418 So. 2d 51 (Miss. 1982).

§ 6.09 STATUTORY MODIFICATIONS

SPENCE v. VAUGHT
Arkansas Supreme Court
367 S.W.2d 238 (1963)

JOHNSON, JUSTICE.

This cases involves the Arkansas guest statutes, Ark. Stats. §§ 75-913-75-915. The action was instituted by appellees DeWitt Vaught and Georgia Vaught, his wife, against appellant Lucy Spence for damages resulting from an automobile accident occurring on February 11, 1962. Appellant and appellee Mrs. Vaught had attended Sunday school and church at Houston, Arkansas, although they lived in Perryville. Mrs. Vaught had gone to Houston with her daughter, who left early. Mrs. Vaught asked appellant, who is Mr. Vaught's aunt, for a ride back to Perryville. About two miles out of Houston the automobile veered to the right off the road and into a ditch. The automobile turned over, injuring appellee severely.

Trial of the case before a jury resulted in a verdict in favor of appellees. For reversal of the judgment on the verdict, appellant contends that there is no evidence of willful and wanton misconduct on the part of the appellant and a verdict for the appellant should have been directed by the trial court.

The Arkansas guest statute referred to above, Ark. Stats. § 75-913, reads as follows:

No person transported as a guest in any automotive vehicle upon the public highways or in aircraft being flown in the air, or while upon the ground, shall have a cause of action against the owner or operator of such vehicle, or aircraft, for damage on account of any injury, death or loss occasioned by the operation of such automotive vehicle or aircraft unless such vehicle or aircraft was wilfully and wantonly operated in disregard of the rights of others.

The operative portion of § 75-915 is as follows:

No person transported or proposed to be transported by the owner or operator of a motor vehicle as a guest, without payment for such transportation, nor the husband, widow, executors, administrators or next of kin of such person, shall have a cause of action for damages against such owner or operator, or other persons responsible for the operation of such car, for personal injury, including death resulting there-from, by persons while in, entering, or leaving such motor vehicle, unless such injury shall have been caused by the willful misconduct of such owner or operator.

Each personal injury case involving the guest statutes must be examined on its own. As we said in *Harkrider v. Cox*, 230 Ark. 155, 321 S.W.2d 226,

[I]t is a question in each case whether the particular facts therein made a jury question as to willful and wanton negligence.

. . . In *McAllister, Administrator v. Calhoun*, 212 Ark. 17, 205 S.W.2d 40, 42, we quoted with approval from *Splawn, Administratix v. Wright*, 198 Ark. 197, 128 S.W. 2d 248: 'Whether an automobile is being operated in such a manner as to amount to wanton and willful conduct in disregard of the rights of others must be determined by the facts and circumstances of each individual case.

The evidence presented in the case at bar is, naturally, controverted. According to Mrs. Vaught's testimony, the car had began to make a singing noise, then a grinding noise, and then a swerve lasting over some period of time, with Mrs. Vaught making warnings to appellant to slow down to see what the trouble was, and with appellant ignoring her warnings. According to appellant, the accident happened very quickly, with there being a sudden swerve and the car veering into the ditch, and at no time were there any warnings from Mrs. Vaught. Appellee Vaught and another witness testified that there was a rim cut on the highway and rubber marks about 3/10ths of a mile or more long leading up to the rim cut. Appellant's husband testified to a gouge or cut in the highway made by a tire rim about 15 or 20 feet from where the car ended up, but would swear to no other marks. Mrs. Vaught testified appellant was driving 50 to 60 miles per hour and did not slow up. Appellant testified that her speed was 45 to 50, that the accident was instantaneous and that she never could find the tire or wheel marks.

Appellant moved for a directed verdict at the close of appellees' testimony, which was overruled. The criterion for trial courts in considering motions for directed verdicts is well-stated in *Smith v. McEachin*, 186 Ark. 1132, 57 S.W.2d 1043:

It is a rule of universal application that, where the testimony is undisputed and from it all reasonable minds must draw the same conclusion of fact, it is the duty of the court to declare as a matter of law the conclusion to be reached, but, where there is any substantial evidence to support the verdict, the question must be submitted to the jury. In testing whether or not there is any substantial evidence in a given case, the evidence and all reasonable inferences deducible there-from should be viewed in the light most favorable to the party against whom the verdict is directed, and, if there is any conflict in the evidence, or where the evidence is not in dispute but is in such a state that fair-minded men might draw different conclusions there-from, it is error to direct a verdict.

Examining the record to determine "the state of the evidence", it is relevant to review the types of negligence and their standards for determination. Negligence is the failure to use ordinary care. *Johnson v. Coleman*, 179 Ark. 1087, 20 S.W.2d 186. Gross negligence is the failure to use even slight care. *Memphis & L. R. R. R. v. Sanders*, 43 Ark. 225. Willful negligence is the same as gross negligence with the added factor that the actor knows, or the situation is so extremely dangerous that he should know, that his act or failure to act will probably cause harm. *Scott v. Shairrick*, 225 Ark. 59, 279 S.W.2d 39.

Applying these standards to the situation as testified to by appellee, it is not illogical to conclude that appellant was negligent when she failed to slow down after the car started humming; she was grossly negligent when she failed to slow down after the car began swerving; and she was wilfully or wantonly negligent in failing to slow down after the grinding noise started, the car swerved more violently, she was twice warned to slow down, and she still continued to drive at the same speed of about fifty miles per hour. Viewing the evidence and all reasonable inferences deducible there-from in the light most favorable to the party against whom the directed verdict was sought, we find that fair-minded men might draw different conclusions there-from, and that therefore the trial court did not err in failing to direct a verdict for appellant.

Appellant's remaining point urged for reversal is that the giving of plaintiffs' (appellees') instruction No. 5 constituted prejudicial error.

Plaintiffs' requested instruction No. 5 reads as follows:

The plaintiffs have alleged that the defendant was negligent in one or more of the following respects:

(2) failing to keep her vehicle under proper control and

(3) in operating the automobile at a speed in excess of that which was reasonable and prudent under the circumstances then existing.

You are instructed that under the laws of the State of Arkansas it was the duty of the defendant, Lucy Spence, to exercise ordinary care in the operation of her vehicle to avoid injury to others, and that a failure on her part to exercise such care would be evidence of negligence. Ordinary care requires every person who operates a motor vehicle upon a public highway to keep his or her vehicle under such control as will enable him or her to check its speed, or to stop it absolutely, if necessary to avoid injury where danger is apparent or reasonably to be anticipated by the exercise of ordinary care. Further, it was the duty of the defendant to exercise ordinary care to operate her vehicle at a speed no greater than was reasonable and prudent under the circumstances, and that a failure to do so would be evidence of negligence.

You are further instructed in that connection that the lawful maximum speed at which the defendant's vehicle might have been operated at the time and place of the accident here involved was that speed which was reasonable and prudent under the circumstances, but not to exceed 60 miles per hour in any event, and should you find that defendant's vehicle was being operated at the time and place of the accident here involved at a speed which was not reasonable and prudent under the circumstances this would be evidence of negligence to be considered along with other circumstances in the case.

Appellant forceably contends that the giving of this instruction was error because it refers to the duty to exercise ordinary care, and, this being a guest statute case, this instruction could only lead to the confusion of the jury and probably caused the jury to conclude that appellant was under a duty to exercise ordinary care rather than under a duty to avoid being guilty of willful and wanton misconduct.

A careful review of the record reveals that not only was willful and wanton negligence or misconduct defined or required in plaintiffs' instructions No. 1, No. 3,

No. 9 and No. 11, but also in plaintiffs' instruction No. 6, given immediately after the alleged erroneous instruction. Instruction No. 6 reads as follows:

Now should you find from a preponderance of the evidence that the defendant, Lucy Spence, was guilty of negligence in one or more of the respects alleged by the plaintiff, as just related to you, this negligence, without more, would not entitle the plaintiffs to maintain this action, or to recover their damages, if any. As you have previously been instructed, to recover in this action, if at all, plaintiffs must prove by a preponderance of the evidence that the defendant was guilty of willful and wanton conduct. They must prove not only that the defendant was negligent, but also that she knew, or had reason to believe, that her act of negligence was about to inflict injury, and that she continued in this course of conduct with a conscious indifference to the consequences thereof, exhibiting a wanton disregard of the rights and safety of others.

When all the instructions are thus considered, we cannot say that they incorrectly presented the law, or that the jury could have been misled thereby. *Pinkerton v. Davis*, 212 Ark. 706, 207 S.W.2d 742.

Affirmed.

HARRIS, CHIEF JUSTICE (dissenting).

In my opinion, the present decision by the court greatly weakens the effectiveness of the Guest Statutes. Appellee, in arguing for affirmance of this case, makes a statement in her brief with which I entirely agree. After reviewing a number of cases, decided under the Guest Statutes, she states, "This review also indicates a trend of the Court toward allowing guest cases to go to the jury under more liberal requirements of proof than in the earlier cases decided immediately after passage of the Guest Statutes." Certainly, I cannot believe that the verdict for appellee would have been upheld under earlier decisions.

. . .

I certainly agree that Mrs. Spence was guilty of ordinary negligence, but I cannot agree that her negligence reached the category of willful and wanton misconduct. It is obvious from the proof that a tire on the Spence automobile was losing air, which occasioned the "humming" sound that was heard. The majority state:

". . . it is not illogical to conclude that appellant was negligent when she failed to slow down after the car started humming; she was grossly negligent when she failed to slow down after the car began swerving; and she was wilfully or wantonly negligent in failing to slow down after the grinding noise started, the car swerved more violently, she was twice warned to slow down, and she still continued to drive at the same speed of about fifty miles per hour."

From the evidence, all of the above took place in less than a minute, and, as far as willful and wanton negligence is concerned, (according to the majority, "when the grinding noise started") this only lasted for a very few seconds! On a clear day and straight highway, Mrs. Spence was driving at a moderate and legal rate of speed. Because of her inability to recognize that the tire was going flat, the accident occurred. I reiterate my belief that she was guilty of ordinary negligence, but I do not consider that these circumstances establish willful and wanton negligence.

I, therefore, respectfully dissent.

NOTES AND QUESTIONS

(1) Not all states enacted guest statutes shielding drivers of automobiles against ordinary negligence vis-a-vis gratuitous guest passengers. A court in one of the states that did not has said that:

> The driver of a motor vehicle is required to exercise reasonable and ordinary care to avoid injury to his gratuitous guest passengers. He is required to exercise a greater degree of care when children are involved. He is not bound to exercise the highest practicable degree of care, as is a common carrier, however, nor is he an insurer of the safety of his passengers. The guest passenger is entitled to rely on the assumption that the driver will use ordinary and reasonable care for his safety, and any act of negligence or fault on the part of the driver which causes injury to such a passenger gives rise to an action for damages under the general tort law of this state.

Murray v. Volkswagen Mid-American, Inc., 297 So. 2d 236 (La. App. 1974).

(2) Guest statutes have proved to be unpopular. Some states have repealed them, and a few have been rendered unconstitutional by the courts. See, *e.g., Brown v. Merlo*, 506 P.2d 212 (Cal. 1973).

(3) As *Spence v. Vaught* illustrates, guest statutes typically lower the standard of care of an operator of a motor vehicle to impose liability to a gratuitous guest occupant only for gross negligence, or willful and wanton negligence. These criteria raise issues about the meanings of the term "guest" and of those various definitions of negligence. See *Roe v. Lewis*, 416 So. 2d 750 (Ala. 1982), for a discussion of the meanings of the former term and *Tew v. Jones*, 417 So. 2d 146 (Ala. 1982), for the latter. How does *Spence v. Vaught* define "wanton?" An oft-quoted definition is:

> Wantonness [is] the conscious doing of some act or omission of some duty under knowledge of the existing conditions and conscious that from the doing of such act or omission of such duty injury will likely or probably result. Before a party can be said to be guilty of wanton conduct, it must be shown that with reckless indifference to the consequences he consciously and intentionally did some wrongful act or omitted some known duty which produced the injury.

See, *e.g., Garreans v. City of Omaha*, 345 N.W.2d 309 (Neb. 1984). See also *Phillips ex rel. Phillips v. United Services Auto. Ass'n*, 988 So. 2d 464 (Ala.2008) which held that a driver's waving to friends outside the car, causing her to lose control and crash, was an "inattentive, thoughtless, or heedless, i.e., negligent" act but that it did not satisfy the "willful or wanton misconduct" standard for liability under the Alabama guest statute.

(4) The following is an example of numerous statutes that modify common law tort rules as they apply in specific contexts. A lawyer must always consult local statutes to ascertain whether there is a statute pertaining to an issue at hand:

> Florida Statutes Annotated. 768.125 Liability for injury or damage resulting from intoxication.

A person who sells or furnishes alcoholic beverages to a person of lawful drinking age shall not thereby become liable for injury or damage caused by or resulting from the intoxication of such person, except that a person who willfully and unlawfully sells or furnishes alcoholic beverages to a person who is not of lawful drinking age or who knowingly serves a person habitually addicted to the use of any or all alcoholic beverages may become liable for injury or damage caused by or resulting from the intoxication of such minor or person.

(5) Some courts apply a lower standard of care as to injuries suffered while participating in sporting activities. See, *e.g.*, *Marchetti v. Kalish*, 559 N.E. 2d 699, 704 (Ohio 1990), holding: "We join the weight of authority . . . and require that before a party may be provided with a cause of action involving injury resulting from a recreational or sports activity, reckless or intentional conduct must exist." By contrast *Lestina v. West Bend Mutual Insurance Company*, 501 N.W. 2d 901, 912 (Wis. 1993), held: "We see no need for the court to adopt a recklessness standard for recreational team contact sports when the negligence-standard, properly understood and applied is appropriate."

Chapter 7

CAUSE-IN-FACT

§ 7.01 INTRODUCTORY PROBLEM

Plaintiff owned and operated a hotel that lay 400 feet north-north-east of defendant's saw mill. Included in the mill was an incinerator to burn sawdust, bark and other wood wastes. The hotel burned down on October 15, 1997. Eighteen years earlier, in 1979, the mill's incinerator chimney had spewed out a torrent of burning wood particles, some of which were seen to float through the air and land on the top of the house directly across the street from the hotel, setting it afire. That house lay 390 feet from the mill. In 1980, 12 feet were added to the chimney of the mill for the purpose of dispersing the effluent over a broader geographic area, thus to lessen the risk to nearby buildings. All these facts were proved at trial. Also introduced was testimony of several people who had seen burning particles from the heightened chimney light in fields, gardens and yards, setting fire to straw and charring clothes hanging out to dry. None of these occurred on the day the hotel burned. Evidence also was adduced that the mill and incinerator were in operation on the day and hour that the fire in the hotel was first detected. The hotel was totally destroyed by the fire, and no direct evidence proved the cause. The fire chief testified that it was his opinion that the fire had begun either on the roof or in the third floor of the three-floor structure. This was based upon his observation of the location of the fire when he arrived at the scene.

At the close of the plaintiff's case in which the foregoing evidence was adduced, the defendant moved for a directed verdict.

Should it be granted?

§ 7.02 GENERAL

[See cases § 4.03, *supra.*]

NOTE

To encourage precise thinking and a clear understanding of the distinguishable concepts, this text divides causation into the two elements, cause-in-fact and proximate cause. Regrettably, however, some courts fail to employ this distinction in the language they use in deciding cases. Consequently, some courts use the term "proximate cause" or the more general term "legal cause" to mean cause-in-fact on some occasions, proximate cause as that term is used in this text on other occasions, and a composite concept based upon consideration of both factors in still others. The opinions in *Magarian v. Bessoni*, 280 A.2d 357 (Conn. 1971), and in *Asgrow-Kilgore Co. v. Milford Hickerson Corp.*, 301 So.2d 441 (Fla. 1974), illustrate this kind of imprecision. In the interest of clear analysis, these concepts should be distinguished with precision in evaluating causation in any context.

§ 7.03   CIRCUMSTANTIAL PROOF

ZINNEL v. BERGHUIS CONSTRUCTION CO.
Minnesota Supreme Court
274 N.W.2d 495 (1979)

PETERSON, JUSTICE.

Plaintiff E. Lester Zinnel and his family were involved in a two-automobile collision on a bypass of a highway under construction by defendants Berghuis Construction Company and Minnesota Valley Improvement Company near Madelia, Minnesota, on January 2, 1973. Plaintiff and his two children were injured, and his wife died as a result of the collision. Third-party defendant, Albert M. Teigum, driver of the second automobile, also died as a result of the collision. Plaintiff alleged negligence by defendants in the signing, striping, and barricading of the highway construction project.

The trial court granted defendants' motion for a directed verdict on the ground that there was not sufficient evidence to find that the alleged negligence of defendants proximately caused the accident. We affirm.

. . .

The collision between the Zinnel and Teigum vehicles occurred on January 2, 1973, at about 2:45 p.m., near the east end of the temporary connection outside of Madelia. It was a clear, sunny winter day. The Teigum vehicle was apparently proceeding east to west, heading into Madelia, and the Zinnel vehicle was coming out of Madelia, proceeding west to east. The head-on collision of the two automobiles occurred in the Zinnel vehicle's lane. An accident reconstuction expert testified for plaintiff that the Teigum vehicle would have traveled onto the blacktop connection via the east-bound lane if the Zinnel vehicle had not been there.

There is minimal evidence as to how the accident happened. There were no eyewitnesses to the accident, and Teigum died at the scene. Plaintiff did not remember anything about the accident except "something red." (The Teigum vehicle was maroon.) He did not recall whether that "something red" was in his lane. Plaintiff's son, Jeffrey, was in the front passenger seat and only remembered looking up and seeing a "red flash."

The layout and markings of the highway require brief description as they relate to plaintiff's claim of causal negligence. The collision occurred at the east end of the temporary connection which was in the shape of a gentle "S" curve from west to east, a distance of 1,000 feet. At each end of the temporary connection there were two 400-foot, 2-degree curves which were connected by a straightaway tangent of 200 feet. Approaching the scene of the accident from the direction traveled by the Teigum vehicle, a driver would have first seen a 65-mile-per-hour speed limit sign, and then he would have seen a curve sign with a combination yellow advisory 50-mile-per-hour speed limit marking. This curve sign was located approximately 700 feet east of the accident and 620 feet from the curve. The next sign was a 50-mile-per-hour maximum speed sign located about 500 feet from the accident and 420 feet from the curve. The new concrete pavement continued past the temporary connection and dead ended. At this point two barricades were placed in each lane of traffic, and on the northernmost barricade there was an arrow pointing toward the direction of the temporary connection. On the new concrete pavement there were dashed yellow centerlines which continued past the temporary connection to the barricades. Just prior to where the temporary connection began, a double, solid yellow do-not-pass line was painted on the concrete facility extending in a curve to the right through the temporary connection. This formed the left-hand side of the lane the driver was to use. Additionally, a solid white edge line was painted on the concrete facility extending in a curve through the temporary connection; this edge line formed the right-hand side of the lane the driver was to use. . . .

The crucial issue was whether plaintiff introduced sufficient evidence that any inadequacies in these traffic control devices proximately caused the collision. Photographs admitted into evidence demonstrated that there were no obstructions to a driver's view of the curve. It was uncontroverted that at the time of the accident the day was sunny, and the road was dry. Because there were no eyewitnesses, and occupants in the Zinnel vehicle recalled seeing only "something red," it was not known what each vehicle was doing before impact. There was no testimony indicating either plaintiff or Teigum was ever confused or misled by these traffic control devices. Teigum was familiar with this road. Because he had a daily routine of driving into Madelia to pick up a newspaper, Teigum traveled on this temporary connection nearly every day during mid-to-late afternoon from August 7, 1972, to the date of the accident. Therefore, a reasonable inference was that Teigum knew about the upcoming curve and understood he was to follow the double centerlines and not the dashed centerlines which extended into the barricades.

A motion for a directed verdict presents a question of law regarding the sufficiency of the evidence to present a fact question for the jury to decide. Jacoboski v. Prax, 290 Minn. 218, 187 N.W.2d 125 (1971). The motion should be granted in those unequivocal cases where in the light of the evidence as a whole, it would clearly be the duty of the trial court to set aside a contrary verdict as being manifestly against the entire evidence. J. N. Sullivan & Assoc. v. F. D. Chapman Const. Co., 304 Minn. 334, 231 N.W.2d 87 (1975). The motion for directed verdict admits for the purposes of the motion the credibility of the evidence for the adverse party and every inference which may be fairly drawn from such evidence. Nevertheless, ". . . court should direct a verdict in favor of the party in whose favor the evidence overwhelmingly preponderates even though there is some evidence in favor of the adverse party. Not every conflict in the evidence gives rise to a jury question." 304 Minn. 336, 231 N.W.2d 89.

Plaintiff claims Teigum strayed into his lane either because he was not given sufficient advance warning of the curve or because he was misled by the continuation of the dashed centerline. Plaintiff has the burden of proving defendants were guilty of negligent conduct and that such negligence was the proximate cause of the accident. While circumstantial evidence can provide sufficient proof of causal connection, such proof must be something more than merely consistent with plaintiff's theory of the case. As we expressed it in E. H. Renner & Sons, Inc. v. Primus, 295 Minn. 240, 243, 203 N.W.2d 832, 835 (1973):

Where the entire evidence sustains, with equal justification, two or more inconsistent inferences so that one inference does not reasonably preponderate over the others, the complainant has not sustained the burden of proof on the proposition which alone would entitle him to recover. It becomes the duty of the trial court to direct a verdict because failing to do so would cause any verdict to the contrary to be based on pure speculation and conjecture.

We agree with the trial court that an examination of the evidence shows that plaintiff's theory is no more supported by or consonant with the facts than other theories which could be developed, theories which would relieve defendants of liability. Plaintiff's theory as to the cause of this accident is no more consistent with the facts than a theory which speculates Teigum was inattentive, took the curve in too wide a fashion, failed to keep his vehicle under control, swerved to avoid something on the road, misjudged the situation, or did anything else to establish he was solely negligent and the sole direct cause of the accident. There is not a sufficient factual basis for concluding traffic control devices proximately caused this accident.

From the evidence as a whole, it would be conjecture for a jury to find inadequate traffic control devices proximately caused this accident. Therefore, the trial court properly granted defendants' motion for a directed verdict.

. . .

NOTES AND QUESTIONS

(1)   What is the standard of proof of causation applied in Zinnel? If applied to the following hypotheticals, what should be the outcome? For similar outcomes on similar facts, see *Cuthbert v. City of Philadelphia*, 417 Pa. 610, 209 A.2d 261 (1965), and *Townsend v. State Department of Highways*, 322 So.2d 139 (La. 1975). *Wall v. Fairview Hosp. and Healthcare Services*, 584 N.W.2d 395, 405 (Minn.1998), reconfirmed the Zinnel ruling that "when all of the evidence will sustain 'two or more inconsistent inferences so that one inference does not reasonably preponderate over the others,' the court must direct a verdict because the plaintiff has not sustained the burden of proof."

Plaintiff fell while descending steps at a race track. She testified only that she fell, and no eye witness could testify as to why. Plaintiff did present evidence that the risers and steps of the staircase were of irregular dimensions, and an architect testified that good practice would require all of them to conform to an unvarying standard dimension. On the strength of that evidence, should the jury be permitted to render a verdict for the plaintiff? See *Majeske v. Palm Beach Kennel Club*, 117 So. 2d 531 (Fla. App. 1960).

Plaintiff was forced off a road by a motor bus during the early morning hours of a Sunday but was unable to identify the bus. Plaintiff introduced evidence that the defendant was the only bus company licensed to operate buses in that town at that time of day, and that defendant had a bus scheduled to pass through the town within 30 minutes of the reported time of the incident. Defendant moved for a directed verdict. Should it be granted? See *Smith v. Rapid Transit, Inc.*, 58 N.E.2d 754 (Mass. 1945).

This raises the question as to whether causation ought ever be pinned on pure probability alone. Should it?

(2)   Courts are less likely to impose specialized burdens of proof in circumstantial evidence cases than perhaps they once were. A large number of jurisdictions hold that circumstantial evidence is as probative as direct evidence and that the only test is whether it is of sufficient weight and credibility to permit a reasonable trier

of fact to draw the rational conclusion that it was adduced to establish. See, e.g., *Berchtold v. Maggi*, 191 Conn. 266, 464 A.2d 1 (1983); *Kuyper v. Gulf Oil Corp.*, 410 A.2d 164 (Del. 1980); *Porter v. Black*, 289 N.W.2d 760 (Neb. 1980); *Rogers v. Dorchester Associates*, 32. N.Y.2d 553, 347 N.Y.S.2d 22, 300 N.E.2d 403 (1973); *Van Zee v. Sioux Valley Hospital*, 315 N.W.2d 489 (S.D. 1982) (need not exclude remote possibilities); *Jesco, Inc. v. Shannon*, 451 So.2d 694 (Miss. 1984)(must be reasonable and legitimate inferences); *Ex Parte Travis*, 414 So.2d 956 (Ala. 1982) (need not establish one inference as stronger than another); *Jacques v. Montana Nat'l Guard*, 649 P.2d 1319 (Mont. 1982) (need not exclude other reasonable hypothesis); and *Mort v. Walker*, 457 N.E.2d 18 (Ill. 1983).

Other courts cling to more rigorous standards of proof when only circumstantial evidence is available. *Bismarck Baptist Church v. Wiedemann Industries, Inc.*, 201 N.W.2d 434 (N.D. 1972) (must exclude equally reasonable inferences); *Lacey v. Louisiana Coca-Cola Bottling Company Ltd.*, 452 So.2d 162 (1984) (must exclude every other reasonable hypothesis with a fair amount of certainty but need not negate all possible causes); and *Gilbert v. Korvette, Inc.*, 457 Pa. 602, 327 A.2d 94 (1974). The latter case adopted Restatement, Torts, Second, § 328(D), which includes the following statement: "(b) other responsible causes, including the conduct of the plaintiff and third persons [must be] sufficiently eliminated by the evidence."

(3)　Does the following case apply the rule of *Zinnel* or some other rule?

NEW YORK LIFE INSURANCE CO. v. McNEELY
Arizona Supreme Court
79 P.2d 948 (1939)

LOCKWOOD, JUDGE.

This is an appeal by New York Life Insurance Company, a corporation, hereinafter called defendant, from a judgment on an insurance policy issued by it on the life of Howard B. McNeely, and in favor of Lillian McNeely, hereinafter called plaintiff. There is singularly little dispute in the actual facts shown by the evidence, the real question being as to the permissible inferences to be drawn there from. These facts, so far as material to a decision, may be stated as follows:

On August 8, 1930, defendant issued to Howard B. McNeely a policy of life insurance, in the amount of three thousand dollars, payable upon receipt of due proof of death, and three thousand dollars, in addition, payable upon due proof that the death resulted from accident as defined under the provisions of the policy relating to such double indemnity. These provisions, so far as material to the case, read as follows:

The Double Indemnity provided on the first page hereof shall be payable upon receipt of due proof that the death of the Insured resulted directly and independently of all other causes from bodily injury effected solely through external, violent and accidental means and occurred within ninety days after such injury.

Double Indemnity shall not be payable if the Insured's death resulted from self-destruction, whether sane or insane; from the taking of poison or inhaling of gas, whether voluntary or otherwise; from committing an assault or felony; from war or any act incident thereto; from engaging in riot or insurrection; from participation as a passenger or otherwise in aviation or aeronautics; or, directly or indirectly, from infirmity of mind or body, from illness or disease, or from any bacterial infection other than bacterial infection occurring in consequence of accidental and external bodily injury. . . .

On Friday, April 19, 1935, McNeely's wife, now Mrs. Geneva Damant, met him in the afternoon at their home in Prescott, and about ten or fifteen minutes later he left in his automobile. About ten or eleven o'clock that night he telephoned her, and was neither seen nor heard from again during his lifetime. On the morning of Saturday, April 20th, his automobile was found on the Prescott-Phoenix highway, about two miles south of Congress Junction, and about one hundred yards north of the Sunrise Service Station. This highway runs in a general north and south direction, and a culvert crosses under the road at the point where the car was found. At each end of said culvert is a concrete abutment which extends about six inches above the highway grade. The car was headed in a northeasterly direction, partially resting on or against the abutment on the east side of the highway, the left front wheel hanging over the concrete abutment. This wheel and the front axle were bent, and a fender somewhat damaged. No glass was broken nor were there any marks of collision; the steering wheel was not damaged, and there was no evidence of any injury on the inside of the car. On the next morning the body of insured was discovered about two hundred fifteen feet from the highway where the car was found. Decomposition had commenced, discoloration was setting in, and flies and maggots were already at work. There was no evidence of any bruise, bump, contusion or abrasion on the head or other part of the body, except a slight discoloration near his right ear and on the back of his right hand. There were bubbles of froth or blood of some kind coming from his lips, and a little dried blood on his face that had apparently come from the right ear. In the pocket of his clothing were found two letters and a will, in his own handwriting. These documents were offered in evidence by defendant, but were excluded by the court, and we shall refer to them later in this opinion. An inquest was thereafter held and a death certificate filed by the coroner, which stated among other things:

The principal cause of death and related causes of importance were as follows: Automobile accident.

. . .

Manner of Injury — back of head.

. . . The case was tried to a jury which rendered a verdict in favor of plaintiff, and from the verdict this appeal was taken.

There are a number of assignments of error, but we think it necessary to discuss only two at length, which are that the court erred in refusing to admit the letters and will, and that the evidence is not sufficient to show that the insured met his death under circumstances covered by the double indemnity provisions of the policy.

It will be seen by referring to the double indemnity provision above set forth, that it was payable only on proof that the death of the insured resulted directly and independently of all other causes from bodily injury effected solely by external, violent and accidental means. Under a provision of this kind, it is necessary not only that the beneficiary of the policy prove the death of the insured, but also prove affirmatively, by a preponderance of the evidence, that such insured came to his death by reason of the specific causes set forth in the policy, and from those causes only. . . .

. . .

[Description of certain letters and hand-written will found on the body of the decedent omitted. Various words implying suicide included the statement, "This is certainly the hardest, if the shortest way out." This evidence was not admitted by the trial court.]

. . . We are of the opinion that where an insurance policy insures only against death from a specified cause, and the complaint alleges that the insured came to his death from that cause, the insurer may, under a general denial, offer any evidence which reasonably tends to show that the cause of death was other than that set forth in the policy. The trial court, therefore, erred in refusing to admit in evidence the letters and will above referred to if they reasonably tend to show that insured committed suicide. . . .

As we said above, it is incumbent upon the plaintiff not only to plead, but to prove, that the insured came to his death by "bodily injury effected solely through external, violent and accidental means." Is there sufficient evidence in the record to sustain a verdict to that effect? No one saw him die, and there is no direct evidence as to the cause of death. Any conclusion as to such cause must be based upon circumstantial evidence. It is the contention of defendant in this case that while circumstantial evidence is admissible to prove the ultimate fact of death from "bodily injury effected solely through external, violent and accidental means", that the circumstances shown by the evidence were not sufficient to justify such a conclusion on the part of the jury, for the reason that in order to draw the ultimate inference of accidental death, it was necessary to pile inference upon inference, and presumption upon presumption, and that this may not be done under the law. The proof of an ultimate fact may be made in two manners, the one by direct or, as it is sometimes called, testimonial evidence, and the other by indirect or, as it is frequently denominated, circumstantial evidence. But it is the rule of law that while a conclusion as to an ultimate fact may be based upon an inference from circumstantial evidence, in reaching such conclusion the inference as to the ultimate fact may not be based on an inference as to the existence of the circumstantial facts.

This rule has been stated in the case of United States v. Ross, 92 U.S. 281, 23 L. Ed. 707, in the following language (page 283): ". . . They are not legitimate inferences, even to establish a fact; much less are they presumptions of law. They are inferences from inferences; presumptions resting on the basis of another presumption. Such a mode of arriving at a conclusion of fact is generally, if not universally, inadmissible. No inference of fact or of law is reliable drawn from premises which are uncertain. Whenever circumstantial evidence is relied upon to prove a fact, the circumstances must be proved, and not themselves presumed. Starkie on Ev. p. 80, lays down the rule thus: 'In the first place, as the very foundation of indirect evidence is the establishment of one or more facts from which the inference is sought to be made, the law requires that the latter should be established by direct evidence, as if they were the very facts in issue.' It is upon this principle that courts are daily called upon to exclude evidence as too remote for the consideration of the jury. The law requires an open, visible connection between the principal and evidentiary facts and the deductions from them, and does not permit a decision to be made on remote inferences. Best on Evid. 95," and the same rule has been repeatedly declared by innumerable decisions. And yet some of the most prominent text writers on the law of evidence attack the rule most vigorously as being unsound in logic and unsustained by practical consideration. 1 Wigmore on Ev. par. 41. As was said by Dean Wigmore:

. . . There is no such rule; nor can be. If there were, hardly a single trial could be adequately prosecuted. For example, on a charge of murder, the defendant's gun is found discharged; from this we infer that he discharged it; and from this we infer that it was his bullet which struck and killed the deceased. Or, the defendant is shown to have been sharpening a knife; from this we argue that he had a design to use it upon the deceased; and from this we argue that the fatal stab was the result of this design. In these and innumerable daily instances we build up inference upon inference, and yet no Court ever thought of forbidding it. All departments of reasoning, all scientific work, every day's life and every day's trials, proceed upon such data.

What is the cause of this sharp divergence between the text writers on the one hand, and the courts on the other? After a careful examination of both the cases and the texts, we are of the opinion that the divergence is more in the form of stating the rule than the application thereof. As Dean Wigmore has frequently pointed out in his monumental work, the rules of evidence applied by the courts are not, and never have been, governed strictly by the principles of logic as taught and applied in the schools. These principles are frequently modified or even set aside on account of practical reasons, which experience shows should govern the trial of controverted issues in the courts. It is true, of course, that in everyday life, all men frequently act as the result of the repeated piling of inferences upon inferences, and, as a matter of strict logic, if an inference has any probative value whatever in aiding one to determine the ultimate question of fact, it should be considered. The principle which is applied by the average man in his own private affairs usually is that no matter how many inferences are piled on each other, it is only necessary that each successive inference should be more probable than any other which might be drawn under all the circumstances. The courts, however, have always insisted that the life, liberty and property of a citizen should not be taken away on possibilities, conjectures, or even, generally speaking, a bare probability. In criminal cases, they demand that when a conviction is to be based on a chain of inferences, each and every link in that chain must exclude every other reasonable hypothesis. In civil cases, involving only property rights, the rule is not so strict, and it is sufficient, if the ultimate fact is to be determined by an inference from facts which are established by direct evidence, that it be more probable than any other inference which could be drawn from the facts thus proven. But when an inference of the probability of the ultimate fact must be drawn from facts whose existence is itself based only on an inference or a chain of inferences, it will be found that the courts have, with very few exceptions, held in substance, although usually not in terms, that all prior links in the chain of inferences must be shown with the same certainty as is required in criminal cases, in order to support a final inference of the probability of the ultimate fact in issue. We think that this is the true meaning of the "inference upon inference" rule in civil cases is borne out by a careful analysis of the majority of cases in which it has been applied, and that the courts do not mean that under no circumstances may an inference be drawn from an inference, but rather that the prior inferences must be established to the exclusion of any other reasonable theory rather than merely by a probability, in order that the last inference of the probability of the ultimate fact may be based thereon. This rule is not based on an application of the exact rules of logic, but upon the pragmatic principle that a certain quantum of proof is arbitrarily required when the courts are asked to take away life, liberty or property.

Let us apply the rule to the facts of the given case. We have the following facts shown by direct evidence: An automobile belonging to the insured was found which had run off the road in such a manner that the left front wheel and the front axle were bent, and a fender damaged. No other injury to the car appeared, and it evidently had not upset. Between twenty-four and forty-eight hours after the car had been thus injured, the body of the insured was found some two hundred feet away from the automobile. It was already advancing in decomposition and showed a discoloration, some of which was on the back of the head and the hand, and some blood and froth were observed exuding from the nose and mouth at the time the body was discovered, while flies and maggots were at work. There were no marks of any kind of bodily injury, or violent death, and the letters above referred to were found on his body. How could reasonable men, on this evidence, have reached the ultimate conclusion that insured met his death by "bodily injury effected solely through external, violent and accidental means"? The only imaginable theory of any cause of death which would bring it within the terms of the policy, was that death was the result of physical injury received in some form of an automobile accident. To reach this conclusion it must have been inferred first that the insured was riding in his car at the time it was injured; second, that he did not voluntarily drive the car into the culvert in an attempt to commit suicide, but did so accidentally; third, that he was violently thrown against some part of the car or thrown from it by reason of the accident; fourth, that by reason thereof he sustained a bodily injury; and fifth, that such bodily injury, independently of all other causes, resulted in his death. As we have pointed out previously, while it is permissible to draw successive inferences, each inference, except the last one, in order to be used as a link in a chain of inferences, must be established to the exclusion of any other reasonable theory, rather than merely by a probability. Let us apply this test. We think the inference that the deceased was riding in the car at the time of the accident comes within the rule. It was his car, in which he left Prescott late the preceding day, and his body was found within a few hundred feet of it. It, therefore, may be used as an inference upon which to base the next inference. This was that he did not voluntarily drive the car into the culvert. In order to draw the third inference that he was thrown violently against some part of the car, or else upon the ground, it is necessary that the second inference must come within the rule. If it does not, the chain breaks. We think this second inference does not satisfy the rule so that a third may be based thereon, in view of the undisputed evidence in regard to the letters found upon his person. It is true these letters were not admitted in evidence, but they should have been, and since they must be at a new trial, we shall consider them in determining whether there is evidence in the record sufficient to sustain a verdict in favor of plaintiff. Judging from those letters, it would appear to any reasonable man that it is as probable that he damaged his car in an attempt to commit suicide as that he did it accidentally.

But even assuming that the inference that he did not voluntarily drive the car into the culvert is established with sufficient certainty to form the second link of the chain, we think the third inference that he was thrown violently against some part of the car or the ground is not permissible under the rule. There is nothing except speculation upon which this inference can be based, for no broken bones were found, no bruises or contusions upon any part of his body, no shattered glass nor broken steering wheel, nor anything which would show to a reasonable certainty that he came violently into contact with any portion of the car or the ground near there. It is true that if this were the ultimate inference to be drawn, it would not be necessary that it be shown with the certainty to which we have previously referred, but it is not. The fourth link in the chain is the inference that he sustained some bodily injury by reason of being thrown against the car or the ground, and this inference may not be drawn unless the inference of his being thrown against the car or the ground is established with the certainty required by the rule, or else there is some direct evidence of a bodily injury. The only direct evidence tending to show bodily injury is a general discoloration of the skin and bloody froth oozing from the ear, mouth and nose. In view of the time the insured had been dead, and the general condition of the body, it is at least as probable that these things were due to the presence of the flies and maggots, and the natural result of decomposition, as that it was the result of a bodily injury effected by external and violent means. But even assuming that the inference of bodily injury effected by violent means were permissible, it is not the ultimate one necessary to sustain plaintiff's case. There must be a further inference that the bodily injury, independently of all other causes, caused his death. It will thus be seen that, in order to reach the ultimate conclusion necessary to sustain the verdict, there must be at least five links in the chain of inferences; that only the first may be considered to be established by a reasonable certainty; that the second, at best, is but a probability, and that the third, fourth and fifth are not even probabilities, but merely possibilities.

. . .

There are a number of other questions raised by the assignments of error, but we think it unnecessary to discuss them, although we have considered them.

The judgment of the superior court of Yavapai County is reversed and the case remanded for a new trial in accordance with the principles set forth herein.

MCALISTER, C. J., and ROSS, J., concur.

NOTES AND QUESTIONS

(1)   Accord on strikingly similar facts, *Voelker v. Combined Insurance Co. of America*, 73 So.2d 403 (Fla. 1954). Does McNeely unnecessarily complicate the application of the rule it espouses? The Arizona Supreme Court subsequently eliminated the distinction between direct and circumstantial evidence, at least in criminal cases. *State v. Harvill*, 476 P.2d 841 (Ariz. 1970) held:

> It is the opinion of this court that the probative value of direct and circumstantial evidence are intrinsically similar; therefore, there is no logically sound reason for drawing a distinction as to the weight to be assigned each. . . . A proper instruction on 'reasonable doubt' as applied to all kinds of evidence gives the jury an appropriate standard upon which to make a determination of guilt or innocence; to instruct further is to invite the confusion of semantics.

It is necessary, therefore, for us to expressly overrule the many decisions of this court which have held that it is fundamental error for the trial court to fail to instruct on the probative force of circumstantial evidence if the prosecution must rely exclusively thereon for a conviction. . . . Consequently, we find no merit in appellant's contention that the trial judge erred in instructing the jury that the law makes no distinction between circumstantial and direct evidence.

(2) Does it occur to you that issues such as those seen in *McNeely* rarely, if ever, would be raised in a negligence action except in connection with proof of cause-in-fact? This reflects the different conceptual meanings of the terms "negligence" (i.e., breach of duty) and "cause-in-fact." Negligence is a legal fact or conclusion. Its determination requires a measuring of evidence against a standard of care that is somewhat abstract. By contrast, cause-in-fact is supposed to reflect a historical, physical certainty.

(3) According to *McNeely*, what standard must circumstantial evidence satisfy before a jury should be permitted to infer cause-in-fact in a criminal case? In a civil case? Why should the rule differ in the two contexts?

Courts differ as to the rule applied in civil cases. Some apply the rule of criminal cases. See, e.g., *Cuthbert v. City of Philadelphia*, 209 A.2d 261 (Pa. 1961). Some apply the rule of *McNeely*. And some apply a more liberal rule to the effect that the inference sought need merely be a reasonable inference from the facts and not that it excludes or preponderates over competing inferences. *Paine v. Gamble Stores, Inc.*, 279 N.W. 257 (Minn. 1938). Which position best conforms to the rule applied in Zinnel? All courts would agree that in the absence of exceptional circumstances, such as those present in the cases of the next section, that the failure to present any evidence as to cause requires a verdict for the defendant. See, e.g., *Tice v. Tice*, 361 So.2d 1053 (Ala. 1978).

COMMENTARY: CORRELLATION AS CAUSE

Some Law and Economics proponents believe courts should decide an act "caused" a particular injury if it significantly raised the probability that it would occur. Suppose a driver drove too fast and crashed on an icy and foggy night? Which factor was a cause? The ice? The fog? The night? Or the speeding? In any event, speeding would surely raise the probability of injury, given a crash. Is this enough to conclude that it was a cause of the injury?

How can causation be distinguished from mere correlation? Suppose competent studies show that the frequency of heart attacks is several times higher in smoker populations than in non-smoker populations? Should a court conclude that smoking "causes" heart attacks? Suppose the studies also show that smokers exercise less than non-smokers? Should a court require smoking heart attack victims to separate the two factors before concluding that smoking is a cause? Suppose studies also show that in populations that follow an identical exercise regime, smokers still have a much higher frequency of heart attacks? Should a court then conclude that smoking "causes" heart attacks?

What if smokers drink more alcohol than non-smokers? Or, smokers live under more stress than non-smokers? Must these factors be neutralized before a court may conclude that smoking is a cause of heart attacks? How would a court go about disentangling all these factors?

§ 7.04   SHIFTING THE BURDEN OF PROOF

OLIVER v. MILES
Mississippi Supreme Court
110 So. 666 (1927)

ETHRIDGE, J.

Lee Miles, the appellee, was plaintiff in the court below and filed suit against the appellant, L. S. Oliver, and Gordon Shamburger, for $199, his damage for an injury inflicted upon his son, Lavell Miles. The suit originated in a justice of the peace court, and judgment was rendered there in favor of Lee Miles for the amount sued for, from which judgment both Shamburger and Oliver appealed to the circuit court, where the case was tried anew.

It appears from the evidence that Shamburger and Oliver had gone out into the country near Collinsville, northwest of Meridian, to hunt birds. They were traveling in a car and passed the boy, Lavell Miles, a short distance from where they stopped the car and got out and went in a westerly direction from the highway, to a point where their dogs had located a covey of partridges. When they approached this place, the partridges, instead of flying in the opposite direction, flew over their heads and across the public highway, and Oliver and Shamburger fired back towards the highway in shooting at the birds and struck Lavell Miles, who was traveling along the edge of the highway in a footpath running along the outer ditches, but between the right of way of the highway. One of the shots fired struck the boy in the eye, resulting in its loss and the necessity of its removal; and the expense of the father in having this done, and the loss of time of the boy from his work during the period he was disabled, and the cost of an artificial eye, and the inconvenience and loss of time caused Miles, the father, constitute the subject-matter of this suit.

Lavell Miles testified that he was traveling along, as above stated, when the guns fired; that he saw the smoke coming from the guns in his direction, and was struck by the shot, one in the eye and some in the leg, but that he was unable to say from which gun the shot that struck him came. At the conclusion of the plaintiff's evidence, the defendants moved for a directed verdict on the ground that the proof did not show which one did the damage, and it devolved upon the plaintiff to show this, as a condition for recovery. The special judge who tried the case below announced that, unless he would elect one or the other, he would grant this peremptory instruction. Thereupon the plaintiff elected a nonsuit as to Shamburger and to proceed against Oliver, but no order was entered upon the minutes of the court in reference thereto. The suit instituted against Oliver resulted in a verdict in favor of the plaintiff for the amount sued for, and, upon this judgment, this appeal is prosecuted.

It is contended by the appellant that the recovery cannot be upheld, first, because this amendment or order was not entered upon the minutes showing nonsuit, and that the declaration stands as though no amendment had been made thereto, under the holdings of this court in Lackey v. Railroad Co., 102 Miss. 339, 59 So. 97, and that the rule is that no recovery can be had, where the suit is a suit for a joint tort and not for a several tort; and, having brought suit for a joint tort, plaintiff cannot recover from one alone, and that the action of the defendants below was not joint, but was several, and therefore that one could not be held responsible for the act of the other. While the stenographer's notes show that the plaintiff elected to nonsuit as to Shamburger, the case of Lackey v. Railroad, 102 Miss. 339, 59 So. 97, holds that the order must be entered upon the minutes, that the court can only speak through its minutes, and we must treat the case as being one of joint suit against the two defendants.

. . .

In 20 R. C. L. p. 149, section 122, it is said:

If two or more persons united in the joint prosecution of a common purpose, under such circumstances that each has authority, express or implied, to act for all, in respect to the control of the means and agencies employed to execute such common purpose, the negligence of one in the management thereof will be imputed to the others. Accordingly, it has been held that where two persons are engaged in a joint enterprise in operating an automobile, the contributory negligence of one will bar a recovery by either, if it is a matter within the scope of the joint agreement (citing Beaucage v. Mercer, 206 Mass. 492, 92 N. E. 774, 138 Am. St. Rep. 401).

In Cullinan v. Tetrault, 123 Me. 302, 122 A. 770, 31 A. L. R. 1330, the court held, in a case where a person left a boy in a drug store incompetent to take charge and sell drugs, that the proprietor would be liable for the injuries caused by the boy's mistakes in attempting to sell drugs, although he was not instructed to sell drugs; but it also held that if two persons enter a drug store to procure an extract for beverage purposes, and one undertakes to make the purchase, his negligence in doing so is imputed to his companion, so as to defeat the action on the ground of contributory negligence; and that the two persons purchasing, being engaged in a joint enterprise in purchasing the beverage, the negligence of one was attributable to the other, so as to make the contributory negligence of one defeat the right of the other.

In Lucey v. John Hope & Sons Engraving & Mfg. Co. et al., 45 R. I. 103, 120 A. 62, the court held that, where an automobile owned by a corporation, in which only two persons were interested, was being driven by one, accompanied by the other, on a mutual pleasure trip, they were engaged in a common enterprise, so as to make the negligence of the driver in injuring a third person in a collision chargeable to the passenger, and to render them jointly liable for such injuries.

In the present case, the parties were engaged in hunting jointly, and both fired across a public highway, which was a negligent act. We think that they were jointly engaged in the unlawful enterprise of shooting at birds flying over the highway; that they were in pursuit of a common purpose; that each did an unlawful act, in the pursuit thereof; and that each is liable for the resulting injury to the boy, although no one can say definitely who actually shot him. To hold otherwise would be to exonerate both from liability, although each was negligent, and the injury resulted from such negligence. We therefore are of the opinion that the court below did not err in this respect.

We do not think there is any merit in the other contentions, and the judgment of the lower court will be affirmed.

Affirmed.

NOTE AND QUESTION

Oliver v. Miles should be closely compared with the more famous *Summers v. Tice*, discussed in the next case. Which of the two cases reaches further to assist a party to prove causation-in-fact? Which of the two is the more manageable doctrine?

SINDELL v. ABBOTT LABORATORIES
California Supreme Court
26 Cal.3d 588, 163 Cal.Rptr. 132, 607 P.2d 924 (1980)

Mosk, Justice.

This case involves a complex problem both timely and significant: may a plaintiff, injured as the result of a drug administered to her mother during pregnancy, who knows the type of drug involved but cannot identify the manufacturer of the precise product, hold liable for her injuries a maker of a drug produced from an identical formula?

Plaintiff Judith Sindell brought an action against eleven drug companies and Does 1 through 100, on behalf of herself and other women similarly situated. The complaint alleges as follows:

Between 1941 and 1971, defendants were engaged in the business of manufacturing, promoting, and marketing diethylstilbesterol (DES), a drug which is a synthetic compound of the female hormone estrogen. The drug was administered to plaintiff's mother and the mothers of the class she represents, for the purpose of preventing miscarriage. In 1947, the Food and Drug Administration authorized the marketing of DES as a miscarriage preventative, but only on an experimental basis, with a requirement that the drug contain a warning label to that effect. DES may cause cancerous vaginal and cervical growths in the daughters exposed to it before birth, because their mothers took the drug during pregnancy. The form of cancer from which these daughters suffer is known as adenocarcinoma, and it manifests itself after a minimum latent period of 10 or 12 years. It is a fast-spreading and deadly disease, and radical surgery is required to prevent it from spreading.

DES also causes adenosis, precancerous vaginal and cervical growths which may spread to other areas of the body. The treatment for adenosis is cauterization, surgery, or cryosurgery. Women who suffer from this condition must be monitored by biopsy or colposcopic examination twice a year, a painful and expensive procedure. Thousands of women whose mothers received DES during pregnancy are unaware of the effects of the drug.

In 1971, the Food and Drug Administration ordered defendants to cease marketing and promoting DES for the purpose of preventing miscarriages, and to warn physicians and the public that the drug should not be used by pregnant women because of the danger to their unborn children.

During the period defendants marketed DES, they knew or should have known that it was a carcinogenic substance, that there was a grave danger after varying periods of latency it would cause cancerous and precancerous growths in the daughters of the mothers who took it, and that it was ineffective to prevent miscarriage. Nevertheless, defendants continued to advertise and market the drug as a miscarriage preventative. They failed to test DES for efficacy and safety; the tests performed by others, upon which they relied, indicated that it was not safe or effective. In violation of the authorization of the Food and Drug Administration, defendants marketed DES on an unlimited basis rather than as an experimental drug, and they failed to warn of its potential danger.

Because of defendants' advertised assurances that DES was safe and effective to prevent miscarriage, plaintiff was exposed to the drug prior to her birth. She became aware of the danger from such exposure within one year of the time she filed her complaint. As a result of the DES ingested by her mother, plaintiff developed a malignant bladder tumor which was removed by surgery. She suffers from adenosis and must constantly be monitored by biopsy or colposcopy to insure early warning of further malignancy.

The first cause of action alleges that defendants were jointly and individually negligent in that they manufactured, marketed and promoted DES as a safe and efficacious drug to prevent miscarriage, without adequate testing or warning, and without monitoring or reporting its effects.

A separate cause of action alleges that defendants are jointly liable regardless of which particular brand of DES was ingested by plaintiff's mother because defendants collaborated in marketing, promoting and testing the drug, relied upon each other's tests, and adhered to an industry-wide safety standard. DES was produced from a common and mutually agreed upon formula as a fungible drug interchangeable with other brands of the same product; defendants knew or should have known that it was customary for doctors to prescribe the drug by its generic rather than its brand name and that pharmacists filled prescriptions from whatever brand of the drug happened to be in stock.

Other causes of action are based upon theories of strict liability, violation of express and implied warranties, false and fraudulent representations, misbranding of drugs in violation of federal law, conspiracy and "lack of consent."

Each cause of action alleges that defendants are jointly liable because they acted in concert, on the basis of express and implied agreements, and in reliance upon and ratification and exploitation of each other's testing and marketing methods.

Plaintiff seeks compensatory damages of $1 million and punitive damages of $10 million for herself. For the members of her class, she prays for equitable relief in the form of an order that defendants warn physicians and others of the danger of DES and the necessity of performing certain tests to determine the presence of disease caused by the drug, and that they establish free clinics in California to perform such tests.

Defendants demurred to the complaint. While the complaint did not expressly allege that plaintiff could not identify the manufacturer of the precise drug ingested by her mother, she stated in her points and authorities in opposition to the demurrers filed by some of the defendants that she was unable to make the identification, and the trial court sustained the demurrers of these defendants without leave to amend on the ground that plaintiff did not and stated she could not identify which defendant had manufactured the drug responsible for her injuries. Thereupon, the court dismissed the action. This appeal involves only five of ten defendants named in the complaint.

We begin with the proposition that, as a general rule, the imposition of liability depends upon a showing by the plaintiff that his or her injuries were caused by the act of the defendant or by an instrumentality under the defendant's control. The rule applies whether the injury resulted from an accidental event (e.g., Shunk v. Bosworth (6th Cir. 1964) 334 F.2d 309) or from the use of a defective product. . . .

There are, however, exceptions to this rule. Plaintiff's complaint suggests several bases upon which defendants may be held liable for her injuries even though she cannot demonstrate the name of the manufacturer which produced the DES actually taken by her mother. The first of these theories, classically illustrated by Summers v. Tice (1948) 33 Cal.2d 80, 199 P.2d 1, places the burden of proof of causation upon tortious defendants in certain circumstances. The second basis of liability emerging from the complaint is that defendants acted in concert to cause injury to plaintiff. There is a third and novel approach to the problem, sometimes called the theory of "enterprise liability," but which we prefer to designate by the more accurate term of "industry-wide" liability, which might obviate the necessity for identifying the manufacturer of the injury-causing drug. We shall conclude that these doctrines, as previously interpreted, may not be applied to hold defendants liable under the allegations of this complaint. However, we shall propose and adopt a fourth basis for permitting the action to be tried, grounded upon an extension of the Summers doctrine.

I

Plaintiff places primary reliance upon cases which hold that if a party cannot identify which of two or more defendants caused an injury, the burden of proof may shift to the defendants to show that they were not responsible for the harm. This principle is sometimes referred to as the "alternative liability" theory.

The celebrated case of Summers v. Tice, supra, 33 Cal.2d 80, 199 P.2d 1, a unanimous opinion of this court, best exemplifies the rule. In Summers, the plaintiff was injured when two hunters negligently shot in his direction. It could not be determined which of them had fired the shot which actually caused the injury to the plaintiff's eye, but both defendants were nevertheless held jointly and severally liable for the whole of the damages. We reasoned that both were wrongdoers, both were negligent toward the plaintiff, and that it would be unfair to require plaintiff to isolate the defendant responsible, because if the one pointed out were to escape liability, the other might also, and the plaintiff-victim would be shorn of any remedy. In these circumstances, we held, the burden of proof shifted to the defendants, "each to absolve himself if he can." (Id., p. 86, 199 P.2d p. 4.) We stated that under those or similar circumstances a defendant is ordinarily in a "far better position" to offer evidence to determine whether he or another defendant caused the injury.

In Summers, we relied upon Ybarra v. Spangard (1944) 25 Cal.2d 486, 154 P.2d 687. There, the plaintiff was injured while he was unconscious during the course of surgery. He sought damages against several doctors and a nurse who attended him while he was unconscious. We held that it would be unreasonable to require him to identify the particular defendant who had performed the alleged negligent act because he was unconscious at the time of the injury and the defendants exercised control over the instrumentalities which caused the harm. Therefore, under the doctrine of res ipsa loquitur, an inference of negligence arose that defendants were required to meet by explaining their conduct.

The rule developed in Summers has been embodied in the Restatement of Torts. (Rest.2d Torts, § 433B, subsec. (3).)[1] Indeed, the Summers facts are used as an illustration (p. 447).

Defendants assert that these principles are inapplicable here. First, they insist that a predicate to shifting the burden of proof under Summers-Ybarra is that the defendants must have greater access to information regarding the cause of the injuries than the plaintiff, whereas in the present case the reverse appears.

Plaintiff does not claim that defendants are in a better position than she to identify the manufacturer of the drug taken by her mother or, indeed, that they have the ability to do so at all, but argues, rather, that Summers does not impose such a requirement as a condition to the shifting of the burden of proof. In this respect we believe plaintiff is correct.

In Summers, the circumstances of the accident themselves precluded an explanation of its cause. To be sure, Summers states that defendants are "[o]rdinarily . . . in a far better position to offer evidence to determine which one caused the injury" than a plaintiff (33 Cal.2d 80, at p. 86, 199 P.2d 1 at p. 4), but the decision does not determine that this "ordinary" situation was present. Neither the facts nor the language of the opinion indicate that the two defendants, simultaneously shooting in the same direction, were in a better position than the plaintiff to ascertain whose shot caused the injury. As the opinion acknowledges, it was impossible for the trial court to determine whether the shot which entered the plaintiff's eye came from the gun of one defendant or the other. Nevertheless, burden of proof was shifted to the defendants.

Here, as in Summers, the circumstances of the injury appear to render identification of the manufacturer of the drug ingested by plaintiff's mother impossible by either plaintiff or defendants, and it cannot reasonably be said that one is in a better position than the other to make the identification. Because many years elapsed between the time the drug was taken and the manifestation of plaintiff's injuries she, and many other daughters of mothers who took DES, are unable to make such identification. Certainly there can be no implication that plaintiff is at fault in failing to do so — the event occurred while plaintiff was in utero, a generation ago.

On the other hand, it cannot be said with assurance that defendants have the means to make the identification. In this connection, they point out that drug manufacturers ordinarily have no direct contact with the patients who take a drug prescribed by their doctors. Defendants sell to wholesalers, who in turn supply the product to physicians and pharmacies. Manufacturers do not maintain records of the persons who take the drugs they produce, and the selection of the medication is made by the physician rather than the manufacturer. Nor do we conclude that the absence of evidence on this subject is due to the fault of defendants. While it is

---

[1] Section 433B, subsection (3) of the Restatement provides: "Where the conduct of two or more actors is tortious, and it is proved that harm has been caused to the plaintiff by only one of them, but there is uncertainty as to which one has caused it, the burden is upon each such actor to prove that he has not caused the harm." The reason underlying the rule is "the injustice of permitting proved wrongdoers, who among them have inflicted an injury upon the entirely innocent plaintiff, to escape liability merely because the nature of their conduct and the resulting harm has made it difficult or impossible to prove which of them has caused the harm." (Rest.2d Torts, § 433B, com. f, p. 446.)

alleged that they produced a defective product with delayed effects and without adequate warnings, the difficulty or impossiblity of identification results primarily from the passage of time rather than from their allegedly negligent acts of failing to provide adequate warnings. Thus Haft v. Lone Palm Hotel (1970) 3 Cal.3d 756, 91 Cal.Rptr. 745, 478 P.2d 465, upon which plaintiff relies, is distinguishable.

It is important to observe, however, that while defendants do not have means superior to plaintiff to identify the maker of the precise drug taken by her mother, they may in some instances be able to prove that they did not manufacture the injury-causing substance. In the present case, for example, one of the original defendants was dismissed from the action upon proof that it did not manufacture DES until after plaintiff was born.

Thus we conclude that the fact defendants do not have greater access to information which might establish the identity of the manufacturer of the DES which injured plaintiff does not per se prevent application of the Summers rule.

Nevertheless, plaintiff may not prevail in her claim that the Summers rationale should be employed to fix the whole liability for her injuries upon defendants, at least as those principles have previously been applied. There is an important difference between the situation involved in Summers and the present case. There, all the parties who were or could have been responsible for the harm to the plaintiff were joined as defendants. Here, by contrast, there are approximately 200 drug companies which made DES, any of which might have manufactured the injury-producing drug.

Defendants maintain that, while in Summers there was a 50 percent chance that one of the two defendants was responsible for the plaintiff's injuries, here since any one of 200 companies which manufactured DES might have made the product which harmed plaintiff, there is no rational basis upon which to infer that any defendant in this action caused plaintiff's injuries, nor even a reasonable possibility that they were responsible.

These arguments are persuasive if we measure the chance that any one of the defendants supplied the injury-causing drug by the number of possible tortfeasors. In such a context, the possibility that any of the five defendants supplied the DES to plaintiff's mother is so remote that it would be unfair to require each defendant to exonerate itself. There may be a substantial likelihood that none of the five defendants joined in the action made the DES which caused the injury, and that the offending producer not named would escape liability altogether. While we propose, infra, an adaptation of the rule in Summers which will substantially overcome these difficulties, defendants appear to be correct that the rule, as previously applied, cannot relieve plaintiff of the burden of proving the identity of the manufacturer which made the drug causing her injuries.

II

The second principle upon which plaintiff relies is the so-called "concert of action" theory. Preliminarily, we briefly describe the procedure a drug manufacturer must follow before placing a drug on the market. Under federal law as it read prior to 1962, a new drug was defined as one "not generally recognized as . . . safe." (s 102, 76 Stat. 781 (Oct. 10, 1962).) Such a substance could be marketed only if a new drug application had been filed with the Food and Drug

Administration and had become "effective." [FN19] If the agency determined that a product was no longer a "new drug," i. e., that it was "generally recognized as . . . safe," (21 U.S.C.A. s 321, subd. (p) (1)) it could be manufactured by any drug company without submitting an application to the agency. According to defendants, 123 new drug applications for DES had been approved by 1952, and in that year DES was declared not to be a "new drug," thus allowing any manufacturer to produce it without prior testing and without submitting a new drug application to the Food and Drug Administration. With this background we consider whether the complaint states a claim based upon "concert of action" among defendants. The elements of this doctrine are prescribed in section 876 of the Restatement of Torts. The section provides, "For harm resulting to a third person from the tortious conduct of another, one is subject to liability if he (a) does a tortious act in concert with the other or pursuant to a common design with him, or (b) knows that the other's conduct constitutes a breach of duty and gives substantial assistance or encouragement to the other so to conduct himself, or (c) gives substantial assistance to the other in accomplishing a tortious result and his own conduct, separately considered, constitutes a breach of duty to the third person." With respect to this doctrine, Prosser states that "those who, in pursuance of a common plan or design to commit a tortious act, actively take part in it, or further it by cooperation or request, or who lend aid or encouragement to the wrongdoer, or ratify and adopt his acts done for their benefit, are equally liable with him. (P) Express agreement is not necessary, and all that is required is that there be a tacit understanding. . . . " (Prosser, Law of Torts (4th ed. 1971), sec. 46, p. 292.)

. . . .

In our view, this litany of charges is insufficient to allege a cause of action under the rules stated above. The gravamen of the charge of concert is that defendants failed to adequately test the drug or to give sufficient warning of its dangers and that they relied upon the tests performed by one another and took advantage of each others' promotional and marketing techniques. These allegations do not amount to a charge that there was a tacit understanding or a common plan among defendants to fail to conduct adequate tests or give sufficient warnings, and that they substantially aided and encouraged one another in these omissions.

The complaint charges also that defendants produced DES from a "common and mutually agreed upon formula," allowing pharmacists to treat the drug as a "fungible commodity" and to fill prescriptions from whatever brand of DES they had on hand at the time. It is difficult to understand how these allegations can form the basis of a cause of action for wrongful conduct by defendants, acting in concert. The formula for DES is a scientific constant. It is set forth in the United States Pharmacopoeia, and any manufacturer producing that drug must, with exceptions not relevant here, utilize the formula set forth in that compendium. (21 U.S.C.A. s 351, subd. (b).)

What the complaint appears to charge is defendants' parallel or imitative conduct in that they relied upon each others' testing and promotion methods. But such conduct describes a common practice in industry: a producer avails himself of the experience and methods of others making the same or similar products. Application of the concept of concert of action to this situation would expand the doctrine far beyond its intended scope and would render virtually any manufacturer liable for the defective products of an entire industry, even if it could be demonstrated that the product which caused the injury was not made by the defendant.

. . .

[Note: The concert of action theory is perhaps best exemplified by unlawful drag racing on public highways. Under the theory, one drag racer who directly caused no harm is liable to innocent victims who were struck by the other drag racer. See *Bierczynski v. Rogers*, 239 A.2d 218 (Del. 1968).]

A third theory upon which plaintiff relies is the concept of industry-wide liability, or according to the terminology of the parties, "enterprise liability." This theory was suggested in Hall v. E. I. Du Pont de Nemours & Co., Inc. (E.D.N.Y. 1972) 345 F.Supp. 353. In that case, plaintiffs were 13 children injured by the explosion of blasting caps in 12 separate incidents which occurred in 10 different states between 1955 and 1959. The defendants were six blasting cap manufacturers, comprising virtually the entire blasting cap industry in the United States, and their trade association. There were, however, a number of Canadian blasting cap manufacturers which could have supplied the caps. The gravamen of the complaint was that the practice of the industry of omitting a warning on individual blasting caps and of failing to take other safety measures created an unreasonable risk of harm, resulting in the plaintiffs' injuries. The complaint did not identify a particular manufacturer of a cap which caused a particular injury.

The court reasoned as follows: there was evidence that defendants, acting independently, had adhered to an industry-wide standard with regard to the safety features of blasting caps, that they had in effect delegated some functions of safety investigation and design, such as labelling, to their trade association, and that there was industry-wide cooperation in the manufacture and design of blasting caps. In these circumstances, the evidence supported a conclusion that all the defendants jointly controlled the risk. Thus, if plaintiffs could establish by a preponderance of the evidence that the caps were manufactured by one of the defendants, the burden of proof as to causation would shift to all the defendants. The court noted that this theory of liability applied to industries composed of a small number of units, and that what would be fair and reasonable with regard to an industry of five or ten producers might be manifestly unreasonable if applied to a decentralized industry composed of countless small producers.

Plaintiff attempts to state a cause of action under the rationale of Hall. She alleges joint enterprise and collaboration among defendants in the production, marketing, promotion and testing of DES, and "concerted promulgation and adherence to industry-wide testing, safety, warning and efficacy standards" for the drug. We have concluded above that allegations that defendants relied upon one another's testing and promotion methods do not state a cause of action for concerted conduct to commit a tortious act. Under the theory of industry-wide liability, however, each manufacturer could be liable for all injuries caused by DES by virtue of adherence to an industry-wide standard of safety.

In the Fordham Comment, the industry-wide theory of liability is discussed and refined in the context of its applicability to actions alleging injuries resulting from DES. The author explains causation under that theory as follows, ". . . [T]he industry-wide standard becomes itself the cause of plaintiff's injury, just as defendants' joint plan is the cause of injury in the traditional concert of action plea. Each defendant's adherence perpetuates this standard, which results in the manufacture of the particular, unidentifiable injury-producing product. Therefore, each industry member has contributed to plaintiff's injury." (Fordham Comment, supra, at p. 997.)

The Comment proposes seven requirements for a cause of action based upon industry-wide liability,[2] and suggests that if a plaintiff proves these elements, the burden of proof of causation should be shifted to the defendants, who may exonerate themselves only by showing that their product could not have caused the injury.

We decline to apply this theory in the present case. At least 200 manufacturers produced DES; Hall, which involved 6 manufacturers representing the entire blasting cap industry in the United States, cautioned against application of the doctrine espoused therein to a large number of producers. (345 F.Supp. at p. 378.) Moreover, in Hall, the conclusion that the defendants jointly controlled the risk was based upon allegations that they had delegated some functions relating to safety to a trade association. There are no such allegations here, and we have concluded above that plaintiff has failed to allege liability on a concert of action theory.

Equally important, the drug industry is closely regulated by the Food and Drug Administration, which actively controls the testing and manufacture of drugs and the method by which they are marketed, including the contents of warning labels. To a considerable degree, therefore, the standards followed by drug manufacturers are suggested or compelled by the government. Adherence to those standards cannot, of course, absolve a manufacturer of liability to which it would otherwise be subject. (Stevens v. Parke, Davis & Co. (1973) 9 Cal.3d 51, 65, 1017 Cal.Rptr. 45, 507 P.2d 653.) But since the government plays such a pervasive role in formulating the criteria for the testing and marketing of drugs, it would be unfair to impose upon a manufacturer liability for injuries resulting from the use of a drug which it did not supply simply because it followed the standards of the industry.

Where, as here, all defendants produced a drug from an identical formula and the manufacturer of the DES which caused plaintiff's injuries cannot be identified through no fault of plaintiff, a modification of the rule of Summers is warranted. As we have seen, an undiluted Summers rationale is inappropriate to shift the burden of proof of causation to defendants because if we measure the chance that any particular manufacturer supplied the injury-causing product by the number of producers of DES there is a possibility that none of the five defendants in this case produced the offending substance and that the responsible manufacturer, not named in the action, will escape liability.

---

[2] The suggested requirements are as follows:

1. There existed an insufficient, industry-wide standard of safety as to the manufacture of the product.

2. Plaintiff is not at fault for the absence of evidence identifying the causative agent but, rather, this absence of proof is due to defendant's conduct.

3. A generically similar defective product was manufactured by all the defendants.

4. Plaintiff's injury was caused by this defect.

5. Defendants owed a duty to the class of which plaintiff was a member.

6. There is clear and convincing evidence that plaintiff's injury was caused by a product made by one of the defendants. For example, the joined defendants accounted for a high percentage of such defective products on the market at the time of plaintiff's injury.

7. All defendants were tortfeasors.

But we approach the issue of causation from a different perspective: we hold it to be reasonable in the present context to measure the likelihood that any of the defendants supplied the product which allegedly injured plaintiff by the percentage which the DES sold by each of them for the purpose of preventing miscarriage bears to the entire production of the drug sold by all for that purpose. Plaintiff asserts in her briefs that Eli Lilly and Company and 5 or 6 other companies produced 90 percent of the DES marketed. If at trial this is established to be the fact, then there is a corresponding likelihood that this comparative handful of producers manufactured the DES which caused plaintiff's injuries, and only a 10 percent likelihood that the offending producer would escape liability.

If plaintiff joins in the action the manufacturers of a substantial share of the DES which her mother might have taken, the injustice of shifting the burden of proof to defendants to demonstrate that they could not have made the substance which injured plaintiff is significantly diminished. While 75 to 80 percent of the market is suggested as the requirement by the Fordham Comment (at p. 996), we hold only that a substantial percentage is required.

The presence in the action of a substantial share of the appropriate market also provides a ready means to apportion damages among the defendants. Each defendant will be held liable for the proportion of the judgment represented by its share of that market unless it demonstrates that it could not have made the product which caused plaintiff's injuries. In the present case, as we have seen, one DES manufacturer was dismissed from the action upon filing a declaration that it had not manufactured DES until after plaintiff was born. Once plaintiff has met her burden of joining the required defendants, they in turn may cross-complaint against other DES manufacturers, not joined in the action, which they can allege might have supplied the injury-causing product.

Under this approach, each manufacturer's liability would approximate its responsibility for the injuries caused by its own products. Some minor discrepancy in the correlation between market share and liability is inevitable; therefore, a defendant may be held liable for a somewhat different percentage of the damage than its share of the appropriate market would justify. It is probably impossible, with the passage of time, to determine market share with mathematical exactitude. But just as a jury cannot be expected to determine the precise relationship between fault and liability in applying the doctrine of comparative fault (Li v. Yellow Cab Co. (1975) 13 Cal.3d 804, 119 Cal.Rptr. 858, 532 P.2d 1226) or partial indemnity (American Motorcycle Ass'n v. Superior Court (1978) 20 Cal.3d 578, 146 Cal.Rptr., 182, 578 P.2d 899), the difficulty of apportioning damages among the defendant producers in exact relation to their market share does not seriously militate against the rule we adopt. As we said in Summers with regard to the liability of independent tortfeasors, where a correct division of liability cannot be made "the trier of fact may make it the best it can." (33 Cal.2d at p. 88, 199 P.2d at p. 5.)

We are not unmindful of the practical problems involved in defining the market and determining market share, but these are largely matters of proof which properly cannot be determined at the pleading stage of these proceedings. Defendants urge that it would be both unfair and contrary to public policy to hold them liable for plaintiff's injuries in the absence of proof that one of them supplied the drug responsible for the damage. Most of their arguments, however, are based upon the assumption that one manufacturer would be held responsible for the products of another or for those of all other manufacturers if plaintiff ultimately prevails. But under the rule we adopt, each manufacturer's liability for an injury would be approximately equivalent to the damages caused by the DES it manufactured.

The judgments are reversed.

BIRD, C. J., and NEWMAN and WHITE, JJ., concur.

RICHARDSON, JUSTICE, dissenting.

I respectfully dissent. In these consolidated cases the majority adopts a wholly new theory which contains these ingredients: The plaintiffs were not alive at the time of the commission of the tortious acts. They sue a generation later. They are permitted to receive substantial damages from multiple defendants without any proof that any defendant caused or even probably caused plaintiff's injuries.

Although the majority purports to change only the required burden of proof by shifting it from plaintiffs to defendants, the effect of its holding is to guarantee that plaintiffs will prevail on the causation issue because defendants are no more capable of disproving factual causation than plaintiffs are of proving it. "Market share" liability thus represents a new high water mark in tort law. The ramifications seem almost limitless, a fact which prompted one recent commentator, in criticizing a substantially identical theory, to conclude that "Elimination of the burden of proof as to identification [of the manufacturer whose drug injured plaintiff] would impose a liability which would exceed absolute liability." (Coggins, Industry-Wide Liability (1979) 13 Suffolk L.Rev. 980, 998, fn. omitted; see also, pp. 1000–1001.) In my view, the majority's departure from traditional tort doctrine is unwise.

The applicable principles of causation are very well established. A leading torts scholar, Dean Prosser, has authoritatively put it this way: "An essential element of the plaintiff's cause of action for negligence, or for that matter for any other tort, is that there be some reasonable connection between the act or omission of the defendant and the damage which the plaintiff has suffered." (Prosser, Torts (4th ed. 1971) § 41, p. 236, italics added.) With particular reference to the matter before us, and in the context of products liability, the requirement of a causation element has been recognized as equally fundamental.

It is clear that any holding that a producer, manufacturer, seller, or a person in a similar position, is liable for injury caused by a particular product, must necessarily be predicated upon proof that the product in question was one for whose condition the defendant was in some way responsible. Thus, for example, if recovery is sought from a manufacturer, it must be shown that he actually was the manufacturer of the product which caused the injury; . . .

(1 Hursh & Bailey, American Law of Products Liability (2d ed. 1974) § 1:41, p. 125, italics added; accord, Prosser, supra, § 103, at pp. 671-672; 2 Dooley Modern Tort Law (1977) § 32.03, p. 243.) Indeed, an inability to prove this causal link between defendant's conduct and plaintiff's injury has proven fatal in prior cases brought against manufacturers of DES by persons who were situated in positions identical to those of plaintiffs herein. . . .

The majority now expressly abandons the foregoing traditional requirement of some causal connection between defendants' act and plaintiffs' injury in the creation of its new modified industry-wide tort. Conceptually, the doctrine of absolute liability which heretofore in negligence law has substituted only for the requirement of a breach of defendant's duty of care, under the majority's hand now subsumes the additional necessity of a causal relationship. . . .

The majority attempts to justify its new liability on the ground that defendants herein are "better able to bear the cost of injury resulting from the manufacture of a defective product." (Ante, p. 144 of 163 Cal. Rptr., p. 936 of 607 P.2d.) This "deep pocket" theory of liability, fastening liability on defendants presumably because they are rich, has understandable popular appeal and might be tolerable in a case disclosing substantially stronger evidence of causation than herein appears. But as a general proposition, a defendant's wealth is an unreliable indicator of fault, and should play no part, at least consciously, in the legal analysis of the problem. In the absence of proof that a particular defendant caused or at least probably caused plaintiff's injuries, a defendant's ability to bear the cost thereof is no more pertinent to the underlying issue of liability than its "substantial" share of the relevant market. A system priding itself on "equal justice under law" does not flower when the liability as well as the damage aspect of a tort action is determined by a defendant's wealth. The inevitable consequence of such a result is to create and perpetuate two rules of law — one applicable to wealthy defendants and another standard pertaining to defendants who are poor or who have modest means. Moreover, considerable doubts have been expressed regarding the ability of the drug industry, and especially its smaller members, to bear the substantial economic costs (from both damage awards and high insurance premiums) inherent in imposing an industry-wide liability. . . .

I am not unmindful of the serious medical consequences of plaintiff's injuries, and the equally serious implications to the class which she purports to represent. In balancing the various policy considerations, however, I also observe that the incidence of vaginal cancer among "DES daughters" has been variously estimated at one-tenth of 1 percent to four-tenths of 1 percent. (13 Suffolk L.Rev., supra, p. 999, fn. 92.) These facts raise some penetrating questions. Ninety-nine plus percent of "DES daughters" have never developed cancer. Must a drug manufacturer to escape this blanket liability wait for a generation of testing before it may disseminate drugs? If a drug has beneficial purposes for the majority of users but harmful side effects are later revealed for a small fraction of consumers, will the manufacturer be absolutely liable? If adverse medical consequences, wholly unknown to the most careful and meticulous of present scientists, surface in two or three generations, will similar liability be imposed? In my opinion, common sense and reality combine to warn that a "market share" theory goes too far. Legally, it expects too much.

I believe that the scales of justice tip against imposition of this new liability because of the foregoing elements of unfairness to some defendants who may have had nothing whatever to do with causing any injury, the unwarranted preference created for this particular class of plaintiffs, the violence done to traditional tort principles by the drastic expansion of liability proposed, the injury threatened to the public interest in continued unrestricted basic medical research as stressed by the Restatement, and the other reasons heretofore expressed.

The majority's decision effectively makes the entire drug industry (or at least its California members) an insurer of all injuries attributable to defective drugs of uncertain or unprovable origin, including those injuries manifesting themselves a generation later, and regardless of whether particular defendants had any part whatever in causing the claimed injury. Respectfully, I think this is unreasonable overreaction for the purpose of achieving what is perceived to be a socially satisfying result.

Finally, I am disturbed by the broad and ominous ramifications of the majority's holding. The law review comment, which is the wellspring of the majority's new theory, conceding the widespread consequences of industry-wide liability, openly acknowledges that "The DES cases are only the tip of an iceberg." (Comment, DES and a Proposed Theory of Enterprise Liability (1978) 46 Fordham L.Rev. 963, 1007.) Although the pharmaceutical drug industry may be the first target of this new sanction, the majority's reasoning has equally threatening application to many other areas of business and commercial activities.

Given the grave and sweeping economic, social, and medical effects of "market share" liability, the policy decision to introduce and define it should rest not with us, but with the Legislature which is currently considering not only major statutory reform of California product liability law in general, but the DES problem in particular. (See Sen. Bill No. 1392 (1979–1980 Reg. Sess.), which would establish and appropriate funds for the education, identification, and screening of persons exposed to DES, and would prohibit health care and hospital service plans from excluding or limiting coverage to persons exposed to DES.) An alternative proposal for administrative compensation, described as "a limited version of no-fault products liability" has been suggested by one commentator. (Coggins, supra, 13 Suffolk L.Rev. at pp. 1019–1021.) Compensation under such a plan would be awarded by an administrative tribunal from funds collected "via a tax paid by all manufacturers." (P. 1020, fn. omitted.) In any event, the problem invites a legislative rather than an attempted judicial solution.

I would affirm the judgments of dismissal.

CLARK and MANUEL, JJ., concur.

NOTES

(1) Some courts have declined to adopt the "market share" theory of causation even in DES cases. See *Zafft v. Eli Lilly & Co.*, 676 S.W.2d 241, 246 (Mo. 1984) (unfair, unworkable and contrary to public policy); *Mulcahy v. Eli Lilly & Co.*, 386 N.W.2d 67, 75 (Iowa 1986) (inappropriate legal "social engineering"); and *Smith v. Eli Lilly & Co.*, 560 N.E.2d 324 (Ill. 1990) (not sound in theory). Although it had applied the market share theory in the *Sindell* context, the New York Court of Appeals refused to extend the theory to benefit "third generation" plaintiffs; i.e., children of daughters who had defective uteruses as a result of their mother's (grandmothers of the plaintiff) having taken DES while the mother of the plaintiff was in utero. *Enright v. Eli Lilly & Company*, 570 N.E.2d 198 (N.Y. 1991).

(2) Several jurisdictions have followed the lead of *Sindell* to apply some version of the "market share" causation theory in DES litigation. No particular preferred formulation has emerged but, instead each court seems to adopt a customized rule. Some of the variations are described below.

(a) In *Collins v. Eli Lilly Co.*, 116 Wis.2d 166, 342 N.W.2d 37 (Wis. 1984), the Wisconsin Supreme Court rejected *Sindell*:

> The primary factor which prevents us from following Sindell is the practical difficulty of defining and proving market share. As noted earlier, it appears many drug companies simply do not have records available from which a fact finder could determine how much DES a given defendant produced or marketed, or when and where the DES was produced and marketed. Even assuming that some drug companies have records, the fact finder still may not be able to compose an accurate assessment of the total market of which those companies were a part. There are several reasons for this: The DES market apparently was quite fluid, with companies entering and leaving the market over the years; some companies no longer exist and some that still exist may not have relevant records; and apparently there are no accurate nationwide records pertaining to the overall production and marketing of DES. We view defining the market and apportioning market share as a near impossible task if it is to be done fairly and accurately in order to approximate the probability that a defendant caused the plaintiff's injuries.
>
> Further, we conclude that the waste of judicial resources which would be inherent in a second "mini-trial" to determine market share militates against its adoption by this court. We emphasize, however, that we do not totally reject the market share theory. Rather, as we explain below, we consider market share, if determinable, to be a relevant factor in apportioning liability among defendants.

342 N.W.2d 49.

Not to be outdone, the court prescribed the following procedure in DES cases:

> Thus, the plaintiff need commence suit against only one defendant and allege the following elements: that the plaintiff's mother took DES; that DES caused the plaintiff's subsequent injuries; that the defendant produced or marketed the type of DES taken by the plaintiff's mother; and that the defendant's conduct in producing or marketing the DES constituted a breach of a legally recognized duty to the plaintiff. In the situation where the plaintiff cannot allege and prove what type of DES the mother took, as to the third element the plaintiff need only allege and prove that the defendant drug company produced or marketed the drug DES for use in preventing miscarriages during pregnancy. Applying the rules of liberal construction to complaints, we construe the plaintiff's second amended complaint as satisfying these required allegations.
>
> At the trial of this case the plaintiff will have to prove each of these elements to the satisfaction of the trier of fact. We emphasize, however, that the plaintiff need not prove that a defendant produced or marketed the precise DES taken by the plaintiff's mother. Rather, the plaintiff need only establish by a preponderance of the evidence that a defendant produced or marketed the type (e.g., color, shape, markings, size, or other identifiable characteristics) of DES taken by the plaintiff's mother; the plaintiff need not allege or prove any facts related to the time or geographic distribution of the subject DES. If the plaintiff is able to prove these elements, the plaintiff may recover all damages from the one defendant. If, however,

more than one defendant is joined, the plaintiff should recover from each defendant damages proportionate to the jury's assignment of liability under the comparative negligence scheme developed below.

Although we hold that it is sufficient for the plaintiff to sue only one defendant, we recognize that the plaintiff may find it preferable to sue as many defendants as can be identified as having possible liability. Simple self-interest should encourage the plaintiff to sue more than one defendant drug company. If the plaintiff cannot prove the case against the single defendant, an action against other potentially liable defendants may be barred by the statute of limitations. A suit against more than one defendant, besides giving the plaintiff more opportunities to establish liability, also ensures that the plaintiff will have a better chance of actually recovering damages, because there is always the possibility that the single defendant will be judgment proof.

342 N.W.2d 51, 52.

(b) In *Martin v. Abbott Laboratories*, 689 P. 2d 368, 382–382 (Wash. 1984), the Supreme Court of Washington applied market share causation theory in this version:

We hold that plaintiff need commence suit against only one defendant and allege the following elements: that the plaintiff's mother took DES; that DES caused the plaintiff's subsequent injuries; that the defendant produced or marketed the type of DES taken by the plaintiff's mother; and that the defendant's conduct in producing or marketing the DES constituted a breach of a legally recognized duty to the plaintiff. At the trial, the plaintiff will have to prove each of these elements to the satisfaction of the trier of fact. We emphasize, however, that the plaintiff need not prove that a defendant produced or marketed the precise DES taken by the plaintiff's mother. Rather, the plaintiff need only establish by a preponderance of the evidence that a defendant produced or marketed the type (e.g., dosage, color, shape, markings, size, or other identifiable characteristics) of DES taken by the plaintiff's mother; the plaintiff need not allege or prove any facts related to the time or geographic distribution of the subject DES. While the type of DES ingested by the mother should be within the domain of her knowledge, facts relating to time and distribution should be particularly within the domain of knowledge of the DES manufacturers and distributors.

We reject the Sindell requirement of joinder of a "substantial share" of the market because it does not alter the probability under our market-share alternate liability theory that a particular defendant caused the injury. As will be demonstrated, a particular defendant's potential liability is proportional to the probability that it caused plaintiff's injury.

Individual defendants are entitled to exculpate themselves from liability by establishing, by a preponderance of the evidence, that they did not produce or market the particular type DES taken by the plaintiff's mother; that they did not market the DES in the geographic market area of plaintiff mother's obtaining the drug; or that it did not distribute DES in the time period of plaintiff mother's ingestion of the drug.

The defendants that are unable to exculpate themselves from potential liability are designated members of the plaintiffs' DES market; defined by the specificity of the evidence as to geographic market area, time of ingestion, and type of DES. These defendants are initially presumed to have equal shares of the market and are liable for only the percentage of plaintiff's judgment that represents their presumptive share of the market. These defendants are entitled to rebut this presumption and thereby reduce their potential liability by establishing their respective market share of DES in the plaintiff's particular geographic market. Upon proof of a market share by a preponderance of the evidence, that particular defendant is only liable for its share of the market as it relates to the total judgment. To the extent that other defendants fail to establish their actual market share, their presumed market share is adjusted so that 100 percent of the market is accounted for.

Application of this rule of apportionment is illustrated by the following hypotheticals. Assume that plaintiff's damages are $100,000 and defendants X and Y remain subject to liability after exculpation by other named defendants. If neither establishes its market share then they are presumed to have equal shares of the market and are liable respectively for 50 percent of the total judgment, X, $50,000 and Y, $50,000. Assume defendant X establishes that it occupies 20 percent of the relevant market, and defendant Y fails to prove its market share. Defendant X is then liable for 20 percent of the damages, or $20,000, and defendant Y is subject to the remaining 80 percent, or $80,000. Assume that defendant X establishes a market share of 20 percent and defendant Y a 60 percent market share. Then defendant X is subject to 20 percent of the judgment, $20,000, and defendant Y to 60 percent of the judgment, $60,000. The plaintiff does not recover her entire judgment because the remaining 20 percent of the market share is the responsibility of unnamed defendants.

The defendants may implead third party defendants in order to reduce their presumptive share of the market or in order to establish an actual reduced market share. This ability of a defendant to reduce its liability reduces the disproportion between potential liability that a particular defendant caused the injury by imposing liability according to respective market shares. In the case where each party carries its burden of proof, no defendant will be held liable for more harm than it statistically could have caused in the respective market.

We recognize that the elimination of individual causal responsibility as an element of plaintiff's case is liability enhancing. However, it is also liability limiting insofar as it permits the defendants to apportion liability according to respective market share and further provides that the plaintiff may not be able to recover her entire damages. Under this market share alternate liability theory, the dilution of causal blame that is attributable to a given defendant may be counterbalanced by the corresponding dilution of liability.

Conley v. Boyle Drug Co., 570 So.2d 275 (Fla. 1990), adopted the Martin market share formulation for application in DES cases.

(3) Which is a more powerful tool for plaintiffs, *Sindell*, *Collins*, or *Martini*? Which is legally soundest?

(4) The student should be mindful that market share theory does not constitute a cause of action of itself but is merely a device to assist plaintiffs to prove (or avoid having to prove) the causation-in-fact element of a tort cause of action. With few exceptions, courts have declined to apply the doctrine beyond the rigorous conditions specified in *Sindell*. DES cases have been its almost exclusive field of application. *Smith v. Cutter Biological, Inc.*, 823 P.2d 717 (Haw. 1991), applied the doctrine in a "blood component" case, but *Doe v. Cutter Biological*, 852 F.Supp 909 (D. Idaho 1994), rejected it. *Morris v. Parke Davis & Company*, 667 F.Supp. 1332 (C.D.Cal. 1987), applied the theory to DPT vaccine. Numerous courts have declined to apply the doctrine to asbestosis cases. See, e.g., *Celotex Corp. v. Copeland*, 471 So.2d 533 (Fla. 1985).

(5) *In the Matter of DES Market Share Litigation*, 591 N.E.2d 226 (N.Y. 1992), held that plaintiffs have a state constitutional right of trial by jury in market share DES litigation.

(6) Suppose the plaintiff's complaint is that the particular specimen of an otherwise harmless fungible product such as an anti-polio vaccine was defective and dangerous because of the defect and not because of a common inherent property of the product? If the plaintiff cannot identify the manufacturer of the defective specimen, should market share theory apply? *Shieffield v. Eli Lilly and Company*, 192 Cal. Rptr. 870 (Cal. App. 1983), rejected it. Do you agree?

(7) *Hall v. E. I. Du Pont de Nemours & Co., Inc.*, 345 F.Supp. 353 (E.D.N.Y.1972) supplied a rationale to justify the concert of action cases: a common capacity to control the risk that caused the harm. Does this explain *Summers v. Tice* discussed in *Sindell*? Do you agree that it cannot be applied in *Sindell* itself?

ANDERSON v. SOMBERG

New Jersey Supreme Court

67 N.J. 291, 338 A.2d 1 (1974), *cert. denied,*423 U.S. 929 (1975)

PASHMAN, JUSTICE.

These negligence-products liability actions had their inception in a surgery performed in 1967 on the premises of defendant St. James Hospital (Hospital). Plaintiff was undergoing a laminectomy, a back operation, performed by defendant Dr. Somberg. During the course of the procedure, the tip of cup of an angulated pituitary rongeur, a forceps-like instrument, broke off while the tool was being manipulated in plaintiff's spinal canal. The surgeon attempted to retrieve the metal but was unable to do so. After repeated failure in that attempt, he terminated the operation. The imbedded fragment caused medical complications and further surgical interventions were required. Plaintiff has suffered significant and permanent physical injury proximately caused by the rongeur fragment which lodged in his spine.

Plaintiff sued: (1) Dr. Somberg for medical malpractice, alleging that the doctor's negligent action caused the rongeur to break; (2) St. James Hospital, alleging that it negligently furnished Dr. Somberg with a defective surgical instrument; (3) Reinhold-Schumann, Inc. (Reinhold), the medical supply distributor which furnished the defective rongeur to the hospital, on a warranty theory and (4) Lawton Instrument Company (Lawton), the manufacturer of the rongeur, on a strict liability in tort claim, alleging that the rongeur was a defective product. In short, plaintiff sued all who might have been liable for his injury, absent some alternative explanation such as contributory negligence.

Dr. Somberg testified that he had not examined the rongeur prior to the day of surgery. He inspected it visually when the nurse handed it to him during the operation, and manipulated its handles to make certain it was functional. The doctor stated that he did not twist the instrument, and claimed that the manner in which the instrument was inserted in plaintiff's body precluded the possibility of twisting. He noted the absence of one of the rongeur's cups when he withdrew the instrument from plaintiff's spinal canal, but his efforts to retrieve the fragment proved of no avail.

Dr. Graubard, a general surgeon, testified as an expert witness for plaintiff. He stated that the rongeur was a delicate instrument, a tool not to be "used incorrectly or with excessive force or to be used against hard substances." He claimed that a twisting of the instrument might cause it to break at the cups. Dr. Graubard stated that a "rongeur used properly and not defective would not break."

The deposition of the operating room supervisor of defendant hospital, Sister Carmen Joseph, was read into the record. She was responsible for visually examining and sterilizing all instruments prior to surgery. The rongeur in question was used about five times a year, and had been used about 20 times before this operation. She did not know who had taken out the rongeur for this operation; she had not worked the day of plaintiff's operation.

The hospital's purchasing agent testified that the rongeur had been purchased from the distributor, Reinhold, about four years prior to plaintiff's surgery and was received in a box bearing the name of the manufacturer, Lawton. The owner of Reinhold testified that the rongeur was not a stock item and had to be specially ordered from Lawton upon receipt of the hospital purchase order. The box was opened at Reinhold's warehouse, to verify that it was a rongeur and it was then forwarded to the hospital.

Defendant Lawton called a metallurgist, a Mr. John Carroll, as an expert witness. He testified that an examination of the broken rongeur revealed neither structural defect nor faulty workmanship. He said that the examination (conducted at an optical magnification 500 times normal size) revealed a secondary crack near the main crack but he could not suggest how or when the crack formed. Mr. Carroll offered an opinion as to the cause of the instrument's breaking: the instrument had been strained, he said, probably because of an improper "twisting" of the tool. The strain, however, could have been cumulative, over the course of several operations, and the instrument could conceivably have been cracked when handed to Dr. Somberg and broken in its normal use.

In short, when all the evidence had been presented, no theory for the cause of the rongeur's breaking was within reasonable contemplation save for the possible negligence of Dr. Somberg in using the instrument, or the possibility that the surgeon had been given a defective instrument, which defect would be attributable to a dereliction of duty by the manufacturer, the distributor, the hospital or all of them.

The case was submitted to a jury on special interrogatories, and the jury returned a finding of no cause as to each defendant. On appeal, the entire Appellate panel concurred in an order for a new trial. A majority held that the verdict represented a miscarriage of justice, and that on the facts of this case it was clear that one of the parties was liable and the jury should have been told that it had to return a verdict against at least one of the defendants. The concurring opinion writer argued that the jury had not been properly instructed on its prerogatives to find for plaintiff; but he felt that the order for a directed verdict against an unnamed defendant was an invitation to the jury to guess which defendant was liable. Accordingly, the concurrence urged that the case be remanded for trial, and that the jury be instructed that plaintiff had made out a very strong prima facie case. Certification was granted. 63 N.J. 586, 311 A.2d 8 (1973).

First, we note that the suggestion in the concurring opinion that the case be sent back on "strengthened" instructions is little more than a pretext for giving plaintiff a second chance before a jury. Neither in the Appellate Division nor before this Court has it been alleged, let alone demonstrated, that the charge did not comport with the standard charge for a "strong" prima facie case made out by res ipsa loquitur (thought to be appropriate here). Indeed, the trial judge very adequately explained to the jury that plaintiff, given all favorable inferences, could be said to have proved his case.

The position adopted by the Appellate Division majority seems to us substantially correct: that is, at the close of all the evidence, it was apparent that at least one of the defendants was liable for plaintiff's injury, because no alternative theory of liability was within reasonable contemplation. Since defendants had engaged in conduct which activated legal obligations by each of them to plaintiff, the jury should have been instructed that the failure of any defendant to prove his nonculpability would trigger liability; and further, that since at least one of the defendants could not sustain his burden of proof, at least one would be liable. A no cause of action verdict against all primary and third-party defendants will be unacceptable and would work a miscarriage of justice sufficient to require a new trial.

In the ordinary case, the law will not assist an innocent plaintiff at the expense of an innocent defendant. However, in the type of case we consider here, where an unconscious or helpless patient suffers an admitted mishap not reasonably foreseeable and unrelated to the scope of the surgery (such as cases where foreign objects are left in the body of the patient), those who had custody of the patient, and who owed him a duty of care as to medical treatment, or not to furnish a defective instrument for use in such treatment can be called to account for their default. They must prove their nonculpability, or else risk liability for the injuries suffered.

This case resembles the ordinary medical malpractice foreign-objects case, where the patient is sewn up with a surgical tool or sponge inside him. In those cases, res ipsa loquitur is used to make out a prima facie case.

The rule of evidence we set forth does not represent the doctrine of res ipsa loquitur as it has been traditionally understood. Res ipsa loquitur is ordinarily impressed only where the injury more probably than-not has resulted from negligence of the defendant, Germann v. Matriss, 55 N.J. 193, 260 A.2d 825 (1970), and defendant was in exclusive control of the instrument. The doctrine has been expanded to include, as in the instant matter, multiple defendants, Jackson v. Magnavox Corp., 116 N.J. Super. 1, 17, 280 A.2d 692 (App.Div.1972); Ybarra v. Spangard, 25 Cal.2d 486, 154 P.2d 687 (Sup.Ct.1948), although even this expansion has been criticized. It has also been expanded to embrace cases where the negligence cause was not the only or more probable theory in the case, but where the alternate theories of liability accounted for the only possible causes of injury. That is the situation in this case, where we find negligence, strict liability in tort and breach of warranty all advanced as possible theories of liability. In such cases, defendants are required to come forward and give their evidence. The latter development represents a substantial deviation from earlier conceptions of res ipsa loquitur and has more accurately been called "akin to res ipsa loquitur," NOPCO Chem. Div. v. Blaw-Knox Co., 59 N.J. 274, 281 A.2d 793 (1971), or "conditional res ipsa loquitur," Quintal v. Laurel Grove Hospital, 62 Cal.2d 154, 166, 41 Cal.Rptr. 577, 397 P.2d 161 (Sup.Ct. 1965); cf. the dissent of Chief Justice Weintraub in Jakubowski v. Minnesota Mining and Manufacturing Co., 42 N.J. 177, 188, 199 A.2d 826 (1964).

. . .

The California cases have taken that turn despite some language to the contrary, and defendants have been required to make: "an affirmative showing (1) of a definite cause for the accident in which cause no element of negligence on the part of the defendant inheres; or (2) of such care in all possible respects as necessarily to lead to the conclusion that the accident could not have happened from want of care, but must have been due to some unpreventable cause, although the exact cause is unknown," Dierman v. Providence Hospital, supra, 188 P.2d at 15, quoting Bourguignon v. Peninsular Ry. Co., 40 Cal.App. 689, 694, 695, 181 P. 669, 671 (1919). Cf. Justice Traynor's dissent in that case argues that the majority's rule could make plaintiff's medical attendants insurers of his safety. We accept the approach of the Dierman majority, which reversed a no cause verdict against plaintiff, and remanded for trial, apparently upon new instructions that defendants in this type of medical malpractice case should be made to exculpate themselves where clearly plaintiff was not at fault. See Louisell and Williams, Res Ipsa Loquitur — Its Future In Medical Malpractice Cases, 48 Cal.L.Rev. 252, 256 (1960), suggesting that in unconscious-patients cases a res lpsa-like charge ought to shift the actual burden of proof. At least one writer has argued that the burden of proof rule should be adopted on the basis of an explicit recognition that the risk of unexplained injuries in these unconscious-patient situations should lie with those who were in custody of the body or who owed a duty to the patient (e.g., as the manufacturers of surgical tools). Thode, The Unconscious Patient: Who Should Bear The Risk Of Unexplained Injuries to A Healthy Part Of His Body?, 1969 Utah L.Rev. 1. See Seavey, Res Ipsa Loquitur: Tabula in Naufragio, supra, 63 Harv.L.Rev. at 646–647.

The imposition of the burden of proof upon multiple defendants, even though only one could have caused the injury, is no novelty to the law, as where all defendants have been clearly negligent. Summers v. Tice, 33 Cal.2d 80, 199 P.2d 1 (1948). As against multiple defendants where there is no evidence as to where culpability lies, the rule is not generally available, according to Prosser, because it might impose an equal hardship on an innocent defendant as on an innocent plaintiff. Prosser notes exceptional special. cases, as where defendant owes a special responsibility to plaintiff, and in those instances the burden of proof can in fact be shifted to defendants. Prosser, Torts (4 ed. 1973), pp. 243–244, 231, 223. The facts of this case disclose just such a special responsibility, and require a shifting of the burden of proof to defendants.

We hold that in a situation like this, the burden of proof in fact does shift to defendants. All those in custody of that patient or who owed him a duty, as here, the manufacturer and the distributor, should be called forward and should be made to prove their freedom from liability. The rule would have no application except in those instances where the injury lay outside the ambit of the surgical procedure in question; for example, an injury to an organ, when that organ was itself the object of medical attention, would not by itself make out a prima facie case for malpractice or shift the burden of proof to defendants. Farber v. Olkon, 40 Cal.2d 503, 254 P.2d 520, 524 (1953).

Further, we note that at the close of all the evidence, no reasonable suggestion had been offered that the occurrence could have arisen because of plaintiff's contributory negligence, or some act of nature; that is, there was no explanation for the occurrence in the case save for negligence or defect on the part of someone connected with the manufacture, handling, or use of the instrument. (Any such proof would be acceptable to negative plaintiff's prima facie case.) Since all parties had been joined who could reasonably have been connected with that negligence or defect, it was clear that one of those parties was liable, and at least one could not succeed in his proofs.

In cases of this type, no defendant will be entitled to prevail on a motion for judgment until all the proofs have been presented to the court and jury. The judge may grant any motion bearing in mind that the plaintiff must recover a verdict against at least one defendant. Inferences and doubts at this stage are resolved in favor of the plaintiff. If only one defendant remains by reason of the court's action, then, in fact, the judge is directing a verdict of liability against that defendant.

. . .

The judgment of the Appellate Division is hereby affirmed, and the cause remanded for trial upon instructions consonant with this opinion.

. . .

MOUNTAIN, J., dissenting.

This Court has reached an extraordinary result in a very remarkable way. As I shall hope to make clear, the structure of argument as presented in the Court's opinion is rested upon an assumed factual premise which does not exist. In part because of this, the concluding and most significant part of the argument suffers from the defect of visiting liability, in a wholly irrational way, upon parties who are more probably than not totally free of blame. I respectfully dissent.

. . .

I of course agree with the Court that it is most unfortunate that this plaintiff should go uncompensated. Every humanitarian instinct impels the hope that when an unconscious patient is injured in some unforeseen and unforeseeable way, due reparation will be forthcoming. It is to the manner in which the Court would seek to fulfill this hope that I object.

As the opinion of the Court has been careful to point out, (P. 8), plaintiff's claims against the surgeon, Dr. Somberg, and against the hospital sound in negligence; his claims against the manufacturer and distributor, on the other hand, are stated as arising from alleged breach of warranty or as resting upon a theory of strict liability in tort. At the conclusion of the plaintiff's case it had become apparent that with respect to his negligence claims he was entitled to invoke the doctrine of res ipsa loquitur. The fracture of the rongeur in the wound bespoke negligence on the part of someone, the instrument was at the time within the control of a defendant and the injury was clearly not attributable to any fault or neglect on the part of the plaintiff.

The opinion takes the view that at this point the burden of proof shifted to defendants. This, as is apparently conceded, has not hitherto been the law of this State. "The operation of this rule of evidence [res ipsa loquitur] does not shift the burden of persuasion. [citing authorities]." Bornstein v. Metropolitan Bottling Co., 26 N.J. 263, 269, 139 A.2d 404, 408 (1958). Nevertheless this alteration in the law may be entirely reasonable and justified — at least if limited to this kind of medical malpractice case. 1 Louisell & Williams, Medical Malpractice sec. 15.02 et seq. In any event the argument as to the procedural effect to be given the rule of res ipsa has well been called "a tempest in a teapot." 2 Harper & James, The Law of Torts (1956) sec. 19.11, p. 1104. Parenthetically, it may be pointed out that the duty of explanation on the part of a surgeon, when unforeseen injury occurs, is always inherent in the relationship between physician and patient. 1 Louisell & Williams, Medical Malpractice, supra, sec. 15.01. Thus far, as to the negligence claims, I might be persuaded to agree with the Court.

But certainly no farther. At this point the effect to be given a shift in the burden of proof becomes the crucial issue. The authorities which have adopted or espoused the view that res ipsa shifts the burden of proof have, as far as I can discover, understood this to mean that upon such a shift taking place, a defendant becomes obliged to offer evidence explaining his own conduct or throwing light upon the circumstances attending plaintiff's injury, which will be of sufficient probative force to establish his lack of fault by a preponderance of the evidence. The fact finder will then be called upon to decide whether the defendant's proofs have met this test or whether they have fallen short.

The view expressed by the Court in this case as to the effect of shifting the burden of proof appears to be something quite different. Under this new rule it is no longer enough that a defendant meet the standard described above. His role is no longer simply that of one who may hope to succeed if his proofs justify a verdict. Rather he now finds himself one of a band of persons from among whom one or more must be singled out to respond in damages to the plaintiff's claim. He is now a member of a group who must collectively, among themselves, play a game of sauve qui peut — and play it for rather high stakes. With all due respect I submit that at this point there has been complete departure from the rule of reason; the argument is now stripped of all rational basis:

Note, first, the role the jury is being called upon to play. The judge will give to the jury two potentially contradictory instructions. First the jurors will be told to arrive at a verdict by a preponderance of the evidence, each defendant having the burden of exculpating himself. Then a further direction will be given that they must bring in a verdict against some one or more of the defendants. But suppose the members of the jury cannot agree that the evidence will sustain a verdict against any defendant. What then! Each juror has taken an oath — no small matter — to reach a verdict only "according to the evidence." What does he now do? Presumably he poses his problem to the judge. And upon seeking the aid of the court, what further instructions is he to be given?

What is to be the posture of the judge if he is thereafter called upon to rule upon a motion for judgment notwithstanding the verdict or for a new trial, and it is perfectly clear to him that the verdict could not be supported by the evidence and was rendered only in response to the compulsion of this proposed charge? I leave the answers to these questions to those jurors and judges who must in the future act under the shadow of this decision.

Consider further the hypothesis last suggested, that a jury does undertake, despite a failure of adequate proof, to carry out the mandate of this instruction. How is a verdict to be reached? The absence of sufficient evidence upon which a verdict might justly rest, coupled with the compulsion to reach a verdict against someone, removes from the case any semblance of rationality. It then becomes a mere game of chance. There being no rational guide, each jury may proceed as the whimsy of the moment dictates. Thus we have trial by lot, or by chance — no more a rational process than were trial by ordeal or trial by combat. And yet it is the very essence of the judicial process that a determination reached by a court shall be the result of a rational study and analysis of applicable fact and law.[3]

Nor can it be seriously contended that in following the course outlined by the Court there would not be instances — perhaps many — where liability would be visited upon wholly innocent persons. I cannot concur in a decision announcing a rule of law which invites such a result.

It is, of course, generally accepted as axiomatic in a society dedicated to the values of individualism, that no person shall be made to answer for an event, unless his responsibility for it has been convincingly proved by due process of law.

[Fleming, Developments in the English Law of Medical Liability, 12 Vand.L. Rev. 633, 646 (1959).]

Finally it may be asked whether a trial such as is here projected may in any true sense be termed either a trial by jury or an exercise of the judicial process, as those concepts are generally understood.

I would vote to reverse the judgment of the Appellate Division and to reinstate the judgment of the trial court.

---

[3] Justice (now Chief Judge) Breitel has expressed the point well:

The primary internal characteristic of the judicial process is that it is a rational one. The judicial process is based on reasoning and presupposes — all anti-rationalists to the contrary notwithstanding — that its determinations are justified only when explained or explainable in reason. No poll, no majority vote of the affected, no rule of expediency, and certainly no confessedly subjective or idiosyncratic view justifies a judicial determination.

. . .

The rational judicial process is not permitted to rove generally over the scene of human affairs. Instead, it must be used, on pain of violating the proprieties, within the framework of a highly disciplined special system of legal rules characteristic of the legal order. No principle of the moral order or any other by itself may demand recognition in the judicial process of dispute determination except as it is incorporated or can be incorporated into the system of legal rules. [Breitel, The Lawmakers, 65 Colum.L.Rev. 749, 772–3 (1965)]

CLIFFORD, J., and JUDGE COLLESTER join in this dissenting opinion.

NOTES AND QUESTIONS

(1)   How, specifically, does *Anderson v. Somberg* differ from *Summers v. Tice*? From *Sindell*? See also *Ferrigno v. Eli Lilly & Co.*, 75 N.J. Super. 551, 420 A.2d 1305 (1980). Could the plaintiff in *Zinnell*, § 7.02 *supra*, have appropriately invoked the *Anderson* rule?

(2)   In *NOPCO Chemical Div. v. Blaw Knox Co.*, 281 A.2d 793 (N.J. 1971), the New Jersey supreme court applied a similar theory to a series of processors and handlers of a defective product, all of whom owed the plaintiff a duty of care. In NOPCO, however, the court merely shifted the burden of persuasion of non-liability to each defendant, and did not require the jury to find at least one of the defendants to be liable, thus permitting it to exonerate all defendants if it so found. Apparently, no other court has applied the most aggressive aspect of *Anderson v. Somberg*.

(3)   Would punitive damages ever be appropriate in a market share liability case? See *Morris v. Parke, Davis & Co.*, 573 F. Supp. 1324 (C.D. Cal.1983).

§ 7.05   MODIFIED SUBSTANTIAL FACTOR

Sindell applied the market share theory of causation to DES, a product that was fungible as to risk whoever manufactured it. Accordingly, some courts have held that a plaintiff must establish all *Sindell* factors including risk-fungibility to invoke market share causation. *Thomas ex rel. Grambling v. Mallett*, 701 N.W.2d 523 (Wis. 2005) extended *Sindell* to lead paint poisoning. As to fungibility in its "risk-contribution" theory, the Wisconsin court requires the plaintiff to prove that each defendant produced the "specific type of white lead carbonate" the plaintiff ingested. Cf., *Smith v. Butter Biological, Inc., a Div. of Miles Inc.*, 823 P.2d 717 (Haw. 1991) (market share applied to blood product despite absence of risk-fungibility).

Several courts have declined to apply market share causation in asbestos cases because different asbestos products pose different risks of producing injury. See *Celotex Corp. v. Copeland*, 471 So.2d 533 (Fla. 1985), *Ferris v. Gatke Corp.*, 132 Cal.Rptr.2d 819 (Cal. Appl. 2003), and *Black v. Abex Corp.*, 603 N.W.2d 182 (N.D. 1999). Could some cases that fail the "but-for" test and the requirements of market share causation or any of the other theories discussed in *Sindell* be salvaged by modifying a different theory of causation? Assume a worker is exposed to asbestos products manufactured by companies D1, D2, D3, . . . Dn, all of which are carcinogens but of markedly different levels of risk. After years of exposure, W contracts a lung cancer indisputably caused by the inhalation of asbestos particles, but cannot prove which defendant produced the product that caused the cancer. Application of the but-for test denies a remedy and *Sindell* does not apply for lack of fungibility. Should the plaintiffs be permitted to recover?

RUTHERFORD v. OWENS-ILLINOIS, INC.
Supreme Court of California
16 Cal. 4th 953, 941 P.2d 1203 (1977)

BAXTER, JUSTICE.

In this consolidated action for asbestos-related personal injuries and wrongful death brought and tried in Solano County, defendant Owens-Illinois, Inc. (Owens-Illinois) contends the trial court erred in instructing the liability phase jury pursuant to Solano County Complex Asbestos Litigation General Order No. 21.00. This instruction shifts the burden of proof to defendants in asbestos cases tried on a products liability theory to prove that their products were not a legal cause of the plaintiff's injuries, provided the plaintiff first establishes certain predicate facts, chief among them that the defendant manufactured or sold defective asbestos-containing products to which plaintiff was exposed, and that plaintiff's exposure to asbestos fibers generally was a legal cause of plaintiff's injury. The Court of Appeal concluded the trial court erred in giving the burden-shifting instruction.

The Court of Appeal further held that the judgment in this case must be reversed because the trial court erred in refusing to permit Owens-Illinois to present a "tobacco company defense." The Court of Appeal's judgment in this regard was error requiring reversal under our recent holding in Richards v. Owens-Illinois, Inc. (1997) 14 Cal.4th 985, 988–989, 60 Cal.Rptr.2d 103, 928 P.2d 1181, a case consolidated and tried with the instant action and three others. However, because the Court of Appeal alternatively determined the trial court erred in giving the burden-shifting instruction, and because plaintiffs here additionally sought review of that aspect of the Court of Appeal's judgment, we must also in this case review the Court of Appeal's holding that it was error to give the burden-shifting instruction.

We conclude the Court of Appeal correctly determined that the burdenshifting instruction should not have been given in this case. For reasons to be explained, we hold that in cases of asbestos-related cancer, a jury instruction shifting the burden of proof to asbestos defendants on the element of causation is generally unnecessary and incorrect under settled statewide principles of tort law. Proof of causation in such cases will always present inherent practical difficulties, given the long latency period of asbestos-related disease, and the occupational settings that commonly exposed the worker to multiple forms and brands of asbestos products with varying degrees of toxicity. In general, however, no insuperable barriers prevent an asbestos-related cancer plaintiff from demonstrating that exposure to the defendant's asbestos products was, in reasonable medical probability, a substantial factor in causing or contributing to his risk of developing cancer. We conclude that plaintiffs are required to prove no more than this. In particular, they need not prove with medical exactitude that fibers from a particular defendant's asbestos-containing products were those, or among those, that actually began the cellular process of malignancy. Instruction on the limits of the plaintiff's burden of proof of causation, together with the standardized instructions defining cause-in-fact causation under the substantial factor test (BAJI No. 3.76) and the doctrine of concurrent proximate legal causation (BAJI No. 3.77) will adequately apprise the jury of the elements required to establish causation. No burden-shifting instruction is necessary on the matter of proof of causation, and in the absence of such necessity, there is no justification or basis for shifting part of the plaintiff's burden of proof to the defendant to prove that it was not a legal cause of plaintiff's asbestos-related disease or injuries. (See Summers v. Tice (1948) 33 Cal.2d 80, 86, 199 P.2d 1 (Summers) [burden shift justified because without it all tortfeasors might escape liability and the injured plaintiff be left "remediless."].)

. . . .

In conclusion, our general holding is as follows. In the context of a cause of action for asbestos-related latent injuries, the plaintiff must first establish some threshold exposure to the defendant's defective asbestos-containing products, FN12 and must further establish in reasonable medical probability that a particular exposure or series of exposures was a "legal cause" of his injury, i.e., a substantial factor in bringing about the injury. In an asbestos-related cancer case, the plaintiff need not prove that fibers from the defendant's product were the ones, or among the ones, that actually began the process of malignant cellular growth. Instead, the plaintiff may meet the burden of proving that exposure to defendant's product was a substantial factor causing the illness by showing that in reasonable medical probability it was a substantial factor contributing to the plaintiff's or decedent's risk of developing cancer. The jury should be so instructed.FN13 The standard instructions on substantial factor and concurrent causation (BAJI Nos. 3.76 and 3.77) remain correct in this context and should also be given.

[The court also held that the giving of the Summers v. Tice burden shifting instruction was harmless error and upheld the judgment for the plaintiff.]

FAIRCHILD v. GLENHAVEN FUNERAL SERVICES LTD. AND OTHERS
House of Lords
[2003] 1 A.C. 32

LORD BINGHAM OF CORNHILL

My Lords, on 16 May 2002 it was announced that these three appeals would be allowed. I now give my reasons for reaching that decision.

The essential question underlying the appeals may be accurately expressed in this way. If (1) C was employed at different times and for differing periods by both A and B, and (2) A and B were both subject to a duty to take reasonable care or to take all practicable measures to prevent C inhaling asbestos dust because of the known risk that asbestos dust (if inhaled) might cause a mesothelioma, and (3) both A and B were in breach of that duty in relation to C during the periods of C's employment by each of them with the result that during both periods C inhaled excessive quantities of asbestos dust, and (4) C is found to be suffering from a mesothelioma, and (5) any cause of C's mesothelioma other than the inhalation of asbestos dust at work can be effectively discounted, but (6) C cannot (because of the current limits of human science) prove, on the balance of probabilities, that his mesothelioma was the result of his inhaling asbestos dust during his employment by A or during his employment by B or during his employment by A and B taken together, is C entitled to recover damages against either A or B or against both A and B? To this question (not formulated in these terms) the Court of Appeal (Brooke, Latham and Kay LJJ), in a reserved judgment of the court reported at [2002] 1 WLR 1052, gave a negative answer. It did so because, applying the conventional "but for" test of tortious liability, it could not be held that C had proved against A that his mesothelioma would probably not have occurred but for the breach of duty by A, nor against B that his mesothelioma would probably not have occurred but for the breach of duty by B, nor against A and B that his mesothelioma would probably not have occurred but for the breach of duty by both A and B together. So C failed against both A and B. The crucial issue on appeal is whether, in the special circumstances of such a case, principle, authority or policy requires or justifies a modified approach to proof of causation.

[Lengthy discussion of cases from English, American, Australian, Canadian and European cases dealing with the limits of the but-for test omitted.]

Policy

The present appeals raise an obvious and inescapable clash of policy considerations. On the one hand are the considerations powerfully put by the Court of Appeal [2002] 1 WLR 1052, 1080, para 103 which considered the claimants' argument to be not only illogical but "also susceptible of unjust results. It may impose liability for the whole of an insidious disease on an employer with whom the claimant was employed for quite a short time in a long working life, when the claimant is wholly unable to prove on the balance of probabilities that that period *67 of employment had any causative relationship with the inception of the disease. This is far too weighty an edifice to build on the slender foundations of McGhee v National Coal Board [1973] 1WLR 1, and Lord Bridge has told us in Wilsher v Essex Area Health Authority [1988] AC 1074 that McGhee established no new principle of law at all. If we were to accede to the claimants' arguments, we would be distorting the law to accommodate the exigencies of a very hard case. We would be yielding to a contention that all those who have suffered injury after being exposed to a risk of that injury from which someone else should have protected them should be able to recover compensation even when they are quite unable to prove who was the culprit. In a quite different context Lord Steyn has recently said in Frost v Chief Constable of Yorkshire Police [1999] 2 AC 455, 491 that our tort system sometimes results in imperfect justice, but it is the best the common law can do."

The Court of Appeal had in mind that in each of the cases discussed in paragraphs 14–21 above (Wardlaw, Nicholson, Gardiner, McGhee) there was only one employer involved. Thus there was a risk that the defendant might be held liable for acts for which he should not be held legally liable but no risk that he would be held liable for damage which (whether legally liable or not) he had not caused. The crux of cases such as the present, if the appellants' argument is upheld, is that an employer may be held liable for damage he has not caused. The risk is the greater where all the employers potentially liable are not before the court. This is so on the facts of each of the three appeals before the House, and is always likely to be so given the long latency of this condition and the likelihood that some employers potentially liable will have gone out of business or disappeared during that period. It can properly be said to be unjust to impose liability on a party who has not been shown, even on a balance of probabilities, to have caused the damage complained of. On the other hand, there is a strong policy argument in favour of compensating those who have suffered grave harm, at the expense of their employers who owed them a duty to protect them against that very harm and failed to do so, when the harm can only have been caused by breach of that duty and when science does not permit the victim accurately to attribute, as between several employers, the precise responsibility for the harm he has suffered. I am of opinion that such injustice as may be involved in imposing liability on a duty-breaking employer in these circumstances is heavily outweighed by the injustice of denying redress to a victim. Were the law otherwise, an employer exposing his employee to asbestos dust could obtain complete immunity against mesothelioma (but not asbestosis) claims by employing only those who had previously been exposed to excessive quantities of asbestos dust. Such a result would reflect no credit on the law. It seems to me, as it did to Lord Wilberforce in McGhee [1973] 1 WLR 1, 7 that:

> "the employers should be liable for an injury, squarely within the risk which they created and that they, not the pursuer, should suffer the consequence of the impossibility, foreseeably inherent in the nature of his injury, of segregating the precise consequence of their default."

CONCLUSION

To the question posed in paragraph 2 of this opinion I would answer that where conditions (1)-(6) are satisfied C is entitled to recover against both A and B. That conclusion is in my opinion consistent with principle, and also with authority (properly understood). Where those conditions are satisfied, it seems to me just and in accordance with common sense to treat the conduct of A and B in exposing C to a risk to which he should not have been exposed as making a material contribution to the contracting by C of a condition against which it was the duty of A and B to protect him. I consider that this conclusion is fortified by the wider jurisprudence reviewed above. Policy considerations weigh in favour of such a conclusion. It is a conclusion which follows even if either A or B is not before the court. It was not suggested in argument that C's entitlement against either A or B should be for any sum less than the full compensation to which C is entitled, although A and B could of course seek contribution against each other or any other employer liable in respect of the same damage in the ordinary way. No argument on apportionment was addressed to the House. I would in conclusion emphasise that my opinion is directed to cases in which each of the conditions specified in (1)-(6) of paragraph 2 above is satisfied and to no other case. It would be unrealistic to suppose that the principle here affirmed will not over time be the subject of incremental and analogical development. Cases seeking to develop the principle must be decided when and as they arise. For the present, I think it unwise to decide more than is necessary to resolve these three appeals which, for all the foregoing reasons, I concluded should be allowed.

[The appeal was allowed. Extended judgments of other Judges omitted.]

Chapter 8

PROXIMATE CAUSATION

In jure non remota causa, sed proxima spectatur. It were infinite for the law to judge the cause of causes, and their propulsion of one another; therefore it contenteth itself with the immediate cause and judgeth of actions by that, without looking to any further degree.

> Bacon, *Maxims of the Law*, Reg. 1, quoted in *Wing v. Morse*, 300 A.2d 491 (Me. 1973). [In law the near cause is looked to, not the remote one.]

§ 8.01 INTRODUCTION

Every negligence case must be analyzed in four steps: duty; breach; causation, including cause-in-fact and proximate cause; and damages. If the plaintiff fails, or is unable, to establish any one of the elements, the defendant will be exonerated. Unfortunately, applying the analysis is often difficult, and courts sometimes botch it. The next case demonstrates the difficulty. It underscores the need to be on guard about the slipperiness of proximate causation, especially when it is considered simultaneously with the duty question. The ensuing sections of this chapter attempt to unravel the doctrine with more clarity.

What usually creates the confusion is deciding whether a negligent actor is to be held responsible for all consequences of a wrongful act. Metaphorically, the doctrine of cause-in-fact is like a fishing net with very fine apertures. It gathers in many fish that are too small to be wisely harvested. Likewise, cause-in-fact attaches liability to consequences that are thought too far removed from the negligent act or too improbable a consequence to be the basis of liability. For example, if a farmer sets a fire to burn his fields and the fire escapes and burns adjoining buildings, the setting of the fire is a cause-in-fact. Moreover, destruction of more remote buildings set afire through a chain of progression is also a cause-in-fact. Even so, is the farmer necessarily to be held responsible for the burning of the adjoining buildings, or, more troublesome, of the remote buildings? As to owners of the adjoining buildings, courts are likely to say that a reasonable farmer should have foreseen the unreasonable risk created by the fire and should have taken reasonable precautions to avoid them. But for the negligent act the adjoining buildings would not have been destroyed, and there is no policy reason not to hold the farmer accountable for failing to do what an ordinarily prudent person would have done in the same situation.

Whether there should be liability for the destruction of remote buildings is more difficult. Cause-in-fact surely is present, but the potential liability for all buildings that might wind up burned as a result of a highly fortuitous string of events is enormous. Is the poor farmer to be held liable for all the far-fetched losses for an act of simple negligence? Feeling instinctively that there must be some end to the scope of liability, at least in some cases, courts have searched for formulae to separate from the whole bulk of cause-in-fact consequences those that are also the "proximate cause" or "legal cause" consequences. Only to these does liability attach.

The following cases illustrate how successful the courts have been in this quest. The cases have been placed under subcategories because of the penchant of courts to do that whenever they can as a means of resolving difficult issues. In all instances, however, the true question remains whether or not the chain of causation-in-fact has been broken. The categories have not in general taken on the concreteness of the various no-duty rules examined earlier. In part, of course, this reflects the fact that proximate causation is a jury question rather than one of law.

PROBLEM

Under contract with the authorities, defendant installed and maintained emergency fire extinguishing equipment in a highway tunnel. Several maintenance periods were missed, and the charge of the fire extinguishers bled off. On the day of the event at issue, plaintiff was driving his vehicle with due care through the tunnel, when he was struck by a speeding soybean truck that overtook him and crashed into the rear of his car. The crash ruptured the gasoline tank in plaintiff's car, and a small fire broke out. Grabbing the nearby fire extinguisher, plaintiff attempted to put out the fire but could not because of low pressure. Before help arrived, plaintiff's car was consumed by flames. Plaintiff sued the defendant for the value of the destroyed vehicle.

At the close of the trial, the defendant requested that the jury be instructed on the legal effects of independent intervening agencies but was refused. Was that refusal in error?

CITY OF SCOTTSDALE v. KOKASKA
Arizona Court of Appeals
17 Ariz. App. 120, 495 P.2d 1327 (1972)

EUBANK, JUDGE.

This appeal arises out of an automobile collision that occurred between a vehicle driven by the plaintiff-appellee, Francene Kokaska and a City of Scottsdale police car driven by Officer Dwight Edwards. Both the City of Scottsdale and Officer Edwards were defendants in the trial court and are appellants here. We will refer to the plaintiff-appellee as the "Plaintiff", to the defendant City of Scottsdale as the "City", and to the defendant police officer Edwards as "Edwards."

The accident occurred in the early morning hours of February 23, 1964, on Scottsdale Road approximately one-half mile north of the intersection of Scottsdale Road and Vista Drive. Scottsdale Road is a four-lane highway at this point consisting of two southbound and two northbound lanes separated only by double painted lines. Just prior to the accident the Plaintiff had been at Joe Hunt's Restaurant and had left there to return to her home. She traveled north on Scottsdale Road at a speed of approximately 35 m.p.h.

Defendant Edwards was employed as a patrolman for the City of Scottsdale and was working the late evening shift on February 23rd. Prior to going on patrol, and for several days previously, Edwards was aware that the brakes on his patrol car were in poor condition. Edwards had advised his immediate supervisor of this fact on the night of the accident, and had even refused to drive the vehicle. His supervisor had ordered him to do so anyway, which he did. The particular defective conditions of the brakes were that they had to be depressed almost to the floorboard before taking hold, and that they would fade and grab.

Edwards went out on patrol and at about 1:15 A.M., on February 23rd he was traveling south on Scottsdale Road in the 200 block. At this point he observed a vehicle traveling north on Scottsdale Road at an excessive rate of speed. Edwards turned his car around and started to chase the speeder. There was conflicting testimony as to whether Edwards was using the red lights and siren during the ensuing chase. He had to stop at the intersection of Camelback Road and Scottsdale Road because of the traffic. At this point the speeder was moving steadily away from him, heading north on Scottsdale Road. Edwards continued the chase at an estimated speed of 60 to 65 m.p.h. with the speeder continuing to outdistance him. As he approached the 5300 block of Scottsdale Road, Edwards saw the Plaintiff's vehicle in the center lane move to the outside, northbound lane, revealing a Vespa motor scooter northbound in the center lane. He also observed two other vehicles in close proximity approaching in the two southbound lanes of Scottsdale Road and then he observed that the motor scooter had stopped in the center lane to make a left-hand turn. At this point Edwards applied the brakes and swerved left across the centerline in order to avoid colliding with the motor scooter. His patrol car sideswiped the left side of a Mercedes driven by Leonard Burkland which was heading south in the center lane. The rear end of the patrol car fishtailed to the right and then back to the left, continuing into the left rear side of the Plaintiff's vehicle. Plaintiff was injured as a result of the collision. The investigating officer reported that the night was dark, the weather was clear, the road was level, and the surface condition of the road was dry.

The operator of the motor scooter, Jan Sturgeon, testified by deposition that she did not hear a siren until after Edwards' patrol car had gone around her motor scooter. The driver of the Mercedes vehicle, Leonard Burkland, also testified by deposition, that he did not see the patrol car until it swung into his southbound lane and at that point the flashing red lights came on. A passenger in Mr. Burkland's auto, his wife, also testified by deposition that she had changed the radio station on the car radio and sat back and saw the defendant's patrol car in their lane with red lights flashing. Neither of them heard a siren. The Plaintiff testified that she did not see flashing red lights or hear a siren before impact. Edwards and his partner testified that the red light was flashing and the siren was operating during the chase, and the City contends that this patrol car was an authorized emergency vehicle as defined by A.R.S. § 28-624.

The cause was tried to a jury which returned a verdict for the Plaintiff against the defendants in the amount of $90,000. This was later remitted to $70,000 by the trial judge. Both defendant Edwards and the City appeal from the judgment.

FORESEEABILITY INSTRUCTIONS

Edwards requested two instructions relating to "foreseeability" both of which are substantially cited in full and approved by the Supreme Court in *Tucker v. Collar*, 79 Ariz. 141, 285 P.2d 178 (1955). The trial court refused both instructions and Edwards objected, stating, in part:

. . . These instructions set forth a test of *foreseeability as the test of negligence*, and I do not believe that the instruction to be given by Your Honor upon negligence gives any test as to foreseeability, and since one of the crucial issues in this case is whether or not the defendant Edwards should have foreseen that an unlighted motor scooter would be stopped in the center lane of the highway, the question of foreseeability is a crucial question and the jury should be instructed thereon. . . . (Emphasis added.)

The Plaintiff counters this by arguing that Edwards failed to raise foreseeability as an issue in the "pre-trial statement" filed pursuant to Rule XVI(c), Uniform Rules of Practice, 17 A.R.S. by defining Plaintiff's issues as "negligence, damages, if any and proximate cause;" and, further argues, in effect, that this case is not a "foreseeability" type case requiring such instructions for the reason that it is bottomed on Edwards' violation of specific statutes and involves a question of negligence *per se* or negligence as a matter of law. The first argument is without substance because the question *is* preserved by the pre-trial statement; the second argument is valid, in part.

Since negligence, as it has developed as a separate tort, is based upon the concept of fault, neither Edwards nor the City, through him, is legally responsible merely because his conduct injured the Plaintiff. 12 Am.Jur.2d Negligence, § 4 (1971 ed.). In order for *actionable* negligence to exist three elements must be satisfied. They are:

1. There must exist a duty on the part of the defendant to protect the plaintiff from the injury of which he complains;

2. The defendant must fail to perform that duty; and

3. An injury to the plaintiff must proximately result from such failure.

A fourth element is always understood to consist of the proof of an actual loss or damages. The first element is the *duty* issue; the second is the *negligence* issue; the third element is the causal relation or *proximate cause* issue; while the fourth element is the *damage* issue. To which issue is the question of foreseeability directed? Edwards says that it is the test for the second issue — *negligence.* However, our Supreme Court has said that it is an element of the first issue — *duty.* For instance in *Mountain States Telephone & Telegraph Co. v. Kelton*, 79 Ariz. 126, 285 P.2d 168 (1955), the court said that the duty the defendants owed plaintiff included the duty to take reasonable precautions to prevent injuring the plaintiff and that the reasonable precautions must be measured by the risk of anticipated harm (foreseeable harm). In *Morris v. Ortiz*, 103 Ariz. 119, 437 P.2d 652 (1968), our Supreme Court analyzes the foreseeability aspect of duty as follows:

To put it another way, to constitute actionable negligence the defendant must owe a duty to the plaintiff, the breach of which results proximately in plaintiff's injury. *Crouse v. Wilbur- Ellis Co.*, 77 Ariz. 359, 272 P.2d 352. So, the question which must be answered is, "What duty did Ortiz owe as the supervising instructor, the breach of which resulted in Morris' injury?" To hold that Ortiz had to anticipate Gillmor's act and somehow circumvent it is to say that it is the responsibility of a school teacher to anticipate the myriad of unexpected acts which occur daily in and about schools and school premises, the penalty for failure of which would be financial responsibility in negligence. We do not think that either the teacher or the district should be subject to such harassment nor is there an invocable legal doctrine or principle which can lead to such an absurd result. (103 Ariz. at 121, 437 P.2d at 654.)

In *Morris* the court held as a matter of law that the circumstances of injury were not foreseeable and consequently no duty was owed plaintiff.

"Duty" is defined by Professor Prosser, in his work on Torts, 2nd edition (1955), page 166, § 36, as one's obligation recognized by the law to conform to a particular standard of conduct toward another. In 1 Restatement of Torts 2nd, p. 7, § 4 (1965) "duty" is used,

. . . to denote the fact that the actor is required to conduct himself in a particular manner at the risk that if he does not do so he becomes subject to liability to another to whom the duty is owed for any injury sustained by such other, of which that actor's conduct is a legal cause.

These definitions, the foregoing cases, and the cases cited hereafter illustrate that three aspects of foreseeability have developed in Arizona law: first, the determination by the court as a matter of law whether as a part of duty, the injury to the Plaintiff was foreseeable under the circumstances; second, as in *Tucker v. Collar, supra*, where the Supreme Court held that foreseeability was a proper question for the jury on the issue of negligence; and third, where the court views foreseeability as an element of proximate or legal causation in intervening force-superseding cause situations as in *Salt River Valley Water Users' Ass'n v. Cornum*, 49 Ariz. 1, 63 P.2d 639 (1937). There seems to be a conflict in these three positions. Arizona, however, is not unique in this conflict as it is a common problem in most states. *See*, Annot., 155 A.L.R. 157, *Foreseeability as an Element of Negligence and Proximate Cause* (1945), and the supplemented Annot., 100 A.L.R. 2d 942 (1965).

[Discussion of a number of cases omitted.]

We believe that the foregoing conflict concerning foreseeability is more apparent than real. A close reading of the cases supports Judge Molloy's statement in *Wilson v. City of Tucson* [446 P.2d 504 (Ariz. App. 1968)], where he said:

There can be no liability in a negligence case unless there is negligent conduct on the part of one which invades a protected legal interest of another who is "within the range of apprehension" and which is the proximate cause of the injuries for which such other person claims damages. These three elements — negligence, an apprehensible interest, and proximate causation — blend into each other. Foreseeability plays a role in determining the presence or absence of all three elements. It is in many case[s] difficult, if not impossible to consider one of the elements apart from the others. With that in mind, we prefer to rest our decision here on the threshold question of whether the facts in this case disclose any breach of duty to the plaintiff's decedent on the part of the police officers. (8 Ariz.App. at 402, 446 P.2d at 508.)

We analyze the cases as saying that in the first instance foreseeability is always a question of law for the court. The court must determine the duty issue of whether an obligation is recognized by the law requiring the defendant to conform to a particular standard of conduct toward the plaintiff. This includes the question of whether the injury to the particular plaintiff was foreseeable. If it is not foreseeable then the trial judge usually disposes of the matter by dismissal, summary judgment, or the directed verdict route. If it is foreseeable and the duty is found by the trial court to exist, the trial court may or may not refer the foreseeability question to the jury by instruction on the issue of negligence. This issue is usually presented to the jury, as in *Tucker v. Collar, supra*, where there is a *debatable question* whether the injury to plaintiff was within the foreseeable scope of the risk or whether defendant was required to recognize the risk or take precautions against it.

In the case at bar the Plaintiff's theory of Edwards' duty to her was based upon Edwards' violation of numerous statutory rules of the road and his failure to use his siren which resulted in her injury. The trial court in permitting the case to go to the jury must have determined the duty issue and the foreseeability question in plaintiff's favor. Thereafter, in a negligence *per se* case such as this, the issues of negligence and proximate cause remained to be determined by the jury under proper instruction. In our opinion, under the circumstances of this case, the trial court properly refused the *Tucker v. Collar, supra*, foreseeability instructions. They were properly rejected because as a matter of law the accident was foreseeable. As the Plaintiff very succinctly puts it — this is not a foreseeability case.

Judgment is affirmed.

NOTES AND QUESTIONS

(1)   To which elements of a plaintiff's prima facie case of negligence does foreseeability pertain? Do not the earlier materials in this book and the initial parts of the *Kokaska* case suggest that duty, breach, and proximate causation all are affected, the first in determinations of the judges, and the latter two in the determination of the finder of fact? Is the court's conclusion necessary? Is it sound?

(2)   Some opinions seem to hold that the entire proximate causation issue comes down to a question of foreseeability. Examine with care, however, other factors that appear in the following cases. By contrast, at least one court has held on occasion that foreseeability is not a factor in proximate causation; all that counts is an unbroken string of events, each following the other without an "intervening efficient cause." *Dellwo v. Pearson*, 107 N.W. 2d 859 (Minn. 1961).

(3)   The two "foreseeability" instructions alluded to in *City of Scottsdale v. Kokaska* were:

> 5. I further instruct you that the duty to exercise care arises from probabilities, rather than from bare possibilities of danger. Consequently, in order for the plaintiff to establish the liability of the defendant for harm, the plaintiff must show by a preponderance of the evidence that the alleged negligent conduct of the defendant was such that, acting as a reasonable and prudent man, the defendant should have recognized that his acts created an appreciable chance of causing the harm done, rather than a bare possibility thereof; and, failing therein, the plaintiff cannot recover in this action.

> 6. I charge you that the defendant was required by law only to anticipate and foresee and guard against what usually happens or is likely to happen, but that he was not required to foresee and provide against that which is unusual and not likely to happen, or, in other words, that which is only remotely and slightly probable and that the proper test in cases of this kind is not whether the injurious result or consequence was possible but whether it was likely to occur according to the usual experience of persons.

Tucker v. Collar, 285 P.2d 178, 179, 180 (Ariz. 1955). The Arizona Supreme Court later repudiated number 6 on the ground that it is error to instruct a jury that the mere fact that a matter was "unusual or unlikely" made it unforeseeable as a matter of law. *Rosen v. Knaub*, 857 P.2d 381, 384 (Ariz. 1993). Does this strengthen the role of the judges or the juries?

§ 8.02　UNFORESEEN PLAINTIFFS

PALSGRAF v. LONG ISLAND RAILROAD
New York Court of Appeals
248 N.Y. 339, 162 N.E.99 (1928)

CARDOZO, C.J.: (See opinion § 4.02, *supra*.)

ANDREWS, J. (dissenting).

Assisting a passenger to board a train, the defendant's servant negligently knocked a package from his arms. It fell between the platform and the cars. Of its contents the servant knew and could know nothing. A violent explosion followed. The concussion broke some scales standing a considerable distance away. In falling, they injured the plaintiff, an intending passenger.

Upon these facts, may she recover the damages she has suffered in an action brought against the master? The result we shall reach depends upon our theory as to the nature of negligence. Is it a relative concept — the breach of some duty owing to a particular person or to particular persons? Or, where there is an act which unreasonably threatens the safety of others, is the doer liable for all its proximate consequences, even where they result in injury to one who would generally be thought to be outside the radius of danger? This is not a mere dispute as to words. We might not believe that to the average mind the dropping of the bundle would seem to involve the probability of harm to the plaintiff standing many feet away whatever might be the case as to the owner or to one so near as to be likely to be struck by its fall. If, however, we adopt the second hypothesis, we have to inquire only as to the relation between cause and effect. We deal in terms of proximate cause, not of negligence.

Negligence may be defined roughly as an act or omission which unreasonably does or may affect the rights of others, or which unreasonably fails to protect one's self from the dangers resulting from such acts. Here I confine myself to the first branch of the definition. Nor do I comment on the word "unreasonable." For present purposes it sufficiently describes that average of conduct that society requires of its members.

There must be both the act or the omission, and the right. It is the act itself, not the intent of the actor, that is important. *Hover v. Barkhoof*, 44 N.Y. 113; *Mertz v. Connecticut Co.*, 217 N.Y. 475, 112 N.E. 166. In criminal law both the intent and the result are to be considered. Intent again is material in tort actions, where punitive damages are sought, dependent on actual malice — not on merely reckless conduct. But here neither insanity nor infancy lessens responsibility. *Williams v. Hays*, 143 N.Y. 442, 38 N.E. 449, 42 Am. St. Rep. 743, 26 L.R.A. 153.

As has been said, except in cases of contributory negligence, there must be rights which are or may be affected. Often though injury has occurred, no rights of him who suffers have been touched. A licensee or trespasser upon my land has no claim to affirmative care on my part that the land be made safe. *Meiers v. Fred Koch Brewery*, 229 N.Y. 10, 127 N.E. 491, 13 A.L.R. 633. Where a railroad is required to fence its tracks against cattle, no man's rights are injured should he wander upon the road because such fence is absent. *Di Caprio v. New York Cent. R. Co.*, 231 N.Y. 94, 131 N.E. 746, 16 A.L.R. 940. An unborn child may not demand immunity from personal harm. *Drobner v. Peters*, 232 N.Y. 220, 133 N.E. 567, 20 A.L.R. 1503.

But we are told that "there is no negligence unless there is in the particular case a legal duty to take care, and this duty must be one which is owed to the plaintiff himself and not merely to others." Salmond Torts (6th Ed.) 24. This I think too narrow a conception. Where there is the unreasonable act, and some right that may be affected there is negligence whether damage does or does not result. That is immaterial. Should we drive down Broadway at a reckless speed, we are negligent whether we strike an approaching car or miss it by an inch. The act itself is wrongful. It is a wrong not only to those who happen to be within the radius of danger, but to all who might have been there — a wrong to the public at large. Such is the language of the street. Such the language of the courts when speaking of contributory negligence. Such again and again their language in speaking of the duty of some defendant and discussing proximate cause in cases where such a discussion is wholly irrelevant on any other theory. *Perry v. Rochester Line Co.*, 219 N.Y. 60, 113 N.E. 529, L.R.A. 1917B, 1058. As was said by Mr. Justice Holmes many years ago:

The measure of the defendant's duty in determining whether a wrong has been committed is one thing, the measure of liability when a wrong has been committed is another. *Spade v. Lynn & B. R. Co.*, 172 Mass. 488, 491, 52 N.E. 747, 748 (43 L.R.A. 832, 70 Am. St. Rep. 298).

Due care is a duty imposed on each one of us to protect society from unnecessary danger, not to protect A, B, or C alone.

It may well be that there is no such thing as negligence in the abstract. "Proof of negligence in the air, so to speak, will not do." In an empty world negligence would not exist. It does involve a relationship between man and his fellows, but not merely a relationship between man and those whom he might reasonably expect his act would injure; rather, a relationship between him and those whom he does in fact injure. If his act has a tendency to harm some one, it harms him a mile away as surely as it does those on the scene. We now permit children to recover for the negligent killing of the father. It was never prevented on the theory that no duty was owing to them. A husband may be compensated for the loss of his wife's services. To say that the wrongdoer was negligent as to the husband as well as to the wife is merely an attempt to fit facts to theory. An insurance company paying a fire loss recovers its payment of the negligent incendiary. We speak of subrogation — of suing in the right of the insured. Behind the cloud of words is the fact they hide, that the act, wrongful as to the insured, has also injured the company. Even if it be true that the fault of father, wife, or insured will prevent recovery, it is because we consider the original negligence, not the proximate cause of the injury. Pollock, Torts (12th Ed.) 463.

In the well-known *Polemis* Case, [1921] 3 K.B. 560, Scrutton, L.J., said that the dropping of a plank was negligent, for it might injure "workman or cargo or ship." Because of either possibility, the owner of the vessel was to be made good for his loss. The act being wrongful, the doer was liable for its proximate results. Criticized and explained as this statement may have been, I think it states the law as it should be and as it is. *Smith v. London & S.W.R. Co. R.R.* (1870-71) L.R. 6 C.P. 14; *Anthony v. Staid*, 52 Mass. (11 Metc.) 290; *Wood v. Pennsylvania R. Co.*,

177 Pa. 306, 35 A. 699, 55 Am. St. Rep. 728, 35 L.R.A. 199; *Trashansky v. Hershkovitz*, 239 N.Y. 452, 147 N.E. 63.

The proposition is this: Every one owes to the world at large the duty of refraining from those acts that may unreasonably threaten the safety of others. Such an act occurs. Not only is he wronged to whom harm might reasonably be expected to result, but he also who is in fact injured, even if he be outside what would generally be thought the danger zone. There needs be duty due the one complaining, but this is not a duty to a particular individual because as to him harm might be expected. Harm to some one being the natural result of the act, not only that one alone, but all those in fact injured may complain. We have never, I think, held otherwise. Indeed in the *Di Caprio* Case we said that a breach of a general ordinance defining the degree of care to be exercised in one's calling is evidence of negligence as to every one. We did not limit this statement to those who might be expected to be exposed to danger. Unreasonable risk being taken, its consequences are not confined to those who might probably be hurt.

If this be so, we do not have a plaintiff suing by "derivation or succession." Her action is original and primary. Her claim is for a breach of duty to herself — not that she is subrogated to any right of action of the owner of the parcel or of a passenger standing at the scene of the explosion.

The right to recover damages rests on additional considerations. The plaintiff's rights must be injured, and this injury must be caused by the negligence. We build a dam, but are negligent as to its foundations. Breaking, it injures property down stream. We are not liable if all this happened because of some reason other than the insecure foundation. But, when injuries do result from our unlawful act, we are liable for the consequences. It does not matter that they are unusual, unexpected, unforeseen, and unforeseeable. But there is one limitation. The damages must be so connected with the negligence that the latter may be said to be the proximate cause of the former.

These two words have never been given an inclusive definition. What is a cause in a legal sense, still more what is a proximate cause, depend in each case upon many considerations, as does the existence of negligence itself. Any philosophical doctrine of causation does not help us. A boy throws a stone into a pond. The ripples spread. The water level rises. The history of that pond is altered to all eternity. It will be altered by other causes also. Yet it will be forever the resultant of all causes combined. Each one will have an influence. How great only omniscience can say. You may speak of a chain or, if you please, a net. An analogy is of little aid. Each cause brings about future events. Without each the future would not be the same. Each is proximate in the sense it is essential. But that is not what we mean by the word. Nor on the other hand do we mean sole cause. There is no such thing.

Should analogy be thought helpful, however, I prefer that of a stream. The spring, starting on its journey, is joined by tributary after tributary. The river, reaching the ocean, comes from a hundred sources. No man may say whence any drop of water is derived. Yet for a time distinction may be possible. Into the clear creek, brown swamp water flows from the left. Later, from the right comes water stained by its clay bed. The three may remain for a space, sharply divided. But at last inevitably no trace of separation remains. They are so commingled that all distinction is lost.

As we have said, we cannot trace the effect of an act to the end, if end there is. Again, however, we may trace it part of the way. A murder at Serajevo may be the necessary antecedent to an assassination in London twenty years hence. An overturned lantern may burn all Chicago. We may follow the fire from the shed to the last building. We rightly say the fire started by the lantern caused its destruction.

A cause, but not the proximate cause. What we do mean by the word "proximate" is that, because of convenience, of public policy, of a rough sense of justice, the law arbitrarily declines to trace a series of events beyond a certain point. This is not logic. It is practical politics. Take our rule as to fires. Sparks from my burning haystack set on fire my house and my neighbor's. I may recover from a negligent railroad. He may not. Yet the wrongful act as directly harmed the one as the other. We may regret that the line was drawn just where it was, but drawn somewhere it had to be. We said the act of the railroad was not the proximate cause of our neighbor's fire. Cause it surely was. The words we used were simply indicative of our notions of public policy. Other courts think differently. But somewhere they reach the point where they cannot say the stream comes from any one source.

Take the illustration given in an unpublished manuscript by a distinguished and helpful writer on the law of torts. A chauffeur negligently collides with another car which is filled with dynamite, although he could not know it. An explosion follows. A, walking on the sidewalk nearby, is killed. B, sitting in a window of a building opposite, is cut by flying glass. C, likewise sitting in a window a block away, is similarly injured. And a further illustration: A nursemaid, ten blocks away, startled by the noise, involuntarily drops a baby from her arms to the walk. We are told that C may not recover while A may. As to B it is a question for court or jury. We will all agree that the baby might not. Because, we are again told, the chauffeur had no reason to believe his conduct involved any risk of injuring either C or the baby. As to them he was not negligent.

But the chauffeur, being negligent in risking the collision, his belief that the scope of the harm he might do would be limited is immaterial. His act unreasonably jeopardized the safety of any one who might be affected by it. C's injury and that of the baby were directly traceable to the collision. Without that, the injury would not have happened. C had the right to sit in his office, secure from such dangers. The baby was entitled to use the sidewalk with reasonable safety.

The true theory is, it seems to me, that the injury to C, if in truth he is to be denied recovery, and the injury to the baby, is that their several injuries were not the proximate result of the negligence. And here not what the chauffeur had reason to believe would be the result of his conduct, but what the prudent would foresee, may have a bearing — may have some bearing, for the problem of proximate cause is not to be solved by any one consideration. It is all a question of expediency. There are no fixed rules to govern our judgment. There are simply matters of which we may take account. We have in a somewhat different connection spoken of "the stream of events." We have asked whether that stream was deflected — whether it was forced into new and unexpected channels. *Donnelly v. H. C. & A. I. Piercy Contracting Co.*, 222 N.Y. 210, 118 N.E. 605. This is rather rhetoric than law. There is in truth little to guide us other than common sense.

There are some hints that may help us. The proximate cause, involved as it may be with many other causes, must be, at the least, something without which the event would not happen. The court must ask itself whether there was a natural and continuous sequence between cause and effect. Was the one a substantial factor in producing the other? Was there a direct connection between them, without too many intervening causes? Is the effect of cause on result not too attenuated? Is the cause likely, in the usual judgment of mankind, to produce the result? Or, by the exercise of prudent foresight, could the result be foreseen? Is the result too remote from the cause, and here we consider remoteness in time and space. *Bird v. St. Paul & M. Ins. Co.*, 224 N.Y. 47, 120 N.E. 86, 13 A.L.R. 875, where we passed upon the construction of a contract — but something was also said on this subject. Clearly we must so consider, for the greater the distance either in time or space, the more surely do other causes intervene to affect the result. When a lantern is overturned, the firing of a shed is a fairly direct consequence. Many things contribute to the spread of the conflagration — the force of the wind, the direction and width of streets, the character of intervening structures, other factors. We draw an uncertain and wavering line, but draw it we must as best we can.

Once again, it is all a question of fair judgment, always keeping in mind the fact that we endeavor to make a rule in each case that will be practical and in keeping with the general understanding of mankind.

Here another question must be answered. In the case supposed, it is said, and said correctly, that the chauffeur is liable for the direct effect of the explosion, although he had no reason to suppose it would follow a collision. "The fact that the injury occurred in a different manner than that which might have been expected does not prevent the chauffeur's negligence from being in law the cause of the injury." But the natural results of a negligent act — the results which a prudent man would or should foresee — do have a bearing upon the decision as to proximate cause. We have said so repeatedly. What should be foreseen? No human foresight would suggest that a collision itself might injure one a block away. On the contrary, given an explosion, such a possibility might be reasonably expected. I think the direct connection, the foresight of which the courts speak, assumes prevision of the explosion, for the immediate results of which, at least, the chauffeur is responsible.

It may be said this is unjust. Why? In fairness he should make good every injury flowing from his negligence. Not because of tenderness toward him we say he need not answer for all that follows his wrong. We look back to the catastrophe, the fire kindled by the spark, or the explosion. We trace the consequences, not indefinitely, but to a certain point. And to aid us in fixing that point we ask what might ordinarily be expected to follow the fire or the explosion.

This last suggestion is the factor which must determine the case before us. The act upon which defendant's liability rests is knocking an apparently harmless package onto the platform. The act was negligent. For its proximate consequences the defendant is liable. If its contents were broken, to the owner; if it fell upon and crushed a passenger's foot, then to him; if it exploded and injured one in the immediate vicinity, to him also as to A in the illustration. Mrs. Palsgraf was. standing some distance away. How far cannot be told from the record — apparently 25 or 30 feet, perhaps less. Except for the explosion, she would not have been injured. We are told by the appellant in his brief, "It cannot be denied that the explosion was the direct cause of the plaintiff's injuries." So it was a substantial factor in producing the result — there was here a natural and continuous sequence — direct connection. The only intervening cause was that, instead of blowing her to the ground, the concussion smashed the weighing machine which in turn fell upon her. There was no remoteness in time, little in space. And surely, given such an explosion as here, it needed no great foresight to predict that the natural result would be to injure one on the platform at no greater distance from its scene than was the plaintiff. Just how no one might be able to predict. Whether by flying fragments, by broken glass, by wreckage of machines or structures no one could say. But injury in some form was most probable.

Under these circumstances I cannot say as a matter of law that the plaintiff's injuries were not the proximate result of the negligence. That is all we have before us. The court refused to so charge. No request was made to submit the matter to the jury as a question of fact, even would that have been proper upon the record before us.

The judgment appealed from should be affirmed, with costs.

NOTES AND QUESTIONS

(1)   To what extent does Judge Andrews's view of proximate causation comport with that of the Maine Supreme Court in *Wing v. Morse*, § 4.05, *supra*?

(2)   *Palsgraf* is famous because of the debate between Cardozo and Andrews as to whether the unforeseen plaintiff raises a fundamental question of duty or a question of proximate causation. Cardozo won that debate in *Palsgraf* and has been widely followed in truly similar circumstances. Examine Andrews's opinion carefully for what he said about proximate causation. Is it plain that he thought Mrs. Palsgraf necessarily should recover? Would he have affirmed a directed verdict for her? What is the basic proximate causation question, according to Andrews? Does he agree with *Kokaska*, for example?

(3)   Although Wisconsin purports to follow Justice Andrews' view of duty, it imposes a judicial limit on liability by applying court-policed "public policy" considerations. *Fandrey v. American Family Mutual Insurance Company*, 680 N.W.2nd 345 (Wis. 2004). These decisions may be made either pre-or-post trial. *Smaxwell v. Bayard*, 682 N.W.2d 923 (Wis. 2004). Since trial judges makes these decisions as questions of law, the decisions are reviewable *de novo* as if they were duty decision in orthodox tort law. *Fandrey*, 680 N.W.2nd at 358. Wisconsin also holds that this public policy analysis supersedes jury consideration of foreseeability of harm in proximate causation analysis. *Pfeifer v. Standard Gateway Theater, Inc.*, 55 N.W.2d 29 (Wis.1952)

§ 8.03   UNFORESEEN CONSEQUENCES

IN RE POLEMIS v. FURNESS, WITHY AND COMPANY
3 K.B. 560 (C.A. 1921)[1]

SCRUTTON, L.J.

---

[1]   [Ed. — King's Bench Division Law Reports of the principal English trial court, appeals there-from, certain criminal appeals and other cases; decision of the Court of Appeal.]

The steamship *Thrasyvoulos* was lost by fire while being discharged by workmen employed by the charterers. Experienced arbitrators, by whose findings of fact we are bound, have decided that the fire was caused by a spark igniting petrol vapour in the hold, the vapour coming from leaks from cargo shipped by the charterers, and that the spark was caused by the Arab workmen employed by the charterers negligently knocking a plank out of a temporary staging erected in the hold, so that the plank fell into the hold, and in its fall by striking something made the spark which ignited the petrol vapour.

On these findings the charterers contend that they are not liable for two reasons: first, that they are protected by an exception of "fire" which in the charter is "mutually excepted"; secondly, that as the arbitrators have found that it could not be reasonably anticipated that the falling of the board would make a spark, the actual damage is too remote to be the subject of a claim. In my opinion both these grounds of defence fail.

[Discussion of the excepted perils contract question omitted.]

The second defence is that the damage is too remote from the negligence, as it could not be reasonably foreseen as a consequence. On this head we were referred to a number of well known cases in which vague language, which I cannot think to be really helpful, has been used in an attempt to define the point at which damage becomes too remote from, or not sufficiently directly caused by, the breach of duty, which is the original cause of action, to be recoverable. For instance, I cannot think it useful to say the damage must be the natural and probable result. This suggests that there are results which are natural but not probable, and other results which are probable but not natural. I am not sure what either adjective means in this connection; if they mean the same thing, two need not be used; if they mean different things, the difference between them should be defined. And as to many cases of fact in which the distinction has been drawn, it is difficult to see why one case should be decided one way and one another. Perhaps the House of Lords will some day explain why, if a cheque is negligently filled up, it is a direct effect of the negligence that some one finding the cheque should commit forgery: *London Joint Stock Bank v. Macmillan*; while if some one negligently leaves a libellous letter about, it is not a direct effect of the negligence that the finder should show the letter to the person libelled: *Weld-Blundell v. Stephens*. In this case, however, the problem is simpler. To determine whether an act is negligent, it is relevant to determine whether any reasonable person would foresee that the act would cause damage; if he would not, the act is not negligent. But if the act would or might probably cause damage, the fact that the damage it in fact causes is not the exact kind of damage one would expect is immaterial, so long as the damage is in fact directly traceable to the negligent act, and not due to the operation of independent causes having no connection with the negligent act, except that they would not avoid its results. Once the act is negligent, the fact that its exact operation was not foreseen is immaterial. This is the distinction laid down by the majority of the Exchequer Chamber in *Smith v. London and South Western Ry. Co.*, and by the majority of the Court in banc in *Rigby v. Hewitt* and *Greenland v. Chaplin*, and approved recently by Lord Sumner in *Weld-Blundell v. Stephens* and Sir Samuel Evans in *H.M.S. London*. In the present case it was negligent in discharging cargo to knock down the planks of the temporary staging, for they might easily cause some damage either to workmen, or cargo, or the ship. The fact that they did directly produce an unexpected result, a spark in an atmosphere of petrol vapour which caused a fire, does not relieve the person who was negligent from the damage which his negligent act directly caused.

OVERSEAS TANKSHIPS (U.K.) LTD. v. MONKS DOCK & ENGINEERING CO. LTD. (THE WAGON MOUND)
[1961] App. Cas. 388 (P.C.)[2]

While an oil-burning vessel, of which the appellants were the charterers, was taking in bunkering oil in Sydney Harbour a large quantity of the oil was, through the carelessness of the appellants' servants, allowed to spill into the harbour. During that and the following day the escaped furnace oil was carried by wind and tide beneath a wharf owned by the respondents, shipbuilders and ship repairers, at which was lying a vessel which they were refitting, and for which purpose their employees were using electric and oxyacetylene welding equipment. Some cotton waste or rag on a piece of debris floating on the oil underneath the wharf was set on fire by molten metal falling from the wharf, and the flames from the cotton waste or rag set the floating oil afire either directly or by first setting fire to a wooden pile coated with oil and thereafter a conflagration developed which seriously damaged the wharf and equipment on it.

In an action by the respondents to recover from the appellants compensation for the damage it was found by the trial judge on the evidence that the appellants "did not know and could not reasonably be expected to have known that it [the furnace oil] was capable of being set afire when spread on water"; and that apart from the damage by fire the respondents had suffered some damage in that oil had congealed upon and interfered with the use of their slipways, which was "damage which beyond question was a direct result of the escape of the oil": —

1961. January 18. The judgment of their Lordships was delivered by Viscount Simonds, who stated the facts set out above and continued: The trial judge also made the all-important finding, which must be set out in his own words: "The raison d'étre of furnace oil is, of course, that it shall burn, but I find the defendant did not know and could not reasonably be expected to have known that it was capable of being set afire when spread on water." This finding was reached after a wealth of evidence, which included that of a distinguished scientist, Professor Hunter. It receives strong confirmation from the fact that at the trial the respondents strenuously maintained that the appellants had discharged petrol into the bay on no other ground than that, as the spillage was set alight, it could not be furnace oil. An attempt was made before their Lordships' Board to limit in some way the finding of fact, but it is clear that it was intended to cover precisely the event that happened.

One other finding must be mentioned. The judge held that apart from damage by fire the respondents had suffered some damage from the spillage of oil in that it had got upon their slipways and congealed upon them and interfered with their use of the slips. He said "the evidence of this damage is slight and no claim for compensation is made in respect of it. Nevertheless it does establish some damage, which may be insignificant in comparison with the magnitude of the damage by fire, but which nevertheless is damage which, beyond question, was a direct result of the escape of the oil." It is upon this footing that their Lordships will consider

---

[2] [Ed. — Appeal Cases Law Reports, decision of the Judicial Committee of the Privy Council.]

the question whether the appellants are liable for the fire damage. That consideration must begin with an expression of indebtedness to Manning J. for his penetrating analysis of the problems that today beset the question of liability for negligence. In the year 1913 in the case of *H.M.S. London*, a case to which further reference will be made, Sir Samuel Evans P. said:

The doctrine of legal causation, in reference both to the creation of liability and to the measurement of damages, has been much discussed by judges and commentators in this country and in America. Vast numbers of learned and acute judgments and disquisitions have been delivered and written upon the subject. It is difficult to reconcile the decisions; and the views of prominent commentators and jurists differ in important respects. It would not be possible or feasible in this judgment to examine them in anything approaching detail.

In the near half-century that has passed since the learned President spoke those words the task has not become easier, but it is possible to point to certain landmarks and to indicate certain tendencies which, as their Lordships hope, may serve in some measure to simplify the law.

It is inevitable that first consideration should be given to the case of *In re Polemis and Furness Withy & Co. Ltd.* which will henceforward be referred to as *Polemis*. For it was avowedly in deference to that decision and to decisions of the Court of Appeal that followed it that the Full Court was constrained to decide the present case in favour of the respondents. In doing so Manning J., after a full examination of that case, said:

To say that the problems, doubts and difficulties which I have expressed above render it difficult for me to apply the decision in *In re Polemis* with any degree of confidence to a particular set of facts would be a grave understatement. I can only express the hope that, if not in this case, then in some other case in the near future, the subject will be pronounced upon by the House of Lords or the Privy Council in terms which, even if beyond my capacity fully to understand, will facilitate, for those placed as I am, its everyday application to current problems.

This cri de coeur would in any case be irresistible, but in the years that have passed since its decision *Polemis* has been so much discussed and qualified that it cannot claim, as counsel for the respondents urged for it, the status of a decision of such long standing that it should not be reviewed.

There can be no doubt that the decision of the Court of Appeal in *Polemis* plainly asserts that, if the defendant is guilty of negligence, he is responsible for all the consequences whether reasonably foreseeable or not. The generality of the proposition is perhaps qualified by the fact that each of the Lords Justices refers to the outbreak of fire as the direct result of the negligent act. There is thus introduced the conception that the negligent actor is not responsible for consequences which are not "direct," whatever that may mean. It has to be asked, then, why this conclusion should have been reached. The answer appears to be that it was reached upon a consideration of certain authorities, comparatively few in number, that were cited to the court. Of these, three are generally regarded as having influenced the decision. The earliest in point of date was *Smith v. London & South Western Railway Co.* In that case it was said that "when it has been once determined that there is evidence of negligence, the person guilty of it is equally liable for its consequences, whether he could have foreseen them or not": see *per* Channell B. Similar observations were made by other members of the court. Three things may be noted about this case: the first, that for the sweeping proposition laid down no authority was cited; the second, that the point to which the court directed its mind was not unforeseeable damage of a different kind from that which was foreseen, but more extensive damage of the same kind; and the third, that so little was the mind of the court directed to the problem which has now to be solved that no one of the seven judges who took part in the decision thought it necessary to qualify in any way the consequences for which the defendant was to be held responsible.

Before going forward to the cases which followed *Polemis*, their Lordships think it desirable to look back to older authorities which appear to them to deserve consideration.

[Review of older cases cast doubt on *Polemis* rule.]

Before turning to the cases that succeeded it, it is right to glance at yet another aspect of the decision in *Polemis*. Their Lordships, as they have said, assume that the court purported to propound the law in regard to tort. But up to that date it had been universally accepted that the law in regard to damages for breach of contract and for tort was, generally speaking, and particularly in regard to the tort of negligence, the same. Yet *Hadley v. Baxendale* was not cited in argument nor referred to in the judgments in *Polemis*. This is the more surprising when it is remembered that in that case, as in many another case, the claim was laid alternatively in breach of contract and in negligence. If the claim for breach of contract had been pursued, the charterers could not have been held liable for consequences not reasonably foreseeable. It is not strange that Sir Frederick Pollock said that Blackburn and Willes JJ. would have been shocked beyond measure by the decision that the charterers were liable in tort: see Pollock on Torts, 15th ed., p. 29. Their Lordships refer to this aspect of the matter not because they wish to assert that in all respects today the measure of damages is in all cases the same in tort and in breach of contract, but because it emphasises how far *Polemis* was out of the current of contemporary thought. The acceptance of the rule in *Polemis* as applicable to all cases of tort directly would conflict with the view theretofore generally held. . . .

Enough has been said to show that the authority of *Polemis* has been severely shaken though lip-service has from time to time been paid to it. In their Lordships' opinion it should no longer be regarded as good law. It is not probable that many cases will for that reason have a different result, though it is hoped that the law will be thereby simplified, and that in some cases, at least, palpable injustice will be avoided. For it does not seem consonant with current ideas of justice or morality that for an act of negligence, however slight or venial, which results in some trivial foreseeable damage the actor should be liable for all consequences however unforeseeable and however grave, so long as they can be said to be "direct." It is a principle of civil liability, subject only to qualifications which have no present relevance, that a man must be considered to be responsible for the probable consequences of his act. To demand more of him is too harsh a rule, to demand less is to ignore that civilized order requires the observance of a minimum standard of behaviour.

This concept applied to the slowly developing law of negligence has led to a great variety of expressions which can, as it appears to their Lordships, be harmonised with little difficulty with the single exception of the so-called rule in

Polemis. For, if it is asked why a man should be responsible for the natural or necessary or probable consequences of his act (or any other similar description of them) the answer is that it is not because they are natural or necessary or probable, but because, since they have this quality, it is judged by the standard of the reasonable man that he ought to have foreseen them. Thus it is that over and over again it has happened that in different judgments in the same case, and sometimes in a single judgment, liability for a consequence has been imposed on the ground that it was reasonably foreseeable or, alternatively, on the ground that it was natural or necessary or probable. The two grounds have been treated as coterminous, and so they largely are. But, where they are not, the question arises to which the wrong answer was given in *Polemis.* For, if some limitation must be imposed upon the consequences for which the negligent actor is to be held responsible — and all are agreed that some limitation there must be — why should that test (reasonable foreseeability) be rejected which, since he is judged by what the reasonable man ought to foresee, corresponds with the common conscience of mankind, and a test (the "direct" consequence) be substituted which leads to nowhere but the never-ending and insoluble problems of causation. "The lawyer," said Sir Frederick Pollock, "cannot afford to adventure himself with philosophers in the logical and metaphysical controversies that beset the idea of cause." Yet this is just what he has most unfortunately done and must continue to do if the rule in *Polemis* is to prevail. A conspicuous example occurs when the actor seeks to escape liability on the ground that the "chain of causation" is broken by a "nova causa" or "novus actus interveniens." . . .

It is, no doubt, proper when considering tortious liability for negligence to analyse its elements and to say that the plaintiff must prove a duty owed to him by the defendant, a breach of that duty by the defendant, and consequent damage. But there can be no liability until the damage has been done. It is not the act but the consequences on which tortious liability is founded. Just as (as it has been said) there is no such thing as negligence in the air, so there is no such thing as liability in the air. Suppose an action brought by A for damage caused by the carelessness (a neutral word) of B, for example, a fire caused by the careless spillage of oil. It may, of course, become relevant to know what duty B owed to A, but the only liability that is in question is the liability for damage by fire. It is vain to isolate the liability from its context and to say that B is or is not liable, and then to ask for what damage he is liable. For his liability is in respect of that damage and no other. If, as admittedly it is, B's liability (culpability) depends on the reasonable foreseeability of the consequent damage, how is that to be determined except by the foreseeability of the damage which in fact happened — the damage in suit? And, if that damage is unforeseeable so as to displace liability at large, how can the liability be restored so as to make compensation payable?

But, it is said, a different position arises if B's careless act has been shown to be negligent and has caused some foreseeable damage to A. Their Lordships have already observed that to hold B liable for consequences however unforeseeable of a careless act, if, but only if, he is at the same time liable for some other damage however trivial, appears to be neither logical nor just. This becomes more clear if it is supposed that similar unforeseeable damage is suffered by A and C but other foreseeable damage, for which B is liable, by A only. A system of law which would hold B liable to A but not to C for the similar damage suffered by each of them could not easily be defended.

Fortunately, the attempt is not necessary. For the same fallacy is at the root of the proposition. It is irrelevant to the question whether B is liable for unforeseeable damage that he is liable for foreseeable damage, as irrelevant as would the fact that he had trespassed on White-acre be to the question whether he has trespassed on Black-acre. Again, suppose a claim by A for damage by fire by the careless act of B. Of what relevance is it to that claim that he has another claim arising out of the same careless act? It would surely not prejudice his claim if that other claim failed: it cannot assist it if it succeeds. Each of them rests on its own bottom, and will fail if it can be established that the damage could not reasonably be foreseen. We have come back to the plain common sense stated by Lord Russell of Killowen in *Bourhill v. Young*. As Denning L.J. said in *King v. Phillips*: "there can be no doubt since *Bourhill* v. *Young* that the test *of liability for shock* is foreseeability of *injury by shock*." Their Lordships substitute the word "fire" for "shock" and endorse this statement of the law.

Their Lordships conclude this part of the case with some general observations. They have been concerned primarily to displace the proposition that unforeseeability is irrelevant if damage is "direct." In doing so they have inevitably insisted that the essential factor in determining liability is whether the damage is of such a kind as the reasonable man should have foreseen. This accords with the general view thus stated by Lord Atkin in *Donoghue v. Stevenson*. "The liabililty for negligence, whether you style it such or treat it as in other systems as a species of 'culpa,' is no doubt based upon a general public sentiment of moral wrongdoing for which the offender must pay." It is a departure from this sovereign principle if liability is made to depend solely on the damage being the "direct" or "natural" consequence of the precedent act. Who knows or can be assumed to know all the processes of nature? But if it would be wrong that a man should be held liable for damage unpredictable by a reasonable man because it was "direct" or "natural," equally it would be wrong that he should escape liability, however "indirect" the damage, if he foresaw or could reasonably foresee the intervening events which led to its being done: cf. *Woods v. Duncan*. Thus foreseeability becomes the effective test. In reasserting this principle their Lordships conceive that they do not depart from, but follow and develop, the law of negligence as laid down by Baron Alderson in *Blyth v. Birmingham Waterworks Co.*

Their Lordships will humbly advise Her Majesty that this appeal should be allowed, and the respondents' action so far as it related to damage caused by the negligence of the appellants be dismissed with costs, but that the action so far as it related to damage caused by nuisance should be remitted to the Full Court to be dealt with as that court may think fit. The respondents must pay the costs of the appellants of this appeal and in the courts below.

NOTES AND QUESTIONS

(1) What, fundamentally, is the difference in approach between *In re Polemis* and *The Wagon Mound*? Does it remind you of the debate between Cardozo and Andrews in *Palsgraf*? Just as Cardozo drew more adherents than Andrews, so has *Wagon Mound* drawn more than *In re Polemis*. Where does *Petition of Kinsman Transit Co.*, 338 F.2d 708 (2nd Cir. 1964) fit?

(2) Later cases arose out of the same episode that gave rise to *The Wagon Mound*. In at least one of them the plaintiffs were able to adduce expert testimony

to the effect that it is a known fact that oil of the type involved can be set afire while floating on water. What effect should this have on the litigation? On its outcome? *Overseas Tankship (U.K.), Ltd. v. Miller Steamship Co. Pty Ltd*, [1967] 1 A.C. 617 (P.C.).

(3) Does the rule stated in the following quotation from *Schafer v. Hoffman*, 831 P.2d 897, 899, 900 (Colo. En Banc. 1992), constitute an exception to the principle of *The Wagon Mound*? If so, why?

The term "thin skull," or "eggshell skull," is derived from illustrations appearing in English cases wherein a plaintiff with an "eggshell skull" suffers death as a result of a defendant's negligence where a normal person would only suffer a bump on the head. *Dulieu v. White & Sons*, 2 K.B. 669, 679 (1901); W. Page Keeton et al., Prosser and Keaton on the Law of Torts § 43, at 292 (5th ed. 1984) [hereinafter "Prosser"] (citing Glanville Williams, *The Risk Principle*, 77 L.Q.Rev. 179, 193-97 (1961)). The negligent defendant is liable for the resulting harm even though the harm is increased by the particular plaintiff's condition at the time of the negligent conduct. Prosser § 43, at 291; see also Restatement (Second) of Torts § 461 cmt. a (1965) ("A negligent actor must bear the risk that his liability will be increased by reason of the actual physical condition of the other toward whom his act is negligent.").

As Prosser notes, there is almost universal agreement on this rule. Prosser § 43, at 291 ("There is almost universal agreement upon liability beyond the risk, for quite unforeseeable consequences, when they follow an impact upon the person of the plaintiff."). Liability "beyond the risk," however, is not solely premised on the existence of ascertainable pre-existing physical conditions: The defendant is held liable when the defendant's negligence operates upon a concealed physical condition, such as pregnancy, or latent disease, or susceptibility to disease, to produce consequences which the defendant could not reasonably anticipate. The defendant is held liable for unusual results of personal injuries which are regarded as unforeseeable, such as tuberculosis, paralysis, pneumonia, heart or kidney disease, blood poisoning, cancer, or the loss of hair from fright. Prosser § 43, at 291-92. Some scholars have interpreted the thin skull doctrine to encompass the plaintiff's physical, mental, or financial condition. 4 Fowler Harper et al., The Law of Torts § 20.3 (2d ed. 1986). "And these preexisting conditions may have the greatest bearing on the extent of the injury actually suffered by any particular plaintiff in a given case. Thus the same slight blow in the abdomen might cause only fleeting discomfort to a man but a miscarriage to a pregnant woman." *Id.* Under Colorado law, it is fundamental that a tortfeasor must accept his or her victim as the victim is found. . . .

Accordingly, under the thin skull doctrine, a tortfeasor "may not seek to reduce the amount of damages [owed to the victim] by spotlighting the physical frailties of the injured party at the time the tortious force was applied to him." *Id.* A thin skull instruction is appropriately given when the defendant seeks to avoid liability by asserting that the victim's injuries would have been less severe had the victim been an average person.

(4) Judge Calabresi, concurring in *Moore v. PaineWebber, Inc.*, 189 F.3d 165, 178 (2d Cir. 1999), cited *Petition of Kinsman Transit Company*, § 5.05 *supra*, for the proposition that the "reasoning" of *Wagon Mound. #1* is not the rule in American law. By contrast *Needham v. Gaylor*, 1996 WL 531596, o, 7 (Ohio App. 2 Dist.1996) opined, "Since Wagon Mound, most commentators have believed that the Polemis

rule is gone for good. American courts have similarly rejected the Polemis rule in ordinary negligence cases. . . . ". Could both be correct? Judge Calabresi seemed to be referring to the doctrine discussed in note (3) above.

ZEIGLER v. BLOUNT BROTHERS CONSTRUCTION CO.
Alabama Supreme Court
364 So. 2d 1163 (1978)

BEATTY, JUSTICE.

This is an appeal from the grant of motions to dismiss filed by the defendants. We affirm.

The plaintiffs brought this action seeking to represent a class of persons who purchase electric power from Alabama Power Company (APCO). The action is grounded upon the failure in 1975 of the Walter Bouldin Dam which is located on the Coosa River in Elmore County, and which is part of the hydroelectric generating system of APCO. In their complaint the plaintiffs alleged that during 1963 or 1964 the defendant Blount Brothers Construction Company (Blount) as general contractor agreed with APCO to construct Walter Bouldin Dam. The defendant, Southern Services, Inc., allegedly prepared the plans and specifications for the dam. Harbert Construction Company (Harbert), another defendant, was a sub-contractor for the powerhouse excavation and embankments, and Harry Hendon & Associates (Hendon), another co-defendant, contracted with APCO to furnish inspections and to advise of possible construction defects. The complaint alleged that Southern Services improperly designed and prepared the plans and specifications, and that Blount and Harbert breached their contracts by failing to construct the dam in accord with the plans and specifications, causing it to collapse. Hendon's inspections, it further alleged, did not detect the deficiencies which resulted in the collapse. These failures, the plaintiffs continued, resulted in APCO, under Alabama law, Public Service Commission's regulations, and the "fuel adjustment clause," increasing the price it charged its customers proportionately by the price it was required to pay for electricity it otherwise would have generated using Walter Bouldin Dam.

. . .

The gist of plaintiffs' negligence action is that these defendants owed a duty of care to the plaintiffs because the defendants could have anticipated that the collapse of the Bouldin Dam would cause subscribers to pay increased utility bills. They cite, *inter alia*, the cases of *Havard v. Palmer & Baker Engineers, Inc.*, 293 Ala. 301, 302 So.2d 228 (1974) for the proposition that "the ultimate test of the existence of a duty to use care is found in the foreseeability that harm may result if care is not exercised." This Court posed the test of foreseeability in the following manner:

[w]ould an ordinary man in defendant's position, knowing what they knew or should have known, anticipate that injury of the nature of that suffered was likely to result. . . .

Havard dealt with a contract between an engineering firm and the City of Mobile. Under that contract the firm was to make annual inspections and recommendations pertaining to the safe operation of a vehicular tunnel operated by the city. This Court held that a duty to the plaintiff was alleged in a complaint which charged that the defendant knew that petroleum fires were to be reasonably anticipated and that the purpose of fire equipment located in the tunnel was to provide emergency protection to the traveling public:

It could be foreseen or anticipated by Palmer & Baker that a fire could break out in the Tunnel and when it did break out, good and workable fire-fighting equipment would be needed to fight the fire. Otherwise, if a fire could not be foreseen or anticipated, why have any such equipment at all in the Tunnell . . . *Havard* at 307, 302 So.2d at 232.

By analogy the plaintiffs conclude that the defendants, being construction and engineering firms, could have foreseen that the collapse of Bouldin Dam would have a "tremendous effect on the generating capacity of the Company system" and "would ultimately mean higher costs to power company customers." Such an analogy, of course, assumes a foreseeable relationship between the construction of the dam and higher costs to consumers because of the imposition of the "fuel adjustment clause."

We disagree with that analogy. The foreseeability aspect of *Havard* was premised upon the relationship between the ultimate risk of harm and the professional knowledge of the engineer defendants. The availability of emergency firefighting equipment was viewed as a subject within the scope of their expertise, and it was foreseeable that the particular harm suffered would necessitate the use of such equipment. But the situation here is materially different. The defendants here are construction and engineering firms. They might, indeed, be held to have foreseen the loss of generating capacity due to a collapse of the dam. They are not, however, utility rate makers nor do the facts otherwise suggest that they have any knowledge with respect to that technical subject. For aught that appears the "fuel adjustment clause" is a rate-fixing device authorized by the Public Service Commission. That body, as we have shown, possesses the authority to fix rates, and their power includes the power to allow the imposition of the "fuel adjustment clause." If APCO has been allowed by the Public Service Commission to adjust its rates upward on account of the failure of Bouldin Dam, it is conceivable that APCO will be required by that Commission to adjust them downward should it recover damages in its lawsuit against some of these defendants. Such an issue is for the Commission to decide, not the courts. . . . Accordingly, we are persuaded that the application of the "fuel adjustment clause" was not a matter reasonably foreseeable by the defendants, but was a remote result. . . .

Let the judgment granting the defendants' motions to dismiss be affirmed. *Affirmed.*

QUESTIONS

Is *Zeigler* a no-duty rule case? Or, is it an adherent of *The Wagon Mound* view of proximate causation? Does it make any difference?

§ 8.04   NOVUS ACTUS INTERVENIENS

[See *Wing v. Morse*, § 4.05, *supra* and *City of Scottsdale v. Kokaska*, § 8.01, *supra*.]

MOUM v. MAERCKLEIN
North Dakota Supreme Court
201 N.W.2d 399 (1972)

STRUTZ, CHIEF JUSTICE, on reassignment.

Evan Dockter, deceased, was an employee of the defendant Soo Line Railway Company, working as a probationary brakeman out of Harvey, North Dakota. He lived in Minot, a distance of approximately seventy miles from Harvey, and traveled to and from his work by car over U. S. Highway No. 52.

On the morning of December 22, 1969, the yard clerk of the defendant called Dockter in Minot, at approximately 7:15 o'clock, and asked him to report in Harvey at 9:10 a. m., to work as an extra on a train traveling from Harvey to Portal, North Dakota. The yard clerk was not a witness at the trial, having died between the time of the accident described in the complaint and the time of trial.

The record discloses that Dockter left Minot at 7:40 a. m. It was snowing when he left home. Enroute to Harvey, he encountered adverse weather conditions and was involved in an automobile accident near Drake, and was killed. Also fatally injured in the collision were the father, the mother, and the baby sister of the minor plaintiff, who herself suffered personal injuries. She brings this action for the wrongful death of her parents and for the personal injuries which she sustained in the mishap.

The plaintiff claims that a severe blizzard was raging between Minot and Harvey at the time that the defendant Soo Line ordered Dockter to report for work; that it was snowing in Minot when Dockter was contacted; and that it was cloudy and snowing, with a brisk southeast wind blowing, in Harvey at the time that the yard clerk of the defendant Soo Line made his call to Dockter. Visibility on the highway was bad and there was some wind and blowing snow, making travel extremely hazardous. The plaintiff further asserts that the deceased, Dockter, notwithstanding the hazardous conditions and the limited visibility prevailing, attempted to pass an automobile traveling in the same direction and failed to give the right of way to the vehicle in which the minor plaintiff was riding with her parents and her baby sister; that an accident resulted, due to the negligence of Dockter, in which the plaintiff's parents and her baby sister were killed and the minor plaintiff was injured; and that the collision in which the plaintiff's parents and her sister were killed and the plaintiff was injured resulted proximately from the negligent act of the Soo Line in ordering its employee to report for work under the conditions and from the negligence of its employee, the deceased Evan Dockter.

The plaintiff alleges that the negligence of the Soo Line consisted, as stated, in ordering the deceased employee, at 7:15 a. m., to report for work in Harvey by 9:10 a. m., knowing the unsafe and hazardous weather, road, and driving conditions then existing, and knowing that the said employee would have to travel approximately seventy miles under such conditions in less than two hours, if he were to report on time; that the defendant Soo Line knew, or should have known, that the deceased employee, in complying with the defendant's order to report for work, would have to drive his automobile in an unsafe manner in order to report on time, and further knowing that in spite of conditions then existing the deceased would endeavor to follow orders because as a probationary employee he would be afraid of losing his job if he did not report on time.

Plaintiff also alleges numerous acts of negligence on the part of the deceased Evan Dockter. A study of the record brings to light that the estate of the deceased Evan Dockter was given a covenant not to sue before the trial of the action began, leaving as the only issue in the trial the negligence of the defendant Soo Line in ordering its employee to report for work under the circumstances and conditions set forth above.

The plaintiff demanded judgment for damages for the wrongful death of her parents and for damages for personal injuries suffered by her as a result of the defendant's negligence. The case was tried to a jury, which returned a verdict for the plaintiff, and judgment was entered on such verdict. The defendant Soo Line thereupon moved for judgment notwithstanding the verdict or, in the alternative, for a new trial. This motion was denied, and the defendant has appealed from the judgment and from the order denying motion for judgment notwithstanding the verdict or for a new trial.

. . .

The defendant Soo Line Railway Company can be held liable to the plaintiff only if it has in some way failed to exercise that degree of care demanded by the circumstances. *Gallagher v. Great Northern Ry. Co.*, 55 N.D. 211, 212 N.W. 839 (1927).

The term "negligence" is relative, and its application depends on the situation of the party and the degree of care that the circumstances reasonably impose. *Halverson v. Zimmerman*, 60 N.D. 113, 232 N.W. 754 (1930). Negligence is not actionable unless it was the proximate cause of the injury complained of.

To constitute actionable negligence, there must be a causal connection between the negligence and the injury sustained; and for the negligence to be the proximate cause of the injury, the defendant must owe to the plaintiff a duty, and the injury to the plaintiff must have resulted as a direct consequence of the negligent breach of that duty. *Bowers* v. *Great Northern Ry. Co.*, 65 N.D. 384, 259 N.W. 99, 99 A.L.R. 1443 (1935).

"Proximate cause" of an injury is a cause which in natural and continuous sequence, unbroken by any controlling, intervening cause, produces injury, and without which it would not have occurred. *Olson v. Cass County Electric Co-operative, Inc.*, 94 N.W.2d 506 (N.D. 1959).

Thus, to render the defendant liable, it must appear not only that the injury complained of was a natural and probable consequence of the negligent act of the defendant, but that such consequence ought reasonably to have been anticipated by a person of ordinary intelligence in the light of attending circumstances.

"Proximate cause" arises when the injury is the natural and probable result of the negligent act or omission and must be of such character as an ordinarily prudent person ought to have foreseen as likely to occur as a result of the negligence, although it is not necessary that the person charged with negligence should have foreseen the precise injury which resulted from his negligent act. *Johnston v. City of East Moline*, 405 Ill. 460, 91 N.E.2d 401 (1950).

One of the tests of "proximate cause" is the defendant's duty to reasonably foresee the consequence of his negligence. If the person had no knowledgeable ground to anticipate that his act would or might result in injury to anyone, the act is not negligent at all. But if the act is negligent, then the person guilty of it is liable for the natural, proximate, and probable consequences, whether he foresaw them or not.

Therefore, to warrant a finding that the negligence is a proximate cause of an injury, it must appear that the injury complained of was the natural and probable result of a negligent act and that it ought to have been foreseen by the defendant. An injury which could not have been foreseen or reasonably anticipated as a probable result of the act is not actionable. The law requires that a person reasonably guard against probabilities — not against all possibilities. The law will not hold a person liable for the unusual. *Ulwelling* v. *Crown Coach Corp.*, 206 Cal.App.2d 96, 23 Cal.Rptr. 631 (1962).

The mere fact that an injury did result from a negligent act is not sufficient to create liability. Such result must have been probable. Liability cannot be based on some prior, remote cause which furnished the condition for the injury resulting from an intervening, unrelated, efficient cause. *Pepsi-Cola Bottling Co. v. Von Brady*, 386 P.2d 993 (Okl.1963). Thus a party is not chargeable with all possible consequences of his negligent act, and he is not responsible for a consequence which is possible according to occasional experiences. He is liable only for the consequences which are probable according to the ordinary, usual experiences of mankind.

In this case, the employee, Dockter, resided in Minot, approximately seventy miles from Harvey, where he was to report for work. He was given less than two hours to make the trip. It was snowing and blowing, and at times visibility was almost zero, while at other times it was fair. He was requested to report for work under these circumstances. Did the action of the Soo Line in requesting him to report for work constitute negligence, and, if so, was such negligent act the proximate cause of the accident which occurred? We believe that the act of the defendant in asking its employee to report for work was a remote cause, and not the proximate cause of the accident. It was an act which created a condition which was followed by an independent, unforeseeable act, that of the employee, Dockter, in trying to pass another car without due care, which caused the injury complained of. Even though the Soo Line's requesting the employee to report for work indirectly resulted in injury to the plaintiff, such injury was not a probable result of the defendant's order, but was only a possible result. Even where the negligence of a party results in injury to another, there can be no liability if the cause is remote and not a "proximate cause," as that term has been defined above. *Tanzi v. New York Central R. Co.*, 155 Ohio St. 149, 98 N.E.2d 39 (1951).

Where the negligence complained of only creates a condition which thereafter is acted upon by a subsequent, independent, unforeseeable act which produces the injury — in this case, Dockter's trying to pass a vehicle on the highway when visibility was very poor — the original negligence is remote and not the proximate cause, even if the injury never would have happened but for the original negligence. Here, the collision would not have happened if the Soo Lines had not requested Dockter to report for work, but that does not make the Soo Line liable for the remote result of its order. The term "proximate cause" contemplates an immediate cause which in natural and probable sequence produces the injury complained of. It excludes the idea of legal liability based on speculative possibilities, or circumstances and conditions remotely connected with the events leading up to the injury. *Mulder v. Tague*, 186 N.W.2d 884 (S.D. 1971).

There were many cars on the highway on the day of the accident. If being on the road was so hazardous that merely driving on the highway under existing conditions and circumstances in itself was negligence, then the plaintiff's parents were negligent for venturing out under such conditions. Such a view, of course, would be untenable. Although the accident which occurred would not have occurred if the defendant Soo Line had not ordered Dockter to report for work, and although the accident which took place was possible, it was not a probable result of the act of the defendant; and an alleged wrongdoer is responsible only for the probable results of his wrongful act. We find that the yard clerk of the defendant could not reasonably have foreseen that the deceased would recklessly try to pass a car at a moment when visibility was poor and thus cause an accident. In other words, we conclude that there was no evidence upon which the jury could find that the action of the yard clerk in telephoning Dockter, the employee of the defendant, to report for work was the proximate cause of the accident. Liability cannot be based upon a prior remote cause which may have provided the conditions that resulted in injury, where the injury itself was the result of an intervening, unrelated cause, which in this case was the negligence of Dockter.

For reasons stated, the judgment of the trial court is reversed, and the complaint of the plaintiffs is ordered dismissed.

NOTES AND QUESTIONS

(1)   Examine with care the facts and the precise holdings of *Wing v. Morse, Kokaska* and *Moum*. See also *Pilgrim v. Fortune Drilling Company*, 653 F.2d 982 (5th Cir. 1981). Can the outcomes be justified, or is there a fundamental difference in the various conceptions of an efficient intervening force (novus actus interveniens)? Two statements that suggest a practical way to examine the effect of negligent acts that intervene between the original negligent act and the harm done are these: "The dust had long settled and the reverberations had long since ceased," said a Missouri court in *Greenwood v. Vanarsdall*, 356 S.W.2d 109 (Mo. App. 1962), wherein almost an hour had elapsed between the original act of negligent driving and the intervening negligent act that caused the harm. "In a traffic mix-up due to negligence, before the disturbed waters have become placid and normal again, the unfolding of events between the culpable act and the plaintiff's eventual injury may be bizarre indeed; yet the defendant may be liable for the result," said the First Circuit in *Marshall v. Nugent*, 222 F.2d 604 (1955), wherein the intervening negligence followed close on the heels of the initial negligent act. Applying those practical tests to the three cases above, what outcomes do you reach? See also *Department of Transportation v. Anglin*, 502 So.2d 896 (Fla. 1987).

(2)   What should be the effect of an intervening negligent act? Suppose a criminal driver causes an automobile crash, rendering several passengers unconscious. Before help arrives, a thief comes upon the scene and takes all the money

and valuables from the helpless victims. Is the original negligent driver responsible for these losses? Is the outcome so clear that it should be decided by the trial judge, or should a jury be permitted to make the decision?

Some cases stand for the proposition that intervening criminal acts of the sort described break the chain of proximate causation as a matter of law. See, *e.g.*, *Galbraith v. Levin*, 81 N.E.2d 560 (Mass. 1948) ("[T]he conduct of the thief [of an automobile left with keys over the visor that was stolen by thief who ran over plaintiff] was an intervening cause which the defendants were not bound to anticipate and guard against."); *McAllister v. Driever*, 318 F.2d 513 (4th Cir. 1963) (defendant left keys in unattended tow truck which was stolen by an unknown person and later abandoned without lights on in travelled portion of a highway. Held: Acts of thief broke the chain of causation between defendant's negligent act and plaintiff's injuries.); and *Watson v. Kentucky & Indiana Bridge Co.*, 126 S.W. 146 (Ky. 1910) (gasoline ran into street from derailed tank car. Resulting explosion injured plaintiff. Held: Defendant was not bound to foresee the criminal act of an unknown person in intentionally setting fire to the spilled gasoline.). There is a decided trend, however, to permit a jury decision where the context is suggestive of a high risk of criminal activity, such as where an automobile left unattended with the key in the ignition is stolen by a thief who runs over another person. See, *e.g.*, *Gaither v. Meyers*, 404 F.2d 216 (D.C. Cir. 1968), and *Vining v. Avis Rent-A-Car Systems, Inc.*, 354 So.2d 54 (Fla. 1978).

(3)   A house painter who was negligently run down by an automobile sustained an injury which left him with a "trick knee" that collapses from time to time. While the painter's tort action for the first injury was pending, the damaged knee folded up and threw the painter off a ladder. He suffered additional separable injuries. May the painter add a claim for the additional injuries to the existing action? If so, will the claim be successful? See *Stephenson v. Air Products & Chemicals, Inc.*, 114 Ill. App. 124, 252 N.E.2d 366 (1969). Suppose the original suit had already been settled at the time of the second injury.

(4)   Suppose in *Moum v. Maerklein* the decedent Dockter, while driving cautiously, had skidded on ice and crashed into the plaintiffs' car due to no fault of his own? Should that change the outcome of the case?

§ 8.05   FREAKISH SEQUENCE OF EVENTS

TOLIN v. TERRELL
Kentucky Court of Appeals
133 Ky. 210, 117 S.W. 290 (1909)

OPINION OF THE COURT BY WILLIAM ROGERS CLAY, COMMISSIONER — Reversed.

Plaintiff, L. R. Terrell, instituted this action against defendant, S. W. Tolin, to recover damages for personal injuries alleged to have been caused by the negligence of defendant. The jury returned a verdict in his favor in the sum of $5,500, and from the judgment based thereon this appeal is prosecuted.

At the time of plaintiff's injury, and for some time prior thereto, S. W. Tolin owned and operated a ferryboat between a point near Petersburg, Ky., and Lawrenceburg, Ind. The boat was about 60 or 65 feet in length, and in the general form of a parallelogram. Its width, however, was greatest in the center, and from that point it gradually narrowed as the ends were approached. The boat was operated by horse power; there being an inclined treadway upon each side of the boat, upon which the horses stood while propelling the boat. These treadways were fenced about with framework of about the same height as the shoulders of the horses. There was a drive or gangway in the center of the boat, about 9 feet 10 inches wide, between the treadways. The front feet of the horses were raised about 2 1/2 feet from the floor of the gangway. When a team drove on the gangway, it would be from 2 to 3 feet from the inclined treadway. At about 7:30 o'clock on the morning of November 6, 1905, plaintiff drove his wagon, which was hitched to a team of mules, on the ferryboat. According to the testimony of plaintiff's witnesses, he drove the team to a position where they could not be reached by either one of the ferry horses; but, owing to the leaky condition of the boat, he was told by one Hartman, who was in charge of the boat, to back his team to a position that brought them alongside, and in biting distance, of a gray mare engaged in operating the inclined treadway on the right side of the boat. After driving his team to this position, plaintiff unhitched the mules, as he claims, for the purpose of having them free in case any accident happened to the boat. Accompanying Terrell were four children, three boys and one girl; the oldest boy being about 15 years of age. After unhitching the team, plaintiff went to the end of the boat where the ferryman was steering, and from that time on he (Terrell) steered the boat. During the passage over the river, a [crew member] by the name of Thornton was placed at the pump, which was a few feet ahead of the team, and continued to use the pump until the boat had about crossed the river. When the boat was within a few feet of the Indiana shore, Hartman took charge of the rudder and relieved plaintiff, who then proceeded to hitch up his team. While he had gone, his lines had dropped on the floor. As he picked up the lines and was attaching them to the brake, the gray mare stuck out her head, bit the right-hand mule on her rump, and the mule then kicked plaintiff, severely and permanently injuring him.

It is the contention of plaintiff that the failure of defendant to have a screen or guard between the gray mare and stock that might be upon the boat, coupled with the fact of the vicious tendency of the mare, of which knowledge was brought home to the agent and manager of the boat, was the direct and proximate cause of paintiff's injury. Upon one point all the witnesses in the case agree; *i.e.*, that plaintiff was engaged in taking up and tying his lines at the time he was injured. In order to hold defendant liable in this case, his negligence must have been such that, without it, the injury would not have happened. While it is true that the question of proximate cause is ordinarily one for the jury, yet, where the evidence connecting the plaintiff's injuries with the defendants alleged negligence amounts to mere speculation or conjecture, no case for the jury is presented. No one could tell, from the evidence before us, whether plaintiff was injured as the result of walking behind his mule without warning and raising the lines, or because the gray mare bit the mule. The mule in question was three years old. In spite of the fact that there was testimony to show that this mule was of so gentle a disposition the children could play at its heels, it is a matter of common knowledge and common experience that there is no telling when or under what circumstances a mule will or will not kick. The only way to escape danger from the feet of a mule is not to go within the radius of its heels. He who goes within these limits assumes the risk of being kicked; and especially so when, without warning to the mule, he picks up the lines, which have been lying on the floor, passes them across the mule, and attempts to tie them at the brake.

Our conclusion in this case is that the evidence for the plaintiff utterly fails to show that the negligence of defendant was the proximate cause of plaintiff's injury. If the gray mare had bitten or kicked the plaintiff, and injured him, such act on the part of the mare might have been within the contemplation of the owner of the boat; but certainly it could not have been reasonably anticipated that, because there was no screen on the boat, the old gray mare would reach a distance of at least three feet and bite a mule on the rump, and that the mule would kick. We therefore conclude that the court erred in not giving the peremptory instruction asked for by the defendant. If the evidence be substantially the same upon a retrial, the court will instruct the jury to find for the defendant.

Judgment reversed, and cause remanded for a new trial consistent with this opinion.

NOTES AND QUESTIONS

(1) Was this case decided on the ground that the plaintiff had not proved causation-in-fact, or that the plaintiff had "assumed the risk," or on ground that the chain of causation was so freakish that the defendant should not be held responsible for the consequences of his original negligent act? Point to the precise language of the court that suggests your conclusion.

(2) *Tolin v. Terrell* represents a class of cases in which no efficient force intervenes, but the entire string of occurrences — each following directly from its predecessor — is unusual or bizarre. As might be expected, neither the outcomes of the cases nor whether they are decided as questions of law or of fact can be explained on any reliable theoretical grounds. Nevertheless, Professor Morris believes that putting the question, "Were the particular accident and the resulting damages foreseeable," permits one to classify most of the cases into one of three categories: typical occurrences; wildly freakish; and, "neither typical nor wildly freakish." Morris on Torts, Second at 163, 164. How should each class be disposed of?

(3) A few courts develop approaches that remove some of the difficulty in disposing of these cases. Already mentioned is the Minnesota approach of rejecting foreseeability as the test. All that matters is that each step in the chain follow directly from its predecessor without intervention. This makes proximate causation a question of hindsight rather than of foresight. *Dellwo v. Pearson*, 107 N.W. 2d 859 (Minn. 1961). See also *Busta v. Columbus Hospital Corporation*, 916 P.2d 122 (Mont. 1996), and cases cited therein. In total opposition to this is the approach sometimes employed by Florida courts, as exemplified by the following statement: ". . . 'natural and probable' consequences are those that a person by prudent human foresight can anticipate as likely to result from an act, because they happen so frequently from the commission of such an act that in the field of human experience they may be expected to happen again." *Pinkerton-Hays Lumber Co. v. Pope*, 127 So.2d 441 (Fla. 1961). Would this test break the chain of proximate causation of the negligence of driver *A* who stops his car in the middle of a highway to sleep off a drunk, when driver *B*, who stops behind *A* to avoid hitting the stopped

car, is crashed into by *C*, who is driving his car negligently? See *Gibson v. Avis Rent-A-Car System, Inc.*, 386 So.2d 520 (Fla. 1980).

(4)   Courts and lawyers continue to be victims of careless analysis in the use of the term "foreseeability" in connection with the various elements of the negligence cause of action. The basic fault is to consider "foreseeability" as if it were an element of the prima facie cause instead of a mere factor to be considered. As *Palsgraf* and other cases teach us, judges consider foreseeability as a threshold issue in determining whether the defendant owed a duty to the plaintiff. This is nothing more than a finding that a jury might find the defendant liable, not that it must or that it should. The jury then factors in "foreseeability," or something like it, to decide the breach question. Thereafter, if breach is determined, the jury might consider the same factor again to consider whether certain elements of damages are simply too far removed from the meaningful act to be recoverable. Nevertheless, some courts have held the "dual" or repetitive use of "foreseeability" is confusing. Hence, *Busta v. Columbus Hospital Corporation*, n. 3 *supra*, eliminated foreseeability from a jury's consideration of causation except in intervening cause cases. In all other cases, a jury's use of foreseeability is to be limited to the breach issue. Do you think this will have a practical effect upon verdicts?

Chapter 9

DEFENSES

§ 9.01 CONTRIBUTORY NEGLIGENCE

Contributory negligence means any negligence of the plaintiff directly and proximately contributing to the cause of the accident.[1]

[See *Butterfield v. Forrester*, § 4.07, *supra.*]

NOTES

(1)   An American court has summed up the defense of contributory negligence as follows:

> . . . Contributory negligence is defined as plaintiff's conduct which falls below the standard of care to which he should perform for his own protection. The standard is determined by reasonableness of behavior under the circumstances. The party relying upon the contributory negligence defense has the burden of proving it. . . .

Bridgewater v. State Through Dept. of Corrections, 434 So. 2d 383, 384–5 (La. 1983).

To the same effect is this statement from *Wing v. Morse*, 300 A.2d 491, 499 (Me. 1973) (see § 4.05, *supra*):

> At common law, negligence is defined as a breach of duty owed to a foreseeable plaintiff to exercise reasonable care for the plaintiff's safety. . . . . Contributory negligence did not at common law presuppose a duty of care owed to someone else. It only presupposed a general duty based upon policy considerations to exercise reasonable care for one's own safety.

(2)   As to whether contributory negligence applies in malpractice cases, the Alabama Supreme Court said in *Ott v. Smith*, 413 So. 2d 1129, 1134–1135 (1982):

> Appellant contends that the trial court also erred in submitting to the jury the issue of contributory negligence. Appellant states that it is rarely proper for such a defense to be allowed in an attorney malpractice case, because the relationship between the attorney and client is a fiduciary one and of a confidential nature. Appellant further contends that contributory negligence has been allowed only (1) where the client was also an attorney and/or otherwise insisted on active participation in the conduct of the case, (2) where the client failed to follow the attorney's advice or instructions, and (3) where the client fails to disclose all relevant facts to the attorney. Appellant states that none of these three instances applies here. We cannot agree with that contention.

---

[1]   McCall v. Weeks, 164 N.W.2d 206, 209 (Neb. 1969).

. . .

In *Theobald v. Byers*, 193 Cal. App. 2d 147 13 Cal. Rptr. 864 (1961), the California Court of Appeals discussed in detail the rationale for permitting contributory negligence in attorney negligence cases. That court stated:

> The rule is well established that an attorney is liable to his client for negligence in rendering professional services. The courts have consistently held that liability will be imposed for want of such skill, prudence and diligence as lawyers of ordinary skill and capacity commonly possess and exercise. . . . The lawyer can thus properly be classified with members of various other professions who are considered to possess knowledge, skill or even intelligence superior to that of an ordinary man and are, as a consequence, held to a higher minimum standard of conduct. . . . Doctors and dentists are held to this higher standard of care and their services can also be said to be of a fiduciary and confidential nature. Hence it would seem clear that similar rules of law would be applicable to all three professions. In actions against doctors and dentists for medical malpractice, courts have held the doctrine of contributory negligence to be a proper defense. . . . A patient will thus be barred from recovery for medical malpractice where the patient has disobeyed medical instructions given by a doctor or dentist or has administered home remedies to an injury without the aid of medical advice. There would seem to be no reason whatever why the same rule should not be applicable in a legal malpractice action where there is evidence that a client chose to disregard the legal advice of his attorney. In our opinion, any other rule would be grossly unfair.

193 Cal. App. 2d at 150, 13 Cal. Rptr. 864. In an action against an attorney for negligence in executing his professional duties, the elements are essentially no different from those of any other negligence suit. To recover, the party seeking damages must prove a duty owed, a breach of that duty, that the breach was the proximate cause of the injury, and damages. . . . [w]e see no reason why contributory negligence should not be applicable in a legal malpractice action where the client has failed to follow the attorney's advice or instructions.

The contributory negligence defense (and comparative negligence apportionment) is also permitted in medical malpractice cases where appropriate. *See, e.g., Gray v. Ford Motor Company*, 914 S.W.2d 464 (Tenn. 1996).

DAVIES v. MANN
Exchequer, 1842 10 M. & W. 547, 152 Eng. Rep. 588.[2]

At the trial, before Erskine, J., at the last Summer Assizes for the county of Worcester, it appeared that the plaintiff, having fettered the fore feet of an ass belonging to him, turned it into a public highway, and at the time in question the ass was grazing on the off side of the road about eight yards wide, when the defendant's waggon, with a team of three horses, coming down a slight descent, at what the witness termed a smartish pace, ran against the ass, knocked it down, and the wheels passing over it, it died soon after. The ass was fettered at the time, and

---

[2] [Ed. — English Reports, general reporter of older English cases, decision of Court of Exchequer; Meeson and Welsby's reports.]

it was proved that the driver of the waggon was some little distance behind the horses. The learned Judge told the jury, that though the act of the plaintiff, in leaving the donkey on the highway so fettered as to prevent his getting out of the way of carriages travelling along it, might be illegal, still, if the proximate cause of the injury was attributable to the want of proper conduct on the part of the driver of the waggon, the action was maintainable against the defendant; and his Lordship directed them, if they thought that the accident might have been avoided by the exercise of ordinary care on the part of the driver, to find for the plaintiff. The jury found their verdict for the plaintiff, damages 40s.

Godson now moved for a new trial, on the ground of misdirection.

LORD ABINGER, C. B. I am of opinion that there ought to be no rule in this case. The defendant has not denied that the ass was lawfully in the highway, and therefore we must assume it to have been lawfully there; but even were it otherwise, it would have made no difference, for as the defendant might, by proper care, have avoided injuring the animal, and did not, he is liable for the consequences of his negligence, though the animal may have been improperly there.

PARKE, B. This subject was fully considered by this Court in the case *of Bridge v. The Grand Junction Railway Company* (3 M. & W. 246), where, as appears to me, the correct rule is laid down concerning negligence, namely, that the negligence which is to preclude a plaintiff from recovering in an action of this nature, must be such as that he could, by ordinary care, have avoided the consequences of the defendant's negligence. I am reported to have said in that case, and I believe quite correctly, that "the rule of law is laid down with perfect correctness in the case of *Butterfield v. Forrester*, that, although there may have been negligence on the part of the plaintiff, yet unless he might, by the exercise of ordinary care, have avoided the consequences of the defendant's negligence, he is entitled to recover; if by ordinary care he might have avoided them, he is the author of his own wrong." In that case of *Bridge v. Grand Junction Railway Company*, there was a plea imputing negligence on both sides; here it is otherwise; and the Judge simply told the jury, that the mere fact of negligence on the part of the plaintiff in leaving his donkey on the public highway, was no answer to the action, unless the donkey's being there was the immediate cause of the injury; and that, if they were of opinion that it was caused by the fault of the defendant's servant in driving too fast, or, which is the same thing, at a smartish pace, the mere fact of putting the ass upon the road would not bar the plaintiff of his action. All this is perfectly correct; for, although the ass may have been wrongfully there, still the defendant was bound to go along the road at such a pace as would be likely to prevent mischief. Were this not so, a man might justify the driving over goods left on a public highway, or even over a man lying asleep there, or the purposely running against a carriage going on the wrong side of the road.

ODEKIRK v. AUSTIN
Arizona Supreme Court
366 P.2d 80 (1961)

BERNSTEIN, VICE CHIEF JUSTICE.

The sole question presented by this appeal is whether the trial court erred in refusing to instruct the jury as to the doctrine of last clear chance.

In determining whether the plaintiff's-appellant's request for submission of a last clear chance issue to the jury was properly refused we will consider the facts in the light most favorable to plaintiff-appellant together with the logical inferences which reasonably flow from such facts. *Casey v. Marshall*, 64 Ariz. 232, 168 P.2d 240 (1946).

The facts are: about 5:15 P.M. on April 17, 1957, plaintiff Cleland P. Odekirk, an eighteen year old college student, disembarked from a friend's automobile at the northeast corner of Seventh Avenue and West McDowell Road in Phoenix. It was a clear, dry day. He proceeded west across the intersection on the north side of West McDowell Road and began running west on the sidewalk. The plaintiff did not remember having left the sidewalk.

A motorist, Mr. O'Brien, driving in the eastbound lane at the time of the collision, testified that he first observed the plaintiff running down the street in a westerly direction in the westbound lane. At this time the plaintiff was a foot and a half from the north curb of West McDowell Road running parallel to the curb. The plaintiff then moved another foot to the south into the street at which time Mr. O'Brien observed the defendant's automobile coming from behind the plaintiff at approximately fifteen or sixteen miles per hour. Mr. O'Brien did not see the actual collision because he had passed the point of impact, but estimated that it was between five to seven seconds from the time he first observed the plaintiff until the collision.

The defendant stated that he did not see the plaintiff until an instant before the impact and that he immediately put on his brakes but could not stop in time. The point of impact was a little over four feet south of the north curb.

The plaintiff brought this action alleging negligence on the part of the defendant. The defendant answered setting up the affirmative defense of contributory negligence. The case was tried before a jury who returned a verdict for the defendant. Thereafter judgment was entered, motion for new trial denied, and this appeal followed.

From the evidence adduced at the trial the jury might have believed the defendant did not see the plaintiff until an instant before the injury, but that he, in the exercise of reasonable care, should have seen the plaintiff as he proceeded from the sidewalk onto the street. Therefore the evidence would sustain a finding that the defendant was negligent in failing to keep a proper lookout. *Pacific Greyhound Lines v. Uptain*, 81 Ariz. 359, 306 P.2d 281 (1957).

There are few, if any, legal doctrines that are more difficult of logical application to varied and ever varying situations than that known as the doctrine of last clear chance, and there is accordingly a vast amount of case law dealing with the subject. Wide research has revealed that the experience of the state courts in applying the doctrine has presented similar problems. Beginning with broad statements, they have found that they are too broad and have modified them only to find that the rules laid down do not apply to the ever varying situations and must be explained and modified again. This process has not yet been completed.

The doctrine of last clear chance is applied for the purpose of determining the legal proximate cause of the injury. The reasoning behind the doctrine is that although the negligence of both plaintiff and defendant continues up to the time of the injury, plaintiff's negligence is remote while the defendant's conduct is the proximate cause of the accident. But "the biggest problem for both the trial and appellate courts necessarily arises in attempting to determine whether the negligent acts of both parties concur as proximate cause. If so, then clearly defendant cannot be guilty of having had the last clear opportunity to avoid the accident." *Hirsh v. Manley*, 81 Ariz. 94, 300 P.2d 588, 591 (1956).

We have heretofore stated that we will follow the principles set forth in the American Law Institute's Restatement of the Law except in cases where a different rule has been laid down by this Court. . . . Under Restatement of the Law, Torts, §§ 479, 480, there are two situations to which the doctrine of last clear chance is applicable.

First, where the defendant did not actually see the peril of the plaintiff, but by keeping a reasonable careful lookout should have seen the peril of the plaintiff and by the exercise of reasonable care have thereafter avoided the injury. In this situation the doctrine only applies when the plaintiff's negligence has terminated or culminated in a situation of peril from which he could not, by the exercise of reasonable care, extricate himself. *Gray v. Woods*, 84 Ariz. 87, 324 P.2d 220 (1958); *Hirsh v. Manley, supra*; Restatement of the Law, Torts, § 479.

It is significant to note that the situation of danger or position of danger referred to in the authorities dealing with the last clear chance doctrine is reached only when a plaintiff, moving toward the path of an oncoming object, has reached a position from which he cannot escape by the exercise of ordinary care.

. . . Where the defendant does not actually know of the plaintiff's situation of peril, the doctrine can only properly be applied where the plaintiff has gotten into a position of inextricable peril. An illustration of this is where a person has caught his foot in a railroad switch, or is in some other similar predicament, so that he is thereafter unable to avert the injury. In such a situation, the plaintiff's negligence has come to rest. In such circumstances the defendant may be held responsible if he either knows, or in the exercise of reasonable care should know, of the plaintiff's helpless situation in time to avoid the injury and fails to do so.

In regard to the application of this principle, the plaintiff here is faced with a dilemma: she was either in inextricable peril or she was not. If she was not in inextricable peril, then at any instant up to the time she got into such predicament, by the exercise of reasonable care, she could have observed the oncoming car and have avoided being hit. On the other hand, she could only have gotten into inextricable peril by getting into the path of the defendant's car, and her peril could be considered inextricable only if the defendant was then too close to avoid striking her. Thus, by the very description of the situation, he did not have the "last clear chance" to avoid the injury. As the phrase indicates, it must be a fair and clear opportunity and not a mere possibility that the collision could have been avoided. *Fox v. Taylor*, 10 Utah 2d 174, 350 P.2d 154, 156–157 (1960).

Certainly, in this case, plaintiff's negligence had not terminated and it would seem equally certain that it had not culminated in a situation of peril from which he could not extricate himself. The facts disclose that plaintiff, without looking, left the sidewalk and was running, with his back to oncoming traffic, up the right side of the street at about a foot and a half from the curb and then angled over a few more feet into the street before being struck by the defendant's automobile. If he had been vigilant it would have been his duty to have stepped off the street at any instant and to have avoided the injury. Plaintiff's negligence therefore never terminated nor culminated in a situation of peril from which he could not extricate himself by the exercise of ordinary care.

It is argued that one who is oblivious to his danger is, in effect, as unable to extricate himself as one who is physically unable to do so. In applying the doctrine of last clear chance we are not exclusively concerned with the negligence of the defendant in the action. We are primarily concerned with the party who seeks to have his own negligence excused by the application of the doctrine. The negligence of the man who is physically unable to extricate himself, after getting his foot stuck in the road, has terminated. But the man walking or running on the wrong side of the road and not on the sidewalk in disobedience to the statute A.R.S. § 28-796 and oblivious to his danger in so proceeding is negligent, *Coe v. Hough*, 42 Ariz. 293, 25 P.2d 547 (1933), until and at the very moment of his injury. If we were to accept the theory urged it would mean that a plaintiff should be in a better position to have his negligence excused under the last clear chance rule if he took no care whatsoever for his own safety than if he kept careful watch for cars coming from behind. We cannot accept the theory that one who is oblivious to his danger is as unable to extricate oneself as one who is physically unable to do so.

Second, an oblivious or inattentive plaintiff not in a position of danger can only avail himself of the doctrine of last clear chance where the defendant *actually saw* the plaintiff or the peril of the plaintiff and should have appreciated the danger and thereafter fails to exercise reasonable care to avoid the injury. Restatement of the Law, Torts, § 480. Under this section of the Restatement dealing with an inattentive plaintiff we are only concerned with whether the defendant actually saw the plaintiff. If a defendant actually sees the plaintiff the doctrine applies although the plaintiff's negligence continues up to the instant of the injury and never terminates or culminates in a position of peril. The application of the rule in a situation such as this needs no support outside of simple considerations of humanity. Any other view would condone wilful and wanton injury.

We conclude that the doctrine of last clear chance is applicable in this jurisdiction under the following circumstances: 1. (a) The plaintiff has negligently subjected himself to a danger and such negligence has terminated or culminated in a situation of peril from which he could not, by the exercise of reasonable care, extricate himself; (b) the defendant saw or ought to have seen the peril of the plaintiff, and (c) the defendant thereafter has a last clear chance to avoid injuring the plaintiff by the exercise of reasonable care and fails to do so. 2. (a) The plaintiff has negligently subjected himself to a danger which he could have avoided by the exercise of reasonable vigilance; (b) the defendant actually saw or knew of the plaintiff's situation and realized or ought to have realized that the plaintiff was inattentive, and (c) the defendant thereafter has a last clear chance to avoid injuring the plaintiff by the exercise of reasonable care and fails to do so.

In this case, the evidence is undisputed that the defendant did not actually see the inattentive plaintiff until an instant before the injury. Under this situation the defendant did not then have an existing ability to avoid harming the plaintiff.

If the defendant does not discover the plaintiff's situation, but merely might do so by proper vigilance, it is obvious that neither party can be said to have a "last clear" chance. The plaintiff is still in a position to escape, and his lack of attention continues up to the point of the accident, without the interval of superior opportunity of the defendant which has been considered so important. The plaintiff may not demand of the defendant greater care for his own protection than he exercises himself. All courts except those of Missouri hold that there can be no recovery. Prosser, Torts, 2d Ed., p. 294.

Such being the case, the plaintiff's negligence was proximate as it was continuous and contributory with that of the defendant and thus the ordinary rules of negligence and contributory negligence were applicable, rather than the exceptional doctrine of last clear chance.

In so far as *Layne v. Hartung*, 87 Ariz. 88, 348 P.2d 291 (1960), is inconsistent with the views expressed herein, it is expressly overruled.

Judgment affirmed.

NOTES

(1) The doctrine of last clear chance has the sole purpose of excusing the plaintiff of negligence. It reflects, in part, the antipathy to the all or nothing character of the common law; the plaintiff wins all, or loses all. Last clear chance permits the plaintiff to win. (As discussed in § 9.04 *infra*, most courts no longer follow the common law rule that a plaintiff's contributory negligence is a total bar to recovery and incorporate the facts that would have given rise to a last clear chance instruction into a general comparative negligence instruction. Is this beneficial to plaintiffs?)

One can create a matrix of facts depending upon whether the negligent plaintiff is helpless (unable to save himself) or inattentive (able to save himself if he "snaps" out of his inattentiveness) and whether the defendant is aware of the plaintiff's plight or is himself inattentive. To which set of circumstances does *Odekirk v. Austin* hold that the defendant must take the last clear chance to prevent the harm?

Most courts refuse to apply the doctrine when both plaintiff and defendant are merely inattentive, either person being able to snap out of it and prevent the harm. Missouri was an exception, having applied what is known as the humanitarian doctrine before the law of comparative fault was adopted in that state. *Womack v. Missouri Pacific Railroad*, 88 S.W.2d 368 (Mo. 1935). Similarly, most courts have refused to exonerate a plaintiff of negligence when a defendant is helpless to avoid the injury, despite the fact that he was negligent in getting into the dangerous fix. Prosser, Law of Torts (4th ed. 1971), at 432. Some courts apply last clear chance only when the defendant has actual knowledge of the plaintiff's position of peril. *See, e.g., Treadway v. Brantley*, 437 So. 2d 93, 97 (Ala. 1983).

(2) Other means courts have used to prevent contributory negligence from defeating a plaintiff's claim are to hold that the plaintiff's act was not negligent as to the particular risk that caused harm, *Smithwick v. Hall Upson & Co.*, 91 A. 924

(Conn. 1890), and to refuse to apply the defense to intentional torts and those involving wanton and reckless behavior, *Kasanovich v. George*, 34 A. 523 (Pa. 1943). Of far more consequence in most jurisdictions is the abrogation of contributory negligence bar to recovery in favor of a comparative negligence apportioned recovery. See § 9.04 *infra*.

§ 9.02　VOLENTI NON FIT INJURIA (ASSUMPTION OF RISK)

PROBLEM

An appellate opinion begins as follows: On the morning of the accident in the instant case, the plaintiff, Emetilde Guillotte, a seventy-eight-year-old widow, had received her pension check and was walking around her small town paying her monthly bills. She planned to stop last at the Town Hall for the purpose of paying her water bill. She approached the building using the main sidewalk adjacent to the street. It was her intent to turn in and go up the entrance walkway leading to the Town Hall's front door. When she turned into the walkway, she was confronted by a string of Christmas lights which town employees had stretched across the walkway at a height of about sixteen to twenty inches. Being somewhat startled, because a box hedge bordering the entrance walkway made it physically impossible for her to view the wire before turning into the walkway, Mrs. Guillotte hesitated momentarily, but then decided to step over it. She got one foot over, but her other foot caught the string, causing her to fall and suffer a serious fracture of her arm.

Plaintiff filed suit against the town and its insurer. After a jury trial, judgment was rendered in her favor, and the defendants appealed. The court of appeal reversed and rendered judgment for the defendants. We granted certiorari to determine whether the court of appeal was correct in reversing the jury verdict on the ground that the plaintiff had assumed the risk.

Complete the opinion, reversing or affirming and clearly explaining your position. Assume that the following colloquy between the defendant's lawyer and the plaintiff is part of the record.

Q. "Mrs. Guillotte, isn't it correct that when you started to cross over that wire you thought you could make it?"

A. "I thought I could, because I wouldn't have started if I didn't know that I could."

LAMBERT v. WILL BROTHERS COMPANY
United States Court of Appeals, Eighth Circuit
596 F.2d 799 (1979)

LAY, CIRCUIT JUDGE.

Mark Lambert brought this diversity suit against Will Brothers Co. to recover damages for personal injuries suffered by Lambert during the course of his employment when using a hydraulic trim press manufactured by the defendant Will Brothers. The case was submitted to a jury on both negligence and strict liability under Arkansas law and the jury returned a general verdict against the plaintiff. This appeal followed. The plaintiff urges that the trial court erred in giving instructions on assumption of risk and independent intervening cause. We find the court erred in submitting the issue of assumption of risk to the jury and reverse and remand the case for a new trial on that basis.

Will Brothers sold the hydraulic trim press in May of 1965 to the Michigan Division of Hoover Ballbearing Co., the parent company of Glenvale Products Co., plaintiff's employer. The press, which is used to fabricate and trim die castings, is activated by depressing two palm control buttons located on the front of a stationary platform at a level slightly below the waistline of a person standing in front of the machine. There are separate buttons to start and stop the electric motor which provides power to the hydraulic system of the press. A red light located just above the start and stop buttons glows when the electrical power system of the press is turned on. When the press was sold in 1965 it did not have ring guards around the palm control buttons. Sometime after Glenvale Products obtained the press it attached ring guards around the palm control buttons.

At the time of plaintiff's injury, however, the ring guard around the right palm control button was missing. Glenvale Products also added a safety jack to the press which would prevent its operation when in place. This safety jack was not working at the time of the accident.

Approximately three months after his employment with Glenvale Products plaintiff was assigned the job of changing dies on the trim presses. Lambert had received approximately two weeks training and had worked three or four months on mechanical trim presses prior to the injury. The particular injury occurred on the first day that the plaintiff had worked on a hydraulic press. Plaintiff's supervisor testified that Lambert and a swing man changed the die on a trim press at the beginning of the shift. The injury occurred when Lambert was changing a die on the trim press near the end of his scheduled work shift. The evidence showed that he had positioned a mobile work table at a right angle to the front of the trim press, his intention being to place the die on the table once he removed it from the machine. Lambert then lowered the upper portion of the press to a closed position. Lambert testified that he then turned off the electrical power, loosened the bolts securing the two die sections to the upper and lower platens, turned the power on and then raised the upper platen to its highest or open position. He testified that he then turned off the power, although he acknowledged that he unknowingly may have pressed the wrong button. In any event when he attempted to remove the die, the upper platen suddenly descended, crushing his right hand. An inspection immediately after the injury revealed that the electrical power to the machine was on, that a corner of the mobile work table had penetrated the ring guard around the left palm control button and that the safety jack attached to the right side of the press was not operable. As previously mentioned the ring guard around the right palm control button was missing.

Based on the above evidence plaintiff's expert testified that in his opinion the injury occurred when plaintiff failed to turn off the electrical power and activated the machine by inadvertently engaging the unguarded right palm control button, a corner of the mobile work table having penetrated the left ring guard and engaged the left palm control button. The expert testified that at the time it was sold the machine was defectively designed in that it did not have ring guards around the palm control buttons, a safety jack and improperly designed buttons which turned the machine's electrical power on and off.

THE CHALLENGED INSTRUCTIONS.

Plaintiff challenges the instructions on assumption of risk and independent intervening cause. The assumption of risk instruction reads:

Furthermore, in this case, Will Brothers contends that Mark Lambert assumed the risk of his own injuries. To establish that defense, Will Brothers, Inc., has the burden of proving each of the following propositions: First, that a dangerous situation existed which was inconsistent with the safety of Mark Lambert. Second, that Mark Lambert knew the dangerous situation existed and realized the risk of damage from it. In determining whether Mark Lambert knew of the dangerous situation and realized the risk of damage from it, you may take into consideration whether the danger was obvious.

The third element to be proved, that Mark Lambert voluntarily exposed himself to the dangerous situation which proximately caused his claimed damages.

The independent intervening cause instruction reads:

If, following any event or omission of a party, an event intervened which in itself caused any damage, completely independent of the conduct of that party, then his act or omission was not a proximate cause of the damage.

Plaintiff urges on appeal that there was no evidence in the record to support either instruction.

ASSUMPTION OF RISK.

In Arkansas

[a]ssumption of risk occurs only when the injured person actually knows and appreciates the danger. The standard is a subjective one, being based upon what the particular person in fact sees, knows, understands, and appreciates. *McDonald v. Hickman*, 252 Ark. 300, 478 S.W.2d 753 (1972).

Price v. Daugherty, 253 Ark. 421, 486 S.W.2d 528, 529 (1972).

In *McDonald v. Hickman*, 252 Ark. 300, 478 S.W.2d 753 (1972), the Arkansas Supreme Court observed:

Assumption of risk, a harsh doctrine, depends upon actual knowledge and appreciation of the danger. As Prosser puts it: "Knowledge of the risk is the watchword of assumption of risk.' Under ordinary circumstances the plaintiff will not be taken to assume any risk of either activities or conditions of which he is ignorant. Furthermore, he must not only know of the facts which create the danger, but he must comprehend and appreciate the danger itself." Prosser on Torts, § 68 (4th ed., 1971). See also the Restatement of Torts (2d), § 496 D (1965), where it is stated: "The standard to be applied is a subjective one, of what the particular plaintiff in fact sees, knows, understands and appreciates. In this it differs from the objective standard which is applied to contributory negligence."

Id. at 302, 478 S.W.2d at 754–55.

Applying the above standard plaintiff argues there must be evidence from which the jury could conclude:

[T]hat plaintiff, as he attempted to remove the die from the press, was *actually* aware (1) that the electrical power to the press was on, (2) that the corner of his work table had penetrated the left ring guard, making contact with the left palm control button, (3) that there was a safety jack on the press for use in changing dies, and (4) that the ring guard around the right palm control was missing.

The defendant initially argues that plaintiff need only understand and appreciate the general nature of the risk of changing the dies and, since Lambert was an experienced die setter, the submission of assumption of risk to the jury was fully warranted. If this contention were true it would alter the subjective standard of assumption of risk under Arkansas law. The mere operation of dangerous machinery which may cause injury when the operator fails to use reasonable care does not invoke the doctrine of assumption of risk. The doctrine requires that the risk assumed be specifically known, understood and appreciated. See *Price v. Daugherty, supra; McDonald v. Hickman, supra*; see also *Rhoads v. Service Machine Co.*, 329 F. Supp. 367, 378–79 (E.D. Ark.1971). The doctrine of assumption of risk was not designed to bar recovery simply because there exists a general risk of injury through accidental misuse. The specific danger must be known and the plaintiff with such knowledge must voluntarily expose him or herself to it.

A more serious argument proffered by the defendant is that there existed sufficient evidence from which the jury could have concluded that the plaintiff was fully aware of an obvious danger and the faulty design of the machine. In *Harris v. Hercules, Inc.*, 455 F.2d 267 (8th Cir. 1972), this court held that the trial court properly submitted assumption of risk to the jury where the plaintiff, who was working with a crane near a high voltage line, "knew and appreciated that the high voltage line was in the area in which the crane was working and that it was dangerous to allow the crane to come into contact with it." *Id.* at 269. This court rejected plaintiff's contention that it was also necessary for him to know that the crane had been moved so close to the line that the potential risk had become an immediate and imminent danger. See *Woodruff Electric Cooperative Corp. v. Daniel*, 251 Ark. 468, 472 S.W.2d 919, 923 (1971). The *Harris* case is an application of the doctrine that a "plaintiff will not be heard to say that he did not comprehend a risk which must have been quite clear and obvious to him." W. Prosser, Law of Torts § 68, at 448 (1971). *Accord, Gilbertson v. Tryco Manufacturing Co.*, 492 F.2d 958, 962 (8th Cir. 1974) ("The situation . . . is no different than a person voluntarily walking across a rifle range during target practice and then claiming he did not know of the projection of the specific bullet that hit him.").

We find the present facts, however, clearly distinguishable and conclude that it was error for the trial court to instruct on assumption of risk. Here there was only evidence of a possible risk from which an injury might conceivably occur rather than evidence that plaintiff knew and appreciated the actual danger which caused his injury. It would appear that Lambert knew, or at least should have known, that the power to the machine was not turned off. If he failed to exercise sufficient caution to turn it off, he was guilty of negligence. This evidence does not, however, alter the fact that Lambert believed the power to be turned off. *Cf. Gilbertson, supra.* Without knowledge that the power was left on it is impossible to say that plaintiff knowingly appreciated the risk and voluntarily chose to undertake it.

Defendant argues that the jury could disbelieve Lambert's statement about turning off the power. Defendant contends it was obvious from the warning light that the power was still on when he removed the die. It is further urged that Lambert was fully aware the right ring guard was missing and therefore the risk was obvious that a person working near the right control button might accidentally engage it. *Cf. Rhoads v. Service Machine Co.*, 329 F. Supp. at 379. Assuming the above facts to be true, there is no evidence that plaintiff had the necessary knowledge that the press would activate. The evidence is undisputed that Lambert knew for the press to be activated that both the left palm control button *and* the right palm control button had to be engaged at the same time. Unless Lambert had the specific knowledge that the left control button was actually engaged, he had a right to assume, even with the power on, that if he accidentally engaged only the right palm control button the platens would not close on his hand.

A similar factual situation appears in *Lambertson v. Cincinnati Corp.*, 257 N.W.2d 679 (Minn. 1977). There

plaintiff was assisting a coemployee in the operation of the press brake. The coemployee was controlling the foot pedal, and plaintiff was placing long metal strips between the ram and the bed and removing them after they had been bent. As the ram was being raised after one cycle, a piece of metal which had been bent fell to the side of the bed opposite to the side where plaintiff was working. Plaintiff reached through the jaws of the machine to retrieve the piece of metal, but his coemployee had kept his foot on the pedal, thus permitting the ram to descend again, crushing plaintiff's arm between the ram and the bed.

Id. at 682.

In rejecting the manufacturer's claim that the trial court erred in failing to instruct the jury on assumption of risk the court wrote:

The employee testified that he did not know that his coemployee's foot was still on the pedal and that he did not know that the machine could double cycle without stopping. While the employee did exclaim in the moments immediately following his injury that he should not have reached through the machine, the manufacturer points to no evidence that would permit a jury to infer that he was fully aware of how the machine operated and yet tried to reach in and out fast enough to avoid the ram.

Id. at 683.

The same reasoning applies here. The defendant points to no evidence that would permit the jury to infer that plaintiff knew the work table had penetrated the left ring guard and that the machine was in a position to be activated by engaging the right palm control button. Absent evidence that the plaintiff was aware of the specific danger, it was error for the trial court to submit to the jury the defense of assumption of risk.

Perhaps Lambert as a reasonable, prudent person should have exercised more caution concerning the electrical power and inspected the location of the mobile work table in relation to the left palm control button. His failure to do so, however, relates only to the issue of his contributory negligence and comparative fault and does not constitute evidence which would support a complete bar to his recovery under the doctrine of assumption of risk.[3]

---

[3] Under the new Arkansas Model Jury Instruction 612, the Arkansas assumption of risk instruction reads:

In view of the necessity for a new trial it is unnecessary to pass on the court's abbreviated instruction on intervening cause. Assuming the evidence warrants the giving of an instruction on independent intervening cause, we feel it should be enlarged to inform the jury that an independent intervening cause[4]

The judgment of the district court is reversed and remanded for a new trial.

NOTES AND QUESTIONS

(1)   How does assumption of risk differ conceptually from contributory negligence? Is there a genuine difference between "foolhardy venturesomeness" and "unreasonable imprudence?" Which is which? Whereas contributory negligence is itself the product of the law of negligence as it absorbed and coalesced its antecedents into a coherent theory, assumption of the risk had crystallized much earlier in the form of the doctrine *volenti non fit injuria.* The general idea is that one who consents to injury will not be heard by the courts to complain. Where contributory negligence is followed in its pristine form, negating all liability, both semantic and conceptual differences may be largely unimportant. Where comparative negligence has supplanted contributory negligence, however, the difference may determine the outcome of a law suit. This will be more understandable after the reader has examined the comparative negligence materials in § 9.04 of this chapter, but *Lambert v. Will Brothers* exemplifies the point. Under the Arkansas comparative negligence statute, Lambert's contributory negligence would diminish but not bar his recovery, whereas assumption of risk would defeat recovery totally. Although most comparative fault jurisdictions permit limited application of assumption of risk as an absolute bar to recovery (See § 9.04), West Virginia requires all cases to treated comparatively. *See Blake v. Wendy's International, Inc.,* 413 S.E.2d 414 (W. Va. 1991).

(2)   Some courts maintain that to say the plaintiff assumed certain risks is simply a contorted way of saying that the defendant was not negligent. For example, it might be said that a worker assumes the inevitable risks of a well run workshop and a passenger on a railroad train assumes the inevitable starts, bumps,

---

ASSUMPTION OF RISK — GENERAL

[Defendant] contends that [plaintiff] assumed the risk of his own (injuries) (damages). To establish that defense, [defendant] has the burden of proving each of the following propositions:

First: That a dangerous situation existed which was inconsistent with the safety of [plaintiff]. . .

Second: That [plaintiff] knew the dangerous situation existed and realized the risk of (injury) (damage) from it. In determining whether [plaintiff] knew of the dangerous situation and realized the risk of (injury) (damage) from it you may take -into consideration whether the danger was (open and) (obvious).

Third: That [plaintiff] voluntarily exposed himself to the dangerous situation which proximately caused his claim (injuries) (damages).

[4] We seriously question whether the instruction should have been given under the circumstances of this case. The general principle governing intervening cause is well set forth by Professor Prosser.

Obviously the defendant cannot be relieved from liability by the fact that the risk, or a substantial and important part of the risk, to which he has subjected the plaintiff has indeed come to pass. Foreseeable intervening forces are within the scope of the original risk, and hence of the defendant's negligence. The courts are quite generally agreed that intervening causes which fall fairly in this category will not supersede the defendant's responsibility. Prosser, *supra,* § 44, at 273.

See Dulin v. Circle F Industries, Inc., 558 F.2d 456, 467 (8th Cir. 1977); Cowrt v. Casey Jones, Contractor, Inc., 250 Ark. 881, 467 S.W.2d 710 (1971), is one not foreseeable to the original tortfeasor. *Price v. Daugherty, supra.*

and lurches on a well run train operated on a well maintained road bed. *Meistrich v. Casino Arena Attraction*, 155 A.2d 70 (N.J. 1959), pushes this line of reasoning to the point of holding that certain implied assumptions of risk are merely applications of contributory negligence in another guise. *Meistrich* treats them all as contributory negligence. This does not apply to express assumptions, however. *Meistrich* has been followed by *Blackburn v. Dorta*, 348 So. 2d 267 (Fla. 1977), but expressly rejected by *Kennedy v. Providence Hockey Club, Inc.*, 376 A.2d 329 (R.I. 1977). Although assumption of risk is not a "favored" defense and "the trend in the law has been toward abolishing it," *Larson v. Pacesetter Systems, Inc.*, 837 P.2d 1273, 1290 (Haw. 1992), many courts maintain a clear doctrinal line between the two defenses in appropriate cases, especially in comparative negligence jurisdictions. See § 9.04 *infra*.

(3)   In *Hackbart v. Cincinnati Bengals, Inc.*, 435 F. Supp. 352 (D. Colo. 1977), the plaintiff, a professional football player, was injured by a blow received while he was kneeling after a play had ended during a regular season game. Does a player assume the risk of all blows during the course of the game? Or, only those within some definable range of severity or connection with the movement of the ball? Does the dichotomy between intentional and unintentional blows help? After examining the matter in detail, the trial court concluded that the "civil courts cannot be expected to control the violence in professional football" and dismissed the case. This holding was reversed on appeal in a decision in which the court stated: The general customs of football do not approve the intentional punching or striking of others. That this is prohibited was supported by the testimony of all of the witnesses. They testified that the intentional striking of a player in the face or from the rear is prohibited by the playing rules as well as the general customs of the game. Punching or hitting with the arms is prohibited. Undoubtedly these restraints are intended to establish reasonable boundaries so that one football player cannot intentionally inflict a serious injury on another. Therefore, the notion is not correct that all reason has been abandoned, whereby the only possible remedy for the person who has been the victim of an unlawful blow is retaliation.

Hackbart v. Cincinnati Bengals, Inc., 601 F.2d 516. 521 (10th Cir. 1979), *cert. denied*, 100 S. Ct. 275 (1979). A number of courts have concluded that there is no liability for injuries suffered in physical contact sports, not by virtue of assumption of risk, but by holding that no duty is owed as to risks inherent in the sport. *See, e.g., Knight v. Jewett*, 834 P.2d 696 (Cal. En Banc 1992). These inherent risks do not include injuries intentionally or recklessly inflicted. *See Marchetti v. Kalish*, 559 N.E.2d 699 (Ohio 1990).

(4)   Some courts conclusively presume that a plaintiff assumes the risk of a particular danger that is "open and obvious" to anyone who might come into contact with it. The rule, sometimes referred to as the "patent danger" rule, precludes the offering of evidence to prove that the plaintiff in fact did not see the hazardous condition or did not appreciate the danger posed by it. The rule apparently first emerged with the New York Court of Appeals' decision in *Campo v. Scofield*, 301 N.Y. 468, 95 N.E.2d 802 (1950), a case which was expressly repudiated by *Micallef v. Miehle Co.*, 39 N.Y.2d 376, 348 N.E.2d 571 (1976). A trend to repudiate the rule has developed. *See, e.g., Brown v. North American Manufacturing Co.*, 576 P.2d 711 (Mont. 1978); *Auburn Machine Works v. Jones*, 366 So. 2d 1167 (Fla. 1979); *Parker v. Highland Park, Inc.*, 565 S.W.2d 512 (Tex. 1978); *Casey v. Gifford Wood Co.*, 61 Mich. App. 208, 232 N.W.2d 360 (1975); and *Holbert v. Slaughter*, 227 Ark.

144, 296 S.W.2d 402 (1957). Contra., *Bemis Co. v. Rubush*, 427 N.E.2d 1058 (Ind. 1981). To what extent, if at all, is the "patent danger rule" embodied in the assumption of risk instruction referred to in *Lambert v. Will Brothers Company*?

In fact, the "open and obvious" danger rule was akin to the implied assumption of risk rule denounced in *Meistrich v. Casino Arena Attraction* and *Blackburn v. Dorta*. The United States Supreme Court explained the old rule in *Arizona Copper Co. v. Hammer*, 250 U.S. 400, 39 S. Ct. 553, 556 (1918), as follows:

> . . . it is to be borne in mind that the matter of the assumption of the risks of employment and the consequences to flow there from has been regulated time out of mind by the common law, with occasional statutory modifications. The rule existing in the absence of statute, as usually enunciated is that all consequences of risk inherent in the occupation and normally incident to it are assumed by the employee and afford no ground of action by him or those claiming under him, in the absence of negligence by the employer; and even risks arising from or increased by the failure of the employer to take the care that he ought to take for the employee's safety are assumed by the latter if he is aware of them or if they are so obvious that any ordinarily prudent person under the circumstances could not fail to observe and appreciate them; but if the employee, having become aware of a risk arising out of a defect attributable to the employer's negligence, makes complaint or objection and obtains a promise of reparation, the common law brings into play a new set of regulations requiring the employer to assume the risk under certain circumstances, the employee under others.

Nevertheless, the tendency of courts to abrogate the "patent danger" rule as a complete defense does not mean that the fact that a particular risk was "open and obvious" to causal observation has no bearing on tort liability. *Bucheleleres v. The Chicago Park District*, 665 N.E.2d 826 (Ill. 1996), referred to the "open and obvious" character of the risk as a major consideration in its holding that the defendant Park District owed no duty to a park patron who dived from a sea wall into Lake Michigan and struck an underwater obstacle. The court also considered the social utility of the parks, the costs of instituting effective warning systems and other duty considerations to conclude: "[with exceptions] the law does not require persons to protect or warn against possible injuries from open or obvious conditions, which by their nature carry their own 'warning' of potential harm." Does this illustrate how a single fact may have heavy bearing both as to the prima facie case and as to defenses? See, for example, *Mazzeo v. City of Sebastian*, 550 So. 2d 1113 (Fla. 1989), involving legally indistinguishable facts, in which the court focussed on assumption of risk and not duty (held: plaintiff's dive must be treated as negligence subject to comparative negligence apportionment.)

(5) Some states have enacted statutes to impose assumption of risk as a complete defense as to injuries sustained while engaging in specified activities. *Kelleher v. Big Sky Montana*, 642 F. Supp. 1128 (D. Mont. 1988), upheld the following statutes against constitutional challenge:

Section 23-2-736(1), Mont. Code Ann.:

A skier assumes the risk and all legal responsibility for injury to himself or loss of property that results from participating in the sport of skiing by virtue of his participation. The assumption of risk and responsibility includes but is not limited to injury or loss caused by the following: variations in terrain, surface or subsurface snow or ice conditions, bare spots, rocks, trees, other forms of forest growth or debris, lift towers and components thereof, pole lines, and plainly marked or visible snowmaking equipment.

Section 23-2-731, Mont. Code Ann.:

It is the purpose of 23-2-7 through 23-2-737 to define those areas of responsibility and affirmative acts for which the ski area operator is liable for loss, damage, or injury and those risks for which the skier expressly assumes or shall be considered to have voluntarily assumed the risk of loss or damage and for which there can be no recovery.

Nevertheless, *Brewer v. Ski-Lift, Inc.*, 762 P.2d 226, 231 (Mont. 1988), limited the defense to those risks within the scope of this jury instruction propounded by the court:

A skier assumes the risk and all legal responsibility for injury to himself or loss of property resulting from the inherent risks in the sport of skiing that are essentially impossible to eliminate by the ski operator.

Under this instruction does a skier assume the risk that a ski operator will locate a maintenance shed too close to a ski trail?

(6)   Assumption of risk is not recognized as a defense in FELA cases, *see, e.g., Taylor v. Burlington Northern Railroad Company*, 787 F.2d 1309 (9th Cir. 1986), nor in maritime law, *see, e.g., DeSole v. United States*, 947 F.2d 1169 (4th Cir. 1991) (some dispute exists on this point in connection with recreational boating accidents).

§ 9.03   FELLOW SERVANT RULE

PRIESTLY v. FOWLER
Michaelmas Term, I Victoriae 3 M. & W. 1, 150 Eng. Rep. 1030 (Ex. 1837)[5]

CASE. — The declaration stated that the plaintiff was a servant of the defendant in his trade of a butcher; that the defendant had desired and directed the plaintiff, so being his servant, to go with and take certain goods of the defendant's, in a certain van of the defendant then used by him, and conducted by another of his servants, in carrying goods for hire upon a certain journey; that the plaintiff, in pursuance of such desire and direction, accordingly commenced and was proceeding *and being carried and conveyed by the said van*, with the said goods; and it became the duty of the defendant, on that occasion, to use due and proper care that the said van should be in a proper state of repair, that it should not be overloaded, and that the plaintiff should be safely and securely carried thereby: nevertheless, the defendant did not use proper care that the van should be in a sufficient state of repair, or that it should not be overloaded, or that the plaintiff should be safely and securely carried thereby, in consequence of the neglect of all and each of which duties the van gave way and broke down, and the plaintiff was

---

[5] [Ed. — English Reports, general reporter of older English cases; decision of the Court of Exchequer; Meeson and Welsby's reports.]

thrown with violence to the ground and his thigh was thereby fractured, &c. Plea, not guilty.

At the trial before *Park*, J., at the Lincolnshire Summer Assizes, 1836, the plaintiff, having given evidence to show that the injury arose from the overloading of the van, and that it was so loaded with the defendant's knowledge, had a verdict for 100 *l.* In the following Michaelmas Term, *Adams*, Serjt., obtained a rule to show cause why the judgment should not be arrested, on the ground that the defendant was not liable in law, under the circumstances stated in the declaration. In Hilary Term,

LORD ABINGER, C. B.

This was a motion in arrest of judgment, after verdict for the plaintiff, upon the insufficiency of the declaration. [His lordship stated the declaration.] It has been objected to this declaration, that it contains no premises from which the duty of the defendant, as therein alleged, can be inferred in law; or, in other words, that from the mere relation of master and servant no contract, and therefore no duty, can be implied on the part of the master to cause the servant to be safely *and* securely carried, or to make the master liable for damage to the servant, arising from any vice or imperfection, unknown to the master, in the carriage, or in the mode of loading and conducting it. For, as the declaration contains no charge that the defendant knew any of the defects mentioned, the Court is not called upon to decide how far such knowledge on his part of a defect unknown to the servant, would make him liable.

It is admitted that there is no precedent for the present action by a servant against a master. We are therefore to decide the question upon general principles, and in doing so we are at liberty to look at the consequences of a decision the one way or the other.

If the master be liable to the servant in this action, the principle of that liability will be found to carry us to an alarming extent. He who is responsible by his general duty, or by the terms of his contract, for all the consequences of negligence in a matter in which he is the principal, is responsible for the negligence of all his inferior agents. If the owner of the carriage is therefore responsible for the sufficiency of his carriage to his servant, he is responsible for the negligence of his coachmaker, or his harness-maker, or his coachman. The footman, therefore, who rides behind the carriage, may have an action against his master for a defect in the carriage, owing to the negligence of the coachmaker, or for a defect in the harness arising from the negligence of the harness-maker, or for drunkenness, neglect, or want of skill in the coachman; nor is there any reason why the principle should not, if applicable in this class of cases, extend to many others. The master, for example, would be liable to the servant for the negligence of the chambermaid, for putting him into a damp bed; for that of the upholsterer, for sending in a crazy bedstead, whereby he was made to fall down while asleep and injure himself; for the negligence of the cook, in not properly cleaning the copper vessels used in the kitchen; of the butcher, in supplying the family with meat of a quality injurious to the health; of the builder, for a defect in the foundation of the house, whereby it fell, and injured both the master and the servant by the ruins.

The inconvenience, not to say the absurdity of these consequences, affords a sufficient argument against the application of this principle to the present case.

But, in truth, the mere relation of the master and the servant never can imply an obligation on the part of the master to take more care of the servant than he may reasonably be expected to do of himself. He is, no doubt, bound to provide for the safety of his servant in the course of his employment, to the best of his judgment, information, and belief. The servant is not bound to risk his safety in the service of his master, and may, if he thinks fit, decline any service in which he reasonably apprehends injury to himself: and in most of the cases in which danger may be incurred, if not in all, he is just as likely to be acquainted with the probability and extent of it as the master. In that sort of employment, especially, which is described in the declaration in this case, the plaintiff must have known as well as his master and probably better, whether the van was sufficient, whether it was overloaded, and whether it was likely to carry him safely. In fact, to allow this sort of action to prevail would be an encouragement to the servant to omit that diligence and caution which he is in duty bound to exercise on the behalf of his master, to protect him against the misconduct or negligence of others who serve him, and which diligence and caution, while they protect the master, are a much better security against any injury the servant may sustain by the negligence of others engaged under the same master, than any recourse against his master for damages could possibly afford.

We are therefore of opinion that the judgment ought to be arrested.

Rule absolute.

NOTE

Because most work injuries to employees are now compensated under workers' compensation laws, which are examined in Chapter 16, *infra*, the fellow servant rule is rarely seen in modern litigation. Many other statutes, including FELA (Federal Employers Liability Act) have abrogated the fellow servant defense in their scope of application. Notwithstanding that, the defense was raised as late as 1982 in New York, leading the New York Court of Appeals to abrogate the defense as serving no valid purpose. *Buckley v. City of New York*, 56 N.Y.2d 300, 437 N.E.2d 1088 (1982). See also *Crenshaw Bros. Produce Co. v. Harper*, 194 So. 353, 361 (Fla. 1940).

§ 9.04 COMPARATIVE NEGLIGENCE

[A] Overview

HOFFMAN v. JONES
Florida Supreme Court
280 So. 2d 431 (1973)

ADKINS, JUSTICE.

The question certified by the District Court of Appeal is:

Whether or not the Court should replace the contributory negligence rule with the principles of comparative negligence?

. . .

All rules of the common law are designed for application to new conditions and circumstances as they may be developed by enlightened commercial and business intercourse and are intended to be vitalized by practical application in advanced society. One of the most pressing social problems facing us today is the automobile accident problem, for the bulk of tort litigation involves the dangerous instrumentality known as the automobile. Our society must be concerned with accident prevention and compensation of victims of accidents. The Legislature of Florida has made great progress in legislation geared for accident prevention. The prevention of accidents, of course, is much more satisfying than the compensation of victims, but we must recognize the problem of determining a method of securing just and adequate compensation of accident victims who have a good cause of action.

The contemporary conditions must be met with contemporary standards which are realistic and better calculated to obtain justice among all of the parties involved, based upon the circumstances applying between them at the time in question. The rule of contributory negligence as a complete bar to recovery was imported into the law by judges. Whatever may have been the historical justification for it, today it is almost universally regarded as unjust and inequitable to vest an entire accidental loss on one of the parties whose negligent conduct combined with the negligence of the other party to produce the loss. If fault is to remain the test of liability, then the doctrine of comparative negligence which involves apportionment of the loss among those whose fault contributed to the occurrence is more consistent with liability based on a fault premise.

We are, therefore, of the opinion that we do have the power and authority to reexamine the position we have taken in regard to contributory negligence and to alter the rule we have adopted previously in light of current "social and economic customs" and modern "conceptions of right and justice."

Use of the terms "contributory negligence" and "comparative negligence" is slightly confusing. The two theories now commonly known by these terms both recognize that negligence of a plaintiff may play a part in causing his injuries and that the damages he is allowed to recover should, therefore, be diminished to some extent. The "contributory negligence" theory, of course, *completely* bars recovery, while the "comparative negligence" theory is that a plaintiff is prevented from recovering only that proportion of his damages for which he is responsible.

The demise of the absolute-bar theory of contributory negligence has been urged by many American scholars in the law of torts. It has been abolished in almost every common law nation in the world, including England — its country of origin — and every one of the Canadian Provinces. Some form of comparative negligence now exists in Austria, France, Germany, Portugal, Switzerland, Italy, China, Japan, Persia, Poland, Russia, Siam and Turkey. Maloney, *supra*, page 154.

Also, our research reveals that sixteen states have so far adopted some form of the comparative negligence doctrine.

One reason for the abandonment of the contributory negligence theory is that the initial justification for establishing the complete defense is no longer valid. It is generally accepted that, historically, contributory negligence was adopted "to protect the essential growth of industries, particularly transportation." Institute of Judicial Administration, Comparative Negligence — 1954 Supplement, at page 2. Modern economic and social customs, however, favor the individual, not industry.

We find that none of the justifications for denying any recovery to a plaintiff, who has contributed to his own injuries to any extent, has any validity in this age.

Perhaps the best argument in favor of the movement from contributory to comparative negligence is that the latter is simply a more equitable system of determining liability and a more socially desirable method of loss distribution. The injustice which occurs when a plaintiff suffers severe injuries as the result of an accident for which he is only slightly responsible, and is thereby denied any damages, is readily apparent. The rule of contributory negligence is a harsh one which either places the burden of a loss for which two are responsible upon only one party or relegates to Lady Luck the determination of the damages for which each of two negligent parties will be liable. When the negligence of more than one person contributes to the occurrence of an accident, each should pay the proportion of the total damages he has caused the other party.

In an effort to ameliorate the harshness of contributory negligence, other doctrines have evolved in tort law such as "gross, willful, and wanton" negligence, "last clear chance" and the application of absolute liability in certain instances. Those who defend the doctrine of contributory negligence argue that the rule is also not as harsh in its practical effect as it is in theory. This is so, they say, because juries tend to disregard the instructions given by the trial judge in an effort to afford some measure of rough justice to the injured party. We agree with Dean Maloney that,

[T]here is something basically wrong with a rule of law that is so contrary to the settled convictions of the lay community that laymen will almost always refuse to enforce it, even when solemnly told to do so by a judge whose instructions they have sworn to follow.

. . .

[T]he disrespect for law engendered by putting our citizens in a position in which they feel it is necessary to deliberately violate the law is not something to be lightly brushed aside; and it comes ill from the mouths of lawyers, who as officers of the courts have sworn to uphold the law, to defend the present system by arguing that it works because jurors can be trusted to disregard that very law. 11 U. Fla. L. Rev. 135, pp. 151–152 (1958).

Since we definitely consider the problem to be a judicial one, we feel the time has come for this Court to join what seems to be a trend toward almost universal adoption of comparative negligence. A primary function of a court is to see that legal conflicts are equitably resolved. In the field of tort law, the most equitable result that can ever be reached by a court is the equation of liability with fault. Comparative negligence does this more completely than contributory negligence, and we would be shirking our duty if we did not adopt the better doctrine.

Therefore, we now hold that a plaintiff in an action based on negligence will no longer be denied any recovery because of his contributory negligence.

If it appears from the evidence that both plaintiff and defendant were guilty of negligence which was, in some degree, a legal cause of the injury to the plaintiff, this does not defeat the plaintiff's recovery entirely. The jury in assessing damages would in that event award to the plaintiff such damages as in the jury's judgment the negligence of the defendant caused to the plaintiff. In other words, the jury should apportion the negligence of the plaintiff and the negligence of the defendant; then, in reaching the amount due the plaintiff, the jury should give the plaintiff only such an amount proportioned with his negligence and the negligence of the defendant. See *Florida Cent. & P. R. Co. v. Foxworth*, 41 Fla. 1, 25 So. 338, 79 Am. St. Rep. 149 (1899).

This rule should not be construed so as to entitle a person to recover for damage in a case where the proof shows that the defendant could not by the exercise of due care have prevented the injury, or where the defendant's negligence was not a legal cause of the damage. Stated differently, there can be no apportionment of negligence where the negligence of the defendant is not directly a legal cause of the result complained of by the plaintiff. A plaintiff is barred from recovering damages for loss or injury caused by the negligence of another only when the plaintiff's negligence is the sole legal cause of the damage, or the negligence of the plaintiff and some person or persons other than the defendant or defendants was the sole legal cause of the damage.

If plaintiff and defendant are both at fault, the former may recover, but the amount of his recovery may be only such proportion of the entire damages plaintiff sustained as the defendant's negligence bears to the combined negligence of both the plaintiff and the defendant. For example, where it is found that the plaintiff's negligence is at least equal to that of the defendant, the amount awarded to the plaintiff should be reduced by one-half from what it otherwise would have been.

The doctrine of last clear chance would, of course, no longer have any application in these cases. *See Martin v. Sussman*, 82 So. 2d 597 (Fla. 1955).

We decline herein to dissect and discuss all the possible variations of comparative negligence which have been adopted in other jurisdictions. Countless law review commentaries and treatises can be found which have covered almost every conceivable mutation of the basic doctrine. Suffice it to say that we consider the "pure form" of comparative negligence — as we have phrased it above — to be the most equitable method of allocating damages in negligence actions.

In the usual situation where the negligence of the plaintiff is at issue, as well as that of the defendant, there will undoubtedly be a counterclaim filed. The cross-plaintiff (just as plaintiff in the main suit) guilty of some degree of negligence would be entitled to a verdict awarding him such damages as in the jury's judgment were proportionate with his negligence and the negligence of cross-defendant. This could result in two verdicts — one for plaintiff and one for cross-plaintiff. In such event the court should enter one judgment in favor of the party receiving the larger verdict, the amount of which should be the difference between the two verdicts. This is in keeping with the long recognized principles of "set off in contract litigation. The Court's primary responsibility is to enter a judgment which reflects the true intent of the jury, as expressed in its verdict or verdicts.

In rare cases the net result of two such claims will be that the party more responsible for an accident will recover more than the party less responsible. On the surface, this might seem inequitable. However, using an extreme example, let us assume that a plaintiff is 80 per cent responsible for an automobile accident and suffers $20,000 in damages, and that the defendant — 20 per cent responsible — fortunately suffers no damages. The liability of the defendant in such a case should not depend upon what damages he *suffered*, but upon what damages he *caused*. If a jury found that this defendant had been negligent and that his negligence, in relation to that of the plaintiff, was 20 per cent responsible for causing the accident then he should pay 20 per cent of the total damages, regardless of the fact that he has been fortunate enough to not be damaged personally.

We are fully confident that the trial court judges of this State can adequately handle any problems created by our change to a comparative negligence rule as these problems arise. The answers to many of the problems will be obvious in light of the purposes for which we adopt the rule stated above:

(1) To allow a jury to apportion fault as it sees fit between negligent parties whose negligence was part of the legal and proximate cause of any loss or injury; and

(2) To apportion the total damages resulting from the loss or injury according to the proportionate fault of each party.

In accomplishing these purposes, the trial court is authorized to require special verdicts to be returned by the jury and to enter such judgment or judgments as may truly reflect the intent of the jury as expressed in any verdict or verdicts which may be returned.

. . .

ROBERTS, JUSTICE (dissenting).

. . .

The sovereign powers of this State are divided into three coordinate branches of government — legislative, judicial and executive — by the Constitution of Florida, Article II, Section 3. Our Constitution specifically prohibits a person belonging to one of such branches from exercising any powers "appertaining to either of the other branches unless expressly provided herein." This Court has been diligent in preserving and maintaining the doctrine of separation of powers, which doctrine was imbedded in both the state and federal constitutions at the threshhold of constitutional democracy in this country, and under which doctrine the judiciary has no power to make statutory law.

. . .

In fine, the primary question is not whether or not the law of contributory negligence should be changed, but rather, who should do the changing. Contributory negligence was recognized in the common law as far back as A.D. 1606 and made a part of the statute law of this State in A.D. 1829, and thus far not changed by statute. If such a fundamental change is to be made in the law, then such modification should be made by the legislature where proposed change will be considered by legislative committees in public hearing where the general public may have an opportunity to be heard and should not be made by judicial fiat. Such an excursion into the field of legislative jurisdiction weakens the concept of separation of powers and our tripartite system of government.

For the foregoing reasons, I respectfully dissent.

[B]   History and Status

Although the British Parliament enacted a pure comparative negligence statute in 1945, most American states clung to the contributory negligence rule much longer. As late as the middle 1960s only ten American states had adopted comprehensive comparative negligence schemes. Despite this, some American states had turned to comparative negligence much sooner. The earliest judicial versions were adopted in Georgia and Tennessee in the nineteenth century, and the earliest comprehensive statutes were enacted in South Dakota, Wisconsin, Mississippi and Nebraska between 1907 and 1913. Arkansas, Puerto Rico, the Virgin Islands, and Maine enacted statutes between that date and 1965; and seventeen additional states adopted comprehensive statutes between 1969 and 1973. South Carolina also adopted a limited statute that was soon invalidated on constitutional grounds.

The truly seminal event of 1973 was the judicial adoption of comparative negligence by the Florida Supreme Court in *Hoffman v. Jones.* Since that occurrence, ten more state supreme courts have adopted comparative negligence by judicial fiat (Texas adopted a rule of limited application judicially) and eight more state legislatures have enacted statutes. In addition, New Zealand, all the states of Australia, and all the provinces of Canada have adopted comparative negligence. (In some states the form of comparative negligence first adopted by judicial decree has been modified by statute: see, *e.g.,* Florida and Illinois.) As of the date of the publication of this book, only Alabama, Maryland, North Carolina, Virginia, and the District of Columbia have not adopted comprehensive comparative negligence plans of some description. Thus, the rule of *Butterfield v. Forrester* continues to hold sway without modification in only a small part of the common law world.

[C]   Varieties of Comparative Negligence

[1]   Pure Comparative Negligence

Hoffman v. Jones adopted what is known as pure comparative negligence. Under this approach no quantum of contributory negligence will bar a plaintiff's recovery unless it constitutes the sole proximate cause of the harm. Or, in other words, unless the plaintiff's own negligence constituted 100% of the causative fault and the defendant's 0%.

Example 1:

Plaintiffs share of negligence: 50%

Defendant's share of negligence: 50%

Plaintiff's full damages: $10,000

Plaintiff's recoverable damages:

$10,000 × 0.50 = $5,000

States that employ pure comparative negligence include Alaska, Arizona, California, Florida, Iowa, Kentucky, Louisiana, Michigan, Mississippi, Missouri, New Mexico, New York, Rhode Island, and Washington.

[2] Modified Comparative Negligence

Between the *Butterfield v. Forrester* rule that any contributory negligence bars all recovery and pure comparative negligence lies the view that some degree of contributory negligence bars all recovery and a lesser degree merely diminishes recovery. States that support this middle view have adopted one of three kinds of modified comparative negligence rules.

[a] The 50% Rule

States that employ the 50% Rule bar a plaintiff's recovery if the plaintiff's share of the negligence is greater than that of the defendant. If the plaintiff's share of the negligence is equal to or less than that of the defendant, the plaintiff's action is permitted, but any recovery is reduced in proportion to the plaintiff's own percentage of fault.

The facts of Example 1 would render the same result in a 50% Rule state as in a pure comparative negligence state. Because the plaintiff's negligence does not *exceed* that of the defendant, the action would not be barred but the full damages would be diminished by 50%.

Example 2:

Plaintiffs share of negligence: 51%

Defendant's share of negligence: 49%

Plaintiff's full damages: $10,000

Plaintiff's recoverable damages: Barred

In Example 2, the plaintiff's contributory negligence, being greater than that of the defendant, bars all recovery.

States that employ the 50% Rule include Connecticut, Delaware, Hawaii, Illinois Indiana, Massachusetts, Minnesota, Montana, Nevada, New Hampshire, New Jersey, Ohio, Oklahoma, Oregon, Pennsylvania, South Carolina, Texas, Vermont, and Wisconsin.

[b] The 49% Rule

States that employ the 49% Rule bar a plaintiff's recovery if the plaintiff's share of the negligence is equal to or more than that of the defendant. If the plaintiff's share of the negligence is 49% or less of all-the causative negligence, the plaintiff's action is permitted, but recovery is reduced in proportion to the plaintiff's own percentage of fault.

Under the 49% Rule, the facts of Examples 1 and 2 would bar a plaintiff's action. In both examples, the plaintiff's share of negligence is not less than the defendant's share.

Example 3:

Plaintiffs share of negligence: 49%

Defendant's share of negligence: 51%

Plaintiff's full damages: $10,000

Plaintiff's recoverable damages:

$10,000 \times 0.51 = \$5,100$

States that employ the 49% Rule comparative negligence include Arkansas, Colorado, Georgia, Idaho, Kansas, Maine, North Dakota, Tennessee, Utah, West Virginia, and Wyoming.

[c]   Slight/Gross Rules

Three states follow some version of what is known as the Slight/Gross Rule. The Nebraska approach is best described by the name. There a plaintiff's contributory negligence does not bar the action if the plaintiff's negligence is slight and the defendant's is gross by comparison. If the action is not barred, the plaintiff's damages are reduced in proportion to the degree of negligence attributed to the plaintiff.

South Dakota at one time followed the Nebraska model directly but now requires only a determination as to whether the plaintiff's contribution negligence was a "slight" factor in causing the harm. If more than slight, the contributory negligence stands as a total bar. If only slight, the plaintiff's recovery is reduced in proportion to its relative portion of the entire causative negligence.

The Tennessee rule is the oldest. Beginning as a judge made rule in the nineteenth century, the novel Tennessee rule was reaffirmed by the Tennessee Supreme Court in 1976. *Street v. Calvert*, 541 S.W.2d 576 (Tenn. 1976). Under this rule, contributory negligence does not bar an action if it was only a "remote factor" in the cause of the harm. If the nexus is more than remote, contributory negligence bars the action. If only remote, it causes the recovery to be reduced proportionately. In 1992 Tennessee abandoned this approach in favor of the 49% rule. See *McIntyre v. Balentine*, 833 S.W.2d 52 (Tenn. 1992).

Although questions of "slight/gross" "slight," and "remote" are for the juries, it may be supposed that the facts underlying Examples 1 through 3 all would result in a bar to recovery under all these rules. That is, negligence in amounts 51%, 50% and 49% would not appear to be slight by contrast to gross, or slight in the abstract, or remote, as those terms have been employed by the courts. By contrast, causative contributory negligence of say, 10%, might not impose the bar, leaving a diminished recovery in the amount of $9000.

[D]   Effect on Other Common Law Doctrines

The adoption of comparative negligence has a direct effect on related common law doctrines, particularly last clear chance, assumption of risk, the patent danger rule, and gross negligence application of special rules. Because of the divergence among the states, no consensus treatment of these points has emerged, and because of the large number of comparative negligence states, an inclusive state-by-state analysis cannot be made. Instead, this treatment will examine the most common approaches to resolving these issues, leaving it to you to explore the law of a particular jurisdiction.

[1]   Last Clear Chance

To ameliorate the harsh "all or nothing" regime of contributory negligence, many common law courts applied the doctrine of last clear chance in special circumstances to save the plaintiff's recovery. Rather than recover nothing, he recovered all. For this reason, to abrogate last clear chance upon the advent of comparative negligence cannot be deemed to be a pro-plaintiff measure.

Although last clear chance has several variations, the most typical is that a plaintiff negligently places himself in a position of danger from which he is helpless to extricate himself (*e.g.*, falls asleep on a railroad track) and a defendant thereafter negligently fails to take action open to him to prevent harm (*e.g.*, fails to stop the train upon discovering the plaintiff's presence.) The theory is that the last wrongdoer who had a clear opportunity to avert the harm ought to be totally responsible for all of it. For this reason, the doctrine is sometimes referred to as "the last wrongdoer's rule." As colorfully stated by the Mississippi Supreme Court, " . . .it must follow, as night the day, that the party who has the last opportunity to avoid the injury is the one upon whom the blame shall fall."[6]

In this light, last clear chance can be viewed as a particularized application of the law of proximate causation; that is, the defendant's supervening negligent act severs the operation of the plaintiff's preceding negligence as a proximate cause of the harm. No matter how the issue is viewed, however, it leaves a delicate question of offsetting one negligent act against another. This is the essential heart of comparative negligence and, therefore, makes most last clear chance situations amenable to comparison.

Some comparative negligence statutes expressly abolish the doctrine of last clear chance,[7] but where they do not, the courts have split on their rulings. Nebraska holds that the doctrine remains available for consideration of juries,[8] whereas a Texas appellate court[9] held that the doctrine is now subsumed under comparative negligence. In general, however, courts that abrogate contributory negligence subsume last clear chance within the comparative negligence doctrine. The *Hoffman v. Jones* statement that last clear chance "no longer [has] any application in these cases"[10] is illustrative.

[2]   Assumption of Risk

Whether or not common law assumption of risk remains as a separate complete defense varies among the comparative negligence jurisdictions. Some statutes expressly "abolish" assumption of risk as a defense,[11] which means that behavior that formally constituted assumption of risk now is to be deemed to be contributory negligence and, as such, subject to comparison under the statute.

---

[6] Fuller v. Illinois Cent. R. Co., 100 Miss. 705, 56 So. 783, 786 (1911).

[7] *See, e.g.*, Conn. Gen. Stats. § 52-572(h) (1973); Ark. Stat. § 16-24-122(c).

[8] Roby v. Auker, 151 Neb. 421, 37 N.W.2d 799 (1949).

[9] de Anda v. Blake, 562 S.W.2d 497 (Tex. Ct. App. 1978).

[10] Hoffman v. Jones, 280 So. 2d 431, 438 (1973). *See also* Li v. Yellow Cab Co., 119 Cal. Rptr. 858, 532 P.2d 1226, 1242 (1975), and Alvis v. Ribar, 85 Ill. 2d 1, 421 N.E.2d 886 (1981).

[11] *See, e.g.*, Conn. Gen. Stat. § 52-572(h) (1973), and Mass. GLC 281, § 85 (1969).

Similarly, the Arkansas statute[12] is representative of a group that prescribes a comprehensive comparative *fault* plan in which "risk assumed" is defined as one form of fault. Among the states that have judicially abrogated contributory negligence in favor of comparative negligence, some have also reclassified assumption of risk as a category of negligence, which, as such, is subject to comparison.[13]

Typically, however, the assumption of risk bar has not been disturbed in instances where the plaintiff has expressly consented to take a risk. The following statement of the California Supreme Court is illustrative:

We think it clear that the adoption of a system of comparative negligence should entail the merger of the defense of assumption of risk into the general scheme of assessment of fault in those particular cases in which the form of assumption of risk is no more than a variant of contributory negligence.[14]

Many comparative negligence statutes literally apply only to "negligence" actions and are silent on the treatment of assumption of risk as an independent total bar to recovery. This view rejects the argument that assumption of risk is a mere variant of contributory negligence. As stated by the Nebraska Supreme Court:

. . .There is a clear distinction between the defense of assumption of risk and the defense of contributory negligence, notwithstanding they may arise under the same set of facts and may sometimes overlap. There is a line of demarcation which, if carefully scrutinized and followed, will allow the court to differentiate between them. Assumption of risk rests in contract or in the principle expressed by the ancient maxim, 'volenti non fit injuria,' whereas contributory negligence rests in tort. The former involves a choice made more or less deliberately and negatives liability without reference to the fact that defense of contributory negligence implies the failure of the plaintiff to exercise due care. As stated in some decisions, assumption of risk is a mental state of willingness, whereas contributory negligence is a matter of conduct.[15]

Other courts, led by *Maiestrich v. Casino Arena Enterprise, Inc.*[16] hold to the contrary on the ground that most forms of behavior that have been treated by courts as assumption of risk are truly negligent rather than consential in character. Hence, they are considered to be negligence and must be compared under the comparative negligence statute.

Both sides of the assumption of the risk debate have some merit, and, in fact, may be closer to agreement than appears on the surface. The Nebraska court required a "mental state of willingness," to evidence assumption, and the *Maiestrich* court did not purport to abrogate the bar in cases of express assumptions, which presumably would require a "mental state of willingness."

---

[12] Ark. Stat. § 16-24-122 (c).

[13] *e.g.*, Blackburn v. Dorta, 348 So. 2d 287 (Fla. 1977). *See also Gustafson v. Benda*, 661 S.W.2d 11 (Mo. 1983), in which the Missouri Supreme Court abrogated the novel humanitarian last clear chance rule in adopting comparative negligence.

[14] Li v. Yellow Cab Co., 119 Cal. Rptr. 858, 532 P.2d 1226, 1241 (1975).

[15] Brackman v. Brackman, 169 Neb. 650, 100 N.W.2d 774, 780 (1960).

[16] 155 A.2d 90 (N.J. 1959).

The disagreement might be removed, to the extent it is semantic, by employing the term *volenti non fit injuria* to describe the defense that constitutes a total bar to recovery in a negligence action. Although this old common law nomenclature has been largely abandoned by American courts, it is still in use in England.[17]

Its strength lies in the connotation of consent to harm, avoiding the difficulty experienced by some courts in distinguishing contributory negligence from so-called *implied* assumption of risk. To be *volens* a plaintiff must expose himself to a known and appreciated risk and he must do it voluntarily, meaning that no undue material external pressure not of his own making impelled him to do so against better judgment. The volenti defense should permit no presumption that the plaintiff was *volens.* The defendant's job would be to adduce objective facts to persuade the jury that the plaintiff did know, did appreciate, and did proceed without undue compulsion. If this view is accepted, no other defense by any name should be permitted to bar a recovery. All other forms of fault should be treated as forms of contributory negligence and, as such, subject to comparison.[18]

The *Meistrich, Blackburn* position is supported by Restatement, Torts, Second, § 496A, which acknowledges four types of assumptions:

a. Express assumption of a known risk.

b. Implied assumption of a known risk.

c. Reasonable encounter of a risk created by the defendant.

d. Unreasonable encounter of a risk created by the defendant.

Under this view, the first two categories stand firm as assumptions, defeating a plaintiff's action. The first would be exemplified by a contract to indemnify the defendant of his negligence, and the second by voluntarily participating in a contact sport. But the latter categories would be considered to be a species of contributory negligence, merely diminishing but not defeating recovery in comparative negligence jurisdictions. They are exemplified by the following hypotheticals. A man comes home to find his house afire, caused by the defendant's negligence.

He rushes into the flames to save his infant trapped inside. Under similar circumstances a second man rushes in to save his torts casebook. According to the drafters of the Restatement, the first man has reasonably encountered a risk created by the defendant; the second man unreasonably has done so. The jury may allocate an appropriate quantum of negligence to each of them.

A more traditional approach to distinguish these situations is to treat the first as an involuntary assumption and the second as voluntary. Thus, the man attempting to save his child has no choice: the risk is known and appreciated, but the assumption is *involuntary* and, therefore, no defense. By contrast, the man saving Little & Lidsky on Torts assumes the risk and defeats his claim. Precisely where the line dividing voluntary from involuntary assumptions is to be drawn will, of

---

[17] *See, e.g.,* Imperial Chem. Ind. Ltd. v. Shatwell, [1965] App. Cas. 683 (HL).

[18] For example, the Florida Supreme Court that authored *Hoffman v. Jones,* later held that implied assumption of risk was thereafter to be treated as a form of comparative negligence. Blackburn v. Dorta, 348 So. 2d 287 (Fla. 1977). In *Kuehner v. Green,* 436 So. 2d 78 (Fla. 1983), the court clarified that a voluntary consensual assumption of risk, *subjectively* known and appreciated by the plaintiff, would constitute a complete bar to recovery at least as to injuries arising out of participating in contact sports.

course, vary. *See, e.g., Morrison & Conklin Construction Co. v. Cooper,* 256 S.W.2d 505 (Ky. 1953). *Scott v. Pacific West Mountain Resort,* 834 P.2d 6, 14 (Wash. 1992), rejected this "traditional approach" in favor of the analysis described above saying:

In contrast, implied reasonable and unreasonable assumption of risk arise where the plaintiff is aware of a risk that already has been created by the negligence of the defendant, yet chooses voluntarily to encounter it. In such a case, plaintiff's conduct is not truly consensual, but is a form of contributory negligence, in which the negligence consists of making the wrong choice and voluntarily encountering a known unreasonable risk.

Are you persuaded that foolhardy exposure of oneself to a subjectively known and appreciated risk is merely a form of negligence? *Blake v. Wendy's International, Inc.,* 413 S.E.2d 414, 418 (W.Va. 1991), apparently holds that all forms of assumption of risk are to be treated as comparative negligence subject to apportionment and not as a bar to recovery per se.

[3] Patent Danger Rule

The "patent danger" rule operated as a complete bar to recovery on the theory that no duty is owed to persons who encounter dangerous conditions that are "open and obvious" to view. This doctrine, in its pure form, is not a variant of assumption of risk because no burden of proof is placed upon the defendant. Nevertheless, the Texas Supreme Court used the advent of the comparative negligence statute as vehicle for abolishing the rule.[19]

Other courts, considering the doctrine to be unjustifiably harsh, have abolished the doctrine on the more general ground that the obviousness of danger ought merely be a part of the jury's consideration of whether the plaintiff exercised the degree of care of a reasonable person under the circumstances.[20]

Abolition of the "patent danger" rule is not laden with the conceptual difficulties of abolishing assumption of risk. The rule had nothing to do with consent to harm, but imposed a conclusive presumption, as a matter of law, that a defendant owed the plaintiff no duty of care if the danger the defendant created was "open and obvious." Abrogating that presumption and permitting a jury to decide what actions reasonable defendants and plaintiffs would have taken under similar circumstances rightfully brings the issue into the mainstream of the law of comparative negligence. Nevertheless, not every jurisdiction has abrogated the rule in all its forms. *See, e.g., Bemis Co. v. Rubush,* 427 N.E.2d 1058 (Ind. 1981).

[4] Res Ipsa Loquitur

How should the advent of comparative negligence affect the invocation of the doctrine of res ipsa loquitur? *Dyback v. Weber,* 500 N.E.2d 8, 10–12 (Ill. 1986), addressed this issue as follows:

---

[19] Parker v. Highland Park, Inc, 565 S.W.2d 512 (Tex. 1978). Texas also subsumed what was known as the "imminent peril" doctrine into comparative negligence, Davila v. Sanders, 557 S.W.2d 770 (Tex. 1977).

[20] *See, e.g.,* Micallef v. Michele Co., 384 N.Y.S.2d 115, 348 N.E.2d 571 (1976), and Auburn Mach. Works v. Jones, 366 So. 2d 1167 (Fla. 1979).

The res ipsa loquitur doctrine permits the trier of fact to infer negligence based on circumstantial evidence, and in our State the doctrine traditionally had required the plaintiff to demonstrate three elements: (1) that the occurrence is one that ordinarily would not happen in the absence of negligence; (2) that the defendant had exclusive control of the instrumentality that caused the event; and (3) that the occurrence was not caused by the plaintiff's own negligent acts or omissions. . . .

. . . We consider that the appellate court here correctly concluded that a plaintiff's freedom from contributory negligence should no longer be a requirement in order to make out a prima facie case under the doctrine. At least five other comparative fault jurisdictions have considered the question and have decided that proof of a plaintiff's freedom from negligence is no longer required under res ipsa loquitur. [Ed. — Omitted citations are from New Mexico, Vermont, Colorado, and Wisconsin.] One of these jurisdictions — New Mexico — has a pure form of comparative negligence, as we adopted in *Alvis [v. Ribar*, 421 N.E.2d 886 (Ill. 1981)], while the other four States operate under a modified form of the comparative fault doctrine. The jurisdictions that operate under a modified comparative fault doctrine, of course, bar recovery on negligence claims, and also now under res ipsa loquitur claims, where the plaintiff is found more than 50% negligent. In addressing the effect of pure comparative fault principles on res ipsa loquitur, the Supreme Court of New Mexico stated that "[t]he mere existence of concurrent negligence does not preclude a particular finding of negligence of one or more tortfeasors through reliance on the res ipsa loquitur doctrine. Otherwise, 'we would effectively erect a complete bar to recovery in cases where a plaintiff must rely on res ipsa loquitur to establish a prima facie case of negligence. * * * Such a result would be in direct contravention of the concept of comparative negligence.'

. . . The defendants argue that, since the plaintiff in a res ipsa loquitur situation is given the benefit of an inference of general negligence, it is appropriate to continue requiring the plaintiff to show his freedom from negligence. They argue that the doctrine, founded on an inference of general negligence, differs so significantly from specific negligence cases that comparative fault should not apply to the former. We disagree because "[t]he analysis, from the viewpoint of comparative negligence, focuses on whether a 'defendant's inferred negligence was, more probably than not, a cause of the injury * * * though [the] plaintiff's [or third party's] negligent acts or omissions may also have contributed to the injury' ". . .This extension of comparative fault principle to res ipsa loquitur cases is consistent with our recent decision in *Casey v. Baseden* (1986), 111 Ill. 2d 341, 95 Ill. Dec. 531, 490 N.E.2d 4. We held there that a plaintiff in a comparative negligence case does not carry the burden of proving his freedom from negligence because "both logic and fairness dictate that the defendant, who stands to benefit from a showing that the plaintiff was negligent, should have the burden of persuading the trier of fact on that issue." . . .Thus, a plaintiff relying on the res ipsa loquitur doctrine should no longer be required to plead and prove freedom from contributory negligence. . . .

A plaintiff need not conclusively prove all the elements of res ipsa loquitur in order to invoke the doctrine. He need only present evidence reasonably showing that elements exist that allow an inference that the occurrence is one that ordinarily does not occur without negligence. . . .

The inference that there was negligence does not disappear if the defendant simply presents direct evidence to the contrary, but the defendant's evidence.

(Note: *Giles v. City of New Haven*, 636 A.2d 1335 (Conn. 1994), adopted the same position, apparently in keeping with all of the decisions on the point at the time. The Illinois legislature enacted a modified form of comparative negligence statute after *Dyback v. Weber* was decided. What effect should that change have on the application of res ipsa loquitur in that state?)

[5] Gross Negligence

Although the prototypical statement that a "plaintiff's negligence, however slight, bars his recovery," rejected the idea of comparative negligence in the common law,[21] some courts refused to consider mere negligence as a defense to more egregious wrongs, including actions founded on "gross" negligence.[22]

It was also generally held that behavior exhibiting elements of wilfullness, wantonness, and intention was more blameworthy and not barred by mere contributory negligence.

Although some jurisdictions experimented with degrees of negligence — slight, ordinary, gross — the approach proved elusive of practical application. Even those states that applied the hierarchy have widely abandoned it except in application to special undertakings, such as those of electricity suppliers and common carriers, and in guest statutes that require a plaintiff to prove the defendant guilty of "gross negligence," "wilful and wanton" behavior or the like.[23]

Even there it must be decided whether the gross negligence makes the defendant responsible for all the plaintiff's damages, despite the plaintiff's contributory negligence, or whether comparative negligence is to apply.[24]

[E] Computation Principles and Issues

Examples 1 through 3 above reveal the facts that must be found to apply comparative negligence principles and demonstrate basic applications under the most common comparative negligence systems. Beneath the simple veneer, however, lurks a maze of difficult issues that arise in applying comparative negligence principles. The most important of these are briefly examined below:

---

[21] *See* Prosser, Law of Torts (4th ed.), at 421.

[22] *See, e.g.*, Li v. Yellow Cab Co., 119 Cal. Rptr. 858, 532 P.2d 1226 (1975).

[23] *See, e.g.*, Ark. Stat. §§ 75-913, 915 (1947).

[24] *See, e.g.*, Amoco Pipeline Co. v. Montgomery, 487 F. Supp. 1268, 1271 (1980). holding that all forms of negligence must be compared under the Arkansas statute and *Li v. Yellow Cab, Co.*, n. 17, *supra*, holding that all forms of "misconduct" short of intentional must be compared under the California system.

[1]   Approaches to Apportioning Damages

American jurisdictions have developed three basic approaches to apportioning damages in comparative fault actions. One is the equally divided property damages rule of admiralty; a second is strict apportionment of damages in proportion to precise percentages of negligence, the whole of which must sum to 100%; and the third is to allocation damages in a manner that appears "just and equitable to the factfinder." As the following discussion shows, most jurisdictions follow the middle course; the admiralty rule has been abandoned; and the third course is followed by only two states.

[a]   Admiralty Equal Division of Damages

Of the three approaches, the admiralty rule was simplest. In all actions in which both parties were at fault, the factfinder determined the property damages suffered by both, added them together, and divided the total into 50% shares. Each party was thus liable for exactly half the total damages without regard to the relative degrees of fault of the two.[25] This twelfth century rule[26] had the very practical value of not requiring a precise apportionment of fault.[27] (If there were more than two parties at fault, the damages of all were aggregated and divided in equal shares.)

The divided damages rule of admiralty apparently remained robust until the Brussels Collision Liability Convention of 1910[28] retreated from it in favor of apportionment in proportion to degrees of fault. The United States did not accept the rule until 1975, when the United States Supreme Court adopted it by judicial fiat.[29] Consequently, the American admiralty rule now conforms to the comparative negligence approach employed in most American states, calling for apportionment of damages in proportion to the degrees of fault of the parties, expressed as percentages summing to 100%.[30]

[b]   Apportionment by Degrees of Negligence

By far the preponderate approach for apportioning damages in American jurisdictions is what may be referred to as the Degrees of Negligence Rule. In all pure comparative negligence states, and in all modified comparative negligence states except Maine and Oregon, a sum total of 100% of causative negligence must be determined by the factfinder and assigned in precise percentages to the persons whose combined fault caused the harm. In many states 100% fault must be allocated to the parties to the action, ignoring the negligence of so-called phantom tortfeasors such as hit and run drivers and others not joined as parties. Other states, however, do require the factfinder to allocate a portion of the 100% to

---

[25] *See* United States v. Reliable Transfer Co., 421 U.S. 397, 95 S. Ct. 1708, 1710–12, 44 L. Ed. 2d 251 (1975) (abrogating the divided damages rule and supplanting it with apportionment in relation to degrees of comparative fault).

[26] *Id.*, at 95 S. Ct. 1711, 421 U.S. 403, n.3.

[27] *Id.*, at 95 S. Ct. 1714, 421 U.S. 407.

[28] *Id.*, at 95 S. Ct. 1712, 421 U.S. 404, n.6.

[29] *Id.*, at 95 S. Ct. 1715, 421 U.S. 411.

[30] *Id.*

phantoms, thus reducing the percentages allocated to the parties. The sum remains 100%.

Once it is determined that a plaintiff's claim is not barred by a threshold (and in all cases in pure comparative negligence states), the process of calculation is virtually the same under all Degrees of Negligence Rule comparative negligence laws. Typically, a plaintiff's recovery is the amount of total damages "diminished in the proportion the amount of negligence attributable to the plaintiff bears to the total negligence of all the parties." Literally, this formulation requires the plaintiff's total damages to be diminished by the product of the plaintiff's total damages and the plaintiff's share of the negligence, expressed as a percentage of the total of 100%. Judgment = (Plaintiff's total damages) — (Plaintiff's total damages × Plaintiff's share of the negligence.) In all states wherein the total negligence of the parties must sum to 100% and in all cases in which there is but one plaintiff and one defendant (and no phantom tortfeasors), this calculation reduces, simply, to the product of the plaintiff's total damages and the defendant's share of the negligence, expressed as a percentage. Judgment = (Plaintiff's total damages x Defendant's percentage of the negligence.) This form of the computation was used in Examples 1 through 3.

[c]　Just and Equitable Apportionment

The Maine[31] Just and Equitable Rule of apportionment permits factfinders to apportion damages as they deem just and equitable without any division into percentages attributable to the various parties.

Maine juries are not required to prescribe degrees of negligence even in determining the threshold question of whether all recovery is barred because the plaintiff was "equally at fault." Instead, the juries must merely adjudge the "relative responsibility" of the parties and the action is barred only if the jury deems the plaintiff to be equally or more responsible than the defendant.[32]

Oregon[33] follows a slightly different approach under which the juries must quantify, in percentages, the amount of deviation of each party's actions from a conceptual datum defined as the standard of care of the ordinary person of reasonable prudence.[34] The sum of the deviations need not (and, indeed, ordinarily would not) sum to 100%. Thus, if the plaintiff deviated 20% and the defendant deviated 30%, the plaintiff would be entitled to an apportioned recovery under the Oregon 50% Rule statute. If the foregoing deviations were reversed, the plaintiff's action would be barred.

Thus, especially Maine, and to a lesser extent, Oregon, have sought to avoid the conceptually mechanistic but realistically highly artificial requirement of having juries measure negligence in precise packages summing to 100%. These approaches openly give juries far more discretion in rendering comparative negligence verdicts.[35]

---

[31]　Me. Rev. Stats. Ann. tit. 14 § 156.

[32]　Wing v. Morse, 300 A.2d 491, 496–7 (Me. 1973).

[33]　Or. Rev. Stats. § 18.470 et seq.

[34]　Sandford v. Chevrolet Div. of General Motors, 642 P.2d 624, 633–4 (Or. 1982).

[35]　*See generally* Aiken, *Proportioning Comparative Negligence — Problem of Theory and Special Verdict Formulation*, 53 Marq. L. Rev. 293 (1970), Wade, *Products Liability and Plaintiff's Fault —*

[2]   Use of Special Verdicts and Other Devices to Simplify the Calculations

[a]   In General

By contrast to issuing verdicts under the "all-or-nothing" regimen of the common law, the job imposed upon factfinders in comparative negligence litigation is complex and conceptually elusive.

Many comparative negligence states have sought to reduce the confusion and chance of mistake by providing for special verdicts and general verdicts accompanied by interrogatories. These devices permit a jury to decide the independent elements of a comparative negligence verdict item-by-item before the comparative law is applied to produce an apportioned judgment. Indeed, some courts have viewed these devices as part of the foundation upon which a judicially adopted comparative negligence system could be built.[36] Nevertheless, the use of special verdicts or similar devices is not a universal *sine qua non* to the adoption of comparative negligence principles. In Oklahoma,[37] for example, general verdicts are required by the state constitution, and in a number of states, including Arkansas, one of the earliest comparative negligence states, submission of comparative negligence cases to general verdicts is the preferred practice, notwithstanding the fact that trial judges possess the discretion to obtain special verdicts.[38]

Although special verdict practice varies markedly among the comparative negligence states, the basic legal issues boil down to these few: Are special verdicts and similar devices to be used in comparative negligence cases? Is the use mandatory or discretionary, and, if discretionary, at whose discretion? What is the form of the special verdicts? Does the court or the jury apply the law to the special findings to produce apportioned judgments? Is the jury to be told of the consequences of its special findings of percentages of negligence upon the right of the parties to recover? May juries return verdicts by a less than unanimous verdict? And, if so, must each element of the comparative negligence verdict be supported by the same common core of jurors making up the necessary majority? These issues are briefly examined in the following subsections.

[b]   Forms of Verdicts Permitted in Comparative Negligence Actions

Comparative negligence verdicts may be rendered in three basic forms: by general verdict, by special verdict and by general verdict accompanied by answers to special interrogatories.

The Uniform Comparative Fault Act, 29 Mercer L. Rev. 373 (1973), and Pearson, *Apportionment of Losses Under Comparative Fault Laws — An Analysis of the Alternatives*, 40 La. L. Rev. 346 (1980).

[36] Alvis v. Ribar, 85 Ill. 2d 1, 421 N.E.2d 886, 889 (1981).

[37] Okla. Const. Art. 7 § 15.

[38] Ark. R. Civ. Proc. No. 49.

[i] General verdicts

The general verdict bestows maximum discretion upon the jury and is, therefore, conceptually most consonant with the right of trial by jury. It also permits a single decision maker, the jury itself, to make all the findings and apply the law to produce apportioned damages verdicts.

This latter characteristic, however, is also a weakness of the general verdict, particularly in comparative negligence actions involving multiple parties. The number of individual findings that must be made in producing an apportioned general verdict, the complex manipulation of findings to create the general verdict, and, especially, the volume of instructions that must be given, collectively impose prodigious burdens upon juries. Thus, the chance of error by reason of confusion, misunderstanding and simple mistake may be high.

Notwithstanding these pitfalls, general verdicts are required in some states,[39] are preferred in others,[40] and are permitted in the discretion of the judge in still others. A few grant the jury the prerogative to return either a general verdict or a special verdict.[41]

[ii] Special verdicts

Special verdicts permit juries to return independent answers to particular questions, leaving to the judge the job of synthesizing an apportioned damages judgment. Thus, special verdicts may considerably lighten a court's burden of instructing the jury and the jury's burden of making findings.[42] Moreover, when the judge makes the calculations to fashion verdicts, the parties are enabled to review the details of the arithmetic, thus lessening the chances of error through misunderstanding or simple mistake.

The main weakness of special verdicts — erosion of the right of trial by jury — is the mirror image of the main strength of general verdicts. Thus, jurisdictions that place a very high value on the total discretion of the jury will be less enthusiastic about special verdicts.

Several states require special verdicts in comparative negligence actions,[43] some by court decrees[44] and others by statute.[45] Another large group of states requires the use of special verdicts at the request of any party,[46] and at least two states[47] grant juries the discretion to return either general or special verdicts in

---

[39] Including New Hampshire and Vermont.

[40] Including Arkansas, Connecticut, Georgia, Mississippi, and Nebraska.

[41] Including Washington and Nebraska.

[42] *See, e.g.*, Commentaries, Fed. Rules Civ. Proc. Rule 49, 28 USCA.

[43] These include Florida, Louisiana, Michigan, New Mexico, Hawaii, New Jersey, Wisconsin (unless general verdict requested), Colorado, Kansas, and West Virginia (general verdict plus special interrogatories.)

[44] *See, e.g.*, Lawrence v. Florida East Coast Railroad Co., 346 So. 2d 1012 (Fla. 1977), and Placek v. City of Sterling Heights, 405 Mich. 638, 275 N.W.2d 511, 528 (1979).

[45] *See, e.g.*, Kan. Stat. Ann. § 60-258a(b) and N.J. 2A. 15-5.2.

[46] These include Illinois, Minnesota, Oregon, Idaho, North Dakota, Utah, and Wyoming.

[47] Nebraska and Utah.

comparative negligence actions. A larger number of states grant a trial judge discretion to require special verdicts.[48]

[iii]   General verdict accompanied by answers to interrogatories

General verdicts accompanied by special questions (or interrogatories) balance the respective advantages of general verdicts and special verdicts. Under this approach, the jury is fully instructed and charged to return a general verdict and is also charged to make special written findings on each of the elements that is a necessary constituent of the final verdict. From these special answers, the judge and the parties can redo the comparative negligence computations and determine whether the jury's various special answers were internally consistent with each other and whether the general verdict was internally consistent with the special answers. Thus, this approach provides a means to oversee the work of the jury and to correct errors, if any. The weakness of a general verdict accompanied by interrogatories is that it requires a jury to do more that it must do merely to return special verdicts. Indeed, under this approach, the jury must receive all the instructions, make all the findings, and do all the calculations that are required for general verdicts.

[c]   Must the Jury be Informed of the Consequences of its Special Findings

Whether or not a jury is to be informed of the consequences to the parties of its special verdicts has split the states into two camps. (The issue arises only in modified comparative negligence jurisdictions where proscribed proportions of fault will bar a plaintiff's recovery *in toto*.) One group holds that although comparative negligence permits (or requires) juries to return precise answers to specific questions, the avoidance of verdicts produced by sympathy or prejudice[49] requires the court to apply the comparative law to apportion damages. This view supports withholding the information from the jury. Wisconsin[50] is the leading proponent of the few remaining adherents[51] to this view.

A much larger group holds that the issue of who is to recover and who is not remains a jury question and, therefore, to withhold the information infringes the right of a jury trial. This preponderate view plainly requires presenting the information to the jury. Adherents to this view fall into three groups: those that require the jury to be informed;[52] those that require the jury to be informed unless, in the opinion of the judge, confusion or prejudice would result;[53] and those that require or permit the jury to be informed upon the request of a party.[54]

---

[48] These include Alaska, California, Iowa, New York, Rhode Island, Massachusetts, Tennessee, and Washington. Many of these apply some form of Rule 49 of the Federal Rules of Civil Procedure.

[49] *See, e.g.,* Peair v. Home Ass'n of Enola Legion No. 751, 430 A.2d 665, 671 (Pa. Super. 1981).

[50] Fehrman v. Smirl, 20 Wis. 2d 1, 121 N.W.2d 255, *reh. den.,* 20 Wis. 2d 11, 122 N.W.2d 439 (1963).

[51] Others are Arkansas, Argo v. Blackshear, 242 Ark. 817, 416 S.W.2d 314 (1967), Hawaii, Hawaii Rev. Stats. § 663-31(b), and Massachusetts, Mass. Laws Ann., ch. 231 § 85.

[52] These include Michigan, Nevada, Oklahoma, Pennsylvania, Colorado, Georgia, and Wyoming.

[53] These include New Jersey, Idaho, and Kansas.

[54] These include North Dakota and Utah.

[d]   Civil Verdicts Permitted by Less than A Unanimous Vote of the Jury

Many states permit the return of civil verdicts by a vote of a less than unanimous jury. Some states permit a three-fourths vote of the jury;[55] some a five-sixths vote;[56] at least one permits a two-thirds vote,[57] at least three permit the parties to stipulate the required majority.[58]

Among these states that permit civil verdicts by less than a unanimous vote, two different comparative negligence rules have emerged. The apparent minority view is that the vote on each comparative negligence issue, *e.g.*, threshold questions, allocations of negligence and damages, must be supported by the identical core of jurors amounting to the required supermajority. Although this "common core"[59] rule was once the favored view, more states now follow the view that a comparative negligence judgment can be issued without a common core of jury support so long as the required supermajority of the jury voted favorably on each issue.[60] This view rejects the contention that a juror outvoted on one issue cannot honestly debate and vote on other issues[61] and strongly promotes the practical reasons given, in the first place, for permitting the return of civil verdicts by less than unanimous jury votes.

§ 9.05   IMMUNITIES

An immunity . . . avoids liability in tort under all circumstances, within the limits set by the immunity itself; it is conferred, not because of the particular facts, but because of the status or position of the favored defendant; and it does not deny the tort, but the resulting liability.

Prosser, Torts (4th ed.), at 970.

A sovereign is exempt from suit, not because of any formal conception or obsolete theory, but on the logical and practical ground that there can be no legal right as against the authority that makes the law on which the right depends.

O.W. Holmes, *Kawananakoa v. Polyblank*, 205 U.S. 349, 353 (1907).

---

[55] These include Arkansas, Idaho, Ohio, Oklahoma, and Oregon.

[56] These include Massachusetts, Michigan, Minnesota, Nebraska, New Jersey, New York, Pennsylvania, Rhode Island, Washington, and Wisconsin.

[57] Montana.

[58] Louisiana (if not stipulated, a three-fourth vote is required), Tennessee, and Vermont.

[59] It is attributed to *Biersach v. Wechselberg*, 238 N.W. 905 (Wis. 1931). *Klanseck v. Anderson Sales & Service, Inc.*, 356 N.W.2d 275 (Mich. App. 1984), adopted the common rule and referred to it as the majority rule.

[60] Among them are: Arkansas, McChristian v. Hooten, 245 Ark. 1045, 436 S.W.2d 844 (1969); Idaho, Tillman v. Thomas, 95 Idaho 569, 585 P.2d 1280 (1978); New Jersey, Ward v. Weeks, 107 A.2d 379, 107 N.J. Super. 351 (1969); New Mexico, Naumburg v. Wagner, 81 N.M. 242, 465 P.2d 521 (1970); New York, Forde v. Ames, 93 Misc. 2d 723, 401 N.Y.S.2d 965 (Sup. Ct. Nassau County 1978); and Oklahoma, Fields v. Volkswagen of America, Inc., 555 P.2d 48 (Okla. 1976).

[61] *See, e.g.*, Ward v. Weekes, 107 N.J. Super. 351, 258 A.2d 379, 381 (1969).

ENGHAUSER MFG. CO. v. ERIKSSON ENGINEERING
Ohio Supreme Court
451 N.E.2d 228 (1983)

WILLIAM B. BROWN, JUSTICE.

The case presents this court with the question of whether the doctrine of governmental immunity from tort liability for municipalities should be sustained in Ohio. With the limitations set forth in this opinion, this court overrules *Dayton v. Pease* (1854), 4 Ohio St. 80, wherein the sovereign immunity doctrine was extended to encompass local governmental units, and all other decisions which support this doctrine, and holds that immunity from tort liability heretofore judicially conferred upon local governmental units is hereby abrogated. Henceforth, so far as municipal governmental responsibility for torts is concerned, the rule is liability — the exception is immunity.

The abolition of this doctrine in Ohio is long overdue. There are probably few tenets of American jurisprudence which have been so unanimously berated as the governmental immunity doctrine. It has been the subject of thousands of learned dissertations; the highest courts of numerous other states, test writers, and law review writers have all been unusually articulate in castigating the existing rule. A quick review of Ohio case law reveals that this court has many times had the matter under consideration.

In light of the comprehensive nature of discussion on this subject, there is little new this court can now add. But because this court is charting a new course in Ohio jurisprudence with this decision, a brief summary of the nature of governmental immunity is appropriate.

Various reasons have been assigned for perpetuation of the doctrine of municipal immunity from liability for torts. The reason adduced most frequently to support the doctrine is that "if there is to be a departure from the rule the policy should be declared and the extent of liability fixed by the legislature." *Conway v. Humbert* (1966), 82 S.D. 317, 323, 145 N.W.2d 524. This type of argument begs the question of the desirability of the doctrine and relegates the whole problem to a discussion of who should change the doctrine.

In Ohio, there is no doubt that the municipal immunity doctrine was judicially created. . . .

Having established that this doctrine is a creature of the courts, this court not only has the power but the duty and responsibility to evaluate the doctrine of municipal immunity in light of reason, logic, and the actions, functions and duties of a municipality in the twentieth century in order to determine whether it should adhere to its own rule of municipal tort immunity.

The courts which have adhered to the rule cite few reasons for that position, other than the longevity of the doctrine and its firmly established position. It is commonly accepted that the doctrine by which municipal corporations are held immune from liability in tort originated with the case of *Russell v. Men of Devon* (1788), 100 Eng. Rep. 359, 362, wherein the immunity was supported because (1) since the group was unincorporated, there was no fund from which the judgment could be paid and (2) "it is better that an individual should sustain an injury than that the public should suffer an inconvenience."

As Justice Traynor stated in *Muskopf, supra,* 56 Cal. 2d at 216, 11 Cal. Rptr. 89, 359 P.2d 457, "[i]f the reasons for *Russell v. Men of Devon* and the rule of county or local district immunity ever had any substance they have none today."

In scarifying the second justification for immunity as set forth in *Russell, supra,* the Supreme Court of New Hampshire stated in *Merrill v. Manchester* (1975), 114 N.H. 722, 724–725, 332 A.2d 378, 380, as follows:

That an individual injured by the negligence of the employees of a municipal corporation should bear his loss himself as advocated in the *Russell* case, *supra,* instead of having it borne by the public treasury to which he and all other citizens contribute, offends the basic principles of equality of burdens and of elementary justice. *Becker v. Beaudoin,* 106 R.I. 562, 568, 261 A.2d 896, 900 (1970); *Molitor v. Kaneland Community Unit Dist. No. 302,* 18 Ill. 2d 11, 21, 163 N.E.2d 89, 93 (1959). It is foreign to the spirit of our constitutional guarantee that every subject is entitled to a legal remedy for injuries he may receive in his person or property. . . . It is also contrary to the basic concept of the law of torts that liability follows negligence and that individual corporations are responsible for the negligence of their agents, servants and employees in the course of their employment. *Spencer v. General Hosp.,* 425 F.2d 479, 487 (D.C. Cir.1969) (Wright, J., concurring).

It would indeed be a sad commentary on our concept of justice if this court continued to endorse the belief that an individual should sustain an injury rather than the municipality be inconvenienced.

The other justification for immunity set forth in *Russell* has likewise lost its validity and vitality. The widespread availability and use of insurance or other modern funding methods render an argument based on economics invalid. Further, there is no empirical data to support the fear that governmental functions would be curtailed as a result of imposing liability for tortious conduct. *Ayala v. Philadelphia Bd. of Pub. Edn.* (1973), 453 Pa. 584, 596, 305 A.2d 877; Note (1973), 26 U. Fla. L. Rev. 89, 90.

Even though the reasons behind the municipal immunity doctrine have vanished and its construction renders an injustice to all people wronged by the local governmental unit or its agents, it has been suggested that the rule be retained because of the principle of *stare decisis.*

As to the fundamental nature and the importance of *stare decisis,* there is no doubt. It lies at the heart of the common law. By this rule, our society has preserved the best of the wisdom and the morality of past ages. Wisdom and morality, however, are not immutable universals of the scholastic philosophers; they are to be modified by each new generation.

When, however, a rule of law is judge-made, and the reasons for its use have vanished, the court should not perpetuate it until petrification. A rule that has outlived its usefulness should be changed. Greater justification is needed for a rule of law than that it has been part of the common law for a few hundred years.

The judicial conscience must no longer permit us to tolerate a principle of human behavior which, out of hand, denies the injured, the maimed and representatives of the deceased a right of action against a wrongdoing simply because the wrongdoer is an employee or agent of a municipality. If municipalities are to expose the people and their property to negligent acts, then they must expect to respond to suit. Municipal corporations in Ohio should no longer receive protection from a doctrine whose only claim to judicial integrity is that it is ancient.

This court's abrogation of municipal immunity does not mean that a municipal entity is liable for all harm that results from its activities; it is only to those harms which are torts that municipalities may now be held liable. This decision merely subjects municipal entities to the same rules as private persons or corporations if a duty has been violated and a tort has been committed.

Nor will a municipality be subject to liability where a statute provides for immunity.

Most importantly, this decision should not be interpreted as abolishing immunity to those certain acts which go to the essence of governing. *Accord Kitto v. Minot Park Dist.* (N.D. 1974), 224 N.W.2d 795; *Parrish v. Pitts* (1968), 244 Ark. 1239, 429 S.W.2d 45; *Spanel v. Mounds View School District No. 621* (1962), 264 Minn. 279, 118 N.W.2d 795. This court does not contemplate that the essential acts of governmental decision-making be the subject of judicial second-guessing or harassment by the actual or potential threat of litigation. The appropriate dividing line falls between those functions which rest on the exercise of judgment and discretion and represent planning and policy-making and those functions which involve the implementation and execution of such governmental policy or planning.

This is indeed proper, for as the Supreme Judicial Court of Massachusetts stated in *Whitney v. Worcester* (1977), 373 Mass. 208, 218–219, 366 N.E.2d 1210:

When the particular conduct which caused the injury is one characterized by the high degree of discretion and judgment involved in weighing alternatives and making choices with respect to public policy and planning, governmental entities should remain immune from liability. "To inquire into such decisions in a tort suit might 'jeopardiz[e] the quality and efficiency of government itself,' and endanger the creative exercise of political discretion and judgment through 'the inhibiting influence of potential legal liability asserted with the advantage of hindsight.'

"*Spencer* v. *General Hosp.*, 425 F.2d 479, 488 (D.C. Cir. 1969) (Wright, J., concurring), quoting from *Elgin* v. *District of Columbia*, 337 F.2d 152, 154–155 (D.C. Cir. 1964). On the other hand, when the particular conduct claimed to be tortious involves rather the carrying out of previously established policies or plans, such acts should be governed by the established standards of tort liability applicable to private individuals or entities and the governmental entity in question held liable for the injuries resulting from such acts.

Accordingly, this court holds that no tort action will lie against a municipal corporation for those acts or omissions involving the exercise of a legislative or judicial function, or the exercise of an executive or planning function involving the making of a basic policy decision which is characterized by the exercise of a high degree of official judgment or discretion. However, once the policy has been made to engage in a certain activity or function, municipalities will be held liable, the same as private corporations and persons, for the negligence of their employees in the performance of the activities. *Accord Superior Uptown v. Cleveland* (1974), 39 Ohio St. 2d 36, 40–41, 313 N.E.2d 820 [68 O.O.2d 21].

. . .

For the foregoing reasons, this court holds that the trial court erred in granting the motion for judgment notwithstanding the verdict based on the applicability of the doctrine of municipal immunity and the jury verdict awarding damages to the appellant is hereby reinstated.

Judgment reversed.

HOLMES, JUSTICE, dissenting.

I have previously stated in numerous occasions my disagreement with the judicial abrogation of municipal immunity. I continue to adhere to that belief, so I must strenuously dissent from the judgment here and, particularly, paragraph one of the syllabus. However, I write here to comment on the manner in which the majority abrogates municipal immunity.

In my opinion in *King v. Williams* (1983), 5 Ohio St. 3d 137, 141, 449 N.E.2d 452, I raised certain questions relating to the abandonment of municipal immunity. While the majority partially responds to these questions, it neglects to address what I consider to be of paramount importance: should this court's decision be prospective or retroactive. In my opinion, the doctrine should be abrogated prospectively.

Generally, decisions of this court which overrule former decisions are applied retroactively. Nevertheless, there are instances where this court has decided to apply a new rule of law prospectively only. *See, e.g., Wolfe v. Wolfe* (1976), 46 Ohio St. 2d 399, 421–422, 350 N.E.2d 413 [75 O.O.2d 474]. It is my opinion that if the defense of sovereign immunity must be abrogated at all, it should be done prospectively only.

The doctrine of sovereign immunity has been a long standing principle of law in this state. To abolish it retroactively would deny municipalities that have relied upon it the opportunity to make arrangements to meet the new liability to which they are subject. The availability of liability insurance has been used in recent years to justify the dramatic expansion of tort liability. Yet, we impose liability on municipalities without allowing them the opportunity to obtain liability insurance. Further, this immunity should be annulled prospectively so that the General Assembly will be given an opportunity to act upon our decision. It is that branch of government which is best equipped to balance competing considerations of public policy. Lastly, the prospective abolition of this defense would be in line with the overwhelming weight of authority from other jurisdictions that have considered this question.

The second area upon which I wish to comment is the attempt of the majority to limit the abolition of municipal immunity. This is in line with other jurisdictions.

The majority correctly determines here that a municipality is immune when it acts legislatively or judicially. Also, I agree that actions which are characterized as "discretionary" should be immunized, but the ambiguity of the language utilized by the majority in this regard does not accomplish this desired result.

The majority describes this latter group of immunized actions as ". . . an executive or planning function involving the making of a basic policy decision which is characterized by the exercise of a high degree of official judgment or discretion." Little practical guidance is given to bench and bar by the adoption of such a nebulous standard, nor are municipal employees informed with any specificity when they will be "second-guessed."

It is difficult for the judiciary by way of decisional law to comprehensively deal with these matters of practical public policy. No reported decision has been found which does more than set slippery standards in this area. This necessarily vague stance of the majority further demonstrates the weakness of this court's actions in the area of governmental immunity. Decisions in this area should have been left to the General Assembly, or, barring that, the General Assembly should have been given the opportunity to enact a practical, comprehensive solution before the court's decisions abrogating municipal immunity became effective.

This court's decisions in the area of governmental immunity cry out for a legislative response. I, for one, hopefully anticipate that the General Assembly will proceed as have the legislative bodies in other states, and enact responsive laws. *See, e.g., Cal. Govt. Code Anno., Sections 810 et seq.*

LOCHER, J., concurs in the foregoing dissenting opinion.

NOTES AND QUESTIONS

(1) Although the doctrine of sovereign immunity was once applied vigorously to protect state and local governments, it has now been largely eroded almost everywhere to a greater or lesser extent either by legislation or by judicial action. The courts tend to be more willing to abrogate immunity for municipal governments than for state governments, political subdivisions of states and state agencies.

The erosion of municipal immunity is said to have begun with *Hargrove v. Town of Cocoa Beach*, 96 So. 2d 130 (Fla. 1957), which eliminated immunity for all actions of a municipality except legislative, quasi-legislative, judicial and quasi-judicial functions. What does that leave? How does it compare with the rule of *Enghauser? See also Commercial Carrier Corp. v. Indian River Cty.*, 371 So. 2d 1010 (Fla. 1979).

(2) Not every court has been willing to abrogate sovereign immunity, even of municipalities. *See, e.g., Gressett By and Through Gressett v. Newton Separate Mun. School*, 697 So. 2d 444 (Miss. 1997) (recounting history of judicial abrogation of sovereign immunity followed by legislative reinstatement followed by judicial limitation.). Even those that have, commonly protect certain classes of discretionary governmental decisions against tort actions. New York, for example, follows the rule "that a municipality cannot be held liable for negligence in the performance of a governmental function, including fire and police protection, unless a special relationship existed between the municipality and the injured party." *DeLong v. County of Erie*, 60 N.Y.2d 296, 469 N.Y.S.2d 611, 615 (1983). Would the survivors of a person who called "911" seeking emergency police protection, who was assured that help was on the way, but who was thereafter "forgotten" by the authorities be entitled to a wrongful death recovery because of the ensuing murder? What issues must be resolved? The Federal Tort Claims Act also contains a discretionary function exception to the waiver of immunity. *United States v. S.A. Empresa DeViacao Aerea Rio Grandense*, 467 U.S. 797 104 S. Ct. 2755, 81 L. Ed. 2d 660 (1984).

(3) Consult the sovereign immunity statute of your state. How much relief does it afford?

BEATTIE v. BEATTIE
Supreme Court of Delaware, En Banc
630 A.2d 1096 (1993)

VEASEY, CHIEF JUSTICE:

In this case we review a decision of the Superior Court granting defendant husband's motion for summary judgment in a negligence action initiated by his plaintiff wife. She is seeking damages for paralyzing injuries she sustained in an automobile accident where her husband was the driver. The trial court properly followed the prior precedents of this Court and relied on the common law doctrine of interspousal immunity ("the Doctrine") which prevents one spouse from suing the other in tort. We have concluded, however, that the Doctrine is no longer a viable concept and no longer meets the needs of modern society. Accordingly, we hereby overrule our prior precedents and REVERSE and REMAND to the Superior Court for proceedings not inconsistent with this opinion.

I. FACTS

On July 15, 1991 defendant-appellee, Michael Beattie ("Husband"), struck the back of a slow moving truck engaged in weed spraying operations on the median of Route 1 near Milford, Delaware. At the time of the collision he was driving a 1991 Oldsmobile Cutlass in which his wife, plaintiff-appellant, Margaret Beattie ("Wife"), was a passenger. His wife sustained serious injuries in the accident which have rendered her a quadriplegic. Her medical bills and expenses are in excess of $286,000. On December 17, 1991, Wife filed a negligence action against her Husband. At the time of the accident, he was covered by a substantial liability insurance policy on the vehicle. Despite the suit, the Beatties have remained married and have no plans to divorce.

II. PROCEEDINGS IN THE SUPERIOR COURT

On February 25, 1992, Husband filed a motion for summary judgment against his wife claiming that the Doctrine barred her negligence claim. The trial court granted the motion, but requested that an amended motion for summary judgment be filed. On June 23, 1992, the Superior Court issued an order granting the amended motion for summary judgment. Thereafter, the wife appealed the decision. Following oral argument before a panel of three justices, the matter was scheduled for re-hearing en Banc and amicus curiae briefing was permitted. The sole issue before this Court is whether the Doctrine should be abrogated and, if so, to what extent.

III. RATIONALE OF THE TRIAL COURT'S DECISION

The trial court's decision granting summary judgment is based upon the Doctrine. This antiquated doctrine was first applied by Delaware courts in the seminal case of *Plotkin v. Plotkin*, Del. Super., 32 Del. 455, 125 A. 455 (1924). In *Plotkin*, the Superior Court adopted the Doctrine primarily on the belief that upon marriage, the identity of the wife merged with that of the husband. The Doctrine's continued existence in Delaware since 1924 has been justified as a means of promoting family harmony and discouraging collusion and fraud upon insurance companies. *Saunders v. Hill, Del.Supr.*, 57 Del. 519, 202 A.2d 807, 808 (1964) (the "absolute legal unity of husband and wife has been substantially eroded by the Married Women's Property Acts" and instead the Doctrine is justified as a means to promote family harmony and discourage collusion and fraud). After most recently reviewing the Doctrine in 1979, this Court held that "it retains sufficient merit to warrant continued adherence." *Alfree v. Alfree*, Del. Supr., 410 A.2d 161, 162 (1979).

IV. STANDARD AND SCOPE OF REVIEW

The issue is whether the Doctrine remains a viable concept in Delaware jurisprudence. The trial court's decision is supported by existing Delaware case law which recognizes the antiquated Doctrine. The validity of the Doctrine has been called into question. Accordingly, this issue poses a legal question which is subject to de novo review. . . .

V. ABROGATION OF THE DOCTRINE

It is well settled that the judiciary has the power to overturn judicially-created doctrine, so long as that doctrine has not been codified in a statute. . . . Furthermore, it is the duty of this Court to review common law rules to ensure that the conditions and policy objectives that justify the rules remain relevant and valid. Relying on the case of *Saunders v. Hill*, Husband argues, conversely, that changes in well-settled public policy must be effected by the General Assembly. . . . This reliance is misplaced, however, because the case is factually distinguishable. In *Saunders* the General Assembly had enacted controlling legislation. In the present case, there is no statute that directly applies to the Doctrine. Therefore, it is within the authority of this Court to abrogate the common law doctrine if it no longer merits recognition. . . . ("The strength and genius of the common law lies in its ability to adapt to the changing needs of the society it governs.").

This Court refused to abrogate the Doctrine in *Alfree*, 410 A.2d at 162, despite the renunciation of the parental immunity doctrine in *Williams v. Williams*, Del. Supr., 369 A.2d 669 (1976). *Williams* held that the promotion of family harmony and the discouragement of collusive and fraudulent claims were unacceptable justifications for the parental immunity doctrine "in light of contemporary conditions and modern concepts of fairness." *Id.* at 671. The *Alfree* Court declined to abrogate the Doctrine because it was then perceived that the effects would be far-reaching and the problem was "more appropriate for legislative solution than for judicial determination." *Alfree*, 410 A.2d at 163 (citation omitted).

The *Alfree* Court's rationale for retaining the Doctrine included: 1) the preservation of family harmony and 2) the prevention of fraud and collusion. *Id.* at 162. These were the same rationales that were rejected with regard to parental immunity in *Williams*. It is inconceivable that suits between children and parents are less likely to disrupt family harmony than interspousal suits. This is also true with respect to property claims and actions for breach of contract, which are actionable in the family context.

In our view, the Doctrine is more likely to have the effect of disrupting family harmony rather than preserving it. Denying a person compensation for injuries arising from the negligence of his or her spouse can be very disruptive (*e.g.*, large medical bills and loss of wages often result from serious accidents). Under the Doctrine, the married couple will have to pay these huge expenses, instead of relying on insurance proceeds. This added financial burden could well promote marital discord. Any destruction of family harmony that is prevented by the Doctrine is likely to be minimal due to the prevalence of liability insurance. In addition, the Doctrine may actually promote divorces because a person who suffers an injury at the hands of his or her spouse, but who has since divorced the spouse, may maintain a tort action against the former spouse. *Hudson v. Hudson*, Del.Super., 532 A.2d 620, 624, appeal refused, Del.Supr., 527 A.2d 281 (1987). Accordingly, it is conceivable that spouses may decide to divorce solely to bypass the restrictions of a Doctrine which putatively is designed to preserve marital harmony. Such a result is repugnant to public policy.

Because of the prevalence of liability insurance, Husband argues that collusion and fraud will increase if spouses are able to sue each other. It is true that the adversarial system may be subject to tension because it is in the defendant spouse's interest for his or her injured spouse to receive some compensation, especially when the insurance company is the "real" party being sued. Such tension could potentially lead to a threat of corruption. Although the possibility of collusion exists in various situations such as intrafamily cases and suits between friends, the judicial system is adept at ferreting out frivolous and unfounded cases.[62] It is unnecessary and unwise to deny legitimate claims in order to prevent fraudulent and collusive suits because the judicial system contains numerous safeguards and deterrents against fraudulent claims such as perjury charges and modern discovery procedures. . . . Cf., *Daubert v. Merrell Dow Pharmaceuticals, Inc.*, 509 U.S. 579 , 113 S. Ct. 2786, 125 L. Ed. 2d 469 (1993) (holding that Federal Rule of Evidence 702 supersedes the "general acceptance" rule regarding scientific evidence, and that the adversarial process, including "vigorous cross-examination," provides safeguards against admission of "junk science" evidence).

The conclusion that the abrogation of the Doctrine will not lead to the destruction of family harmony or the proliferation of fraudulent suits is amply supported by empirical evidence.[63] Delaware is the only state in the nation which recognizes the doctrine solely on common law grounds. Four other states also recognize the Doctrine,[64] but do so pursuant to a statute or a perceived statutory prohibition of judicial abrogation of the Doctrine.

In addition to arguing that the Doctrine should be abrogated because it is no longer a viable concept, Wife also argues that the Doctrine violates the Delaware Financial Responsibility Laws, 21 Del. C. Ch. 29 and 21 Del. C. § 2118 (hereinafter

---

[62] The Supreme Court of West Virginia abrogated the Doctrine in 1978. The court explained: "[w]e do an injustice not only to the intelligence of jurors, but to the efficacy of the adversary system, when we express undue concern over the quantum of collusive or meritless law suits." *Coffindaffer v. Coffindaffer*, W. Va. Supr., 161 W. Va. 557, 244 S.E.2d 338, 343 (1978).

[63] For example, the amicus curiae brief of the Delaware Trial Lawyers Association ("DTLA") provides data which suggest that abrogation of the doctrine has had no negative effects on insurance premiums, thus indicating that the number of fraudulent or collusive suits has not risen dramatically. DTLA Brief at exhibits A-D.

[64] Prior to an opinion by the Florida Supreme Court dated May 27, 1993, five states other than Delaware recognized the Doctrine. *Waite v. Waite*, 618 So. 2d 1360–61 (1993) ("[T]here no longer is a sufficient reason warranting a continued adherence to the doctrine of interspousal immunity.").

"§ 2118"). Section 2118, Delaware's no-fault statute, states that coverage on automobiles must be provided against all liability and injuries. Section 2118(f) further states that once a plaintiff recovers from the insurer, the insurer is subrogated to the plaintiff's right to sue the insured. Thus, recovery of insurance proceeds by the plaintiff is based on the plaintiff's right of action against the insured. Application of the Doctrine renders § 2118 unenforceable in full. Construing the coverage provisions of the Delaware Financial Responsibility Laws, specifically 21 Del. C. § 2118 and 21 Del. C. § 2902, this Court has held that "neither statute restricts liability coverage to certain claims based upon the relationship of the plaintiff to the defendant. Rather, both provisions are drafted in broad language which provides for liability coverage for all claims up to the stated limits, regardless of the identity of the plaintiff." *State Farm Mut. Auto Ins. Co. v. Wagamon*, Del. Supr., 541 A.2d 557, 560 (1988). This holding strongly supports a finding that the General Assembly intended to extend coverage to an injured spouse.

We agree with the Supreme Court of Kansas and the vast majority of other jurisdictions which have found the Doctrine to be "a judicial anachronism that no longer merits recognition." *Flagg v. Loy*, Kan.Supr., 241 Kan. 216, 734 P.2d 1183, 1190 (1987). Accordingly, we hold that the Doctrine no longer meets the needs of society and must be abrogated.

VI. EXTENT OF THE ABROGATION

We now focus our attention on the extent to which the Doctrine should be abrogated. Amicus curiae briefs advocating various theories were filed. This Court must, however, confine its ruling to the case presently before it. Our decision to abrogate the Doctrine applies to any injury which is negligently caused.[65]

Accordingly, we overrule *Alfree* and abrogate the Doctrine.

For the most part, interspousal lawsuits typically are initiated when the tortfeasor has sufficient insurance coverage to provide for the damages. From this fact, Wife argues that the Doctrine should be abrogated only to the extent that liability insurance coverage protects the negligent spouse. Under this theory, a negligent spouse is immune from tort liability for damages in excess of his or her liability insurance coverage. One reason for the limit is that it avoids the problem of one spouse executing on marital property to satisfy an excess judgment. In the absence of a statute, the Court finds no reason to limit suits between married persons to insurance coverage while imposing no restrictions upon other suits. Also, making insurance coverage the limit on liability may have the practical effect of leaving the injured spouse far from compensated for his or her suffering. In the present case, the Husband was covered by substantial insurance, but in cases where the tortfeasor spouse has very little or no insurance, the injured spouse will be limited to recovering insufficient damage awards or no award at all. Having concluded that the Doctrine is no longer based on sound public policy grounds, this Court should not retain restrictions that would have the effect, at least in some

---

[65] The vast majority of jurisdictions that have abrogated the Doctrine have not limited it to automobile torts. Excluding Florida's recent abrogation of the Doctrine, thirty-eight out of forty-four states have not limited the abrogation to automobile torts. Wayne F. Foster, Annotation, *Modern Status of Interspousal Tort Immunity In Personal Injury and Wrongful Death Actions*, 92 A.L.R.3d 901 (1979). See also *Hack v. Hack*, Pa. Supr., 495 Pa. 300, 433 A.2d 859, 869 (1981).

instances, of preserving the Doctrine. In our view, it is not appropriate to deny or limit a right based upon the existence of insurance coverage. In addition, although the present case involves the rule of interspousal immunity for negligence rather than an intentional tort, it is reasonable to conclude that there is "no logical or legal reason for drawing a distinction between the two." *Klein v. Klein*, Cal. Supr., 58 Cal. 2d 692, 26 Cal. Rptr. 102, 103, 376 P.2d 70, 71 (1962). We realize that marital harmony is lacking where spouses intentionally harm one another. There is logic to the argument that, in cases where the parties have since divorced, there is little, if any, justification for barring an injured spouse from suing for intentional torts as well.[66]

The case before us is a negligence case, however, and the intentional tort case is not before us. Nevertheless, it appears that the rationale underlying the abrogation of the Doctrine in the context of negligence actions would apply to intentional torts.

VII. CONCLUSION

We find that the Doctrine is a relic from the common law that is no longer a viable concept and no longer meets the needs of modern society. The overwhelming majority of states in this nation have already abrogated the Doctrine without negative repercussions. Accordingly, we overrule *Alfree* and reject the Doctrine as a defense in this case.

NOTES AND QUESTIONS

(1) *Beattie v. Beattie* made the argument that interspousal immunity is disruptive to family harmony because it might force a divorce to eliminate the immunity and permit an action between former spouses arising out of a tort committed during the marriage. By contrast, some jurisdictions follow the rule that the immunity holds even after divorce as to torts committed during the marriage (but not as to torts committed *prior* to the marriage). Should interspousal immunity be abolished in a state that follows this rule? Florida was such a state until *Waite v. Waite*, 618 So. 2d 1360 (Fla. 1993), abolished the rule in all applications.

(2) Although making an accurate catalog of the status of interspousal immunity requires a meticulous examination of the law of each state, the opinion in *Waite v. Waite, supra,* suggests that over 30 jurisdictions have completely abrogated the doctrine. Others have limited abrogation to motor vehicle cases or intentional tort cases. See Karp and Karp, *Domestic Torts*, Family Law Series, January 1996 Cumulative Supplement. In some decisions the doctrine is abrogated only when liability insurance is provided. Should this make a difference? After *Waite* the trend to abolish this immunity continued. *See, e.g., Boxman v. Bozman*, 830A.2d 450 (Md. 2003).

Despite the robust trend against the doctrine, at least a handful of jurisdictions

---

[66] The amicus curiae brief of the Section on Women and the Law of the Delaware State Bar Association ("DSBA") argues that abrogation of the Doctrine with respect to intentional torts is necessary because neither Delaware divorce law nor Delaware criminal law provide adequate remedies for intentional torts committed against spouses. Assuming the existing law is inadequate, it does not necessarily follow that abrogation of the Doctrine is the sole answer. Other methods of reform include a modification of existing criminal or divorce law through legislative initiative.

continue to apply it. See, *e.g.*, *Eisenhardt v. Snook*, 986 So. 2d 700 (La. App. 2008) (declining to apply Louisiana's interspousal immunity statute to bar an action by a live-in girl friend), and *Gates v Gates*, 587 S.E.2d 32 (Ga. 2003) (applying Georgia's codified interspousal immunity doctrine to bar a spouse's action against her spouse for a pre-marital tort even though she had filed for divorce.). See also *Larkin v. Larkin*, 601 S.E.2d 487 (Ga. App. 2004), holding that the immunity barred the action by an estate of one spouse against the estate of the other, whose negligent driving killed both.

SEARS, ROEBUCK & CO. v. HUANG
Supreme Court of Delaware, En Banc
652 A.2d 568 (1995)

HOLLAND, JUSTICE:

This is an interlocutory appeal from the Superior Court. The plaintiff-appellee, Hsu-Nan Huang, guardian ad litem for Stephanie Huang ("Huang"), a minor, seeks damages from the defendants-appellants, Sears, Roebuck & Co. ("Sears") and Otis Elevator Co, ("Otis"). Huang's suit is based on the alleged negligence of Sears and Otis, with regard to an incident in which Huang's hand became caught in an escalator.

This appeal arises from the Superior Court's ruling, which granted Huang's motion in limine, to preclude reference at trial to the alleged negligent conduct of Huang's mother. The Superior Court certified that ruling to this Court . . . : first, it concluded that this Court's recent decision in *Beattie v. Beattie*, Del.Supr., 630 A.2d 1096 (1993), placed the continued viability of Delaware's limited parental immunity doctrine in question . . . This Court accepted the interlocutory appeal. . . .

The defendants, Sears and Otis, have raised two arguments. First, according to the defendants, the parental immunity doctrine should now be abrogated entirely for reasons similar to those that recently persuaded this Court to abrogate completely the interspousal immunity doctrine. See *Beattie v. Beattie*, 630 A.2d 1096. Second, the defendants argue alternatively that the Superior Court erred, as a matter of law, in ruling that Delaware's limited parental immunity doctrine precludes the presentation of evidence or argument regarding its allegation of negligent supervision by Huang's mother as a supervening cause of Huang's injury.

This Court has decided to retain the current Delaware law which recognizes a limited parental immunity doctrine. *Schneider v. Coe*, Del. Supr., 405 A.2d 682 (1979) ("*Schneider I*"). This Court has also decided to adhere to its prior holding in *McKeon* that evidence of a parent's negligent supervision may be presented to establish that such negligence was a supervening cause of a minor child's personal injury. *McKeon v. Goldstein*, 164 A.2d at 262–63. Because we find the Superior Court's ruling is inconsistent with *McKeon*, the interlocutory judgment of the Superior Court must be reversed.

Substantive Facts

On October 5, 1991, Huang, then four years old, along with her younger brother, accompanied their mother, Cheung-Hua Mei (hereinafter "Mother"), while she shopped in the Sears retail outlet at Price's Corner. After hearing an announcement on the store's public address system, the Mother and her children took the ascending escalator from the first floor to the second floor to see a presentation on jewelry. The presentation took place on the second floor within a few feet of the escalator. The jewelry presentation was given before more than twenty people by Valerie Carroll ("Carroll") on behalf of her employer, Classic Contemporary Designs. During the presentation, Huang's brother was in a stroller. Huang stood next to her Mother. The Huang family was somewhere in the middle of the crowd.

The Mother stood watching the jewelry presentation approximately six feet from the escalator. At times, Huang either held her Mother's hand or held the stroller next to her Mother. Carroll stated that as she got into the beginning of the demonstration, about 5 minutes into it, the little girl went towards the escalator. "The very first time she did that I stopped and asked the mother to get the child; that was the only time I asked her." According to Carroll, Huang went to the escalator and had to be brought back by her Mother more than two or three times.

At the conclusion of the presentation, Carroll was handing out free pendants to those in attendance when she heard Huang scream. Carroll rushed over and stopped the escalator. She then called for a security guard who came and removed Huang's hand and arm from the nippoint between the escalator handguard and handrail.

The Mother does not remember her daughter walking away from her and toward the escalator several times during the fifteen minute jewelry presentation. The Mother recalls Huang standing next to her, holding the stroller, as she approached Carroll to accept a pendant. As she went around the display table to receive the gift, she heard Huang's scream. The Mother believes the time lapse was approximately thirty seconds between the time when she last remembered Huang holding onto the stroller and when she heard Huang's scream.

. . .

Procedural Facts

The amended complaint alleges negligence in the construction, maintenance, and operation of the Otis manufactured escalator system in place in the Sears retail location in Price's Corner. This negligence allegedly resulted in the injury to Huang. The complaint, as amended, states that the:

[m]inor plaintiff was at all times reasonably supervised by her mother who kept a proper lookout for minor plaintiff's safety.

Sears and Otis seek to assert the defense of supervening cause based on the Mother's negligent supervision of her child, Huang. On April 8, 1993, Sears filed its answer to Huang's amended complaint, alleging as part of its Fifth Affirmative Defense that:

if the plaintiff was damaged in any manner whatsoever, that said damage was a direct and proximate result of the intervening and superseding actions on the part of other persons and not of this defendant, and that such intervening and superseding action on the part of the other person or persons bars recovery herein on behalf of the plaintiff due to the doctrine of intervening, superseding causation.

Sears and Otis have not asserted third party claims for contribution. They seek to introduce evidence regarding the Mother's conduct in order to show that her negligence, not theirs, was the sole (supervening) proximate cause of Huang's injury. The Superior Court ruled that no reference or argument could be made at trial to the negligence of Huang's mother. This decision was based on the doctrine of parental immunity which bars children from suing their parents, and third parties from suing parents for contribution, in cases in which an unemancipated child is negligently injured.

History in Delaware Parental Immunity Doctrine

The doctrine of parental immunity was first recognized in Delaware by the Superior Court in the case of *Strahorn v. Sears, Roebuck & Co.*, Del. Super., 50 Del. 50, 123 A.2d 107 (1956). The facts *of Strahorn* are similar to the facts in the case sub judice. A little boy evaded his father's grasp, ran to an escalator, fell, and injured his fingers in the escalator apparatus. In *Strahorn*, the Superior Court noted, "the majority rule is that an unemancipated minor cannot sue a parent in tort in a case of ordinary negligence." *Id.* 123 A.2d at 108 (citations omitted). The Superior Court adopted the majority rule, relying in part on the public policy of "preserv[ing] the peace and harmony of the home." *Id.* Accordingly, the Superior Court held the action was barred by the doctrine of parental immunity, notwithstanding the fact that the action was for contribution from the minor child's parent, as opposed to a direct action against the parents for damages by the minor child. *Id.* 123 A.2d at 109–10.

This Court first addressed the doctrine of parental immunity in the case of *Williams v. Williams*, Del. Supr., 369 A.2d 669 (1976). In *Williams*, a father, as next friend of the child, brought a direct action against the minor child's mother for injuries the child sustained in an automobile accident. This Court held that "an absolute rule of parental immunity in tort has no rational basis under modern day conditions and circumstances" and allowed the minor's suit to stand. *Id.* at 673. This Court did not completely abrogate the doctrine of parental immunity in *Williams* and was careful to point out that *Strahorn* had not been overruled. The holding in *Williams* was limited. It only permitted an unemancipated minor child to sue an insured parent for negligence arising from an automobile accident. In *Williams*, we stated, "[w]hether this Court will adopt the doctrine of parental immunity when . . . issues of parental authority and discretion are presented must await another case." *Id.*

Three years later, in *Schneider v. Coe*, Del. Supr., 405 A.2d 682 (1979) ("*Schneider I*"), this Court decided the question that *Williams* left unresolved. In *Schneider I*, a minor child ventured into a neighbor's yard and was kicked by a pony. The issue presented was whether a "parent who negligently supervises his unemancipated child can be liable for the resulting injury to his child." *Id.* at 682. This Court ruled that evidence regarding the parent's negligence was inadmissible. *Williams* was distinguished because "[u]nlike driving an automobile, supervision of one's children involves issues of parental control, authority, and discretion that are uniquely matters of a very personal type of judgment." *Id.* at 684:

Reciprocal rights and duties inhere in the parent-child relationship. Anything creating conflict between parent and child, or interfering with the authority, discretion, or control that a parent has the right to exercise in supervising his child is repugnant to the institution of the family, and therefore is against public policy. Parental immunity will not be abrogated where the duty arises from the family relationship, for to do so would manifestly tend to disturb domestic tranquility. *Id.*

In *Schneider I*, this Court explicitly declined to extend the holding in *Williams* to abrogate entirely the doctrine of parental immunity. After recognizing the exception to the parental immunity doctrine in *Williams*, this Court held that "where parental control, authority, or discretion is involved, the rule of parental immunity must be preserved." *Id.* . . .

Limited Parental Immunity Delaware Retains Doctrine

Otis and Sears contend that this Court should no longer retain the doctrine of parental immunity. That argument is based, by analogy, on this Court's recent decision to abrogate the doctrine of interspousal tort immunity. *Beattie v. Beanie*, Del. Supr., 630 A.2d 1096 (1993). While the national trend has been toward eroding the doctrine of parental immunity, only ten states have completely abrogated the doctrine for all torts.

The majority of states, thirty-three, have not abrogated the parental immunity doctrine altogether, but have only recognized certain exceptions and still provide partial immunity. *Id.* at 630 n. 88. Twenty-nine states, for example, have abandoned the doctrine in the instance of automobile accidents, such as in the *Williams* decision. *Id.* at 632 n. 100. Twenty-six states have abrogated the doctrine for negligent torts. *Id.* at 631. Many states, however, have not abrogated the doctrine or have reserved judgment when the facts before them involve parental discretion, control and authority. We have decided to adhere to all of our prior precedents with regard to the issue of parental immunity. . . . Therefore, "where parental control, authority, or discretion is involved, the rule of parental immunity [is] preserved" in Delaware. *Schneider I*, 405 A.2d at 684.

If Parent's Negligence Relevant Admissible As Supervening Cause

Otis and Sears second argument is that, even if the Mother is immune from direct liability or liability for contribution, they should be allowed to present evidence to establish that the Mother's negligent supervision (control) was a supervening cause of her minor child's injuries. This Court responded affirmatively to a similar argument in *McKeon v. Goldstein*, Del. Supr., 53 Del. 24, 164 A.2d 260 (1960). In *McKeon*, this Court stated that "the determination of proximate cause is a question of fact for the trier of facts." *Id.* 164 A.2d at 263.

Thus, in *McKeon*, we held that even when the parent was not (and could not be) a named defendant, the trier of fact must decide whether the parent's negligent supervision was the sole proximate cause, *i.e.*, supervening cause, of her minor child's injury. If the parent's negligence was a supervening cause of the child's injury, the named defendants' negligence would be a remote cause, rather than a proximate cause, and the defendants would not be liable as tortfeasors.[67]

---

[67] In *McKeon*, this Court allowed a jury to hear evidence of parental conduct for the issue of proximate causation. The case involved a mother who left her child on a bed adjacent to a hot steam pipe

We adhere to that holding in this case.

Huang contends that the holding in *McKeon* was modified in 1980, when the *Schneider* litigation came before this Court a second time in *Coe v. Schneider*, Del.Supr., 424 A.2d 1 (1980) ("*Schneider II*"). The question presented in *Schneider II* was whether evidence of the parent's

negligent supervision of a child was admissible in a suit based on the "attractive nuisance" doctrine. This Court held that any reference to the parent's negligent conduct was inadmissible, even with regard to the issue of proximate cause.

In *Schneider II*, this Court held that "[g]iven Delaware's adherence to the rule of Restatement [of Torts] (2d) § 339 [Ed. — See section 5.04[B] *supra.*], under the facts of this case, parental supervision is immaterial to the question of the defendants' liability." *Id.* at 2. . . . "Notably, § 339 and the official comments thereto do not make the possessor's liability contingent upon a showing that the child's trespass was not due to parental negligence in failing to properly supervise the child." *Schneider II*, 424 A.2d at 2. Thus our holding in *Schneider II*, regarding the immateriality of the parent's negligent control, was explicitly based on the attractive nuisance doctrine theory of liability.

Delaware's recognition of a limited parental immunity doctrine in *Schneider I* is completely consistent with the recognition that, when parental negligence is relevant but not actionable, a defendant may introduce evidence to establish that parental negligence was the supervening cause of a minor child's injury.

This Case Delaware Jurisprudence Limited Parental Immunity

This Court has held that Delaware's enactment of a comparative negligence statute did not change the common law doctrine of proximate cause. *Culver v. Bennett*, 588 A.2d at 1098. Multiple defendants may be liable as joint tortfeasors if each defendant's negligence is found to be a proximate cause of a plaintiff's injury. *Id.* If one defendant's negligence is found to be the sole proximate cause of the plaintiff's injury, it is a supervening cause which shields the other defendants from liability. . . .

In cases where the parental immunity doctrine applies, defendants who decide to assert the parent's negligence as a supervening cause adopt essentially an "all or nothing" legal strategy. The trier of fact may decide that the parent's negligence and the negligence of one or more defendants were all proximate causes of the child's injury. In such an event, since the parent is immune from direct liability or liability for contribution, by definition the parent cannot be a joint tortfeasor. . . . Therefore, the non-parent tortfeasors will be held jointly and severally liable for the entire amount of the minor child's damages.

Because this case is in the pre-trial stage and will be remanded for further proceedings, we will summarize our holdings seriatim. First, where parental control, authority, or discretion is involved, *e.g.*, in potential actions against parents for negligent supervision of their children, the rule of parental immunity is preserved in Delaware and precludes direct claims by a minor child, as well as third-party claims for contribution. . . . Second, if the parent's negligence is

---

from the heating system. The mother placed the child on her bed after noticing a bulge in the ceiling over the child's crib which appeared to be from a water leak. The child was subsequently discovered severely burned lying on the floor near the pipe.

relevant[68] to the minor child's theory of liability, but not actionable,[69] a defendant may introduce evidence to establish that the parent's negligence was a supervening cause of the minor child's injury. . . . Third, if the parent's negligence was a proximate cause but not a supervening cause, the parent's negligence does not provide a basis for reducing full payment to the minor child or the basis for a claim of contribution by any defendant determined to be a tortfeasor, since by definition the parent cannot be a joint tortfeasor.

Conclusion

The interlocutory judgment of the Superior Court, which granted the plaintiff's motion in limine, is reversed. This matter is remanded for further proceedings in accordance with this opinion.

NOTES AND QUESTIONS

(1) *Broadbent v. Northbrook Indemnity Company*, 907 P.2d 43, 45–46 (Ariz. 1995), provided this additional information about the background of the parental immunity doctrine:

I. History and Purpose of the Parental Immunity Doctrine

A. The Origins of Parental Immunity

We begin by stating a few basic facts about the treatment of children under the law and family immunities. Under common law, a child has traditionally been considered a separate legal entity from his or her parent. . . . Children have generally been allowed to sue their parents in property and contract actions. *Goller v. White*, 20 Wis. 2d 402, 122 N.W.2d 193, 197 (1963). . . . In contrast, at common law the courts merged the identity of husband and wife; therefore, spousal immunity prohibited any action by a wife against her husband because to do so would have been to sue herself . . . see. *Windauer v. O'Connor*, 13 Ariz. App. 442, 442–45, 477 P.2d 561, 562–65 (1970) (holding that doctrine of spousal immunity did not bar action by former wife against divorced husband for personal injuries sustained when husband shot wife during marriage). The doctrine of spousal immunity has been abolished and there has not been a prohibition against siblings suing each other.

The doctrine of parental immunity is an American phenomenon unknown in the English common law. . . . Courts in Canada and Scotland have held that children may sue their parents in tort. *See Gibson*, 92 Cal. Rptr. at 289, 479 P.2d at 649 . . .

In early American history, children were viewed as "evil and in need of strict discipline," and the courts recognized wide parental discretion. . . . There was a strong presumption that parental discipline was proper. *See, e.g.*, S.C. Code Ann. § 16-3-40 (Law.Co-op.1976) (statute originating from 1712 that provided a defense to "[k]illing by stabbing or thrusting" if done while chastising or correcting your child). Only recently has the state intervened to protect children. *See, e.g.*, A.R.S. §§ 8-501 to -550.01 (child

---

[68] *See Schneider II*, 424 A.2d 1.

[69] *See Schneider I*, 405 A.2d 682.

welfare and placement). Viewed against this backdrop, it is not surprising that no American child had sought recovery against a parent for tortious conduct until the late nineteenth century. In *Hewlett v. George*, 68 Miss. 703, 711, 9 So. 885, 887 (1891), the Supreme Court of Mississippi held, without citation to legal authority, that a child could not sue her parent for being falsely imprisoned in an insane asylum because of parental immunity, a doctrine which that court created from whole cloth. As its rationale, the court stated:

> [S]o long as the parent is under obligation to care for, guide and control, and the child is under reciprocal obligation to aid and comfort and obey, no such action as this can be maintained. The peace of society, and of the families composing society, and a sound public policy, designed to subserve the repose of families and the best interests of society, forbid to the minor child a right to appear in court in the assertion of a claim to civil redress for personal injuries suffered at the hands of the parent.

Hewlett, 68 Miss. at 711, 9 So. at 887.

Hewlett was followed by two cases that were also decided on parental immunity grounds, and these came to be known as the "great trilogy" of cases establishing the parental immunity doctrine. In *McKelvey v. McKelvey*, the Tennessee Supreme Court held that a minor child could not sue her father for "cruel and inhuman treatment" allegedly inflicted by her stepmother with the consent of her father. 111 Tenn. 388, 77 S.W. 664, 664–65 (1903). *McKelvey* cited *Hewlett* as the only authority for the doctrine of parental immunity and analogized the parent-child relationship to that of the husband-wife relationship, noting that the basis for the spousal immunity was, in part, the fact that husband and wife are a legal entity. *McKelvey*, 77 S.W. at 664–65.

In *Roller v. Roller*, the Supreme Court of Washington cited *Hewlett* and held that a minor child could not sue her father for rape, even though he had been convicted of the criminal violation, because of the doctrine of parental immunity. . . . The *Roller* court argued that if the child recovered a money judgment from the parent and then died, the parent would then become heir to the property that had been taken from him. . . . In addition, *Roller* argued that "the public has an interest in the financial welfare of other minor members of the family, and it would not be the policy of the law to allow the estate, which is to be looked to for the support of all the minor children, to be appropriated by any particular one."

This " 'great trilogy' " was the inauspicious beginning of the doctrine of parental immunity, which was soon embraced by almost every state. However, the courts soon began fashioning several exceptions to the doctrine, and in several states the doctrine has been abolished. Saying, "We want to protect the right of parents to raise their children by their own methods and in accordance with their own attitudes and beliefs," *Id.* at 907 P.2d 49, *Broadbent* expressed similar concern about the right of parents to control their children without state intervention as the Delaware court did in *Huang*, but declined to restrict the abrogation of parental immunity as *Huang* did. Instead, *Broadbent* held: "A parent is not immune from liability for tortious conduct directed toward his child solely by reason of that relationship. . . . And, a parent is not liable for an act or omission that injured his child if the parent acted as a reasonable and prudent parent in the situation would." *Id.* 907 P.2d at 50.

Broadbent held that the parent was *not* immune. What would be the outcome in Delaware? Which is the better result? Should it depend upon whether or not liability insurance is available to pay the judgment?

(2)   As *Huang* and *Broadbent* suggest, the parental immunity doctrine has been abrogated or limited almost everywhere. A 1996 compilation indicated that it has been abolished (or never existed) in 35 states (including the District of Columbia), is limited to negligence actions in 12 states, and is in effect with exceptions in only 4 states. Karp and Karp, *Domestic Torts*, Family Law Series, January 1996 Cumulative Supplement.

(3)   Should immunity apply when a parent sues an unemancipated minor child, as when the child drives negligently and injures a parent passenger? Or when an unemancipated sibling injures an unemancipated sibling? For understandable reasons these actions have arisen much less frequently than have parental liability actions. *Ales v. Ales*, 650 So. 2d 484 (Miss. 1995), permitted an exception to the family immunity doctrine to permit a parent to sue an unemancipated child for injuries suffered by the parent in a motor vehicle crash to the same extent that its ruling in *Glaskox v. Glaskox*, 614 So. 2d 906 (Miss. 1992), had acknowledged an exception to the doctrine to permit an unemancipated child to sue a parent in motor vehicle cases. What is the rule in your state on these points?

(4)   Some courts have taken half-steps of abolishing interfamily immunities as to intentional torts, *see, e.g., Robinson v. Robinson*, 914 S.W.2d 292 (Ark. 1996) (immunity precludes a daughter's negligence claim against her mother for having failed to prevent her father from sexually abusing her but does not preclude an intentional tort claim against her father), or to the extent that liability insurance is available to indemnify the defendant family member. See, *e.g., Unah v. Martin*, 676 P.2d 1366 (Okla. 1984) (parental immunity waived to extent of insurance); *Ard v. Ard*, 414 So. 2d 1066 (Fla. 1982) (parental immunity waived to extent of insurance); and *Dorsey v. State Farm Mut. Auto. Ins. Co.*, 9 Ohio St. 2d 27, 457 N.E.2d 1169 (1984) (parental immunity does not bar action against estate of deceased parent and liability insurance carrier), but Oregon flatly rejected interjecting insurance into the liability issue. *Norwest v. Presbyterian Intercommunity Hospital*, 293 Or. 543, 552, 652 P.2d 318 (1982) ("A person's liability in our law still remains the same whether or not he has liability insurance; properly, the provision and cost of such insurance varies with potential liability under our law, not the law with the cost of insurance.") Instead, the Oregon Supreme Court adopted Restatement policies expressed as follows:

(1) A parent or child is not immune from tort liability to the other solely by reason of that relationship.

(2) Repudiation of general tort immunity does not establish liability for an act or omission that because of the parent-child relationship, is otherwise privileged or not tortious.

Restatement, Torts, Second § 895G (1979). Is this the same rule as applied in *Broadbent* note 1 *supra?* Is a parent's negligent driving a privileged act? If not, what is? *See Winn v. Gilroy*, 681 P.2d 776 (Or. 1984).

(5) Not everyone agrees with the abolition of parent-child immunity. For example, in *Balts v. Balts*, 142 N.W.2d 66 (Minn. 1966), Judge Sheran dissented from the abolition of parent child immunity reasoning:

> The effect of the majority opinion is to eliminate the doctrine of family immunity in actions for tort. Although the rule announced applies only to actions by a parent against a child, acceptance of the reasoning which supports this decision forecasts the end of immunity with respect to actions for damages incurred by a child and caused by the negligence of a parent, and suits for tort between husband and wife as well.
>
> I dissent from this determination because it represents a reversal, without adequate reason or compelling necessity, of long established law based upon significant considerations of public policy.
>
> It seems to me that before changing the rule with respect to suits of this kind, there are a number of questions, some involving social mores and others economic considerations, which should be answered, including these:
>
> > (1) Are there significant numbers among the people of this state who, apart from the exigencies of a particular case in which they may at the moment be involved, feel that the social interest is advanced by encouraging litigation between members of the same family?
> >
> > (2) To what extent do people who have been injured in accidents consider themselves deprived of justice because of our rule which forbids the use of the courts to recover money damages from their children, or their parents, or their spouses?
> >
> > (3) Given a choice, would people generally prefer to insure against loss occasioned by accidents of this kind through forms of insurance which provide benefits without the necessity of proving fault on the part of a family member?
> >
> > (4) To what extent is it presently the practice on the part of those obtaining liability insurance to avail themselves of the advantage of lower premium rates by securing coverage which does not apply to members of the same family residing in the same household, and what will be the effect of our decision in this case upon persons who prefer that kind of coverage?
> >
> > (5) To what extent will persons now immune from direct suit be exposed to claims for contribution on account of which their policies of liability insurance issued in reliance on our prior decisions afford no coverage?
> >
> > (6) Will the elimination of the doctrine of family immunity lead to collusive suits and simulated adversity? Will those scrupulously forthright in the courtroom and those who prefer not to sue their close relatives be compelled through higher insurance premiums to pay the bill for those not so restrained who may exploit the opportunities afforded by the rule now adopted?

(7) Is it good social policy to let members of the same family work out their problems between themselves? Or has the experience of our court system in dealing with sensitive domestic matters been so distinctively successful as to assure us that it is ready now to assume new responsibilities in this area? The fact that there are no certain answers to at least some of these questions in the scholarly majority opinion proves only that this court is not equipped to provide such answers.

(6) *Zellmer v. Zellmer*, 188 P.3d 497 (Wash. 2008) continued to apply parental immunity to negligence actions, but not those predicated on wilful or wanton misconduct. *Zellman* approved immunity for a step parent who was *in loco parentis* to an injured child, leaving a factual determination as to whether that status applied. Alexander, C. J., dissenting in part and concurring in part, gave this report on the status of parental immunity generally:

> The parental immunity doctrine, which we first recognized in *Roller v. Roller*, 37 Wash. 242, 79 P. 788 (1905), has heretofore applied only to a birth or adoptive parent (hereinafter parent). . . . This doctrine should not be extended to stepparents for several reasons. The first is that support for the general concept of parental immunity has been steadily eroding over the last several decades in jurisdictions around the nation. We noted this very point over 25 years ago. . . . , saying: "The trend of many modern cases is to limit or entirely abolish parental immunity." Indeed, the highest courts in six jurisdictions, Hawaii, Nevada, North Dakota, Utah, Vermont, and the District of Columbia, declined to adopt the doctrine in the first place. Furthermore, courts of last resort in 11 states that once recognized the doctrine have subsequently abolished it. Of the remaining states where parental immunity is still recognized, many have limited the circumstances under which the doctrine can be applied by creating exceptions to its application. Finally, courts in four jurisdictions that recognize the parental immunity doctrine have explicitly refused to extend the same immunity to stepparents.

Id., 188 P.3d at 508, 509.

COWAN v. HOSPICE SUPPORT CARE, INC.
Supreme Court of Virginia
268 Va. 482, 603 S.E.2d 916 (2004)

Opinion by Justice BARBARA MILANO KEENAN.

In this appeal, we consider whether a plaintiff's claims of gross negligence and willful and wanton negligence against a charity are barred by the doctrine of charitable immunity.

For purposes of this appeal, the facts relevant to this issue of law and question of first impression are not in dispute. On July 9, 2001, the plaintiff, Ingrid H. Cowan, placed her mother, Ruth D. Hazelwood (the decedent), in Harbor House, a residential facility that provides temporary care for very ill persons when their primary caregiver seeks respite. Harbor House is operated by the defendant, Hospice Support Care, Inc. (Hospice), "a non-profit, non-medical volunteer hospice support corporation."

The decedent was bedridden and required the assistance of two persons to move her from her bed to a bedside commode. During the decedent's first night at Harbor House, a single volunteer lifted her from the bed. When the decedent's right leg became "caught" in the bed, the volunteer heard a loud "popping-cracking" noise in the leg. That evening, and for the remainder of the decedent's week-long stay at Harbor House, the decedent received morphine for pain in her leg, but she was not provided any other medical treatment.

Cowan returned to Harbor House on July 16, 2001. After she and her mother left the facility, Cowan discovered that the decedent's leg was swollen and that she appeared to be in pain. As a result, Cowan took the decedent to a nearby hospital emergency room. The decedent was diagnosed as having a shattered right femur, which required amputation of her leg above the knee. The decedent died four days later from complications resulting from the surgery.

Cowan filed an amended motion for judgment in the circuit court against Hospice alleging wrongful death of the decedent based on claims of simple negligence, gross negligence, willful and wanton negligence, and negligent hiring and retention. Upon consent of the parties, the circuit court dismissed the simple negligence count. Hospice filed a plea in bar of charitable immunity to the counts of gross negligence and willful and wanton negligence, and a demurrer to the negligent hiring and retention count. The circuit court sustained the plea in bar and demurrer and dismissed these remaining counts with prejudice. Among other things, the circuit court concluded that the charitable immunity doctrine barred recovery for acts or omissions of gross negligence and willful and wanton negligence. Cowan appeals.

On appeal, Cowan argues that this Court has not applied the charitable immunity doctrine to shield a charity from liability for acts of gross negligence or willful and wanton negligence. She asserts that because gross negligence and willful and wanton negligence are different in degree and kind from simple negligence, the charitable immunity doctrine should not be defined as including immunity for those more extreme acts. Cowan also contends that the charitable immunity doctrine should not be applied to acts of gross negligence or willful and wanton negligence because, in instances of such extreme conduct, the public's interest in encouraging charitable activities is outweighed by the need to deter such acts of "reckless and harmful behavior."

In response, Hospice argues that charities should be immune from liability for all degrees of negligence because the absence of such immunity would discourage them from performing their beneficial activities. Hospice asserts that this Court, in its prior decisions, has discussed charitable immunity from liability for negligence without specifically limiting that immunity to claims of simple negligence. Thus, Hospice contends, because gross negligence and willful and wanton negligence are simply different degrees of negligence, charitable immunity extends to shield charities from liability for those categories of negligent conduct as well.

Hospice also asserts that Code § 8.01-226.4, which effectively subjects hospice volunteers to liability for acts of gross negligence and willful and wanton negligence, is evidence of the General Assembly's intent to shield charities from similar liability by providing*486 a remedy against the individuals who actually commit such acts.[70] We disagree with Hospice's arguments.

Under the doctrine of limited immunity applied to charities in this Commonwealth, a charitable institution is immune from liability to its beneficiaries for negligence caused by acts or omissions of its servants and agents, provided that the charity has exercised due care in their selection and retention. *Straley v. Urbanna Chamber of Commerce*, 243 Va. 32, 35, 413 S.E.2d 47, 49 (1992); . . . While this immunity shields a charity from claims made by its beneficiaries, the immunity does not extend to protect the charity from claims made by persons who have no beneficial relationship to the charity but are merely invitees or strangers. . . .

We adopted this doctrine of limited charitable immunity based on public policy considerations. *Moore v. Warren*, 250 Va. 421, 424, 463 S.E.2d 459, 460 (1995), . . . *Weston v. Hospital of St. Vincent*, 131 Va. 587, 609–10, 107 S.E. 785, 792 (1921). These considerations rest on the premise that the services charities extend to their beneficiaries also benefit the public by alleviating a public burden. . . . When charities are required to expend funds to litigate negligence claims, the charities' ability to perform services for their beneficiaries is restricted. . . .

These public policy considerations provide the framework for resolving the issue before us. In deciding this question, we focus on the nature of the conduct involved in the differing degrees of negligence and the extent to which each type of conduct deviates from the role of charities and their contribution to the public welfare.

As our decisions have recognized, there are three levels of negligence. The first level, simple negligence, involves the failure to use the degree of care that an ordinarily prudent person would exercise under similar circumstances to avoid injury to another. . . . The second level, gross negligence, is a degree of negligence showing indifference to another and an utter disregard of prudence that amounts to a complete neglect of the safety of such other person. This requires a degree of negligence that would shock fair-minded persons, although demonstrating something less than willful recklessness. . . .

The third level of negligent conduct is willful and wanton negligence. This conduct is defined as "acting consciously in disregard of another person's rights or acting with reckless indifference to the consequences, with the defendant aware, from his knowledge of existing circumstances and conditions, that his conduct probably would cause injury to another." *Etherton v. Doe*, 268 Va. 209, 213–14, 597 S.E.2d 87, 90 (2004). . . .

As these definitions illustrate, there are fundamental distinctions separating acts or omissions of simple negligence from those of gross negligence and willful and wanton negligence. When we consider these distinctions in the context of the charitable immunity doctrine, their differing applications to the doctrine become apparent.

Acts or omissions of simple negligence may occur routinely in the performance of the activities of any charitable organization. Employees or volunteers, in carrying out their duties, may fail to understand or to adequately follow

---

[70] [Fn.2 in the opinion.] Hospice additionally argues that even if it can be sued for gross negligence or willful and wanton negligence, Cowan has failed to plead sufficient facts to state a claim for either. However, we do not consider this argument because the circuit court did not rule on the sufficiency of the facts pleaded in the amended motion for judgment. Thus, the issue is not before us in this appeal.

instructions of a supervisor, may exercise poor judgment, or may have a lapse in attention to an assigned task. While serious consequences may result from these deficiencies in performance, they ordinarily do not involve an extreme departure from the charity's routine actions in conducting its activities.

In contrast, gross negligence involves conduct that "shocks fair-minded people," and willful and wanton negligence involves such recklessness that the actor is aware that his conduct probably would cause injury to another. *Etherton*, 268 Va. at 213–14, 597 S.E.2d at 900;. . . . Thus, unlike simple negligence, these two levels of negligence are characterized by conduct that represents an unusual and marked departure from the routine performance of a charity's activities.

As a practical matter, a charity's performance of its mission may be thwarted by litigation directed at the charity's failure to perform its activities in accordance with standards of ordinary care. For this reason, our Commonwealth's public policy in favor of promoting the activities of charitable organizations has been employed to shield charities from liability for their acts of simple negligence.

This rationale, however, is inapplicable to conduct involving gross negligence and willful and wanton negligence. Unlike acts or omissions giving rise to claims of simple negligence, such conduct can never be characterized as an attempt, albeit ineffectual, to carry out the mission of the charity to serve its beneficiaries. Therefore, we conclude that the public policy rationale that shields a charity from liability for acts of simple negligence does not extend to acts of gross negligence and willful and wanton negligence.

This conclusion does not represent a departure from our often-stated preference for legislative rather than judicial action to "abolish or relax" the charitable immunity doctrine. Instead, our present holding, like several of our earlier decisions, serves to define the contours of the doctrine with regard to a subject we have not previously addressed. See, e.g., *Moore*, 250 Va. at 424, 463 S.E.2d at 460–61 (volunteer of charity is immune from liability to charity's beneficiaries while engaged in performance of charity's work); *Straley*, 243 Va. at 37, 413 S.E.2d at 50–51 (community member only generally served by charity is not beneficiary); *Weston*, 131 Va. at 610, 107 S.E. at 792 (one who pays for charity's services can be beneficiary of charity).

We also observe that our holding today is consistent with the General Assembly's enactment of Code § 8.01-226.4. That statute provides civil immunity for the acts or omissions of hospice volunteers who render care to terminally ill patients, provided that the volunteers act in good faith and in the absence of gross negligence or willful misconduct. In enacting this section, the General Assembly has expressed a clear preference for excluding from the protection of charitable immunity acts or omissions of gross negligence and willful misconduct.

For these reasons, we conclude that the circuit court erred in sustaining the defendant's plea of charitable immunity to Counts II and III of Cowan's amended motion for judgment. We will reverse the circuit court's judgment and remand the case for further proceedings consistent with the principles expressed in this opinion.

Reversed and remanded.

NOTES AND QUESTIONS

(1)   Not every organization that claims to be a charity is entitled to immunity. The Virginia Supreme Court has applied a ten-factor test to ascertain entitlement:

(1) Does the entity's charter limit the entity to a charitable or eleemosynary purpose?

(2) Does the entity's charter contain a not-for- profit limitation?

(3) Is the entity's financial purpose to break even or earn a profit?.

(4) Does the entity in fact earn a profit and, if so, how often does that occur?.

(5) If the entity earns a profit (a surplus beyond expenses) must that be used for a charitable purpose?

(6) Does the entity depend on contributions and donations for a substantial portion of its existence?

(7) Is the entity exempt from federal income tax and/or local real estate tax?

(8) Does the entity's provision of services take into consideration a person's ability to pay for such services?

(9) Does the entity have stockholders or others with an equity stake in its capital?

(10) Are the directors and officers of the entity compensated and, if so, on what basis?

Ola v. YMCA of South Hampton Roads, Inc., 621 S.E.2d 70, 73, n.1 (Va. 2005). Applying these tests, the Virginia court determined that a not-for-profit corporation that was created to improve the billing and collection processes of physicians at the University of Virginia Medical Center was not entitled to the immunity. *University of Virginia Health Services Foundation v. Morris ex rel. Morris*, 657 S.E.2d 512 (Va.2008)

(2)   English and American courts once deemed charitable corporations (though not charitable individuals) to be immune from torts committed in rendering institutional charitable acts — for example, malpractice in the rendering of hospital services. The so-called rule of charitable immunity has been abrogated or severely restricted in a large number of jurisdictions. *See Howle v. Camp Amon Carter*, 470 S.W.2d 629, 630 (Tex.1971) (abolished common-law doctrine of charitable immunity and held that a charitable enterprise is subject to vicarious liability under the same rule applicable to business organizations operated for profit); *Brown v. Anderson County Hosp. Assoc.*, 234 S.E.2d 873 (1977) (modified doctrine of charitable immunity to make charitable hospitals liable only for heedless and reckless acts). *See also President & Directors of Georgetown College v. Hughes*, 130 F.2d 810 (D.C. Cir. 1942), for a history and criticism of charitable immunity. *See also Albritton v. Neighborhood Centers Ass'n. for Child Development*, 466 N.E.2d 867(Ohio 1984). *But see Abramson v. Reiss*, 638 A.2d 743, 750 (Md. 1994) ("the doctrine of charitable immunity remains alive, and reasonably well in Maryland, despite its fall into disfavor elsewhere in the country"), and *Sowders v. St. Joseph's Mercy Health Center*, 368 Ark. 466, 247 S.W.3d 514 (Ark. 2007) (held that the doctrine of

charitable immunity was not unconstitutional, declined to abolish it, but called on the legislature to consider whether the doctrine should be abolished.

The doctrine does not preclude an action against an employee of a charity, *Moore v. Warren*, 463 S.E.2d 459 (Va. 1995) (a case of first impression holding that volunteer workers who carry out the charity's work are also immune.) In some jurisdictions, immunity statutes have been enacted to encourage designated volunteer activities, *see, e.g., Szarzynsti v. YMCA*, 517 N.W.2d 135 (Wis.1994) (statute provided immunity to landowners who opened land for recreational uses). In at least one jurisdiction, judicial abrogation of immunity was followed by partial legislative restoration. *See Harvey v. Ocowee Memorial Hospital*, 416 S.E.2d 623 (S.C. 1992).

Chapter 10

DAMAGES

§ 10.01 PERSONAL INJURY

[A] Elements of Recovery

PROBLEM

Tom was a 24-year-old male, newly married with plans for starting a family. He was handsome, athletic, a college graduate, and employed as a well-paid junior manager by an international computer firm. As a result of the defendant's negligence, Tom suffered severe physical injuries. He was hospitalized for eight months, during which he underwent a series of surgical procedures and hours of physical and occupational therapy. His injuries rendered him a permanent quadriplegic with no ability to walk or sit upright. He has no bowel or bladder control, is sexually impotent, and has but limited use of his extremities. He cannot perspire below the neck. He is on continual medication and constant prophylactic care must be taken to guard against respiratory and urinary tract infection and breakdown of skin tissue. He is unable to bathe, shave, or groom his hair and cannot be left alone for any extended period of time. The future will be the same. Tom lives in fear that his wife will abandon him, and he feels degraded by need of intimate bodily care.

Tom's employer continued to pay his wages for one year, then stopped. Tom's health insurance company paid $100,000 of the $200,000 medical costs accrued the first year. Tom's mother has provided him with personal nursing care for the four months he has been at home since his discharge from the hospital.

What losses has Tom suffered that can be recompensed by money damages? What specific elements of loss should be considered? How are the losses to be proved? How is the loss to be evaluated in dollars?

RUSH v. SEARS, ROEBUCK AND CO.
New York Supreme Court, Appellate Division
92 A.D.2d 1072, 461 N.Y.S.2d 559 (1983)

Before MAHONEY, P.J., and CASEY, WEISS, LEVINE and SWEENEY, JJ.

MEMORANDUM DECISION.

Appeal from a judgment of the Supreme Court in favor of plaintiffs, entered January 4, 1982 in Albany County, upon a verdict rendered at Trial Term.

On April 29, 1973, a tent that had been sold by defendant in 1966 caught fire in the yard where it had been set up for the use and enjoyment of the neighborhood children. Alone in the tent when the fire started, Bobbie Jo Rush, a little girl then aged five, sustained third-degree burns over 95% of her body, resulting in her death 15 days later. Her older sister, Donna Rush, a plaintiff herein, entered the tent in an attempt to rescue Bobbie Jo and suffered second and third-degree burns over approximately 42% of her body, resulting in long and painful periods of hospitalization and treatment, skin grafting, debridement, permanently disfiguring scars and excruciating pain and suffering. The cause of the fire was never definitely determined. Opinions ranged from the improper use of a hibachi that was said to have been used inside for cooking and warming purposes, to the discovery of lighter fluid cans in the area after the fire. In any event, plaintiffs did not attempt to prove the cause of the fire but relied in theory on the failure of defendant to treat the tent with any kind of fire retardancy, knowing it would be used and occupied by persons for living and recreational purposes.

After a trial, a jury awarded $300,000 to plaintiff Lloyd T. Rush, as administrator of the estate of Bobbie Jo, and $4,000,000 to Donna, who is now sui generis, as well as $12,265.35 for medical expenses incurred on behalf of both girls. There is no argument concerning the award for medical expenses. The excessiveness of the awards of $4,000,000 and $300,000 is the principal reason for reversal raised by defendant on this appeal.

We hold that the award of $300,000 made to plaintiffs in the conscious pain and suffering action brought on behalf of Bobbie Jo is not excessive and should be sustained. In our opinion, such an award is not disproportionate to the community and judicial consensus of prior cases (see Senko v. Fonda, 53 A.D.2d 638, 639, 384 N.Y.S.2d) or shocking to the conscience of the court (Petosa v. City of New York, 63 A.D.2d 1016, 1016–17, 406 N.Y.S.2d 354). Nor is there indication that passion, partiality, prejudice or some other improper motive led the jury astray (Jennings v. Van Schaick, 13 Daly 7, 8–9) in awarding such amount on behalf of a five-year-old girl who received third-degree burns over almost her entire body which caused her death 15 days later. Accordingly, the verdict of $300,000 to plaintiffs on behalf of Bobbie Jo should be sustained.

As to the $4,000,000 award to Donna, however, we are of the view that it is excessive, and that the remarks of plaintiffs' counsel in his summation contributed to the excessiveness as discussed ante. Conceding and considering the nature and extent of the injuries received by Donna, the terrible pain and suffering, past, present and future, which attends those injuries, the hospitalization and treatments necessitated by such injuries, their permanency, their disfigurement of a girl who was just entering puberty, and the psychological and emotional impact inflicted by such injuries, we are unable to sustain a verdict in the amount of $4,000,000. Despite the severity of her injuries, and in no way minimizing their gravity, Donna was able to return to school in September following the fire and was a student at the State University at Brockport studying computer science and math at the time of trial. She sings in her college choir and with several area dance bands. She was employed at Sherman's Amusement Park on Caroga Lake during the summer before trial. She is not bedridden, shut in, or in need of constant custodial care, or helpless. She is able to attend to her own needs and her mental faculties remain unimpaired. She is an active member of society and will be able to pursue gainful employment when she completes her education.

In these circumstances, we are of the opinion that $1,500,000 would more realistically represent fair and just compensation for the injuries she sustained. This conclusion is reached with some consideration of the reduction of the award made by us in Caprara v. Chrysler Corp., 71 A.D.2d 515, 423 N.Y.S.2d 694, affd. 52 N.Y.2d 114, 436 N.Y.S.2d 251, 417 N.E.2d 545, where a verdict of $3,600,000 in favor of a young man rendered a quadriplegic was reduced to $2,000,000. Furthermore, we find no authority in which similar injuries approximated an award of $4,000,000 (see Broder, Trial Tactics, Techniques, NYLJ, Feb. 10, 1983, p. 1, col. 1, and authorities cited therein).

. . .

Finally, contrary to defendant's claim, plaintiffs' attorney's summation does not require reversal. Inasmuch as no objection was taken to the summation, this court may reverse only in the interests of justice (Martin v. City of Cohoes, 37 N.Y.2d 162, 165, 371 N.Y.S.2d 687, 332 N.E.2d 867). Under this standard, the summation is not so prejudicial as to require unconditional reversal. Certain statements of plaintiffs' counsel on summation, however, may well have contributed to the verdict's excessiveness, especially the statement, repeated 12 times, that defendant, seated in its industrial "tower", selected a non-flame retardant fabric to save a trifling five cents a yard. Plaintiffs' counsel also disclosed to the jury the amounts demanded by plaintiffs as damages in the complaint, which were the amounts that the jury awarded after only 63 minutes of deliberation. Such disclosure, however, was permissible and the Trial Judge promptly and properly instructed the jury not to use those figures in determining damages, but to reach a figure based on the evidence and the jury's judgment (Tate v. Colabello, 58 N.Y.2d 84, 87, 459 N.Y.S.2d 422, 445 N.E.2d 1011; Rice v. Ninacs, 34 A.D.2d 388, 392, 312 N.Y.S.2d 246). Although the comments of plaintiff's counsel do not require unconditional reversal, we cannot say that the comments did not contribute in some degree to the excessiveness of the verdict (see Kusisto v. McLean, 52 A.D.2d 674, 382 N.Y.S.2d 146).

. . .

Judgment modified, on the law and the facts, by reversing so much thereof as awarded plaintiff Donna Rush $4,000,000, and a new trial ordered only with respect to the issue of damages that were awarded plaintiff Donna Rush, unless, within 20 days after the service of a copy of the order to be entered herein, plaintiff Donna Rush shall stipulate to reduce the amount of the verdict in her favor to $1,500,000, in which event, the judgment, as so reduced; is affirmed with costs to plaintiffs.

MAHONEY, P.J., and CASEY, WEISS and LEVINE, JJ., concur.

SWEENEY, Justice (concurring in part and dissenting in part).

I regret that I am unable to fully agree with the result reached by the majority. While my disagreement is a narrow one, it is, I believe, significant, necessitating a brief explanation. Where, as here, the court is to sustain the verdict on the issues of liability but concludes that the verdict is excessive and recommends a 62% reduction in the damages, I am of the view that the better procedure is to remand for retrial on the question of damages. To adopt the majority's method unfairly deprives plaintiff Donna Rush of her entitlement to a jury assessment of damages.

NOTES AND QUESTIONS

(1)   Are you satisfied that the court had the power to reduce the amount of damages as determined by the jury? Does this interfere with the right of trial by jury? Like many states, West Virginia has a state constitutional provision, quoted in the excerpt below, modelled after the Seventh Amendment to the United States Constitution. In *Addair v. Majectic Petroleum Co. Inc.*, 232 S.E.2d 821 (W. Va. 1977), the court made reference to that provision and approved a challenged jury verdict with the following admonition to the courts:

[First, the court quoted the common law rule, as follows:]

We desire to be understood that this Court does not say, or lay down any rule that there never can happen a case of such excessive damages in tort where the Court may not grant a new trial; but in that case the damages must be monstrous and enormous indeed, and such as all mankind must be ready to exclaim against, at first blush. Beardmore v. Carrington, 2 Wilson, K.B. 244, 250, 95 Eng. Rep. 790, 793, (1764).

[Then the court criticized judicial interference with jury verdicts, as follows:]

The books are full of attempts by this and other courts to carefully review trial records to determine whether trial judges should have set aside jury verdicts as excessive. Implicit in all these cases is the substitution of judges' judgment about the amount that should have been awarded for the judgment of juries. . . .

We are thus brought to the nub of the matter of setting aside "excessive" verdicts and awarding new trials: Are there state and federal constitutional restrictions that prohibit court's interference with jury verdicts claimed to be excessive? . . .

Our own state constitution restates the federal constitution's Seventh Amendment prohibition against reexamination of facts tried by juries. Article 3, Section 13 prescribes that "No fact tried by a jury shall be otherwise reexamined in any case than according to the rules of the common law." However, this court has never decided an excessive jury verdict case upon the constitutional basis. . . .

The first West Virginia decision dealing with the question was Sweeney v. Baker, 13 W.Va. 158 (1878). . . . Sweeney introduced into West Virginia law the [following] words of Chief Justice Kent [quoted from Coleman v. Southwick, 9 Johns 45, 52 (N.Y. 1812)] which seem to be the basis for the American rule about award of new trials because of excessive jury verdicts:

. . . The damages, therefore, must be so excessive as to strike mankind, at first blush, as being beyond all measure, unreasonable and outrageous, and such as manifestly show the jury to have been actuated by passion, partiality, prejudice, or corruption. In short, the damages must be flagrantly outrageous and extravagant, or the court cannot undertake to draw the line; for they have no standard by which to ascertain the excess. The common law recognized that a different rationale was applicable to determine courts' authority to interfere with jury verdicts where the damages were readily ascertainable, and courts' authority to interfere with verdicts where the damages were indeterminate. When the amount was capable of exact proof, and thus left nothing for the jury to have opinion about, the courts did not hesitate to adjust the verdicts to the proved damages.

. . .

The courts then and now have never hesitated to correct mistaken verdicts where sums certain were involved. Some of our cases . . . have stated that "mistake" was a basis for reducing excess verdicts where indeterminate damages were being tested. These seem incorrect based upon our examination of the common law precedents. Every adjective and phrase Kent used to describe the excessiveness necessary to be present in a verdict to allow judicial interference, came from the English cases he cited. And in addition we found "monstrous" in Beardmore, a word we particularly admire and recommend to our brethren to encourage their restraint in setting aside verdicts claimed to be too large. Through the years courts have emasculated the common law interdiction. Now all that remains is the "mealy-mouth" caution against setting aside a verdict unless it indicates that the jury was influenced by passion, partiality, prejudice or corruption, or entertained a mistaken view of the case. . . .

How meek and mild has become the rule since Kent first proclaimed it, using as his precedent the common law to which our federal and state constitutions refer us! We believe too much of the force has been lost from the original admonitions in the old cases and that the constitutions require us not to interfere with jury verdicts claimed to be excessive where the amount is in Kent's words a "matter of opinion," 9 Johns. at 52, unless the verdict is monstrous and enormous, at first blush beyond all measure, unreasonable and outrageous, and such as manifestly shows jury passion, partiality, prejudice, or corruption. This rule is no more objective than our former mild-mannered measure. Affixing it to the constitutions and returning the heady language that was originally its expression, does not of course remove the final judgment from the judges. But we are hereby admonishing our judges and ourselves, in the same manner as did Lord Camden in Beardmore, not to interfere in the jury's domain except with extreme reluctance. The constitutional scriveners did not repose in the bench the responsibility for finding facts, but in the peers of those seeking justice.

Most state constitutions do not include the provision pertaining to judicial review of facts found by juries adopted in the United States and West Virginia constitutions, which means that federal judges are more restricted than state judges in most states in this regard. Nevertheless, *Gasperini v. Center for Humanities, Inc.*, 116 S. Ct. 2211, 135 L.Ed.2d 659 (1996), held that federal courts might apply the New York practice that permits judges to overturn jury verdicts on excessiveness grounds if the verdicts "deviate materially from what would be reasonable compensation" when the federal jury was deciding an issue under New York state law.

(2) A more typical approach was employed in *Junior Food Stores, Inc. v. Rice*, 671 So. 2d 67 (Miss. 1996), as follows:

> A court in Mississippi can disturb a jury verdict if the court finds that the damages are excessive or inadequate for the reason that the jury was influenced by bias, prejudice, or passion, so as to shock the conscience or that the damages awarded were contrary to the overwhelming weight of credible evidence. . . . This Court is not authorized to disturb a jury verdict as to damages because it "seems too high" or "seems too low." . . .

> It matters not that some members of this Court, had they been sitting as triers of fact, probably would have assessed damages at a lower amount, because this Court reviews jury awards within the constraints of rules of

law. . . . Rather, the question is whether considering the evidence in the light most favorable to [the plaintiff], together with all reasonable inferences which may be drawn there-from, this Court can say that no reasonable jury could, on the facts in this case, have concluded that [the plaintiff's] damages were in the amount [fixed by the jury].

(3)   Is there a systematic difference that matters in the two approaches? As applied to the principal case?

HELFEND v. SOUTHERN CALIFORNIA RAPID TRANSIT DISTRICT
California Supreme Court
2 Cal. 3d 1, 84 Cal. Rptr. 173, 465 P.2d 61 (1970)

TOBRINER, ACTING CHIEF JUSTICE.

Defendants appeal from a judgment of the Los Angeles Superior Court entered on a verdict in favor of plaintiff, Julius J. Helfend, for $16,400 in general and special damages for injuries sustained in a bus-auto collision that occurred on July 19, 1965, in the City of Los Angeles.

We have concluded that the judgment for plaintiff in this tort action against the defendant governmental entity should be affirmed. The trial court properly followed the collateral source rule in excluding evidence that a portion of plaintiff's medical bills had been paid through a medical insurance plan that requires the refund of benefits from tort recoveries.

1. The facts

Shortly before noon on July 19, 1965, plaintiff drove his car in central Los Angeles east on Third Street approaching Grandview. At this point Third Street has six lanes, four for traffic and one parking lane on each side of the thoroughfare. While traveling in the second lane from the curb, plaintiff observed an automobile driven by Glen A. Raney, Jr., stopping in his lane and preparing to back into a parking space. Plaintiff put out his left arm to signal the traffic behind him that he intended to stop; he then brought his vehicle to a halt so that the other driver could park.

At about this time Kenneth A. Mitchell, a bus driver for the Southern California Rapid Transit District, pulled out of a bus stop at the curb of Third Street and headed in the same direction as plaintiff. Approaching plaintiff's and Raney's cars which were stopped in the second lane from the curb, Mitchell pulled out into the lane closest to the center of the street in order to pass. The right rear of the bus sideswiped plaintiff's vehicle, knocking off the rearview mirror and crushing plaintiff's arm, which had been hanging down at the side of his car in the stopping signal position.

An ambulance took plaintiff to Central Receiving Hospital for emergency first aid treatment. Upon release from the hospital plaintiff proceeded to consult Dr. Saxon, an orthopedic specialist, who sent plaintiff immediately to the Sherman Oaks Community Hospital where he received treatment for about a week. Plaintiff underwent physical therapy for about six months in order to regain normal use of his left arm and hand. He acquired some permanent discomfort but no permanent disability from the injuries sustained in the accident. At the time of the injury plaintiff was 67 years of age and had a life expectancy of about 11 years. He owned the Jewel Homes Investment Company which possessed and maintained small rental properties. Prior to the accident plaintiff had performed much of the minor maintenance on his properties including some painting and minor plumbing. For the six-month healing period he hired a man to do all the work he had formerly performed and at the time of the trial still employed him for such work as he himself could not undertake.

Plaintiff filed a tort action against the Southern California Rapid Transit District, a public entity, and Mitchell, an employee of the transit district. At trial plaintiff claimed slightly more than $2,700 in special damages, including $921 in doctor's bills, a $336.99 hospital bill, and about $45 for medicines.[1] Defendant requested permission to show that about 80 percent of the plaintiff's hospital bill had been paid by plaintiff's Blue Cross insurance carrier and that some of his other medical expenses may have been paid by other insurance. The superior court thoroughly considered the then very recent case of City of Salinas v. Souza & McCue Construction Company (1967) 66 Cal. 2d 217, 57 Cal. Rptr. 337, 424 P.2d 921, distinguished the Souza case on the ground that Souza involved a contract setting, and concluded that the judgment should not be reduced to the extent of the amount of insurance payments which plaintiff received. The court ruled that defendants should not be permitted to show that plaintiff had received medical coverage from any collateral source.

After the jury verdict in favor of plaintiff in the sum of $16,300, defendants appealed, raising only two contentions: (1) The trial court committed prejudicial error in refusing to allow the introduction of evidence to the effect that a portion of the plaintiff's medical bills had been paid from a collateral source. (2) The trial court erred in denying defendant the opportunity to determine if plaintiff had been compensated from more than one collateral source for damages sustained in the accident.

We must decide whether the collateral source rule applies to tort actions involving public entities and public employees in which the plaintiff has received benefits from his medical insurance coverage.

2. The collateral source rule

The Supreme Court of California has long adhered to the doctrine that if an injured party receives some compensation for his injuries from a source wholly independent of the tortfeasor, such payment should not be deducted from the damages which the plaintiff would otherwise collect from the tortfeasor. (See, e.g., Peri v. Los Angeles Junction Ry. Co. (1943) 22 Cal. 2d 111, 131, 137 P.2d 441.) As recently as August 1968 we unanimously reaffirmed our adherence to this doctrine, which is known as the "collateral source rule.". . . .

Although the collateral source rule remains generally accepted in the United States, nevertheless many other jurisdictions[2] have restricted[3] or repealed it. In

---

[1] The plaintiff claimed special damages of $2,737.99 of which $1,302.99 represented medical expenses, $35 repair of plaintiff's watch, about $1,350 expenses and costs incurred as a result of hiring another man to do the work plaintiff normally performed, and $50 plaintiff's share of the automobile repair costs.

[2] After a period in which it appeared that the courts of the United Kingdom, the country of the rule's

this country most commentators have criticized the rule and called for its early demise. In Souza we took note of the academic criticism of the rule, characterized the rule as "punitive," and held it inapplicable to the governmental entity involved in that case.

[Souza was a breach of contract case. Certain payments made by a supplier to the contractor- plaintiff were set off against the liability of the city-defendant.]

We held that the trial court improperly determined damages against the city by refusing to allow the city to show that the supplier had recompensed Souza for some of the damages caused by the city's breach. In this contract setting in which the supplier did not constitute a wholly independent collateral source,[4] we held that the collateral source rule cannot be applied against public entities because the collateral source rule appears punitive in nature and punitive damages cannot be imposed on public entities.

Although Souza's reasoning as to punitive damages might appear to apply to private tortfeasors as well as public entities and to torts as well as contract actions, we did not there consider the collateral source rule in contexts different from the specific contractual setting and particular relationship of the parties involved. We distinguish the present case from Souza on the ground that in Souza the plaintiff received payments from his subcontractor which, in the contractual setting of that case, did not constitute a truly independent source. Obviously, such a "source" differs entirely from the instant one, which derives from plaintiff's payment of insurance premiums. Here plaintiff received benefits from his medical insurance coverage only because he had long paid premiums to obtain them. Such an origin does constitute a completely independent source. Hence, although we affirm the holding in Souza, we do not believe that its reasoning either compels the abolition of the collateral source rule in all cases or requires an unwarranted exemption

---

origin, would disavow it (see Browning v. War Office (1963) 1 Q.B. 750), the House of Lords in Parry v. Cleaver (1969) 2 W.L.R. 821, has recently reaffirmed the rule and applied it to a case of a tort victim who, following the automobile accident in which he was disabled, received a pension. (See Bradburn v. Great Western Ry. (1874) L.R. 10 Ex. I; Atiyah, Collateral Benefits Again (1969) 32 Mod. L. Rev. 397.) Most other western European nations have repudiated the rule. (See Fleming, The Collateral Source Rule and Loss Allocation in Tort Law, supra, 54 Cal. L. Rev. 1478, 1480–1484, 1516–1523, 1535–1540.)

[3] The New York Court of Appeals has, for example, quite reasonably held that an injured physician may not recover from a tortfeasor for the value of medical and nursing care rendered gratuitously as a matter of professional courtesy. (See Coyne v. Campbell (1962) 11 N.Y.2d 372, 230 N.Y.S.2d 1, 183 N.E.2d 891.) The doctor owed at least a moral obligation to render gratuitous services in return, if ever required; but he had neither paid premiums for the services under some form of insurance coverage nor manifested any indication that he would endeavor to repay those who had given him assistance. Thus this situation differs from that in which friends and relatives render assistance to the injured plaintiff with the expectation of repayment out of any tort recovery; in that case, the rule has been applied.

. . . On the other hand, New York has joined most states in holding that a tortfeasor may not mitigate damages by showing that an injured plaintiff would receive a disability pension. . . . In these cases the plaintiff had actually or constructively paid for the pension by having received lower wages or by having contributed directly to the pension plan.

[4] In Laurenzi v. Vranzian (1945) 25 Cal. 2d 806, 813, 155 P.2d 633, 637, this court held that "payments by one tortfeasor on account of a harm for which he and another are each liable, diminish the amount of the claim against the other whether or not it was so agreed at the time of payment and whether the payment was made before or after judgment. Since the plaintiff can have but one satisfaction, evidence of such payments is admissible for the purpose of reducing pro tanto the amount of the damages he may be entitled to recover." Hence, the rule applies only to payments that come from a source entirely independent of the tortfeasor and does not apply to payments by joint tortfeasors or to benefits the plaintiff receives from a tortfeasor's insurance coverage.

from the rule of public entities and their employees involved in tort actions. Souza does not even suggest that public employees should be charged with the extra liability which an exemption for public entities might imply.

The collateral source rule as applied here embodies the venerable concept that a person who has invested years of insurance premiums to assure his medical care should receive the benefits of his thrift. The tortfeasor should not garner the benefits of his victim's providence.

The collateral source rule expresses a policy judgment in favor of encouraging citizens to purchase and maintain insurance for personal injuries and for other eventualities. Courts consider insurance a form of investment, the benefits of which become payable without respect to any other possible source of funds. If we were to permit a tortfeasor to mitigate damages with payments from plaintiff's insurance, plaintiff would be in a position inferior to that of having bought no insurance, because his payment of premiums would have earned no benefit. Defendant should not be able to avoid payment of full compensation for the injury inflicted merely because the victim has had the foresight to provide himself with insurance.

Some commentators object that the above approach to the collateral source rule provides plaintiff with a "double recovery," rewards him for the injury, and defeats the principle that damages should compensate the victim but not punish the tortfeasor. We agree with Professor Fleming's observation, however, that "double recovery is justified only in the face of some exceptional, supervening reason, as in the case of accident or life insurance, where it is felt unjust that the tortfeasor should take advantage of the thrift and prescience of the victim in having paid the premiums." (Fleming, Introduction of the Law of Torts (1967) p. 13i.) As we point out infra, recovery in a wrongful death action is not defeated by the payment of the benefit on a life insurance policy.

Furthermore, insurance policies increasingly provide for either subrogation or refund or benefits upon a tort recovery, and such refund is indeed called for in the present case. (See Fleming, The Collateral Source Rule and Loss Allocation in Tort Law, supra, 54 Cal. L. Rev. 1478, 1479.) Hence, the plaintiff receives no double recovery; the collateral source rule simply serves as a means of by-passing the antiquated doctrine of non-assignment of tortious actions and permits a proper transfer of risk from the plantiff's insurer to the tortfeasor by way of the victim's tort recovery. The double shift from the tortfeasor to the victim and then from the victim to the insurance carrrier normally occur with little cost in that the insurance carrier is often intimately involved in the initial litigation and quite automatically receives its part of the tort settlement or verdict.[5]

Even in cases in which the contract or the law precludes subrogation or refund of benefits, or in situations in which the collateral source waives such subrogation or refund, the rule performs entirely necessary functions in the computation of damages. For example, the cost of medical care often provides both attorneys and juries in tort cases with an important measure for assessing the plaintiff's general

---

[5] In personal injury cases in which the tort victim is unwilling to sue, subrogation subjects the tort victim to additional trouble and incurs further cost. A provision for refund of benefits, such as in the present case, avoids these difficulties by permitting the tort victim to decide whether to undertake litigation against the tortfeasor. (See Fleming, The Collateral Source Rule and Loss Allocation in Tort Law, supra, 54 Cal. L. Rev. 1478, 1526, 1536–1537.)

damages. . . . To permit the defendant to tell the jury that the plaintiff has been recompensed by a collateral source for his medical costs might irretrievably upset the complex, delicate, and somewhat indefinable calculations which result in the normal jury verdict.

. . .

We also note that generally the jury is not informed that plaintiff's attorney will receive a large portion of the plaintiff's recovery in contingent fees or that personal injury damages are not taxable to the plaintiff and are normally deductible by the defendant.[6] Hence, the plaintiff rarely actually receives full compensation for his injuries as computed by the jury. The collateral source rule partially serves to compensate for the attorney's share and does not actually render "double recovery" for the plaintiff. Indeed, many jurisdictions that have abolished or limited the collateral source rule have also established a means for assessing the plaintiff's costs for counsel directly against the defendant rather than imposing the contingent fee system.[7] In sum, the plaintiff's recovery for his medical expenses from both the tortfeasor and his medical insurance program will not usually give him "double recovery," but partially provides a somewhat closer approximation to full compensation for his injuries.[8]

If we consider the collateral source rule as applied here in the context of the entire American approach to the law of torts and damages, we find that the rule presently performs a number of legitimate and even indispensable functions. Without a thorough revolution in the American approach to torts and the consequent damages, the rule at least with respect to medical insurance benefits has become so integrated within our present system that its precipitous judicial nullification would work hardship. In this case the collateral source rule lies between two systems for the compensation of accident victims: the traditional tort

---

[6] Section 104(a) (2) of the Internal Revenue Code of 1954 (26 U.S.C. § 22(b) (5)) permits the tort victim to exclude from his gross income the amount of damages he receives from a tort verdict or settlement on account of his personal injuries or illness. (See generally, as to the tax consequences of tort cases, Guardino, Tax Aspects of Recoveries and Damages in Lawsuits (April-May 1969) 5 Trial 34.) The plaintiff who had been in a high tax bracket and who recovers for loss of earnings on a pretax basis is placed in a better position than if he had earned the same income. (See Note (1964) 77 Harv. L. Rev. 741, 747.) The United States Court of Appeals for the Second Circuit recently observed that:

> In "the great mass of litigation at the lower or middle reach of income scale, where future income is fairly predictable, added exemptions or deductions drastically affect the tax and . . . the plaintiff is almost certain to be under-compensated for loss of earning power in any event." The under compensation would arise from the erosion of the recovery due to the failure to award attorneys' fees, almost always high in this type of litigation because of their contingent nature, and to continuing inflation; . . . [I]n cases "at the opposite end of the income spectrum," failure to deduct for taxes would result in an award that "would be plainly excessive even after taking full account of the countervailing factors we have mentioned."

(*Petn. of Marina Mercante Nicaraguense, S.A.* (2d Cir. 1966 (Friendly, C.J.)) 364 F.2d 118, 125; . . .

[7] Under workmen's compensation subrogation normally prevents double recovery by shifting the loss to the tortfeasor.

. . .

[8] Of course, only in cases in which the tort victim has received payments or services from a collateral source will he be able to mitigate attorney's fees by means of the collateral source rule. Thus the rule provides at best only an incomplete and haphazard solution to providing all tort victims with full compensation. Depriving some tort victims of the salutary protections of the collateral source rule will, short of a thorough reform of our tort system, only decrease the available compensation for injuries. (See *McWeeney v. New York*, N. H. & H. R. R. Co., supra, 282 F.2d 34, 38; but cf. Schwartz, The Collateral Source Rule, supra, 41 B.U.L. Rev. 348, 351–352.)

recovery based on-fault and the increasingly prevalent coverage based on non-fault insurance. Neither system possesses such universality of coverage or completeness of compensation that we can easily dispense with the collateral source rule's approach to meshing the two systems. (Cf., e.g., Bilyeu v. State Employees' Retirement System (1962) 58 Cal. 2d 618, 629, 25 Cal. Rptr. 562, 375 P.2d 442 (concurring opn. of Peters, J.).) The reforms which many academicians propose cannot easily be achieved through piecemeal common law development; the proposed changes, if desirable, would be more effectively accomplished through legislative reform. In any case, we cannot believe that the judicial repeal of the collateral source rule, as applied in the present case, would be the place to begin the needed changes.

Although in the special circumstances of Souza we characterized the collateral source rule as "punitive" in nature, we have pointed out the several legitimate and fully justified compensatory functions of the rule. In fact, if the collateral source rule were actually punitive, it could apply only in cases of oppression, fraud, or malice and would be inapplicable to most tort, and almost all negligence, cases regardless of whether a governmental entity were involved. (See Civ. Code, § 3294; Note (1967) 55 Cal. L. Rev. 1059, 1165.) We therefore reaffirm our adherence to the collateral source rule in tort cases in which the plaintiff has been compensated by an independent collateral source — such as insurance, pension, continued wages, or disability payments — for which he had actually or constructively (see fns. 5 and 14, supra) paid or in cases in which the collateral source would be recompensed from the tort recovery through subrogation, refund of benefits, or some other arrangement. Hence, we conclude that in a case in which a tort victim has received partial compensation from medical insurance coverage entirely independent of the tortfeasor the trial court properly followed the collateral source rule and foreclosed defendant from mitigating damages by means of the collateral payments.

3. The collateral source rule, public entities, and public employees

Having concluded that the collateral source rule is not simply punitive in nature, we hold, for the reasons set out infra, that the rule as delineated here applies to government entities as well as to all other tortfeasors. We must therefore disapprove of any indications to the contrary in City of Salinas v. Souza & McCue Constr. Co., supra, 66 Cal. 2d 217, 226–228, 57 Cal. Rptr. 337, 424 P.2d 921.

Defendants would have this court create a special form of sovereign immunity as a novel exception to the collateral source rule for tortfeasors who are public entities or public employees. (Cf. Muskopf v. Corning Hosp. Dist. (1961) 55 Cal. 2d 211, 221, 11 Cal. Rptr. 89, 359 P.2d 457.) We see no justification for such special treatment. In the present case the nullification of the collateral source rule would simply frustrate the transfer of the medical costs from the medical insurance carrier, Blue Cross, to the public entity. The public entity or its insurance carrier is in at least as advantageous a position to spread the risk of loss as is the plaintiff's medical insurance carrier. To deprive Blue Cross of repayment for its expenditures on plaintiff's behalf merely because he was injured by a public entity rather than a private individual would constitute an unwarranted and arbitrary discrimination.

NOTES AND QUESTIONS

(1)   Elements of personal injury damages are initially categorized as either special or general damages. The division can be critical in both pleading and proof-making; generally, special damages must be specially pleaded and proved with particularity, whereas general damages need not be specially pleaded and are provable under more flexible evidential standards. The following statement of Fullagar, J. in *Paff v. Speed*, 105 C.L.R. 549 (High Court, Australia) succinctly sums up the distinctions:

> . . . it may be well, elementary though the subject may be, to begin by briefly stating what I conceive to be the general basis on which damages are awarded at common law for personal injuries. The orthodox direction to a jury in such begins, even though it may not use those very terms, by drawing and explaining a distinction between "special damages" and "general damages." Special damages are awarded in such cases in respect of monetary loss actually suffered and expenditure actually incurred. Their two characteristics are (1) that they are assessed only up to the date of verdict, and (2) that they are capable of precise arithmetical calculation or at least of being estimated with a close approximation to accuracy. The familiar examples are medical and surgical fees paid or payable, ambulance and hospital expenses, and loss of income. Where the plaintiff has been employed at a fixed wage or salary, his loss of income can commonly be calculated with exactness. Where the plaintiff has not been employed, but is, for example, a professional man, his monetary loss can be estimated without difficulty by reference to his past earnings. In a high proportion of cases, the amount of the "special damages" is agreed between counsel for the plaintiff and counsel for the defendant.
>
> "General damages" on the other hand, are, of their very nature, incapable of mathematical calculation, and (although the expression is apt to be misleading) commonly very much "at large." They are at large in the sense that a jury has, in serious cases, a wide discretion in assessing them. Also, general damages may be assessed not with reference to any limited period, but with reference to an indefinite future. Damages may be awarded for "pain and suffering" and such damages are assessable for past, present and future pain and suffering. But here calculation is obviously impossible, and damages for pain and suffering should clearly be regarded as "general" and not "special damages." In fact, the question of general damages is generally, I think, put to a jury under three heads (1) "economic loss", (2) loss of "amenities" or "enjoyment of life", and (3) pain and suffering.
>
> "Economic loss" may include expenditure (for, e.g., medical expenses) which it is shown that the plaintiff will probably incur in the future as a result of his injuries. But the major item of a claim under this head is usually put as "loss of wages" or "loss of income." It would be more accurately described as "loss of earning capacity." Actual loss of wages or loss of income will have been already taken into account in assessing special damages, and what the plaintiff must receive in respect of the future is compensation for total or partial incapacity to earn income. The whole system on which general damages are awarded is open to criticism, but the direction to a jury to award a lump sum is too well established to be now

challenged, and the awarding of periodical payments subject to review is, of course, quite impracticable.

(2)   Recovery for pain and suffering is both the most important and most controversial element of damages for personal injury. Many scholars deem it to be inappropriate mainly because pain and suffering bears no rational relationship to a true economic loss. See, e.g., J. O'Connell, A Proposal to Abolish Defendants' Payment for Pain and Suffering in Return for Payment of Claimants' Attorneys' Fees, 1981 Ill. L. Rev. 333 (1981); M. Plant, Damages for Pain and Suffering, 19 Ohio St. L. J. 200 (1958), Morris, Liability for Pain and Suffering, 59 Col. L. Rev. 476 (1959). Jaffe, Damages for Personal Injury: The Impact of Insurance, 18 Law & Contemp. Prob. 219 (1953) and Peck, Compensation for Pain: A Reappraisal in Light of New Medical Evidence, 72 Mich. L. Rev. 1355 (1974). Thus, according to this view, this element of recovery has no logical part in the compensatory theory of general tort recovery. That being the case, the argument is sometimes advanced that pain and suffering damages are punitive in character. What rejoinder does Helfend make to that?

Despite the scholarly criticism of it, all American courts permit pain and suffering recoveries. See, e.g., *Thompson v. National R.R. Passenger Corp.*, 621 F.2d 824 (6th Cir. 1980). Courts are happy to assume that pain and suffering has economic consequences. For example, in 1917, the North Carolina Supreme Court said, "As all pain is mental and centers in the brain, it follows that as an element of damage for personal injury the injured party is allowed to recover for actual suffering of mind and body when they are immediate and necessary consequences of the negligent injury." *Hargis v. Knoxville Power Co.*, 175 N.C. 31, 94 S.E. 702, 703 (1917). And, in 1955, the Minnesota Supreme Court added, "The reasonableness of an award for damages can be appraised only in the light of the elementary principle that plaintiff should be given neither more nor less than a sum which leaves him financially whole to the same extent as he would have been had not injury occurred." *Hallada v. Great Northern Ry.*, 244 Minn. 81, 69 N.W.2d 673, 686 (1955). Indeed, pain and suffering recovery is so well accepted that Professor Morris, in calling for reform, warned that "nothing in the public sense of justice challenges awards of damages for pain and suffering."

Is the public sense of justice offended by the award of $300,000 to the estate of Bobbie Jo Rush, the five-year-old who died after 15 days? Who will enjoy the use of the money? What about an award of $50,000 to an estate for ten hours of suffering by the decedent? See *Estate of King v. Aetna Cas. & Sur. Co.*, 427 So. 2d 902 (La. App. 3 1983). The award of $1.5 million to Donna Rush? What of an award of $6 million for the pain and suffering of Tom, whose injuries were described in the Problem beginning this section? See *City of Tamarac v. Garchar*, 398 So. 2d 889 (Fla. App. 1981). If the public would be offended, how do you account for the jury awards?

Somewhat surprisingly, whether or not plaintiffs are entitled to recover for loss of enjoyment of life as an element of recovery separate and distinct from physical and mental pain and suffering is not well developed in American law. See Loss of Enjoyment of Life — Should It Be a Compensable Element of Personal Injury Damages? 11 Wake Forest Law R. 459 (1975). For example, if two men are rendered quadriplegic, one in a permanent coma and the other perfectly aware of his condition, should one be permitted a larger recovery than the other? Thompson permitted a separate charge on this element. Another approach is to include the element in a general instruction, such as: "Plaintiff is entitled to recovery for pain and suffering resulting from bodily injury, disability, mental anguish and loss of capacity for the enjoyment for life experienced in the past or to be experienced in the future." *Powell v. Hegney*, 239 So. 2d 599, 600 (Fla. App. 1970). A third view, said by the foregoing law review commentary to be the minority view, is to deny recovery. See, e.g., *Hogan v. Santa Fe Trail Transportation Co.*, 85 P.2d 38 (Kans. 1938), and *Flannery v. United States*, 718 F.2d 108 (4th Cir. 1983) (holding that the Federal Tort Claims Act did not permit this element of recovery). British courts permit recovery for this element of loss, but only in the amount of a "conventional sum" that is small by standards of American pain and suffering recoveries. See, e.g., *Lim v. Camden Health Authority*, [1980] App. Cas. 182 (H.L.)

(3)   A late twentieth century reform movement made a determined and somewhat successful effort to "reform" tort law in a number of respects, including placing fixed statutory caps on the recovery of damages for pain and suffering. Although these measures are detailed in content, a 1996 survey compiled these caps: Alaska ($500,000); Colorado ($250,000); Hawaii ($375,000); Maryland ($500,000); Minnesota ($400,000); Idaho ($400,000); Kansas ($250,000); Oregon ($500,000); and, Illinois ($500,000). See American Tort Reform Association, Tort Reform Record, December 31, 1995. Some states have invalidated similar caps as violations of state constitutional guarantees of access to the courts for redress of injuries. See, e.g., *Smith v. Department of Insurance*, 507 So. 2d 1080 (Fla. 1982). Courts in other states have upheld cap statutes against similar attacks. See, e.g., *Balter v. Flint Goodrich Hospital of Dillard University*, 607 So. 2d 517 (La. 1992) (upholding $500,000 statutory cap on general damages in a medical malpractice action.)

(4)   Ordinarily, the expense of medical diagnosis undertaken for the purpose of ruling out the existence of an internal injury that might have resulted from a physical impact is compensable. For example, if a motorist negligently knocks over a bicyclist resulting in a hard blow to the head, the bicyclist's expenses in being examined for internal head injuries would be compensable even if no injury existed. What if a defendant negligently exposes a plaintiff to a fatal but treatable disease? May the plaintiff recover the expense of continual medical monitoring even if the disease is not contracted? *Potter v. Firestone Tire and Rubber Company*, 863 P.2d 795, 824, 825 permitted recovery under these conditions:

> [we] hold that the cost of medical monitoring is a compensable item of damages where the proofs demonstrate, through reliable medical expert testimony, that the need for future monitoring is a reasonably certain consequence of a plaintiff's toxic exposure and that the recommended monitoring is reasonable. In determining the reasonableness and necessity of monitoring, the following factors are relevant: (1) the significance and extent of the plaintiff's exposure to chemicals; (2) the toxicity of the chemicals; (3) the relative increase in the chance of onset of disease in the exposed plaintiff as a result of the exposure, when compared to (a) the plaintiff's chances of developing the disease had he or she not been exposed, and (b) the chances of the members of the public at large of developing the disease; (4) the seriousness of the disease for which the plaintiff is at risk; and (5) the clinical value of early detection and diagnosis. Under this holding, it is for the trier of fact to decide, on the basis of competent medical testimony, whether and to what extent the particular

plaintiff's exposure to toxic chemicals in a given situation justifies future periodic medical monitoring.

(5) Despite the variation in the law concerning recovery for the loss of enjoyment in one's own life, the law is well settled that a husband may recover for loss of enjoyment of the comforts and services provided by his spouse. This recovery traditionally was composed of two parts: first, for the value of the services actually provided the husband by his wife, and, second, the intangible losses accruing from diminished love, companionship, sexual relations and the like. The entire element of recovery is usually referred to as loss of consortium. In the early common law, only a man could complain of loss of consortium, a gender based artifact that may now have been completely expunged. See, e.g., *Gates v. Foley*, 247 So. 2d 40 (Fla. 1971), and *Moran v. Quality Aluminum Casting Co.*, 34 Wis. 2d 542, 150 N.W.2d 137 (1967), for modern cases that equate the rights of men and women on this point. Should a spouse be permitted to sustain a cause of action for loss of consortium stemming from an injury that occurred before marriage? *Gillespie-Linton v. Miles*, 473 A.2d 947 (Md. App. 1984). During an engagement? See *Sawyer v. Bailey*, 413 A.2d 165 (Me. 1980).

(6) Fathers, and perhaps mothers, would also be entitled to claim loss of services of a minor child who was hurt by another person. Indeed, this was a branch of the common law rule actio per quod servitium amisit (a master can recover for economic losses he suffered because of physical harm done his servant), a rule that has lost much of its force. See, e.g., *Inland Revenue Commissioners v. Hornbrook*, [1956] 2 Q.B. 641 (C.A.); but see *Commissioner for Railroads (N.S.W.) v. Scott*, (1959) 102 C.L.R. 392 (Aust. H.C.). American courts have generally not permitted loss of consortium recovery for parents of injured children, limiting recovery to the value of lost services. See *Jordan v. Bero*, 210 N.E.2d 618 (W. Va. 1974), infra. and In the Matter of Certification of Questions of Law From the United States Court of Appeals, 544 N.W.2d 183 (S.Dak. 1996). Contra, *Shockley v. Prier*, 66 Wis. 2d 394, 225 N.W.2d 495 (Wis. 1975). Similarly, many courts refuse to permit loss of consortium actions by the children of injured parents. See, e.g., *Thompson v. Love*, 661 So.2d 1131 (Miss. 1995) and *Guenther v. Stollberg*, 495 N.W.2d 286 (Neb. 1993), But see *Williams v. Hook*, 804 P.2d 1131 (Okla. 1990), *Hibpshman v. Prudhoe Bay Supply, Inc.*, 734 P.2d 991 (Alaska 1987) and *Theama by Bichler v. City of Kenosha*, 117 Wis. 2d 508, 344 N.W.2d 513 (1984). What legitimate objections can be made to these actions?

(7) The orthodox view is that consortium actions are derivative in nature and are thus subject to the same limitations and defenses that apply to the injured person's action. Some jurisdictions apparently view consortium actions to be founded on "independent rights." See *Herold v. Burlington Northern, Inc.*, 761 F.2d 1241 (8th Cir. (N.D.) 1985) (holding that a wife's consortium recovery would not be diminished on account of her injured husband's negligence), and *Bowen v. Kil-Kare, Inc.*, 585 N.E.2d 384, 392 (Ohio 1992) (acknowledging the action to be "derivative" in sense of existing on the basis of a right of action of the directly injured spouse and subject to apportionment of liability based upon the spouses's negligence but holding "that an action for loss of consortium occasioned by a spouse's injury is a separate and distinct cause of action that cannot be defeated by a contractual release of liability which has not be signed by the spouse who is entitled to maintain the action.")

(8) Suppose a defendant negligently hurls a thimble that strikes the plaintiff in the head. Owing to a congenital defect in the plaintiff's skull, unknown either to the plaintiff or defendant, the plaintiff had an unusual susceptibility to harm from the blow and suffered extremely severe injuries from it. Is the defendant liable for only the superficial damage that would have been inflicted upon a normal person or the full damages suffered by the unfortunate person with the "egg shell" skull?

This matter is extensively examined in Minzer, et al., 2 Damages in Tort Actions, Chap. 15, "Aggravation of Injury" (Matthew Bender & Co.), from which the following adapted excerpts are taken. See also the discussion of avoidance of damages examined in Note 5, § 10.01[C], *infra*.

A well-settled doctrine of the common law which has been embraced by every American jurisdiction is that a tortfeasor is liable not only for damages resulting from direct and unique injuries inflicted on the victim but also for damages resulting from the aggravation of the victim's pre-existing disease, condition, or predisposition to injury. The aggravation doctrine applies even though the victim's pre-existing condition might have made the damages more extensive than could have been foreseen or ordinarily would have been expected.[9] The rule often appears in an abbreviated form — a tortfeasor, whether acting from negligence or intent, must take his victim as he finds him[10] — and is sometimes labeled as the "enhancement," "special sensitivity," "thin skull," or "eggshell skull"[11] rule.

Although generally couched in the language of proximate cause and liability, the aggravation rule functions primarily as a rule of damages. If the alleged tortfeasor's act would not have resulted in any injury to an ordinary person, the fact that the injured party was a person of peculiar susceptibility will not affect the liability issue,[12] unless the tortfeasor was on notice of the susceptibility or weakness.[13]

However, if the misconduct charged would have constituted a breach of duty to a person of ordinary susceptibility, liability is thereby established and the peculiar susceptibilities of the injured party become relevant to the damages determination.[14]

---

[9] *See, e.g., Whatley v. Henry*, 65 Ga. App. 668, 16 S.E.2d 214 (1941). "The sick or diseased, as well as the healthy, may recover for injuries proximately caused by the negligence of another. The recovery may be not only for those independent of, but also in aggravation of, such sickness or disease."

[10] *See, e.g., Fischer v. Moore*, 183 Colo. 392, 517 P.2d 458 (1973). "[I]t is axiomatic that the tortfeasor must accept the plaintiff as he finds him and may not seek to reduce the amount of damages by spotlighting the physical frailties of the injured party at the time the tortious force was applied to him."

[11] *See, e.g., Draisma v. United States*, 492 F. Supp. 1317 (W.D. Mich. 1980); *Dulieu v. White*, 2 K.B. 669 (1901).

[12] *See, e.g., Lockwood v. McCaskill*, 262 N.C. 663, 138 S.E.2d 541 (1964), rule stated.

[13] *See, e.g., Spade v. Lynn & Boston R.R.*, 172 Mass. 488, 52 N.E.747, 43 L.R.A. 832 (1899), by way of clarification; [I]f the defendant's servant [railroad conductor] did not commit an unjustifiable battery on the plaintiff's person [while removing a drunken man from the car in which plaintiff was riding], the defendant must answer for the actual consequences of that wrong to her as she was, and cannot cut down her damages by showing that the effect would have been less upon a normal person. . . . The measure of a defendant's duty in determining whether a wrong has been committed is one thing; the measure of liability when a wrong has been committed is another.

[14] *See, e.g., Johnson v. Bender*, 369 N.E.2d 936 (Ind. App. 1977), sheriff's not being aware of prisoner's alcoholism, which increased danger that prisoner would vomit and aspirate gastric content

Two interrelated policies undergird the affirmative dimension of the aggravation rule — (1) to discourage persons from acting negligently in the mistaken anticipation that any consequent liability will necessarily be minimal, and (2) to assure that innocent victims have full recourse for injuries they would not have suffered but for the tortfeasor's negligence.

. . .

Consistent with the same policies, it is well-settled that a tortfeasor can also be held liable for subsequent aggravation of the injuries inflicted on the victim; provided that the aggravated injuries can be shown to have been proximately caused by the initial injuries. This application of the aggravation doctrine most often arises where the tortfeasor's victim sustains additional injuries either (1) as a result of a weakened condition caused by the original injuries,[15] or (2) as a result of treatment or aid rendered by a third party to whom the victim reasonably turns, or upon whom the victim reasonably relies, for assistance in dealing with the initial injuries.[16] Liability may attach whether the assistance thus provided is rendered prudently or negligently, since, in either case, the adverse result is considered a foreseeable consequence of the initial injuries. However, where the subsequent injury results from the injured party's own negligence or from a distinct intervening cause, damages for the subsequent injury are not chargeable against the initial tortfeasor.

If [on the other hand] a defendant can establish that injuries for which the plaintiff seeks recovery are attributable to a pre-existing condition, then the defendant's liability will be limited to only that portion of the total harm attributable to the aggravation, if any, of the original condition.[17] An injured person may not recover damages for an adverse condition as it existed prior to the defendant's alleged intervention.

(9)　Does the collateral source rule considered in *Helfend* overcompensate plaintiffs who collect from two sources (or more) for the same injury: once from a health insurance company and a second time from the tortfeasor?[18] Maybe, but

---

after forcible administration of paraldehyde by two deputies no defense to liability for prisoner's death; sheriff need only have foreseen deceased's nausea and need not have foreseen the greater injury.

[15] *See, e.g., Hartnett v. Tripp*, 231 Mass. 382, 121 N.E. 17 (1918), plaintiff, who had been injured by defendant's negligence, fell and refractured the femur of his right leg when he was trying to get out of his wheelchair with the aid of his crutches; evidence of second injury properly admitted; jury question presented since plaintiff "was performing a natural and necessary act, which it could not be ruled was negligent or so distinct from his original injury as to be a separate and independent act."

[16] *See, e.g., Atherton v. Devine*, 602 P.2d 634 (Okla. 1979), original tortfeasor must bear risk involved in transporting injured victim to place where treatment is available; trial court erred in holding that initial tortfeasor could not be held liable for subsequent injuries sustained when ambulance which was carrying plaintiff to the hospital from the scene of the first accident was involved in a second collision; such result was reasonably foreseeable as a natural consequence of the original wrong; judgment for defendant reversed.

[17] *See, e.g., Henderson v. United States*, 328 F.2d 502 (5th Cir. [Ala.] 1964), an appropriate discount must be made for damages that would have been suffered even in the absence of the defendant's negligence.

[18] If there is a subrogation clause both the tortfeasor and the insurance company could argue that the other should pay the victim's losses. The key issue is which party - the insurance company or the tortfeasor — should pay for the victim's losses? As between the insurance company and the tortfeasor, surely the tortfeasor should pay. They are the one that committed the Tort, after all, and they are the

consider these factors:

1. Plaintiffs typically pay 1/3 of the Tort recoveries to attorneys as legal fees and sometimes must pay costs of litigation (such as expert witness fees) as well.

2. Tort cases do not award prejudgment interest or adjust for inflation. A plaintiff who suffers damages in the amount of $100 and receives $100 years later may not be fully compensated. For example, the injury in *Helfend* occurred in in 1965 but the Tort judgment was not issued until 1970. This particular five year period experienced inflation of slightly more than 23% inflation. Hence, a victim that lost $100 in 1965 would need to receive $123 in 1970 merely to compensate for inflation.

3. We can combine these adjustments and apply them to a hypothetical plaintiff who supposedly was overcompensated by being paid twice for a $100 loss. Reduce the $100 Tort recovery by 1/3 paid to the lawyer. This leaves a net of $67. To this add the $100 recovered from the health insurance company.[19] This brings the net to $167. But if recovery was delayed in the *Helfend* 5 year period, it must be divided by 1.23 to adjust for inflation, leaving a net of $135 in terms of constant dollars.

4. Health insurance policies ordinarily compensate only economic losses, such as medical expenses and maybe wage losses. Hence, the pain and suffering portion of a Tort recovery is seldom, if ever, subject to the risk of double recovery. Often this is the largest portion of a Tort award. The subtraction of legal fees from this portion may reduce the net recovery to much less than actual losses.

5. Health insurance policies ordinarily have deductibles, co-payments, and limits. These further reduce payments to victims, thus minimizing the risk of double recovery.

[B]   Nature of Proof

JORDAN v. BERO

West Virginia Supreme Court of Appeals

210 S.E.2d 618 (1974)

[Plaintiff Russell Jordan, a minor, and his father brought an action against the Beros for harm done the boy when he was struck by defendant's automobile. The boy recovered $20,000 for general damages, including future medical expenses, earnings losses, and pain and suffering. His father recovered $6,000 for medical expenses and loss of services and future medical expenses and loss of services up to the boy's majority. The defendants appeal, alleging errors in instruction given and expert testimony permitted.]

Without a doubt, the most troublesome problem presented on this appeal involves the proof of permanent injuries and the instructions given and refused by the court in clarification of this issue. Defendants' Instruction No. 19 which was

---

one that should be sent a economic message by the Tort system not to be negligent again.

[19] This assumes the victim does not have to hire an attorney to help recover their damages from their own insurance company.

refused by the court would have told the jury that there was not sufficient evidence of permanent injury suffered by the plaintiff resulting from the accident which would permit a lawful recovery of damages therefor. Consequently, even though the jury determined to find for the plaintiffs, it would have been instructed by the court not to award any damages for permanent injuries.

On the other hand, Plaintiffs' Instruction Nos. 14 and 15, given by the court, made the question of the existence and amount of permanent injuries one for the jury's determination. In both instructions the jury was permitted, after resolution of the issue of liability, to allocate a portion of its award of damages to permanent injuries. Neither Plaintiffs' Instruction No. 14 nor Plaintiffs' Instruction No. 15 required that the jury find as a part of its award that plaintiff was entitled to permanent damages. The language used was merely permissive or suggestive to the jury that it could award such damages "if any" they found to be warranted under the circumstances and evidence of the case.

In Plaintiffs' Instruction No. 14, the jury was instructed that Norman Jordan, the infant plaintiff's father, would be entitled to recover from a negligent defendant, specials representing doctor, drug and hospital bills expended to date in the amount of $1,022.53. In addition, and forming the basis for the defendants' objection, the jury was also permitted to give consideration to injuries, permanent in nature, allocable to Norman Jordan, as represented by:

(1) Future doctor, drug and medical bills to be incurred, if any, on behalf of Russell Jordan;

(2) Any future labor or wages of Russell Jordan that his father, Norman D. Jordan, would be entitled to in the future, if any. (Emphasis supplied).

And in considering the above, you may take into consideration the age and physical condition of the Plaintiff, Russell Jordan, at the time of his injuries, but in no event shall your verdict in this case exceed the sum of $12,000.00. (The amount demanded in the ad damnum clause of the complaint).

In Plaintiffs' Instruction No. 15, the jury was instructed that the infant plaintiff, Russell Jordan, could recover from a negligent defendant for the physical and mental pain to date that he had suffered as a result of the accident, and further — again forming the basis for the defendants' objection — the jury could consider any of plaintiff's injuries resulting from the accident which were permanent in nature, and make an award in such sum as would compensate him for:

(1) Future physical and mental pain and suffering, if any.

(2) Loss of future earnings, if any, which he may sustain in the future.

(3) Any residuals, if any, that he may sustain in the future. (Emphasis supplied).

And in considering the above, you (the jury) may take into consideration the age and physical condition of the Plaintiff at the time of his injuries, but in no event shall your verdict in this case exceed the sum of $50,000.00 (The amount demanded in the ad damnum clause of the complaint).

The defendants objected to both instructions on the basis that they, in allowing the jury to consider the amount sued for, $12,000 and $50,000, respectively, amounts not proven in evidence, constituted prejudicial error from that standpoint alone.

While we agree with the thrust and implication of the defendants' objection in this regard, that such sums are normally relevant only in limitation of the amount of the jury's award to a plaintiff, we do not find error on this assignment.

Certainly, the better practice would be to withhold any monetary figure from the jury's consideration which might be suggestive of amounts of damage not proven in evidence. However, recognizing the proper function of the jury and, also, that damage awards in personal injury actions are necessarily somewhat indeterminate in character and amount, this Court, while not approving exposition of ad damnum clauses to the jury, does not reverse a case for this impropriety alone.

. . .

Moving to the substantial and troublesome bases of defendants' objections — to the court's refusal in giving Defendants' Instruction No. 19, and to the court's granting of Plaintiffs' Instructions Nos. 14 and 15 — , we must squarely confront the question of permanency of injuries and the proof adduced in support thereof. In a nutshell, defendants assert, and correctly so, that to form a basis of a legal recovery for the future permanent consequences of the wrongful infliction of a personal injury, it must appear with reasonable certainty that such consequences will result from the injury. Contingent or merely possible future injurious effects are too remote and speculative to support a lawful recovery. Wilson v. Fleming, 89 W.Va. 553, 109 S.E. 810 (1921). To meet the contention, the plaintiffs, while recognizing the validity of the foregoing rule in this jurisdiction, seek to avoid the thrust of this objection on the basis that the inclusion of the crucial language, "if any" vitiates the objection. Plaintiffs say that inasmuch as the instructions allowing an award of permanent injuries are couched in merely permissive language rather than in the form of a binding directive to the jury, the giving of the same does not constitute reversible error.

. . .

The drafter of this opinion would be fortunate indeed if the problem were susceptible of such a simple solution. Unfortunately, it is not.

We are confronted once again with the problem of determining how much evidence is necessary to meet the standard of reasonable certainty which will support instructions to the jury that that body properly might give consideration in its award of damages to lasting and permanent effects of an injury suffered at the hands of a negligent defendant. At the outset, we must review the evidence of permanency in the case and then decide whether the rules applicable to the evidence sustain the recovery given the plaintiffs in the court below, or whether these rules necessarily require the reversal of the results of this case and the award of a new trial to the defendants.

The medical evidence in this case tells us that Russell Jordan was rendered unconscious by a blow or blows sustained in his vehicular accident with Wayne Bero.

. . .

We hold that plaintiff introduced sufficient proof from expert testimony that the contusion which rendered him unconscious for a period of six days was a severe brain injury which is permanent in nature.

. . .

Although the past medical expenses arising from the accident occurrence were proved to be both necessary and reasonable, no effort was made by the plaintiffs to prove the necessity for future medical expenses or their projected reasonable cost.

We also note that the plaintiffs made no substantial effort to adduce explicit proof which would support a finding that the boy's future earning capacity would be impaired by reason of his brain injury. The only evidence bearing on this aspect of damages was the father's testimony that the infant plaintiff did not perform his daily chores with the same alacrity and concentration as he had demonstrated prior to the accident.

. . .

The boy's father, also a plaintiff in the action, testified to several instances which tended to demonstrate his son's lack of proper memory as to events occurring before the accident, his lack of ability to concentrate since the accident on matters requiring both mental and physical attention, and the general deterioration of the boy's grade point average in school work occurring since the accident.

On these basic facts we are asked whether sufficient evidence of future consequences from the negligent act of the defendant was proven to lawfully permit the jury to make an award for the future effects of the permanent injury.

The permanency or future effect of any injury must be proved with reasonable certainty in order to permit the injured party to recover future damages. . . . Future damages are those sums awarded to an injured party for, among other things: (1) Residuals or those future effects of an injury which have reduced the capability of an individual to function as a whole man; (2) future pain and suffering; (3) loss or impairment of earning capacity; and (4) future medical expenses.

As indicated from the case references to permanency of injuries and sufficiency of proof thereof, supra, many such cases are tested on appeal from the aspect of who was qualified to give testimony as to the reasonable certainty of the future effects of injuries. The general rules of sufficiency on this point have been developed with reference to the apparency of the injury to the beholder.

Where the injury is of such a character as to be obvious, the effects of which are reasonably common knowledge, it is competent to prove either by lay testimony from the injured litigant or others who have viewed his injuries, or by expert testimony — medical, forensic, actuarial, and the like — or from both lay and expert testimony. . . .

On the other hand, where the injury is obscure, that is, the effects of which are not readily ascertainable, demonstrable, or subject of common knowledge, mere subjective testimony of the injured party or other lay witnesses does not prove the future effect of the injury to a reasonable certainty. In such situation, medical or other expert opinion testimony is required to establish the future effects of the injury to a reasonable degree of certainty. . . .

Brain injury cases exemplify those in which both the injury itself and more often, the future effects of the injury fall into the classification of "obscure" injuries. Physicians, courts and juries all have particular trouble with evaluations of these injuries.

In fairness to the plaintiff, courts and juries tend to give the benefit of the doubt to the injured plaintiff when the effects of the injury are such that they may very well be serious, permanent, and functionally disabling, when their possible manifestations are latent and often hidden from the view of both the qualified surgeon and the layman juror. On the other hand, in fairness to a defendant who may be called upon to pay a very large sum to compensate for an injury which may, in fact, not be present, courts remain circumspect and necessarily severe in the application of the reasonable certainty rule.

Once, however, permanency is established by competent testimony to a degree of reasonable certainty, proof of foreseeable consequences is less difficult. In all of the following cases upon proof of permanency, the jury was permitted to infer the extent and value of the future effects of head and brain injuries and make award therefor to the plaintiff. . . .

In summary, these cases adopt the salutary view that where, as with brain injuries, the manifestation of a permanent injury may be latent, unpredictable in the time of its appearance and obscure, positive medical evidence that the injury is permanent is usually sufficient to take the question to the jury and to support an award of damages for the future effects of the injury. . . . This rule has been recognized and applied by this jurisdiction to claims for "residuals" or future effects of proved permanent injuries. See, Shreve v. Faris, supra; Walker v. Robertson, supra; Bragg v. C. I. Whitten Transfer Co., 125 W. Va. 722, 26 S.E.2d 217 (1943); Bailey v. De Boyd, supra. We now reaffirm its validity to the facts at hand.

As an element of future damages, pain and suffering may be an item of recovery where it is reasonably certain that such will result from the injury received. . . . The rule was summarized by Judge Haymond in the case of Shreve v. Faris, supra, at page 827 of the West Virginia Report, 111 S.E.2d at page 174:

As to future pain and suffering in general, such pain and suffering on the part of the injured person, in consequence of the injury, are a proper element of damages which may be allowed if there is reasonable certainty that such pain and suffering will result. 15 Am. Jur., Damages, Section 73.

Again, on this point, where the injury has been shown to be permanent with a reasonable degree of certainty and symptoms as to pain and suffering persist at the time of trial, coupled with the presence of other residuals as documented by law and expert testimony in the case of an obscure injury, such future pain and suffering may be reasonably inferred by the jury from the very fact or existence of the permanent injury.

. . .

In this case we recognize and apply the rule of Collins v. Skaggs, 110 W. Va. 518, 159 S.E. 515 (1931), which held:

The law furnishes no measure of damages for pain and suffering. In such case, the decision of the jury upon the amount is generally conclusive, unless it is so large or small as to induce the belief that the jury was influenced by passion, partiality, corruption, or prejudice, or misled by some mistaken view of the case. Id. at page 520, 159 S.E. at page 516.

As we have indicated, this Court favorably views reasonable inferences arising from the evidence in proof of future effects of permanent injury. This approach, however, cannot be extended to unreasonable lengths in support of instant claims for impairment of earning capacity and future medical expenses, which in this trial were proffered on a paucity of evidence in one instance and on no evidence in the other.

Future medical expenses and impairment of earning capacity are proper elements of recovery when a plaintiff has suffered a permanent injury and it has been shown that these particular results are reasonably certain to occur and ensue from the injury. . . .

Undoubtedly, even an infant plaintiff who has never been gainfully employed may recover damages for impairment of his future earning capacity. During his minority, his parents or guardians may also recover damages for such impairment or loss of earning capacity occurring during the infant plaintiff's minority proximately resulting from the negligent conduct of a defendant. . . . Nevertheless, impairment of earning capacity is an item of permanent damages which again must be proved to a reasonable degree of certainty; it cannot be left to sheer speculation or surmise.

In this case, the testimony from plaintiff's father that his son did not perform his chores with the same degree of concentration and diligence as he did previous to the injuries sustained in the accident cannot, standing alone, support an award of impairment of earning capacity. This evidence, while competent, is of such slight inferential value as to be deficient when it is asserted in support of a permissive instruction allowing the jury to make an award for impairment of earning capacity to his father and guardian and to the infant himself. On the other hand, we believe, consistent with our holding in respect to future pain and suffering and residuals, where the permanent injury is proven, reasonable inferences based upon sufficient evidence are all that is necessary to carry this question to the jury for its consideration. Here, however, the evidence was de minimis and was not sufficient to raise a proper inference for the jury's consideration.

On the question of permitting the jury to consider an award for future medical expenses, the plaintiff's reach also exceeds his grasp. As noted previously, the record is absolutely devoid of any attempt to prove that plaintiff or his father will incur future medical expenses from the injury.

. . .

. . .To support a relevant instruction on the recovery of future medical expenses, the plaintiff must offer proof to a degree of reasonable certainty which will indicate costs within an approximate range, as well as the necessity and reasonableness of such prospective medical charges.

With the foregoing principles firmly in mind, we sustain the award of $20,000 to the infant plaintiff for the injuries suffered by him proximately resulting from the negligent conduct of the defendant Wayne Bero on the highways of this State.

In determining whether the verdict of a jury is supported by the evidence, every reasonable and legitimate inference, fairly arising from the evidence in favor of the party for whom the verdict was returned, must be considered, and those facts, which the jury might properly find under the evidence, must be assumed as true.

Syllabus point 5, Poe v. Pittman, 150 W. Va. 179, 144 S.E.2d 671 (1965); syllabus point 3, Walker v. Monongahela Power Company, 147 W. Va. 825, 131 S.E.2d 736 (1963).

The verdict in favor of the infant plaintiff was attacked as excessive, and as not supported by the evidence. We must reject this attack. There was ample evidence of permanency of an injury which was obscure only in its final and ultimate effects. Lay and medical evidence adduced in support of the plaintiff's case demonstrated that in addition to the permanent injury, plaintiff had suffered deleterious effects from the automobile accident from which a jury may have reasonably inferred he will so suffer in the future and that such suffering and residuals will effect his capacity to function as a whole man in the future. Consequently, we hold that the giving of the permissive Instruction No. 15, offered by the plaintiffs, was a lawful instruction supported by the evidence of this case.

. . .

[The father's award of $6,000 was found to be excessive because of the lack of evidence to establish future medical expenses for the boy and future loss of services from him.]

Both parties to this litigation have engaged in the expense and time involved in trial. They should not have to repeat the process if it can be avoided and still be served by an outcome fair to their respective adversary interests. If this case were reversed and remanded for a new trial it would be for the sole reason that Plaintiffs' Instruction No. 14 constituted reversible error and permitted a recovery in favor of Norman Jordan in excess of the medical expenses in the amount of $1,022.53 proved by him as necessary and reasonable for his son's care. We have struck as improper from that instruction a suggestion to the jury that it could award damages for impairment of Russell Jordan's earning capacity and for future medical expenses.

Consequently, to avoid the necessity and cost of a new trial of this case for a single issue, we choose to reverse on this point and remand the case and to direct that the trial court give the plaintiff Norman Jordan a period of thirty days to decide whether he will accept a remittitur in the amount of $4,977.47 resulting in a total verdict payable to him in the amount of $1,022.53, plus interest and costs. "Where the amount in excess in an excessive verdict is definitely ascertainable, a remittitur may be properly employed." Syllabus point 3, Fortner v. Napier, 153 W. Va. 143, 168 S.E.2d 737 (1969); Accord, Bragg v. C. I. Whitten Transfer Company, supra. If he chooses to accept this reduced award without the necessity of a new trial, the case may be so concluded under the procedure recently approved in Earl T. Browder, Inc. v. County Court of Webster County, supra:

"When the illegal part of the damages ascertained by the verdict of a jury is clearly distinguishable from the rest, and may be ascertained by the court without assuming the functions of the jury and substituting its judgment for theirs, the court may allow plaintiff to enter a remittitur for such part, and then refuse a new trial." Point 4, Syllabus, Chapman v. Beltz & Sons Co., 48 W. Va. 1, 35 S.E. 1013.

Syllabus point 2, id. Otherwise, the plaintiffs must submit to a new trial. See Carlin, Remittiturs and Additurs, 49 W. Va. Law Q. 1 (1942).

. . .

Affirmed in part; reversed in part; and remanded with directions.

NEELY, JUSTICE (concurring):

I concur in the result in this case but I respectfully differ from the majority with regard to the reasoning of syllabus points 7, 9, 12, 13 and 15, all relating to the level of proof necessary to sustain a claim for future damages as a result of personal injury. The majority opinion articulates the traditional rule that future damages must be proved to a reasonable degree of medical certainty, but then recognizes that in an area such as brain injury where it is difficult to predict the ultimate effects of an injury it is almost impossible to comply with the rule.

It appears that the traditional rule requiring future damages to be proved to a reasonable degree of medical certainty was developed at a time when lawyers and judges had substantially less sophistication with probability theory and statistics than they have today. Accordingly the rule has been stated in relatively vague language and has been even more vaguely applied to various factual situations. I believe that the real rule which is in practice applied in the courts and which has been applied by this Court in the case at bar is far different from the enigma of supposed logic which is presented as the formal rule. . . .

. . .

The fact that a person is confronted with a ten percent, fifteen percent, or twenty percent probability (in the mathematical sense) that he will suffer future injuries should be sufficient to permit him to recover for those future injuries at least in proportion to the probability of such injuries occurring. Therefore, in a hypothetical case, if a man can demonstrate that there is a twenty percent probability that he will have future injuries which would, if they occurred, result in damage to him in the amount of a hundred thousand dollars, he should be able to recover twenty thousand dollars from the defendant, which recovery would represent the injury of incurring a twenty percent probability of suffering one hundred thousand dollars worth of damages.

. . .

In keeping with the traditional rule, the probability, in the mathematical sense, of future injury must be proved to a reasonable degree of medical certainty. Accordingly a doctor should be permitted to testify that on the basis of his experience and his evaluation of statistical information from recorded cases of similar injuries he believes that there is to a reasonable degree of medical certainty a twenty percent probability of suffering a particular disability. Once it is determined that there is a probability of loss, evidence should then be admitted concerning the maximum expected loss should the victim completely lose in the game of chance he is playing with the fates.

Accordingly the jury would be instructed that from all the evidence they should determine what the overall probability is that the plaintiff will suffer future damages, and that from all of the evidence they should determine the amount of monetary damages to which the plaintiff would be entitled if the disabilities which doctors reasonably believe are possible actually come to pass. The jury would then be instructed to multiply the amount of future damages reasonably to be expected times the probability of those damages actually occurring and arrive at a figure which will compensate the plaintiff for the possibility of future injuries. It would appear that in a major damage suit the jury could be aided by expert testimony with regard to probability analysis to make the problem comprehensible to the average layman.

NOTES AND QUESTIONS

(1) How should the negligent failure to diagnose a fatal, but curable, illness be treated when the evidence does not conclusively establish that but-for the negligence the illness would have been cured? Some courts hold that the victim (or survivors) must prove that it is more probable than not that the victim would have been cured in order to maintain a "lost chance to survive" action. See e.g., *Gooding v. University Hospital*, 445 So. 2d 1015 (Fla. 1984). Others hold that the plaintiff need prove only that the defendant's negligence was a substantial factor in the loss of chance. See, e.g., *Ehrlinger v. Sipes*, 454 N.W.2d 754 (Wis. 1990) and *McKellips v. Saint Francis Hospital, Inc.*, 741 P.2d 467, 475 (Okla. 1987)("[t]he new standard of sufficiency of proof lowers a plaintiff's burden of production . . . to establish a jury question on the issue of causation on a showing of substantial decrease in the chance of survival. . . . The jury would be required to determine whether the increase in risk under the circumstances was a substantial factor in causing harm.")

(2) Suppose a defendant negligently exposes a plaintiff to an enhanced risk of cancer or AIDS or some other fatal disease? May an action be maintained for emotional damage if the disease has not yet been contracted? *Potter v. Firestone Tire and Rubber Co.*, 863 P.2d 795, 816 (Cal. En Banc 1993), permitted an action under these strictures:

> [w]e hold with respect to negligent infliction of emotional distress claims arising out of exposure to carcinogens and/or other toxic substances: Unless an express exception to this general rule is recognized: in the absence of a present physical injury or illness, damages for fear of cancer may be recovered only if the plaintiff pleads and proves that (1) as a result of the defendant's negligent breach of a duty owed to the plaintiff, the plaintiff is exposed to a toxic substance which threatens cancer; and (2) the plaintiff's fear stems from a knowledge, corroborated by reliable medical or scientific opinion, that it is more likely than not that the plaintiff will develop the cancer in the future due to the toxic exposure. Under this rule, a plaintiff must do more than simply establish knowledge of a toxic ingestion or exposure and a significant increased risk of cancer. The plaintiff must further show that based upon reliable medical or scientific opinion, the plaintiff harbors a serious fear that the toxic ingestion or exposure was of such magnitude and proportion as to likely result in the feared cancer.

Does the "more probable than not" threshold destroy a plaintiff's action? When would it not be justified? See, *Hagerty v. L&L Marine Services, Inc.*, 788 F.2d 315, 318 (5th Cir. 1986), modified 797 F.2d 256 (1986). See also *Potter* in connection with intentional torts.

Macy's California, Inc. v. Superior Court, 48 Cal. Rptr. 2d 496 (Cal. App. 1996), applied the *Potter* "more probable that not" threshold to a case involving fear of contracting AIDS. Macy's also considered whether, when the fear of contracting AIDS arose out of a negligently inflicted needle puncture, the emotional distress arising out of fear of contracting AIDS could be recovered as "parasitic damages" to the slight physical injury caused by the needle puncture. The court held, "For parasitic recovery of emotional distress damages, the plaintiff must have sustained physical injury, meaning detrimental change to the body.' Id., at 505. Is this in keeping with the traditional "impact rule" examined in Chapter 5?

O'DOWD v. LINEHAM
Supreme Court of Michigan
189 N.W.2d 333 (1971)

ADAMS, JUSTICE:

. . .

II

OF THE TESTIMONY AND OPINIONS OF EXPERTS

Few lawsuits can be tried in this, the age of experts, without the use of expert testimony. Criminal cases frequently require testimony by a fingerprint expert, a handwriting expert, or a lab technician. Cases involving lands often turn on the expert testimony of land surveyors. Lawsuits over the performance or non-performance of construction contracts almost invariably involve the testimony of experts in the field of engineering or structural design. Seldom is a malpractice case tried without expert testimony from doctors. Products liability cases depend in large part upon expert testimony for plaintiff and defendant. Other examples can be drawn from almost every kind of litigation.

Yet distrust of the expert persists. This is particularly the case when, as a witness, he undertakes to give his opinion. His expertise, when used to supplement facts for the benefit of the jury, is less often subject to objection.

The problem can be illustrated if we take the simple case of a French witness who is unable to speak English and whose testimony must be presented to the jury through a translator. If the translator is fluent in both French and English, if he faithfully gives to the jury the statements of the witness, no one questions such a procedure. However, if the translator is inept, incompetent or biased in favor of one of the parties so that there is an unfaithful or speculative translation of the words of the witness, the procedure becomes subject to attack. The jury is better off without such testimony. The use of an expert is similar to that of a translator — the evidence which has been presented to the jury cannot be adequately comprehended, analyzed and weighed by it without the aid of the special knowledge of the expert as to the meaning and significance of the facts in evidence.

It is well understood nowadays that fingerprints found at the scene of a crime, if they can be identified as being the same as those taken from a defendant, may be a vital link in establishing his guilt. Fingerprints are like a foreign language. It takes the work of the fingerprint expert and his opinion with regard to identification to forge that vital link.

Since the testimony of experts is frequently used and is often vital to assist a jury in ascertaining the true facts of a case, what are the rules governing the admissibility of such testimony?

1. There must be an expert. In the professions and in most scientific disciplines, specific areas of expertise are readily recognized. The test of an expert presents no difficulty. In other areas, it is quite as easy to recognize that no valid expertise exists. A water dowser who purports to find water with the aid of a willow wand could scarcely qualify as an expert on subterranean waters, while a scientifically trained and experienced student of the subject might do so. A policeman with an eighth grade education who has been on traffic duty for 10 years and has investigated innumerable traffic accidents may have limited credentials as a traffic expert, while a laboratory technician, never at the scene of an accident, who has analyzed paint samples taken from cars at the scene may be qualified to testify as to whether the cars came into contact.

2. There must be facts in evidence which require or are subject to examination and analysis by a competent expert. Fingerprints must have been found at the scene of the crime and must also have been taken from the defendant before an expert can present his findings to the jury. The X-ray of plaintiff's chest must be identified as such, also as to the date when taken, etc., before the radiologist can give his reading of it to the jury.

3. Finally, there must be knowledge in a particular area that belongs more to an expert than to the common man. This is the most difficult test of all. The application of it depends upon the relation of expert knowledge to common knowledge at a given time. We need no expert today to tell us that the world is round — or that disease is spread by germs — or that man can travel to the moon. Yet certain experts will be much more capable than the common man of measuring the speed of an oncoming automobile, of calculating the stresses and strains upon a given roof at a given time and in a given place, and of determining the location of a section corner.

NOTES AND QUESTIONS

(1) The need for expert testimony permeates modern personal injury litigation, especially where losses are to accrue in futero. The one place where it has no part, however, except to lay a foundation for the existence of it, is in setting the amount of the award for pain and suffering. Unlike the convention of English law, American law, as stated in *Jordan v. Bero*, "furnishes no measure" of pain and suffering damages, but instead leaves the measurement to the "high order of human judgment" reposed in the "enlightened conscience" of the jury. *Braddock v. Seaboard Air Line Railroad Company*, 80 So. 2d 662 (Fla. 1955). Generally, jury verdicts will not be disturbed unless they are so "grossly excessive [or, rarely, small] as to evince passion, bias and prejudice on the part of the jury so as to shock the conscience." *Woods v. Nichols*, 416 So. 2d 659, 672 (Miss. 1982). See, also, *Lamke v. Louden*, 269 N.W.2d 53 (Minn. 1978) (affirming $450,000 verdict for loss of one leg), and *Fruit v. Schreiner*, 502 P.2d 133 (Alaska 1972) (affirming $650,000 for loss of one leg). This loose expansiveness of the pain and suffering element of recovery can cover up deficiencies in evidence as to the tangible losses. Was this evident in the Jordan boy's recovery in *Jordan v. Bero*?

Plaintiffs' lawyers are prone to argue to the jury along these lines: "How much money would you demand to agree voluntarily to suffer for one day the pain that this plaintiff has suffered and will hereafter suffer for the remainder of her life?" Many courts reject this so-called "per diem" or "golden rule" approach as inflammatory and prejudicial against the defendant. Why? See, e.g., *Ahlstrom v. Minneapolis St. Pa. & Sault Ste. Marie R. Co.*, 244 Minn. 1, 68 N.W.2d 873 (1955). Do you agree?

Typically when a court deems a verdict to be excessive, it orders a remittitur as was done in regard to the father's recovery in *Jordan v. Bero*. Was it proper to make affirmance of the son's award depend upon his father's acceptance of a remittitur? The remittitur is a device used by the courts to control juries. Many courts deem it to be an inherent judicial power, but legislatures sometimes step in to expand the power or otherwise particularize it. See, e.g., Fla. Stat. § 768.043. The counterpart order is an additur, when the court deems the award to be too low in light of the evidence. Courts have traditionally been less willing to employ the additur than the remittitur. Why?

How is a trial court to adjudge whether a jury's award is too much or too little? One court has said that the following factors should be considered:

1) the severity of the injury;

2) whether the injury is supported by objective physical evidence or only by subjective evidence;

3) whether the injury is permanent;

4) the plaintiff's ability to continue his employment;

5) the disparity between the amount of out-of-pocket expenses and the amount of the verdict; and

6) the damages a plaintiff requested in his complaint.

Feld v. Merriam, 461 A.2d 225, 234 (Pa. Super. 1983). Can you suggest others? See generally Minzer, et al., Damages in Tort Actions (9 vols., Matthew Bender & Co.) for materials relevant to analysis of the adequacy or inadequacy of a verdict.

(2) As to lost income, actual wage loss is a measure, but not the measure, of recovery. One court has expressed the typical rule as follows:

> What plaintiff earned before and after the injury does not constitute the measure. Even if he had been unemployed at the time of the injury he is entitled to an award for impairment or diminution of earning power. And while his earning capacity at the time of the injury is relevant, it is not necessarily determinative of his future ability to earn. . . . Damages should be estimated on the injured person's ability to earn money, rather than what he actually earned before the injury.

Toolse v. Fakouri, 371 So. 2d 1120 (La. 1979).

Another court has stated:

> It is settled law . . . that loss of earning capacity, as distinct from loss of wages, salary, or earnings, is a separate element of damage. It is equally well settled that a loss of past earnings is an item of special damage and must be specifically pleaded and proved. Impairment of earning capacity is an item of general damage and proof may be had under general allegations of injury and damage. . . . Proof of an actual loss of earnings or wages is not essential to recovery for loss of earning capacity.

Washington v. American Community Stores Corp., 244 N.W.2d 286, 289 (Neb. 1976). Is there a difference between these two statements?

Ascertaining future losses is hard enough when a seasoned wage earner with an established employment history is permanently injured. Juries must consider prospects of pay increases and promotions, probable duration of working life, and the like. Much harder are cases such as would be posed by *Jordan v. Bero*, supra, if the young boy had been permanently injured without a foreseeable shortening of his life expectancy. What sorts of evidence could be adduced to establish diminution of earning capacity for the duration of an infant plaintiff's expectable working life? Does expert testimony have a place in such a case? How?

Suppose an NCAA heavyweight wrestling champion is rendered permanently and totally disabled as a result of an automobile crash. Should he be permitted to prove the earnings of the best professional wrestlers? Of the typical collegiate wrestling coach? See *Washington v. American Community Stores Corp.*, 244 N.W.2d 286 (Neb. 1976), where it is stated, "Recovery for loss or diminution of the power to earn in the future is based upon such factors as the plaintiff's age, life expectancy, health, habits, occupation, talents, skill, experience, training, and industry." Suppose a high school sophomore is rendered permanently and totally disabled by a crash. If her parents were college graduates, should she be permitted to prove the earnings of the typical female college graduate? If her hope was to have been a veterinarian, should she be permitted to prove the earnings of a typical veterinarian? See *Gilborges v. Wallace*, 379 A.2d 269 (N.J. 1977).

Suppose a housewife is injured or killed. Should the value of lost housewife services be recoverable? By whom? How would they be proved? See *DeLong v. County of Erie*, 60 N.Y.2d 296, 469 N.Y.S.2d 611 (1983). Should the demand for future losses of an injured housewife be couched in terms of lost services or in some other way? See *Florida Grayhound Lines, Inc. v. National Indemnity Co.*, 5 Wis. 2d 231, 92 N.W.2d 884 (1958), and *Jesco, Inc. v. Shannon*, 451 So.2d 694 (Miss. 1984).

For a thorough discussion of loss of future earning capacity, see 2 Minzer, et al., Damages in Tort Actions, Chapter 10, "Loss of Time or Earnings and Impairment of Earning Capacity" (Matthew Bender & Co.).

[C]   Adjustments to Recoveries

[See *Helfend v. Southern California Rapid Transit Dist.*, § 10.01[A], *supra.*]

NOTES AND QUESTIONS

(1) The collateral source rule, which was an issue in *Helfend v. Southern California Rapid Transit System*, supra, generally applies in American jurisdictions. A basic statement of the rule is "that compensation due a party from an independent source other than the wrongdoer does not operate to lessen damages recoverable from the wrongdoers." *Tebo v. Havlik*, 109 Mich. App. 413, 415 (1981). The rule represents a judicial resolution of two conflicting premises of recovery for tortious wrongs: that a plaintiff should receive one complete recovery and no more, and that a wrongdoer should be made to pay for all harm done. The collateral source rule resolves the conflict by siding with the innocent victim. In

short, the rule holds that it is better for a victim than for a tortfeasor to receive a windfall.

The rule routinely applies when a benefit is received that the plaintiff has paid for through insurance premiums, attributes of employment and the like. In those cases it is said that "to allow the defendant to reduce his liability because the plaintiff's exercise of contract right of recovery against their insurer . . . would be an unjust enrichment.. . . " *Beaird v. Brown*, 373 N.E.2d, 1055, 1057 (Ill. App. 1978). When the plaintiff receives a gratuitous benefit and later seeks to collect the value of it from the defendant, is it so obvious that the plaintiff should prevail? For example, may an injured physician recover from the tortfeasor the value of medical services provided gratis by a fellow physician? See, e.g., *Coyne v. Campbell*, 183 N.E.2d 891 (N.Y. 1962). See generally, Anno., 11 A.L.R. 2d 1115 (1967). Suppose the collateral source of benefits is a public welfare program. See *Horton v. Brooks*, 325 So. 2d 912 (Miss. 1976), and *Nelson v. Trinity Medical Center*, 419 N.W.2d 886 (N.D. 1988) (holding that the collateral source rule precludes admitting evidence of the receipt of public benefits).

While the collateral source rule is, perhaps, fair in favoring victims over tortfeasors, the duplication of recoveries by victims is costly. Consequently, to hold back on the rising costs of liability insurance, some legislatures have abrogated the rule and given the benefit of the collateral sources to defendants. See, e.g., Fla. Stat. § 627.7372.

(2) The tort reform movement has prompted the enactment of statutes in many states to permit the introduction of collateral sources into evidence and to permit offsets from damage awards. As of 1996, at least 21 states have enacted some version of these statutes. American Tort Reform Association, Tort Reform Record, December 31, 1995. The statutes vary widely as to what evidence may be admitted and as to how the offset is to be made. Does your state have a collateral source statute? Does it provide a fairer system than the common law rule of full recovery? Compare with the following:

Indiana Code § 34-4-36

SEC. 1. The purpose of this chapter is:

(1) To enable the trier of fact in a personal injury or wrongful death action to determine the actual amount of the prevailing party's pecuniary loss; and

(2) To provide that a prevailing party not recover more than once from all applicable sources for each item of loss sustained.

Sec. 2. In a personal injury or wrongful death action the court shall allow the admission into evidence of:

(1) proof of collateral source payments, other than:

(A) payments of life insurance or other death benefits;

(B) insurance benefits for which the plaintiff or members of the plaintiff's family have paid for directly; or

(C) payments made by the state or the United States, or any agency, instrumentality, or subdivision thereof, that have been made before trial to a plaintiff as compensation for the loss or injury for which the action is brought;

(2) proof of the amount of money that the plaintiff is required to repay, including worker's compensation benefits, as a result of the collateral benefits received; and

(3) proof of the cost to the plaintiff or to members of the plaintiff's family of collateral benefits received by the plaintiff or the plaintiff's family.

Sec. 3. Proof of payments under section 2 of this chapter shall be considered by the trier of fact in arriving at the amount of any award and shall be considered by the court in reviewing awards that are alleged to be excessive.

NOTES AND QUESTIONS

(1) § 768.76 Florida Statutes. Collateral sources of indemnity

1. In any action to which this part applies in which liability is admitted or is determined by the trier of fact and in which damages are awarded to compensate the claimant for losses sustained, the court shall reduce the amount of such award by the total of all amounts which have been paid for the benefit of the claimant, or which are otherwise available to him, from all collateral sources; however, there shall be no reduction for collateral sources for which a subrogation or reimbursement right exists. Such reduction shall be offset to the extent of any amount which has been paid, contributed, or forfeited by, or on behalf of, the claimant or members of his immediate family to secure his right to any collateral source benefit which he is receiving as a result of his injury.

2. For purposes of this section:

(a) "Collateral sources' means any payments made to the claimant, or made on his behalf, by or pursuant to:

1. The United States Social Security Act, [Ed. — and similar programs as described with exceptions.].

2. Any health, sickness, or income disability insurance; automobile accident insurance that provides health benefits or income disability coverage; and any other similar insurance benefits, except life insurance benefits available to the claimant, whether purchased by him or provided by others.

3. Any contract or agreement of any group, organization, partnership, or corporation to provide, pay for, or reimburse the costs of hospital, medical, dental, or other health care services.

4. Any contractual or voluntary wage continuation plan provided by employers or by any other system intended to provide wages during a period of disability.

(Exemptions and implementing provisions omitted.)

(2) The common law "once and for all" rule, see *The Darley Main Colliery Company v. Mitchell*, § 4.05 *supra*, creates massive evidentiary and computational difficulties for tort litigants and jurors, primarily because the award must often compensate losses that have not yet been experienced. Not only must the evidence establish that it is more probable than not that losses will accrue in the future, which was an issue in *Jordan v. Bero*, but it must also establish the amount of the future damages, which is a harder job.

In addition, the value of a loss that will occur in the future must be converted to present value in making the "once and for all" award. Take as a simple case the recovery needed to offset a one dollar loss to happen one year from now. The present value is the amount of money that must be placed in a bank today that, when added to the interest accruing at the market rate of interest over the ensuing year, will add up to one dollar a year from today. If the market rate of interest is 9%, that amount is 91%; if it is 5%, the amount is 95%, and so on. In this application the appropriate market rate of interest is commonly referred to as the discount rate.

The variation of present value with different discount rates creates disputes as to the exact size of the rate to be used. Will defendants favor high or low discount rates? This is an evidential question creating the need of expert testimony of a different kind from that pertaining to the existence and nature of injuries. How would the appropriate rate be determined? Actuarial tables greatly simplify the job of making present value calculations after the discount rate and amounts of future losses have been determined.

(3) If defendants may insist that the value of future losses be reduced to present value, is it fair to plaintiffs to evaluate future losses in terms of today's value of similar losses? Or, ought plaintiffs be permitted to introduce evidence as to the expectable rate of inflation and its effect upon the value of losses to be accrued in the future? To illustrate, if the inflation rate is 7%, then the value in current dollars of a loss to be incurred one year from today would be $1.07, assuming it would be valued at one dollar if it occurred today. To determine the present value of that future loss, the inflated sum would be discounted as described above. Thus, if the discount rate is 10%, the present value of that particular future loss would be about 97%.

Until the decade of the 70s, annual inflation rates in the United States tended to be small, and few courts instructed juries on the effect of inflation. Traditionally, courts considered "that future inflation or deflation is speculative and that the injured person can, in any event, invest his recovery in equities such as land and thus have the benefit of both inflation and the income." *Schnebly v. Baker*, 217 N.W.2d 708 (Iowa 1974). With the onset of "double digit" inflation (greater than 10%), this was no longer tolerable. As one court said, ". . . we have taken the position that inflation is a fact of life that cannot fairly and realistically be ignored." *Ossenfort v. Associated Milk Producers, Inc.*, 254 N.W.2d, 672, 684 (Minn. 1977). Consequently, many, if not most, courts now permit the introduction of evidence and argument about inflation.

Exactly how inflation is to be taken into account has received no uniform answer. Among techniques employed are to instruct the jury not to discount future losses, *Beaulieu v. Elliott*, 434 P.2d 665 (Alaska, 1967), and to use an artificially small discount rate such as one or two percent. *Bush v. Busch Constr. Inc.*, 262 N.W.2d 377 (Minn. 1977). Perhaps the most thorough judicial canvassing of the subject was done by the High Court of Australia in *Pennant Hills Restaurant Pty Ltd. v. Barrell Insurances Pty. Limited*, 34 A.L.R. 162 (H.C. 1980).

(4) The United States Internal Revenue Code does not tax "the amount of any damages received (whether by suit or agreement) on account of personal injuries or sickness. . . " I.R.C. § 104(a) (2). Accordingly, a plaintiff who receives a damages award for lost earnings based upon the gross amount that would have been earned but-for the injury may thereby receive a windfall to the extent of the taxes which would have been ordinarily assessed on taxable income in the amount

of the damages award. See, e.g., Comment, Income Tax Effects on Personal Injury Recoveries, 30 La. L. Rev. 672 (1970). Nevertheless, courts commonly do not permit evidence or instruction on taxation of damages on grounds that the future effect of taxation is too speculative. See, e.g., *Raines v. New York Central R. Co.*, 283 N.E.2d 230 (Ill. 1972). The United States Supreme Court broke step with this tradition in *Norfolk & W. Ry. Co. v. Liepelt*, 100 S. Ct. 755 (1980), and held that defendants are entitled to have juries instructed on the taxation question in personal injury and wrongful death actions brought under the Federal Employers' Liability Act, a federal statute that does not control state law tort actions.

(5) Defendant and plaintiff are preparing to go on a hunting trip together when defendant negligently gashes plaintiff's arms with a hunting knife, causing a severe wound. Competent medical aid is immediately available but, despite defendant's urgings, plaintiff refuses to avail himself of it. Defendant specifically states, "You'd better go have a tetanus shot now. That's an old, worn knife that's been in many an animal carcass." Plaintiff steadfastly refused, saying, "I don't want to delay the trip."

Defendant contracted tetanus and suffered extensive medical costs in treating it. The medical opinion is that had he been inoculated immediately after the injury, he would not have contracted the disease. To what extent is the defendant liable to the plaintiff? Suppose the plaintiff had sought immediate inoculation; would the plaintiff have been liable for the costs of that preventative treatment?

This matter is examined extensively in Minzer, et. al., 3 Damages in Tort Actions, Chap. 16, "Doctrine of Avoidable Consequences." (Matthew Bender & Co.), from which the following adapted excerpts are taken.

It is well established that an injured party may not recover damages from a wrongdoer for any consequences of the injury which could have been reasonably avoided.[20] In practice, the rule focuses on the injured party's efforts to minimize those damages proximately flowing from the injury-producing event.[21] The scope of the minimization effort is circumscribed by these factors:

(1) it must be in good faith;

(2) it must be executed with reasonable skill, prudence, and efficiency;

(3) it must be reasonably warranted by, and in proportion to, the injury and consequences to be averted; and

(4) it must be undertaken in a reasonably justified belief that it will avoid or reduce the damage otherwise to be expected from the wrongdoing.

The rule applies whether the injury be to person or to property, in both settings precluding as a matter of policy those recoveries which either would be unjust[22] or

---

[20] *See, e.g., Chesapeake & Ohio Ry. v. Kelly*, 241 U.S. 485, 36 S. Ct. 630, 60 L. Ed. 417 (1915). "Ordinarily a person seeking to recover damages for the wrongful act of another must do that which a reasonable man would do under the circumstances to limit the amount of the damages."

[21] *See, e.g., Crowson v. Bayou State Oil Corp.*, 367 So.2d 417 (La. App. 1979), judgment amended by reducing award by one-half where plaintiff failed to minimize loss to herd of cattle resulting from ingestion of oil-contaminated water.

[22] *See, e.g., Tatum v. Morton*, 386 F. Supp. 1308 (D. D.C. 1974), court disallowed damages for prolongation of detention resulting from plaintiff's refusal to post $10 collateral; court quoted *Ellerman Lines, Ltd. v. The President Harding*, 288 F.2d 288, 290 (2d Cir. [NY] 1961): " 'The community's notions

would contribute to an unnecessary increase in the overall costs of accidents.[23] Moreover, the doctrine of avoidable consequences applies with equal force whether the action is in tort or for breach of contract.

Importantly, the rule does not foreclose all recovery and should not be confused with the doctrine of contributory negligence.[24] Contributory negligence, which may serve as a bar to any recovery by the injured party [or to diminish damages in a comparative law jurisdiction], focuses on the cause of the initial injury — producing event. Minimization of damages, in contrast, focuses on the injured party's action or inaction subsequent to the initial injury.[25]

Generally, the doctrine of avoidable consequences will not operate against an injured party where the failure to minimize damages occurs subsequent to some intentional or reckless act on defendant's part, or where the tort is positive and continuous,[26] or constitutes a nuisance.[27]

. . .

Generally, the doctrine of avoidable consequences functions as a negative rule, disallowing recovery of damages which the injured party could reasonably have avoided. The doctrine, however, encompasses an important affirmative dimension as well, permitting recovery of costs reasonably expended by an injured party in an effort to minimize losses.[28] Illustratively, interest charges on loans,[29] as well as attorney and other professional fees not associated with the litigation expenses of the lawsuit,[30] are recoverable from the wrongdoer.

---

of fair compensation to an injured plaintiff do not include wounds which in a practical sense are self-inflicted.' "

[23] Note, Medical Care, Freedom of Religion, & Mitigation of Damages, 87 Yale L.J. 1466 (1978).

[24] *See e.g., Bill C. Harris Constr. Co. v. Powers,* 554 S.W.2d 332 (Ark. 1977), damage to bulldozer submerged in rising waters; "Failure to mitigate damages does not relieve a tortfeasor of liability. It is a consideration, only, in the computation of the amount of damages."

[25] *See, e.g., Blair v. Eblen,* 461 S.W.2d 370 (Ky. 1970), judgment for defendant-doctor in hand injury case rev'd; trial court erred in submitting contributory negligence instruction to the jury where the plaintiff's alleged negligent conduct occurred after the hand had been permanently injured, part of it amputated, and the defendant's treatment of it had ceased; defendant only entitled to an instruction on minimization.

[26] *See, e.g., Allen v. Morris Bldg. Co.,* 360 Mich. 214, 103 N.W.2d 491 (1960), willful grading of adjoining lots led to permanent drainage of surface water onto plaintiffs' property; judgment for plaintiffs affirmed; rule cited and applied; plaintiffs not required to raise the grade of their own lot to minimize damages.

[27] *See, e.g., Desimone v. Mutual Materials Co.,* 162 P.2d 808 (Wash. 1945), damage to crops and land from flooding resulting from defendant's sand operation; plaintiffs need not show reasonable efforts to minimize damages in order to recover, since that requirement ". . . does not apply to cases of nuisances. . . . "

[28] *See, e.g., Robbins v. Farmers Union Grain Terminal Ass'n,* 552 F.2d 788 (8th Cir. [SD] 1977), costs of extra feed supplement to offset weight loss and increase value of cattle were recoverable; judgment for plaintiff affirmed.

[29] *See, e.g., Rodrigues v. State,* 52 Hawaii 156, 472 P.2d 509 (1970), "interest charges, an incidental expense of a loan which is incurred by the claimant in good faith to mitigate damages, may be recovered as an item of compensatory damages"; homeowners permitted to recover interest charges expense on loan, incurred to effect repairs to their flooded house and its furnishings, made necessary by defendant's negligent failure to keep a culvert clear of obstructions.

[30] *See, e.g., Tulsa Mun. Airport Trust v. National Gypsum Co.,* 551 P.2d 304 (Okla. App. 1976), plaintiffs stated a cause of action for the recovery of reasonable fees for services rendered by roofing expert and attorney in an effort to reduce losses resulting from defendants' alleged creation of a faulty

Importantly, recovery of costs may be had even where the effort to minimize damages proves unsuccessful,[31] or actually increases the loss,[32] or where less costly alternatives might later be shown to have been available.[33]

§ 10.02   PUNITIVE DAMAGES

ROGINSKY v. RICHARDSON-MERRILL, INC.
United States Court of Appeals, Second Circuit
378 F.2d 832 (1967)

FRIENDLY, J:

[This was a product liability action to recover for personal injuries suffered by the plaintiff, primarily the development of cataracts, a consequence of taking a medicine MER/29 manufactured by the defendant to lower blood cholesterol levels. The plaintiff also claimed punitive damages on grounds that the defendant was consciously indifferent to damaging side effects of the drug in the manner it conducted its testing program. Applying the law of New York, the federal district court awarded both compensatory and punitive damages. The appeals court is aware that several hundred similar actions have been filed against the manufacturer.]

IV.

We thus come to the issue of punitive damages, an issue of extreme significance not only in monetary terms to this defendant in view of the hundreds of pending MER/29 actions and to the plaintiff as well, but from a longer range, to the entire pharmaceutical industry and to all present and potential users of drugs. Plaintiff, of course, does not claim that defendant intended to harm him; his contention is that defendant's negligence rose to such a level of irresponsibility or worse as to invite this extraordinary sanction.

The remedy has a long history. Its first articulation in England came in a case of illegal entry. The jury was held justified in going beyond "the small injury done to the plaintiff" because of the desirability of taking account of "a most daring public attack made upon the liberty of the subject" through entry and imprisonment pursuant to "a nameless warrant." Huckle v. Money, 2 Will.K.B. 206, 95 Eng. Rep. 768 (1763). See also Wilkes v. Wood, Lofft 1, 18, 19, 98 Eng. Rep. 489, 498–99 (C.P.

---

aircraft hangar roof; court distinguished between costs of litigation" and "costs of mitigation"; judgment dismissing plaintiffs action reversed.

[31] *See, e.g., Texas & Pac. Ry. v. Mercer*, 90 S.W.2d 557 (Tex. App. 1936), plaintiff-farmer entitled to recover for wear and tear to truck which he had to drive over narrow, rough, dirt road to get to produce market because defendant blocked graveled highway for 4 months; "the expenses incurred in an effort to mitigate damages are not to aggravate, but to lessen, the amount for which the wrongdoer might be held liable. If the effort is successful, the defendant reaps the benefit thereof. If it turns out otherwise, it is but just that he should sustain the loss."

[32] *See, e.g.*, Elgin, J. & E. Ry. v. American Commercial Line, Inc., 317 F. Supp. 175 (N.D. Ill. 1970), bridge struck by barge being pushed by defendant's vessel; safety of bridge reasonable justification for plaintiff's acceptance of higher repair bid where highest bidder could begin work 3 months sooner than low bidder; judgment for plaintiff.

[33] *See, e.g.*, Elgin, J. & E. v. American Commercial Line, Inc., 317 F. Supp. 175 (N.D. Ill. 1970).

1763). Later decisions reflect a variety of rationales: redressing affronts to personal feelings not susceptible of measurement, cf. Tullidge v. Wade, 3 Wils. K.B. 18, 95 Eng. Rep. 909 (1769), financing the cost of deserving litigation where only small compensatory damages can be expected, diverting the plaintiff's desire for revenge into peaceful channels, and serving as punishment for and deterrence from socially disapproved conduct. "Typical of the torts for which such damages may be awarded are assault and battery, libel and slander, deceit, seduction, alienation of affections, malicious prosecution, and intentional interferences with property such as trespass, private nuisance, and conversion." Prosser, Torts § 2 at 10-11 (1964). What strikes one is not merely that these torts are intentional but that usually there is but a single victim; a punitive recovery by him ends the matter, except for such additional liability as may be provided by the criminal law.

There is no doubt, however, that the remedy has been extended to cases where, although the defendant did not intend to harm the plaintiff, he showed "such a conscious and deliberate disregard of the interests of others that his conduct may be called willful or wanton." Prosser, Torts § 2 at 10 (1964). Such an extension was altogether natural: from a moral standpoint there is not too much difference between the driver who heads his car into a plaintiff and the driver who takes the wheel knowing himself to be so drunk that he probably will hit someone and not caring whether he does or not; and it is as important to deter the latter type of conduct as the former. But such cases still resemble those first considered in an important respect — a high probability that the number of plaintiffs will be few and that they will join, or can be forced to join in a single trial.

The legal difficulties engendered by claims for punitive damages on the part of hundreds of plaintiffs are staggering. If all recovered punitive damages in the amount here awarded these would run into tens of millions, as contrasted with the maximum criminal penalty of "imprisonment for not more than three years, or a fine of not more than $10,000, or both such imprisonment and fine", 21 U.S.C. § 333(b), for each violation of the Food, Drug and Cosmetic Act with intent to defraud or mislead. We have the gravest difficulty in perceiving how claims for punitive damages in such a multiplicity of actions throughout the nation can be so administered as to avoid overkill. Judge Croake did all that he could here, instructing the jury that it "may consider the potentially wide effect of the actions of the corporation and, on the other hand, . . . the potential number of actions similar to this one to which that wide effect may render the defendant subject." Yet it is hard to see what even the most intelligent jury would do with this, being inherently unable to know what punitive damages, if any, other juries in other states may award other plaintiffs in actions yet untried. We know of no principle whereby the first punitive award exhausts all claims for punitive damages and would thus preclude future judgments; if there is, Toole's judgment in California, see fn. 3, which plaintiff's brief tells us came earlier, would bar Roginsky's. Neither does it seem either fair or practicable to limit punitive recoveries to an indeterminate number of first-comers, leaving it to some unascertained court to cry, "Hold, enough," in the hope that others would follow. While jurisprudes might comprehend why Toole in California should walk off with $250,000 more than a compensatory recovery and Roginsky in the Southern District of New York and Mrs. Ostopowitz in Westchester County with $100,000, most laymen and some judges would have some difficulty in understanding why presumably equally worthy plaintiffs in the other 75 cases before Judge Croake or elsewhere in the country should get less or none. And, whatever the right result may be in strict theory, we think it somewhat unrealistic to expect a judge, say in New Mexico, to tell a jury that their fellow townsman should get very little by way of punitive damages because Toole in California and Roginsky and Mrs. Ostopowitz in New York had stripped that cupboard bare, even assuming the defendant would want such a charge, and still more unrealistic to expect that the jury would follow such an instruction or that, if they didn't, the judge would reduce the award below what had become the going rate. There is more to be said for drastic judicial control of the amount of punitive awards so as to keep the prospective total within some manageable bounds. This would require, for example, a reduction of the instant $100,000 award to something in the $5000-$10,000 range, still leaving defendant exposed to several million dollars of exemplary damages. We perceive nothing in the New York decisions that would prevent our reducing a punitive damage award because of the large number of suits arising out of the same conduct by the defendant. But there is equally nothing to indicate that New York would follow such a course, and a state otherwise willing to impose such self-denying limits might be disinclined to do so until assured that others would follow suit.

Although multiple punitive awards running into the hundreds may not add up to a denial of due process, nevertheless if we were sitting as the highest court of New York we would wish to consider very seriously whether awarding punitive damages with respect to the negligent — even highly negligent — manufacture and sale of a drug governed by federal food and drug requirements, especially in the light of the strengthening of these by the 1962 amendments, 76 Stat. 780 (1962), and the present vigorous attitude toward enforcement, would not do more harm than good. A manufacturer distributing a drug to many thousands of users under government regulation scarcely requires this additional measure for manifesting social disapproval and assuring deterrence. Criminal penalties and heavy compensatory damages, recoverable under some circumstances even without proof of negligence, should sufficiently meet these objectives, see Note, supra note 6, 41 N.Y.U.L. Rev. at 1171, and the other factors cited as justifying punitive awards are lacking. Many awards of compensatory damages doubtless contain something of a punitive element, and more would do so if a separate award for exemplary damages were eliminated. Even though products liability insurance blunts the deterrent effect of compensatory awards to a considerable extent, the total limited, bad experience is usually reflected in future rates, and insurance affords no protection to the damage to reputation among physicians and pharmacists which an instance like the present must inevitably produce. On the other hand, the apparent impracticability of imposing an effective ceiling on punitive awards in hundreds of suits in different courts may result in an aggregate which, when piled on large compensatory damages, could reach catastrophic amounts. If liability policies can protect against this risk as several courts have held, the cost of providing this probably needless deterrence, not only to the few manufacturers from whom punitive damages for highly negligent conduct are sought but to the thousands from whom it never will be, is passed on to the consuming public; if they cannot, as is held by other courts and recommended by most commentators, a sufficiently egregious error as to one product can end the business life of a concern that has wrought much good in the past and might otherwise have continued to do so in the future, with many innocent stockholders suffering extinction of their investments for a single management sin.

However, the New York cases afford no basis for our predicting that the Court of Appeals would adopt a rule disallowing punitive damages in a case such as this, and the Erie doctrine wisely prevents our engaging in such extensive law-making on local tort liability, a subject which the people of New York have entrusted to their legislature and, within appropriate limits, to their own courts, not to us. Our task is the more modest one of assessing the sufficiency of the evidence within the framework of New York decisions on the award of punitive damages for recklessness. As to this, we are convinced that the consequences of imposing punitive damages in a case like the present are so serious that the New York Court of Appeals would subject the proof to particularly careful scrutiny.

V.

The parties are in substantial agreement on one point — that New York does not impose punitive damages on a corporation unless, as charged by Judge Croake, "the officers or directors, that is, the management" of the company or the relevant division "either authorized, participated in, consented to or, after discovery, ratified the conduct" giving rise to such damages. . . . New York, in other words, adheres to the "complicity rule," holding the corporate master liable for punitive damages "only when superior officers either order, participate in, or ratify outrageous conduct."

The New York courts have used a variety of phrases to describe the "moral culpability," Walker v. Sheldon, 10 N.Y.2d 401, 404–405, 223 N.Y.S.2d 488, 491, 179 N.E.2d 497 (1961), which will support punitive damages for nonintentional torts. In Caldwell v. New Jersey Steamboat Co., 47 N.Y. 282, 296 (1872), the Court of Appeals spoke of "utter recklessness." Later it said the conduct "must be reckless and of a criminal nature, and clearly established." Cleghorn v. New York Cent. & H. R.R.R., 56 N.Y. 44, 48 (1874). It has also used such terms as "wanton or malicious, or gross and outrageous," Powers v. Manhattan Ry., 120 N.Y. 178, 182, 24 N.E. 295, 296 (1890), and "conscious indifference to the effect of his acts." Gostkowski v. Roman Catholic Church of the Sacred Hearts, 262 N.Y. 320, 323, 186 N.E. 798, 799 (1933). Very recently the Third Department has spoken of action "'committed recklessly or wantonly, i.e., without regard to the rights of the plaintiff, or of people in general,'" Soucy v. Greyhound Corp., 27 A.D.2d 112, 113, 276 N.Y.S.2d 173, 175 (3d Dept. 1967), quoting Magagnos v. Brooklyn Heights R. R., 128 App. Div. 182, 112 N.Y.S. 637, 638 (2d Dept. 1908). In an earlier decision that court had held that "culpable negligence" was not enough to warrant punitive damages. Noonan v. Luther, 119 App. Div. 701, 104 N.Y.S. 684 (3d Dept. 1907). What comes through from a study of these and many other New York decisions is that the recklessness that will give rise to punitive damages must be close to criminality, see 14 N.Y. Jur., Damages § 181 p. 41, and that, like criminal conduct, it must be "clearly established." It therefore seems appropriate to look to the latest authoritative New York definition of recklessness, that expressed by the legislature in the Revised Penal Law, McKinney's Consol. Laws, c. 40, § 15.05, subd. 3:

A person acts recklessly with respect to a result . . . when he is aware of and consciously disregards a substantial and unjustifiable risk that such result will occur or that such circumstance exists. The risk must be of such nature and degree that disregard thereof constitutes a gross deviation from the standard of conduct that a reasonable person would observe in the situation.

Obviously this definition would be met if a manufacturer placed a drug on the market without any test program, a practice now rendered unlawful by federal legislation, or when its management knew the program had disclosed dangers of serious mischance or was incomplete in some material respect. Sufficient proof would also be furnished if, after the drug had been placed on the market, the manufacturer was shown to have become aware of danger and to have done nothing, deliberately closing its eyes. On the other hand, error in failing to make what hindsight demonstrates to have been the proper response — even "gross" error — is not enough to warrant submission of punitive damages to the jury.

[The court examines the evidence pertaining to the defendant's conduct in evaluating the risks of MER/29.]

Plaintiff places heavy reliance on the argument that even though no one of the incidents we have analyzed would itself warrant a finding of recklessness, their combination permits an inference of a plan which not only heightens the significance of each item but would permit consideration of other acts we have not detailed including those of subordinates. We have no quarrel with this as a general principle; indeed we have said quite recently that, even in a criminal case, "The trier is entitled, in fact bound, to consider the evidence as a whole; and, in law as in life, the effect of this generally is much greater than of the sum of the parts." United States v. Bottone, 365 F.2d 389, 392 (2 Cir.), cert. denied, 385 U.S. 974, 87 S. Ct. 514, 17 L. Ed. 2d 437 (1966). Still the burden devolves on the court to see that when all the evidence is thus considered, there is enough to warrant the finding that the law requires. And here we think plaintiff fails. The thorough discovery by his industrious and able counsel has unearthed countless instances of carelessness and even of wilfulness by subordinate officials and of failure to exercise proper supervision and possible bad judgment by higher ones. Granted that few human endeavors would escape without blemish from such searching scrutiny, the picture is not a pretty one. But there was no proof from which a jury could properly conclude that defendant's officers manifested deliberate disregard for human welfare; what it shows as to this, apart from negligence in policing subordinates and a somewhat stiff-necked attitude toward the FDA, is rather that they were so convinced of the value of the drug both to the public welfare and to the company's finances that they maintained a sanguine view longer than prudence warranted.

. . .

The judgment as to compensatory damages is affirmed; the judgment as to punitive damages is reversed. No costs.

NOTES AND QUESTIONS

(1) Awarding punitive damages clearly departs from the typical tort goal of restoring a plaintiff to status quo ante as nearly as can be done by an award of money. The justification for it is "to punish wrongdoers and deter the commission of wrongful acts." *Pistorius v. Prudential Ins. Co. of America*, 176 Cal. Rptr. 660, 667 (Cal. App. 1981). The Roginsky opinion canvasses most of the tests employed to determine whether punitive damages ought to be awarded. The case is easiest when the basic tort involves an intentional wrong or malicious misbehavior and is most difficult when the basic tort is simple negligence without any coloration of improper motivation. Courts are wary about turning every compensation claim into one for punitive damages. Thus, according to the Georgia Court of Appeal:

> . . . To authorize the imposition of punitive damages, there must be affirmative evidence of facts showing "willful misconduct, malice, fraud, wantonness, or oppression, or that entire want of care which would raise the presumption of a conscious indifference to consequences. . . . If this be not the law, then practically every case of negligent injury can be the vehicle of submitting to the jury the question of willfulness and wantonness, by merely using adjectives in describing the character of the negligence. . . . Negligence, although gross, will not alone authorize the recovery of punitive damages.

Mills v. Mangum, 107 Ga. App. 614, 617 (1963). Similarly, *Chrysler Corporation v. Wolmer*, 499 So.2d 823, 825 (Fla. 1986), confirmed that in Florida personal injury actions, "punitive damages are warranted only where the egregious conduct of the defendant, although perhaps not covered by criminal law constitutes a public wrong by [exhibiting] a reckless disregard for human life equivalent to manslaughter. . . ", and *Roboserve, Incorporated v. Kato Kagabu Company, Limited*, 78 F.2d 266, 276 (7th Cir. 1996), applying Illinois law, held that punitive damages were disfavored in fraud actions in that state and would be awarded only upon a showing of "an intent to injure constituting gross misconduct or malicious behavior."

Courts usually impose special rules before awarding punitive damages on the basis of vicarious liability. For example, *Mattyasovszky v. West Towns Bus Co.*, 330 N.E.2d 509 (Ill. 1975), applied the rule of Restatement (Second) of Agency Section 217C which states:

> Punitive damages can properly be awarded against a master or other principal because of an act by an agent if, but only if: (a) the principal authorized the doing and the manner of the act, or (b) the agent was unfit and the principal reckless in employing him, or (c) the agent was employed in managerial capacity and was acting within the scope of employment, or (d) the principal or a managerial agent of the principal ratified or approved the act.

Despite this cautious approach, at least two courts have authorized punitive damages in automobile crash cases solely on grounds that the defendant was driving while intoxicated as long as a prima facie case of simple negligence was otherwise made out. See *Taylor v. Superior Court*, 598 P.2d 854 (Cal. 1979), and *Ingram v. Pettit*, 340 So. 2d 922 (Fla. 1976). Even granting that drunk drivers constitute a danger of unusual gravity upon the highways, does this fact justify singling out individual defendants for civil punishment in the form of punitive damages without holding the plaintiff to the usual standards of proof? Do punitive damages constitute a windfall to plaintiffs? How else might the goals of punitive damages be satisfied?

(2) Numerous attempts have been made to overturn punitive damage awards on the ground that they permit the deprivation of property without due process of law. Most have been unsuccessful, but *BMW of North America v. Gore*, 116 S. Ct. 1589 (1996), held that a $2,000,000 punitive damage award arising out of a $4,000 compensatory award in a fraudulent concealment case did constitute a deprivation of property without due process of law because the defendant was not on notice of the potential legal consequences of his actions. In adjudging the issue, the Supreme Court focussed on three factors that it deemed to be indicators of punitive damages excessiveness: (a) the egregiousness of the defendant's actions; (b) the ratio

between compensatory damages and the amount of punitive damages; and (c) the difference between the punitive damage award and the civil and criminal penalties imposed for comparable misconduct that is positively outlawed by statute or regulation.

The Supreme Court extended its *BMW* due process analysis in *State Farm Mut. Auto. Ins. Co. v. Campbell*, 538 U.S. 408, 123 S. Ct. 1513 (2003). After observing that *BMW* required courts to consider these three guideposts in reviewing jury punitive damage awards,

(1) the degree of reprehensibility of the defendant's misconduct;

(2) the disparity between the actual or potential harm suffered by the plaintiff and the punitive damages award; and

(3) the difference between the punitive damages awarded by the jury and the civil penalties authorized or imposed in comparable cases.

Id., 123 S. Ct. at 1520, the Supreme Court applied them to hold that a $145 million punitive award could not stand in a case of an $1 million compensatory award. The Court suggested that a 1:1 ratio of punitive to compensatory awards would "likely" be justified in that case. Id., 123 S. Ct. at 1526. The Supreme Court further extended its analysis in *Exxon Shipping Co. v. Baker*, 128 S. Ct. 2605 (2008). There, a jury returned a verdict of $507.5 million in compensatory damages and $5 billion in punitive damages. The trial court entered judgment in the amount of the compensatory award and entered a punitive damages judgment of $2.5 billion (after remitting half of the jury's verdict). Applying maritime law (not constitutional principles) the Supreme Court held that the maximum ratio of punitive to compensatory damages in the case should be 1:1. Examining statistical studies of compensatory and punitive awards in many decisions, the Court found that the mean ratio was about 0.7:1 punitive to compensatory. That being so, the Court held that the upper limit in maritime cases is 1:1 punitive to compensatory and directed the lower courts to remit the punitive award to the amount of the compensatory award.

(3) The tort reform movement has accounted for the enactment of some kind of punitive damages statutes in about 80% of the states. See American Tort Reform Association, Tort Reform Record, December 31, 1995. In an appendix to *BMW of North America v. Gore*, note 2 supra., the Supreme Court compiled these statutes in three categories: I. Caps on Punitive Damages (16 states); II. Allocation of Punitive Damages to State Agencies (13 states); and III. Mandatory Bifurcation of Liability and Punitive Damages Determinations (13 states). (Some states have adopted more than one measure.) Does a statute regulate punitive damages in your state?

(4) If punitive damages are to be awarded in a tort case, what guidelines ought to be followed in assessing how much? In the criminal law, statutes authorize incarceration and fines within ranges that the legislators believe satisfy the various retributive, deterrent and rehabilitative goals of the law. In the common law of torts no guidelines are provided apart from the admonitions of appellate courts. One court listed guidelines "all of which are grounded in the purpose and function of punitive damages" as follows:

One factor is the particular nature of the defendant's acts in light of the whole record; clearly, different acts may be of varying degrees of reprehensibility, and the more reprehensible the act, the greater the appropriate punishment, assuming all other factors are equal. Another relevant yardstick is the amount of compensatory damages awarded; in general, even an act of considerable reprehensibility will not be seen to justify a proportionally high amount of punitive damages if the actual harm suffered thereby is small. Also to be considered is the wealth of the particular defendant; obviously, the function of deterence will not be served if the wealth of the defendant allows him to absorb the award with little or no discomfort. By the same token, of course, the function of punitive damages is not served by an award which, in light of the defendant's wealth and the gravity of the particular act, exceed the level necessary to properly punish and deter.

Neal v. Farmers Ins. Exchange, 582 P.2d 980 (Cal. 1978).

Within the stated guidelines the amount of punitive damages is discretionary with the jury and will not be disturbed on appeal absent a showing that the jury was influenced by passion or prejudice, or that the award bears no relationship to the harm done, or that it imposes a hardship out of proportion to the injury suffered. *Tallcott v. Hall*, 224 So. 2d 420, 422 (Fla. App. 1969).

In *Bould v. Touchett*, 349 So. 2d 1181 (Fla. 1977), the Florida Supreme Court repudiated the common rule that punitive damages should bear some proportionate relationship to the amount of compensatory damages in favor of the more flexible rule that the goal should be to "hurt but not to bankrupt." Following this approach, the court approved an $800,000 punitive damages award in a $65,000 compensatory damages case. The amount of the award would not bankrupt the defendant. What recommends this rule more highly than one, say, that punitive damages may not exceed compensatory damages? For extended discussions of punitive damages, see *BMW of North America, Inc. v. Gore*, note 2 supra. and 5 Minzer et al., Damages in Tort Actions, Chapter 40, "Punitive Damages" (Matthew Bender & Co.).

(5) Some read Judge Friendley's *Roginsky* opinion as cautioning against awards of punitive damages in so-called mass tort litigation. That caution has not stopped the courts from awarding punitive damages in mass tort cases, notably those against tobacco manufacturers and in the notorious *Exxon Valdez* cases. *See, e.g., Exxon Shipping Co. v. Baker*, 128 S. Ct. 2605 (2008). The court in *Johns-Manville Sales Corp v. Janssens*, 463 So. 2d 242, 254 (Fla. 1st DCA 1988), stated: "The arguments against allowing punitive damages in mass product litigation made by Judge Friendly in *Roginsky v Richardson Merrill, Inc.*, . . . are pure dictum and have not been accepted by any other court." Nevertheless, *Baker* and *Janssens* involved a single defendant and many plaintiffs. By contrast, cases involving classes of defendants and plaintiffs often raise difficult issues of class certification that are beyond the scope of this study and that often fail. *See, e.g., Engle v. Liggett Group, Inc.*, 945 So. 2d 1246 (Fla. 2006).

§ 10.03   PROPERTY DAMAGES

[See *Livingston v. The Rawyards Coal Co.*, § 4.06, *supra.*]

NOTES AND QUESTIONS

(1) Having no general damages element and usually wholly determinable at the time of trial, property damages ordinarily are not as difficult to assess as personal injury damages. The following black letter statement from McCormick on Damages[34] sums up the usual rules.

124. When personal property is wrongfully destroyed, the normal measure of damages is its value at the time of destruction, with interest.

When personal property is wrongfully injured —

(a) The normal standard of recovery is the difference between the value just before, and just after, the injury.

(b) But if the damaged property is reasonably susceptible of repair, the owner may recover the reasonable cost of repair, plus the difference between the value of the property before the injury and after the repair, unless the value is enhanced, in which event the increase in value would be deducted from the cost of repair.

(c) And if recovery is based upon the cost of repair, the owner may recover, in addition, for the loss of the use of the property during the time necessary for repair. In case of a vehicle or vessel which is customarily rented out by the owner, the usable value may be measured by the market rental value; and, in cases where a substitute has actually been employed, the reasonable cost of the substitute may be recovered as special damage due to the deprivation of use.

(2) Occasionally property may be destroyed that has virtually no market value, yet might have had considerable sentimental value or use value to its owner. As to property of this class one court said:

> It is often impossible to place what is a current market value on such articles but the law does not contemplate that this be done with mathematical exactness. The law guarantees every person a remedy when he has been wronged. If the damage is to personal property as in this case, it may be impossible to show that all of it had a market value. In fact it may be very valuable so far as the owner is concerned but have no value so far as the public is concerned. It would be manifestly unfair to apply the test of market value in such cases.

> When the wrong is shown it becomes the duty of court and jury to apply a test that will reasonably compensate the person wronged rather than one that makes it impossible to do so.

Florida Public Utilities Co. v. Wester, 7 So. 2d 788, 89 (Fla. 1942).

Another court has applied a three tier test of damages to personal property: (1) Market value in the case of destruction of property with market value; (2) cost to replace or reproduce if there is no market value and the thing can be replaced or reproduced; and (3) value to the owner if the thing has no market value and cannot be replaced or reproduced. *McCurdy v. Union Pac. R.R.*, 413 P.2d 617 (Wash. 1966). Under this view, value attributable to pure sentiment, meaning "indulging in feeling to an unwarranted extent" or "affectedly or mawkishly emotional" is not

---

[34] Reprinted from McCormick on Damages with permission of the West Publishing Company. Copyright 1935.

recoverable. *Mieske v. Bartell Crug Co.*, 593 P.2d 1308, 1311 (Wash. 1979).

The subject of recovery for injury to property is explored in detail in 4 Minzer, et al., Damages in Tort Actions, Chapter 37, "Damages to and Destruction of Personal Property" (Matthew Bender & Co.).

Chapter 11

MULTIPLE PARTIES

§ 11.01 INTRODUCTION

The presence of more than two parties in a tortious episode poses additional difficulties in the application of tort doctrines. The issues most often appearing are treated in four separate subsections: § 11.02, Vicarious Liability, examines circumstances where one person will be held responsible for the negligence of another; § 11.03, Settlement Issues, examines factors that impinge upon a plaintiff's willingness to settle with only one of two or more tortfeasors; § 11.04, Special Considerations in Comparative Negligence Actions, examines special problems raised by comparative fault in multi-party actions; and § 11.05, Contribution and Indemnity, examines adjustment of liabilities among tortfeasors. In addition to matters of substantive law, these issues frequently involve sophisticated questions of civil procedure and trial practice, which can only be touched upon here.

§ 11.02 VICARIOUS LIABILITY

Under what circumstances, if any, should one person be held legally responsible in tort for the wrongful acts of another? For the purposes here, you should approach this question with two assumptions: (1) that the person sought to be held liable was completely free of wrongful behavior of any kind, and (2) that the person who actually caused the harm was actively negligent. What is the rationale of vicarious liability? Vindication of wrong, deterrence, or something else entirely?

PERDUE v. MITCHELL
Alabama Supreme Court
373 So. 2d 650 (1979)

Shores, Justice.

This is a suit for injuries allegedly arising from the negligent operation of an automobile. Defendant Mitchell, the operator of the car, was served but failed to appear at trial; and the court entered a default judgment against him in the amount of $10,000. That judgment is not contested on appeal. At the close of testimony, the trial court entered a directed verdict in favor of the owner of the car, defendant/ Mrs. Eloise Smith. The plaintiffs appealed and argue that two rulings require reversal: . . .

2) The trial court's granting Mrs. Smith's motion for a directed verdict.

The accident involved occurred when Mrs. Smith's automobile, driven by Mitchell, made a left turn in front of a van owned and operated by plaintiffs, Tillman and Patricia Perdue. Mrs. Smith was not in the car at the time of the collision. Plaintiffs base their claim against her on two theories: 1) Vicarious liability and 2) negligent entrustment.

The record shows that Mrs. Smith is elderly and infirm and depends on friends and relatives to chauffeur her about. On the day of the accident, she arranged for defendant Mitchell, a seventeen-year-old boy, to drive her to her brother's house in Coldwater, Alabama, where she intended to preserve peaches. Before leaving Montgomery, Mrs. Smith and the Mitchell boy stopped at the farmers' market where Mrs. Smith was to buy the peaches. While she was inside the market, Mitchell drove off in the car and collided with plaintiffs' van. Mrs. Smith was left stranded at the farmers' market and, after trying to locate her car for two hours, she got a ride home. She testified that she attempted to have the Mitchell boy arrested but was told by the police that she would have to report it to the juvenile authorities. She testified that she did so. She learned of the accident during the afternoon. Her automobile was a total loss. Plaintiffs contend that Mitchell had permission to use Mrs. Smith's car at the time of the accident and was, therefore, acting as her agent.

. . .

Because no evidence whatever was presented on the issue of negligent entrustment, we are concerned here solely with the issue of vicarious liability.

A directed verdict is proper in two circumstances:

> . . . First, where there is a complete absence of pleading or proof on an issue or issues material to the cause of action or defense, and second, where there are not any controverted issues of fact upon which reasonable men could differ [Citation Omitted]. *Loeb and Co., Inc. v. Martin*, 295 Ala. 262, 264, 327 So. 2d 711, 712 (1976).

ARCP 50, which establishes the directed verdict device, specifically incorporates the scintilla rule. The appellate court must, therefore, examine the record to see if there exists " . . . a mere gleam, glimmer, spark, the least particle, the smallest trace, or a scintilla in support of the theory of the complaint. . . . " *Kilcrease v. Harris*, 288 Ala. 245, 252, 259 So. 2d 797, 802 (1972).

An examination of the record reveals that the plaintiffs failed to introduce any testimony which would support their contention that Mitchell was operating the vehicle with Mrs. Smith's permission at the time of the accident. Mrs. Smith does not contest plaintiffs' assertion that Mitchell was operating the vehicle as her agent while she was with him in the car. She does contend, however, that she did not authorize him to take the car while she was inside the farmers' market, and that he was performing no business for her when he did so. To recover for damages for injuries sustained in an automobile accident against the driver's employer upon a theory of respondent superior, it is incumbent upon plaintiff to prove that the collision occurred while the driver was within the scope of its employment, and happened while he was in the accomplishment of objectives within the line of his duties. . . .

The facts establish only that Mitchell was authorized to drive Mrs. Smith to Coldwater, not to use the car in her absence The only testimony introduced on that subject was that of Mrs. Smith and Sandra Judy, Mitchell's mother. Mrs. Smith denied that she had given Mitchell permission to use the car. Mrs. Judy testified that Mrs. Smith telephoned her home asking for Mitchell's whereabouts, stating that he was supposed to be waiting for her at the market.

Plaintiffs are forced to fall back on an administrative presumption of agency raised by proof of Mrs. Smith's ownership of the car. They cite *Alabama Power Co. v. McGehee*, 228 Ala. 505, 509, 154 So. 105, 108 (1934), to the effect that:

> . . . proof of ownership of an automobile causing injury raises an administrative presumption that the person in possession and control of the automobile is the agent or servant of the owner, and is acting within the line and scope of his employment. (Citations Omitted)

The effect of these presumptions as stated in *Tullis v. Blue*, 216 Ala. 577, 578, 114 So. 185, 187 is: " . . . They are prima facie presumptions merely, or, as they are sometimes called, administrative presumptions, based upon considerations of fairness and convenience in placing the burden of proof. They are not in themselves evidence, and in practice their effect is merely to impose upon the defendant (the owner of the car) the burden of showing that the driver was not his agent, or that, if he was, he was not acting within the scope of his authority or in the course of his employment. If the evidence thereon is in conflict, or leads to doubtful inference only, the issue should go to the jury. If, however, the evidence, without dispute, rebuts the facts thus presumed, there is no issue for the jury, and the general affirmative charge should be given for the defendant on request. *Dowdell v. Beasley*, 205 Ala. 130, 87 So. 18."

The holding of *McGehee, supra*, has been reaffirmed as recently as *Cook v. Fullbright, supra*, and *Teague v. Motes*, 57 Ala. App. 609, 330 So. 2d 434 (1976). Both decisions postdate the passage of the new Rules which substitute the directed verdict for the affirmative charge mentioned in *McGehee*, Rule 50, Committee Comments.

By proving Mrs. Smith's ownership of the vehicle, plaintiffs passed to her the burden of showing that Mitchell was not acting as her agent at the time of the accident. She testified that Mitchell was not acting on her behalf; that, to the contrary, he stole her automobile and left her stranded. This testimony was clear and undisputed. The plaintiffs did not offer any evidence that Mitchell was acting within the scope of his employment, or that he was a permissive user of the car at the time of the accident. In these circumstances, a directed verdict was appropriate.

. . .

Affirmed.

NOTES AND QUESTIONS

(1) Perhaps the doctrine of *respondeat superior* is the most frequently applied form of vicarious liability. Why did it fail in *Perdue v. Mitchell?* Most applications involve negligent operation of motor vehicles.

Under what circumstances should the owner of, say, a Coca Cola delivery truck, not be liable for the negligent driving of the employee-operator of the truck?

(2) What is the basis of *respondeat superior* liability? According to the speech of Lord Pearce in *Imperial Chemical Indus. Ltd. v. Shatwell* [1965] App. Cas. 683 [H.L.],

The doctrine of vicarious liability has not grown from any very clear, logical or legal principle but from social convenience and rough justice. The master having (presumably for his own benefit) employed the servant, and being (presumably) better able to make good any damage which may occasionally result from the arrangement, is answerable to the world at large for all the torts committed by his servant within the scope of it. The doctrine maintains that liability even in respect of acts which the employers had expressly prohibited . . . and even when the employers are guilty of no fault themselves. . . .

Is this law or economics?

(3)   The requirement of a master (employer)-servant (employee) relationship as a basis for *respondeat superior* liability frequently injects principles of the law of agency into tort actions. Ordinarily, vicarious liability does not apply when one person hires an independent contractor to perform some job when the contractor is not under that person's direct control in performing the details of the work. For example, is a person who contracts with building contractor X to have a home built ordinarily liable for X's wrongful acts in building the home? Why?

In distinguishing between servants to whose acts *respondeat superior* applies, and independent contractors to whose acts the doctrine does not apply, most courts apply Restatement Agency Second § 220:[1]

Definition of Servant

(1) A servant is a person employed to perform services in the affairs of another and who with respect to the physical conduct in the performance of the services is subject to the other's control or right to control.

(2) In determining whether one acting for another is a servant or an independent contractor, the following matters of fact, among others, are considered:

(a) the extent of control which, by the agreement, the master may exercise over the details of the work;

(b) whether or not the one employed is engaged in a distinct occupation or business;

(c) the kind of occupation, with reference to whether, in the locality, the work is usually done under the direction of the employer or by a specialist without supervision;

(d) the skill required in the particular occupation;

(e) whether the employer or the workman supplies the instrumentalities, tools, and the place of work for the person doing the work;

(f) the length of time for which the person is employed;

(g) the method of payment, whether by the time or by the job;

(h) whether or not the work is a part of the regular business of the employer;

---

[1] Copyright 1965 by The American Law Institute. Reprinted with the permission of The American Law Institute.

(i) whether or not the parties believe they are creating the relation of master and servant; and

(j) whether the principal is or is not in business.

Do occasions exist in which a contracting party should be liable for the torts of a genuine independent contractor?

(4)　An exception to the general rule that an owner or contracting party is not liable for the negligence of an independent contractor in performing a contract is that the contracting party remains liable for negligence connected with the performance of a *nondelegable duty.* Consider this excerpt from *Chiani v. Board of Education of the City of New York,* 663 N.E.2d 283, 287–88 (N.Y. 1995), in which parents of a child struck by a car after leaving a school bus at an unauthorized stop sued the school board on theories of direct and vicarious liability for the negligence of the independent contractor school transportation company:

Plaintiffs contend that the schools are vicariously liable . . . because the task delegated was inherently dangerous. [W]e decline plaintiffs' invitation to extend liability to the schools.

Ordinarily, a principal is not liable for the acts of independent contractors in that, unlike the master-servant relationship, principals cannot control the manner in which the independent contractors' work is performed. Of numerous exceptions to this general rule, the one plaintiffs advance is the nondelegable duty — that the defendants were not free to delegate to a contractor the responsibility for transporting school children. . . . The "nondelegable duty" exception may be invoked where a particular responsibility is imposed upon a principal by statute or regulation . . . or where the task at issue is inherently dangerous. . . . [W]e [cannot] agree with plaintiffs that vicarious liability should be imposed because the duty delegated is inherently dangerous. . . . This State has long recognized an exception from the general rule where, generically, the activity involved is "dangerous in spite of all reasonable care" . . . This exception applies when it appears both that "the work involves a risk of harm inherent in the nature of the work itself [and] that the employer recognizes, or should recognize, that risk in advance of the contract" . . . Familiar examples of inherently dangerous activities are blasting, certain types of construction and working with high tension electric wires. . . .

Demanding though it may be, the activity of transporting children by bus to and from school — successfully accomplished countless times daily — does not involve that sort of inherent risk for the nonnegligent driver and is simply not an inherently dangerous activity so as to trigger vicarious liability. Plaintiffs contend that a particularized version of this same exception applies where the employer knows or has special reason to know that the work for which the independent contractor was hired creates a "peculiar unreasonable risk" in the absence of special precautions and the employer takes no steps to minimize the risk. (Restatement [Second] of Torts § 413;[2] see, . . . Prosser and Keeton, Torts § 71, at 512 [neither "inherently

---

[2]　Restatement (Second) of Torts § 413 reads in full:

One who employs an independent contractor to do work which the employer should recognize as likely to create, during its progress, a peculiar unreasonable risk of physical harm to others unless special precautions are taken, is subject to liability for physical harm caused to them by the absence of such precautions if the employer (a) fails to provide in the contract

dangerous" nor "peculiar unreasonable risk" has been well defined and have been used by courts interchangeably]). The school's failure to inform students that they were prohibited from crossing Route 209 and to instruct bus drivers not to pick up students who crossed the highway, according to plaintiffs, resulted in a "peculiar unreasonable risk" for which the school should be vicariously liable because it did not take adequate precautions. We have not previously adopted or rejected this Restatement exception and find it unnecessary to do so here.

[S]ection 413 rests on both the principal's knowledge of a peculiar unreasonable risk created by the work of the independent contractor and the principal's failure to take any steps to minimize that risk, though in the best position to do so. . . . Here, there was no evidence that the school knew of the students' unsafe practice of crossing the highway to undesignated stops; the school took measures to minimize any risk by designating stops on both sides of the road; and the bus company, which did know of the students' practice, was itself in a position to reduce the risk by refusing to receive passengers except at their designated stops.

There is, in short, no basis for direct or vicarious liability of defendant schools.

More generally, the court in *Alcock v. Wraith*, 59 Builder L.R. 16 (1991) (Court of Appeal), listed the "main exceptions" to the "general principle" in English law that a person who employs an independent contractor is not vicariously liable for the contractor's torts; as follows:

(a) Cases where the employer is under some statutory duty which he cannot delegate.

(b) Cases involving the withdrawal of support from neighboring land.

(c) Cases involving the escape of fire.

(d) Cases involving the escape of substances, such as explosives, which have been brought on to the land and which are likely to do damage if they escape; liability will attach under the rule in Rylands v. Fletcher (1868) LR3 HL330.

(e) Cases involving operations on the highway which may cause danger to persons using the highway.

(f) Cases involving non-delegable duties of an employer for the safety of his employees.

(g) Cases involving extra-hazardous acts.

(5)   In what may be the strongest theory of vicarious liability is the doctrine that the possessor of a "dangerous instrumentality" who consents to its use by another person is vicariously liable for negligence in the consensual use. In an apparently novel position, the Florida Supreme Court has held that an ordinary automobile is a dangerous instrumentality when used on the public highways. *Anderson v. Southern Cotton Oil Co.*, 74 So. 975 (Fla. 1917). The Florida court has acknowledged only exceedingly narrow exceptions to this doctrine. *See, e.g., Ady v. American Honda Finance Corporation*, 675 So. 2d 577 (Fla. 1996). Compare the reach of this doctrine in connection with the use of borrowed or rented motor vehicles on the highway to that of the doctrine employed in *Perdue v. Mitchell.* The Florida legislature enacted a statute that limited the amount of the vicarious liability of

---

that the contractor shall take such precautions, or (b) fails to exercise reasonable care to provide in some other manner for the taking of such precautions.

commercial rental car companies under the Florida dangerous instrumentality doctrine. § 324.021 Fla. Stat. Thereafter, Congress enacted a statute known as the Graves Amendment, 49 U.S.C.A. § 30106, that prohibits the application of such a rule of vicarious liability to commercial rental car companies. *Garcia v. Vanguard Car Rental USA, Inc.*, 540 F.3d 1242 (11th Cir. 2008) affirmed a decision that held the Graves Amendment required that such an action against a commercial rental car company be dismissed. These statutes do not purport to affect application of the doctrine to those who are not commercial rental car companies.

Several states apply a more limited "family purpose" doctrine of imputed liability. *See, e.g., State Farm Mutual Automobile Insurance Co. v. Duran*, 93 N.M. 489, 601 P.2d 722 (App. 1979), and *Williams v. Wachovia Bank & Trust Co.*, 292 N.C. 416, 233 S.E.2d 589 (1977). Under this doctrine the owner of a family car is liable for the negligent torts of family members who, with the owner's consent, use the car for family purposes. What issues would this doctrine engender? What underlying legal and social factors establish the need for the doctrine? Ordinarily, are parents legally responsible for the torts of their children? *See, e.g., Snow v. Nelson*, 450 So. 2d 269 (Fla. App. 1984). A number of states have enacted automobile consent statutes, making owners vicariously liable for negligent torts committed by users who have the owner's consent.

(6) Care must always be taken to distinguish direct negligence from vicarious responsibility. For example, to permit an openly drunken person to operate one's automobile would be an act of direct negligence. (Hence, in Florida, the owner would be directly liable for the negligence of the drunken driver and also vicariously liable under the Florida dangerous instrumentality rule.) In *Matkin v. County Skillet Poultry Company*, 514 So. 2d 1356, 57, 58 (Ala. 1987), a landowner sued the defendant for having negligently entrusted 66,000 live chickens to a farmer (Smith) who permitted the wastes to encroach upon the plaintiff's land. The appellate court affirmed a summary judgment for the defendant, as follows:

[As this Court has held, it is] the bailee's incompetence, and not necessarily his negligence, [that] is the dispositive issue. This view was explained in *Brown v. Vanity Fair Mills*, 291 Ala. 80, 82–83, 277 So. 2d 893, 896 (1973), where the Court adopted the following definition of "negligent entrustment" from Restatement (Second) of Torts § 390 (1986):

One who supplies directly or through a third person a chattel for the use of another whom the supplier knows or has reason to know to be likely because of his youth, inexperience, or otherwise, to use it in a manner involving unreasonable risk of physical harm to himself and others whom the supplier should expect to share in or be endangered by its use, is subject to liability for physical harm resulting to them.

The Court then listed the elements of negligent entrustment as:

(1) Proof that the entrustee was incompetent, inexperienced or reckless; (2) that the entrustor "knew or had reason to know" of the entrustee's condition [or] proclivities; (3) that there was an entrustment of the chattel; (4) that the entrustment created an appreciable risk of harm to the plaintiff and a relational duty on the part of the defendant; (5) that the harm to the plaintiff was "proximately" or "legally" caused by the negligence of the defendant.

Under this definition, the question is whether Country Skillet knew or had reason to know that the entrustment of 66,000 chickens to Smith created an appreciable risk of harm to the Matkins and a duty to them on the part of Country Skillet. Although the Matkins argue that the term "chattel" in the above quoted language is broad enough to include chickens, we agree with the trial court's conclusion that chickens confined in wire cages are not "dangerous instrumentalities" as required by the doctrine of negligent entrustment. All of the Alabama cases heretofore applying the doctrine of negligent entrustment have related to vehicles, boats, firearms, or explosives. *Wilbanks*, 425 So. 2d at 1125. The delivery of chickens to Smith in the present case can hardly be compared to the entrustment of these dangerous instrumentalities to an incompetent. Indeed, the Matkins readily admitted, in their memorandum in opposition to defendant's motion for summary judgment, that "This is not a case involving killer chickens. . . . "

Although aware that 66,000 chickens can produce a prodigious amount of dung, we are of the opinion that it is not negligent to entrust them to a poultry farmer. If this were negligence, then wholesale producers, such as Country Skillet, could not use their poultry for its intended purpose. *See Wilbanks, supra.* The trial court did not err in granting summary judgment for Country Skillet Poultry.

SCOTT v. McGAUGH
Kansas Supreme Court
506 P.2d 1155 (1973)

FROMME, JUSTICE:

This action was brought by C. Kirk Scott, a passenger in a vehicle owned and operated by Dennis McClure, for personal injuries sustained by him in a collision between the McClure vehicle and a vehicle driven by the defendant, Leon L. McGaugh. Scott appeals from a judgment in favor of the defendant McGaugh entered on a jury verdict.

During the trial in the court below the judge ruled as a matter of law the plaintiff and his driver were engaged in a joint venture at the time of the collision, and the jury was instructed that the negligence of the driver, if any, was imputable to the plaintiff passenger. The questioned instruction reads as follows:

No. 18

The Court finds that as a matter of law the plaintiff and his driver, Dennis McClure, were engaged in a joint venture at the time of this collision so that any negligence on the part of the driver, Dennis McClure, is imputed to the plaintiff, C. Kirk Scott.

The appellant Scott contends the evidence at the trial conclusively showed that the relationship and understanding between the driver (McClure) and the passenger (Scott) was insufficient in law to impose vicarious liability on Scott for the negligence, if any, of the driver. He contends the relationship and understanding of the parties did not result in a joint venture with the requisite mutual right of control over the vehicle being used at the time of the accident.

Before discussing the law, evidentiary facts of the case bearing upon the relationship and understanding of McClure and Scott will be detailed. These facts were uncontroverted.

Prior to and at the time of the accident in question the Equitable Life Insurance Company in Wichita had employed several trainee salesmen. These trainee salesmen were employed on a salary plus a commission basis. They were required to furnish their own transportation in calling on prospects for insurance. They were not compensated by the company for the use of their personal cars. A list of insurance prospects was available at the company office in Wichita. These prospects were obtained from the "Welcome Wagon" list of newcomers in the city. The company encouraged the trainee salesmen to work in pairs. When two trainees participated in making a sale of insurance the usual commission to be earned was credited one half to each trainee. The company kept the records on these sales.

McClure and Scott were trainee salesmen employed by Equitable. They had previously joined forces in calling on insurance prospects. In some instances Scott had driven his car and in other instances McClure drove his car. They were not compensated by the company or by other trainees for the use of their personal cars. Each took turns driving his own car so he would not be "freeloading" on the other trainees. McClure and Scott did not always work together, both had worked with other trainees.

On the morning of the accident Scott and McClure arrived at the company office in their own separate cars. They looked over the list of prospects together and decided to join forces that day in making certain calls on prospects. One prospect chosen had been previously approached by McClure and Scott as a team. When McClure and Scott left the office McClure's car was parked nearby so they took McClure's car at his suggestion. McClure drove, and on the way to the home of their mutual prospect the collision occurred. McClure's car collided with a car driven by the defendant McGaugh in an open intersection in a residential district in Wichita. Further details of the collision are unnecessary to determine this question presented on appeal.

We will assume for the purpose of examining the question that both drivers were negligent in some particular and that their concurrent acts of negligence were a direct cause of the collision.

Now, as a preliminary matter, let us consider what is generally considered to amount to contributory negligence by a passenger. In the absence of vicarious responsibility (imputed contributory negligence) a passenger in an automobile is required to use reasonable care for his own safety.

No exact yardstick can be provided for cases of failure to control the conduct of a driver but in the new draft Restatement, Torts, Second, § 495, it is said:

A plaintiff is barred from recovery if the negligence of a third person is a legally contributing cause of his harm, and the plaintiff has been negligent in failing to control the conduct of such person. (p. 556.)

An instruction was given in this case on contributory negligence of a passenger, absent vicarious responsibility, as originally set forth in PIK, Civil, § 8.91. It was as follows:

It is the duty of a passenger while riding in an automobile driven by another person, to use that care which a reasonably careful person would use for his own protection under the circumstances then existing.

A passenger may properly rely upon the driver to attend to the operation of the vehicle, in the absence of knowledge of danger, or of facts which would give him such knowledge.

It is for the jury to say from the evidence whether a passenger exercised such care as a reasonably careful person would exercise under the existing circumstances. (p. 248.)

We note the form of this suggested instruction has been revised in the 1968 Supplement of PIK, Civil.

Now let us consider the primary question raised in this appeal, imputed contributory negligence. In this opinion the terms imputed negligence and imputed contributory negligence are used interchangeably and without implying any difference in meaning. As a general proposition imputed negligence will bar plaintiff's recovery. It does so not from culpability or wrongful act by plaintiff but from liability for another person's wrongful act. Such liability is an artificial creation of the law arising out of the relationship of parties and is referred to as vicarious responsibility. Such responsibility or liability is imposed by reason of the relationship. One such relationship giving rise to imputed negligence is loosely referred to as a joint adventure or joint enterprise. These two terms will be used interchangeably herein without attempting to connote any difference.

The fiction which gives rise to imputable negligence has been criticized and it is said to find small favor with the courts (*Reading Township v. Telfer*, 57 Kan. 798, 48 P. 134) but it persists in almost all of the states. (Prosser, Law of Torts [3rd Ed. HB], § 71, p. 494.) The Minnesota Supreme Court found the doctrine of imputed negligence so distasteful in automobile cases that it refused in 1966 to continue to recognize it.

In Kansas if vicarious liability is to be imposed upon a passenger in an automobile for the culpable acts of his driver because of their relationship as joint adventurers, the liability must arise by reason of a contract, agreement or understanding of the parties. Such agreement or understanding may be either expressed or implicit. In *Schmid v. Eslick*, 181 Kan. 997, 317 P.2d 459, it is said:

The essential question is whether, under the facts and circumstances, the driver and the passenger can be found by implication to have agreed to have an equal privilege and right to manage and control the vehicle. . . . (p. 1003, 317 P.2d p. 464.)

To constitute a joint venture which will impose vicarious liability four things must be established before the relationship of the parties will give rise to an application of the doctrine of imputed negligence. There must be (1) an agreement, (2) a common purpose, (3) a community of interest and (4) an equal right to a voice, accompanied by an equal right of control over the instrumentality (the automobile). (*Bedenbender v. Walls*, 177 Kan. 531, 535, 280 P.2d 630; Prosser, Law of Torts [3rd Ed. HB], § 71, p. 490.)

It should be noted that the fourth essential, the right of control, must be present in the relationship of the parties before negligence can be imputed to the passenger. This right of control is necessary to confer agency upon the driver and like any other agency it must be based upon agreement. A right of control of a vehicle may not be required to carry out the common purpose in some joint adventures, since mutual use and operation of an automobile may not be considered necessary to carry on the joint adventure. In such cases there is no vicarious liability from the operation of a vehicle.

. . .

When no express agreement for mutual "right of control" is present an agreement may be implied if the facts and circumstances will support such an understanding.

The following factual situations have been held not to support such an understanding between the parties.

In the Restatement, Torts, Second, § 491, on the subject of contributory negligence arising from joint enterprise the following illustration is given on page 550:

2. A, as attorney for B, is engaged in the trial of a case in the town of X. C is retained by B to assist A. Both A and C live in the same village, which is at some distance from the town of X. On the day of the trial A offers to drive C to X. While on the way to X, A drives the car carelessly and a collision ensues in which C is injured. A's negligent driving does not bar C from recovering against the driver of the negligently driven vehicle with which A's car collides.

. . .

We have been unable to find a case with a factual situation identical to our present case. It is noteworthy that in our research we have failed to find any alleged joint enterprise case in which this court has held a trial court was justified under the evidence in imposing vicarious liability upon the passenger as a matter of law. In the future there may arise such a case but instances, no doubt, will be rare in the absence of an express agreement for mutual "right of control."

In several cases this court has held that under the facts of those cases "right of control" was a jury question. In *Heiserman v. Aikman*, 163 Kan. 700, 186 P.2d 252, the question of alleged agency of the driver was held to be a jury question but on the separate issue of alleged joint adventure imposing vicarious liability this court held the evidence was insufficient to establish plaintiff's mutual "right of control." On this latter issue it was held error to submit the question to the jury.

In the recent case of *Kelty v. Best Cabs, Inc.*, 206 Kan. 654, 481 P.2d 980, we had a strong factual basis for supporting a jury finding on mutual "right of control." Mr. and Mrs. Kelty (the driver and passenger) were engaged in the paperhanging business. They worked together. He ran the business and she worked as his helper and assistant. The accounts and records of the business were kept jointly. The income from their mutual efforts went into a joint account. Joint income tax returns were filed. The title to the truck, in which they were riding at the time of the accident, was held jointly. The accident occurred on the way to work.

There can be little doubt in the *Kelty* case that a joint adventure was established. The question of mutual "right of control" over the use and operation of the jointly owned truck, however, was held to be a question of fact for the jury. The jury entered a verdict in favor of the plaintiff passenger, and in effect found either the driver was not negligent or the passenger had no mutual "right of control." This court in affirming the judgment held the question was properly submitted to the jury and indirectly we held this strong factual situation, which included joint ownership of the truck, did not establish mutual "right of control" of the vehicle as a matter of law.

By way of comparison let us examine the factual situation in the present case. As between McClure and Scott there were no joint tax returns, no ongoing business, no joint bookkeeping, and no joint ownership of the vehicle. McClure and Scott were separately employed by Equitable as salesmen. Both owned separate automobiles. Any common purpose or community of interest between them was entirely dependent upon their employment by Equitable. Their community of interests did not exist separate and apart from their employment. Equitable kept the records and paid them separately.

Although a plaintiff passenger and a driver of an automobile are co-workers or fellow employees of a common employer and both are acting in the course of and in the furtherance of the business, this alone does not make them participants in a joint enterprise which will impose vicarious liability under the "right of control" test; and this is true irrespective of whether the vehicle is owned by the employer, the fellow driver or by the plaintiff himself.

In our present case McClure was the owner and operator of the car. The passenger Scott claimed no interest therein. There was no evidence that Scott had ever driven McClure's car or exercised any control over either the car or the driver. There was no understanding between the parties which might authorize Scott to use or control the operation of the McClure vehicle. In the absence of McClure it would appear that Scott had no right to be in the vehicle. The sharing of transportation was gratuitous and the sharing arose from a common desire to save personal expenses. There was nothing in the nature of the undertaking to sell insurance which dictated the use of the McClure vehicle. These two co-employees might as well have used some means of public transportation to call on this prospect. In such case their common purpose and community of interest would have been the same.

In determining vicarious responsibility of a passenger for the culpable negligence of a driver in connection with an alleged joint enterprise the "right of control" test must be applied and the test must be met before contributory negligence may be imputed to the passenger.

Where evidence of the relationship and understanding of the parties is undisputed and the facts and circumstances clearly show a passenger does not have an equal privilege and right to control the operation of the vehicle under the "right of control" test, the issue of joint enterprise to support vicarious liability becomes one of law for the court's determination; and, the court should instruct the jury that negligence of the driver, if any, is not imputable to the plaintiff passenger.

After carefully reviewing the evidence in the record this court fails to find any evidence from which an understanding may be implied that McClure and Scott had an equal right of control and were possessed of equal authority to prescribe the conditions of use and operation of the McClure vehicle under the "right of control" test enunciated in *Schmid v. Eslick, supra.* Accordingly, it is held that the trial court erred (1) in determining the driver and passenger in this case were engaged in a joint enterprise imposing vicarious liability and (2) in instructing the jury that any negligence on the part of the driver, McClure, was imputed to the plaintiff Scott.

NOTES AND QUESTIONS

(1)   The joint venture theory of *Scott v. McGough* would apply in appropriate cases irrespective of the type of negligent act one of the joint venturers undertook. By contrast, some forms of vicarious responsibility are directly related to particular instrumentalities of harm. In *Perdue v. Mitchell*, for example, the defendant sought to raise a presumption of agency between the driver of a motor vehicle and its owner (the equivalent of the master-servant relationship as far as vicarious responsibility is concerned) from the mere fact that the negligent driver was operating the vehicle with the consent of the owner. Why did that argument fail?

(2)   The joint venture theory of vicarious liability is based upon the same economic premises that under-gird master-servant respondeat superior vicarious liability. Viewed from this perspective, does the decision in *Oliver v. Miles*, § 7.04 *supra*, appear to stretch the doctrine? Another related version of the theory is that members of a partnership are vicariously liable for the negligent acts of other partners, employees, and agents of the partnership. This potential liability sometimes influences the legal form adopted to operate businesses and also has lead to the enactment of statutes in many states to limit the liability of members of professional services partnerships, such as those composed of physicians, accountants and lawyers.

WEBER v. STOKELY-VAN CAMP, INC.
Minnesota Supreme Court
144 N.W.2d 540 (1966)

Knutson, Chief Justice.

This is an appeal from an order denying plaintiff's motion for judgment notwithstanding the verdict or a new trial.

Plaintiff, Joseph C. Weber, is engaged in the business of supplying and servicing vending machines and coin-operated games in an area in Minnesota involving part of Martin County. Maynard S. Sunken was employed by Weber in such business.

Warren Curtis Musser was an employee of defendant, Stokely-Van Camp, Inc.

On September 18, 1963, while Sunken was driving Weber's 1962 Chevrolet pickup truck in the scope of his employment he was involved in a collision with a 1963 Ford pickup truck owned by defendant and driven by Musser, also engaged in the scope of his employment. Weber, riding with Sunken at the time of the collision, suffered personal injuries along with damage to his truck. He sued defendant for the negligence of its agent Musser. Defendant answered, denying any negligence on the part of Musser, and alleged the contributory negligence of Weber's employee which, when imputed to Weber, would bar recovery.

It is admitted that while Sunken would usually drive when he and Weber were on business trips together, Weber frequently told him where to go and what route to take. Sunken testified that Weber did not direct him in his driving but that he would have obeyed any order had it been given.

The court instructed the jury that as a matter of law the negligence of Sunken would be imputed to Weber under these circumstances. The jury returned an 11 to 1 verdict for defendant and this appeal followed.

The questions presented are whether the court erred in the above instruction, and whether certain members of the jury were guilty of such misconduct as to demand a new trial. The facts pertinent to this latter issue will be stated when the issue is discussed.

1. It must be conceded that based on existing case law the trial court's instruction concerning imputed negligence was correct, and if Sunken was found to be contributorily negligent, Weber cannot recover. The rule is based on the right of control, not the exercise of it; and illogical as the rule may be, the master has a theoretical right to control under the facts of this case, even though he does not exercise it and has little or no opportunity to do so. Essentially, imputation of the negligence of a servant to a master rests on a so-called "both-way test" — that is, if the master is vicariously liable to a third party due to the agent's negligence, he is also barred from recovery because his agent's negligence is imputed to him. In *Frankle v. Twedt*, 234 Minn. 42, 45, 47 N.W.2d 482, 486, we said:

. . . On the basis of an agency relationship, the negligence of an agent is imputed to his principal as a bar to the latter's right of recovery, in an action which he brings against a third party, *only* when the nature of the agency relationship is such that the principal would be subject to a vicarious liability as a defendant to another who may have been injured by the agent's negligence.

While plaintiff does not seriously dispute the existing rule, he argues that the rule is unjust and ought to be abandoned. There is much merit in his position. In *Christensen v. Hennepin Transp. Co., Inc.*, 215 Minn. 394, 10 N.W.2d 406, 147 A.L.R. 945, we held the negligence of a bailee was not to be imputed to a bailor in an action by the plaintiff-bailor against a third party to recover damages for personal injuries; even though under our Financial Responsibility Act, Minn. St. 170.54, the bailor would be liable to a third party injured by the negligence of the bailee.

The whole doctrine of imputed negligence probably had its inception in an "unfortunate" English decision, *Thorogood v. Bryan* [1849] 8 C.B. 115, 137 Eng. Rep. 452, holding that the negligence of an omnibus driver was imputed to a passenger precluding the right of the passenger to recover for injuries caused by the negligent operation of another vehicle. That decision met with little favor in this country and was likewise subsequently repudiated in England. Many of the cases refusing to follow Thorogood are collected in *Little v. Hackett*, 116 U.S. 366, 371, 6 S. Ct. 391, 393, 29 L. Ed. 652, 654, where the court said:

That one cannot recover damages for an injury to the commission of which he has directly contributed is a rule of established law and a principle of common justice. And it matters not whether that contribution consists in his participation in the direct cause of the injury, or in his omission of duties which, if performed, would have prevented it. If his fault, whether of omission or commission, has been the proximate cause of the injury, he is without remedy against one also in the wrong. It would seem that the converse of this doctrine should be accepted as sound — that when one has been injured by the wrongful act of another, to which he has in no respect contributed, he should be entitled to compensation in damages from the wrongdoer. And such is the generally received doctrine, unless a contributory cause of the injury has been the negligence or fault of some person towards whom he sustains the relation of superior or master, in which case the negligence is imputed to him, though he may not have personally participated in or had knowledge of it; and he must bear the consequences.

From that statement and others like it the rule has evolved that where a certain relationship exists between parties, such as master and servant, the negligence of the one, that is the servant, is imputed to the master barring his right of recovery even though he is completely innocent of any fault. If negligence is based on fault, it is difficult to rationalize imputed negligence where the party seeking recovery is without fault. Many of the reasons for imputing negligence of a servant to a master in a suit by an injured third party — that is, making the master vicariously liable to the injured third party — are discussed in Prosser, Torts (3 ed.) § 68. It would serve no useful purpose to elaborate on them here. Probably the most popular reason is to provide the injured person with a "deep pocket." In other words, vicarious liability is attached to the master-servant relationship, providing the injured person with a defendant who in all likelihood can respond in damages if he establishes a right thereto. There may be some justification for the rule of vicarious liability even though the master is without fault; but from vicarious liability has come the companion rule imputing to the master the negligence of the servant when the master seeks to recover for his own damage and injury, even though the master was not at fault. There is no necessity for creating a solvent defendant in that situation, nor can any of the reasons given for holding a master vicariously liable in a suit by third persons be defended on any rational ground when applied to imputing negligence of a servant to a faultless master who seeks recovery from a third person for his own injury or damage. Why should the negligent third person escape liability under these circumstances? Here the logic, if there is any, for imputing negligence to a faultless plaintiff in a suit by him against a third party is completely lacking. Yet, regardless of the illogic of the rule, it has been universally accepted in this country.

This rule has become known as the both-ways rule. It has come under increasing criticism in recent years. Originally the contributory negligence of a bailee was imputed to a bailor the same as the contributory negligence of a servant was imputed to a master. Many of the courts throughout the country have repudiated this doctrine long ago. We did so in *Christensen v. Hennepin Transp. Co., Inc.*, 215 Minn. 394, 10 N.W.2d 406, 147 A.L.R. 945, which was followed in *Jacobsen v. Dailey*, 228 Minn. 201, 36 N.W.2d 711, 11 A.L.R.2d 1429. There are other equally inconsistent applications of the rule. For instance, the negligence of the servant is not imputed to the master in a suit by the master against the servant, but when he sues a third-party joint tortfeasor, he is barred from recovery from such third party. In the case of a joint enterprise, the negligence of one of those so engaged is imputed to all in a suit against a third person but not in a suit inter se. *Berlin v. Koblas*, 183 Minn. 278, 236 N.W. 307; *Murphy v. Keating*, 204 Minn. 269, 283 N.W. 389, 23 Minn. L. Rev. 666.

. . .

The original Restatement, Torts, adopted the both-ways test where a master-servant relationship exists, and also included imputed negligence in several other relationships. Section 485 read:

Except as stated in §§ 493 and 494, a plaintiff is barred from recovery by the negligent act or omission of a third person if, but only if, the relation between them is such that the plaintiff would be liable as defendant for harm caused to others by such negligent conduct of the third person.

Section 486 of the original Restatement specifically adopted the both-ways test where a master-servant relationship exists. It read:

A master is barred from recovery against a negligent defendant by the contributory negligence of his servant acting within the scope of his employment.

However, with respect to § 486 the rule remains the same.

In areas where vicarious liability did not apply, § 495 of the original Restatement provided:

A plaintiff is barred from recovery if the negligence of a third person is a legally contributing cause of his harm, and the plaintiff

(a) has the ability to control the conduct of the third person, and

(b) knows or has reason to know that he has such ability, and

(c) knows or should know

(i) that it is necessary to exercise his control, and

(ii) that he has an opportunity to do so, and

(d) fails to utilize such opportunity with reasonable care.

In the new draft § 495 reads:

A plaintiff is barred from recovery if the negligence of a third person is a legally contributing cause of his harm, and the plaintiff has been negligent in failing to control the conduct of such person.

Had § 495 in the original draft been adopted in cases involving the master-servant relationship and others where contributory negligence is imputed to a faultless plaintiff it would have been more in harmony with our concept of negligence based on fault. In view of the fact that imputed negligence has now been abandoned in Restatement, Torts (2d) as to relationships where it formerly applied, it is difficult to find any tenable reason why it should be retained in a master-servant relationship where the master is entirely without fault.

The whole problem of imputed contributory negligence needs reexamination. In automobile accident cases it is doubtful if the both-ways test, or any test creating a bar to recovery by a person vicariously liable, is now necessary in this state. Our Financial Responsibility Act makes the owner of any automobile liable for the negligence of the operator using it with the owner's consent. Conceivably an agent or servant might be using an automobile of his own in his master's business and the master be vicariously liable for the negligence of the servant while so engaged in the scope of his business; but except in a case of that kind the master under our Financial Responsibility Act would be liable for the negligence of the servant if engaged in the scope of his business, without the rule of imputed negligence. Minnesota, in the *Christensen* and *Jacobsen* cases, as mentioned above, is one of the few states where the logic of the both-ways test has been analyzed in the light of our Financial Responsibility Act.

Application of the rule imputing contributory negligence of a servant to a master in a suit by the master to recover against a negligent third party, when the master is not present in the car at all, is hard to justify on any theory. When the master is present as a passenger, as he was in the case before us, there may be some chance that he could exercise his theoretic control over the operation of the car if he saw fit to do so. But even here, unless it can be shown that he actually tried to take over manual operation of the vehicle, what chance does he have to exercise this right? As the court aptly stated in *Jenks v. Veeder Contracting Co., Inc.*, 177 Misc. 240, 243, 30 N.Y.S.2d 278, 281, affirmed, 264 App. Div. 979, 37 N.Y.S.2d 230, appeal dismissed, 289 N.Y. 787, 46 N.E.2d 848:

Parties having equal legal title to a motor vehicle cannot be permitted to contend for the wheel in moving traffic and hence the imputation of negligence to the joint owner present upon the theory of equal legal right to domination or control is untenable when applied to the facts of this case.

The realities of the actual operation of vehicles on highways cannot be entirely overlooked in dealing with the rights and obligations of those present with the driver.

We can think of nothing more dangerous in these days of congested travel on high-speed highways than to permit a master riding as a passenger in a car driven by his servant constantly to interfere with the servant's driving, or his attempt to exercise a theoretic right of control. To do so would be the clearest evidence of active negligence on the part of the master, for which he would be chargeable without imputing to him the negligence of his servant. Imputed negligence, on the other hand, presupposes that the master is innocent of any fault. How, then, can we reconcile the theory of right to control, the exercise of which would charge the master with negligence and imputed negligence based on the theory that he is free from any fault? The two just do not hang together.

We are convinced the time has come to discard this rule which is defensible only on the grounds of its antiquity. In doing so we realize we may stand alone, but a doctrine so untenable should not be followed so as to bar recovery of one entitled to damages. We limit this decision to automobile negligence cases. There may be other situations where the same result should follow, but we leave those decisions for the future as they come before us. We also limit the retrospective effect of the decision to this case so as not to impose unjustly liability on defendants who have relied on the rule without notice of a departure from it. In view of the fact that the matter has been brought before us by this appeal, it would be unjust not to apply the rule to those involved here.

. . .

NOTES AND QUESTIONS

(1) What is the rationale of the "both-ways" test of imputed negligence? Does the defendant's argument for barring the claim of the plaintiff in *Weber* have exactly the same grounding in theory as the plaintiff's argument for holding the defendant liable in *Perdue v. Mitchell*?

(2) Although the *Weber* court thought that it might "stand alone" in abrogating (partially) the doctrine of imputed contributory negligence, the fact is that the doctrine was never popular. In the years since *Weber*, many other courts have wholly or partially repudiated the doctrine. Perhaps most notable is *Kalechman v. Drew Auto Rental, Inc.*, 33 N.Y.2d 397, 308 N.E.2d 886 (1973). Some courts, however, have declined to follow *Weber's* lead. *See, e.g., Hoeft v. Friedal*, 70 Wis. 2d 1022, 235 N.W.2d 918 (1975), *and Altimari v. Campbell*, 56 Ohio App. 2d 253, 382 N.E.2d 1187 (1978). *See generally* F. James, *Imputed Negligence and Vicarious Liability: The Study of a Paradox*, 10 U. Fla. L. Rev. 48 (1957). See also Restatement, Torts, Second § 485 and commentary.

STOPPLEWORTH v. REFUSE HIDEAWAY, INC.

Supreme Court of Wisconsin 546 N. W. 870 (Wis. 1996)

GESKE, JUSTICE.

John and Jacqueline Stoppleworth petitioned this court for review of an unpublished decision of the court of appeals affirming an order of the Circuit Court for Dane County which dismissed their negligence action against defendants, John W. DeBeck, Thomas G. DeBeck, Refuse Hideaway, Inc., and Bituminous Fire and Marine Insurance Co. Circuit Court Judge Mark A. Frankel entered the judgment following the jury's verdict finding that, although the DeBecks and Refuse Hideaway's negligent operation of the Refuse Hideaway Landfill contaminated surrounding well water consumed by John Stoppleworth, the defendants' negligence was not causal of his basal cell carcinoma.

The issue before this court is the propriety of the circuit court's order precluding any mention to the jury of the identity of the insurer, Bituminous, as a party to the action. Stoppleworth contends that he is entitled to a new trial because the prohibition on disclosure of Bituminous' position as defendant violated a substantial right — that of the right to a "Jury trial inviolate."

Although we conclude that there is neither a constitutional right nor a statutory requirement to name all parties, we hereby adopt a procedural rule that, in a jury trial, the court shall identify all joined parties to the jury panel. We do not disturb the jury's verdict in the case at hand, however, because we conclude that the order of the circuit court did not affect any of the plaintiffs' substantial rights. Therefore, we affirm the court of appeals' decision.

FACTS

The defendants in this action, John and Tom DeBeck, and Refuse Hideaway, Inc., owners and operators of the Refuse Hideaway Landfill in the Town of Middleton, Wisconsin, are insured by Bituminous Fire and Marine Insurance Co. (Bituminous). The plaintiff, John Stoppleworth, initiated a toxic tort claim against the defendants in which he asserted that their negligent operation of the landfill resulted in contamination of his parents' well. Stoppleworth claimed that he was personally injured by this negligence through exposure to chemical contaminants in the well water which he asserted was a substantial factor in causing his basal cell carcinoma, a form of skin cancer.

The defendants filed a motion in limine, requesting that there be no mention of Bituminous before the jury and that the insurer's name be removed from the caption and the jury verdict. The defendants argued that the fact that the DeBecks and Refuse Hideaway, Inc. were insured was irrelevant to the issues before the court, and that to inform the jury of the insurer's role as a defendant would be unduly prejudicial. They based these arguments on studies of jury behavior indicating that when juries are aware defendants are insured, they tend to award higher damages.[3] The plaintiffs countered that any potential prejudice would be allayed by instructing the jurors that their knowledge of the existence of an insurance company as a defendant should have no bearing on their determination of liability or nonliability.[4] The circuit court granted the defendants' motion and ordered that the identity of Bituminous as a defendant not be revealed to the jury in any manner. The court reasoned that, although the insurer was a party, "they're only a party really for purposes that don't concern the jury."

Uncontroverted evidence showed that the Stoppleworths' well contained volatile organic chemical contaminants. The defendants proceeded on the theory that John Stoppleworth's skin cancer was not caused by exposure to any of these chemicals, but rather by chronic exposure to the sun. The defense presented evidence that, despite Stoppleworth's claims that because of his fair skin he never went out in the sun without sun screen, he had been sunburned numerous times. Childhood photographs showed him outdoors without sun protection and with varying degrees of sunburn. John Stoppleworth testified that about once a year, while he was a teenager, he would burn to the point of peeling. Testimony by family members revealed that he did quite a bit of outdoor work landscaping at his home. John Stoppleworth also spent time on the lake in his pontoon boat and water-skiing. He and his wife honeymooned in Jamaica and had recently taken a seven-day Caribbean cruise.

The defense presented two expert witnesses who testified to a reasonable degree of medical probability that John Stoppleworth's cancer was not caused by exposure to the contaminants in his parents' well water. Defense witness, toxicologist Dr. Gots, testified that of the chemicals found in the Stoppleworths' well only one, vinyl chloride, is a known human carcinogen. No epidemiological studies have linked vinyl chloride to human basal cell carcinoma. A second expert witness for the defense, Dr. Barnett, is a board certified dermatologist who testified that he had treated more than 1,400 basal cell carcinomas over the previous ten years. He testified that, based on his own experience and an extensive search of the medical research literature, there were no indications that toxins

---

[3] The defendants relied upon the following sources: Dale W. Broader, *The University of Chicago Jury Project*, 38 Neb. L. Rev. 744, 754 (1959) (damage awards are lowest when jury is not aware defendant has insurance and are highest when that information is revealed and a correctional instruction is given in response to an objection); James K. Hammitt et al., *Tort Standards and Jury Decisions*, 14 J. Legal Studies 751, 755 (1985) (defendants who can be presumed to be heavily insured tend to be assessed larger damage awards). . . .

[4] This admonition is found in Wis JI — Civil 125: References to an insurance company have been made in this case. The title to this case included an insurance company as a defendant. There is no question as to insurance in the special verdict, however. This is because no dispute of fact concerning insurance is involved in this case. In addition, the liability or nonliability of (defendant) for the damages claimed is exactly the same, whether (defendant) is or is not covered by insurance. Under your oath as jurors, you are duty bound to be impartial toward all the parties to this case. So, you should answer the questions in the verdict as you would if thee were no insurance company in this case.

such as vinyl chloride had ever been linked to development of basal cell skin cancer. Finally, on cross-examination of the plaintiffs' expert, Dr. Bryan, the defense elicited confirmation that if exposure to vinyl chloride in the well water were a substantial factor in causing John Stoppleworth's basal cell carcinoma, it "would be the first case that [Dr. Bryan was] aware of in the world."

The jury returned a verdict finding the defendants negligent in the operation of Refuse Hideaway Landfill. However, the jury determined that this negligence was not a cause of John Stoppleworth's skin cancer. The circuit court thereby issued an order for judgment dismissing the Stoppleworths' action and subsequently denied their motion for a new trial. The court of appeals affirmed on the basis that, even if precluding mention of Bituminous was erroneous, the Stoppleworths had not demonstrated that they were prejudiced by the circuit court's ruling or that their substantial rights were affected and, therefore, they were not entitled to a new trial. This court accepted the plaintiffs' petition for review.

I.

This court must determine whether there exists a statutory or constitutional right to name all parties joined in a lawsuit. This is a question of law which we review de novo. . . .

The Stoppleworths argue that they have both a statutory and constitutional right to reveal the identities of joined parties to the jury. They find support for their statutory claim in Wis. Stat. § 632.24 (direct action against insurer)[5] and Wis. Stat. § 803.04(2) (a) (permitting plaintiff to join insurer as a party defendant).[6]

The Stoppleworths assert that by creating these statutory mechanisms the legislature expressed a public policy to facilitate the joinder of insurers as party defendants in negligence actions and that the identity of the insurer as a defendant is pivotal. Further, they argue that these statutes implicitly confer on plaintiffs the right to disclose the identity of all defendants. They cite the lack of statutory provisions explicitly allowing an insurer to "secrete or exclude" its identity from the jury as indicative of legislative intent that no such "privilege" should be recognized.

In contrast, the defendants posit that the primary legislative purpose behind the direct action statutes is one of judicial economy — to protect successful plaintiffs from having to pursue insolvent defendants before proceeding against the

---

[5] Wis. Stat. § 632.24, reads:

> Direct action against insurer. Any bond or policy of insurance covering liability to others for negligence makes the insurer liable, up to the amount stated in the bond or policy, to the persons entitled to recover against the insured for the death of any person or for injury to persons or property, irrespective of whether the liability is presently established or is contingent and to become fixed or certain by final judgment against the insured.

[6] Wis. Stat. § 803.04(2) (a), reads in relevant part:

> In any action for damages caused by negligence, any insurer which has an interest in the outcome of such controversy adverse to the plaintiff or any of the parties to such controversy, or which by its policy of insurance assumes or reserves the right to control the prosecution, defense or settlement of the claim or action, or which by its policy agrees to prosecute or defend the action brought by plaintiff or any of the parties to such action, or agrees to engage counsel to prosecute or defend said action or agrees to pay the costs of such litigation, is by this section made a proper party defendant in any action brought by plaintiff in this state on account of any claim against the insured.

defendants' insurers. In support of this interpretation, they cite *Decade's Monthly Fund v. Whyte & Hirschboeck*, 173 Wis. 2d 665, 495 N.W.2d 335 (1993), in which we traced the history of Wisconsin's direct action statutes. There, we noted that, as early as 1927, the legislative purposes had been identified as including the desire to: save litigation and reduce the expense by determining the rights of all parties in a single action which is usually defended by the insurance carrier. [To] expedite the final settlement of litigation and the final payment to the injured person, if he be entitled to recovery. [To] place the burden upon the insurance carrier who has been compensated in advance for its liability to pay the damage assessed for such injuries to person and damage to property as have been caused by actionable negligence on the part of the person insured. . . .

Thus we have recognized that the core-functions of these statutes are to expedite the litigation process and to facilitate a successful claimant's access to compensation.

We find the defendants' arguments most persuasive on this point — what the jury knows or doesn't know of the identities of the various parties is not even contemplated by these statutes. We conclude that there is no support for the plaintiffs' claim that a statutory right exists to name all joined parties. The legislative history does not indicate an intent to convey such a right, nor has this court previously recognized such a statutory right. We decline to do so now.

The Stoppleworths contend that this court implicitly recognized the right to name all parties in *Vuchetich v. General Casualty Co.*, 270 Wis. 552, 72 N.W.2d 389 (1955). Specifically, they argue that *Vuchetich* established precedent that the identity of an insurer defendant must always be revealed to the jury. There, we reversed a circuit court order enjoining the plaintiff from making any reference to the defendant insurance company, stating:

The proposition that, while one may have his action against a designated defendant, he may not refer to that defendant or divulge its name during the litigation presents a paradox so startling that only the most direct and positive authority will convince us of its truth. *Id.* at 555, 72 N.W.2d 389. Although we found error in that case, this court did not base its decision on the existence of a "right" to have the parties' identities revealed to the jury. Rather, we concluded that the order, which prohibited any voir dire questioning of the jurors or witnesses as to connections with the defendant insurer, was erroneous because it prevented the plaintiff from investigating potential bias.

Here, however, the circuit court permitted exploration during voir dire as to whether any of the jurors had been previously involved in any litigation involving insurance companies. Additionally, the court "was prepared to go further if there was any indication that there might be any connection between any of the jurors and the defendant insurance company." We do not find *Vuchetich* controlling.

II.

The Stoppleworths next contend that the circuit court's order barring mention of Bituminous violated their right to a "jury trial inviolate" as guaranteed under the Wisconsin Constitution, art. I, § 5. They argue that "certainly the fundamental right to a jury trial must include the right of a plaintiff to identify to a jury those parties to the litigation who appear and participate in the proceeding." The plaintiffs cite no authority in support of their claim that the circuit court's order violated the constitutional right to trial by jury. Their argument is based on inference and assumption and we do not find it convincing.[7]

Although we find neither a statutory nor a constitutional right to have all parties identified, we conclude that in a jury trial, as a procedural rule, the court should apprise the jurors of the names of all the parties to the lawsuit.[8] This rule shall apply in all cases, not just those involving insurance companies.

The defendants based their motion to exclude mention of Bituminous on the statutes controlling rules of evidence in Wisconsin. The name of any given joined party simply is not evidence.[9] Therefore, the rules of evidence should not be used to analyze the potential effect of advising the jury of the existence of a specific party to a lawsuit. However, just as trial judges are frequently confronted with the potential prejudicial effect on the jury of extraneous information, a circuit court can always give a cautionary instruction when it wants to protect against unfair prejudice. In a situation such as this case, we agree with the Stoppleworths' contention that any potential for prejudice is aptly addressed by use of the curative instruction, Wis JI — Civil 125, which reminds jurors that they must be impartial because a defendant's liability or nonliability is unaffected by whether he or she is insured.

III.

The Stoppleworths argue that the failure to mention Bituminous to the jury entitles them to a new trial. We may not order a new trial unless, after consideration of the entire proceeding, we determine that a party's substantial rights have been affected. Wis. Stat. § 805.18(2). We conclude that no substantial rights of the Stoppleworths were affected and therefore we affirm the order of the circuit court dismissing their negligence claim in accordance with the jury's verdict.

The only specific harm that the Stoppleworths claim to have suffered because of the circuit court's order was that they were restricted from conducting a meaningful cross-examination of the defense's expert witness, Dr. Gots, as to

---

[7] Additionally, the defendants argued that plaintiffs' constitutional claim was fatally flawed because this court has held that "[t]he right preserved in Art. I., sec. 5 of the Wisconsin Constitution is simply the right as it existed at the time of the adoption of [the] constitution in 1848." *In Interest of N.E.*, 122 Wis. 2d 198, 203, 361 N.W.2d 693 (1985) (finding juvenile's right to jury trial in delinquency proceedings strictly statutory, not constitutional); *see also Bergren v. Staples*, 263 Wis. 477, 481–83, 57 N.W.2d 714 (1953) (finding no constitutional right to jury trial in action against third-party tortfeasor by worker's compensation insurer). Thus, a claim that the state constitution prevents infringement upon the right to a jury trial in actions that did not exist in 1848 will be unavailing. The first statute permitting direct action against an insurer was not enacted until 1925. See 1925 Wis. Laws ch. 341 (creating Wis. Stat. § 85.25). Because we conclude that identification of parties does not impact the right to jury trial, we need not further pursue this argument.

[8] A practical reason for this rule was illustrated during oral argument in the following hypothetical: if a circuit court issued an order similar to the one issued here in a direct action suit where the claim had been brought only against the insurer and not the alleged tortfeasor, there would be no defendant to be named to the jury.

[9] According to Black's Law Dictionary 555 (6th ed. 1990), "evidence" is defined as: Testimony, writings, or material objects offered in proof of an alleged fact or proposition. That probative material, legally received, by which the tribunal may be lawfully persuaded of the truth or falsity of a fact in issue.

possible prejudice or bias. They argue that their attempts to impeach Dr. Gots' credibility were substantially curtailed because they could not establish his "close association" with the insurance industry.[10] The Stoppleworths acknowledge that the court's order did not expressly forbid them to mention insurance in general or even Dr. Gots' previous work for insurance defendants in particular. However, they contend that such a line of questioning was not pursued because it would have been "meaningless" to a jury unaware that there was an insurer defendant in the instant action.

After an examination of the entire proceeding as reflected in the record, we are not convinced by this argument. The Stoppleworths not only had ample opportunity to impeach Dr. Gots' credibility by painting him as a mouthpiece for the defense, but they ably exercised that opportunity. The jury was made aware: that Dr. Gots specializes in the area of forensic toxicology; that he has published articles in that area; that his company is a member of the Defense Research Institute which is devoted to litigation defense; that he has given many presentations for that organization aimed at advising attorneys on how to defend toxic tort cases; and that he has previously testified for the defense in cases in which cancer causation is an issue. Additionally,

Dr. Gots testified that, in this case, he had been hired by the defense and was being paid at the rate of $275 per hour. This record does not support the claim that the plaintiffs' right to cross-examination was substantially affected.

Because we conclude that the order prohibiting the identification of Bituminous as a defendant did not affect the Stoppleworths' substantial rights, they are not entitled to a new trial and we affirm the decision reached by the court of appeals.

NOTES AND QUESTIONS

(1) *Stoppleworth* touches upon several issues. One is, when does a liability insurance company become liable to the plaintiff who was the victim of the insured defendant's negligence? The insurance company's liability is determined by the insurance contract with the insured person, and liability insurance contracts traditionally merely impose an obligation upon the insurance company to indemnify the insured person after the insured person has been found liable to the plaintiff. Hence, traditionally, liability insurance companies would not be proper parties in a plaintiff's negligence action against an insured defendant.

As *Stoppleworth* proves, numerous states have enacted what are known as "direct action" statutes that authorize the plaintiff to join the liability insurance company as a named defendant in the action against the insured defendant. What advantages does this provide the plaintiff?

(2) Note the provisions of the Wisconsin direct action statutes as quoted in *Stoppleworth*. Some direct action statutes are quite limited. *See, e.g., Giroux v. Purington Building Systems, Inc.,* 670 A.2d 1227 (R.I. 1996) (direct action permitted when insured person has filed for bankruptcy); and *National Bank of Commerce v. Quirk,* 918 S.W.2d 138 (Ark. 1996) (direct action statute limited to

---

[10] The Stoppleworths did not make an offer of proof detailing what specific testimony they were precluded from introducing regarding Dr. Gots' connection to the insurance industry.

insurers of certain governmental agencies and other entities not subject to law suits).

Many jurisdictions do not authorize direct actions. *See, e.g., Hamilton v. Blackmun*, 915 P.2d 1210 (Alaska 1996), and *Nationwide Mutual Insurance Co. v. Regional Electric Contractors, Inc.*, 680 A.2d 547 (Md. 1996).

(3) *Shingleton v. Bussey*, 223 So. 2d 713 (Fla. 1969), is apparently the only judicial decision to authorize direct actions by judicial decree (on a third party beneficiary theory). This decision was promptly overruled by a statute, restoring the traditional rule with some exceptions. *Van Bibber v. Hartford Accident and Idemn. Ins. Co.*, 439 So. 2d 880 (Fla. 1983).

(4) The second question raised in *Stoppleworth* is whether the jury is to be informed that the defendant is insured in regard to the action. Why would defendants object? The orthodox rule (at least in the absence of direct action statute) is that the mere mention of "insurance" is grounds for mistrial. Does the prophylactic instruction referred to in *Stoppleworth* eliminate the prejudice that a defendant might suffer from directly informing a jury of the presence of insurance? Would jurors ordinarily assume that insurance is a factor if nothing is said? *Government Employees Insurance Company v. Krawzak*, 675 So. 2d 118 (Fla. 1996), also held that the jury should be informed that an insurance company that is a defendant under Florida's limited direct action statute is a defendant to the action.

§ 11.03   SETTLEMENT ISSUES

Four elements of common law tort liability guided settlement negotiations in predictable paths: first, the rule that a plaintiff's contributory negligence barred recovery; second, the rule that joint tortfeasors were jointly and severally liable for all damages; third, the rule that the release of one joint tortfeasor released all; and, fourth, the rule of no contribution among joint tortfeasors. Most of these elements have been modified to one degree or the other in virtually every jurisdiction and, perhaps, no jurisdiction applies all the common law rules in there pristine forms.

Chapter 9 described the various forms of comparative negligence that have supplanted the common law bar of contributory negligence in most jurisdictions. Apart from that, modification of the theory of joint and several liability has perhaps been the most widely successful undertaking of the tort reform movement. One source reported that as of 1996 joint and several liability was not applied in four states (Alabama, Indiana, Kansas and Oklahoma) and had been abolished or modified to one degree or another in 34 others. American Tort Reform Association, Tort Reform Update, December 31, 1995. Unlike the movement to adopt comparative negligence, which was propelled by the strength of its perceived intrinsic fairness to protect plaintiffs as a class from the common law bar of contributory negligence, the movement to abolish joint and several liability has been a concerted effort to protect well heeled defendant classes from being required to pay all damages a plaintiff suffered as a result of the aggregated negligence of multiple defendants, some of whom might be judgment proof. *See, e.g., Newville v. State*, 883 P.2d 793, 799 (Mont. 1994) ("The stated aim . . . was to protect 'deep pockets' defendants such as municipal and county governments when they were faced with minimal percentages of negligence assigned to them by juries but nonetheless required to pay large judgments under joint and several liability principles.")

The doctrine of joint and several liability of multiple tortfeasors permits a plaintiff to extract judgment from any one of several tortfeasors or some from one and some from another until the entire judgment is satisfied. See notes, § 4.02 *infra*. This gives plaintiffs an undeniable advantage. Nevertheless, the corollary rule that the release of one joint and several tortfeasor releases all imperils unsuspecting plaintiffs.

Thus, *P* might obtain a joint and several judgment of $1000 against *A* and *B*. *P* collects $500 from *A* and, in exchange, executes a document releasing *A* of "all" liability. *P* then approaches *B* to collect the remaining $500. *B* refuses on the strength of the release given *A*, and the action is dismissed. Why?

As with many common law doctrines that originated in ancient practice, the true reason is lost in antiquity. But plausible explanations can be found. In *Cheetham v. Ward*,[11] for example, a 1797 case in the Court of Common Pleas, Eyre, C.J. ruled against the plaintiff on the acknowledged principle "that where a personal action is once suspended by the voluntary act of the party entitled to it, it is forever gone and discharged."[12] The style of the courts of that day was to adhere strictly to precedence, rather than search for reason. Thus, Eyre felt no compunction to say:[13]

The very point in issue was . . . decided in the year-book: and Brian there gives excellent reasons for it. In fact there is but one duty extending to both obligors; and it was pointedly put that a discharge of one, or the satisfaction made by one, is a discharge of both. This puts an end to the argument that the action is not necessarily suspended as to both: for it is the effect of the suspension as to one that releases, discharges, and extinguishes the action as to both. This case, therefore, must be decided by the year-book, and the principle there laid down, which has never been doubted since, whether founded in reason or not.

Both English and American courts applied this rule to joint and several tort obligations, including those based upon independent negligent acts that merged to produce an indivisible injury. The Maine Supreme Court stated the rule as follows:[14]

In a joint trespass or tort each is considered as sanctioning the acts of all the others, thereby making them his own. Each is therefore liable for the whole damage, as occasioned by himself, and it may be recovered by a suit against him alone. There can be no separate estimate of the injury committed by each, and a recovery accordingly. The difficulty in maintaining the suit against the others is that the law considers that the one who has paid for the injury occasioned by him, and has been discharged, committed the whole trespass and occasioned the whole injury, and that he has therefore satisfied the plaintiff for the whole injury which he received.

The release-of-one-releases-all rule was a trap for unversed plaintiffs. A layman might, in common sense, believe that if two defendants jointly injured him, he could accept a settlement from one and still pursue the other for the unpaid remainder of the loss. But such was not the law, and many plaintiffs were disappointed. The rule

---

[11] 126 Eng. Rep. 1102, 1 Bos & Pul 630 (1779).

[12] *Id.* at 126, Eng. Rep. 1104.

[13] *Id.*

[14] Gilpatrick v. Hunter, 41 Am. Dec. 370, 371 (Me.), quoted in ABB v. Northern Pac. Ry. Co., 65 P. 954, 955 (Wash. 1902).

also clearly stood as an inhibition to settlement. A knowledgeable plaintiff, or one represented by a lawyer, would simply spurn any attempt of one defendant to settle, absent a satisfactory consideration of all the damages. Thus, ignorant plaintiffs entered partial settlements to their grief, and informed plaintiffs often persevered to trial even against defendants who, individually, were willing to settle.

A rule so contrary to expectations and fair administration of justice was understandably unpopular with the courts. Relief valves emerged in the forms of covenants not to sue and covenants not to enforce judgment. Thus, if a plaintiff received payment of $100 from one of two joint tortfeasors and released him, that release discharged the other. But if the plaintiff took the same $100 in exchange for a promise (covenant) not to sue (or not to enforce judgment), then there was no discharge and no inhibition upon a suit against the other joint tortfeasor. This rule was adopted in English[15] and American courts.[16]

The reasoning underlying this odd result was that the covenant created a contract right; it did not discharge the underlying tort right of the plaintiff. The plaintiff had the capacity to breach the covenant and sue anyway. Such an act would itself give rise to a breach of contract action for damages in the covenantee, measured presumably by the amount of the tort remedy against the covenantee plus litigation expenses. But in any case, the tort was not discharged. In other words, the plaintiff's original tort cause of action remained, and the defendant now possessed a counter-claim in breach of contract.

As might be expected, this paradox — a covenant does not discharge but a release does — created a new legal issue. What words constitute a release, and what words constitute a covenant? This issue revived one of the evils that the covenant not to sue was supposed to avoid; it set a trap for plaintiffs who did not understand the import of the words used. Two lines of cases evolved, one applying a rigid standard of construction to the detriment of plaintiffs[17] and the other applying a more forgiving standard to the benefit of plaintiffs.[18] The key in all cases, as expressed by an English court, was the intention of the parties to the covenant:[19]

In determining whether the document be a covenant not to sue, the intention of the parties was to be carried out; and, if it were clear that the right against a joint debtor was intended to be preserved, in as much as the right would not be preserved if the document were held to be a release, the proper construction, where this was sought to be done, was that it was a covenant not to sue, and not a release.

Notwithstanding this view, some courts continued to smash the hopes of plaintiffs on the strength of subtle phrasings in the covenants.[20]

---

[15] *See, e.g.,* Duck v. Mayeu, 2 QB 511 (1892).

[16] *See, e.g.,* Gilbert v. Finch, 66 N.E. 133 (N.Y. 1903); ABB v. Northern Pac. Ry. Co., 68 P. 954 (Wash. 1902); L & N R R Co. v. Allen, 67 Fla. 257 (1914).

[17] *See, e.g.,* ABB v. Northern Pac. Ry. Co., 68 P. 954 (Wash. 1902).

[18] *See, e.g.,* Gilbert v. Finch, 66 N.E. 133 (N.Y. 1903).

[19] Duck v. Mayen, 2 QB 511 (1892).

[20] *See, e.g.,* Sands v. Wilson, 140 Fla. 18, 191 So. 21 (1939).

According to Prosser, the idea of the release of a liability was confused with the idea of the satisfaction of a judgment for liability.[21] The release of one tortfeasor was assumed to have satisfied the claim against all when it clearly was intended to do no such thing. As noted above, many courts[22] ameliorated the harsh rule by recognizing covenants not to sue. A valid covenant required only that the judgment against the non-settling tortfeasor be reduced *pro tanto* by the amount of the consideration paid for the covenant not to sue.[23] This carried out the true expectations of the contracting parties.

Some courts have flatly repudiated the rule that release of one releases all. *See, e.g., Kussler v. Burlington Northern, Inc.*, 606 P.2d 520 (Mont. 1980). Instead, the true intention of the parties is to be given effect. This view deems the old rule to be unsupportable by any modern view of policy. Much more commonly, legislatures have statutorily modified the old rule. These statutes are typified by § 4 of the Uniform Contribution Among Tortfeasors Act reproduced in the next section.

The availability of limited releases and covenants not to sue creates new settlement opportunities for plaintiffs, as demonstrated by the next case.

VERMONT UNION SCHOOL DISTRICT v. H.P. CUMMINGS CONSTRUCTION CO.
Vermont Supreme Court
469 A.2d 742 (1983)

HILL, JUSTICE.

The Vermont Union School District No. 21 (school district) instituted this action on July 26, 1976, against its general contractor, the H.P. Cummings Construction Company (Cummings), and Cummings' roofing subcontractor, Major L. Rodd, Inc. (Rodd), for alleged defects in the school district's Blue Mountain School roof. Its complaint alleged that the new roof had widespread leakage problems caused by the roof's blistering and bubbling surface. The complaint further alleged that both defendants had been negligent, had breached warranties, and had failed to construct the roof in a workmanlike manner. In response, Cummings and Rodd sought indemnity from the GAF Corporation (GAF), Rodd's supplier of roofing materials for the Blue Mountain School.

. . .

After extensive review of the documents secured from GAF through discovery, the parties took several procedural steps which significantly altered the posture of this action. On March 3, 1980, and June 6, 1980, the trial court permitted Rodd and the school district to amend their pleadings to seek direct relief and punitive damages against GAF. The school district, Rodd and Cummings then negotiated an agreement detailing each party's liabilities and obligations. In the agreement, which was later memorialized and filed with the trial court on November 10, 1980,

---

[21] Prosser, Law of Torts (5th Ed.), 332. Prosser states that, at common law, release were executed under seal, a formality that the tort cases ignored.

[22] Prosser, Law of Torts (4th Ed.), 303. Prosser states that only Washington and Virginia refused to recognize covenants not to sue. Despite this statement, *ABB v. Northern Pac. Ry. Co.*, 68 P. 954 (Wash. 1902), acknowledges the existence of covenants not to sue, properly drawn.

[23] Prosser, Law of Torts (5th Ed.), 335–36.

Rodd and Cummings waived all defenses to the school district's complaint and admitted all liability. The school district then agreed that the judgments stipulated to would be fully satisfied and discharged in return for the good faith prosecution by Cummings and Rodd of all claims pending against GAF. The agreement further outlined a distribution formula for all damages ultimately collected from GAF.

In response, GAF moved to have the agreement declared void, to have all claims against it dismissed as being extinguished by the agreement, and again to have the claims of Rodd and the school district dismissed on statute of limitation grounds. On January 7, 1981, GAF's motion was denied. GAF then cross-claimed against Rodd, seeking indemnity for improper application of the roof, alleging that Rodd breached warranties and negligently failed to follow GAF's specifications.

The trial commenced on February 3, 1981. On March 25, 1981, the jury, in answer to special interrogatories, returned an award of approximately $2,295,000 against GAF, of which $1,600,000 constituted punitive damages (to be split evenly, according to the agreement, between the school and Rodd). Of the remainder, $195,000 was awarded to the school for the cost of roof replacement, and approximately $500,000 was awarded to Rodd as compensatory and indemnity damages. GAF moved for remittitur of all punitive damages and all further damages awarded to Rodd, and additionally moved for a new trial. In a post trial order dated May 7, 1981, the trial court denied the motions, and GAF subsequently filed a timely notice of appeal. We reverse.

[Perhaps uniquely, Vermont law requires two non-lawyer assistant judges to participate in trial with a regular judge. This case was conducted without assistant judges. The Supreme Court held that to be grounds of mistrial and reversed the judgment on that account.]

Although we are precluded from reviewing many of the issues of law presented in this appeal. it is appropriate that we review one of these issues because it is likely to recur at retrial. *State v. Carmody*, 140 Vt. 631, 637, 442 A.2d 1292, 1295 (1982). That issue concerns the validity of the agreement between the school, Rodd, and Cummings. On November 10, 1980, the school, Cummings and Rodd entered into a written stipulation which was filed with the court on that date, sanctioned by the court in its pretrial order of January 7, 1981, and ultimately admitted into evidence during the course of the trial. Although the stipulation was not reduced to writing until November, the parties to it had orally agreed to its terms in the summer of 1980. On August 12, 1980, GAF filed interrogatories inquiring into the nature and substance of the agreement and, in its answer, dated September 15, 1980, the school disclosed the essential terms of the stipulation. Thus, GAF was aware of the stipulation and apprised of its terms at least five months prior to the commencement of trial.

The written stipulation briefly recounted the factual background of the case, and asserted that the roofing materials provided by GAF "were defective, in part because they contained excessive moisture." The stipulation also acknowledged the legal liability of Cummings and Rodd to the school "for such compensatory damages as are finally determined in this litigation to have been proximately caused by the fact that the roof . . . contained such defective materials. . . . " Rodd, in turn, acknowledged liability to Cummings "for the same reason." The school then asserted that it would not seek punitive damages against Cummings or Rodd as a consequence of their liability. In consideration of Cummings' and Rodd's stipulation, the school agreed that any judgments in its favor against Cummings and Rodd would be "fully satisfied and discharged" by the good faith prosecution by Cummings and Rodd of all claims of the school and of Cummings and Rodd against GAF, and the payment over to the school of all amounts which were ultimately recovered and collected from GAF by Cummings and Rodd in compensation for the school's damages. The stipulation then outlined that such good faith prosecution would include investigating, providing witnesses and retaining experts, presenting evidence relating to all triable claims, and appealing and retrying the case, if necessary, to obtain a final determination of the school's damages.

The final provisions of the stipulation were as follows:

6. If H.P. Cummings or Rodd recover and collect from GAF any amounts for the said School District damages, whether by negotiation and settlement or by verdict and judgment, said amounts shall be paid over to the School District, less offsets if any, and the School District shall accept such sum in full payment, satisfaction and discharge of the judgments in its favor against H.P. Cummings and Rodd stipulated to herein and H.P. Cummings and Rodd and each of them will thereupon be fully released and discharged from any and all liability to the School District for the said School District damages. Such payment shall also be in full payment, discharge and satisfaction of the judgment in favor of H.P. Cummings against Rodd stipulated to herein for said School District damages. It is agreed that such payments to the School District shall be conditioned upon, limited to and payable from and only from any sums actually collected from GAF by H.P. Cummings or Rodd for said School District damages and if no collection is obtained for said School District damages by H.P. Cummings or Rodd from GAF the attempts by H.P. Cummings or Rodd to collect and recover from GAF for such amounts shall constitute payment, satisfaction and discharge of the judgments stipulated to herein and H.P. Cummings and Rodd shall be fully released and discharged from any liability to the School, and Rodd shall be fully released and discharged from any liability to H.P. Cummings, in connection with the construction of the school building. It is understood and agreed that neither H.P. Cummings or Rodd are under any obligation to pay over to the School District any sums they or either of them may collect from GAF which are not for the said School District damages but rather for other compensatory damages sustained by H.P. Cummings or Rodd, whether obtained by negotiation and settlement or verdict and judgment, and that distribution of any punitive damages which may be recovered by any of the parties to this stipulation shall be governed by the provisions of the next paragraph.

7. The School District, H.P. Cummings and Rodd may each present any claim they have for punitive damages against GAF. All punitive damages recovered from GAF, whether by negotiation and settlement or by verdict and judgment, shall be divided evenly between the School District and Rodd. In the event the jury should find punitive damages separately, the parties hereby agree that the court may combine said punitive damages and divide them evenly between the School District and Rod. In the event the Court should not approve this division of punitive damages, it shall not negate this stipulation but it shall be viewed separately and may be subject to separate amendment by the parties hereto.

8. It is not the intention of the parties that this agreement be viewed as a waiver of any of the terms and provisions of the contracts between the parties, nor is it a release, but rather an agreement which stipulates the liability of certain

defendants and provides a method for those defendants to discharge that liability.

GAF moved to declare the stipulation void as adverse to GAF's right to a fair trial and violative of public policy. By an order dated January 7, 1981, the court denied this motion, finding that the agreement underlying the stipulation was valid. However, the court refused to accept the provisions of paragraph 7 regarding the division of any punitive damage award between Rodd and the school, and cautioned the jury that the clause was not binding. The court also acknowledged that because of the stipulation, trial procedure would have to be modified; ultimately, all the parties to the stipulation were designated as plaintiffs for the purposes of trial, and the entire stipulation was introduced as evidence, used by GAF in examining witnesses, and submitted to the jury as Exhibit 1.

On appeal GAF renews its argument that, by failing to declare the stipulation void as a matter of law, the court denied GAF's right to a fair trial. It characterizes the stipulation as a "Mary Carter agreement," a term coined by a Florida court in the case of *Maule Industries, Inc. v. Rountree*, 264 So. 2d 445 (Fla. Dist. Ct. App. 1972), rev'd on other grounds, 284 So.2 d 389 (Fla. 1973), (referring to the agreement in *Booth v. Mary Carter Paint Co.*, 202 So. 2d 8 (Fla. Dist. Ct. App. 1967)). Plaintiffs contend that the stipulation is not a Mary Carter agreement, that neither its provisions nor its spirit contravenes public policy, and that GAF's right to a fair trial was not compromised. Since this question is one of first impression for this Court, to pass on it we must review both the current state of the law regarding Mary Carter agreements, and the policy considerations underlying their use.

Although this Court has not yet addressed the validity of Mary Carter agreements, the issue has been litigated extensively in other jurisdictions, *see, e.g.*, *Breitkreutz v. Baker*, 514 P.2d 17 (Alaska 1973); . . . and has been the subject of much commentary.

[*See, e.g.*, Freedman, *The Expected Demise of "Mary Carter": She Never Was Well!*, 633 Ins. L. J. 602 (1975).]

In essence, a Mary Carter agreement is a contract by which one or more defendants in a multi- party case secretly align themselves with the plaintiff and agree to continue as active defendants in the suit while working to aid in the plaintiff's case; in exchange, their own maximum liability will be diminished proportionately by increasing the liability of the nonagreeing defendant or defendants. *Cox v. Kelsey-Hayes Co., supra*, 594 P.2d at 357 (citing *Ward v. Ochoa, supra*, 284 So. 2d 385). The agreements themselves take a variety of forms; however, four features are commonly considered to be essential:

1. The agreeing defendants must remain in the action in the posture of defendants.

2. The agreement must be kept secret.

3. The agreeing defendants guarantee to the plaintiff a certain monetary recovery regardless of the outcome of the lawsuit.

4. The agreeing defendants' liability is decreased in direct proportion to the increase in the nonagreeing defendants' liability.

. . .

The facts of a Nevada decision, *Lum v. Stinnett*, [488 P.2d 347 (Nev. 1977)], typify such arrangements. In *Lum*, plaintiff and two co-defendant physicians effectively conspired to shift the malpractice liability to a third defendant physician. Under the Mary Carter agreement, the two physicians agreed to pay plaintiff $20,000 if the jury awarded plaintiff nothing or less than $20,000; but if the jury verdict exceeded $20,000, these two physicians would pay nothing. Plaintiff further agreed not to settle with the third defendant physician for less than $20,000 without the written consent of the two signing physicians. The two physicians were present as defendants at trial, but plaintiff virtually disregarded them. At the close of his case, plaintiff dismissed all charges against them and recovered a judgment of $50,000 against the remaining physician. That judgment was ultimately reversed on appeal, in an opinion which caustically denounced Mary Carter agreements and declared them void per se as against public policy.

Not surprisingly, Mary Carter agreements have been widely criticized as champertous, violative of public policy, and a distortion of the adversary relationship between plaintiffs and defendants which results in a collusive proceeding adversely affecting the nonagreeing defendant's right to a fair trial.

In effect, the "Mary Carter agreement" is a *partial* settlement of a dispute between a plaintiff and at least one of the defendants. The role of the contracting defendant is comparable to that of the role of an actor in a real play. He is a favored party to the litigation as he hides behind his mask, thereby precluding the court, the jury, and the noncontracting defendant or defendants from recognizing what has conspiratorily transpired to their detriment. The contracting defendant or defendants are defendants in name only, since they, by "agreement," actively promote the plaintiff's case. They may very well abandon or not even assert certain obvious defenses, such as contributory negligence, assumption of the risk, or even misuse of the product. They may readily admit the reasonableness of the damages claimed by the plaintiff. In either event, the "conduct" of the contracting defendant or defendants must influence the judge and jury, especially in those situations where the judge and jury are unaware of the executed "Mary Carter agreement." Therefore, any recovery by the plaintiff is tainted because it also accrues to the benefit of the contracting defendant or defendants at the expense of the noncontracting defendant or defendants. Freedman, *supra*, at 610. On the issue of secrecy, one court noted.

Secrecy is the essence of such an arrangement, because the court or jury as trier of the facts, if apprised of this, would likely weigh differently the testimony and conduct of the signing defendant as related to the non-signing defendants. By painting a gruesome testimonial picture of the other defendant's misconduct or, in some cases, by admissions against himself and the other defendants, he could diminish or eliminate his own liability by use of the secret "Mary Carter Agreement."

Ward v. Ochoa, *supra*, 284 So. 2d at 387.

Although Mary Carter agreements are frequently denounced, only two states have condemned their use outright by ruling them void per se. See generally Freedman, *supra*, and Miller, *supra*, who argue that all such agreements should be held illegal per se. The majority of jurisdictions regard such agreements cautiously, choosing to treat them on a case by case basis rather than by categorical condemnation or absolute approval. In this regard, the reasoning of the

Florida court in *Maule Industries, Inc. v. Rountree, supra*, is instructive:

We are not inclined to paint with a brush that broad [as per se illegality]. Obviously the number of variations of the so-called "Mary Carter Agreement" is limited only by the ingenuity of counsel and the willingness of the parties to sign, and we therefore feel that we can neither condone nor condemn such agreements generically. We simply say that we do not find the agreement in this case to be void.

264 So. 2d at 447. . . .

As one commentator noted, "[t]he better solution is to attack only those aspects of the typical agreement that unfairly prejudice the nonagreeing defendant" and skew the results of trial. Grant, *supra*, at 1410. Thus, a majority of those jurisdictions considering the issue have fashioned a rule requiring that such agreements be subject to pretrial discovery and, with some qualifications, admitted into evidence. Some jurisdictions allow admission for the sole purpose of attacking the credibility of witnesses, and require a limiting jury instruction to that effect. *See, e.g., Bedford School District v. Caron Construction Co., supra*, 116 N.H. at 805–06, 367 A.2d at 1054–55. Others allow the agreements in to prove the fact of their existence but require the excission of any inculpatory or self-serving statements and statements concerning the monetary amount of settlement, recognizing the inherently prejudicial nature of such information. . . . Still other jurisdictions leave the extent of the agreement's admissibility to the discretion of the trial court.

Having thus considered the policies and law surrounding Mary Carter agreements, we do not agree with GAF that the stipulation entered into here between the school, Cummings and Rodd was such a collusive instrument. The agreement was not secret; GAF was apprised of its essential terms a full five months before trial, and the document was filed with the court and incorporated into the court's pretrial order two months before trial. Nor did the parties to the agreement attempt to deceive the court by masquerading Rodd or Cummings as nominal defendants; once the stipulation was entered into, these two parties were explicitly realigned as plaintiffs, and so conducted themselves throughout the trial. Finally, the school was not guaranteed a fixed monetary recovery by the stipulation, regardless of the outcome of trial. Rather, its recovery, if any, was left wholly to the determination of the fact finder.

The only questionable provision in the stipulation pertained to the splitting of any punitive damage award between the school and Rodd. To the extent that this provision was valid, it effectively decreased Rodd's liability in direct proportion to the increase in GAF's liability. However, as noted above, the trial court rejected this provision. Moreover, the parties to the agreement themselves acknowledged the questionable validity of this clause by declaring it to be severable. We agree that the propriety of this provision is dubious, and we approve the trial court's rejection of it. See Grant, *supra*, at 1415-17.

Since the trial court rejected the provision to split the punitive damage award, the agreement as limited thereby had none of the characteristics of a Mary Carter agreement, and threatened none of the interests sought to be preserved when such overt contracts exist. Moreover, even if we were to consider the stipulation as akin to a Mary Carter agreement, we would not be compelled to agree with GAF that its rights were unduly prejudiced thereby. As noted above, the majority of courts do not apply a per se prohibition of such agreements, but rather fashion a procedure for safeguarding the rights of the noncontracting defendant. In part this reflects a determination that such agreements are not wholly without salutary effect. As one court noted, "they encourage out-of-court settlements and help solve the economic need of an injured person confronted with the delays in the court system." *Grillo v. Burke's Paint Co., supra*, 275 Or. at 427, 551 P.2d at 452.

In this case, all the procedures used to minimize the prejudice to a noncontracting defendant were employed: the agreement was disclosed to GAF upon proper discovery motions; the document was filed in court; and Rodd and Cummings were realigned as plaintiffs at the trial. Finally, the questionable provision regarding punitive damages splitting was rejected by the court.

Thus, on the particular facts before us, we find nothing illegal or improper about the pretrial stipulation entered into here. We recognize, however, the exclusion of evidence regarding settlement agreements. *See* V.R.E. 408; *Slayton v. Ford Motor Co.*, 140 Vt. 27, 29, 435 A.2d 946, 947 (1981) (jury may not be informed of a settlement agreement between one of several defendants and a plaintiff); *see also Griffith v. Nielsen* 141 Vt. 423, 428, 449 A.2d 965, 968 (1982) ("[u]naccepted offers of settlement or compromise are inadmissible since public policy strongly favors settlement of disputed claims without litigation") (citing *Dutch Hill Inn, Inc. v. Patten*, 131 Vt. 187, 192, 303 A.2d 811, 814 (1973)). Therefore, on retrial, the agreement should not be admitted into evidence, nor should the jury be advised of its existence, since the jury might draw improper inferences if it is informed of the settlement. See *Slayton, supra.*

Reversed and remanded.

NOTES AND QUESTIONS

(1)　Do you agree that Mary Carter agreements in the pure form are not *per se* unfair? Arizona refers to them as "Gallagher" agreements, *City of Tuscon v. Gallagher*, 108 Ariz. 140, 493 P.2d 1197 (1972), and Illinois permits a particular version known as "loan agreements." *Palmer v. Avco Distributing Co.*, 75 Ill. App. 3d 598, 31 Ill. Dec. 278, 398 N.E.2d 480 (1979).

(2)　The action from which the term "Mary Carter Agreement" derives, *Booth v. Mary Carter Paint Co.*, 202 So. 2d 8 (Fla. App. 1967), involved an agreement with in essence the following provisions:

First, that the maximum liability, exposure or financial contribution of defendant X shall be $12,500.00.

Second, that in the event of a joint verdict against defendant X and the Mary Carter Paint Company exceeding $37,500.00, the plaintiff will satisfy said judgment against Mary Carter Paint Company entirely, with no contribution from defendant X. Provided, however, that if the Mary Carter Paint Company is not financially responsible to the extent of $37,500.00, defendant X will contribute an amount of money between Mary Carter Paint Company's actual responsibility and the figure of $37,500.00, but not to exceed $12,500.00.

Third, that in the event of a verdict for all the defendants, defendant X will pay the plaintiff $12,500.00; and in the event of a verdict against Mary

Carter Paint Company less than $37,500.00, defendant X will contribute the sum of $12,500.00.

Fourth, that defendant X shall continue as an active defendant in the defense of said litigation until all questions of liability and damages are resolved between the plaintiff and all defendants.

Fifth, that should the conditions laid down in the agreement result in any financial responsibility on the part of defendant X, defendant X will pay the plaintiff within five days after the questions of liability and damages between the plaintiff and all defendants are settled or concluded.

Sixth, that the parties intend this agreement to be construed as a conditional agreement between them as to financial responsibility only, and that it shall not constitute, or be construed to constitute, a release, settlement, admission of liability, or otherwise, and shall have no effect upon the trial of this case as to liability or extent of damages, nor shall said agreement be revealed to the jury.

. . .

Eighth, that the contents of this agreement shall be furnished to no one, unless so ordered by the court, and

Ninth, that the terms and conditions specified in the agreement, which are dependent upon a jury verdict, shall be equally applicable to and binding on the parties in the event plaintiff amicably settles the issues of liability and damages with Mary Carter Paint Company.

Explain the purpose of each term. What would happen if the jury were to return a verdict in the exact amount of $12,500? In *Dosdourian v. Carsten*, 624 So. 2d 241 (Fla. 1993), the Florida Supreme Court held that all agreements that require a settling defendant to remain as an apparently active defendant in a continuing action against nonsettling defendants are void as against public policy. Do you agree? This killed the use of classic Mary Carter agreements in Florida. Does this discourage or encourage settlements?

§ 11.04 SPECIAL CONSIDERATIONS IN COMPARATIVE NEGLIGENCE

[A] Liability of Multiple Defendants

A crucial comparative negligence question is whether multiple defendants are jointly and severally liable for a plaintiff's apportioned damages, or whether each defendant is individually liable only for his proportionate share of the harm done. The effect of the answer can be illustrated, as follows:

Example 1. Joint and Several Liability

Plaintiff's Share of Negligence:	20%
Defendant A's Share of Negligence:	40%
Defendant B's Share of Negligence:	30%
Defendant C's Share of Negligence:	10%
Plaintiff's Damages:	$10,000

Example 1. Joint and Several Liability

Plaintiff's Apportioned Judgment:
$$\$10,000 \times 0.80 = \qquad\qquad \$8,000$$

Under the rule of joint and several liability, a plaintiff who receives a judgment of \$8,000 against Defendants A, B and C can execute the judgment in any manner, collecting all from one or some from each until the judgment is satisfied.

Example 2. (Individual) Liability

[Damages and percentages as in Example 1]
Defendant A's Individual Liability:
$$\$10,000 \times 0.40 = \qquad\qquad \$4,000$$
Defendant B's Individual Liability:
$$\$10,000 \times 0.30 = \qquad\qquad \$3,000$$
Defendant C's Individual Liability:
$$\$10,000 \times 0.10 = \qquad\qquad \$1,000$$

Under the rule of apportioned individual liability, no defendant is liable for more than a proportionate share of the plaintiff's total damages. The plaintiff also stands the risk of judgment proof tortfeasors and the burden of multiple executions.

[1]   Joint and Several Liability

CONEY v. J.L.G. INDUSTRIES, INC.
Supreme Court of Illinois
97 Ill.2d 104, 454 N.E.2d 197 (1983)

THOMAS J. MORAN, JUSTICE:

Clifford M. Jasper died as a result of injuries sustained on January 24, 1978, while operating a hydraulic aerial work platform manufactured by defendant, J.L.G. Industries, Inc. Plaintiff, Jack A. Coney, administrator of Jasper's estate, filed a two-count complaint in the circuit court of Peoria County under the wrongful death and survival acts (Ill.Rev.Stat.1977, ch. 70, par. 1 et seq., ch. 110 1/2, par. 27-6) . . . Defendant filed two affirmative defenses. The first asserted that Jasper was guilty of comparative negligence or fault in his operation of the platform. The second contended that Jasper's employer, V. Jobst & Sons, Inc., was also guilty of comparative negligence in failing to instruct and train Jasper on the operation of the platform and by failing to provide a "groundman." In these defenses, defendant requested that its fault, if any, be compared to the total fault of all parties and any judgment against defendant reflect only its percentage of the overall liability, i.e., that defendant not be held jointly and severally liable.

On plaintiff's motion, the trial court struck the defenses, but it certified three questions for appeal pursuant to Supreme Court Rule 308 (73 Ill. 2d R. 308). . . .

[One of the three certified questions is]:

. . . .

Whether the doctrine of comparative negligence or fault eliminates joint and several liability?

. . . .

JOINT AND SEVERAL LIABILITY

The common law doctrine of joint and several liability holds joint tortfeasors responsible for the plaintiff's entire injury, allowing plaintiff to pursue all, some, or one of the tortfeasors responsible for his injury for the full amount of the damages. Paul Harris Furniture Co. v. Morse (1956), 10 Ill. 2d 28, 43, 139 N.E.2d 275; Nordhaus v. Vandalia R.R. Co. (1909), 242 Ill. 166, 174, 89 N.E. 974; Wabash, St. Louis & Pacific Ry. Co. v. Shacklet (1883), 105 Ill. 364, 381.

Defendant asserts joint and several liability is a corollary of the contributory negligence doctrine. Prior to *Alvis*, a plaintiff who was guilty of even slight contributory negligence was barred from recovery. Defendant maintains that joint and several liability balanced this inequity by permitting a faultless plaintiff to collect his entire judgment from any defendant who was guilty of even slight negligence. With the adoption of comparative negligence where damages are apportioned according to each party's fault, defendant argues it is no longer rational to hold a defendant liable beyond his share of the total damages. Defendant relies primarily on a line of cases where joint and several liability was abolished or limited in the course of construing a statutory scheme of liability. *Brown v. Keill* (1978), 224 Kan. 195, 580 P.2d 867; *Laubach v. Morgan* (Okl.1978), 588 P.2d 1071; *Howard v. Spafford* (1974), 132 Vt. 434, 321 A.2d 74; and *Bartlett v. New Mexico Welding Supply, Inc.* (1982), 98 N.M. 152, 646 P.2d 579.

The vast majority of jurisdictions, however, which have adopted comparative negligence have retained joint and several liability as a part of their comparative negligence doctrine:

[Citations omitted from Alaska, Arkansas, California, Colorado, Connecticut, Florida, Georgia, Idaho, Maine, Michigan, Minnesota, Nebraska, New Jersey, New York, North Dakota, Washington, and Wisconsin.]

Generally, four reasons have been advanced for retaining joint and several liability:

(1) The feasibility of apportioning fault on a comparative basis does not render an indivisible injury "divisible" for purposes of the joint and several liability rule. A concurrent tortfeasor is liable for the whole of an indivisible injury when his negligence is a proximate cause of that damage. In many instances, the negligence of a concurrent tortfeasor may be sufficient by itself to cause the entire loss. The mere fact that it may be possible to assign some percentage figure to the relative culpability of one negligent defendant as compared to another does not in any way suggest that each defendant's negligence is not a proximate cause of the entire indivisible injury.

(2) In those instances where the plaintiff is not guilty of negligence, he would be forced to bear a portion of the loss should one of the tortfeasors prove financially unable to satisfy his share of the damages.

(3) Even in cases where a plaintiff is partially at fault, his culpability is not equivalent to that of a defendant. The plaintiff's negligence relates only to a lack of

due care for his own safety while the defendant's negligence relates to a lack of due care for the safety of others; the latter is tortious, but the former is not.

(4) Elimination of joint and several liability would work a serious and unwarranted deleterious effect on the ability of an injured plaintiff to obtain adequate compensation for his injuries. . . .

In adopting comparative negligence, this court eliminated the total bar to recovery which a plaintiff had faced under contributory negligence. In return for allowing a negligent plaintiff to recover, this court said fairness requires that a plaintiff's damages be "reduced by the percentage of fault attributable to him." (Emphasis added.) (*Alvis v. Ribar* (1981), 85 Ill. 2d 1, 25, 52 Ill. Dec. 23, 421 N.E.2d 886.) Were we to eliminate joint and several liability as the defendant advocates, the burden of the insolvent or immune defendant would fall on the plaintiff; in that circumstance, plaintiff's damages would be reduced beyond the percentage of fault attributable to him. We do not believe the doctrine of comparative negligence requires this further reduction. Nor do we believe this burden is the price plaintiffs must pay for being relieved of the contributory negligence bar. The quid pro quo is the reduction of plaintiff's damages. What was said in *American Motorcycle Association v. Superior Court* (1978), 20 Cal. 3d 578, 590, 146 Cal. Rptr. 182, 189, 578 P.2d 899, 906, is applicable here: "[F]airness dictates that the 'wronged party should not be deprived of his right to redress,' * * * '[t]he wrongdoers should be left to work out between themselves any apportionment.' "

Further support for retaining joint and several liability is found in "An Act in relation to contribution among joint tortfeasors" (Act) (Ill. Rev. Stat.1979, ch. 70, par. 301 et seq.). Although the instant case accrued prior to its effective date, the Act expresses the intent of our legislature concerning joint and several liability:

> "Sec. 4 Rights of Plaintiff Unaffected. A plaintiff's right to recover the full amount of his judgment from any one or more defendants subject to liability in tort for the same injury to person or property, or for wrongful death, is not affected by the provisions of this Act." Ill.Rev.Stat.1979, ch. 70, par. 304.

Moreover, under the Act, it is the defendant or defendants who must bear the burden of the insolvent or immune defendant:

> "Sec. 3. Amount of Contribution. The pro rata share of each tortfeasor shall be determined in accordance with his relative culpability. However, no person shall be required to contribute to one seeking contribution an amount greater than his pro rata share unless the obligation of one or more of the joint tortfeasors is uncollectible. In that event, the remaining tortfeasors shall share the unpaid portions of the uncollectible obligation in accordance with their pro rata liability.

If equity requires, the collective liability of some as a group shall constitute a single share." Ill. Rev. Stat.1979, ch. 70, par. 303.

Defendant concedes that where the plaintiff is free from fault each defendant should still be held jointly and severally liable. It also admits in its reply brief that the Act leaves unaffected the common law doctrine of joint and several liability. Defendant points out, however, that it was subsequent to the enactment of the Act that this court adopted comparative negligence. Now, under *Alvis*, damages are allocated according to fault. As such, defendant argues, *Alvis* mandates that a tortfeasor should be liable only to the extent that his negligent acts or omissions produced the damages.

We find nothing in *Alvis* which mandates either a shift in who shall bear the risk of the insolvent defendant or the elimination of joint and several liability. Defendant has not cited nor have we found persuasive judicial authority for the proposition that comparative negligence compels the abolition of joint and several liability. On the contrary, most jurisdictions which have adopted comparative negligence have retained the doctrine. Therefore, we hold that our adoption of comparative negligence in *Alvis* does not change the long-standing doctrine of joint and several liability.

. . . . The doctrine of joint and several liability, like contribution, operates only where two or more persons are subject to liability in tort arising out of the same injury to a plaintiff. (See Ill. Rev. Stat.1979, ch. 70, par. 302; *Paul Harris Furniture Co. v. Morse* (1956), 10 Ill. 2d 28, 43, 139 N.E.2d 275.) Such is not the case here, and the doctrine of joint and several liability has no application.

Therefore, in response to the questions posed, we conclude that . . . comparative fault does not eliminate joint and several liability. . . . The order of the circuit court striking the affirmative defenses is affirmed, and the cause is remanded to the circuit court of Peoria County with directions to allow defendant to amend his first defense so as to be consistent with the views expressed herein.

NOTES AND QUESTIONS

(1) The joint and several liability holding of *Coney v. J.L.G. Industries, Inc.* was superseded by statute:

§ 2-1116. Limitation on recovery in tort actions; fault.

(a) The purpose of this Section is to allocate the responsibility of bearing or paying damages in actions brought on account of death, bodily injury, or physical damage to property according to the proportionate fault of the persons who proximately caused the damage.

(b) As used in this Section:

"Fault" means any act or omission that (i) is negligent, willful and wanton, or reckless, is a breach of an express or implied warranty, gives rise to strict liability in tort, or gives rise to liability under the provisions of any State statute, rule, or local ordinance and (ii) is a proximate cause of death, bodily injury to person, or physical damage to property for which recovery is sought.

"Contributory fault" means any fault on the part of the plaintiff (including but not limited to negligence, assumption of the risk, or willful and wanton misconduct) which is a proximate cause of the death, bodily injury to person, or physical damage to property for which recovery is sought.

"Tortfeasor" means any person, excluding the injured person, whose fault is a proximate cause of the death, bodily injury to person, or physical damage to property for which recovery is sought, regardless of whether that person is the plaintiff's employer, regardless of whether that person is joined as a party to the action, and regardless of whether that person may have settled with the plaintiff.

(c) In all actions on account of death, bodily injury or physical damage to property in which recovery is predicated upon fault, the contributory fault chargeable to the plaintiff shall be compared with the fault of all tortfeasors whose fault was a proximate cause of the death, injury, loss, or damage for which recovery is sought. The plaintiff shall be barred from recovering damages if the trier of fact finds that the contributory fault on the part of the plaintiff is more than 50% of the proximate cause of the injury or damage for which recovery is sought. The plaintiff shall not be barred from recovering damages if the trier of fact finds that the contributory fault on the part of the plaintiff is not more than 50% of the proximate cause of the injury or damage for which recovery is sought, but any economic or non-economic damages allowed shall be diminished in the proportion to the amount of fault attributable to the plaintiff.

735 ILCS 5/2-1116. *See Freislinger v. Emro Propane Co.*, 99 F.3d 1412 (7th Cir 1996).

During the 1990's most state legislatures enacted statutes altering joint and several liability in some manner in some contexts. In ordinary negligence actions about one-third of the states now follow "pure apportioned liability," about one-third "pure" joint and several liability, and the remainder employ some mixed system.

(2) Prior to the widespread enactment of statutes modifying joint and several liability, most pure comparative negligence schemes applied the common law rule of joint and several liability,[24] as did many modified comparative negligence jurisdictions led by the notable example in Wisconsin.[25]

True to the comparative fault principle, all comparative negligence states that employed joint and several liability also employed some form of contribution among joint tortfeasors. Although some prescribed contribution in equal pro rata shares,[26] the modern trend is to prescribe contribution in proportion to degrees of negligence.[27]

[2]   Individual Apportioned Liability[28]

Repudiating joint and several liability in favor of apportioned individual liability (which is often referred to as "several liability") in direct proportion to a particular defendant's allocation of negligence carries the principle of liability in proportion to fault to its logical end. In theory, it permits a plaintiff to recover from each tortfeasor in exact proportion to that tortfeasor's wrong, and, similarly, each

---

[24] This was consistent with the view of the Uniform Comparative Fault Act (ULA), § 2.

[25] *See, e.g.*, Kingston v. C & N. W. Ry., 191 Wis. 610, 211 N.W. 913 (1927); Bielski v Schulze, 16 Wis. 2d 1, 114 N.W. 2d 105, 107 (1962).

[26] As specified by the Uniform Contribution Among Tortfeasors Act (ULA), § 2.

[27] As specified by the Uniform Comparative Fault Act (ULA), § 2.

[28] Among the states that employed individual apportioned liability at an early phase of the modem tort reform movement were Indiana, Kansas, and Ohio. *See especially Brown v. Kiell*, 224 Kan. 195, 580 P.2d 867 (1968). V.T.C.A. §§ 33.001; 33.011; 33.013.

tortfeasor is liable for no more than a proportionate share of wrong. It also eliminates the need for contribution. The flaw in the theory is its assumption that the abstract but false idea that a person's fault "caused" a distinguishable portion of an indivisible injury has real meaning. (Remember, if any particular injury can be allocated solely to a single defendant then that defendant, and no one else is responsible for it.) In fact, it does not. Each negligent act that is the cause of an indivisible harm is a cause in fact; but-for it, the injury would not have happened. Even with apportioned individual liability, any defendant whose negligence was not a cause in fact of an indivisible injury is entitled to be wholly exonerated.

The premise of the common law was that each negligent person should be responsible for all the harm caused by the negligence, and was innocent of all harm not caused by it. Which is sounder? The common law view? Or apportioned liability?

[B]   Threshold Comparisons

Under pure comparative negligence, a plaintiff's contributory negligence will not bar recovery unless it is the sole proximate cause of the plaintiff's harm, but modified comparative negligence systems continue to bar all recovery unless the plaintiff's negligence is less than the prescribed threshold (49% Rule, 50% Rule, Slight/Gross Rule). Consequently, multiple defendant actions raise this basic question in modified comparative negligence jurisdictions: in determining whether the plaintiff's action is barred, is the plaintiff's contributory negligence to be compared to that of all defendants collectively, or must it be compared to that of each defendant individually?

Two basic rules, with variations, have developed. The "Unit Rule"[29] compares the negligence of the plaintiff to the aggregated negligence of all the defendants, and the "Individual Rule"[30] compares the negligence of the plaintiff to that of each party from whom recovery is sought. The right to recover against each defendant is independently determined. A plaintiff who is permitted to recover under the Unit Rule recovers against all defendants, including those whose individual negligence is less than that of the plaintiff. By contrast, the Individual Rule may permit a recovery against one or more defendants while barring it against others.

In sum, the Individual Rule states will permit no recovery against a particular defendant whose negligence is exceeded (or equaled in 49% Rule states) by that of the plaintiff; whereas the Unit Rule states will permit a plaintiff to recover against all defendants who are negligent in any degree so long as the plaintiff's negligence is not greater than the aggregate of that of all the defendants (or not equal to it in 49% Rule states).

Some states follow modified versions of these two rules. Under the Modified Unit Rule, the determination of whether the plaintiff's contributory negligence bars recovery follows the Unit Rule, except that the plaintiff's recovery is joint and several only as to those defendants whose negligence was equal to or more than that of the plaintiff. A defendant whose negligence was of such a proportion that

---

[29] Unit Rule states include Arkansas, Connecticut, Hawaii, Maine, Massachusets, Nevada, New Jersey, Oregon, Pennsylvania, Texas, Vermont and West Virginia.

[30] Individual Rule states include Georgia, Idaho, Minnesota, Montana, North Dakota, Utah, Wisconsin and Wyoming.

the plaintiff could not recover had that defendant been the sole tortfeasor is liable only for the product of the plaintiff's total damages and that defendant's allocated share of negligence.[31]

[C]   Phantom Tortfeasors

Sometimes when harm is caused by the concurrent (or joint) fault of several persons, one or more actual tortfeasors will not be joined in the ensuing tort action. Unknown persons, such as hit and run drivers, and immune persons, such as spouses or sovereigns, are examples of "phantom tortfeasors.[32] When a phantom is not joined, the factfinder must specify whether the aggregate of negligence apportioned to the parties adds up to 100%, or whether some part may be apportioned to the non-party tortfeasor.

Example 3

Plaintiff's Share of Total Negligence:	25%
Defendant's Share of Total Negligence:	25%
Phantom's Share of Total Negligence:	50%

If in Example 3 the phantom's negligence is included in the apportionment, plaintiff would, under the law in some states, obtain a recovery of 75% of full damages against the defendant. If, by contrast, the phantom's negligence were excluded from the apportionment, a different allocation of percentages between the plaintiff and the defendant would be required. For example, the allocation might be: Plaintiff, 50%; Defendant, 50%. Under that allocation, the plaintiff would recover only 50% of full damages from the defendant.

How phantom negligence is treated in modified comparative negligence jurisdictions can determine whether recovery will be permitted at all. No jurisdiction, except perhaps one employing the Slight/Gross Rule, would bar the plaintiff's action under the allocations of Example 3. By contrast, a 50%-50% allocation reached by excluding phantom negligence would bar a plaintiff's action in a 49% Rule jurisdiction.

Many states that followed the rule of joint and several liability of multiple joint tortfeasors do not apportion negligence to a phantom tortfeasor.[33] Nevertheless, a few joint and several liability states and some apportioned individual liability states 1112 do apportion negligence to phantoms.

Instructing juries to apportion a percentage of fault to persons who are not parties tends to be disadvantegeous to plaintiffs and can unnecessarily complicate the litigation. For example, a plaintiff may be injuried in a multiple vehicle crash in which potential defendant X is plainly at fault but in which the fault of defendants Y and Z is less certain or even doubtful. What must a plaintiff do to avoid having defendant X adopt a trial strategy of placing the blame upon Y and Z who are not parties? This is called "trying the empty chair." Would it not be preferable to

---

[31] Modified Unit Rule States include Indiana, Kansas, Ohio, Oklahoma and Vermont.

[32] This approach is exemplified by the Uniform Comparative Fault Act (ULA), § 2.

[33] *See, e.g., American Motorcycle Ass'n v. Superior Court*, 146 Cal. Rptr. 182, 578 P.2d 899, 906 n.2 (1978); *Walker v Droger Grocery & Baking Co.*, 214 Wis. 519, 252 N.W. 721 (1934); *Ferguson v. Northern States Power Co.*, 307 Minn. 26, 239 N W 2d 190 (1976); and, *Board of County Commissioners v. Redenour*, 623 P.2d 1174, 1191, 1192.

allocate negligence only to parties to the action, and permit defendant X to implead Y and Z as co-defendants if that seemed to be a strong defense tactic? *Newville v. State*, 883 P.2d 793, 802 (Mont. 1994), invalidated a statute that required the allocation of fault to nonparties, saying:

> [The statute in question, Section 27-1-703(4), MCA (1987), provides in pertinent part:
>
> (4) . . . For purposes of determining the percentage of liability attributable to each party whose action contributed to the injury complained of, the trier of fact shall consider the negligence of the claimant, injured person, defendants, third-party defendants, persons released from liability by the claimant, persons immune from liability to the claimant, and any other persons who have a defense against the claimant. The trier of fact shall apportion the percentage of negligence of all such persons. . . .]
>
> In the case before us, plaintiffs contend that § 27-1-703, MCA (1987), arbitrarily prejudices plaintiffs by requiring them to exonerate nonparties. They contend there is no reasonable basis to require any plaintiff to prepare a defense at the last minute for nonparties whom defendants seek to blame for the injury, but who have not been joined as defendants; and that there is no reasonable basis for requiring plaintiffs to examine jury instructions, marshal evidence, make objections, argue the case, and examine witnesses from the standpoint of unrepresented parties, particularly when they do not know until the latter part of the trial that defendants will seek to place blame on unrepresented persons. These procedural problems form the bases for our holding that § 27-1-703, MCA (1987), in part violates substantive due process.
>
> We conclude that § 27-1-703(4), MCA (1987), unreasonably mandates an allocation of percentages of negligence to nonparties without any kind of procedural safeguard. As a result, plaintiffs may not receive a fair adjudication of the merits of their claims. It imposes a burden upon plaintiffs to anticipate defendants' attempts to apportion blame up to the time of submission of the verdict form to the jury. Such an apportionment is clearly unreasonable as to plaintiffs, and can also unreasonably affect defendants and nonparties.

A number of other courts have adopted rules similar to the one invalidated in *Newville v. State* without consideration of the constitutional premises deemed controlling therein. *See, e.g., Fabre v. Marin*, 623 So. 2d 1182 (Fla. 1993).[34]

§ 11.05 CONTRIBUTION AND INDEMNIFICATION

[A] Common Law Rule

As noted in § 4.07, *supra,* the common law adopted the rule of no contribution among tortfeasors at least as early as 1799 when the celebrated case *of Merryweather v. Nixan*[35] was decided. Years later, Judge Cooley[36] explained the rule, as follows:

---

[34] *See, e.g.,* Ind. Stats. Ann. § 34-4-33-5(b) (1).

[35] 8 TR 186, 101 Eng. Rep. 1337 (1799).

[36] Cooley on Torts (3d ed.), 261, 262.

The discouragement of all illegal transactions by distinctly apprising every person who engages in them that the risk he incurs is not merely of being compelled to share with the others the loss that may follow, for this, in many cases would be insignificant, and in all cases would be small in proportion to the size and formidable character of the combination. He is, therefore, given to understand that whoever takes part in an illegal transaction must do so under a responsibility only measured by the whole extent of the injury or loss; an understanding very well calculated to make men hesitate who, under a different rule, would be disposed to give full scope to evil inclinations . . . The State, from a consideration of its own pecuniary interests, and of the interests of other litigants, may wisely refuse to assist in adjusting equities between persons who have been engaged in unlawful action. The expense of administering justice is always a large item in the State's expenditures, and one which must be borne by the common contributions of the people. Where one has suffered from participation in an unlawful undertaking, what justice can there be in any demand on his part that the State shall supply courts and officers and incur expense to indemnify him against a loss he has encountered through a disregard of its laws. Here the question is not merely one of what is right, as between himself and his associates, but what is best for the interest of the State. When that question is up for consideration, the fact is not to be overlooked that there are unavoidable difficulties and necessary evils connected with litigation which multiply rapidly as the cases increase in number. Courts and juries, at the best, are but imperfect instruments for the accomplishment of justice; and the greater the volume of litigation, the less is the attention which any particular case is likely to receive, and the greater the probability, that right may be overcome by artifice, or by a false and deceptive exposition of the facts. Trusty justice must follow after wrong with deliberate and measured tread; and every honest litigant in seeking it must be more or less impeded, when those who have no just claim on the consideration of the court are allowed to push their complaints before it. It is not necessary to look further for reasons in support of the rule to which attention has been directed.

Despite Judge Cooley's rousing justification of the no-contribution rule, many courts developed exceptions to it. Perhaps the most common was that when one tortfeasor was not truly at fault, but only vicariously liable on policy grounds, such as *respondeat superior*, then the technically liable tortfeasor might be wholly indemnified in an action against the actual wrongdoer.[37]

Another exception was recognized in instances in which both of two defendants were wrongdoers as to the plaintiff but as between themselves were not wrongdoers.[38] For example, two lumberjacks in a joint venture to harvest wood might trespass on A's land believing it to be their own. If A recovered damages against one of the two, that one could have contribution (not indemnity) against the other because, as between the two, the law would not deem them to be wrongdoers. Hence, the no contribution rule would not apply. By contrast, if the two men were intending to steal A's wood, then they would be wrongdoers as between each other and neither contribution nor indemnity would be permitted. According to Cooley,

---

[37] Cooley on Torts (3d ed.), 255. On the other hand, Cooley observes that if a servant batters a person, upon the order of the master, knowing the act to be wrongful, then the servant could not be indemnified or have contribution from the master. In such a case, the servant would be an actual and not merely a technical wrongdoer, and the no contribution rule would apply.

[38] Cooley on Torts (3d ed.), 258.

"If [the contribution plaintiff] knew the act was illegal, or if the circumstances were such as to render ignorance of the illegality inexcusable, then he will be left by the law where his wrongful action has placed him."[39]

Furthermore, the no-contribution rule does not rule out actions for indemnification in appropriate cases. Indemnification shifts all, not part, of the burden of the judgment to the actual tortfeasor. Most indemnification cases involve technical vicarious liability, such as *respondeat superior* under which an innocent master is held liable to the plaintiff for the negligent acts of a servant.[40] The basic justification of respondeat superior is mutuality: The master who receives the benefit of the servant's productive acts should stand the risks of the servant's negligent acts. Other examples of technical vicarious liability include contracting parties who are liable for the negligence of independent contactors involved in the performance of a non-delegable duty,[41] and owners of dangerous instrumentalities lent to borrowers who thereafter negligently use them to injure a third person.[42] In cases such as these, the common law did not deny a vicariously liable tortfeasor upon whom the injured plaintiff executed judgment the right of *indemnity* against the actual wrongdoer.

By far the most flexible relief valve to the no-contribution rule was the widely adopted view that a "passively" negligent tortfeasor might have indemnity (not contribution) from an "actively" negligent tortfeasor. Cooley attributed this doctrine to *Old Colony R.R. v. Slavens*,[43] but the facts of *Nashua Iron Steel Co. v. Worcester, etc., R.R. Co.*[44] are most instructive. The plaintiff was hit by a runaway horse, which had been frightened by a negligently operated train. The court held that if the horse owner from whom the plaintiff recovered had been negligent only in leaving his horse at an improper place, and the train operator negligently frightened the horse, then the horse owner could seek indemnity from the train operator. Applied in this manner, the "active-passive" theory of indemnification was flexible enough, contrary to what some courts said, to permit indemnification in favor of a slightly negligent defendant against a more negligent one.

---

[39] Cooley cites *Adamson v. Jarvis*, 4 Bing 66, 73, 130 Eng. Rep. 693, 696 (1827), per Best, C.J. as "concisely" stating the rule: (" . . . the rule that the wrong-doers cannot have redress or contribution against each other is confined to cases where the person seeking redress must be presumed to have known that he was doing an unlawful act.")

[40] Cooley on Torts (3d ed.), 255.

[41] *See, e.g., Bartlett v. Davis Corp.*, 219 Kan. 148, 547 P.2d 800 (1976) (contractual indemnity), and *Maule Industries v. Messana*, 62 So. 2d 737 (Fla. 1953) (farmer contracted with operator to irrigate land. Operator negligently flooded adjoining land. Held: farmer cannot escape liability where where he had actual notice of danger posed to neighbor).

[42] *See, e.g., Anderson v. Southern Cotton Oil Co.*, 74 So. 975, 978 (1917) ("The principles of the common law do not permit the owner of an instrumentality that is not dangerous per se, but is peculiarly dangerous in its operation, to authorize another to use such instrumentality on the public highways without imposing upon such owner liability for negligent use. The liability grows out of the obligation of the owner to have the vehicle, that is not inherently dangerous per se, but peculiarly dangerous in its use, properly operated when it is by his authority on the public highway.").

[43] 148 Mass. 363, 19 N.E. 372 (1889) (plaintiff injured upon entering a railroad station as a consequence of obstruction negligently created by mail contractors; railroad was permitted indemnity against the mail contractors).

[44] 62 N.H. 159 (1882). The case appears to apply, in effect, the rule of last clear chance among defendants. That is, the horse owner was helpless to avoid the runaway, and the train operator could have, with due care, avoided it, but did not.

[B]   Modern Contribution Rules

Wisconsin was the first state to depart by judicial decision from the no-contribution rule. In *Ellis v. Chicago & N. W. Railway*,[45] a 1918 case, the Wisconsin Supreme Court relied upon earlier cases permitting contribution "where the element of moral turpitude is not involved and there is no willful or conscious wrong between the parties against whom a judgment in a tort action is recovered"[46] to permit contribution in equal pro rata shares where "the inadvertent acts of both [defendants] concurred in producing the injuries."[47] Thus, *Ellis* broke through the doctrinal no-contribution rule and permitted contribution when independent negligent acts coverged to produce an indivisible injury.

In 1919, Virginia enacted a contribution statute modeled after *Ellis.* Under that statute, "Contribution among wrongdoers may be enforced where the wrong is a mere act of negligence, and involves no moral turpitude."[48] This statute left virtual complete discretion to the courts to work out the amounts and conditions of contribution.

In 1939, the first Uniform Contribution Among Tortfeasors Act was promulgated. That act permitted contribution in equal pro rata shares among joint tortfeasors, defined as "two or more persons jointly or severally liable in tort for the same injury to person or property . . ."[49] The 1939 uniform act was spare in its operational specifications and was superseded in 1955 by the current fully developed model. At the time of the 1955 revision, eight jurisdictions had adopted the 1939 act,[50] eight jurisdictions employed statutes that applied only to joint tortfeasors,[51] six jurisdictions applied simpler contribution statutes such as the one in Virginia,[52] and six jurisdictions permitted contribution without a statute.[53] Wisconsin, of course, fell into the latter group.

In 1962, the Wisconsin Supreme Court decided *Bielski v. Schulze*[54] prescribing contribution on the basis of relative degrees of fault. This was done over a vigorous dissenting assertion that allocating negligence in percentages among tortfeasors would unduly burden litigation. The majority brushed it aside, saying:[55]

It is true under present practice, if the plaintiff is not found causally negligent, no apportionment need be made, but at that point in the lawsuit the form of the verdict has included a comparison question and the jury has been instructed in its use. In the minority of cases which would not have a comparison question, the new

---

[45] 167 Wis. 392, 167 N.W. 1048 (1918) (A railroad train and street car crashed, injuring a claimant. Each of the operators was negligent. The claimant recovered against the street car company which sought contribution from the railroad company. Contribution granted.).

[46] *Id.* at 167 N.W. 1053.

[47] *Id.*

[48] Section 5779, Code Va. 1919.

[49] Uniform Contribution Among Tortfeasors Act (1939) (ULA) § 1.

[50] Arkansas (1941), Delaware (1949) (later modified), Hawaii (1941), Maryland (1941), New Mexico (1947), Pennsylvania (1951), Rhode Island (1940), and South Dakota (1945). 12 ULA 59.

[51] Michigan, Mississippi, Missouri, New Jersey, Virginia, and Wisconsin. 12 ULA 59.

[52] Georgia, Kentucky, Louisiana, New Jersey, Virginia, and Wisconsin. 12 ULA 59.

[53] District of Columbia, Minnesota, Pennsylvania, Tennessee, Wisconsin and Maine. 12 ULA 60.

[54] 16 Wis. 2d 1, 114 N.W.2d 105 (1962).

[55] 114 N.W.2d 110.

rule would require the jury to determine an additional inquiry on the relative degrees of negligence for comparison purposes. Any change requires some adjustments, but those which we foresee are not sufficient grounds to deny the benefits of the new rule.

Deeming contribution to be rooted in equity, the majority saw "no reason in logic or in natural justice why the shares of common liability of joint tortfeasors should not be translated into the percentage of causal negligence which contributed to the injury."[56]

Other courts have more recently abrogated the no-contribution rule and permitted contribution based upon pure comparative fault. In 1972, the Court of Appeals of New York expanded the active-passive indemnification rule to permit contribution in negligence cases[57] and later in the same year imposed the "fairer rule . . . to distribute the loss in proportion to the allocable concurring fault."[58] In 1978, the Illinois Supreme Court repudiated the no-contribution rule in a pair of product liability cases and permitted contribution on the basis of relative fault.[59] And, in 1978, the California Supreme Court built upon the active-passive indemnification rule (referred to in California as equitable indemnification)[60] to impose contribution based on relative fault. The California rule is referred to as "equitable partial indemnity."[61] In the same year, the Missouri Supreme Court acknowledged an equitable right of contribution among concurrent tortfeasors (also called indemnity) based upon relative degrees of fault.[62]

In sum, in apparent isolation from comparative negligence developments (but surely not independent of them), two streams of contribution rules have developed: the equal pro rata shares approach now attributable to the Uniform Contribution Among Tortfeasors Act; and the contribution on the basis of relative degrees of fault approach attributable to the revised Wisconsin view and incorporated in the Uniform Comparative Fault Act. As demonstrated in § 11.05[C], *infra*, comparative negligence schemes often incorporate contribution.

The Uniform Contribution Among Tortfeasors Act is set forth below. Applicable provisions of the Uniform Comparative Fault Act are presented in § 11.05[C], *infra*.

---

[56] 114 N.W.2d 107.

[57] *Dole v. Dow Chem. Co.*, 30 N.Y.2d 143, 331 N.Y.S.2d 382, 282 N.E.2d 288 (1972).

[58] *Kelly v. Long Island Lighting Co.*, 31 N.Y.2d 25, 286 N.E.2d 241, 243 (1972).

[59] *Skinner v. Reed-Prentice Division*, 70 Ill. 2d 1, 374 N.E.2d 437 (1978); *Stevens v. Silver Mfg. Co.*, 70 Ill. 2d 41, 374 N.E.2d 455 (1978).

[60] *City & County of San Francisco v. Ho Sing*, 51 Cal. 2d 127, 330 P.2d 802 (1952).

[61] *American Motorcycle Ass'n v. Superior Court*, 146 Cal. Rptr. 182, 578 P.2d 899 (1978).

[62] *Missouri Pac. R.R. v. Whitehead & Kales Co.*, 566 S.W.2d 466 (Mo. 1978).

UNIFORM CONTRIBUTION AMONG TORTFEASORS ACT[63]

§ 1 [Right to Contribution]

(a) Except as otherwise provided in this Act, where two or more persons become jointly or severally liable in tort for the same injury to person or property or for the same wrongful death, there is a right of contribution among them even though judgment has not been recovered against all or any of them.

(b) The right of contribution exists only in favor of a tortfeasor who has paid more than his pro rata share of the common liability, and his total recovery is limited to the amount paid by him in excess of his pro rata share. No tortfeasor is compelled to make contribution beyond his own pro rata share of the entire liability.

(c) There is no right of contribution in favor of any tortfeasor who has intentionally [willfully or wantonly] caused or contributed to the injury or wrongful death.

(d) A tortfeasor who enters into a settlement with a claimant is not entitled to recover contribution from another tortfeasor whose liability for the injury or wrongful death is not extinguished by the settlement nor in respect to any amount paid in a settlement which is in excess of what was reasonable.

(e) A liability insurer, who by payment has discharged in full or in part the liability of a tortfeasor and has thereby discharged in full its obligation as insurer, is subrogated to the tortfeasor's right of contribution to the extent of the amount it has paid in excess of the tortfeasor's pro rata share of the common liability. This provision does not limit or impair any right of subrogation arising from any other relationship.

(f) This Act does not impair any right of indemnity under existing law. Where one tortfeasor is entitled to indemnity from another, the right of the indemnity obligee is for indemnity and not contribution, and the indemnity obligor is not entitled to contribution from the obligee for any portion of his indemnity obligation.

(g) This Act shall not apply to breaches of trust or other fiduciary obligation.

§ 2 [Pro Rata Shares]

In determining the pro rata shares of tortfeasors in the entire liability (a) their relative degrees of fault shall not be considered; (b) if equity requires the collective liability of some as a group shall constitute a single share; and (c) principles of equity applicable to contribution generally shall apply.

§ 3 [Enforcement]

(a) Whether or not judgment has been entered in an action against two or more tortfeasors for the same injury or wrongful death, contribution may be enforced by separate action.

---

[63] This Act has been printed through the permission of the National Conference of Commissioners on Uniform State Laws, and copies of the Act may be ordered from them at a cost of $2.00 at 645 North Michigan Avenue, Suite 510, Chicago, IL 60611.

(b) Where a judgment has been entered in an action against two or more tortfeasors for the same injury or wrongful death, contribution may be enforced in that action by judgment in favor of one against other judgment defendants by motion upon notice to all parties to the action.

(c) If there is a judgment for the injury or wrongful death against the tortfeasor seeking contribution, any separate action by him to enforce contribution must be commenced within one year after the judgment has become final by lapse of time for appeal or after appellate review.

(d) If there is no judgment for the injury or wrongful death against the tortfeasor seeking contribution, his right of contribution is barred unless he has either (1) discharged by payment the common liability within the statute of limitations period applicable to claimant's right of action against him and has commenced his action for contribution within one year after payment, or (2) agreed while action is pending against him to discharge the common liability and has within one year after the agreement paid the liability and commenced his action for contribution.

(e) The recovery of a judgment for an injury or wrongful death against one tortfeasor does not of itself discharge the other tortfeasors from liability for the injury or wrongful death unless the judgment is satisfied. The satisfaction of the judgment does not impair any right of contribution.

(f) The judgment of the court in determining the liability of the several defendants to the claimant for an injury or wrongful death shall be binding as among such defendants in determining their right to contribution.

§ 4 [Release or Covenant Not to Sue]

When a release or a covenant not to sue or not to enforce judgment is given in good faith to one of two or more persons liable in tort for the same injury or the same wrongful death:

(a) It does not discharge any of the other tortfeasors from liability for the injury or wrongful death unless its terms so provide; but it reduces the claim against the others to the extent of any amount stipulated by the release or the covenant, or in the amount of the consideration paid for it, whichever is the greater; and,

(b) It discharges the tortfeasor to whom it is given from all liability for contribution to any other tortfeasor.

[C]   Effect of Comparative Negligence

[1]   Comparative Negligence with Joint and Several Liability

The adoption of comparative negligence with joint and several liability as to the plaintiff's apportioned damages does not of itself require abrogation of the no-contribution rule. A jurisdiction might still refuse to aid the tortfeasor who pays the judgment. Nevertheless, the same equitable arguments that ultimately undermined the common law bar of contributory negligence also undermined the no-contribution rule. The question becomes, which rule applies: the equal pro rata shares rule or the relative degrees of fault rule?

As noted in § 11.05[B], *supra*, Section 5 of the Uniform Contribution Among Tortfeasors Act prescribes contribution in equal pro rata shares.[64] By contrast, the more recent. (1977) Uniform Comparative Fault Act prescribes a right of "equitable" contribution, as follows:[65]

(a) A right of contribution exists between or among two or more persons who are jointly and severally liable upon the same indivisible claim for the same injury, death, or harm, whether or not judgment has been recovered against all or any of them. It may be enforced either in the original action or by a separate action brought for that purpose. The basis for contribution is each person's equitable share of the obligation, including the equitable share of a claimant at fault, as determined in accordance with the provisions of Section 2.

(b) Contribution is available to a person who enters into a settlement with a claimant only (1) if the liability of the person against whom contribution is sought has been extinguished, and (2) to the extent that the amount paid in settlement was reasonable.

The Commissioners' comments to the Uniform Comparative Fault Act indicate that the foregoing provisions should replace the pro rata shares provision in the Uniform Contribution Among Tortfeasors Act. Thus, the Uniform Comparative Fault Act divides the whole of the fault between the plaintiff and all the defendants and then subdivides the defendants' portion among them.[66]

The Uniform Comparative Fault Act prescribes enforcement procedures both for actions in which all tortfeasors joined as defendants and for actions in which some are not joined:

(a) If the proportionate fault of the parties to a claim for contribution has been established previously by the court, as provided by Section 2, a party paying more than his equitable share of the obligation, upon motion, may recover judgment for contribution.

(b) If the proportionate fault of the parties to the claim for contribution has not been established by the court, contribution may be enforced in a separate action, whether or not a judgment has been rendered against either the person seeking contribution or the person from whom contribution is being sought.

(c) If a judgment has been rendered, the action for contribution must be commenced within [one year] after the judgment becomes final. If no judgment has been rendered, the person bringing the action for contribution either must have (1) discharged by payment the common liability within the period of the statute of limitations applicable to the claimant's right of action against him and commenced the action for contribution within [one year] after payment, or (2) agreed while action was pending to discharge the common liability and, within [one year] after the agreement, have paid the liability and commenced an action for contribution.

---

[64] Uniform Contribution Among Tortfeasors Act (ULA) § 2. Subsection (b) permits, for example, a servant and a vicariously liable master to be treated as a single tortfeasor for contribution purposes. Thus, if defendants *A, B* and *C* are jointly and severally liable, but *B* and *C* are servant and vicariously liable master, *A* would be entitled to contribution of + from *B* and *C* collectively, and not.

[65] Uniform Comparative Fault Act (ULA) § 4.

[66] 12 ULA 43 (1984 pocket part).

The operation of these provisions and the meaning of "equitable" contribution are illustrated in the comments, as follows:

Example 1.[67]

Plaintiff's Share of Negligence:	40%
Defendant A's Share of Negligence:	30%
Defendant B's Share of Negligence:	10%
Plaintiff's Damages:	$20,000
Plaintiff's Apportioned Damages:	
$20,000 × 0.60 =	$12,000

Plaintiff executes against Defendant A:
On proper motion, Defendant A is entitled to contribution:

From Defendant B:	
$12,000 × 0.20/0.60	$4,000
From Defendant C:	
$12,000 × 0.10/0.60	$2,000

Example 2.[68]

(Same as Example 1, except plaintiff sues only Defendant *A* and the division of negligence is Plaintiff, 40%, Defendant *A*, 60%. Defendant *A* pays the $12,000 judgment).

Defendant *A* brings a separate action against Defendants *B* and *C* and the following allocation of fault of the collective fault of the defendants is made:

Defendant A:	50%
Defendant B:	33.3%
Defendant C:	16.7%
Defendant A receives judgments from:	
Defendant B:	
$12,000 × 0.333 =	$4,000
Defendant C:	
$12,000 × 0.167 =	$2,000

The Uniform Comparative Fault Act thus prescribes a coherent fault-based system of contribution.

To achieve administrative and evidential economy, courts might prefer to employ the equal pro rata shares contribution rule of the Uniform Contribution Among Joint Tortfeasors Act. Although an allocation of negligence between the plaintiff and the defendants collectively must be made, the further allocation among defendants is unnecessary.[69] Under this approach, Examples 1 and 2 would be

---

[67] 12 ULA 44 (1984 pocket part). Adapted from original Illustration No. 9.

[68] 12 ULA 44 (1984 pocket part). Adapted from original Illustration No. 10.

[69] Except in the modified comparative negligence states that apply the Individual Rule and in hybrid states, like Texas, that hold a tortfeasor whose negligence is less than that of the plaintiff liable only for his proportionate share of the plaintiff's harm.

Defendant A:	$12,000

resolved as follows:

Example 3:

Plaintiff's Share of Negligence:	40%
Defendant A, B, and C's collective share of negligence:	60%
Plaintiff's Damages:	$20,000
Plaintiff's Apportioned Damages: $20,000 × 0.60 =	$12,000
Defendant Executes Against Defendant A:	$12,000
On proper motion, Defendant A obtains contribution from: Defendant B $12,000 × 1/3 =	$4,000
Defendant C $12,000 × 1/3 =	$4,000

[2]   Comparative Negligence with Apportioned Individual Liability

The application of apportioned individual liability to apportioned comparative negligence judgments eliminates the need of contribution, except in special cases. Each defendant is apportioned an exact judgment that adheres individually and to no other person.[70]

Example 4:

(Same as Example 1 as to damages and allocations of negligence).	
Plaintiff's Apportioned Individual Judgments:	
Defendant A: $20,000 × 0.30 =	$6,000
Defendant B: $20,000 × 0.20 =	$4,000
Defendant C: $20,000 × 0.10 =	$2,000

On proper motion, Defendant A obtains contribution from:	
Defendant B $12,000 × 1/3 =	$4,000
Defendant C $12,000 × 1/3 =	$4,000

The equal pro rata shares approach in theory favors those greater in fault at the expense of those lesser in fault. It implicitly recognizes, however, the difficulty, artificiality and cost of allocating negligence in exact percentages.

[70] *See, e.g.,* Ind. Stats. Ann. 34-4-33-5(b)4.

Defendant A would be liable for $6,000 and would have no additional liability even if the judgments against Defendants B and C proved to be uncollectable. Nor would Defendant A be entitled to seek contribution for any portion of the $6,000. The apportioned individual judgments are independent and create no rights and obligations except between the plaintiff and the individual judgment debtors.

An exception arises when all tortfeasors are not joined, and the jurisdiction ignores the negligence of phantom defendants. For example, in Example 4, if only Defendant A were joined in the action, then the division of fault would presumably be as in Example 2 and Defendant A would be liable for $12,000. Defendant A should be permitted to bring a contribution action against Defendants B and C.

A second exception arises when two tortfeasors are treated as one for the purpose of the allocating fault between the plaintiff and the defendants collectively. Suppose in Example 1, Defendants B and C are master and servant and are treated as one for the purposes of comparative fault. And suppose the two are found responsible for 30% of the harm. Plaintiff executes against Defendant B and recovers $6,000 ($20,000 $\times$ 0.30). Defendant B should be permitted to bring a contribution (or indemnification) action against Defendant C under the prevailing contribution rule.

[3]   Indemnity Under Comparative Negligence

The adoption of comparative negligence and contribution does not logically or equitably require the elimination of indemnification. Both the 1939[71] and the 1955[72] Uniform Contribution Among Tortfeasors Acts expressly preserve independent indemnification actions as they exist in a particular jurisdiction. And the 1977 Uniform Comparative Fault Act acknowledges that in appropriate cases two or more persons may be treated as a single person in allocating percentages of negligence. Nothing in the 1977 Act precludes indemnification among these tortfeasors.

As a general matter, statutes and court decrees continue to recognize indemnity as a separate right independent of any newly created right of contribution.[73] Nevertheless, given the availability of contribution, some courts have narrowed the scope of indemnity. Both Florida[74] and Kansas[75] have merged "active-passive"

---

[71] Uniform Contribution Among Tortfeasors Act (1939) (ULA) § 6: "This Act does not impair any right of indemnity under existing law."

[72] Uniform Contribution Among Tortfeasors Act (1955) (ULA) § 1(f):

This Act does not impair any right of indemnity under existing law. Where one tortfeasor is entitled to indemnity from another, the right of the indemnity obligee is for indemnity and not contribution, and the indemnity obligor is not entitled to contribution from the obligee for any portion of his indemnity obligation.

[73] *See, e.g.*, Connecticut, *Gomean v. Forrest*, 176 Conn. 523, 409 A.2d 1006 (1979) (passive tortfeasor may be indemnified by active tortfeasor); Texas, Tex. Rev. Civ. Stats. Art. 2212; Kansas, *Kennedy v. Sawyer*, 228 Kan. 439, 619 P.2d 788 (Kan. 1980); Florida, *Houdaille Industries v. Edwards*, 374 So. 2d 450 (Fla. 1979).

[74] *Houdaille Industries v. Edwards*, 374 So. 2d 490 (Fla. 1979) (Manufacturer's defective product killed a workman. The workman recovered in tort from the manufacturer and from the employer under workers' compensation. The manufacturer brought an indemnification action against the employer. Relief denied. The manufacturer was not technically liable. Its only claim for contribution was as a passive tortfeasor, which theory was abrogated.)

[75] *Kennedy v. City of Sawyer*, 228 Kan. 439, 618 P.2d 788 (1980) (Retains the theory of "hold

indemnification into the rules of contribution, leaving indemnity only where the indemnified tortfeasor was vicariously liable on technical grounds and wholly innocent of actual fault.

[D]   Contribution and Immunities

Suppose a family composed of father, mother and five-year-old child are making a pleasure trip in the family car with Mother driving. Owing to the combined negligence of Mother and Defendant, driver of another car, a crash ensues between the two vehicles. Father and Child are both injured and each brings an action against Defendant. Under a statute modeled on the Uniform Contribution Among Tortfeasors Act, Defendant brings a contribution action against Mother in respect of both the claim by Father and Child. In a jurisdiction that would immunize Mother against a direct action by Father or Child, (See § 9.05 *supra*), should the contribution actions be permitted? *See, e.g., Bedell v. Reagan*, 159 Me. 292, 192 A.2d 24 (1983); *Puller v. Puller*, 380 Pa. 219, 110 A.2d 175 (1955); and *Shor v. Paoli*, 353 So. 2d 825 (Fla. 1977). May a distinction be made between contribution in Father's action and Child's? *See, e.g., Joseph v. Quest*, 414 So. 2d 1003 (Fla. 1982). Should it matter whether Mother is covered by liability insurance or not? *See, e.g., Ard v. Ard*, 414 So. 2d 1066 (Fla. 1982). Should it matter whether Father was killed, resulting in a wrongful death action against Defendant, or whether Father was only injured and is suing Defendant for personal injuries? *See, e.g., Moser v. Hampton*, 67 Or. App. 716, 679 P.2d 1379 (1984), and *Dressler v. Tubbs*, 435 So. 2d 792 (Fla. 1983).

---

harmless" contractual indemnity and indemnity for vicarious liability, but subsumes "active-passive" indemnity into fault apportionments under the Kansas several liability statute.)

Chapter 12

INTENTIONAL TORTS TO THE PERSON

§ 12.01 INTRODUCTION

PROBLEMS

(1) Kate, a female law student, fell asleep with her head resting on the desk of her carrel. Bob, a timid male law school student who was secretly in love with her, gently kissed the back of her neck and scampered away. Unknown to Bob, some of his classmates saw the kiss. When told of it, Kate was enraged because she "despised the thought of being kissed by that ugly little worm."

(2) Hearing of Kate's reaction, Bob was mortified and wanted to make amends. Although he was extremely embarrassed to do so, he made up his mind to apologize to Kate face to face and then try to put her and the episode out of his mind. His roommate advised him, "If you're going to do it, don't delay, and when you do it, do it in a hurry."

Later that morning, Bob saw Kate drinking from a water fountain in an empty corridor. Screwing up his courage to the fullest, he walked toward her as determinedly and as fast as he could. Clutched tightly in his hand was a statement he had carefully written out. It read: "Kate, I am deeply embarrassed and sorry for the discomfort I have caused you and apologize sincerely. If you can, please forgive me. In any case, I promise never to be a bother to you again."

In his nervous state, Bob could control neither the timing nor the modulation and volume of his address to Kate. While still walking fast, he blurted out the first word, "Kate," in a shrill, loud voice. Kate looked up from the fountain, saw him coming, and fainted, falling forward onto the fountain. The blow broke several of her teeth, and the emotional trauma caused her to drop out of law school for a term.

(3) Three of Bob's classmates ribbed him mercilessly about the secret kiss. He begged them to stop, but his pleas only heightened their barbs. They then began to post signs about the premises with pictures depicting people in vulnerable positions and carrying the message, "Never sleep or tarry. You may be the next target of the Secret Kisser." Bob would tear down the signs as fast as they appeared, but they kept cropping up. Finally, the three law students collected a sum of money and ran several of the posters as advertisements in the student newspaper.

After reading the advertisements, Bob became hysterical, seized sharp scissors, and slashed his wrists. Fortunately quick emergency treatment saved Bob's life but the injury and mental collapse caused him to stay in a hospital for several weeks. He could not bring himself to return to law school, and he was advised by his psychiatrists to abandon the idea of becoming a lawyer, which he did.

(4) Bob lost consciousness as a result of his suicide attempt. He was found in his room by a friend who immediately called for emergency help. Still unconscious, Bob

was rolled into the emergency operating room at Mercy Hospital where Dr. Abel immediately began emergency surgery. After the emergency was abated, Dr. Abel removed from Bob's hand several large warts that were not involved in the emergency.

While recovering, Bob suffered a virulent staph infection of a type that occurs only in operating rooms. Bob was hospitalized for two additional weeks because of the infection, incurring additional medical expenses of $8,500. Bob wants to sue for the infection and the unauthorized removal of the warts.

(5) Upon being discharged from the hospital, Bob was presented with an itemized bill of charges. Reviewing them, Bob saw a list of services that he believed he had not received. He complained to the hospital's business manager who asserted that the "services were delivered or they would not be on the bill." Bob refused to pay the charges or verify their validity. The business manager angrily said, "Okay, in that case you cannot be discharged from the hospital under the law in this state." Bob was sitting in a wheelchair and permitted himself to be wheeled back to his room, where he immediately returned to bed and fell asleep in exhaustion. The next morning, he telephoned his lawyer and was soon thereafter released from the hospital without paying the bill or signing anything. It was later determined that none of the contested charges was valid, and also that there was no state law concerning discharge. The manager's statement reflected a hospital policy adopted by the Board of Directors. A copy was posted on the back of the door of each hospital room.

Bob was later presented with a new bill in the amount of $250 for the extra day he spent in the hospital. He refused to pay it and also wants to sue the hospital on some ground if he can.

(6) Suppose Bob paid the $250 and checked out of the hospital. He consulted his lawyer, who determined that the purported law on hospital discharges did not exist. Bob brought an action against the hospital and recovered the $250 upon a finding that the charges had been erroneous.

Bob then filed an action against the business manager, seeking to recover the attorney's fees and other unreimbursed expenses of the preceding suit, damages for emotional distress and embarrassment, and punitive damages.

(7) A statute in Bob's state contains the following provision:

Stat. Ann. 1-7a. Theft of services. It is punishable as a misdemeanor for any person to accept services of any kind in this state with the intention not to pay for said services if said services have reasonable value of $200 or less, and punishable as a felony of the second degree for any person to accept services of any kind in this state with the intention not to pay for said services if said services have reasonable value of more than $200.

Suppose Bob tore up the $250 bill for extra services and returned it with an angry note stating a firm refusal to pay the bill. Upon receiving that letter, the hospital manager immediately drove to the state attorney's office and swore out a complaint under Stat. Ann. 1-7a. The hospital manager then telephoned Bob and told him that the complaint had been filed. The manager also said, "I know the state attorney well; if you'll pay the $250 bill, he will drop this prosecution; if not, he will prosecute as hard as he can." Bob hung up the phone without replying. Two weeks later, the prosecutor began formal proceedings against him.

(8) Upon his recovery, Bob organized a jazz combo named the "Mellow Shysters." The group became popular with students and was booked by a number of social groups and clubs, including the Law Student Organization for the Rule of Law (SORL). Hearing of this, Bob's former law school tormentors immediately commenced a boycott against the SORL event, demanding that the Mellow Shysters be dropped in favor of some other group. Because of a pressing need to make money, SORL cancelled the agreement, and Bob was unable to get another booking for the date. Two other law student organizations broke off booking negotiations with Bob, fearing similar disruption.

(9) Fed up with his tormentors, Bob confronted Joe, the ringleader, grabbed him by the lapels of his coat and yelled, "Get off my back, you son-of-a-bitch!" Bill, Joe's co-hort, got on his knees behind Bob and Joe and pushed Bob down. Bob hit his head on the sidewalk, suffered a concussion, and was hospitalized for three weeks.

How many causes of action can be well pleaded on the facts in these problems? For whom? Against whom? If each and every fact stated and no others could be proved, how many cases should be won by the plaintiff?

§ 12.02   ELEMENTS OF THE PRIMA FACIE CASE

The torts examined in this chapter are of three sorts: those that derive from the ancient tort of trespass vi et armis and that have not been swallowed up by the law of negligence; those that have a common law origin independent of trespass vi et armis; and those that have more modem origins. Of the first category are battery, assault, and false imprisonment (and false arrest).

Of the second are deceit, malicious prosecution (which may be subdivided into malicious criminal prosecution and malicious civil prosecution) and abuse of process. And of the third are intentional interference with contractual relations and intentional infliction of mental distress. Common to all of these is a willful or the equivalent (or worse) state of mind possessed by the defendant in regard to the impact of his actions upon the plaintiff. Apart from that, the torts vary markedly, perhaps making it novel to present this particular array of torts in a single chapter. The goal is to examine the essential points with a minimum of duplication. To avoid confusion, you must fix in your mind the elements of each tort. To that end, a summary of the elements of the prima facie case of each of them is presented below. These are the definitions found in the Restatement, Torts, Second, and they would find approval in many but not all courts. In general, each element ("intention," "malice," "consent" and the like) is itself subject to varying meanings. Succeeding sections of this chapter examine some of them.

Certain torts that sometimes evoke a willful mental state do not appear in this chapter. These include the surviving descendants of trespass quare clasum frigit and trespass de bonis asportatis, and conversion, which are examined in Chapter 15, and defamation and invasion of privacy, examined in Chapters 19 and 20. In addition, the Restatement describes torts that may be categorized as sub-classifications of others, which you can identify by examining the Table of Contents of the Restatement, Torts, Second.

Restatement, Torts, Second[1]

Battery

§ 13 Battery: Harmful Contact

An actor is subject to liability to another for battery if

(a) he acts intending to cause a harmful or offensive contact with the person of the other or a third person, or an imminent apprehension of such a contact, and

(b) a harmful contact with the person of the other directly or indirectly results.

§ 18 Battery: Offensive Contact

(1) An actor is subject to liability to another for battery if

(a) he acts intending to cause a harmful or offensive contact with the person of the other or a third person, or an imminent apprehension of such a contact, and

(b) an offensive contact with the person of the other directly or indirectly results.

(2) An act which is not done with the intention stated in Subsection (1,a) does not make the actor liable to the other for a mere offensive contact with the other person although the act involves an unreasonable risk of inflicting it and, therefore, would be negligent or reckless if the risk threatened bodily harm.

Assault

§ 21 Assault

(1) An actor is subject to liability to another for assault if

(a) he acts intending to cause a harmful or offensive contact with the person of the other or a third person, or an imminent apprehension of such a contact, and

(b) the other is thereby put in such imminent apprehension.

(2) An action which is not done with the intention stated in Subsection (1,a) does not make the actor liable to the other for an apprehension caused thereby although the act involves an unreasonable risk of causing it and, therefore, would be negligent or reckless if the risk threatened bodily harm.

False Imprisonment

§ 35 False Imprisonment

(1) An actor is subject to liability to another for false imprisonment if

(a) he acts intending to confine the other or a third person within boundaries fixed by the actor, and

(b) his act directly or indirectly results in such a confinement of the other, and

(c) the other is conscious of the confinement or is harmed by it.

---

[1] Copyright 1965 by The American Law Institute. Reprinted with the permission of The American Law Institute.

(2) An act which is not done with the intention stated in Subsection (1,a) does not make the actor liable to the other for a merely transitory or otherwise harmless confinement, although the act involves an unreasonable risk of imposing it and therefore would be negligent or reckless if the risk threatened bodily harm.

Deceit

§ 525 Liability for Fraudulent Misrepresentation

One who fraudulently makes a misrepresentation of fact, opinion, intention or. law for the purpose of inducing another to act or to refrain from action in reliance upon it, is subject to liability to the other in deceit for pecuniary loss caused to him by his justifiable reliance upon the misrepresentation.

§ 526 Conditions Under Which Misrepresentation is Fraudulent (Scienter)

A misrepresentation is fraudulent if the maker

    (a) knows or believes that the matter is not as he represents it to be,

    (b) does not have the confidence in the accuracy of his representation that he states or implies, or

    (c) knows that he does not have the basis for his representation that he states or implies.

Malicious Prosecution

§ 653 Elements of A Cause of Action [Malicious Criminal Prosecution]

A private person who initiates or procures the institution of criminal proceedings against another who is not guilty of the offense charged is subject to liablity for malicious prosecution if

    (a) he initiates or procures the proceedings without probable cause and primarily for a purpose other than that of bringing an offender to justice, and

    (b) the proceedings have terminated in favor of the accused.

Wrongful Use of Civil Procedings

§ 674 General Principle [Malicious Civil Prosecution]

One who takes an active part in the initiation, continuation or procurement of civil proceedings against another is subject to liability to the other for wrongful civil proceedings if

    (a) he acts without probable cause, and primarily for a purpose other than that of securing the proper adjudication of the claim in which the proceedings are based, and

    (b) except when they are ex parte, the proceedings have terminated in favor of the person against whom they are brought.

Abuse of Process

§ 682 General Principle

One who uses a legal process, whether criminal or civil, against another primarily to accomplish a purpose for which it is not designed, is subject to liability to the other for harm caused by the abuse of process.

Intentional Interference with Contractual Relations

§ 766 Intentional Interference With Performance of Contract By Third Person

One who intentionally and improperly interferes with the performance of a contract (except a contract to marry) between another and a third person by inducing or otherwise causing the third person not to perform the contract, is subject to liabililty to the other for the pecuniary loss resulting to the other from the failure of the third person to perform the contract.

§ 766A Intentional Interference with Another's Performance of His Own Contract

One who intentionally and improperly interferes with the performance of a contract (except a contract to marry) between another and a third person, by preventing the other from performing the contract or causing his performance to be more expensive or burdensome, is subject to liability to the other for the pecuniary loss resulting to him.

§ 766B Intentional Interference with Prospective Contractual Relation

One who intentionally and improperly interferes with another's prospective contractual relation (except a contract to marry) is subject to liability to the other for the pecuniary harm resulting from loss of the benefits of the relation, whether the interference consists of

(a) inducing or otherwise causing a third person not to enter into or continue the prospective relation or

(b) preventing the other from acquiring or continuing the prospective relation.

Intentional Infliction of Emotional Distress

§ 46 Outrageous Conduct Causing Severe Emotional Distress

(1) One who by extreme and outrageous conduct intentionally or recklessly causes severe emotional distress to another is subject to liablity for such emotional distress, and if bodily harm to the other results from it, for such bodily harm.

(2) Where such conduct is directed at a third person, the actor is subject to liability if he intentionally or recklessly causes severe emotional distress

(a) to a member of such person's immediate family who is present at the time, whether or not such distress results in bodily harm, or

(b) to any other person who is present at the time, if such distress results in bodily harm.

§ 12.03   MENTAL STATE OF THE DEFENDANT

[A]   Intent

The following is the official comment to § 16, Restatement, Torts, Second. If this view is correct, is the *Clayton* case, infra, rightly or wrongly decided?

> In order that the actor shall be liable [in battery] it is not necessary that he intend to bring about the harmful contact which results from his act. It is enough that he intends to bring about an offensive contact or an apprehension of either a harmful or offensive contact, and that the bodily harm results as a legal consequence from such offensive contact or from such apprehension. The interest in freedom from either form of contact or from the apprehension of it so far a part of the other's interest in his bodily security that the intention to inflict an offensive contact or to create an apprehension of either a harmful or offensive contact is sufficient to make the actor liable for a harmful contact resulting therefrom, even though such harmful contact was not intended.[2]

Vosburg v. Putney, 50 N.W. 403 (Wis. 1891), supports the comment. Is the comment also supported by this statement: " . . . a man who does an unlawful act is liable for the consequences, although they may not have been intended." *Mercer v. Corbin*, 20 N.E. 132, 134 (Ind. 1889).

CLAYTON v. NEW DREAMLAND ROLLER SKATING RINK
New Jersey Supreme Court
82 A.2d 458 (1951)

EASTWOOD, J.A.D.

This is an appeal from a judgment of dismissal entered by the Essex County Court, Law Division, at the end of the plaintiffs' case, on motion of the defendants in an action for damages for injuries sustained by Alice Clayton arising out of a fall in the defendants' premises.

On October 9, 1948, plaintiff, Alice Clayton, and her husband, entered defendants' premises as paying patrons for the purpose of roller skating. While skating, Mrs. Clayton fell, allegedly caused by chewing gum negligently permitted to remain on the main skating rink floor. She

sustained a fracture of her left arm and was taken to the first aid room of defendants' premises where one Victor J. Brown, an officer of the defendant corporation, attempted to set Mrs. Clayton's arm.

. . .

After her fall, Mrs. Clayton was assisted to her feet by her husband and a guard and skated off the main floor, through the observation area in which there was a refreshment stand, to the first aid room. Mr. Brown was summoned and upon arrival proceeded to administer first aid to Mrs. Clayton. He manipulated plaintiff's fractured arm and applied traction to it and when asked whether or not

---

[2] Copyright 1965 by The American Law Institute. Reprinted with the permission of The American Law Institute.

he was a doctor, Brown replied in the negative, stating that as a prize fight manager he had experience in such matters. A splint was applied to Mrs. Clayton's arm by Brown, and she was taken to Fitkin Hospital where efforts were made to set her arm with the aid of fluoroscopic and X-ray examination. Efforts to reduce the fracture proving insufficient, bone grafts had to be performed in addition to the use of plates and screws.

In the plaintiffs' complaint they charge the defendants with (1) negligence in the operation and conduct of their premises; that (2) the defendant, Victor J. Brown, for and on behalf of himself and as servant, agent and employee of the defendant corporation, unlawfully attempted to set the left arm of the plaintiff and acted in a capacity for which he had no skill, causing an aggravation of the injury of the plaintiff, Alice Clayton; that (3) the defendant, Victor J. Brown, individually, and as servant, agent and employee of the defendant corporation, committed an assault and battery upon the plaintiff, Alice Clayton; that (4) the defendant, Victor J. Brown, had no medical experience or capacity to treat the plaintiff for her injuries and although she requested the defendant to cease any further treatment, Brown, acting individually and as an employee of the defendant corporation, maliciously continued to mistreat the plaintiff, Alice Clayton, causing the injuries for which she brought her action; and (5), the plaintiff, James F. Clayton, as husband of Alice Clayton, sued for his damages per quod.

The plaintiffs contend that the trial court erred in dismissing the complaint, in that jury questions were presented as to the defendants' negligence in the maintenance and operation of the roller skating rink; that the acts of defendant, Brown, were acts of negligence or assault and battery; that the trial court erroneously decided that plaintiff assumed the risks involved in the enterprise in which she was engaged; and improperly refused to allow Mrs. Clayton to testify as an expert as to proper standards of care for roller skating rinks of a size comparable to the one in question; and erroneously refused to allow the hypothetical question propounded to plaintiff's doctor.

[Discussion of Negligence Action Omitted.]

We are of the opinion that the trial court erred in dismissing the plaintiffs' action of assault and battery against the defendants as asserted in count three of their complaint. The defendants contend that the acts performed by Brown were an attempt to administer aid to an injured skater, barren of any intent to inflict bodily harm and in an effort to assist recovery by the injured patron. The least manual touching of the body of another against his will constitutes an "assault and battery." Moore v. Camden & Trenton Railway Co., 74 N.J.L. 498, 65 A. 1021 (E. & A. 1907); Central R.R. Co. of N.J. v. Simandl, 124 N.J.Eq. 207, 1 A.2d 312 (Ch. 1938); affirmed 125 N.J.Eq. 91, 4 A.2d 281 (E. & A. 1939). "The fact that the defendants were actuated by no improper motives in doing as they did, could not be material in a case where only compensative damages were sought to be recovered. That which is, essentially, a trespass, cannot become lawful from being done with good intentions, neither can the manner of doing the thing affect its intrinsic character. If unlawful in its own nature, it must continue to be so, however carefully or skillfully it may be done." Bruch v. Carter, 32 N.J.L. 554 at page 562 (E. & A. 1867), Moore v. Camden & Trenton Railway Co., supra; 4 Am. Jur., Assault and Battery, sec. 5, p. 128. The defendant, Victor J. Brown, concededly was not a medical doctor nor one authorized to administer bodily treatment for one suffering an injury. In the face of the protestations of Mrs. Clayton and her husband, he manipulated and pulled her arm with "heavy force" causing her pain. Although his acts may have been performed with the best of intentions, it is clear that plaintiffs' proofs raised a jury question as to the unlawfulness of his acts, particularly in view of the fact that he did not obtain the consent of Mrs. Clayton. Consequently, the jury might well have found that Brown's conduct constituted an assault and battery upon her and would have warranted a verdict against Brown and his employer for the consequential damages occasioned thereby. Such is the settled rule with respect to even those who are skilled in medical science and licensed to practice as such. Mr. Justice Garrison, speaking for the Supreme Court in Bennan v. Parsonnet, 83 N.J.L. 20 at pages 22, 23, 83 A. 948, at page 949, (1912), stated the prevailing rule in this State: "The trial judge in his charge followed the opinion of Judge Brown in Mohr v. Williams, decided by the Supreme Court of Minnesota (95 Minn. 261, 104 N.W. 12), which, as annotated in 1 L.R.A. (N.S.) 439, correctly presents the common law rule upon the subject. That rule is thus stated in 1 Kinkead on Torts, § 375: 'The patient must be the final arbiter as to whether he shall take his chances with the operation or take his chances of living without it. Such is the natural right of the individual which the law recognizes as a legal right. Consent therefore of an individual must be either expressly or impliedly given before a surgeon may have the right to operate.'" In Barnett v. Bachrach, 34 A.2d 626, 627 (Mun.Ct. of App., D.C. 1943), the New Jersey rule was given emphasis. "We recognize and follow the rule announced in a number of cases, including the celebrated case of Schloendorff v. Society of New York Hospital, 211 N.Y. 125, 105 N.E. 92, 93, 52 L.R.A., N.S., 505, Ann. Cas. 1915C, 581, in which Justice Cardozo said 'Every human being of adult years and sound mind has a right to determine what shall be done with his own body; and surgeon who performs an operation without his patient's consent commits an assault, for which he is liable in damages. . . . This is true, except in cases of emergency when the patient is unconscious, and where it is necessary to operate before consent can be obtained.' "Nolan v. Kechijian, 75 R.I. 165 64 A.2d 866 (Sup. Ct. R.I. 1949). The court must accept as true all evidence which supports the view of the party against whom the motion is made and must give him the benefit of all inferences which may logically and legitimately be drawn therefrom in his favor. McKinney v. Public Service Interstate Transp. Co., 4 N.J. 229, 243, 72 A.2d 326 (1950). Where fair-minded men might honestly differ as to the conclusions to be drawn from the facts, whether controverted or uncontroverted, the question at issue should be submitted to the jury. Antonio v. Edwards, 5 N.J. 48, 74 A.2d 307 (1950). The plaintiffs' case should have been submitted to the jury on the question of the defendants' liability for the alleged assault and battery. Under the foregoing rules the plaintiffs' proofs also raised factual issues for the determination of the jury with respect to the allegations of the second and fourth counts of the complaint.

. . .

The judgment of dismissal is reversed with respect to the issues raised by the second, third and fourth counts of the complaint. A new trial is directed on these issues. In all other respects the judgment is affirmed. Costs to abide the event.

NOTES AND QUESTIONS

(1) What is the gravamen of intent? See also, *Vosburg v. Putney*, 50 N.W. 403 (Wis. 1891), and *Garratt v. Dailey*, 279 A.2d 1091 (Wash. 1955). Cf., *Spivey v. Battaglia*, 258 So.2d 815 (Fla. 1972).

(2)   For sport, a teenage boy lights the fuse of a firecracker and throws it into the crowded stands at a football game. The firecracker lands successively upon the heads of A, B, and C, each of whom instinctively flings the sparkling object away. Flying out of C's hand it hits the face of D, exploding and putting out his eye. Who, if anyone, is liable to D and on what ground? See *Scott v. Shepard*, 3 Wils. K.B. 403, 95 Eng. Rep. 1124 (1773).

(3)   Where is the line to be drawn between mere negligence and an intentional wrong, given the meaning of intent as defined in Clayton? In *Gollins v. Gollins*, [1964] A.C. 644 (H.L. (E) 1963), the meaning of intent was raised in a proceeding by a wife against her spouse seeking an order on non-cohabitation on grounds of persistent cruelty. Lord Reid delivered a long judgment in which he said, at 664:

> Sometimes it is said that a person must be presumed to have intended the natural and probable result of what he did. That, if taken literally, must mean that it would be irrelevant to prove that in fact he did not intend that result: it would introduce a purely objective standard not depending at all on the state of his mind. In fact people often intend something quite different from what they know to be the natural and probable result of what they are doing. To take a trivial example, if I say I intend to reach the green, people will believe me although we all know that the odds are ten to one against my succeeding: and no one but a lawyer would say that I must be presumed to have intended to put my ball in the bunker because that was the natural and probable result of my shot. Irrebuttable presumptions have had a useful place in the law of tort in facilitating the change from a subjective to an objective standard. For a long time it was thought that, at least in theory, intention or mental state of some kind was a necessary ingredient in negligence. But life would be impossible in modern conditions unless on the highway and in the market place we were entitled to rely on the other man behaving like a reasonable man. So we now apply a purely objective standard. The other man may have been doing his best and he may not realize that his best is not good enough, but if he causes damage by falling short of the ordinary standard he must pay. In matrimonial affairs we are not dealing with objective standards, and it is not a matrimonial offence to fall below the standard of the reasonable man (or the reasonable woman). We are dealing with this man and this woman.

What application does this have to the law of intentional torts?

Not all courts require intent as an element of battery. See note (4) after *Letang v. Cooper*, Chapter 3, *supra*. Canada is another of these jurisdictions. See *Eisner v. Maxwell*, [1951] 1 D.L.R. 816, 823.

MASTERS v. BECKER
N.Y. Supreme Court, Appellate Division
22 A.D. 2d 118, 254 N.Y.S.2d 633 (1964)

CHRIST, JUSTICE.

The single question is whether, with respect to a cause of action for assault, the definition of intent given by the trial court in its charge and in its ruling on an exception and a request to charge constituted reversible error. The court stated that the plaintiffs were required to establish that the infant defendant intended the act that resulted in injury, that she intended to commit an injury, and that she intended the very injury sustained by the infant plaintiff. The court also posed the question: "Can a nine-year old, by her action, intend the injury which resulted in this case?" To all this plaintiffs' counsel took an exception and requested the court to charge that plaintiffs were required to establish only that "the act was done with intent to inflict an offensive bodily contact." The court refused such request to charge and adhered to its previous instructions.

When the injury occurred, the infant plaintiff Susan Masters was about six years of age and the infant defendant Claudia Becker was about nine years of age. They, together with Claudia's sister, were playing on a motor truck in an empty lot, and Susan was standing on a narrow ledge on the outside of the truck's tailgate. Claudia told or at least urged Susan to get off; and Susan refused and cried, saying she was frightened. Then Claudia pried Susan's fingers off the tailgate and Susan fell to the ground, sustaining severe injuries. Claudia's testimony indicated that the reason for her act was to force Susan to give Claudia and her sister their turns to get onto the ledge so that they could jump off.

The correct rule as to intent is set forth in the American Law Institute's Restatement of the Law (Restatement of the Law of Torts, vol. 1, § 16, subd. 1), namely: that intent is established "If an act is done with the intention of inflicting upon another an offensive but not a harmful bodily contact or of putting another in apprehension of either a harmful or offensive bodily contact, and such act causes a bodily contact to the other . . . although the act was not done with the intention of bringing about the resulting bodily harm." . . .

The law as thus stated has been followed in Baldinger v. Banks, 26 Misc.2d 1086, 201 N.Y.S.2d 629 which case was approved by this court in a subsequent connected case. . . .

A plaintiff in an action to recover damages for an assault founded on bodily contact must prove only that there was bodily contact; that such contact was offensive; and that the defendant intended to make the contact. The plaintiff is not required to prove that defendant intended physically to injure him. Certainly he is not required to prove an intention to cause the specific injuries resulting from the contact.

Hence, the trial court's rulings and instructions were not in harmony with the law. On the facts a jury could well find that Claudia intended only to force Susan off the truck, without any thought of injuring her. It could also find that Claudia intended the bodily contact she was forcing upon Susan; and that, although this was not harmful in itself, it was offensive to Susan. Under a correct instruction, findings of the presence of such intent would be sufficient for holding Claudia responsible for the ensuing injury. In requiring plaintiffs to establish that Claudia in fact intended an injury and even the very injury that Susan sustained, the trial court was in error. Such instruction imposed on plaintiffs an excessive burden and made it highly improbable that the jury would find in favor of plaintiffs.

In Baldinger v. Banks, supra, where the correct rule was applied, liability was found against an even younger child than Claudia. There, the act of a six-year old boy was not significantly dissimilar to Claudia's. He resented the four-year-old infant plaintiff's presence on a lawn where he was playing and he pushed her. She fell to the ground and sustained severe injuries. A substantial recovery was awarded against the boy.

As the error in the instant case was highly prejudicial the judgment should be reversed on the law, and a new trial granted, with costs to plaintiffs to abide the event.

Judgment reversed on the law and new trial granted as between the plaintiffs and the infant defendant, with costs to the plaintiffs to abide the event.

PETERSON v. HAFFNER
Indiana Supreme Court
59 Ind. 130, 26 Am. Rpts. 81 (1877)

PERKINS, J.

Suit by Haffner against Peterson, for damages occasioned by an assault and battery.

Answer: the general denial, and a special paragraph. A demurrer was sustained to the latter; but, as the facts stated in it were admissible under the general denial, the action of the court upon the demurrer is unimportant.

Trial; verdict for the plaintiff, in the sum of one thousand dollars, and judgment, over a motion for a new trial, on the verdict; exception. Errors are properly assigned.

The facts of the case are as follows:

On the 25th of April, 1874, Fred Haffner, a boy five years old, and his brother Willie, who was between six and seven years old, were seated in front of their father's house, in Lafayette, upon a sand-heap, beside a bed of mortar.

We will let William Peterson, the defendant, a boy between thirteen and fourteen years of age at the time of committing the assault and battery, make his own statement of the transaction. He testified:

Me and Thomas A. Cunningham, George Gladden, William Winehart and Frank Robinson were up in the Hollow, where we had a fire roasting apples. We then came down on Fifth street; Haffner's boys were on a pile of sand by a box of mortar; we were all playing there in the street, throwing pebbles, chips and mortar at each other; had been there about twenty or thirty minutes; I was sitting on one corner of the mortar-box, and Willie Haffner on the opposite corner; Willie Winehart had just thrown some mortar at me, and I picked up some mortar and said to Willie Haffner, "Run or I will hit you," and he started to run, and Freddie with him, and I threw the mortar at Willie, and a part hit him on the back of his head, and just as I threw Freddie turned to look back, and a part of the mortar flew off and hit him above the eye; we were laughing and playing; was not mad; all in fun, and just as we were in the habit of playing; Freddie went to wipe the mortar off and commenced to cry, and Willie Haffner took hold of him and commenced to try to rub the mortar off; Willie Haffner had been dabbling in the mortar with his hands, same as I had, but I do not recollect that he threw any at me or any of the other boys; I was not mad at Willie or Freddie Haffner, and did not intend to hurt either of them; it was all in play and fun; we were all laughing; I stayed until Mrs. Haffner and Mr. Sheehan came round to where Freddie was crying, inside of the gate, and then went home; Willie and Freddie Haffner were in the habit of being with us boys in the street, and frequently came to our house and played in our yard with me; never had any quarrel or difficulty with them; was always on good terms with them until after this happened; I was in Haffner's house on next Sunday after the accident; Mrs. Haffner called me to come in, and asked me if I had done it on purpose; I told her that I had not, that I did not want to hurt Freddie; she asked me if I was not going to pay the doctor's bill; we were playing by throwing chips, pebbles and things at each other, as we were daily in the habit of doing.

. . .

Freddie was placed under the treatment of different oculists. It was of no avail. His eye went out.

The testimony above copied, fully and fairly presents the case.

. . .

It were well that domestic training and discipline of children should prevent such barbarous and dangerous sports as that described in the testimony in this cause. They may be attended by most unhappy and serious consequences. This case furnishes a sad instance. But, where domestic government does not prevent, the law must intervene to redress, in proper cases, injuries inflicted in them.

It is clear that an assault and battery was committed. It was unprovoked. Neither Willie nor Freddie Haffner had thrown any thing at any of the other boys, or in any way interfered with them, during the day, and they were at the time, as we may say, at their own home. There is no question of contributory negligence, or "of mutual consent to engage in play of a dangerous character," in this case. The assault was rudely, purposely and wilfully committed. The appellant, defendant below, notified the Haffner boys of his intention to commit the acts. He did not intend to inflict the injury, but he intended to do the wrongful act from which the injury resulted, and he is answerable for that result. 3 Cooley Bl. Com. 120, n. 4. The fact that the act was done in sport, it having been intentionally done, will not relieve the perpetrator from liability. See Adams v. Waggoner, 33 Ind. 531.

Infancy is not a defence to this action. An infant is liable for his torts, though not generally upon his contracts. In Reeve's Domestic Relations, it is said: "Where the minor has committed a tort with force, he is liable at any age." Page 386, and note 2 by Parker & Baldwin . . .

. . .

What we have already said renders it unnecessary, that we should extend this opinion by special comment on the instructions given and refused, and the ruling on the motion for a new trial.

The judgment is affirmed, with costs.

NOTES AND QUESTIONS

(1) Whom did the defendant intend to hit with the mortar? Assuming that the court did not make a mistake in that regard, what does the *Peterson v. Haffner* holding teach about the law of tortious intent?

(2) Why was the intent wrongful? Was the particular act not authorized by common practice of the boys' mode of play?

(3) Negligence law employs a child's standard of care in appropriate cases. Do not the same policy considerations call for similar treatment in the law of intentional torts? The *Peterson* holding is commonly accepted, as explained by this statement from *Ellis v. D'Anglo*, 253 P.2d 675, 677-78 (Cal. App. 1953):

> From . . . authorities and the cases which they cite it may be concluded generally that an infant is liable for his torts even though he lacks the mental development and capacity to recognize the wrongfulness of his conduct so long as he has the mental capacity to have the state of mind necessary to the commission of the particular tort which he is charged. Thus as between a battery and negligent injury an infant may have the capacity to intend the violent contact which is essential to the commission of battery when the same infant would be incapable of realizing that his heedless conduct might foreseeably lead to injury to another which is the essential capacity of mind to create liability for negligence.

> [The court concluded that the four-year-old could not be guilty of negligence].

> When it comes to the count charging battery, a very different question is presented. We certainly cannot say that a four year old child is incapable of intending the violent or the harmful striking of another. Whether a four year old child had such intent presents a fact question; and in view of section 41 of the Civil Code which makes the recognition of the wrongful character of the tort immaterial so far as the liability for compensatory damages is concerned, we must hold that the count charging battery states a cause of action.

Accord, *Garrett v. Dailey*, 279 P.2d 1091 (Wash. 1955).

[B]   Malice

SANDERS v. DANIEL INTERNATIONAL CORPORATION
Supreme Court of Missouri, En Banc
682 S.W.2d 803 (Mo. 1984)

WELLIVER, JUDGE.

This case involves a malicious prosecution action brought by respondent, Robert A. Sanders. At trial, the jury returned a verdict in favor of respondent, awarding him $100,000 in actual damages and $250,000 in punitive damages. We ordered the cause transferred after the Southern District affirmed the judgment. We reverse and remand.

The criminal prosecution forming the basis for this malicious prosecution action was a misdemeanor case in which respondent was charged with the attempted theft of tools and gauges valued over fifty dollars. Respondent was one of seven persons charged with that crime. [Respondent Sanders] and the other six were workmen at Daniel's worksite. All had been arrested and charged with stealing tools and gauges from the worksite. The information was sworn to by the prosecutor following a conversation in his office with agents of appellant, Daniel International Corporation. The prosecutor dismissed the misdemeanor action because he believed that insufficient evidence existed to proceed with the [criminal] trial. Respondent [Sanders] then filed this action for malicious prosecution.

. . .

Appellant [Daniel] raises a number of issues on appeal. First, we must address appellant's argument that respondent failed to establish all of the elements of the tort of malicious prosecution, particularly the requisite "malice." This involves examining whether MAI 16.01 (1981) correctly defines malice for a malicious prosecution. MAI 16.01 provides, in part, that malice is "the doing of a wrongful act intentionally without just cause or excuse." . . .

Actions for malicious prosecution have never been favorites of the law. There is almost universal agreement that sound public policy dictates that the law should encourage the uncovering and prosecution of crime. Any "policy that discourages citizens from reporting crime or aiding in prosecution would be undesirable and detrimental to society in general." Cates v. Eddy, 669 P.2d 912, 917-18 (Wyo.1983). Courts have always recognized that "[m]alicious prosecution is an action which tends to dilute the public policy of encouraging persons having knowledge of possible crimes to cooperate with public officers." Seelig v. Harvard Cooperative Society, 1 Mass.App. 341, 296 N.E.2d 825 (1973). . . . We believe that this public policy coupled with current crime rates mandates that we reexamine the element of malice in a malicious prosecution as it is defined for the jury in our present MAI 16.01.

A person suing on a theory of malicious prosecution must plead and prove six elements: (1) the commencement of a prosecution against the plaintiff; (2) the instigation by the defendant; (3) the termination of the proceeding in favor of the plaintiff; (4) the want of probable cause for the prosecution; (5) the defendant's conduct was actuated by malice; and (6) the plaintiff was damaged. S. Greenleaf, II Greenleaf on Evidence §§ 449-59 (2nd ed. 1844). See also Stafford v. Muster, 582 S.W.2d 670, 675 (Mo. banc 1979). We focus our attention on the fifth and crucial element of malice; and, because malice also justifies a punitive damage award, we must address the connection between the type of malice necessary to establish liability and that which is necessary to sustain an award of punitive damages.

The word "malice" connotes a culpable mental state, but the term lacks any uniform definition. In a well-researched opinion in 1917, the Arizona Supreme Court observed that "[t]here are different kinds and degrees of malice as well as the nature of the evidence going to prove its existence." Griswold v. Home, 19 Ariz. 56, 165 P. 318, 323 (1917). Indeed, one eminent scholar commented that the term is so "slippery" that it should be banished from the law. Ames, How Far an Act May Be A Tort Because of the Wrongful Motive of the Actor, 18 Harv.L.Rev. 411, 422 n. 1 (1905). We have retained the term and, not surprisingly, the different kinds and degrees of malice have often been confused throughout the development of the law in Missouri. The result is that we now utilize a single definition of malice and it is highly questionable whether it properly describes either the malice required to sustain a malicious prosecution or that required to sustain punitive damages in a malicious prosecution.

In general, the law recognizes three degrees of malice. First, there is malice in its universal sense as understood in the popular mind, which means "ill will, spite, personal hatred, or vindictive motives." Peasley v. Puget Sound Tug & Barge Co., 13 Wash.2d 485, 125 P.2d 681, 689 (1942). Such malicious conduct is founded in ill will, "and is evidenced by an attempt to vex, injure, or annoy another." Davis v.

Hearst, 160 Cal. 143, 116 P. 530, 537 (1911). . . . This type of malice is commonly referred to as "malice in fact" or "actual malice."

A second degree of malice is malice in its legal sense. The definition of legal malice has a broader meaning than the popularly understood definition of malice in fact. Malice in its enlarged legal sense embraces any improper or wrongful motive — that is, malo animo. . . . Some courts also have included within legal malice conduct which is so reckless or wantonly and willfully in disregard of one's rights that a trier of fact could infer from such conduct bad faith or malo animo. . . . Although he incorrectly termed it "malice in law," Newell aptly defined this type of malice as something less than malice in fact and "simply . . . a general wickedness or intent on the part of a person; a depraved inclination to do harm, or to disregard the rights or safety of mankind generally." . . .

Third, there is "malice in law." This degree of malice is properly defined as a wrongful act done intentionally without just cause or excuse. . . . The law imputes malice "to a wrongdoer from the mere intentional doing of a wrongful act to the injury of another without legal justification or excuse." Freezer v. Miller, 163 Va. 180, 176 S.E. 159, 168 (1934). . . . For example, [i]f one gives a perfect stranger unaware a blow with a deadly weapon likely to produce death, he does it of malice, because he does it intentionally without just cause or legal excuse. If he maims cattle without knowing whose they are, if he poisons a well of drinking water without knowing who is likely to drink of it, he does it of malice, because it is a wrongful act and done intentionally without any legal justification or excuse. This is the malice of the law — a malice of pleading and proof made necessary by definitions of offenses against the law or the exigencies of the case. It is established by a conclusive legal presumption, and proof of malice in fact is not required. Griswold v. Horne, supra, 165 P. at 323. An all-too-often unrecognized difference exists between this type of malice in law and malice in its legal sense. The former rests upon a legal presumption independent of any proof concerning a defendant's mental state, while the latter requires either direct or indirect proof of a mental state somewhat less culpable than malice in fact. . . .

The weight of authority clearly indicates that a malicious prosecution action can be supported only by either actual or legal malice. Malice in law is insufficient. A plaintiff must establish that the defendant acted either with ill will toward the plaintiff or from any other improper motive. Treatise writers are in general agreement that, at the very least, an improper or wrong motive is essential. Justice Holmes, for example, commented upon the relevancy of a defendant's moral condition in such suits: Such a limitation would stand almost alone in the law of civil liability. But the nature of the wrong is peculiar, and, moreover, it is quite consistent with the theory of liability here advanced that it should be confined in any given instance to actual wrongdoing in a moral sense. O. Holmes, The Common Law Tradition 113 (M. Howe ed. 1963). Over one hundred years later, Prosser and Keeton wrote: The plaintiff has the burden of proving that the defendant instituted the proceeding "maliciously." This unfortunate word, which has so much vexed the kindred law of defamation, requires no less in the way of definition here. It means something more than the fictious "malice in law" which has been developed in defamation cases as a cloak for strict liability. There must be "malice in fact." At the same time it does not necessarily mean that the defendant was inspired by hatred, spite or ill will; and there is authority that if his purpose was otherwise a proper one, the addition of the incidental fact that he felt indignation or resentment toward the plaintiff will not make him liable. As in the cases of qualified privilege in defamation, the courts seem to have looked to the primary purpose behind the defendant's action. If he is found to have acted chiefly to give vent to motives of ill will, "malice" is established. But it is found also where his primary purpose was merely something other than the social one of bringing an offender to justice. . . . W. Prosser & W. Keeton, supra, at 882-83. Other similar expressions may be found concerning the required type of malice. Ordinarily, in order to constitute malice supporting an action for malicious prosecution, there must be malus animus, denoting that the person who instituted the original proceeding was actuated by wrong motives. . . . [Accepted] authorities illustrate that while ill will, hatred or spite may not be necessary to establish the cause of action, the plaintiff must prove that the defendant was at least actuated by an improper or wrongful motive.

Decisions from numerous state courts are no less forceful in asserting that more than malice in law is needed to establish the elements of a malicious prosecution. Some courts require actual malice, while other courts hold that malice in its legal sense is sufficient. . . .

Some of these courts hold that legal malice also encompasses conduct which is "wrongful and willfully done, with a consciousness that it is not according to law or duty." Wiggin v. Coffin, 29 Fed.Cas. 1157, 1159 (C.C.D.Me.1836) (No. 17,634). . . . Care must be taken to distinguish this type of malice from negligence: Malice is distinguishable from mere negligence in that it arises from absence of purpose. The characteristic of negligence is inadvertence or an absence of an intent to injure. This does not imply that the act was done involuntarily or unconsciously, but merely that the person doing it was not conscious that the act constituted a want of reasonable care. If so conscious the act becomes malicious. The books agree that the prosecution need not have been prompted by malevolence or any corrupt design, nor necessarily involve spite or hatred toward the person accused. It is enough if it be the result of any improper or sinister motive and in disregard of the rights of other . . . , or if done willfully and purposely. . . . But to constitute malice there must have been (1) a motive or purpose, and (2) it must have been an improper one. Enkins v. Gilligan, 131 Iowa 176, 108 N.W. 237, 238 (1906) (citations omitted). In short, the conduct must be such that a jury could infer and find an improper motive. . . .

Contrary to the weight of authority, Missouri has retained a malice in law standard for the definition of malice in malicious prosecution actions. "The element of malice in malicious prosecution is defined as the intentional doing of a wrongful act without legal justification. It may be inferred from the absence of probable cause and does not necessarily involve hatred or ill will." Parthenopoulos v. Maddox, 629 S.W.2d 563, 571 (Mo.App.1981). . . . This is essentially the definition found in MAI 16.01: The term ["malice"] ["malicious"] ["maliciously"] as used in this [these] instruction[s] does not mean hatred, spite or ill will, as commonly understood, but means the doing of a wrongful act intentionally without just cause or excuse. Although Missouri has dubbed and titled this definition "legal malice," it is in fact what we have described as "malice in law." The instruction does not require the jury to find that the defendant acted with an improper purpose .. . .

The Court in [its] early cases erroneously assumed that the definition of malice could be culled from defamation cases where malice served as a cloak for strict liability. . . .

The case at bar leaves us no choice but to clarify the element of malice in malicious prosecution actions. In so doing we resolve the misunderstanding that has plagued this state's law for many years. We can no longer in good conscience sanction the use of MAI 16.01. The instruction reflects a definition of malice in law and does not indicate to the jury that the defendant had to have acted with the requisite culpable mental state. In the past the jury has been told that malice exists when the defendant does a "wrongful act intentionally without just cause." The "wrongful act" "without just cause" is committed when the defendant acts without probable cause, an entirely separate element of the tort. All that has remained for the jury to determine is that the defendant act "intentionally." To a jury this suggests, as counsel for respondent argued in closing argument, that the initiation of the prosecution was "not an accident." This fails to recognize the distinction between intention and malice. Intention refers to the defendant's intent to commit the act which causes the harm. . . . The type of intent embraced in the concept of malice is quite different . . . [For malice there] must be intent to cause the harm and not merely to commit the act which causes the harm. The effect of MAI 16.01 is to place a premium on the absence of probable cause thereby relegating malice to a mere legal fiction, a legal inference or presumption. This is contrary to the weight of authority and we believe was never intended by our prior decisional law.

MAI 16.01 is further misleading because it states that malice "does not mean hatred, spite or ill will." Hatred, spite or ill will is necessary to establish malice in fact. . . . By informing the jury that malice does not mean hatred, spite or ill will instead of informing the jury that malice does not necessarily mean hatred, spite or ill will, MAI 16.01 goes one step further in suggesting to a jury that mere intent to do an act that the law subsequently classifies as wrongful is sufficient.

In Haswell v. Liberty Mutual Insurance Co., 557 S.W.2d 628 (Mo. banc 1977), this Court discussed adopting the Restatement definition of malice for malicious prosecution of civil proceedings. The passing years, the ever increasing problem of crime, and the need for effectively carrying out the public policy of urging citizens to aid in the prosecution of crime now mandates that we reach a different result with respect to malicious prosecution actions arising from a criminal proceeding. The Restatement of Torts (Second) § 668 (1965) provides: "To subject a person to liability for malicious prosecution, the proceedings must have been initiated primarily for a purpose other than that of bringing an offender to justice." This definition, while not requiring proof of malice in fact, will require proof of legal malice and bring Missouri back into step with the majority of jurisdictions.

Having held that MAI 16.01 improperly defines the element of malice in malicious prosecution actions, MAI 23.07 (1981) should be modified so as to incorporate the Restatement definition.[3] We believe that respondent should be afforded a new trial to determine whether or not appellant acted with the degree of malice necessary to sustain the cause of action. . . .

To the extent that either our prior cases or MAI 16.01 conflict with the degrees of malice we have found necessary to support malicious prosecution. . . , they can

---

[3] The second paragraph of MAI 23.07 should be amended as follows: "Second, in so doing defendant acted primarily for a purpose other than that of bringing an offender to justice and acted without reasonable grounds, . . . " The term "reasonable grounds" still requires definition. MAI 16.05 (1981).
. . .

no longer be followed. The need to encourage citizen assistance and participation in the enforcement of our criminal laws compels this long overdue reexamination of the law of malicious prosecution.

The cause is reversed and remanded for retrial consistent with this opinion.

NOTES AND QUESTIONS

(1)   The different kinds of malice have been acknowledged at least since *Mitchell v. Jenkins*, 5B & AD 588, 110 Eng. Rep. 908 (1833), was decided. In *Mitchell v. Jenkins* the judges held that malice in the legal sense (i.e., improper motive or purpose) was sufficient to establish the malice element of a malicious prosecution action, but malice in law (i.e., malice presumed from the absence of probable cause) would not. Most modern American courts agree. The judges in *Mitchell v. Jenkins* also agreed that the " 'probable cause' "element of the malicious prosecution action is a question of law to be determined by the judge; whereas, the "malice" question is a fact question for the jury. Most, if not all, modern American courts agree. Think about what these elements denote. Why should "probable cause" be deemed to be a question of law?

(2)   Who has the burden of proof on the various elements of a malicious prosecution action? See Restatement, Torts, Second, § 672. What damages should be recoverable? It is generally held that a plaintiff may recover for damages to reputation and emotional distress in this action, Id., § 670.

(3)   Other Restatement positions on malicious prosecution of criminal actions include the following:[4]

§ 657 Plaintiff's Guilt As Bar to Recovery

The fact that the person against whom criminal proceedings are instituted is guilty of the crime charged against him, is a complete defense against liability for malicious prosecution.

§ 659 Manner of Termination

Criminal proceedings are terminated in favor of the accused by

(a) a discharge by a magistrate at a preliminary hearing, or

(b) the refusal of a grand jury to indict, or

(c) the formal abandonment of the proceedings by the public prosecutor, or

(d) the quashing of an indictment or information, or

(e) an acquittal, or

(f) a final order in favor of the accused by a trial or appellate court.

---

[4] Copyright 1965 by The American Law Institute. Reprinted with the permission of The American Law Institute.

§ 662 Existence of Probable Cause

One who initiates or continues criminal proceedings against another has probable cause for doing so if he correctly or reasonably believes

(a) that the person whom he accuses has acted or failed to act in a particular manner, and

(b) that those acts or omissions constitute the offense that he charges against the accused, and

(c) that he is sufficiently informed as to the law and the facts to justify him in initiating or continuing the prosecution.

§ 669 Lack of Probable Cause As Evidence of An improper Purpose

Lack of probable cause for the initiation of criminal proceedings, in so far as it tends to show that the accuser did not believe in the guilt of the accused, is evidence that he did not initiate the proceedings for a proper purpose.

CHAPMAN v. HONIG
2 Q.B. 502 [1963] (C.A.)[5]

On June 22, 1962, the tenant of a flat in a tenement house gave evidence on subpoena in an action by a former fellow-tenant against their common landlord for trespass and conversion of goods. The fellow-tenant was awarded £193 10s. by the county court judge. On the following day the landlord served notice to quit on the tenant who had given evidence, to expire on July 28, 1962. The tenant stayed on, and on August 15 attempts were made on behalf of the landlord to padlock the doors of his flat. The tenant obtained an injunction from the county court to restrain further action by the landlord, but difficulties continued, and eventually the tenant vacated the flat. He brought an action against the landlord alleging trespass and breach of the covenant for quiet enjoyment, and alleging also that the landlord's action in giving him notice was in contempt of court, but not claiming damages therefor. The county court judge (who had tried the former tenant's action) found that the landlord's motive in serving the notice to quit was to punish and victimise the tenant for giving evidence, and held that the legal consequences were that, whether or not the notice to quit was valid, the tenant, having been the victim of contempt of court and injured thereby, was entitled to damages without proof of any special pecuniary loss; and he awarded the tenant, £50 damages. On appeal by the landlord: —

LORD REID:

. . .

The plaintiff's counsel has relied upon passages in the judgment of Lord Denning M.R. in Attorney-General v. Butterworth. He said: "I have no hesitation in declaring that the victimization of a witness is a contempt of court, whether done whilst the proceedings are still pending or after they have finished. Such a

---

[5] [Ed. — Queen's Bench Law Reports of the principal English trial court, appeals therefrom, and certain criminal appeals, decision of the Court of Appeal.]

contempt will be punished by the court itself, before which he has given evidence, and, so that those who think of doing such things may be warned where they stand, I would add that if the witness has been damnified by it, he may well have redress in a civil court for damages."

After referring to the Witnesses (Public Inquiries) Protection Act, 1892, the Master of the Rolls said: "Why were courts of justice thus excluded? Not because the victimization of witnesses before the court was any less reprehensible, but because the courts have their own machinery at hand for dealing with victimization, namely, their power to bring offenders before them for contempt of court, and, I would add, the remedy to a person aggrieved of bringing an action for the wrong done."

Those passages were clearly obiter dicta because no question of civil liability arose for decision in that case. As obiter dicta, when read together and fairly construed, they contain a warning of the risks incurred by a person who acts in contempt of court and do not in my view say or imply that there is necessarily in every case of contempt of court of the kind which we are considering a civil right of action for damages. In many cases there would be such a right. The act of victimization may be itself a tort or a breach of contract, for instance, trespass, assault, libel, slander, wrongful dismissal or breach of covenant for quiet enjoyment. In some cases the vindictive motive would of itself render unlawful an act which without such motive would have been lawful. For instance, in a defamation action the vindictive motive would be malice defeating a plea of privilege; it would make a prosecution "malicious": it might cause some act by an occupier of land, which would otherwise have been a lawful use of the land, to be an act of nuisance (Christie v. Davey; Hollywood Silver Fox Farm Ltd. v. Emmett); and it might cause some concerted activity, which might otherwise have been an innocent combination in defence or furtherance of trade interests, to be an actionable conspiracy. On the facts of Attorney-General v. Butterworth there was a possibility that Greenlees might have had a cause of action for conspiracy, but it did not arise for decision and was not investigated. There might well be other cases in which the vindictive motive would render unlawful some act which would otherwise be lawful.

There is a special difficulty in the present case. The act complained of, the service of the notice to quit, was on the face of it a lawful exercise of a contractual right, duly implemented in accordance with the provisions of the tenancy agreement and effective to terminate the tenant's estate and to convert the landlord's interest from an estate in reversion to an estate in possession. Common experience is that, when the validity of an act done in purported exercise of a right under a contract or other instrument is disputed, the inquiry is limited to ascertaining whether the act has been done in accordance with the provisions of the contract or other instrument. I cannot think of any case in which such an act might be invalidated by proof that it was prompted by some vindictive or other wrong motive. Motive is disregarded as irrelevant. A person who has a right under a contract or other instrument is entitled to exercise it and can effectively exercise it for a good reason or a bad reason or no reason at all. If the rule were different, if the exercise of such a right were liable to be overthrown, in an action brought at any time within the limitation period, by proof that the act was done with a wrong motive, there would be a great unsettlement of property titles and commercial transactions and relationships. I think it was conceded by the plaintiff's counsel in the course of his argument that the notice to quit must be considered to have been valid for the purpose of terminating the tenant's estate. I am not insisting on the concession, because it may have been withdrawn in later discussion. In any case that is in my judgment the right conclusion the point.

What follows? The notice to quit was valid: it was effective for its purpose of requiring the plaintiff to quit the premises: it terminated the tenant's right of possession: the defendant was entitled under the tenancy agreement to give the notice and he gave it in all respects in conformity with the provisions of the tenancy agreement. For those purposes, in those connections, in those aspects, the giving of the notice was a lawful act. How then could it be unlawful for some other purpose or in some other connection or in some other aspect as between the same parties? Of course it could be lawful as between these parties, the plaintiff and the defendant, and yet unlawful as between the defendant and the court on the ground that it was calculated to interfere with the administration of justice. But in my view the same act cannot be as between the same parties both a lawful exercise of a contractual right and at the same time unlawful as being tortious and giving rise to an action for damages. No such complication has yet existed in the law and it is not necessary or desirable to introduce it.

LORD DENNING, M.R. (Dissenting):

. . .

The principle upon which this case falls to be decided is simply this. No system of law can justly compel a witness to give evidence and then, on finding him victimized for doing it, refuse to give him redress. It is the duty of the court to protect the witness by every means at its command. Else the whole process of the law will be set at naught. If a landlord intimidates a tenant by threatening him with notice to quit, the court must be able to protect the tenant by granting an injunction to restrain the landlord from carrying out his threat. If the landlord victimises a tenant by actually giving him notice to quit, the court must be able to protect the tenant by holding the notice to quit to be invalid. Nothing else will serve to vindicate the authority of the law. Nothing else will enable a witness to give his evidence freely as he ought to do. Nothing else will empower the judge to say to him: "Do not fear. The arm of the law is strong enough to "protect you."

. . .

The truth is, however, that this is a new case. None like it has ever come before the courts so far as I know. But that is no reason for us to do nothing. We have the choice before us. Either to redress a grievous wrong, or to leave it unremedied. Either to protect the victim of oppression, or to let him suffer under it. Either to uphold the authority of the law, or to watch it being flouted. Faced with this choice I have no doubt what the answer should be. We cannot stand idly by. The law which compels a witness to give evidence is in duty bound to protect him from being punished for doing it. That was the view of Judge Sir Alun Pugh when he granted an injunction. It was the view of Judge Baxter when he gave damages of £50. It is my view too. I would not turn the tenant away without remedy. I would dismiss this appeal.

[The appeal was granted and the case dismissed.]

NOTES AND QUESTIONS

Should the doing of an act that causes harm to another person solely as an expression of spite or ill will make the action tortious if it were otherwise entirely lawful and within the discretion of the actor? This issue has arisen most frequently in instances in which employers fire "at-will" employees for a reason having nothing to do with job performance. An "at-will" employee is one who has no contract for a fixed term of employment or that permits discharge only for just cause. The law is settled in most jurisdictions that employers may fire at-will employees for any reason, good or bad, at any time or for no reason at all. Similarly, at-will employees may quit without legal consequences when they please. Despite this strong rule of law, most courts now acknowledge a narrow "public policy" exception to the at will doctrine and permit fired employees to sue employers who maliciously fire them from at-will jobs for reasons that violate "clear mandates of public policy." See, e.g., *Lawrence Chrysler Plymouth Corporation v. Brooks*, 465 S.E.2d 800 (Va. 1996). Courts strictly confine the exception to clearly established mandates of public policy that protect public interests rather than the mere private or proprietary interests of the plaintiff. The landmark case is *Peterman v. International Brotherhood of Teamsters*, 344 P.2d 25 (Cal. 1955) (against public policy to fire employee who refuses to commit perjury to protect employer). Other cases include applying the narrow exception include *Framton v. Central Indiana Gas Co.*, 297 N.E. 2d 425 (Ind. 1973) (retaliatory discharge of employee who filed a workers compensation claim against the employer violated public policy) and *Nees v. Hocks*, 536 P.2d 512 (Or. En Banc 1975) (firing of employee who missed work to serve on jury duty violated public policy).

ECKENRODE v. LIFE OF AMERICA INSURANCE COMPANY
United States Court of Appeals, Seventh Circuit
470 F.2d 1 (1972)

KILEY, CIRCUIT JUDGE.

Plaintiff, a resident of Pennsylvania, filed this three count diversity complaint to recover damages for severe emotional injury suffered as a result of the deliberate refusal of Life of America Insurance Company (Insurer), of Chicago, to pay her the proceeds of Insurer's policy covering the life of her husband. The district court dismissed the suit. Plaintiff has appealed. We reverse.

In Count I plaintiff sought recovery of the face amount of the policy. In Count II she sought compensatory damage for Insurer's "outrageous conduct" in refusing to pay her the policy proceeds when its duty was clear and when it knew of plaintiff's and her family's financial distress. In Count III she sought compensatory and punitive damages 1) because Insurer allegedly defrauded decedent into the insurance contract by its promise of payment of benefits immediately upon proof of the insured's death from "accidental causes," while at the time its practice was not to pay meritorious claims; and 2) because Insurer allegedly sought by "economic coercion" to compel plaintiff — so increasingly financially distressed — to accept less than the face value of the policy or be forced to sue for payment of the proceeds.

. . .

Only Counts II and III, therefore, are before us on this appeal.

I.

Taking the allegations, properly pleaded in Counts II and III, as true, the following facts are stated:

. . .

[Defendant insurance company refused to pay the face amount of a valid policy of insurance on the life of the plaintiff's deceased husband; defendant knew of the plaintiff's impecunious straits for herself and several children and attempted to make her take less than the face amount as a condition of payment.]

II.

The issue before us with respect to Counts II and III is whether plaintiff beneficiary of her husband's life insurance policy — may on the foregoing "facts" recover damages for severe mental distress allegedly suffered as a result of Insurer's conduct. Illinois law controls our decision, and, in anticipation that the Illinois Supreme Court would hold as we do, we decide the issue in favor of plaintiff.

We have no doubt, in view of Knierim v. Izzo, 22 Ill.2d 73, 174 N.E.2d 157 (1961), that the Illinois Supreme Court would sustain plaintiff's complaint against Insurer's motion to dismiss.

In Knierim, plaintiff filed a wrongful death action alleging, inter alia, that defendant Izzo threatened her with the murder of her husband, carried out the threat, and thereby proximately caused her severe emotional distress. The trial court dismissed her complaint, but the Illinois Supreme Court reversed and held that plaintiff had stated a cause of action for an intentional causing of severe emotional distress by Izzo's "outrageous conduct."

The court recognized the "new tort" of intentional infliction of severe emotional distress, following similar recognition by an "increasing number of courts," and cited several state decisions. 174 N.E.2d at 163. The court rejected reasons given by other courts not recognizing the "new tort." As to the reason that mental disturbance is incapable of financial measurement, the court pointed out that "pain and suffering" and "mental suffering" are elements of damage, respectively, in personal injury and malicious prosecution cases. 174 N.E.2d at 163. As to the reason that mental consequences are too evanescent for the law to deal with, the court noted that psychosomatic medicine had learned much in the past "thirty years" about the bodily effects of man's emotions, and that symptoms produced by "stronger emotions" are now visible to the professional eye. 174 N.E.2d at 164. As to the reason that recognizing the "new tort" would lead to frivolous claims, the court observed that triers of fact from their own experiences would be able to draw a line between "slight hurts" and "outrageous conduct." Id. And finally, as to the reason that mental consequences vary greatly with the individual so as to pose difficulties too great for the law, the court adopted an objective standard against which emotional distress could be measured. The court thought that the standard of "severe emotional distress to a person of ordinary sensibilities, in the absence of special knowledge or notice" would be a sufficient limit for excluding "mere vulgarities . . . as meaningless abusive expressions." 174 N.E.2d at 165. The court noted that the "reasonable man" is well known to triers of fact who are also well acquainted with "the man of ordinary sensibilities."

The court added a cautionary note, expressing confidence that Illinois trial judges would not permit litigation to introduce "trivialities and mere bad manners" under the cloak of the "new tort." The court concluded — with implications from the famous Warren-Brandeis article on the "new tort" or privacy — that peace of mind is a personal interest of sufficient importance to receive the law's protection against intentional invasion by "outrageous conduct," and that the allegations in Mrs. Knierim's complaint stated a cause of action.

In Knierim the court, inter alia, relied upon State Rubbish Collectors Association v. Siliznoff, 38 Cal. 2d 330, 240 P.2d 282 (1952), and Restatement, Torts § 46 (1948 Supp.). In Siliznoff the California Supreme Court, in an opinion by Justice Roger Traynor, recognized the "new tort" for the first time and held that Siliznoff could recover from the cross-defendant Rubbish Collectors Association for mental distress caused by the Association's severe threats to beat him up, destroy his truck and put him out of business unless Siliznoff offered to pay over certain proceeds to the Association. Later, the California Supreme Court en banc affirmed a trial court judgment against an insurance company, including $25,000 for mental suffering caused by the insurance company's earlier unreasonable refusal to accept a settlement within the limits of the liability policy. Crisci v. Security Ins. Co. of New Haven, 66 Cal.2d 425, 58 Cal. Rptr. 13, 426 P.2d 173 (1970). There Mrs. Crisci's mental distress claim was in addition to her loss of property caused by the insurance company's failure to settle. The court thought that where there were substantial damages apart from the mental distress, the danger of fictitious claims was reduced.

Subsequently in Fletcher v. Western National Life Ins. Co., 10 Cal. App.3d 376, 89 Cal.Rptr. 78 (1970), an appellate court relying upon Siliznoff and Crisci, held that the defendant insurance company's threatened and actual bad faith refusals to make payments under the disability policy were essentially tortious in nature and could legally be the basis for an action against the company for intentional infliction of emotional distress. The decision rested on the finding that the refusals were maliciously employed by the company in concert with false and threatening communications directed to the badly injured plaintiff-insured for the purpose of causing him to surrender his policy or disadvantageously settle a nonexistent dispute. 89 Cal.Rptr. at 93. The court found sufficient evidence showing emotional distress of the "requisite severity" (i.e., outrageousness), and thus affirmed the trial court's denial of judgment N.O.V.

We think that the California court in Fletcher, supra, set out correctly the elements of a prima facie case for the tort of "intentional infliction of severe emotional distress":

(1) Outrageous conduct by the defendant;

(2) The defendant's intention of causing, or reckless disregard of the probability of causing emotional distress;

(3) The plaintiff's suffering severe or extreme emotional distress; and

(4) Actual and proximate causation of the emotional distress by the defendant's outrageous conduct.G4452

See Knierim, supra: Restatement 2d Torts, § 46(1); Prosser, Torts § 11 (3d Ed. 1964).

It is our view that were this case before the Illinois Supreme Court, that court would find the foregoing elements substantially correct; and that plaintiff here has sufficiently pleaded the elements.

It is recognized that the outrageous character of a person's conduct may arise from an abuse by that person of a position which gives him power to affect the interests of another; and that in this sense extreme "bullying tactis" and other "high pressure" methods of insurance adjusters seeking to force compromises or settlements may constitute outrageous conduct. Restatement 2d Torts § 46 Comment (e): Prosser, Torts § 11 at 49-50. It is also recognized that the extreme character of a person's conduct may arise from that person's knowledge that the other is peculiarly susceptible to emotional distress by reason of some physical or mental condition or peculiarity. Restatement 2d Torts § 46 Comment (f); Prosser, Torts § 11. See Keenan, The Insurer and the Tort of the Intentional Infliction of Mental Distress, Insurance Counsel Journal 335 (1972).

Here Insurer's alleged bad faith refusal to make payment on the policy, coupled with its deliberate use of "economic coercion" (i.e., by delaying and refusing payment it increased plaintiff's financial distress thereby coercing her to compromise and settle) to force a settlement, clearly rises to the level of "outrageous conduct" to a person of "ordinary sensibilities."

Furthermore, it is common knowledge that one of the most frequent considerations in procuring life insurance is to ensure the continued economic and mental welfare of the beneficiaries upon the death of the insured. See Crisci, 66 Cal.2d 425, 58 Cal.Rptr. at 19, 426 P.2d at 179. The very risks insured against presuppose that upon the death of the insured the beneficiary might be in difficult circumstances and thus particularly susceptible and vulnerable to high pressure tactics by an economically powerful entity. Fletcher, 89 Cal.Rptr. at 95. In the case before us Insurer's alleged high pressure methods (economic coercion) were aimed at the very thing insured against, and we think that the insurance company was on notice that plaintiff would be particularly vulnerable to mental distress by reason of her financial plight.

In deciding as we do, we note that insurance business affects a great many people, is subject to substantial governmental regulation and is stamped with a public interest. Memorial Gardens Ass'n, Inc. v. Smith, 16 Ill.2d 116, 156 N.E.2d 587 (1959); People ex rel. Bolton v. Progressive Gen. Ins. Co., 85 Ill.App.2d 427, 229 N.E.2d 350 (1967); Crisci, supra; Fletcher, supra. We also note that insurance contracts are subject to the same implied conditions of good faith and fair dealing as are other contracts. Appleman, Insurance § 1612 (1967); I.L.P., Insurance §§ 101, 141 et seq. (1956).

It is true that settlement tactics may be privileged under circumstances where an insurer has done no more than insist upon his legal rights in a permissible way. But we do not think that a refusal to make payments based on a bad faith insistence on a non-existent defense is privileged conduct against the complaint here.

III.

We hold, however, that plaintiff may not recover punitive damages because in our view Knierim v. Izzo, supra, will not support an anticipation that the Illinois Supreme Court would sustain a judgment allowing punitive damages.

. . .

NOTES AND QUESTIONS

(1) The tort of "outrage" is difficult to maintain both because of the extremity of the behavior required to establish a prima facie case and also because of the severity of the harm that must be shown to be compensable. Why impose these elevated standards? What would happen to the great care the law has taken to constrain the scope of the tort of negligent infliction of emotional distress if they were lowered? Many of the cases that permit recovery involve circumstances in which the plaintiff was intentionally or recklessly exposed to acts of extreme brutality or indecency committed against another person.

(2) *Eckenrode* demonstrates that insurance companies sometimes fail to honor their contracts with insureds. What does it take to turn a mere breach of contract into a tort?

(3) Perhaps more common than the situation in *Eckenrode* are cases in which a liability insurance company has an opportunity to settle a tort action against the company's insured for the limits of the policy or less, but refuses to do so. For example, suppose the policy covers liabilities of up to $10,000 and the company ignores an offer to settle for $2500, even though it had reserved $4500 to pay the claim, because it estimated that the injured party had only a 20-30% chance of recovering anything in court. Later the injured party recovered a judgment of $18,500 against the insured. Can the insurance company be required to pay more than the contractual obligation of $10,000?

A number of jurisdictions have awarded damages against the insurance companies in "excess judgment" cases. For example, in *Auto Mutual Indemnity Co. v. Shaw*, 134 Fla. 815, 184 So. 852 (1938), the court laid down a rule that it later described as follows:

> In [*Auto Mutual*] it was held an insurance company owed an obligation to its insured by virtue of its contract to negotiate with claimant in good faith, and that its decision not to settle must be the result of weighing of probabilities in a fair and honest way; and that its decision should be honest and intelligent and a good faith conclusion based upon a knowledge of the facts and circumstances upon which liability was predicated and upon a knowledge of the nature and extent of the injuries as far as they reasonably could be ascertained.

Campbell v. Government Employees Insurance Co., 306 So.2d 525, 528 (Fla. 1975). According to *Campbell*, the standard is "bad faith rather than negligence." Id, at 530. Although *Campbell* laid out no specific criteria of bad faith, the court in *National Security Fire & Cas. Co. v. Bowen*, 417 So.2d 179, 183 (Ala. 1982), specified the following:

(a) an insurance contract between the parties and a breach thereof by the defendant;

(b) an intentional refusal to pay the insured's claim;

(c) the absence of any reasonably legitimate or arguable reason for that refusal (the absence of a debatable reason);

(d) the insurer's actual knowledge of the absence of any legitimate or arguable reason;

(e) if the intentional failure to determine the existence of a lawful basis is relied upon, the plaintiff must prove the insurer's intentional failure to determine whether there is a legitimate or arguable reason to refuse to pay the claim.

In short, plaintiff must go beyond a mere showing of nonpayment and prove a bad faith nonpayment, a nonpayment without any reasonable ground for dispute. Or, stated differently, the plaintiff must show that the insurance company had no legal or factual defense to the insurance claim.

The "debatable-reason" under (c) above means an arguable reason, one that is open to dispute or question. Webster's Third New International Dictionary (1931) at 116.

On facts identical to those described above, Campbell permitted the insured to recover compensatory damages of $9,384 and punitive damages of $25,000 against the insurance company. Is that justifiable under the Bowen critieria?

[C]   Scienter

DERRY v. PEEK
[1889] 14 A.C. 337 (H.L.)[6]

A special act incorporating a tramway company provided that the carriages might be moved by animal power, and, with the consent of the Board of Trade, by steam power. The directors issued a prospectus containing a statement that by their special Act the company had the right to use steam power instead of horses. The plaintiff took shares on faith of this statement. The Board of Trade afterwards refused their consent to the use of steam power and the company was wound up. The plaintiff having brought an action of deceit against the directors founded upon the false statement:

[The action was decided for defendants after a trial, but the dismissal was reversed by the Court of Appeals.]

LORD HERSCHELL: —

My Lords, in the statement of claim in this action the respondent, who is the plaintiff, alleges that the appellants made in a prospectus issued by them certain statements which were untrue, that they well knew that the facts were not as stated in the prospectus, and made the representations fraudulently, and with the view to induce the plaintiff to take shares in the company.

"This action is one which is commonly called an action of deceit, a mere common law action." This is the description of it given by Cotton L.J. in delivering judgment. I think it important that it should be borne in mind that such an action

---

[6] [Ed. — Appeal Cases Law Reports, decision of House of Lords.]

differs essentially from one brought to obtain rescission of a contract on the ground of misrepresentation of a material fact. The principles which govern the two actions differ widely. Where rescission is claimed it is only necessary to prove that there was misrepresentation; then, however honestly it may have been made, however free from blame the person who made it, the contract, having been obtained by misrepresentation, cannot stand. In an action of deceit, on the contrary, it is not enough to establish misrepresentation alone; it is conceded on all hands that something more must be proved to cast liablity upon the defendant, though it has been a matter of controversy what additional elements are requisite. I lay stress upon this because observations made by learned judges in actions for rescission have been cited and much relied upon at the bar by counsel for the respondent. Care must obviously be observed in applying the language used in relation to such actions to an action of deceit. Even if the scope of the language used extend beyond the particular action which was being dealt with, it must be remembered that the learned judges were not engaged in determining what is necessary to support an action of deceit, or in discriminating with nicety the elements which enter into it.

. . .

In the Court below Cotton L.J. said: "What in my opinion is a correct statement of the law is this, that where a man makes a statement to be acted upon by others which is false, and which is known by him to be false, or is made by him recklessly, or without care whether it is true or false, that is, without any reasonable ground for believing it to be true, he is liable in an action of deceit at the suit of anyone to whom it was addressed or anyone of the class to whom it was addressed and who was materially induced by the misstatement to do an act to his prejudice." About much that is here stated cannot, I think, be two opinions. But when the learned Lord Justice speaks of a statement made recklessly or without care whether it is true or false, that is without any reasonable ground for believing it to be true, I find myself, with all respect, unable to agree that these are convertible expressions. To make a statement careless whether it be true or false, and therefore without any real belief in its truth, appears to me to be an essentially different thing from making, through want of care, a false statement, which is nevertheless honestly believed to be true. And it is surely conceivable that a man may believe that what he states is the fact, though he has been so wanting in care that the Court may think that there were no sufficient grounds to warrant his belief. I shall have to consider hereafter whether the want of reasonable ground for believing the statement made is sufficient to support an action of deceit. I am only concerned for the moment to point out that it does not follow that it is so, because there is authority for saying that a statement made recklessly, without caring whether it be true or false, affords sufficient foundation for such an action.

That the learned Lord Justice thought that if a false statement were made without reasonable ground for believing it to be true an action of deceit would lie, is clear from a subsequent passage in his judgment. He says that when statements are made in a prospectus like the present, to be circulated amongst persons in order to induce them to take shares, "there is a duty cast upon the director or other person who makes those statements to take care that there are no expressions in them which in fact are false; to take care that he has reasonable ground for the material statements which are contained in that document which he prepares and circulates for the very purpose of its being acted upon by others."

The learned judge proceeds to say: "Although in my opinion it is not necessary that there should be what I should call fraud, yet in these actions, according to my view of the law, there must be a departure from duty, that is to say, an untrue statement made without any reasonable ground for believing that statement to be true; and in my opinion when a man makes an untrue statement with an intention that it shall be acted upon without any reasonable ground for believing that statement to be true he makes a default in a duty which was thrown upon him from the position he has taken upon himself, and he violates the right which those to whom he makes the statement have to have true statements only made to them."

Now I have first to remark on these observations that the alleged "right" must surely be here stated too widely if it is intended to refer to a legal right, the violation of which may give rise to an action for damages. For if there be a right to have true statements only made, this will render liable to an action those who make untrue statements, however innocently. This cannot have been meant. I think it must have been intended to make the statement of the right correspond with that of the alleged duty, the departure from which is said to be making an untrue statement without any reasonable ground for believing it to be true. I have further to observe that the Lord Justice distinctly says that if there be such a departure from duty an action of deceit can be maintained, though there be not what he should call fraud. I shall have by-and-by to consider the discussions which have arisen as to the difference between the popular understanding of the word "fraud" and the interpretation given to it by lawyers, which have led to the use of such expressions as "legal fraud," or "fraud in law;" but I may state at once that, in my opinion, without proof of fraud no action of deceit is maintainable. When I examine the cases which have been decided upon this branch of the law, I shall endeavour to shew that there is abundant authority to warrant this proposition.

[Examination of cases omitted.]

In my opinion making a false statement through want of care falls far short of, and is a very different thing from, fraud, and the same may be said of a false representation honestly believed though on insufficient grounds. Indeed Cotton L.J. himself indicated, in the words I have already quoted, that he should not call it fraud. But the whole current of authorities, with which I have so long detained your Lordships, shews to my mind conclusively that fraud is essential to found an action of deceit, and that it cannot be maintained where the acts proved cannot properly be so termed. And the case of Taylor v. Ashton appears to me to be in direct conflict with the dictum of Sir George Jessel, and inconsistent with the view taken by the learned judges in the Court below. I observe that Sir Frederick Pollock, in his able work on Torts (p. 243, note), referring, I presume, to the dicta of Cotton L.J. and Sir George Jessel M.R., says that the actual decision in Taylor v. Ashton is not consistent with the modern cases on the duty of directors of companies. I think he is right. But for the reasons I have given I am unable to hold that anything less than fraud will render directors or any other persons liable to an action of deceit.

At the same time I desire to say distinctly that when a false statement has been made the questions whether there were reasonable grounds for believing it, and what were the means of knowledge in the possession of the person making it, are most weighty matters for consideration.

The ground upon which an alleged belief was founded is a most important test of its reality. I can conceive many cases where the fact that an alleged belief was destitute of all reasonable foundation would suffice of itself to convince the Court that it was not really entertained, and that the representation was a fraudulent one. So, too, although means of knowledge are, as was pointed out by Lord Blackburn in Brownlie v. Campbell a very different thing from knowledge, if I thought that a person making a false statement had shut his eyes to the facts, or purposely abstained from inquiring into them, I should hold that honest belief was absent, and that he was just as fraudulent as if he had knowingly stated that which was false.

I have arrived with some reluctance at the conclusion to which I have felt myself compelled, for I think those who put before the public a propectus to induce them to embark their money in a commercial enterprise ought to be vigilant to see that it contains such representations only as are in strict accordance with fact, and I should be very unwilling to give any countenance to the contrary idea. I think there is much to be said for the view that this moral duty ought to some extent to be converted into a legal obligation, and that the want of reasonable care to see that statements, made under such circumstances, are true, should be made an actionable wrong. But this is not a matter fit for discussion on the present occasion. If it is to be done the legislature must intervene and expressly give a right of action in respect of such a departure from duty. It ought not, I think, to be done by straining the law, and holding that to be fraudulent which the tribunal feels cannot properly be so described. I think mischief is likely to result from blurring the distinction between carelessness and fraud, and equally holding a man fraudulent whether his acts can or cannot be justly so designated.

It now remains for me to apply what I believe to be the law to the facts of the present case. The charge against the defendants is that they fraudulently represented that by the special Act of Parliament which the company had obtained they had a right to use steam or other mechanical power instead of horses. The test which I purpose employing is to inquire whether the defendants knowingly made a false statement in this respect, or whether, on the contrary, they honestly believed what they stated to be a true and fair representation of the facts.

. . .

I agree with the Court below that the statement made did not accurately convey to the mind of a person reading it what the rights of the company were, but to judge whether it may nevertheless have been put forward without subjecting the defendants to the imputation of fraud, your Lordships must consider what were the circumstances. By the General Tramways Act of 1870 it is provided that all carriages used on any tramway shall be moved by the power prescribed by the special Act, and where no such power is prescribed, by animal power only. In order, therefore, to enable the company to use steam-power, an Act of Parliament had to be obtained empowering its use. This had been done, but the power was clogged with the condition that it was only to be used with the consent of the Board of Trade. It was therefore incorrect to say that the company had the right to use steam; they would only have that right if they obtained the consent of the Board of Trade. But it is impossible not to see that the fact which would impress itself upon the minds of those connected with the company was that they had, after submitting the plans to the Board of Trade, obtained a special Act empowering the use of steam. It might well be that the fact that the consent of the Board of Trade was

necessary would not dwell in the same way upon their minds, if they thought that
the consent of the Board would be obtained as a matter of course if its
requirements were complied with, and that it was therefore a mere question of
expenditure and care. The provision might seem to them analogous to that
contained in the General Tramways Act, and I believe in the Railways Act also,
prohibiting the line being opened until it had been inspected by the Board of Trade
and certified fit for traffic, which no one would regard as a condition practically
limiting the right to use the line for the purpose of a tramway or railway. I do not
say that the two cases are strictly analogous in point of law, but they may well have
been thought so by business men.

I turn now to the evidence of the defendants. I will take first that of Mr. Wilde,
whose conduct in relation to the promotion of the company is free from suspicion.
He is a member of the Bar and a director of one of the London tramway
companies. He states that he was aware that the consent of the Board of Trade was
necessary, but that he thought that such consent had been practically given,
inasmuch as, pursuant to the Standing Orders, the plans had been laid before the
Board of Trade with the statement that it was intended to use mechanical as well
as horsepower, and no objection having been raised by the Board of Trade, and the
Bill obtained, he took it for granted that no objection would be raised afterwards,
provided the works were properly carried out. He considered, therefore, that,
practically and substantially they had the right to use steam, and that the
statement was perfectly true. [Lord Herschell reviewed the testimony of four other
defendants and found it to be of the same effect on the point in question.]

. . .

Stirling J. gave credit to these witnesses, and I see no reason to differ from him.
What conclusion ought to be drawn from their evidence? I think they were
mistaken in supposing that the consent of the Board of Trade would follow as a
matter of course because they had obtained their Act. It was absolutely in the
discretion of the Board whether such consent should be given. The prospectus was
therefore inaccurate. But that is not the question. If they believed that the consent
of the Board of Trade was practically concluded by the passing of the Act, has the
plaintiff made out, which it was for him to do, that they have been guilty of a
fraudulent misrepresentation? I think not. I cannot hold it proved as to any one of
them that he knowingly made a false statement, or one which he did not believe to
be true, or was careless whether what he stated was true or false. In short, I think
they honestly believed that what they asserted was true, and I am of opinion that
the charge of fraud made against them has not been established.

I quite admit that the statements of witnesses as to their belief are by no means
to be accepted blindfold. The probabilities must be considered. Whenever it is
necessary to arrive at a conclusion as to the state of mind of another person, and to
determine whether his belief under given circumstances was such as he alleges, we
can only do so by applying the standard of conduct which our own experience of the
ways of men has enabled us to form; by asking ourselves whether a reasonable
man would be likely under the circumstances so to believe. I have applied this test,
with the result that I have a strong conviction that a reasonable man situated as
the defendants were, with their knowledge and means of knowledge, might well
believe what they state they did believe, and consider that the representation made
was substantially true.

Adopting the language of Jessel M.R. in Smith v. Chadwick, I conclude by saying that on the whole I have come to the conclusion that the statement, "though in some respects inaccurate and not altogether free from imputation of carelessness, was a fair, honest and bona fide statement on the part of the defendants, and by no means exposes them to an action for deceit."

I think the judgment of the Court of Appeal should be reversed.

Order of the Court of Appeal reversed . . .

NOTES AND QUESTIONS

(1)   *Derry v. Peek* set out a state of mind required for deceit that is commonly referred to as scienter. In the second paragraph of his opinion, Lord Herschell quoted authority to the effect that misrepresentation of a kind less culpable than scienter might be the basis of a recission of contract. Why did the plaintiff not proceed along that line in *Derry v. Peek?*

Derry v. Peek hardened the law of torts into the mold that no duty is owed for mere negligent or innocent misrepresentations. Bit by bit this no-duty rule has eroded and many jurisdictions now permit negligence actions for negligent misrepresentation in limited circumstances. See § 5.05, supra. Before courts were willing to substitute negligence for scienter, some developed what might be referred to as special scienter, as illustrated in the statement below:

> The knowledge, by the maker of the representation, of its falsity, or, in technical phrase, the scienter, can be established by either one of the three following phrases of proof: (1) That the representation was made with actual knowledge of its falsity; (2) without knowledge either of its truth or falsity; (3) under circumstances in which the person making it ought to have known, if he did not know, of its falsity. Under the first phase the proof must show actual knowledge of the falsity of the representation. Under the second phase it should show that the representation was made in such absolute, unqualified, and positive terms as to imply that the party making it had knowledge of its truth, and that he made such absolute unqualified and positive assertion on a subject of which he was ignorant, and that he had no knowledge whether his assertion in reference thereto was true or false. Under the third phase the proof should show that the party occupied such a special situation or possessed such means of knowledge as made it his duty to know as to the truth or falsity of the representation made. If the proof establishes either one of these three phases, the scienter is sufficiently made out.

Joiner v. McCullers, 158 Fla. 562, 28 So.2d 823 (1947).

This statement has been cited as authority for the proposition that "[i]n this state, a negligent representation is considered tantamount to actionable fraud." *Ostreyko v. B.C. Morton Organization, Inc.*, 310 So.2d 316, 137 (Fla. App. 1975). Michigan is said to be the primary jurisdiction that permits an action for mere negligent misrepresentation. See *United States Fidelity and Guaranty Co. v. Black*, 313 N.W.2d 77 (Mi. 1981) (setting out elements of "minority" rule of "innocent" misrepresentation.) Most courts continue to require scienter. See, e.g., *Onita Pacifica Corporation v. Bronson*, 843 P.2d 890 (Or. 1992) (holding that economic losses arising from negligent misrepresentation in arms length negotiations are not actionable.)

(2)   Obtaining relief from contractual obligations because of misrepresentations typically is easier than obtaining damages, as is demonstrated by this summary:

> Even innocent misrepresentation may be grounds for recission of contract. According to the weight of authority, misrepresentation of material facts, although innocently made, if acted on by the other party to his detriment, will constitute a sufficient ground for recission and cancellation in equity. The real inquiry is not whether the party making the representation knew it to be false, but whether the other party believed it to be true and was misled by it in making the contract; and, whether the misrepresentation is made innocently or knowingly, the effect is the same. It is as conclusive a ground of relief in equity as a willful and false assertion, for it operates as a surprise and imposition on the other party; and in such case the party must be held to his representations.

96 Corpus Juris, § 23, p. 1169, quoted in *Langly v. Irons Land & Development Co.,* 114 So. 769, 771 (Fla. 1927).

(3)   Even in jurisdictions that permit a tort action for mere negligent misrepresentation, might there be some advantage to proceed in deceit? In *Ex Parte Smith,* 416 So.2d 1222 (Ala. 1982), a car dealer sold a car to the plaintiff knowing that the dealership could not deliver a good title. Might that be a ground for recission, apart from the law of torts? What more advantageous remedy might deceit supply? According to the Alabama court, at 1223:

The law should and does permit the imposition of punitive damages under these facts. It is true, as the Court of Civil Appeals correctly notes, that not all actionable wrongs permit the imposition of punitive damages. But some do. At 22 Am. Jur.2d Damages, § 249 (1965), the rule is summarized as follows:

> Exemplary damages, if recoverable at all, may be recovered only in cases where the wrongful act complained of is characterized by, or partakes of, some circumstances of aggravation, such as wilfulness, wantonness, maliciousness, gross negligence or recklessness, oppression, outrageous conduct, indignity and contumely, insult, or fraud or gross fraud. . . .

> One or more of the conditions under which exemplary damages are recoverable is sufficient. For example, if the act is done with a fraudulent, malicious, or oppressive motive on the part of the wrongdoer, there is ground for exemplary damages, although the act is done without rudeness or insult. Exemplary damages may be also recovered, although there is no malice, fraud, or intent to oppress on the part of the wrongdoer, if the act is done in a rude, insulting, or reckless manner, in disregard of social obligations, or with such gross negligence as to amount to positive misconduct.

> The elements are disjunctive. One need not prove each of them, but must prove at least one of them, to justify an award of punitive damages. Thus, the question is: Has any one of the foregoing been proved by the plaintiff in this case? Clearly so. It has been proved without contradiction that Big Three willfully and intentionally represented that it owned the car when it knew that it did not own the car. It represented that it had good title when,

in fact, the car was encumbered by a prior lien. Ala. Code 1975, § 6-5-103. This we think is enough to meet the burden which the law casts on a plaintiff seeking exemplary damages.

. . .

. . .[I]f the misrepresentation is shown to have been made knowing that it is false then the law permits punitive damages by way of punishment. Without knowledge of its falseness, the law allows only compensatory damages (Ala. Code 1975, § 6-5-101), unless the misrepresentation is made so recklessly and heedlessly as to amount to the same thing as knowledge of its falseness.

[D]   Probable Cause

COBLYN v. KENNEDY'S, INC.
Massachusetts Supreme Judicial Court
359 Mass. 319, 268 N.E.2d 860 (1971)

SPIEGEL, JUSTICE.

This is an action of tort for false imprisonment. At the close of the evidence the defendants filed a motion for directed verdicts which was denied. The jury returned verdicts for the plaintiff in the sum of $12,500. The case is here on the defendants' exceptions to the denial of their motion and to the refusal of the trial judge to give certain requested instructions to the jury.

We state the pertinent evidence most favorable to the plaintiff. On March 5, 1965, the plaintiff went to Kennedy's Inc. (Kennedy's), a store in Boston. He was seventy years of age and about five feet four inches in height. He was wearing a wollen shirt, which was "open at the neck," a topcoat and a hat. "[A]round his neck" he wore an ascot which he had "purchased . . . previously at Filenes." He proceeded to the second floor of Kennedy's to purchase a sport coat. He removed his hat, topcoat and ascot, putting the ascot in his pocket. After purchasing a sport coat and leaving it for alterations, he put on his hat and coat and walked downstairs. Just prior to exiting through the outside door of the store, he stopped, took the ascot out of his pocket, put it around his neck, and knotted it. The knot was visible "above the lapels of his shirt." The only stop that the plaintiff made on the first floor was immediately in front of the exit in order to put on his ascot.

Just as the plaintiff stepped out of the door, the defendant Goss, an employee, "loomed up" in front of him with his hand up and said: "Stop. Where did you get that scarf?" The plaintiff responded, "[W]hy?" Goss firmly grasped the plaintiff's arm and said: "[Y]ou better go back and see the manager." Another employee was standing next to him. Eight or ten other people were standing around and were staring at the plaintiff. The plaintiff then said, "Yes, I'll go back in the store" and proceeded to do so. As he and Goss went upstairs to the second floor, the plaintiff paused twice because of chest and back pains. After reaching the second floor, the salesman from whom he had purchased the coat recognized him and asked what the trouble was.

The plaintiff then asked: "[W]hy 'these two gentlemen stop me?'" "The salesman confirmed that the plaintiff had purchased a sport coat and that the ascot belonged to him.

The salesman became alarmed by the plaintiff's appearance and the store nurse was called. She brought the plaintiff into the nurse's room and gave him a soda mint tablet. As a direct result of the emotional upset caused by the incident, the plaintiff was hospitalized and treated for a "myocardial infarct."

Initially, the defendants contend that as a matter of law the plaintiff was not falsely imprisoned. They argue that no unlawful restraint was imposed by either force or threat upon the plaintiff's freedom of movement. Wax v. McGrath, 255 Mass. 340, 342, 151 N.E. 317. However, "[t]he law is well settled that '[a]ny genuine restraint is sufficient to constitute an imprisonment, . . . and '[a]ny demonstration of physical power which, to all appearances, can be avoided only by submission, operates as effectually to constitute an imprisonment, if submitted to, as if any amount of force had been exercised.' 'If a man is restrained of his personal liberty by fear of a personal difficulty, that amounts to a false imprisonment' within the legal meaning of such term." Jacques v. Childs Dining Hall Co., 244 Mass. 438, 438-439, 138 N.E. 843.

We think it is clear that there was sufficient evidence of unlawful restraint to submit this question to the jury. Just as the plaintiff had stepped out of the door of the store, the defendant Goss stopped him, firmly grasped his arm and told him that he had "better go back and see the manager." There was another employee at his side. The plaintiff was an elderly man and there were other people standing around staring at him. Considering the plaintiff's age and his heart condition, it is hardly to be expected that with one employee in front of him firmly grasping his arm and another at his side the plaintiff could do other than comply with Goss's "request" that he go back and see the manager. The physical restraint imposed upon the plaintiff when Goss grasped the plaintiff's arm readily distinguishes this case from Sweeney v. F. W. Woolworth Co., 247 Mass, 277, 142 N.E. 50, relied upon by the defendants.

In addition, as this court observed in the Jacques case, supra, at p. 441, 138 N.E. at p. 844, the "honesty and veracity [of the plaintiff] had been openly . . . challenged. If she had gone out before . . . [exonerating herself], her departure well might have been interpreted by the lookers on as an admission of guilt, or of circumstances from which guilt might be inferred. The situation was in the control of the defendant. The restraint or duress imposed by the mode of investigation . . . the jury could say was for the accomplishment of the defendant's purpose, even if no threats of public exposure or of arrest were made, and no physical restraint of . . . [the plaintiff] was attempted." . . .

The defendants next contend that the detention of the plaintiff was sanctioned by G.L. c. 231, § 94B, inserted by St.1958, c. 337. This statute provides as follows: "In an action for false arrest or false imprisonment brought by any person by reason of having been detained for questioning on or in the immediate vicinity of the premises of a merchant, if such person was detained in a reasonable manner and for not more than a reasonable length of time by a person authorized to make arrests or by the merchant or his agent or servant authorized for such purpose and if there were reasonable grounds to believe that the person so detained was committing or attempting to commit larceny of goods for sale on such premises, it shall be a defence to such action. If such goods had not been purchased and were concealed on or amongst the belongings of a person so detained it shall be presumed that there were reasonable grounds for such belief."

The defendants argue in accordance with the conditions imposed in the statute that the plaintiff was detained in a reasonable manner for a reasonable length of time and that Goss had reasonable grounds for believing that the plaintiff was attempting to commit larceny of goods held for sale.

It is conceded that the detention was for a reasonable length of time. See Proulx v. Pinkerton's Natl. Detective Agency, Inc., 343 Mass. 390, 392-393, 178 N.E.2d 575. We need not decide whether the detention was effected in a reasonable manner for we are of opinion that there were no reasonable grounds for believing that the plaintiff was committing larceny and, therefore, he should not have been detained at all. However, we observe that Goss's failure to identify himself as an employee of Kennedy's and to disclose the reasons for his inquiry and actions, coupled with the physical restraint in a public place imposed upon the plaintiff, an elderly man who had exhibited no aggressive intention to depart, could be said to constitute an unreasonable method by which to effect detention.. . .

The pivotal question before us as in most cases of this character is whether the evidence shows that there were reasonable grounds for the detention. At common law in an action for false imprisonment, the defence of probable cause, as measured by the prudent and cautious man standard, was available to a merchant. Standish v. Narragansett S.S. Co., 111 Mass. 512, 517. Jacques v. Childs Dining Hall Co., 244 Mass. 438, 439, 138 N.E. 843, Muniz v. Mehlman, 327 Mass. 353, 358, 99 N.E.2d 37. In enacting G.L. c. 231, § 94B, the Legislature inserted the words, "reasonable grounds." Historically, the words "reasonable grounds" and "probable cause" have been given the same meaning by the courts. In the case of United States v. Walker, 7 Cir., 246 F.2d 519, 526, it was said: "'Probable cause' and 'reasonable grounds' are concepts having virtually the same meaning." The following cases have expressly stated that the words may be used interchangeably and without distinction .. . .

In the case of Lukas v. J.C. Penney Co., . . . at p. 361, 378 P.2d 717, the Oregon Supreme court construed the meaning of the words "reasonable grounds" in its "shoplifting statute" as having the same meaning as they have in a statute authorizing arrest without a warrant and applied the probable cause standard to the facts before it.

The defendants assert that the judge improperly instructed the jury in stating that "grounds are reasonable when there is a basis which would appear to the reasonably prudent, cautious, intelligent person." In their brief, they argue that the "prudent and cautious man rule" is an objective standard and requires a more rigorous and restrictive standard of conduct than is contemplated by G.L. c. 231, § 94B. The defendants' requests for instructions, in effect, state that the proper test is a subjective one, viz., whether the defendant Goss had an honest and strong suspicion that the plaintiff was committing or attempting to commit larceny.[7]

---

[7] The bill of exceptions recites that "[t]he defendants duly excepted to the failure of the Court to give their requested instructions 1, 2 and 3." These requests are as follows: "1. If the defendant Goss had a belief to the extent of an honest and strong suspicion that the plaintiff had committed larceny or was attempting to commit larceny of goods for sale on Kennedy's premises, the jury should find that he acted reasonably . . . 2. If the jury find the ascot . . . was concealed on or amongst the belongings of the plaintiff, they must find that the defendants had reasonable grounds to believe that larceny had been attempted or committed. 3. If the jury find that the defendant Goss reasonably suspected the plaintiff

. . .

We do not agree. As we have attempted to show, the words "reasonable grounds" and "probable cause" have traditionally been accorded the same meaning.

If we adopt the subjective test as suggested by the defendants, the individual's right to liberty and freedom of movement would become subject to the "honest . . . suspicion" of a shopkeeper based on his own "inarticulate hunches" without regard to any discernible facts. In effect, the result would be to afford the merchant even greater authority than that given to a police officer. In view of the well established meaning of the words "reasonable grounds" we believe that the Legislature intended to give these words their traditional meaning. This seems to us a valid conclusion since the Legislature has permitted an individual to be detained for a "reasonable length of time."

. . .

We also note that an objective standard is the criterion for determining probable cause or reasonable grounds in malicious prosecution and false arrest cases. Bacon v. Towne, 4 Cush. 217, 238-239. Wax v. McGrath, 255 Mass. 340, 343, 151 N.E.317. We see no valid reason to depart from this precedent in regard to cases involving false imprisonment.

Applying the standard of reasonable grounds as measured by the reasonably prudent man test[8] to the evidence in the instant case, we are of opinion that the evidence warranted the conclusion that Goss was not reasonably justified in believing that the plaintiff was engaged in shoplifting. There was no error in denying the motion for directed verdicts and in the refusal to give the requested instructions.

Exceptions overruled.

NOTES AND QUESTIONS

(1) Is this formulation consistent with *Coblyn*?

> "Probable cause" as the term is employed in actions for malicious prosecution, is such a state of facts in the mind of the prosecutor as would lead a man of ordinary caution and prudence to believe or entertain an honest and strong suspicion that the person is guilty.

Birwood Paper Co. v. Damsky, 229 So.2d 521 (Ala. 1969).

(2) Does it appear to you that merchants are at a considerable disadvantage in attempting to control shoplifting? Is the probable cause requirement so stringent

---

of theft or failing to pay for goods belonging to Kennedy's, they must return verdicts for the defendants on all counts."

The defendant's brief refers only to request No. 1 although their argument appears to touch on the periphery of the remaining two requests.

[8] . . .

We also note here that the defendants incorrectly rely on certain language in the case of Pihl v. Morris, 319 Mass, 577, 580, 66 N.E.2d 804, 806 to support their argument that only "an honest and strong suspicion" is needed rather than "reasonable grounds." That case states that "an honest and strong suspicion" is a necessary part of probable cause (emphasis supplied).

that many shoplifters will be successful because merchants are fearful of making a mistake in challenging a suspected person? Many legislatures have thought so and have enacted statutes that provide additional protection. Although there is no standard enactment, the Massachusetts statute in *Coblyn* and the Montana statute below illustrate the elements commonly included in them:

Montana Code Annotated:

46-6-502. Arrest by private person

(1) A private person may arrest another when there is probable cause to believe that the person is committing or has committed an offense and the existing circumstances require the person's immediate arrest.

(2) A private person making an arrest shall immediately notify the nearest available law enforcement agency or peace officer and give custody of the person arrested to the officer or agency.

46-6-506. Temporary detention by merchant — liability

(1) A merchant, as defined in 30-11-301, who has reason to believe that a person has committed or is in the process of committing the offense of theft may stop and temporarily detain that person. The merchant:

(a) shall promptly inform the person that the stop is for investigation of shoplifting and that upon completion of the investigation, the person will be released or turned over to the custody of a peace officer;

(b) may demand the person's name and present or last address and question the person in a reasonable manner for the purpose of ascertaining whether or not the person is guilty of shoplifting;

(c) may take into possession any merchandise for which the purchase price has not been paid and that is in the possession of the person or has been concealed from full view; and

(d) may detain the person or request the person to remain on the premises until a peace officer arrives.

(2) A stop, detention, questioning, or recovery of merchandise under this section must be done in a reasonable manner and time. Unless evidence of concealment is obvious and apparent to the merchant, this section does not authorize a search of the detained person other than a search of the person's coat or other outer garments and any package, bag, or other container. After the purpose of a stop has been accomplished or 30 minutes have elapsed, whichever occurs first, the merchant shall allow the person to go unless the person is arrested and turned over to the custody of a peace officer.

(3) A merchant stopping, detaining, or arresting a person on the belief that the person is shoplifting is not liable for damages to the person unless the merchant acts in a manner contrary to this section.

(2) Any stop, detention, questioning, or recovery of merchandise under 46-6-502(3) and this section shall be done in a reasonable manner and time. Unless evidence of concealment is obvious and apparent to the merchant, 46-6-502 and this section shall not authorize a search of his coat or other outer garments and any package, briefcase, or other container, unless the search is done by a peace officer

under proper legal authority. After the purpose of a stop has been accomplished or 30 minutes have elapsed, whichever occurs first, the merchant shall allow the person to go unless the person is arrested and turned over to the custody of a police officer.

(3)   Such stop and temporary detention, with or without questioning or removal of merchandise, when done by a merchant in compliance with the law, shall not constitute an unlawful arrest or search. A merchant stopping, detaining, or arresting a person on the belief that such person is shoplifting is not liable for damages to such person unless the merchant acts with malice, either actual or implied, or contrary to the provisions of this law.

(3)   In *Duran v. Buttrey Food, Inc.*, 616 P.2d 327 (Mont. 1980) the Montana Supreme Court invalidated the statutory grant of a 30-minute restraining period without an arrest on grounds that the provision violated Art. II, § 10, 1972 Mont. Const. as follows:

The right of individual privacy is essential to the well-being of a free society and shall not be infringed without the showing of a compelling state interest.

The court held:

> We fail to discern a compelling state interest which would justify the very serious invasion of a person's privacy which occurs when she is publicly stopped and detained for up to thirty minutes by private individuals who search her purse and cause her great indignity and embarrassment, all under the immunity ostensibly granted by Section 46-6-503, MCA. While it is true that merchants and their employees as private individuals have a right to defend their property, that right does not amount to a compelling state interest which would justify allowing the merchant or his employee to invade the privacy of another individual to the extent permitted under Section 46-6-503, MCA. Therefore, insofar as it permits a merchant with immunity to stop and temporarily detain an individual suspected of shoplifting for up to thirty minutes without making an arrest, we hold Section 46-6-503, MCA, unconstitutional as an invasion of the right to privacy guaranteed by 1972 Mont. Const. Art. II, § 10, as it applies in this case.

616 P.2d at 333. What protection for merchants remains under the statute?

(4)   Is "probable cause" a question of fact or a question of law? As noted earlier, at least since *Mitchell v. Jenkins*, 5 B & AD 588, 110 Eng. Rep. 908 (1833), was decided, most, if not all courts have held that the "probable cause" element of the malicious prosecution prima facie case is a question of law to be determined by the judge. When the facts are in dispute, the issue would ordinarily be submitted to the jury as a mixed question of fact and law. By contrast, the "malice" element would ordinarily be considered to be a fact question for the jury.

(5)   Courts use the terms "false arrest" and "false imprisonment" interchangeably. As stated in *Kraft v. City of Bettendorf*, 359 N.W.2d 466, 469 (Ia. 1984), "False arrest is indistinguishable from false imprisonment." § 12.03 supra. See, e.g. *Cleveland, C., C. & St. L. Ry. v. Dixon*, 51 Ind. App. 658, 96 N.E. 815 (1911).

§ 12.04   MENTAL STATE OF THE PLAINTIFF

[A]   Unconsented to Touchings

McDONALD v. FORD

Florida District Court of Appeal

223 So. 2d 553 (1969)

HOBSON, ACTING CHIEF JUSTICE.

Plaintiff-appellant, Marie McDonald, appeals a final judgment entered pursuant to the trial court's granting of defendant-appellee's motion for directed verdict.

This appeal involves an action for personal injuries received by Marie McDonald which she alleged was caused by the negligent conduct of Mr. Ford, the defendant-appellee herein, while she was a social guest in his home and while he attempted to make love to her.

The incident complained of occurred in the early morning hours of April 26, 1965, in a home owned by the defendant. Prior to this date, plaintiff and defendant had seen each other socially and on occasion even contemplated getting married. They had spent the evening prior to the incident in question together, during which time defendant consumed several alcoholic drinks. In the early morning hours which followed the two of them went to defendant's home where plaintiff agreed to prepare coffee for them. While the coffee was heating, plaintiff went into the living-room where she knelt before a stereo set sorting through some records which were stacked on the floor. Defendant had gone to another part of the house to remove his overcoat and tie. While plaintiff was still looking through the records, defendant came up behind her, laughingly embraced her, and though she resisted, kissed her hard. As defendant was hurting plaintiff physically by his embrace, plaintiff continued to struggle violently and defendant continued to laugh and pursue his love-making attempts. In the process plaintiff struck her face hard upon an object that she is unable to specifically identify and in so doing injured her jaw. When she was able to break away, she grabbed her purse, left his house and went home.

At the close of plaintiff's case the defendant moved for a directed verdict on the ground that plaintiff's proof conclusively showed a battery had been committed and that this showing precluded submission of the case to the jury on the issue of negligence as charged in the complaint.

The lower court in granting the motion for a directed verdict in favor of the defendant stated:

THE COURT: It's my finding in this case that I'm going to grant this motion for a directed verdict. I feel that if this case has any basis in fact, it is in the basis of an intentional tort, due to the testimony of the plaintiff in this case, and that there is nothing to submit this case to the jury on the negligence count.

At trial, Marie McDonald's testimony on the issue of the negligence of Mr. Ford was as follows:

So I knelt on the floor, and I was picking out one more record to put on, when Mr. Ford came back into the room, and I didn't pay any attention at first, because

I was trying to pick out a record, till I heard him laugh, and he grabbed a hold of me and he crushed me so hard — he's so strong and big, and — and I'm not so big, and I tried to push away from him, and the harder I struggled to get away from him, trying to tell him that he was hurting me, the harder he pushed me to him, and he kissed me real hard. He came down on me so hard, and, of course, I was struggling. We were bending and twisting, and something banged me awfully hard on my face, and as soon as I could get free, I grabbed my pocketbook and left.

Q. Mrs. McDonald, he was in fact hurting you as he squeezed you?

A. Yes, sir.

Q. And you say that you tried to pull away when he was squeezing you there?

A. Yes, I tried to push away, and the harder I tried to push, the more he tried to get hold of me, the more he tried to kiss me, and we were bending and twisting and turning around, and I was pushing and shoving, and he was so strong, and I just — I don't know what happened, but I was just — he was too strong on me, you know, I just — you just — I was just banged and bumped all over, but my face was just — just hurt terribly.

Q. This happened while he was trying to kiss you and you were trying to get away?

A. Yes, sir.

On cross examination, Marie McDonald testified as follows:

A. — Mr. Ford came into the room while I was kneeling down, and I didn't pay much attention, you know, he just walked in, was off to the side of me here, and I heard a noise behind me, and I sort of half got up to look around. He was laughing and he grabbed a-hold of me, and he just crushed me when he grabbed a hold of me.

Q. What did you say when he grabbed hold of you?

A. Well, I tried to push away, you know, I tried to say, "Let go of me." I suppose I said that, and he just brought his mouth down real hard on my face and kissed me, and the harder I struggled to get away, the harder he held me, and he's extremely strong, and the more I pushed and bended and twisted to get away from him, the more he kept pulling me toward him and crushing me against him, and we struggled and struggled, and I got bumped and — until I could get away from him.

Q. While you were struggling, were you knocked to the floor at any time?

A. I was bent over, and we were struggling so hard, I don't know whether I was knocked to the floor or whether —

Q. You say you were bent over this way struggling?

A. Yes, we were struggling.

Q. And where was he, in back of you or in front of you at this time?

A. Well, he had got to one side, and I twisted to one side, and I don't know whether my jaw could have hit on his knee or his elbow or the side of the stereo. It was a fierce struggle. I was trying to get away from him. He didn't realize that he was crushing me so hard. He was laughing and I was struggling to get away from him.

In view of the above testimony, it is clear that what actually occurred here was an assault and battery. The initial stages of this incident did not constitute assault and battery as "an assault is an intentional, unlawful offer of corporal injury to another by force, or force unlawfully directed toward the person of another, under such circumstances as to create a fear of imminent peril, coupled with the apparent present ability to effectuate the attempt. The essential element of an assault is the violence offered, and not actual physical contact," and "a battery is defined as an unlawful touching or striking or the use of force against the person of another with the intention of bringing about a harmful or offensive contact or apprehension thereof. The degree of force used is immaterial, except upon the question of damages." 3 Fla. Jr., Assault and Battery, § 3.

Dean Prosser has further described an action for battery in the following terms (Prosser, Law of Torts, 35 [3d ed. 1964]):

The gist of the action for battery is not the hostile intent of the defendant, but rather the absence of consent to the contact on the part of the plaintiff.

Specifically, and more helpful with regard to the instant case, Prosser asserts that the defendant may be liable for battery "where an unappreciative woman is kissed without her consent." And, further, Prosser recognizes that:

Taking indecent liberties with a woman without her consent is of course a battery.

In the latter stages of this incident when plaintiff tried to free herself and get away, the conduct on defendant's part, by definition, became assault and battery.

The parties have not cited, nor has our research disclosed any Florida case directly on point. However, the Court of Appeals of Ohio in Williams v. Pressman, 113 N.E. 2d 395 (Ohio App. 1953) held at page 396:

. . . An assault and battery is not negligence for such action is intentional, while negligence connotes an unintentional act.

As plaintiff sued on a negligence theory, the lower court must be and hereby is Affirmed.

NOTES AND QUESTIONS

Suppose Marie McDonald had succumbed without struggle to the amorous offerings of her pursuer and suppose further that a statute created a felonious crime of statutory rape, defined as the act of sexual intercourse with a female of age less than 16 years. Should the existence of that statute affect whether or not Marie, who was 15 years old, would have a valid cause of action in battery against the defendant? What public policies come into conflict in resolving that issue? See *Barton v. BeeLine, Inc.*, 265 N.Y.S. 284 (1933), and Restatement, Torts, Second § 829.

WILKINSON v. VESEY
Supreme Court of Rhode Island
110 R.I. 1606, 295 A.2d 676 (1972)

KELLEHER, JUSTICE.

These are medical malpractice actions brought by a husband and wife against the defendant physicians each of whom has specialized in the field of diagnostic and therapeutic radiology. The wife is the victim of the alleged malpractice. The husband has sued for consequential damages. A jury trial was held in the Superior Court. At the end of eight days of testimony, the plaintiffs concluded their case. At that juncture, the trial justice first refused them permission to amend their complaints and then granted the defendants' motion for a directed verdict. The plaintiffs seek a reversal of each of these adverse decisions.

. . .

[The wife suffered grievous injury from certain radiation treatments administered to her. Portions of the opinion dealing with erroneous diagnosis are omitted.]

The Failure to Disclose the Possible Risks Involved in the Treatment Prescribed

One-half century ago, Justice Cardozo, in the oft-cited case of Schloendorff v. Society of New York Hospital, 211 N.Y. 125, 105 N.E. 92 (1914), made the following observation:

Every human being of adult years and sound mind has a right to determine what shall be done with his own body; and a surgeon who performs an operation without his patient's consent, commits an assault, for which he is liable in damages. (cites omitted) This is true except in case of emergency where the patient is unconscious and where it is necessary to operate before consent can be obtained. Id. at 129-130, 105 N.E. at 93.

We adhered to this principle in Nolan v. Kechijian, supra, where we said a surgeon could be liable in an action of trespass for the unauthorized removal of a patient's spleen where the evidence showed that the consent given was limited to surgery which was designed to strengthen the ligaments supporting the spleen.

Shortly after the Schloendorff case, there began to appear on the judicial scene a doctrine wherein courts with increasing frequency began to rule that a patient's consent to a proposed course of treatment was valid only to the extent he had been informed by the physician as to what was to be done, the risk involved and the alternatives to the contemplated treatment. This theory, which today is known as the doctrine of informed consent, imposes a duty upon a doctor which is completely separate and distinct from his responsibility to skillfully diagnose and treat the patient's ills.

The trial justice recognized the concept of informed consent but ruled it was inapplicable to the case at bar.

There is no unanimity as to the theory of recovery which a plaintiff must adopt when his suit alleges a failure by a physician to adequately disclose the risks and alternatives of a proposed diagnostic, therapeutic or surgical procedure. Some courts have held that any treatment or procedure given without informing the patient of its inherent risks vitiates the consent and allows suit based upon the theory that a battery has been committed. The prevailing view, however, classifies the physician's duty in this regard as a question of negligence because of the absence of the elements of any willful intent by the physician to injure his patient. . . . We think that where the lack of informed consent is alleged, the battery concept should not be recognized. Recovery under the battery theory will be allowed only where the procedure is completely unauthorized. Where, as here, the procedure is authorized but the patient claims a failure to disclose the risks involved to a course of therapy, the claim sounds in negligence.

Likewise, there is a divergence of opinion as to the necessity for and the use of expert testimony in determining the scope of the physician's duty to warn or inform his patient of the risks inherent in any proposed course of therapy or surgery. Most jurisdictions treat informed consent in the same manner as medical malpractice. As a result, plaintiff is required to establish (1) by expert medical testimony what a reasonable practitioner, under the same or similar circumstances, would have disclosed to his patient concerning risks incident to a proposed procedure; and (2) that the physician has deviated from this standard to the injury of the plaintiff. Proof of these two elements is required in instances where there has been a partial disclosure as well as in instances of no disclosure. The trial justice, in granting a direction on the informed consent count, pointed to the lack of expert testimony.

The plaintiff recognizes the majority view but asks that we adopt a modified version of the majority view as expressed in Natanson v. Kline, supra.

In that case, the plaintiff brought suit to recover damages which she allegedly suffered as the result of her receiving radiation therapy using radioactive cobalt. One of the grounds for her charges of negligence was the defendant's failure to warn the plaintiff that the proposed course of treatment involved grave consequences, including the risk of bodily injury or even death.

As explicated in Collins v. Meeker, 198 Kan. 390, 424 P.2d 488 (1967), the Natanson rule provides that, in absence of an emergency, a physician has an obligation to make a reasonable explanation and disclosure to his patient of the risks and hazards involved in a proposed course of treatment to the end that whatever consent given by the patient to the prescribed treatment may be an informed and intelligent consent, that where a physician is silent and makes no disclosure whatever, he has failed in the duty owed to the patient and the patient is not required to produce expert testimony to show that the doctor's failure was contrary to accepted medical practice but rather than it devolves upon the doctor to establish that his failure to make any disclosure did in fact conform under the existing conditions to accepted medical standards; and that where actual disclosures have been made and are ascertainable, the patient then must produce expert medical testimony to establish that the disclosures made were not in accord with those which reasonable medical practitioners would have divulged under the same or like circumstances.

While there may be strength in numbers as one views the many courts which require expert testimony as to the community standard of revelation by one seeking to recover on the basis of informed consent, we shall go one step beyond Natanson and join hands with Canterbury v. Spence, 464 F.2d 772 (D.C. Cir. 1972), where the Circuit Court of Appeals ruled that there was no necessity for expert testimony since the jury could determine, without recourse to a showing by the plaintiff of what the medical fraternity in the community tells its patients, the reasonableness or unreasonableness of the extent of a physician's communication with a patient. Our reasoning, however, may be somewhat different than that of the court in Canterbury.

The requirement that a patient obtain an expert to evaluate the disclosures made in the light of the prevailing practice in the locality undermines the very basis of the informed consent theory — the patient's right to be the final judge to do with his body as he wills. Blind adherence to local practice is completely at odds with the undisputed right of the patient to receive information which will enable him to make a choice — either to take his chances with the treatment or operation recommended by the doctor or to risk living without it. As will be noted later, the patient is entitled to receive material information upon which he can base an informed consent. The decision as to what is or is not material is a human judgment in our opinion, which does not necessarily require the assistance of the medical profession. The patients' right to make up his mind should not be delegated to a local medical group — many of whom have no idea as to his informational needs. The doctor-patient relationship is a one-on-one affair. What is a reasonable disclosure in one instance may not be reasonable in another. This variability negates the need of the plaintiff showing what other doctors may tell other patients.

The jury can decide if the doctor has disclosed enough information to enable the patient to make an intelligent choice without the necessity of the plaintiff's expert. The plaintiff, of course, must present evidence as to the undisclosed facts and their materiality. If the jury finds the undisclosed information immaterial, the doctor has acted reasonably in withholding it. If it finds the nondisclosure is material, the doctor may have acted unreasonably and will be held liable for his failure to obtain the patient's informed consent.

By our absolving the patient of the need to present medical testimony reflecting a community standard of disclosure, we do not mean to prevent the physician from introducing evidence of such a standard, if one exists, nor does it eliminate the need for a witness with the proper expertise whose testimony will establish the known risks involved in the procedure in controversy. Mason v. Ellsworth, supra.

In stressing the patient's right to make a choice, we are aware that a patient may hear solely what he wants to hear, or be completely inattentive to what he is being told or after an adverse result forget what he was told. Such matters are issues of credibility to be resolved by the trier of fact. Mason v. Ellsworth, supra. We have every confidence that a juror will adhere to his oath and "give a true verdict . . . according to law and the evidence given you."

. . .

Having established defendants' duty to disclose we will now delineate the extent of the disclosure which should be made. Obviously there is no need to disclose risks that are likely to be known by the average patient or that are in fact known to the patient usually because of a past experience with the procedure in question. . . . It is not necessary that a physician tell the patient any and all of the possible risks and dangers of a proposed procedure. Getchell v. Mansfield, Or. 439 P.2d 953 (1971). As we noted earlier, materiality is to be the guide. It is our belief that, in due deference to the patient's right to self determination, a physician is bound to disclose all the known material risks peculiar to the proposed procedure. Materiality may be said to be the significance a reasonable person, in what the physician knows or should know is his patient's position, would attach to the disclosed risk or risks in deciding whether to submit or not to submit to surgery or treatment. Waltz and Scheuneman, Informed Consent to Therapy, 64 Nw. U.L.Rev. 628, 640 (1970). Among the factors which point to the dangerousness of a medical technique are the severity of the risk and the likelihood of its occurrence. A very small chance of death or serious disablement may well be significant; a potential disability which dramatically outweighs the potential benefit of therapy or the detriments of the existing malady may require appropriate discussions with the patient. Canterbury v. Spence, supra. A physician's liability in this area is to be judged on the basis of what he told the patient before treatment began. Liability should be imposed only if the trier of fact finds the physician's communication to be unreasonably inadequate. Canterbury v. Spence, supra. The imposition of a duty of making disclosure is tempered by the recognition that there may be a situation where a disclosure should not be made because it would unduly agitate or undermine an unstable patient. . . .

There was evidence in the record as to the risk involved in a nonnegligent administration of the radiation therapy. When Dr. Hunt was on the witness stand, he was asked whether, if no deviation had been taken from the procedures he had described, the treatment would have produced the result that it did. His first reply was, "I can't say that." Later, in reply to another question, he said that the treatment as described was "not expected" to produce the result experienced by Winifred. His answers, which are at odds with his later testimony that the treatment, if properly given, would cause no harm, are susceptible to the inference that the damage caused to Winifred's chest area was a known possible risk even if the procedures were followed to the letter. In order to prevail in an action, where recovery is based upon the doctrine of informed consent, the plaintiff must prove that if he had been informed of the material risk, he would not have consented to the procedure and that he had been injured as a result of submitting to the procedure. . . . It is obvious from the record that Winifred was prepared to offer evidence that she would have refused to undergo the proposed therapy had she been properly informed.

Since this is the first time that we have considered the doctrine of informed consent, it is fitting that we conclude this phase of the present appeal by quoting the following exhortation found in Morris and Moritz, Doctor and Patient and The Law (5th ed. 1971):

Accordingly, prudent advice to the doctor would seem to be as follows: All medical procedures have risks (the patient not allergic to penicillin yesterday may be violently so today); the greater the risk, the greater the duty to inform. Rule of thumb: unless therapeutic reasons contraindicate, make a simple, quiet, but honest disclosure commensurate with the risk in all cases and let the patient choose what risks he wishes to run with his body. . . .

Besides being good medicine, good humanity, good public relations, and good medico-legal defense, the preceding advice has a therapeutic value all its own. The informed and consenting patient, aware of the risk, is not so shocked should the risk turn up in his case and, if patient-physician rapport is high, is much less likely to sue his doctor in the first instance.

The text to which we have just referred can be found in the library of the Rhode Island Medical Society. One of its authors is an attorney and the other, Dr. Allen R. Moritz, is a physician who has specialized in pathology. We have cited this work to emphasize the thought shared by many that "more communication" between doctor and patient means "less litigation" between patient and doctor.

There was error in directing the verdict on the issue of the lack of Winifred's informed consent.

[B]   Apprehension of Battery

STEPHENS v. MYERS
[1830] 4 Car. & P. 350, 172 Eng. Rep. 73[9]

It appeared, that the plaintiff was acting as chairman, at a parish meeting, and at the head of a table, at which table the defendant also sat, there being about six or seven persons between him and the plaintiff. The defendant having, in the course of some angry discussion, which took place, been very vociferous, and interrupted the proceedings of the meeting, a motion was made, that he should be turned out, which was carried by a very large majority. Upon this, the defendant said, he would rather pull the chairman out of the chair, than be turned out of the room; and immediately advanced with his fist clenched toward the chairman, but was stopped by the churchwarden, who sat next but one to the chairman, at a time when he was not near enough for any blow he might have meditated to have reached the chairman; but the witnesses said, that it seemed to them that he was advancing with an intention to strike the chairman.

Spankie, Serjt., for the defendant, upon this evidence, contended, that no assault had been committed, as there was no power in the defendant, from the situation of the parties, to execute his threat — there was not a present ability — he had not the means of executing his intention at the time he was stopt.

Tindal, C.J., in his summing up, said — It is not every threat, when there is no actual personal violence, that constitutes an assault, there must, in all cases, be the means of carrying the threat into effect. The question I shall leave to you will be, whether the defendant was advancing at the time, in a threatening attitude, to strike the chairman, so that his blow would almost immediately have reached the chairman, if he had not been stopt; then, though he was not near enough at the time to have struck him, yet if he was advancing with that intent, I think it amounts to an assault in law. If he was so advancing, that, within a second or two of time, he would have reached the plaintiff, it seems to me it is an assault in law. If you think he was not advancing to strike the plaintiff, then only can you find your verdict for the defendant; otherwise you must find it for the plaintiff, and give him such damages as you think the nature of the case requires.

Verdict of the plaintiff — Damages Is.

----

[9] [Ed. — English Reports, general reporter of older English cases, Nisi Prius decision; Carlington and Payne's reports.]

NOTES AND QUESTIONS

A and B have a furious argument over a debt. Finally, A says to B, "You've cheated and coerced people weaker than you all your lousy life. If you weren't so old and weak, I'd smash your evil face to a bloody pulp with these hard but honest hands of mine!" Is it an actionable assault? See Speech of Pollock, C. B. in *Corbett v. Grey*, 4 Ex. 729, 744, 154 E.R. 1409, 1415 (1849).

[C]   Extreme Emotional Upset

[See § 12.03[B], *Eckenrode v. Life of America Insurance Company*, 470 F.2d (1972).]

[D]   Reasonable Reliance

SHARP v. IDAHO INVESTMENT CORP.
Idaho Supreme Court
504 P.2d 386 (1972)

[Plaintiff brought an action in deceit against the Idaho Investment Corporation and its officers to recover damages arising out of a failed investment. Plaintiff claimed fraud in the inducement of the investment and certain statutory violations. The plaintiff recovered below.]

COMMON LAW FRAUD

Dr. Sharp, the respondent, alleged in his complaint[10] that Idaho Investment Corporation, through its agents, misrepresented material facts about the condition of the company. The district court found that there had been material misstatements and omissions by Idaho Investment.

Corporation and its agents in the stock sale to Dr. Sharp and concluded that Idaho Investment Corporation and its officers were liable for fraud.

. . .

---

[10] In summary, paragraph 9 of the complaint alleges:

A. That the prospectus misstated investments by appellant in its subsidiaries, and that the stated figures were false, fraudulent and untrue, inasmuch as the book value of the subsidiaries was materially less.

B. That the prospectus stated the expense of the stock sales would not exceed 171/2%, which was untrue.

C. That certain bonuses, loans and gifts were paid to its officers.

D. That the appellants used a "pitch kit" using illustrations of the major insurance companies of America and the profits derived by them as examples of profits that purchasers of stock could expect, if they invested in appellant corporation. That the pitch kit was compiled with the intent to mislead purchasers.

E. That appellant by its agent told respondents that appellant corporation owned "certain valuable properties, manufacturing plants and savings and loan association which were of a great value and were operating at a profit" but that such statements were untrue.

[Note: this footnote appears at a different place in the opinion.]

The district court concluded that Idaho Investment Corporation through its agents had misstated and omitted material facts in the sale of the stock to Dr. Sharp. To support this conclusion the district court made exhaustive findings of fact on the issue of fraud. The numerous findings of fact relate to alleged misstatements and omissions in Neilson's conversations with the plaintiff and various written material disseminated to the respondents by Idaho Investment Corporation through its agent, Neilson. Before we may sustain the district court's conclusion there must be clear and convincing evidence of the facts establishing the elements of an action in fraud.

To establish fraud the plaintiff has a difficult burden of proof. This Court in Walker v. Nunnenkamp, 84 Idaho 485, 373 P.2d 559 (1962), outlined the elements essential to prove fraud:

To establish the allegation of fraud, a party must prove by a preponderance of the evidence all of the elements which are inherently contained in such allegation.

. . . Comprehensively stated, the elements of actionable fraud consist of: (1) A representation. (2) Its falsity. (3) Its materiality. (4) The speaker's knowledge of its falsity or ignorance of its truth. (5) His intent that it should be acted on by the person and in the manner reasonably contemplated. (6) The hearer's ignorance of its falsity. (7) His reliance on its truth. (8) His right to rely thereon. (9) And his consequent and proximate injury. . . .

. . .

A party alleging fraud has the burden of proof. All elements of such allegation must be established by clear and convincing evidence. . . . Generally, all of these ingredients must be found to exist, and the absence of any one of them is fatal to recovery.

In reviewing the record this court is not convinced that there is proof to sustain the finding of (1) a false representation or omission of a material fact, and (2) the hearer's reliance thereon.

Critical to this case is the discovery of facts sustaining the district court's findings of misrepresentations. A false representation is the cornerstone to an action in fraud. There are three bases for laying the "cornerstone" in this case: oral misrepresentations, written false statements, and material omissions.

The only oral statements at issue are those made by the sales agent, Neilson, to the respondent. Moreover, the only witness to these statements is the respondent, Dr. Sharp. Dr. Sharp testified that in 1965 he purchased stock from the Idaho Investment Corporation. During October of 1965, Neilson contacted Dr. Sharp on three different occasions within a two week period. During Neilson's three visits Dr. Sharp was shown at least twice a "pitch kit" in a loose-leaf binder entitled "How to make your money make money while you sleep." This "pitch kit" consisted of numerous printed cardboard sheets containing statements, figures, and charts suggesting generally the profitability of life insurance companies as an investment. Neilson's "spiel" indicated that Idaho Investment Corporation would in the future attempt to put together the largest life insurance company in the western United States. From these statements it is impossible to find a misrepresentation of present or past existing fact.

According to Dr. Sharp, Neilson also described the business and profitability of Idaho Investment Corporation's subsidiaries. Dr. Sharp characterized these statements as intentional misrepresentations. Accepting this argument, the district court found these statements to be intentional false representations. We believe this to be error for two reasons. First, the evidence is far from being clear and convincing that these statements were in fact false. Second, there is no evidence that these statements were about present or past existing facts, but the statements pertained to anticipated corporate performance. Without elaborating on the later point there is a general rule in law of deceit that a representation consisting of promise or a statement as to a future event will not serve as basis for fraud, even though it was made under circumstances as to knowledge and belief which would give rise to an action for fraud had it related to an existing or past fact. Pocatello Security Trust Co. v. Henry, 35 Idaho 321, 206 P. 175 (1922); 37 Am.Jur.2d, Fraud & Deceit, § 57.

As in many cases the general rule has almost become the exception. Idaho recognizes two exceptions to the general rule about statements or promises in futuro: (1) fraud may be predicated upon the nonperformance of a promise in certain cases where the promise is the device to accomplish the fraud. Pocatello Security Trust Co. v. Henry, supra; Miller-Cahoon Co. v. Wade, 38 Idaho 484, 221 P. 1102 (1923); (2) in cases where promises are blended or associated with misrepresentation of fact, there is fraud if a promise is accompanied with statements of existing facts showing the ability of the promisor to perform the promise without which it would not have been accepted or acted upon. Pocatello Security Trust Co. v. Henry, supra; Keane v. Allen. Opinions or predictions about the anticipated profitability of a business are usually not actionable as fraud. However, when there is an affirmative promise or statement that a certain act will be undertaken, such a statement is actionable providing the other elements of fraud are shown. Assuming that Neilson's statements were in fact promises or statements that a certain act would be done, we can find no evidence establishing any of the elements of fraud, i.e. intent, knowledge of falsity, etc. Actually, these statements of Neilson can be characterized as "puffing."

We turn now to certain written materials disseminated by Idaho Investment Corporation which may contain false representations of fact. Although the district court found that misrepresentations had been made in the "pitch kit," prospectus, sales material, bulletins and "other written material," there is no indication of which statements in particular were false. In reviewing the numerous exhibits we conclude that there are no misrepresentations. True enough, optimism and enthusiasm pervade the sales material. However, the respondent has not carried his burden of producing clear and convincing evidence of the falsity of any statement in the written material supposedly relied on by Dr. Sharp. The record fails to support the finding that Idaho Investment Corporation issued written material containing intentional misrepresentations.

As a final basis for imposing liability on Idaho Investment Corporation we must consider the omission of facts material to the transaction which deprived the respondent of exercising his business investment judgment. The district court found that Idaho Investment Corporation "omitted certain facts" which deprived the respondents of a "fair and honest" opportunity to evaluate the stock. First, we are unable to determine whether such omissions were intentional or negligent. Second, we are unable to discover the extent or exact nature of the omissions.

Third, there is no evidence showing that such omissions, if there were any, were material. Indeed, the respondents never alleged in the complaint that material facts had been omitted. There is no evidence in the record which supports a conclusion that omissions concerning the financial status of Idaho Investment Corporation were of such a nature that Dr. Sharp would not have purchased the stock had the omissions been revealed. Furthermore, Dr. Sharp did not read the prospectus or offering circular until after he had purchased the stock. Thus, any omission in the prospectus was not material to his decision to purchase.

Finally, the element of reliance merits discussion in this case. The district court found that the respondents relied on the oral statements made by Neilson and the prospectus circulated to buyers by Idaho Investment Corporation. Reliance is a fundamental element of fraud which must be proven by clear and convincing evidence. In order for the respondent, Dr. Sharp, to secure redress he must have, in fact, relied upon a statement or representation as an inducement to purchase the stock. We find a notable absence of the element of reliance supporting the district court's finding of fraud.

On direct examination Dr. Sharp was asked: "Doctor, would you tell me why you purchased stock in the Idaho Investment Corporation?" Dr. Sharp replied, "Because I believed Mr. Neilson. I was acquainted with Mr. Frazier and other officers of Sierra Life. I knew the officers and expected it to be a profitable venture." This answer reveals a common theme which appears throughout the record. Dr. Sharp was an investor in Sierra Life Insurance Company, an Idaho corporation. By coincidence most of the officers of Idaho Investment Corporation were officials of Sierra Life Insurance Company. For example, Fred Frazier was president of both Idaho Investment Corporation and Sierra Life Insurance Company. Although this inter-locking feature of corporate officials was publicized extensively by Idaho Investment Corporation in its sales materials and company news bulletins, neither the respondents nor the district court chose to attach any significance to its connection with the element of reliance. From Dr. Sharp's own testimony it is evident that rather than relying on representations or misstatements by Idaho Investment Corporation and its agents he relied on expectations based on his experience with another corporation.

There is also no evidence in the record to support the finding that Dr. Sharp relied on the offering circular. Dr. Sharp testified that he never read the offering circular until after he purchased the stock. To be actionable the representation must have been relied on at the time of the transaction. We conclude that there is no evidence in the record to support a finding of reliance.

In summarizing the fraud count respondents have failed to establish the falsity of alleged misrepresentations or the existence of a material omission. Furthermore, without discussing the other elements necessary to sustain an action in fraud, we can find no evidence of reliance on an oral misrepresentation written false statement, or an omission of a material fact.

Judgment reversed. Costs to appellants.

NOTES AND QUESTIONS

(1) Two women are having a luncheon. A says to B, "My broker, C, advised me to buy XYZ stock immediately, because of an unannounced oil strike it made yesterday." After lunch, B quickly calls her broker, D, and purchases $10,000 of the shares of XYZ. XYZ soon thereafter goes into bankruptcy, and B loses her entire investment. Suppose C had substantial holdings in XYZ and had fabricated the story to attempt to strengthen the market for XYZ stock so that he could sell his shares before XYZ failed. What action, if any, would B have against A, C and D? Or, suppose C had mistakenly said "XYZ" to A, when he had meant to say "XYD," a company that did in fact strike oil, causing its stock to soar in price. "XYZ" failed. What action would B have against A, C or D? See Section 5.05 supra.

(2) Related to reliance is the requirement of detriment. Suppose a debtor has incurred a liability of undetermined amount to a bank. The bank president calls in the debtor and demands that he sign a check for $5000 and execute a new note for the unpaid balance "to be determined by an independent audit." The debtor inquires, "How much more do I owe?" The banker replies, "I believe this payment will discharge your obligation but sign this note just in case." The banker actually knows that the total debt is at least $8500 and also knows that the debtor has only $5056 in his checking account. Later, the bank brings an action to collect the new note, and the debtor counterclaims in deceit, seeking $5000 compensatory damages — saying he would not have paid the $5000 had he been honestly informed about the state of his indebtedness — and punitive damages. Should the debtor's action prevail? See *Amason v. First State Bank of Lineville*, 369 So.2d 547, 551 (Ala. 1979).

BESSETT v. BASNETT
Florida Supreme Court
389 So.2d 995 (1980)

ALDERMAN, JUSTICE.

The respondents, Mr. and Mrs. Basnett, the appellants in the district court and the plaintiffs in the trial court, were Connecticut residents interested in resettling in Florida. They obtained information about Redfish Lodge from its owners, the Besetts, and the Besetts' real estate broker, Czerwinski. As prospective buyers, they made several trips to Florida to inspect the lodge. They allege that the sellers misrepresented the size of the land offered for sale to be approximately 5.5 acres, when, in fact, the sellers knew it to be only 1.44 acres. They allege that the sellers knowingly misrepresented the amount of the lodge's business for 1976 to be $88,000 and that the roof on a building was brand new, when, in fact, the business income was substantially lower and the roof was not new and leaked. They also allege the defendants misrepresented to them the availability of additional land for expansion. Relying on these misrepresentations, which they allege were made to induce them to buy, they bought the lodge and the land.

Upon the motion of the defendants, the trial court, relying on Potakar v. Hurtak, dismissed the complaint for failing to state a cause of action. The district court reversed on the authority of its decision in Upledger v. Vilanor, Inc., 369 So.2d 427 (Fla.2d DCA 1979) cert. denied, 378 So.2d 350 (Fla.1979). These cases represent the two divergent lines of authority on this issue which have developed in Florida.

Potakar v. Hurtak was also a fraudulent misrepresentation action. Potakar alleged that he had asked Hurtak if the previous lessees of a restaurant had made a profit, and Hurtak replied they had, even though he knew the previous lessees had lost money for several years. Potakar alleged the misrepresentations were made to defraud, deceive, and influence him to lease the business. In affirming the trial court's dismissal of the complaint for failure to state a cause of action, the court observed that there were "no allegations as to the past profits, no showing as to the right of the plaintiff to rely on past statement, no fact stated as to the diligence on the plaintiff's part in investigating, or failing to investigate such facts, or how he was prevented from investigating the past profits of the said business." 82 So.2d at 503. The Court looked to 23 Am.Jur., Fraud and Deceit § 155, at 960-61 (1940), for a statement of the general rule that "a person to whom false representations have been made is not entitled to relief because of them if he might readily have ascertained the truth by ordinary care and ascertained the truth by ordinary care and attention, and his failure to do so was the result of his own negligence." 82. So.2d at 503. The Court concluded that Potakar's complaint did not state a cause of action.

The district court, in Upledger, reached a different result. In that case, Upledger, who was purchasing an apartment building from Vilanor, relied upon misrepresentations made by Vilanor concerning the amounts for which the apartments rented and the duration of the leases. Upledger admitted that he did not undertake an independent investigation, and he claimed that he would not have completed the purchase if he had known the true facts. In reversing the trial court's dismissal of Upledger's complaint, the district court, recognizing that there are conflicting lines of authority concluded:

[W]hen a specific false statement is knowingly made and reasonably relied upon, we choose to align ourselves with the growing body of authorities which holds that the representee is not precluded from recovery simply because he failed to make an independent investigation of the veracity of the statement. . . .

369 So.2d at 430.

The district court, we believe, made the correct choice. A person guilty of fraudulent misrepresentation should not be permitted to hide behind the doctrine of caveat emptor. The principle of law which we adopt is expressed in Sections 540 and 541 of Restatement (Second) of Torts (1976) as follows:

§ 540 Duty to Investigate.

The recipient of a fraudulent misrepresentation of fact is justified in relying upon its truth, although he might have ascertained the falsity of the representation had he made an investigation.

COMMENT:

a. The rule stated in this Section applies not only when an investigation would involve an expenditure of effort and money out of proportion to the magnitude of the transaction, but also when it could be made without any considerable trouble or expense. Thus it is no defense to one who has made a fraudulent statement about his financial position that his offer to submit his books to examination is rejected. On the other hand, if a mere cursory glance would have disclosed the falsity of the representation, its falsity is regarded as obvious under the rule stated in § 541.

b. The rule stated in this Section is applicable even though the fact that is fraudulently represented is required to be recorded and is in fact recorded. The recording acts are not intended as a protection for fraudulent liars. Their purpose is to afford a protection to persons who buy a recorded title against those who, having obtained a paper title, have failed to record it. The purpose of the statutes is fully accomplished without giving them a collateral effect that protects those who make fraudulent misrepresentations from liability.

§ 541 Representation Known to Be or Obviously False.

The recipient of a fraudulent misrepresentation is not justified in relying upon its truth if he knows that it is false or its falsity is obvious to him.

COMMENT:

a. Although the recipient of a fraudulent misrepresentation is not barred from recovery because he could have discovered its falsity if he had shown his distrust of the maker's honesty by investigating its truth, he is nonetheless required to use his senses, and cannot recover if he blindly relies upon a misrepresentation the falsity of which would be patent to him if he had utilized his opportunity to make a cursory examination or investigation. Thus, if one induces another to buy a horse by representing it to be sound, the purchaser cannot recover even though the horse has but one eye, if the horse is shown to the purchaser before he buys it and the slightest inspection would have disclosed the defect. On the other hand, the rule stated in this Section applies only when the recipient of the misrepresentation is capable of appreciating its falsity at the time by the use of his senses. Thus a defect that any experienced horseman would at once recognize at first glance may not be patent to a person who has had no experience with horses.

A person guilty of fraud should not be permitted to use the law as his shield. Nor should the law encourage negligence. However, when the choice is between the two — fraud and negligence — negligence is less objectionable than fraud. Though one should not be inattentive to one's business affairs, the law should not permit an inattentive person to suffer loss at the hands of a misrepresenter. As the Michigan Supreme Court said many years ago:

There may be good, prudential reasons why, when I am selling you a piece of land, or a mortgage, you should not rely upon my statement of the facts of the title, but if I have made that statement for the fraudulent purpose of inducing you to purchase, and you have in good faith made the purchase in reliance upon its truth, instead of making the examination for yourself, it does not lie with me to say to you, "It is true that I lied to you, and for the purpose of defrauding you, but you were guilty of negligence, of want of ordinary care, in believing that I told the truth; and because you trusted to my word, when you ought to have suspected me of falsehood, I am entitled to the fruits of my falsehood and cunning, and you are without a remedy."

Bristol v. Braidwood, 28 Mich. 191, 196 (1873).

We hold that a recipient may rely on the truth of a representation, even though its falsity could have been ascertained had he made an investigation, unless he knows the representation to be false or its falsity is obvious to him. We recede from *Potakar v. Hurtak* insofar as it is inconsistent with our present holding, and we disapprove all other decisions inconsistent with our holding in this case.

As was the case in *Upledger*, the petitioners in this case, as owners of the property being sold, had superior knowledge of its size, condition, and business income. As prospective purchasers, the respondents were justified in relying upon the representations that were made to them although they might have ascertained the falsity of the representations had they made an investigation. From the complaint, it does not appear that the respondents knew that the alleged misrepresentations were false, nor can we conclude from that complaint as a matter of law that the misrepresentations were obviously false.

Accordingly, we approve the decision of the district court.

It is so ordered.

NOTES AND QUESTIONS

(1) Suppose the seller of a house knows that the house suffered structural damage as a result of a termite infestation. The buyer is free to, and does, examine the house with some care but fails to find the evidence of the termites. Seller makes no effort to conceal the evidence but says nothing about it. The buyer asks no questions about termites or structural defects. After the purchase, the buyer finds the defects and spends $10,000 to correct them. Will plaintiff prevail in an action of deceit against the buyer? Compare *Sanders v. White*, 476 So.2d 84 (Ala. 1985) (seller of a home does not commit tort of deceit by keeping silent about known defects in the absence of active concealment), and *Johnson v. Davis*, 480 So.2d 625 (Fla. 1985) (seller of a home who knows of defects that materially affect the value of the home and which are not readily observable and not known to the buyer is under a duty to disclose them to the buyer.) See also the discussion of "silent fraud" in *United States Fidelity and Guaranty Co. v. Black*, 313 N.W.2d 77 (Mi. 1981).

(2) Law and Economics judges would be likely to place the duty of uncovering and revealing the crucial information on the party who could do it best or at least cost. Would imposing the duty to reveal information create a disincentive for sellers to collect information in the future? How could the *Bessett* buyer have obtained the needed information?

§ 12.05   PHYSICAL EFFECT ON THE PLAINTIFF

[A]   Harmful or Offensive Touching

[See *McDonald v. Ford*, § 12.04[A], *supra.*]

[B]   Confinement

[See *Coblyn v. Kennedy*, § 12.03[D], *supra.*]

QUESTION

Is *Coblyn* consistent with the following Restatement rules?

Restatement, Torts, Second[11]

§ 36 What Constitutes Confinement

(1) To make the actor liable for false imprisonment, the other's confinement within the boundaries fixed by the actor must be complete.

(2) The confinement is complete although there is a reasonable means of escape, unless the other knows of it.

(3) The actor does not become liable for false imprisonment by intentionally preventing another from going in a particular direction in which he has a right or privilege to go.

§ 42 Knowledge of Confinement

Under the rule stated in § 35, there is no liability for intentionally confining another unless the person physically restrained knows of the confinement or is harmed by it.

----

§ 12.06　ECONOMIC EFFECT ON THE PLAINTIFF

[See *Frank Coulson, Inc.-Buick v. General Motors Corp.*, § 12.07[D], infra.].

NOTE AND QUESTION

Should the theory of tortious interference with economic interests be limited to contractual interests? Some courts acknowledge that an intentional interference with an expectancy to receive an inheritance or bequest is actionable. See, e.g., *Peffer v. Bennett*, 523 F.2d 1323 (10th Cir. 1975), and *Holt v. First National Bank of Mobile*, 418 So.2d 77 (Ala. 1982).

§ 12.07　DEFENSES

[A]　Defense of Life and Limb

WATTS v. AETNA CASUALTY & SURETY COMPANY
Louisiana Court of Appeals
309 So.2d 402 (1975)

DENNIS, JUDGE.

This tort action results from an altercation between plaintiff Butler Watts and defendant Robert B. Baker, Jr., which occurred on August 21, 1972 at Baker's place of employment, an automobile agency in Shreveport. Baker was a service advisor for the agency, and it was his job to make arrangements for automobile

----

[11] Copyright 1965 by The American Law Institute. Reprinted with the permission of The American Law Institute.

mechanical work between customers and the agency's repair shop.

On an earlier occasion, about twelve days before the incident in question here, Watts had dealt with Baker about some work done on his car. Watts felt that he had been charged for some unnecessary work on that occasion. On August 21, 1972 Watts brought his car back to the shop because of a different mechanical problem. He again dealt with Baker, and the two immediately disagreed about the possible cause of the automobile trouble. Watts snatched a work order pad from Baker's hand and wrote some instructions of his own to the shop mechanics. Baker retrieved the tablet and scratched out Watts' notations on the work order. Heated words were spoken, but Watts left the car at the shop and departed without further incident. Later that day, after a mechanic had discovered the cause of the problem, Baker called Watts and asked him to come to the shop to verify the mechanic's determination before any repair work was begun. When Watts arrived, Baker showed him the car. In the presence of other shop employees Baker emphatically stated that he had been right and Watts had been wrong about the cause of the car trouble. Watts and Baker then engaged in a heated argument about the events which transpired on this and the previous occasion when his car had been in the shop. The dispute culminated in Baker striking Watts twice and rendering his unconscious for several minutes. Watts was taken to the hospital and received treatment and medication from physicians for a period of time.

Watts sued Baker, his employer and its insurer for damages. The principal issues litigated were: whether Watts provoked the attack; whether Baker used excessive force; and the extent of injury to Watts caused by the incident.

After a jury trial below, a verdict was rendered against Baker, his employer and its insurer in favor of Watts in the amount of $27,500. The trial judge entered a judgment in accordance with the verdict and denied motions for new trials by plaintiff and defendants. All parties appealed.

. . .

Defendants' first three specifications of error question whether the jury acted within its discretion in determining that Baker committed a battery upon Watts. The plaintiff, Watts, testified that during his argument with Baker, he did not curse or threaten Baker. The defendant, Baker, testified that Watts cursed him vilely and repeatedly during the dispute and that he struck Watts in the face twice because Watts drew back his fist as if to hit him. The other witnesses, all Baker's co-employees, generally corroborated his version of the altercation. There were significant differences in their testimony as to the exact number and wording of the epithets used by Watts. The witnesses generally agreed, however, that Watts several times referred to Baker by appellations which, if taken literally, accused him of incest and derogatorily described his maternal descent, and which were preceded by a term Baker may have considered sacrilegious. More importantly, these witnesses differed a great deal on whether Watts had drawn back his hand, whether he made a fist with the hand, or whether any motion by Watts appeared to be hostile. During the witnesses' testimony regarding this issue the attorneys asked them to demonstrate with arms and hands how Watts had moved, and the attorneys also used demonstrative movements of their own during the interrogations. Of course, none of this demonstrative evidence, which must have been very helpful to the jury, could be incorporated in the written record to which our review is limited.

The principles of law governing the trial of actions for damages for battery are well settled. Mere words, no matter how calculatedly they are used to excite or irritate, cannot justify a battery. . . . Provocation by words, however, can be considered in mitigation of damages although rejected as justification for an unlawful act. Morneau v. American Oil Company, supra. Even where there is an aggressive act, justifying a battery, the person retaliating may use only so much force as is necessary to repel the aggression, and if he goes beyond this, using force in excess of what would have been reasonably necessary, he is liable for damages for injury caused by employment of such unnecessary force. . . .

Without question Baker struck Watts twice in the face without receiving a blow himself. It is undisputed that after the second blow Watts fell to the shop floor and lost consciousness for several minutes. Beyond these facts, however, we cannot be certain what the jury found, since written interrogatories were not submitted. In our opinion the jury should have decided that Watts cursed and reviled Baker. From a reading of the record we find that a determination for either party would have been reasonable on the other crucial issues involving the altercation itself, viz., whether Watts appeared to move his hand in such a manner as to physically threaten Baker; and whether, under the circumstances, and given the age, size, and physical characteristics of the parties, Baker used more force than reasonably appeared necessary to repel the aggression. Furthermore, we are mindful of the fact that much of the evidence which would have been important to a correct determination of these issues consisted of demeanor and demonstrative evidence which was available to the jury but not to us.

We cannot find manifest error in either one of two conclusions which the jury could have reached as a basis for its verdict. The jury reasonably could have found there was no aggressive act or appearance of a hostile movement on Watts' part justifying retaliation by Baker; or, it could have reasonably found that, although Watts provoked the attack by an antagonistic movement of his hand, Baker used excessive force under the circumstances. Therefore, we conclude, from the transcript of the conflicting testimony of the witnesses, that the jury acted within its authority in finding for the plaintiff, on the issue of liability.

Although plaintiff did not object to the jury's award in his specifications of errors, he devoted a major portion of his oral and written argument to the subject. Therefore, we will consider his complaint that the award was inadequate along with the defendants' specification that the jury erred in returning an excessive verdict.

. . .

[History of treatment omitted.]

We cannot say that the jury abused its discretion when it returned an award for $27,500, because from the evidence it would have been justified in compensating plaintiff for pain, suffering, permanant brain damage, permanent change of personality, permanent loss of sexual potency, temporary worsening of his heart condition, loss of one month's pay, and loss of past and future earnings as a used car buyer. Much less are we prepared to find that the jury failed to exercise its discretion properly with regard to the question of mitigation of damages. The Supreme Court, in Morneau v. American Oil Company, supra, merely stated that "[p]rovocation by words . . . can be considered in mitigation of damages . . . " and held that the words used in the context of the incident involved in that case were insufficient to merit any mitigation of damages. Our search of the jurisprudence has failed to disclose a statement of a more definite standard for deciding when and how much damages should be mitigated. We are, therefore, led to the conclusion that both questions are peculiarly within the discretion of the trier of facts.

In our view, the evidence of the words used by Watts in this case was sufficient to provide a basis for mitigation. But we also conclude that a refusal by the jury to mitigate, or a refusal to mitigate more drastically, in this case would not have been an abuse of its vast discretion pertaining to this issue.

On the other hand, we are unable to find that the jury abused its discretion in assessing an inadequate amount in damages. Even without mitigation of the damages we find that the award was within the much discretion that must be left to the jury. Considering that it was permissible for the jury to mitigate the damages, it is very clear that the verdict does not represent an inadequate award.

. . .

For the reasons assigned, the judgment rendered in accordance with the jury verdict is affirmed, at the cost of the defendants-appellants.

Affirmed.

NOTES AND QUESTIONS

(1)   Is *Watts* consistent with the following statements from Restatement of the Law, Torts (Second)?[12]

§ 63 Self-Defense By Force Not Threatening Death or Serious Bodily Harm

(1) An actor is privileged to use reasonable force, not intended or likely to cause death or serious bodily harm, to defend himself against unprivileged harmful or offensive contact or other bodily harm which he reasonably believes that another is about to inflict intentionally upon him.

(2) Self-defense is privileged under the conditions stated in Subsection (1), although the actor correctly or reasonably believes that he can avoid the necessity of so defending himself,

(a) by retreating or otherwise giving up a right or privilege, or

(b) by complying with a command with which the actor is under no duty to comply or which the other is not privileged to enforce by the means threatened.

§ 70 Character and Extent of Force Permissible

(1) The actor is not privileged to use any means of self-defense which is intended or likely to cause a bodily harm or confinement in excess of that which the actor correctly or reasonably believes to be necessary for his protection.

. . .

---

[12] Copyright 1965 by The American Law Institute. Reprinted with the permission of The American Law Institute.

§ 82 Effect of Excessive Force

If the actor applies a force to or imposes a confinement upon another which is in excess of that which is privileged.

(a) the actor is liable for so much of the force or confinement as is excessive;

. . .

(c) the other has the privilege to defend himself against the actor's use or attempted use of excessive force or confinement.

(2) The courts have long been divided over whether a person may stand and fight when his only defense is deadly force, or whether he must flee to avoid using it. There is some authority that western and southern states permit a holding of ground whereas other states do not permit it. All states, however, impose no duty to retreat when one is in his own home. What would be the justification of a no-duty to retreat rule in the home? *State v. Bobbitt*, 415, So.2d 724 (Fla. 1982), took away even that privilege in a criminal case where both the assailant and the person defending with deadly force are legal residents of the same abode. Should that rule be applied in civil cases?

(3) The idea that provocation will mitigate damages but not excuse an intentional tort is old. See, e.g., *Railroad v. Fleming*, 82 Tenn. 128, 14 LRA 128 (1884).

[B]   Assault and Battery

BRADLEY v. HUNTER
Louisiana Court of Appeal
413 So.2d 674 (1982)

Cutrer, Judge.

This is a wrongful death and survival suit arising out of the fatal shooting of J. W. Bradley.

The shooting death of J. W. Bradley (J. W.) took place at approximately 9:00 P.M., on May 14, 1980, in Campti, Louisiana. J. W. was shot by defendant, Aurila F. Hunter (Aurila), in front of the "Honeydripper Cafe" which is operated by Aurila and her mother, Ora Edwards (Ora), also named as a defendant in this suit.

. . .

This is a non-jury trial and after plaintiff had presented her evidence, the trial court granted defendants' motion for a directed verdict, dismissing plaintiff's suit. Plaintiff appeals. We affirm.

The substantial issue on appeal is whether defendant, Aurila, was justified in shooting J. W. in self-defense.

. . .

FACTS

Aurila testified that J. W., a twenty-eight-year-old man, came into the "Honeydripper" around 9:00 to 9:30 P.M., May 14, 1980, wanting to purchase a soft drink ("coke"). Aurila is sixty-five years old, not in particularly good health (she is under a doctor's care), unmarried and lives with her eighty-two-year-old mother, Ora, who owns the cafe. Ora, a widow, also in poor health and under a doctor's care, works in the cafe with Aurila. No one else is employed in the restaurant. The cafe sells food, a little beer and no hard liquor.

Aurila testified at trial that she has had trouble with J. W. on at least two prior occasions and told him not to come into the cafe. That night J. W. entered wanting his "coke" but Aurila refused to serve him. Ora offered J. W. the "coke" but he refused. J. W. began to threaten and curse Aurila who restrained herself despite his cursing the two old women. She told him to go home. He did not leave until he had finished cursing and threatening Aurila.

A Smith & Wesson Model 10.38 caliber revolver was kept under the counter near the cash register. While J. W. remained in the store Aurila did not pick up the gun but she did so after he had left. J. W. walked out of the cafe cursing and threatening the women. After he had left, Ora went outside to see if J. W. had gone. Aurila went out onto the porch to see about her mother. As she stood on the porch, Aurila saw J. W. coming toward her, walking rapidly, as she said he had a tendency to do, with his arms flailing away, fists clenched, and cursing and threatening her. She then pulled the gun from her blouse pocket and told J. W. not to come to the cafe. She fired one warning shot (probably two, as three shots were fired but only one hit J. W.), and fired again whenever J. W. kept coming, walking fast, cursing and threatening Aurila. She fired from about thirty feet away; the bullet struck J. W. in the head, killing him.

Aurila testified that J. W. had threatened her two weeks before the incident in question, after she had refused to sell him some beer. She stated that he threatened to "get her" should she go outside to the mailbox. From that time until the incident in question, Aurila stated that she did not go to the mailbox for fear of J. W. She stated that she had known J. W. since he was a small child and knew of his reputation in the community. Aurila stated that she knew J. W. had previously shot a man in the back with a shotgun. Also, she saw him strike another person across the back with a crutch for refusing him a drink of wine. J. W.'s "wife" and aunt both stated that he had spent considerable periods of time in jail. Plaintiff stated that since they began living together in 1972 or 1973, he had spent over one-half of the time in prison. Deputy Dowden, an investigating officer, stated that he had known the decedent due to having received calls about him and his prior arrests. He further testified that J. W. was very belligerent toward the law enforcement officers; he had made threats to them and felt he was capable of carrying them out. His testimony in this regard is as follows:

Q. Where did these occur?

A. These were, as I said, in the past throughout my career and at times, I've picked up the subject.

Q. Have you ever picked him up in the Campti area?

A. Yes, sir.

Q. Where in Campti?

A. It's been quite a few occasions. It would be hard to say. Mostly in the area around the Campti Short Stop.

Q. And was he cooperative with you? Do you recall his attitude?

A. Very few occasions was he cooperative.

Q. Okay. Now, how was he uncooperative?

A. He was usually very belligerent towards officers.

Q. Did he ever threaten you?

A. Yes, sir.

Q. Okay. How did he threaten you?

A. He made numerous threats throughout his conversation as to what he would do

Q. Do you feel that he was capable of carrying out these threats if he had the chance to do so?

A. I would say so, in my opinion, yes, sir.

As can be gleaned from the testimony presented by plaintiff, J. W. was considered to be less than a model citizen. He was known to have a quick temper and violent propensities. He was a young man of twenty-eight who had threatened, cursed and intimidated two old women aged sixty-five and eighty-two. At the time of the shooting J. W. was walking rapidly toward the two women, who were standing on their porch. He was cursing and throwing his arms about in a threatening manner. A warning both verbally and by a discharge of the gun failed to dissuade J. W. from his continued harassment of Aurila and Ora. Aurila fired again in fear of her and her mother's safety, killing J. W. Aurila stated that she was really fearful for her and her mother's safety at the time of the incident.

John Kirkendoll testified that he was about fifty yards away from the scene at the time of the shooting. He stated that at the time of the shooting, J. W. was standing in the middle of the highway. This testimony was not accepted by the trial court. Kirkendoll stated that he did not "run with" J. W. but was an "associate" of his. Deputy Dowden stated that Kirkendoll had been drinking at the time of the incident. The trial court committed no error in rejecting this testimony.

The law applicable to a case of this kind is clear and well settled. In the case of Roberts v. American Employers Ins. Co., Boston, Mass., 221 So.2d 550 (La.App. 3rd Cir. 1969), this court stated as follows:

The privilege of self-defense in tort actions is now well recognized by our jurisprudence. Where a person reasonably believes he is threatened with bodily harm, he may use whatever force appears to be reasonably necessary to protect against the threatened injury. . . . Of course, each case depends on its own facts, such as, for instance, the relative size, age and strength of the parties, their reputations for violence, who was the aggressor, the degree of physical harm reasonably feared and the presence or absence of weapons. (Citations omitted.)

In summary, the trial judge found decedent, J. W. Bradley, to be a man "of a pugnacious and aggressive nature, with a long record, ever since he had been an adult, and perhaps even before, a long record of violence, which brought him into contact with the law." The trial judge pointed out that J. W. had spent about four of the last nine years in prison. J. W. had been warned on prior occasions to stay out of the "Honeydripper Cafe," yet he refused; he entered the cafe that fateful night cursing and threating the two elderly women who operated it. He refused to leave, despite their request, until he had sufficiently cursed them. Aurila took the gun with her when she went onto the porch to see about her mother who had gone out to see if J. W. had left.

Then, with the passage of some period of time, here he comes back again, rushing at her with his fists balled up and walking at her and threatening her, while she stood on her own porch. She warned him. Her testimony was that she told him, "Go away." She fired a warning shot. Even Mr. Kirkendoll, who was cold sober, according to his testimony, testified that the first shot did not hit Bradley. And his testimony was that Bradley was not hit and said something to her, or something of that nature. But, this didn't slow him down. He kept on coming at her. The evidence, as a whole, indicates to me that the decedent made Mrs. Hunter shoot him. And the finding of the Court is that this was a case of justifiable self-defense and the motion for the directed verdict is granted in favor of the defendant. The case is dismissed.

From our perusal of the record, we conclude that the trial court was correct in finding that Aurila acted in self-defense.

Plaintiff cites the case of Brasseaux v. Girouard, 269 So.2d 590 (La.App. 3rd Cir. 1972), writ den., 271 So.2d 262 (La.1973), as a basis for the contention that Aurila did not shoot in selfdefense. We disagree. In Brasseaux, self-defense was disallowed. It is, however, clearly distinguishable from the case at hand.

In Brasseaux, the plaintiff and defendant were involved in a boundary dispute. On the day in question, during daylight hours, plaintiff and defendant each drove their vehicles to an open pasture. A fence separated the parties. Accompanying defendant in his pickup truck were four men; defendant's brother-in-law, a son-in-law and two nephews. Brasseaux was accompanied by one person who remained in the vehicle during the incident. Defendant got out of his truck with a shotgun and stood behind his truck as Brasseaux walked from his vehicle toward the fence. When Brasseaux was near the fence, defendant shot him while he was thirty-five feet away and had made no effort to cross the fence. The court observed as follows:

. . . Girouard's position behind the truck near four relatives and armed with an automatic shotgun was ample protection from Brasseaux who was at least 35 feet away, alone and not making an attempt to cross the fence. To the argument that Girouard feared that Brasseaux's hidden hand concealed a weapon, we state that Girouard had the drop on Brasseaux and could have readily ascertained that Brasseaux was unarmed. . . .

The court concluded that:

. . . We do not feel that under the circumstances presented here a reasonable person would or could have believed in good faith that it was necessary for him to shoot plaintiff in self defense.

In the case at hand, Aurila and her mother did not have the protection of four men, the fence or truck. Under the circumstances of this case, Aurila, as a reasonable person, could have believed in good faith that it was necessary for her to shoot J. W. to prevent bodily harm to her and/or her mother.

The trial judge, after hearing plaintiff's testimony and proof, ruled that she had not proved her case by a preponderance of the evidence. As a factual determination we cannot reverse the trial court's ruling absent manifest error or the decision being clearly wrong. No such error appears in this record.

Affirmed.

QUESTION

Is *Bradley v. Hunter* consistent with the following statements of the Restatement, Torts, Second?[13]

§ 65 Self-Defense by Force Threatening Death or Serious Bodily Harm

(1) Subject to the statement in Subsection (3), an actor is privileged to defend himself against another by force intended or likely to cause death or serious bodily harm, when he reasonably believes that

(a) the other is about to inflict upon him an intentional contact or other bodily harm, and that

(b) he is thereby put in peril of death or serious bodily harm or ravishment, which can safely be prevented only by the immediate use of such force.

(2) The privilege stated in Subsection (1) exists although the actor correctly or reasonably believes that he can safely avoid the necessity of so defending himself by

(a) retreating if he is attacked within his dwelling place, which is not also the dwelling of the other, or

(b) permitting the other to intrude upon or dispossess him of his dwelling place, or

(c) abandoning an attempt to effect a lawful arrest.

(3) The privilege stated in Subsection (1) does not exist if the actor correctly or reasonably believes that he can with complete safety avoid the necessity of so defending himself by

(a) retreating if attacked in any place other than his dwelling place, or in a place which is also the dwelling of the other, or

(b) relinquishing the exercise of any right or privilege other than his privilege to prevent intrusion upon or dispossession of his dwelling place or to effect a lawful arrest.

§ 76 Defense of Third Person

The actor is privileged to defend a third person from a harmful or offensive contact or other invasion of his interests of personality under the same conditions and by the same means as those under and by which he is privileged to defend

---

[13] Copyright 1965 by The American Law Institute. Reprinted with the permission of The American Law Institute.

himself if the actor correctly or reasonably believes that

(a) the circumstances are such as to give the third person a privilege of self-defense, and

(b) his intervention is necessary for the protection of the third person.

(2) Do you agree with the duty-to-retreat policy incorporated in the foregoing statements?

(3) Why is the provision pertaining to the defender's state of mind posited differently in § 65 than in § 76?

[C]   Defense of Property

KATKO v. BRINEY
Iowa Supreme Court
183 N.W.2d 657 (1971)

Moore, Chief Justice.

The primary issue presented here is whether an owner may protect personal property in an unoccupied boarded-up farm house against trespassers and thieves by a spring gun capable of inflicting death or serious injury.

We are not here concerned with a man's right to protect his home and members of his family. Defendants' home was several miles from the scene of the incident to which we refer infra.

Plaintiff's action is for damages resulting from serious injury caused by a shot from a 20-gauge spring shotgun set by defendants in a bedroom of an old farm house which had been uninhabited for several years. Plaintiff and his companion, Marvin McDonough, had broken and entered the house to find and steal old bottles and dated fruit jars which they considered antiques.

At defendants' request plaintiff's action was tried to a jury consisting of residents of the community where defendants' property was located. The jury returned a verdict for plaintiff and against defendants for $20,000 actual and $10,000 punitive damages.

After careful consideration of defendants' motions for judgment notwithstanding the verdict and for new trial, the experienced and capable trial judge overruled them and entered judgment on the verdict. Thus we have this appeal by defendants.

. . .

II. Most of the facts are not disputed. In 1957 defendant Bertha L. Briney inherited her parents' farm land in Mahaska and Monroe Counties. Included was an 80-acre tract in southwest Mahaska County where her grandparents and parents had lived. No one occupied the house thereafter. Her husband, Edward, attempted to care for the land. He kept no farm machinery thereon. The outbuildings became dilapidated.

For about 10 years, 1957 to 1967, there occurred a series of trespassing and housebreaking events with loss of some household items, the breaking of windows and "messing up of the property in general". The latest occurred June 8, 1967, prior to the event on July 17, 1967 herein involved.

Defendants through the years boarded up the windows and doors in an attempt to stop the intrusions. They had posted "no trespass" signs on the land several years before 1967. The nearest one was 35 feet from the house. On June 11, 1967 defendants set "a shotgun trap" in the north bedroom. After Mr. Briney cleaned and oiled his 20-gauge shotgun, the power of which he was well aware, defendants took it to the old house where they secured it to an iron bed with the barrel pointed at the bedroom door. It was rigged with wire from the doorknob to the gun's trigger so it would fire when the door was opened. Briney first pointed the gun so an intruder would be hit in the stomach but at Mrs. Briney's suggestion it was lowered to hit the legs. He admitted he did so "because I was mad and tired of being tormented" but "he did not intend to injure anyone". He gave no explanation of why he used a loaded shell and set it to hit a person already in the house. Tin was nailed over the bedroom window. The spring gun could not be seen from the outside. No warning of its presence was posted.

Plaintiff lived with his wife and worked regularly as a gasoline station attendant in Eddyville, seven miles from the old house. He had observed it for several years while hunting in the area and considered it as being abandoned. He knew it had long been uninhabited. In 1967 the area around the house was covered with high weeds. Prior to July 16, 1967 plaintiff and McDonough had been to the premises and found several old bottles and fruit jars which they took and added to their collection of antiques. On the latter date about 9:30 p. m. they made a second trip to the Briney property. They entered the old house by removing a board from a porch window which was without glass. While McDonough was looking around the kitchen area plaintiff went to another part of the house. As he started to open the north bedroom door the shotgun went off striking him in the right leg above the ankle bone. Much of his leg, including part of the tibia, was blown away. Only by McDonough's assistance was plaintiff able to get out of the house and after crawling some distance was put in his vehicle and rushed to a doctor and then to a hospital. He remained in the hospital 40 days.

Plaintiff's doctor testified he seriously considered amputation but eventually the healing process was successful. Some weeks after his release from the hospital plaintiff returned to work on crutches. He was required to keep the injured leg in a cast for approximately a year and wear a special brace for another year. He continued to suffer pain during this period.

There was undenied medical testimony plaintiff had a permanent deformity, a loss of tissue, and a shortening of the leg.

The record discloses plaintiff to trial time had incurred $710 medical expense, $2056.85 for hospital service, $61.80 for orthopedic service and $750 as loss of earnings. In addition thereto the trial court submitted to the jury the question of damages for pain and suffering and for future disability.

III. Plaintiff testified he knew he had no right to break and enter the house with intent to steal bottles and fruit jars therefrom. He further testified he had entered a plea of guilty to larceny in the nighttime of property of less than $20 value from a private building. He stated he had been fined $50 and costs and paroled during good behavior from a 60-day jail sentence. Other than minor traffic charges this was plaintiff's first brush with the law. On this civil case appeal it is not our prerogative to review the disposition made of the criminal charge against him.

The main thrust of defendants' defense in the trial court and on this appeal is that "the law permits use of a spring gun in a dwelling or warehouse for the purpose of preventing the unlawful entry of a burglar or thief".

. . .

In the statement of issues the trial court stated plaintiff and his companion committed a felony when they broke and entered defendants' house. In instruction 2 the court referred to the early case history of the use of spring guns and stated under the law their use was prohibited except to prevent the commission of felonies of violence and where human life is in danger. The instruction included a statement breaking and entering is not a felony of violence.

Instruction 5 stated: "You are hereby instructed that one may use reasonable force in the protection of his property, but such right is subject to the qualification that one may not use such means of force as will take human life or inflict great bodily injury. Such is the rule even though the injured party is a trespasser and is in violation of the law himself."

Instruction 6 stated: "An owner of premises is prohibited from willfully or intentionally injuring a trespasser by means of force that either takes life or inflicts great bodily injury; and therefore a person owning a premise is prohibited from setting out 'spring guns' and like dangerous devices which will likely take life or inflict great bodily injury, for the purpose of harming trespassers. The fact that the trespasser may be acting in violation of the law does not change the rule. The only time when such conduct of setting a 'spring gun' or a like dangerous device is justified would be when the trespasser was committing a felony of violence or a felony punishable by death, or where the trespasser was endangering human life by his act."

Instruction 7, to which defendants made no objection or exception, stated: "To entitle the plaintiff to recover for compensatory damages, the burden of proof is upon him to establish by a preponderance of the evidence each and all of the following propositions:

1. That defendants erected a shotgun trap in a vacant house on land owned by defendant, Bertha L. Briney, on or about June 11, 1967, which fact was known only by them, to protect household goods from trespassers and thieves.

2. That the force used by defendants was in excess of that force reasonably necessary and which persons are entitled to use in the protection of their property.

3. That plaintiff was injured and damaged and the amount thereof.

4. That plaintiff's injuries and damages resulted directly from the discharge of the shotgun trap which was set and used by defendants."

The overwhelming weight of authority, both textbook and case law, supports the trial court's statement of the applicable principles of law.

Prosser on Torts, Third Edition, pages 116-118, states:

. . . the law has always placed a higher value upon human safety than upon mere rights in property, it is the accepted rule that there is no privilege to use any force calculated to cause death or serious bodily injury to repel the threat to land or chattels, unless there is also such a threat to the defendant's personal safety as to justify a self-defense. . . . spring guns and other man-killing devices are not justifiable against a mere trespasser, or even a petty thief. They are privileged only against those upon whom the landowner, if he were present in person would be free to inflict injury of the same kind.

Restatement of Torts, section 85, page 180, states: "The value of human life and limb, not only to the individual concerned but also to society, so outweighs the interest of a possessor of land in excluding from it those whom he is not willing to admit thereto that a possessor of land has, as is stated in § 79, no privilege to use force intended or likely to cause death or serious harm against another whom the possessor sees about to enter his premises or meddle with his chattel, unless the intrusion threatens death or serious bodily harm to the occupiers or users of the premises. . . . A possessor of land cannot do indirectly and by a mechanical device that which, were he present, he could not do immediately and in person. Therefore, he cannot gain a privilege to install, for the purpose of protecting his land from intrusions harmless to the lives and limbs of the occupiers or users of it, a mechanical device whose only purpose is to inflict death or serious harm upon such as may intrude, by giving notice of his intention to inflict, by mechanical means and indirectly harm which he could not, even after request, inflict directly were he present."

In Volume 2, Harper and James, The Law of Torts, section 27.3, pages 1440, 1441, this is found: "The possessor of land may not arrange his premises intentionally so as to cause death or serious bodily harm to a respasser. The possessor may of course take some steps to repel a trespass. If he is present he may use force to do so, but only that amount which is reasonably necessary to effect the repulse. Moreover if the trespass threatens harm to property only — even a theft of property — the possessor would not be privileged to use deadly force, he may not arrange his premises so that such force will be inflicted by mechanical means. If he does, he will be liable even to a thief who is injured by such device."

. . .

[Examination of other authorities omitted.]

In addition to civil liability many jurisdictions hold a land owner criminally liable for serious injuries or homicide caused by spring guns or other set devices.

. . .

In Wisconsin, Oregon and England the use of spring guns and similar devices is specifically made unlawful by statute. 44 A.L.R., section 3, pages 386, 388.

The legal principles stated by the trial court in instructions 2, 5 and 6 are well established and supported by the authorities cited and quoted supra. There is no merit in defendants' objections and exceptions thereto. Defendants' various motions based on the same reasons stated in exceptions to instructions were properly overruled.

V. Plaintiff's claim and the jury's allowance of punitive damages, under the trial court's instructions relating thereto, were not at any time or in any manner challenged by defendants in the trial court as not allowable. We therefore are not presented with the problem of whether the $10,000 award should be allowed to stand.

. . .

This opinion is not to be taken or construed as authority that the allowance of punitive damages is or is not proper under circumstances such as exist here. We hold only that question of law not having been properly raised cannot in this case be resolved.

Study and careful consideration of defendants' contentions on appeal reveal no reversible error.

Affirmed.

LARSON, JUSTICE, dissenting.

I respectfully dissent, first, because the majority wrongfully assumes that by installing a spring gun in the bedroom of their unoccupied house the defendants intended to shoot any intruder who attempted to enter the room. Under the record presented here, that was a fact question. Unless it is held that these property owners are liable for any injury to an intruder from such a device regardless of the intent with which it is installed, liability under these pleadings must rest upon two definite issues of fact, i.e., did the defendants intend to shoot the invader, and if so, did they employ unnecessary and unreasonable force against him?

It is my feeling that the majority over-simplifies the impact of this case on the law, not only in this but other jurisdictions, and that it has not thought through all the ramifications of this holding.

. . .

As previously indicated, this appeal presents two vital questions which are as novel as they are difficult. They are, (1) is the owner of a building in which are kept household furniture, appliances, and valuables, but not occupied by a person or persons, liable in damages to an intruder who in the nighttime broke into and entered the building with the intent to steal and was shot and seriously injured by a spring gun allegedly set by the owner to frighten intruders from his property, and (2) if he is liable for compensatory damages, is this a proper case for the allowance of exemplary or punitive damages?

The trial court overruled all objections to the instructions and denied defendants' motion for a new trial. Thus, the first question to be resolved in the status of the law in this jurisdiction as to the means of force a property owner is privileged to use to repel (1) a mere trespasser, (2) a criminal invader, thief or burglar, where he presents no threat to human life or safety, and (3) an intruder or criminal breaking and entering a dwelling which poses a threat to human life and safety. Overlooked by the majority is the vital problem relating to the relevancy and importance of the owner's intent in placing the device.

I have been unable to find a case exactly like the case at bar, although there have been many cases which consider liability to a mere trespasser for injuries incurred by a spring gun or other dangerous instruments set to protect against intrusion and theft.

. . .

It appears there are cases and some authority which would relieve one setting a spring gun on his premises of any liability if adequate warning had been given an intruder and he ignores the warning. In all of these cases there is a question as to the intent of the property owner in setting the device. Intent, of course, may be determined from both direct and indirect evidence, and it is true the physical facts may be and often are sufficient to present a jury issue. I think they were here, but no clear instruction was given in this regard.

If, after proper instructions, the finder of fact determined that the gun was set with an intent and purpose to kill or inflict great bodily injury on an intruder, then and only then may it be said liability is established unless the property so protected is shown to be an occupied dwelling house. Of course, under this concept, if the finder of fact determines the gun set in an unoccupied house was intended to do no more than to frighten the intruder or sting him a bit, no liability would be incurred under such pleadings as are now presented. If such a concept of the law were adopted in Iowa, we would have here a question for the fact-finder or jury as to whether the gun was willfully and intentionally set so as to seriously injure the thief or merely scare him away.

I feel the better rule is that an owner of buildings housing valuable property may employ the use of spring guns or other devices intended to repel but not seriously injure an intruder who enters his secured premises with or without a criminal intent, but I do not advocate its general use, for there may also be liability for negligent installation of such a device. What I mean to say is that under such circumstances as we have here the issue as to whether the set was with an intent to seriously injure or kill an intruder is a question of fact that should be left to the jury under proper instructions, and that the mere setting of such a device with a resultant serious injury should not as a matter of law establish liability.

In the case of a mere trespass able authorities have reasoned that absolute liability may rightfully be fixed on the landowner for injuries to the trespasser because very little damage could be inflicted upon the property owner and the danger is great that a child or other innocent trespasser might be seriously injured by the device. In such matters that say no privilege to set up the device should be recognized by the courts regardless of the owner's intent. I agree.

On the other hand, where the intruder may pose a danger to the inhabitants of a dwelling, the privilege of using such a device to repel has been recognized by most authorities, and the mere setting thereof in the dwelling has not been held to create liability for an injury as a matter of law. In such cases intent and the reasonableness of the force would seem relevant to liability.

Although I am aware of the often-repeated statement that personal rights are more important than property rights, where the owner has stored his valuables representing his life's accumulations, his livelihood business, his tools and implements, and his treasured antiques as appears in the case at bar, and where the evidence is sufficient to sustain a finding that the installation was intended only as a warning to ward off theives and criminals, I can see no compelling reason why the use of such a device alone would create liability as a matter of law. . . .

I would, therefore, conclude there is merit in appellants' contention that the law was not made clear to the jury as to whether the act of placing a spring gun on this premise was prohibited by law, or whether the act of placing such a device requires a finding of intention to shoot the intruder or cause him great bodily injury to establish liability. I cannot tell whether the jury found liability on the mere act of placing the gun as Mr. Briney did in his house or on the fact that he did so with the intent to seriously harm a trespasser.

In the case at bar, I have pointed out, there is a sharp conflict in the evidence. The physical facts and certain admissions as to how the gun was aimed would tend to support a finding of intent to injure, while the direct testimony of both defendants was that the gun was placed so it would "hit the floor eventually" and that it was set "low so it couldn't kill anybody." Mr. Briney testified, "My purpose in setting up the gun was not to injure somebody. I thought more or less that the gun would be at a distance of where anyone would grab the door, it would scare them", and in setting the angle of the gun to hit the lower part of the door, he said, "I didn't think it would go through quite that hard."

If the law in this jurisdiction permits, which I think it does, an explanation of the setting of a spring gun to repel invaders of certain private property, then the intent with which the set is made is a vital element in the liability issue.

In view of the failure to distinguish and clearly give the jury the basis upon which it should determine that liability issue, I would reverse and remand the entire case for a new trial.

. . .

[Judge Larson also would disallow punitive damages on these facts.]

NOTES AND QUESTIONS

(1) *Molliter manus imposuit* is an old plea of justification meaning roughly, "He gently laid hands on." Black's Law Dictionary (4 ed.), 1156. In modern terms it means that a person is entitled to use non-harmful force to defend himself, protect his property or keep the peace. Who is to distinguish between a justified "light" touching and an unjustified battery? If a light touching is justified, does the person being touched have a right to respond in kind?

As to forcible recapture of chattels, see Restatement of Torts (Second) §§ 100-106. As to force that may be used to defend property, the Restatement, Torts (Second) provides:[14]

§ Defense of Possession By Force Not Threatening Death or Serious Bodily Harm

An actor is privileged to use reasonable force, not intended or likely to cause death or serious bodily harm, to prevent or terminate another's intrusion upon the actor's land or chattels, if

(a) the intrusion is not privileged or the other intentionally or negligently causes the actor to believe that it is not privileged, and

(b) the actor reasonably believes that the intrusion can be prevented or terminated only by the force used, and

(c) the actor has first requested the other to desist and the other has disregarded

---

[14] Copyright 1965 by The American Law Institute. Reprinted with the permission of The American Law Institute.

the request, or the actor reasonably believes that a request will be useless or that substantial harm will be done before it can be made.

§ 79 Defense of Possession By Force Threatening Death or Serious Bodily Harm

The intentional infliction upon another of a harmful or offensive contact or other bodily harm by a means which is intended or likely to cause death or serious bodily harm, for the purpose of preventing or terminating the other's intrusion upon the actor's possession of land or chattels, is privileged if, but only if, the actor reasonably believes that the intruder, unless expelled or excluded, is likely to cause death or serious bodily harm to the actor or to a third person whom the actor is privileged to protect.

§ 81 Amount of Force Permissible

(1) The actor is not privileged to use any means of defending his land or chattels from intrusion which are intended or likely to cause bodily harm or confinement in excess of that which the actor correctly or reasonably believes to be necessary to prevent or terminate the other's intrusion.

(2) The actor is privileged in defense of his land or chattels against intrusion to do an act which is intended to put another in immediate apprehension of a harmful or offensive contact or other bodily harm or confinement which is in excess of that which the actor is privileged to inflict, if his act is intended and reasonably believed by him to be likely to do no more than to create such an apprehension.

(2) What is the defense of "probable cause" in a false imprisonment action? See *Coblyn v. Kennedy's, Inc.*, § 12.03[D], supra., and notes. How does probable cause in that context differ from probable cause in a malicious prosecution action? The orthodox answer is that proof of lack of probable cause is an element of the plaintiff's prima facie case in a malicious prosecution action; whereas, it is an element of a defendant's affirmative defense in a false arrest action. The difference affects who has the burden of proof. Most courts agree that the determination of probable cause is a mixed question of fact and law in a false arrest action. Accordingly, if the facts are in dispute, the jury decides the issue; otherwise it is a question of law for the court. See, e.g., *Dyson v. City of Pawtucket*, 670 A.2d 233 (R.I. 1996) and *Jones v. City of Columbia*, 389 S.E.2d 662, 663 (S.C. 1990). A few courts appear to treat the probable cause defense as a jury question in all cases. See, e.g., *Prison v. Delchamps Store No.11*, 507 So.2d 478 (Ala. 1987).

[D]   Defense of Economic Interests

FRANK COULSON, INC.—BUICK v. GENERAL MOTORS CORP.
United States Court of Appeals, Fifth Circuit
488 F.2d 202 (1974)

GEWIN, CIRCUIT JUDGE:

The mutually profitable relationship between an automobile manufacturer and its dealer sometimes ends in an unpleasant separation. In this particular instance, like numerous other disputatious counterparts, litigation ensued. Frank Coulson,

Inc.—Buick (Coulson), formerly a Buick dealer in Florida, brought suit in the Florida state courts against the General Motors Corporation (GM). Coulson asserted two independent grounds for relief: (1) Through duress and undue influence wrongfully exerted by GM, Coulson was forced to sell its dealership assets; and (2) GM had maliciously interfered with the contractual negotiations between

Coulson and the dealership purchaser. General Motors removed the case to federal district court because of diversity of citizenship. On the basis of special interrogatories, a jury found against Coulson on its first theory — forced sale. It awarded damages of $25,000, however, on the second theory — interference with contractual negotiations. The trial judge set aside the jury verdict by granting GM's motion for judgment notwithstanding the verdict and Coulson appeals. We vacate and remand with directions.

Coulson had been at least a moderately successful dealership enjoying steadily increasing sales. In 1970 GM received two letters highly critical of the dealership. The letters allegedly had a substantial influence on Buick executives and shortly after their receipt Coulson received a series of visits from GM representatives. Frank Coulson, corporation president, claimed that the visits were part of plan by GM to force a sale of the dealership assets.

GM representatives apparently suggested that Frank Coulson, age 65, was getting old and should bring a younger man into the business. Coulson agreed to negotiate the sale of his dealership assets, and authorized GM to solicit buyers. In the course of finding buyers GM apparently "spread the word" that Coulson was going out of business. Coulson testified that dessemination of this information caused a decline in sales. He maintained that GM also coerced his sale by demands for unnecessary repairs on his facilities. Furthermore, Gene Miller, the Zone Manager for GM, allegedly intimated that the Coulson franchise would not be renewed. Nevertheless, the franchise was renewed in November 1970, one month before the eventual sale.

Coulson did enter into negotiations for the sale of the dealership assets with Glenn Ralph, a Buick dealer from New York. Frank Coulson testified that in April 1970 he and Ralph agreed on a sales price of $100,000. Gene Miller, however, notified Ralph and Coulson that as GM's Zone Manager he would not approve a sale for any amount in excess of $50,000. GM's approval was essential because without it a purchaser would not receive the necessary Buick franchise.

Coulson testified that $50,000 was the value of the corporation's tangible assets alone — $25,000 in parts and $25,000 in equipment. Thus, a sale at that price would allow nothing for intangible goodwill. Expert testimony was presented by Coulson that the dealership's goodwill might be worth as much as $400,000. Even GM's expert admitted that Coulson's good-will was worth between $35,000 and $50,000. Moreover, GM recognized that Coulson's parts were worth $25,000. Although GM contends that the dealership's furniture, fixtures and equipment had been depreciated to zero, Mr. Miller seemed to recognize the value of $25,000. On cross examination Miller testified that the way he "looked at it" all Coulson had to sell were tangible assets.

Coulson and Ralph eventually consummated a sales transaction. In the written documents the sales price was stated to be $50,000. Additionally, Mr. and Mrs. Coulson entered into a $35,000 transaction with Kengle Realty, a New York corporation owned by Glen Ralph and his brother. This transaction, in a rather complex manner, related to real estate improvements upon the premises in which the Coulson dealership was located. Ralph testified that the two transactions were actually part of the sale, and thus the actual price of the dealership was $85,000. According to Ralph, the second agreement, which related to the real estate, was designed to keep the true price concealed from GM. In response to a special interrogatory the jury found that the $35,000 transaction was indeed separate from the sale of the dealership assets.[15]

The district court submitted each of Coulson's grounds for recovery to the jury. The first theory of recovery, that GM had coerced Coulson in bad faith into a sale, was contained in the following interrogatory:

Do you find from a preponderance of the evidence that the defendant, General Motors, was guilty of bad faith in its dealing with plaintiff?

The jury responded in the negative. Coulson's second ground, that GM maliciously interfered with its negotiations once they were under way, was embodied in another interrogatory:

Do you find from a preponderance of the evidence that the defendant, General Motors, is guilty of malicious interference with the plaintiff's contract negotiations with Ralph?

The jury answered "Yes." The jury, therefore, found that although GM did not coerce Coulson to sell, it had interfered with negotiations for the sale.

The district court granted GM's motion for judgment notwithstanding the verdict assigning three reasons as a basis for its decision: (1) the jury's finding of no bad faith indicated that there was no substantial evidence of malicious interference; (2) GM was privileged to intervene and there was no substantial evidence that it overreached this privilege; (3) the evidence was clear and overwhelming that Coulson had suffered no damage from GM's alleged interference in the contract negotiations. GM has properly urged us to judge the correctness of the result reached by the trial court, not the reason relied upon. Since we view the result as error, however, we must necessarily explain our differences with the lower court.

The district court's first assigned reason was based upon the inconsistency of a finding of no "bad faith" with a finding of "maliciousness." As we understand Florida law, however, a strict legalistic concept of maliciousness is not an element of an action based on interference with a prospective contractual relationship. In Florida, malice will be inferred where the interference is shown to be intentional. Furthermore, we are convinced that the jury was entirely justified in treating the bad faith interrogatory as applicable to Coulson's first theory — forced sale. Coulson's second theory was contained in the malicious interference interrogatory.

---

[15] The jury answered special interrogatory No. 1:

Do you find from a preponderance of the evidence that the $35,000.00 promissory note which was executed and delivered by Kengle Realty, Inc. to Mr. and Mrs. Coulson was part of the purchase price which Ralph paid to the Coulson corporation for the purchase of the dealership business?

Answer "yes" or "no."

ANSWER "No."

We find that the jury's answers are consistent with its award to Coulson Corporation.

. . .

The trial court's final motion for granting the judgment notwithstanding the verdict was the lack of substantial evidence that GM overreached its privilege to intervene. The scope of the privilege to intervene in contractual negotiations is not clearly defined under Florida law. We find no reason to presume, however, that Florida is not in accord with the weight of authority. It is generally recognized that tort liability exists for interference with prospective contractual relationship. The cause of action has run parallel to that for interference with existing contracts. As is the case with existing contracts any manner of intentional invasion of the plaintiff's interests may be sufficient if the purpose is not a privileged one. When the plaintiff proves a prima facie case of interference, the defendant has the burden of avoiding liability by showing that his conduct is privileged or justified.

This branch of the law, unlike others, has not crystallized a complete set of definite rules as to the existence or non-existence of a privilege. Various important factors have been identified, however, which relate to an appraisal of the private interests of the parties involved as well as to a consideration of the social utility of these private interests. The principal issue thus becomes whether the social benefits derived in permitting acts of intervention outweigh the harm to be expected therefrom. Therefore, if Coulson established a prima facie case of interference, GM had the burden of justifying its activity based upon social policy.

On the basis of all the evidence presented, the jury certainly could have believed that GM's zone manager, Miller, stated to Frank Coulson and Glenn Ralph that he would not approve a sale for a price exceeding $50,000. Furthermore, the jury could have concluded that such statements disrupted contractual negotiations and reduced Coulson's sale price. Proof of intentional interference and resulting damage are sufficient to establish Coulson's prima facie case.

GM has a strong private interest in the success of its dealerships. This interest will justify intervention for proper business purposes. GM is privileged to approve or disapprove a purchaser, for example, because it can demonstrate strong and legitimate business interests to justify such action. It will deal with the purchaser in the future and he will represent Buick to the public. The purchaser's integrity is justifiably important.

GM's privilege to intervene as to the dealer's sale price is similarly limited to justifiable business interests. It has been recognized that manufacturers, like GM, have an interest in ensuring that new dealers are financially sound. Such an interest does not grant GM an absolute privilege, however, to limit a dealer's sales price. An expansive construction would give GM the privilege to impose undue economic pressure on its outgoing dealer, in whose business its interest is terminated, and to unduly benefit the incoming dealer's financial strength by exercising a powerful veto and refusing to approve a proposed sale of the dealership except at a grossly inadequate price. In the instant the case the limitation imposed by GM's zone manager was $50,000, the value of the tangible assets. As stated earlier, GM's own expert accountant testified that Coulson's good will was worth between $35,000 and $50,000. Coulson's witness would have placed it much higher. Furthermore, GM's zone manager had no knowledge of Ralph Buick's financial condition when the $50,000 limit was set. It is apparent that the

$50,000 limitation bore no reasonable relation to the future financial solvency of Glenn Ralph Buick, Inc.

After giving due consideration to all of the evidence disclosed in the record, we hold that there was indeed substantial evidence to support the findings of the jury. Accordingly, the jury's verdict in favor of Coulson Corporation must be reinstated. The judgment of the district court is vacated and the case is remanded for proceedings consistent with this opinion.

NOTES AND QUESTIONS

(1)   Is *Coulson* consistent with the following statement on the privilege point?

The law recognizes that a contracting party has a justification or privilege to interfere where necessary to protect that party's own contractual rights provided such interference is without malice. 45 Am.Jur.2d, Interference, Section 29. And, although the texts and cases are somewhat imprecise in their treatment of the subject of privilege, the following statement by the Ohio courts appears to bring the subject into proper focus:

> One who purposely causes a third person not to enter into or continue a business relation with another in order to influence the other's policy in the conduct of his business is privileged if (1) the actor has an economic interest in the matter with reference to which he wishes to influence the policy of the other, (2) the desired policy does not illegally restrain competition or otherwise violate a defined public policy, and (3) the means employed are not improper. *Petty v. Dayton Musicians' Assoc.*, 153 N.E.2d 218 (Ohio Com. Pl. 1958), aff'd. 153 N.E.2d 223 (Ohio App.).

Serafino v. Palm Terrace Apts., 343 So.2d 851, 852 (Fla. App. 1976).

(2)   It is generally agreed that a defendant may interfere to protect his own, existing legally protectable economic interests. Thus, if two parties have an enforceable contract with a third, either of the two may insist upon performance with the third, even though it disables him from performing the other contract. Should a contract terminable at will be protectable under this course of action? Should an injunction against the interferer ever be permitted? Against the third party? See, e.g., *Heavener, Ogier Services v. R. W. Fla. Region*, 418 So.2d 1074 (Fla. App. 1982).

[E]   Insanity and Childhood

In *Williams v. Hays*, 38 N.W. 449, 450-51 (N.Y. 1894), the following statement appears:

> The important question for us to determine, then, is whether the insanity of the defendant furnishes a defense to the plaintiff's claim, and I think it does not. The general rule is that an insane person is just as responsible for his torts as a sane person, and the rule applies to all torts, except, perhaps, those in which malice, and therefore intention, actual or imputed, is a necessary ingredient, like libel, slander, and malicious prosecution. In all other torts, intention is not an ingredient, and the actor is responsible, although he acted with a good and even laudable purpose, without any malice.

The law looks to the person damaged by another, and seeks to make him whole, without reference to the purpose or the condition, mental or physical, of the person causing the damage. The liability of a lunatic for his torts, in the opinions of judges, has been placed upon several grounds. The rule has been invoked that, where one of two innocent persons must bear a loss, he must bear it whose act caused it. It is said that public policy requires the enforcement of the liability, that the relatives of a lunatic may be under inducement to restrain him, and that tortfeasors may not simulate or pretend insanity to defend their wrongful acts, causing damage to others. The lunatic must bear the loss occasioned by his torts, as he bears his other misfortunes, and the burden of such loss may not be put upon others. In Buswell on Insanity (section 355) it is said: "Since, in a civil action for a tort, it is not necessary to aver or prove any wrongful intent on the part of the defendant, it is a rule of the common law that, although a lunatic may not be punishable criminally, he is liable in a civil action for any tort he may commit." In Cooley on Torts (page 98) the learned author says: "A wrong is an invasion of right, to the damage of the party who suffers it. It consists in the injury done, and not commonly in the purpose or mental or physical capacity of the person or agent doing it. It may or may not have been done with bad motive. The question of motive is usually a question of aggravation only. Therefore, the law, in giving redress, has in view the case of the party injured, and the extent of his injury, and makes what he suffers the measure of compensation." . . . There is consequently no anomaly in compelling one who is not chargeable with wrong intent to make compensation for an injury committed by him, for, as is said in an early case, "the reason is because he that is damaged ought to be recompensed." And at page 100 he says: "Undoubtedly, there is some appearance of hardship, even of injustice, in compelling one to respond for that which, for want of the control of reason, he was unable to avoid; that it is imposing upon a person already visited with the inexpressible calamity of mental obscurity an obligation to observe the same care and precaution respecting the rights of others that the law demands of one in the full possession of his faculties. But the question of liability in these cases, as well as in others, is a question of policy; and it is to be disposed of as would be the question whether the incompetent person should be supported at the expense of the public, or of his neighbors, or at the expense of his own estate. If his mental disorder makes him dependent, and at the same time prompts him to commit injuries, there seems to be no greater reason for imposing upon the neighbors or the public one set of these consequences, rather than the other; no more propriety or justice in making others bear the losses resulting from his unreasoning fury, when it is spent upon them or their property, than there would be in calling upon them to pay the expense of his confinement in an asylum, when his own estate is ample for the purpose." In Shearman and Redfield on Negligence (section 57), it is said: "Infants and persons of unsound mind are liable for injuries caused by their tortious negligence; and, so far as their responsibility is concerned, they are held to the same degree of care and diligence as persons of sound mind and full age. This is necessary, because otherwise there would be no redress for injuries committed by such persons; and the anomaly might be witnessed of a child, having abundant wealth, depriving another of his property without compensation." In Reeves' Domestic Relations (page 386), it is said: "Where the minor has committed a tort with force, he is liable at any age; for in case of civil injuries, with force, the intention is not regarded, for in such case a lunatic is as liable to compensate in damages as a man in his right mind." The doctrine of these authorities is illustrated in many interesting cases.

Apart from the law of negligence in which most jurisdictions do acknowledge a child's standard of care of some version, the foregoing statement describes the continuing antipathy of the law to insanity (and childhood as to intentional torts) as a defense to tortious acts. See, e.g., *Shelter Mutual Insurance Company v. Williams*, 804 P.2d 1374 (Kan. 1991). Although *Williams v. Hay* acknowledges that a defendant may be so devoid of reason as to be incapable of forming the intention to do the act that is alleged to have been an intentional tort, very few cases seem to have been decided on that point. See, e.g., *Globe American Casualty Company v. Lyons*, 641 P.2d 251 (Ariz. App. 1982) (holding that a defendant who suffered a "mental derangement which deprived her of her capacity to act in accordance with reason and while in that condition acted on an irrational compulsion to drive her vehicle into oncoming traffic" did not commit an intentional act). Most courts have disagreed with this conclusion. See, e.g., *Johnson v. Insurance Company of North America*, 350 S.E.2d 616 (Va. 1986) (holding that the intentional shooting of another was an intentional act even though the defendant believed God ordered him to do it, but acknowledging that the intention might have been missing had the defendant insanely believed that he was merely "peeling a banana"), and *Williams v. Kearbey*, 775 P.2d 670, 674 (Kan. App. 1989) ("In finding for the plaintiffs, the jury necessarily found that [the defendant] touched or struck the plaintiffs with the intent of bringing about either a contact or an apprehension of contact, that is 'harmful or offensive.' The fact that [he] did not 'understand the nature of his acts' or did not 'understand that what he was doing was prohibited by law' does not preclude the jury from finding that [he] acted intentionally in discharging a weapon [to injure the plaintiff]").

Many of these insanity cases involve the question of whether the insane defendant's liability insurance carrier is responsible for the defendant's tort under a policy that excludes coverages of injuries caused by the defendant's "intentional" acts. *Home Insurance Company v. Aetna Life and Casualty Company*, 644 A.2d 933, 938 (Conn. App. 1994), states, "The rule that mentally infirm persons face civil liability for intentional torts does not . . . preclude a holding that the actions of such persons are regarded as unintentional for the purposes of an intentional action exclusion clause of an insurance policy because the principles have different justifications." Again, most courts seem to disagree. See, *Prasad v. Allstate Insurance Company*, 644 So.2d 992 (Fla. 1994).

[F] Parens Patriae — Intentional Corporal Punishment

THOMAS v. BEDFORD
Louisiana Court of Appeals
389 So. d 405 (1980)

FRED W. JONES, JR., JUDGE.

Anna Spear Goff Thomas, as the natural tutrix of her minor son, Joseph A. Goff, filed this suit against Carter Bedford, a Caddo Parish school teacher, the Caddo Parish School Board, and the latter's liability insurance carrier, Reliance Insurance Company, for injuries allegedly sustained by the minor because of a battery committed by Bedford at a Caddo Parish School.

Plaintiff appeals from a district court judgment rejecting her demands. We reverse and render judgment for plaintiff.

The incident in question occurred in February 1979 at the Northwood High School in Caddo Parish. Goff, a student at the school, was 14 years of age, weighed between 95 and 100 pounds, and was 4 feet 9 inches in height. Bedford, a teacher at the school, was 26 years of age, weighed between 135 and 140 pounds, and was 5 feet 9 inches in height. The two had become acquainted the previous year when Goff was in one of Bedford's classes. The record indicated that, although not a serious disciplinary problem, Goff tended to engage in mischievious behavior, some of which had been occasionally directed at Bedford.

On the afternoon of February 15, 1979, while Bedford was standing outside a classroom at the high school conversing with two other teachers, Goff came up and struck Bedford a light blow in the back with his hand. Instead of going to his class as instructed by Bedford, Goff picked up a rubber band and from a distance of about two feet propelled it into Bedford's face. Goff then turned and ran into his classroom, chased by Bedford who threw a two foot long 1 by 2 board at the youngster, but missed him.

Bedford left and went to his classroom where he remained for ten or fifteen minutes. He then returned to Goff's classroom and pulled the youngster into an adjoining vacant "project" room where the altercation in question took place. Bedford testified that he gave Goff a "severe shaking."

On the other hand, Goff stated that Bedford struck him three or four times on the body with his fist. The statement of the physician who examined Goff, finding that the youngster had contusions of the chest, arms and back, tended to corroborate Goff's version of the incident.

It is now recognized that "corporal punishment, reasonable in degree, administered by a teacher to a pupil for disciplinary reasons, is permitted in Louisiana." Roy v. Continental Insurance Co., 313 So.2d 349 (La.App.3rd Cir. 1975). Further elaborating, the court in Roy commented:

It is also a well established rule in general tort law that a teacher is immune from civil liability for physical corporal punishment, reasonable in degree, administered to a student. But it is likewise clear under tort law that this discretionary right of a teacher to use physical punishment is a limited one and immunity or privilege from liability requires a showing that said punishment was administered neither unreasonably nor excessively, measured in part by such factors as the nature of the punishment itself, the misconduct of the child, the teacher's motive in the discipline, and the age and physical condiction of the pupil. The question of "reasonableness" or "excessiveness" is determined on a case by case basis. . . .

    . . .

The rationale of these cases, which we adopt, is that a minor's school teacher, while the youngster is attending school, stands in the place of the parent for the purpose of enforcing discipline and, in connection therewith, may use a reasonable degree of corporal punishment. The factual question presented by each individual case is whether the punishment was unreasonable or excessive under the circumstances.

In his written reasons for judgment in this case the trial judge concluded that "although the teacher's action greatly exceeded reasonable force (emphasis added), nevertheless, there is sufficient provocation by plaintiff for Mr. Bedford to have lost his temper in rendering corporal punishment on Joseph Goff." In a previous portion of that opinion the minor had been characterized as the "aggressor."

The "aggressor doctrine" contemplates an altercation provoked by the aggressor against a party who defends himself. Even if, under the facts of this case, Goff's striking Bedford in the back and hitting him with a rubber band rendered him an aggressor, it is obvious that the subsequent altercation in the "project" room, some 10 or 15 minutes later after Bedford had admittedly calmed down, was in fact a separate incident and not a spontaneous reaction to the original provocation. Therefore, the "aggressor doctrine" is inapplicable. The pivotal issue here is whether the corporal punishment meted out by Bedford was unreasonable. The trial judge explicitly answered that question in the affirmative. Since this is a factual question and our review of the record does not show that the trial judge was clearly wrong in his conclusion, we must accept that ruling. Consequently, under our jurisprudence Bedford, his employer and the latter's insurance carrier are liable for Goff's injuries.

Legitimate concern for disciplinary problems in our schools ably articulated by the conscientious trial judge, does not permit us to disregard our responsibility to accord due deference to the rights of all those participants in the educational process, students as well as teachers and administrators. Needless to say, our law does not by any means render the latter impotent in the face of rule infractions. Where appropriate, corporal punishment may be administered in a reasonable manner as a measured, rational response to serious acts of misconduct.

On the issue of quantum it is obvious that the injuries sustained by Goff were relatively minor, consisting of bruises which remained sore for a week or two. No classes were missed. Under the circumstances, we conclude that the sum of $500.00 will adequately compensate the plaintiff for her son's injuries.

For the reasons set forth, we reverse the judgment of the trial court and render judgment in favor of the plaintiff and against the defendants, in solido, for the sum of $500.00 together with legal interest as provided for by law and court costs in the lower court and on appeal.

NOTES AND QUESTIONS

(1) *Setliff v. Raides Parish School Board*, 888 So.2d 1156 (La. App. 2004) applied the following statute and local policy to deny a recovery:

LSA-RS§ 223. Discipline of pupils; suspension from school, corporal punishment A. Every teacher is authorized to hold every pupil to a strict accountability for any disorderly conduct in school or on the playground of the school, or on any school bus going to or returning from school, or during intermission or recess. Each parish and city school board shall have discretion in the use of corporal punishment. In those cases in which a parish or city school board decides to use corporal punishment, each parish or city school board shall adopt such rules and regulations as it deems necessary to implement and control any form of corporal punishment in the schools in its district.

(2) As stated by the United States Supreme Court in *Ingraham v. Wright*, 430 U.S. 651, 659, 97 S.Ct. 1401, 1406, 51 L.Ed. 2d 711 (1977):

The use of corporal punishment in this country as a means of disciplining school children dates back to the colonial period. It has survived the transformation of primary and secondary education from the colonials' reliance on optional private arrangements to our present system of compulsory education and dependence on public schools. Despite the general abandonment of corporal punishment as a means of punishing criminal offenders, the practice continues to play a role in the public education of school children in most parts of the country. Professional and public opinion is sharply divided on the practice, and has been for more than a century. Yet we can discern no trend toward its elimination.

Spacek v. Charles, 928 S.W.2d 88, (Tex. App. 1996), cited Ingraham for this proposition: "Corporal punishment is but one form of discipline that the common law sanctions, providing that teachers impose reasonable but not excessive force in disciplining a child." See also *Rinehart v. Board of Education, Western Local School District*, 621 N.E. 1365 (Ohio App. 1993), holding a school teacher to be immune from tort liability under the Ohio statutes.

[G]   Apprehension of a Fleeing Felon

Although the rule has been criticized in modern times, the common law generally permitted peace officers to use deadly force to apprehend a person suspected of the commission of a felony where necessary to make the apprehension, despite the fact that the suspected person was not threatening the life of anyone at the moment. See, e.g., *Werner v. Hartfelder*, 113 Mich. App. 747 (1982). Whether or not the common law permits private citizens to use deadly force in the same circumstances is more disputed. Id. The Model Penal Code would limit the use of deadly force to occasions wherein it is essential to the protection of human life and bodily security or where violence was used in committing the felony, but that rule has been adopted in comparatively few jurisdictions. Id., 750, 751.

In England, the rule has been described as follows:

The power of arrest is confided by the common law both to constables and to private individuals. The constable has power within his district to arrest a person on reasonable suspicion of his having committed a felony. The private individual has power on two conditions: (1) that a felony has actually been committed; (2) that there is reasonable and probable cause of suspecting the person arrested. In these cases the grounds for suspicion must be brought before the court, the onus is on the person who arrested to prove the reasonable grounds, and the issue whether the cause is reasonable or not is to be determined by the judge. These propositions will be found in any elementary text book. I will refer to authority that the defendant in an action for false imprisonment based on unlawful arrest is entitled to succeed if he pleads and proves that the imprisonment was legally justifiable . . . that he must show the cause of suspicion so that the court may judge of the reasonableness . . . that a man directing a constable to act on a suggestion of felony is bound to show probable cause of suspicion . . . that the plea must show reasonable and probable ground for suspicion, i.e., facts which raise a reasonable suspicion, not all the evidence (per Lord Campbell C.J.), and it is for the court to say whether the facts pleaded shew reasonable cause . . . that it is a good plea that the man was arrested on a reasonable suspicion of felony, but not enough that the suspicion was bona fide . . . that the civilian defendant must make out a reasonable ground of suspicion and that a felony has actually been committed. . . . In all these cases it is obvious that the courts were dealing with an objective fact to be proved before them by the defendant, and that their pronouncements would be nonsense if the inquiry had only been whether the defendant believed that he had reasonable ground.

Liverside v. Sir John Anderson, 1942 App. Cas. 206, 228, 229 (H.L.).

Most fleeing felon cases involve governmental defendants (e.g., police officers) and often invoke constitutional law questions in addition to torts issues. These questions are beyond the scope of this text. See *Tennessee v. Garner*, 478 U.S. 1, 105 S.Ct. 1094, 85 L.Ed. 2d 1 (1985) (invalidating a Tennessee statute that authorized the use of deadly force against an unarmed and not dangerous fleeing felon).

Chapter 13

COMMON LAW STRICT LIABILITY PROBLEM

Each year the students of a principal state university hold a homecoming extravaganza that includes an elaborate nighttime fireworks display in the football stadium. This event is formally sanctioned and supported by the university's administration. Great Explosions, Inc. is the manufacturer of the fireworks.

In the year in question certain of the sky rockets were packed with more explosive than called for in the specifications. The organizers had ordered and used the product defined by the manufacturer's specifications for ten previous years. Although more than 1000 of the particular product had been set off in the display during those years, no part of any of them was ever known to have escaped from the safety zone employed by the organizers of the event. Furthermore, there is no record that any other user of this particular product had found them to be charged with explosives in excess of the specifications.

On this occasion, one of the over-charged rockets flew onto a nearby divided highway and, while still burning fiercely, lighted on the top of a tank truck of gasoline owned by Star Oil Transporting Company, a major transporter of motor fuels. The truck was driven by Mike Malone, an employee of Star Oil. Seeing the bright flames in the side mirror of the truck, Malone pulled the truck off the highway and leaped out of the cab, fire extinguisher in hand. By that time the flames had ignited the rubber gasket on a secured opening on the top of the truck, and Malone quickly perceived that the fire was out of his control. He immediately began running down the highway waving his arms in an attempt to stop on-coming traffic.

The tank truck exploded sending out a great ball of flame that overtook Malone and severely burned him. Other supercharged missiles landed on the property of the university, causing substantial property damage.

The vibrations in the earth produced by the explosion also knocked over cages on nearby land owned by the Exotic Pharmaceutical Company. The cages contained poisonous snakes from which venom was to be extracted to make medicines. These cages were bolted to concrete piers and were designed to be safe against the strongest earthquake anyone ever predicted for the area. One of the snakes escaped and bit John Locke, a pedestrian, who became extremely ill and was hospitalized.

Several lawsuits ensue: Malone sues Star Oil, the university, and Great Explosions, Inc. for damages flowing from his personal injuries. Star Oil sues the university and Great Explosions, Inc. for the loss of its truck and cargo and to recoup workers' compensation payments made to Malone. The university sues Great Explosions, Inc. to recover for damages done the stadium by others of the overcharged rockets and to be indemnified against any judgment that might be executed against it by Malone or Star Oil. Exotic Pharmaceutical Company sues

Star Oil Company, the university, and Great Explosions, Inc. seeking damages for its losses and indemnity against its liability, if any, to Locke. Locke sues Exotic Pharmaceutical Company, Star Oil Company, the university, and Great Explosions, Inc. seeking damages stemming from his personal injuries.

Assume the cases have been tried and sufficient evidence adduced to prove each and every one of the foregoing facts and no others. You are the trial court judge. For each case, write a jury instruction that states the appropriate standard of liability of each defendant to each plaintiff. Assume that the state university is an independent legal entity, capable of being sued and not entitled to sovereign immunity.

FLETCHER v. RYLANDS
L.R.I. Ex. 265, 159 Eng. Rep. 737 (Ex. 1866)[1]

BLACKBURN, J.

This was a special case stated by an arbitrator, under an order of nisi prius, in which the question for the Court is stated to be, whether the plaintiff is entitled to recover any, and, if any, what damages from the defendants, by reason of the matters there-in-before stated.

In the Court of Exchequer, the Chief Baron and Martin, B., were of opinion that the plaintiff was not entitled to recover at all, Bramwell, B., being of a different opinion. The judgment in the Exchequer was consequently given for the defendants in conformity with the opinion of the majority of the court. The only question argued before us was, whether this judgment was right, nothing being said about the measure of damages in case the plaintiff should be held entitled to recover. We have come to the conclusion that the opinion of Bramwell, B., was right, and that the answer to the question should be that the plaintiff was entitled to recover damages from the defendants, by reason of the matters stated in the case, and consequently, that the judgment below should be reversed, but we cannot at present say to what damages the plaintiff is entitled.

It appears from the statement in the case, that the plaintiff was damaged by his property being flooded by water, which, without any fault on his part, broke out of a reservoir constructed on the defendants' land by the defendants' orders, and maintained by the defendants.

It appears from the statement in the case that the coal under the defendants' land had, at some remote period, been worked out; but this was unknown at the time when the defendants gave directions to erect the reservoir, and the water in the reservoir would not have escaped from the defendants' land, and no mischief would have been done to the plaintiff, but for this latent defect in the defendants' subsoil. And it further appears, that the defendants selected competent engineers and contractors to make their reservoir, and themselves personally continued in total ignorance of what we have called the latent defect in the subsoil; but that these persons employed by them in the course of the work became aware of the existence of the ancient shafts filled up with soil, though they did not know or suspect that they were shafts communicating with old workings.

---

[1] [Ed. — English reports, general reporter of older English cases, decision of Exchequer Division Court of Appeal; Law Reports, Exchequer Court.]

It is found that the defendants, personally, were free from all blame, but that in fact proper care and skill was not used by the persons employed by them, to provide for the sufficiency of the reservoir with reference to these shafts. The consequence was, that the reservoir when filled with water burst into the shafts, the water flowed down through them into the old workings, and thence into the plaintiff's mine, and there did the mischief.

The plaintiff, though free from all blame on his part, must bear the loss, unless he can establish that it was the consequence of some default for which the defendants are responsible. The question of law therefore arises, what is the obligation which the law casts on a person who, like the defendants, lawfully brings on his land something which, though harmless whilst it remains there, will naturally do mischief if it escapes out of his land. It is agreed on all hands that he must take care to keep in that which he has brought on the land and keeps there, in order that it may not escape and damage his neighbours, but the question arises whether the duty which the law casts upon him, under such circumstances, is an absolute duty to keep it in at his peril, or is, as the majority of the Court of Exchequer have thought, merely a duty to take all reasonable and prudent precautions, in order to keep it in, but no more. If the first be the law, the person who has brought on his land and kept there something dangerous, and failed to keep it in, is responsible for all the natural consequences of its escape. If the second be the limit of his duty, he would not be answerable except on proof of negligence, and consequently would not be answerable for escape arising from any latent defect which ordinary prudence and skill could not detect.

. . .

We think that the true rule of law is, that the person who for his own purposes brings on his lands and collects and keeps there anything likely to do mischief if it escapes, must keep it in at his peril, and, if he does not do so, is prima facie answerable for all the damage which is the natural consequence of its escape. He can excuse himself by showing that the escape was owing to the plaintiff's default; or perhaps that the escape was the consequence of vis major, or the act of God; but as nothing of this sort exists here, it is unnecessary to inquire what excuse would be sufficient. The general rule, as above stated, seems on principle just. The person whose grass or corn is eaten down by the escaping cattle of his neighbour, or whose mine is flooded by the water from his neighbour's reservoir, or whose cellar is invaded by the filth of the neighbour's privy, or whose habitation is made unhealthy by the fumes and noisome vapours of his neighbour's alkali works, is damnified without any fault of his own; and it seems but reasonable and just that the neighbour, who has brought something on his own property which was not naturally there, harmless to others so long as it is confined to his own property, but which he knows to be mischievous if it gets on his neighbour's, should be obliged to make good the damage which ensues if he does not succeed in confining it to his own property. But for his act in bringing it there no mischief could have accrued, and it seems but just that he should at his peril keep it there so that no mischief may accrue, or answer for the natural and anticipated consequences. And upon authority, this we think is established to be the law whether the things so brought be beasts, or water, or filth, or stenches.

. . .

RYLANDS v. FLETCHER
LR 3, H.L. 352 (1868)[2]

THE LORD CHANCELLOR (LORD CAIRNS): —

. . .

My Lords, the principles on which this case must be determined appear to me to be extremely simple. The Defendants, treating them as the owners or occupiers of the close on which the reservoir was constructed, might lawfully have used that close for any purpose for which it might in the ordinary course of the enjoyment of land be used and if, in what I may term the natural user of that land, there had been any accumulation of water, either on the surface or underground, and if, by the operation of the laws of nature, that accumulation of water had passed off into the close occupied by the Plaintiff, the Plaintiff could not have complained that that result had taken place. If he had desired to guard himself against it, it would have lain upon him to have done so, by leaving, or by interposing, some barrier between his close and the close of the Defendants in order to have prevented that operation of the laws of nature.

. . .

On the other hand if the Defendants, not stopping at the natural use of their close, had desired to use it for any purpose which I may term a non-natural use, for the purpose of introducing into the close that which in its natural condition was not in or upon it, for the purpose of introducing water either above or below ground in quantities and in a manner not the result of any work or operation on or under the land, — and if in consequence of their doing so, or in consequence of any imperfection in the mode of their doing so, the water came to escape and to pass off into the close of the Plaintiff, then it appears to me that that which the Defendants were doing they were doing at their own peril; and, if in the course of their doing it, the evil arose to which I have referred, the evil, namely, of the escape of the water and its passing away to the close of the Plaintiff and injuring the Plaintiff, then for the consequence of that, in my opinion, the Defendants would be liable.

. . .

My Lords, these simple principles, if they are well founded, as it appears to me they are, really dispose of this case.

The same result is arrived at on the principles referred to by Mr. Justice *Blackburn* in his judgment, in the Court of Exchequer Chamber.

. . .

My Lords, in that opinion, I must say I entirely concur. Therefore, I have to move your Lordships that the judgment of the Court of Exchequer Chamber be affirmed, and that the present appeal be dismissed with costs.

---

[2] [Ed. — Law Reports Court of Exchequer, decision of House of Lords.]

Lord Cransworth: —

My Lords, I concur with my noble and learned friends in thinking that the rule of law was correctly stated by Mr. Justice Blackburn in delivering the opinion of the Exchequer Chamber. If a person brings, or accumulates, on his land anything which, if it should escape, may cause damage to his neighbor, he does so at his peril. If it does escape, and cause damage, he is responsible, however careful he may have been, and whatever precautions he may have taken to prevent the damage.

. . .

I concur, therefore, with my noble and learned friends in thinking that the judgment below must be affirmed, and that there must be judgment for the Defendant in Error.

Judgment of the Court of Exchequer Chamber affirmed.

Lords' Journals, 17th July, 1868.

QUESTIONS

Is the Lord Chancellor's apparent approval of the judgment of Blackburn, J. a total validation of its *ratio decidendi*? If not, is the difference of practical importance?

CLARK-AIKEN COMPANY v. CROMWELL-WRIGHT COMPANY
Massachusetts Supreme Court
323 N.E.2d 876 (1975)

Tauro, Chief Justice.

. . .

The plaintiff brought an action in tort in two counts; the first alleging negligence, the second in strict liability. It seeks to recover for damage caused when water allegedly stored behind a dam on the defendant's property was released and flowed onto its property. A Superior Court judge sustained the defendant's demurrer on the ground that "Count II . . . does not allege a cause of action under the law of this Commonwealth." He held that, "in order to recover for damage caused by the water which escaped from the dam owned by the Defendants, the Plaintiffs must allege and prove that the escape was caused by intentional or negligent fault of some person or entity." The sole issue before us is whether a cause of action in strict liability exists in this Commonwealth regardless of considerations of fault on the part of the defendant. After careful consideration, we conclude that strict liability as enunciated in the case of *Rylands v. Fletcher*, [1868] L.R. 3 H.L. 330, is, and has been, the law of the Commonwealth.

. . .

The lower appellate court considered two possible courses in the case: it could be decided on the basis of negligence, in which case the court would be required to face the issue of whether a defendant would be liable for the acts of its contractors, or it could be viewed as a strict liability case, thereby obviating the need for making such a determination.

[Discussion of opinions in *Rylands v. Fletcher* omitted. The present defendant argued that liability there was in negligence.]

There is, then, nothing in either opinion in the *Rylands* case which would support the defendant's contention that the case is founded on negligence. Furthermore, the English courts have never regarded it as anything but one of strict liability. . . .

. . . Finally, there is no basis to conclude that this court has adopted anything but the broad strict liability rule of the case, and Massachusetts case law follows and supports this view.

In the instant case the defendant contends (and the Superior Court judge agreed) that none of the Massachusetts cases which purportedly apply the rule of strict liability are in fact premised on that doctrine. Furthermore, the defendant disputes the authority of those cases which seemingly approve the doctrine, recognizing it as the law of the Commonwealth, and argues that the citing of the *Rylands* case as authority in them is either in an improper context or unnecessary to the decision. We cannot agree with this analysis. We think that logic and reason permit these cases to be read consistently with the existence of strict liability as a rule of law in this Commonwealth. We proceed to an examination of these cases to illustrate the point.

[Examination of cases omitted]

In light of what we have said, it becomes necessary to examine the parameters of the strict liability doctrine to determine whether it is applicable to the facts as pleaded in count 2 of the declaration in this case. As previously stated, Lord Cairns in *Rylands v. Fletcher, supra,* narrowed the applicability of strict liability to those uses of one's property which could be termed "non-natural." This limitation subsequently developed into the requirement that, in order to subject a landowner to strict liability, he must be using his property in an "unusual and extraordinary" way. . . .

In *United Elec. Light Co. v. Deliso Constr. Co., Inc.,* 315 Mass. 313, 322, 52 N.E.2d 553, 558 (1943), this court characterized a proper subject for imposition of strict liability as "an unusual undertaking or one of such an extremely dangerous nature that it must be performed at the sole risk of the one therein engaged." Thus, while upholding the strict liability doctrine, we held nonetheless that a mixture of cement and water used in underground tunnelling which escaped onto the plaintiff's property, was not a proper subject for imposition of strict liability, on the ground that "[t]hey were ordinary materials widely used in construction work." *Ibid.* To the same effect is a water tank or pressing system in a commercial building, *Fibre Leather Mfg. Corp. v. Ramsay Mills, Inc.,* 329 Mass. 575, 109 N.E.2d 910 (1952); *Brian v. B. Sopkin & Sons, Inc.,* 314 Mass. 180, 49 N.E.2d 894 (1943), and a chemical widely used in cleaning, *Kaufman v. Boston Dye House, Inc.,* 280 Mass. 161, 182 N.E. 297 (1932). Conversely, we found the useless wall of a burned out structure left standing to be an appropriate subject for strict liability, *Ainsworth v. Lakin, supra,* and the same is true of dams and dikes in certain circumstances. . . .

This formulation of strict liability is in accord with the proposed revision of Restatement 2d: Torts (Tent. Draft No. 10, April 20, 1964), § 519, which provides that "[o]ne who carries on an abnormally dangerous activity is subject to liability for harm . . . resulting from the activity, although he has exercised the utmost care to prevent such harm." Section 520 then sets out the factors to be considered in determining whether the activity in question is to be considered "abnormally dangerous." These are: "(a) Whether the activity involves a high degree of risk of some harm to the person, land or chattels of others; (b) Whether the gravity of the harm which may result from it is likely to be great; (c) Whether the risk cannot be eliminated by the exercise of reasonable care; (d) Whether the activity is not a matter of common usage; (e) Whether the activity is inappropriate to the place where it is carried on: and (f) The value of the activity to the community." Comment f to . . . § 520 states in part, "In general, abnormal dangers arise from activities which are in themselves unusual, or from unusual risks created by more usual activities under particular circumstances. . . . The essential question is whether the risk created is so unusual, either because of its magnitude or because of the circumstances surrounding it, as to justify the imposition of strict liability for the harm which results from it, even though it is carried on with all reasonable care."

The tentative draft cautions against defining a type of activity as "abnormally dangerous" in and of itself, however, and advocates considering the activity in light of surrounding circum- stances on the facts of each case. This, in essence, shifts consideration from the nature of the activity to the nature and extent of the risk. As an example, it distinguishes cases where large quantities of water are stored "in dangerous location in a city" from those in which "water is collected in a rural area, with no particularly valuable property near," imposing strict liability in the former but not the latter case. § 520(3). We believe this approach is sound and comports well with the basic theory underlying the strict liability rule. Additionally, it finds support in our prior case law, and accordingly we choose to follow it.

This case is before us on a report by a judge of the Superior Court and technically requires us only to answer the question reported. However, the defendant's demurrer to count 2 (strict liability) was sustained below on the theory that strict liability is not the law of the Common- wealth. We must examine the plaintiff's declaration, then, to determine whether the facts pleaded are sufficient to state a cause of action in strict liability.

The relevant portion of count 2 of the plaintiff's declaration. . . . can be construed as setting forth sufficient facts to support all the elements of the plaintiff's claim. It alleges that the defendant carried on the challenged activity for its own benefit, that said activity was dangerous and created a risk of harm to the plaintiff, that the danger thus created in fact ensued, and that the plaintiff was damaged thereby.

It is not for this court, at this juncture, to decide whether the ultimate facts established at the trial will make out a case for imposition of strict liability. "Whether the activity is an abnormally dangerous one is to be determined by the [trial] court, upon consideration of all the factors listed . . . and the weight given to each which it merits upon the facts in evidence." Restatement 2d:

Torts (Tent. Draft No. 10, April 20, 1964), § 520, comment, p. 68. Moreover, the real issue is not the *sufficiency of the pleadings* but rather one of substantive law, namely the existence of strict liability as the law of Massachusetts. We decide merely that the plaintiff's declaration is sufficient to set forth a cause of action under Massachusetts law. Accordingly, (a) we answer the reported question in the affirmative and (b) we reverse the order below sustaining the defendant's demurrer.

So ordered.

NOTES AND QUESTIONS

(1)   As to the effect to be given to a determination that an activity is abnormally dangerous, the Restatement, Torts, Second prescribes:[3]

§ 519 General Principle

(1) One who carries on an abnormally dangerous activity is subject to liability for harm to the person, land or chattels of another resulting from the activity, although he has exercised the utmost care to prevent the harm.

(2) This strict liability is limited to the kind of harm, the possibility of which makes the activity abnormally dangerous.

(2)   Should the doctrine of *Rylands v. Fletcher* as adopted in *Clark-Aiken Co.* be applied to either of the following cases?

a. Drilling oil in Texas occasions the building of ponds to store briny fluids that come up from the wells during drilling. Creating ponds of fresh water is common in Texas because of the aridity of most of the state and the need to store water for livestock and irrigation. This practice began early in the history of the state. Suppose a brine pond levee should collapse, ruining a farmer's pasture with the flood of salty water. Must the plaintiff prove negligence by the defendant?

b. Central Florida is the site of a rich lode of phosphate ore. Converting the natural ore to usable product produces massive quantities of a slimy colloid that remains in suspension for years. Thus, producers must construct huge ponds to store the slime. Suppose a slime pond dike bursts, releasing billions of gallons of the colloid into a river that abounded with fish, fishers, swimmers, boaters and other users. The slime destroyed practically all life in the river and rendered the water unpotable. Should appropriate plaintiffs be required to prove negligence by the defendant?

Compare *Turner v. Big Lake Oil Co.*, 96 S.W.2d 221 (Tex. 1936), and *Cities Service Co. v. State*, 312 So. 2d 799 (Fla. App. 1975).

(3)   In answering the questions posed in the preceding note, consider that not all courts have receded from an early American tendency to reject the doctrine of *Rylands v. Fletcher.* For example, in *Moulton v. Groveton Papers Company*, 289 A.2d 68 (N.H. 1972), the court refused to extend the strict liability notions it had adopted for defective products (*See* Chapter 14 *infra)* to breaking dams. Said the court, at 72:

---

[3] Copyright 1965 by The American Law Institute. Reprinted with the permission of The American Law Institute.

We are of the opinion that the history and the considerations which have led this court to adopt strict liability in products actions are substantially different from those which prevail in the case of dams.

For almost a century this court has followed a consistent policy against imposing absolute liability except in very few instances. . . . The rule of absolute liability for trespass "appears to have been. repudiated in England, where it was born, and it is safe to say that it is almost at its last gasp in the United States." Prosser, Torts § 13, at 64 (4th ed. 1971); *see* Restatement (Second) of Torts, § 166 (1965). The above is not a strong inducement for changing our long established policy against imposing absolute liability.

Although the reported demise of common law strict liability referred to in the foregoing quotation is certainly exaggerated, it remains true that some United States jurisdictions have never acknowledged it. *See, e.g., Wyrulec Company v. Schutt*, 866 P.2d 756, 761 (Wyo. 1993), and *Barras v. Monsanto Company*, 831 S.W.2d 859, 865 (Tex. App. 1992). The English repudiation is untrue, *see, e.g., Cambridge Water Co. Ltd. v. Eastern Counties Leather plc*, [1994] A.C. 264 (House of Lords), but it is apparently true that *Rylands v. Fletcher* has never been incorporated into Scot law. *See, e.g., RHM Bakeries (Scotland) Ltd. v. Strathclyde Regional Council*, The Times (January 1985) (House of Lords).

KLEIN v. PYRODYNE CORPORATION
Supreme Court of Washington, En Banc
810 P.2d 917, as amended, 817 P.2d 1359 (1991)

GUY, JUSTICE.

The plaintiffs in this case are persons injured when an aerial shell at a public fireworks exhibition went astray and exploded near them. The defendant is the pyrotechnic company hired to set up and discharge the fireworks. The issue before this court is whether pyrotechnicians are strictly liable for damages caused by fireworks displays. We hold that they are.

Defendant Pyrodyne Corporation (Pyrodyne) is a general contractor for aerial fireworks at public fireworks displays. Pyrodyne contracted to procure fireworks, to provide pyrotechnic operators, and to display the fireworks at the Western Washington State Fairgrounds in Puyallup, Washington on July 4, 1987. All operators of the fireworks display were Pyrodyne employees acting within the scope of their employment duties. As required by Washington statute, Pyrodyne purchased a $1,000,000 insurance policy prior to the fireworks show. The policy provided $1,000,000 coverage for each occurrence of bodily injury or property damage liability. Plaintiffs allege that Pyrodyne failed to carry out a number of the other statutory and regulatory requirements in preparing for and setting off the fireworks. For example, they allege that Pyrodyne failed to properly bury the mortar tubes prior to detonation, failed to provide a diagram of the display and surrounding environment to the local government, failed to provide crowd control monitors, and failed to keep the invitees at the mandated safe distance.

During the fireworks display, one of the 5-inch mortars was knocked into a horizontal position. From this position a shell inside was ignited and discharged. The shell flew 500 feet in a trajectory parallel to the earth and exploded near the crowd of onlookers. Plaintiffs Danny and Marion Klein were injured by the explosion. Mr. Klein's clothing was set on fire, and he suffered facial burns and serious injury to his eyes. The parties provide conflicting explanations of the cause of the improper horizontal discharge of the shell. Pyrodyne argues that the accident was caused by a 5-inch shell detonating in its above-ground mortar tube without ever leaving the ground.[4] Pyrodyne asserts that this detonation caused another mortar tube to be knocked over, ignited, and shot off horizontally. In contrast, the Kleins contend that the misdirected shell resulted because Pyrodyne's employees improperly set up the display. They further note that because all of the evidence exploded, there is no means of proving the cause of the misfire.

The Kleins brought suit against Pyrodyne under theories of products liability and strict liability.[5] Pyrodyne filed a motion for summary judgment, which the trial court granted as to the products liability claim. The trial court denied Pyrodyne's summary judgment motion regarding the Kleins' strict liability claim, holding that Pyrodyne was strictly liable without fault and ordering summary judgment in favor of the Kleins on the issue of liability. Pyrodyne appealed the order of partial summary judgment to the Court of Appeals, which certified the case to this court. Pyrodyne is appealing solely as to the trial court's holding that strict liability is the appropriate standard of liability for pyrotechnicians. A strict liability claim against pyrotechnicians for damages caused by fireworks displays presents a case of first impression in Washington.

ANALYSIS

I

FIREWORKS DISPLAYS AS ABNORMALLY DANGEROUS ACTIVITIES

The Kleins contend that strict liability is the appropriate standard to determine the culpability of Pyrodyne because Pyrodyne was participating in an abnormally dangerous activity. This court has addressed liability for fireworks display injuries on one prior occasion. In *Callahan v. Keystone Fireworks Mfg. Co.*, 72 Wash. 2d 823, 435 P.2d 626 (1967), this court held that a pyrotechnician could maintain a negligence suit against the manufacturer of the defective fireworks. The issue as to whether fireworks displays are abnormally dangerous activities subject to strict liability was not raised before the court at that time, and hence remains open for this court to decide.

The modern doctrine of strict liability for abnormally dangerous activities derives from *Fletcher v. Rylands*, 159 Eng. Rep. 737 (1865), *rev'd*, 1 L.R.-Ex. 265, [1866] All E.R. 1, 6, *aff'd sub nom. Rylands v. Fletcher*, 3 L.R.- H.L. 330, [1868] All E.R. 1, 12, in which the defendant's reservoir flooded mine shafts on the plaintiff's adjoining land. *Rylands v. Fletcher* has come to stand for the rule that "the defendant will be liable when he damages another by a thing or activity unduly dangerous and inappropriate to the place where it is maintained, in the light of the

---

[4] Plaintiffs note that Pyrodyne's argument is based upon an affidavit made by Pyrodyne's President, Jerry Elrod, who was not present at the display.

[5] Defendants kept no record as to the manufacturer of the aerial bombs used in the July 4, 1987 display; thus, the manufacturer was not identifiable.

character of that place and its surroundings." W. Keeton, D. Dobbs, R. Keeton & D. Owen, *Prosser and Keeton on Torts* § 78, at 547–48 (5th ed. 1984).

The basic principle of *Rylands v. Fletcher* has been accepted by the Restatement (920 Second) of Torts (1977). *See generally Prosser and Keeton* § 78, at 551 (explaining that the relevant Restatement sections differ in some respects from the *Rylands* doctrine). Section 519 of the Restatement provides that any party carrying on an "abnormally dangerous activity" is strictly liable for ensuing damages. The test for what constitutes such an activity is stated in section 520 of the Restatement. Both Restatement sections have been adopted by this court, and determination of whether an activity is an "abnormally dangerous activity" is a question of law. . . .

Section 520 of the Restatement lists six factors that are to be considered in determining whether an activity is "abnormally dangerous". The factors are as follows:

> (a) existence of a high degree of risk of some harm to the person, land or chattels of others;
>
> (b) likelihood that the harm that results from it will be great;
>
> (c) inability to eliminate the risk by the exercise of reasonable care;
>
> (d) extent to which the activity is not a matter of common usage;
>
> (e) inappropriateness of the activity to the place where it is carried on; and
>
> (f) extent to which its value to the community is outweighed by its dangerous attributes.

Restatement (Second) of Torts § 520 (1977). As we previously recognized in *Langan v. Valicopters, Inc., supra,* 88 Wash. 2d at 861–62, 567 P.2d 218 (citing Tent. Draft No. 10, 1964, of comment (f) to section 520), the comments to section 520 explain how these factors should be evaluated:

> Any one of them is not necessarily sufficient of itself in a particular case, and ordinarily several of them will be required for strict liability. On the other hand, it is not necessary that each of them be present, especially if others weigh heavily. Because of the interplay of these various factors, it is not possible to reduce abnormally dangerous activities to any definition. The essential question is whether the risk created is so unusual, either because of its magnitude or because of the circumstances surrounding it, as to justify the imposition of strict liability for the harm that results from it, even though it is carried on with all reasonable care.

Restatement (Second) of Torts § 520, comment *f* (1977). Examination of these factors persuades us that fireworks displays are abnormally dangerous activities justifying the imposition of strict liability.

We find that the factors stated in clauses (a), (b), and (c) are all present in the case of fireworks displays. Any time a person ignites aerial shells or rockets with the intention of sending them aloft to explode in the presence of large crowds of people, a high risk of serious personal injury or property damage is created. That risk arises because of the possibility that a shell or rocket will malfunction or be misdirected. Furthermore, no matter how much care pyrotechnicians exercise, they cannot entirely eliminate the high risk inherent in setting off powerful explosives such as fireworks near crowds. The dangerousness of fireworks displays is evidenced by the elaborate scheme of administrative regulations with which pyrotechnicians must comply. Pyrotechnicians must be licensed to conduct public displays of special fireworks. . . . The necessity for such regulations demonstrates the dangerousness of fireworks displays.

Pyrodyne argues that if the regulations are complied with, then the high degree of risk otherwise inherent in the displays can be eliminated. Although we recognize that the high risk can be reduced, we do not agree that it can be eliminated. Setting off powerful fireworks near large crowds remains a highly risky activity even when the safety precautions mandated by statutes and regulations are followed. The Legislature appears to agree, for it has declared that in order to obtain a license to conduct a public fireworks display, a pyrotechnician must first obtain a surety bond or a certificate of insurance, the amount of which must be at least $1,000,000 for each event.[6] RCW 70.77.285,.295.

The factors stated in clauses (a), (b), and (c) together, and sometimes one of them alone, express what is commonly meant by saying an activity is ultrahazardous. Restatement (Second) of Torts § 520, comment *h* (1977). As the Restatement explains, however, "[l]iability for abnormally dangerous activities is not . . . a matter of these three factors alone, and those stated in Clauses (d), (e), and (f) must still be taken into account." Restatement (Second) of Torts § 520, comment *h* (1977); *see also New Meadows Holding Co. v. Washington Water Power Co., supra,* 102 Wash. 2d at 504, 687 P.2d 212 (Pearson, J., concurring) ("strict liability . . . may not be imposed absent the presence of at least one of the factors stated in clauses (d), (e), and (f)").

The factor expressed in clause (d) concerns the extent to which the activity is not a matter "of common usage". The Restatement explains that "[a]n activity is a matter of common usage if it is customarily carried on by the great mass of mankind or by many people in the community." Restatement (Second) of Torts § 520, comment *i* (1977). As examples of activities that are not matters of common usage, the Restatement comments offer driving a tank, blasting, the manufacture, storage, transportation, and use of high explosives, and drilling for oil. The deciding characteristic is that few persons engage in these activities. Likewise, relatively few persons conduct public fireworks displays. Therefore, presenting public fireworks displays is not a matter of common usage.

Pyrodyne argues that the factor stated in clause (d) is not met because fireworks are a common way to celebrate the 4th of July. We reject this argument. Although fireworks are frequently and regularly enjoyed by the public, few persons set off special fireworks displays. Indeed, the general public is prohibited by statute from making public fireworks displays insofar as anyone wishing to do so must first obtain a license. RCW 70.77.255.

The factor stated in clause (e) requires analysis of the appropriateness of the activity to the place where it was carried on. In this case, the fireworks display was conducted at the Puyallup Fairgrounds. Although some locations — such as over

---

[6] The fact that the Legislature requires a liability policy for an activity does not in itself imply that the Legislature views the activity as being abnormally dangerous for purposes of imposing strict liability. The fact that the Legislature has mandated a $1,000,000 liability policy for pyrotechnicians, however, does suggest that the Legislature views public fireworks displays as involving a high risk even when the appropriate safety precautions are taken.

water — may be safer, the Puyallup Fairgrounds is an appropriate place for a fireworks show because the audience can be seated at a reasonable distance from the display. Therefore, the clause (e) factor is not present in this case.

The factor stated in clause (f) requires analysis of the extent to which the value of fireworks to the community outweighs its dangerous attributes. We do not find that this factor is present here. This country has a long-standing tradition of fireworks on the 4th of July. That tradition suggests that we as a society have decided that the value of fireworks on the day celebrating our national independence and unity outweighs the risks of injuries and damage.

In sum, we find that setting off public fireworks displays satisfies four of the six conditions under the Restatement test; that is, it is an activity that is not "of common usage" and that presents an ineliminably high risk of serious bodily injury or property damage. We therefore hold that conducting public fireworks displays is an abnormally dangerous activity justifying the imposition of strict liability. This conclusion is consistent with the results reached in cases involving damages caused by detonating dynamite. This court has recognized that parties detonating dynamite are strictly liable for the damages caused by such blasting. . . . There are a number of similarities between fireworks and dynamite. Both activities involve licensed experts intentionally igniting for profit explosives that have great potential for causing damage. Moreover, after the explosion no evidence remains as to the original explosive. The notable difference between fireworks and dynamite is that with fireworks the public is invited to watch the display and with dynamite the public is generally prohibited from being near the blasting location. Because detonating dynamite is subject to strict liability, and because of the similarities between fireworks and dynamite, strict liability is also an appropriate standard for determining the standard of liability for pyrotechnicians for any damages caused by their fireworks displays.

II

PUBLIC POLICY AND STRICT LIABILITY FOR FIREWORKS DISPLAYS

Policy considerations also support imposing strict liability on pyrotechnicians for damages caused by their public fireworks displays, although such considerations are not alone sufficient to justify that conclusion. Most basic is the question as to who should bear the loss when an innocent person suffers injury through the nonculpable but abnormally dangerous activities of another. In the case of public fireworks displays, fairness weighs in favor of requiring the pyrotechnicians who present the displays to bear the loss rather than the unfortunate spectators who suffer the injuries. In addition,

> [t]he rule of strict liability rests not only upon the ultimate idea of rectifying a wrong and putting the burden where it should belong as a matter of abstract justice, that is, upon the one of the two innocent parties whose acts instigated or made the harm possible, but it also rests on problems of proof:

> One of these common features is that the person harmed would encounter a difficult problem of proof if some other standard of liability were applied. For example, the disasters caused by those who engage in abnormally

dangerous or extra-hazardous activities frequently destroy all evidence of what in fact occurred, other than that the activity was being carried on. Certainly this is true with explosions of dynamite, large quantities of gasoline, or other explosives.

Siegler v. Kuhlman, 81 Wash. 2d 448, 455, 502 P.2d 1181 (1972), *cert. denied*, 411 U.S. 983, 93 S. Ct. 2275, 36 L. Ed. 2d 959 (1973). In the present case, all evidence was destroyed as to what caused the misfire of the shell that injured the Kleins. Therefore, the problem of proof this case presents for the plaintiffs also supports imposing strict liability on Pyrodyne.

. . .

III

STATUTORY STRICT LIABILITY FOR FIREWORKS

As well as holding Pyrodyne strictly liable on the basis that fireworks displays are abnormally dangerous activities, we also hold that RCW 70.77.285 imposes statutory strict liability.[7] The statute, which mandates insurance coverage to pay for *all* damages resulting from fireworks displays, establishes strict liability for any ensuing injuries.

An example of a statute which the appellate court has held to be a strict liability statute is RCW 16.08.040, which reads in part:

> The owner of any dog which shall bite any person . . . shall be liable for such damages as may be suffered by the person bitten, regardless of the former viciousness of such dog or the owner's knowledge of such viciousness.

See Beeler v. Hickman, 50 Wash. App. 746, 750–51, 750 P.2d 1282 (1988). The court in *Beeler* held that the language of the statute clearly established strict liability for the owner of the dog. Although RCW 70.77.285 does not establish strict liability in the same language as the dog bite statute, it nonetheless provides that pyrotechnicians shall pay for all damages to persons or property resulting from fireworks displays.

. . . .

---

[7] RCW 70.77.285 states: "Except as provided in RCW 70.77.355, the applicant for a permit under RCW 70.77.260(2) for a public display of fireworks shall include with the application evidence of a bond issued by an authorized surety company. The bond shall be in the amount required by RCW 70.77.295 and shall be conditioned upon the applicant's payment of all damages to persons or property resulting from or caused by such public display of fireworks, or any negligence on the part of the applicant or its agents, servants, employees, or subcontractors in the presentation of the display. Instead of a bond, the applicant may include a certificate of insurance evidencing the carrying of appropriate public liability insurance in the amount required by RCW 70.77.295 for the benefit of the person named therein as assured, as evidence of ability to respond in damages. The local fire official receiving the application shall approve the bond or insurance if it meets the requirements of this section."

IV

POSSIBLE NEGLIGENT MANUFACTURE AS AN INTERVENING FORCE

Pyrodyne argues that even if there is strict liability for fireworks, its liability under the facts of this case is cut off by the manufacturer's negligence, the existence of which we assume for purposes of evaluating the propriety of the trial court's summary judgment. According to Pyrodyne, ashell detonated without leaving the mortar box because it was negligently manufactured. This detonation, Pyrodyne asserts, was what caused the misfire of the second shell, which in turn resulted in the Kleins' injuries. Pyrodyne reasons that the manufacturer's negligence acted as an intervening or outside force that cuts off Pyrodyne's liability.

In support of its position, Pyrodyne relies upon *Siegler v. Kuhlman, supra,* and *New Meadows Holding Co. v. Washington Water Power Co.,* 102 Wash. 2d 495, 687 P.2d 212 (1984). In *Siegler,* a young woman was killed in an explosion when the car she was driving encountered a pool of thousands of gallons of gasoline spilled from a gasoline truck. This court held that transporting gasoline in great quantities along public highways and streets is an abnormally dangerous activity that calls for the application of strict liability. *Siegler,* 81 Wash. 2d at 459–60, 502 P.2d 1181. Justice Rosellini concurred, but stated:

> I think the opinion should make clear, however, that the owner of the vehicle will be held strictly liable only for damages caused when the flammable or explosive substance is allowed to escape without the apparent intervention of any outside force beyond the control of the manufacturer, the owner, or the operator of the vehicle hauling it. I do not think the majority means to suggest that if another vehicle, negligently driven, collided with the truck in question, the truck owner would be held liable for the damage.

Siegler, at 460, 502 P.2d 1181 (Rosellini, J., concurring).

In *New Meadows Holding Co.,* the plaintiff was injured when he attempted to light an oil stove and unwittingly ignited natural gas leaking from a damaged gas line several blocks away. The leak allegedly was caused several years earlier when workers laying a telephone cable damaged the gas line. This court held that the transmission of natural gas through underground lines is not an abnormally dangerous activity justifying the imposition of strict liability. *New Meadows Holding Co.,* 102 Wash. 2d at 503, 687 P.2d 212. In *dicta,* we also stated that the rule of strict liability should not apply where there is the intervention of an outside force beyond the defendant's control, and that the gas leak was caused by such an outside force. *New Meadows Holding Co.,* at 503, 687 P.2d 212. Pyrodyne reasons that the shell manufacturer's negligence in supplying a defective shell, like the actions of the cable-laying workers who damaged the gas line in *New Meadows Holding Co.,* provided an outside force beyond Pyrodyne's control, and that therefore strict liability should not apply.

We note that the Restatement (Second) of Torts takes a position contrary to that advocated by Pyrodyne. Section 522 of the Restatement provides that:

> One carrying on an abnormally dangerous activity is subject to strict liability for the resulting harm although it is caused by the unexpectable

> (a) innocent, negligent or reckless conduct of a third person . . .

Restatement (Second) of Torts § 522 (1977). The comment to section 522 explains that "[i]f the risk [from an abnormally dangerous activity] ripens into injury, it is immaterial that the harm occurs through the unexpectable action of a human being". Restatement (Second) of Torts § 522, comment *a* (1977).

Thus, on the one hand, Pyrodyne urges us to adopt the view that any intervention by an outside force beyond the defendant's control is sufficient to relieve the defendant from strict liability for an abnormally dangerous activity. On the other hand, section 522 provides that no negligent intervention by a third person will relieve the defendant from strict liability for abnormally dangerous activities. We reject both positions. Contrary to section 522, we hold that a third person's intervening acts of negligence will sometimes provide a defense from liability for those carrying on an abnormally dangerous activity. Contrary to the implication Pyrodyne would have us draw from the dicta in *New Meadows Holding Co.* and the *Siegler* concurrence, we hold that a defendant may be held strictly liable for injuries arising from an abnormally dangerous activity even when those injuries were in part caused by the intervening acts of a third person over whom the defendant had no control.

A basic principle regarding the scope of legal liability for strict liability is that the sequence of events between the defendant's conduct and the plaintiff's injury must have occurred without the intervention of some unexpected, independent cause:

> The sequence of events must have been such that it is not unfair to hold the defendant liable therefor. Here we find the ordinary rules governing legal causation quite adequate to state the law. Thus, although accumulation of water is extra-hazardous because its escape involves a risk of serious damage to adjoining property holders, nevertheless the escape must occur in the ordinary course of nature, and if some superseding cause occasions the escape there is no liability. *We have such a superseding cause where the escape is caused by the act of God or by a vis major which defendant is not bound as a reasonable man to anticipate.* Even the gnawing of a rat may be such an unexpected independent cause as to make it unjust to hold defendant liable. *So, also, if the escape of the water is brought about by the intervening wrongful act of a third person which was not foreseeable under the circumstances, the defendant is relieved from liability.*

(Italics ours; citations omitted.) Harper, *Liability Without Fault and Proximate Cause*, 30 Mich. L. Rev. 1001, 1009–10 (1932); *see also, Prosser and Keeton* § 79, at 563–64. Conversely, if the damage or injury to the plaintiff was brought about in a manner that *was* foreseeable under the circumstances, then the defendant is not relieved from liability. *See Galbreath v. Engineering Constr. Corp.*, 149 Ind. App. 347, 273 N.E.2d 121, 56 A.L.R.3d 1002 (1971) (blasting is an extrahazardous activity that gives rise to liability for all resulting foreseeable injuries).

We hold that intervening acts of third persons serve to relieve the defendant from strict liability for abnormally dangerous activities only if those acts were unforeseeable in relation to the extraordinary risk created by the activity. *Cf. Herberg v. Swartz*, 89 Wash. 2d 916, 578 P.2d 17 (1978) (intervening but foreseeable acts of third persons are no defense to liability in negligence); Restatement (Second) of Torts § 447 (1977) (same). The rationale for this rule is that it encourages those who conduct abnormally dangerous activities to anticipate and take precautions against the possible negligence of third persons. Where the third person's negligence is beyond the actor's control, this rule, unlike the *Siegler* dicta, nonetheless imposes strict liability if the third person negligence was reasonably foreseeable. Such a result allocates the economic burden of injuries arising from the forseeable negligence of third persons to the party best able to plan for it and to bear it — the actor carrying on the abnormally dangerous activity.[8]

In the present case, negligence on the part of the fireworks manufacturer is readily foreseeable in relation to the extraordinary risk created by conducting a public fireworks display. Therefore, even if such negligence may properly be regarded as an intervening cause, an issue we need not decide, it cannot function to relieve Pyrodyne from liability.[9] This is not to say, however, that in a proper case a defendant in a strict liability action could not pursue a claim against a third party and enforce a right of contribution to an extent proportionate to that party's fault.

CONCLUSION

We hold that Pyrodyne Corporation is strictly liable for all damages suffered as a result of the July 1987 fireworks display. Detonating fireworks displays constitutes an abnormally dangerous activity warranting strict liability. Public policy also supports this conclusion. . . . This establishes the standard of strict liability for pyrotechnicians. Therefore, we affirm the decision of the trial court.

NOTES AND QUESTIONS

(1)   Do you conclude that the question of intervening force is one that must be considered in determining whether common law strict liability is to be invoked? Or, does it go to a "proximate causation" element of the prima facie case of common law strict liability? Or, is it an affirmative defense to such an action? For example, suppose vibrations produced by blasting in a gold mine so disturbed mother minks at a nearby commercial mink farm that in a frenzy they ate their valuable young. Should the defendant be absolutely liable for the losses suffered by the mink farmer? Should the blaster's possession of actual knowledge of the minks' delicate constitution and the risk thereby imposed make a difference to that determination? *See Foster v. Preston Mill Co.*, 268 P.2d 645 (Wash. 1954), and *Williams v. Amoco Production Company*, 734 P.2d 1113 (Kan. 1987) (common law strict liability is limited to kind of harm whose risk of occurrence makes the activity abnormally dangerous.) *See, also*, Restatement, Torts, Second, § 519(2).

(2)   *See also, Cambridge Water Co. Ltd. v. Eastern Counties Leather plc*, [1994] A.C. 264 (House of Lords), a case of first impression in which the court held that common law strict liability could be invoked only as to damages the defendant

---

[8] By this analysis we do not license the imposition of negligence concepts onto the law of strict liability. We merely recognize a limited defense to liability for abnormally dangerous activities where the injury resulted from the unforeseeable intervention of a third person.

[9] An intervening cause may be defined as a force that actively operates to produce harm to another after the actor's act or omission has been committed. See Restatement (Second) of Torts § 441(1) (1977) (defining "intervening cause" in negligence context). The manufacturer's alleged negligence occurred prior to Pyrodyne's fireworks display, but it actively operated to produce harm only after the aerial shells had been ignited.

foresaw or reasonably could have foreseen at the time a particular act was committed. The court also held, however, that an ordinary industrial operation, such as a tannery operation, could qualify as a non-natural use of the land despite a long presence at its site.

(3)   In blasting cases some courts initially held that only damage done by debris thrown onto the plaintiff's property invoked common law strict liability and that the plaintiff must prove negligence as to damage caused by concussion alone. Some of those same courts now apply the doctrine both to debris and concussion damages. *See, e.g., Spano v. Perini Corporation*, 250 N.E. 2631 (N.Y. 1967), holding that common law strict liability may be invoked in either instance. Should this affect the result in the mink case in note 1? Should a pile driver engaged in building a highway bridge be held to the strict liability standard? *See Caporale v. C.W. Blakeslee & Sons, Inc.*, 175 A.2d 561 (Conn. 1961), and *Hutchinson v. Capeletti Bros., Inc.*, 397 So. 2d 952 (Fla. App. 1981).

(4)   *In re Hanford Nuclear Reservation Litigation*, 534 F.3d 986 (9th Cir. 2008), an action in which plaintiffs alleged that certain plutonium producers were strictly liable for cancers caused by carcinogenic emissions during World War II, considered the "public policy" exception that failed in *Pyrodyne*:

> Defendants' final defense is that even if their conduct constituted an abnormally dangerous activity, they are exempted from strict liability under Washington law pursuant to the "public duty" exception. See Restatement (Second) of Torts § 521. While this issue presents a close question, we conclude that Defendants do not qualify for the exception.

> Section 521 of the Restatement provides:

>> The rules as to strict liability for abnormally dangerous activities do not apply if the activity is carried on in pursuance of a public duty imposed upon the actor as a public officer or employee or as a common carrier.

>> Id. . . . Although widely adopted, the courts that have applied the public duty exception have generally done so only to the extent a defendant was legally required to perform the ultrahazardous activity. See Restatement (Second) of Torts, § 521, cmt. a. The Washington Supreme Court's decision in *Siegler v. Kuhlman*, 81 Wash. 2d 448, 502 P.2d 1181 (1972), supports such an application of the public duty doctrine here. The defendants in Siegler were a trucking company for Texaco and its driver, and the company was not legally obligated as a common carrier to carry materials that eventually caused an explosive, fatal accident on a highway. The Washington court held that the activity was abnormally dangerous and that the defendants could be held strictly liable for the accident. It is therefore most likely that the Washington Supreme Court would apply strict liability when the defendant was performing a dangerous activity for "his own purpose," and would apply the public duty exception only in the appropriate case when the defendant was engaged in a legally-obligated activity, such as a regulated common carrier bound to carry hazardous substances.

> Defendants argue that in light of the exceptional and patriotic circumstances under which they operated Hanford, we should treat them as analogous to public employees who would qualify for the

exception. . . . Defendants do not satisfy the exception's purpose in this case. Defendants are not public officers or employees or common carriers, see Restatement (Second) of Torts § 521, and they were not legally obligated to operate Hanford.

The prototypical example of a defendant entitled to the public duty exception is a utility company that is legally required to transport an ultrahazardous good, such as electricity, and causes injury to someone during transport. Courts have recognized a public duty exception in such cases, because common carriers must accept, carry, and deliver all goods offered to them for transport within the scope of the operating authority set forth in their permits. *See, e.g.*, 16 U.S.C. § 824 et. seq. (granting the Federal Energy Regulatory Commission authority to establish guidelines for common carriers of electricity in interstate commerce); *United States v. W. Processing Co.*, 756 F. Supp. 1416, 1421 (W.D. Wash. 1991). They cannot discriminate against customers or refuse to accept commodities that may be dangerous for transport. *Id.*

The case law therefore illustrates that the duty involved is the legal obligation to perform the abnormally dangerous activity in accordance with government orders. See, e.g., *EAC Timberlane v. Pisces, Ltd.*, 745 F.2d 715, 721 n. 12 (1st Cir. 1984) (noting that the public duty must be one imposed on the actor). . . . *Town of East Troy v. Soo Line R.R. Co.*, 409 F. Supp. 326, 329 (E.D. Wis. 1976) (no strict liability for spillage of carbolic acid by derailment of common carrier train); . . . . Qualifying entities must be operating pursuant to the mandate and control of the government; they must have little discretion over the manner in which they conduct their activities.. . .

There was no government mandate here. The events giving rise to this litigation occurred before the government developed rules or the ability to control nuclear facilities. The government was relying on the expertise of defendants and not vice versa.

We should not confuse the legal concept of a public duty with popular notions of patriotic duty taken at personal sacrifice. Defendants may well have been acting at the government's urging during wartime. The public duty exception, however, was developed under state law in recognition of the need to protect private actors who are legally required to engage in ultrahazardous activities. No matter how strongly Defendants may have felt a patriotic duty, they had no legal duty to operate Hanford, and they are, therefore, not entitled to the public duty exception. The district court correctly found defendants subject to strict liability.

PECAN SHOPPE OF SPRINGFIELD, MISSOURI, INC. v.
TRI-STATE MOTOR TRANSIT CO.
Missouri Court of Appeals
573 S.W.431 (1978)

FLANIGAN, JUDGE.

Defendant Tri-State Motor Transit Co. is a motor carrier licensed by the state of Missouri and the Department of Transportation. On September 14, 1970, the union employees of Tri-State went on strike. In the early morning hours of September 30, 1970, a tractor-trailer unit, owned by Tri-State and driven by its non-striking employee John A. Galt, was transporting a load of dynamite, for shipper DuPont Company, from Joplin, Missouri, to a mining site at Boss, Missouri.

As the unit was traveling on Interstate Highway 44 in Greene County, Missouri, it approached an overpass on which stood Bobby Shuler, one of the striking employees. Using a 30–30 rifle, Shuler fired three shots at the unit, thereby causing a "tremendous" explosion which resulted in the death of Galt[10] and the destruction of the unit. The explosion caused heavy damage to nearby improved land owned by plaintiff Pecan Shoppe of Springfield, Missouri, Inc., on which it conducted a restaurant and service station business.

Plaintiff brought this action for damages against Tri-State and the union. Prior to the trial plaintiff settled its claim against the union. The amount of that settlement did not fully compensate plaintiff for its damages and the case proceeded to trial against Tri-State. The jury returned a verdict in favor of Tri-State. Plaintiff appeals.

Plaintiff's principal "point relied on" is that the trial court erred in failing to direct a verdict for plaintiff on the issue of liability. It is plaintiff's position that the doctrine of strict liability was applicable to the admitted facts and that the sole province of the jury was to determine the extent of plaintiff's uncompensated damages and to render the appropriate award.

It is the position of Tri-State that the trial court did not err in the manner claimed because "the theory of strict liability does not apply to a common carrier engaged in transporting explosives," and further, that the cause of the explosion "was the intervening criminal act of convicted murderer Bobby Shuler."

Where the undisputed facts establish as a matter of law that the plaintiff is entitled to recover, the trial court may and should direct a verdict in his favor. . . . Plaintiff's contention is that certain basic facts, conceded to be true by Tri-State, required the trial court to direct a verdict in plaintiff's favor. Those facts are:

1. Tri-State was operating its truck, loaded with dynamite, on the highway;

2. The dynamite exploded;

3. As a direct result of the explosion, plaintiff sustained damage for which it was not fully compensated.

---

[10] The conviction of Shuler for the second degree murder of Galt was affirmed in *State v. Shuler*, 486 S.W.2d 505 (Mo. 1972).

The facts recited above were undisputed. The parties also agree that after the commencement of the strike and prior to the explosion, various acts of violence were committed against Tri-State by "persons known and unknown."

Witnesses for Tri-State testified that the nighttime movement of explosives was safer than daytime movement because of less traffic. Plaintiff, however, attempted to show that the risk of violence was lower during daytime. After the commencement of the strike Tri-State vehicles moved in convoys, usually accompanied by security guards as escorts. The FBI, the highway patrol, and local sheriffs, were informed of movements of the convoys.

The unit driven by Galt was one of a two-unit convoy. Prior to its departure from Tri-State's premises at Joplin, the sheriffs of Lawrence County and Greene County were notified of the movement. This information was relayed to deputy sheriffs and other patrol officers. Several law enforcement vehicles were assigned the duty of protecting the convoy. There are six overpasses in Greene County and deputy sheriff Lindsey had checked the overpass used by Shuler a few minutes before the explosion occurred. Officer Lindsey was checking another overpass, a quarter of a mile away, when he heard the explosion.

In submitting the case the jury the court, at the instance of the plaintiff, gave two verdict- directing instructions. Instruction No. 2, in essence, required a verdict in favor of the plaintiff if the jury found these facts: Tri-State operated a truck that carried dynamite; the dynamite exploded; "Such use by (Tri-State) of its property was unreasonable"; and plaintiff sustained damage as a result.

Instruction No. 3 required the jury to return a verdict for the plaintiff if they found that plaintiff was damaged as a result of defendant's conduct in two alternative respects and if the jury found that such conduct was negligent. The alternative grounds were: (1) Tri-State "operated its truck carrying dynamite at night when incidents of shooting were occurring at night and such truck could have been operated during the day," and (2) Tri-State "operated its truck carrying dynamite at a time when it knew that such truck might be fired upon and could cause an explosion."

Plaintiff argues that the transportation of dangerous commodities in interstate commerce by motor carrier requires a special certification by the Interstate Commerce Commission and that Tri-State, having sought that certification, exercised its free choice to transport explosives. Approximately 50 percent of Tri-State's business consists of the hauling of explosives, ammunition and nuclear waste. Accordingly, says plaintiff, Tri-State should not be entitled to avail itself of those principles which exempt a common carrier from liability for injuries caused by the explosion of commodities in its custody where there is no showing that the carrier was negligent or maintained a nuisance. Plaintiff also argues that the acts of violence which antedated the explosion made the criminal conduct of Shuler foreseeable.

Tri-State argues that plaintiff was accorded a decision on the issues of negligence and unreasonable use and that, under the instant facts, the doctrine of strict liability should not be invoked. Tri-State relies upon its status as a "common carrier by motor vehicle" as defined in 49 U.S.C.A. § 303(a) (14) and seeks to avail itself of those principles of liability which pertain to the transportation of explosives by such carriers. Tri-State points out that the Restatement of Torts, Second, Vol. 3, Chapter 21 (§§ 519-524(a)) contains certain principles concerning "abnormally dangerous activities." Section 521 is to the effect that "the rules as to strict liability for abnormally dangerous activities" do not apply if the activity is carried on in pursuance of a public duty imposed upon the actor as a common carrier.[11] Tri-State advances the alternative argument that the criminal conduct of Shuler serves to exculpate it, even assuming that liability would otherwise attach.

None of the foregoing arguments totally lacks appeal. Neither side, in their respective and excellent briefs, has cited any authority which is factually similar. This case, viewed in all of its aspects, seems to be one of first impression and the disposition of this appeal has not been free of difficulty.

This court concludes that the trial court did not err in refusing to direct a verdict for the plaintiff.

Counsel have cited no Missouri cases dealing with the liability of a transporter for damages caused by the explosion of dangerous substances in its custody. Missouri courts have dealt with the liability of persons who use explosives in blasting activities and with the liability of storers of dangerous substances.

In *Summers v. Tavern Rock Sand Co.*, 315 S.W.2d 201, 203 (1, 2) (Mo. 1958), our supreme court said: " '[B]lasting is regarded as a work which one may lawfully do, providing he avoids injuring persons or property, and subject to his obligation to pay damages for any injury inflicted by his blasting.' . . . And in this state when damage to property is by vibration or concussion from blasting there is an invasion of the premises and liability irrespective of negligence quite as if the blasting had cast rocks or debris thereon."

When persons or property, located in populated areas and off the premises of the storer of dangerous substances, are injured as a result of an explosion of the substances, the storer incurs liability "regardless of the question of the degree of care he exerted to prevent an explosion." *Scalpino v. Smith*, 154 Mo. App. 524, 135 S.W. 1000, 1004 (5) (1911). The court there said:

"The act of defendant in storing a dangerous quantity of dynamite on his premises was an invasion of the personal and property rights of his neighbors who dwelt within the range of its destructive force." Similar holdings are found in *Schnitzer v. Excelsior Powder Mfg. Co.*, 160 S.W. 282 (Mo. App. 1912). . . .

In *Schnitzer* the court held that the defendant was guilty of maintaining a public nuisance in storing on its premises combustible and explosive materials in such large quantities that their mere presence constituted a continuous menace to persons living in the vicinity. In *French* the court held that the storer of nitroglycerin was liable to a plaintiff whose nearby home was damaged by an explosion and that liability attached whether the substance "exploded by pure accident or by negligence." The court added: "He who made it possible for the damage to be done should bear [the] loss.".:

Courts in other jurisdictions are not in agreement on the issue of whether a transporter of dangerous substances, in the absence of negligence or facts

---

[11] Section 522 of the Restatement of Torts, Second, provides that one carrying on an abnormally dangerous activity is subject to strict liability for the resulting harm although it is caused by three enumerated "unexpectable" sources, one of which is "innocent, negligent, or reckless conduct of a third person." However, a "caveat" to § 522 reads: "The Institute expresses no opinion as to whether the fact that the harm is done by an act of a third person that is not only deliberate but also intended to bring about the harm, relieves from liability one who carries on an abnormally dangerous activity."

supporting a finding of nuisance, is liable for injuries caused by their explosion. Authorities denying liability in such circumstances include *Pope v. Edward M. Rude Carrier Corp.*, 138 W. Va. 218, 75 S.E.2d 584 (1953) and *Christ Church Parish v. Cadet Chem. Corp.*, 25 Conn. Sup. 191, 199 A.2d 707 (1964). The foregoing authorities represent the majority view. 31 Am. Jur. 2d *Explosions and Explosives* § 86, p. 855; 35 C.J.S. *Explosives* § 9, p. 283; Restatement of Torts, Second, § 521. On the other hand, strict liability was imposed upon the carrier in *Siegler v. Kuhlman*, 81 Wash. 2d 448, 502 P.2d 1181 (1972) and *Chavez v. So. Pac. Trans. Co.*, 413 F. Supp. 1203 (E.D. Cal. 1976). In *Pope*, a leading authority in the field, a shipment of dynamite was being transported on a public highway by a licensed contract carrier (Rude) on behalf of a manufacturer and shipper (DuPont). The injured plaintiff sought recovery against Rude and DuPont on two theories, the maintenance of a public nuisance and the doctrine of absolute liability. In rejecting both theories, the court emphasized the distinction between the liability of the transporter of such substances and that of a storer or a user for blasting purposes. The court said, 138 W. Va. 218, 75 S.E.2d at p. 595: "With respect to the liability of a common carrier or other carrier who transports high explosives the rule is that in the absence of negligence on its part such carrier is not liable to third persons who are injured by an explosion which occurs during the transportation by it of such explosives but that it is liable for injuries caused by its negligence or where it has so handled a shipment that it has become a nuisance which causes injury."

The court quoted, with approval, the following language from *Actiesselskabet Ingrid v. Central Railroad Company of New Jersey*, 216 F. 72, 78 (C.A. 2 1914): "It certainly would be an extraordinary doctrine for courts of justice to promulgate to say that a common carrier is under legal obligation to transport dynamite and is an insurer against any damage which may result in the course of transportation, even though it has been guilty of no negligence which occasioned the explosion which caused the injury. It is impossible to find any adequate reason for such a principle."

In *Christ Church Parish*, Defendant's tractor-trailer unit, loaded with 20 tons of chemical substances, exploded. Recognizing that Connecticut applied the doctrine of absolute liability to users of explosives for blasting purposes, the court stated 25 Conn. Sup. 191, 199 A.2d at p. 709:

"The liability of the carrier should be predicated upon its knowledge of the dangerous propensities of the substance it is transporting, together with its use of a standard of care commensurate with the dangerous character of the substance." On the other hand, in *Siegler*, the doctrine of strict liability was applied to render the owner of a gasoline truck liable for the death of a motorist who was killed when her automobile encountered a pool of spilled gasoline on the highway. The trailer of defendant's tractor-trailer unit separated from the tractor and overturned. The cause of the separation was unknown. The court said, 81 Wash. 2d 448, 502 P.2d at p. 1184:

Dangerous in itself, gasoline develops even greater potential for harm when carried as freight, extraordinary dangers deriving from sheer quantity, bulk and weight, which enormously multiply its hazardous properties. . . . It is quite probable that the most important ingredients of proof will be lost in a gasoline explosion and fire. Gasoline is always dangerous whether kept in large or small quantities because of its volatility, inflammability and explosiveness. But when several thousand gallons of it are allowed to spill across a public highway that is, if, while in transit as freight, it is not kept impounded the hazards to third persons are so great as to be almost beyond calculation. . . . The rule of strict liability rests not only upon the ultimate idea of rectifying a wrong and putting the burden where it should belong as a matter of abstract justice, that is, upon the one of the two innocent parties whose acts instigated or made the harm possible, but it also rests on problems of proof.

Referring to explosions of "dynamite, large quantities of gasoline, and other explosives," the court pointed out that persons harmed thereby encounter difficult problems of proof if some standard of liability, other than strict liability, is applied. The court stated that the transportation of large quantities of gasoline on the public highway was "more highly hazardous" than the storage of it in commercial quantities.[12]

Some courts have imposed liability upon the storer of dangerous substances when the explosion was caused by lightning. . . .

In *Chavez*, 18 boxcars, loaded with bombs, exploded in a railroad yard. The boxcars and bombs were owned by the United States and were being hauled by Southern Pacific under a contract with the Navy. The cause of the explosion is not stated in the opinion. Southern Pacific sought dismissal of those claims against it which were predicated on the theory of strict liability. The court said, at p. 1208:

Notwithstanding Southern Pacific's protestations to the contrary, one public policy now recognized in California as justifying the imposition of strict liability for the miscarriage of an ultrahazardous activity is the social and economic desirability of distributing the losses, resulting from such activity, among the general public.

The court said, at p. 1209:

[T]he risk distribution justification for imposing strict liability is well suited to claims arising out of the conduct of ultrahazardous activity. The victims of such activity are defenseless. Due to the very nature of the activity, the losses suffered as a result of such activity are likely to be substantial an "overwhelming misfortune to the person injured." . . . By indirectly imposing liability on those that benefit from the dangerous activity, risk distribution benefits the social-economic body in two ways: (1) the adverse impact of any particular misfortune is lessened by spreading its cost over a greater population and over a larger time period, and (2) social and economic resources can be more efficiently allocated when the actual costs of goods and services (including the losses they entail) are reflected in their price to the consumer. Both of these benefits may be achieved by subjecting Southern Pacific to strict liability.

The court in *Chavez* rejected the doctrines of *Actiesselskabet Ingrid, Pope* and *Christ Church Parish*, all discussed *supra*, and said there was no sound basis for exempting carriers from the doctrine of strict liability. The court said at p. 1214:

---

[12] In *Siegler* the concurring opinion of Judge Rosellini espoused the risk distribution argument supported by the *Chavez* Case. However, he stated that the principal opinion "should make clear . . . that the owner of the vehicle will be held strictly liable only for damages caused when the flammable or explosive substance is allowed to escape without the apparent intervention of any outside force beyond the control of the manufacturer, the owner, or the operator of the vehicle hauling it. I do not think the majority means to suggest that if another vehicle, negligently driven, collided with the truck in question, the truck owner would be held liable for the damage. But where, as here, there was no outside force which caused the trailer to become detached from the truck, the rule of strict liability should apply."

[T]here is no logical reason for creating a "public duty" exception when the rationale for subjecting the carrier to absolute liability is the carrier's ability to distribute the loss to the public. Whether the carrier is free to reject or bound to take the explosive cargo, the plaintiffs are equally defenseless. Bound or not, Southern Pacific is in a position to pass along the loss to the public. Bound or not, the social and economic benefits which are ordinarily derived from imposing strict liability are achieved. Those which benefit from the dangerous activity bear the inherent costs. The harsh impact of inevitable disasters is softened by spreading the cost among a greater population and over a larger time period. . . .

Siegler lends support to plaintiff's argument that transporting dynamite on public highways is even more dangerous than storing it and Missouri has imposed absolute liability upon storers thereof. *Chavez* advances the "risk distribution" justification and challenges the majority view granting exemptions to carriers. There is much to be said in favor of these holdings but in neither *Siegler* nor *Chavez* was the court confronted with a situation involving the criminal act of a third person as the immediate cause of the explosion.

Other jurisdictions have dealt with the liability of a storer or transporter of dangerous substances where the explosion was caused by the intentional misconduct of a third person. [The court examined a number of negligence cases in which an intervening criminal act was held to have severed the chain of proximate causation.]

On the other hand, even if the immediate cause of plaintiff's injuries was the criminal act of a third person, defendant is not always relieved of liability. In *Gaines v. Property Servicing Co.*, 276 S.W.2d 169 (Mo. 1955), plaintiff was a tenant in an apartment building owned by the defendant. Plaintiff was injured as a result of a fire in the building. The building was not equipped with a fire escape as required by statute. The fire was lit by one Haley who was convicted of arson for setting it. The defendant asserted that he was relieved of liability by reason of Haley's intervening intentional criminal act. In holding the defendant liable, the court pointed out that he was guilty of negligence per se in failing to comply with the statute. The purpose of the statute was to furnish protection against injury from any fire, regardless of its origin. The court held it was immaterial whether the fire "had its origin in accident, act of God, negligence, or willful, intentional, and wrongful conduct." A jury was entitled to find that defendant's negligence concurred "with the intentionally set fire" to cause the injuries and the trial court did not err in denying defendant's request for a directed verdict.

The case at bar is distinguishable from *Gaines*. Plaintiff made no showing that Tri-State violated any statute or regulation dealing with the transportation of dynamite. There was nothing unlawful in Tri-State's operation of the unit which exploded.

In order for this court to uphold plaintiff's contention it must adopt the minority view, exemplified by *Siegler* and *Chavez*, which refuses to recognize the general rule of non-liability of common carriers for explosions occurring in the absence of negligence and elements of nuisance. Plaintiff has cited no authority to support the view that a carrier which devotes most of its business to the transportation of explosives is entitled to less favorable consideration than the ordinary common carrier. In the absence of a clear legislative intent, the granting of a specific classification to a carrier should not create a liability where otherwise none exists.

Further, this court would have to take the additional step, not taken by *Siegler* or *Chavez*, of invoking the doctrine of absolute liability where the undisputed evidence shows that the explosion was caused by the criminal act of a third person. This it is unwilling to do. Plaintiff's principal point has no merit. . . .

The judgment is affirmed.

NOTES AND QUESTIONS

(1)   Extrapolation of the *Rylands v. Fletcher* doctrine to cover activities that are not directly associated with the "non-natural user" of the defendant's land has not been widely accepted. In part this may be a consequence of the close historical connection between the tort and other ancient theories of liability connected with damage to interests in land, such as nuisance and trespass to land. These theories are examined in Chapter 15. Nevertheless, as *Tri-State Motor Transit Co.* demonstrates, a few decisions have applied the doctrine to damages caused by mishaps on public highways or in railroad facilities. Even in England, the doctrine has apparently been applied in a few "highway cases." *See Crown River Cruises Ltd. v. Kimbolton Fireworks Ltd.*, The Times, 6 March 1996 (Q.B. Div.), declining to apply common law strict liability as to a fireworks display conducted on a barge moored in the Thames River in central London both because other causes of action would provide a remedy and also because "of the current judicial and academic reserve which appears detectible towards extension of the principle of *Rylands v. Fletcher* beyond its present limits." Nevertheless, the court's decision suggests that common law strict liability would have been applied had the fireworks display emanated from the defendants's private property instead of from a navigable river.

In contrast to the few "highway cases" that have applied common law strict liability, the more orthodox approach applies the doctrine only when the owner or occupier of a site of land uses it to conduct an abnormally dangerous activity that "escapes" and does some damage on neighboring property. Accordingly, most courts routinely decline to apply the doctrine to actions brought by owners of land who have been damaged by the residue (*e.g.*, toxic pollution of the soil or buildings) of activities carried on by preceding occupiers of the same land. *See, e.g., Rosenblatt v. Exxon Company*, U.S.A., 642 A.2d 180, 188 (Md. 1994); *325–342 E. 56th Street Corporation v. Mobil Oil Corporation*, 906 F. Supp. 669, 677 (D.C. 1995); *Dartron Corporation v. Uniroyal Chemical Company Inc.*, 917 F. Supp. 1173 (N.D. Oh. 1996); and, *Hydro-Manufacturing, Inc. v. Kayser-Roth Corp.*, 640 A.2d 950 (R.I. 1994). *Contra, Prospect Industries Corp., v. Singer Company*, 569 A.2d 908 (N.J. Super. 1989) and *Russell-Stanley Corp. v. Plant Industries, Inc.*, 595 A.2d 534 (N.J. Super. 1991).

(2)   Suppose carbon monoxide in the exhaust from a delivery truck that is parked with the engine running is taken into the air intake to an apartment house, making the occupants ill. Would the delivery company be liable for the harm done without proof of negligence? The court in *McDonald v. Associated Fuels Ltd.*, [1954] 3 D.L.R. 775, 783 (S. Ct. Brit. Col.) declined to apply the doctrine saying: "I find it difficult to accept the extension of the rule in *Rylands v. Fletcher* to an action for personal injuries." This is consistent with English decisions beginning with *Read v. Lyons & Co. Ltd.*, [1947] App. Cases 156 (House of Lords), which have declined to apply common law strict liability as a cause of action to remedy bodily injuries.

(3)   Note that *Tri-State Motor Transit Co.* contained some discussion about whether common law strict liability is a better "risk distribution" principle than negligence. In *Indiana Harbor Belt Railroad Company v. American Cyanamid Company*, 916 F.2d 1174, 1181 (7th Cir. 1990), a small railroad company sued a shipper of a chemical that had escaped from the railroad company's yards and caused damage in abutting residential neighborhoods. The district court had permitted the railroad company to invoke common law strict liability against the shipper who had turned the product over to the railroad company at the shipper's plant and had exercised no further control over it. The appellate court reversed, stating in part:

The relevant activity is transportation, not manufacturing and shipping. This essential distinction the plaintiff ignores. But even if the plaintiff is treated as a transporter and not merely a shipper, it has not shown that the transportation of acrylonitrile in bulk by rail through populated areas is so hazardous an activity, even when due care is exercised, that the law should seek to create — perhaps quixotically — incentives to relocate the activity to nonpopulated areas, or to reduce the scale of the activity, or to switch to transporting acrylonitrile by road rather than by rail, perhaps to set the stage for a replay *of Siegler v. Kuhlman*. It is no more realistic to propose to reroute the shipment of all hazardous materials around Chicago than it is to propose the relocation of homes adjacent to the Blue Island switching yard to more distant suburbs. It may be less realistic. Brutal though it may seem to say it, the inappropriate use to which land is being put in the Blue Island yard and neighborhood may be, not the transportation of hazardous chemicals, but residential living. The analogy is to building your home between the runways at O'Hare.

The briefs hew closely to the Restatement, whose approach to the issue of strict liability is mainly allocative rather than distributive. By this we mean that the emphasis is on picking a liability regime (negligence or strict liability) that will control the particular class of accidents in question most effectively, rather than on finding the deepest pocket and placing liability there. At argument, however, the plaintiff's lawyer invoked distributive considerations by pointing out that Cyanamid is a huge firm and the Indiana Harbor Belt Railroad a fifty-mile-long switching line that almost went broke in the winter of 1979, when the accident occurred. Well, so what? A corporation is not a living person but a set of contracts the terms of which determine who will bear the brunt of liability. Tracing the incidence of a cost is a complex undertaking which the plaintiff sensibly has made no effort to assume, since its legal relevance would be dubious. We add only that however small the plaintiff may be, it has mighty parents: it is a jointly owned subsidiary of Conrail and the Soo line.

The case for strict liability has not been made. Not in this suit in any event. We need not speculate on the possibility of imposing strict liability on shippers of more hazardous materials, such as the bombs carried in *Chavez v. Southern Pacific Transportation Co., supra*, any more than we need differentiate (given how the plaintiff has shaped its case) between active and passive shippers. We noted earlier that acrylonitrile is far from being the most hazardous among hazardous materials shipped by rail in highest volume. Or among materials shipped, period.

(4)   As to the proximate causation issue, contrast *Tri-State Motor Transit Co.* and *Yukon Equipment, Inc. v. Fireman's Fund Insurance Company*, 585 P.2d 1206, 1211, 1212 (Alaska 1978), wherein two thieves intentionally detonated a bomb

storage site to obliterate evidence of their thievery. The plaintiffs, neighbors whose property had been destroyed by the blast, sued under the strict liability theory and the defendant denied liability on proximate causation grounds. The court held:

> The reasons for imposing absolute liability on those who have created a grave risk of harm to others by storing or using explosives are largely independent of considerations of locational appropriateness. We see no reason for making a distinction between the right of a homesteader to recover when his property has been damaged by a blast set off in a remote corner of the state, and the right to compensation of an urban resident whose home is destroyed by an explosion originating in a settled area. In each case, the loss is properly to be regarded as a cost of the business of storing or using explosives. Every incentive remains to conduct such activities in locations which are as safe as possible, because there the damages resulting from an accident will be kept to a minimum.

II

The next question is whether the intentional detonation of the storage magazine was a superseding cause relieving petitioners from liability. In *Sharp v. Fairbanks North Star Borough*, 569 P.2d 178 (Alaska 1977), a negligence case, we stated that a superseding cause exists where "after the event and looking back from the harm to the actor's negligent conduct, it appears to the court highly extraordinary that it should have brought about the harm." 569 P.2d at 182, quoting from Restatement (Second) of Torts § 435 (1965). We further explained in *Sharp*, [w]here the defendant's conduct threatens a particular kind of result which will injure the plaintiff and an intervening cause which could not have been anticipated changes the situation but produces the same result as originally threatened, such a result is within the scope of the defendant's negligence. *Id.* at 183 n. 9.

The considerations which impel cutting off liability where there is a superseding cause in negligence cases also apply to cases of absolute liability. Prior to the explosion in question the petitioners' magazines had been illegally broken into at least six times. Most of these entries involved the theft of explosives. Petitioners had knowledge of all of this.

Applying the standards set forth in *Sharp, supra*, to these facts we find there to have been no superseding cause. The incendiary destruction of premises by thieves to cover evidence of theft is not so uncommon an occurrence that it can be regarded as highly extraordinary.[13] Moreover, the particular kind of result threatened by the defendant's conduct, the storage of explosives, was an explosion at the storage site. Since the threatened result occurred it would not be consistent with the principles stated in *Sharp, supra*, to hold there to have been a superseding cause. Absolute liability is imposed on those who store or use explosives because they have created an unusual risk to others. As between those who have created the risk for the benefit of their own enterprise and those whose only connection

---

[13] *See Chicago, Wilmington & Vermillion Coal Co. v. Glass*, 34 Ill. App. 364 (1889), where the court stated with reference to stored explosives:

It is because no human skill can tell when or where the fatal spark from the clouds or the incendiary's torch may light this dangerous mass and involve everything within its reach in instant destruction that its presence and close contact with human habitation will not be tolerated. 34 Ill. App. at 370.

with the enterprise is to have suffered damage because of it, the law places the risk of loss on the former. When the risk created causes damage in fact, insistence that the precise details of the intervening cause be foreseeable would subvert the purpose of that rule of law.

Can *Tri-State* and *Yukon* be satisfactorily distinguished? If not, which is the sounder view in light of the premises of common law strict liability? Which, if either, is consistent with *Pyrodyne*? Consider again this question: is the intervening force issue one factor to consider in determining whether strict liability applies, a causation issue, or a defense?

ISAACS v. POWELL
Florida Supreme Court
267 So. 2d 861 (1972)

McNulty, Judge.

This is a case of first impression in Florida. The question posed is whether Florida should adopt the general -rule that the owner or keeper of a wild animal, in this case a chimpanzee, is liable to one injured by such animal under the strict liability doctrine, *i.e.*, regardless of negligence on his part, or whether his liability should be predicated on his fault or negligence.[14]

Plaintiff-appellant Scott Isaacs was two years and seven months old at the times material herein. His father had taken him to defendants-appellees' monkey farm where, upon purchasing an admission ticket, and as was usual and encouraged by appellees, he also purchased some food to feed the animals. While Scott was feeding a chimpanzee named Valerie she grabbed his arm and inflicted serious injury.

The exact details of how Valerie was able to grab Scott's arm are in dispute. Appellees contend that Scott's father lifted the boy above reasonably sufficient protective barriers to within Valerie's reach, while appellants counter that the barriers and other protective measures were insufficient. But in any case, appellants do not now, nor did they below, rely on any fault of appellees. Rather, they rely solely on the aforesaid generally accepted strict or, as it is sometimes called, absolute liability doctrine under which negligence or fault on the part of the owner or keeper of an animal *ferae naturae* is irrelevant. Appellees, on the other hand, suggest that we should adopt the emerging, though yet minority, view that liability should depend upon negligence, *i.e.*, a breach of the duty of care reasonably called for taking into account the nature and specie of the animal involved. We will consider this aspect of the problem first and will hereinafter discuss available defenses under the theory we adopt.

The trial judge apparently agreed with the appellees that fault or negligence on the part of the owners of a wild animal must be shown. He charged the jury on causation as follows:

---

[14] Although the precise question has never been decided in Florida, our sister court in the third district recognized the general rule in dictum while deciding that the bees involved in that case were not wild animals and thus the rule of negligence applied regardless. *Ferreira v. D'Asaro* (Fla. App. 1963), 152 So. 2d 736.

The issues for your determination are whether the proximate cause of Scott Isaacs' injuries was the improper protection for paying customers of the defendants in the condition of the cage, and whether the approximate cause of (sic) the placing of Scott by his father, Howard Isaacs, within the barrier placed by the defendants for the protection of customers of the defendant.

In other words the trial judge asked the jury to decide whether Scott was injured through the fault of defendants-appellees and/or through the fault of his father. The jury returned a verdict for the defendants; but obviously, it's impossible for us to determine whether, under the foregoing charge, the jury so found because they were unable to find fault on defendants' part, or whether they so found because they believed the cause of Scott's injury to be the fault of the father. If, of course, we adopt the negligence theory of liability there would be no error in submitting both issues to the jury. But we are of the view that the older and general rule of strict liability, which obviates the issue of the owner's negligence, is more suited to the fast growing, populous and activity-oriented society of Florida. Indeed, our society imposes more than enough risks upon its members now, and we are reluctant to encourage the addition of one more particularly when that one more is increasingly contributed by those who, for profit, would exercise their "right" to harbor wild animals and increase exposure to the dangers thereof by luring advertising. Prosser puts it this way:

. . . [Liability] has been thought to rest on the basis of negligence in keeping the animal at all; but this does not coincide with the modern analysis of negligence as conduct which is unreasonable in view of the risk, since it may not be an unreasonable thing to keep a tiger in a zoo. *It is rather an instance of the strict responsibility placed upon those who, even with proper care, expose the community to the risk of a very dangerous thing.* While one or two jurisdictions insist that there is no liability without some negligence in keeping the animal, by far the greater number impose strict liability. (Italics supplied)

Additionally, we observe that Florida has enacted [a statute] relating to dogs, which abrogates the permissive "one bite" rule of the common law. That rule posited that an owner of a dog is liable to one bite by such dog only if he is chargeable with "scienter," *i.e.*, prior knowledge of the viciousness of the dog. Necessarily, of course, the cause of action therefor was predicated on the negligence of the owner in failing to take proper precautions with knowledge of the dog's vicious propensities. Our statute, however, has in effect imposed strict liability on a dog owner (from which he can absolve himself only by complying with the warning proviso of the statute). It would result in a curious anomaly, then, if we were to adopt the negligence concept as a basis for liability of an owner or keeper of a tiger, while § 767.04, *supra*, imposes potential strict liability upon him if he should trade the tiger for a dog. We are compelled to adopt, therefore, the strict liability rule in these cases.

Concerning, now, available defenses under this rule we share the view, and emphasize, that "strict or absolute liability" does not mean the owner or keeper of a wild animal is an absolute insurer in the sense that he is liable regardless of any fault on the part of the victim. Moreover, we do not think it means he is liable notwithstanding an intervening, efficient independent fault which *solely* causes the result, as was possibly the case here if fault on the part of Scott's father were the sole efficient cause.

As to the fault of the victim himself, since the owner or keeper of a wild animal is held to a rigorous rule of liability on account of the danger inherent in harboring such animal, it has generally been held that the owner ought not be relieved from such liability by slight negligence or want of ordinary care on the part of the person injured. The latter's acts must be such as would establish that, with knowledge of the danger, he voluntarily brought the calamity upon himself. This general rule supports the Restatement of Torts, § 515 which we now adopt and set forth as follows:

(1) A plaintiff is not barred from recovery by his failure to exercise reasonable care to observe the propinquity of a wild animal or an abnormally dangerous domestic animal or to avoid harm to his person, land or chattels threatened by it.

(2) A plaintiff is barred from recovery by *intentionally and unreasonably* subjecting himself to the risk that a wild animal or an abnormally dangerous domestic animal will do harm to his person, land or chattels. (Italics supplied)

With regard to an intervening fault bringing about the result we have no hesitancy in expanding the foregoing rule to include as a defense the willful or intentional fault of a third party provided such fault is of itself an efficient cause and is the sole cause. If a jury were to decide in this case, therefore, that the *sole efficient* cause of Scott's injury was the intentional assumption of the apparent risks on the part of the boy's father and his placing of the boy within reach of the danger, it would be a defense available to appellees. Clearly, though, this defense would be related only to causation and is not dependent upon any theory of imputation of the father's fault to the son, which is now irrelevant in view of the extent of strict liability in these cases and the limited defenses available there under.

The judgment is reversed and the cause is remanded for a new trial on the theory of strict liability, and the defenses thereto, as enunciated above.

Reversed.

NOTES AND QUESTIONS

(1) On a "dare" the plaintiff stuck his hand into a barrel of rattlesnakes possessed by the defendant, suffering grievous illness as a consequence. What should be the outcome of the case if it is determined that the plaintiff disbelieved that the barrel contained rattlesnakes? See *Keyser v. Phillips Petroleum Co.*, 287 So. 2d 364 (Fla. App. 1973). *See also Overstreet v. Gibson Product Co., Inc. of Del Rio*, 558 S.W.2d 58 (Tex. App. 1977), in which the court declined to apply strict liability as to a rattlesnake that had entered the defendant's premises from the natural environment without the defendant's knowledge. Restatement (Second) Torts § 515 provides:

§ 515. Plaintiff's Conduct

(1) Except as stated in Subsection (2), the contributory negligence of the plaintiff is not a defense to the strict liability of the possessor of an animal.

(2) The plaintiff's contributory negligence in knowingly and unreasonably subjecting himself to the risk that a wild animal or an abnormally dangerous domestic animal will do harm to his person, land or chattels, is a defense to the strict liability.

(3) The plaintiff's assumption of the risk of harm from the animal is a defense to the strict liability.

(2)   The meaning of "scienter" used in this context is elaborated by the following extracts from *Johnston v. Ohls*, 457 P.2d 1941, 196–198 (Wash. 1967), a case in which an attacking dog caused a motorcycle crash:

> Common law liability for injuries caused by vicious or dangerous dogs is based upon a form of strict liability. One who keeps a dog, who knows or reasonably should know that the dog has vicious or dangerous propensities likely to cause the injury complained of, has a duty to kill the animal or confine it. Any injury caused by such an animal subjects the owner to prima facie liability without proof of negligence.
>
> . . .
>
> The courts in various jurisdictions appear to be about evenly divided upon the issue of whether contributory negligence is a defense to this common law liability. *See* 66 A.L.R.2d, *supra*, 924–939.
>
> However, we are already aligned with those courts which hold that contributory negligence is not a defense in a common law action based upon scienter. *Brewer v. Furtwangler, supra*, 171 Wash. 620, 18 P.2d 838:
>
>> The terms "negligence" and "contributory negligence" are employed, for convenience and not in a strictly legal sense, in actions of the class in which the case at bar falls. The ground of liability in an action for injuries caused by a vicious dog is not negligence in the ordinary sense; hence, in its ordinary meaning, contributory negligence is not a defense.
>
> . . .
>
> Of course if plaintiff's own actions comprise such "essential fault" as to constitute the proximate cause of his injury, or if plaintiff provoked the animal, such behavior might constitute a defense. *See Muller v. McKesson*, 73 N.Y.195, 29 Am. Rep. 123 (1878); 66 A.L.R.2d 916, 931, *supra*. But such behavior can and should be distinguished from that which merely contributes to the accident in the usual negligence concept.
>
> Defendants contend that, in addition to the common law ground for recovery based upon scienter, plaintiffs alleged negligence in their complaint, and that contributory negligence is a defense for that cause of action. Even though negligence was alleged in the complaint, the jury was instructed that plaintiffs were not to recover absent a showing that defendants knew or should have known of their dog's vicious tendencies. Defendants do not object to this instruction. This requirement of knowledge or scienter is the only prerequisite to the application of common law strict liability. Therefore, even though plaintiffs alleged negligence, they could only have recovered by proving the elements of a common law action based on scienter — to which contributory negligence is not a defense.
>
> . . .
>
> Plaintiffs also assign error to the failure of the trial court to give their proposed instruction No. 9 which read:

In considering whether defendants knew or should have known facts sufficient to put them on notice that their dog might injure other persons, you are instructed that the injury complained of doe s not have to be the exact same injury that the dog has inflicted before in order to hold the defendants liable. It is sufficient if the plaintiffs were injured by the conduct of a dog the defendants knew was dangerous or vicious.

Plaintiffs contend that defendants' arguments plus the trial court's instruction No. 13 misled the jury into understanding that the dog's previous manifestations of viciousness must have been nearly identical to those causing the accident before knowledge of viciousness will result in liability to the owner.

Instruction No. 13 reads:

An owner of a dog is not liable for injuries caused by it unless: the dog has a vicious propensity or dangerous tendency as those terms are herein defined; the owner knows or by the exercise of reasonable care should know of the same; and the vicious propensity or dangerous tendency is similar to the type involved in the accident of which the plaintiff complains.

Therefore, unless you find that: the defendant's dog, Timmy, possessed vicious propensities or dangerous tendencies that the defendants knew or in the exercise of reasonable care should have known of such propensities; and the propensities were of the type which, in the light of ordinary human experience, would be likely to cause the type of accident which plaintiff complains of, then your verdict must be for the defendants and against the plaintiff.

This instruction is not challenged on appeal; so the question is whether plaintiffs' proposed instruction No. 9 should have also been given.

Plaintiffs correctly point out that it is not necessary for a dog to have previously bitten someone before its owner will be charged with knowledge that it is likely to do so. *See Mailhot v. Crowe, supra.* Nor will the owner of a vicious dog be excused from liability when the dog knocks a woman down merely because the dog is muzzled. *See Hicks v. Sullivan*, 122 Cal. App. 635, 10 P.2d 516 (1932). However, there is the requirement that the owner have knowledge of a trait or propensity of the animal which would be likely to cause the accident complained of. *See* Prosser, Torts 515 (3d ed. 1964). Under plaintiffs' proposed instruction, an owner would be liable for *any* damage caused by a dog he knew to be dangerous or vicious. Under the court's instruction, the owner must have knowledge of propensities which "in the light of ordinary human experience, would be likely to cause the type of accident which plaintiff complains of." We believe the instruction as given is a correct statement of the law. There was no error in refusing to give plaintiffs' requested instruction No. 9.

(3) The law pertaining to wild and vicious animals varies widely among the states both as to when strict liability pertains and also as to whether contributory negligence and assumption of risk constitute defenses to actions brought under that theory. Although generalizations are bound to be misleading as to specific applications, a review of cases suggests that contributory negligence would not be a

defense to common law strict liability actions but that assumption of risk would be. *See, e.g., Franken v. City of Sioux Center*, 272 N.W. 422 (Ia. 1978), and *Marshall v. Ranne*, 511 S.W.2d 255 (Tex. 1974). With the advent of comparative fault, however, comparative fault statutes in many jurisdictions require that both contributory negligence and assumption of risk be treated as comparative defenses. *See, e.g., Mills v. Smith*, 673 P.2d 117 (Kans. App. 1983), and *Johnson v. Swain*, 787 S.W.2d 36 (Tex. 1989) (applying the Texas comparative causation statute).

(4)   Which animals are wild animals for the purpose of invoking strict liability can be disputatious. For example, *Ollhof v. Peck*, 503 N.W.2d 323 (Wis. App. 1993), held that a muskellunge (a fish) kept in a petting zoo did not invoke strict liability as to a bite delivered to the hand of an adult petter. One decision catalogues five classes of animals as follows without indicating which invokes strict liability:

> For the purpose of determining the rules of law applicable to case involving injuries committed by animals, they may be divided in five general classes, namely: (1) Animals ferae naturae, of known savage and vicious nature, as bears, lions, tigers; (2) animals ferae naturae which generally may be domesticated or tamed as to lose their native ferocity, as bees, monkeys, etc.; (3) domestic animals which are known by their owner or keeper to be vicious; (4) domestic animals not known by their owner or keeper to be vicious, and (5) domestic herbivorous animals prone to wander and consume crops, grass and herbage.

Whitfield v. Stewart, 577 P.2d 1295, 1297 (Ok. 1978), quoting 3 Corpus Juris 82. (5) Many jurisdictions have enacted statutes pertaining to dog bites. *See, e.g., DeRobertis v. Randazzo*, 462 A.2d 1260 (N.J. 1983). These statutes vary widely in their coverages and consequences.

HOUSE v. THORNTON
Washington Supreme Court
457 P.2d 199 (1969)

HALE, JUDGE

Fraud is so easy to claim that the law makes it hard to prove. When the basement, walls, floors and foundation of a house plaintiffs had bought from defendants slipped and cracked and the supporting terrain slid away from the foundation, plaintiffs brought this suit to rescind the sale. Plaintiffs Homer and Noreen House charged the sellers with overt false misrepresentations and deceit but the court granted the rescission although expressly finding that these allegations were not clearly, cogently and convincingly proved. Defendant sellers appeal, and we perceive the major issue to be whether, in the sale of a brand-new house to its first buyer and occupant, the law impresses the transaction with a warranty that the foundation is firm and secure.

. . .

Homes and Noreen House, plaintiffs, first saw the house in August, 1964. At the time, it was virtually complete and the upstairs was ready for occupancy but some partitions and plasterboard had yet to be installed in the basement. Landscaping was largely uncompleted. Plaintiffs noticed ruts and crevices in the rockery and ditches in the backyard apparently caused by erosion. A few weeks later, in

September, 1964, they bought the house and lot 9 plus an adjoining 10 feet on lot 10 for $32,583.38, making a down payment of $12,583.38 and financing the $20,000 balance through a mortgage with the University Federal Savings and Loan Association.

About 3 months later, in December, 1964, following a period of heavy rains, the Houses observed a three-eights inch crack open up in the earth outside of but running the length of and parallel to the east wall of the house and on into the adjacent lot. Water accumulated in the yard, and Mr. House, on the advise of Mr. Thornton, the builder, dug a trench to drain it. In digging this trench, Mr. House first discovered the existence of the old foundation.

During the following winter, 1965, another crack in the yard opened up and Mr. House dug another trench to drain the water away from it and found that the earth beneath it settled for about 3 inches near the north end of the house. Then the steps and basement wall separated, and the seam between the chimney and house opened so that daylight showed through it into the living room. Earth supporting the end of the concrete patio dropped 4 to 6 inches and the walkway to the patio separated 4 to 5 inches for a distance of 20 feet. Mr. Thorton brought in a machine, cracked up and removed the patio, and discovered that the east wall of the basements had budged. A crack developed in the basement floor running up into a section of the concrete basement wall. The floor of the basement dropped about 6 inches and another crack opened up in the basement wall.

. . .

[The cracks worsened and efforts to remedy them failed.]

Plaintiffs brought this suit for rescission. The trial court granted a decree rescinding the sale on tender of a deed by plaintiffs to the defendants, awarded plaintiffs judgment in the sum of $11,685.69, and ordered the defendants to hold plaintiffs harmless from any further liability on the mortgage. In allowing plaintiffs rescission and arriving at damages of $11,685.69 for moneys paid in and expended by them, the court deducted from their award a reasonable rental for their occupancy fixed at $200 per month for 39 months, or a total reduction in the judgment of $7,800.

Plaintiffs, as earlier stated, brought this suit for rescission on the basis of deceit and misrepresentation concerning the stability of the house, lot and surrounding terrain. They testified that the appearance of the lot and slope on which the house rested and the appearance of the higher surrounding terrain and that of the rockery and patio prompted them to make inquiries of the defendant sellers before completing the purchase as to the security of the lot. They said the defendants assured them that there could be no problems as to the hill on which the house stood, that sewers had been installed to replace the old septic tanks in the area, and that, if there had been any problems of slides, the trees in the vicinity would have shown it. Defendants, they said, pointed to some standing trees and piling, all completely erect, which they said would have been leaning had there been slippage.

. . .

The trial court granted plaintiffs a decree of rescission but not on the main grounds of false and misleading representations. It categorically exonerated defendants of overt misrepresentation and deceit in an express finding that there was insufficient proof of positive, fraudulent misstatements and that no fraudulent misstatements were "established by clear, cogent and convincing evidence." Further obviating the idea of fraud, the court found that the defendants "believed that the foundations which had been established for the house . . . were adequate to support it," and that "defendants Thornton took all the steps they felt were necessary to comply with a difficult soil situation." The court found, too, that the defendants knew there had been a house on the same lot and that, because of "some type of earth movement, the concrete foundation had cracked and the house had to be removed."

Again, in summarizing the case in an oral opinion, the court categorically stated that its judgment was not to be based on concepts of fraud and deceit. Finally, to make it clear that actionable fraud and deceit were not the basis for the relief granted, the trial judge, favoring the record with a memorandum opinion, said:

Plaintiffs alleged fraud as grounds for their requested rescission. However, the Court found, after the presentation of all the evidence, that the plaintiffs had failed to sustain their burden to prove by clear, convincing and cogent evidence that any affirmative misrepresentation had been made to Mr. House concerning the soil stability.

Rescission was thus granted and judgment awarded the buyers, as we understand the learned judge's opinion, on the basis that the defendants knew of the earlier soil slippage and removal of the house some 15 years earlier from lot 9; that this possible instability would not be evident to a purchaser even on careful examination unless he were a soil expert; and that this knowledge, even though the vendor conscientiously and for good reason believed the foundation and soil to be firm and secure, gave rise to a duty to disclose it to the buyer. The failure to make such a disclosure, concluded the trial court, engendered the same right to rescission in this case as would actionable fraud and deceit.

Fraud and deceit, being so easy to assert, must be proved by clear, cogent and convincing evidence. . . . Despite the absence of actionable fraud, deceit and misrepresentation, however, we think that the trial court reached the right conclusion. Our reasons differ in some degree from those of the trial court although it should be said that the doctrines upon which we affirm have not, we think, been heretofore squarely stated in this jurisdiction in cases arising from the sale and purchase of realty.

In two cases, the issues concerning the sale of or construction upon real estate have approached, but not quite reached, the determinative issues now before us. *Hoye v. Century Builders, Inc.*, 52 Wash. 2d 830, 329 P.2d 474 (1958), held that when a contractor undertook to construct a house for and upon the land of another, there was an implied warranty that the house would be fit for human habitation. In *Fain v. Nelson*, 57 Wash. 2d 217, 356 P.2d 302 (1960), we again held that, where a building is sold in the course of construction, there can be an implied warranty that on completion it will be fit for the intended purpose, but that a defective but reparable roof was not such a fatal defect or deficiency as to vitiate the contract since it did not render the building unfit for its intended purpose and did not amount to a breach of the implied warranty.

The rule of implied warranty of fitness covering new construction or the sale of a partially constructed building, although closely related to the sale of a brand new residence, falls short of meeting the precise issues in the instant case. Frequently, the prospective purchaser of a house buys it with knowledge of its defects and makes no point whatever of their existence before consummating the deal; and if the defects or deficiencies or conditions do not render the house unfit for habitation, the question of whether an implied warranty covers them could be said to depend on whether they are of such magnitude as to prevent the house from being used for the purpose for which it was purchased. *See Fain v. Nelson, supra.* But the present trend is toward the implied warranty of fitness and away from caveat emptor when it comes to the things which vitally affect the structural stability or preclude the occupancy of the building.

Nothing, of course, can be said to be more vital to a dwelling than the stability of its foundation. When the foundation of a house cracks, slips, shifts or deteriorates to such an extent that a person of reasonable prudence would reasonably assume that the house is unsafe for occupancy, it is no longer fit for its intended purpose, *i.e.*, a place of residence for the owner and his family. This, of course, is true whether the danger arises from instability of the land and terrain on which the foundation rests or from defects in the foundation's design, installation, fabrication or composition. There can be little doubt that the house which plaintiffs bought from the defendants met this test of unsuitability. The evidence amply supported the court's conclusion that the sliding, slipping, and cracking of the foundation and floors, and the cracking and shifting of the walls, although due not to faulty design, installation or workmanship but rather to the instability of the ground and terrain upon which the house stood, rendered the premises unusable as a dwelling.

Although the court found that the defendants were free of fraud and misrepresentation, and there was no proof that the defendants failed to properly design and erect the building, or that they used defective materials or in any respect did an unworkman like job, and that they were innocent of any intentional wrong, the fact remains that they sold, and turned over to plaintiffs a brand-new $32,000 residence which turned out to be unfit for occupancy. As between vendor and purchaser, the builder-vendors, even though exercising reasonable care to construct a sound building, had by far the better opportunity to examine the stability of the site and to determine the kind of foundation to install. Although hindsight, it is frequently said, is 20–20 and defendants used reasonable prudence in selecting the site and designing and constructing the building, their position throughout the process of selection, planning and construction was markedly superior to that of their first purchaser-occupant. To borrow an idea from equity, of the innocent parties who suffered, it was the builder-vendor who made the harm possible. If there is a comparative standard of innocence, as well as of culpability, the defendants who built and sold the house were less innocent and more culpable than the wholly innocent and unsuspecting buyer. Thus, the old rule of caveat emptor has little relevance to the sale of a brand-new house by a vendor-builder to a first buyer for purposes of occupancy.

We apprehend it to be the rule that, when a vendor-builder sells a new house to its first intended occupant, he impliedly warrants that the foundations supporting it are firm and secure and that the house is structurally safe for the buyer's intended purpose of living in it.

. . .

NOTES

(1)   A number of decisions have acknowledged the existence of a warranty of habitability or similar warranty in the sale of new homes. The exact criteria of the warranties differ widely. *See, e.g., Kirk v. Ridgway*, 373 N.W.2d 491 (Iowa 1985) (implied warranty of workmanship); *Stiles v. Evans*, 683 S.W.2d 481 (Tex. App. 1985) (implied warranty of workmanship and habitability); *Conklin v. Hurley*, 428 So. 2d 654 (Fla. 1983) (implied warranty of amenability or merchantability); *Gamble v. Main*, 300 S.E.2d 110 (W. Va. 1983); *Redarowicz v. Orlendorf*, 441 N.E.2d 324 (Ill. 1982) (implied warranty of habitability extends beyond first purchaser); *Loch Hill Construction Co., Inc. v. Fricke*, 399 A.2d 883 (Md. App. 1979) (implied warranty that home is fit for habitation); *McDonald v. Mianicki*, 398 A.2d 1283 (N.J. 1979) (implied warranty of habitability of new home applies to all developers, not just mass developers); *Tavares v. Horstman*, 542 P.2d 1275 (Wyo. 1975) (implied warranty of habitability); *Yepson v. Burgess*, 525 P.2d 1019 (Or. En Banc 1974) (implied warranty of workmanship and habitability in new house); *Pollard v. Saxe & Yolles Development Co*, 525 P.2d 88 (Cal. 1974) (vendors and builders of new home impliedly warrant workmanlike manner); *Padula v. J.J. Deb Cin Homes, Inc.*, 298 A.2d 529 (R.I. 1973); *Smith v. Old Watson Development Co.*, 479 S.W.2d 795 (Mo. En Banc 1972); *Weeks v. Slavick Builders*, 180 N.W.2d 503 (Mich. App. 1970); *Shearman v. Centex Homes*, 78 Cal. App. 4th 611, 92 Cal. Rptr. 2d 761 (2000) (builder of "mass produced homes" is strictly liable for construction defects that damage the home itself); and *Moglia v. McNeil Co., Inc.*, 700 N.W.2d 606 (Neb. 2005) (acknowledges that one who designs and constructs a home owes a warranty of workmanlike performance that extends to subsequent buyers; but declines to recognize a warranty of habitability under the circumstances.)

(2)   *Eastern Steel Constructors, Inc. v. City of Salem*, 549 S.E.2d 266 (W. Va. 2001) held that the professional designer of a commercial building owed a warranty of plans and specifications to the contractor who obtained the contract to construct the building even though the two were not in privity of contract. The court applied a duty analysis similar to the analysis that applies in negligence actions for pure economic loss. *See* § 5.05[A] *supra*.

(3)   California initially adopted a theory of strict liability as to the condition of premises in landlord-tenant leases of residential property, *Becker v. IRM Corporation*, 698 P.2d 116 (Cal. 1985), but later overruled that decision as being unsound. *Peterson v. Superior Court*, 899 P.2d 905 (Cal. 1995). *Acosta-Mestre v. Hilton Intern. of Puerto Rico, Inc.*, 156 F.3d 49 (1st Cir. 1998), applying Puerto Rico law, relied upon *Peterson* to conclude that an innkeeper is not strictly liable to patrons as to the condition of furniture in a hotel. The court stated, "Other courts in the United States that have considered the issue have reached the same conclusion." *Id.*, 156 F.3d at 55, n.5.

Chapter 14

PRODUCT LIABILITY

The cases in this chapter trace the remarkable course of product liability law from the negligence no-duty rule of *Winterbottom v. Wright*, to the breach of warranty doctrines that courts applied to provide an alternative remedy to offset the initial impotence of the negligence cause of action in this field, and finally to the product strict liability rule of *Greenman v. Yuba Power Products, Inc.* As a result of the development reflected herein, the modern product liability lawyer must be prepared to consider negligence, breach of warranties, and strict liability as alternative or cumulative causes of action. After you have reviewed the materials in this chapter, propose the best approach to plead the case in the problem below:

PROBLEM

Bob Roberts, an employee of Ace Contracting Company, attempted to drive an asphalt roller up an inclined ramp onto the bed of a transporter truck. Roberts had already driven a paving machine onto the transporter and parked it at the front. The loading ramp was permanently affixed to the bed of the transporter. After the transporter was loaded, the ramp was pulled and folded at the front. Ample room remained to park the roller on the back of the transporter.

Roberts had worked for Ace for ten years and had driven the machines off and on the transporter hundreds of times. On the morning in question a heavy dew had fallen, making the oak surface of the ramp somewhat slick. This reduced the friction between the steel rollers of the rolling machine and the oak ramp.

An eyewitness who happened to be an experienced roller operator but who was not employed by Ace will testify as follows. As Roberts drove up the ramp, he stood up on the deck of the roller, although a seat was provided. When the roller reached the deck of the transporter, it was going too fast for Roberts to stop it. It hit the paver with a moderate jolt and bounced back. The roller started back down the ramp, and Roberts gunned the engine to bring it back onto the transporter. Again, the roller hit the paver and bounced back. This time Roberts let the machine go back down the ramp, apparently with the intention of starting over from the ground.

The rolling machine weighed about 16 tons and had two rollers. The driver was about five feet and the steerer about three feet in diameter. The roller was backing with the driving roller downhill. The ramp was "paved" with oak boards two inches thick. The ramp was hinged in the middle and folded when retracted. When the ramp was extended, a gap of 15 inches was left between the oak boards on each side of the hinge. There was no support between the hinged joint in the ramp and the ground. As the roller backed down, the big driving roller rolled over the gap with a slight bump, but when the small roller reached the hinge it "fell" into the 2-inch-deep, 15-inch-wide gap with a severe jolt produced by the natural elasticity of the unsupported hinged joint.

Then standing, Roberts lost his footing and was thrown backwards onto the metal surface covering the top of the large roller. He tried desperately to cling to the surface but skidded off onto the ground in the path of the descending roller. The machine ran over Roberts, killing him instantly.

Expert investigation produced the following evidence. The rolling machine was manufactured by XYZ Company two years before the date of the accident. It had no safety rails and hand holds of any kind around the operator's platform. Of twenty other roller models manufactured at that time, eleven had safety rails and the remainder did not. No statute or government regulation required safety rails on rollers, but the American Association of Automotive Engineers standards "recommended" safety rails on all heavy construction equipment as good practice.

The transporter with ramp had been manufactured for Ace by Fuge Trailers, Inc. eighteen months prior to the accident. The drawings for the trailer called for a five-inch gap between the oak boards at the hinge. Without consulting the designee, the manufacturing crew had arbitrarily enlarged the gap during manufacture when it was found that the boards rubbed together as the ramp folded. Enlarging the gap to six inches would have eliminated the problem.

Fuge also made no elasticity analysis of the ramp. A mechanical design expert will testify that the natural elasticity of the unsupported hinged joint was three times that of a typical loading ramp, and this caused the jolt to be greatly amplified when the small roller fell into the gap. He will also testify that the resulting bounce would have been minimized had the ramp been designed with stiffeners or with supports that extended to the ground.

Ace had no policy on whether operators should sit or stand when operating a roller. Ace was aware that some operators stood and deemed the decision to sit or stand to be one of operator discretion as long as all other safety precautions were observed. No statute, governmental regulation or professional standard addressed the matter. Some safety experts will testify that operators should always sit; others will testify that operators should exercise discretion. Some operators will testify that they always sit; a smaller number will testify they always stand; and some will testify they sometimes stand.

1. Draft a complaint for Roberts's widow, his only survivor.

2. Draft an answer for: (a) XYZ, (b) Fuge.

3. Draft proposed instructions for the plaintiff.

4. Draft proposed instructions for: (a) XYZ, (b) Fuge.

§ 14.01 NEGLIGENCE AND PRIVITY: THE DOCTRINE THAT OUGHT NEVER HAVE BEEN

WINTERBOTTOM v. WRIGHT
[1842] 10 M. & W. 109, 152 Eng. Rep. 402[1]

[The plaintiff was employed by the Postmaster General to drive a mail coach. The defendant was under contract to the Postmaster General to repair and maintain all the mail coaches. A coach driven by the plaintiff collapsed, allegedly because of defective maintenance, and the plaintiff was injured. The plaintiff brought an action against the defendant alleging that the defendant "improperly and negligently conducted himself" in the performance of his duties, thereby causing harm to the plaintiff. To this complaint the defendant demurred.

What follows are arguments for (Byles) and against (Peacock), the demurrer and the judgments of the judges. Note with care the arguments made by the plaintiff's lawyer, especially the allusion to Levy v. Langridge.]

Byles, for the defendant, objected that the declaration was bad in substance. — This is an action brought, not against Atkinson and his co-contractors, who were the employers of the plaintiff, but against the person employed by the Postmaster-General, and totally unconnected with them or with the plaintiff. Now it is a general rule, that wherever a wrong arises merely out of the breach of a contract, which is the case on the face of this declaration, whether the form in which the action is conceived be ex contractu or ex delicto, the party who made the contract alone can sue: Tollit v. Sherstone, 5 M. & W. 283. If the rule were otherwise, and privity of contract were not requisite, there would be no limit to such actions. If the plaintiff may, as in this case, run through the length of three contracts, he may run through any number or series of them; and the most alarming Sherstone, 5 M. & W. 283. If the rule were otherwise, and privity of one of the sufferers by such an accident as that which recently happened on the Versailles railway, might have his action against the manufacturer of the defective axle. So, if the chain-cable of an East Indiaman were to break, and the vessel went aground, every person affected, either in person or property, by the accident, might have an action against the manufacturer, and perhaps against every seller also of the iron. Again, suppose a gentleman's coachman were injured by the breaking down of his carriage, if this action be maintainable, he might bring his action against the smith or the coach-maker, although he could not sue his master, who is the party contracting with him: Priestly v. Fowler, 3 M. & W. 1. There is no precedent to be found of such a declaration, except one in 8 Wentworth, 397, which has been deemed very questionable. Rapson v. Cubitt, 9 M. & W. 710, is an authority to show that the party injured by the negligence of another cannot go beyond the party who did the injury, unless he can establish that the latter stood in the relation of a servant to the party sued. In Witte v. Hague, 2 Dowl. & Ry. 33, where the plaintiff sued for an injury produced by the explosion of a steam-engine boiler, the defendant was personally present managing the boiler at the time of the accident. Levy v. Langridge, 4 M. & W. 337, will probably be referred to on the other side. But that case was expressly decided on the ground that the defendant, who sold the gun by which the plaintiff was injured, although he did not personally contract with the plaintiff, who was a minor, knew that it was bought to be used by him. Here there

---

[1] [Ed. — English Reports, general reporter of old English cases; Meeson and Welsby's reports.]

is no allegation that the defendant knew that the coach was to be driven by the plaintiff. There, moreover, fraud was alleged in the declaration, and found by the jury: and there, too, the cause of injury was a weapon of a dangerous nature, and the defendant was alleged to have had notice of the defect in its construction. Nothing of that sort appears upon this declaration.

Peacock, contra. — This case is within the principle of the decision in Levy v. Langridge. Here the defendant entered into a contract with a public officer to supply an article which, if imperfectly constructed, was necessarily dangerous, and which, from its nature and the use for which it was destined, was necessarily to be driven by a coachman. That is sufficient to bring the case within the rule established by Levy v. Langridge. In that case the contract made by the father of the plaintiff with the defendant was made on behalf of himself and his family generally, and there was nothing to show that the defendant was aware even of the existence of the particular son who was injured. Suppose a party made a contract with government for a supply of muskets, one of which, from its misconstruction, burst and injured a soldier: there it is clear that the use of the weapon by a soldier would have been contemplated, although not by the particular individual who received the injury, and could it be said, since the decision in Levy v. Langridge, that he could not maintain an action against the contractor? So, if a coach-maker, employed to put on the wheels of a carriage, did it so negligently that one of them flew off, and a child of the owner were thereby injured, the damage being the natural and immediate consequence of his negligence, he would surely be responsible. So, if a party entered into a contract to repair a church, a workhouse, or other public building, and did it so insufficiently that a person attending the former, or a pauper in the latter, were injured by the falling of a stone, he could not maintain an action against any other person than the contractor; but against him he must surely have a remedy. It is like the case of a contractor who negligently leaves open a sewer, whereby a person passing along the street is injured. It is clear that no action could be maintained against the Postmaster-General: Hall v. Smith, 2 Bing. 156; Humphreys v. Mears, 1 Man. & R. 187; Priestly v. Fowler. But here the declaration alleges the accident to have happened through the defendant's negligence and want of care. The plaintiff had no opportunity of seeing that the carriage was sound and secure. [Alderson, B. — The decision in Levy v. Langridge proceeds upon the ground of the knowledge and fraud of the defendant.] Here also there was fraud: the defendant represented the coach to be in a proper state for use, and whether he represented that which was false within his knowledge, or a fact as true which he did not know to be so, it was equally a fraud in point of law, for which he is responsible.

Lord ABINGER, C. B. — I am clearly of opinion that the defendant is entitled to our judgment. We ought not to permit a doubt to rest upon this subject, for our doing so might be the means of letting in upon us an infinity of actions. This is an action of the first impression, and it has been brought in spite of the precautions which were taken, in the judgment of this Court in the case of Levy v. Langridge, to obviate any notion that such an action could be maintained. We ought not to attempt to extend the principle of that decision, which, although it has been cited in support of this action, wholly fails as an authority in its favour; for there the gun was bought for the use of the son, the plaintiff in that action, who could not make the bargain himself, but was really and substantially the party contracting. Here the action is brought simply because the defendant was a contractor with a third person; and it is contended that thereupon he became liable to every body who might use the carriage. If there had been any ground for such an action, there certainly would have been some precedent of it; but with the exception of actions against innkeepers, and some few other persons, no case of a similar nature has occurred in practice. That is a strong circumstance, and is of itself a great authority against its maintenance. It is however contended, that this contract being made on the behalf of the public by the Postmaster-General, no action could be maintained against him, and therefore the plaintiff must have a remedy against the defendant. But that is by no means a necessary consequence — he may be remediless altogether. There is no privity of contract between these parties; and if the plaintiff can sue, every passenger, or even any person passing along the road, who was injured by the upsetting of the coach, might bring a similar action. Unless we confine the operation of such contracts as this to the parties who entered into them, the most absurd and outrageous consequences, to which I can see no limit, would ensue. Where a party becomes responsible to the public, by undertaking a public duty, he is liable, though the injury may have arisen from the negligence of his servant or agent. So, in cases of public nuisances, whether the act was done by the party as a servant, or in any other capacity, you are liable to an action at the suit of any person who suffers. Those, however, are cases where the real ground of the liability is the public duty, or the commission of the public nuisance. There is also a class of cases in which the law permits a contract to be turned into a tort; but unless there has been some public duty undertaken, or public nuisance committed, they are all cases in which an action might have been maintained upon the contract. Thus, a carrier may be sued either in assumpsit or case; but there is no instance in which a party, who was not privy to the contract entered into with him, can maintain any such action. The plaintiff in this case could not have brought an action on the contract; if he could have done so, what would have been his situation, supposing the Postmaster-General had released the defendant? that would, at all events, have defeated his claim altogether. By permitting this action, we should be working this injustice, that after the defendant had done every thing to the satisfaction of his employer, and after all matters between them had been adjusted, and all accounts settled on the footing of their contract, we should subject them to be ripped open by this action of tort being brought against him.

ALDERSON, B.

I am of the same opinion. The contract in this case was made with the Postmaster-General alone; and the case is just the same as if he had come to the defendant and ordered a carriage, and handed it at once over to Atkinson. If we were to hold that the plaintiff could sue in such a case, there is no point at which such actions would stop. The only safe rule is to confine the right to recover to those who enter into the contract: if we go one step beyond that, there is no reason why we should not go fifty. The only real argument in favour of the action is, that this is a case of hardship; but that might have been obviated, if the plaintiff had made himself a party to the contract. Then it is urged that it falls within the principle of the case of Levy v. Langridge. But the principle of that case was simply this, that the father having bought the gun for the very purpose of being used by the plaintiff, the defendant made representations by which he was induced to use it. There, a distinct fraud was committed on the plaintiff; the falsehood of the representation was also alleged to have been within the knowledge of the defendant who made it, and he was properly held liable for the consequences. How are the facts of that case applicable to those of the use it. There, a distinct fraud was committed on the plaintiff; the falsehood declaration? It shows nothing of the kind. Our judgment must therefore be for the defendant.

GURNEY, B., concurred.

ROLFE, B.

The breach of the defendant's duty, stated in this declaration, is his omission to keep the carriage in a safe condition; and when we examine the mode in which that duty is alleged to have arisen, we find a statement that the defendant took upon himself, to wit, under and by virtue of the said contract, the sole and exclusive duty, charge, care, and burden of the repairs, state, and condition of the said mail-coach, and, during all the time aforesaid, it had become and was the sole and exclusive duty of the defendant, to wit, under and by virtue of his said contract, to keep and maintain the said mail-coach in a fit, proper, safe, and secure state and condition. The duty, therefore, is shown to have arisen solely from the contract; and the fallacy consists in the use of that word "duty." If a duty to the Postmaster-General be meant, that is true; but if a duty to the plaintiff be intended, (and in that sense the word is evidently used,) there was none. This is one of those unfortunate cases in which there certainly has been damnum, but it is damnum absque injuria; it is, no doubt, a hardship upon the plaintiff to be without a remedy, hut, by that consideration we ought not to be influenced. Hard cases, it has been frequently observed, are apt to introduce bad law.

Judgment for the defendant.

NOTE

Winterbottom v. Wright is now history, but exactly how broadly its application has been abrogated in any particular jurisdiction depends upon how far it has been receded from in that jurisdiction. The next two cases are typical and well known milestones in the recession. The third, *Donoghue v. Stevenson*, which we have seen before, commemorates the effective burial of *Winterbottom v. Wright* in English negligence law. Most United States jurisdictions have a counterpart.

THOMAS v. WINCHESTER
New York Court of Appeals *6 N.Y. 397,*
57 Am. Dec. 455 (1852)

RUGGLES, CH. J.

APPEAL from the general term of the Supreme Court, in the sixth district, where a motion for a new trial, made upon a bill of exceptions, had been denied, and judgment entered upon a verdict in favor of the plaintiffs.

This action was brought by Samuel Thomas and Mary Ann, his wife, against the defendants, Winchester and Gilbert, to recover damages for negligently putting up, labelling and selling, as and for extract of dandelion, a simple and harmless medicine, a jar of extract of belladonna, a deadly poison; by means whereof, the plaintiff, Mary Ann Thomas, to whom a dose of dandelion had been prescribed by a physician, and to whom a portion of the contents of the jar of belladonna had been administered, as and for extract of dandelion, had been greatly injured.

The complaint alleged, that the defendants, from the year 1843, to the 1st January 1849, were engaged in putting up and vending certain vegetable extracts, at a store in the city of New York, designated as "108 John Street," and that the defendant, Gilbert, had, for a long time previously thereto, been so engaged, at the same place. That among the extracts so prepared and sold by them, were those respectively known as the "extract of dandelion," and the "extract of belladonna;" the former a mild and harmless medicine, and the latter a vegetable poison, which, if taken as a medicine in such quantity as might be safely administered of the former, would destroy the life, or seriously impair the health, of the person to whom the same might be administered. That, at some time between the periods above mentioned, the defendants put up and sold to James S. Aspinwall, a druggist in the city of New York, a jar of the extract of belladonna, which had been labelled by them as the extract of dandelion, and was purchased of them as such, by Aspinwall. That Aspinwall afterwards, on the 10th May 1845, relying upon the label so affixed by the defendants, sold the said jar of belladonna to Alvin Foord, a druggist of Cazenovia, in the county of Madison, as the extract of dandelion. That afterwards, on the 27th March 1849, the plaintiff, Mrs. Thomas, being sick, a portion of the extract of dandelion was prescribed for her, by her physician, and the said Alvin Foord, relying upon the label affixed by the defendants to said jar of belladonna, and believing the same to be the extract of dandelion, did, on the application of the plaintiff, Samuel Thomas, sell and deliver to him, from the said jar of belladonna, a portion of its contents, which was administered to the plaintiff, Mrs. Thomas, under the belief that it was the extract of dandelion; by which she was greatly injured, so that her life was despaired of, &c. The plaintiffs also averred that the whole injury was occasioned by the negligence and unskilfulness of the defendants in putting up and falsely labelling the jar of belladonna as the extract of dandelion, whereby the plaintiffs, as well as the druggists, and all other persons through whose hands it passed, before being administered as aforesaid, were induced to believe, and did believe, that it contained the extract of dandelion.

The defendants, in their answers, severally denied the allegations of the complaint, and insisted that they were not liable for the medicines sold by Aspinwall and Foord.

It was proved, on the trial, before Mason, J., that Mrs. Thomas being in ill health, her physician prescribed for her a dose of dandelion. Her husband purchased what was believed to be the medicine prescribed, at the store of Dr. Foord, a physician and druggist in Cazenovia, Madison county, where the plaintiffs resided. A small quantity of the medicine thus purchased was administered to Mrs. Thomas, on whom it produced very alarming effects; such as coldness of the surface and extremities, feebleness of circulation, spasms of the muscles, giddiness of the head, dilation of the pupils of the eyes, and derangement of mind. She recovered, however, after some time, from its effects, although, for a short time, her life was thought to be in great danger.

The medicine administered was belladonna, and not dandelion. The jar from which it was taken was labelled "½ lb. dandelion, prepared by A. Gilbert, No. 108 John Street, N.Y. Jar 8 oz." It was sold for, and believed by Dr. Foord to be, the extract of dandelion, as labelled. Dr. Foord purchased the article, as the extract of dandelion, from James S. Aspinwall, a druggist at New York. Aspinwall bought it of the defendant, as extract of dandelion, believing it to be such.

The defendant, Winchester, was engaged at No. 108 John Street, New York, in the manufacture and sale of certain vegetable extracts for medicinal purposes, and in the purchase and sale of others. The extracts manufactured by him were put up in jars for sale, and those which he purchased were put up by him in like manner. The jars containing extracts manufactured by himself and those containing extracts purchased by him from others, were labelled alike. Both were labelled like the jar in question, as "prepared by A. Gilbert." Gilbert was a person employed by the defendant at a salary, as an assistant in his business. The jars were labelled in Gilbert's name, because he had been previously engaged in the same business, on his own account, at No. 108 John Street, and, probably, because Gilbert's labels rendered the articles more saleable.

The extract contained in the jar sold to Aspinwall, and by him to Foord, was not manufactured by the defendant, but was purchased by him from another manufacturer or dealer. The extract of dandelion and the extract of belladonna resemble each other in color, consistence, smell and taste; but may, on careful examination, be distinguished the one for the other by those who are well acquainted with these articles. Gilbert's labels were paid for by Winchester, and used in his business, with his knowledge and assent.

At the close of the testimony, the defendants' counsel moved for a nonsuit, on the following grounds:

1. That the action could not be sustained, as the defendant was the remote vendor of the article in question; and there was no connection, transaction or privity between him and the plaintiffs, or either of them.

. . .

The learned judge overruled the motion for a nonsuit, and the defendants' counsel excepted.

. . .

RUGGLES, C. J. (after stating the facts.)

The action was properly brought in the name of the husband and wife, for the personal injury and suffering of the wife; and the case was left to the jury, with the proper directions on that point. (1 Chit. Plead. 62.)

The case depends on the first point taken by the defendant, on his motion for a nonsuit; and the question is, whether the defendant, being a remote vendor of the medicine, and there being no privity or connection between him and the plaintiffs, the action can be maintained. If, in labelling a poisonous drug with the name of a harmless medicine, for public market, no duty was violated by the defendant, excepting that which he owed to Aspinwall, his immediate vendee, in virtue of his contract of sale, this action cannot be maintained.

If A. builds a wagon and sells it to B., who sells it to C., and C. hires it to D., who in consequence of the gross negligence of A., in building the wagon, is overturned and injured, D. cannot recover damages against A., the builder. A.'s obligation to build the wagon faithfully, arises solely out of his contract with B.; the public have nothing to do with it. Misfortune to third persons, not parties to the contract, would not be a natural and necessary consequence of the builder's negligence; and such negligence is not an act imminently dangerous to human life. So, for the same reason, if a horse be defectively shod by a smith, and a person hiring the horse from the owner, is thrown and injured, in consequence of the smith's negligence in shoeing; the smith is not liable for the injury. The smith's duty in such case grows exclusively out of his contract with the owner of the horse; it was a duty which the smith owed to him alone, and to no one else. And although the injury to the rider may have happened, in consequence of the negligence of the smith, the latter was not bound, either by his contract, or by any considerations of public policy or safety, to respond for his breach of duty to any one except the person he contracted with.

This was the ground on which the case of Winterbottom v. Wright (10 Mees. & Welsb. 109) was decided. A. contracted with the postmaster-general to provide a coach to convey the mail-bags along a certain line of road, and B. and others also contracted to horse the coach along the same line. B. and his co-contractors hired C., who was the plaintiff, to drive the coach. The coach, in consequence of some latent defect, broke down; the plaintiff was thrown from his seat and lamed. It was held, that C. could not maintain an action against A., for the injury thus sustained. The reason of the decision is best stated by Baron ROLFE: A.'s duty to keep the coach in good condition, was a duty to the postmaster-general, with whom he made his contract, and not a duty to the driver employed by the owners of the horses.

But the case in hand stands on a different ground. The defendant was a dealer in poisonous drugs; Gilbert was his agent in preparing them for market. The death or great bodily harm of some person, was the natural, and almost inevitable, consequence of the sale of belladonna by means of the false label. . . .

. . . In the present case, the sale of the poisonous article was made to a dealer in drugs, and not to a consumer; the injury, therefore, was not likely to fall on him, or on his vendee, who was also a dealer; but much more likely to be visited on a remote purchaser, as actually happened. The defendant's negligence put human life in imminent danger. Can it be said, that there was no duty on the part of the defendant, to avoid the creation of that danger, by the exercise of greater caution? Or that the exercise of that caution was a duty only to his immediate vendee, whose life was not endangered? The defendant's duty arose out of the nature of his business, and the danger to others incident to its mismanagement. Nothing but mischief like that which actually happened could have been expected, from sending the poison falsely labelled into the market; and the defendant is justly responsible for the probable consequences of the act. The duty of exercising caution in this respect did not arise out of the defendant's contract of sale to Aspinwall; the wrong done by the defendant was in putting the poison, mislabelled, into the hands of Aspinwall; as an article of merchandise, to be sold and afterwards used, as the extract of dandelion, by some person then unknown.

The owner of a horse and cart, who leaves them unattended in the street, is liable for any damage which may result from his negligence. (Lynch v. Nurdin, 1 Ad. & Ellis, N. S., 29; Illidge v. Goodwin, 5 Car. & Payne 190.) The owner of a loaded gun, who puts it into the hands of a child, by whose indiscretion it is discharged, is liable for the damage occasioned by the discharge. (5 Maule & Sel. 198.) The defendant's contract of sale to Aspinwall does not excuse the wrong done to the plaintiffs' it was a part of the means by which the wrong was effected. The plaintiffs' injury and their remedy would have stood on the same principle, if the defendant had given the belladonna to Dr. Foord, without price, or if he had put it in his shop, without his knowledge, under circumstances which would probably have led to its sale on the faith of the label.

In Longmeid v. Holliday (6 Exch. 761), the distinction is recognised between an act of negligence imminently dangerous to the lives of others, and one that is not so. In the former case, the party guilty of the negligence is liable to the party injured, whether there be a contract between them or not; in the latter, the negligent party is liable only to the party with whom he contracted, and on the ground that negligence is a breach of the contract.

The defendant, on the trial, insisted that Aspinwall and Foord were guilty of negligence, in selling the article in question for what it was represented to be in the label; and that the suit, if it could be sustained at all, should have been brought against Foord. The judge charged the jury that, if they, or either of them, were guilty of negligence in selling the belladona for dandelion, the verdict must be for the defendant; and left the question of their negligence to the jury, who found on that point for the plaintiff. If the case really depended on the point thus raised, the question was properly left to the jury; but I think, it did not. The defendant, by affixing the label to the jar, represented its contents to be dandelion; and to have been "prepared" by his agent Gilbert. The word "prepared" on the label, must be understood to mean that the article was manufactured by him, or that it had passed through some process, under his hands, which would give him personal knowledge of its true name and quality. Whether Foord was justified in selling the article upon the faith of the defendant's label, would have been an open question, in an action by the plaintiffs against him, and I wish to be understood as giving no opinion on that point. But it seems to me, to be clear, that the defendant cannot, in this case, set up as a defence, that Foord sold the contents of the jar, as and for what the defendant represented it to be. The label conveyed the idea distinctly to Foord, that the contents of the jar was the extract of dandelion; and that "the defendant knew it to be such; so far as the defendant is concerned, Foord was under no obligation to test the truth of the representation. The charge of the judge in submitting to the jury the question in relation to the negligence of Foord and Aspinwall, cannot be complained of by the defendant.

Gardiner, J., concurred in affirming the judgment, on the ground that selling the belladonna without a label indicating that it was a poison, was declared a misdemeanor by statute (2 R. S. 694, § 23), but expressed no opinion upon the question whether, independent of the statute, the defendant would have been liable to these plaintiffs.

Gridley, J., was not present when the cause was decided. All the other members of the court concurred in the opinion delivered by Ruggles, Ch. J.

Judgment affirmed.

NOTE

Among the early cases in agreement was *Davis v. Guarniere*, 15 N.E. 350 (Ohio 1887).

MACPHERSON v. BUICK MOTOR CO.
New York Court of Appeals
111 N.E. 1050 (1916)

CARDOZO, J.

The defendant is a manufacturer of automobiles. It sold an automobile to a retail dealer. The retail dealer resold to the plaintiff. While the plaintiff was in the car it suddenly collapsed. He was thrown out and injured. One of the wheels was made of defective wood, and its spokes crumbled into fragments. The wheel was not made by the defendant; it was bought from another manufacturer. There is evidence, however, that its defects could have been discovered by reasonable inspection, and that inspection was omitted. There is no claim that the defendant knew of the defect and willfully concealed it. The case, in other words, is not brought within the rule of Kuelling v. Lean Mfg. Co., 183 N.Y. 78, 75 N.E. 1098, 2 L.R.A. (N.S.) 303, 111 Am. St. Rep. 691, 5 Ann. Cas. 124. The charge is one, not of fraud, but of negligence. The question to be determined is whether the defendant owed a duty of care and vigilance to any one but the immediate purchaser.

The foundations of this branch of the law, at least in this state, were Thomas v. Winchester, 6 N.Y. 397, 57 Am. Dec. 455.

[Discussion of Thomas and intervening cases omitted.]

We hold, then, that the principle of Thomas v. Winchester is not limited to poisons, explosives, and things of like nature, to things which in their normal operation are implements of destruction. If the nature of a thing is such that it is reasonably certain to place life and limb in peril when negligently made, it is then a thing of danger. Its nature gives warning of the consequences to be expected. If to the element of danger there is added knowledge that the thing will be used by persons other than the purchaser, and used without new tests, then, irrespective of contract, the manufacturer of this thing of danger is under a duty to make it carefully. That is as far as we are required to go for the decision of this case. There must be knowledge of a danger, not merely possible, but probable. It is possible to use almost anything in a way that will make it dangerous if defective. That is not enough to charge the manufacturer with a duty independent of his contract. Whether a given thing is dangerous may be sometimes a question for the court and sometimes a question for the jury. There must also be knowledge that in the usual course of events the danger will be shared by others than the buyer. Such knowledge may often be inferred from the nature of the transaction. But it is possible that even knowledge of the danger and of the use will not always be enough. The proximity or remoteness of the relation is a factor to be considered. We are dealing now with the liability of the manufacturer of the finished product, who puts it on the market to be used without inspection by his customers. If he is negligent, where danger is to be foreseen, a liability will follow.

We are not required, at this time, to say that it is legitimate to go back of the manufacturer of the finished product and hold the manufacturers of the component parts. To make their negligence a cause of imminent danger, an independent cause must often intervene; the manufacturer of the finished product must also fail in his duty of inspection. It may be that in those circumstances the negligence of the earlier members of the series is too remote to constitute, as to the ultimate user, an actionable wrong. . . . We leave that question open. We shall have to deal with it when it arises. The difficulty which it suggests is not present in this case. There is here no break in the chain of cause and effect. In such circumstances, the presence of a known danger, attendant upon a known use, makes vigilance a duty. We have put aside the notion that the duty to safeguard life and limb, when the consequences of negligence may be foreseen, grows out of contract and nothing else. We have put the source of the obligation where it ought to be. We have put its, source in the law.

From this survey of the decisions, there thus emerges a definition of the duty of a manufacturer which enables us to measure this defendant's liability. Beyond all question, the nature of an automobile gives warning of probable danger if its construction is defective. This automobile was designed to go 50 miles an hour. Unless its wheels were sound and strong, injury was almost certain. It was as much a thing of danger as a defective engine for a railroad. The defendant knew the danger. It knew also that the car would be used by persons other than the buyer. This was apparent from its size; there were seats for three persons. It was apparent also from the fact that the buyer was a dealer in cars, who bought to resell. The maker of this car supplied it for the use of purchasers from the dealer just as plainly as the contractor in Devlin v. Smith supplied the scaffold for use by the servants of the owner. The dealer was indeed the one person of whom it might be said with some approach to certainty that by him the car would not be used. Yet the defendant would have us say that he was the one person whom it was under a legal duty to protect. The law does not lead us to so inconsequent a conclusion. Precedents drawn from the days of travel by stagecoach do not fit some approach to certainty that by him the car would not be used. Yet the imminent does not change, but the things subject to the principle do change. They are whatever the needs of life in a developing civilization require them to be. . . .

[Discussion of contrary decisions from other jurisdictions omitted. As to England, Cardozo said, "In England the limits of the rule are still unsettled." Winterbottom v. Wright, page 666, supra, is often cited.]

In this view of the defendant's liability there is nothing inconsistent with the theory of liability on which the case was tried. It is true that the court told the jury that "an automobile is not an inherently dangerous vehicle." The meaning, however, is made plain by the context. The meaning is that danger is not to be expected when the vehicle is well constructed. The court left it to the jury to say whether the defendant ought to have foreseen that the car, if negligently constructed, would become "imminently dangerous." Subtle distinctions are drawn by the defendant between things inherently dangerous and things imminently dangerous, but the case does not turn upon these verbal niceties. If danger was to be expected as reasonably certain, there was a duty of vigilance, and this whether you call the danger inherent or imminent. In varying forms that thought was put before the jury. We do not say that the court would not have been justified in ruling as a matter of law that the car was a dangerous thing. If there was any error, it was none of which the defendant can complain.

We think the defendant was not absolved from a duty of inspection because it bought the wheels from a reputable manufacturer. It was not merely a dealer in automobiles. It was a manufacturer of automobiles. It was responsible for the finished product. It was not at liberty to put the finished product on the market without subjecting the component parts to ordinary and simple tests. Richmond & Danville R.R. Co. v. Elliott, 149 U.S. 266, 272, 13 Sup. Ct. 837, 37 L. Ed. 728. Under the charge of the trial judge nothing more was required of it. The obligation to inspect must vary with the nature of the thing to be inspected. The more probable the danger the greater the need of caution. . . .

The judgment should be affirmed, with costs.

WILLARD BARTLETT, C. J. (dissenting).

The theory upon which the case was submitted to the jury by the learned judge who presided at the trial was that, although an automobile is not an inherently dangerous vehicle, it may become such if equipped with a weak wheel; and that if the motor car in question, when it was put upon the market was in itself inherently dangerous by reason of its being equipped with a weak wheel, the defendant was chargeable with a knowledge of the defect so far as it might be discovered by a reasonable inspection and the application of reasonable tests. This liability, it was further held, was not limited to the original vendee, but extended to a subvendee like the plaintiff, who was not a party to the original contract of sale.

I think that these rulings, which have been approved by the Appellate Division, extend the liability of the vendor of a manufactured article further than any case which has yet received the sanction of this court. It has heretofore been held in this state that the liability of the vendor of a manufactured article for negligence arising out of the existence of defects therein does not extend to strangers injured in consequence of such defects, but is confined to the immediate vendee. The exceptions to this general rule which have thus far been recognized in New York are cases in which the article sold was of such a character that danger to life or limb was involved in the ordinary use thereof; in other words, where the article sold was inherently dangerous. As has already been pointed out, the learned trial judge instructed the jury that an automobile is not an inherently dangerous vehicle.

The late Chief Justice Cooley of Michigan, one of the most learned and accurate of American law writers, states the general rule thus:

The general rule is that a contractor, manufacturer, vendor or furnisher of an article is not liable to third parties who have no contractual relations with him, for negligence in the construction, manufacture, or sale of such article.

2 Cooley on Torts (3d Ed.), 1486.

The leading English authority in support of this rule, to which all the later cases on the same subject refer, is Winterbottom v. Wright, 10 Meeson & Welsby, 109,. . . .

[Remainder of dissenting opinion omitted.]

———————

DONOGHUE v. STEVENSON
[1932] App. Cas. 562 [H.L.][2]

[The plaintiff was made ill when she consumed a bottle of ginger beer that allegedly contained the decomposed remains of a snail. The lower court the action on grounds of no duty owed by the bottler to one not in privity. The following judgment of Lord Atkin is generally taken to reflect the consensus view of the Lords.]

LORD ATKIN.

My Lords, the sole question for determination in this case is legal: Do the averments made by the pursuer in her pleading, if true, disclose a cause of action? I need not restate the particular facts. The question is whether the manufacturer of an article of drink sold by him to a distributor, in circumstances which prevent the distributor or the ultimate purchaser or consumer from discovering by inspection any defect, is under any legal duty to the ultimate purchaser or consumer to take reasonable care that the article is free from defect likely to cause injury to health. I do not think a more important problem has occupied your Lordships in your judicial capacity; important both because of its bearing on public health and because of the practical test which it applies to the system under which it arises. . . . In the present case we are not concerned with the breach of the duty; if a duty exists, that would be a question of fact which is sufficiently averred and for present purposes must be assumed. We are solely concerned with the question whether, as a matter of law in the circumstances alleged, the defender owed the present case we are not concerned with the breach of the duty; if a duty exists, that would be a question of fact which is sufficiently averred and for present purposes must be assumed. We are solely concerned with the question whether, as a matter of law in the circumstances alleged, the defender owed any duty to the pursuer to take care.

It is remarkable how difficult it is to find in the English authorities statements of general application defining the relations between parties that give rise to the duty. The Courts are concerned with the particular relations which come before them in actual litigation, and it is sufficient to say whether the duty exists in those circumstances. The result is that the Courts have been engaged upon an elaborate classification of duties as they exist in respect of property, whether real or personal, with further divisions as to ownership, occupation or control, and distinctions based on the particular relations of the one side or the other, whether manufacturer, salesman or landlord, customer, tenant, stranger, and so on. In this way it can be ascertained at any time whether the law recognizes a duty, but only where the case can be referred to some particular species which has been examined and classified. And yet the duty which is common to all the cases where liability is established must logically be based upon some element common to the cases where it is found to exist. To seek a complete logical definition of the general principle is probably to go beyond the function of the judge, for the more general the definition the more likely it is to omit essentials or to introduce non-essentials. . . .

---

[2] [Ed. — Appeal Cases Law Reports, decision of House of Lords.]

At present I content myself with pointing out that in English law there must be, and is, some general conception of relations giving rise to a duty of care, of which the particular cases found in the books are but instances. . . .

[Lord Atkin's formulation of his "neighbour" principle of proximity omitted. See § 4.01 supra.]

There will no doubt arise cases where it will be difficult to determine whether the contemplated relationship is so close that the duty arises. But in the class of case now before the Court I cannot conceive any difficulty to arise. A manufacturer puts up an article of food in a container which he knows will be opened by the actual consumer. There can be no inspection by any purchaser and no reasonable preliminary inspection by the consumer. Negligently, in the course of preparation, he allows the contents to be mixed with poison. It is said that the law of England and Scotland is that the poisoned consumer has no remedy against the negligent manufacturer. If this were the result of the authorities, I should consider the result a grave defect in the law, and so contrary to principle that I should hesitate long before following any decision to that effect which had not the authority of this House. I would point out that, in the assumed state of the authorities, not only would the consumer have no remedy against the manufacturer, he would have none against any one else, for in the circumstances alleged there would be no evidence of negligence against any one other than the manufacturer; and, except in the case of a consumer who was also a purchaser, no contract and no warranty of fitness, and in the case of the purchase of a specific article under its patent or trade name, which might well be the case in the purchase of some articles of food or drink, no warranty protecting even the purchaser-consumer. There are other instances than of articles of food and drink where goods are sold intended to be used immediately by the consumer, such as many forms of goods sold for cleaning purposes, where the same liability must exist. The doctrine supported by the decision below would not only deny a remedy to the consumer who was injured by consuming bottled beer or chocolates poisoned by the negligence of the manufacturer, but also to the user of what should be a harmless proprietary medicine, an ointment, a soap, a cleaning fluid or cleaning powder. I confine myself to articles of common household use, where every one, including the manufacturer, knows that the articles will be used by other persons than the actual ultimate purchaser — namely, by members of his family and his servants, and in some cases his guests. I do not think so ill of our jurisprudence as to suppose that its principles are so remote from the ordinary needs of civilized society and the ordinary claims it makes upon its members as to deny a legal remedy where there is so obviously a social wrong.

It will be found, I think, on examination that there is no case in which the circumstances have been such as I have just suggested where the liability has been negatived. There are numerous cases, where the relations were much more remote, where the duty has been held not to exist. There are also dicta in such cases which go further than was necessary for the determination of the particular issues, which have caused the difficulty experienced by the Courts below. I venture to say that in the branch of the law which deals with civil wrongs, dependent in England at any rate entirely upon the application by judges of general principle also formulated by judges, it is of particular importance to guard against the danger of stating propositions of law in wider terms than is necessary, lest essential factors be omitted in the wider survey and the inherent adaptability of English law be unduly restricted. For this reason it is very necessary in considering reported cases in the law of torts that the actual decision alone should carry authority, proper weight, of course, being given to the dicta of the judges. . . .

[Lord Atkin distinguished Langridge v. Levy on the ground that it was an action in fraud and Winterbottom v. Wright on the ground that it had been pleaded in contract not tort, and as such, was "manifestly right."]

I do not find it necessary to discuss at length the cases dealing with duties where the thing is dangerous, or, in the narrower category, belongs to a class of things which are dangerous in themselves. I regard the distinction as an unnatural one so far as it is used to serve as a logical differentiation by which to distinguish the existence or nonexistence of a legal right. In this respect I agree with what was said by Scrutton L.J. in Hodge & Sons v. Anglo-American Oil Co., a case which was ultimately decided on a question of fact. "Personally, I do not understand the difference between a thing dangerous in itself, as poison, and a thing not dangerous as a class, but by negligent construction dangerous as a particular thing. The latter, if anything, seems the more dangerous of the two; it is a wolf in sheep's clothing instead of an obvious wolf." The nature of the thing may very well call for different degrees of care, and the person dealing with it may well contemplate persons as being within the sphere of his duty to take care who would not be sufficiently proximate with less dangerous goods; so that not only the degree of care but the range of persons to whom a duty is owed may be extended. But they all illustrate the general principle. In the Dominion Natural Gas Co., Ld. v. Collins and Perkins, the appellants had installed a gas apparatus and were supplying natural gas on the premises of a railway company. They had installed a regulator to control the pressure and their men negligently made an escape-valve discharge into the building instead of into the open air. The railway workmen — the plaintiffs — were injured by an explosion in the premises. The defendants were held liable. Lord Dunedin, in giving the judgment of the Judicial Committee (consisting of himself, Lord Macnaghton, Lord Collins, and Sir Arthur Wilson), after stating that there was no relation of contract between the plaintiffs and the defendants, proceeded:

There may be, however, in the case of anyone performing an operation, or setting up and installing a machine, a relationship of duty. What that duty is will vary according to the subject-matter of the things involved. It has, however, again and again been held that in the case of articles dangerous in themselves, such as loaded firearms, poisons, explosives, and other things ejusdem generis, there is a peculiar duty to take precaution imposed upon those who send forth or install such articles when it is necessarily the case that other parties will come within their proximity.

This, with respect, exactly sums up the position. The duty may exist independently of contract. Whether it exists or not depends upon the subject-matter involved; but clearly in the class of things enumerated there is a special duty to take precautions. This is the very opposite of creating a special category in which alone the duty exists. . . .

It is always a satisfaction to an English lawyer to be able to test his application of fundamental principles of the common law by the development of the same doctrines by the lawyers of the Courts of the United States. In that country I find that the law appears to be well established in the sense in which I have indicated.

The mouse had emerged from the ginger-beer bottle in the United States before it appeared in Scotland, but there it brought a liability upon the manufacturer. I must not in this long judgment do more than refer to the illuminating judgment of Cardozo J. in MacPherson v. Buick Motor Co. in the New York Court of Appeals, in which he states the principles of the law as I should desire to state them, and reviews the authorities in other States than his own. Whether the principle he affirms would apply to the particular facts of that case in this country would be a question for consideration if the case arose. It might be that the course of business, by giving opportunities of examination to the immediate purchaser or otherwise, prevented the relation between manufacturer and the user of the car being so close as to create a duty. But the American decision would undoubtedly lead to a decision in favour of the pursuer in the present case.

My Lords, if your Lordships accept the view that this pleading discloses a relevant cause of action you will be affirming the proposition that by Scots and English law alike a manufacturer of products, which he sells in such a form as to show that he intends them to reach the ultimate consumer in the form in which they left him with no reasonable possibility of intermediate examination, and with the knowledge that the absence of reasonable care in the preparation or putting up of the products will result in an injury to the consumer's life or property, owes a duty to the consumer to take that reasonable care.

It is a proposition which I venture to say no one in Scotland or England who was not a lawyer would for one moment doubt. It will be an advantage to make it clear that the law in this matter, as in most others, is in accordance with sound common sense. I think that this appeal should be allowed.

NOTES AND QUESTIONS

(1)　Viewing the preceding four cases strictly from the point of view of the negligence cause of action, do you see how courts initially went astray when they accepted, as they did, the holding of *Winterbottom v. Wright*? These courts interpreted *Winterbottom* as barring all actions for personal injuries or property damage against any particular defendant unless that plaintiff was in privity of contract with the defendant. These cases depict the tortuous path taken by the courts in unshackling themselves from the privity notion that never should have insinuated itself into the theory of negligence.

Does it appear to you that Lord Atkin's judgment in *Donoghue v. Stevenson* completely eliminates privity as a consideration in negligence actions involving defective products? Does he not squarely and appropriately turn the issue into one of duty, not privity? Is his judgment more or less comprehensive and decisive than that of Judge Cardozo in *MacPherson*, for which Lord Atkin expressed such admiration? If *MacPherson* were to be controlling precedent in any jurisdiction, could you say that privity as such would never be an issue in a negligence cause of action stemming from a defective product? If *Donoghue* were controlling?

(2)　Lord Atkin's judgment in *Donoghue* not only did great service in ridding English negligence law of an unnatural and troublesome dogma, but it also turned inside out some of the judicial conventions in the use of precedent. Examine very carefully the differing views of Lord Abinger in *Winterbottom v. Wright* and Lord

Atkin in *Donoghue* as to the meaning to be given the absence of precedent on any issue. Examine, too, Lord Atkin's view of the relative value to be given judicial rhetoric and the actual holding of a case. For example, does the precedential value of *Langridge v. Levy* shift from *Winterbottom* to *Donoghue*? Finally, although it may be true, as Lord Atkin asserts, that the judges in *Winterbottom v. Wright* treated that case as one sounding in contract, is it not also true that the lawyer Peacock made at least a lame attempt to argue the case on ex delicto grounds?

§ 14.02 EXPRESS AND IMPLIED WARRANTIES AND PRIVITY

Negligence is not the only cause of action that might be available to a defendant in a case involving harm caused by a defective product. In the olden days, a plaintiff might have had a cause of action, if any, in trespass (of some variety) or in trespass on the case, but not both. The plaintiff who went forward with the incorrect theory was often doomed to lose. Under modern rules of procedure and joinder, a plaintiff need not single out one action to the exclusion of the others but may simultaneously proceed on alternative grounds. Although the rules of damages might differ for different causes of action, the plaintiff need succeed on only one to be entitled to recover something. By contrast, to avoid liability, a defendant must prevail on all counts.

We have already seen several different grounds of tort liability: that the defendant intentionally caused harm; that the defendant negligently caused harm; and that the defendant caused harm under conditions of "non-natural" use of land that will lead the courts to impose strict liability without any showing of negligence or intention. To these grounds may be added two more variants of strict liability that do not require a plaintiff to prove that the defendant's behavior was faulty in any sense. Indeed, proof by the defendant that the challenged behavior conformed to the highest standard of care would not constitute a defense. The first of these grounds is breach of contract: that the defendant broke a promise and the harm complained of was caused by the breach. The second, commonly known as strict liability in tort, rests not on the notion of "non-natural" use of land but on the economic concept that the commercial enterprise that profits from the sale of a product ought to bear the cost of harm caused by defects in products sold for profit.

After privity was erroneously (according to Lord Atkin in *Donoghue*) introduced into the negligence cause of action in the aftermath of *Winterbottom v. Wright*, courts regularly and apparently inevitably confused the elements of negligence and contract actions. Although the jurisprudence in many jurisdictions remains hopelessly fouled, we may now simply divide these causes of action as follows.

A negligence action must rest upon a breach of duty of care as defined by negligence concepts. Privity of contract has no proper role to play except as one of many factors to be assessed in determining whether a duty exists. Liability will be imposed only if the defendant's performance fails to equal or exceed that of a reasonable person of ordinary prudence under the same circumstances.

Contract promises define the precise nature of the duties in a breach of contract action. Although contract doctrine includes circumstances in which privity is not necessary, the plaintiff must usually be in privity of contract with the defendant because the contractual duties run not to the world but only to those to whom the promise was made. That the defendant breached the contract is the only wrongful behavior that must be shown by a plaintiff. The reason for the defendant's breach is ordinarily of no moment and to show that the defendant did all that could be done to perform would be no defense. Ordinarily, given a breach, liability is strict.

Harking back to *Winterbottom v. Wright*, we might ask whether the defendant expressly promised to be responsible for personal injuries caused by poorly maintained coaches. The answer would be, "no." How then does a personal injury action arise out of a contract to repair coaches or, indeed, out of a contract for sale of an article that turns out to do some harm because of a defect, even if privity exists? The answer lies in contractual theories of incidental and consequential damages that are properly the subject of a different course. Suffice it for present purposes to say that this aspect of contract law has not been a stumbling block to recovery.

A more troublesome aspect of many contracts, especially those involving the sale of goods, is that often a seller has made no promises to convey the goods to the buyer. Buyers are on notice to inspect the goods, and they get what they see and nothing more. "Let the buyer beware" became a dogma of contract law. In time, however, the law of merchants developed trade practices to make commercial dealings more fluid and less costly. These ultimately insinuated themselves into the general law of contracts. Thus if the seller did not deny its existence, the sale of goods carried with it an implied warranty that the goods were of merchantable quality, meaning at least the average quality of goods a buyer would be expected to buy. Moreover, if a buyer stated its requirements and reasonably depended upon the seller to supply a product to fit the particular purpose, the sale would additionally carry an implied warranty of fitness for the particular purpose, unless negatived by the seller. Later, in the cases of food-stuffs, many courts adopted an implied warranty of fitness of human consumption. A few courts have also applied an implied warranty of habitability to sales or even leases of residential premises. (See *House v. Thornton*, § 12.04 *supra*.) Nevertheless, it was in the law governing merchant transactions that implied warranty theories gained a foothold as an alternative cause of action to negligence.

Warranties can also be created by the express words and actions of the parties. The next case is perhaps the most renowned example of this. Still, implied warranties have generated much more litigation and confusion than express warranties. The second case demonstrates how they can be created, how negatived, how negation can be nullified, and how the requirement of privity can sometimes be avoided.

BAXTER v. FORD MOTOR CO.
Washington Supreme Court
12 P.2d 409 (1932)

HERMAN, J.

During the month of May, 1930, plaintiff purchased a model A Ford town sedan from defendant St. John Motors, a Ford dealer, who had acquired the automobile in question by purchase from defendant Ford Motor Company. Plaintiff claims that representations were made to him by both defendants that the windshield of the automobile was made of nonshatterable glass which would not break, fly, or shatter. October 12, 1930, while plaintiff was driving the automobile through

Snoqualmie pass, a pebble from a passing car struck the windshield of the car in question, causing small pieces of glass to fly into plaintiff's left eye, resulting in the loss thereof. Plaintiff brought this action for damages for the loss of his left eye and for injuries to the sight of his right eye. The case came on for trial, and, at the conclusion of plaintiff's testimony, the court took the case from the jury and entered judgment for both defendants. From that judgment, plaintiff appeals. . . .

The second assignment of error is that the court refused to admit in evidence certain catalogues and printed matter furnished by respondent Ford Motor Company to respondent St. John Motors for distribution and assistance in sales. When the car was sold to appellant, a written purchase order was entered into between the seller and the purchaser. Ford Motor Company was not a party to this agreement. Certain reading matter was printed on the back of the purchase contract, which printing purported to tell what constituted the Lincoln Motor Company warranty and the Ford Motor Company warranty. There was nothing in connection with the sales agreement which indicates that either the Lincoln Motor Company warranty or the Ford Motor Company warranty there set forth was made to, or accepted by, appellant or any other person. The instrument in question was devoid of any provision which would have given appellant the right to sue the Lincoln Motor Company or the Ford Motor Company, if privity of contract be a condition precedent to a suit predicated on misrepresentations perpetrated by a manufacturer upon the public, resulting in the sale of products put forth as possessing qualities which the victim of such misrepresentations later discovers, to his damage, were lacking. Hence respondent Ford Motor Company cannot successfully maintain that, so far as appellant is concerned, its warranties to appellant were set forth in the purchase agreement between appellant and the respondent dealer. So far as that respondent St. John Motors is concerned, the written contract limits its responsibility to appellant. The purchase order stated that it contained the entire contract, and there was contained therein the following agreement: "It is further agreed that no warranty either express or implied is made by the dealer under this order or otherwise covering said car."

To have permitted the introduction of the testimony in question as against respondent St. John Motors would have been to have countenanced an attempt to vary the terms of the written instrument by parol testimony. Such evidence was not competent against respondent St. John Motors, and there was not sufficient evidence against that respondent to justify submission of the cause to the jury. Judgment was properly entered for respondent St. John Motors.

The principal question in this case is whether the trial court erred in refusing to admit in evidence, as against respondent Ford Motor Company, the catalogues and printed matter furnished by that respondent to respondent St. John Motors to be distributed for sales assistance. Contained in such printed matter were statements which appellant maintains constituted representations or warranties with reference to the nature of the glass used in the windshield of the car purchased by appellant. A typical statement, as it appears in appellant's exhibit for identification No. 1, is here set forth:

Triplex Shatter-Proof Glass Windshield. All of the new Ford cars have a Triplex shatter-proof glass windshield — so made that it will not fly or shatter under the hardest impact. This is an important safety factor because it eliminates the dangers of flying glass — the cause of most of the injuries in automobile accidents. In these days of crowded, heavy traffic, the use of this Triplex glass is an absolute necessity. Its extra margin of safety is something that every motorist should look for in the purchase of a car — especially where there are women and children.

Respondent Ford Motor Company contends that there can be no implied or express warranty without privity of contract, and warranties as to personal property do not attach themselves to, and run with, the article sold.

Mazetti v. Armour & Co., 75 Wash. 622, 135 P. 633, 634, 48 L. R. A. (N. S.) 213, Ann. Cas. 1915C, 140, was a case brought against Armour & Co. by proprietors of a restaurant. The complaint alleged that in the course of their business they purchased from the Seattle Grocery Company a carton of cooked tongue, relying upon the representations of Armour & Co. that its goods were pure, wholesome, and fit food for human beings; that in the center of the carton was a foul, filthy, nauseating, and poisonous substance; that during the due course of trade plaintiffs served one of their patrons a portion of the tongue, the customer ate of it, became sick and nauseated, and proceeded publicly to denounce service of such foul and poisonous food; that the incident became generally known; that plaintiffs had no knowledge of or means of learning the character of the food served; that its condition could not be discovered until it was served for use; and that, as a result thereof, plaintiffs were damaged. The trial court sustained a demurrer to the complaint. In the course of an opinion reversing the case, the court said:

It has been accepted as a general rule that a manufacturer is not liable to any person other than his immediate vendee; that the action is necessarily one upon an implied or express warranty, and that without privity of contract no suit can be maintained; that each purchaser must resort to his immediate vendor. To this rule certain exceptions have been recognized: (1) Where the thing causing the injury is of a noxious or dangerous kind. (2) Where the defendant has been guilty of fraud or deceit in passing off the article. (3) Where the defendant has been negligent in some respect with reference to the sale or construction of a thing not imminently dangerous. . . .

Although the cases differ in their reasoning, all agree that there is a liability in such cases irrespective of any privity of contract in the sense of immediate contract between the parties. . . .

To the old rule that a manufacturer is not liable to third persons who have no contractual relations with him for negligence in the manufacture of an article should be added another exception, not one arbitrarily worked by the courts, but arising, as did the three to which we have heretofore alluded, from the changing conditions of society. An exception to a rule will be declared by courts when the case is not an isolated instance, but general in its character, and the existing rule does not square with justice. Under such circumstances a court will, if free from the restraint of some statute, declare a rule that will meet the full intendment of the law. No case has been cited that is squarely in point with the instant case; but there is enough in the adjudged cases to warrant us in our conclusion. . . .

We would be disposed to hold on this question that, where sealed packages are put out, and it is made to appear that the fault, if any, is that of the manufacturer, the product was intended for the use of all those who handle it in trade as well as those who consume it.

In the case at bar the automobile was represented by the manufacturer as having a windshield of nonshatterable glass "so made that it will not fly or shatter under the hardest impact." An ordinary person would be unable to discover by the usual and customary examination of the automobile whether glass which would not fly or shatter was used in the windshield. In that respect the purchaser was in a position similar to that of the consumer of a wrongly labeled drug, who has bought the same from a retailer, and who has relied upon the manufacturer's representation that the label correctly set forth the contents of the container. For many years it has been held that, under such circumstances, the manufacturer is liable to the consumer, even though the consumer purchased from a third person the commodity causing the damage. Thomas v. Winchester, 6 N.Y. 397, 57 Am. Dec. 455. The rule in such cases does not rest upon contractual obligations, but rather on the principle that the original act of delivering an article is wrong, when, because of the lack of those qualities which the manufacturer represented it as having, the absence of which could not be readily detected by the consumer, the article is not safe for the purposes for which the consumer would ordinarily use it.

The vital principle present in the case of Mazetti v. Armour & Co., supra, confronts us in the case at bar. In the case cited the court recognized the right of a purchaser to a remedy against the manufacturer because of damages suffered by reason of a failure of goods to comply with the manufacturer's representations as to the existence of qualities which they did not in fact possess, when the absence of such qualities was not readily discoverable, even though there was no privity of contract between the purchaser and the manufacturer.

Since the rule of caveat emptor was first formulated, vast changes have taken place in the economic structures of the English speaking peoples. Methods of doing business have undergone a great transition. Radio, billboards, and the products of the printing press have become the means of creating a large part of the demand that causes goods to depart from factories to the ultimate consumer. It would be unjust to recognize a rule that would permit manufacturers of goods to create a demand for their products by representing that they possess qualities which they, in fact, do not possess, and then, because there is no privity of contract existing between the consumer and the manufacturer, deny the consumer the right to recover if damages result from the absence of those qualities, when such absence is not readily noticeable.

. . .

We hold that the catalogues and printed matter furnished by respondent Ford Motor Company for distribution and assistance in sales (appellant's exhibits for identification Nos. 1, 2, 3, 4 and 5) were improperly excluded from evidence, because they set forth representations by the manufacturer that the windshield of the car which appellant bought contained Triplex nonshatterable glass which would not fly or shatter. The nature of nonshatterable glass is such that the falsity of the representations with reference to the glass would not be readily detected by a person of ordinary experience and reasonable prudence. Appellant, under the circumstances shown in this case, had the right to rely upon the representations made by respondent Ford Motor Company relative to qualities possessed by its products, even though there was no privity of contract between appellant and respondent Ford Motor Company. . . .

The trial court erred in taking the case from the jury and entering judgment for respondent Ford Motor Company. It was for the jury to determine, under proper instructions, whether the failure of respondent Ford Motor Company to equip the windshield with glass which did not fly or shatter was the proximate cause of appellant's injury.

We have considered the other assignments of error, and find them to be without merit.

Reversed, with directions to grant a new trial with reference to respondent Ford Motor Company; affirmed as to respondent St. John Motors.

HENNINGSEN v. BLOOMFIELD MOTORS, INC.
New Jersey Supreme Court
161 A.2d 69 (1960)

The opinion of the court was delivered by FRANCIS, J.

Plaintiff Claus H. Henningsen purchased a Plymouth automobile, manufactured by defendant Chrysler Corporation, from defendant Bloomfield Motors, Inc. His wife, plaintiff Helen Henningsen, was injured while driving it and instituted suit against both defendants to recover damages on account of her injuries. Her husband joined in the action seeking compensation for his consequential losses. The complaint was predicated upon breach of express and implied warranties and upon negligence. At the trial the negligence counts were dismissed by the court and the cause was submitted to the jury for determination solely on the issues of implied warranty of merchantability." Verdicts were returned against both defendants and in favor of the plaintiffs. Defendants appealed and plaintiffs cross-appealed from the dismissal of their negligence claim. The matter was certified by this court prior to consideration in the Appellate Division.

The facts are not complicated, but a general outline of them is necessary to an understanding of the case.

On May 7, 1955 Mr. and Mrs. Henningsen visited the place of business of Bloomfield Motors, Inc., an authorized De Soto and Plymouth dealer, to look at a Plymouth. They wanted to buy a car and were considering a Ford or a Chevrolet as well as a Plymouth. They were shown a Plymouth which appealed to them and the purchase followed. The record indicates that Mr. Henningsen intended the car as a Mother's Day gift to his wife. He said the intention was communicated to the dealer. When the purchase order or contract was prepared and presented, the husband executed it alone. His wife did not join as a party.

The purchase order was a printed form of one page. On the front it contained blanks to be filled in with a description of the automobile to be sold, the various accessories to be included, and the details of the financing. The particular car selected was described as a 1955 Plymouth, Plaza "6", Club Sedan. The type used in the printed parts of the form became smaller in size, different in style, and less readable toward the bottom where the line for the purchaser's signature was placed. The smallest type on the page appears in the two paragraphs, one of two and one-quarter lines and the second of one and one-half lines, on which great stress is laid by the defense in the case. These two paragraphs are the least legible and the most difficult to read in the instrument, but they are most important in the evaluation of the rights of the contesting parties. They do not attract attention and there is nothing about the format which would draw the reader's eye to them. In fact, a studied and concentrated effort would have to be made to read them. De-emphasis seems the motive rather than emphasis. More particularly, most of the printing in the body of the order appears to be 12 point block type, and easy to read. In the short paragraphs under discussion, however, the type appears to be six point script and the print is solid, that is, the lines are very close together.

The two paragraphs are:

The front and back of this Order comprise the entire agreement affecting this purchase and no other agreement or understanding of any nature concerning same has been made or entered into, or will be recognized. I hereby certify that no credit has been extended to me for the purchase of this motor vehicle except as appears in writing on the face of this agreement. I have read the matter printed on the back hereof and agree to it as a part of this order the same as if it were printed above my signature. I certify that I am 21 years of age, or older, and hereby acknowledge receipt of a copy of this order.

On the right side of the form, immediately below these clauses and immediately above the signature line, and in 12 point block type, the following appears:

CASH OR CERTIFIED CHECK ONLY ON DELIVERY.

On the left side, just opposite and in the same style type as the two quoted clauses, but in eight point size, this statement is set out:

This agreement shall not become binding upon the Dealer until approved by an officer of the company.

The two latter statements are in the interest of the dealer and obviously an effort is made to draw attention to them.

The testimony of Claus Henningsen justifies the conclusion that he did not read the two fine print paragraphs referring to the back of the purchase contract. And it is uncontradicted that no one made any reference to them, or called them to his attention. With respect to the matter appearing on the back, it is likewise uncontradicted that he did not read it and that no one called it to his attention.

The reverse side of the contract contains 8½ inches of fine print. It is not as small, however, as the two critical paragraphs described above. The page is headed "Conditions" and contains ten separate paragraphs consisting of 65 lines in all. The paragraphs do not have head-notes or margin notes denoting their particular subject, as in the case of the "Owner Service Certificate" to be referred to later. In the seventh paragraph, about two-thirds of the way down the page, the warranty, which is the focal point of the case, is set forth. It is. as follows:

7. It is expressly agreed that there are no warranties, express or implied, made by either the dealer or the manufacturer on the motor vehicle, chassis, of parts furnished hereunder except as follows.

The manufacturer warrants each new motor vehicle (including original equipment placed thereon by the manufacturer except tires), chassis or parts manufactured by it to be free from defects in material or workmanship under normal use and service. Its obligation under this warranty being limited to making good at its factory any part or parts thereof which shall, within ninety (90) days after delivery of such vehicle to the original purchaser or before such vehicle has been driven 4,000 miles, whichever event shall first occur, be returned to it with transportation charges prepaid and which its examination shall disclose to its satisfaction to have been thus defective; this warranty being expressly in lieu of all other warranties expressed or implied, and all other obligations or liabilities on its part, and it neither assumes nor authorizes any other person to assume for it any other liability in connection with the sale of its vehicles. . . . (Emphasis ours.)

The new Plymouth was turned over to the Henningsens on May 9, 1955. No proof was adduced by the dealer to show precisely what was done in the way of mechanical or road testing beyond testimony that the manufacturer's instructions were probably followed. Mr. Henningsen drove it from the dealer's place of business in Bloomfield to their home in Keansburg. On the trip nothing unusual appeared in the way in which it operated. Thereafter, it was used for short trips on paved streets about the town. It had no servicing and no mishaps of any kind before the event of May 19. That day, Mrs. Henningsen drove to Asbury Park. On the way down and in returning the car performed in normal fashion until the accident occurred. She was proceeding north on Route 36 in Highlands, New Jersey, at 20–22 miles per hour. The highway was paved and smooth, and contained two lanes for northbound travel. She was riding in the right-hand lane. Suddenly she heard a loud noise "from the bottom, by the hood." It "felt as if something cracked." The steering wheel spun in her hands; the car veered sharply to the right and crashed into a highway sign and a brick wall. No other vehicle was in any way involved. A bus operator driving in the left-hand lane testified that he observed plaintiffs' car approaching in normal fashion in the opposite direction; "all of a sudden [it] veered at 90 degrees . . . and right into this wall." As a result of the impact, the front of the car was so badly damaged that it was impossible to determine if any of the parts of the steering wheel mechanism or workmanship or assembly were defective or improper prior to the accident. The condition was such that the collision insurance carrier, after inspection, declared the vehicle a total loss. It had 468 miles on the speedometer at the time.

The insurance carrier's inspector and appraiser of damaged cars, with 11 years of experience, advanced the opinion, based on the history and his examination, that something definitely went "wrong from the steering wheel down to the front wheels" and that the untoward happening must have been due to mechanical defect or failure; "something down there had to drop off or break loose to cause the car" to act in the manner described.

As has been indicated, the trial court felt that the proof was not sufficient to make out a prima facie case as to the negligence of either the manufacturer or the dealer. The case was given to the jury, therefore, solely on the warranty theory, with results favorable to the plaintiffs against both defendants.

I.

The Claim of Implied Warranty Against the Manufacturer.

In the ordinary case of sale of goods by description an implied warranty of merchantability is an integral part of the transaction. R.S. 46:30-20, N.J.S.A. If the buyer, expressly or by implication, makes known to the seller the particular purpose for which the article is required and it appears that he has relied on the seller's skill or judgment, an implied warranty arises of reasonable fitness for that purpose. R.S. 46:30-21(1), N.J.S.A. The former type of warranty simply means that the thing sold is reasonably fit for the general purpose for which it is manufactured and sold. . . .

Ryan v. Progressive Grocery Stores, 255 N.Y. 388, 175 N.E. 105, 74 A.L.R. 339 (Ct. App. 1931); 1 Williston on Sales, § 243 (Rev. ed. 1948). As Judge (later Justice) Cardozo remarked in Ryan, supra, the distinction between a warranty of fitness for a particular purpose and of merchantability in many instances is practically meaningless. In the particular case he was concerned with food for human consumption in a sealed container. Perhaps no more apt illustration of the notion can be thought of than the instance of the ordinary purchaser who informs the automobile dealer that he desires a car for the purpose of business and pleasure driving on the public highway. . . .

Of course such sales, whether oral or written, may be accompanied by an express warranty. Under the broad terms of the Uniform Sale of Goods Law any affirmation of fact relating to the goods is an express warranty if the natural tendency of the statement is to induce the buyer to make the purchase. R.S. 46:30-18, N.J.S.A. And over the years since the almost universal adoption of the act, a growing awareness of the tremendous development of modern business methods has prompted the courts to administer that provision with a liberal hand. Vold, Law of Sales, § 86, p. 429 (2d ed. 1959). Solicitude toward the buyer plainly harmonizes with the intention of the Legislature. That fact is manifested further by the later section of the act which preserves and continues any permissible implied warranty, despite an express warranty, unless the two are inconsistent. R.S. 46:30-21(6), N.J.S.A.

The uniform act codified, extended and liberalized the common law of sales. The motivation in part was to ameliorate the harsh doctrine of caveat emptor, and in some measure to impose a reciprocal obligation on the seller to beware. The transcendent value of the legislation, particularly with respect to implied warranties, rests in the fact that obligations on the part of the seller were imposed by operation of law, and did not depend for their existence upon express agreement of the parties. And of tremendous significance in a rapidly expanding commercial society was the recognition of the right to recover damages on account of personal injuries arising from a breach of warranty. . . .

The particular importance of this advance resides in the fact that under such circumstances strict liability is imposed upon the maker or seller of the product. Recovery of damages does not depend upon proof of negligence or knowledge of the defect. . . .

As the Sales Act and its liberal interpretation by the courts threw this protective cloak about the buyer, the decisions in various jurisdictions revealed beyond doubt that many manufacturers took steps to avoid these ever increasing warranty obligations. Realizing that the act governed the relationship of buyer and seller, they undertook to withdraw from actual and direct contractual contact with the buyer. They ceased selling products to the consuming public through their own employees and making contracts of sale in their own names. Instead, a system of independent dealers was established; their products were sold to dealers who in turn dealt with the buying public, ostensibly solely in their own personal capacity as sellers. In the past in many instances, manufacturers were able to transfer to the dealers burdens imposed by the act and thus achieved a large measure of immunity for themselves. But, as will be noted in more detail hereafter, such marketing practices, coupled with the advent of large scale advertising by manufacturers to promote the purchase of these goods from dealers by members of the public, provided a basis upon which the existence of express or implied warranties was predicated, even though the manufacturer was not a party to the contract of sale.

The general observations that have been made are important largely for purposes of perspective. They are helpful in achieving a point from which to evaluate the situation now presented for solution. Primarily, they reveal a trend and a design in legislative and judicial thinking toward providing protection for the buyer. It must be noted, however, that the sections of the Sales Act, to which reference has been made, do not impose warranties in terms of unalterable absolutes. R.S. 46:30-3, N.J.S.A., provides in general terms that an applicable warranty may be negatived or varied by express agreement. As to disclaimers or limitations of the obligations that normally attend a sale, it seems sufficient at this juncture to say they are not favored, and that they are strictly construed against the seller. . . .

With these considerations in mind, we come to a study of the express warranty on the reverse side of the purchase order signed by Claus Henningsen. At the outset we take notice that it was made only by the manufacturer and that by its terms it runs directly to Claus Henningsen. On the facts detailed above, it was to be extended to him by the dealer as the agent of Chrysler Corporation. The consideration for this warranty is the purchase of the manufacturer's product from the dealer by the ultimate buyer. . . .

The terms of the warranty are a sad commentary upon the automobile manufacturers' marketing practices. Warranties developed in the law in the interest of and to protect the ordinary consumer who cannot be expected to have the knowledge or capacity or even the opportunity to make adequate inspection of mechanical instrumentalities, like automobiles, and to decide for himself whether they are reasonably fit for the designed purpose. . . .

But the ingenuity of the Automobile Manufacturers Association, by means of its standardized form, has metamorphosed the warranty into a device to limit the maker's liability. To call it an "equivocal" agreement, as the Minnesota Supreme Court did, is the least that can be said in criticism of it. Federal Motor Truck Sales Corporation v. Shamus, 190 Minn. 5, 250 N.W. 713, 714 (Sup. Ct. 1933).

[Description of warranty omitted. The effect was to eliminate liability for personal injury, leaving the manufacturer liable only for defects in the vehicle itself.]

Putting aside for the time being the problem of the efficacy of the disclaimer provisions contained in the express warranty, a question of first importance to be decided is whether an implied warranty of merchantability by Chrysler Corporation accompanied the sale of the automobile to Claus Henningsen.

. . .

Chrysler points out that an implied warranty of merchantability is an incident of a contract of sale. It concedes, of course, the making of the original sale to Bloomfield Motors, Inc., but maintains that this transaction marked the terminal point of its contractual connection with the car. Then Chrysler urges that since it was not a party to the sale by the dealer to Henningsen, there is no privity of contract between it and the plaintiffs, and the absence of this privity eliminates any such implied warranty.

[Discussion of privity omitted.]

We see no rational doctrinal basis for differentiating between a fly in a bottle of beverage and a defective automobile. The unwholesome beverage may bring illness to one person, the defective car, with its great potentiality for harm to the driver, occupants, and others, demands even less adherence to the narrow barrier of privity. . . .

Under modern conditions the ordinary layman, on responding to the importuning of colorful advertising, has neither the opportunity nor the capacity to inspect or to determine the fitness of an automobile for use; he must rely on the manufacturer who has control of its construction, and to some degree on the dealer who, to the limited extent called for by the manufacturer's instructions, inspects and services it before delivery. In such a marketing milieu his remedies and those of persons who properly claim through him should not depend "upon the intricacies of the law of sales. The obligation of the manufacturer should not be based alone on privity of contract. It should rest, as was once said, upon 'the demands of social justice.' "Mazetti v. Armour & Co., 75 Wash. 622, 135 P. 633, 635, 48 L.R.A., N.S., 213 (Sup. Ct.1913). . . .

Accordingly, we hold that under modern marketing conditions, when a manufacturer puts a new automobile in the stream of trade and promotes its purchase by the public, an implied warranty that it is reasonably suitable for use as such accompanies it into the hands of the ultimate purchaser. Absence of agency between the manufacturer and the dealer who makes the ultimate sale is immaterial.

II.

The Effect of the Disclaimer and Limitation of Liability Clauses on the Implied Warranty of Merchantability . . .

The warranty before us is a standardized form designed for mass use. It is imposed upon the automobile consumer. He takes it or leaves it, and he must take it to buy an automobile. No bargaining is engaged in with respect to it. In fact, the dealer through whom it comes to the buyer is without authority to alter it; his function is ministerial — simply to deliver it. The form warranty is not only standard with Chrysler but, as mentioned above, it is the uniform warranty of the Automobile Manufacturers Association. Members of the Association are: General Motors, Inc., Ford, Chrysler, Studebaker-Packard, American Motors (Rambler), Willys Motors, Checker Motors Corp., and International Harvester Company. Automobile Facts and Figures (1958 Ed., Automobile Manufacturers Association) 69. Of these companies, the "Big Three" (General Motors, Ford, and Chrysler) represented 93.5% of the passenger-car production for 1958 and the independents 6.5%. Standard & Poor (Industrial Surveys, Autos, Basic Analysis, June 25, 1959) 4109. And for the same year the "Big Three" had 86.72% of the total passenger vehicle registrations. Automotive News, 1959 Almanac (Slocum Publishing Co., Inc.) p. 25.

The gross inequality of bargaining position occupied by the consumer in the automobile industry is thus apparent. There is no competition among the car makers in the area of the express warranty. Where can the buyer go to negotiate for better protection? Such control and limitation of his remedies are inimical to the public welfare and, at the very least, call for great care by the courts to avoid injustice through application of strict common-law principles of freedom of contract. Because there is no competition among the motor vehicle manufacturers with respect to the scope of protection guaranteed to the buyer, there is no incentive on their part to stimulate good will in that field of public relations. Thus, there is lacking a factor existing in more competitive fields, one which tends to guarantee the safe construction of the article sold. Since all competitors operate in the same way, the urge to be careful is not so pressing. . . .

Although the courts, with few exceptions, have been most sensitive to problems presented by contracts resulting from gross disparity in buyer-seller bargaining positions, they have not articulated a general principle condemning, as opposed to public policy, the imposition on the buyer of a skeleton warranty as a means of limiting the responsibility of the manufacturer. They have endeavored thus far to avoid a drastic departure from age-old tenets of freedom of contract by adopting doctrines of strict construction, and notice and knowledgeable assent by the buyer to the attempted exculpation of the seller. . . .

Public policy at a given time finds expression in the Constitution, the statutory law and in judicial decisions. In the area of sale of goods, the legislative will has imposed an implied warranty of merchantability as a general incident of sale of an automobile by description. The warranty does not depend upon the affirmative intention of the parties. It is a child of the law; it annexes itself to the contract because of the very nature of the transaction. . . .

The judicial process has recognized a right to recover damages for personal injuries arising from a breach of that warranty. The disclaimer of the implied warranty and exclusion of all obligations except those specifically assumed by the express warranty signify a studied effort to frustrate that protection. True, the Sales Act authorizes agreements between buyer and seller qualifying the warranty obligations. But quite obviously the Legislature contemplated lawful stipulations (which are determined by the circumstances of a particular case) arrived at freely by parties of relatively equal bargaining strength. The lawmakers did not authorize the automobile manufacturer to use its grossly disproportionate bargaining power to relieve itself from liability and to impose on the ordinary buyer, who in effect has no real freedom of choice, the grave danger of injury to himself and others that attends the sale of such a dangerous instrumentality as a defectively made automobile. In the framework of this case, illuminated as it is by the facts and the many decisions noted, we are of the opinion that Chrysler's attempted disclaimer of an implied warranty of merchantability and of the obligations arising there-from is so inimical to the public good as to compel an adjudication of its invalidity. . . .

III.

The Dealer's Implied Warranty.

The principles that have been expounded as to the obligation of the manufacturer apply with equal force to the separate express warranty of the dealer. This is so, irrespective of the absence of the relationship of principal and agent between these defendants, because the manufacturer and the Association establish the warranty policy for the industry. The bargaining position of the dealer is inextricably bound by practice to that of the maker, and the purchaser must take or leave the automobile, accompanied and encumbered as it is by the uniform warranty.

For the reasons set forth in Part I hereof, we conclude that the disclaimer of an implied warranty of merchantability by the dealer, as well as the attempted elimination of all obligations other than replacement of defective parts, are violative of public policy and void. . . .

IV.

Proof of Breach of the Implied Warranty of Merchantability.

Both defendants argue that the proof adduced by plaintiffs as to the happening of the accident was not sufficient to demonstrate a breach of warranty. Consequently, they claim that their motion for judgment should have been granted by the trial court. We cannot agree. In our view, the total effect of the circumstances shown from purchase to accident is adequate to raise an inference that the car was defective and that such condition was causally related to the mishap . . . [The court supported this conclusion by referring to evidence of expert testimony, testimony of Mr. and Mrs. Henningsen, and holdings of various negligence cases that had permitted juries to find for plaintiffs on the basis of slight evidence even when res ipsa loquitur did not technically apply.]

Thus, determination by the jury was required. . . .

V.

The Defense of Lack of Privity Against Mrs. Henningsen.

Both defendants contend that since there was no privity of contract between them and Mrs. Henningsen, she cannot recover for breach of any warranty made by either of them. On the facts, as they were developed, we agree that she was not a party to the purchase agreement. . . . Her right to maintain the action, therefore, depends upon whether she occupies such legal status there-under as to permit her to take advantage of a breach of defendants' implied warranties.

For the most part the cases that have been considered dealt with the right of the buyer or consumer to maintain an action against the manufacturer where the contract of sale was with a dealer and the buyer had no contractual relationship with the manufacturer. In the present matter, the basic contractual relationship is between Claus Henningsen, Chrysler, and Bloomfield Motors, Inc. The precise issue presented is whether Mrs. Henningsen, who is not a party to their respective warranties, may claim under them. In our judgment, the principles of those cases and the supporting texts are just as proximately applicable to her situation. We are convinced that the cause of justice in this area of the law can be served only by recognizing that she is such a person who, in the reasonable contemplation of the parties to the warranty, might be expected to become a user of the automobile. Accordingly, her lack of privity does not stand in the way of prosecution of the injury suit against the defendant Chrysler. . . .

Harper and James suggest that this remedy ought to run to members of the public, bystanders, for example, who are in the path of harm from a defective automobile. 2 Harper & James, supra, note 6, p. 1572. Section 2–318 of the Uniform Commercial Code-proposes that the warranty be extended to "any natural person who is in the family or household of his buyer or who is a guest in his home if it is reasonable to expect that such person may use, consume or be affected by the goods and who is injured in person by breach of the warranty." And the section provides also that "A seller may not exclude or limit the operation" of the extension. A footnote thereto says that beyond this provision "the section is neutral and is not intended to enlarge or restrict the developing case law on whether the seller's warranties, given to his buyer, who resells, extend to other persons in the distributive chain." Uniform Commercial Code, supra, at P. 100.

It is not necessary in this case to establish the outside limits of the warranty protection. For present purposes, with respect to automobiles, it suffices to promulgate the principle set forth above. . . .

VII.

Under all of the circumstances outlined above, the judgments in favor of the plaintiffs and against the defendants are affirmed.

NOTES AND QUESTIONS

(1) As the cases in § 14.01 showed, the *Winterbottom v. Wright* privity requirement in negligence product liability law has been largely eroded in actions for bodily injury and property damage. Although absence of privity should never have been the basis for a firm no duty rule in negligence actions, privity of contract is a core element of a contract (i.e., warranty) action. Why do the courts sometimes find it appropriate to avoid the privity requirement in warranty actions where, given the contractual basis of the action, the doctrine is conceptually sound?

(2) All states except Louisiana have accepted some version of the Uniform Commercial Code, thereby codifying the law of express and implied warranties. The most important provisions are § 2-302 (Unconscionable Contract or Clause), § 2-313 (Express Warranty by Affirmation, Promise, Description, Sample), § 2-314 (Implied Warranty; Merchantability; Usage of Trade), § 2-315 (Implied Warranty: Fitness for Particular Purpose), § 2-316 (Exclusion or Modification of Warranties), and § 2-318, reproduced below. Note the alternatives that the drafters provide in § 2-318 as to the privity question. Which one was adopted by the legislature of your state? Would it be proper for your state courts to extend the reach of the no-privity requirement in sales situations farther than the statute itself does?

Uniform Commercial Code[3]

§ 2-318. Third-Party Beneficiaries of Warranties and Obligations.

(1) In this section:

(a) "Immediate buyer" means a buyer that enters into a contract with the seller.

(b) "Remote purchaser" means a person that buys or leases goods from an

---

[3] Copyright by The American Law Institute and the National Conference of Commissioners on Uniform State Laws. Reprinted with permission of the Permanent Editorial Board for the Uniform Commercial Code.

immediate buyer or other person in the normal chain of distribution.

Alternative A to subsection (2)

(2) A seller's warranty to an immediate buyer, whether express or implied, a seller's remedial promise to an immediate buyer, or a seller's obligation to a remote purchaser under Section 2-313A or 2-313B extends to any individual who is in the family or household of the immediate buyer or the remote purchaser or who is a guest in the home of either if it is reasonable to expect that the person may use, consume, or be affected by the goods and who is injured in person by breach of the warranty, remedial promise, or obligation. A seller may not exclude or limit the operation of this section.

Alternative B to subsection (2)

(2) A seller's warranty to an immediate buyer, whether express or implied, a seller's remedial promise to an immediate buyer, or a seller's obligation to a remote purchaser under Section 2-313A or 2-313B extends to any individual who may reasonably be expected to use, consume, or be affected by the goods and who is injured in person by breach of the warranty, remedial promise, or obligation. A seller may not exclude or limit the operation of this section.

Alternative C to subsection (2)

(2) A seller's warranty to an immediate buyer, whether express or implied, a seller's remedial promise to an immediate buyer, or a seller's obligation to a remote purchaser under Section 2-313A or 2-313B extends to any person that may reasonably be expected to use, consume, or be affected by the goods and that is injured by breach of the warranty, remedial promise, or obligation. A seller may not exclude or limit the operation of this section with respect to injury to the person of an individual to whom the warranty, remedial promise, or obligation extends.

Do the implied warranties of merchantability under 2–318 create liability only for the immediate seller or do they also extend to manufacturers of defective products when the manufacturer is not in privity of contract with the plaintiff? The Supreme Court of Indiana considered this question in *Hyundai Motor America, Inc. v. Goodin*, 822 P.2d 947 (Ind. 2005). *Goodin* involved a claim for loss of bargain damages against the manufacturer, which resulted in an award of a $3000 for manufacturing defects in a used car which the plaintiff had purchased from a used car dealer. The action was maintained under the implied warranty of merchantability in the sales contract between the original owner and the new car dealer. *Goodin* acknowledged that Indiana law did not require privity between a manufacturer and a consumer (i.e., the second purchaser in this case) if the defect constituting the breach of implied warranty of merchantability caused bodily injury or damage to other property (i.e., not the vehicle itself). By contrast, whether privity was required between a user and a manufacturer (which the court referred to as "vertical privity") in a case involving loss of bargain economic damages was a novel issue Indiana. Stating that most courts that had considered the issue agreed, the Indiana court held that vertical privity was not required. *Kovach v. Alpharma, Inc.*, 800 N.E.2d 55 (Ind. App. 2008) declined to extend *Goodin* to a claim for breach of warranty of fitness of particular purpose because fitness of purpose claims require that the seller have actual knowledge of the specific needs of a buyer and proceed to supply a product that satisfies them. The manufacturer did not have this knowledge. In direct contrast to *Goodin, Clemens v. DaimlerChrysler Corp.*, 534

F.3d 1017 (9th Cir. 2008) held that the California commercial code requires vertical privity in the *Goodin* circumstances. *Clemens* acknowledged that "state courts have split on this privity question," Id., 534 F.3d at 1024.

§ 14.03   STRICT LIABILITY FOR DEFECTIVE PRODUCTS

GREENMAN v. YUBA POWER PRODUCTS, INC.
California Supreme Court
377 P.2d 897 (1962)

TRAYNOR, JUSTICE.

Plaintiff brought this action for damages against the retailer and the manufacturer of a Shopsmith, a combination power tool that could be used as a saw, drill, and wood lathe. He saw a Shopsmith demonstrated by the retailer and studied a brochure prepared by the manufacturer. He decided he wanted a Shopsmith for his home workshop, and his wife bought and gave him one for Christmas in 1955. In 1957 he bought the necessary attachments to use the Shopsmith as a lathe for turning a large piece of wood he wished to make into a chalice. After he had worked on the piece of wood several times without difficulty, it suddenly flew out of the machine and struck him on the forehead, inflicting serious injuries. About ten and a half months later, he gave the retailer and the manufacturer written notice of claimed breaches of warranties and filed a complaint against them alleging such breaches and negligence.

After a trial before a jury, the court ruled that there was no evidence that the retailer was negligent or had breached any express warranty and that the manufacturer was not liable for the breach of any implied warranty. Accordingly, it submitted to the jury only the cause of action alleging breach of implied warranties against the retailer and the causes of action alleging negligence and breach of express warranties against the manufacturer. The jury returned a verdict for the retailer against plaintiff and for plaintiff against the manufacturer in the amount of $65,000. The trial court denied the manufacturer's motion for a new trial and entered judgment on the verdict. The manufacturer and plaintiff appeal. Plaintiff seeks a reversal of the part of the judgment in favor of the retailer, however, only in the event that the part of the judgment against the manufacturer is reversed.

Plaintiff introduced substantial evidence that his injuries were caused by defective design and construction of the Shopsmith. His expert witnesses testified that inadequate set screws were used to hold parts of the machine together so that normal vibration caused the tailstock of the lathe to move away from the piece of wood being turned permitting it to fly out of the lathe. They also testified that there were other more positive ways of fastening the parts of the machine together, the use of which would have prevented the accident. The jury could therefore reasonably have concluded that the manufacturer negligently constructed the Shopsmith. The jury could also reasonably have concluded that statements in the manufacturer's brochure were untrue, that they constituted express warranties, and that plaintiff's injuries were caused by their breach.

The manufacturer contends, however, that plaintiff did not give it notice of breach of warranty within a reasonable time and that therefore his cause of action for breach of warranty is barred by section 1769 of the Civil Code. . . .

[The court held against the manufacturer on this technical point on the law of warranties.]

Moreover, to impose strict liability on the manufacturer under the circumstances of this case, it was not necessary for plaintiff to establish an express warranty as defined in section 1732 of the Civil Code. A manufacturer is strictly liable in tort when an article he places on the market, knowing that it is to be used without inspection for defects, proves to have a defect that causes injury to a human being. Recognized first in the case of unwholesome food products, such liability has now been extended to a variety of other products that create as great or greater hazards if defective. . . .

Although in these cases strict liability has usually been based on the theory of an express or implied warranty running from the manufacturer to the plaintiff, the abandonment of the requirement of a contract between them, the recognition that the liability is not assumed by agreement but imposed by law and the refusal to permit the manufacturer to define the scope of its own responsibility for defective products . . . make clear that the liability is not one governed by the law of contract warranties but by the law of strict liability in tort. Accordingly, rules defining and governing warranties that were developed to meet the needs of commercial transactions cannot properly be invoked to govern the manufacturer's liability to those injured by their defective products unless those rules also serve the purposes for which such liability is imposed.

We need not recanvass the reasons for imposing strict liability on the manufacturer. They have been fully articulated . . . [previously]. . . . The purpose of such liability is to insure that the costs of injuries resulting from defective products are borne by the manufacturers that put such products on the market rather than by the injured persons who are powerless to protect themselves. Sales warranties serve this purpose fitfully at best. . . . In the present case, for example, plaintiff was able to plead and prove an express warranty only because he read and relied on the representations of the Shopsmith's ruggedness contained in the manufacturer's brochure. Implicit in the machine's presence on the market, however, was a representation that it would safely do the jobs for which it was built. Under these circumstances, it should not be controlling whether plaintiff selected the machine because of the statements in the brochure, or because of the machine's own appearance of excellence that belied the defect lurking beneath the surface, or because he merely assumed that it would safely do the jobs it was built to do. It should not be controlling whether the details of the sales from manufacturer to retailer and from retailer to plaintiff's wife were such that one or more of the implied warranties of the sales act arose. (Civ. Code, § 1735.) "The remedies of injured consumers ought not to be made to depend upon the intricacies of the law of sales." . . . To establish the manufacturer's liability it was sufficient that plaintiff proved that he was injured while using the Shopsmith in a way it was intended to be used as a result of a defect in design and manufacture of which plaintiff was not aware that made the Shopsmith unsafe for its intended use. . . .

The judgment is affirmed.

NOTES AND QUESTIONS

(1)   The strict liability doctrine of Greenman as applied to manufacturers of products was accepted by American courts with amazing celerity. By contrast, it did not catch a foothold in England until Parliament adopted a product strict liability statute in 1988 to conform English law to a product liability directive of the European Economic Community. Although the theory has been applied in some context by most state courts, any theory so newly crystallized is bound to have gaps in coverage, produce inconsistencies in application, and have unanswered questions about defenses and how joint tortfeasors are to work out liability among themselves under modern theories of contribution and indemnification. The next case demonstrates errors that can be made by trying to answer too many of these questions too fast. Isolate each important question addressed by the opinion and criticize the court's handling of it.

(2)   Before turning to the next case, you should examine the widely accepted version of strict liability for sellers (note the broadened scope of that term) of products formulated in Restatement, Torts, Second § 402A. This language may have been adopted verbatim by more courts than any other section of any Restatement. Nevertheless, one must be mindful of Lord Atkin's observation in *Donoghue v. Stevenson* (§ 14.01, supra): It is the holdings of the cases that are of true precedential value, not the rhetoric of the judges. In most instances, when a court applies the doctrine of § 402A, only a portion of the formulation is necessary to the decision. Thus, in the best common law tradition, only that portion is true precedent; the remainder is dictum.

The American Law Institute statement and some of its commentary follow:

Restatement, Torts, Second[4]

§ 402A Special Liability of Seller of Product for Physical Harm to User or Consumer

(1) One who sells any product in a defective condition unreasonably dangerous to the user or consumer or to his property is subject to liability for physical harm thereby caused to the ultimate user or consumer, or to his property, if

(a) the seller is engaged in the business of selling such a product, and

(b) it is expected to and does reach the user or consumer without substantial change in the condition in which it is sold.

(2) The rule stated in Subsection (1) applies although

(a) the seller has exercised all possible care in the preparation and sale of his product, and

(b) the user or consumer has not bought the product from or entered into any contractual relation with the seller.

Caveat:

The Institute expresses no opinion as to whether the rules stated in this Section may not apply

---

[4] Copyright 1965 by The American Law Institute. Reprinted with the permission of The American Law Institute.

(1) to harm to persons other than users or consumers;

(2) to the seller of a product expected to be processed or otherwise substantially changed before it reaches the user or consumer; or

(3) to the seller of a component part of a product to be assembled.

. . .

c. On whatever theory, the justification for the strict liability has been said to be that the seller, by marketing his product for use and consumption, has undertaken and assumed a special responsibility toward any member of the consuming public who may be injured by it; that the public has the right to and does expect, in the case of products which it needs and for which it is forced to rely upon the seller, that reputable sellers will stand behind their goods; that public policy demands that the burden of accidental injuries caused by products intended for consumption be placed upon those who market them, and be treated as a cost of production against which liability insurance can be obtained; and that the consumer of such products is entitled to the maximum of protection at the hands of someone, and the proper persons to afford it are those who market the products.

d. The rule stated in this Section is not limited to the sale of food for human consumption, or other products for intimate bodily use, although it will obviously include them. It extends to any product sold in the condition, or substantially the same condition, in which it is expected to reach the ultimate user or consumer. Thus the rule stated applies to an automobile, a tire, an airplane, a grinding wheel, a water heater, a gas stove, a power tool, a riveting machine, a chair, and an insecticide. It applies also to products which, if they are defective, may be expected to and do cause only "physical harm" in the form of damage to the user's land or chattels, as in the case of animal food or a herbicide.

e. Normally the rule stated in this Section will be applied to articles which already have undergone some processing before sale, since there is today little in the way of consumer products which will reach the consumer without such processing. The rule is not, however, so limited, and the supplier of poisonous mushrooms which are neither cooked, canned, packaged, nor otherwise treated is subject to the liability here stated.

COMMENTARY: A LAW AND ECONOMICS PERSPECTIVE ON STRICT LIABILITY

In his concurring opinion in *Escola v. Cola Cola Bottling Company*, § 6.02 *infra.*, Judge Traynor proposed that "a manufacturer incurs absolute liability when an article he had placed on the market, knowing it is to be used without inspection, proves to have a defect that causes injury to human beings." Judge Traynor finally won his point in *Greenman v. Yuha Power Products*, and his idea quickly "caught on" and spread throughout the industrial world.

The *Escola* facts may be used to apply Law and Economics analysis to this movement. Suppose out of every 100,000,000 soft drink bottles, one explodes and causes a $1,000,000 injury to the user? Suppose the bottler had done everything a reasonable bottler could do to eliminate the risk and that further reducing the risk would add at least one-dollar to the selling price of each bottle? Should this expenditure be made? If not, who should bear the loss when the one-in-100 million injury occurs?

Was the bottler's conduct negligent under the Hand formula? Compare B (the $1.00 cost per bottle to further reducing the risk) to the expectation of harm from the one-in-100 million risk that a bottle will explode and cause a $1,000,000 injury. If we assume risk neutrality, the expectation of harm would be $0.01. Because the cost to prevent the harm ($1.00) would be much greater than the expectation of harm to be avoided ($0.01), the analysis would conclude that the bottler was not negligent.

Who should pay or absorb the $1,000,000 loss when it occurs? We could require the victim to absorb the loss by denying Tort Recovery.[5] We could (at least in theory) decide that soft drinks are too dangerous and remove them from the market.[6] We could decide these losses should be paid by some form of national health insurance. Or, we could make bottlers strictly liable to pay the losses - with full knowledge that expected future costs would be passed-on on to consumers. Strict liability would require the bottler to pay $1,000,000 to the victim and the bottler would increase the price of the product by one cent per bottle to fund future liabilities. Although the rare losses would still occur, the Tort system would have effectively bundled a mini-insurance policy into each bottle. Instead of paying $1.00 per bottle, consumers would pay $1.01 and also receive an implicit insurance policy making the bottler strictly liable when the rare bottle explodes.

Which is the better rule: negligence, leaving the victims without recovery? Or strict liability, placing all the costs upon bottlers? Consider these factors.

Advantages of Strict Liability

1. Risk spreading. The price of the rare loss is spread among all consumers in small increments in price. Because most are risk avoiders, consumers would tend to prefer this rule.

2. Lower litigation and judicial costs. The difficult negligence "breach" issue would no longer be litigated, thus saving costs. These savings would arise whether the cases were litigated under traditional negligence standards or under cost/benefit standards.

3. Deception analogy. Because most people do not reasonably expect soft drink bottles to explode, consumers may view the rare failures as market deception. Strict liability provides a surer remedy, thus mitigating consumer dissatisfaction.

4. Behavior modification. Which party could better prevent the losses? Consumers could do nothing to avoid the explosions and a negligence cost/benefit analysis absolves bottlers from doing more. Imposing strict liability would create an incentive for bottlers to do more. Would it be beneficial to require bottlers to provide this warning: "There is one-in-100 million chance a bottle might explode and injure you." Would consumers read such warning? How could those who did read it alter their behavior for safety?

5. Certainty. Strict liability is more certain than negligence liability. Bottlers know that they will pay when the rare bottle explodes and will plan accordingly. By

---

[5] Some soft drink purchasers would, however, have insurance.

[6] If we seriously considered this option, wouldn't it be likely that many or even most modern products similarly would be found to cause at least some accidents? Do we really want to ban, for example, all automobiles and pharmaceuticals just because these products could cause harm to 1/100,000,000 users?

contrast, negligence liability is more uncertain, thus introducing contingencies in planning.

6. Most of the poor do not have insurance. Few victims would have the resources to absorb the rare $1,000,000 loss. Strict liability favors all victims and closes the gap between the poor and the wealthy.

Disadvantages of Strict Liability

1. Consumers ultimately pay the costs of strict liability payouts. In exploding bottle cases, it matters little whether consumers pay $1.01 for soft drinks instead of $1.00. Suppose, however, the product were an irreplaceable pharmaceutical and imposing strict liability on manufacturers would raise the retail price from $5.00 a day to $50.00 a day? Poor consumers and those without insurance would suffer disadvantage in a strict liability regime.

2. Less innovation and bankruptcy. Some manufacturers might not be able to predict expected future losses and embed them in prices charged consumers. Or, the expectation of harm might be so high that prices would not bear them or insurance would be too expensive. Fear of paying out huge sums might chill innovation in some industries, such as pharmaceuticals, and could even force some manufacturers out of business.

3. Allow consumers to take risks. We have a well developed insurance market. Risk averse consumers may avail themselves of it for protection and risk seekers may take the risk. Strict liability forces higher prices upon all of them, but a negligence scheme permits risk takers to purchase cheaper products without paying an insurance premium. Why should the Tort system eliminate less safe, but less costly, options from the marketplace?

4. Behavior modification. In exploding bottle cases consumers can do nothing to avoid the rare harm, but with many other products consumers could prevent injuries for the least cost. Can you think of such a product? In these cases, Law and Economics analysis may select negligence as the preferred regime.

5. Poor consumers would "subsidize" rich consumers. Strict liability imposes higher prices on all consumers, but wealthy victims of the rare harms would tend to recover greater Tort awards than poor victims. For example, an injured lawyer who lost a year's income of $300,000 would obtain an award 10 times greater than would an injured victim who earned $30,000 per year. Does this mean poor victims would subsidize wealthy victims in a strict liability regime?

6. From a moral perspective the manufacturer did nothing wrong. Even the safest company in an industry may be perceived as a wrongdoer when it is held strictly liable for the rare harm. Does this potential unwarranted injury to reputation outweigh the positive attributes of strict liability?

7. Overall, which do you deem to be preferable in product cases: strict liability? Or negligence? Why?

WEST v. CATERPILLAR TRACTOR COMPANY
Florida Supreme Court
336 So. 2d 80 (1976)

ADKINS, JUSTICE.

This case is presented on certificate as authorized by Fla. Stat. § 25.031, F.S.A., and in Rule 4.61, Florida Appellate Rules, 32 F.S.A., from the United States Court of Appeals for the Fifth Circuit, 504 F.2d 967, in an appeal from a final judgment of the trial court which applied the doctrine of strict liability in a products liability suit.

The court states that:

A caterpillar grader operated by an employee of Houdaille Industries struck and ran over, with its left rear tandem wheel, Gwendolyn West on a street under construction in Miami, Florida, on September 1, 1970. Gwendolyn West died of massive internal injuries after six days in the hospital. As a result, the deceased's husband, Leon West, individually and as administrator of the estate of his deceased wife, claimed a right to damages against Houdaille Industries and Caterpillar Tractor Company, Inc., the manufacturer of the machine. He ultimately settled with Houdaille Industries for $35,000 damages and brought a products liability suit against the manufacturer of the grader, Caterpillar Tractor Company, Inc., in the United States District Court, in and for the Southern District of Florida bottomed on diversity of citizenship jurisdiction.

West's Complaint contained two counts: (1) negligent design of the grader by failure to provide an audible warning system for use while backing the grader, by failure to provide adequate rear view mirrors, and by manufacturing the grader with a blind spot created by obstructions when looking to the rear while driving in reverse, and (2) a breach of implied warranty or strict liability based upon the same design defects.

At trial, the evidence indicated that preceding the accident Gwendolyn West had walked to the corner, stood on the west curb of the street which was under construction, speaking to a friend, for a period while the grader operated in a forward manner, southward and proceeded to pass her. The machine reached the end of its southward operation and commenced to back up. In the meantime, Mrs. West began walking across the street intersecting the path of the grader while it was traveling in reverse. She had been waiting for a bus, and as it approached she commenced to walk across the street, looking to her left; and then she looked into her purse; and continued to look into her purse until the time of the accident. She did not look to her right at any time toward the approaching grader. Both West and Caterpillar presented extensive conflicting expert testimony about the alleged defects in the design of the caterpillar. . . .

In answer to special interrogatories, the jury found Caterpillar liable on all three theories of recovery and determined that damages totalled $125,000. The jury also concluded that Mrs. West's negligence contributed to the accident to a degree of 35 percent.

The Court entered judgment for West and disregarded comparative negligence on the basis of strict liability and concluded that contributory (comparative) negligence was no defense to strict liability in Florida. The Court thus awarded damages of $90,000 which represented the full jury award of $125,000 set off by the earlier $35,000 settlement. This appeal followed.

3. Questions to be Certified.

1. (a) Under Florida law, may a manufacturer be held liable under the theory of strict liability in tort, as distinct from breach of implied warranty of merchantability, for injury to a user of the product or a bystander?

(b) If the answer to 1(a) is in the affirmative, what type of conduct by the injured party would create a defense of contributory or comparative negligence?

(1) In particular, under principles of Florida law, would lack of ordinary due care, as found by the jury in this case, constitute a defense to strict tort liability?

2. Assuming Florida law provides for liability op behalf of a manufacturer to a user or bystander for breach of implied warranty, what type of conduct by an injured person would constitute a defense of contributory or comparative negligence?

(a) In particular, does the lack of ordinary due care, as found by the jury in the case, constitute such a defense? Products liability deals with recourse for personal injury or property damage resulting from the use of a product and, in the past, has covered actions for negligence, breach of express warranty, breach of implied warranty, and fraud. These theories of recovery have been refined and consolidated to such an extent that the distinctions frequently have more theoretical than practical significance. As a result the theory of strict liability has evolved to complement the traditional conditional warranty and negligence theories. A statement of this theory appears in the American Law Institute Restatement (Second) of Torts § 402A, as follows:

(1) One who sells any product in a defective condition unreasonably dangerous to the user or consumer or to his property is subject to liability for physical harm thereby caused to the ultimate user or consumer, or to his property, if

(a) the seller is engaged in the business of selling such a product, and

(b) it is expected to and does reach the user or consumer without substantial change in the condition in which it is sold.

(2) The rule stated in Subsection (1) applies although

(a) the seller has exercised all possible care in the preparation and sale of his product, and

(b) the user or consumer has not bought the product from or entered into any contractual relation with the seller.

[Analysis of prior cases omitted.]

From the foregoing analysis it is apparent that the Florida courts in many instances have imposed an absolute or strict liability in tort upon a manufacturer for placing a product on the market knowing that it is to be used without inspection for defects which cause injury to a human being. The manufacturer, by placing on the market a potentially dangerous product for use and consumption and by inducement and promotion encouraging the use of these products, thereby undertakes a certain and special responsibility toward the consuming public who may be injured by it. We believe that the prior decisions of this Court are in conformity with the principles set forth in the Restatement (Second) of Torts § 402A, quoted above. Such a recognition by the Court is no great new departure from present law and, in most instances, accomplishes a change of nomenclature. We should take a realistic view of the doctrine of products liability in Florida, as our distinctions frequently have been of more theoretical than practical significance. See Keeton, Products Liability, 49 Va. L. Rev. 675, 676 (1963).

The court in Royal v. Black and Decker Mfg. Co., 205 So. 2d 307, 309 (Fla. App. 3d 1967), discussing the trend of Florida decisions toward strict liability, said:

At the heart of each theory is the requirement that the plaintiff's injury must have been caused by some defect in the product. Generally, when the injury is in no way attributable to a defect, there is no basis for imposing product liability upon the manufacturer. It is not contemplated that a manufacturer should be made the insurer for all physical injuries caused by his products.

In other words strict liability should be imposed only when a product the manufacturer places on the market, knowing that it is to be used without inspection for defects, proves to have a defect that causes injury to a human being. The user should be protected from unreasonably dangerous products or from a product fraught with unexpected dangers. In order to hold a manufacturer liable on the theory of strict liability in tort, the user must establish the manufacturer's relationship to the product in question, the defect and unreasonably dangerous condition of the product, and the existence of the proximate causal connection between such condition and the user's injuries or damages.

We adopt the doctrine of strict liability as stated by the A.L.I. Restatement (Second) of Torts § 402A. In this, we are not alone.

[In reply to the argument that the legislature's adoption of the UCC's warranties barred the court from adopting another theory of strict liability for sellers of products, the court concluded:]

We recognize that there are two parallel but independent bodies of products liability law. One, strict liability, is an action in tort; the other, implied warranty, is an action in contract. An action under the strict liability doctrine eliminates the notice requirement, restricts the effectiveness of disclaimers to situations where it can be reasonably said that the consumer has freely assumed the risk, and abolishes the privity requirement. The doctrine of strict liability does not introduce a notion of "defective condition unreasonably dangerous to the user or consumer or to his property" which is different from the notion of "unmerchantability" as applied in warranty law. With the continued increase of products liability cases, the strict liability doctrine adapts the law to the marketing condition of today's marketing consumer. . . .

At the present time there is no legislative impediment to the adoption of this doctrine.

We next turn to the question of whether the doctrine of strict liability should be extended to a foreseeable bystander who comes within range of the danger.

The manufacturer unquestionably intends that its product will be used by the public. There would appear to be no logic or reason in denying a right of relief to persons injured by defective merchandise solely on the ground that he was not himself a user of the merchandise. Many products in the hands of the consumer are sophisticated and even mysterious articles, frequently a sealed unit with an alluring exterior rather than a visible assembly of component parts. In today's world it is often only the manufacturer who can fairly be said to know and understand when an article is suitably designed and safely made for its intended purpose. *See* Codling v. Paglia, 32 N.Y.2d 330, 345 N.Y.S.2d 461, 298 N.E.2d 622 (1973).

Toombs v. Ft. Pierce Gas Co., 208 So. 2d 615 (Fla. 1968), was an action by the customer of a gas company, his family and bystanders for injuries sustained in the explosion of a propane gas storage tank. The Court held that, with respect to bystanders injured by the explosion, the dangerous instrumentality exception to privity requirement extended the liability of the company to persons one should expect to be in the vicinity of the proper use of the chattel.

The framers of the Restatement did not express an opinion on whether the doctrine should apply where harm befalls persons other than users or consumers. A majority of the courts have said that there is no adequate rationale or theoretical explanation why nonusers and nonconsumers should be denied recovery. . . .

The public policy which protects the user and the consumer of a manufactured article should also protect the innocent bystander. Of course, the duty of a manufacturer for breach of which liability will attach runs only to those who suffer personal injury or property damage as the result of using or being within the vicinity of the use of the dangerous instrumentality furnished by a manufacturer which fails to give notice of the danger. Injury to a bystander is often feasible. A restriction of the doctrine to the users and consumers would have to rest on the vestige of the disappearing privity requirement. This requirement has been often applied, and frequently mutilated, in cases where a supplier of chattels was held liable on some theory of warranty.

We now hold that a manufacturer may be held liable under the theory of strict liability in tort, as distinct from breach of implied warranty of merchantability, for injury to a user of the product or a bystander, thereby answering question 1(a) in the affirmative.

We now turn to question 1(b) which reads as follows:

(b) If the answer to 1(a) is in the affirmative, what type of conduct by the injured party would create a defense of contributory or comparative negligence?

(1) In particular, under principles of Florida law, would lack of ordinary due care, as found by the jury in this case, constitute a defense to strict tort liability?

It has been held generally that simple, contributory negligence is not a defense in a strict liability action, . . . if such a defense is based upon the failure of the user to discover the defect in the product or the failure of the user to guard against the possibility of its existence.

Strict liability does not make the manufacturer or seller an insurer. Strict liability means negligence as a matter of law or negligence per se, the effect of which is to remove the burden from the user of proving specific acts of negligence.

The gist of the doctrine of contributory negligence is that the person injured should not recover when it appears that the injury would have been avoided if the injured person had exercised reasonable care. In other words, the injured person must act as a reasonable person in exercising for his own safety the caution commensurate with the potential danger. This defense has been recognized where a products liability action is based on negligence. . . .

Under the "reasonable man" standard the failure of the consumer or user, in the absence of warning, to discover a defect in the product or the failure to guard against the possibility of its existence would not bar recovery under the doctrine of contributory negligence. . . .

As stated in the Restatement (Second) of Torts § 402A, comment at 356.

Contributory negligence. Since the liability with which this Section deals is not based upon negligence of the seller, but is strict liability, the rule applied to strict liability cases (see § 524) applies. Contributory negligence of the plaintiff is not a defense when such negligence consists merely in a failure to discover the defect in the product, or to guard against the possibility of its existence. On the other hand the form of contributory negligence which consists in voluntarily and unreasonably proceeding to encounter a known danger, and commonly passes under the name of assumption of risk, is a defense under this Section as in other cases of strict liability. If the user or consumer discovers the defect and is aware of the danger, and nevertheless proceeds unreasonably to make use of the product and is injured by it, he is barred from recovery.

We recognize that contributory negligence of the user or consumer or bystander in the sense of a failure to discover a defect, or to guard against the possibility of its existence, is not a defense. Contributory negligence of the consumer or user by unreasonable use of a product after discovery of the defect and the danger is a valid defense. Prior to the adoption of the comparative negligence doctrine, a plaintiff's conduct as the sole proximate cause of his injuries would constitute a total defense. . . .

The defendant manufacturer may assert that the plaintiff was negligent in some specified manner other than failing to discover or guard against a defect, such as assuming the risk, or misusing the product, and that such negligence was a substantial proximate cause of the plaintiff's injuries or damages. . . . The fact that plaintiff acts or fails to act as a reasonable prudent person, and such conduct proximately contributes to his injury, constitutes a valid defense. In other words, lack of ordinary due care could constitute a defense to strict tort liability.

We now have comparative negligence, so the defense of contributory negligence is available in determining the apportionment of the negligence by the manufacturer of the alleged defective product and the negligent use made thereof by the consumer. The ordinary rules of causation and the defenses applicable to negligence are available under our adoption of the Restatement rule. If this were not so, this Court would, in effect, abolish the adoption of comparative negligence. . . .

The last certified question reads as follows:

2. Assuming Florida law provides for liability on behalf of a manufacturer to a user or bystander for breach of implied warranty, what type of conduct by an injured person would constitute a defense of contributory or comparative negligence?

(a) In particular, does the lack of ordinary due care, as found by the jury in the case, constitute such a defense?

The adoption of the doctrine of strict liability in tort does not result in the demise of implied warranty. If a user is injured by a defective product, but the circumstances do not create a contractual relationship with a manufacturer, then the vehicle for recovery could be strict liability in tort. If there is a contractual relationship with the manufacturer, the vehicle of implied warranty remains.

Contributory negligence is generally considered to be a doctrine of the law of torts. However, breach of warranty actions retain certain aspects of the law of torts and frequently a given set of facts could support either an action for breach of implied warranty or an action for negligence. As a consequence questions have arisen as to whether a defense of contributory negligence may properly be asserted in an action for breach of warranty. . . .

In Coleman v. American Universal of Florida, Inc., 264 So. 2d 451 (Fla. App. 1st 1972), the sole question under consideration was whether the trial court correctly instructed the jury that the plaintiff's contributory negligence constituted a bar to his recovery in an action for breach of implied warranty. The court pointed out that the authorities were "pretty evenly divided on the question before us." The court then said:

In this legal situation, with the authorities fairly evenly divided, we are inclined to the view that contributory negligence is available as a defense in an action for breach of an implied warranty, even though it may superficially look as though we are thereby approving a tortious defense in an action ex contractu.

Our philosophy in this matter was well expressed by Schreiber and Rheingold in their "Products Liability" (Chap. 5, page 32) in their concluding remarks, as follows:

As is readily apprehended, contributory negligence in the defense of a product liability action is a can of worms. But, if it is recognized that there is not [sic] such thing as "contributory negligence" and that the defense contemplated is that of abnormal, unintended, or unforeseen use, or is that of assumed risk, or that of lack of due care, then there may perhaps be order brought out of the chaos. However, it is strongly suggested that even these defenses are, in the absence of uncontrovertible facts, no panacea for defendants. There are much better ways to beat a product liability claim than relying on contributory negligence, an illusory defense. 264 So.2d 454.

We approve this decision. Unreasonable exposure to a known and appreciated risk should bar recovery in an action based upon implied warranty just as it bars recovery in negligence. However, it is unreasonable to require the noncommercial consumer to make any sort of detailed or expert inspection. If the injured person's conduct is a proximate cause of the injuries, the defendant would have the right to a charge on comparative negligence in an action for breach of implied warranty. If the injured person failed to use that degree of care which a reasonably careful person would use under like circumstances then he is guilty of some negligence. If this negligence was a proximate contributing cause of the injuries, the defendant would be entitled to raise the defense of contributory or comparative negligence. In other words, lack of ordinary due care could constitute such a defense.

To summarize, we recognize that in the present day marketing milieu treatment of the manufacturer's liability to ultimate purchasers or consumers in terms of implied warranty is simply using a convenient legal device to accomplish some recourse for an injured person. Traditionally, warranty has had its source in contract. Ordinarily there is no contract in a real sense between a manufacturer and an ultimate consumer of its product. As a result, warranty law in Florida has become filled with inconsistencies and misapplications in the judiciary's attempt to provide justice to the injured consumer, user, employee, bystander, etc., while still maintaining the contract principles of privity.

The obligation of the manufacturer must become what in justice it ought to be — an enterprise liability, and one which should not depend upon the intricacies of the law of sales. The cost of injuries or damages, either to persons or property, resulting from defective products, should be borne by the makers of the products who put them into the channels of trade, rather than by the injured or damaged persons who are ordinarily powerless to protect themselves. We therefore hold that a manufacturer is strictly liable in tort when an article he places on the market, knowing that it is to be used without inspection for defects, proves to have a defect that causes injury to a human being. This doctrine of strict liability applies when harm befalls a foreseeable bystander who comes within range of the danger.

Contributory or comparative negligence is a defense in a strict liability action if based upon grounds other than the failure of the user to discover the defect in the product or the failure of the user to guard against the possibility of its existence. The consumer or user is entitled to believe that the product will do the job for which it was built. On the other hand, the consumer, user, or bystander is required to exercise ordinary due care.

The adoption of the doctrine of strict liability in tort does not result in the demise of implied warranty. In an action upon implied warranty the defense of contributory or comparative negligence may be interposed, for the injured person is required to exercise "ordinary due care."

Having answered the questions certified, we return the case to the United States Court of Appeals for a decision as to the evidentiary and procedural issues which remain.

It is so ordered.

NOTES AND QUESTIONS

(1) What difficulties lurk in the following statement of the court: "Strict liability means negligence as a matter of law or negligence per se, the effect of which is to remove the burden from the user of proving specific acts of negligence"? Compare this statement, "Strict liability is not a development in the law of negligence; it evolved separately." *Lewis v. Timeco*, 716 F.2d 1425, 1433 (5th Cir. 1983).

(2) Numerous courts employed the doctrines of *Greenman v. Yuba Power Product*, § 402A as applied in *West v. Caterpillar Tractor Company* to make radical changes in the law of product liability, mostly to expand liability in the form of strict liability upon industry. In response to what people some considered an alarming expansion of liability and the concomitant emergence of numbers of collateral legal issues pertaining to what defenses should be acknowledged, how multi-party issues should be resolved and the like, the American Law Institute adopted the following sections of Restatement of the Law (Third) of Torts. To what extent courts apply these principles to supplant earlier § 402A must be determined state by state.

§ 1. Liability Of Commercial Seller Or Distributor For Harm Caused By Defective Products

One engaged in the business of selling or otherwise distributing products who sells or distributes a defective product is subject to liability for harm to persons or property caused by the defect.

§ 2. Categories Of Product Defect

A product is defective when, at the time of sale or distribution, it contains a manufacturing defect, is defective in design, or is defective because of inadequate instructions or warnings. A product:

(a) contains a manufacturing defect when the product departs from its intended design even though all possible care was exercised in the preparation and marketing of the product;

(b) is defective in design when the foreseeable risks of harm posed by the product could have been reduced or avoided by the adoption of a reasonable alternative design by the seller or other distributor, or a predecessor in the commercial chain of distribution, and the omission of the alternative design renders the product not reasonably safe;

(c) is defective because of inadequate instructions or warnings when the foreseeable risks of harm posed by the product could have been reduced or avoided by the provision of reasonable instructions or warnings by the seller or other distributor, or a predecessor in the commercial chain of distribution, and the omission of the instructions or warnings renders the product not reasonably safe.

§ 3. Circumstantial Evidence Supporting Inference Of Product Defect

It may be inferred that the harm sustained by the plaintiff was caused by a product defect existing at the time of sale or distribution, without proof of a specific defect, when the incident that harmed the plaintiff:

(a) was of a kind that ordinarily occurs as a result of product defect; and

(b) was not, in the particular case, solely the result of causes other than product defect existing at the time of sale or distribution.

§ 4. Noncompliance And Compliance With Product Safety Statutes Or Regulations

In connection with liability for defective design or inadequate instructions or warnings:

(a) a product's noncompliance with an applicable product safety statute or administrative regulation renders the product defective with respect to the risks sought to be reduced by the statute or regulation; and

(b) a product's compliance with an applicable product safety statute or administrative regulation is properly considered in determining whether the product is defective with respect to the risks sought to be reduced by the statute or regulation, but such compliance does not preclude as a matter of law a finding of product defect.

§ 5. Liability Of Commercial Seller Or Distributor Of Product Components For Harm Caused By Products Into Which Components Are Integrated

One engaged in the business of selling or otherwise distributing product components who sells or distributes a component is subject to liability for harm to persons or property caused by a product into which the component is integrated if:

(a) the component is defective in itself, as defined in this Chapter, and the defect causes the harm; or

(b)(1) the seller or distributor of the component substantially participates in the integration of the component into the design of the product; and

(b)(2) the integration of the component causes the product to be defective, as defined in this Chapter; and

(b)(3) the defect in the product causes the harm.

§ 6. Liability Of Commercial Seller Or Distributor For Harm Caused By Defective Prescription Drugs And Medical Devices

[Omitted.]

§ 7. Liability Of Commercial Seller Or Distributor For Harm Caused By Defective Food Products

One engaged in the business of selling or otherwise distributing food products who sells or distributes a food product that is defective under § 2, § 3, or § 4 is subject to liability for harm to persons or property caused by the defect. Under § 2(a), a harm-causing ingredient of the food product constitutes a defect if a reasonable consumer would not expect the food product to contain that ingredient.

§ 8. Liability Of Commercial Seller Or Distributor Of Defective Used Products

One engaged in the business of selling or otherwise distributing used products who sells or distributes a defective used product is subject to liability for harm to persons or property caused by the defect if the defect:

(a) arises from the seller's failure to exercise reasonable care; or

(b) is a manufacturing defect under § 2(a) or a defect that may be inferred under § 3 and the seller's marketing of the product would cause a reasonable person in the position of the buyer to expect the used product to present no greater risk of defect than if the product were new; or

(c) is a defect under § 2 or § 3 in a used product remanufactured by the seller or a predecessor in the commercial chain of distribution of the used product; or

(d) arises from a used product's noncompliance under § 4 with a product safety statute or regulation applicable to the used product.

A used product is a product that, prior to the time of sale or other distribution referred to in this Section, is commercially sold or otherwise distributed to a buyer not in the commercial chain of distribution and used for some period of time.

§ 9. Liability Of Commercial Product Seller Or Distributor For Harm Caused By Misrepresentation

One engaged in the business of selling or otherwise distributing products who, in connection with the sale of a product, makes a fraudulent, negligent, or innocent misrepresentation of material fact concerning the product is subject to liability for harm to persons or property caused by the misrepresentation.

§ 10. Liability Of Commercial Product Seller Or Distributor For Harm Caused By Post-Sale Failure To Warn

(a) One engaged in the business of selling or otherwise distributing products is subject to liability for harm to persons or property caused by the seller's failure to provide a warning after the time of sale or distribution of a product if a reasonable person in the seller's position would provide such a warning.

(b) A reasonable person in the seller's position would provide a warning after the time of sale if:

(1) the seller knows or reasonably should know that the product poses a substantial risk of harm to persons or property; and

(2) those to whom a warning might be provided can be identified and can reasonably be assumed to be unaware of the risk of harm; and

(3) a warning can be effectively communicated to and acted on by those to whom a warning might be provided; and

(4) the risk of harm is sufficiently great to justify the burden of providing a warning.

§ 11. Liability Of Commercial Product Seller Or Distributor For Harm Caused By Post-Sale Failure To Recall Product

One engaged in the business of selling or otherwise distributing products is subject to liability for harm to persons or property caused by the seller's failure to recall a product after the time of sale or distribution if:

(a)(1) a governmental directive issued pursuant to a statute or administrative regulation specifically requires the seller or distributor to recall the product; or

(a)(2) the seller or distributor, in the absence of a recall requirement under Subsection (a)(1), undertakes to recall the product; and

(b) the seller or distributor fails to act as a reasonable person in recalling the product.

§ 12. Liability Of Successor For Harm Caused By Defective Products Sold Commercially By Predecessor

A successor corporation or other business entity that acquires assets of a predecessor corporation or other business entity is subject to liability for harm to persons or property caused by a defective product sold or otherwise distributed commercially by the predecessor if the acquisition:

(a) is accompanied by an agreement for the successor to assume such liability; or

(b) results from a fraudulent conveyance to escape liability for the debts or liabilities of the predecessor; or

(c) constitutes a consolidation or merger with the predecessor; or

(d) results in the successor becoming a continuation of the predecessor.

§ 13. Liability Of Successor For Harm Caused By Successor's Own Post-Sale Failure To Warn

(a) A successor corporation or other business entity that acquires assets of a predecessor corporation or other business entity, whether or not liable under the rule stated in § 12, is subject to liability for harm to persons or property caused by the successor's failure to warn of a risk created by a product sold or distributed by the predecessor if:

(1) the successor undertakes or agrees to provide services for maintenance or repair of the product or enters into a similar relationship with purchasers of the predecessor's products giving rise to actual or potential economic advantage to the successor, and

(2) a reasonable person in the position of the successor would provide a warning.

(b) A reasonable person in the position of the successor would provide a warning if:

(1) the successor knows or reasonably should know that the product poses a substantial risk of harm to persons or property; and

(2) those to whom a warning might be provided can be identified and can reasonably be assumed to be unaware of the risk of harm; and

(3) a warning can be effectively communicated to and acted on by those to whom a warning might be provided; and

(4) the risk of harm is sufficiently great to justify the burden of providing a warning.

§ 14. Selling Or Distributing As One's Own A Product Manufactured By Another

One engaged in the business of selling or otherwise distributing products who sells or distributes as its own a product manufactured by another is subject to the same liability as though the seller or distributor were the product's manufacturer.

§ 15. General Rule Governing Causal Connection Between Product Defect And Harm

Whether a product defect caused harm to persons or property is determined by the prevailing rules and principles governing causation in tort.

§ 16. Increased Harm Due To Product Defect

(a) When a product is defective at the time of commercial sale or other distribution and the defect is a substantial factor in increasing the plaintiff's harm beyond that which would have resulted from other causes, the product seller is subject to liability for the increased harm.

(b) If proof supports a determination of the harm that would have resulted from other causes in the absence of the product defect, the product seller's liability is limited to the increased harm attributable solely to the product defect.

(c) If proof does not support a determination under Subsection (b) of the harm that would have resulted in the absence of the product defect, the product seller is liable for all of the plaintiff's harm attributable to the defect and other causes.

(d) A seller of a defective product that is held liable for part of the harm suffered by the plaintiff under Subsection (b), or all of the harm suffered by the plaintiff under Subsection (c), is jointly and severally liable or severally liable with other parties who bear legal responsibility for causing the harm, determined by applicable rules of joint and several liability.

§ 17. Apportionment Of Responsibility Between Or Among Plaintiff, Sellers And Distributors Of Defective Products, And Others

[Omitted.]

§ 18. Disclaimers, Limitations, Waivers, And Other Contractual Exculpations As Defenses To Products Liability Claims For Harm To Persons

Disclaimers and limitations of remedies by product sellers or other distributors, waivers by product purchasers, and other similar contractual exculpations, oral or written, do not bar or reduce otherwise valid products-liability claims against sellers or other distributors of new products for harm to persons.

§ 19. Definition Of "Product"

For purposes of this Restatement:

(a) A product is tangible personal property distributed commercially for use or consumption. Other items, such as real property and electricity, are products when the context of their distribution and use is sufficiently analogous to the distribution and use of tangible personal property that it is appropriate to apply the rules stated in this Restatement.

(b) Services, even when provided commercially, are not products.

(c) Human blood and human tissue, even when provided commercially, are not subject to the rules of this Restatement.

§ 20. Definition Of "One Who Sells Or Otherwise Distributes"

For purposes of this Restatement:

(a) One sells a product when, in a commercial context, one transfers ownership thereto either for use or consumption or for resale leading to ultimate use or consumption. Commercial product sellers include, but are not limited to, manufacturers, wholesalers, and retailers.

(b) One otherwise distributes a product when, in a commercial transaction other than a sale, one provides the product to another either for use or consumption or as a preliminary step leading to ultimate use or consumption. Commercial nonsale product distributors include, but are not limited to, lessors, bailors, and those who provide products to others as a means of promoting either the use or consumption of such products or some other commercial activity.

(c) One also sells or otherwise distributes a product when, in a commercial transaction, one provides a combination of products and services and either the transaction taken as a whole, or the product component thereof, satisfies the criteria in Subsection (a) or (b).

§ 21. Definition Of "Harm To Persons Or Property": Recovery For Economic Loss

For purposes of this Restatement, harm to persons or property includes economic loss if caused by harm to:

(a) the plaintiff's person; or

(b) the person of another when harm to the other interferes with an interest of the plaintiff protected by tort law; or

(c) the plaintiff's property other than the defective product itself.

(3)   In 1985, the European Economic Community issued Directive 85/374/EEC which required member states to adopt a product liability law that complied with these requirements:

Article 1. The producer shall be liable for damage caused by a defect in his product.

Article 2. For the purpose of this Directive "product" means all movables, with the exception of primary agricultural products and game, even though incorporated into another movable or into an immovable. "Primary agricultural products" means the products of the soil, of stock-farming and of fisheries, excluding products which have undergone initial processing. "Product" includes electricity.

Article 3. (1) "Producer" means the manufacturer of a finished product, the producer of any raw material or the manufacturer of a component part and any person who, by putting his name, trade mark or other distinguishing feature on the product presents himself as its producer. (2) Without prejudice to the liability of the producer, any person who imports into the Community a product for sale, hire, leasing or any form of distribution in the course of his business shall be deemed to be a producer within the meaning of this Directive and shall be responsible as a producer. (3) Where the producer of the product cannot be identified, each supplier of the product shall be treated as its producer unless he informs the injured person, within a reasonable time, of the identity of the producer or of the person who supplied him with the product. The same shall apply, in the case of an imported product, if this product does not indicate the identity of the importer referred to in paragraph 2, even if the name of the producer is indicated.

Article 4. The injured person shall be required to prove the damage, the defect and the causal relationship between defect and damage.

Article 5. Where, as a result of the provisions of this Directive, two or more persons are liable for the same damage, they shall be liable jointly and severally, without prejudice to the provisions of national law concerning the rights of contribution or recourse.

Article 6. (1) A product is defective when it does not provide the safety which a person is entitled to expect, taking all circumstances into account, including: (a) the presentation of the product; (b) the use to which it could reasonably be expected that the product would be put; (c) the time when the product was put into circulation. (2) A product shall not be considered defective for the sole reason that a better product is subsequently put into circulation.

Article 7. The producer shall not be liable as a result of this Directive if he proves: (a) that he did not put the product into circulation; or (b) that, having regard to the circumstances, it is probable that the defect which caused the damage did not exist at the time when the product was put into circulation by him or that this defect came into being afterwards; or (c) that the product was neither manufactured by him for sale or any form of distribution for economic purpose nor manufactured or distributed by him in the course of his business; or (d) that the defect is due to compliance of the product with mandatory regulations issued by the public authorities; or (e) that the state of scientific and technical knowledge at the time when he put the product into circulation was not such as to enable the existence of the defect to be discovered; or (f) in the case of a manufacturer of a component, that the defect is attributable to the design of the product in which the component has been fitted or to the instructions given by the manufacturer of the product.

Article 8. (1) Without prejudice to the provisions of national law concerning the right of contribution or recourse, the liability of the producer shall not be reduced when the damage is caused both by a defect in product and by the act or omission of a third party. (2) The liability of the producer may be reduced or disallowed when, having regard to all the circumstances, the damage is caused both by a defect in the product and by the fault of the injured person or any person for whom the injured person is responsible.

Article 9. For the purpose of Article 1, "damage" means: (a) damage caused by death or by personal injuries; (b) damage to, or destruction of, any item of property other than the defective product itself, with a lower threshold of 500 ECU, provided that the item of property: (i) is of a type ordinarily intended for private use or consumption, and (ii) was used by the injured person mainly for his own private use or consumption. This Article shall be without prejudice to national provisions relating to non-material damage. [Various sections omitted.]

Article 12. The liability of the producer arising from this Directive may not, in relation to the injured person, be limited or excluded by a provision limiting his liability or exempting him from liability. [Remainder omitted.]

Is the plan of the directive more or less beneficial to plaintiffs than § 402A? Than the Restatement of the Law (Third) of Torts? The British Parliament enacted the substance of the EEC directive into law in 1988. See Consumer Protection Act 1987 (c43).

WOODERSON v. ORTHO PHARMACEUTICAL CORP.
Kansas Supreme Court
681 P.2d 1038 (1984)

MILLER, JUSTICE:

Plaintiff, Carol Lynn Wooderson, brought this action in the District Court of Sedgwick County for damages for personal injuries which she claims resulted from her ingestion, over a period of years, of the oral contraceptive Ortho-Novum 1/80, manufactured by the defendant, Ortho Pharmaceutical Corporation (Ortho). At the conclusion of a six-week trial, the jury returned a verdict and the court entered judgment for plaintiff and against Ortho for actual damages of $2,000,000 and punitive damages of $2,750,000. Ortho appeals. The primary issues are whether there was sufficient competent evidence to support the verdict, and whether the trial court properly submitted the matter of punitive damages to the jury. Other issues will be stated in the opinion.

Carol Lynn Wooderson consulted Dr. Richard L. Hermes of Lawrence, Kansas, a physician specializing in obstetrics and gynecology, in the fall of 1972. She was planning to be married and wanted some method of contraception. Dr. Hermes prescribed an oral contraceptive (o.c.), Ortho-Novum 1/80, manufactured by the defendant. This is an "ethical" drug, one obtainable only upon prescription, as distinguished from a "proprietary" or "patent" drug, one sold over the counter. Plaintiff was in good health at that time; her blood pressure was 100/56, and she had never had any problems with her kidneys or with high blood pressure.

[Plaintiff later suffered from hypertension, hemolytic uremic syndrome (HUS), and renal failure. The evidence established that these were predictable side effects of the drug in some patients. Neither the plaintiff nor her physician had been informed of the potential side effects. On appeal, defendant argues, in part, that it had no duty to warn of the side effects.]

DUTY TO WARN

Ortho contends that it had no duty to add to the prescribing instructions for Ortho-Novum 1/80 a statement that there might be an association between the use of that product and HUS, malignant hypertension, or acute renal failure. In support of this contention, it cites Restatement (Second) of Torts § 402A (1965), including the comments thereto, and Lindquist v. Ayerst Laboratories, Inc., 227 Kan. 308, 319, 607 P.2d 1339 (1980). Lindquist was a products liability and medical malpractice case brought against Ayerst Laboratories, Inc., the manufacturer of an anesthetic which had been administered to the decedent, and the two physicians who had administered the anesthetic. Verdict had been entered for the defendants and plaintiff appealed. In the course of the opinion, we said:

[T]he jury was properly instructed regarding the doctrine of strict liability expressed in Restatement (Second) of Torts § 402A (1965). The jury was instructed to find Ayerst liable provided they found the drug was in a defective condition and unreasonably dangerous to persons who might be expected to use it, where that defect caused or contributed to the death of Lindquist. The defective condition is the failure of Ayerst to properly warn and instruct the medical profession with respect to the use and possible consequences of the use of Fluothane. 227 Kan. at 319, 607 P.2d 1339.

[Comment j to § 402 A provides, in part]

j. Directions or warning. . . . Where, however, the product contains an ingredient to which a substantial number of the population are allergic, and the ingredient is one whose danger is not generally known, or if known is one which the consumer would reasonably not expect to find in the product, the seller is required to give warning against it, if he has knowledge, or by the application of reasonable, developed human skill and foresight should have knowledge, of the presence of the ingredient and the danger. Likewise in the case of poisonous drugs, or those unduly dangerous for other reasons, warning as to use may be required. (Emphasis supplied.)

Defendant seizes upon that portion of the comment reading "if he has knowledge, or by the application of reasonable, developed human skill and foresight should have knowledge. . . . " Ortho contends, in essence, that an ethical (prescription) drug manufacturer is not bound to provide warnings until the occurrence of side effects is so frequent and the evidence of causation so clear-cut that the drug maker is itself convinced that the drug causes or contributes to such problems. This, we conclude, is not the law. A drug manufacturer's duty to warn is discussed and the rules are stated in numerous cases. A leading case in this field is McEwen v. Ortho Pharmaceutical, 270 Or. 375, 528 P.2d 522 (1974). Plaintiff McEwen brought suit against Ortho and Syntex for their alleged failure to give appropriate warning to the medical profession of dangers which the manufacturers knew or had reason to know were inherent in the use of their products. Plaintiff recovered judgment and defendants appealed. In affirming the judgment, the court said:

I. DEFENDANTS' DUTY TO WARN PLAINTIFF'S DOCTORS

1. There is no question here of any defect in the manufacture of defendants' oral contraceptives, nor of their efficacy when taken as prescribed. It is well settled, however, that the manufacturer of ethical drugs bears the additional duty of making timely and adequate warnings to the medical profession of any dangerous side effects produced by its drugs of which it knows, or has reason to know. . . .

The duty of the ethical drug manufacturer to warn is limited to those dangers which the manufacturer knows, or has reason to know, are inherent in the use of its drug. However, the drug manufacturer is treated as an expert in its particular field, and is under a "continuous duty . . . to keep abreast of scientific developments touching upon the manufacturer's product and to notify the medical profession of any additional side effects discovered from its use." Schenebeck v. Sterling Drug, Inc., 423 F.2d 919, 922 (8th Cir. 1970); accord O'Hare v. Merck & Co., 381 F.2d 286, 291 (8th Cir. 1967). The drug manufacturer's duty to warn is, therefore, commensurate not only with its actual knowledge gained from research and adverse reaction reports but also with its constructive knowledge as measured by scientific literature and other available means of communication.

Although the duty of the ethical drug manufacturer is to warn the doctor, rather than the patient, the manufacturer is directly liable to the patient for a breach of such duty. . . . The manufacturer's compliance with this duty enables the prescribing physician to balance the risk of possible harm against the benefits to be gained by the patient's use of that drug. Moreover, as observed by the court in Sterling Drug, Inc. v. Cornish, *supra* 370 F.2d at 85:

. . . [T]he purchaser's doctor is a learned intermediary between the purchaser and the manufacturer. If the doctor is properly warned of the possibility of a side effect in some patients, and is advised of the symptoms normally accompanying the side effect, there is an excellent chance that injury to the patient can be avoided. This is particularly true if the injury takes place slowly. . . .

Although the ethical drug manufacturer's duty to warn has been discussed most often with reference to the prescribing physician, the above reasoning applies with equal force to the treating physician. It is especially important that the treating doctor receive the manufacturer's warnings where it is impossible to predict in advance whether a particular patient is apt to suffer adverse effects from a drug, since the treating doctor may be more likely to observe the actual symptoms of the drug's untoward consequences. If the prescribing physician is entitled to make an informed choice in deciding whether the patient should begin taking a prescription drug, it follows that a treating physician should have the same information in making his decision as to whether the patient should stop taking that drug.

The duty of the ethical drug manufacturer to warn extends, then, to all members of the medical profession who come into contact with the patient in a decision-making capacity. To satisfy this duty, the manufacturer must utilize methods of warning which will be reasonably effective, taking into account both the seriousness of the drug's adverse effects and the difficulties inherent in bringing such information to the attention of a group as large and diverse as the medical profession. . . . The warning should be sufficient to apprise the general practitioner as well as the "unusually sophisticated medical man" of the dangerous propensities of the drug. . . . In short, "it is incumbent upon the manufacturer to bring the warning home to the doctor." . . .

It has been suggested, however, that the manufacturer of a prescription drug should be under no duty to warn the medical profession that its product is dangerous when used by certain allergic or hypersensitive users. It is unreasonable, so the argument runs, to impose upon the manufacturer a duty to warn doctors of dangers threatening a statistically insignificant number of users. We find this argument unpersuasive.

In the field of negligence, the duty to warn is limited to those dangerous propensities of the drug of which the manufacturer knows, or has reason to know. If allergic reactions are harder to anticipate, this should be taken into account in evaluating the manufacturer's knowledge. It must be remembered that the negligence liability of the ethical drug manufacturer is restricted to those dangers which are foreseeable.

Furthermore, to simply conclude that it is unreasonable to impose liability where the known danger threatens only a statistically small percentage of the drug's users is to beg the very question of negligence. The size of the class of endangered persons is one — albeit only one — of the factors to be considered in deciding whether the manufacturer's warnings were, in fact, reasonable.

The ethical drug manufacturer is, then, subject to a duty to warn the medical profession of untoward effects which the manufacturer knows, or has reason to know, are inherent in the use of its drug. . . .

In Ortho Pharmaceutical v. Chapman, 180 Ind. App. 33, 388 N.E.2d 541 (1979), the Court of Appeals of Indiana, Fourth District, said:

We are persuaded that the duty to warn under Comment k does not arise until the manufacturer knows or should know of the risk. [Citations omitted.] In the case of drug manufacturers, the standard of constructive knowledge is that of an expert in that particular field. . . . [D]ates are "vitally important" with respect to the duty to warn. Because a manufacturer cannot be required to warn of a risk unknown to science, the knowledge chargeable to him must be limited to that of the period during which the plaintiff was using the product in question. [Citations omitted.]

A second important limitation on liability . . . applies to manufacturers of ethical [prescription] drugs. Since such drugs are available only by prescription, a manufacturer's duty to warn extends only to the medical profession, and not the ultimate users. . . . The rationale for this exception to the Restatement's general rule is that "Prescription drugs are likely to be complex medicines, esoteric in formula and varied in effect. As a medical expert, the prescribing physician can take into account the propensities of the drug, as well as the susceptibilities of his patient. His is the task of weighing the benefits of any medication against its potential dangers. The choice he makes is an informed one, an individualized medical judgment bottomed on a knowledge of both patient and palliative." . . .

The court in Terhune v. A.H. Robins Co., supra, elaborates further:

The reasons for this rule should be obvious. Where a product is available only on prescription or through the services of a physician, the physician acts as a "learned intermediary" between the manufacturer or seller and the patient. It is his duty to inform himself of the qualities and characteristics of those products which he prescribes for or administers to or uses on his patients, and to exercise an independent judgment, taking into account his knowledge of the patient as well as the product. The patient is expected to and, it can be presumed, does place primary reliance upon that judgment. The physician decides what facts should be told to the patient. Thus, if the product is properly labeled and carries the necessary instructions and warnings to fully apprise the physician of the proper procedures for use and the dangers involved, the manufacturer may reasonably assume that the physician will exercise the informed judgment thereby gained in conjunction with his own independent learning, in the best interest of the patient. It has also been suggested that the rule is made necessary by the fact that it is ordinarily difficult for the manufacturer to communicate directly with the consumer. (Footnote omitted.)

In summary, a proper warning under Comment k in the context of the facts at bar, communicates a risk attendant on the use of the product which is known to experts in the field during the period in which the product is used. It need only be directed to doctors, not patients who are the ultimate users.

Again, with reference to the manufacturer's duty to warn, the Second Circuit in Lindsay v. Ortho Pharmaceutical Corp., 637 F.2d 87 (2d Cir. 1980), said:

The manufacturer's duty is to warn of all potential dangers which it knew, or in the exercise of reasonable care should have known, to exist. . . . The duty is a continuous one, requiring the manufacturer to keep abreast of the current state of knowledge of its products as gained through research, adverse reaction reports, scientific literature, and other available methods. . . . Except where FDA regulations otherwise provide, the manufacturer's duty is to warn the doctor, not the patient. The doctor acts as an "informed intermediary" between the manufacturer and the patient, evaluating the patient's needs, assessing the risks and benefits of available drugs, prescribing one, and supervising its use. Wolfgruber v. Upjohn Co., *supra*, 72 App. Div. 2d [59] at 61, 423 N.Y.S.2d 95. 637 F.2d at 91.

One other case is illuminating. In Seley v. G.D. Searle & Co., 67 Ohio St. 2d 192, 423 N.E.2d 831 (1981), the Supreme Court of Ohio discussed the adequacy of warnings. It said:

A jury may find that a warning is inadequate and unreasonable even where the existence of a "risk," i.e., a causal relationship between use of the product and resulting injury, has not been definitely established. . . . Thus, where scientific or medical evidence exists tending to show that a certain danger is associated with use of the drug, the manufacturer may not ignore or discount that information in drafting its warning solely because it finds it to be unconvincing. . . .

. . .

During the times relevant to this lawsuit, the label which accompanied Ortho-Novum 1/80, when purchased by the patient, instructed the patient not to take the drugs without her doctor's continued supervision. It warned that the drug could cause side effects, but it did not elaborate upon those side effects except to say that the most serious known side effect was abnormal blood clotting. The "package insert" which is sent to the physician and which contains the information included in the Physicians' Desk Reference (PDR), an annual volume provided for use by physicians, presented detailed instructions, contraindications, warnings, and precautions. It is undisputed, however, that none of these warned of any possible association between the use of the product and HUS, malignant hypertension, or acute renal failure. Dr. Hermes, plaintiff's gynecologist, testified in substance that he probably would have lowered the dosage had he been informed by Ortho of these potential dangers. Ortho had access to literature that should have prompted it to inform Dr. Hermes of what he needed to know. The expert testimony and the exhibits in this case disclose that there was an abundance of published information in the medical journals, prior to and during the years when plaintiff was taking Ortho-Novum 1/80, which linked the use of oral contraceptives with HUS, malignant hypertension, and acute renal failure. We agree with the McEwen and Seley courts. The available scientific literature clearly tended to show that there was danger of HUS, malignant hypertension and acute kidney failure attendant to the use of the drug. Ortho, as an expert in the field, knew or should have known of the risk. We conclude that, on the basis of the evidence, Ortho had a duty to warn the prescribing physician, and the trial court properly submitted to the jury the issue of the adequacy of Ortho's published warning.

We hold that the manufacturer of an ethical drug has a duty to warn the medical profession of dangerous side effects of its products of which it knows, has reason to know, or should know, based upon its position as an expert in the field, upon its research, upon cases reported to it, and upon scientific development, research, and publications in the field. This duty is continuing. We do not need to determine, in this case, what duty, if any, such a manufacturer has to warn the ultimate consumer, the patient. Here, neither was warned by Ortho, but Ortho's failure to warn the physician is sufficient to sustain the finding of negligence or breach of duty against it in this case.

Ortho also argues that the FDA has determined that contraceptive-induced HUS does not merit warnings, and that the courts of Kansas must defer to the FDA's determination. This argument centers around a letter from the FDA to Searle Laboratories. Searle had proposed fifteen or more package insert changes, covering many and varied subjects. Only one of those mentioned the inclusion of HUS as a possible side effect. The FDA responded that it did not concur with the additional changes included in that proposal. This letter cannot be construed as a clear determination by the FDA that contraceptive-induced HUS does not merit warnings, and thus this argument has no merit.

NOTES AND QUESTIONS

(1) Is proof of a defect based upon lack of warning different from proof of negligent failure to warn? Do you agree with the proposition that prescription drugs should be the subject of product strict liability actions? This issue has been hotly disputed and at least two lines of authority have developed. One is referred to as the "blanket immunity" approach and is exemplified by *Brown v. Superior Court*, 751 P.2d 470 (Cal. 1988). Another is the so-called "risk\benefit" approval and is exemplified by *Toner v. Lederle Laboratories*, 732 P.2d 297 (Id. 1987). Although the theories expressed in these and many other cases are too detailed and specific to be addressed in this text, the student might attempt to identify the theory incorporated in Restatement of the Law Torts (Third): Product Liability, which states:

§ 6. Liability Of Commercial Seller Or Distributor For Harm Caused By Defective Prescription Drugs And Medical Devices

(a) A manufacturer of a prescription drug or medical device who sells or otherwise distributes a defective drug or medical device is subject to liability for harm to persons caused by the defect. A prescription drug or medical device is one that may be legally sold or otherwise distributed only pursuant to a health-care provider's prescription.

(b) For purposes of liability under Subsection (a), a prescription drug or medical device is defective if at the time of sale or other distribution the drug or medical device:

(1) contains a manufacturing defect as defined in § 2(a); or

(2) is not reasonably safe due to defective design as defined in Subsection (c); or

(3) is not reasonably safe due to inadequate instructions or warnings as defined in Subsection (d).

(c) A prescription drug or medical device is not reasonably safe due to defective design if the foreseeable risks of harm posed by the drug or medical device are sufficiently great in relation to its foreseeable therapeutic benefits that reasonable health-care providers, knowing of such foreseeable risks and therapeutic benefits, would not prescribe the drug or medical device for any class of patients.

(d) A prescription drug or medical device is not reasonably safe due to inadequate instructions or warnings if reasonable instructions or warnings regarding foreseeable risks of harm are not provided to:

(1) prescribing and other health-care providers who are in a position to reduce the risks of harm in accordance with the instructions or warnings; or

(2) the patient when the manufacturer knows or has reason to know that health-care providers will not be in a position to reduce the risks of harm in accordance with the instructions or warnings.

(e) A retail seller or other distributor of a prescription drug or medical device is subject to liability for harm caused by the drug or device if:

(1) at the time of sale or other distribution the drug or medical device contains a manufacturing defect as defined in § 2(a); or

(2) at or before the time of sale or other distribution of the drug or medical device the retail seller or other distributor fails to exercise reasonable care and such failure causes harm to persons.

(2) What sort of warning should have been given to make the product non-defective? Does the following statement provide suitable guidelines?

An adequate warning is one which, if followed, would make the product safe for the user, that is, had the injured person complied with the warning, there could have been no accident. . . . The warning must be given in such a manner that it can reasonably be brought to the attention of the user, such as placing it on the container in which the product comes, placing it on the product itself or, where appropriate, providing an instruction or operational manual.

Quattlebaum v. Hy-Reach Equipment, 453 So. 2d 578, 586 (La. App. 1984).

(3) Suppose a manufacturer learns of a dangerous defect after products have been sold. Does it have a product strict liability duty to search out the product and warn potential users? *See, e.g., Feldman v. Lederle Laboratories*, 97 N.J. 429, 479 A.2d 374 (1984).

(4) Should punitive damages awards be permitted in product strict liability cases? If so, is it necessary that the evidence prove more than that the product was defective and unreasonably dangerous?

§ 14.04 PRODUCT LIABILITY: RATIONALIZATION OF THEORIES

[A] The Prima Facie Case

The law of product liability is confused and complex. As the preceding materials show, the reasons are mainly historical and doctrinal. The tortuous untangling of the notion of privity from the negligence cause of action demonstrates the historical connection. The process by which warranty theories and enterprise strict liability were built onto the underlying negligence cause of action demonstrates the doctrinal connection. Although the courts have acknowledged that each of these theories constitutes a separate cause of action, they have had great difficulty in clearly differentiating the elements of one from those of the others. The purpose of this section is to suggest an analytical structure to eliminate this conceptual confusion. The goal is to find ways to try cases in a manner that will confuse jurors as little as possible. The section also examines some additional aspects of the strict liability cause of action.

The principal assertion of this section is that the elements of the negligence cause of action as presented in this text — namely duty, breach, causation and damages — may be generalized and applied to both warranty and strict liability causes of action.

[1] Duty

In negligence, duty derives from notions of relationship, foreseeability, and proximity as developed in *Palsgraf, Donoghue v. Stevenson* and others of the preceding cases. The matter was grievously confused by *Winterbottom v. Wright*, which was erroneously treated as the ratio decidendi for a non-privity no-duty rule. This no-duty posture was gradually flushed away by *MacPherson, Donoghue* and a myriad of other cases.

In the warranty cause of action, duty derives from contract either expressly, as in Baxter, or implicitly, as in the implied warranties of merchantability, fitness for a particular purpose, and fitness for human consumption. Because of the contractual basis of warranty liability, privity of contract makes conceptual sense. Remedies are provided to promisees against promisors. Nevertheless, as the Uniform Commercial Code provisions and *Henningsen v. Bloomfield Motors show*, some legislatures and courts have extended the warranty duty not only to those in privity of contract but also to certain users and consumers.

The duty question in the enterprise strict liability cause of action must be resolved into two sub-questions: duty of and duty to. As to "duty of," the formulation of Restatement, Torts, Second § 402A applies enterprise strict liability to "one who sells" and who is also in the business of selling. This imposes liability throughout the economic web to manufacturers, distributors and retailers. All are "sellers." Nevertheless, the basic rationale of enterprise liability — that is, that the price of all products spreads the cost of harm done by defective ones — does not fit all cases. Should it apply to a small independent retailer? Does it fit large, chain retailers better or worse than it fits small independent manufacturers? Unless the goal is to force every seller into an insurance scheme, the enterprise theory of itself does not justify relieving the plaintiff of the burden of proving negligence in every application. Courts have split on where the line should be drawn. Some have applied enterprise strict liability to all business sellers, but others have not. Which category does *West v. Caterpillar Tractor* fall into?

Some courts have also applied the enterprise liability doctrine in certain settings that do not involve a sale. *See, e.g., Cintrone v. Hertz Truck Leasing & Rental Serv.*, 212 A.2d 769 (N.J. 1965), and *W.E. Johnson Equip. Co. v. United Air Lines*, 238 So. 2d 98 (Fla. 1959). Is this a perversion of theory?

As to "duty to," the Restatement formulation extends liability to "the ultimate user or consumer, or to his property" but expresses no opinion as to a more general class of plaintiffs, commonly referred to as "bystanders." In *West v. Caterpillar Tractor*, the Florida Supreme Court extended protection to Mrs. West, who was a bystander. Similarly, in *Coding v. Paglia*, 292 N.E.2d 614 (N.Y. 1973), the New York Court of Appeal extended protection to the driver of an automobile that was crashed into by a defective vehicle manufactured by one of the defendants. Thus, some courts do apply the strict liability "duty to" to bystanders. Taking a more general approach, the torts student should see that the notion of "duty to" as developed in negligence would fit nicely at this place. The foreseeability factor is especially appropriate. By contrast, privity of contract has no application to pure tort theory, except as an element in duty analysis and ought otherwise to be eschewed by the courts.

[2]   Breach

A negligence duty is breached when a person owing the duty fails to exercise the care that would be used by an ordinary person of reasonable prudence under the same circumstances. Liability turns on a testing of the quality of what the defendant did or did not do. In short, negligence law tests behavior.

By contrast, neither the warranty nor the strict liability cause of action concerns itself with the quality of the defendant's behavior. The issue is not whether the defendant exercised prudent care or even the utmost care. Instead, these theories test the quality of the product that was the instrument of harm. In warranty actions the template of quality is the substance of the promises made about quality. In clear cases the agreed contract specifications define the standard, but more often the substance of the warranty is fixed impliedly by warranties of merchantability and fitness as understood in a particular trade. This text will not attempt to explicate how the substance of those warranties is determined, which is better left to a course on contracts. Instead, attention will be focused upon the tort theory of strict liability.

The proof of breach in § 402A actions requires showing that the product was sold by the defendant "in a defective condition unreasonably dangerous to the user or consumer or to his property." Although many courts have adopted this "defective — unreasonably dangerous" formulation, the California Supreme Court that gave birth to the theory in *Greenman v. Yuba Power Products* requires proof only that the product was defective. *See Cronin v. J.B.E. Olsen Corp.*, 501 P.2d 1153 (Cal. 1972). The Restatement also requires the plaintiff to prove that after the defendant relinquishes control of the product "it is expected to and does reach the user or consumer without substantial change in the condition in which it is sold." This derives from *MacPherson v. Buick Motor Company* and, conceptually, is more appropriately an issue of proximate causation than of breach. Nevertheless, the requirement suggests that manufacturers of component parts that are to be assembled into a finished product by someone else may have a lesser duty to produce non-defective products than do manufacturers of finished products.

When a product fails because of a flaw in the materials used or because it was incorrectly assembled, proof that it was defective is virtually self-evident. It remains to show only that it was unreasonably dangerous. Thus, the collapsed wheel of the Buick in *MacPherson* and the failed steering mechanism of the Plymouth in *Henningsen* pose no difficult conceptual issues. Flawed products sometimes raise difficult problems of proof but no difficult problems of principle. By contrast, *West v. Caterpillar Tractor* raises a very difficult problem of principle. There, the manufacturer adopted a basic design that itself was claimed to make the products "defective — unreasonably dangerous." The nub of the complaint is that the product is defective because the design is bad. *See* Henderson, Judicial Review of Manufacturer's Conscious Design Choices: The Limits of Adjudication, 73 Col. L. Rev. 1531 (1973).

Bad design may give rise to actions in negligence, in breach of warranty and in enterprise strict liability. In negligence, the plaintiff must prove that the defendant failed to use due care in making his design decisions. Both parties would be permitted to introduce evidence as to the defendant's awareness of potential risks, alternative designs considered and rejected, and alternative designs not considered. The ultimate burden of proof would be upon the plaintiff. What must the plaintiff prove in the strict liability action? How would the plaintiff's burden to prove the gravemen of strict liability differ from the burden in the negligence action? Might a plaintiff carry the strict liability burden by proving the feasibility of safer alternative designs? Would this be different from proving negligence? Why? To make the proof of a strict liability action easier for plaintiffs, many courts have attempted to derive more specific standards to test what makes a product defective and unreasonably dangerous. The following case and notes examine some of them.

THIBAULT v. SEARS, ROEBUCK & CO.
New Hampshire Supreme Court
395 A.2d 843 (1978)

Douglas, Justice.

This is an action to recover damages for harm sustained by the plaintiff when a lawn mower manufactured by the defendant injured the plaintiff's foot. Trial by jury on tort counts sounding in negligence and strict liability before Flynn, J., resulted in verdicts for the defendant. The plaintiff's exceptions concerning his strict liability claim were reserved and transferred. We affirm.

The plaintiff bought a "Craftsman" rotary power mower from the Sears, Roebuck & Company outlet in 1968. He had used similar mowers for over fifteen years and was thoroughly familiar with them. The rear of the housing of plaintiff's mower is embossed with the warning, "Keep Hands & Feet From Under Mower." The instruction booklet twice advises the operator to mow slopes lengthwise, not up and down. Although this advice is not highlighted, the type throughout the booklet is easily readable.

Despite this advice, the plaintiff thought that a long steep slope on his property could be mowed more safely if it were mowed up and down. While mowing in this manner, he lost his balance and fell. He instinctively gripped the handle of the mower as he fell and when he came to rest at the bottom of the slope, his foot was under the housing. Although there was conflicting testimony at the trial, the plaintiff contended that his foot slipped under the housing because the mower lacked a rear trailing guard. The defendant contended that the plaintiff lifted the mower from the ground when he fell, thus bringing the blade down on his foot. The defendant therefore argued that the lack of a guard did not contribute to the accident. Alternatively, the defendant contended that the plaintiff was "contributorily negligent" in mowing up and down contrary to the explicit written instructions.

Before the adoption of the doctrine of strict liability, the injured consumer's recourse at law was "to bring an action based either on the negligence of the manufacturer or, additionally or alternatively, on breach of warranty." Cassidy, Strict Liability in New Hampshire, 18 N.H.B.J. 3, 4 (1976). Consumers may now maintain actions based upon strict liability. Buttrick v. Lessard, 110 N.Y. 36, 260 A.2d 111 (1969); Elliott v. Lachance, 109 N.H. 481, 256 A.2d 153 (1969). Some commentators have suggested that strict liability is in reality a tool of social engineering, and that manufacturers should be required to bear the entire risk and costs of injuries caused by products. "If redistribution [of costs] is desired, there is no reason why the law should retain the requirements of causation and product defect; to the extent that any defendant can rely upon those requirements to defeat a plaintiff's cause of action, this 'policy' of tort law will be defeated." Epstein, Products Liability: The Search for the Middle Ground, 56 N.C.L. Rev. 643, 659 (1978).

We disagree with this approach to the doctrine of strict liability. Unlike workmen's compensation and no-fault automobile insurance, strict liability is not a no-fault system of compensation. The common-law principle that fault and responsibility are elements of our legal system applicable to corporations and individuals alike will not be undermined or abolished by "spreading" of risk and cost in this State. Viewed as a system of spreading the risk, the doctrine of strict liability has had economic consequences. In the fifteen years since Greenman v. Yuba Power Products, Inc., 59 Cal. 2d 57, 27 Cal. Rptr. 697, 377 P.2d 897 (1963), some writers have noted that the doctrine "has led to a decline in consumer 'freedom of choice.' Consumers willing to assume risk and who want to avail themselves of lower product prices, are less able to do so." Sachs, Products Liability: An Economic View, 14 Trial 48, 51 (1978).

. . .

In a strict liability case alleging defective design, the plaintiff must first prove the existence of a "defective condition unreasonably dangerous to the user." Buttrick v. Lessard, 110 N.H. at 38–39, 260 A.2d at 113; Bellotte v. Zayre Corp., 116 N.H. 52, 352 A.2d 723 (1976). In determining unreasonable danger, courts should consider factors such as social utility and desirability. . . . The utility of the product must be evaluated from the point of view of the public as a whole, because a finding of liability for defective design could result in the removal of an entire product line from the market. Some products are so important that a manufacturer may avoid liability as a matter of law if he has given proper warnings. . . . In weighing utility and desirability against danger, courts should also consider whether the risk of danger could have been reduced without significant impact on product effectiveness and manufacturing cost. For example, liability may attach if the manufacturer did not take available and reasonable steps to lessen or eliminate the danger of even a significantly useful and desirable product. *See* Twerski, From Defect to Cause to Comparative Fault: Rethinking Some Product Liability Concepts, 60 Marquette L. Rev. 297, 316–19 (1977) (discussing risk-utility analysis).

Another factor to be considered is the presence or absence of a warning. Of course, some products, such as carving knives, are obviously and inherently dangerous. When a risk is not apparent, however, the user must be adequately and understandably warned of concealed dangers. We do not agree, however, with such cases as Davis, supra, in which the Ninth Circuit held that in the absence of adequate warning a one-in-a-million risk of adverse reaction to a vaccine, known to the manufacturer, was a sufficient basis on which to impose strict liability. We also reject cases that demand that a manufacturer warn against uses which were neither intended by the manufacturer nor within the reasonably foreseeable use of the product. *Cf.* Moran v. Faberge, Inc., 273 Md. 538, 332 A.2d 11 (1975) (perfume manufacturer liable for burns to teenage girl whose companion used cologne to scent a lit candle); Spruill v. Boyle-Midway, Inc., 308 F.2d 79 (4th Cir. 1962) (manufacturer in failure-to-warn case liable when child drank furniture polish). These decisions fail to recognize that individual consumers have certain responsibilities. Manufacturers cannot foresee and warn of all absurd and dangerous uses of their product. Such decisions may harm our economy and unnecessarily encourage legislative intervention. . . .

The duty to warn is concomitant with the general duty of the manufacturer, which "is limited to foreseeing the probable results of the normal use of the product or a use that can reasonably be anticipated." McLaughlin v. Sears, Roebuck & Co., 111 N.H. 265, 268, 281 A.2d 587, 588 (1971). Nevertheless, when an unreasonable danger could have been eliminated without excessive cost or loss of product efficiency, liability may attach even though the danger was obvious or there was adequate warning. . . . A manufacturer "is not obliged to design the safest possible product, or one as safe as others make or a safer product than the one he has designed, so long as the design he has adopted is reasonably safe." Mitchell v. Ford Motor Co., 533 F.2d 19, 20 (1st Cir. 1976) (citations omitted). The obviousness of the danger should be evaluated against the reasonableness of the steps which the manufacturer must take to reduce the danger. Montgomery and Owen, *supra* at 837; Twerski, *supra* at 14.

The plaintiff in a defective design case must also prove causation and foreseeability. He must show that the unreasonably dangerous condition existed when the product was purchased, McLaughlin v. Sears, Roebuck & Co., 111 N.H. at 267, 281 at 588, and that the dangerous condition caused the injury. W. Prosser, The Law of Torts § 41 (4th ed. 1971). The plaintiff must further prove that the purpose and manner of his use of the product was foreseeable by the manufacturer. This requirement is predicated on the manufacturer's duty to design his product reasonably safely for the uses which he can foresee. Foreseeability of use, however, extends beyond the consumer's actual use of the product; for example, a failure to read or follow instructions for product use may not be fatal to the plaintiff's case if he can show that such failure was reasonably foreseeable. . . .

Inquiry into the dangerousness of a product requires a multifaceted balancing process involving evaluation of many conflicting factors. A court will rarely be able to say as a matter of law that a product has no social utility, or that the purpose or manner of its use that caused the injury was not foreseeable. . . . The jury must decide whether the potentiality of harm is open and obvious. . . . Reasonableness, foreseeability, utility, and similar factors are questions of fact for jury determination. We now turn to defenses.

The Restatement (Second) of Torts § 402A, Comment n (1965) states in part that:

. . . [t]he form of contributory negligence which consists in voluntarily and unreasonably proceeding to encounter a known danger, and commonly passes under the name of assumption of the risk, is a defense under this Section as in other cases of strict liability. If the user or consumer discovers the defect and is aware of the danger, and nevertheless proceeds to make use of the product and is injured by it, he is barred from recovery. (Emphasis added).

In Buttrick v. Lessard, 110 N.H. at 40, 260 A.2d at 114, this court pointed out that the phrase in Comment n referring to "assumption of the risk" had led to "some confusion." We saw no difficulty in describing the defense of plaintiff's conduct in voluntarily and unreasonably proceeding to encounter a known danger as one of "contributory negligence" rather than the more commonly known phrase "assumption of the risk." The reason was that this court views "the doctrine of 'assumption of the risk' . . . with distaste. . . . " Id. *See* Cassidy, Strict Liability in New Hampshire, 18 N.H.B.J. 3, 15 (1976). "The problem is largely one of semantics." Buttrick *supra* at 40, 260 A.2d at 114. Of course, product misuse and abnormal uses are defenses to strict liability.

. . .

Other courts have recognized that when fault or negligence concepts are injected into a strict liability case using comparative negligence, semantic and conceptual problems become crucial. In a reversal of some of its earlier "pure" products liability stances, the California Supreme Court attempted to delineate those factors the jury must compare in a strict liability case. In Daly v. General Motors Corp., 20 Cal. 3d 725, 144 Cal. Rptr. 380, 575 P.2d 1162 (1978), a "second collision" action, a single car accident resulted in the decedent being ejected from his car due to what plaintiff alleged was a defectively designed door latch mechanism. The defendant asserted that the decedent had been intoxicated and had failed to use a seat belt or lock on the door (despite warnings in the owner's manual). The California court stated the theoretical question as follows:

Because plaintiff's case rests upon strict products liability based on improper design of the door latch and because defendants assert a failure in decedent's conduct, namely, his alleged intoxication and nonuse of safety equipment, without which the accident and ensuing death could not have occurred, there is thereby posed the overriding issue in the case, should comparative principles apply in strict products liability actions?

Id. at 731–32, 144 Cal. Rptr. at 383, 575 P.2d at 1165.

The court answered in the affirmative and we agree. The California court pointed out that there are semantical and theoretical differences between the "apples" of negligence and the "oranges" of strict liability that should not be mixed. Id. at 734, 144 Cal. Rptr. at 385, 575 P.2d at 1167. The court held, however, that it was not balancing dissimilar concepts by using comparative fault in a strict liability case, reasoning that, "[t]he conduct of one party in combination with the product of another, or perhaps the placing of a defective article in the stream of protected and anticipated use, may produce the ultimate injury." Id. at 736, 144 Cal. Rptr. at 386, 575 P.2d at 1168.

To the extent the California court included negligence concepts in its comparison, we disagree. Semantic and conceptual clarity is essential if the jury is to understand a defective design case, especially if counts in negligence and strict liability are going to the jury. While we note that both counts are permitted, we do not recommend to plaintiffs that counts in both negligence and strict liability against the same defendant be submitted to the jury because of the confusion which is created. Where both counts are submitted to the jury, the charge on the negligence count at the present time is:

Plaintiff's Claim: Defense:
Negligence   Contributory Negligence
Governing Statute:
Comparative Negligence

And on the strict liability count, the jury charge includes:

Plaintiff's Claim: Defense:
Strict Liability   Contributory Negligence
Governing Statute:
Comparative Negligence

The negligence concept in such instructions to a jury of laymen necessarily pervades the entire charge, thus submerging or obliterating the doctrinal impact of strict liability in a welter of verbiage. The jury should not be expected to grasp the extremely fine distinctions the trial court attempts to provide in its explanation that "comparative negligence" in a strict liability case does not really require a comparison of the parties' "negligence." If the trial courts use the term "plaintiff's misconduct" to replace the words "contributory negligence" in the jury charge, this will separate the theories of strict liability and negligence more effectively in the minds of twelve laymen. "Plaintiff's misconduct" will include, where applicable, product misuse or abnormal use, as well as embodying the "negligence" or "assumption of the risk" concepts in our prior cases of voluntarily and unreasonably proceeding to encounter a known danger. The words "plaintiff's misconduct" accurately describe what action by the plaintiff, combined with the interaction of a defendant's product, caused an accident or injury. In Buttrick v. Lessard, supra, we used similar terminology when we said the defendant "would be entitled to have considered [by the jury] the conduct of the plaintiff in stepping on the [dimmer] switch with knowledge of the defect and his operation of the car after the lights failed." Buttrick, 110 N.H. at 40, 260 A.2d at 113, emphasis added. Of course, as before, if the jury finds such conduct to have been the sole cause of the accident, the plaintiff is barred from recovery. See Restatement (Second) of Torts § 402A, Comment n (1965). To state all of the above discussed affirmative defenses to be proven by the defendant as "plaintiff's misconduct" uses a neutral term that avoids erroneously injecting assumption of the risk or the "flavor of negligence into the strict liability doctrine." Hagenbuch v. Snap-On Tools Corp., 339 F.Supp. 676, 682 (D.N.H. 1972).

We judicially recognize the comparative concept in strict liability cases parallel to the legislature's recognition of it in the area of negligence. Accordingly, we hold that the trial court . . . should instruct the jury that it is to compare the causal effect of the defect in the product or design with the affirmative defense of misconduct of the plaintiff and allocate the loss as hereinafter indicated. The trial court should read or paraphrase Restatement (Second) of Torts § 402A (1) and (2) to the jury; the jury should then usually be asked by special verdict if plaintiff's proof has met the requirements of the Restatement. If plaintiff's proof is sufficient, the jury must weigh the plaintiff's misconduct, if any, and reduce the amount of damages by the percentage that the plaintiff's misconduct contributed to cause his loss or injury so long as it is not greater than fifty percent. If the jury concludes that the "misconduct of the plaintiff was the sole cause or greater than one-half the cause of the loss or injury, the verdict must be for the defendant. Of course, if plaintiff's misconduct did not cause the loss of injury, there would be no reduction in damages if the defendant is found liable. In multiple defendant cases, if recovery is allowed against more than one defendant, the jury shall apportion the loss in the ratio to which each liable defendant caused or contributed to the loss or injury to the amount of causation or liability attributed to all defendants against whom recovery is allowed. . . . Use of the special verdict is permissible in strict liability cases despite the language of RSA 507:7-a (Supp. 1977) referring to a general verdict in negligence cases. In any complicated or multiple count negligence or strict liability cases, trial judges have the inherent power to use special questions and verdicts to guide the jury and to aid in post-verdict review. . . .

. . .

In the present case the jury returned a verdict for the defendant and the trial judge entered judgment. There is evidence to support the verdict. *See* Kierstead v. Betley Chevrolet-Buick, Inc., 118 N.H. — , — , 389 A.2d 429, 431 (1978). Even though the jury could have found that the plaintiff's actual use of the lawn mower that caused the injury was foreseeable, a jury could also have found that the warning was adequate, or that the design was not the cause of the accident, or that the plaintiff's misconduct was more than fifty percent responsible for the injury.

The plaintiff also excepted to the admission of the custom and usage standards of the lawn mower industry. The evidence was relevant and correctly admitted. The trial court charged the jury that the standards were evidence, but not binding on them, and that compliance with the standards would not absolve the manufacturer from liability if those standards did not comport with the jury's notion of proper design. The admission of such evidence under the circumstances was not error. . . .

Exceptions overruled.

NOTES AND QUESTIONS

(1)   Does *Thibault* provide a coherent, reliable set of guidelines for determining what makes a product defective and unreasonably dangerous? Compare it with the formulations expressed in the succeeding notes. Focus carefully upon the point of view that the fact finder is required to take in each instance. Can you improve upon the lot of them?

(2)   *Cepada v. Cumberland Engineering Co.*, 386 A.2d 816, 826–827 (N.J. 1978):

Our study of the decisions satisfies us that [a] risk/utility analysis rationalizes what the great majority of the courts actually do in deciding design defect cases where physical injury has proximately resulted from the defect. Several recent cases have expressly referred to and applied the stated analysis. [Citations omitted]

* * *

Dean Wade suggests that before determining whether the case for liability should be given to the jury the trial court should give consideration to whether a balanced consideration of the following factors did not preclude liability as a matter of law:

(1) The usefulness and desirability of the product — its utility to the user and to the public as a whole.

(2) The safety aspects of the product — the likelihood that it will cause injury, and the probable seriousness of the injury.

(3) The availability of a substitute product which would meet the same need and not be as unsafe.

(4) The manufacturer's ability to eliminate the unsafe character of the product without impairing its usefulness or making it too expensive to maintain its utility.

(5) The user's ability to avoid danger by the exercise of care in the use of the product.

(6) The user's anticipated awareness of the dangers inherent in the product and their avoidability, because of general public knowledge of the obvious condition of the product, or of the existence of suitable warnings or instructions.

(7) The feasibility, on the part of the manufacturer, of spreading the loss by setting the price of the product or carrying liability insurance.

[Wade, On The Nature of Strict Tort Liability for Products, 44 Miss L.J. 825 at 837–838 (1973).]

If the case is sent to the jury, since it would not always be appropriate for the court to include in the instructions to the jury all seven of the factors mentioned above, Dean Wade suggests the following model instruction:

A [product] is not duly safe if it is so likely to be harmful to persons [or property] that a reasonably prudent manufacturer [supplier], who had actual knowledge of its harmful character would not place it on the market. It is not necessary to find that this defendant had knowledge of the harmful character of the [product] in order to determine that it was not duly safe. Id., at 839–840.

Subject to substituting the Section 402A language, "defective condition unreasonably dangerous," for the Wade-preferred "not duly safe," we approve and adopt this instruction for incorporation into a charge in an action against a manufacturer for strict liability in tort based upon the design defect of a product.

(3) *Barker v. Lull Engineering Co.*, 20 Cal. 3d 413, 143 Cal. Rptr. 225, 237–238 (1978) 573 P.2d 443:

> Although our cases have thus recognized a variety of considerations that may be relevant to the determination of the adequacy of a product's design, past authorities have generally not devoted much attention to the appropriate allocation of the burden of proof with respect to these matters.
>
> . . .
>
> The allocation of such burden is particularly significant in this context inasmuch as this court's product liability decisions, from Greenman to Cronin, have repeatedly emphasized that one of the principal purposes behind the strict product liability doctrine is to relieve an injured plaintiff of many of the onerous evidentiary burdens inherent in a negligence cause of action. Because most of the evidentiary matters which may be relevant to the determination of the adequacy of a product's design under the "risk-benefit" standard — e.g., the feasibility and cost of alternative designs — are similar to issues typically presented in a negligent design case and involve technical matters peculiarly within the knowledge of the manufacturer, we conclude that once the plaintiff makes a prima facie showing that the injury was proximately caused by the product's design, the burden should appropriately shift to the defendant to prove, in light of the relevant factors, that the product is not defective. Moreover, inasmuch as this conclusion flows from our determination that the fundamental public policies embraced in Greenman dictate that a manufacturer who seeks to escape liability for an injury proximately caused by its product's design on a risk-benefit theory should bear the burden of persuading the trier of fact that its product should not be judged defective, the defendant's burden is one affecting the burden of proof, rather than simply the burden of producing evidence.
>
> . . .
>
> Thus, to reiterate, a product may be found defective in design, so as to subject a manufacturer to strict liability for resulting injuries, under either of two alternative tests. First, a product may be found defective in design if the plaintiff establishes that the product failed to perform as safely as an ordinary consumer would expect when used in an intended or reasonably foreseeable manner. Second, a product may alternatively be found defective in design if the plaintiff demonstrates that the product's design proximately caused his injury and the defendant fails to establish, in light of the relevant factors, that, on balance, the benefits of the challenged design outweigh the risk of danger inherent in such design.

(4) *Welch v. Outboard Marine Corporation*, 481 F.2d 252 (5th Cir. 1973):

> A product is defective and unreasonably dangerous when a reasonable seller would not sell the product if he knew of the risks involved or if the risks are greater than a reasonable buyer would expect.

(5) A primary desire of the proponents of Restatement of the Law of Torts (Third) was to eliminate the consumer expectation test for determination of a design defect. How effectively does this section achieve that purpose?

§ 2. Categories Of Product Defect

A product is defective when, at the time of sale or distribution, it contains a manufacturing defect, is defective in design, or is defective because of inadequate instructions or warnings. A product:

(a) contains a manufacturing defect when the product departs from its intended design even though all possible care was exercised in the preparation and marketing of the product;

(b) is defective in design when the foreseeable risks of harm posed by the product could have been reduced or avoided by the adoption of a reasonable alternative design by the seller or other distributor, or a predecessor in the commercial chain of distribution, and the omission of the alternative design renders the product not reasonably safe;

(c) is defective because of inadequate instructions or warnings when the foreseeable risks of harm posed by the product could have been reduced or avoided by the provision of reasonable instructions or warnings by the seller or other distributor, or a predecessor in the commercial chain of distribution, and the omission of the instructions or warnings renders the product not reasonably safe.

Does the EEC product liability directive appear to permit a consumer expectation test? See Article 6, in note (3) after *West v. Caterpillar Tractor Company*.

(6) In *Lippard v. Houdaille Industries, Inc.*, 715 S.W.2d 491 (Mo. 1986) the Missouri Supreme Court declined to treat contributory negligence as a defense to a product strict liability claim. The Missouri legislature quickly enacted this statute to supersede that holding:

1. Contributory fault, as a complete bar to plaintiff's recovery in a products liability claim, is abolished. The doctrine of pure comparative fault shall apply to products liability claims as provided in this section.

2. Defendant may plead and prove the fault of the plaintiff as an affirmative defense. Any fault chargeable to the plaintiff shall diminish proportionately the amount awarded as compensatory damages but shall not bar recovery.

3. For purposes of this section, "fault" is limited to:

(1) The failure to use the product as reasonably anticipated by the manufacturer;

(2) Use of the product for a purpose not intended by the manufacturer;

(3) Use of the product with knowledge of a danger involved in such use with reasonable appreciation of the consequences and the voluntary and unreasonable exposure to said danger;

(4) Unreasonable failure to appreciate the danger involved in use of the product or the consequences thereof and the unreasonable exposure to said danger;

(5) The failure to undertake the precautions a reasonably careful user of the product would take to protect himself against dangers which he would reasonably appreciate under the same or similar circumstances; or

(6) The failure to mitigate damages.

V.A.M.S. 537.765

[3]   Causation

Most courts have imported cause-in-fact and proximate causation doctrines developed in the law of negligence directly to the law of enterprise strict liability. Nevertheless, two points may be emphasized. One, as noted earlier, is that the Restatement formulation carries a specific proximate causation factor in the requirement that the plaintiff prove that the product "is expected to and does reach the user or consumer without substantial change in the condition in which it is sold." In many settings that specific requirement would pose a more definite block to liability than would typical negligence proximate causation analysis. For example, a manufacturer might in some instances anticipate substantial changes in its product but ought nevertheless to foresee that a particular defect might escape detection or correction in the process that intervenes before the final product gets into the hands of the consumer. This appears unnecessarily restrictive, and courts may avoid turning the criterion into a limited no-duty rule by using it only as a factor to be considered in the determination of proximate causation.

The second point is that many courts are perplexed about what defenses apply to defeat an enterprise strict liability action. How, for example, is the defense of contributory negligence to apply? If the prima facie case against a defendant rests primarily upon policy, it confuses the issue to say that a plaintiff will be defeated because of his own faulty behavior. This has led some courts to focus upon proximate causation as the principal basis upon which a plaintiff's case might fail. For example, if a plaintiff were to use a product in some wildly abnormal manner or, if knowing of a product's dangerous propensities, voluntarily were to use the product with full knowledge of the dangerous propensity, a court might resolve the issue by concluding that the defendant need not have foreseen such events. Thus, the chain of proximate causation would be broken. (Alternatively, might this conduct be treated as assumption of risk? *See Bowling v. Heil Company*, 511 N.E.2d 373 (Ohio 1987).)

One difficulty with the proximate causation approach is that it places upon the plaintiff the burden of proving that the chain of proximate causation was not broken. On the other hand, in a negligence action upon the same facts, the matter might be treated as an affirmative defense, placing the burden upon the defendant to prove that the plaintiff was negligent or assumed the risk of harm. Thus, the proximate causation approach makes it difficult to keep the elements of negligence and strict liability conceptually distinct and evidentially consistent.

[4]   Damages

The question of damages need be addressed only briefly. Because negligence and strict liability are both tort causes of action, no doctrinal reason to formulate different rules of compensatory damages presents itself. Despite this, the formulation of the Restatement is self limiting in that it subjects sellers to liability for physical harm thereby caused to the ultimate user or consumer, or to his property. This leaves unanswered whether various forms of incidental economic loss that would be compensable in negligence would also be compensable in strict liability. No good reason to make such a distinction appears on the face of the matter.

Punitive damages are different. Their basic justification is that wrongdoing more culpable than mere negligence may be punished to make an example of the wrongdoer. Because strict liability requires no proof of a defendant's wrongdoing, it would require a drastic departure from settled jurisprudence to permit punitive damages to be awarded as an elemental part of the enterprise strict liability cause of action. Thus, a plaintiff seeking to recover punitive damages should be required to prove that the defendant's conduct was suitably wrongful and not merely that the defendant's product was defective and unreasonably dangerous. Nevertheless, under appropriate pleadings and proofs, punitive damages have been awarded in product strict liability actions. *See, e.g., Owens-Illinois v. Zenobia*, 601 A.2d 633 (Ohio 1987) (requiring clear and convincing evidence of bad faith.)

Should remedies for warranty actions be shaped by forward looking contract doctrines or by backward looking tort doctrines? The conceptual rules of contract damages were laid down in *Hadley v. Baxendale*, 9 Exch. 341, 156 Eng. Rep. 145 (Ex. 1854), and have been elaborated by some courts and statutes to apply where the breach causes physical injury or property damage. For example, Uniform Commercial Code § 2-715 permits recovery for "incidental and consequential damages," including "injury to person or property proximately resulting from any breach of warranty." This seems to exclude pure economic loss, but it remains possible for a court to elaborate the black letter of the code, as was done in *Henningsen.*

[B]   Affirmative Defenses

Both *West v. Caterpillar Tractor* and *Thibault v. Sears Roebuck & Co.* may be criticized in their conceptual approaches to affirmative defenses in enterprise strict liability actions. In *West*, the Florida Supreme Court referred to strict liability as "negligence as a matter of law or negligence per se." This formulation is conceptually erroneous, but stating it that way permitted the court to apply comparative negligence principles to enterprise strict liability actions. Does this mean that a defendant should be permitted to present evidence that he was not negligent at all? Reread *West* to question that point and also to ascertain what kinds of behavior may be used to reduce a plaintiff's recovery. Contrast *Codling v. Paglia*, 298 N.E.2d 622 (N.Y. 1973), as follows:

We . . . hold that, under a doctrine of strict products liability, the manufacturer of a defective product is liable to any person injured or damaged if the defect was a substantial factor in bringing about his injury or damages; provided: (1) that at the time of the occurrence the product is being used (whether by the person injured or damaged or by a third person) for the purpose and in the manner normally intended, (2) that if the person injured or damaged is himself the user of the product, he would not by the exercise of reasonable care have both discovered the defect and perceived its danger, and (3) that by the exercise of reasonable care the person injured or damaged would not otherwise have averted his injury or damages.

. . .

The contributory fault of a plaintiff could be found in use of the product for other than its normally intended purpose or other than in the manner normally intended. This jury was properly charged on this aspect of the case, and its finding in favor of Paglia as plaintiff cannot be disturbed. Or, contributory fault could be found in the failure to exercise such reasonable care as would have disclosed the defect and the danger attributable thereto. Here again there is no basis for a finding of error in the record in this case. There remains, however, the question whether Paglia independently exercised that degree of care for his own safety that a reasonably prudent person would have exercised under the same circumstances, quite apart from the defective steering mechanism. Thus, in this case, the issue whether Paglia as plaintiff had exercised reasonable care in the operation of his automobile, quite separate and distinct from the defective steering mechanism, and if he did not whether such lack of care was a substantial factor in producing his damages, was never submitted to the jury. Our examination of this record discloses that it cannot fairly be said to be entirely barren of evidence which might have supported a jury verdict against Paglia on this combined issue. Accordingly there must be a new trial. . . .

Thibault attempted to avoid confusing the contributory negligence defense with whatever is to be acknowledged as a defense to a strict liability action. To make the distinction, it accepted "plaintiff's misconduct" as a strict liability defense. Unfortunately, the court imbued the new doctrine with negligence concepts when it said, " 'Plaintiff's misconduct' will include, where applicable, product misuse or abnormal use, as well as embodying the 'negligence' or 'assumption of the risk' concepts in our prior cases of voluntarily and unreasonably proceeding to encounter a known danger."

West and *Thibault* are troublesome, because negligence and strict liability are not perfect equivalents. According to Lord Atkin in *Donoghue v. Stevenson*, "The liability for negligence, whether you style it as such or treat it as in other systems as a species of 'culpa,' is no doubt based upon a general public sentiment of moral wrongdoing for which the offender must pay." This "moral wrongdoing" content of common law negligence makes it conceptually awkward to compare a plaintiff's contributory negligence to a defendant's liability under a theory that requires no proof of wrongdoing, such as implied warranty and product strict liability torts. For this reason, and perhaps others, a number of comparative negligence statutes purport to apply only to negligence actions and have been so applied by the courts. Nevertheless, other statutes have been construed to apply to product strict liability actions, and still others expressly incorporate product strict liability actions within the statutory comparisons or openly prescribe more sweeping doctrines of comparative fault, responsibility or culpability to reach beyond negligence actions.

States that permit a melding of the theories accept the premise that juries will not be confused by the theoretical differences between "the 'apples' of negligence and the 'oranges' of strict liability."[7] They essentially leave it to the good sense of the jury to allocate responsibility in proportions suggested by all the evidence. From a practical point of view, this approach is not subject to serious criticism. Instructing juries on the conceptual differences between negligence and strict liability is not a rewarding exercise. But from a conceptual point of view, clarity is desirable. To achieve this, the supreme courts of Florida[8] and Wisconsin[9] adopted

---

[7] *Thibault v. Sears Roebuck & Co.*, 395 A.2d 843 (N.H. 1978), citing *Daley v. General Motors Corp.*, 144 Cal. Rptr. 380, 575 P.2d 1062 (Cal. 1968).

[8] *West v. Caterpillar Tractor Co.*, 336 So. 2d 80 (Fla. 1976).

the expedient of defining strict liability as a mere species of negligence. Although wrong by generally accepted standards, this merger neatly solves the conceptual problem.

By contrast to the redefinition approach, the Texas Supreme Court formulated a doctrine of comparative causation to apportion responsibility between a strictly liable defendant and a negligent plaintiff. Under the comparative causation approach, "the trier of fact must . . . determine the respective percentages (totalling 100%) by which these two concurring causes contributed to bring about the event.[10] Although comparative causation may be conceptually sounder than comparative fault, it too requires an artificial jury determination. If each of two causes is a necessary cause in the sense that harm would not have occurred in its absence (the "but-for" test), how can it be said that one cause is proportionately greater than the other?

To avoid the problem of matching irreconcilable doctrines, might a system of duty be imposed upon product users to guard potential strict liability defendants against unnecessary liability from defective products? This duty may be referred to as the "plaintiff's duty to prevent harm." Consider the following jury instruction:

Each person has a duty to prevent harm when using or consuming a product supplied by someone else. This includes the duty not to expose suppliers and manufacturers to losses in paying for injuries and damages that would not occur if the duty to prevent harm is observed. The duty may be breached if a plaintiff did not discover a defect that you believe a reasonable person should have discovered under the circumstances, or if the plaintiff discovered the defect and thereafter did not use the care a reasonable person should have used to prevent harm. The burden of proving that the plaintiff breached the duty to prevent harm rests upon the defendant, and if the evidence does not persuade you that the duty was breached, then you must not diminish the plaintiff's damages.

If you find that the plaintiff breached the duty to prevent harm, then you must decide how the losses should be apportioned between the plaintiff and the defendants based upon your evaluation of all the evidence in this case that goes to the justice of the matter. You should express your conclusion in percentage of harm apportioned to the plaintiff and percentage apportioned to the defendants collectively. The sum must be 100%. For example, if you apportion 50% of the harm to the defendants, then 50% would be assigned the plaintiff, and the amount of recovery would be full losses as found by you minus 50%.[11]

Although no state appears to have employed the foregoing proposal in its precise terms for treating this issue, some states do not bar a plaintiff's claim or diminish recovery in a product strict liability action if the plaintiff's only wrong was not to discover a product defect. Those jurisdictions would exclude the words "if a plaintiff did not discover a defect that you believe a reasonable person should have under the circumstances" from the proposed instruction.

The proposed approach would permit juries to award damages ranging from full recovery to nothing. It is essentially a doctrineless approach to comparative

[9] *Dippel v. Sciano*, 37 Wis. 2d 443, 155 N.W.2d 55, 64–65 (1967).

[10] *Duncan v. Cessna Aircraft Co.*, 665 S.W.2d 414 (Tex. 1984).

[11] J. Little, A Rationalization of the Law of Product Liability, 36 Fla. L. Rev. 27 (1984).

responsibility. The comparative fault statutes of Minnesota[12] and Washington[13] definefault to include "unreasonable failure to avoid an injury." Is this equivalent to the proposed approach? Most states follow different approaches.[14]

Numerous courts have concluded that many forms of assumption of risk are nothing more than contributory negligence, and have treated them as comparative defenses rather than as a distinct complete bar to recovery. *See Thibault, supra, Meistrich v. Casino Arena Enterprises, Inc.*, 155 A.2d 90 (N.J. 1959), and *Blackburn v. Dorta*, 348 So. 2d 287 (Fla. 1977). As generous to plaintiffs as that may be, that version of the assumption of risk does not square with its independent historical development.

Among the states that subsume strict liability within the comparisons by adopting a broader comparative fault principle are Arkansas, Maine, Minnesota, Oregon, Washington and Hawaii. The Hawaii approach is notable because although the Hawaii comparative fault statute applies modified comparative principles to negligence actions, the Hawaii Supreme Court imposed pure comparative principles to product strict liability actions. *Larson v. Pacesetter Systems, Inc.*, 837 P.2d 1273, 1289 (Haw. 1992).

Among the states that have applied comparative causation principles in some context are Texas and Utah.

Among states that do not consider contributory negligence to be a defense to product strict liability actions are Georgia, Montana and South Dakota.

Assumption of risk derives from the doctrine volenti non fit injuria, whose common law origins far antedate the law of negligence. The sense of volenti is that one who consents to injury will not be heard to complain in court. In the United States this has become known in negligence law as the voluntary assumption of a known and appreciated risk, but in England it retains its more general common law form. In any event, the concept of consent to harm is clearly independent of the concept of heedlessness or indifference to harm. Consequently, a court might appropriately acknowledge volenti as a separate, total defense to an enterprise strict liability action. Given such a defense, a defendant would be entitled to have the jury instructed that if the plaintiff was volens and consented to the harm, then the plaintiff should recover nothing. Whether the court would use standard assumption of risk phraseology or something else would be a matter of local choice. Whom should the burden of consent be upon? Although a court might adopt the foregoing course, would it also be appropriate to reject such a separate defense in favor of an encompassing comparative negligence defense that runs from all to nothing? The doctrine of assumption of risk as a bar to a product strict liability claim was applied in *Bowling v. Heil Company*, 511 N.E.2d 373 (Ohio 1987).

Although this analysis has focused upon enterprise strict liability, it applies fortiorari to breach of warranty causes of action because of their contractual basis. *See, e.g., Karl v. Bryant Air Conditioning Co.*, 331 N.W.2d 456 (Mich. 1982).

---

[12] 6 Minn. Stats. Ann. § 605.01 Subd. 1a (1978).

[13] Wash. Rev. Code Ann. 4.22.010 (8).

[14] Among the states that apply comparative negligence principles to product strict liability actions are California, Florida, Hawaii, Idaho, Kansas, Louisiana, Mississippi, Nebraska, New Jersey and Wisconsin.

[C]   Contribution and Indemnification

Contrary to the common law, all states now permit contribution among joint defendants in some circumstances. How is the adjustment to be done when the liability of all defendants rests upon enterprise strict liability? And how is it to be done when some defendants are strictly liable but others are liable in negligence or warranty?

Is there a reason to abandon the indemnification theory that did operate at common law? That is, if one tortfeasor is liable solely on technical grounds, as when the owner of a motor vehicle is held vicariously liable for the negligent driving of the operator, should the technically liable but otherwise innocent tortfeasor be permitted to transfer the entire loss to the truly culpable tortfeasor? Most courts have answered this question in the affirmative. Nevertheless, indemnification may seldom apply to aid enterprise strict liability defendants and should not be permitted to undermine enterprise liability. For example, a product might be defective and unreasonably dangerous because an employee of the employer negligently misassembled it. If this could be proved, the plaintiff could maintain a negligence action against the employee and the employer. The latter's liability would be under the doctrine of respondeat superior. Independently, the employer would also be liable under the doctrine of enterprise strict liability. Should a strictly liable employer be permitted to shift the entire loss to the actively negligent employee? How well does the following case address this issue?

SKINNER v. REED-PRENTICE DIVISION
Illinois Supreme Court
70 Ill. 2d 1, 374 N.E.2d 437 (1978)

GOLDENHERSH, JUSTICE:

Plaintiff, Rita Rae Skinner, a minor, by Virginia Skinner, her mother and next friend, filed this action in the circuit court of Cook County seeking to recover damages for personal injuries suffered as the result of the alleged malfunction of an injection molding machine manufactured by defendant, Reed-Prentice Division Package Machinery Co. (hereafter manufacturer). The manufacturer filed a third-party complaint seeking contribution from the third-party defendant, Hinckley Plastic, Inc. (hereafter employer), by whom plaintiff was employed at the time of her injuries. The circuit court allowed the employer's motion to dismiss the third-party complaint, the appellate court affirmed (40 Ill.App.3d 99, 351 N.E.2d 405), and we allowed the manufacturer's petition for leave to appeal. The pleadings are adequately reviewed in the appellate court opinion, and it suffices here to state that plaintiff seeks to recover on the basis of strict liability in tort while the third-party complaint alleges negligence on the part of the employer. The relief asked by the manufacturer in its third-party complaint is "that if judgment be entered in favor of the plaintiff and against it that judgment be entered against the third party defendant and in favor of third party plaintiff in such amount, by way of contribution, as would be commensurate with the degree of misconduct attributable to the third party defendant in causing plaintiff's injuries."

In its dismissal order the circuit court observed that in Gertz v. Campbell, 55 Ill. 2d 84, 302 N.E.2d 40, this court "indicated that it might adopt the New York rule, because it stated, citing the Dole case [Dole v. Dow Chemical Co. (1972), 30 N.Y.2d 143, 331 N.Y.S.2d 382, 282 N.E.2d 288] 'to illustrate, there can and should be a continuing search for better solutions. The Court of Appeals of New York has recently supplanted this active-passive negligence criteria from indemnitee with one founded on equitable principles.' "It concluded, however, "that there is no decision in this state allowing contribution under the facts pleaded in the third party complaint." In affirming the judgment, the appellate court concluded that "a decision to apply theories of contribution in the instant case would require substantive and procedural formulations beyond the authority of this court" and that the issue presented was "the type of issue which should be decided by the highest court of this State . . . " 40 Ill. App. 3d

The manufacturer argues that no decision of this court prohibits contribution between tortfeasors; that where the tort was not intentionally committed, sound public policy requires that contribution between tortfeasors be permitted; that a manufacturer held liable on the basis of strict liability in tort should have a right of contribution against others who contributed to cause the injuries; and that if this court should adopt a rule of contribution, it should be based on the relative degree of fault rather than on the basis of equal apportionment among the number of wrongdoers. The employer argues that the long-established rule in this jurisdiction among tortfeasors; that the only exception to the general rule is that a "passive" tortfeasor may obtain indemnity from an "active" tortfeasor; and that a manufacturer held strictly liable in tort cannot seek indemnity from the employer for the reason that public policy requires that the manufacturer's liability be considered "active."

. . .

As the court, quoting from Prosser, Torts 278 (3d ed. 1964), observed in Suvada v. White Motor Co., 32 Ill. 2d 612, 624, 210 N.E.2d 182, 188: "There is an important distinction between contribution, which distributes the loss among the tortfeasors by requiring each to pay his proportionate share, and indemnity, which shifts the entire loss from one tortfeasor who has been compelled to pay it to the shoulders of another who should bear it instead." In Nelson v. Cook, 17 Ill. 443, an action by a sheriff against a judgment creditor to recover the sum he was compelled to pay for the conversion of another's property, this court, considering the distinction for the first time, said: "The principle laid down in Merryweather v. Nixan [(1799), 101 Eng. Rep. 1337], 8 Term R. 186, that there is no right of contribution as between tortfeasors, or trespassers, has been, and still is, recognized as unquestionable law. But this does not affect the right of indemnity where a right of indemnity exists." (17 Ill. 443, 449.) Based on the facts before it the court held that the sheriff had no right of implied indemnity.

This court has candidly recognized that the concept of implied indemnity, based on the active- passive negligence-doctrine, "has been utilized to mitigate the harsh effects that could result from an inflexible application of this judicially created bar to contribution." (Muhlbauer v. Kruzel, 39 Ill. 2d 226, 230, 234 N.E.2d 790, 792.) The application of this all or nothing liability based on terms of active-passive negligence, which "have not obtained precise judicial definition" (see Carver v. Grossman, 55 Ill. 2d 507, 511, 305 N.E.2d 161, 163), to the ever increasing situations where there is some fault attributable to both parties produces harsh effects without uniformity of result.

. . .

We are of the opinion that there is no valid reason for the continued existence of the no- contribution rule and many compelling arguments against it. We agree with Dean Prosser that "[t]here is obvious lack of sense and justice in a rule which permits the entire burden of a loss, for which two defendants were equally, unintentionally responsible, to be shouldered onto one alone, according to the accident of a successful levy of execution, the existence of liability insurance, the plaintiff's whim or spite, or his collusion with the other wrongdoer, while the latter goes scot free." (Prosser, Torts sec. 50, at 307 (4th ed. 1971).

The employer argues that the abolition of the no-contribution rule would produce substantial change in the fabric of tort law and substantial changes are best left to the General Assembly. Where this court has created a rule or doctrine which, under present conditions, we consider unsound and unjust, we have not only the power, but the duty, to modify or abolish it. For the purposes of the motion to dismiss, the allegations of fact in the third-party complaint must be taken as true (Acorn Auto Driving School, Inc. v. Board of Education, 27 Ill. 2d 93, 96, 187 N.E.2d 722), and on these facts the governing equitable principles require that ultimate liability for plaintiff's injuries be apportioned on the basis of the relative degree to which the defective product and the employer's conduct proximately caused them. . . .

Citing Texaco, Inc. v. McGrew Lumber Co., 117 Ill. App. 2d 351, 254 N.E.2d 584, Kossifos v. Louden Machinery Co., 22 Ill. App. 3d 587, 317 N.E.2d 749, and Burke v. Sky Climber, Inc., 57 Ill. 2d 542, 316 N.E.2d 516, the employer argues that a defendant held strictly liable in tort is precluded from seeking contribution "because public policy requires that its liability to an original plaintiff be considered active" and that the duty imposed in strict liability is more stringent than in cases involving negligence. We do not agree. The public policy considerations which motivated the adoption of strict liability (see Suvada v. White Motor Co., 32 Ill. 2d 612, 210 N.E.2d 182) were that the economic loss suffered by the user should be imposed on the one who created the risk and reaped the profit, including everyone from the manufacturer on through to the seller or any one of them. When the economic loss of the user has been imposed on a defendant in a strict liability action the policy considerations of Suvada are satisfied and the ordinary equitable principles governing the concepts of indemnity or contribution are to be applied. Thus, in Liberty Mutual Insurance Co. v. Williams Machine & Tool Co., 62 Ill. 2d 77, 338 N.E.2d 857, where the assembler of the product, who had settled strict liability actions against it, filed an indemnity action against the producer of the defective component part, the court adopted a rule for indemnification in the manufacturer-distributor-seller chain. After noting that the policy reasons for adopting strict liability in Suvada were not the same as those determining the ultimate liability in the manufacturer-distributor chain, the court, in effect, put the assembler in the shoes of the user and the producer into the shoes of the assembler in order for the assembler to shift the full economic loss to the producer. The court said: "In our judgment, the rule we are adopting is a logical and necessary [and equitable] extension of the principles enunciated in Suvada and Williams. It does not impose an undue burden on defendant and those similarly situated, for it is they who originated the defective product. Nor does it make them absolute insurers of the safety of their products. Plaintiffs in such indemnity actions must still prove the necessary elements of a strict liability action — that the product contained a defective condition which existed at the time it left defendant's control, rendering the product unreasonably dangerous and proximately causing the injury resulting in plaintiff's liability to the injured party. [Suvada theory of strict liability from seller through manufacturer.] And while proof of an indemnitee's negligence will not serve to bar a strict liability indemnity claim, proof that he misused the product or assumed the risk of the defect will be an effective bar to recovery." 62 Ill. 2d 77, 84–85, 338 N.E.2d 857, 861.

Misuse of the product or assumption of the risk by a user will serve to bar his recovery . . . and indemnity is not available to one who misuses the product or assumes the risk of its use . . . We are of the opinion that if the manufacturer's third-party complaint alleges that the employer's misuse of the product or assumption of the risk of its use contributed to cause plaintiff's injuries, the manufacturer has stated a cause of action for contribution. The fact that the employee's action against the employer is barred by the Workmen's Compensation Act (Ill. Rev. Stat.1975, ch. 48, pars. 138.5, 138.11) would not preclude the manufacturer's third-party action against the employer for indemnification (Miller v. DeWitt, 37 Ill. 2d 273, 226 N.E.2d 630) and should not serve to bar its action for contribution.

We hold that the third-party complaint, although pleaded in terms of negligence, alleges misuse of the product and assumption of risk on the part of the employer and states a cause of action for contribution based on the relative degree to which the defective product and the employer's misuse of the product or its assumption of the risk contributed to cause plaintiff's injuries. For the reasons stated, the judgments of the appellate and circuit courts are reversed and the cause is remanded to the circuit court of Cook County for further proceedings consistent with this opinion.

Reversed and Remanded.

WARD, CHIEF JUSTICE, dissenting:

I must dissent from the judgment of the court . . . reversing the dismissal of the third-party complaints.

The situation in which the doctrine of contribution properly has been applied is that in which the independent acts of two or more tortfeasors (among whom there exists no antecedent express or implied agreement of indemnity) combine to produce a single, indivisible injury, and where each party, unlike the situation here, is liable to the plaintiff in tort on the ground of negligence or of strict liability. (Prosser, Torts 309 (4th ed. 1971).) The majority correctly observes that such cases do not lend themselves readily to a qualitative analysis of tortious conduct as "active" or "passive," as the indemnity theory requires.

Yet in Skinner the majority predicates its proposal for allowance of contribution among tortfeasors on the theory that the "ultimate liability for plaintiff's injuries be apportioned on the basis of the relative degree to which the defective product and the employer's conduct proximately caused them." (70 Ill. 2d at 14, 15 Ill. Dec. at 834, 374 N.E.2d at 442.) Although the majority opinion does not elaborate on its meaning, this standard suggests some quantitative comparison, such as 60 percent to 40 percent, instead of the qualitative comparison of active and passive made in the indemnity cases. The majority does not show that the determination of what percentage of the plaintiff's damages should be attributable to each tortfeasor will prove any more manageable than the active-passive test used for indemnity.

There are a few jurisdictions in which the amount of the contribution between joint tortfeasors is based on the relative fault of each tortfeasor. . . . As Prosser observes, the usual method of distributing the loss, however, has been to divide the total damages pro rata without regard to comparative fault. That is the method adopted under the current provisions of the Uniform Contribution Among Tortfeasors Act as revised in 1955. (12 Uniform Laws Annotated secs. 1(b), (2).) Of the 18 jurisdictions which have adopted either the 1955 uniform act or its 1939 predecessor, some 13 appear to use the pro rata approach. . . . The conceptual basis for pro rata contribution is of course that one tortfeasor has discharged an obligation for which the other tortfeasor was also liable.

In any event, the majority's rule of apportionment should not have application in these cases. The plaintiffs are proceeding against the defendant manufacturers on the theory of strict liability, and of course negligence or its absence is not a factor in determining the liability of the defendants. These defendants thus may be without culpability in the sense that they were non-negligent. The majority says that the extent of liability among tortfeasors should be determined by their relative roles in proximately causing the plaintiffs' injuries, but it seems to me that this formula cannot properly be applied in the absence of common standard of comparison. The plaintiffs seek to recover on the ground of strict liability; the defendants in their third-party complaints allege negligence by the employers. What will be the method of comparison, with negligence not a factor in determining the defendants' liability?

. . .

UNDERWOOD, JUSTICE, dissenting:

. . .

DOOLEY, JUSTICE, dissenting:

Today we have buried a great body of Illinois law. . . .

Contribution and indemnity have been commingled as if they were identical. Each is a precept wholly different from the other. . . .

. . .

That strict liability is not based on fault is well recognized. In Suvada v. White Motor Co. (1965), 32 Ill. 2d 612, 210 N.E.2d 182, where this State adopted the doctrine as well as section 402A of the Restatement (Second) of Torts (1965), such considerations as public interest in human life and health, the manufacturer's solicitations to purchase, and the justice of imposing liability on one who creates the risk and reaps the profit, are described as the motivating forces for the adoption of the doctrine. . . .

. . .

Under strict liability, responsibility is imposed because of the character of the product, not because of fault. . . . Under the Restatement of the Law of Torts, it is immaterial that the manufacturer has "exercised all possible care in the preparation and sale of his product." Restatement (Second) of Torts sec. 402A(2) (a) (1965) . . .

. . .

Contributory negligence on the part of the user is not an issue. . . . It should be crystal clear that negligence or any other concept of fault is anathematic to the tenets of strict liability.

It is clear that the objectives of the doctrine are to protect the consumer and to make responsible the manufacturers who put in commerce unreasonably dangerous products which cause injury. If these goals are to be accomplished, ultimate liability for injury from the defective product must rest on the manufacturer. Thus, liability has been permitted to flow from the retailer . . . to reach the manufacturer or from the manufacturer of the defective product to the manufacturer of the component part which made the finished product defective. . . .

These were the compelling reasons why the obligation to produce a reasonably safe product was made nondelegable. . . . Non-delegable means that the obligation cannot be transferred to others.

It would frustrate the intent of strict liability to permit the manufacturer of the unreasonably dangerous, injury-causing product to pass on his liability to another so that the maker might either be indemnified or obtain some contribution.

The majority opinion treats strict liability as if the manufacturer's responsibility were predicated upon negligence concepts. All cases and surveys referred to in the majority opinion to support its position involve negligent tortfeasors. Dole v. Dow Chemical Co. (1972), 30 N.Y.2d 143, 331 N.Y.S.2d 382, 282 N.E.2d 288, the only products case cited, was an action predicated against the manufacturer on negligence not strict liability. Plaintiff's action there was against a chemical company for negligently labeling a fumigant used by an employer. The manufacturer's third-party action against the employer was for breach of an independent duty owed plaintiff.

. . .

The third-party complaint alleges that plaintiff's injuries resulted from a combination of the conduct of both defendants, so that they were co-tortfeasors. As we have seen, the manufacturer's liability arises not from his conduct but from putting into commerce an unreasonably dangerous product. Nor, as has been pointed out, can an employer be a co-tortfeasor under the Workmen's Compensation Act.

I am realistic enough to know that in every instance where an employee is injured, the manufacturer of a defective, injury-causing product, to avoid liability or spread the risk, will charge the employer with multiple aspects of negligence. The negligence may be in failing to instruct the employee as to the use of the product or in not having an adequate number of persons engaged in the operation in which the product was employed. Again, it may be in not inspecting the product for defects, although such inspection is not required under the doctrine of strict liability. (Restatement (Second) of Torts sec. 402A, Comment n (1965); Sweeney v. Max A. R. Matthews Co, (1968), 94 Ill. App. 2d 6, 21, 236 N.E.2d 439, aff'd (1970), 46 Ill. 2d 64, 264 N.E.2d 170.) Or it may be in buying a machine which the manufacturer saw fit to sell without protective components as was the case in Robinson v. International Harvester Co. (1977), 70 Ill. 2d 47, 15 Ill. Dec. 850, 374 N.E.2d 458. Yet this is but an example of putting into commerce an unreasonably dangerous product. The aspects of negligence which the fertile mind of the skilled trial lawyer will conjure are countless.

. . .

While the majority's position may appear to demonstrate "kitchen equity," it clashes with those precepts which govern our actions, those of inferior courts, and last, but certainly not least, those of the litigants. Legal principles are not mere hollow sounds. They create rights, define obligations, and determine the mechanics for the realization of such rights and obligations. Principles, it must never be forgotten, have a pragmatic effect on the law in action. The admissibility of all evidence is determined by principles, common law or statutory, which control the particular action. So also the fact-finder, be it court or jury, is governed by principles in arriving at its conclusion.

The underlying concept of the majority is that equity and fairness dictate its conclusion. Apart from the fact that principles must control, one court, in denying the manufacturer of a defective product indemnity against the employer of injured employees, made these pithy observations:

It is argued that if indemnity is not allowed the result is manifestly inequitable since the jury found Outboard to be only twenty-five percent at fault while the employers each were found to be thirty-seven and one-half percent at fault. Consequently, as a matter of fairness, the employers should not be insulated completely. Although this contention has some appeal, it is one to be submitted to the legislature rather than to us. To date, the legislature has insulated the contributing employer and has voided indemnity absent an independent duty owing from the employer to the third party. (Outboard Marine Corp. v. Schupbach) (1977), Nev., 561 P.2d 450, 454.

Many will undoubtedly urge that the contentions of the majority are for the legislature. I only know they are not for us. We must be governed by reason, not sentiment. We have no license to experiment with novel concepts because they might appeal to a personal sense of justice.

. . .

Contribution is the distribution or the spreading of a loss between two or more persons who are jointly liable for having committed a tort against a third party. In accordance with the general rule, one who is compelled to pay the whole or more than his just share of the loss, upon which several persons are liable, is entitled to contribution against the others from the payment of their respective shares. . . .

Indemnity, on the other hand, shifts the entire loss from one tortfeasor to another who, by express contract or by operation of law, is deemed responsible for making full payment. . . .

We have already noted how contribution and indemnity, two distinct concepts, are often confused. . . .

The apparent effect of the majority is to abolish indemnity. "Total indemnification" (Robinson), "partial indemnification" (Skinner and Stevens) and "contribution" are all treated interchangeably.

Absent from the majority opinion is any definition of what constitutes contribution or "partial indemnity." Wanting also are guidelines for what the court holds. Standards will be impossible to formulate in the absence of some clear definition of the position of the majority other than the abolition of the rule of no contribution. An opinion so wide-sweeping in character must offer something constructive. Opened up, but unresolved, are a series of important queries.

What is the status of the tortfeasor who had a right to bona fide indemnity, not contribution? Has this right been impaired? Has the active-passive criterion of implied indemnity been abolished?

Suppose one tortfeasor enters into a settlement with the plaintiff. Is he entitled to recover contribution from other defendants whose liability remains vital, notwithstanding the settlement? Or what about the insurer who discharges the liability of its tortfeasor insured? Is it subrogated to a right of contribution?

What will be the vehicle of apportionment of damages between wrongdoers? Will it be by third-party action, by counterclaim between defendants, by independent actions, or by all such vehicles?

What is the basis of contribution? Will it be according to a payment of more than a pro rata share? Or will it be on the basis of "pure" contribution with the amount of fault being determined at 100%? The majority opinion has an ethereal mystique so that neither judges nor lawyers can know how to give it meaning.

When a court undertakes to announce a new doctrine which is a departure from the past not only in principle but in practice, it would seem it has the obligation to spell out in detail how this new teaching shall be put into practice. *See* Hoffman v. Jones (Fla. 1973), 280 So. 2d 431, and Li v. Yellow Cab Co. (1975), 13 Cal. 3d 804, 119 Cal. Rptr. 858, 532 P.2d 1226, where the Florida and California Supreme Courts, in adopting by judicial fiat comparative negligence, spelled out in detail how the doctrine shall be applied.

I predict that this trio, Skinner, Stevens and Robinson, will generate a proliferation of much merit-less litigation. Every action against the manufacturer or retailer in strict liability in tort will mean another action whereby the manufacturer or retailer will seek "indemnity" or "contribution" against some third party outside the distributive chain, so that the manufacturer's responsibility may be taken over or at least shared.

Proliferation of such litigation is unwholesome. The trial of a lawsuit against the manufacturer in strict liability, with the manufacturer focusing on the negligence of the employer, will be complex. The manufacturer will use the employer's negligence as a defense to the original action — the objective of the third-party actions before us. More than that, such litigation will fill the halls of justice with obstacles, make litigation an even rarer luxury, and add additional trial days to a docket already struggling under a near fatal burden.

Like Jefferson, I believe "law and institutions must go hand in hand with the progress of the human mind." Like Jefferson, I do not believe in deviation from recognized principles for expediency. This is far too violent a wrench in the law.

The effect of the majority's opinion will be far reaching unless the General Assembly manifests greater wisdom than this court. A statute insulating the employer from all liability to the employee other than for workmen's compensation benefits, including third-party actions is needed for the preservation of the employer. He should not be saddled with the responsibilities of the manufacturers.

NOTE AND QUESTION

Skinner merely brushes the surface of the difficulty allocations that may arise when multiple defendants have been found liable to a product liability claimant, perhaps on different theories. How do you apportion liability among, for example, a negligent retailer, a strictly liable distributor and a strictly liable manufacturer? Under its "comparative causation" principles the Texas Supreme Court has said: "Comparative causation does not affect the right of a retailer or other member of the marketing chain to receive indemnity from the manufacturer of the defective product when the retailer or other member of the marketing chain is merely a conduit for the defective product and is not independently culpable." *Duncan v. Cessna Aircraft Co.*, 665 S.W.2d 414 (Tex. 1984). The modern apportionment statutes in many states prescribe rules to be followed. In general, the Restatement of the Law of Torts (Third) provides this guidance:

§ 17. Apportionment Of Responsibility Between Or Among Plaintiff, Sellers And Distributors Of Defective Products, And Others

(a) A plaintiff's recovery of damages for harm caused by a product defect may be reduced if the conduct of the plaintiff combines with the product defect to cause the harm and the plaintiff's conduct fails to conform to generally applicable rules establishing appropriate standards of care.

(b) The manner and extent of the reduction under Subsection (a) and the apportionment of plaintiff's recovery among multiple defendants are governed by generally applicable rules apportioning responsibility.

Does this help?

Chapter 15

TORTIOUS DAMAGE TO INTERESTS IN PROPERTY

§ 15.01 TRESPASS

PROBLEM A

Tom Smith, a cabbie who owned and operated his own taxi under the name "Smith Cab," picked up a passenger at the bus station in downtown Anytown. The passenger, a 30-to-35-year-old male of about "average size," loaded himself and a duffel bag into the back seat and asked to be taken to 206 York Road. Upon arriving at the address, which was in a sparsely populated area of town, Smith drove the cab into the driveway. Before Smith could switch off the key and engage the parking brake, the passenger jammed a hard cold object into the back of his neck and said "Don't move or talk! Get out of the car and leave your cash on the seat." Glancing in the mirror, Smith saw that it was an umbrella handle that was against his neck. He then tried to grab the umbrella but missed it and then was struck with a hard object. Smith was knocked unconscious, and the unbraked car rolled down the driveway, picking up speed until it struck the house. The gas line on the cab ruptured, and the gas spilled onto the hot car engine and ignited. The fire quickly spread to the house, which was destroyed.

Smith was saved by John Jarman, owner of the house, who pulled him out before flames engulfed the cab. The passenger broke his leg trying to get out of the moving cab and was captured by the police soon thereafter. He was later convicted of several crimes.

Jarman brings an action against Smith in trespass, seeking compensation for damage done to his property. Who should prevail? Why?

[A]   Introduction

Letang v. Cooper, Chapter 3, *supra*, examined the historic separation of the law of negligence and the law of intentional wrongs, as applied in bodily injury actions, as the two emerged from their ancestors, *trespass vi et armis* and trespass on the case. As Denning, M.R. observed, modern law generally permits one cause of action, not two, depending upon the quality of the defendant's state of mind. Thus, in personal injury actions, the old common law distinction between direct harm and consequential harm has been rendered legally obsolete in favor of the new distinction between negligence and intention.

As the cases in this section demonstrate, a fully equivalent modernization of the law has not occurred in *trespass quare clasum fregit* and *trespass vi et armis*, as they apply to real property interests, and *trespass de bonis asportatus*, as it applies to personal property. Although the complete Latin names are seldom used nowadays, the underlying causes of action survive under the designations trespass to land and trespass to chattel, or the equivalent. It remains true, however, that most property damage actions are brought under the law of negligence, indicating at least a permissive absorption of the old trespass cases into the law of negligence. Nevertheless, a remedy may be available in trespass under circumstances in which negligence would fail. When would a negligence action fail?

[B] The Gravamen of Trespass

DUMONT v. MILLER
[1873] 4 A.J.R. 152 (Vic. S.Ct. F.C.)[1]

The respondent, Thomas Miller, was sued by M. Dumont, a vigneron at Nunawading, for a trespass on the plaintiff's property. It was proved that the defendant had, with a pack of beagles, entered upon the plaintiff's property in pursuit of a hare, but no actual damage had been done to the plaintiff. At the County Court a verdict was returned for the defendant, but it was submitted that this verdict was wrong, and that as the defendant was proved to have trespassed, the verdict should be for the plaintiff.

The Court concurred with this view, and directed a verdict for the plaintiff, damages 1s.

(1) See also *Wernberg v. Matanuska Elec. Ass'n*, 494 P.2d 790 (Alaska 1972) holding that a jury need not award actual damages to remedy a "technical trespass" that was "nondeliberate" and caused not actual damages. Similarly, *Hawke v. Maus*, 226 N.E.2d 713 (Ind. App. 1967) stated this rule:

> In an action of trespass quare clausum fregit, it is necessary for the plaintiff to prove only that he was in possession of the land and that the defendant entered thereon without right, such proof entitling the plaintiff to nominal damages without proof of injury, and upon additional proof of injury to products of the soil, the plaintiff is entitled to compensatory damages.

Id., 226 N.E. at 717.

(2) Nevertheless, a trespasser's motivation for intentionally entering the land of another is ordinarily legally irrelevant. *Hawke v. Maus* also stated these principles:

> It is true that in an action of trespass the intention of the defendant in making the entry or intrusion is immaterial. This proposition is strongly urged by appellee who cites two Indiana cases as authority. There are many decisions in Indiana setting forth this cardinal principle of trespass. However, a careful reading of these decisions will disclose that in each the entry was based upon a voluntary act of the defendant. This distinction is best described by the scholars.
>
> > 'In order to be liable for a trespass on land under the rule stated in s 158, it is necessary only that the actor intentionally be upon any part of the land in question. It is not necessary that he intend to invade the possessor's interest in the exclusive possession of his land and, therefore, that he know his entry to be an intrusion.' 1 Restatement, Second, Torts, s 164, Comment (a), p. 296 (1965).

---

[1] [Ed. — Australian Juridical Reporter, decision of the Full Court of the Supreme Court of Victoria.]

'The intention which is required to make the actor liable under the rule stated in this Section is an intention to enter upon the particular piece of land in question, irrespective of whether the actor knows or should know that he is not entitled to enter.' 1 Restatement, Second, Torts, s 163, Comment (b), p. 294 (1965); 1 Restatement, Second, Torts, s 158, p. 277 (1965).

Id., 226 N.E. at 715, 716. In *Goulding v. Cook*, 661 N.E. 1322 (Mass. 1966), a plaintiff in good faith and supported by objective facts built a septic tank on land whose ownership was disputed and then in litigation. The septic tank was to serve the plaintiff's home which was located on property that the plaintiff undisputably owned. The litigation proved that the other person was the true owner. Under these facts, the court required the landowner to remove the septic tank and pay damages caused by the trespass. The court indicated that a landowner might be required to accommodate a slight innocent intrusions even if permanent but held that this was not such a case.

In contrast, where the entry is entirely negligent, as when a driver is involved in a collision and the crash impels a car onto the property of another, there is no trespass and recovery is governed by the law of negligence. *Hawke v. Maus, supra.*

(3) Suppose a person is required to enter the land of another in order to avoid a threat of eminent injury? *Rossi v. DelDuca*, 181 N.E.2d 591 (Mass. 1962) involved an eight year old girl who was being chased by a vicious dog. She attempted to escape by running through the land of the defendant to the safety of her home. The defendant's vicious great Danes attached and mauled her until she was rescued by her father. The eight year old sued the owner of the great Danes who defended on the grounds that the girl was a trespasser. The court rejected this defense:

This evidence brings the case, we think, within the principle that one is privileged to enter land in the possession of another if it is, or reasonably appears to be, necessary to prevent serious harm to the actor or his property. Restatement 2d: Torts, Tent. draft no. 2, 1958, § 197. This privilege not only relieves the intruder from liability for technical trespass (*Carter v. Thurston*, 58 N.H. 104; *Ploof v. Putnam*, 81 Vt. 471, 71 A. 188, 20 L.R.A., N.S., 152; *Boutwell v. Champlain Realty Co.*, 89 Vt. 80, 94 A. 108. . . . but it also destroys the possessor's immunity from liability in resisting the intrusion. *Ploof v. Putnam*, 81 Vt. 471, 71 A. 188, 20 L.R.A.,N.S., 152. See Bohlen, Incomplete Privilege to Inflict Intentional Invasions of Interests of Property & Personality, 39 Harv.L.Rev. 307. 'The important difference between the status of one who is a trespasser on land and one who is on the land pursuant to an imcomplete privilege is that the latter is entitled to be on the land and therefore the possessor of the land is under a duty to permit him to come and remain there and hence is not privileged to resist.' Restatement 2d: Torts, Tent. draft no. 2, 1958, § 197, comment k.

Id., 181 N.E.2d 593, 594. The sparse authority on the subject suggests that although a landowner may not exclude another from entering property under such an emergency, the landowner may recover for actual injury the unauthorized entry inflicts upon the landowner's interests. *Campbell v. Race*, 61 Mass. 408 (1851) and *Vincent v. Lake Erie Transp. Co.*, 124 N.W. 221 (Minn. 1910).

HUDSON v. NICHOLSON
[1839] 5 M. & W. 437, 151 Eng. Rep. 185[2]

[To shore up the walls of his own building, the defendant placed a supporting structure upon the land of another person. No consent was received from the second person. Subsequently, that land came into the possession of the plaintiff, who demanded of the defendant that the structure be removed from his property. The defendant refused. Thereafter, the plaintiff brought an action, which the defendant contested on grounds, in part, that the cause of action had arisen in favor of the plaintiff's predecessor in possession and should not be enforced by the present plaintiff. This reflected a general rule that certain causes of action are personal and cannot be assigned to or enforced by anyone else. The defendant also objected that the plaintiff had mispleaded the action in case. The plaintiff prevailed at trial, and on appeal the defendant sought a rule in arrest of judgment.]

LORD ABINGER, C.B.

I was at first disposed to think that the judgment ought to be arrested in this case, on the ground I have already stated in the course of the argument. I still adhere to the opinion that this is properly the ground of an action of trespass, and not case. It is not similar to those cases that have been cited, of trespass to a person, chattel, where trespass and case are concurrent remedies, and where a party may waive the trespass and go for the consequential damage; as for instance in the case of an asportation of goods, where trover may at all times be maintained. A party may even bring trover to try the right to coal mines; but those cases contain distinct causes of action, and are not analogous to an action brought for a trespass to the soil, which is continued. The whole of this declaration shows that these timbers were put into the soil of the plaintiff for the purpose of supporting the defendant's house, and they were continued there by the defendant himself, rendering him substantially a trespasser, as much as if he had stuck a pole in the land of the plaintiff. It is specially assigned as ground of complaint that the plaintiff could not remove the shores without pulling down the deffendant's house; but it is for the defendant to show that his house would be thereby injured. I think, therefore, that this is substantially a trespass. Then it is ingeniously argued by Mr. Rawlinson, that this count is a good count in trespass after verdict; that the declaration, although not in artificial language a declaration of trespass, yet contains in reality a charge of trespass. Then the only difficulty on this point is the writ of summons being described on the record as being in an action on the case. I am not, however, aware of any case in which this has been considered at all material; and I think a variance between the writ and declaration is no ground for arresting the judgment. In practice it is well known that such objections are cured by the subsequent pleadings. That being so, and no authority being cited for the defendant which bears upon the point, we may treat this declaration as what it really is, *viz* a declaration in trespass without the words "vi et armis." After verdict, the omission of those words is of no importance. We must now look to the substances; and, substantially, this is a count in trespass. The rule must therefore be discharged.

---

[2] [Ed — English Reports, general reporter of older English cases, decision of Exchequer Division Court of Appeal; Meeson and Welsby's reports.]

Gurney, B., concurred.

Maule, B. — I am of the same opinion, and think that this declaration states a continuing act of wrong by the defendant, and not such an injury as in the subject of an action upon the case, but of trespass.

. . .

Rule discharged

GARRETT v. SEWELL
Alabama Supreme Court
18 So. 737 (1895)

[Plaintiff, Garrett, alleged that the defendant, Sewell, removed a portion of a fence that was situated on the boundary between their lands. Sometime later, livestock of unknown ownership invaded plaintiff's land through the opening and destroyed a substantial portion of the growing crops. It may be assumed that plaintiff discovered the break in the fence before the invasion of the livestock but did nothing to replace it before the livestock entered. The plaintiff brought an action in trespass and on other grounds. The defendant denied the allegations and may be assumed to have alleged contributory negligence as an affirmative defense. At the trial, plaintiff was not permitted to prove that the livestock came into the exposed land and destroyed the crop on grounds that the damage was too remote from the trespass.]

McClellan, J.

. . .

The verdict of the jury was for the plaintiff on all the issues presented, with assessment of damages in this language: "We, the jury, find the issues in favor of the plaintiff, and assess the damages at three and 26/100 dollars." There was judgment for plaintiff for this sum as damages, and for an equal sum as costs, and for the defendant for the balance of the costs (Code, § 2838); and from the judgment plaintiff prosecutes this appeal.

All the issues having been found in favor of the plaintiff, it is manifest that she has no ground of complaint against the judgment below, except in respect of the assessment of damages, and errors [in exclusion of testimony.]

The plaintiff proposed to show by a witness that he (the witness) saw stock in the field from around which the defendant had removed the fence, and on the crop there growing. The court refused to allow this proof to be made. Had the plaintiff been allowed to pursue this line of evidence, we cannot know but that material damage to the crop would have been shown. Such damage is an element of recovery under the counts in trespass. The rule is thus stated: "The wrongdoer is responsible for the consequences which flow immediately from his wrongful or negligent acts and the responsibility is not relieved by the fact that the consequences of the injurious act could have been prevented by the care or skill of the injured party." 26 Am. & Eng. Enc. Law, p. 677. This fence was there, and the plaintiff, according to the verdict of the jury, had a right to have it remain there, for the sole purpose of protecting her fields and crops from the incursions and depredations of live stock. Its wrongful removal defeated this sole object of its existence, and was the direct cause of the depredations sought to be proved, and these the immediate, not remote, uncertain, and speculative, consequences of the wrong. The court erred to plaintiff's prejudice in the exclusion of this testimony.

. . .

The only argument made here for the appellee goes to the proposition that on the undisputed evidence the general charge should have been given for the defendant, and that, of consequence, any error committed by the trial court was without injury to the plaintiff. This argument is based upon two assumptions of fact, neither of which, we think, is supported by the record. In the first place, it is insisted that the evidence without conflict shows that the land upon which the fence stood in part was in the possession of a tenant of the plaintiff at the time of the alleged trespass. If this were so, of course the plaintiff could not recover under the second and third counts. But the evidence is in conflict on the point. Garrett, the plaintiff's husband, testifies that no part of the land inclosed on one side by this fence was rented at the time the fence was removed, but that a tenant for the previous year, who was living in the house at the time, was there only temporarily, until he could get another place for the current year, occupied for this purpose only by permission of the plaintiff, and in accordance with this purpose moved out, and left the premises, a few days after the removal of the fence. If the jury believed this evidence, they should have found that the plaintiff, and not this former tenant, was in possession of the land from which the fence was removed. Garrett further testified that tenants cultivating the cleared land on that tract did not rent the woodland through which this fence ran, and, if this were true, the plaintiff could maintain trespass for entry upon and wrong done upon the woodland, though a tenant were then in possession of the house and open land, as was decided when the case was here before. *Garrett v. Sewell*, 95 Ala. 456, 10 South. 226.

The second assumption of fact in this position of appellee is that there is no evidence that the defendant ever entered upon the land of the plaintiff in the removal of the fence, but, to the contrary, the evidence affirmatively shows that he did not. This assumption is also, we think, gratuitous. There is abundant evidence that the fence was on the line between the parties, — a partition fence, established and recognized as such for more than 10 years before its removal. It was, therefore, necessarily partly on the land of both the adjoining proprietors. In removing this fence, in taking away the rails of which it was built, and which rested in part in actual contact with the soil which belonged to the plaintiff, and were supported thereby equally with defendant's land, the defendant necessarily "entered upon" the plaintiff's land, though he may have all the while stood and walked upon his side of the line, and though his feet may not have touched the earth on plaintiff's side. We attach no importance to the fact that in going to the place where the fence stood for the purpose of removing it the defendant and his employees passed over another part of the plaintiff's land. The trespass charged was not committed upon this other land; it may have been only a few yards wide and 10 miles away; and, if the fact of entry upon plaintiff's land depended upon this testimony, we should say there was no evidence of the fact. Though the whole case will be opened up for trial below, we deem it unnecessary to pass upon other rulings made in the court below. Some of them, we do not doubt, the circuit judge will have no hesitancy in reversing if the points are again presented, and others he will, with equal facility and certainty of correctness, repeat. For the error pointed out, — the only one of which plaintiff can complain on this appeal, — the judgment below must be reversed. The cause is remanded.

NOTES AND QUESTIONS

(1) What would be too "remote" to be considered an element of damages in trespass? Suppose a motorist negligently drove a motor vehicle upon the plaintiff's premises without consent, lost control, struck the plaintiff's house, and damaged the stairs into the house. Nine days later, before repairs were made, the plaintiff momentarily forgot about the damage and fell from the stairs because of the damage. What benefit does the plaintiff gain by suing in trespass? As to the distinction between recoverable "immediate" harm and unrecoverable "collateral harm," one court has said:

> The terms "immediate" and "consequential" should . . . be understood, not in reference to the time which the act occupies, or the space through which it passes, or the place from which it is begun, or the intention with which it is done, or the instrument or agent employed, or the lawfulness or unlawfulness of the act; but in reference to the progress and termination of the act, to its being done on the one hand, and its having been done on the other. If the injury is inflicted by the act at any moment of its progress, from the commencement to the termination thereof, then the injury is direct or immediate; but if it arises after the act has been completed, though occasioned by the act, then it is consequential or collateral, or, more exactly, a collateral consequence.

Jordan v. Wyatt, 45 Va. 151, 47 Am. Dec. 720, 722 (1847). Does this test resolve the issue in the broken steps case? See *Leonard v. Nat Harrison Associates, Inc.*, 122 So.2d 432 (Fla. App. 1966).

In *Jackson v. Bohlin*, 75 So. 697, 700 (Ala. 1917), the court elaborated the distinctions as follows:

> Where the trespass is attended by only constructive or implied force, in an action of trespass for the injury resulting therefrom, the plaintiff can only recover such damages as directly result from the trespass, and for any consequential damages he may suffer must resort to an action on the case.

> . . .

> But when the act complained of was attended by such force as will support an action of trespass vi et armis, all the damages suffered by the plaintiff, whether direct or consequential, or whether occurring immediately or some time after the trespass, may be recovered; but where the damages are such as are not the usual consequence of the act, they must be specially claimed.

How does this differ from the case in note (2), *infra*?

(2) In *Wyant v. Crouse*, 86 N.W. 527 (Mich. 1901), the defendant broke into a blacksmith shop, built a fire in the forge and did some work for himself. When he left, the fire escaped through defects in the chimney, destroying both real and personal property. Because no evidence was adduced to show that the defendant had been negligent in the handling of the fire, the principal issue was whether he was liable for the consequential damages in trespass *quare clausum fregit*. The Michigan court said, "when one trespasses on land he is liable for the direct injury

to the freehold, and the consequences naturally to be expected arising therefrom, in an action of trespass." *Id.* at 528. The court said also at 522:

> The liability of the defendant is based upon a wrongful act, and the nature of the act, and not the consequences, determines his liability. He was engaged in an unlawful act, and therefore was liable for all of the consequences, indirect and consequential as well as direct, and there is no occasion to discuss the degree of his negligence in permitting the shop to burn, if the fire was caused by the fire he built. This accountability for the consequences is not affected by the form of action.

Are those two statements consistent? See also *Insurance Company of North America v. Cuevas*, 199 N.W.2d 681, 682 (Mich. 1972), where it is said:

> It must be remembered that under Michigan law a trespasser is liable for all of the consequences, indirect and consequential, as well as direct damages resulting from his trespass, irrespective of his negligence. *Wyant v. Crouse*, 127 Mich. 158, 86 N.W. 527 (1901).

(3) The preceding three cases illustrate trespasses that overtly invade the possessor's right of exclusive possession. From them it should be clear that the trespass action does not require that the defendant actually be challenging the state of the possessor's title or attempting to wrest it away by force, although actions of that kind would be trespasses. Instead the possessory interest protected is the right not to have another "break the close" and enter the property under any auspices except consent of the possessor.

(4) Would it make a difference if the entry was not of a person but of an object thrown or placed upon the property by someone other than the possessor? How does *Hudson v. Nicholson* speak to that? See commentary in *Rushing v. Hooper-McDonald, Inc.*, § 15.01[c], *infra*. More difficult are cases in which less substantial objects are wafted upon the possessor's property, settling down to cause damage of some kind. This class of invasion forces the law to draw lines of two kinds — one is to differentiate the tort of trespass from the tort of nuisance, and the second is to differentiate tortious invasions from invasions that must be tolerated. The problems are well posited by the following excerpt from *Hennessy v. Carmony*, 25 A. 374, 376-77 (N.J. 1892):

> Upon reason and authority I think there is a clear distinction between that class of nuisances which affect air and light merely, by way of noises and disagreeable gases, and obstruction of light, and those which directly affect the land itself, or structures upon it. Light and air are elements which mankind enjoy in common, and no one person can have an exclusive right in any particular portions of either; and, as men are social beings, and by common consent congregate, and need fires to make them comfortable and to cook their food, it follows that we cannot expect to be able to breathe air entirely free from contamination, or that our ears shall not be invaded by unwelcome sounds. Thus, my neighbor may breathe upon my land from his, and the smoke from his house fire and the vapor from his kitchen may come onto my land, or he may converse in audible tones while standing near the dividing line, and all without giving me any right to complain. So my neighbor and I may build our houses on the line between our properties, or have a party wall in common, so that we are each liable to hear and be more or less disturbed by the noise of each other's family, and cannot complain

of it. In all these matters of the use of the common element air we give and take something of injury and annoyance, and it is not easy to draw the line between reasonable and unreasonable use in such cases, affecting, as they do, mainly the comfort, and, in a small degree only, the health, of mankind. In attempting to draw this line, we must take into consideration the character which has been impressed upon the neighborhood by what may be called the "common consent" of its inhabitants. But when we come to deal with what is individual property, in which the owner has an exclusive right, the case is different. While my neighbor may stand by my fence on his own lot, and breathe across it over my land, and may permit the smoke and smell of his kitchen to pass over it, and may talk, laugh, and sing or cry, so that his conversation and hilarity or grief is heard in my yard, he has no right to shake my fence ever so little, or to throw sand, earth, or water upon my land in ever so small a quantity. To do so is an invasion of property, and a trespass, and to continue to do so constitutes a nuisance; and, if he may not shake my fences or my house by force directed immediately against them, I know of no principle by which he may be entitled to do it by indirect means. I think the distinction between the two classes of injury is clear.

Citing English case authority, *Hennessy* distinguished between invasions that caused material injury to property as actionable and those that cause only personal discomfort as nonactionable. Does that distinction conform to your judgment?

Judges in the early cases found it difficult to comprehend that invading odors, smoke and fine particles of matter could constitute trespasses. Those cases had to be brought in nuisance or not at all. In modern times, however, more courts have acknowledged that invasion of particles of only microscopic size can be the basis for trespass. *Lubin v. Iowa City*, 131 N.W.2d 765, 768 (Iowa, 1964), canvassed a number of these cases as follows:

Many recent cases have applied strict liability on the theory of trespass. *Casanover v. Villanova Realty Co.* (1948), Mo. App., 209 S.W.2d 556, 559 (surface water and sediment case upon land by regrading); *Martin v. Reynolds Metals Co.* (1959) 221 Or. 86, 342 P.2d 790 (fluoride particles escaping from aluminum reduction plant); *Hall v. DeWeld Mica Corp.*, 244 N.C. 182, 93 S.E.2d 56 (invisible particles of silicon dioxide); *United Electric Light Co. v. Deliso Const. Co.* 315 Mass. 343, 348, 52 N.E.2d 553 (grout escaping through the earth); *Sheppard Envelope Co. v. Arcade Malleable Iron Co.* (1956) 335 Mass 180, 138 N.E.2d 777 (soot and grit); *Gregg v. Dellai Taylor Oil Corp.* (1961) 162 Tex. 26, 344 S.W.2d 411 ("cracking sand" under surface to produce more natural gas); *Reynolds Metal Co. v. Lampert* (9 Cir.1963) 316 F.2d 272 (fluoride particles). *Mairs v. Manhattan Real Estate Ass'n* (1882) 89 N.Y. 498 (water seepage); *Loo v. Lenhardt* (1961) 227 Or. 242, 362 P.2d 312 (spraying of chemicals from airplane held an extrahazardous activity).

Many other cases might be added to the list including *Edwood v. City of New York*, 450 F. Supp. 846 (S.D.N.Y. 1978), involving damage done to the rights of riparian owners by the thermal pollution of the river, and *McDonald v. Associated Fuels* (1954) 3 D.L.R. 775 (Brit. Col.), involving introduction of carbon monoxide into a ventilation system. *Martin v. Reynolds Metals Co., supra,* extended the reach of the tort of trespass, relying in part upon Einstein's equations relating matter and energy. Does that imply that a beam of light might constitute a trespass as it passes over a parcel of land?

(5) Does an overflying aircraft constitute a trespass or, perhaps, a nuisance? Before Federal regulation preempted many issues involving the flight of aircraft, this question was often addressed in tort actions. The common law maxim *"cujus est solum ejus est usque ad coelum"* meant roughly that the owner of land has the right to possess, and thus exclude others, from the top of the sky to the bottom of the earth. Although this maxim gave rise to nice historical arguments about rights, common practice showed that it had no practical application to overflights so high that the possessor of the soil could not conceivably control the airspace and that would not interfere with the possessor's use of the surface. Moreover, flights that are low enough to interfere with the possessor's use are more likely to be treated as nuisances than trespasses. See, *e.g., Antonik v. Chamberlain,* 78 N.E.2d 752 (Ohio 1947). In addition, when a governmental entity is a proper defendant in overflight cases, a constitutional theory of inverse condemnation recognized by the United States Supreme Court in *United States v. Causby,* 382 U.S. 256 (1940), and later cases, provides a more suitable remedy. In sum, very few aircraft flyovers would be a proper basis for a trespass action nowadays. Although this does not necessarily mean that no remedy is available, it does suggest that the issue is more likely to be joined under one of the more flexible causes of action noted above.

(6) Why would litigants prefer that a cause of action be treated as trespass rather than nuisance? You should be able to answer this question after examining the nuisance materials in § 15.01[C], *infra.*

[C]   Nature of Defendant's Act of Entry

SEROTA v. M. & M. UTILITIES, INC.
New York District Court, Nassau County
55 Misc.2d 286, 285 N.Y.S.2d 121 (1967)

DECISION ON MOTION

BERNARD TOMSON, JUDGE

The plaintiff has brought suit against the defendant corporation, a supplier of fuel oil, for damages sustained to the lawn and shrubbery on his property by reason of defendant's alleged unauthorized delivery of fuel oil to his home. The claimed damages were apparently sustained because of spillage. Plaintiff's complaint in its first cause of action alleges a trespass and the unauthorized deposit of fuel oil upon the lawn and shrub beds surrounding plaintiff's home, and in its second cause of action, alleges negligence on the part of the defendant in delivering the oil. It appears that the defendant corporation had a contract with the former owner of plaintiff's premises to deliver fuel oil. The defendant claims that he had no notice of cancellation of the contract; that the spillage was caused by the fact that defendant was not aware that plaintiff's tank contained the amount that it did actually contain; that defendant assumed that the amount of oil he intended to deliver would not have caused an overflow but for the fact that an intervening delivery of oil had taken place between the time he had last delivered oil and the time the delivery complained of took place. Plaintiff has moved for summary judgment.

"Trespass" is defined in 87 C.J.S. Trespass § 1 as follows:

In a general sense any invasion of another's rights is a trespass. In the law "trespass" has a well ascertained and fixed meaning, which in its general signification embraces every infraction of a legal right; and so the term "trespass" in its broadest sense has been held to mean any misfeasance, transgression, or offense which damages another's person, health, reputation, or property.

In *Bomptin Realty Co. v. City of New York*, 196 Misc. 218, 219-220, 91 N.Y.S.2d 780, 783 reversed on other grounds 276 A.D. 1094, 96 N.Y.S.2d 414, it was stated, "The right to have one's property in its original condition, not changed by the well-meaning, but wrongful, conduct of others, is a property right, the invasion of which gives the right to damages, . . .

It is apparent from the facts alleged by plaintiff that the defendant's conduct in depositing oil on plaintiff's premises constituted a trespass which is actionable unless the oil delivery was authorized. On defendant's part the affidavit of its secretary-treasurer admits the delivery complained of and seems to rely on defendant's authority in making the delivery upon his contract with the former owner and a "right" to have been notified that the oil delivery contract was cancelled. The difficulty with such a proposition is that although defendant claims the existence of a contract with the former owner of plaintiff's premises, he makes no claim of any agreement with plaintiff. Lacking privity between the parties, his claimed "right" to a cancellation notice from plaintiff is without substance.

Although plaintiff's papers in support of his motion do not allege any facts tending to prove that the defendant intended to commit a trespass, it is our view that no such proof is necessary. . . .

In the *Socony-Vacuum* case it was stated (pp. 366-367, 109 N.Y.S.2d pp. 801-802):

It was not necessary, however, that the trespasser intend to commit a trespass or even that he know that his act will constitute a trespass, *Winteringham v. Lafoy*, 1827, 17 Cow. 735. The actor may be innocent of moral fault, but there must be an intent to do the very act which results in the immediate damage. In other words, trespass requires an intentional act. Harper on Torts, (1932) § 27.

Obviously, the defendant intended to come upon plaintiff's land and make an oil delivery and did not intend to commit a trespass or intentionally to cast oil upon plaintiff's land. His innocence and his mistaken belief that his visit was authorized is of no moment since his intent is clearly shown to have been to deliver oil. This unauthorized act, resulting in whatever damages which may have occurred, rendered him liable. The Court in *Phillips v. Sun Oil Co.*, 307 N.Y. 328, 331, 121 N.E.2d 249, 250-251 stated:

Trespass is an intentional harm at least to this extent: while the trespasser, to be liable, need not intend or expect the damaging consequence of his intrusion, he must intend the act which amounts to or produces the unlawful invasion, and the intrusion must at least be the immediate or inevitable consequence of what he willfully does, or which he does so negligently as to amount to willfulness. . . .

To constitute such a trespass, the act done must be such as "will to a substantial certainty result in the entry of the foreign matter." Restatement, Torts, *supra*, 158, comment h.

Plaintiff's motion for summary judgment on the first cause of action for trespass is granted and the matter is set down for hearing on January 10, 1968 in this part to assess damages. The plaintiff's motion for summary judgment on the second cause of action sounding in negligence is denied as moot since summary judgment is here granted on the first cause of action.

. . .

RUSHING v. HOOPER-McDONALD, INC.
Alabama Supreme Court
300 So.2d 94 (1974)

HEFLIN, CHIEF JUSTICE.

This case arose and was tried before the implementation of the new Alabama Rules of Civil Procedure. The appeal is from a judgment in favor of the defendant after the trial judge gave the general affirmative charge with hypothesis.

Appellant-plaintiff — Burl Rushing's amended complaint contained eight counts, each alleging a trespass to "the fish pond and surrounding banks and lands known as Bonners Fish Pond." Each count claimed damages in the sum of $30,000.00 and asked for punitive damages.

Count One alleged a trespass in April, 1968; Count Two, in May, 1969; Count Three, in July, 1969; Count Four, in September, 1969; Count Five in August, 1970; Count Six, in January, 1971; Count Seven, in March, 1971; and Count Eight alleged a continuing trespass during the period from April 1, 1968, to March 31, 1971.

Plaintiff Burl Rushing does not own the pond or the surrounding land, but claimed possession as a sublessee from his brother Lawrence Rushing, who had leased the property from its owner. Plaintiff claimed to have gone into possession of the pond in 1965 or 1966 as sublessee to his brother; he testified that his brother held under a written lease at that time, but no written lease was introduced covering the period prior to January 1, 1969.

There was introduced a written lease from the owner of the pond, Mrs. Mary Alice Thames (whose maiden name was Bonner), to Plaintiff's brother, Lawrence Rushing, which recited that the lease would cover a 5-year period from January 1, 1969, to December 31, 1974 [The dates indicate a 6-year period]. The terms of the lease covered " . . . a fish pond in the City of Andalusia, Alabama, known as Bonners Fish Pond . . . ," and the lease contained the following condition:

3. This lease covers the right to ingress and regress over and across surrounding lands for the purpose of allowing the free use of said fish pond and the banks thereof by Lessee, his guests and licensees.

The lease made no mention of any other part of the Thames tract of land on which the pond was located.

Appellee, Hooper-McDonald, Inc. (Defendant), owned land uphill from and bordering the Thames tract on which the fish pond was located. Plaintiff testified that on seven occasions the defendant emptied asphalt or asphalt-type materials so that they ran downhill onto the Thames tract and thence into a stream which carried them to the pond, with the results that the pond was polluted and fish were killed or otherwise rendered unmerchantable.

Plaintiff Rushing testified that some of the asphalt was dumped on the defendant's property, some on the Thames property, and some on a dedicated public street (which was grown up in woods) between the properties. However, there was no evidence that the defendant dumped any of the asphalt directly into the pond or onto the banks of the pond, except in one clean-up effort.

At the close of the plaintiff's evidence the trial judge gave the general affirmative charge with hypothesis.

[The trial court judge dismissed the action, saying that it should have been brought in negligence rather than trespass.]

Thus, the plaintiff presents this question: Can a trespass be committed by one who discharges asphalt in such a manner that it will in due course invade a neighbor's realty and thereby cause harm? This court answers in the affirmative.

A trespass may be committed by disturbing the possession of the occupant, though the person committing the trespass does not actually go on the premises, as by throwing water or missiles on the land, or removing a partition fence, though the trespasser does not place his foot on the land. . . .

In 87 C.J.S. Trespass, § 13c, it is stated:

The entry need not be in person but may be by the projection of force beyond the boundary of the land where the projecting instrument is employed. Thus, the trespass may be committed by casting earth, or other substances, upon another's land, by projecting anything into, over, or upon the land; by discharging water thereon, or by felling trees so that they fall upon the land . . .

Restatement, Second, Torts, § 158, Liability for Intentional Intrusions on Land, recites:

One is subject to liability to another for trespass, irrespective of whether he thereby causes harm to any legally protected interest of the other, if he intentionally

(a) *enters land* in the possession of the other, *or causes a thing* or a third person *to do so,* or

(b) remains on the land, or

(c) fails to remove from the land a thing which he is under a duty to remove. (Emphasis supplied)

In the Comments under this Restatement section appears the following:

i. *Causing entry of a thing.* The actor, without himself entering the land, may invade another's interest in its exclusive possession by throwing, propelling, or placing a thing either on or beneath the surface of the land or in the air space above it. Thus, in the absence of the possessor's consent or other privilege to do so, it is an actionable trespass to throw rubbish on another's land, even though he himself uses it as a dump heap, or to fire projectiles or to fly an advertising kite or balloon through the air above it, even though no harm is done to the land or to the possessor's enjoyment of it. *In order that there may be a trespass under the rule stated in this Section, it is not necessary that the foreign matter should be thrown directly and immediately upon the other's land. It is enough that an act is done with knowledge that it will to a substantial certainty result in the entry of the foreign matter.* Thus one who so piles sand close to his boundary that by force of gravity alone it slides down on to his neighbor's land, or who so builds an enbankment that during ordinary rainfalls the dirt from it is washed upon adjacent lands, becomes a trespasser on the other's land. (Emphasis supplied)

This court holds that it is not necessary that the asphalt or foreign matter be thrown or dumped directly and immediately upon the plaintiff's land but that it is sufficient if the act is done so that it will to a substantial certainty result in the entry of the asphalt or foreign matter onto the real property that the plaintiff possesses. Therefore the trial court erred in giving the general affirmative charge.

The defendant contends that the injury here is not direct and immediate but is a mere consequence of the acts complained of. It argues from the cases of *City of Fairhope v. Raddcliffe*, 48 Ala.App. 224, 263 So.2d 682 (1972) and *Howell v. City of Dothan*, 234 Ala. 158, 174 So. 624 (1937) to show that injuries from consequential acts must be remedied in an action based on trespass on the case rather than in trespass. In *Raddcliffe* the damages claimed against the city were for allegedly causing or allowing its sewer line to overflow and flood the plaintiff's house. The sewer line was stopped up by rags and clothing at a point below the house, causing the sewage to back into and flood the plaintiff's house. Speaking to the complaint, the court in *Raddcliffe*, stated:

This is not a charge of application of direct force against the property of plaintiff. It has been held that the Supreme Court of Alabama in a long line of cases that an action for overflow of land by obstructing the flow of drainage is one of trespass on the case. . . . The sustaining of demurrer to appellant's plea of the statute of limitations of one year to Count One was error.

Raddcliffe is distinguishable from the case at bar in that here there was no obstruction that caused the flow of asphalt onto the plaintiff's possessed realty; rather the flow was direct. The *Howell* case involved a bill in equity to enjoin a nuisance and the failure of the plaintiff to file claims against the City of Dothan within a statutory time limit. Likewise, as in *Raddcliffe*, obstructions caused the flow of pollution onto the plaintiff's property. That case is clearly distinguishable from the one under review. The obstructions in these were not intentional as was the damming of a stream that backed up water on another's property in *W. T. Ratliff Co. v. Purvis, supra*, where such was held to constitute wantonness.

Under the facts of the instant case the jury should have the right to determine whether there was an intentional intrusion onto the realty of which the plaintiff claimed that he was in possession.

. . .

Reversed and Remanded.

NOTES AND QUESTIONS

(1) Does it appear that the defendant in *Rushing v. Hooper-McDonald, Inc.* knew that it was substantially certain that the asphalt would flow into the plaintiff's property? Would it still be trespass if the defendant did not know it, but ought to have? If no reasonable person would have known it?

(2) *Serota* and *Rushing* are among numbers of cases that can be cited for the general proposition that trespass is an absolute liability tort. Yet, even these

opinions convey a limitation on that proposition. What is it? As seen earlier, the law of trespass as it applies to personal injuries has now evolved into the independent torts of intentional wrongs and negligence, whereas, as applied to entry onto the land, the old distinction between direct (trespass) and consequential (case) injuries retains some viability. Does this mean that a negligent entry is as much a trespass as an intentional entry, as defined by the preceding cases, as long as direct injury occurs? This point remains unclarified in many jurisdictions, although the drafters of the Restatement, Torts, Second, § 165 recognize negligent trespass, as follows:[3]

> One who recklessly or negligently, or as a result of an extra hazardous activity, enters land in the possession of another or causes a thing or third person so to enter is subject to liability to the possessor if, but only if, his presence or the presence of the thing or third person upon the land causes harm to the land, to the possessor thereof or to a thing or a third person in whose security the possessor has a legally protected interest.

Among cases applying this section to recognize a negligent trespass is *Zimmer v. Stephenson*, 403 P.2d 343 (Wash. 1965).

A different view was expressed, as follows, in *Harris v. Baden*, 17 So.2d 608, 612 (Fla. 1944).

> At common law, every entry upon another's land, except by consent, was deemed a trespass for which satisfaction would lie. Every man's land was considered, as a matter of law, to be enclosed and set apart from his neighbor's, either by a visible and material fence or by an ideal boundary existing only in contemplation of the law.

Among cases that hold the defendant strictly liable for harm done for unintentional entry without proof that the entry was negligent is *Lubin v. Iowa City*, 131 N.W.2d 765 (Iowa 1964).

(3) What legal interest in the trespassed-upon land was claimed by the plaintiff in *Rushing?* The outcome of that case demonstrates that the law of trespass protects not bare legal title but the right to possess and excludes others who have no right of possession. The right to exclude may be asserted by tenants, holders of easements and holders of other recognized possessory property interests and may be held jointly with other persons. See, for example, *Hale v. DeWeld Mica Corp.*, 93 S.E.2d 56 (N.C. 1956), and *Norris v. City of Miami*, 367 So.2d 1038 (Fla. App. 1978).

[D] Defenses

FLORIDA PUBLISHING CO. v. FLETCHER
Florida Supreme Court
340 So.2d 914 (1976)

ROBERTS, JUSTICE.

. . .

---

[3] Copyright 19 — by The American Law Institute. Reprinted with the permission of The American Law Institute.

The facts supported by the record are succinctly stated in the summary final judgment of the trial judge who determined that there was no real dispute as to the material facts. Respondent, Mrs. Fletcher, left Jacksonville for New York on September 15, 1972, to visit a friend. She left in Jacksonville her three young daughters, including seventeen-year-old Cindy. A "baby sitter" was to spend the nights with the children, but there was no one with them in the home during the daytime except a young man who had a room in the house and whom Mrs. Fletcher described as Cindy's "boy friend." On the afternoon of September 15, 1972, while Cindy was alone in the house, a fire of undetermined origin did large damage to the home, and Cindy died.

The fire and police departments were called by a neighbor who discovered the fire, but too late to save the child. A large group of firemen, news media representatives, and onlookers gathered at the scene and on Mrs. Fletcher's property.

When the Fire Marshal and Police Sergeant Short entered the house to make their official investigation, they invited the news media to accompany them, as they deposed was their standard practice. The media representatives entered through the open door; there was no objection to their entry; they entered quietly and peaceably; they did no damage to the property; and their entry was for the purpose of their news coverage of this fire and death.

The Fire Marshal desired a clear picture of the "silhouette" left on the floor after the removal of Cindy's body. He and Sergeant Short in their depositions explained that the picture was important for their respective investigations to show that the body was already on the floor *before* the heat of the fire did any damage in the room. The Fire Marshal took one polaroid picture of the silhouette, but it was not too clear, he had no further film, and he requested photographer Cranford to take the "silhouette" picture which was made a part of the official investigation file of both the Fire and Police.

This picture was not only a part of the investigation but News Photographer Cranford turned it and his other pictures over to the defendant newspaper. It and several other pictures appeared in the news story of The Florida Times-Union on September 16, 1972.

Respondent first learned of the facts surrounding the death of her daughter by reading the newspaper story and viewing the published photographs.

Respondent filed an amended complaint against petitioner alleging (1) trespass and invasion of privacy, (2) invasion of privacy, (3) wrong intentional infliction of emotional distress — seeking punitive damages.

The trial court dismissed Count II and granted final summary judgment for petitioner as to Counts I and III. Relative to the granting of summary judgment for Petitioner as to Count I, the trial judge cogently explicated:

As to Count I, the question raised by the motion for summary judgment is one of law as there is no genuine issue of material fact. The question raised is whether the trespass alleged in Count I of the complaint was consented to by the doctrine of common custom and usage.

The law is well settled in Florida and elsewhere that there is no unlawful trespass when peaceable entry is made, without objection, under common custom and usage.

In *Martin* v. *Struthers* (1943) 319 U.S. 141, 149 [63 S.Ct. 862, 87 L.Ed. 1313], the Court struck down as unconstitutional and "invalid in conflict with the freedom of speech and press" a city ordinance which made it unlawful trespass to knock on doors and ring doorbells to distribute literature. In so doing, at pages 147-149 [63 S.Ct.862] it made the far reaching pronouncement followed by the Florida Supreme Court in *Prior v. White* (Fla. 1938) 132 Fla. 1, 180 So. 347, 356:

Traditionally the American law punishes persons who enter onto the property of another after having been warned by the owner to keep off . . . We know of no state which, as does the Struthers ordinance in effect, makes a person a criminal trespasser if he enters the property of another for an innocent purpose without an explicit command from owners to stay away.

In *McKee v. Gratz* (1922) 262 [260] U.S. 127 [43 S.Ct. 16, 67 L.Ed. 167], the Supreme Court recognized the rule that it was not trespass when under the "habits of the country" entry was commonly made.

. . .

Not only did the Fire Marshal and Detective Sergeant Short testify it was common custom and usage to permit the news media to enter under the circumstances here, and of the great number of times they had permitted it in private homes, but many affidavits were filed to the same effect, including those of Duval County Sheriff Carson and Florida Attorney General Shevin.

. . .

Plaintiff filed no affidavits except her own; she makes no attempt to qualify as an expert; and she simply states her personal belief generally, without going into the situation involving coverage of a news story of public interest. She shows no qualifications to make an affidavit on the custom and usage in such matters.

In Mrs. Fletcher's deposition, she stated she was in New York at the time of the fire; there was no one at the scene who objected to the entry; and she makes it clear she does not contend there was any force used for entry, or any physical damage done to the premises.

Plaintiff likewise concedes that it was perfectly proper for the Fire and Police to enter without permission. The Fire and Police used the picture as part of their official investigation and actually requested that such picture be taken and would have made such request even had the Plaintiff been there and objected. There is no evidence that any restriction was placed upon the Defendant's photographer in the use of the photographs he took at the request of the Police and Fire Marshal.

Numerous affidavits, as above set forth, have been filed by the Defendant in support of its motion for summary judgments. All these affidavits attest to the fact that it is common usage, custom and practices for news media to enter private premises and homes to report on matters of public interest or a public event. The court therefore finds that there is no genuine issue of material fact and that as a matter of law an entry, that may otherwise be an actionable trespass, becomes lawful and non-actionable when it is done under common usage, custom and practice. The court further finds that the entry complained of in Count I of the plaintiff's complaint was one permitted by common usage, custom and practice, and that the Defendant is entitled to a summary judgment as a matter of law as to matters alleged in Count I of the Plaintiff's complaint.

On appeal, the District Court of Appeal reversed as to the granting of summary judgment on Count I, stating:

We do not here hold that a trespass or "intrusion" did in fact occur sub judice: We simply find that such is alleged in Count I of the amendment complaint and that the proofs before the learned trial judge are insufficient to resolve the point by summary judgment.

Although recognizing that consent is an absolute defense to an action for trespass and that the defense of custom and usage is but another way of expressing consent by implication — that is consent may be implied from custom, usage or conduct — the District Court commented that the emergency of the fire was over and that there was no contention that petitioner's employees entered the premises to render assistance, explained that respondent did not either impliedly or expressly invite petitioner's employees into her home, and concluded that the proofs before the court were not sufficient to show that there was no genuine issue of material fact as to whether implied consent by custom and usage authorized entry into the premises without invitation by appellant.

As to the other points on appeal, the District Court of Appeal, First District, determined that although punitive damages are recoverable in a proper case for trespass resulting in invasion of privacy, the trial judge did not err in granting summary judgment for petitioner on issue of punitive damages, held that the trial court correctly dismissed Count II with prejudice, and correctly granted summary judgment for petitioner as to Count III.

The District Court erred in reversing summary judgment for petitioners as to Count I. The trial court properly determined from the record before it that there was no genuine issue of material fact insofar as the entry into respondent's home by petitioner's employees became lawful and non-actionable pursuant to the doctrine of common custom, usage, and practice and since it had been shown that it was common usage, custom and practice for news media to enter private premises and homes *under the circumstances present here.*

Judge McCord in the dissenting opinion could not agree with the majority that the news photographer who entered the burned out home was a trespasser or that the photograph published by petitioner and the news story resulting from the entry were an actionable invasion of privacy. We agree with explication by Judge McCord in his dissenting opinion:

. . .

An analysis of the cases on implied consent by custom and usage, indicates that they do not rest upon the previous nonobjection to entry by the particular owner of the property in question but rest upon custom and practice generally. Implied consent would, of course, vanish if one were informed not to enter at that time by the owner or possessor or by their direction. But here there was not only no objection to the entry, but *there was an invitation to enter by the officers investigating the fire.* The question of implied consent to news media personnel to enter premises in a circumstance such as this appears to be one of first impression not only in this jurisdiction but elsewhere. This, in itself, tends to indicate that the practice has been accepted by the general public since it is a widespread practice of long-standing. Due to such widespread and long-standing custom, reason and logic support the application of implied consent to enter the premises in the case before us. It, therefore, was not a trespass, and I would affirm the trial court." (emphasis supplied)

Accordingly, that portion of the decision of the District Court of Appeal, First District, reversing summary judgment for petitioner as to Count I is quashed, and the cause is remanded for further proceedings consistent herewith.

It is so ordered.

NOTES AND QUESTIONS

(1)   See also, *Smith v. Voncannon*, 197 S.E.2d 524 (N.C. 1973), a case implying consent to enter under more ordinary circumstances. Compare *Miller v. National Broadcasting Co.*, 232 Cal. Rptr. 668 (Cal.App. 1986), which without discussion of consent by custom permitted a trespass action against television reporters who entered a private residents without consent along with medical emergency personnel, and *Desnick v. American Broadcasting Companies, Inc.*, 44 F.2d 1345 (7th Cir. 1995), which denied a trespass action against reporters who entered a physician's office as patients under false pretenses in order to investigate allegations of quackery.

(2)   Although the case authority is skimpy, it seems clear that genuine emergencies not of the intruder's own making will justify an entry against the consent of an owner of land to protect the life and limb of the entrant. *Ploof v. Putnam*, 71 A. 188 (Vt. 1908), held the landowner liable for harm done when he cast adrift a boat that was seeking refuge from a violent storm. By the same token, it appears settled, again on little authority, that the intruder must pay for actual harm done by his unconsented to intrusion. See *Vincent v. Lake Erie Transportation Co.*, 124 N.W. 221 (Minn. 1910).

Many ancillary questions are largely untested. For example, suppose the emergency is genuine but it is of the intruder's own making? Or, suppose the interests to be protected by the intrusion are light compared to the risk posed to the landowner by the intrusion?

[E]   Remedies

TURNER v. SOUTHERN EXCAVATION, INC.
Louisiana Court of Appeal, Second Circuit
322 So.2d 326 (1975)

HALL, JUDGE.

Plaintiff, Theresa M. Turner, sued defendant, Southern Excavation, Inc., for property damage and mental anguish and humiliation resulting from willful and wanton trespass by defendant on plaintiff's property. Judgment was rendered awarding plaintiff $1,500 for property damage, $3,500 for mental anguish and humiliation, and $75 for the cost of a survey of the property, or a total award of $5,075. Expert witness fees for plaintiff's two experts were set at $50 each.

Plaintiff appeals seeking an increase in the award for property damage and mental anguish and humiliation, and for an increase of the fee of each expert witness to $100. Defendant appeals seeking a reduction of the property damage and mental anguish award, and for disallowance of the cost of the survey.

The record shows that Mrs. Turner is the owner of a 100' × 100' corner lot located several miles north of Coushatta, Louisiana, in Red River Parish. There was located on the lot a small, rundown old house which is admittedly uninhabitable. Mrs. Turner resides in Shreveport and does not live on the property, nor had anyone else for some period of time prior to the alleged trespass beginning in October of 1973. The lot was covered with small trees and shrubbery, and there was a small concrete slab located thereon that possibly could be used as a foundation. Trees identified specifically as having been growing on the property included cedar, plum, peach and crepe myrtle. Many of the fruit trees were bearing.

The defendant corporation was doing some construction work for the Highway Department and in this connection leased property adjoining on plaintiff's property as a site for an asphalt plant. Defendant also wanted to use plaintiff's lot for this purpose. Prior to going onto plaintiff's property, defendant's agent, Mr. Kirkpatrick, contacted Mrs. Turner by telephone to ask if his company could level and clear the lot and use it as a storage place for its equipment and as a parking lot for its trucks while doing construction work in the area. Defendant may have offered a small rental fee at this time. Mrs. Turner declined the offer.

. . .

[Contrary to Mrs. Turner's express wishes the defendant entered the property, leveled it, and made use of it.]

Mrs. Turner's lot is now stripped bare of vegetation. The trial judge found the actions of the defendant in clearing and bulldozing Mrs. Turner's property and continuing to use it over her objection, to be a willful and wanton trespass and in legal and moral bad faith. Although contested at trial, defendant does not now contest this aspect of the decision, which is manifestly correct. Thus, we are only faced with an issue of quantum.

Plaintiff seeks an increase in the award for property damage from $1,500 to $10,000, which she alleges is the amount it would take to restore the property to its prior condition. She also seeks to have the award for mental anguish increased to $15,000. Defendant seeks to have the $1,500 award reduced contending that where restoration costs are out of all proportion to the value of the property they do not provide an adequate method for measuring damages. Defendant argues that the proven diminution in market value of the property or the value of timbers removed would be a correct method of evaluating damages in cases such as this, and that, in any event, property damages should not exceed the market value of the property. Defendant further argues that $3,500 is beyond the limits of discretion of the trial judge as reflected by the jurisprudence as compensation for plaintiff's mental anguish and humiliation.

. . .

Defendant's trespass was deliberate, willful, wanton, illegal and forcible. It was done without any vestige of legal right and in legal and moral bad faith.

Replacement or restoration cost, before and after market value, and other usual methods of measuring property damage are of little value in measuring plaintiff's damages in this case. It is difficult to separate and make specific awards for property damage and for damage resulting from mental anguish and the like. Plaintiff's pecuniary loss is negligible but her damages are considerable.

Plaintiff offered testimony by an expert in the landscaping business who estimated the cost of replacing the topsoil and planting new trees and shrubs similar to those destroyed at over $8,900. Replacement cost is unrealistic as a measure of damages in this case as such cost is out of proportion with the value of the property, either in terms of market value or aesthetic or sentimental value. The lot's highest and best use is commercial, and the lot would not and could not be restored to its condition prior to the trespass.

Likewise, diminution in market value is not an appropriate measure of damages. There was testimony by an expert real estate appraiser that the property had a market value of $1,600 and, its highest and best use being commercial, the trees and shrubs added nothing to the market value. Yet, it cannot be denied that plaintiff's property was damaged. The trees and shrubs, which had aesthetic and sentimental value to plaintiff, were destroyed and cannot be replaced.

The courts of Louisiana have consistently recognized the right of property owners to recover damages done to the aesthetic value of their property. *Curole v. Acosta*, 303 So.2d 530 (La.App. 1st Cir. 1974); *City of New Orleans* v. *Shreveport Oil Co.*, 170 La. 432, 128 So. 35 (1930). In *Curole*, an award of $750 was made to a plaintiff whose rural property was partially cleared when the defendant used it as a turnaround spot for his bulldozer which was clearing adjoining property. In the *City of New Orleans* case, one tree was destroyed and could not be replaced and the Supreme Court awarded $750. In that case, the Supreme Court made the distinction between ordinary and wanton trespasses. In each of these cases the destroyed trees and shrubs were found to be irreplaceable and their value to the owners not discernible on the open market. There, as here, neither the replacement costs nor the diminution in fair market value could reasonably be used to determine the amount to be awarded for the property damage.

Likewise, the courts of Louisiana have consistently awarded damages in cases of deliberate, forcible trespass for "invasion of property rights" and "mental anguish" or the like. The nature of such damages is most clearly described in *Loeblich v. Garnier*, 113 So.2d 95 (La.App. 1st Cir. 1959) as follows:

The often found general statement that only compensatory and not punitive damages are awardable in Louisiana is in apparent conflict with the awards often made for damages for mental anguish and embarrassment caused by an illegal and deliberate violation of property rights or for such violation itself irrespective of any pecuniary damage caused thereby (which damages, according to the definition above cited, are regarded in other states as exemplary or punitive damages). The key to resolution of this conflict seems to be that in such circumstances such awards in Louisiana are regarded as compensatory for violations of a recognized property right, rather than punitory.

. . .

There is no hard and fast rule for measuring damages in a case of willful and wanton trespass and destruction of private property. The court must adopt an approach in each case that will do substantial justice between the parties. *East v. Pan American Petroleum Corporation*, 168 So.2d 426 (La.App. 3d Cir. 1964); *City of New Orleans v. Shreveport Oil Co., supra.*

. . .

For the reasons assigned, the judgment appealed from is affirmed. All costs of this appeal are assessed to the defendant-appellant.

Affirmed.

NOTES AND QUESTIONS

(1)   What if there had been no physical damage done to the plaintiff's real property or his chattels? *Dumont v. Miller, supra,* stands for the universally accepted rule that damages as such are not a necessary element of the plaintiff's prima facie case. This emphasizes that the gravamen of the wrong is intrusion onto the right of exclusive possession. Nevertheless, as also illustrated in *Dumont,* some cases may award nominal damages only. See, also, Restatement, Torts, Second, § 158. For example, *Hampton v. Portland General Electric Co.,* 519 P.2d 89 (Ore. 1974), was a case with facts quite similar to those in *Turner* as far as what the defendant did but he entered innocently. Despite the trespass, the jury found that no actual harm was done and awarded no damages. The appellate court sustained the verdict.

(2)   At one time trespass actions would be used to try the disputed titles to land. Today, these actions would more typically be litigated under a statutory procedure for trying title, which is more properly a subject of property law rather than torts. They will not be examined here.

(3)   As noted in *Turner,* the most commonly accepted measure of actual damages for trespass to property is the diminution of market value caused by the invasion. *Turner* also demonstrates that courts may deviate from that theory when it does not supply a just result, but the Louisiana rules permitting damage to "aesthetic value of the property" and for mental anguish may be unusual. Perhaps the facts of *Turner* would justify a recovery under the separate tort of intentional infliction of mental distress, but apart from intentional wrongdoing, does it not seem strange to permit recovery for mental anguish in trespass cases when the law has so restricted that remedy in negligence personal injury cases?

For example, a later Louisiana case cited *Turner* for the proposition:

> It is in those cases where the trespass is aggravated by circumstances of gross recklessness and deliberate disregard of the victim's right that it is said that mental anguish is reasonably calculated or expected to result to the victim. . . . In other cases, where the trespass is not aggravated by such circumstances, the burden of proving actual mental anguish damages, of course, is much greater because of the absence of reasonably expected mental anguish. But where the burden is met and actual damages are proved — even though not reasonably expected — the victim should be allowed the damages.

Adams v. State Dept. of Highways, 357 So.2d 1239 (La. App. 1978). Under this rationale the Louisiana Supreme Court permitted damages for mental anguish to stand in light of evidence that the plaintiff was upset over the loss of "real good squirrel [hunting] territory" as a consequence of the defendant's trespass. *Boswell v. Roy O. Martin Lumber Co.,* 363 So.2d 506 (La. 1978).

(4)   Cases arise in which the nature of the property is changed by the trespass. For example, in *Livingstone v. The Rawyards Coal Co.*, § 4.05, *supra*, the coal was transposed from real property as it reposed *in situ* to personal property when severed from the earth. Although the identity of what has been damaged is usually not an issue in property damage cases, *Livingstone* proves that this is not always so. The various measures discussed there are quite typical.

A similar question was raised about cut timber in *Skeels v. Starrett*, 24 N.W. 98 (Mich. 1885). *Skeels* permitted the plaintiff to recover the market value of the harvested timber less actual costs of harvesting it. Does that unfairly reward the plaintiff? In reply to the defendant's argument that the plaintiff ought not recover unless he could prove his damages to a certainty, the court quoted *Gilbert v. Kennedy*, 22 Mich. 117, as follows:

> . . . to deny the injured party the right to recover any actual damages in such cases, because they are of a nature which cannot be thus certainly measured, would be to enable parties to profit by and speculate upon their own wrongs, encourage violence, and invite depredation; . . . and where, from the nature of the case, adequate damages cannot be measured with certainty by a fixed rule, all the facts and circumstances tending to show such damages as are claimed in the declaration, or their probable amount, should be submitted to the jury to enable them to form, under proper instructions from the court, such reasonable and probable estimate as, in the exercise of good sense and sound judgment, they shall think will produce adequate compensation.

Under this ruling it was admissible to introduce evidence as to the value of the finished lumber made of the timber as well as expert testimony as to the value of the timber on the stump.

When would it be appropriate to measure damages by cost to restore rather than either by diminution of the value of the land or the value of the timber as measured in *Skeels?* See, *e.g., Fiske v. Moczik*, 329 So.2d 35 (Fla. App. 1976), and *Session Pulpwood, Inc. v. Martin*, 416 So.2d 1040 (Ala. Civ. App. 1982).

(5)   Most often a trespass is a one time affair, leaving the plaintiff with a need only of damages. In some instances, however, the trespass continues either in the sense that the defendant comes back or in the sense that some trespassory object remains on the plaintiff's property. May the plaintiff obtain an equitable order from the court to have the trespass abated? Although it is said that courts will employ their equity powers only when a legal remedy is inadequate, a finding of inadequacy often is perfunctory when an interest in real property is at stake, no matter how much it costs the defendant to remove the offending object. See, *e.g., Crushed Stone v. Moore*, 369 P.2d 811 (Okla. 1962). On the other hand, fine distinctions sometimes separate trespass from the nuisance, a tort in which equitable remedies are applied more flexibly. Examples of this are seen in § 15.02, *infra.* If the action is merely of nuisance, many courts will "balance the equities" and require the plaintiff to accept damages rather than abatement.

Other courts permit a similar remedy. For example, in *Rushing v. Hooper-McDonald, Inc., supra*, the Alabama Court permitted recovery for mental suffering, "if the trespass was committed under circumstances of insult or contumely." Is this formulation more or less restrictive than that of the independent tort of intentional infliction of mental distress? If there is a difference, what explains it?

See also *Miller v. National Broadcasting Co.*, 232 Cal. Rptr. 668, 677 (Cal.App. 1986) (under California law the "consequences flowing from an intentional act such as trespass may include emotional distress neither accompanied by an physical injury to the person to the land.")

(6)   Some cases raise nice questions about the nature of the property actually damaged by the trespass. For example, in *Rushing v. Hooper-McDonald, Inc.*, *supra*, recovery for the fish destroyed by the pollution was in question. In reply to several of the issues raised, the court said, at 99, 100:

> On the retrial of this case, undoubtedly, the question will arise as to whether or not the trial judge may charge the jury pertaining to damages for the destruction of or injury to fish. This involves the inquiry of whether fish are real or personal property.

In *People v. Morrison*, 194 N.Y. 175, 86 N.E. 1120, 128 Ann.St.Rep. 552 (1909), the defendant was charged with larceny of some clams and oysters from a staked area of Jamaica Bay. The court stated:

> When clams or oysters are reclaimed from nature and transplanted to a bed where none grew naturally, and the bed is so marked out by stakes as to show that they are in the possesion of a private owner, they are personal property and may become the subject of larceny. Although in the nature of *ferae naturae to* which a qualified title may be acquired by possession, when reclaimed and transplanted, they need not be confined, for, as they cannot move about, they cannot get away, even when placed in the water, as they must be in order to live.

In *Reese v. Qualtrough*, 48 Utah 23, 156 P. 955 (1916), the Supreme Court of Utah held that fish in a fish pond must be regarded as personal property.

The next question that arises is whether or not in a suit for trespass to land there can be recovery for damaged or destroyed personal property. In *Central of Georgia Ry. v. Barnett*, 220 Ala. 284, 124 So. 868 (1929), the following language appears:

> Nevertheless, if it be shown that not only injury to the real estate was suffered, but that valuable property was taken or destroyed, there is no reason why the plaintiff should not recover for such loss. Any other rule would enable the trespasser to profit by and speculate upon his own wrong . . . Section 162 of Restatement, Second, Torts, is as follows:

> § 162. Extent of Trespasser's Liability of Harm.

> A trespass on land subjects the trespasser to liability for physical harm to the possessor of the land at the trespass, or to the land or *to his things*, caused by any act done, activity carried on, or condition created by the trespasser, irrespective of whether his conduct is such as would subject him to liability were he not a trespasser. (Emphasis supplied.)

> Thus in the instant case the plaintiff is entitled to have a jury pass on the issue of damage to his fish.

(7)   Although the authority for this proposition is thin, the law seems to acknowledge a right of unauthorized entry upon the lands of another to avert injury or to recover property that has been deposited thereon without the fault of the owner, say by a flooded river. See *Carter v. Thurston*, 58 N.H. 104 (1877), a case

involving the recovery of logs that a flood had deposited on the lands of another:

> This right of pursuit and reclamation rests upon the same natural right as that which permits the owner of cattle to pursue into an adjoining field and recover his beasts straying from the highway; but in the pursuit and recovery of his cattle or his logs, the owner must do no unnecessary damage, and is responsible for any excess or abuse of his right. This right of reclaiming stranded logs is a common law right, a natural right, incident to the right of navigation.

Id.

§ 15.02 TRESPASS TO CHATTELS AND CONVERSION

PROBLEM B

Nancy Quincy purchased a used Chevrolet from Anytown Motors. She paid $1500 down and signed a note for the balance of $15,000 to be paid off in monthly installments. In addition, she signed a chattel mortgage giving a security interest in the vehicle to Motors. Among the provisions was this one:

> Buyer (Quincy) agrees that in the event any monthly payment remains unpaid on the expiration of the 10th calendar day after the payment is due Seller (Motors) may without notice enter said vehicle and repossess it. Buyer further agrees that Seller may resell said vehicle applying the sum received to the unpaid balance of the note and holding said Buyer accountable for the remainder.

Nancy also purchased a Chevrolet of the same year, model and color from another dealer, giving her two cars of identical exterior appearances.

Nancy fell into a pattern of making her monthly payment late, often on the 12th or 13th day after the due date. After the third month in a row of accepting late payments, Motors wrote Nancy indicating that the vehicle would be repossessed immediately if payment were not timely at any time in the future.

Nancy failed to make the next payment on time. On the day after the default, Motors sent H.T. Wise to repossess the car. Toward dusk on a stormy day, Wise drove to Nancy's home. Seeing a Chevrolet of the correct description sitting at curbside on the public street, Wise quickly unlocked the door, got in, manipulated the starter mechanism and drove away. He had not gone a block, however, when he noticed that the interior of the car was red, whereas the one he was instructed to repossess was described as white. Wise drove the car around the block, reparked it in the spot he removed it from, and locked the door. All this was seen by a next door neighbor who had tried to call Nancy but had not gotten through because the line was busy.

Wise then saw the second car in Nancy's open garage. He entered the garage, opened the car, which was the correct one, and drove away. Motors sold the car the next day.

As Wise was driving away, a bolt of lightning struck a large tree in Nancy's yard. The tree fell on the Chevrolet parked by the curb, totally destroying it.

Nancy brings an action against Motors for having converted both vehicles. Defendant moves for summary judgment and affidavits are produced to establish all the foregoing facts and no others. Should the motion be granted? If not, what damages should be awarded if Nancy were to sustain the cause of action in the subsequent trial? See *Edwards v. Helm*, 5 Ill. 143 (1843).

FOULDES v. WILLOUGHBY
[1841] 8 M. & W. 540, 151 Eng. Rep. 1153[4]

Trover for two horses. It appeared at the trial that the defendant was the manager of a ferry from B. to L., and that the plaintiff embarked on board the defendant's ferry-boat at B., having with him the horses in question, for the carriage of which he had paid the usual fare. When the defendant came on board, it having been suggested that the plaintiff had behaved improperly on board, he the defendant told the plaintiff he would not carry the horses over the water, and that he must take them on shore. The plaintiff refused to do this, and the defendant took them from the plaintiff and put them on shore, and they were conveyed to an hotel kept by the defendant's brother. The plaintiff remained on board and was conveyed over the water. On the following day the plaintiff sent for the horses, but they were not delivered up; a message was however afterwards sent to the plaintiff that he might have the horses on sending for them and paying for their keep, but that if he did not send for them, they would be sold to pay the expenses. The latter was accordingly done, and this action was brought. The defence set up was, that the plaintiff having misconducted himself on board, the horses were put on shore in order to get rid of the plaintiff by inducing him to follow them.

The learned Judge, in summing up, told the jury that the defendant, by taking the horses from the plaintiff and turning them out of the vessel, had been guilty of a conversion, unless they thought the plaintiff's conduct justified his removal from the steamboat, and he had refused to go without his horses: [The jury returned a verdict for the plaintiff and judgment was entered against the defendant.]

. . .

Lord Abinger, C. B.

This is a motion to set aside the verdict on the ground of an alleged misdirection; and I cannot help thinking that if the learned Judge who tried the cause had referred to the long and frequent distinctions which have been taken between such a simple asportation as will support an action of trespass, and those circumstances which are requisite to establish a conversion, he would not have so directed the jury. It is a proposition familiar to all lawyers, that a simple asportation of a chattel, without any intention of making any further use of it, although it may be a sufficient foundation for an action of trespass, is not sufficient to establish a conversion. I had thought that the matter had been fully discussed, and this distinction established, by the numerous cases which have occurred on this subject; but, according to the agreement put forward by the plaintiff's counsel to-day, a bare asportavit is a sufficient foundation to support an action of trover.

I entirely dissent from this argument; and therefore I think that the learned Judge was wrong, in telling the jury that the simple fact of putting these horses on shore by the defendant, amounted to a conversion of them to his own use. In my

---

[4] [Ed. — English Reports, general reporter of older English cases, decision of Exchequer Division Court of Appeal; Meeson and Welsby's reports.]

opinion, he should have added to his direction, that it was for them to consider what was the intention of the defendant in so doing. If the object, and whether rightly or wrongfully entertained is immaterial, simply was to induce the plaintiff to go on shore himself, and the defendant, in furtherance of that object, did the act in question, it was not exercising over the horses any right inconsistent with, or adverse to, the rights which the plaintiff had in them. Suppose, instead of the horses, the defendant had put the plaintiff himself on shore, and, on being put on shore, the plaintiff had refused to take his horses with him, and the defendant had said he would take them to the other side of the water, and had done so, would that be a conversion? That would be a much more colourable case of a conversion than the present, because, by separating the man from his property, it might, with some appearance of fairness, he said the party was carrying away the horses without any justifiable reason for so doing. Then, having conveyed them across the water, and finding neither the owner nor any one else to receive them, what is he to do with them?

Suppose, under those circumstances, the defendant lands them, and leaves them on shore, would that amount to a conversion? The argument of the plaintiff's counsel in this case must go the length of saying that it would. Then, suppose the reply to be, that those circumstances would amount to a conversion, I ask, at what period of time did the conversion take place? Suppose the plaintiff had immediately followed his horses when they were put on shore, and resumed possession of them, would there be a conversion of them in that case? I apprehend, clearly not. It has been argued, that the mere touching and taking them by the bridle would constitute a conversion, but surely that cannot be: if the plaintiff had immediately gone on shore and taken possession of them, there could be no conversion. Then the question, whether this were a conversion or not, cannot depend on the subsequent conduct of the plaintiff in following the horses on shore.

Would any man say, that if the facts of this case were, that the plaintiff and defendant had had a controversy as to whether the horses should remain in the boat, and the defendant had said, "If you will not put them in shore, I will do it for you," and in pursuant of that threat, he had taken hold of one of the horses to go ashore with it, an action of trover could be sustained against him? There might, perhaps, in such a case, be ground for maintaining an action of trespass, because the defendant may have had no right to meddle with the horses at all: but it is clear that he did not do so for the purpose of taking them away from the plaintiff, or of exercising any right over them, either for himself or for any other person.

The case which has been cited from Strange's Reports, of *Bushell v. Miller*, seems fully in point. There the plaintiff and defendant, who were porters, had each a stand on the Custom-House Quay. The plaintiff placed goods belonging to a third party in such a manner that the defendant could not get to his chest without removing them, which he accordingly did, and forgot to replace them, and the goods were subsequently lost. Now suppose trespass to have been brought for that asportation, the defendant, in order to justify the trespass, would plead, that he removed the parcels, as he lawfully might, for the purpose of coming at his own goods; and the court there said, that whatever ground there might be for an action of trespass, in not putting the package back in its original place, there was none for trover, inasmuch as the object of the party in removing it was one wholly collateral to any use of the property, and not at all to disturb the plaintiff's rights in or dominion over it.

Again, suppose a man puts goods on board of a boat, which the master thinks are too heavy for it, and refuses to carry them, on the ground that it might be dangerous to his vessel to do so. and the owner of the goods says, "if you put my goods on shore, I will go with them," and he does so; would that mount to a conversion in the master of the vessel, even assuming his judgment as to the weight of the goods to be quite erroneous, and that there really would be no danger whatever in taking them? In order to constitute a conversion, it is necessary either that the party taking the goods should intend some use to be made of them, by himself or by those for whom he acts, or that, owing to his act, the goods are destroyed or consumed, to the prejudice of the lawful owner. As an instance of the latter branch of this definition, suppose, in the present case, the defendant had thrown the horses into the water, whereby they were drowned, that would have amounted to an actual conversion; or as in the case cited in the course of the argument, of a person throwing a piece of paper into the water; for, in these cases, the chattel is changed in quality, or destroyed altogether. But it has never yet been held, that the single act of removal of a chattel, independent of any claim over it, either in favour of the party himself or any one else, amounts to a conversion of the chattel.

In the present case, therefore, the simple removal of these horses by the defendant, for a purpose wholly unconnected with any the least denial of the right of the plaintiff to the possession and enjoyment of them, is no conversion of the horses, and consequently the rule for a new trial ought to be made absolute.

With respect to the amount of damages, it was altogether a question for the jury. I am not at all prepared to say, that if the jury were satisfied that there had been a conversion in this case, they would be doing wrong in giving damages to the full value of the horses. I do not at all rest my judgment on that point, but put it aside entirely. If the Judge had told the jury that there was evidence in the case from whence they might infer that a conversion of these horses had taken place at some time, it would have been difficult; but his telling them that the simple act of putting them on shore amounted to a conversion, I think, was a misdirection, on which the defendant is entitled to a new trial.

ALDERSON, B.

I am of the same opinion . . . But the question here is, where a man does an act, the effect of which is not for a moment to interfere with my dominion over the chattel, but on the contrary, recognising throughout my title to it, can such an act as that be said to amount to a conversion? I think it cannot. Why did this defendant turn the horses out of his boat? Because he recognized them as the property of the plaintiff. He may have been a wrong-doer in putting them ashore; but how is that inconsistent with the general right which the plaintiff has to the use of the horses? It clearly is not; it is a wrongful act done, but only like any common act of trespass, to goods with which the party has no right to meddle. Scratching the panel of a carriage would be a trespass; but it would be a monstrous thing to say that it would be a ground for an action of trover; and yet to that extent must the plaintiff's counsel go, if their argument in this case be sound. But such is not the law; and the true principle is that stated by *Chamber* and *Holroyd*, Js., when at the bar, in their argument in the case of *Shipwick v. Blanchard*, 6 T.R. 299, that "In order to maintain trover, the goods must be taken or detained, with intent to convert them to the taker's own use, or to the use of those for whom he is acting." This definition, indeed, requires an addition to be made to it, namely, that the destruction of the goods will also amount to a conversion. For these reasons, I think, in the case before us, the question ought to have been left to the jury, to say, whether the act done by the defendant, of seizing these horses and putting them on shore, was done with the intention of converting them to his own use, *i.e.*, with the intention of impugning, even for a moment, the plaintiff's general right of dominion over them. If so, it would be a conversion; otherwise not.

GURENY, B.

If it had been left to the jury, on the whole of the evidence in this case, to say whether a conversion had taken place or not, I think there was abundant evidence from which they might have drawn an affirmative conclusion. But the Judge only left that question to them on one part of the evidence, namely, that of the defendant's taking these horses out of the boat, and putting them ashore; and I cannot agree to the position, that that act, standing alone, amounts to a conversion.

. . .

ROLFE, B.

. . .

I quite agree with my Brother *Gurney*, that if the learned Judge in the present case had not put the conversion to the jury as founded on the single fact of taking the horses on shore, but had left it for their consideration on the whole case as it stood, not only was there evidence of a conversion, but there was such as would have fully warranted the jury in coming to the conclusion at which they arrived. The question, however, was not so left to the jury, and this rule to set aside the verdict for misdirection must therefore be made absolute.

Rule absolute.

MASONITE CORPORATION v. WILLIAMSON
Mississippi Supreme Court
404 So.2d 565 (1981)

PATTERSON, CHIEF JUSTICE, for the Court:

Marie Tate Williamson and W. B. Tate brought suits in the Chancery Court of Pike County for trespass and conversion of timber on their lands. All parties involved in the timber cutting and resulting sales were made defendants in the suits which were consolidated for trial. The chancellor found in favor of Mrs. Williamson and W. B. Tate. Two defendants, Masonite Corporation and Hilda Hines, appeal, assigning numerous errors, only four of which require discussion.

During the summer of 1976, George Brown entered into a verbal agreement with Hilda Hines to purchase timber owned by Miss Hines. Brown then entered into verbal agreements with other parties to cut and remove the timber. The timber was sold to different lumber mills, principally to mills owned by Masonite Corporation. All these parties — Hilda Hines, George Brown, those who cut, loaded, and hauled the timbers, and the purchasers of the timber — were made defendants in the present action.

The land owned by Hilda Hines is joined on the south by a 40 acre tract of land owned by Marie Williamson. The Bala Chitto Creek meanders back and forth along the southern border, with Miss Hines owning approximately three acres south of this creek. W. B. Tate owned sixty acres involved in this dispute, adjoining the Hines and Williamson properties. This controversy arose over timber cut south of the Bala Chitto Creek.

Miss Hines testified that at the time she contracted with Brown, she was uncertain about the location of her boundary lines, but thought that she owned three acres south of the creek. Although no fence marked the property lines, Brown made only superficial efforts to locate the boundary lines. Under Brown's direction almost the entire 40 acres of timbers belonging to Mrs. Williamson was clear cut. Cutting was also done on W. B. Tate's land, though not as extensively as on the Williamson tract. Cutting stopped when the Williamsons and Tates became aware of the cutting and asserted their ownership of the land. Brown subsequently pled guilty in the circuit court to two counts of malicious trespass arising out of these facts.

Proof of the amount of wood cut and removed came from the testimony of a forester. He made a 100% stump count of the cutting on both the Williamson and Tate lands. Measurements of the diameter and height of each stump were used to compute the volume of board feet in each tree cut. From the calculations the forester determined that 934 trees, with a stumpage value of $26,397.80 and a delivered value of $44,160, were cut off the Williamson land. 220 trees, having a stumpage value of $12,090 and delivered value of $19,039, were found to be cut from W. B. Tate's land.

The chancellor found each defendant who actually received and converted any timber liable for damages. Brown was held liable for damages in the amount of the delivered value of the timber plus the statutory penalty of $15 per tree. Although a conspiracy between Brown, Hines, and Craft, the principal cutter, had been alleged, the chancellor did not find that it had been proven. Miss Hines was held liable for $13,656.38, the amount she was paid by Brown less $343.62, the amount of the timbers on the property she owned south of the creek. Masonite and other purchasers of the converted timber were held liable for the delivered value of the timber they purchased. The damages against Masonite totaled $26,770.21. The chancellor found Masonite entitled, on its cross-bill, to recover against Brown the amount Masonite paid in damages to Mrs. Williamson and W. B. Tate.

Hilda Hines in her primary assignment of error contends that the judgment against her was erroneous because it was granted on the basis of negligence while the pleadings sounded of trespass and conversion based on conspiracy.

. . .

Conversion results from conduct intended to affect property. Conversion requires an intent to exercise dominion or control over goods inconsistent with the true owner's rights . . . In finding that Miss Hines should have realized the timber did not come from her own land, the chancellor found this intent to exercise dominion or control. Thus, when Miss Hines contracted for the cutting and received periodic payments for the timber, she exercised control over the timber inconsistent with the rights of Mrs. Williamson and W. B. Tate. Neither a mistake of fact on the part of Miss Hines concerning the location of the property liens nor the good faith of Miss Hines is a defense to this action of conversion. The chancellor's determination that Miss Hines should have realized the source of the timber is simply a finding that Miss Hines acted in a positive way sufficient to constitute conversion. Thus, we find no merit in this assignment of error.

. . .

The primary assignment of error by Masonite Corporation concerns the measure of damages used by the chancellor. The damages assessed against Masonite were based on the delivered value of the timber, the price paid for the timber delivered to the Masonite mills. Masonite contends that the correct measure of damages is the stumpage value, the value of the standing timber before it is enhanced by cutting, loading, and hauling to the lumber mills.

It is well settled when a trespass is willful, the trespasser is held liable for enhanced damages, the value of the timber as enhanced by the trespasser's labor in cutting, loading, and hauling the timber . . . The chancellor found that Brown, the original trespasser, was willful in his trespass and awarded damages of the delivered value of the timbers against Brown. However, Masonite argues that because it was not the original trespasser and because it acted in good faith in purchasing the timber, the enhanced damages of delivered value was not the appropriate measure of damages.

It is well settled in this state that the measure of damages in an action for conversion is the value of the property at the time and place of its conversion . . . . : Under this rule the delivered value is the appropriate measure of damages. Masonite converted the timber when it purchased the timber cut and delivered to its mill. Thus the value at the time and place of conversion is the delivered value.

Where trees have been cut and removed through inadvertence or mistake, the proper measure of damages is the stumpage value, the value of the standing trees, unenhanced by any labor of the trespasser . . . Masonite argues that because of its good faith in purchasing the timber, the measure of damages should be the stumpage value, the same as that used when the original trespasser acted in good faith. Some states have held that an innocent purchaser from a good faith trespasser is liable only for the stumpage value and not for any enhanced value . . . However this is not the situation in the present case.

While we have not ruled specifically on the measure of damages against an innocent purchaser of converted timber from a willful trespasser, we are of the opinion the delivered value is the appropriate measure of damages. This is the rule enunciated by an early U. S. Supreme Court case, *E. E. Bolles Wooden Ware Co. v. U. S.*, 106 U.S. 432, 1 S.Ct. 398, 27 L.Ed. 230 (1882), and followed in numerous jurisdictions . . . This position is strengthened, we think, by the fact that had the owners been able to identify their timber at the Masonite mills, they could have recovered possession from Masonite, causing Masonite to lose its purchase price, the delivered value. Thus, we are of the opinion that the delivered value of timber is the appropriate measure of damages against one who unknowingly purchased converted timber from a willful trespasser.

. . .

Having considered all the assignments of error, we find them without merit. Thus, this cause is affirmed.

Affirmed.

NOTES AND QUESTIONS

(1)   According to Prosser, the law of trespass to chattels differs markedly in two respects from the law of trespass to land. First, intention to trespass is an element of the tort of trespass to chattels. Actions for damages arising from non-intentional trespasses are now subsumed under the law of negligence. Second, actual damage is also an element of the tort. Still, because the gravamen of the wrong remains interference with the right of exclusive possession, substantial deprivation of that right is actionable even in the absence of physical damage. Should, therefore, the plaintiff have succeeded on a trespass to chattels action in *Foulds v. Willoughby*? If so, what damages should have been awarded?

(2)   Conversion is clearly the more potent tort because of the remedy, in effect a forced sale of the converted chattel to the tortfeasor.

The essential elements of the tort are the intentional exercise of dominion over the property of another and the right of immediate possession in the plaintiff vis-a-vis the defendant who violated the plaintiff's right. See, *e.g., Citizens National Bank v. Osetek*, 353 F. Supp. 958 (S.D.N.Y. 1973). The tort applies only to personal property; there can be no conversion of realty. See, *e.g., Rowe v. Burrup*, 518 P.2d 1386, 1389 (Idaho 1974).

The existence of the alternative remedies of trespass and conversion for the intermeddling with a chattel is explained by the independent historical development of the two torts and not by logic or even by modern conceptions of justice. Preceding materials have examined the evolution of the modern law of trespass. Conversion stems from a very old tort originally known as trover, signifying in Norman French a "finding" by the defendant followed by conversion to his own use. Later the action of detinue was invented for cases in which the defendant rightfully came into possession of a chattel but thereafter wrongfully refused to give it up upon demand of a person with superior right to possess it. All these fact patterns are now generally subsumed under the title conversion. See, *e.g., National Surety Corp. v. Applied Systems*, 418 So.2d 847 (Ala. 1982), explicitly so holding. Nevertheless, the old names do occasionally appear in modern opinions. See for example, *Bryce Hospital Credit Union, Inc. v. Warrior Dodge, Inc.*, 276 So.2d 602 (Ala. 1973), wherein the plaintiff brought an action of detinue against a repair shop owner who refused to release the plaintiff's car that had been brought in for repairs.

(3)   The typical conversion remedy is to award the value of the thing at the date of conversion. In addition, many courts award interest from the date of conversion. See, e.g, *Gillette v. Stapleton*, 336 So.2d 1226 (Fla. App. 1976). Under what circumstances would it also be appropriate to award damages for loss of use of the chattel? See, *e.g., Alexander v. Qwik Change Car Center, Inc.*, 352 So.2d 188 (La. 1977).

Because of the potency of the remedy, *Fouldes v. Willoughby* would not permit an action of conversion for every slight exercise of dominion over a chattel. One of the earliest cases on this point was *Edwards v. Helm*, 5 Ill. 143 (1843), which held that a person who had ridden a horse 15 miles before returning it had not converted it. The position of the Restatement, Torts, Second is as follows:[5]

---

[5] Copyright 1965 by The American Law Institute. Reprinted with the permission of The American Law Institute.

§ 222A:

(1) Conversion is an intentional exercise of dominion or control over a chattel which so seriously interferes with the right of another to control it that the actor may justly be required to pay the other the full value of the chattel.

(2) In determining the seriousness of the interference and the justice of requiring the actor to pay the full value, the following factors are important:

(a) the extent and duration of the actor's exercise of dominion or control;

(b) the actor's intent to assert a right in fact inconsistent with the other's right of control;

(c) the actor's good faith;

(d) the extent and duration of the resulting interference with the other's right of control;

(e) the harm done to the chattel;

(f) the inconvenience and expense caused to the other.

See, *e.g.*, *Mustola v. Toddy*, 456 P.2d 1004 (Ore. 1969).

(4)   Use or destruction of "found" articles may constitute a conversion. Indeed, this was the foundation of the ancient action in trover. Is this rule too burdensome in a "throw-away" culture? Is a person risking liability by picking up and disposing of what appears to be discarded items or even litter in the street? *Boston Educational Research Co. v. American Machine & Foundry Co.*, 488 F.2d 344, 349 (1st Cir. 1973), held that "a possessor faced with material left behind cannot act unreasonably but is entitled to act on appearances." The defendant destroyed certain valuable chattels that appeared to be trash. He was exonerated.

(5)   Plaintiffs will sometimes prefer to repossess a converted chattel than sell it to a wrongdoer. When the wrongdoer had wrongfully taken the chattel, the common law recovery action was known as *replevin*; whereas, if the defendant had rightfully gained possession but wrongfully withheld it at a later time, the recovery action would be *detinue*. Because recovery remedies are usually deemed to be under the purview of property law rather than tort law, no further examination of them will be made here.

(6)   What kinds of things may be converted? Specifically, does the taking of a tangible representation of an intangible asset, such as a stock certificate, make the converter accountable for anything more than the actual value of the paper in the stock certificate? Courts are now more likely to permit recovery of the value of the intangible asset than they once were.

(7)   The problem opening this section is a common risk of modern commercial practices. See, *e.g.*, *Richmond v. Fields Chevrolet Co.*, 493 P.2d 154 (Ore. 1972). The outcomes of the cases are strongly influenced by the terms of the purchase agreements, local statutes, and public policy considerations, particularly in considering whether the terms of harsh agreements are enforceable. Some statutes authorize repossessions that would otherwise constitute conversions. For example, the plaintiff in *Fendler v. Texaco Oil Co.*, 499 P.2d 179 (Ariz. 1972), was unable to recover against a towing company who removed a vehicle from a no parking zone and refused to release it until a towing bill was paid. Nevertheless, where a statute

permits repossession of secured property, failure to comply exactly with the prescribed procedure may nullify any statutory defense to conversion. See, *e.g.,* *Wells v. Central Bank of Alabama,* 347 So.2d 114 (Ala. Civ. App. 1977).

§ 15.03   NUISANCE

Sic Utere Two Ut Alienum Non Laedas

"A nuisance may be merely a right thing in the wrong place — like a pig in the parlor instead of the barnyard."

Sutherland, J. *Village of Euclid v. Ambler Realty Co.,* 272 U.S. 365, 47 S.Ct. 114 (1926).

PROBLEM C

Anytown was a very quiet village. After a valuable mineral was discovered in the surrounding countryside, the population rapidly quadrupled, bringing strange people and odd ways. A private operator began a child care center in a big house purchased from an elderly couple who moved out of town. It was located on Main Street in the middle of a fine old residential area. Twenty-five pre-school age children attended the center, arriving before 8:00 a.m. each morning and departing about 5:00 p.m.

During the day the children played in the yard, sang songs inside, slept and ate. The coming and going, singing and general hubbub destroyed the tranquility of the sleepy neighborhood.

Bus service was instituted to Anytown. The buses had to traverse some lightly paved public streets that heretofore had been used only by passenger cars. The heavy buses soon crumbled the pavement, making the roads extremely rough. In addition, the buses vibrated the earth and rattled windows and dishes in the old homes. The plaster in some of the homes cracked and broke.

A bank with a chiming clock tower came to town. The clock chimed once on quarter past the hour, twice on the half hour, three times on the three quarter hour, and the time plus a catchy tune on the hour. The chiming began at 7:00 a.m. and continued until midnight. Young children were disturbed late at night and during nap time; night workers were disturbed during the morning; elderly people were disturbed during the early morning, midafternoon and late evening; and several church congregations were disturbed during services throughout the day and week.

Tom and Mary Jones, Jim and Betty Smith, and Tim and Grace Taylor brought nuisance actions: against the child care center to enjoin the use of the site for anything but a residence; against the bus company for damages done to their homes; and against the bank to enjoin the chiming of the bells. In addition, the six collectively sought damages for harm done the public street and an injunction against future use of buses on the lightly paved streets.

The defendants demurred to each count of the various actions. Which if any ought to be sustained?

[A] Gravamen of Private Nuisance

BALDWIN v. McCLENDON
Alabama Supreme Court
288 So. 2d 761 (1974)

McCALL, JUSTICE.

The respondents, Robert Baldwin and W. J. Bottcher, appeal from an adverse final decree in equity.

The appellees, James E. McClendon and Ethel McClendon, are husband and wife. Their home, for some fifteen years, has been a forty-seven acre farm, located in a rural agricultural area of Blount County, about seven miles southeast of Oneonta on the road to Springville. In early 1970, the appellants commenced hog production on a large commercial scale on the appellant Baldwin's property which adjoins the appellees. In their business, the appellants operate two hog parlors each with a separate connecting lagoon. One hog parlor will house something over a thousand hogs and a second smaller one will accommodate approximately four hundred. There is also a third servicing lagoon. The hog parlor is a covered shelter with a concrete floor, laid on a plane, slightly declining toward the adjoining lagoon. The hogs are fed and watered in the parlors, and there they live, sleep and grow to a desired weight, when they are topped out. The lagoons which adjoin the hog parlors are related facilities, designed for the purpose of retaining and disposing of the waste material excreted by the hogs on the floor in their parlors. These lagoons are entrenched bodies of water into which the hog waste is flushed down with water in cleaning the parlor floors. In the lagoons, the waste material, comingling with the water, creates a chemical reaction resulting in a disintegration of the waste. This causes the emission of offensive odors. During the trial, the extent and intensity of the odor was the subject of much conflicting testimony. The appellees and witnesses offered by them, in general, said that the odor is so bad that they had to keep the doors and windows in the house closed, that it sickened them at the stomach, caused loss of appetite and practically ruined all outdoor recreation about the homeplace. The appellees' residence was said to be at distances varying from two hundred to a thousand feet from the nearest hog parlor and adjoining lagoon. Witnesses testified that these facilities adjoined the appellees' land near the division line between the parties.

. . .

The court further found that the operation of the hog parlors and lagoons was an obnoxious nuisance subject to abatement by a court of equity, and that the appellees suffered damages from the nuisance because of its proximity to their home, one of the lagoons being about as close to the appellees' property line as it could be built. The court also observed that the appellants had spent some $31,300 in creating the hog parlors and lagoons, and that an injunction would bring a severe blow to them. The court concluded that the appellees were entitled to have the nuisance abated, or else, be compensated in damages, if the nuisance is allowed to continue.

Accordingly, the court ordered and decreed that the appellants be enjoined, prohibited and restrained from operating the hog parlors and lagoons, provided that, if the appellants paid into the court the sum of $3,000 as damages for the use of the appellees, the injunction would not go into effect, and the appellees' only relief would be compensation for damages, but, if not paid within thirty days, the injunction would go into full force and effect without further orders of the court.

The appellants argue that their operation is carried on in a rural community given over almost entirely to agricultural pursuits, such as the growing of farm produce, the raising of turkeys and chickens, the dairy business, and hog and cattle production, and that it follows that fowl and animal odors will permeate the area to some degree. They assert that the appellees should endure some unpleasantness and not be permitted to enjoin a lawful business, the facilities for which were constructed according to approved plans and specifications, and the operation of which is conducted in a reaonable manner.

While these contentions must be considered in deciding the case, we think the decision also hinges on other factors, such as the location and proximity of the operation to the appellees' home, the intensity and volume of the odors, their interference, if any, with the appellees' own well-being and the enjoyment of their home, and any consequential depreciation in value of their home. It appears that the trial judge considered these matters.

In *Grady v. Wolsner*, 46 Ala. 381, the court said that anything constructed on a person's premises which, of itself, or by its intended use, directly injures a neighbor in the proper use and enjoyment of his property, is a nuisance.

In 1 Wood on Nuisances, § 556, quoted in *Hundley v. Harrison*, 123 Ala. 292, 297, 26 So. 294, the author lays down the rule as to a private nuisance to be that a man may do an act on his own land which is not unlawful or wrong — not using it in such manner as to injure another, for he may not so use his property as to injure another. *Hundley, supra*, states:

. . . When he sends on to the lands of his neighbor noxious smells, smoke, etc., then he is not doing an act on his own property only, but he is doing an act on his neighbor's property also; because every man has a right, by the common law, to the pure air and to have no noxious smells sent on his lands, unless by a period of time a man has, by what is called prescriptive right, obtained the power of throwing a burden on his neighbor's property. . . .

The above statement of a principle should be and is qualified in the same decision, where the court said:

. . . "In the case of noisome smells, as with nuisances from smoke or noxious vapors, the stenches must be of such a character as to be offensive to the senses, or as to produce actual physical discomfort, such as materially interfere with the comfortable enjoyment of property within their sphere. It is not necessary that the smells should be hurtful or unwholesome, it is sufficient if they are offensive, or produce such consequences, inconvenience or discomfort, as to impair the comfortable enjoyment of property, by persons of ordinary sensibilities," — such as people generally, in the absence of proof to the contrary, will be presumed to have. "A smell that is simply disagreeable to ordinary persons, is such physical annoyance as makes the use of property producing it a nuisance, whether it be hurtful in its effects or not." . . . § 563; 16 Am. & Eng. Enc.Law, 948; *Campbell v. Seaman*, 63 N.Y. 568, [s.c.] 20 Am.Rep. 567.

On several occasions, we have defined a private nuisance as "any establishment, erected on the premises of one, though for the purposes of trade or business, lawful in itself, which, from the situation, the inherent qualities of the business, or the manner in which it is conducted, directly causes substantial injury to the property of another, or produces material annoyance and inconvenience to the occupants of adjacent dwellings, rendering them physically uncomfortable, is a nuisance. In applying this principle, it has been repeatedly held that smoke, offensive odors, noise, or vibrations, when of such degree or extent as to materially interfere with the ordinary comfort of human existence, will constitute a nuisance."

. . .

Guided by the above statements, whether or not a private nuisance exists depends on the facts in the case, *Martin Bldg. Co. v. Imperial Laundry Co.*, 220 Ala. 90, 124 So. 82, and the weight and credibility that the court gives to the testimony and evidence heard in open court, including the fact that the trial judge made a personal inspection of the subject property and stated his own findings.

The trial court concluded from all the evidence that the odors and gases which came from the hog parlors and lagoons were of such noxious intensity and volume as to interfere with the appellees' enjoyment of their home and made its use physically uncomfortable, less desirable and less valuable than it otherwise would be.

. . .

[Those findings were supported by the evidence in the record.]

Under a prayer for general relief, a court of equity has power to mold its relief to meet the equities developed in the trial . . . that are consistent with the allegations of the bill. . . . Where a court of equity assumes jurisdiction for injunctive relief, it will retain the bill for all purposes necessary to a complete determination and settlement of the matters involved, though they be purely of a legal nature.

. . .

Here, the trial court decreed that the appellees were entitled to have the nuisance abated, or else be compensated in damages, if the nuisance is to continue. No doubt the court deemed such relief appropriate under the facts. We will not undertake to surmise the court's reasons for so decreeing. We do state though that there are facts and law present to support the trial court's decision. The authorities that we have cited above make it clear that the trial court had the power and discretion to make this decision. No cross-appeal has been taken.

The effect of the decree is clear. If the appellants do not pay the $3,000, the nuisance will be abated, and no damages will then be forthcoming, because the court did not award any damages other than to realty. On the other hand, if the appellants pay the damages, they may continue their operation, and this will continue indefinitely the depreciated value of the appellees' property. The damages awarded are measurable for all time, because if paid, the nuisance may be expected to continue. In that case, the measure of damages for the nuisance, is the difference in the value of the property for a home with and without such odor . . .

. . .

Moreover, assuming that the appellants' operation met some set of sanitary standards for similar operations, this would not affect the appellees' right to equitable relief, because the issue is not whether the appellants were negligent . . . or their business lawful, but whether or not from the inherent qualities of the business, or the manner in which it is conducted, it directly causes substantial injury to the properties of the appellees, or produces material annoyance and inconvenience to them in the comfortable enjoyment of their home.

. . .

Having considered those issues that have been sufficiently raised in the appellant's assignments of error and argued by them, and finding no error, we affirm the final decree of the trial court.

Affirmed.

McCARTY v. NATURAL CARBONIC GAS CO.
New York Court of Appeals
189 N.Y. 40, 81 N.E. 549 (1907)

VANN, J.

This action was brought to restrain the defendant from so operating its manufactory as to cause smoke, soot, and dust emitted from its chimneys to gather and settle about the dwelling house of the plaintiff to his annoyance and injury. The trial court found the following facts in substance:

[The defendant burned soft coal in a manufacturing operation. The black smoke and soot damaged the plaintiff's property and interfered with its use.]

The rental value of the plaintiff's house has been injured by the use of soft coal by the defendant to the extent of $800, and he has incurred expense for cleaning rugs to the extent of $18 more. The court, after repeating as conclusions of law its findings of fact in relation to reasonable and necessary use, further found as conclusions of law that "the defendant should be enjoined, restrained, and forbidden from burning soft coal on its said plant in the village of Saratoga Springs, N.Y., for the purpose of generating steam," and that "the plaintiff herein is entitled to the sum of $818 damages, and is also entitled to the costs of the action." Upon appeal to the Appellate Division the judgment was modified by deducting from the damages awarded the sum of $18 as of the date when the judgment was entered, and, as so modified, the judgment was unanimously affirmed.

. . .

The law relating to private nuisances is a law of degree, and usually turns on the question of fact whether the use is reasonable or not under all the circumstances. No hard and fast rule controls the subject, for a use that is reasonable under one set of facts would be unreasonable under another. Whether the use of property to carry on a lawful business, which creates smoke or noxious gases in excessive quantities, amounts to a nuisance, depends on the facts of each particular case. 21 Am. & Eng. Ency. of Law (2d Ed.) 692. Location, priority of occupation, and the fact that the injury is only occasional, are not conclusive, but are to be considered in connection with all the evidence, and the inference drawn from all the facts

proved whether the controlling fact exists that the use is unreasonable. If that fact
is found, a nuisance is established, and the plaintiff is entitled to relief in some
form. Unless that fact is found, or it is an inference of law from other facts found,
no nuisance is established, even if the plaintiff shows that he has suffered some
damage, annoyance, and injury. Those evils are at times incidental to civilized life,
and the sufferer finds compensation in the arts and agencies of civilized society.
. . . What is reasonable is sometimes a question of law and at others a question of
fact. When it depends upon an inference from peculiar, numerous, or complicated
circumstances, it is usually a question of fact. Whether the use of property by one
person is reasonable, with reference to the comfortable enjoyment of his own
property by another, generally depends upon many and varied facts; such as
location, nature of the use, character of the neighborhood, extent and frequency of
the injury, the effect on the enjoyment of life, health, and property, and the like.
Such was the nature of the question in this case which, we think, is one of fact. The
case last cited involved injury to ornamental shrubbery on land adjacent to a
village, from the noxious gases of a brick factory, which dug the clay on its own
premises, and the exhaustive opinion of Judge Earl holds, with the concurrence of
all the judges, that articles of luxury are as much under the protection of the law as
articles of necessity; that it is immaterial that the injury is only occasional; that the
right to an injunction is not affected by the fact that the brick kiln was used before
the plaintiff purchased his land; and that if the use is such "as to produce a tangible
and appreciable injury to neighboring property, or such as to render its enjoyment
specially uncomfortable or inconvenient," it constitutes a nuisance.

. . .

The leading authorities in all jurisdictions hold, that the question is whether the
defendant makes a reasonable, or, as some judges express themselves, a proper
use of his own property? Sometimes negligence is referred to as an element in the
question. Judge Landon once pointedly said: "A lawful business negligently
conducted is not a lawful business lawfully conducted"; but, as the quotation
implies, since a negligent use of one's own property to the injury of another is an
unreasonable use, the ultimate question after all is whether the use is reasonable.
Dunsbach v. Hollister, 2 N.Y. Supp. 94, 49 Hun, 352, 354. Negligence, wrong
business methods, improper appliances, and the like may bear upon, but do not
control, the question of reasonable use. If the use is reasonable, there can be no
private nuisance; but if the use is unreasonable and results in substantial injury, an
actionable nuisance exists. Trifling results are disregarded, for the courts proceed
with great caution and will not interfere with the use of property by the owner
thereof, unless such use is unreasonable, the injury material and actual, not
fanciful or sentimental. "Lex non favet votis delicatorum." *Genet v. Del. & Hud.
Canal Co.*, 122 N.Y. 505, 529, 25 N.E. 922; Wood on Nuisances (3d Ed.) 679;
Jaggard on Torts, 744; Garrett on Law of Nuisances, 146.

The defendant's business is lawful and not a nuisance per se, although it has
been found that as carried on it is a nuisance in fact. The extent more than the
nature of the injury, the quantum, rather than the damnum, constitutes the
nuisance. Some smoke is generally created by the natural and ordinary use of land
near a village or city, and, while this may sometimes be annoying to neighbors, it is
part of the price paid for living where there are neighbors. But when the smoke is
so unusual and excessive as to materially interfere with the ordinary comfort of
human existence, the trier of the facts, taking into account all the circumstances,

such as public utility, locality, immediate surroundings, and the like, may find the use unreasonable. This is not a case where the defendant cannot carry on its business without injury to neighboring property, for all damage can be avoided by the use of hard coal, as is done by one of its competitors in the same kind of business in the same locality, or possibly by the use of some modern appliance such as a smoke consumer, although either would involve an increase in expense. It is better, however, that profits should be somewhat reduced than to compel a householder to abandon his home, especially when he did not "come to the nuisance," but was there before. "The safety of property generally is superior in right to a particular use of a single piece of property by its owner. It renders the enjoyment of all property more secure by preventing such use of one piece by one man as may injure all his neighbours." *Sullivan v. Dunham*, 161 N. Y. 290, 300, 55 N. E. 923, 76 Am. St. Rep. 274, 47 L. R. A. 715. The use made of property may be unpleasant, unsightly, or, to some extent, annoying and disagreeable to the occupants of neighboring property without creating a nuisance. When, however, it not only interferes materially with the physical comfort of persons in their own homes, but also causes some financial injury to the owner, it constitutes a nuisance. That is this case, and the facts found compel an affirmance except in one particular.

The conclusion of law that the defendant should be enjoined from burning soft coal on its premises to make steam is too broad, for it is unlimited as to time or circumstances, and the judgment follows the conclusion. If the defendant, by the use of some appliance now known or which may become known hereafter, can burn soft coal in its factory without injury to the plaintiff, it cannot lawfully be deprived of that right. If the plaintiff should convert his house into a factory, using soft coal, he would not be entitled to an injunction. The defendant, therefore, should be permitted to apply at Special Term, upon proper notice at any time, for a modification of the decree at the foot thereof, permitting it to burn soft coal, upon proof of such a change of facts as to make such use of its property no longer unreasonable. Subject to this modification, the judgment should be affirmed, with costs.

O'BRIEN, J. (dissenting).

The plaintiff recovered a judgment in this case, enjoining the defendant from the transaction of business on its own land. Damages have also been awarded to the plaintiff as compensation for the injury complained of. The question arising upon the appeal is whether the facts found in the case sustain the conclusion of law.

. . .

The contention of the plaintiff in the present case is that the defendant in the operation of its manufacturing plant should have used anthracite coal instead of soft coal. It is found that this change must involve an additional expense upon the defendant. The amount of that additional expense has not been found, but it is found that in order to conduct the defendant's business from 2 1/2 to 4 tons of coal per day must be burned. The defendant cannot carry on its business without observing due economy in its management. If it can be compelled by the plaintiff for his own comfort to impose additional burdens upon the business, the result may be the loss of reasonable profits, and it may be in the destruction of the business entirely. If the plaintiff can legally demand that the defendant must use anthracite coal instead of soft coal, there is no reason why he may not demand other changes that would enhance his own comforts or enjoyment of his property. It is fair to assume from the findings that the defendant consumes on an average of 3 tons of coal per day. In the course of a year it is necessary, therefore, to burn about 1,000 tons, and as the cost of hard coal would be about $2 per ton more than that of soft coal, it would require the defendant to increase the expense of operating its plant in the sum of about $2,000 annually. There is nothing in the record to show that the business which the defendant is conducting is a very profitable one. It may well be that the business has not yet produced any profit whatever, and such an increase in the expense might not only absorb the profits, but result in a loss. It has been said that the power to tax includes the power to destroy, and if the plaintiff or other parties similarly situated, armed with the decree of the court, can compel the defendant to make the changes suggested by the judgment in this case for his own comfort, the application of such a principle might go far to render the defendant's property and business worthless.

It is quite difficult, if not impossible, to state from the findings, with any degree of accuracy, just what the legal injury is of which the plaintiff complains. No injury has been suffered from the use of soft coal to the trees, shrubbery, or the grounds of the plaintiff, nor to his health or that of his family. The smoke and dust have not injured his house either in the interior or exterior, or the furniture or decorations. It was not shown or found that the conduct of the defendant's business discolored the plaintiff's house in any way. The present condition in that respect, whatever it is, is due to ordinary use and the lapse of time. The judgment must stand, if at all, upon that vague and somewhat fanciful claim that his home is not as comfortable as it would have been if the defendant's business was not carried on at all, or carried on in some different manner, or by the use of other materials at greater expense. No tangible legal right of the plaintiff as against the defendant has been or is violated, since whatever effect the operation of the defendant's business and the use of its own property has upon that of the plaintiff in diminishing his personal comfort is one of the results or incidents of residing in a locality where manufacturing is lawfully and necessarily carried on. All the cases hold that the plaintiff or other parties similarly situated must endure some inconvenience or some degree of discomfort, and I am unable to see why the facts of this case as found do not bring it within the operation of that principle.

We are not making law for this case merely. A legal principle is involved of far-reaching importance. Whatever we decide in this case must apply to every manufactory or manufacturing establishment in the state. It is a question of comfort on the part of the plaintiff. On the part of the defendant it may be a question of life or death, and it certainly is a question of the right to conduct a business such as this which the defendant is engaged in with good judgment and reasonable economy. There is no question, such as was involved in the *Bohan* Case, of noxious smells and poisonous vapors due to the use of naphtha, which it was alleged and found was detrimental to health. In the present case it is a question as to how far the defendant may be compelled to increase the expenses of its business in order to secure greater comfort for the plaintiff in the enjoyment of his home. Has he a legal right to demand that his property shall be exempt from smoke, dust, or cinders on certain occasions when the wind is in the right direction, or the atmosphere in the right condition to produce the discomforts of which the plaintiff complains? Unless such a legal right exists, the judgment in this case is wrong, since it imposes a burden upon the defendant's business greatly in excess of any monetary or other loss resulting from the use of soft coal. It seems to me that within the principles announced by this court, and which have been stated, that no such legal right exists, and hence the judgment should be reversed, and a new trial granted, costs to abide the event.

NOTES AND QUESTIONS

(1)   What is the gravamen of private nuisance?

The term *nuisance*, as with the term *trespass*, technically denotes the nature of the harm done a property interest rather than the nature of a defendant's wrongful act. In essence, therefore, to establish the presence of a nuisance is to establish only damages. Still remaining is to establish whether or not the actions of the perpetrator of the nuisance are legally culpable.

It is commonly accepted that a defendant is liable for the nuisance he creates if he was negligent in causing it, if he intentionally caused it, or if he was engaged in an activity that would give rise to strict liability under the general theory of *Rylands v. Fletcher.* See, *e.g., Hero Lands Co. v. Texaco, Inc.*, 310 So.2d 93, 97 (La. 1975), and *Burr v. Adam Eidemiller, Inc.*, 126 A.2d 403, 406 (Pa. 1956). This means that the defendant will not be held responsible for innocently caused nuisances where he was not engaged in an ultra hazardous activity. It also means that a defendant may have an affirmative defense that would ordinarily apply as a foil to the particular theory that underpins the plaintiff's action.

(2)   Do both the preceding cases use a balancing approach that has not been seen before to determine the existence of a cause of action? Is it novel? The Ohio Supreme Court explained the need of it, as follows:

All systems of jurisprudence recognize the requirement of compromises in the social state. Members of society must submit to annoyance consequent upon the reasonable use of property. "Sic utere tuo ut alienum non laedas" is an old maxim which has a broad application. If such rule were held to mean that one must never use his own property in such a way as to do any injury to his neighbor or his property, it could not be enforced in civilized society. People who live in organized communities must of necessity suffer some damage, inconvenience and annoyances from their neighbors. For these annoyances, inconveniences and damages, they are generally compensated by the advantages incident to living in a civilized state.

Antonik v. Chamberlain, 78 N.E.2d 759-60 (Ohio 1947). In *Antonik*, the court refused to enjoin an airport that allegedly would violate the peace and tranquility of a residential neighborhood. Said the court, at 760:

> The case before us presents legal and equitable principles of far-reaching importance. Whatever we decide here has a bearing upon every airport in this state. On the part of the plaintiffs it is in most part a question of comfort. On the part of the defendants it is a question of the life or death of a legitimate and necessary business. The inconvenience to be experienced by the plaintiffs from the erection of the airport does not appear to be any greater than the inconvenience or damage resulting to the owners and occupiers of residential property in the vicinity of or adjacent to any airport erected in this state. *Powell v. Craig*, 113 Ohio St. 245, at page 249, 148 N.E. 607.

(3) Because of the balancing approach, one can find different courts coming to opposite conclusions on what appears to be quite similar factual circumstances. For example, in *Waschak v. Moffat*, 109 A.2d 310 (Pa. 1954), the Pennsylvania Supreme Court denied a remedy on facts similar to those in *McCarty*. Was the fact that Pennsylvania is a major coal mining and consuming state a factor? The Pennsylvania court snidely quoted the statement, "Without smoke, Pittsburgh would have remained a very pretty *village*," which had been uttered by dissenting judge Musmanno in an earlier case. Musmanno himself would have granted a remedy in *Waschak*.

(4) The dividing line between a trespass and a nuisance is sometimes vague and tenuous. At common law wafting smoke, vapor and odors were treated as nuisances. The physical character of the microscopic particles involved was not recognized as a sufficient tangible invading force to constitute a trespass. Although most decisions follow the common law, a few modern decisions have held that the entry of invisible particles with potency to harm (*i.e.*, certain toxic compounds) may constitute a trespass as well as a nuisance. See, *e.g.*, *Martin v. Reynolds Metals Company*, 342 P.2d 790 (Or. 1960), cert.den. 362 U.S. 918, 80 S.Ct. 677, 4 L.Ed.2d 739, *Borland v. Sanders Lead Company, Inc.*, 369 So.2d 523 (Ala. 1979), and *Maryland Heights Leasing, Inc. v. Mallinckbrodt, Inc.*, 706 S.W.2d 218 (Mo.App. 1986) (radioactive gases). *Martin v. Union Pacific Railroad Company*, 474 P.2d 740 (Or. 1970), extended this doctrine to hold that an invading prairie fire constituted a trespass despite the fact that fire had anciently been classified as a "tenuous" substance.

(5) In *McCarty*, Judge Vann observed that the defendant was not engaged in a nuisance per se. This alludes to an infrequent categorization used by some courts, explained as follows:

Nuisances fall into two categories — nuisance *per se* and nuisance *per accidens* or in fact. A nuisance *per se* is an act, instrument, or structure which is a nuisance at all times and under any circumstances. A nuisance *per accidens* or nuisance in fact is an act, instrument, or a structure which becomes a nuisance by reason of surrounding circumstances. (*Dill* v. *Excell Packing Co.*, 183 Kan. 513, 331 P.2d 539; and 66 C.J.S. Nuisances § 3, p. 733.) Obviously, under the above definiton neither a football field nor a baseball diamond, or the operation thereof, can be said to be a nuisance *per se*. (For example see *Riffey* v. *Rush*, 51 N.D. 188, 199 N.W. 523 [baseball]; and *Board of Education of Louisville v. Klein et al.*, 303 Ky. 234, 197 S.W.2d 427 [football].) Since the football field and baseball diamond are not nuisances *per se*, then the critical question for our determination is whether the proposed construction and uses thereof, under all the surrounding circumstances established by the evidence, substantially interferes with the comfortable enjoyment by appellees of the adjacent premises owned by them.

Vickridge 1st & 2nd Addition Homeowners Ass'n v. Catholic Diocese, 510 P.2d 1296 (Kan. 1973). What might constitute a nuisance per se? *Buddy v. State*, 229 N.W.2d 865 (Mich. App. 1975), lists some, and *Rosario v. City of Lansing*, 268 N.W.2d 230 (Mich. 1978), indicates a special context in which a nuisance per se would be actionable but a nuisance per accidens would not.

Nuisance cases number in the hundreds. Some uses that have been found to be nuisances are: Funeral homes ("ordinarily" a nuisance in exclusively residential areas), *Mitchell v. Bearden*, 503 S.W.2d 904 (Ark. 1974); funeral home in "essentially" a residential neighborhood, *Travis v. Moore*, 377 So.2d 609 (Miss. 1979);

keeping of more than 40 dogs in residential areas, *Larson v. McDonald*, 212 N.W.2d 505 (Iowa 1973); gas pipeline next to residences, *Hero Lands Co. v. Texaco, Inc.*, 310 So.2d 93 (La. 1975); vibrations from heavy buses, *D'Amico v. New Orleans Public Service, Inc.*, 348 So.2d 116 (La. App. 1977); ready mix concrete plant in proper zoning but next to residential area, *Morgan County Concrete Co. v. Tanner*, 374 So.2d 1344 (Ala. 1979); noise from striking of shoes on terrazo floor in commons area of a condominium, *Baum v. Coronado Condominium Ass'n*, 376 So.2d 914 (Fla. App. 1979).

Some uses that have been found not to be nuisances are: funeral home with approved zoning in area "not exclusively" residential, *Rigsby v. Burton*, 305 So.2d 366 (Ala. 1974); chiming electronic bell tones, *Acker v. Protective Life Insurance Co.*, 353 So.2d 1150 (Ala. 1978); noise and commotion attendant to increased automobile traffic from proposed real estate development, *Fugazzoto v. Brookwood One*, 325 So.2d 161 (Ala. 1976); the operation of a day nursery next to a guest house, *Beckman v. Marshall*, 85 So.2d 552 (Fla. 1956); and, the erection of a garish Christmas display that attracted large crowds of people into a residential neighborhood, *Rodriguez v. Copeland*, 475 So.2d 1071 (La. 1985).

(6) What effect did the *McCarty* court give the finding that "the plaintiff had owned his property for several years before the defendant erected its factory"? What arguments can be made for and against a proposition that "coming to a nuisance" defeats a plaintiff's action? Although some courts state that "priority of occupation is a circumstance of considerable weight," *Helmkamp v. Clark Ready Mix Concrete*, 214 N.W.2d 126 (Iowa 1974), that factor seldom seems to be determinative. In *Brede v. Minnesota Crushed Stone Co.*, 173 N.W. 805, 808 (Minn. 1919), the Minnesota Supreme Court went so far as to say, "little is now left of the doctrine that a person coming to a nuisance had no right to complain of it." See also *Department of Transp. v. Burnette*, 384 So.2d 916, 922 (Fla. App. 1980), citing Prosser approvingly for the proposition that "coming to a nuisance" has little validity where the new owner "buys in good faith and not for the sole purpose of a vexatious lawsuit."

Nevertheless, an agricultural operation, even the "hog parlors" in *Baldwin v. McClendon*, makes a sympathetic case if it began far in the country and gradually was "grown to" by a city. Acknowledging that such an operation had some equities, *Spur Industries, Inc. v. Del E. Webb Development Co.*, 494 P.2d 700 (Ariz. 1970), required the plaintiff to bear the cost of moving the defendant's cattle feed lot to a more remote location. Does that appear to be a reasonable outcome? What are the limits of the approach?

(7) Is the validity of a plaintiff's nuisance complaint objectively or subjectively tested? The following exempt states what probably is the universal view:

> In dealing with the question of what constitutes a nuisance, the characteristics and temperament of the affected person or persons must be taken into consideration. The test to be applied is the effect of the condition complained of on ordinary persons with a reasonable disposition in ordinary health and possessing the average and normal sensibilities. It is a well-settled principle of law that:

> The test is not what the effect of the matters complained of would be on persons of delicate or dainty habits of living, or of financial or fastidious tastes; or on persons who are delicate, or invalids, afflicted with disease,

bodily ills; or abnormal physical conditions; or on persons who are of nervous temperament, or peculiarly sensitive to annoyance or disturbance of the character complained of; or on persons who use their land for purposes which require exceptional freedom from deleterious influences. 66 C.J.S., Nuisances, § 18(c), p. 765.

Beckman v. Marshall, 85 So.2d 552, 555 (Fla. 1956).

(8)   The *McCarty* opinions contain some of the earliest economic reasoning that can be found in a Tort case. If they had been combined, *McCarty* may have advanced the use of the Learned Hand formula — in 1907!

Judge Vann's majority opinion found that the pollution damaged plaintiff by $818: $800 in a lower rental value of his property and $18 in additional cleaning expenses. Assume these were annual costs. Judge O'Brien's dissenting opinion noted the defendant would incur additional costs of $2,000 annually to burn cleaner coal. How would a modern Law & Economics judge decide whether the defendant had committed a tort to burn the polluting coal? B would be $2000. The product of $P \times L$ would be $818 (the court found the loss to be certain, not just a probability). Since $2000 > $818, a court using the Learned Hand formula would not find the defendant to have been negligent to use the polluting coal and would be unlikely to order defendant to spend $2,000 to avoid only $818 in damages. (Would this mean that a defendant is permitted to harm a plaintiff knowingly and with immunity simply because inflicting the harm is the cheapest way to conduct the defendant's business?) But this assumes that only one home was harmed by the pollution. If even two others also suffered $818 damages, the L from the pollution ($3 \times $818) would exceed the B from the increased coal costs and defendant should be found liable.

(9)   The *McCarty* defendant lost. Did it necessarily have to purchase coal that cost $2000 more per year, even though plaintiff's damages were only $818 per year? Perhaps not. Recall the Coase Theorem provides that in the absence of prohibitive transaction costs the parties will arrive at the most efficient solution no matter which way a court's initial decision comes out. Rational parties with low transaction costs should be able to strike a deal somewhere between $818 and $2000 per year and thereby reach the most efficient solution.[6] Defendant might say to the plaintiff: "If the court's order is enforced, I will have to purchase coal that will cost me an additional $2,000 per year, but the less expensive coal harms you by only $818 per year. I will pay you $1,500 per year not to enforce the court's order against me, if you will permit me to use the less expensive coal. You would make $682 profit per year ($1500 - $818) and I would gain $500 (paying plaintiff $1500 per year instead of spending $2,000 for cleaner coal). We will both be better off." Unless the transaction costs of reaching this solution are too high or the parties are too angry to bargain rationally, the parties should reach the most efficient solution and defendant would not purchase the more expensive coal. (May parties voluntarily agree to ignore a court's order that one of them take a specific action?)

---

[6] This assumes there are no additional negative effects from using the less expensive type of coal.

[B]   Gravamen of Public Nuisance

CULWELL v. ABBOTT CONSTRUCTION COMPANY
Kansas Supreme Court
506 P.2d 1191 (1973)

PRAGER, JUSTICE:

This is an action to recover damages for personal injuries. The plaintiff, Dick Culwell claimed he was injured as the result of his tripping over a "chalk line" placed by the defendant, Abbott Construction Company, Inc. over a sidewalk leading into the Phillips County Hospital at Phillipsbury, Kansas. The case was tried to a jury which found in favor of the defendant. Most of the factual circumstances are not in dispute and are substantially as follows: The defendant, a building contractor, was engaged in construction work on the hospital building. The work involved a certain amount of excavating, and the defendant's employees had placed a "chalk line" or nylon string across the sidewalk and running nearly the length of the building to mark the perimeter of the excavation work. The sidewalk led to the doors of the hospital on the north side. The plaintiff Culwell, while using the sidewalk to enter the hospital, tripped over the "chalk line" and fell against a portion of the building.

. . .

The plaintiff's first point on this appeal is that the trial court erred in refusing to instruct the jury on the theory of nuisance as set forth in plaintiff's requested instruction No. 2.

. . .

Throughout the history of this state there has been an abundance of cases involving claims of injury based upon the maintenance of a nuisance. A reading of the nuisance cases in Kansas and other jurisdictions confirms the statement of Professor William L. Prosser that there is perhaps no more impenetrable jungle in the entire law than that which surrounds the word "nuisance." (Prosser, Law of Torts, 4th Ed., Ch. 15, § 186, p. 571.) In his exhaustive work on the law of torts, Professor Prosser points out that the word "nuisance" has meant all things to all men, and that there is a general agreement that the word is incapable of any exact or comprehensible definition. "Nuisance" in itself means no more than hurt, annoyance or inconvenience. Since the early period of the common law, the word "nuisance" in the tort field has encompassed two separate but often overlapping concepts . . . private nuisance and public nuisance. Private nuisance historically has been and is a tort related to an unlawful interference with a person's use or enjoyment of his land. The concept of a private nuisance does not exist apart from the interest of the landowner. Hence a private nuisance is a civil wrong, based on a disturbance of some right or interest in land. The remedy for it lies in the hands of the individual landowner whose rights have been disturbed. . . .

The concept of a public nuisance developed as an entirely separate principle based upon an infringement of the rights of the state or the community at large. Public nuisance comprehends a miscellaneous and diversified group of minor criminal offenses based on some interference with the interests of the community or the comfort or convenience of the general public. To be considered public, the nuisance must affect an interest common to the general public, rather than peculiar to one individual or only a few.

. . .

Stated in another way, a public nuisance is one which annoys a substantial portion of the community. . . . The earliest cases of public nuisance involved purprestures which were encroachments or obstructions on the public highway or some area of the public domain. Purprestures are held to be nuisances today. . . . At common law a public nuisance was always a crime and punishable as such. Down through the years, the concept of public nuisance has been broadly expanded to include a multitude of acts deemed inimical to public health, safety, comfort, peace, convenience or morals. Some examples of public nuisances are houses of prostitution, gambling dens, hog pens, illegal liquor establishments, indecent exhibitions, bullfights, unauthorized prize fights and the illegal practices of law and medicine.

The problem of distinguishing between public and private nuisances is further complicated by the fact that sometimes an individual may sustain an injury from a public nuisance which differs in kind from that sustained by the community in general. In that situation, the injured citizen may maintain an action and recover damages for his particular injury. . . . Today it is uniformly held that a private individual has no action for the invasion of a purely public right, unless his damage is in some way to be distinguished from that sustained by other members of the general public. It is not enough that he suffers the same inconvenience or is exposed to the same threatened injury as everyone else. In the absence of some peculiar individual injury, redress for a public nuisance must be left to the appointed representatives of the community. . . . The trouble is that once this rule is accepted, the courts have not always found it easy to determine what is a sufficient "peculiar damage" to support the private action. Some rather fine lines have been drawn in the decisions. Where a plaintiff suffers personal injury or harm to his health as a result of a public nuisance, there is no difficulty in finding a different kind of damage which justifies an action by the individual plaintiff. This is the rationale of those cases where cities have been liable for personal injuries caused by a public held nuisance. . . .

It should also be noted that a public nuisance may be a private nuisance as well when it interferes with an individual landowner's enjoyment of his land. This has served to muddle the problem. Professor Prosser points out another factor which causes confusion. Nuisance is a field of tort liability rather than a type of tortious conduct. Nuisance has reference to the interests invaded, to the damage or harm inflicted, and not to any particular kind of act or omission which has led to the invasion. Professor Prosser concludes that the attempt frequently made to distinguish between nuisance and negligence for example, is based entirely upon a mistaken emphasis based upon what the defendant has done rather than the result which has followed, and forgets completely the well-established fact that negligence is merely one type of conduct which may give rise to a nuisance. . . . In other words, a nuisance may result from conduct which is intentional or negligent or conduct which falls within the principle of strict liability without fault. The point is that nuisance is a result and negligence is a cause, and they cannot be distinguished otherwise.

Keeping these principles in mind, let us turn to the factual situation presented in the case at bar to determine whether or not the plaintiff may proceed against the defendant on the theory of *private* nuisance. We think it obvious that plaintiff cannot base his recovery on the theory of private nuisance, since nowhere does it appear that he was injured in relation to a right which he enjoyed by reason of his ownership of an interest in land. The fact of personal injury alone is not enough to give rise to a claim of private nuisance.

. . .

We next consider the question whether or not plaintiff has a claim against the defendant based upon personal injuries suffered as the result of a *public* nuisance. On this point the plaintiff contends that the "chalk line" across the sidewalk was an obstruction of a public highway which materially interfered with its use by the public and therefore constituted a public nuisance. We have held on several occasions that whether or not in a given case a nuisance has been created depends on many factors, such as the type of neighborhood, the nature of the thing or wrong complained of, its proximity to those alleging injury or damage, its *frequency, continuity, or duration,* and the damage or annoyance resulting, and each case must necessarily depend on its particular facts and circumstances.

. . .

We have no hesitancy whatsoever in holding that the "chalk line" across the sidewalk in the case at bar was not a public nuisance. In the first place obstructions of public streets or sidewalks of a temporary nature reasonably necessary for the improvement of private property or incidental to the proper use and enjoyment of the premises are not nuisances. . . . Here the hospital was in exercise of its rights in performing useful construction work on the hospital building and in having such work performed by the defendant construction company. It is undisputed in the evidence that "chalk lines," such as the one over which the plaintiff fell, are customarily used in the construction industry as a means of marking the boundaries of excavation work to be performed. A "chalk line" is an accepted tool used by contractors to carry out contracts of public and private construction. In the second place the undisputed evidence shows that the "chalk line" had been in its position across the sidewalk only a short period of time during the day in which the plaintiff was injured. In a number of cases we have held that one of the requisites of a nuisance is that it has been in existence for some period of time rather than being an isolated instance of a temporary nature. Frequency, continuity and duration are distinguishing factors to be considered in determining whether or not a nuisance exists.

In [an earlier case] a six-year-old boy brought suit to recover for personal injuries sustained when he stepped into hot burning coals resulting from the burning of a tree stump, by school employees on the school playground. We held that the burning tree stump was not a nuisance because of a lack of continuity or duration. In [an earlier case] the ten-year-old plaintiff was attacked and bitten by a coyote which had escaped from its enclosure at the city zoo and was running loose in the area frequented by visitors. We held that this was also an isolated instance of a temporary nature not falling within the definition of a nuisance under the decisions of the court. It was held that the facts presented only an ordinary negligence case.

When we apply the rationale of those cases to the case at bar, it is clear that the placing of the "chalk line" across the sidewalk did not constitute a public nuisance. The most that could be said for the situation is that the employees of the defendant Abbott Construction Company may have negligently and carelessly failed to provide sufficient warnings to pedestrians of the location of the "chalk line". Any right of recovery of necessity would have to be based on a theory of negligence alone. We hold that the trial court did not err in refusing to submit plaintiff's case to the jury on the theory of public nuisance.

. . .

For the reasons set forth above the judgment of the district court is affirmed.

NOTES AND QUESTIONS

(1)   What is the gravamen of a public nuisance? If private citizens cannot maintain actions to abate public nuisances, who can? Would the judicial system be better served if private citizens could maintain the actions? Several states including Michigan and Florida have enacted statutes liberalizing the right to sue under defined circumstances. These reflect the environmental activism of the late 1960s and the 1970s but seem not to have generated much litigation. Why?

(2)   While private citizens may not maintain an action to abate a public nuisance, nothing prevents the proper public official from seeking to abate public nuisance merely because the activity also degrades private property interests. Indeed, widespread interference with private property is one form of public nuisance. See, e.g., *Guillot v. Town of Lutcher*, 373 So.2d 1385 (La. App. 1979), noise, litter, spray and dirt from car wash; *Conley v. City of Montgomery*, 414 So.2d 581 (Ala. 1982), construction of housing units in violation of building code; and *State ex rel Shevin v. Morgan*, 289 So.2d 782 (Fla. App. 1974), operation of noisy mechanical scarecrow next to residential area.

By the same token, the act that constitutes a public nuisance may sometimes single out a particular private person for harm. Must that person depend upon a public official to bring an action for relief? The test enunciated in *Culwell v. Abbott Construction Co.*, 506 P.2d 1191 (Kan. 1973), has widespread, if not universal, acceptance. Applying this test, the court in *Burgess v. M/V Tamano*, 370 F. Supp. 247 (D. Maine 1973), permitted commercial fishermen and clam diggers to recover damages resulting from an oil spill in public waters but would not permit on-shore business operators to recover for loss of trade resulting from a decline in tourist business after the oil spill. *Cf., Pruitt v. Allied Chemical Co.*, 523 F. Supp. 975 (E.D. Va. 1981).

[C]   Remedies

HELMKAMP v. CLARK READY MIX COMPANY
Iowa Supreme Court
214 N.W.2d 126 (1974)

CHLENHOPP, JUSTICE.

The question in this appeal is whether we should enjoin as a nuisance the operation of the cement ready-mix plant of defendant Clark Ready Mix Company in Carroll County, Iowa. We hear the appeal de novo. We give weight to the trial court's fact findings but are not bound by them. . . .

. . .

[The Court concluded that the evidence established a nuisance.]

II. *Relief.* When the tort of nuisance is proved, an essential second step must be taken: fashioning appropriate relief. Plaintiffs asked for an injunction to prohibit operation of the ready- mix plant; they did not seek damages. The trial court refused the injunction asked. Plaintiffs insist injunction is the appropriate relief here.

Three posibilities exist. On the one hand, we can hold that damages are appropriate and turn plaintiffs out of court in this suit. On the other hand, we can hold that injunction is appropriate and prohibit operation of the plant. Between these alternatives, we can grant an injunction relating to the manner of operating the plant or remand with permission for plaintiffs to amend to ask damages as was done in *Riter* v. *Keokuk Electro-Metals Co.*, 248 Iowa 710, 82 N.W.2d 151.

The court has stated, "[T]o justify the abatement of a claimed nuisance the annoyance must be such as would cause physical discomfort or injury to a person of ordinary sensibilities." *Schlotfelt v. Vinton Farmers' Supply Co.*, 252 Iowa at 1108, 109 N.W.2d at 698. We are satisfied this nuisance meets that test. But several other factors must be weighed. The American Law Institute enumerates the main factors in Restatement, Torts 2d, Tentative Draft No. 19, § 936(1):

The appropriateness of injunction against tort depends on a comparative appraisal of all of the factors in the case, including the following primary factors:

(a) the character of the interest to be protected,

(b) the relative adequacy to the plaintiff of injunction and of other remedies,

(c) plaintiff's delay in bringing suit,

(d) plaintiff's misconduct,

(e) the relative hardship likely to result to defendant if injunction is granted and to plaintiff if it is denied,

(f) the interests of third persons and of the public, and

(g) the practicality of framing and enforcing the order of judgment.

In a given case in which a nuisance is shown, the determination of whether injunction shall be granted or the objectors shall be relegated to damages is ultimately a judgment call. Upon consideration of the evidence here and the various factors which we have quoted, we believe that plaintiffs should be granted the injunction they seek.

True, defendant bought unzoned land outside the city, but that land is just outside the city and near the residential area in question. Plaintiffs are not seeking relief for a zoning violation but for nuisance. The harm caused by the plant is as great from an actual standpoint as though defendant were operating at the same distance but within the political boundaries of the city. Defendant knew, when it bought the land and erected the plant, of the proximity of the homes. Defendant cannot successfuly stand on the fact that it is outside the city and say it may therefore operate without regard to the nearby dwellings which were there first. Cf. *Bates v. Quality Ready- Mix Co.*, 261 Iowa 696, 154 N.W.2d 852 (both dwelling and ready-mix plant outside of city); *Jefferson Lumber & Concrete Products, Inc. v. Jimco, Inc.*, 217 So.2d 721 (La. App.); *Muskegon Trust Co. v. Bousma*, 247 Mich. 98, 225 N.W. 611. Plaintiffs acted promptly and are not guilty of laches.

We return the case to district court with directions to let a writ of injunction issue prohibiting operation of the plant, in addition to the injunction previously granted.

Reversed and remanded with directions.

NOTES AND QUESTIONS

(1) *Helmkamp* recites the range of remedies ordinarily applied in nuisance cases. Least controversial is damages for actual physical harm done by a one time episode. Injunctions against an ongoing injunction are more difficult. In deciding whether to issue an injunction, many courts will follow the "balancing of equities" approach seen in *Helmkamp*. The equitable nature of injunction relief leaves the courts considerable leeway to fashion a remedy for the circumstances, especially where the defendant is not an intentional wrongdoer.

In general;

> Injunctions are never granted when they are against good conscience, or productive of hardship, oppression, injustice, or public or private mischief, and it may be said to be the duty of the court whose jurisdiction is invoked to secure injunctive relief, when considering the application, to consider and weigh the relative convenience and inconvenience and the comparative injuries to the public which would result from the granting or refusal of the injunction sought.

42 Am. Jur. 2d, *Injunctions*, § 56, pp. 798, 799 quoted in *Daniels v. Chapius*, 344 So.2d 500, 503 (Ala. 1977).

Brede v. Minnesota Crushed Stone Co., 173 N.W. 805, 808-9 (Minn. 1919), applied this balancing approach. There, the Minnesota Supreme Court would neither deny injunctive relief entirely nor summarily shut down the defendant's limestone operation. Instead, the court remanded with the following instruction:

> The case is one in which relief should be given under the rule that an injunction should never go beyond the requirements of the particular case, nor should it close an industrial plant if it is possible to avoid doing so while giving plaintiff the relief to which he is entitled. Little or no evidence was

introduced to show whether the noise of blasting can or cannot be smothered, or whether its jarring effects may or may not be reduced by using smaller charges of dynamite without seriously interfering with defendant's quarrying operations. The court was not advised as to the possibility of controlling the escape of lime dust from defendant's crusher and dust mill. We should suppose that it is feasible to confine the dust very largely to defendant's own premises, and so remove or substantially mitigate the annoyance to plaintiffs from that source. Further testimony should be taken on these features of the case only, in order that the trial court may be in a position to act intelligently in affording plaintiffs' relief, without destroying defendant's business.

To the same effect is *Martin Bldg. Co. v. Imperial Laundry Co.*, 124 So. 82, 85 (Ala. 1929), where the court also initially refused to approve an injunction, saying:

We are persuaded, therefore, that the question of abatement of the nuisance by improved methods should be by the court given further consideration, to the end that complainant may have relief without material interference with respondent's lawful business. . . . As said in 1 Wood in Nuisances, § 823: "Injunctive orders should be carefully drawn, and in no case should they restrain the defendant from doing more than is necessary to stop the nuisance." In [an earlier case] this court approved the suggestion that in some cases it is well to direct a reference to ascertain if the evil complained of may be remedied by approved appliances or scientific alterations and that the register report thereon. We again approve this method as most advantageous. The order of reference to the register should provide a wide range of investigation as to any practical method for remedying the evil complained of, as it should not be confined merely to those herein discussed.

Would these courts approve an injunction if alternative relief proved impossible? What do you infer to be the rule in the jurisdiction of *Baldwin v. McClendon*? It has been said that "mere diminution of the value of property by a nuisance, without irreparable mischief" is not of itself ample justification for an injunction. *Vickridge 1st and 2nd Addition Homeowners Ass'n v. Catholic Diocese*, 510 P.2d 1296, 1306 (Kan. 1973).

(2) Some courts refuse to adopt the balancing approach once it is determined that a nuisance exists. Given the wrong, these courts will grant relief no matter how costly to the defendant. Still remaining is the possibility that such a court might on balance find that no nuisance exists. That outcome may be more probable in a jurisdiction that will not balance the equities in fashioning relief than in one that will.

New York traditionally enjoined nuisances without any balancing, but *Boomer v. Atlantic Cement Co.*, 257 N.E.2d 870 (N.Y. 1970), receded from this inflexible approach. Instead, *Boomer* permitted an award of "permanent damages" where shutting down the offensive operation would cause disproportionately large economic loss to the community in comparison to the damage done the plaintiff's property. The majority refused to employ the compromise remedy of ordering the defendant to abate the nuisance by a certain date under threat of injunction if the nuisance persisted beyond it.

(3)   What should be the measure of "permanent damages" when a nuisance deprives the owner of all his land? What is the practical effect of such a remedy on the ownership of the plaintiff's property? Does it permit a private defendant to take land from another person against his will? Who usually possesses that power?

(4)   A more difficult issue arises when a plaintiff seeks to enjoin a threatening activity before the nuisance manifests itself. May a court stop the defendant in his tracks? Or must it wait, perhaps until after he has spent a large sum of money, thereby creating an equitable estoppel? *Vickridge 1st and 2nd Addition*

Homeowners Ass'n v. Catholic Diocese, 540 P.2d 1296, 1301 (Kan. 1973), typifies the judicial resolution of this dilemma:

> Generally, injunctions are only granted to restrain actual existing nuisances. However, in some instances a court of equity may enjoin a threatened or anticipated nuisance. With respect to a proposed use of land the rule is stated in 58 Am.Jur.2d. Nuisances, § 147, as follows:

> A proposed use of land will not be restrained where it will not inevitably constitute a nuisance. If the complainant's right is doubtful, or the thing which it is sought to restrain is not a nuisance per se and will not necesarily become a nuisance, but may or may not become such, depending on the use, manner of operation, or other circumstances, equity will not interfere.

> Thus, where the anticipated injury arises from the use to which a proposed structure is to be put, and not from the structure itself, which will not be a nuisance, and is of such nature that it may be put to a lawful use which would not constitute a nuisance, the courts have generally declined to interfere with its erection on the ground that the contemplated use will necessarily be a nuisance. . . . (pp. 725, 726.)

> A court of equity may interfere by injunction to prevent a threatened injury where a proposed structure will be a nuisance *per se*, but a mere prospect, possibility or threat of future annoyance or injury from a structure or instrumentality which is not a nuisance *per se*, is not ground for an injunction and equity will not interfere where the apprehended injury or annoyance is doubtful, uncertain, speculative or contingent.

(5)   In nuisance actions the orthodox rule of damages is the difference in market value of the property with and without the nuisance. For temporary nuisances, this difference is often proved by the economic consequences of loss of use of the property or by diminution of rental value, plus cost to restore actual physical damages, if any. For permanent nuisances, this difference is ordinarily proved by the actual diminution in the market value of the property. See, *e.g., Weinhold v. Wolff*, 555 N.W. 2d 454 (Ia. 1996). Moreover, some courts permit awards of damages for mental suffering, even without impact, because like annoyance, discomfort, inconvenience, and sickness, these damages are of the kind "generally caused by nuisance." *Exxon Corp. USA v. Dunn*, 474 So.2d 1269, 1274 (Fla. App. 1985).

(6)   The *Helmkamp* plaintiff did not want money damages, but wanted — and the court ordered — an injunction "prohibiting operation of the plant." Under the Coase Theorem, what is the practical difference between these alternative remedies? Remember, the parties will attempt to reach the most efficient solution unless the transaction costs of getting there exceed the potential gains.

Suppose the pollution caused plaintiff to suffer $10,000 damages and defendant would incur $1,000,000 added costs to operate without pollution? The least cost (most efficient) solution would be for the defendant to continue to operate and pay plaintiff the $10,000 damages. An order to close the plant appears to take away this option. Rather than close its plant, could defendant offer plaintiff between $10,000 and $1,000,000 to forgo its right to enforce the court's order? If the transaction costs were not excessive, the parties should arrive at a solution that would benefit both of them. By contrast, if the court simply ordered defendant to pay plaintiff's $10,000 damages, that would have been defendant's only cost and it would continue to operate as before.

When should a court order a defendant to close its plant? When it causes irreparable damages? When the damages caused exceed defendant's costs to avoid them? When the court believes a closure order would cause defendant to negotiate with the plaintiff for a bigger recovery? Should the court know that Coase theorem holds that the plant would be unlikely to close if it would be more efficient for defendant to strike a bargain with the plaintiff and continue operating? The only issues would be rational behavior and the amount of the bargain.

§ 15.04 ENVIRONMENTAL TORTS

Trespass to land and public nuisance are the common law tort causes of action most helpful in combatting pollution of the human environment. Nevertheless, the causes of action possess implicit inadequacies when applied to an industrial culture. These include the absence of plaintiffs who possess both the legal capacity to sue and the economic resources to undertake protracted and costly litigation. Moreover, whereas the law of torts is best suited to resolve discrete disputes between individual litigants, the issues of environmental degradation tend to have sweeping societal impact, placing very broad interests (strong economy versus clean environment) into adversarial positions.

Resolving these disputes is more properly the province of legislatures than of judiciaries and that is where the most effective activity has taken place. In the decades of the 1960s and 1970s, the United States Congress and the various state legislatures enacted comprehensive anti-pollution laws. Typically, these are regulatory in thrust, requiring a potential polluter to obtain a permit for his operations before he begins. As a consequence, levels of pollution have fallen, and the need to expand the scope of the common law remedies has substantially abated. Nevertheless, common law remedies generally have not been repealed and may apply to environmental disputes notwithstanding legislative remedies, especially where a private person has been singled out for harm. For example, *Bieheman v. City of Chicago*, 864 F.2d 463, cet denied, 490 U.S. 1080, 109 S. Ct. 2099, 104 L.Ed.2d 661 (1989); held that federal regulation of air traffic did not exclude the law of private nuisance where personal injury resulted, and *Atwater Township Trustees v. B.F.I. Willowcreek Lawfill*, 617 N.E. 2d 1089 (Ohio 1993), held that a foul smelling land dump could be abated under the law of private nuisance despite the presence of state regulations.

Chapter 16

WORKERS' COMPENSATION, NO-FAULT AUTOMOBILE REPARATIONS, AND OTHER STATUTORY MEASURES

§ 16.01 WORKERS' COMPENSATION

In some settings enforcement of administrative remedies has replaced the common law of torts as the legal means for obtaining relief for injuries. By far the most sweeping of these fields is reparation of industrial injuries. As the industrial revolution bloomed in the nineteenth century the capacity of the common law of torts to remedy workers' injuries negligently caused by employers or fellow employees shrank. The trilogy of common law defenses — contributory negligence, assumption of risk and fellow servant — applied with vengeance to defeat the great majority of the claims against employers, leaving most injured workers with no job and no means of cure or support.

Layered on this was the extreme dangerousness of the workplace in the nineteenth and early twentieth centuries. In part, this may have been a product of the virtual immunity employers possessed to liability for workplace injuries. With no economic incentive to make safer workplaces industry was literally financially better off to forego investing in safety and to replace injured and killed workers with new ones. This mode of operation was favored by an ample supply of compliant labor from the masses of immigrants then entering the country in search of work.

A terrific struggle ensued between the forces of capital (management) and the forces of labor (social reformers and unions) to provide relief for injured workers. This occurred not only in the United States but also in England and across what is now considered Western Europe. Early in the twentieth century change began in the United States. (It came earlier in England and Western Europe.) Some state legislatures altered or even abolished the contributory negligence, assumption of risk, and fellow servant defenses in some industries — often so-called "hazardous occupations." In 1908 Congress employed this approach in the Federal Employees Liability Act (FELA) that then applied to railroad employments. In 1930 Congress extended FELA to airline employments. 45 U.S.C. § 181. The relevant current FELA provisions provide:

> **45 U.S.C.A. § 51. Liability of common carriers by railroad, in interstate or foreign commerce, for injuries to employees from negligence; employee defined**
>
> Every common carrier by railroad while engaging in commerce between any of the several States or Territories, or between any of the States and Territories, or between the District of Columbia and any of the States or Territories, or between the District of Columbia or any of the States or Territories and any foreign nation or nations, shall be liable in damages to any person suffering injury while **he is employed by such carrier in such commerce**, or, in case of the death of such employee, to his or her personal

representative, for the benefit of the surviving widow or husband and children of such employee; and, if none, then of such employee's parents; and, if none, then of the next of kin dependent upon such employee, **for such injury or death resulting in whole or in part from the negligence of any of the officers, agents, or employees of such carrier**, or by reason of any defect or insufficiency, due to its negligence, in its cars, engines, appliances, machinery, track, roadbed, works, boats, wharves, or other equipment.

. . . .

45 U.S.C.A. § 53. Contributory negligence; diminution of damages

In all actions on and after April 22, 1908 brought against any such common carrier by railroad under or by virtue of any of the provisions of this chapter to recover damages for personal injuries to an employee, or where such injuries have resulted in his death, **the fact that the employee may have been guilty of contributory negligence shall not bar a recovery**, but the damages shall be diminished by the jury in proportion to the amount of negligence attributable to such employee: Provided, That no such employee who may be injured or killed shall be held to have been guilty of contributory negligence in any case where the violation by such common carrier of any statute enacted for the safety of employees contributed to the injury or death of such employee.

45 U.S.C.A. § 54. Assumption of risks of employment

In any action brought against any common carrier under or by virtue of any of the provisions of this chapter to recover damages for injuries to, or the death of, any of its employees, **such employee shall not be held to have assumed the risks of his employment in any case where such injury or death resulted in whole or in part from the negligence of any of the officers, agents, or employees of such carrier**; and no employee shall be held to have assumed the risks of his employment in any case where the violation by such common carrier of any statute enacted for the safety of employees contributed to the injury or death of such employee.

(Bold added.)

These FELA provisions plainly modify the common law of torts but do not displace them. Most notably, two of the trilogy of common law defenses are abolished and the legal effect of contributory negligence is to diminish but not bar recovery.

Many state legislatures similarly modified the law of torts in actions by injured workers against employers, particularly in hazardous occupations. But a more drastic change was cooking in the late nineteenth century. Social reformers favored a solution that would impose the cost of all workplace injuries upon industry — without regard to fault. "Let the price of the product bear the blood of the workman" was the rallying cry. Concomitantly, it was agreed that industry would receive a *quid pro quo*; to wit, immunity to common law suits, even in cases of negligent injuries.

The British Workman's Compensation Act of 1906 emerged from this movement. As was commonplace at that time, modifications to the common law migrated to the

United States in fits and starts. New York was among the early innovators. In 1910 it enacted a limited workers' compensation law that the Court of Appeals invalidated on constitutional grounds. *Ivers v. Bufalo Ry. Co.*, 201 N.E. 271, 94 N.E. 431 (N.Y. 1911). In 1913 New York amended and reenacted the law in a form modeled closely on the 1906 British statute. The New York courts upheld this statute against constitutional challenges and it was reviewed by the Supreme Court of the United States. That court upheld the act in the decision presented below.

These are notable aspects of this decision. First, it succinctly described the framework of the act, particularly its effect on common law tort claims. And, second, it rejected fundamental constitutional challenges, thereby clearing the way for adoption in all the states of the United States. Thereafter, every state eventually enacted a workers' compensation statute and all trace their ancestry to the 1906 British Act.

NEW YORK CENTRAL RAILROAD v. WHITE
United States Supreme Court
243 U.S. 188, 61 L.Ed. 667 (1916)

MR. JUSTICE PITNEY delivered the opinion of the court.

A proceeding was commenced by defendant in error before the Workmen's Compensation Commission of the State of New York, established by the Workmen's Compensation Law of that State, to recover compensation from the New York Central & Hudson River Railroad Company for the death of her husband, Jacob White, who lost his life September 2, 1914, through an accidental injury arising out of and in the course of his employment under that company. The Commission awarded compensation in accordance with the terms of the law; its award was affirmed, without opinion, by the Appellate Division of the Supreme Court for the Third Judicial Department, whose order was affirmed by the Court of Appeals, without opinion. 169 App. Div. 903; 216 N.Y. 653. Federal questions having been saved, the present writ of error was sued out by the New York Central Railroad Company, successor, through a consolidation of corporations, to the rights and liabilities of the employing company. The writ was directed to the Appellate Division, to which the record and proceedings had been remitted by the Court of Appeals. *Sioux Remedy Co. v. Cope*, 235 U.S. 197, 200.

The errors specified are based upon these contentions: (1) That the liability, if any, of the railroad company for the death of Jacob White is defined and limited exclusively by the provisions of the Federal Employers' Liability Act of April 22, 1908, c. 149, 35 Stat. 65; and (2) that to award compensation to defendant in error under the provisions of the Workmen's Compensation Law would deprive plaintiff in error of its property without due process of law, and deny to it the equal protection of the laws, in contravention of the Fourteenth Amendment.

. . .

We turn to the constitutional question. The Workmen's Compensation Law of New York establishes 42 groups of hazardous employments, defines "employee" as a person engaged in one of these employments upon the premises or at the plant or in the course of his employment away from the plant of his employer, but excluding farm laborers and domestic servants; defines "employment" as including employment only in a trade, business, or occupation carried on by the employer for pecuniary gain, "injury" and "personal injury" as meaning only accidental injuries arising out of and in the course of employment, and such disease or infection as naturally and unavoidably may result there-from; and requires every employer subject to its provisions to pay or provide compensation according to a prescribed schedule for the disability or death of his employee resulting from an accidental personal injury arising out of and in the course of the employment, without regard to fault as a cause except where the injury is occasioned by the willful intention of the injured employee to bring about the injury or death of himself or of another, or where it results solely from the intoxication of the injured employee while on duty, in which cases neither the injured employee nor any dependent shall receive compensation. By § 11, the prescribed liability is made exclusive, except that, if an employer fails to secure the payment of compensation as provided in § 50, an injured employee, or his legal representative in case death results from the injury, may at his option elect to claim compensation under the act or to maintain an action in the courts for damages, and in such an action it shall not be necessary to plead or prove freedom from contributory negligence, nor may the defendant plead as a defense that the injury was caused by the negligence of a fellow servant, that the employee assumed the risk of his employment, or that the injury was due to contributory negligence. Compensation under the act is not regulated by the measure of damages applied in negligence suits, but in addition to providing medical, surgical, or other like treatment, it is based solely on loss of earning power, being graduated according to the average weekly wages of the injured employee and the character and duration of the disability, whether partial or total, temporary or permanent; while, in case the injury causes death, the compensation is known as a death benefit, and includes funeral expenses not exceeding one hundred dollars, payments to the surviving wife (or dependent husband) during widowhood (or dependent widowerhood) of a percentage of the average wages of the deceased, and if there be a surviving child or children under the age of eighteen years, an additional percentage of such wages for each child until that age is reached. There are provisions invalidating agreements by employees to waive the right to compensation, prohibiting any assignment, release, or commutation of claims for compensation or benefits except as provided by the act, exempting them from the claims of creditors, and requiring that the compensation and benefits shall be paid only to employees or their dependents. Provision is made for the establishment of a Workmen's Compensation Commission with administrative and judicial functions, including authority to pass upon claims to compensation on notice to the parties interested. The award or decision of the commission is made subject to an appeal, on questions of law only, to the Appellate Division of the Supreme Court for the Third Department, with an ultimate appeal to the Court of Appeals in cases where such an appeal would lie in civil actions. A fund is created, known as "the state insurance fund," for the purpose of insuring employers against liability under the law and assuring to the persons entitled the compensation thereby provided. The fund is made up primarily of premiums received from employers, at rates fixed by the commission in view of the hazards of the different classes of employment, and the premiums are to be based upon the total payroll and number of employees in each class at the lowest rate consistent with the maintenance of a solvent state insurance fund and the creation of a reasonable surplus and reserve.

. . . .

The scheme of the act is so wide a departure from common-law standards respecting the responsibility of employer to employee that doubts naturally have been raised respecting its constitutional validity. The adverse considerations urged or suggested in this case and in kindred cases submitted at the same time are: (a) that the employer's property is taken without due process of law, because he is subjected to a liability for compensation without regard to any neglect or default on his part or on the part of any other person for whom he is responsible, and in spite of the fact that the injury may be solely attributable to the fault of the employee; (b) that the employee's rights are interfered with, in that he is prevented from having compensation for injuries arising from the employer's fault commensurate with the damages actually sustained, and is limited to the measure of compensation prescribed by the act; and (c) that both employer and employee are deprived of their liberty to acquire property by being prevented from making such agreement as they choose respecting the terms of the employment.

In support of the legislation, it is said that the whole common-law doctrine of employer's liability for negligence, with its defenses of contributory negligence, fellow-servant's negligence, and assumption of risk, is based upon fictions, and is inapplicable to modern conditions of employment; that in the highly organized and hazardous industries of the present day the causes of accident are often so obscure and complex that in a material proportion of cases it is impossible by any method correctly to ascertain the facts necessary to form an accurate judgment, and in a still larger proportion the expense and delay required for such ascertainment amount in effect to a defeat of justice; that under the present system the injured workman is left to bear the greater part of industrial accident loss, which because of his limited income he is unable to sustain, so that he and those dependent upon him are overcome by poverty and frequently become a burden upon public or private charity; and that litigation is unduly costly and tedious, encouraging corrupt practices and arousing antagonisms between employers and employees.

In considering the constitutional question, it is necessary to view the matter from the standpoint of the employee as well as from that of the employer. For, while plaintiff in error is an employer, and cannot succeed without showing that its rights as such are infringed *(Plymouth Coal Co. v. Pennsylvania,* 232 U.S. 531, 544; *Jeffrey Mfg. Co. v. Blagg,* 235 U.S. 571, 576;) yet, as pointed out by the Court of Appeals in the *Jensen* Case, 215 N.Y. 526, the exemption from further liability is an essential part of the scheme, so that the statute, if invalid as against the employee, is invalid as against the employer.

The close relation of the rules governing responsibility as between employer and employee to the fundamental rights of liberty and property is of course recognized. But those rules, as guides of conduct, are not beyond alteration by legislation in the public interest. No person has a vested interest in any rule of law entitling him to insist that it shall remain unchanged for his benefit. . . . .The common law bases the employer's liability for injuries to the employee upon the ground of negligence; but negligence is merely the disregard of some duty imposed by law; and the nature and extent of the duty may be modified by legislation, with corresponding change in the test of negligence. Indeed, liability may be imposed for the consequences of a failure to comply with a statutory duty, irrespective of negligence in the ordinary sense; safety appliance acts being a familiar instance. . . .

The fault may be that of the employer himself, or — most frequently — that of another for whose conduct he is made responsible according to the maxim respondeat superior. In the latter case, the employer may be entirely blameless, may have exercised the utmost human foresight to safeguard the employee; yet, if the alter ego while acting within the scope of his duties be negligent — in, disobedience, it may be, of the employer's positive and specific command — the employer is answerable for the consequences. It cannot be that the rule embodied in the maxim is unalterable by legislation.

The immunity of the employer from responsibility to an employee for the negligence of a fellow employee is of comparatively recent origin, it being the product of the judicial conception that the probability of a fellow workman's negligence is one of the natural and ordinary risks of the occupation, assumed by the employee and presumably taken into account in the fixing of his wages. . . .

The doctrine has prevailed generally throughout the United States, but with material differences in different jurisdictions respecting who should be deemed a fellow servant and who a vice-principal or alter ego of the master, turning sometimes upon refined distinctions as to grades and departments in the employment. . . .

It needs no argument to show that such a rule is subject to modification or abrogation by a State upon proper occasion.

The same may be said with respect to the general doctrine of assumption of risk. By the common law the employee assumes the risks normally incident to the occupation in which he voluntarily engages; other and extraordinary risks and those due to the employer's negligence he does not assume until made aware of them, or until they become so obvious that an ordinarily prudent man would observe and appreciate them, in either of which cases he does assume them, if he continue in the employment without obtaining from the employer an assurance that the matter will be remedied; but if he receive such an assurance, then, pending performance of the promise, the employee does not in ordinary cases assume the special risk. . . . Plainly, these rules, as guides of conduct and tests of liability, are subject to change in the exercise of the sovereign authority of the State.

So, also, with respect to contributory negligence. Aside from injuries intentionally self-inflicted, for which the statute under consideration affords no compensation, it is plain that the rules of law upon the subject, in their bearing upon the employer's responsibility, are subject to legislative change; for contributory negligence, again, involves a default in some duty resting on the employee, and his duties are subject to modification.

It may be added, by way of reminder, that the entire matter of liability for death caused by wrongful act, both within and without the relation of employer and employee, is a modern statutory innovation, in which the States differ as to who may sue, for whose benefit, and the measure of damages.

But it is not necessary to extend the discussion. This court repeatedly has upheld the authority of the States to establish by legislation departures from the fellow-servant rule and other common-law rules affecting the employer's liability for personal injuries to the employee. . . . A corresponding power on the part of Congress, when legislating within its appropriate sphere, was sustained in *Second Employers' Liability Cases*, 223 U.S. 1. And see *El Paso & Northeastern Ry. Co.*

v. Gutierrez, 215 U.S. 87, 97; *Baltimore & Ohio R. R. Co. v. Interstate Commerce Commission*, 221 U.S. 612, 619. . . .

. . . It is true that in the case of the statutes thus sustained there were reasons rendering the particular departures appropriate. Nor is it necessary, for the purposes of the present case, to say that a state might, without violence to the constitutional guaranty of "due process of law," suddenly set aside all common-law rules respecting liability as between employer and employee, without providing a reasonably just substitute. Considering the vast industrial organization of the state of New York, for instance, with hundreds of thousands of plants and millions of wage earners, each employer, on the one hand, having embarked his capital, and each employee, on the other, having taken up his particular mode of earning a livelihood, in reliance upon the probable permanence of an established body of law governing the relation, it perhaps may be doubted whether the state could abolish all rights of action, on the one hand, or all defenses, on the other, without setting up something adequate in their stead.

No such question is here presented, and we intimate no opinion upon it. The statute under consideration sets aside one body of rules only to establish another system in its place. If the employee is no longer able to recover as much as before in case of being injured through the employer's negligence, he is entitled to moderate compensation in all cases of injury, and has a certain and speedy remedy without the difficulty and expense of establishing negligence or proving the amount of the damages. Instead of assuming the entire consequences of all ordinary risks of the occupation, he assumes the consequences, in excess of the scheduled compensation, of risks ordinary and extraordinary. On the other hand, if the employer is left without defense respecting the question of fault, he at the same time is assured that the recovery is limited, and that it goes directly to the relief of the designated beneficiary. And just as the employee's assumption of ordinary risks at common law presumably was taken into account in fixing the rate of wages, so the fixed responsibility of the employer, and the modified assumption of risk by the employee under the new system, presumably will be reflected in the wage scale. The act evidently is intended as a just settlement of a difficult problem, affecting one of the most important of social relations, and it is to be judged in its entirety. We have said enough to demonstrate that, in such an adjustment, the particular rules of the common law affecting the subject matter are not placed by the 14th Amendment beyond the reach of the lawmaking power of the state; and thus we are brought to the question whether the method of compensation that is established as a substitute transcends the limits of permissible state action. . . .

Reduced to its elements, the situation to be dealt with is this: Employer and employee, by mutual consent, engage in a common operation intended to be advantageous to both; the employee is to contribute his personal services, and for these is to receive wages, and, ordinarily, nothing more; the employer is to furnish plant, facilities, organization, capital, credit, is to control and mange the operation, paying the wages and other expenses, disposing of the product at such prices as he can obtain, taking all the profits, if any there be, and, of necessity, bearing the entire losses. In the nature of things, there is more or less of a probability that the employee may lose his life through some accidental injury arising out of the employment, leaving his widow or children deprived of their natural support; or that he may sustain an injury not mortal, but resulting in his total or partial disablement, temporary or permanent, with corresponding impairment of earning capacity. The physical suffering must be borne by the employee alone; the laws of nature prevent this from being evaded or shifted to another, and the statute makes no attempt to afford an equivalent in compensation. But, besides, there is the loss of earning power, — a loss of that which stands to the employee as his capital in trade. This is a loss arising out of the business, and, however it may be charged up, is an expense of the operation, as truly as the cost of repairing broken machinery or any other expense that ordinarily is paid by the employer. Who is to bear the charge? It is plain that, on grounds of natural justice, it is not unreasonable for the state, while relieving the employer from responsibility for damages measured by common-law standards and payable in cases where he or those for whose conduct he is answerable are found to be at fault, to require him to contribute a reasonable amount, and according to a reasonable and definite scale, by way of compensation for the loss of earning power incurred in the common enterprise, irrespective of the question of negligence, instead of leaving the entire loss to rest where it may chance to fall, — that is, upon the injured employee or his dependents. Nor can it be deemed arbitrary and unreasonable, from the standpoint of the employee's interest, to supplant a system under which he assumed the entire risk of injury in ordinary cases, and in others had a right to recover an amount more or less speculative upon proving facts of negligence that often were difficult to prove, and substitute a system under which, in all ordinary cases of accidental injury, he is sure of a definite and easily ascertained compensation, not being obliged to assume the entire loss in any case, but in all cases assuming any loss beyond the prescribed scale.

Much emphasis is laid upon the criticism that the act creates liability without fault. This is sufficiently answered by what has been said, but we may add that liability without fault is not a novelty in the law. The common-law liability of the carrier, of the inn-keeper, of him who employed fire or other dangerous agency or harbored a mischievous animal, was not dependent altogether upon questions of fault or negligence. Statutes imposing liability without fault have been sustained. . . .

We have referred to the maxim respondeat superior. In a well-known English case, *Hall v. Smith*, 2 Bing. 156, 160, this maxim was said by Best, C. J., to be "bottomed on this principle, that he who expects to derive advantage from an act which is done by another for him, must answer for any injury which a third person may sustain from it." And this view has been adopted in New York. *Cardot v. Barney*, 63 N. Y. 281, 287. The provision for compulsory compensation, in the act under consideration, cannot be deemed to be an arbitrary and unreasonable application of the principle, so as to amount to a deprivation of the employer's property without due process of law. The pecuniary loss resulting from the employee's death or disablement must fall somewhere. It results from something done in the course of an operation from which the employer expects to derive a profit. In excluding the question of fault as a cause of the injury, the act in effect disregards the proximate cause and looks to one more remote — the primary cause, as it may be deemed — and that is, the employment itself. For this, both parties are responsible, since they voluntarily engage in it as co-adventurers, with personal injury to the employee as a probable and foreseen result. In ignoring any possible negligence of the employee producing or contributing to the injury, the lawmaker reasonably may have been influenced by the belief that in modern industry the utmost diligence in the employer's service is only in some degree inconsistent with adequate care on the part of the employee for his own safety; that the more intently he devotes himself to the work, the less he can take precautions for his own security. And it is evident that the consequences of a disabling or fatal injury are precisely the same to the parties immediately affected, and to the community, whether the proximate cause be culpable or innocent. Viewing the entire matter, it cannot be pronounced arbitrary and unreasonable for the State to impose upon the employer the absolute duty of making a moderate and definite compensation in money to every disabled employee, or in case of his death to those who were entitled to look to him for support, in lieu of the common-law liability confined to cases of negligence.

This, of course, is not to say that any scale of compensation, however insignificant on the one hand or onerous on the other, would be supportable. In this case, no criticism is made on the ground that the compensation prescribed by the statute in question is unreasonable in amount, either in general or in the particular case. Any question of that kind may be met when it arises.

. . .

Judgment affirmed.

NOTES

(1)   Most workers' compensation laws employ a model that is exemplified by the Workers' Compensation Act and Rehabilitation Law proposed by the Council of State Governments. Excerpts are presented below.

Excerpts from Model Workers' Compensation Statute[1]

PART I COVERAGE AND LIABILITY

Section 1. Liability for Compensation. (a) Every employer subject to this act shall be liable for compensation for injury or death without regard to fault as a cause of injury or death.

. . .

(c) Liability for compensation shall not apply where injury to the employee was occasioned solely by his intoxication or by his willful intention to injure or kill himself or another.

Section 2. Definitions. As used in this act unless the context otherwise requires:

(a) "Injury" means any harmful change in the human organism arising out of and in the course of employment, including damage to or loss of a prosthetic appliance, but does not include any communicable disease unless the risk of contracting such disease is increased by the nature of the employment.

(b) "Death" means death resulting from an injury.

. . .

Section 3. Coverage of Employers. The following shall constitute employers subject to the provisions of this act:

---

[1] Source, Workmen's Compensation Act and Rehabilitation Law, reprinted from suggested State Legislation, The Council of State Governments (1973).

(a) Every person that has in the state one or more employees subject to this act.

(b) The state, any agency thereof, and each country, city, town, township, incorporated village, school district, sewer district, drainage district, public or quasi-public corporation, or any other political subdivision of the state that has one or more employees subject to this act.

Section 4. Coverage of Employees. The following shall constitute employees subject to the provisions of this act, except as exempted under Section 5:

(a) Every person, including a minor, whether lawfully or unlawfully employed, in the service of an employer under any contract of hire or apprenticeship, express or implied, and all helpers and assistants of employees whether paid by the employer or employee, if employed with the knowledge, actual or constructive, of the employer.

(b) Every executive officer of a corporation.

(c) Every person in the service of the state or of any political subdivision or agency thereof, under any contract of hire, express or implied, and every official or officer thereof, whether elected or appointed, while performing his official duties. Every person who is a member of a volunteer fire or police department shall be deemed, for the purpose of this act, to be in the employment of the political subdivision of the state where the department is organized. Every person who is a regularly enrolled volunteer member or trainee of the civil defense corps of this state as established under the [State Civil Defense Act] shall be deemed, for the purposes of this act, to be in the employment of the state.

Section 5. Exemptions. The following employees are exempt from the coverage of this act:

(a) Any person employed as a domestic servant in a private home by an employer who has less than two employees regularly employed 40 or more hours a week in such employment.

. . .

Section 10. Exclusiveness of Liability. (a) If an employer secures payment of compensation as required by this act, the liability of such employer under this act shall be exclusive and in place of all other liability of such employer to the employee, his legal representative, husband or wife, parents, dependents, next of kin, and anyone otherwise entitled to recover damages from such employer at law or in admiralty on account of such injury or death. For purposes of this section, the term "employer" shall include a "contractor" covered by subsection (b) of Section 1, whether or not the subcontractor has in fact, secured the payment of compensation. The liability of an employer to another person who may be liable for or who has paid damages on account of injury or death of an employee of such employer arising out of and in the course of employment and caused by a breach of any duty or obligation owed by such employer to such other shall be limited to the amount of compensation and other benefits for which such employer is liable under this act on account of such injury or death, unless such other and the employer by written contract have agreed to share liability in a different manner. The exemption from liability given an employer by this section shall also extend to such employer's carrier and to all employees, officers or directors of such employer or carrier, provided the exemption from liability given an employee, officer or director of an employer or carrier shall not apply in any case where the injury or death is proximately caused by the willful and unprovoked physical aggression of such employee, officer or director.

(b) If an employer fails to secure payment of compensation as required by this act, an injured employee, or his legal representative in case death results from the injury, may claim compensation under this act and in addition may maintain an action at law or in admiralty for damages on account of such injury or death, provided that the amount of compensation shall be credited against the amount received in such action, and provided that, if the amount of compensation is larger than the amount of damages received, the amount of damages less the employee's legal fees and expenses shall be credited against the amount of compensation. In such action the defendant may not plead as a defense that the injury was caused by the negligence of a fellow servant, that the employee assumed the risks of his employment, or that the injury was due to the contributory negligence of the employee.

Section 11. Third Party Liability. (a) The right to income and other benefits under this act, whether for disability or death, shall not be affected by the fact that the injury or death is caused under circumstances creating a legal liability in some person (other than the employer or another person exempt from liability under Section 10 of this act) to pay damages therefor, such person so liable being hereinafter referred to as the third party.

. . .

PART II MEDICAL, REHABILITATION AND BURIAL SERVICES

Section 12. Medical Services, Appliances and Supplies. (a) For any injury covered by this act, the employee shall be entitled to all medical services, appliances and supplies which are required by the nature of his injury and which will relieve pain and promote and hasten his restoration to health and employment. The employer shall furnish such services, appliances and supplies and necessary replacements or repairs of such appliances unless the need for such replacements or repairs is due to lack of proper care by the employee.

. . .

PART III INCOME BENEFITS

Section 16. Income Benefits for Disability. Income benefits for disability shall be paid to the employee as follows, subject to the maximum and minimum limits specified in Section 17.

(a) *Total Disability:* For total disability, 55 per cent of his average weekly wage during such disability, and 2½ per cent of his average weekly wage for each dependent, up to a maximum of five (5) specified in subsection (t) of Section 2, except a wife living apart from her husband for justifiable cause or by reason of his desertion unless such wife is actually dependent on the employee.

(b) *Partial Disability:* For partial disability, 55 per cent of his decrease in wage-earning capacity during the continuance thereof, and 21/2 per cent of his average weekly wage for each dependent, up to a maximum of five (5), specified in subsection (t) of Section 2, except a wife living apart from her husband for justifiable cause or by reason of his desertion unless such wife is actually dependent on the employee.

(c) *Scheduled Income Benefits:* For total permanent bodily loss or losses herein scheduled, after and in addition to the income benefits payable during the period of recovery, scheduled income benefits in the amount of 55 per cent of the average weekly wage as follows: [Omitted].

(2) In ensuing years the states have adopted a myriad of different rules on coverage, tort immunities, benefits and a myriad of other points. A lawyer must always consult the current version of the act wherever an industrial injury occurs.

§ 16.02   NO-FAULT AUTOMOBILE REPARATIONS

From the beginning of the automobile age highway crashes have caused injuries, deaths, and property damage in ever-ascending numbers. Concomitantly, the role of liability insurance has burgeoned to protect automobile users against liability when things go wrong. Rising insurance rates, clogged court dockets, delays in resolving cases, high legal costs, inequities in case resolutions, and other perceived deficiencies in the tort system stimulated reformers to look for something more efficient than the law of torts as the vehicle to repair these injuries.

No-fault proposals began to appear before World War II but that conflict stilled the movement for almost three-decades. Finally, in 1969, Massachusetts enacted the first automobile no-fault compensation law in the United States. Florida quickly followed suit and another twenty-plus states enacted similar laws in the ensuing years. Nevertheless, unlike workers' compensation, no-fault automobile laws found far less than universal approval. Many states that adopted no-fault laws in the early years later repealed them, leaving only twelve no-fault jurisdictions[2] in 2009.

Although the content of no-fault automobile reparation laws varies widely, two core features are essential. First, automobile owners are required to purchase a prescribed amount of personal injury protection (PIP) insurance to be paid without consideration of fault to any person injured in a crash involving an insured vehicle. Second, PIP insured owners (and drivers) are immunized to tort liability for general damages unless an injury exceeds some prescribed threshold of severity.

The Uniform Motor Vehicle Reparations Act explifies such a no-fault law. Key provisions are printed below. Further examination of the topic is beyond the scope of this book.

UNIFORM MOTOR VEHICLE ACCIDENT REPARATIONS ACT[3]

— ULA —

§ 1 [Definitions]

(a) In this Act:

(1) "Added reparation benefits" means benefits provided by optional added reparation insurance (Section 16).

---

[2] District of Columbia, Florida, Hawaii, Kansas, Kentucky, Massachusetts, Michigan, Minnesota, New Jersey, New York, North Dakota, Pennsylvania, and Utah. Source: Auto Insurance In-Depth LLC.

[3] This Act has been reprinted through the permission of the National Conference of Commissioners on Uniform State Laws, and copies of the Act may be ordered from them at a cost of $2.00 at 645 North Michigan Avenue, Suite 510, Chicago, IL 60611.

(2) "Basic reparation benefits" means benefits providing reimbursement for net loss suffered through injury arising out of the maintenance or use of a motor vehicle, subject, where applicable, to the limits (Section 13), deductibles (Sections 14 and 18), exclusions (Sections 12, 14, and 15), disqualifications (Sections 21 and 22), and other conditions provided in this Act.

(3) "Basic reparation insured" means:

(i) a person identified by name as an insured in a contract of basic reparation insurance complying with this Act (Section 7(d)); and

(ii) while residing in the same household with a named insured, the following persons not identified by name as an insured in any other contract of basic reparation insurance complying with this Act: a spouse or other relative of a named insured; and a minor in the custody of a named insured or of a relative residing in the same household with a named insured. A person resides in the same household if he usually makes his home in the same family unit, even though he temporarily lives elsewhere.

(4) "Injury" and "injury to person" mean bodily harm, sickness, disease, or death.

(5) "Loss" means accrued economic detriment consisting only of allowable expense, work loss, replacement services loss, and, if injury causes death, survivor's economic loss and survivor's replacement services loss. Noneconomic detriment is not loss. However, economic detriment is loss although caused by pain and suffering or physical impairment.

. . .

(7) "Motor vehicle" means:

(i) a vehicle of a kind required to be registered under [the laws of this State relating to motor vehicles] or

(ii) a vehicle, including a trailer, designed for operation upon a public roadway by other than muscular power, except a vehicle used exclusively upon stationary rails or tracks. "Public roadway" means a way open to the use of the public for purposes of automobile travel.

. . .

(9) "Noneconomic detriment" means pain, suffering, inconvenience, physical impairment, and other nonpecuniary damage recoverable under the tort law of this State. The term does not include punitive or exemplary damages.

. . .

§ 2 [Right to Basic Reparation Benefits]

(a) If the accident causing injury occurs in this State, every person suffering loss from injury arising out of maintenance or use of a motor vehicle has a right to basic reparation benefits.

(b) If the accident causing injury occurs outside this State, the following persons and their survivors suffering loss from injury arising out of maintenance or use of a motor vehicle have a right to basic reparation benefits:

(1) basic reparation insureds; and

(2) the driver and other occupants of a secured vehicle, other than (i) a vehicle which is regularly used in the course of the business of transporting persons or property and which is one of 5 or more vehicles under common ownership, or (ii) a vehicle owned by an obligated government other than this State, its political subdivisions, municipal corporations, or public agencies.

§ 3 [Obligation to Pay Basic Reparation Benefits]

(a) Basic reparation benefits shall be paid without regard to fault.

(b) Basic reparation obligors and the assigned claims plan shall pay basic reparation benefits, under the terms and conditions stated in this Act, for loss from injury arising out of maintenance or use of a motor vehicle. This obligation exists without regard to immunity from liability or suit which might otherwise be applicable.

§ 4 [Priority of Applicability of Security for Payment of Basic Reparation Benefits]

[Omitted]

§ 5 [Partial Abolition of Tort Liability]

(a) Tort liability with respect to accidents occurring in this State and arising from the ownership, maintenance, or use of a motor vehicle is abolished except as to:

(1) liability of the owner of a motor vehicle involved in an accident if security covering the vehicle was not provided at the time of the accident;

(2) liability of a person in the business of repairing, servicing, or otherwise maintaining motor vehicles arising from a defect in a motor vehicle caused or not corrected by an act or omission in repair, servicing, or other maintenance of a vehicle in the course of his business;

(3) liability of a person for intentionally caused harm to person or property;

(4) liability of a person for harm to property other than a motor vehicle and its contents;

(5) liability of a person in the business of parking or storing motor vehicles arising in the course of that business for harm to a motor vehicle and its contents;

(6) damages for any work loss, replacement services loss, survivor's economic loss, and survivor's replacement services loss, not recoverable as basic reparation benefits by reason of the limitation contained in the provisions on standard weekly limit on benefits for those losses (Section 13), that occur after the injured person is disabled by the injury for more than [6] months or after his death caused by the injury; and

(7) damages for noneconomic detriment in excess of [$5,000], but only if the accident causes death, significant permanent injury, serious permanent disfigurement, or more than 5 months of complete inability of the injured person to work in an occupation. "Complete inability of an injured person to work in an occupation" means inability to perform, on even a part-time basis, even some of the duties required by his occupation or, if unemployed at the time of injury, by any occupation

for which the injured person was qualified.

. . .

§ 6 [Reparation Obligor's Rights of Reimbursement, Subrogation, and Indemnity]

[Omitted]

§ 7 [Security Covering Motor Vehicle]

[Omitted]

§ 10 [Required Minimum Tort Liability Insurance and Territorial Coverage]

[Omitted]

§ 14 [Optional Deductibles and Exclusions]

[Omitted]

§ 15 [Property Damage Exclusion]

Basic reparation benefits do not include benefits for harm to property.

§ 22 [Intentional Injuries]

A person intentionally causing or attempting to cause injury to himself or another person is disqualified from basic or added reparation benefits for injury arising from his acts, including benefits otherwise due him as a survivor. . . .

§ 23 [Reparation Obligor's Duty to Respond to Claims]

[Omitted]

§ 37 [Penalties]

An owner of a motor vehicle who operates the vehicle or permits it to be operated in this State when he knows or should know that the has failed to comply with the requirement that he provide security covering the vehicle (Section 7) is guilty of a [misdemeanor] and upon conviction may be fined not more than [$300] or imprisoned for not more than [90] days, or both.

§ 16.03   STATUTORY TORTS AND OTHER STATUTORY REVISIONS OF THE COMMON LAW

Legislatures have created numerous statutory causes of action that were never acknowledged in the common law. Many of these provide tort-like remedies and apply tort-like procedures. Although no attempt is made here to catalogue those measures, they are exemplified by 42 U.S.C. § 1983. This statute was enacted by Congress to provide a remedy against persons who wrongfully use state power to deprive other persons of rights "secured by the Constitution and laws" of the United States. That measure provides:

42 U.S.C. § 1983. Civil action for deprivation of rights

Every person who, under color of any statute, ordinance, regulation, custom, or usage, of any State or Territory or the District of Columbia, subjects, or causes to be subjected, any citizen of the United States or other person within the jurisdiction thereof to the deprivation of any rights, privileges, or immunities secured by the Constitution and laws, shall be liable to the party injured in an action at law, suit in equity, or other proper proceeding for redress, except that in any action brought against a judicial officer for an act or omission taken in such officer's judicial capacity, injunctive relief shall not be granted unless a declaratory decree was violated or declaratory relief was unavailable. For the purposes of this section, any Act of Congress applicable exclusively to the District of Columbia shall be considered to be a statute of the District of Columbia.42.

This statute was initially enacted in 1871 to enforce the Fourteenth Amendment, but it was not employed to any great extent until the civil rights movement gained momentum in the second half of the twentieth century. Although not the earliest of the decisions, *Monell v. Department of Social Services of City of New York*, 436 U.S. 658, 98 S.Ct. 2018 (1978) gave the movement great impetus by virtue of its holding that municipalities are "persons" subject to liability under the act. Once "discovered," this statute has been employed in thousands of cases to remedy injuries caused by wrongful actions taken under the "color" of state law. Examining the many legal issues arising out of the field of "constitutional torts" is the subject of specialized courses.

In addition to the creation of statutory torts that did not exist in the common law, legislatures have enacted myriad statutes that modify the common law in content, pleading requirements, standards of proof, measurement and limitations on damages, and otherwise. Examples such as wrongful death statutes, survival statutes, comparative fault acts, "guest statutes," contribution acts, and others are treated in earlier chapters of this text. The medical negligence field has been the subject of extensive treatment of this sort. To determine the current status of the law on these matters a student must consult the laws of the jurisdiction in question.

Chapter 17

DEFAMATION AND INVASION OF PRIVACY

Who steals my purse steals trash;
'tis something, nothing;
'Twas mine, 'tis his, and has been
slave to thousands;
But he that filches from my good name
Robs me of that which not enriches him
And makes me poor indeed.
Shakespeare, "Othello."

§ 17.01 DEFAMATORY CONTENT

PROBLEM

Bernice and Hilda frequently enjoyed an outing at the Metro Dog Track, watching the racing dogs run. Occasionally the two would lay a small bet between them. On the day in question the two approached the pay-out window after the eighth race with a winning ticket in hand, paying 20 to 1 odds on Spiderlegs, a hitherto unknown dog. Paul, the paying agent at the track, looked at the ticket proffered by the two and pushed it back saying, "What man's pocket did you pick this from?"

Flabbergasted, the two women sought out Ralph, assistant security officer for the track and their long time acquaintance. Ralph heard them out and agreed to go with them to talk to Paul. Having listened to what the three had to say, Paul again refused to cash the ticket, saying, "I ain't cashing no ticket for no stoop!"

The two women consult you for legal advice. You are persuaded the facts stated above can be proved irrefutably. What advice do you give the women? Be sure to disclose the especially difficult issues you see. *See, Campbell v. Jacksonville Kennel Club*, 66 So. 2d 495 (Fla. 1953).

VILLERS v. MONSLEY
(1769) 3 Wils. K.B. 403, 95 Eng. Rep. 886 (K.B.)[1]

Case upon a libel, for writing a letter that plaintiff stunk of brimstone, and had the itch.

Action upon the case against the defendant for maliciously writing and publishing a libel upon the plaintiff in the words following, viz.

"Old Villers, so strong of brimstone you smell,

----

[1] [Ed. — English Reports, general reports of older English cases, decision of King's Bench Court of Appeal.]

As if not long since you had got out of hell;
But this damnable smell I no longer can bear,
Therefore I desire you would come no more here;
You old stinking, old nasty, old itchy old toad,
If you come any more, you shall pay for your board,
You'll therefore take this as a warning from me,
And never more enter the doors, while they belong to J. P.

"Wilncoat, December 4, 1767."

The defendant pleaded not guilty: a verdict was found for the plaintiff and sixpence damages, at the last assizes for the county of Warwick. And now it was moved by Sergeant Burland, in arrest of judgment, that this was not such a libel for which an action would lie; that the itch is a distemper to which every family is liable; to have it is no crime, nor does it bring any disgrace upon a man, for it may be innocently caught or taken by infection; the small pox, or a putrid fever, are much worse distempers; the itch is not so detestable or so contagious as either of them, for it is not communicated by the air, but by contact or putting on a glove, or the clothes of one who has the itch, and although it be an infectious distemper, yet it implies no offence in the person having it, and therefore no action will lie for saying or writing that a man has got the itch. It is not like saying writing that a man has got the leprosy, or is a leper, for which an action upon the case will lie, because a leper shall be removed from the society of men by the writ of de leproso amovendo, 1 Roll. Abr. 44. Cro. Jac. 144. Hob. 219, although it be a natural infirmity.

WILMOT LORD C.J. — I think this is such a libel for which an action well lies; we must take it to have been proved at the trial that it was published by the defendant maliciously; and if any man deliberately or maliciously publishes any thing in writing concerning another which renders him ridiculous, or tends to hinder mankind from associating or having intercourse with him, an action well lies against such publisher. I see no difference between this and the cases of the leprosy and plague; and it is admitted that an action lies in those cases. The writ de leproso amovendo is not taken away, although the distemper is almost driven away by cleanliness, or new-invented remedies; the party must have the distemper to such a degree before the writ shall be granted, which commands the sheriff to remove him without delay ad locum solitarium ad habitandum ibidem prout moris est, ne per communem conversationem suam hominibus dampnum vel periculum eveniat quovismodo. The degree of leprosy is not material; if you say he has the leprosy it is sufficient, and the action lies: the reason of that case applies to this. I do not know whether the itch may not be communicated by the air without contact; it is said to be occasioned by animalcula in the skin, and must be cured by outward application. Nobody will eat, drink, or have any intercourse with a person who has the itch and stinks of brimstone; therefore I think this libel actionable, and that judgment must be for the plaintiff.

CLIVE. — I am of the same opinion, that this is a very malicious and scandalous libel.

BATHURST J. — I wish this matter was thoroughly gone into, and more solemnly determined; however, I have no doubt at present but that the writing and publishing any thing which renders a man ridiculous is actionable: and whether the itch be occasioned by a man's fault or misfortune, it is a cruel charge, and renders him both ridiculous and miserable, by being kept out of all company: I repeat it, that I wish there were some more solemn determination, that the writing and publishing any thing which tends to make a man ridiculous or infamous ought to be punished; for saying a man has the itch, without more, perhaps an action would not lie without other malevolent circumstances. I am of the same opinion, that judgment must be for the plaintiff.

GOULD J. — What my brother Bathurst has said is very material; there is a distinction between libels and words; a libel is punishable both criminally and by action, when speaking the words would not be punishable in either way; for speaking the words rogue and rascal of any one, an action will not lie; but if those words were written and published of any one, I doubt not an action would lie. If one man should say of another that he has the itch, without more, an action would not lie; but if he should write those words of another, and publish them maliciously, as in the present case, I have no doubt at all but the action well lies. What is the reason why saying a man has the leprosy or plague is actionable? It is because the having of either cuts a man off from society; so the writing and publishing maliciously that a man has the itch and stinks of brimstone, cuts him off from society. I think the publishing any thing of a man that renders him ridiculous is a libel and actionable, and in the present case am of opinion for the plaintiff. Judgment for the plaintiff per tot. Cur. [Editor's note: per totam curiam.] without granting any rule to shew cause.

QUESTION

What if, instead of printing that plaintiff had "the itch," the defendant had printed that the plaintiff had died? Would this communication be actionable?

SALOMONE v. MACMILLAN PUBLISHING COMPANY
New York Supreme Court
97 Misc. 2d 346, 411 N.Y.S.2d 105 (1978)

EDWARD J. GREENFIELD, JUSTICE:

Remember Eloise, the precocious six year old girl of Kay Thompson's creation who lived at the Plaza? Well, according to a book entitled "Titters", captioned as "The First Collection of Humor by Women", and published by defendants, she is now 26, and has grown into a sophisticated, uninhibited and sexy young woman who still lives at the Plaza.

The updated version of Eloise, entitled "Eloise Returns" is not by the original author, but is credited to Janie Gaynor and Peggy Goldman, who are contributors to the collection of pieces, poems, pictures and parodies designed (with mixed success) to showcase samples of humor by women. Some of its is clever, some of it dull, and some of it in questionable taste, but it is clear that the intent is to be funny. When, however, humor is at the expense of a sensitive person, the right of freedom of expression and the right of privacy and freedom from undue defamation collide. This case raises such an issue.

The plaintiff herein is Alphonse W. Salomone, a flesh and blood person who was in real life the manager of the Plaza Hotel for many years, and is now manager of the New York Hilton Hotel. In the original story, he is referred to by six year old Eloise briefly. She says:

"I am a nuisance in the lobby.
Mr. Salomone said so.
He is the Manager.
I always say 'Good morning, Mr. Salomone'
and he always says 'Good morning, Eloise'."

Accompanying the text is a drawing of Eloise curtseying, and a genial looking man smiling, and bowing low.

In "Eloise Returns," which is obviously a parody of the original, with the text running only four pages, there is also a reference to Mr. Salomone, only this time it is on the cover. On the original cover, a child has climbed up on a chair to scrawl the name "Eloise" with pink lipstick on the mirror above the marble fireplace. On the cover of the updated version, a grown up young lady has scrawled assorted raunchy graffiti on the walls, and on the mirror above the marble fireplace she has written with pink lipstick (in lettering identical to that on the original cover) the words "Eloise Returns." Immediately beneath that, in smaller letters, are the words "Mr. Salomone was a child molester!!"

Mr. Salomone has not found the use of his name in this way at all amusing. He is in fact outraged, and he has brought suit to recover $1,000,000 based on his contention that the statement about him on the cover of "Eloise Returns" is libelous per se.

Defendant Macmillan has moved to dismiss the complaint pursuant to CPLR 3211(a) (7) on the ground that it fails to state a cause of action in that the words taken, in context, are obviously a joke, and do not really convey any defamatory meaning. Plaintiff insists that the words are libelous per se, and could not possibly be construed as humorous, and accordingly he urges that the motion to dismiss be denied.

Plaintiff's complaint does not plead special damages, so unless the language employed be considered libelous per se, the complaint cannot withstand defendant's motion. A statement is defamatory on its face if it is clearly damaging to the reputation of the person to whom it relates. Reputation is a fragile shell which may be injured by words which tend to expose one to public hatred, shame, obloquy, contumely, odium, contempt, ridicule, aversion, ostracism, degradation or disgrace, or to induce an evil opinion of one in the minds of right-thinking persons. The question presented is whether the statement herein cannot possibly be construed as defaming plaintiff, because it is "all in fun."

Clearly the charge that someone is a "child molester" on its face imputes to an individual a crime involving moral turpitude — the carnal abuse of children. It is a charge that, if true, causes revulsion — for even in a society in which there has been a profound change in sexual mores, the use of children as sexual objects is considered a perversion of the lowest kind. There is nothing more likely than such a charge to create aversion and antipathy and destroy a reputation. It is reported that even in our prisons, with a population teeming with murderers, thieves, rapists and pimps, the child molester is on the lowest rung of the social ladder, and is regarded with scorn by his fellow criminals.

Defendant urges that despite the words themselves, no fair-minded person seeing them in context would seriously believe that the real-life Mr. Salomone was in fact a child-molester. "Eloise" was a work of fiction — about a made-up child and what her supposed reactions would be in a sophisticated but actual setting. The name of Mr. Salomone as manager of the hotel was added to lend a dash of verisimilitude to the work. "Eloise Returns" purports to be a parody of the original, echoing some of the phraseology and sentiments of the earlier work, but now through the mouth of a grown-up and thoroughly uninhibited Eloise. In the original she depicts Mr. Salomone as someone who considers her a nuisance. Twenty years later she gets back at him by scribbling that *he* was a child molester. No one, asserts the defendants, would consider this as a genuine, serious accusation for it is obviously designed to be humorous. Mr. Salomone's name is not alone on the cover of "Eloise Returns". Some of the graffiti depicted contain supposedly humorous sexual innuendoes about well-known public figures.

Is there a recognized exception from the laws of libel when words otherwise defamatory are uttered in a humorous context? Of course, common sense tells us there must be. Humor takes many forms — sheer nonsense, biting satire, practical jokes, puns (clever and otherwise), one-liners, ethnic jokes, incongruities and rollicking parodies, among others. Laughter can soften the blows dealt by a cruel world, or can sharpen the cutting edge of truth. Without humor — the ability to recognize the ridiculous in any situation, there can be no perspective. Humor is a protected form of free speech, just as much to be given full scope, under appropriate circumstances, as the political speech, the journalistic exposé, or the religious tract.

The principle is well established that an allegedly libelous statement must be read and understood in the context in which it appears.

Words which standing alone may reasonably be understood as defamatory may be so explained or qualified by their context as to make such an interpretation unreasonable. So, too, words which alone are innocent may in their context clearly be capable of a defamatory meaning and may be so understood. The context of a defamatory imputation includes all parts of the communication which are ordinarily heard or read with it.

Balabanoff v. Hearst Consolidated Publications, 294 N.Y. 351, 355, 62 N.E.2d. 599, 600.

If, taken in context, it is unmistakably clear that a statement otherwise libelous is set forth in jest, in unambiguously jocular, and would be regarded by all who read it as good-natured fun, then it cannot be said that the reputation of the person mentioned has been so undermined as to support a cause of action for libel.

Humor, then, may well be a defense to a suit in libel, but the mere assertion that a statement was meant to be funny does not automatically absolve the utterer. Humor is intensely subjective. Blank looks or even active loathing may be engendered by a statement or cartoon that evokes howls of laughter from another. What is amusing or funny in the eyes of one person may be cruel and tasteless to someone else. There is always a thin line between laughter and tears. Risibility and sensitivity must go hand in hand.

Especially is this true in dealing with parody and satire. Satire employs "irony, derision, or wit in any form to expose folly or wickedness." American Heritage

Dictionary, New College Edition 1976. It works through analogy and allusion to achieve recognition of the ridiculous. Its very essence is understatement. Parody, on the other hand, shuns subtlety. Its aim is to amuse and expose by imitating life, but larger than life. Its essence is distortion and exaggeration. Hence, like the warped and curved mirrors in a carnival fun house, it depends upon the grotesque for its effects.

Thus, the writer resorting to parody must be wary, for his shafts may miss the mark, and be cruel without purpose, inflicting real hurt where only laughter was intended.

However desirable it may be that the readers of and the writers for the public prints shall be amused, it is manifest that neither such readers nor writers should be furnished such amusement at the expense of the reputation or business of another. In the language of Joy, C.B.: "The principle is clear that a person shall not be allowed to murder another's reputation in jest;" or, in the words of Smith, B., in the same case: "If a man in jest conveys a serious imputation, he jests at his peril." *Donoghue v. Hayes* (1831), Hayes, Irish Exchequer, 265, 266.

Triggs v. Sun Printing & Pub. Assn., supra, 179 N.Y. p. 155, 71 N.E. p. 742.

In this case there is a sharp conflict between the contentions of the parties as to whether the work in question is uproariously funny and witty and a clever parody of a well-known work, or whether, as the plaintiff contends, the publication is merely a "collection of obscenity, smut and filth." It is difficult for a court to impose its own opinions as to the intent and impact of a purportedly humorous work. As stated by Botein, P.J. in *University of Notre Dame Du Lac et al., v. Twentieth Century-Fox Film Corporation et al.*, 22 A.D.2d 452, 256 N.Y.S.2d 301:

There is no point whatsoever in disclosing our views as to the artistic merit, good taste or essential decency of the treatment . . .

p. 455, 256 N.Y.S.2d p. 304.

Further, he stated:

We may not import the role of literary or dramatic critic into our functioning as judges in this case; and so for purposes of the law we may not reach a conclusion that the works of fiction involved in this litigation are not artistic or literary works . . . Whether [the work] is good burlesque or bad, penetrating satire or blundering buffoonery, is not for us to decide. It is fundamental that courts may not muffle expression by passing judgment on its skill or clumsiness, its sensitivity or coarseness; nor on whether it pains or pleases.

p. 458, 256 N.Y.S.2d p. 307

While the court, in that case, held that the work in question could not be enjoined in equity, it suggested that the remedy of the party who is the butt of the joke is at law, provided that libel can be proven.

This is precisely the kind of libel case suggested as appropriate by the Appellate Division, with the court having been warned not to impose its own values in measuring the work in question. The issue of whether a matter is harmless humor or cruel and vicious derision is peculiarly a judgmental question. Unless a jury has been waived, the court should not intercede as the ultimate finder of the facts. Just as questions of what is truth, what is reasonable, or what is obscene are left to the collective judgment of a group of laymen serving on a jury, so the question of whether a particular statement is non-actionable humor or compensable libel should appropriately be left to the judgment of a jury.

Public figures may justifiably be considered not only subjects of criticism but even calumny, but the same does not apply to persons who have never sought to thrust themselves into the limelight. The parody and satire to which public figures may be subject does not equally apply to private persons. The manager of the Plaza Hotel or the Hilton Hotel, while at a focal point in public activity, does not ordinarily put his private personality under the spotlight for all to see. In such a case, only a jury should make the ultimate determination as to whether the use of a name for poking fun is within legitimate limits or is so inexcusably over the line as to warrant damages. Application of these principles requires that the defendants' motion to dismiss the complaint be denied, and the matter be determined at a trial.

SALOMONE v. MACMILLAN PUBLISHING COMPANY
New York Supreme Court, Appellate Division
77 A.D.2d 501, 429 N.Y.S.2d 441 (1980)

MEMORANDUM DECISION.

Order, Supreme Court, New York County, entered January 11, 1980, denying the motions of defendants and third party defendants for summary judgment in this libel action, unanimously reversed on the law and the motions for summary judgment granted dismissing the complaint, without costs or disbursements.

. . .

Plaintiff Salomone, now senior vice president of the Hilton Hotels Corporation and managing director of the New York Hilton, was the manager of the Plaza when *Eloise* was published. From the evidence submitted, appellants were as shocked to learn that the Mr. Salomone of the fictional *Eloise* was an actual person as he was to learn of the accusation against him in *Eloise Returns*. Without doubt, plaintiff has suffered embarrassment and anguish. We must, nonetheless, dismiss his complaint because he has suffered no damages that are compensable in law.

Plaintiff pleads no special damage. He concedes that he has sustained no financial loss or physical damage attributable to appellants' publication. He claims damages for loss of reputation and for mental anguish. He has been unable to come forth with any proof of loss of reputation because he knows of no one who believes he was a child molester or thinks less of him due to the publication.

. . .

As to the claim for mental anguish, it has long been held in this state that such damage is compensable only when it is concomitant with loss of reputation (*Terwilliger v. Wands*, 17 N.Y. 54; *Wilson v. Goit*, 17 N.Y. 442). While the U. S. Supreme Court, in *Gertz*, would appear to have allowed the states sufficient latitude to include in the definition of "actual injury" mental anguish unaccompanied by loss of reputation, this has not occurred in this state. (*See Moran v. Hearst Corp.*, 40 N.Y.2d 1071, 392 N.Y.S.2d 253, 360 N.E.2d 932, concurring opinion.)

All concur except KUPFERMAN, J., who concurs in a memorandum as follows:

I concur only on the basis that the work which contains the alleged libel is an obvious parody and not intended to be taken seriously, nor can a reasonable person come to the conclusion that there was serious intent to the statement expressed. *Cf. Berlin v. E. C. Publications, Inc.*, 2 Cir., 329 F.2d 541.

NOTE AND QUESTIONS

(1) What is the essence of defamation? What is it that makes a statement defamatory? The Restatement (Second) of Torts § 559 (1977) defines a defamatory statement as one that tends to harm an individual's reputation by "lower[ing] him in the estimation of the community or [by] deter[ring] third persons from associating or dealing with him." Is this definition consistent with that given in *Villers v. Monsley*? In *Salomone v. Macmillan Publishing Co.*?

(2) Must a defamatory statement be communicated to a third person to be actionable, or is it enough if the defendant makes the statement only to the plaintiff?

(3) The law of defamation is composed of two branches, libel (written defamation) and slander (spoken defamation). The following excerpts explains their similarities and distinctions. "Report on the Committee on Defamation," Cmd.[2] 5909, London (1975).

HISTORY OF DISTINCTION BETWEEN LIBEL AND SLANDER

1. In early times, when few people were literate and printing had not been invented, proceedings for slander quite substantial in volume were entertained in local manorial and seigniorial courts, and also in the ecclesiastical courts. Such proceedings resulted in fines or ecclesiastical pains. The King's courts took no cognizance of defamation except in cases where the statutes about *scandalum magnatum* applied. In the course of the 16th century however, the common law courts began to develop an action on the case for defamation. They may have been concerned with the public order aspect, and no doubt they were, as ever, avid for jurisdiction. As the action was on the case, damages were the gist of it, and it was not generally recognized that defamation was an act wrongful *per se.* No distinction was observed between written and spoken defamation, but it is to be recalled that the first English printed book was published in 1474, and that printing required a license until 1697. The origin of the common law exceptions to the rule that slander required proof of special damage is obscure. [These exceptions are outlined below.] That relating to imputation of crime may well have started from the purpose of delimiting the respective jurisdictions of the common law and the ecclesiastical courts, but it is hard to see what the presence or absence of special damage had to do with this. It may well be that all three exceptional cases were thought so obviously likely to result in damage that no proof of it was necessary. At all events these exceptions were all well established by the middle of the 17th century. The common law jurisdiction proved extraordinarily popular, largely perhaps, because damages were found to be a more useful and attractive remedy than ecclesiastical pains, and during the reigns of Elizabeth I, James I and Charles I there was an

---

[2] Command Paper.

extraordinary flood of litigation. In their attempt to stem this, the courts introduced the rule of *mitior sensus*, whereby no words alleged to be defamatory *per se* were held to be defamatory if non-defamatory meaning could possibly be screwed out of them. The prime example of this is *Holt v. Astgrigg*, [(1868) L.R. 3Q.B. 396] in which Sir Thomas Holt failed in his action, although the defendant had said that he "struck his cook on the head with a cleaver, and cleaved his head; the one part lay on the one shoulder and another part on the other," on the ground that the defendant had not said that Sir Thomas had killed the cook. The rule that in other cases ascertainable "temporal" damage had to be proved was strictly insisted on, and repetition of a slander was not held to be actionable until early in the 19th century.

2. In the meantime, another and distinct line of legal development was opening up. This was connected with the establishment in 1488 of the Court of Star Chamber, which came to be very much concerned with the suppression of duelling and also with the control of printing, particularly in relation to seditious libels. In that court any defamation was a crime, and truth was no defense, except in the case of non-seditious slanders. The remedies available there were thus more efficacious than under an action on the case. The Court of Star Chamber was abolished in 1641. After the Restoration the common law judges, who had been represented in the Court of Star Chamber, took over the rules which had there been formulated and applied and developed them so as to create a new tort of libel, for the constitution of which proof of actual damage was not required. Their purpose, no doubt, was to deal with the same social problems, in particular duelling, which had led the Court of Star Chamber to adopt the rules in the first place. At all events in *King v. Lake*, [15 & 16 V.Ct. c.76] it was held that libel evinced more malice than slander and was therefore actionable per se.

THE PRESENT STATE OF THE LAW

75. A defamatory statement is *libel* if it is in permanent form and *slander* if it consists in significant words or gestures. The practical difference is that *libel* is actionable *per se*, but *slander* is not actionable without proof of special damage, unless it falls within certain exceptional categories.

76. The distinction was evolved at a period when methods of communication were simple and unsophisticated. There was no difficulty in relegating to libel the written word, pictures and statues, and to slander the spoken utterance, mimicry and gestures generally. Modern inventions, however, have rendered the distinction antiquated and given rise to some nice problems. In *Youssoupoff v. Metro-Goldwyn-Mayer Pictures Ltd.* [(1934) 50 T.L.R.581] the Court of Appeal had no difficulty in holding that defamatory matter in a talking cinematograph film was a libel, but it has never been decided whether, for example, such matter recorded on a gramophone record or on tape constitutes libel or slander. The late Sir. A.P. Herbert, in his story *Libel at Sea*, posed the question into which category it is proper to place defamatory messages communicated by flag signals in International Code, which remain hoisted for some period of time and are not like a semaphore message, purely transitory. It is suggested that sky-writing by an aeroplane may be libel, if defamatory, because the vapour takes some little time to disperse. The legislature has, not unnaturally, thought it proper to intervene in relation to certain media of communication. [References to United Kingdom statutes omitted. *See* § 19.6 *supra.*]

77. The exceptional cases where slander is actionable without proof of special damage are as follows: —

(a) imputation of a criminal offense punishable with imprisonment, not including an offense for which imprisonment may be inflicted on non-payment of a fine which has been imposed;

(b) imputation of a contagious or infectious disease likely to prevent other persons from associating with the plaintiff;

(c) imputation of unchastity or adultery to any woman or girl — being statutory exception introduced by the Slander of Women Act 1891, which also provides that "a plaintiff shall not recover more costs than damages unless the judge shall certify that there were reasonable grounds for bringing the action;"

(d) imputation of unfitness, dishonesty or incompetence in any office, profession, calling, trade or business held or carried on by the plaintiff at the time when the slander was published. In relation to this exception it was formerly the law that words which imputed misconduct without actual or implied reference to the office, profession, calling, trade or business were not actionable per *se* even though the imputation would naturally tend to injure the plaintiff therein. Section 2 of the Defamation Act 1952 altered this by providing, "in an action for slander in respect of words calculated to disparage the plaintiff in any office, profession, calling, trade or business held or carried on by him at the time of publication, it shall not be necessary to allege or prove special damage, whether or not the words are spoken of the plaintiff in the way of his office, profession, calling, trade or business."

Paragraphs 1 and 2 above are taken from Appendix VI of the Report; paragraphs 75 through 77 from Chapter 2.

(3) The American law of torts inherited the structure of the English common law of defamation, noted above. When radio, movies and television came along, the distinction between libel and slander created the same kind of difficulties that occurred in England. Basically, the issue became what must be proved and who has the burden of proof. Historically, libel carried with it the presumption of damage, thus obviating the need to plead and prove special damages as a condition to permitting juries to award general damages. By contrast, mere slander carried no such presumption; the pleader had to plead and prove special damages as a part of his prima facie case. Only then could a jury award general damages. Consequently, one plaintiff who was libeled might recover and another of whom the exact same defamation was published, but orally, might not.

Just as in England, American courts were called upon to make hairline distinctions between what is libel and what is slander when publication was through a broadcast medium or the movies. *See, e.g., First Independent Baptist Church v. Southerland*, 373 So. 2d 647 (Ala. 1979), holding a radio broadcast to be libel.

(4)　As is noted in the quotation of Note (2), *supra*, some forms of slander became known as slander *per se* and received the same favored treatment as libel as far as pleading and proving of special damages were concerned. That is, general damages may be obtained when the slander is of one of the *per se* categories even though no special damages are pleaded and proved. What justifies this result?

Adding to the complexity of defamation is a division made by some courts between libel and libel *per quod. See, e.g., Sharratt v. Housing Innovations, Inc.*,

310 N.E.2d 343 (Mass. 1974). Libel *per quod* means essentially that the libel does not plainly show on the face of the published words. Consider, for example, the impact of the words "the Sultan of the Swat hides lead in his lumber" had they been printed about 1930. On their face the words do not appear to be defamatory. If, however, one supplies the reader the additional information that the "Sultan of the Swat" is Babe Ruth, the legendary baseball batter, that "lumber" is jargon for baseball bat, and that it is illegal to imbed lead in bats because of the added force it supplies, then the defamatory meaning emerges. "Babe Ruth is a cheat;" which of course he was not. As is noted in ensuing cases, pleading the additional information is known as the "inducement," pleading the defamatory meaning is known as the "innuendo," and pleading the references that make the defamation of or pertaining to the plaintiff is the "colloquium."

In many American jurisdictions, the distinction between libel and libel per quod is relatively insignificant because all libel is actionable without proof of special damages. Nevertheless, in those jurisdictions that give legal meaning to the distinction between libel and libel *per quod*, libel *per quod* is treated as mere slander, thereby requiring the pleading and proving of special damages as a part of the plaintiff's prima facie case. Because of the complexities in this area, courts sometimes become confused and it would not be useful to present case materials elaborating this distinction. Each reader would be better off to examine the case law of a jurisdiction of interest.

(5) How is damage to reputation to be measured? *Firestone v. Time, Inc.*, 305 So. 2d 172, 176 (Fla. 1974), approved this jury instruction: "If you find the plaintiff is entitled to recover damages you may consider any shame, mortification, mental anguish, or hurt feelings experienced in the past or to be experienced in the future, if any, which you find from the evidence." Does this answer the question? The common law rule is that damage to reputation is presumed from the publication of libel or slander per se and no evidence of actual injury need be introduced to permit an award of compensatory damages. Subject to constitutional limitation, if applicable, as examined in succeeding sections, this rule continues to be applied in many jurisdictions. *Bryson v. News Family Publications, Inc.*, 672 N.E.2d 1207 (Ill. 1996), *Kluss v. Alcan Aluminum Corporation*, 666 N.E.2d 603 (Ohio App. 1995), *Richie v. Paramount Pictures Corporation*, 532 N.W.2d 235, 238 (Minn. App. 1995), and *Keohane v. Stewart*, 882 P.2d 1293, 1304 (Colo. En Banc 1994). *Contra, Gobin v. Globe Publishing Co.*, 649 P.2d 1239, 1243 (Kan. 1982), and *Little Rock Newspapers, Inc. v. Dodrill*, 660 S.W.2d 933, 935 (Ark. 1983) (requiring evidence of actual injury to reputation before "parasitic" emotional damages may be awarded.)

LEWIS v. DAILY TELEGRAPH LTD.
[1964] A.C. 234 (H.L.E.)[3]

Two newspapers, the Daily Telegraph and the Daily Mail, printed the following items on December 23, 1958.

[DAILY TELEGRAPH]

INQUIRY ON FIRM BY CITY POLICE

---

[3] [Ed. — Appeals Cases Law Reports, decision of House of Lords.]

Daily Telegraph Reporter.

Officers of the City of London Fraud Squad are inquiring into the affairs of Rubber Improvement Ltd. and its subsidiary companies. The investigation was requested after criticism of the chairman's statement and the accounts by a shareholder at the recent company meeting.

The chairman of the company, which has an authorized capital of £1 million, is Mr. John Lewis, former Socialist M.P. for Bolton.

[DAILY MAIL]

FRAUD SQUAD PROBE FIRM

The City Fraud Squad, under Superintendent Francis Lea, are inquiring into the affairs of Rubber Improvement Ltd. Chairman of the £4,000,000 group, whose shares have dropped from 22s. last year to 7s. 4½d. yesterday, is Mr. John Lewis, former Socialist M.P.

The company specializes in flexible rubber conveyor belting designed for the National Coal Board.

Lewis and other plaintiffs sued in defamation, setting forth the above reports, alleging that they were "falsely and maliciously printed and published," and alleging specifically in Paragraph 4:

By the said words the defendants meant and were understood to mean that the affairs of the plaintiffs and/or its subsidiaries were conducted fraudulently or dishonestly or in such a way that the police suspected that their affairs were so conducted.

The defendant defended on grounds of justification. The Plaintiff requested that the jury be instructed that they were free to infer the meanings alleged in paragraph 4 of the pleadings. In the action against the Daily Telegraph (referred to below as the first trial) the trial judge refused to strike the innuendos and instructed the jury as follows:

Salmon J., having read the statement in the "Daily Telegraph" to the jury, said in his summing-up: "This case very largely depends on what in your view those words mean. The question is, what would they have meant to the ordinary man and woman when he or she read them on the morning of December 23? It has been said that the ordinary man, with his cup of tea in one hand, reading this paper, does not read it with a suspicious, tortuous and sinister mind. That is very true, you may think. On the other hand, it has been said that when the ordinary man spreads his paper out on the table and reads it with his cup of tea in one hand, he does not necessarily hold the scales of justice in delicate equipoise in the other. You have got to think of the ordinary man. How would the ordinary man understand this? The two views which have been canvassed before you are these: Mr. Faulks has said [Ed. — As counsel for defendants]: Well, the ordinary man is not very suspicious; he would just regard it as a piece of intelligence, the police are looking into it, and it would not really produce any other effect upon his mind. Mr. Milmo says [Ed. — As counsel for plaintiffs]: Well, the ordinary man seeing this "City Police. Officers of the City of London Fraud Squad are inquiring into the affairs of Rubber Improvement Ltd." — the ordinary man, not being any more suspicious than his neighbour, would immediately say to himself, says Mr. Milmo — either he would say to himself: "There is fraud here, or the police would not be looking into it" or, he would say to himself: "At any rate, there is enough in this for the police to suspect that there is fraud." I cannot really help you. Those are the two rival contentions. It is for you to say what it means. When you read the newspapers, what would you have thought when you read that? You see, the only way you can get at what the ordinary man and woman think is by getting a jury of 12 people together, who are ordinary men and women, and asking them what they would have thought. You may ask yourselves, what would people in the City think if they woke up one morning and read that in the paper? Members of the jury, anything is defamatory which tends to lower you in the esteem of right thinking people. But if anyone reading this thought — any ordinary reasonable man reading this thought — that it meant that Mr. Lewis had been guilty of fraud; or that the police suspected that Mr. Lewis had been guilty of fraud; or that he had allowed the affairs of the company to be conducted fraudulently or dishonestly; or the police suspected that he had, would that tend to lower him in the esteem of right thinking people? And as far as the company is concerned, it is suggested by the plaintiffs that these words mean to the ordinary man that the affairs of the company and its subsidiaries were conducted fraudulently or dishonestly; or that the police suspected that they were so conducted. That is what is said by the plaintiffs these words would convey to the ordinary man and woman, and that the ordinary man and woman would not merely say to themselves: 'Oh well, it is a very interesting piece of intelligence: the police are inquiring into it. There may be a routine examination. We do not draw any conclusions at all.' As I say, consider that you get up one morning in a perfectly reasonable frame of mind; you are not feeling suspicious particularly, but you have a look at that: what would it mean to you?" The judge then went on to deal with the issue of justification and to direct the jury that if they thought that the meaning conveyed was no more than that the police were making an inquiry, then they had to consider whether the defendants had proved that an inquiry had been made. The judge reminded the jury of the evidence and said: "Does that constitute an inquiry into these matters by the police? You may think it does: you may think it does not."

At the second trial there was no submission that the innuendo should be struck out. Salmon J. left the alleged innuendo meanings to the jury as possible, natural and ordinary meanings of the words complained of.

The jury brought in large verdicts against both defendants. The Court of Appeal ordered a new trial on grounds of misdirection and excessive damages. Plaintiffs appeal this order to the House of Lords:

LORD DEVLIN. My Lords, the natural and ordinary meaning of words ought in theory to be the same for the lawyer as for the layman, because the lawyer's first rule of construction is that words are to be given their natural and ordinary meaning as popularly understood. The proposition that ordinary words are the same for the lawyer as for the layman is as a matter of pure construction undoubtedly true. But it is very difficult to draw the line between pure construction and implication, and the layman's capacity for implication is much greater than the lawyer's. The lawyer's rule is that the implication must be necessary as well as reasonable. The layman reads in an implication much more freely; and unfortunately, as the law of defamation has to take into account, is especially prone to do so when it is derogatory.

In the law of defamation these wider sorts of implication are called innuendoes. The word explains itself and is very apt for the purpose. In *Rex v. Horne* De Grey

C.J. said: "In the case of a libel which does not in itself contain the crime, without some extrinsic aid, it is necessary that it should be put upon the record, by way of introduction, if it is new matter; or by way of innuendo, if it is only matter of explanation. For an innuendo means nothing more than the words, 'id est,' 'scilicet,' or 'meaning,' or 'aforesaid,' as, explanatory of a subject-matter sufficiently expressed before."

An innuendo had to be pleaded and the line between an ordinary meaning and an innuendo might not always be easy to draw. A derogatory implication may be so near the surface that it is hardly hidden at all or it may be more difficulty to detect. If it is said of a man that he is a fornicator the statement cannot be enlarged by innuendo. If it is said of him that he was seen going into a brothel, the same meaning would probably be conveyed to nine men out of ten. But the lawyer might say that in the latter case a derogatory meaning was not a necessary one because a man might go to a brothel for an innocent purpose. An innuendo pleading that the words were understood to mean that he went there for an immoral purpose would not, therefore, be ridiculous. To be on the safe side, a pleader used an innuendo whenever the defamation was not absolutely explicit. That was very frequent, since scandalmongers are induced by the penalties for defamation to veil their meaning to some extent. Moreover, there were some pleaders who got to think that a statement of claim was somehow made more forceful by an innuendo, however plain the words. So rhetorical innuendoes were pleaded, such as to say of a man that he was a fornicator meant and was understood to mean that he was not fit to associate with his wife and family and was a man who ought to be shunned by all decent persons and so forth. Your Lordships were told, and I have no doubt it is true, that before 1949 it was very rare indeed to find a statement of claim in defamation without an innuendo paragraph.

. . .

My Lords, a system of pleading was built up on this basis which in 1949 was disconcerted by the introduction of a new rule — Ord. 19, r. 6(2). The object of the rule was to require that extrinsic facts must not only be proved but pleaded, thus restoring the position before 1852. The object was simple enough. It is the language of the rule that has caused the difficulties which have recently been brought to a head and have been the subject of three decisions, including the present one, by the Court of Appeal. The sub-rule reads: "(2) In an action for libel or slander if the plaintiff alleges that the words or matter complained of were used in a defamatory sense other than their ordinary meaning, he shall give particulars of the facts and matters on which he relies in support of such sense."

The word "innuendo" is not used. But the effect of the language is that any meaning that does not require the support of extrinsic fact is assumed to be part of the ordinary meaning of the words. Accordingly, an innuendo, however well concealed, that is capable of being detected in the language used is deemed to be part of the ordinary meaning.

This might be an academic matter if it were not for the principle that the ordinary meaning of words and the meaning enlarged by innuendo give rise to separate causes of action.

. . .

[Lord Devlin traces the history of the pleading of innuendos in English law and concludes that defamation cases must be pleaded in three paragraphs: (1) setting out the precise words complained about, (2) setting out the defamation the words import on their face, and (3) setting out a meaning that depends upon knowledge of external facts by the recipient of the words in (1) that render the words defamatory. Lord Devlin refers to (2) as the rhetorical innuendo and notes that it frequently is not needed. He refers to (3) as the legal innuendo and notes that it must always be accompanied by proof of the external facts.]

. . . I must now state how in the light of what I have said generally should decide the point at issue. Paragraph 4 of the statement of claim is as follows: "By the said words the defendants meant and were understood to mean that the affairs of the plaintiffs and/or its subsidiaries were conducted fraudulently or dishonestly or in such a way that the police suspected that their affairs were so conducted."

The Court of Appeal considered this paragraph to be defective, and I agree with them. This does not involve any sort of criticism of the learned pleader, who drafted his statement of claim at a time when it was possible to take almost any view of the points I have been canvassing. It is plain now that paragraph 4 must be treated as in form a plea of a legal innuendo. But in substance it is not a legal innuendo because no extrinsic facts are pleaded: general knowledge is, as I have indicated already, not an extrinsic fact . . . but is matter, not requiring to be proved, in the light of which the jury can interpret the publication. In substance the paragraph is a plea of a popular innuendo and the confusion between substance and form makes it embarrassing.

But I cannot, with respect, agree with the Court of Appeal that the way in which the judge treated this point is by itself a ground for a new trial. He went by the substance of the paragraph and left it to the jury as an ordinary innuendo, not a legal one. Perhaps he ought to have insisted on an amendment in the form, but he stated the course he was going to take and neither counsel offered any objection to it. I cannot think that the jury could have been in any way misled. . . .

I turn now to the main ground for ordering a new trial. This was that the judge misdirected the jury by failing to tell them that the words were not capable of bearing one or more of the defamatory meanings alleged in paragraph 4 of the statement of claim. It is admitted that the words are capable of some defamatory meaning, and I think it is undoubtedly defamatory of a company to say that its affairs are being inquired into by the police. But paragraph 4 alleges that the words meant "that the affairs of the plaintiffs and/or its subsidiaries were conducted fraudulently or dishonestly or in such a way that the police suspected that their affairs were so conducted." This is saying that the words mean either that the plaintiffs were guilty of fraud or that they were suspected of fraud. If it is permissible to distinguish between these two meanings, then for reasons which I shall give as I proceed I should hold that the words are capable of the latter meaning but not of the former, and I should on this basis agree with the Court of Appeal that the jury should have been so directed and that, since they were not, there should be a new trial. But Mr. Milmo has submitted that it is not right so to distinguish.

In the first place, he relies on what are called the "rumour cases." I agree, of course, that you cannot escape liability for defamation by putting the libel behind a prefix such as "I have been told that . . . " or "it is rumoured that . . . ", and then asserting that it was true that you had been told or that it was in fact being rumoured. You have, as Horridge J. said, in a passage that was quoted with approval by Greer L.J. in *Cookson v. Harewood*, "to prove that the subject-matter of the rumour was true." But this is not a case of repetition or rumour. I agree with the distinction drawn by Horridge J. on this point, though not necessarily with his limited view of the effect of the libel in that case. Anyway, even if this is to be treated as a rumour case, it is still necessary to find out what the rumour is. A rumour that a man is suspected of fraud is different from one that he is guilty of it. For the purpose of the law of libel a hearsay statement is the same as a direct statement, and that is all there is to it.

The real point, I think, that Mr. Milmo makes is that whether the libel is looked at as a statement or as a rumour, there is no difference between saying that a man is suspected of fraud and saying that he is guilty of it. It is undoubtedly defamatory, he submits, to say of a man that he is suspected of fraud, but it is defamatory only because it suggests that he is guilty of fraud: so there is no distinction between the two. This is to me an attractive way of putting the point. On analysis I think that the reason for its attraction is that as a maxim for practical application, though not as a proposition of law, it is about three-quarters true. When an imputation is made in a general way, the ordinary man is not likely to distinguish between hints and allegations, suspicion and guilt. It is the broad effect that counts and it is no use submitting to a judge that he ought to dissect the statement before he submits it to the jury . . . A man's reputation can suffer if it can truly be said of him that although innocent he behaved in a suspicious way; but it will suffer much more if it is said that he is not innocent.

It is not, therefore, correct to say as a matter of law that a statement of suspicion imputes guilt. It can be said as a matter of practice that it very often does so, because although suspicion of guilt is something different from proof of guilt, it is the broad impression conveyed by the libel that has to be considered and not the meaning of each word under analysis. A man who wants to talk at large about smoke may have to pick his words very carefully if he wants to exclude the suggestion that there is also a fire; but it can be done. One always gets back to the fundamental question: what is the meaning that the words convey to the ordinary man: you cannot make a rule about that. They can convey a meaning of suspicion short of guilt; but loose talk about suspicion can very easily convey the impression that it is a suspicion that is well founded.

In the libel that the House has to consider there is, however, no mention of suspicion at all. What is said is simply that the plaintiff's affairs are being inquired into. That is defamatory, as is admitted, because a man's reputation may in fact be injured by such a statement even though it is quite consistent with innocence. I dare say that it would not be injured if everybody bore in mind, as they ought to, that no man is guilty until he is proved so, but unfortunately they do not. It can be defamatory without it being necessary to suggest that the words contained a hidden allegation that there were good grounds for inquiry. A statement that a woman has been raped can affect her reputation, although logically it means that she is innocent of any impurity: *Yousoupoff v. Metro-Goldwyn-Mayer Pictures Ltd.* So a statement that a man has been acquitted of a crime with which in fact he was never charged might lower his reputation. Logic is not the test. But a statement that an inquiry is on foot may go further and may positively convey the impression that there are grounds for the inquiry, that is, that there is something to suspect. Just as a bare statement of suspicion may convey the impression that there are grounds for belief in guilt, so a bare statement of the fact of an inquiry may convey the impression that there are grounds for suspicion. I do not say that in this case it does; but I think that the words in their context and in the circumstances of publication are capable of conveying that impression. But can they convey an impression of guilt? Let it be supposed, first, that a statement that there is an inquiry conveys an impression of suspicion; and, secondly, that a statement of suspicion conveys an impression of guilt. It does not follow from these two suppositions that a statement that there is an inquiry conveys an impression of guilt. For that, two fences have to be taken instead of one. While, as I have said, I am prepared to accept that the jury could take the first, I do not think that in a case like the present, where there is only the bare statement that a police inquiry is being made, it could take the second in the same stride. If the ordinary sensible man was capable of thinking that wherever there was a police inquiry there was guilt, it would be almost impossible to give accurate information about anything: but in my opinion he is not. I agree with the view of the Court of Appeal.

There is on this branch of the case a final point to be considered. It is undoubtedly the law that the judge should not leave the question "libel or no libel" to the jury unless the words are reasonably capable of a defamatory meaning. But if several defamatory meanings are pleaded or suggested, can the judge direct the jury that the words are capable of one meaning but not of another? The point is important here because the defendant admits that the words are defamatory in one sense but disputes that they are defamatory in the senses pleaded in the statement of claim and contends that the judge should have so directed the jury. Mr. Milmo and Mr. Duncan appear at one time to have argued in the Court of Appeal that the function of the judge was exhausted when he ruled that the words were capable of being defamatory and that it was not for him to inquire whether they were or were not capable of any particular defamatory meaning. But later they abandoned the point and therefore did not initiate the discussion of it here. Nevertheless there was considerable discussion of it because some of your Lordships at one time felt that it was a point which ought to be considered.

In the result I think that all your Lordships are now clearly of the opinion that the judge must rule whether the words are capable of bearing each of the defamatory meanings, if there be more than one, put forward by the plaintiff.

This supports indirectly my view on the desirability of pleading different meanings. If the plaintiff can get before the jury only those meanings which the judge rules as capable of being defamatory, there is good reason for having the meanings alleged set out precisely as part of the record.

For the reasons I have given earlier, I agree that there must be a new trial on the ground of misdirection: but I should in any event have considered that there should be a new trial on the issue of damages as they are, in my opinion, ridiculously out of proportion to the injury suffered.

E. HULTON & CO. v. JONES
[1910] A.C. 20 (House of Lords)[4]

Mr. Artemus Jones, a barrister in practice, had been at one time on the staff of the *Sunday Chronicle*, a newspaper owned and published by the appellants, and contributed articles signed by himself to some of the appellants' publications. The appellants published in the *Sunday Chronicle* an article defamatory of a person described as "Artemus Jones." The article is set out in the report of the decision below. At the trial before Channell J. and a special jury at Manchester of an action brought by the respondent against the appellants, friends of the respondent gave evidence that they had read the libel and believed it to refer to the respondent. The evidence of the author of the article and of the editor of the *Sunday Chronicle* that they did not know of the existence of the respondent was accepted as true by the respondent's counsel. The jury found a verdict for the plaintiff for 1750 *l.* damages, and judgment was entered for him. Upon an application-by the defendants to set aside the verdict and judgment and to order a new trial, or alternatively to enter judgment for the defendants, the Court of Appeal (Lord Alverstone C.J. and Farwell L.J., Fletcher Moulton L.J. dissenting) affirmed the judgment and dismissed the application. Hence this appeal.

[Further background is provided from the following statement from the report of the trial. (1909) K.B. at 445.]

The article, which was written by the Paris correspondent of the paper, purported to describe a motor festival at Dieppe, and the parts chiefly complained of ran thus: "Upon the terrace marches the world, attracted by the motor races — a world immensely pleased with itself, and minded to draw a wealth of inspiration — and, incidentally, of golden cocktails — from any scheme to speed the passing hour. . . . 'Whist! there is Artemus Jones with a woman who is not his wife, who must be, you know — the other thing!' whispers a fair neighbour of mine excitedly into her bosom friend's ear. Really, is it not surprising how certain of our fellow-countrymen behave when they come abroad? Who would suppose, by his goings on, that he was a churchwarden at Peckham? No one, indeed, would assume that Jones in the atmosphere of London would take on so austere a job as the duties of a churchwarden. Here, in the atmosphere of Dieppe, on the French side of the Channel, he is the life and soul of a gay little band that haunts the Casino and turns night into day, besides betraying a most unholy delight in the society of female butterflies." The plaintiff had in fact received the baptismal name of Thomas only, but in his boyhood he had taken, or had been given, the additional name of Artemus, and from that time he had always used, and had been universally known by, the name of Thomas Artemus Jones or Artemus Jones. He had, up to the year 1901, contributed signed articles to the defendants' newspaper. The plaintiff was not a churchwarden, nor did he reside at Peckham. Upon complaint being made by the plaintiff of the publication of the defamatory statements in the article, the defendants published the following in the next issue of their paper: "It seems hardly necessary for us to state that the imaginary Mr. Artemus Jones referred to in our article was not Mr. Thomas Artemus Jones, barrister, but, as he has complained to us, we gladly publish this paragraph in order to remove any possible misunderstanding and to satisfy Mr. Thomas Artemus Jones we had no intention whatsoever of referring to him."

---

[4] [Ed. — Appeal Cases Law Reports, decision of House of Lords.]

[Judgments of the House of Lords]

Lord Loreburn L.C. My Lords, I think this appeal must be dismissed. A question in regard to the law of libel has been raised which does not seem to me to be entitled to the support of your Lordships. Libel is a tortious act. What does the tort consist in? It consists in using language which others knowing the circumstances would reasonably think to be defamatory of the person complaining of and injured by it. A person charged with libel cannot defend himself by shewing that he intended in his own breast not to defame, or that he intended not to defame the plaintiff, if in fact he did both. He has none the less imputed something disgraceful and has none the less injured the plaintiff. A man in good faith may publish a libel believing it to be true, and it may be found by the jury that he acted in good faith believing it to be true, and reasonably believing it to be true, but that in fact the statement was false. Under those circumstances he has no defence to the action, however excellent his intention. If the intention of the writer be immaterial in considering whether the matter written is defamatory, I do not see why it need be relevant in considering whether it is defamatory of the plaintiff. The writing, according to the old form, must be malicious, and it must be of and concerning the plaintiff. Just as the defendant could not excuse himself from malice by proving that he wrote it in the most benevolent spirit, so he cannot shew that the libel was not of and concerning the plaintiff by proving that he never heard of the plaintiff. His intention in both respects equally is inferred from what he did. His remedy is to abstain from defamatory words.

It is suggested that there was a misdirection by the learned judge in this case. I see none. He lays down in his summing up the law as follows: "The real point upon which your verdict must turn is, ought or ought not sensible and reasonable people reading this article to think that it was a mere imaginary person such as I have said — Tom Jones, Mr. Pecksniff as a humbug, Mr. Stiggins, or any of that sort of names that one reads of in literature used as types? If you think any reasonable person would think that, it is not actionable at all. If, on the other hand, you do not think that, but think that people would suppose it to mean some real person — those who did not know the plaintiff of course would not know who the real person was, but those who did know of the existence of the plaintiff would think that it was the plaintiff — then the action is maintainable, subject to such damages as you think under all the circumstances are fair and right to give to the plaintiff."

I see no objection in law to that passage. The damages are certainly heavy, but I think your Lordships ought to remember two things. The first is that the jury were entitled to think, in the absence of proof satisfactory to them (and they were the judges of it), that some ingredient of recklessness, or more than recklessness, entered into the writing and the publication of this article, especially as Mr. Jones, the plaintiff, had been employed on this very newspaper, and his name was well known in the paper and also well known in the district in which the paper circulated. In the second place the jury were entitled to say this kind of article is to be condemned. There is no tribunal more fitted to decide in regard to publications, especially publications in the newspaper Press, whether they bear a stamp and character which ought to enlist sympathy and to secure protection. If they think that the licence is not fairly used and that the tone and style of the libel is reprehensible and ought to be checked, it is for the jury to say so; and for my part, although I think the damages are certainly high, I am not prepared to advise your

Lordships to interfere, especially as the Court of Appeal have not thought it right to interfere, with the verdict.

Lord Shaw of Dunfermline. My Lords, I concur in the observations which have been made by the Lord Chancellor, but for my own part I should desire in terms to adopt certain language which I will now read from the judgment of the Lord Chief Justice: "The question, if it be disputed whether the article is a libel upon the plaintiff, is a question of fact for the jury, and in my judgment this question of fact involves not only whether the language used of a person in its fair and ordinary meaning is libelous or defamatory, but whether the person referred to in the libel would be understood by persons who knew him to refer to the plaintiff."

My Lords, with regard to this whole matter I should put my propositions in a threefold form, and, as I am not acquainted by training with a system of jurisprudence in which criminal libel has any share, I desire my observations to be confined to the question of civil responsibility. In the publication of matter of a libelous character, that is matter which would be libellous if applying to an actual person, the responsibility is as follows: In the first place there is responsibility for the words used being taken to signify that which readers would reasonably understand by them; in the second place there is responsibility also for the names used being taken to signify those whom the readers would reasonably understand by those names; and in the third place the same principle is applicable to persons unnamed but sufficiently indicated by designation or description.

My Lords, I demur to the observation so frequently made in the argument that these principles are novel. Sufficient expression is given to the same principles by Abbott C.J. in *Bourke v. Warren* (1) (cited in the proceedings), in which that learned judge says: "The question for your consideration is whether you think the libel designates the plaintiff in such a way as to let those who knew him understand that he was the person meant. It is not necessary that all the world should understand the libel; it is sufficient if those who know the plaintiff can make out that he is the person meant." I think it is out of the question to suggest that that means "meant in the mind of the writer" or of the publisher; it must mean "meant by the words employed." The late Lord Chief Justice Coleridge dealt similarly with the point in *Gibson v. Evans* (2), when in the course of the argument he remarked: "It does not signify what the writer meant; the question is whether the alleged libel was so published by the defendant that the world would apply it to the plaintiff."

Appeal Dismissed

NOTES AND QUESTIONS

(1) The following excerpt from *Bowling v. Pow*, 301 So. 2d 55 (Ala. 1974), elaborates the peculiarities in pleading and proving of defamatory meaning:

Words usually, though not always form the basis of actions of defamation. Known better by the parties, men of letters, than by men of law in general, " . . . Words, words, words . . . ", sometimes apparently meaningless, even occasionally indicating "madness" with a "method in't", often have such a variety of meanings that the context of particular words must be examined at times in order to determine their meaning on the occasion of their use. As to speakers or writers in general, the context usually consists of the language that precedes or follows, or both, the words in question. In the law of defamation, however, the field of examination is much broader and includes extrinsic circumstances not found within the contexture of a particular discourse. This to a great extent accounts for the development in common law pleading of subjects referred to as inducement, innuendo and colloquium. . . .

Although variously stated, the inducement is that part of the complaint in action of defamation that sets forth extrinsic facts which the plaintiff deems advisable or appropriate to allege in his effort to show in the complaint that the matter published is defamatory. The innuendo is that part of the complaint wherein the plaintiff seeks to explain the meaning of language as defamatory, which could or would otherwise be considered as innocuous or so ambiguous or uncertain in meaning that a defamatory sense is not clearly revealed. The colloquium is that part of the complaint that in effect charges that the defamatory matter was published of and concerning the plaintiff.

. . .

It is to be readily seen that there can be matter that is so clearly and certainly defamatory and applicable to plaintiff on its face that there was no necessity, even at common law, to set forth in such cases, an inducement, an innuendo, or a colloquium. On the other hand, it is equally observable that at times the contents of an alleged publication are not sufficient in and of themselves to show a defamatory imputation directed at plaintiff and that a showing of extrinsic circumstances, a defamatory meaning or an application to plaintiff — one, two or all — is necessary to show that plaintiff was defamed.

Defamation does not necessarily involve opprobrious or scurrilous language. It is often elegant, refined and scholarly in essence and environment, and some of the best linguists have engaged in and been victims of it. The parties hereto can find distinguished company, as evidenced by *Cooper v. Greeley*, 1 Denio 347 (N.Y. 1845), in which the words of Horace Greeley concerning James Fenimore Cooper, "He will not bring the action in New York, for we are known here, nor in Otsego, for he is known there" were held defamatory as imputing a bad reputation to Cooper in Otsego, an example of defamation indirection by suave implication.

(2)   The job of establishing the colloquium is hard enough in circumstances such as the "Artemus Jones" case. After all, a large number of persons of that name might appear, each claiming to have been defamed. What constitutes the potential limit of liability under such circumstances? Contrast the statement, "One lawyer out of ten is a thief!" As a rule, courts have been unwilling to permit juries to determine that any particular person has been defamed when the plaintiff is merely one member of a fairly sizable group, but the smaller the group and the more universal the attribution the more likely the action will be permitted. *Neiman-Marcus v. Lait*, 13 F.R.D. 311 (S.D.N.Y. 1952), examines the limits of this so-called group defamation in the context of a salacious publication. Who can sustain an action upon the statement, "All lawyers are thieves"?

(3)   Defamation is a wrong to reputation. Dead people cannot be defamed (Why?), and many jurisdictions hold that only natural persons can be defamed.

Does it follow that the statement, "XYZ, Inc. cheats its customers!" is defamatory of no one? Some jurisdictions do permit defamation actions by non-natural persons.

---

§ 17.02 PUBLICATION

COLLERTON v. MACLEAN
[1962] N.Z.L.R. 1045 (Supreme Court)[5]

ACTION for damages for libel.

The plaintiff was the secretary of the Wellington Freezing Works and Related Trades Employees Industrial Union of Workers. The four defendants were members of the Executive Council of the union, the two first-named defendants being members of and councilors for the Petone Branch of the union, and the third and fourth named defendants being members and councilors for the Waingawa Branch of the union. It was alleged that on 27 September 1961 the defendants published or caused to be published of the plaintiff in the way of his office as secretary of the union to members of the union a requisition in writing containing the following words:

Please take note that Petone and Waingawa Branches hereby direct that a Special Meeting of Executive Councillors be called in Wellington on the 9th October 1961 at 10.30 a.m. The authority for this is outlined in Rule 6 Section (e).

BUSINESS: Secretary's repeated under-mining tactics causing unparalleled disharmony throughout the freezing industry.

Secretary's tardiness in carrying out allotted duties.

The required signatures are set out below.

McGREGOR J. [after stating the facts as above]: The plaintiff claims that by the publication of these words he has been injured in his character and reputation, and in the way of his employment as a union secretary, and has been brought into public odium, ridicule and contempt. In his amended statement of claim the plaintiff claims the sum of £5 as damages.

The first questions to be considered are whether the words are defamatory of the plaintiff, and if so, whether there has been publication as alleged by the plaintiff. The defendants plead by way of defence justification in that the words are true in substance and in fact; secondly, that they were published on a privileged occasion to other members of the executive who had a common interest in the matter, and that they were published without malice.

A defamatory statement is a statement which is calculated to lower the plaintiff in the estimation of right thinking men, or cause him to be shunned or avoided or expose him to hatred, contempt or ridicule, or one which is calculated to convey an imputation disparaging to him in his business or office or calling: Gatley on Libel and Slander, 5th ed. In the present case it seems to me that the document is clearly defamatory. The reference to the plaintiff is in respect of his office as secretary of the union. It charges him with repeated undermining tactics causing unparalleled

---

[5] [Ed. — New Zealand Law Reports.]

disharmony throughout the industry. The result of undermining tactics must certainly be disruption and chaos in the union. If a secretary were guilty of such tactics he would obviously be a person unfit to hold such office. The first essential requirement of the holder of such an office would be, in my view, to endeavour to achieve harmony and avoid discord among the members of the union. Likewise tardiness in carrying out allotted duties is a reflection on a person holding the office of secretary of a union, and would make such a person unfitted to continue in office. I agree that the meaning taken from the words by a reasonably minded reader would naturally be that the plaintiff, as alleged by him in his statement of claim, was inefficient, incompetent, unfaithful in his office, and was acting in a manner which was not in the interests of the union, and was therefore unfit to be secretary of the union. It seems to me that the statement in its natural meaning and primary sense is defamatory and that ordinary reasonable people reading the statement and placing the ordinary meaning on the words used would think ill of the plaintiff. I do not think this is seriously contested by the defendants.

I next pass to the question of publication, which is denied by the defendants. It is clear from the evidence that the author of the requisition was the first defendant MacLean. He prepared and typed the requisition. He and the second defendant Dellaway were the representatives on the Executive Council of the union of the Petone Branch of the union, and the third and fourth defendants were likewise representatives of the Waingawa Branch of the union. The first defendant, after preparing the requisition, called a meeting of six members of the Executive Council, the four defendants and two other members, who represented the Ngauranga Branch of the union. This meeting was held at the Midland Hotel in a private room on 27 September 1961. A seventh person named Flynn was also present. He was not a member of the Executive Council, and the explanation given in evidence was that he was invited to take the chair at the meeting. It seems that there was a discussion at the meeting in regard to various activities of the plaintiff. The defendant MacLean seems to have produced another document dated 12 September 1961 stated to be observations regarding certain activities of the plaintiff, and in it he accused the plaintiff of double dealing and following a very dangerous course all to the detriment of progressive freezing workers' business. As a result of the discussion the six persons present other than the chairman signed the notice of requisition. The two Ngauranga members are not defendants in the action, as it seems they have made to the plaintiff a retraction of the allegations contained in the requisition. After this meeting MacLean posted the requisition to the plaintiff. It thereupon became the duty of the plaintiff under the rules of the union to call a special meeting of the Executive. The rules provide that a special meeting of the committee shall be called whenever the secretary receives a requisition to call such meeting, signed by any three Branches. The present requisition complies with this rule, and it thereupon became the duty of the secretary to convene a meeting and give notice in writing thereof to each member of the Executive Committee. On receipt of the requisition the plaintiff gave notice of a special meeting to be held on Wednesday 11 October 1961. The meeting was duly held in accordance with this notice. There were present 13 members of the executive apart from the plaintiff, and such number includes the four defendants in this action, and two observers were permitted to stay at the meeting without voice or vote. On a motion moved and seconded by the first two defendants the standing orders were suspended, and the next matter considered was the business contained in the defendants' requisition, the words of which are recorded in the minutes. A motion was then moved by the second defendant Dellaway that a secret ballot be conducted amongst all financial members of the union for the purpose of determining whether Mr. Collerton's appointment as secretary be terminated. This motion was lost by eight votes to five, with one informal vote. The meeting then proceeded to other business.

In regard to publication by the defendants it seems to me that three separate matters must be considered. First, whether there was a publication by MacLean to the other signatories of the requisition when he produced it for discussion and signature at the meeting at the Midland Hotel on 27 September. The second question is whether there was a publication of the requisition by the defendants to Flynn, a person requested to be present at this meeting and to take the chair thereat. The third question is whether the signatories to the requisition were parties to its publication at the executive committee meeting on 11 October, the production of the requisition being done by the secretary at the meeting in the course of his duties as secretary.

. . .

In regard to the meeting at the Midland Hotel the four defendants, and also Mr. Flynn, the chairman, claim that the requisition was not shown to him. I feel that I cannot accept this denial. Mr. Flynn was specially imported to take the chair at the meeting, and control the meeting. The result of the meeting was that the six others present decided to sign the requisition and forward it to the secretary. I do accept that owing to a leg infirmity Mr. Flynn was not sitting at the table during this meeting, but sitting in an armchair, but I cannot accept his denial that he did not see the document or any copy of it on that occasion. He admits that he knew the copy was at that meeting, but he says it was not read out to him, although he knew these men were signing a document. This explanation, although it is confirmed by the four defendants, seems to my mind too specious. According to the defendant MacLean the requisition had been drafted by him with some help and advice from his seniors, and he had discussed it with Dellaway and Flynn. Mr. Flynn was in control of the meeting as chairman, and I am satisfied that he not only knew the contents of the document, but in his capacity as chairman he actually saw the document. It seems to me that there was a publication to Flynn at this meeting.

I also take the view that the four defendants were parties to the publication at the meeting of the Executive Committee of the union on 11 October. It is stated in Gatley, 5th ed. 81, that by publication is meant the making known of the defamatory matter after it has been written, to some person other than the person of whom it is written. If the statement is sent straight to the person of whom it is written, there is no publication of it. And at page 82 "Publication is effected by any act on the part of the defendant which conveys the defamatory meaning of the matter to the person to whom it is communicated." It seems to me in the present instance that the defamatory matter was made known by MacLean to all the persons present at the meeting at the Midland Hotel, including Flynn, and that the other five signatories then adopted the defamatory words. It is true that the next step in the publication was the act of the plaintiff in forwarding a copy of the requisition to each of the members of the Executive Committee when he gave notice calling the meeting. But this publication, it seems to me, was in the course of his duty, and the defendants knew and must have recognized when they forwarded the requisition to the secretary that he would be required in the course of his duty to publish it to all the members of the Executive Committee. It is said that if it can be proved that the plaintiff expressly or impliedly assented to or acquiesced in the publication of the defamatory matter, no action will lie. But does a person assent to or acquiesce in the publication when he is under a duty to make such publication? Before there can be a publication the defamatory matter must be made known after it has been written to some person other than the person of whom it was written. If the statement is sent straight to the person of whom it is written there is no publication, for you cannot publish a libel of a man to himself. But if the sender of the letter has put it out of his own control and has directed it in such a manner that it might be read by a person other than the person to whom it is addressed there is a publication by the sender of it. The position bears some resemblance to that in *Theaker v. Richardson* [1962] 1 All E.R. 229. There the defendant wrote a highly defamatory letter to the plaintiff, for which he had no justification. The defendant intended to deliver the letter to the plaintiff in person, but changed his mind, and put it through her letter box. It was picked up by the plaintiff's husband, who opened it without looking at the name of the envelope, thinking it was an election address. The jury answered in the affirmative two questions left to them

(1) Did the defendant anticipate that someone other than the plaintiff would open and read the letter? (2) Was it a natural and probable consequence of the defendant's writing and delivery of the letter that the plaintiff's husband would open and read it?

The answers of the jury to the issues and the verdict thereon for the plaintiff were upheld by the majority of the Court of Appeal. Harman L.J. after considering various authorities in regard to publication, says: "It thus appears that the answer to the question of publication of a libel contained in a letter will depend on the state of the defendant's knowledge, either proved or inferred, of the conditions likely to prevail in the place to which the libel is destined. I have considered the rival arguments and am of opinion that these are just the kind of questions of fact which ought to be left to a jury and that the learned Judge was fully justified in doing so" (*ibid.*, 235).

Pearson L.J. says: "The question arising can be put in this form. The plaintiff's husband, acting carelessly and thoughtlessly but meaning no harm, picked up and opened and began to read the letter. Was his conduct something unusual out of the ordinary and not reasonably to be anticipated, or was it something which could quite easily and naturally happen in the ordinary course of events? In my judgment that is a fair formulation of the question, and, when so formulated, it is seen to be a question of fact which in a trial with a jury can and should be left to and decided by the jury, who have observed the witnesses giving evidence and have and are expected to use their own common sense and general knowledge of the world and perhaps some particular knowledge (if they have it) of the locality concerned and the ways of its inhabitants. In my judgment, it would not be right to substitute the opinion of this Court for the opinion of the jury on such a question arising in the course of a trial with a jury" (*ibid.*, 238).

In *Gomersall v. Davies* (1898) 14 T.L.R. 430 a letter was sent to the plaintiff by the defendant and was opened by the clerk of the addressee, the plaintiff, in the ordinary course of business. It was held that there was evidence of publication to go to the jury immediately [if] it was proved that the clerk opened the letter in the ordinary course of his duty and read it.

Questions were left by the Judge to the jury, who answered them in favour of the plaintiff, and the Court of Appeal were of opinion that the questions were rightly left to the jury, because on the facts there was evidence that to the defendant's knowledge letters addressed to the plaintiff and received in the ordinary course of business would be likely to be opened by persons in the plaintiff's employment. This case can be compared with *Huth v. Huth* [1915] 3 K.B. 32 where a letter to the plaintiff was wrongly opened and read by the plaintiff's butler.

In the present case it seems to me the question is one of fact and that I should consider the conduct of the defendants, and it seems to me that it was not out of the ordinary, and was reasonably to be anticipated, that the result of forwarding the requisition to the plaintiff would be publication to all the members of the Executive Committee. The secretary was under a duty to give notice to the members of the Executive Committee of the business of the special meeting requisitioned by the defendants, and this business included the defamatory matter in the requisition. Moreover, the requisition was produced, according to the minutes, and according to the evidence of MacLean, at the meeting of the Executive Committee, and discussed. The defendants in my view were parties to this publication, and it was a publication not only to the members of the Executive Committee present, but was a further publication to the two other persons, Messrs. M. Flynn and S. Arnst, who were permitted to be present as two observers without voice or vote. I therefore conclude that there was publication of the defamatory matter to Flynn at the Midland Hotel meeting, and to all the members of the Executive Committee plus the two observers at the October meeting of the Executive Council. This is sufficient, and I do not, therefore, have to consider whether the act of MacLean in producing the requisition at the Midland Hotel meeting to the other members of the Executive then present and for the purpose of procuring their signatures was a separate publication by him to the other signatories.

NOTES AND QUESTIONS

(1)   As is examined in § 17.05, *infra*, certain defenses and privileges apply in the law of defamation by rough analogy to those that apply in the law of intentional torts. After having examined those defenses, the reader should revisit *Collerton* and consider whether it was important for the plaintiff to have established that M. Flynn and S. Arnst were present at the various meetings.

(2)   Defamation has always been a strict liability tort, having been recognized as such as early as the seventeenth century in *Mercer v. Sparks*, 74 Eng. Rep. 1005. *Mercer* succinctly held that "words themselves are malicious and slanderous," thereby obviating any need for the plaintiff to show ill will, intention to harm or negligence. *See also, Bromage v. Prosser*, 107 Eng. Rep. 1051 (1830). In form, malice was required in common law actions, but in law the publication of the defamatory statement constituted an irrebuttable presumption of malice. *See, e.g., Layne v. The Tribune Co.*, 108 Fla. 177, 146 So. 234 (1933). Thus, whether or not the defendant was reasonable in his belief in the truth of a defamatory statement that was in fact false is simply irrelevant in the common law of defamation. Nevertheless, as is suggested in *Collerton*, the common law did require either an intention to

publish the defamation to someone other than the defamed person or negligent publication. Thus, if one person, taking reasonable precautions to exclude third persons, were to say to another, "You are a thief," then a defamation action could not be maintained if some third person fortuitously overheard the statement. *See, e.g., McKinney v. County of Santa Clara.*, 168 Cal. Rptr. 89 (Ct. App. 1980). At common law, however, a defendant who republished a defamatory statement was liable as if the defendant had been the original publisher. Because of the perceived unfairness of the republication rule, many legislatures have entered this field to provide statutory protection to innocent republishers of defamation. Finally, the United States Supreme Court in *New York Times v. Sullivan, infra,* and *Gertz v. Robert Welch, Inc., infra,* imposed constitutional limitations that apply to most defamations of this kind.

---

§ 17.03   MALICE

[A]   Common Law Malice

[See *Hulton v. Jones,* § 17.01, *supra.*]

[B]   Constitutional Malice

NEW YORK TIMES COMPANY v. SULLIVAN
United States Supreme Court
376 U.S. 254, 84 S. Ct. 710, 11 L. Ed. 2d 686 (1964)

Mr. Justice Brennan delivered the opinion of the Court.

We are required in this case to determine for the first time the extent to which the constitutional protections for speech and press limit a State's power to award damages in a libel action brought by a public official against critics of his official conduct.

Respondent L. B. Sullivan is one of the three elected Commissioners of the City of Montgomery, Alabama. He testified that he was "Commissioner of Public Affairs and the duties are supervision of the Police Department, Fire Department, Department of Cemetery and Department of Scales." He brought this civil libel action against the four individual petitioners, who are Negroes and Alabama clergymen, and against petitioner the New York Times Company, a New York corporation which publishes the New York Times, a daily newspaper. A jury in the Circuit Court of Montgomery County awarded him damages of $500,000, the full amount claimed, against all the petitioners, and the Supreme Court of Alabama affirmed. 273 Ala. 656, 144 So. 2d 25. [Editor's note: — At the time this case was decided, $500,000 was the largest libel judgment in Alabama history.]

Respondent's complaint alleged that he had been libeled by statements in a full-page advertisement that was carried in the New York Times on March 29, 1960. Entitled "Heed Their Rising Voices," the advertisement began by stating that "As the whole world knows by now, thousands of Southern Negro students are engaged in widespread non-violent demonstrations in positive affirmation of the right to live in human dignity as guaranteed by the U. S. Constitution and the Bill of Rights." It went on to charge that "in their efforts to uphold these guarantees, they are being met by an unprecedented wave of terror by those who would deny and negate that document which the whole world looks upon as setting the pattern for modern freedom. . . . " Succeeding paragraphs purported to illustrate the "wave of terror" by describing certain alleged events. The text concluded with an appeal for funds for three purposes: support of the student movement, "the struggle for the right-to-vote," and the legal defense of Dr. Martin Luther King, Jr., leader of the movement, against a perjury indictment then pending in Montgomery.

. . .

Of the 10 paragraphs of text in the advertisement, the third and a portion of the sixth were the basis of respondent's claim of libel. They read as follows:

Third paragraph:

In Montgomery, Alabama, after students sang "My Country, 'Tis of Thee" on the State Capitol steps, their leaders were expelled from school, and truckloads of police armed with shotguns and tear-gas ringed the Alabama State College Campus. When the entire student body protested to state authorities by refusing to re-register, their dining hall was padlocked in an attempt to starve them into submission.

Sixth paragraph:

Again and again the Southern violators have answered Dr. King's peaceful protests with intimidation and violence. They have bombed his home almost killing his wife and child. They have assaulted his person. They have arrested him seven times — for "speeding," "loitering" and similar "offenses." And now they have charged him with "perjury" — *a felony* under which they could imprison him for *ten years*. . . .

[Although these statements did not name him, Sullivan (respondent) argued that they were understood as "of and concerning" him and were libelous *per se.* Sullivan sued the New York Times as publisher and 64 persons whose names appeared as sponsors of the advertisement. The jury was instructed that the statements were libelous *per se* and unprivileged. The jury was also instructed that falsity, malice and general damages are presumed and need not be alleged or proved.]

Respondent relies heavily, as did the Alabama courts, on statements of this Court to the effect that the Constitution does not protect libelous publications. Those statements do not foreclose our inquiry here. None of the cases sustained the use of libel laws to impose sanctions upon expression critical of the official conduct of public officials. The dictum in *Pennekamp v. Florida*, 328 U.S. 331, 348–349, 66 S. Ct. 1029, 1038, 90 L. Ed. 1295, that "when the statements amount to defamation, a judge has such remedy in damages for libel as do other public servants," implied no view as to what remedy might constitutionally be afforded to public officials. In *Beauharnais v. Illinois*, 343 U.S. 250, 72 S. Ct. 725, 96 L. Ed. 919, the Court sustained an Illinois criminal libel statute as applied to a publication held to be both defamatory of a racial group and "liable to cause violence and disorder." But the Court was careful to note that it "retains and exercises authority to nullify action which encroaches on freedom of utterance under the guise of punishing libel"; for "public men, are, as it were, public property," and "discussion cannot be denied and the right, as well as the duty, of criticism must not be stifled." *Id.*, at 263–264, 72 S. Ct. at 734, 96 L. Ed. 919 and n. 18.

. . .

The constitutional guarantees require, we think, a federal rule that prohibits a public official from recovering damages for a defamatory falsehood relating to his official conduct unless he proves that the statement was made with "actual malice" — that is, with knowledge that it was false or with reckless disregard of whether it was false or not. An oft-cited statement of a like rule, which has been adopted by a number of state courts, is found in the Kansas case of *Coleman v. MacLennan*, 78 Kan. 711, 98 P. 281 (1908). The State Attorney General, a candidate for re-election and a member of the commission charged with the management and control of the state school fund, sued a newspaper publisher for alleged libel in an article purporting to state facts relating to his official conduct in connection with a school-fund transaction. The defendant pleaded privilege and the trial judge, over the plaintiff's objection, instructed the jury that where an article is published and circulated among voters for the sole purpose of giving what the defendant believes to be truthful information concerning a candidate for public office and for the purpose of enabling such voters to cast their ballot more intelligently, and the whole thing is done in good faith and without malice, the article is privileged, although the principal matters contained in the article may be untrue in fact and derogatory to the character of the plaintiff; and in such a case the burden is on the plaintiff to show actual malice in the publication of the article.

In answer to a special question, the jury found that the plaintiff had not proved actual malice, and a general verdict was returned for the defendant. On appeal the Supreme Court of Kansas, in an opinion by Justice Burch, reasoned as follows (78 Kan., at 724, 98 P., at 286):

[I]t is of the utmost consequence that the people should discuss the character and qualifications of candidates for their suffrages. The importance to the state and to society of such discussions is so vast, and the advantages derived are so great that they more than counter-balance the inconvenience of private persons whose conduct may be involved, and occasional injury to the reputations of individuals must yield to the public welfare, although at times such injury may be great. The public benefit from publicity is so great and the chance of injury to private character so small that such discussion must be privileged.

The court thus sustained the trial court's instruction as a correct statement of the law, saying:

In such a case the occasion gives rise to a privilege qualified to this extent. Any one claiming to be defamed by the communication must show actual malice, or go remediless. This privilege extends to a great variety of subjects and includes matters of public concern, public men, and candidates for office. 78 Kan., at 723, 98 P., at 285.

Such a privilege for criticism of official conduct is appropriately analogous to the protection accorded a public official when *he* is sued for libel by a private citizen. In *Barr v. Matteo*, 360 U.S. 564, 575, 79 S. Ct. 1335, 1341, 3 L. Ed. 2d 1434, this Court held the utterance of a federal official to be absolutely privileged if made "within the outer perimeter" of his duties. The States accord the same immunity to statements of their highest officers, although some differentiate their lesser officials and qualify the privilege they enjoy. But all hold that all officials are protected unless actual malice can be proved. The reason for the official privilege is said to be that the threat of damage suits would otherwise "inhibit the fearless, vigorous, and effective administration of policies of government" and "dampen the ardor of all but the most resolute, or the most irresponsible, in the unflinching discharge of their duties." *Barr v. Matteo, supra*, 360 U.S., at 571, 79 S. Ct., at 1339, 3 L. Ed. 2d 1434. Analogous considerations support the privilege for the citizen-critic of government. It is as much his duty to criticize as it is the official's duty to administer. As Madison said, see *supra*, p. 723, "the censorial power is in the people over the Government, and not in the Government over the people." It would give public servants an unjustified preference over the public they serve, if critics of official conduct did not have a fair equivalent of the immunity granted to the officials themselves.

We conclude that such a privilege is required by the First and Fourteenth Amendments.

We hold today that the Constitution delimits a State's power to award damages for libel in actions brought by public officials against critics of their official conduct. Since this is such an action, the rule requiring proof of actual malice is applicable. While Alabama law apparently requires proof of actual malice for an award of punitive damages, where general damages are concerned malice is "presumed." Such a presumption is inconsistent with the federal rule. "The power to create presumptions is not a means of escape from constitutional restrictions," *Bailey v. Alabama*, 219 U.S. 219, 239, 31 S. Ct. 145, 151, 55 L. Ed. 191; "[t]he showing of malice required for the forfeiture of the privilege is not presumed but is a matter for proof by the plaintiff . . . " *Lawrence v. Fox*, 357 Mich. 134, 146, 97 N.W.2d 719, 725 (1959). Since the trial judge did not instruct the jury to differentiate between general and punitive damages, it may be that the verdict was wholly an award of one or the other. But it is impossible to know, in view of the general verdict returned. Because of this uncertainty, the judgment must be reversed and the case remanded.

. . .

Since respondent may seek a new trial, we deem that considerations of effective judicial administration require us to review the evidence in the present record to determine whether it could constitutionally support a judgment for respondent. This Court's duty is not limited to the elaboration of constitutional principles; we must also in proper cases review the evidence to make certain that those principles have been constitutionally applied. This is such a case, particularly since the question is one of alleged trespass across "the line between speech unconditionally guaranteed and speech which may legitimately be regulated."

. . .

Applying these standards, we consider that the proof presented to show actual malice lacks the convincing clarity which the constitutional standard demands, and hence that it would not constitutionally sustain the judgment for respondent under the proper rule of law. The case of the individual petitioners requires little discussion. Even assuming that they could constitutionally be found to have authorized the use of their names on the advertisement, there was no evidence whatever that they were aware of any erroneous statements or were in any way reckless in that regard. The judgment against them is thus without constitutional support.

As to the Times, we similarly conclude that the facts do not support a finding of actual malice. The statement by the Times' Secretary that, apart from the padlocking allegation, he thought the advertisement was "substantially correct," affords no constitutional warrant for the Alabama Supreme Court's conclusion that it was a "cavalier ignoring of the falsity of the advertisement [from which], the jury could not have but been impressed with the bad faith of The Times, and its maliciousness inferable there-from." The statement does not indicate malice at the time of the publication; even if the advertisement was not "substantially correct" — although respondent's own proofs tend to show that it was — that opinion was at least a reasonable one, and there was no evidence to impeach the witness' good faith in holding it. The Times' failure to retract upon respondent's demand, although it later retracted upon the demand of Governor Patterson, is likewise not adequate evidence of malice for constitutional purposes. Whether or not a failure to retract may ever constitute such evidence, there are two reasons why it does not here. *First*, the letter written by the Times reflected a reasonable doubt on its part as to whether the advertisement could reasonably be taken to refer to respondent at all. *Second*, it was not a final refusal, since it asked for an explanation on this point — a request that respondent chose to ignore. Nor does the retraction upon the demand of the Governor supply the necessary proof. It may be doubted that a failure to retract which is not itself evidence of malice can retroactively become such by virtue of a retraction subsequently made to another party. But in any event that did not happen here, since the explanation given by the Times' Secretary for the distinction drawn between respondent and the Governor was a reasonable one, the good faith of which was not impeached.

Finally, there is evidence that the Times published the advertisement without checking its accuracy against the news stories in the Times' own files. The mere presence of the stories in the files does not, of course, establish that the Times "knew" the advertisement was false, since the state of mind required for actual malice would have to be brought home to the persons in the Times' organization having responsibility for the publication of the advertisement. With respect to the failure of those persons to make the check, the record shows that they relied upon their knowledge of the good reputation of many of those whose names were listed as sponsors of the advertisement, and upon the letter from A. Philip Randolph, known to them as a responsible individual, certifying that the use of the names was authorized. There was testimony that the persons handling the advertisement saw nothing in it that would render it unacceptable under the Times' policy of rejecting advertisements containing "attacks of a personal character"; their failure to reject it on this ground was not unreasonable. We think the evidence against the Times supports at most a finding of negligence in failing to discover the misstatements, and is constitutionally insufficient to show the recklessness that is required for a finding of actual malice.

. . .

The judgment of the Supreme Court of Alabama is reversed and the case is remanded to that court for further proceedings not inconsistent with this opinion.

Reversed and remanded.

MR. JUSTICE BLACK, with whom MR. JUSTICE DOUGLAS joins (concurring).

. . .

In my opinion the Federal Constitution has dealt with this deadly danger to the press in the only way possible without leaving the free press open to destruction — by granting the press an absolute immunity for criticism of the way public officials do their public duty. . . . An unconditional right to say what one pleases about public affairs is what I consider to be the minimum guarantee of the First Amendment.

I regret that the Court has stopped short of this holding indispensable to preserve our free press from destruction.

NOTES AND QUESTIONS

(1) For an examination of the historical backdrop of the *Sullivan* case, see Anthony Lewis, Make No Law (Random House 1991).

(2) What must a plaintiff show in order to establish actual malice? Is the actual malice standard overly protective of defendants? Many non-United States jurisdictions think so. *Holomisa v. Argus Newspapers Ltd.*, 1996 (2) South Africa 588, *Theophanous v. Herald & Weekly Times Ltd.*, (1994) 124 A.L.R. I (HC, Australia), and *Hill v. Church of Scientology of Toronto* (1995) 126 D.L.R. (4th 129) (Supreme Court, Canada), have all declined to follow *Sullivan*.

GERTZ v. ROBERT WELCH, INC.
United States Supreme Court
418 U.S. 323, 94 S. Ct. 2997, 41 L. Ed. 2d 789 (1974)

MR. JUSTICE POWELL delivered the opinion of the Court.

This Court has struggled for nearly a decade to define the proper accommodation between the law of defamation and the freedoms of speech and press protected by the First Amendment. With this decision we return to that effort. We granted certiorari to reconsider the extent of a publisher's constitutional privilege against liability for defamation of a private citizen.

[Gertz was hired to bring a civil action against a Chicago policeman named Nuccio. The plaintiffs were the parents of a youth named Nelson that Nuccio shot and killed. The defendant printed certain libelous statements, below, about Gertz, who brought a libel action. Gertz recovered in a jury trial but the verdict was reversed by the Court of Appeals on ground that the New York Times standard had not been applied.]

In his capacity as counsel for the Nelson family in the civil litigation, petitioner attended the coroner's inquest into the boy's death and initiated actions for damages, but he neither discussed Officer Nuccio with the press nor played any part in the criminal proceeding. Notwithstanding petitioner's remote connection with the prosecution of Nuccio, respondent's magazine portrayed him as an architect of the "frame-up." According to the article, the police file on petitioner took "a big, Irish cop to lift." The article stated that petitioner had been an official of the "Marxist League for Industrial Democracy, originally known as the Intercollegiate Socialist Society, which has advocated the violent seizure of our government." It labeled Gertz a "Leninist" and a "Communist-fronter." It also stated that Gertz had been an officer of the National Lawyers Guild, described as a Communist organization that "probably did more than any other outfit to plan the Communist attack on the Chicago police during the 1968 Democratic Convention."

These statements contained serious inaccuracies. The implication that petitioner had a criminal record was false. Petitioner had been a member and officer of the National Lawyers Guild some *15* years earlier, but there was no evidence that he or that organization had taken any part in planning the 1968 demonstrations in Chicago. There was also no basis for the charge that petitioner was a "Leninist" or a "Communist-fronter." And he had never been a member of the "Marxist League for Industrial Democracy" or the "Intercollegiate Socialist Society."

The managing editor of American Opinion made no effort to verify or substantiate the charges against petitioner.

. . .

We begin with the common ground. Under the First Amendment there is no such thing as a false idea. However pernicious an opinion may seem, we depend for its correction not on the conscience of judges and juries but on the competition of other ideas. But there is no constitutional value in false statements of fact. Neither the intentional lie nor the careless error materially advances society's interest in "uninhibited, robust, and wide-open" debate on public issues. *New York Times Co. v. Sullivan*, 376 U.S., at 270, 84 S. Ct., at 721. They belong to that category of utterances which "are no essential part of any exposition of ideas, and are of such slight social value as a step to truth that any benefit that may be derived from them is clearly outweighed by the social interest in order and morality." *Chaplinsky v. New Hampshire*, 315 U.S. 568, 572, 62 S. Ct. 766, 769, 86 L. Ed. 1031 (1942).

Although the erroneous statement of fact is not worthy of constitutional protection, it is nevertheless inevitable in free debate. As James Madison pointed out in the Report on the Virginia Resolutions of 1798: "Some degree of abuse is inseparable from the proper use of every thing; and in no instance is this more true than in that of the press." 4 J. Elliot, Debates on the Federal Constitution of 1787, p. 571 (1876). And punishment of error runs the risk of inducing a cautious and restrictive exercise of the constitutionally guaranteed freedoms of speech and press. Our decisions recognize that a rule of strict liability that compels a publisher or broadcaster to guarantee the accuracy of his factual assertions may lead to intolerable self-censorship. Allowing the media to avoid liability only by proving the truth of all injurious statements does not accord adequate protection to First Amendment liberties. As the Court stated in *New York Times Co. v. Sullivan, supra*, 376 U.S., at 279, 84 S. Ct., at 725: "Allowance of the defense of truth, with the burden of proving it on the defendant, does not mean that only false speech will be deterred." The First Amendment requires that we protect some falsehood in order to protect speech that matters.

The need to avoid self-censorship by the news media is, however, not the only societal value at issue. If it were, this Court would have embraced long ago the view that publishers and broadcasters enjoy an unconditional and indefeasible immunity from liability for defamation. Such a rule would, indeed, obviate the fear that the prospect of civil liability for injurious falsehood might dissuade a timorous press from the effective exercise of First Amendment freedoms. Yet absolute protection for the communications media requires a total sacrifice of the competing value served by the law of defamation.

. . .

Theoretically, of course, the balance between the needs of the press and the individual's claim to compensation for wrongful injury might be struck on a case-by-case basis. As Mr. Justice Harlan hypothesized, "it might seem, purely as an abstract matter, that the most utilitarian approach would be to scrutinize carefully every jury verdict in every libel case, in order to ascertain whether the final judgment leaves fully protected whatever First Amendment values transcend the legitimate state interest in protecting the particular plaintiff who prevailed." *Rosenbloom v. Metromedia, Inc.*, 403 U.S., at 63, 91 S. Ct., at 1829 (footnote omitted). But this approach would lead to unpredictable results and uncertain expectations, and it could render our duty to supervise the lower courts unmanageable. Because an *ad hoc* resolution of the competing interests at stake in each particular case is not feasible, we must lay down broad rules of general application. Such rules necessarily treat alike various cases involving differences as well as similarities. Thus it is often true that not all of the considerations which justify adoption of a given rule will obtain in each particular case decided under its authority.

With that caveat we have no difficulty in distinguishing among defamation plaintiffs. The first remedy of any victim of defamation is self-help — using available opportunities to contradict the lie or correct the error and thereby to minimize its adverse impact on reputation. Public officials and public figures usually enjoy significantly greater access to the channels of effective communication and hence have a more realistic opportunity to counteract false statements then private individuals normally enjoy. Private individuals are therefore more vulnerable to injury, and the state interest in protecting them is correspondingly greater.

More important than the likelihood that private individuals will lack effective opportunities for rebuttal, there is a compelling normative consideration underlying the distinction between public and private defamation plaintiffs. An individual who decides to seek governmental office must accept certain necessary consequences of that involvement in public affairs. He runs the risk of closer public scrutiny than might otherwise be the case. And society's interest in the officers of government is not strictly limited to the formal discharge of official duties. As the Court pointed out in *Garrison v. Louisiana*, 379 U.S., at 77, 85 S. Ct., at 217, the public's interest extends to "anything which might touch on an official's fitness for office . . . Few personal attributes are more germane to fitness for office than dishonesty, malfeasance, or improper motivation, even though these characteristics may also affect the official's private character."

Those classed as public figures stand in a similar position. Hypothetically, it may be possible for someone to become a public figure through no purposeful action of his own, but the instances of truly involuntary public figures must be exceedingly rare. For the most part those who attain this status have assumed roles of especial prominence in the affairs of society. Some occupy positions of such persuasive power and influence that they are deemed public figures for all purposes. More commonly, those classed as public figures have thrust themselves to the forefront of particular public controversies in order to influence the resolution of the issues involved. In either event, they invite attention and comment.

Even if the foregoing generalities do not obtain in every instance, the communications media are entitled to act on the assumption that public officials and public figures have voluntarily exposed themselves to increased risk of injury from defamatory falsehood concerning them. No such assumption is justified with respect to a private individual. He has not accepted public office or assumed an "influential role in ordering society." *Curtis Publishing Co. v. Butts*, 388 U.S., at 164, 87 S. Ct., at 1996 (Warren, C. J., concurring in result). He has relinquished no part of his interest in the protection of his own good name, and consequently he has a more compelling call on the courts for redress of injury inflicted by defamatory falsehood. Thus, private individuals are not only more vulnerable to injury than public officials and public figures; they are also more deserving of recovery.

For these reasons we conclude that the States should retain substantial latitude in their efforts to enforce a legal remedy for defamatory falsehood injurious to the reputation of a private individual. The extension of the *New York Times* test proposed by the *Rosenbloom* plurality would abridge this legitimate state interest to a degree that we find unacceptable. And it would occasion the additional difficulty of forcing state and federal judges to decide on an *ad hoc* basis which publications address issues of "general or public interest" and which do not — to determine, in the words of Mr. Justice Marshall, "what information is relevant to self-government." *Rosenbloom v. Metromedia, Inc.*, 403 U.S., at 79, 91 S. Ct., at 1837. We doubt the wisdom of committing this task to the conscience of judges. Nor does the Constitution require us to draw so thin a line between the drastic alternatives of the *New York Times* privilege and the common law of strict liability for defamatory error. The "public or general interest" test for determining the applicability of the *New York Times* standard to private defamation actions inadequately serves both of the competing values at stake. On the one hand, a private individual whose reputation is injured by defamatory falsehood that does concern an issue of public or general interest has no recourse unless he can meet the rigorous requirements of *New York Times*. This is true despite the factors that distinguish the state interest in compensating private individuals from the analogous interest involved in the context of public persons. On the other hand, a publisher or broadcaster of a defamatory error which a court deems unrelated to an issue of public or general interest may be held liable in damages even if it took every reasonable precaution to ensure the accuracy of its assertions. And liability may far exceed compensation for any actual injury to the plaintiff, for the jury may be permitted to presume damages without proof of loss and even to award punitive damages.

We hold that, so long as they do not impose liability without fault, the States may define for themselves the appropriate standard of liability for a publisher or broadcaster of defamatory falsehood injurious to a private individual. This approach provides a more equitable boundary between the competing concerns involved here. It recognizes the strength of the legitimate state interest in compensating private individuals for wrongful injury to reputation, yet shields the press and broadcast media from the rigors of strict liability for defamation. At least this conclusion obtains where, as here, the substance of the defamatory statement "makes substantial danger to reputation apparent." This phrase places in perspective the conclusion we announce today. Our inquiry would involve considerations somewhat different from those discussed above if a State purported to condition civil liability on a factual misstatement whose content did not warn a reasonably prudent editor or broadcaster of its defamatory potential. Such a case is not now before us, and we intimate no view as to its proper resolution.

IV

Our accommodation of the competing values at stake in defamation suits by private individuals allows the States to impose liability on the publisher or broadcaster of defamatory falsehood on a less demanding showing than that required by *New York Times*. This conclusion is not based on a belief that the considerations which prompted the adoption of the *New York Times* privilege for defamation of public officials and its extension to public figures are wholly inapplicable to the context of private individuals. Rather, we endorse this approach in recognition of the strong and legitimate state interest in compensating private individuals for injury to reputation. But this countervailing state interest extends no further than compensation for actual injury. For the reasons stated below, we hold that the States may not permit recovery of presumed or punitive damages, at least when liability is not based on a showing of knowledge of falsity or reckless disregard for the truth.

. . .

We would not, of course, invalidate state law simply because we doubt its wisdom, but here we are attempting to reconcile state law with a competing interest grounded in the constitutional command of the First Amendment. It is therefore appropriate to require that state remedies for defamatory falsehood reach no farther than is necessary to protect the legitimate interest involved. It is necessary to restrict defamation plaintiffs who do not prove knowledge of falsity or reckless disregard for the truth to compensation for actual injury. We need not define "actual injury," as trial courts have wide experience in framing appropriate jury instructions in tort actions. Suffice it to say that actual injury is not limited to out-of-pocket loss. Indeed, the more customary types of actual harm inflicted by defamatory falsehood include impairment of reputation and standing in the community, personal humiliation, and mental anguish and suffering. Of course, juries must be limited by appropriate instructions, and all awards must be supported by competent evidence concerning the injury, although there need be no evidence which assigns an actual dollar value to the injury.

We also find no justification for allowing awards of punitive damages against publishers and broadcasters held liable under state-defined standards of liability for defamation. In most jurisdictions jury discretion over the amounts awarded is limited only by the gentle rule that they not be excessive. Consequently, juries assess punitive damages in wholly unpredictable amounts bearing no necessary relation to the actual harm caused. And they remain free to use their discretion selectively to punish expressions of unpopular views. Like the doctrine of presumed damages, jury discretion to award punitive damages unnecessarily exacerbates the danger of media self-censorship, but, unlike the former rule, punitive damages are wholly irrelevant to the state interest that justifies a negligence standard for private defamation actions.

They are not compensation for injury. Instead, they are private fines levied by civil juries to punish reprehensible conduct and to deter its future occurrence. In short, the private defamation plaintiff who establishes liability under a less demanding standard than that stated by *New York Times* may recover only such damages as are sufficient to compensate him for actual injury.

V

Notwithstanding our refusal to extend the *New York Times* privilege to defamation of private individuals, respondent contends that we should affirm the judgment below on the ground that petitioner is either a public official or a public figure. There is little basis for the former assertion. Several years prior to the present incident, petitioner had served briefly on housing committees appointed by the mayor of Chicago, but at the time of publication he had never held any remunerative governmental position. Respondent admits this but argues that petitioner's appearance at the coroner's inquest rendered him a "de facto public official." Our cases recognized no such concept. Respondent's suggestion would sweep all lawyers under the *New York Times* rule as officers of the court and distort the plain meaning of the "public official" category beyond all recognition. We decline to follow it.

Respondent's characterization of petitioner as a public figure raises a different question. That designation may rest on either of two alternative bases. In some instances an individual may achieve such pervasive fame or notoriety that he becomes a public figure for all purposes and in all contexts. More commonly, an individual voluntarily injects himself or is drawn into a particular public controversy and thereby becomes a public figure for a limited range of issues. In either case such persons assume special prominence in the resolution of public questions.

Petitioner has long been active in community and professional affairs. He has served as an officer of local civic groups and of various professional organizations, and he has published several books and articles on legal subjects. Although petitioner was consequently well known in some circles, he had achieved no general fame or notoriety in the community. None of the prospective jurors called at the trial had ever heard of petitioner prior to this litigation, and respondent offered no proof that this response was atypical of the local population. We would not lightly assume that a citizen's participation in community and professional affairs rendered him a public figure for all purposes. Absent clear evidence of general fame or notoriety in the community, and pervasive involvement in the affairs of society, an individual should not be deemed a public personality for all aspects of his life. It is preferable to reduce the public-figure question to a more meaningful context by looking to the nature and extent of an individual's participation in the particular controversy giving rise to the defamation.

In this context it is plain that petitioner was not a public figure. He played a minimal role at the coroner's inquest, and his participation related solely to his representation of a private client. He took no part in the criminal prosecution of Officer Nuccio. Moreover, he never discussed either the criminal or civil litigation with the press and was never quoted as having done so. He plainly did not thrust himself into the vortex of this public issue, nor did he engage the public's attention in an attempt to influence its outcome. We are persuaded that the trial court did not err in refusing to characterize petitioner as a public figure for the purpose of this litigation.

We therefore conclude that the *New York Times* standard is inapplicable to this case and that the trial court erred in entering judgment for respondent. Because the jury was allowed to impose liability without fault and was permitted to presume damages without proof of injury, a new trial is necessary. We reverse and remand for further proceedings in accord with this opinion.

It *is so ordered.*

Reversed and remanded.

NOTES AND QUESTIONS

(1)   Theoretically, *Sullivan* and *Gertz* do not modify the common law, because the United States Supreme Court has no jurisdiction over state common law, but they clearly overlay it with superior constitutional restraints. Practically, however, state courts must abide by these restraints, thereby effectively embedding them into the law of defamation as applied. Arguably, however, if *Sullivan* and *Gertz* were ever to be overruled, the underlying common law would reemerge. That unlikely happenstance is not much of a reason to learn about the common law of defamation, but the need for a clear understanding of what the law is and why is a powerful one.

Sullivan and *Gertz* add several non-common law issues to defamation law: What are the legal characteristics of a public figure (or public official) that call into play the *Sullivan* "actual malice" standard? (Referred to herein as "constitutional malice" to avoid confusion with common law malice. The constitutional malice standard is identical to common law *scienter* as defined in common law deceit by *Derry v. Peek, supra.* What standard of fault should be applied in cases controlled by *Gertz*? Are cases involving private plaintiffs and defendants who are not in the publishing or broadcasting business subsumed within *Gertz* or does the untrammeled common law of defamation apply? (That is, John Smith sees his arch enemy on the street and within hearing of passersby shouts, "Bill Jones, you scoundrel, your arrant thievery will yet be your undoing!") And, what are the guidelines of "actual damages" within limits permitted by *Gertz*? Some of these questions are touched upon in the following notes.

(2)   The question of who is a public official has not been generally disputatious. Ordinarily, this question of status can be objectively ascertained, but one court has said, "The designation of 'public official' applies, at a minimum, to those persons employed by a public or governmental body who have, or appear to have, substantial responsibility for or control over the conduct of governmental affairs." *Forrest v. Lynch*, 347 So. 2d 1255, 1258 (La. App. 1977), citing, *Rosenblatt v. Baer*, 383 U.S. 75 (1966). Does that help? Conceivably, it remains open for a public official to assert that defamation as to completely private matters should not invoke the constitutional malice standard. Take, for example, the false statement, "Congressman Jones is a child molester." What objection can be made to withholding the constitutional malice standard? Does the objection hold if the plaintiff is an appointed city manager? *Buckley v. Esquire, Inc.*, 344 F. Supp. 1133 (S.D.N.Y. 1972), held that *Sullivan* did not extend the constitutional malice standard to purely private aspects of a widely known public figure's life.

Gertz itself gives considerable guidance as to who is a public figure. What is it? The Supreme Court has subsequently held that the mere fact that the plaintiff has become embroiled by happenstance in a publicized issue is not the decisive factor in determining who is a public figure. See *Time, Inc. v. Firestone*, 424 U.S. 448 (1976), *Hutchinson v. Proxmire*, 443 U.S. 111 (1979), and *Walston v. Reader's Digest Ass'n, Inc.*, 443 U.S. 157 (1979). In *Hutchinson*, the plaintiff was the recipient of a federal research grant who had been awarded Senator Proxmire's "Golden Fleece Award," in recognition of what Proxmire deemed to be a notable waste of public funds. In response to Hutchinson's defamation action, Proxmire argued that by applying for and receiving a federal research grant and through his scientific publications, Hutchinson, who was an academician, was a public person at least for the purpose of the "award." Examining the record, the Supreme Court found Hutchinson's "public profile" to be "much like those of countless members of his profession," and reaffirmed that "those charged with defamation cannot, by their own conduct, create their own defense by making the claimant a public figure." *Id.*, at 2688. *See*, however, *Arnold v. Taco Properties, Inc.*, 427 So. 2d 216 (Fla. App. 1983), and *Ferguson v. Watkins*, 448 So. 2d 271 (Miss. 1984), for cases holding that a person elevates himself to public figure status when he thrusts himself into the "vortex" of a public dispute.

In *Firestone* the fact that the plaintiff who had a famous name by marriage became involved in a scandalous divorce did not make her a public figure. Nor was Wolston, the nephew of a Russian spy, a public figure on that account. For an application of these cases, *see American Ben. Life Ins. Co. v. McIntyre*, 375 So. 2d 239 (Ala. 1979).

(3) The resolution of what constitutes constitutional malice is not without guidelines. As noted above, the "knowledge of falsity or reckless disregard of whether true or false" formulation is the same as *scienter* in common law deceit. Hence, a mass of decisional law is available. In addition to that, a large number of defamation opinions explicating *Sullivan* have been written. In sum, it may be said that the courts assiduously police the facts to assure that mere negligence is not permitted to satisfy the standard.

Herbert v. Lando, 441 U.S. 153 (1979), raised the evidentiary issue of whether a plaintiff might inquire into the thought processes followed by the producer of a television news report in order to prove constitutional malice. The defendant argued that a plaintiff must rely upon objective facts to demonstrate constitutional malice and that the defendant's thought processes were privileged under the First Amendment. In denying such a privilege the Supreme Court said:

> Although defamation litigation, including suits against the press, is an ancient phenomenon, it is true that our cases from *New York Times* to *Gertz* have considerably changed the profile of such cases. In years gone by, plaintiffs made out a prima facie case by proving the damaging publication. Truth and privilege were defenses. Intent, motive and malice were not necessarily involved except to counter qualified privilege or to prove exemplary damages. The plaintiff's burden is now considerably expanded. In every or almost every case, the plaintiff must focus on the editorial process and prove a false publication attended by some degree of culpability on the part of the publisher. If plaintiffs in consequence now resort to more discovery, it would not be surprising; and it would follow that the costs and other burdens of this kind of litigation have escalated and

become much more troublesome for both plaintiffs and defendants. It is suggested that the press needs constitutional protection from these burdens if it is to perform its task, which is indispensable in a system such as ours.

Creating a constitutional privilege foreclosing direct inquiry into the editorial process, however, would not cure this problem for the press. Only complete immunity from liability from defamation would effect this result, and the Court has regularly found this to be an untenable construction of the First Amendment. Furthermore, mushrooming litigation costs, much of it due to pretrial discovery, are not peculiar to the libel and slander area. There have been repeated expressions of concern about undue and uncontrolled discovery, and voices from this Court have joined the chorus, but until and unless there are major changes in the present rules of civil procedure, reliance must be had on what in fact and in law are ample powers of the district judge to prevent abuse. . . .

Furthermore, according to the Supreme Court, when reviewing lower court findings that constitutional malice was present, appellate courts "must exercise independent judgment and determine whether the record establishes actual malice with convincing clarity" rather than apply the clearly erroneous standard pre-scribed for general litigation. *Bose Corp. v. Consumers Union of U.S., Inc.*, 466 U.S. 485, 514 (1984). This requires appellate courts to search the record for "clear and convincing proof" of constitutional malice. *Id. St. Amant v. Thompson*, 390 U.S. 727, 88 S. Ct. 1323, 1325, 20 L. Ed. 2d 262 (1968), held that proof of constitutional malice requires a showing that the defendant entertained "actual doubts" as to the truth.

Independent review is of great benefit to defendants, because federal judges have tended to be more sympathetic to defendants' First Amendment claims than juries have. Does this degree of appellate review abridge the Seventh Amendment guarantee that "no fact tried by a jury, shall otherwise be reexamined by any Court of the United States, than according to the rules of the common law?"

(4)   In cases controlled by *Gertz*, state courts have latitude to apply any standard of culpability they wish so long as they do not impose liability without fault. In *Time, Inc. v. Firestone*, 424 U.S. 448 (1976), the Supreme Court insisted that "at some point in the state proceedings some factfinder has made a conscious determination of the existence or non-existence of [fault]." The Court refused to "canvas the record" to make the finding itself in the first instance, but implied that if a state appellate court "consciously" did so the finding could be affirmed. Nevertheless, findings of fact ordinarily are made in trial courts, and it may be expected that most state courts will follow that practice in defamation cases.

The more important question is what will be the standard of fault applied in *Gertz* cases. Because *Gertz* is but a federal overlay over a common law cause of action, a potent argument can be made that the common law right ought to be eroded the minimum amount to comply with the *Gertz* fault standard. This implies a standard of simple negligence. What advantage, if any, does this have to lawyers and judges?

Most jurisdictions have adopted the negligence standard in *Gertz* cases, *see, e.g. Brown v. Bryan*, 339 So. 2d 577 (Ala. 1976), but some have adopted a more stringent standard, such as gross negligence and even constitutional malice. *See Chapadeau v. Utica Observer Dispatch, Inc.*, 341 N.E.2d 569 (N.Y. 1975), as to the former class, and *Walker v. Colorado Springs Sun, Inc.*, 538 P.2d 450 (Colo. 1975), as to the latter.

(5) In *Philadelphia Newspapers, Inc. v. Hepps*, 475 U.S 767 (1986), the United States Supreme Court held that a private plaintiff bears the burden of proving falsity, at least when the defamatory communication involves an issue of public concern. Perhaps because *Hepps* was a 5-4 decision, the Court's holding was quite narrow, leaving unresolved whether this holding would also apply in cases involving nonmedia defendants and whether the plaintiff must bear the burden of proving falsity in cases not involving matters of public concern. What is the practical effect of shifting the burden of proof on falsity to the plaintiff? Is *Hepps* a significant obstacle to defamation plaintiffs?

---

§ 17.04   DAMAGES

[A]   Under Common Law

GERTZ v. ROBERT WELCH, INC.
United States Supreme Court
418 U.S. 323, 94 S. Ct. 2997, 41 L. Ed. 2d 789 (1974)

[Court's opinion is set out on § 17.03 [B], *supra*]

MR. JUSTICE WHITE, dissenting.

For some 200 years — from the very founding of the Nation — the law of defamation and right of the ordinary citizen to recover for false publication injurious to his reputation have been almost exclusively the business of state courts and legislatures. Under typical state defamation law, the defamed private citizen had to prove only a false publication that would subject him to hatred, contempt, or ridicule. Given such publication, general damage to reputation was presumed, while punitive damages required proof of additional facts. The law governing the defamation of private citizens remained untouched by the First Amendment because until relatively recently, the consistent view of the Court was that libelous words constitute a class of speech wholly unprotected by the First Amendment, subject only to limited exceptions carved out since 1964.

But now, using that Amendment as the chosen instrument, the Court, in a few printed pages, has federalized major aspects of libel law by declaring unconstitutional in important respects the prevailing defamation law in all or most of the 50 States. That result is accomplished by requiring the plaintiff in each and every defamation action to prove not only the defendant's culpability beyond his act of publishing defamatory material but also actual damage to reputation resulting from the publication. Moreover, punitive damages may not be recovered by showing malice in the traditional sense of ill will; knowing falsehood or reckless disregard of the truth will now be required.

. . .

Lest there be any mistake about it, the changes wrought by the Court's decision cut very deeply. In 1938, the Restatement of Torts reflected the historic rule that publication in written form of defamatory material — material tending "so to harm the reputation of another as to lower him in the estimation of the community or to deter third persons from associating or dealing with him" — subjected the publisher to liability although no special harm to reputation was actually proved. Restatement of Torts § 569 (1938). Truth was a defense, and some libels were privileged; but, given a false circulation, general *damage*, to reputation was presumed and damages could be awarded by the jury, along with any special damages such as pecuniary loss and emotional distress. At the very least, the rule allowed the recovery of nominal damages for any defamatory publication actionable *per se* and thus performed a vindicatory function by enabling the plaintiff publicly to brand the defamatory publication as false. The salutary social value of this rule is preventive in character since it often permits a defamed person to expose the groundless character of a defamatory rumor before harm to the reputation has resulted therefrom. *Id.*, § 569, comment b, p. 166.

If the defamation was not libel but slander, it was actionable *per se* only if it imputed a criminal offense; a venereal or loathsome and communicable disease; improper conduct of a lawful business; or unchastity by a woman. *Id.*, § 570. To be actionable, all other types of slanderous statements required proof of special damage other than actual loss of reputation or emotional distress, that special damage almost always being in the form of material or pecuniary loss of some kind. *Id.*, § 575 and comment b, pp. 185–187.

Damages for libel or slander *per se* included "harm caused thereby to the reputation of the person defamed or in the absence of proof of such harm, for the harm which normally results from such a defamation." *Id.*, § 621. At the heart of the libel-and-slander-per-se damage scheme lay the award of general damages for loss of reputation. They were granted without special proof because the judgment of history was that the content of the publication itself was so likely to cause injury and because "in many cases the effect of defamatory statements is so subtle and indirect that it is impossible directly to trace the effects thereof in loss to the person defamed." *Id.*, § 621, comment a, p. 314. Proof of actual injury to reputation was itself insufficient proof of that special damage necessary to support liability for slander not actionable *per se*. But if special damage in the form of material or pecuniary loss were proved, general damages for injury to reputation could be had without further proof. "The plaintiff may recover not only for the special harm so caused, but also for general loss of reputation." *Id.*, § 575, comment a, p. 185. The right to recover for emotional distress depended upon the defendant's otherwise being liable for either libel or slander. *Id.*, § 623. Punitive damages were recoverable upon proof of special facts amounting to express malice. *Id.*, § 908 and comment b, p. 555.

Preparations in the mid-1960's for Restatement (Second) of Torts reflected what were deemed to be substantial changes in the law of defamation, primarily a trend toward limiting *per se* libels to those where the defamatory nature of the publication is apparent on its face, *i.e.*, "where the defamatory innuendo is apparent from the publication itself without reference to extrinsic facts by way of inducement." Restatement (Second) of Torts § 569, p. 29 (Tent. Draft No. 12, Apr. 27, 1966). Libels of this sort and slanders *per se* continued to be recognized as actionable without proof of special damage or injury to reputation. All other defamations would require proof of special injury in the form of material or pecuniary loss. Whether this asserted change reflected the prevailing law was heavily debated, but it was unquestioned at the time that there are recurring situations in which libel and slander are and should be actionable *per se.*

In surveying the current state of the law, the proposed Restatement (Second) observed that "[a]ll courts except Virginia agree that any libel which is defamatory upon its face is actionable without proof of damage. . . . " Restatement (Second) of Torts § 569, p. 84 (Tent. Draft No. 11, Apr. 15, 1965). Ten jurisdictions continued to support the old rule that libel not defamatory on its face and whose innuendo depends on extrinsic facts is actionable without proof of damage although slander would not be. Twenty-four jurisdictions were said to hold that libel not defamatory on its face is to be treated like slander and thus not actionable without proof of damage where slander would not be. *Id.,* § 569, p. 86. The law in six jurisdictions was found to be in an unsettled state but most likely consistent with the Restatement (Second). *Id.,* § 569, p. 88. The law in Virginia was thought to consider libel actionable without proof of special damage only where slander would be regardless of whether the libel is defamatory on its face. *Id.,* § 569, p. 89. All States, therefore, were at that time thought to recognize important categories of defamation that were actionable *per se.* Nor was any question apparently raised at that time that upon proof of special damage in the form of material or pecuniary loss, general damages to reputation could be recovered without further proof.

Unquestionably, state law continued to recognize some absolute, as well as some conditional, privileges to publish defamatory materials, including the privilege of fair comment in defined situations. But it remained true that in a wide range of situations, the ordinary citizen could make out a prima facie case without proving more than a defamatory publication and could recover general damages for injury to his reputation unless defeated by the defense of truth.

The impact of today's decision on the traditional law of libel is immediately obvious and indisputable. No longer will the plaintiff be able to rest his case with proof of a libel defamatory on its face or proof of a slander historically actionable *per se.* In addition, he must prove some further degree of culpable conduct on the part of the publisher, such as intentional or reckless falsehood or negligence. And if he succeeds in this respect, he faces still another obstacle: recovery for loss of reputation will be conditioned upon "competent" proof of actual injury to his standing in the community. This will be true regardless of the nature of the defamation and even though it is one of those particularly reprehensible statements that have traditionally made slanderous words actionable without proof of fault by the publisher or of the damaging impact of his publication. The Court rejects the judgment of experience that some publications are so inherently capable of injury, and actual injury so difficult to prove, that the risk of falsehood should be borne by the publisher, not the victim. Plainly, with the additional burden on the plaintiff of proving negligence or other fault, it will be exceedingly difficult, perhaps impossible, for him to vindicate his reputation interest by securing a judgment for nominal damages, the practical effect of such a judgment being a judicial declaration that the publication was indeed false. Under the new rule the plaintiff can lose, not because the statement is true, but because it was not negligently made.

So too, the requirement of proving special injury to reputation before general damages may be awarded will clearly eliminate the prevailing rule, worked out over a very long period of time, that, in the case of defamations not actionable *per se,* the recovery of general damages for injury to reputation may also be had if some form of material or pecuniary loss is proved. Finally, an inflexible federal standard is imposed for the award of punitive damages. No longer will it be enough to prove ill will and an attempt to injure.

These are radical changes in the law and severe invasions of the prerogatives of the States. They should at least be shown to be required by the First Amendment or necessitated by our present circumstances. Neither has been demonstrated.

. . .

Not content with escalating the threshold requirements of establishing liability, the Court abolishes the ordinary damages rule, undisturbed by *New York Times* and later cases, that, as to libels or slanders defamatory on their face, injury to reputation is presumed and general damages may be awarded along with whatever special damages may be sought. Apparently because the Court feels that in some unspecified and unknown number of cases, plaintiffs recover where they have suffered no injury or recover more than they deserve, it dismisses this rule as an "oddity of tort law." The Court thereby refuses in *any* case to accept the fact of wide dissemination of a *per se* libel as prima facie proof of injury sufficient to survive a motion to dismiss at the close of plaintiff's case.

I have said before, but it bears repeating, that even if the plaintiff should recover no monetary damages, he should be able to prevail and have a judgment that the publication is false. But beyond that, courts and legislatures literally for centuries have thought that in the generality of cases, libeled plaintiffs will be seriously shortchanged if they must prove the extent of the injury to their reputations. Even where libels or slanders are not on their face defamatory and special damage must be shown, when that showing is made, general damages for reputation injury are recoverable without specific proof.

The Court is clearly right when at one point it states that "the law of defamation is rooted in our experience that the truth rarely catches up with a lie." *Ante*, at 3009 n. 9. But it ignores what that experience teaches, *viz.*, that damage to reputation is recurringly difficult to prove and that requiring actual proof would repeatedly destroy any chance for adequate compensation. Eminent authority has warned that it is clear that proof of actual damage will be impossible in a great many cases where, from the character of the defamatory words and the circumstances of publication, it is all but certain that serious harm has resulted in fact.

W. Prosser, Law of Torts § 112, p. 765 (4th ed. 1971).

The Court fears uncontrolled awards of damages by juries, but that not only denigrates the good sense of most jurors — it fails to consider the role of trial and appellate courts in limiting excessive jury verdicts where no reasonable relationship exists between the amount awarded and the injury sustained. Available information tends to confirm that American courts have ably discharged this responsibility.

The new rule with respect to general damages appears to apply to all libels or slanders, whether defamatory on their face or not, except, I gather, when the plaintiff proves intentional falsehood or reckless disregard. Although the impact of the publication on the victim is the same, in such circumstances the injury to reputation may apparently be presumed in accordance with the traditional rule. Why a defamatory statement is more apt to cause injury if the lie is intentional than when it is only negligent, I fail to understand. I suggest that judges and juries who must live by these rules will find them equally incomprehensible.

With a flourish of the pen, the Court also discards the prevailing rule in libel and slander actions that punitive damages may be awarded on the classic grounds of common-law malice, that is, " '[a]ctual malice' in the sense of ill will or fraud or reckless indifference to consequences." C. McCormick, Law of Damages § 118, p. 431 (1935). In its stead, the Court requires defamation plaintiffs to show intentional falsehood or reckless disregard for the truth or falsity of the publication. The Court again complains about substantial verdicts and the possibility of press self-censorship, saying that punitive damages are merely "private fines levied by civil juries to punish reprehensible conduct and to deter its future occurrence." *Ante*, at 3012. But I see no constitutional difference between publishing with reckless disregard for the truth, where punitive damages will be permitted, and negligent publication where they will not be allowed. It is difficult to understand what is constitutionally wrong with assessing punitive damages to deter a publisher from departing from those standards of care ordinarily followed in the publishing industry, particularly if common-law malice is also shown.

I note also the questionable premise that "juries assess punitive damages in wholly unpredictable amounts bearing no necessary relation to the actual harm caused." *Ibid.* This represents an inaccurate view of established practice, "another of those situations in which judges, largely unfamiliar with the relatively rare actions for defamation, rely on words without really going behind them. . . . " While a jury award in any type of civil case may certainly be unpredictable, trial and appellate courts have been increasingly vigilant in ensuring that the jury's result is "based upon a rational consideration of the evidence and the proper application of the law." *Reynolds v. Pegler*, 13 F. Supp. 36, 39 (S.D.N.Y. 1954), *aff'd*, 223 F.2d 429 (CA2), *cert. denied*, 350 U.S. 846, 76 S. Ct. 80, 100 L. Ed. 754 (1955). Moreover, some courts require that punitive damages bear a reasonable relation to the compensatory damages award. Still others bar common-law punitive damages or condition their award on a refusal to print a retraction.

The danger . . . of immoderate verdicts, is certainly a real one, and the criterion to be applied by the judge in setting or reducing the amount is concededly a vague and subjective one. Nevertheless the verdict may be twice submitted by the complaining defendant to the common sense of trained judicial minds, once on motion for new trial and again on appeal, and it must be a rare instance when an unjustifiable award escapes correction.

C. McCormick, *supra*, § 77, p. 278.

The Court points to absolutely no empirical evidence to substantiate its premise. For my part, I would require something more substantial than an undifferentiated fear of unduly burdensome punitive damages awards before retooling the established common-law rule and depriving the States of the opportunity to experiment with different methods for guarding against abuses.

Even assuming the possibility that some verdicts will be "excessive," I cannot subscribe to the Court's remedy. On its face it is a classic example of judicial overkill. Apparently abandoning the salutary *New York Times* policy of case-by-case " 'independent examination of the whole record' . . . so as to assure ourselves that the judgment does not constitute a forbidden intrusion on the field of free expression," the Court substitutes an inflexible rule barring recovery of punitive damages absent proof of constitutional malice. The First Amendment is a majestic statement of a free people's dedication to "uninhibited, robust, and wide-open" debate on public issues, but we do it a grave disservice when we needlessly spend its force. For almost 200 years, punitive damages and the First Amendment have peacefully coexisted. There has been no demonstration that state libel laws as they relate to punitive damages necessitate the majority's extreme response. I fear that those who read the Court's decision will find its words inaudible, for the Court speaks "only [with] a voice of power, not of reason."

. . .

For the foregoing reasons, I would reverse the Court of Appeals and reinstate the jury's verdict.

NOTES AND QUESTIONS

(1) Would it be proper to uphold an award of punitive damages where no compensatory damages were awarded but actual malice was proved? *See, Newson v. Henry*, 443 So. 2d 817 (Miss. 1983).

(2) The United States Supreme Court partially loosened the constitutional restraints on state defamation law in *Dun & Bradstreet, Inc. v. Greenmoss Builders, Inc.*, 472 U.S. 749 (1985). In that case, Dun & Bradstreet, a credit reporting agency, falsely informed five of its subscribers that Greenmoss Builders had filed a voluntary petition for bankruptcy. Even after being informed of its error, Dun & Bradstreet allegedly took inadequate steps to correct it. Greenmoss Builders sued for defamation.

A jury awarded Greenmoss Builders $50,000 in compensatory damages and $300,000 in punitive damages. The trial judge granted defendant's motion for a new trial because the jury instructions given were inconsistent with *Gertz*. The Vermont Supreme Court reversed, holding that *Gertz* only applied to media defendants. In a fractured 5-4 plurality opinion, the United States Supreme Court affirmed, but a majority of the justices rejected the distinction between media and nonmedia defendants. Instead, the Court focused on the fact that, unlike *Gertz*, *Dun & Bradstreet* involved speech on matters of private rather than public concern. Justice Powell, writing for a plurality, framed the issue in the case as follows:

> In *Gertz v. Robert Welch, Inc.,* . . . we held that the First Amendment restricted the damages that a private individual could obtain from a publisher for a libel that involved a matter of public concern. More specifically, we held that in these circumstances the First Amendment prohibited awards of presumed and punitive damages for false and defamatory statements unless the plaintiff shows "actual malice," that is, knowledge of falsity or reckless disregard for the truth. The question presented in this case is whether this rule of *Gertz* applies when the false and defamatory statements do not involve matters of public concern.

> The Court answered this question in the negative, holding that *Gertz* was inapplicable because the speech at issue did not involve a matter of public concern. Justice Powell reasoned that while "speech on 'matters of public concern' []is 'at the heart of the First Amendment's protection' "speech on purely private matters is of less First Amendment significance.

Thus, Powell concluded: "[i]n light of the reduced constitutional value of speech involving no matters of public concern, . . . the state interest [in providing remedies for defamation] adequately supports awards of presumed and punitive damages — even absent a showing of actual malice."

Ultimately, five Justices voted to allow private plaintiffs to recover presumed and punitive damages without a showing of actual malice in cases involving speech of purely private concern. Does the logic of the decision imply that a plaintiff need not prove fault if the speech involves a matter of purely private concern? How should courts distinguish speech of public concern from speech of private concern? Should state courts impose higher obstacles to recovery in defamation cases than the United States Constitution imposes?

[B]   Damages Under Constitutional Restraints

[See *Gertz v. Robert Welch, Inc.*, § 17.03[B], *supra.*]

§ 17.05   DEFENSES

[A]   Justification

TRUTH (N.Z.) LTD. v. AVERY
[1959] N.Z.L.R. 284 (Court of Appeal)[6]

NORTH J. This is an appeal from the judgment of the Chief Justice dismissing a motion for a new trial in a libel suit sought by the appellant (the defendant in the Court below) on the ground that there had been misdirection on three material points of law.

The action was brought by the respondent, who is an inspector employed by the Wellington Society for the Prevention of Cruelty to Animals, as a result of an article which appeared in *New Zealand Truth* on October 1, 1957. The article criticized the respondent's behaviour in shooting a dog which was said to be annoying two goats on a hillside in the Moa Point area. The caption to the article read "Dog's cruel death at hands of S.P.C.A. Inspector." It was claimed that the dog was shot in the stomach at a range of 300 yards, and was left for a quarter-of-an-hour or more struggling in agony on a hillside, while the inspector drove his car to a point above the dog when it took several more shots to kill it. It was said:

The bungling and unnecessarily cruel manner in which this unfortunate animal was destroyed by an official whose primary duty is the prevention of cruelty to animals has caused angry comment and protest among people who knew about the incident; [and that] the hillside looked like a slaughter yard with blood all over it.

According to the article the respondent admitted that at the time he shot the dog he was unaware that he could have driven his car to the top of the hill which would have brought him much closer to the dog; he was said to have justified his

---

[6] [Ed. — New Zealand Law Reports.]

conduct in shooting the dog from the road below on the ground that the countryside was too steep for him to climb as he was wearing smooth-soled shoes. A photograph of the grave of the dog was included carrying the caption:

Tended amid Tears: Jumbo's grave with a cross placed on it by the tear-stricken lad who had regarded him as one of the family.

The respondent in his statement of claim, set out the whole of the article and alleged: that the said article including headlines, photograph and captions was falsely and maliciously printed and published by the defendant and was known or ought to have been known by the defendant to be untrue.

The appellant answered this allegation by two defenses; first, that the whole of the words published were true in substance and in fact, and, secondly, by an alternative plea of fair comment. . . .

It was common ground that the appellant did not prove the charge that the dog was shot at a range of 300 yards, the actual distance being not less than 110 yards or more than 188 yards. At the trial, the appellant called evidence — both expert and lay — in an endeavour to show that, even at the shorter range admitted by the respondent, he ought to have known that he was unlikely to kill the dog outright with his first shot; therefore, in the circumstances, the risk of merely wounding the dog was considerable and likely to be attended by unnecessary pain to the animal. It was also sought to show that, if the respondent had paused to make inquiries from local people, he would have been told that the goats were not in peril, and were well able to look after themselves; but, even if the respondent formed the opinion that the situation called for the killing of the dog, then at least he would have been told that there was another road leading to the top of the hill which would have taken him to the vicinity of the dog, and thus his shot would have been more certain, and there would not, in any event, have been any considerable delay between the time of wounding and the time of destruction. All this evidence presumably was led on behalf of the appellant for the purpose of persuading the jury that the error in range was immaterial, and that the sum of the evidence justified the appellant's criticism that the dog had been destroyed in a bungling and unnecessarily cruel manner.

In this Court, Mr. Cooke for the appellant assured us that senior counsel, Mr. Hardie Boys, in his final address, had told the jury that the appellant did not retract a single word contained in the article and reasserted its contention that the dog had been destroyed in a bungling and unnecessarily cruel manner; that only after he had said this did he go on to deal with the alternative defense of fair comment. Mr. Castle for the respondent, on the other hand, in his final address to the jury, submitted that there were two mis-statements of facts in the article: first, the error in range which he submitted was of major importance in considering the whole tenor of the article; and, secondly, the statement that the: bungling and unnecessarily cruel manner in which this unfortunate animal was destroyed had caused angry comment and protest among people who know about the incident.

When the time came for the learned Chief Justice to sum up, he instructed the jury on the difference between statements of fact and comment, and told them that the statement that the dog had been shot at a range of 300 yards was clearly a statement of fact, and was admittedly untrue. He then went on to say that in his view the words "bungling and unnecessarily cruel manner" were comment and not a statement of fact, but he left it to the jury to determine whether this was so. He said that he agreed, however, that the passage referring to the angry comment and protest among certain people was a statement of fact, but he added that in his view it was a statement of fact which the jury might think have been proved to be true. He then went on to suggest that there was one further statement of fact which had not been referred to by Mr. Castle, and which he thought had not been proved — namely, the words "the hillside looked like a slaughter yard with blood all over it." Once again, however, he left it to the jury to decide whether it was fact or comment.

. . . In his summing-up the learned Chief Justice, of course, dealt separately with the defenses of justification and fair comment, and the first complaint made by Mr. Cooke was that when dealing with the defense of justification, the jury were invited to consider only whether the allegations of fact had been justified and were not asked to consider whether the comments also had been justified, and for that purpose to have regard to the evidence adduced to support the truth of the comments.

[The court examined the trial judge's summing up to the jury in detail. The principal issues were whether the defendant was entitled to have the jury instructed that there could be no action for defamatory *comment if* the comment (as distinguished from statement of fact) was true or if it was "fair" even if not true.]

The defense of justification is concerned with establishing the truth of the statements complained of, whether they be allegations of fact which it is intended to prove to be true, or comment which it is intended to prove to be true, or, as is sometimes said, correct. The defense of fair comment is, of its nature, concerned with comment only: "the defense of fair comment is concerned with expressions of opinion as distinguished from assertions of fact" (20 Halsbury's Laws of England, 2nd ed. 488); and its purpose is to protect the comment, not on the ground that it is true in the sense of being correct but on the ground that, even though untrue, it should nevertheless be protected as an honest expression of opinion on a matter of public interest. If it is desired to assert the truth of the comment there must be a plea of justification, and, conversely, it is not permissible under a plea of fair comment, there being no plea of justification, to assert the truth of the comment as distinct from the truth of the facts on which it is based. . . . It is true that a defendant pleading fair comment is not only entitled but is bound to prove the facts on which the comment is based, and in this respect there is a similarity between the two defenses, but he does so not as an end in itself (as where the plea is justification), but as a foundation for a necessary step towards establishing the plea of fair comment. . . .

[See next case for elaboration of the defense of fair comment.]

The final objection to the summing up was that the learned Chief Justice should not have left it to the jury to determine whether the words "the hillside looked like a slaughter yard with blood all over it" were fact or comment. It cannot be questioned that it is the duty of the Judge to leave all doubtful statements to the jury to decide to which class they belong: . . . Mr. Cooke, however, argued that the introduction of a simile was conclusive and made the statement merely an expression of opinion. We do not agree. It seems to us that the furthest the matter can be taken is that the introduction of the simile assists in a finding that the words were comment only, but we do not think that it would be a correct direction to tell the jury that it would not treat the sentence as a statement of fact. After all, it purports to be a description of the hillside, and usually a misdescription would be regarded as a statement of fact. Mr. Cooke, no doubt, would be entitled to submit strongly to the jury that the use of the simile branded the sentence as comment and not fact, but he cannot ask that the jury should be directed that they are obliged to treat the words as comment only. . . .

The appeal is allowed, the judgment in the Court below is set aside; and an order is made for a new trial.

NOTES AND QUESTIONS

(1) What is meant by justification? Why should it constitute a defense to a defamation action? At one time common law judges refused to accept truth as a defense to the then crime of libel, thus stimulating this poetic outburst from Robert Burns:

Dost know that old Manfield
Who writes like the Bible,
Says the more'tis a truth, sir,
The more'tis a libel.

"The Reproof." Prosser reports that this view was imported into the civil law of defamation by a number of courts but was soon supplanted by statute. Prosser, Law of Torts (4th ed.) 797. What is the effect of the following example?

> In criminal prosecutions and civil actions for defamation the truth may be given in evidence. If the matter charged as defamatory is true and was published with good motives, the party shall be acquitted or exonerated.

Art. 1, § 4, Constitution, State of Florida. Is it permissible for truth to be deemed a complete defense in the absence of good motives?

In the law of Scotland, this defense is known as "Veritas." Report of The Committee on Defamation, Cmd. 5909, § 129, 1975.

(2) What is meant by truth? Literal truth or substantial truth? May a defendant insist that a given publication be tested for truth in its entirety rather than part by part?

[B] Fair Comment

LANE v. RANDOM HOUSE, INC.
United States District Court, District of Columbia.
23 Media L. Rep. 1385 (1995)

LAMBERTH, DISTRICT JUDGE.

Defendant Random House, Inc. has moved for dismissal of Plaintiff Mark Lane's complaint pursuant to Fed. R. Civ. P. 12(b) (6). Alternatively, Random House has moved for summary judgment under Fed. R. Civ. P. 56. Upon consideration of the filings of counsel and the relevant law, Random House's motion for summary judgment is hereby GRANTED on all counts. . . .

I. LEGAL STANDARD

Because the parties have submitted evidence outside of the complaint, including copies of the disputed advertisement and book, the court will treat Random House's motion as one for summary judgment. Fed. R. Civ. P. 12(b) (6). Summary judgment is appropriate where there is no genuine dispute as to any material fact and the moving party is entitled to judgment as a matter of law. *E.g., Celotex Corp. v. Catrett*, 477 U.S. 317, 322–23 (1986).

. . .

II. FACTUAL BACKGROUND

This is a libel case concerning an advertisement that appeared in The New York Times on two occasions in late August, 1993. The advertisement announced publication by Random House of Gerald Posner's Case Closed, a book supporting the Warren Commission's conclusion that Lee Harvey Oswald, acting alone, assassinated President John F. Kennedy. The theme of the book is captured near the bottom of the advertisement — "ONE MAN. ONE GUN. ONE INESCAPABLE CONCLUSION." — followed by the promotional exhortation to "READ: CASE CLOSED BY GERALD POSNER."

Lane's objection is to the body of the advertisement where his photograph appears along with five other literati whose theories about the Kennedy assassination are well-known to American readers and filmgoers. Each photograph is accompanied by a direct quote; and each quote is contrary to the views espoused by Posner in his new book. Above the six photographs is the caption: "GUILTY OF MISLEADING THE AMERICAN PUBLIC."

Immediately after the advertisement appeared, Lane protested to both The New York Times and Random House. His demand for a retraction was rejected. Random House indicated that it would not re-run the advertisement — but only because the pre-publication promotional campaign for Posner's book was finished.

Lane does not deny the quote attributed to him in the advertisement: "There is no convincing evidence that Oswald fired a gun from the sixth-floor window of the Book Depository or anywhere else on the day of the assassination." Still, Lane argues that he was injured in two respects. First, he objects to the unauthorized use of his photograph, name and notoriety in promoting the sale of Case Closed. Second, he seeks damages for the disparagement of his integrity and candor arising from the perceived suggestion in the advertisement that he has been intellectually dishonest with the American people.

III. ISSUES

[I]n count five, Lane claims defamation. According to Lane, Random House knew or could easily have determined that Lane had not been charged with nor convicted of fraud on the American public. Nevertheless, with actual malice or extreme recklessness, Random House twice published the offending advertisement. Because the falsity of the statement, "GUILTY OF MISLEADING THE AMERICAN PUBLIC," was objectively determinable, and because the statement was likely to be believed as factual, Lane contends that he was defamed. The appellation "GUILTY" was untrue; Lane was neither charged with nor convicted of misleading his readers.

As a result, Lane says he has not experienced the demand of previous years for his views and commentary; he has encountered increased difficulty in securing production for his other written works; and he anticipates reduced lecture bookings, fewer opportunities for publication, and diminished ability to attract significant clients for lucrative retainers. These concerns have caused Lane mental anguish and emotional distress. He places a $10 million price tag on these assorted grievances, in the form of actual, compensatory, presumed and punitive damages. Additionally, he requests attorneys' fees and costs.

Random House, in its motion for summary judgment, advances these arguments: (1) the advertisement in question contains protected opinion rather than a verifiably false statement of fact; (2) the advertisement constitutes privileged fair commentary on Lane's conspiracy theory. . . .

VI. DEFAMATION

In his fifth and last count, Lane claims defamation. According to Lane, Random House knew or could easily have determined that Lane had not been charged with nor convicted of misleading the American public. Nevertheless, with actual malice or extreme recklessness, Random House twice published the offending advertisement. Because the falsity of the charge was objectively determinable and likely to be believed as factual, Lane contends he was defamed.

There is, however, a very real risk in sanctioning recovery for libel under these circumstances.

Debate about one of our important historical events could be stifled by threats of costly litigation. As Random House remarked in their motion for summary judgment, "To allow conspiracy theorists to haul book authors into court in an effort to punish written criticism is contrary to our tradition of arriving at truth through a robust exchange of views in the marketplace of ideas." Lane is certainly entitled to his beliefs; but it is not defamatory to criticize him. Books, editorials and talk shows are more appropriate forums than courts for this type of polemic.

Lane is well aware of a judicial disposition in favor of open and unobstructed debate. In his failed libel action as attorney for Willis Carto's Liberty Lobby, Lane and his client were told by the court: "Neither an organization nor a person who sallies forth to espouse a specific creed or conviction can resort to the courts to silence those who disagree with that viewpoint." *Carto v. Buckley*, 649 F. Supp. 502, 508 (S.D.N.Y. 1986).

Both common law and constitutional protections are available to Random House. Ordinarily, an elementary canon mandates that courts not address a constitutional question if there is another ground on which the case can be decided.

. . . However, defamation is inextricably linked with First Amendment concerns. For that reason, courts frequently examine the constitutional implications of libel actions at the summary judgment stage. *See, e.g., Milkovich v. Lorain Journal Co.,* 497 U.S. 1, 3 (1990). . . . " In the First Amendment area, summary procedures are even more essential. . . . The threat of being put to the defense of a lawsuit . . . may be as chilling to the exercise of First Amendment freedoms as fear of the outcome of the lawsuit itself. . . . " *Washington Post Co. v. Keogh,* 365 F.2d 965, 968 (D.C. Cir. 1966), *cert. denied,* 385 U.S. 1011 (1967).

Accordingly, the court will explore the First Amendment ramifications of Lane's complaint. Although the common law fair comment privilege might also be an adequate basis upon which to grant Random House's motion for summary judgment, the court's dismissal of Lane's defamation count is grounded primarily in the First Amendment. Still, as a preliminary matter, the fair comment privilege is worth a cursory review.

A. Fair Comment Privilege

The common law privilege of fair comment applies where the reader is aware of the factual foundation for a comment and can therefore judge independently whether the comment is reasonable. *Milkovich,* 497 U.S. at 30 n. 7 (Brennan, J., dissenting). Fair comments are not actionable in defamation "[b]ecause the reader understands that such supported opinions represent the writer's interpretation of the facts presented, and because the reader is free to draw his or her own conclusions based upon those facts. . . . " *Moldea I,* 15 F.3d at 1144. In the District of Columbia, the fair comment privilege can be invoked even if the underlying facts are not included with the comment. *Fisher v. Washington Post Co.,* 212 A.2d 335, 338 (D.C. 1965) (relying on *Sullivan v. Meyer,* 141 F.2d 21 (D.C. Cir.), *cert. denied,* 322 U.S. 743 (1944)).

Here, application of the privilege is straightforward. Lane's direct quote is included in the Random House advertisement and the reader is urged to read Case Closed (or the works of any or all of the six conspiracists) for a fuller explication of the competing viewpoints. The inclusion of the underlying facts, directly in the form of a quotation and indirectly in the form of a booklist, more than complies with this circuit's criteria for applying the fair comment privilege. *See also, Potomac Valve and Fitting, Inc. v. Crawford Fitting Co.,* 829 F.2d 1280, 1290 (4th Cir. 1987) (challenged statement not actionable because "premises are explicit, and the reader is by no means required to share [defendant's] conclusion").

B. First Amendment Protection

The precepts governing the interrelationship between defamation and First Amendment jurisprudence were recently set forth in *Milkovich,* 497 U.S. at 18–21. To be defamatory, a statement must be "objectively verifiable" as true or false. *Id.,* at 21. To insure room for "imaginative expression" and "rhetorical hyperbole," statements are only actionable if they have an explicit or implicit factual foundation. *Id.* at 20. Full constitutional protection exists for rhetoric that, due to its loose, figurative tone cannot reasonably be interpreted as stating actual facts about an individual, and for imprecise statements that are not susceptible of being proved true or false. *Id.* at 20–21.

The Seventh Circuit expanded upon the *Milkovich* formulation. "[I]f it is plain that the speaker is expressing a subjective view, an interpretation, a theory, conjecture, or surmise, rather than claiming to be in possession of objectively verifiable facts, the statement is not actionable." *Haynes v. Alfred A. Knopf, Inc.*, 8 F.3d 1222, 1227 (7th Cir.1993) (citations omitted).

"GUILTY OF MISLEADING THE AMERICAN PUBLIC," would seem the ideal prototype of a statement that conforms to the *Milkovich-Haynes* model. It is rhetorical hyperbole; it does not state actual facts about an individual; it cannot be proven true or false. The statement in the Random House advertisement "could not reasonably be interpreted as stating anything other than a subjective belief." *Groden* at 14. Gerald Posner's evaluation in Case Closed is that Lane misled the public. That evaluation cannot be objectively verified without resolving thirty years of controversy surrounding the Kennedy assassination. To the extent that Posner's opinion rests on underlying facts, those facts are lodged in his and Lane's books. Events discussed in the two books have resisted objective verification for more than three decades. Readers may believe one book, the other, or neither; but there is no indication that Lane's theories have acquired the imprimatur of received wisdom.

Prior to *Milkovich*, this circuit recognized a strict dichotomy in defamation actions between assertions of opinion and assertions of fact. *See, e.g., Ollman*, 750 F.2d at 971. *Milkovich* rejected this practice. *Post-Milkovich* cases held that opinions can be actionable if they imply a provably false fact. *See, e.g., White*, 909 F.2d at 522. Thus, the task is to "determine as a threshold matter whether a challenged statement is capable of a defamatory meaning; and whether it is verifiable — that is, whether a plaintiff can prove that it is false." *Molded II*, 22 F.3d at 316–17 (citing *Moldea I*, 15 F.3d at 1142–45). The burden of proving falsity rests squarely on the plaintiff. He or she must demonstrate either that the statement is factual and untrue, or an opinion based implicitly on facts that are untrue.

Applying these principles in a context not far removed from the dispute the court grapples with today, the D.C. Circuit concluded: "[W]hen a reviewer offers commentary that is tied to the work being reviewed, and that is a supportable interpretation of the author's work, that interpretation does not present a verifiable issue of fact that can be actionable in defamation." *Moldea II*, 22 F.3d at 313. The context in *Moldea II* was a book review "in which the allegedly libelous statements were evaluations quintessentially of a type readers expect to find in that genre." *Id.* at 315. It was Moldea's book at issue, not his character, reputation or competence as a journalist. While a bad review inevitably injures an author's reputation to some extent, "criticism's long and impressive pedigree persuades us that, while a critic's latitude is not unlimited, he or she must be given the constitutional 'breathing space' appropriate to the genre." *Id.* (citing *Sullivan, 376 U.S. at 272*).

Lane insists that his case against Random House is not about who killed President Kennedy. Instead, Random House has accused Lane in no uncertain terms of being guilty of a public deceit, of duplicity and intellectual dishonesty. Random House implied that Lane has been exposed as a charlatan. Indeed, attests Lane, Random House's charges can be proven false; his veracity, integrity, intellectual honesty and candor can all be plumbed in a trial as a matter of fact.

If Random House had said what Lane said it said, perhaps we would have a more perplexing case. Even then, it is difficult to imagine how the court could assess Lane's deceitfulness, veracity, etc. without examining the assassination itself. Reckless disregard for the truth might qualify Lane for some of Random House's unstated pejoratives; but the "truth" has remained camouflaged since 1963, notwithstanding protracted analysis and debate. In *Milkovich* terms, if the underlying facts are not "objectively verifiable," the opinion based upon those facts is not actionable. 497 U.S. at 21. In *White* terms, "[a]ssertions of opinion on a matter of public concern . . . receive full constitutional protection if they do not contain a provably false factual connotation." 909 F.2d at 522. The challenged Random House statement has no provably false connotation, nor does it imply provable facts.

Moreover, Random House simply did not mention candor, integrity, duplicity, charlatanism or the other colorful terminology conjured up by Lane. The advertisement expressly said: "guilty of misleading the American public." "Guilty" is defined as "justly chargeable with or responsible for a usually grave breach of conduct." Webster's Ninth New Collegiate Dictionary 542 (1990). In this instance, the breach of conduct is misleading the public. "Mislead" is not synonymous with "deceive." The latter implies "imposing a false idea or belief," while the former is merely "a leading astray that may or may not be intentional." *Id.* at 329. Whether or not Lane has been exposed as a charlatan, one would be hard-pressed to pluck that insinuation from the comparatively bland charge in the Random House advertisement. . . .

The contested statement in the Random House advertisement reflects differing interpretations of the murky facts surrounding the Kennedy assassination. By "expressing a point of view only . . . the challenged language is immune from liability." *Phantom Touring*, 953 F.2d at 729.

Groden concurs: "[K]nown evidence concerning the Kennedy assassination and the extensive debate over the Warren Commission's findings demonstrate that the actual facts will never be verifiable to everyone's satisfaction. Thus, the statements in the advertisement are merely statements of Posner's argument or opinion. . . . " Groden at 14–15.

VIII. CONCLUSION

For reasons more fully set forth above, the motion for summary judgment by defendant Random House is granted . . .

Mark Lane might well profit from Jefferson's sage advice: "I laid it down as a law to myself, to take no notice of the thousand calumnies issued against me, but to trust my character to my own conduct, and the good sense and candor of my fellow citizens." If nonetheless Lane is affronted by such minor provocations as the court addresses today, he may elect to minimize his exposure by opting for a lower public profile. More likely, having acknowledged that publicity is the lifeblood of his career, Lane will have to overcome his brittleness — or seek solace elsewhere than from this court.

NOTES AND QUESTIONS

(1) The common law defense of fair comment was explained by *Kotlikoff v. The Community News*, 444 A.2d 1086 (N.J. 1982) as follows:

Traditionally, one could be found liable for defamation if one published an opinion that harmed another's reputation. However, expressions of opinion were privileged if they constituted "fair comment" on a matter of public concern. Restatement (Second) of Torts 566, comment a (1977). This

Court has articulated the following definition of the fair comment privilege:

> In a word, "fair comment" (a) must be based on facts truly stated, and (b) must not contain imputations of corrupt or dishonorable motives on the person whose conduct or work is criticized, save in so far as such imputations are warranted by the facts, and (c) must be the honest expression of the writer's real opinion; and if the comment complies with these conditions, it is fair comment, however incorrect be the views expressed by the critic, or however exaggerated or even prejudiced be the language of the criticism; the "limits of criticism are exceedingly wide." Gatley, Libel and Slander, sections 344, 354. [*Leers v. Green*, 24 N.J. 239, 254–55, 131 A.2d 781 (1957).]

Has common law fair comment been rendered obsolete as a defense? Or, would a defendant be entitled to defend an action on grounds of both common law and constitutional defenses?

(2)   In the 1980s, numerous courts began to recognize a constitutional opinion privilege based on Justice Powell's dictum in *Gertz*, "Under the First Amendment there is no such thing as a false idea." This constitutional opinion privilege was a powerful weapon against defamation plaintiffs because it allowed courts to dismiss a plaintiff's suit at a very early stage of the litigation. Nevertheless, in *Milkovich v. Lorain Journal Co.*, 497 U.S. 1 (1990), the Supreme Court declined "to create a wholesale defamation exemption for anything that might be labeled 'opinion'." Milkovich was a high school wrestling coach. He sued defendants based on a sports column suggesting that he had lied under oath at a judicial hearing about his team's role in a brawl at a wrestling match. After "an odyssey of litigation spanning nearly 15 years," the Ohio Court of Appeals granted the newspaper's motion for summary judgment on the basis that the columnist's statements were constitutionally protected "opinion."

The United Stated Supreme Court reversed, stating:

> If a speaker says, "In my opinion John Jones is a liar," he implies a knowledge of facts which lead to the conclusion that Jones told an untruth. Even if the speaker states the facts upon which he bases his opinion, if those facts are either incorrect or incomplete, or if his assessment of them is erroneous, the statement may still imply a false assertion of fact. Simply couching such statements in terms of opinion does not dispel these implications; and the statement, "in my opinion Jones is a liar," can cause as much damage to reputation as the statement, "Jones is a liar." As Judge Friendly aptly stated: "[It] would be destructive of the law of libel if a writer could escape liability for accusations of [defamatory conduct] simply by using, explicitly or implicitly, the words 'I think.' "[quoting *Cianci v. New Times Pub. Co.*, 639 F.2d 54 (2d Cir. 1980)]. It is worthy of note that at common law, even the privilege of fair comment did not extend to "a false statement of fact, whether it was expressly stated or implied from an expression of opinion." Restatement (Second) of Torts, at 566, Comment a (1977).

. . .

We are not persuaded that, in addition to [existing constitutional] protections, an additional separate constitutional privilege for "opinion" is required to ensure the freedom of expression guaranteed by the First Amendment. The dispositive question in the present case then becomes whether a reasonable factfinder could conclude that the statements in the column imply an assertion that petitioner Milkovich perjured himself in a judicial proceeding. We think this question must be answered in the affirmative. As the Ohio Supreme Court itself observed: "[T]he clear impact in some nine sentences and a caption is that [Milkovich] 'lied at the hearing after . . . having given his solemn oath to tell the truth.' "This is not the sort of loose, figurative, or hyperbolic language which would negate the impression that the writer was seriously maintaining that petitioner committed the crime of perjury. Nor does the general tenor of the article negate this impression.

We also think the connotation that petitioner committed perjury is sufficiently factual to be susceptible of being proved true or false. A determination whether petitioner lied in this instance can be made on a core of the objective evidence by comparing, inter alia, petitioner's testimony before the OHSAA board with his subsequent testimony before the trial court. As the [Ohio Supreme Court noted in another case arising out of the same facts], "[w]hether or not [the plaintiff] did indeed perjure himself is certainly verifiable by a perjury action with evidence adduced from the transcripts and witnesses present at the hearing. Unlike a subjective assertion the averred defamatory language is an articulation of an objectively verifiable event." 496 N.E. 2d, at 707. So too with petitioner Milkovich.

How should courts separate opinions that "imply an assertion of objective fact" from those that do not? Why does the Court think this distinction is constitutionally relevant? Does a statement asserting that an author's book is "horribly written" imply an assertion of objective fact? Why or why not? Why does the Court suggest that rhetorical hyperbole is constitutionally protected but not opinion?

(3) In addition to the defense of "fair comment," which applies generally to critical evaluations of performances and writings, many courts have acknowledged a qualified privilege to make a fair and accurate report of judicial proceedings, including, in some jurisdictions, information recorded in police blotters. *See, e.g., Flanagan v. Nicholson Publishing Company*, 68 So. 964 (Fla. 1917), and *Read v. News-Journal Co.*, 474 A.2d 119 (Del. 1984) (fair and accurate abridgement of judicial proceeding is privileged notwithstanding malice or ill will). The drafters of the Restatement take the position that this privilege operates even when the publisher knows that the accurately reported statements are defamatory and false. Restatement, Torts, Second § 611, comment a (1977). *Contra, Lancourt v. Herald Globe Ass'n*, 17 A.2d 253 (Vt. 1941). Cases on both sides are discussed in *O'Neil v. Tribune Company*, 176 So. 2d 535 (Fla. App. 1965). Is there room for this privilege to operate after *Sullivan* and *Gertz*?

[C]   Absolute Privilege

BARR v. MATTEO
United States Supreme Court
360 U.S. 564, 79 S. Ct. 1335, 3 L. Ed. 2d 1434 (1959)

MR. JUSTICE HARLAN announced the judgment of the Court, and delivered an opinion, in which MR. JUSTICE FRANKFURTER, MR. JUSTICE CLARK, and MR. JUSTICE WHITTAKER join.

. . .

This is a libel suit, brought in the District Court of the District of Columbia by respondents, former employees of the Office of Rent Stabilization. The alleged libel was contained in a press release issued by the office on February 5, 1953, at the direction of petitioner, then its Acting Director.

[The press release read as follows:

"William G. Barr, Acting Director of Rent Stabilization today served notice of suspension on the two officials of the agency who in June 1950 were responsible for the plan which allowed 53 of the agency's 2,681 employees to take their accumulated annual leave in cash.

"Mr. Barr's appointment as Acting Director becomes effective Monday, February 9, 1953, and the suspension of these employees will be his first act of duty. The employees are John J. Madigan, Deputy Director for Administration, and Linda Matteo, Director of Personnel.

" 'In June 1950,' Mr. Barr stated, 'my position in the agency was not one of authority which would have permitted me to stop the action. Furthermore, I did not know about it until it was almost completed.

" 'When I did learn that certain employees were receiving cash annual leave settlements and being returned to agency employment on a temporary basis, I specifically notified the employees under my supervision that if they applied for such cash settlements I would demand their resignations and the record will show that my immediate employees complied with my request.

" 'While I was advised that the action was legal, I took the position that it violated the spirit of the Thomas Amendment and I violently opposed it. Monday, February 9th, when my appointment as Acting Director becomes effective, will be the first time my position in the agency has permitted me to take any action on this matter, and the suspension of these employees will be the first official act I shall take.'

"Mr. Barr also revealed that he has written to Senator Joseph McCarthy, Chairman of the Committee on Government Operations, and to Representative John Phillips, Chairman of the House Subcommittee on Independent Offices Appropriations, requesting an opportunity to be heard on the entire matter."

Matteo was one of the employees who had taken advantage of the plan. No claim was made that the plan was illegal, though it was demonstrably politically unpopular.]

On February 4, 1953, Senator Williams delivered a speech on the floor of the Senate strongly criticizing the plan, stating that "to say the least it is an unjustifiable raid on the Federal Treasury, and heads of every agency in the Government who have condoned this practice should be called to task." The letter above referred to was ordered printed in the Congressional Record. Other Senators joined in the attack on the plan. Their comments were widely reported in the press on February 5, 1953, and petitioner, in his capacity as Acting Director of the agency, received a large number of inquiries from newspapers and other news media as to the agency's position on the matter.

On that day petitioner served upon respondents letters expressing his intention to suspend them from duty, and at the same time ordered issuance by the office of the press release which is the subject of this litigation.

. . .

Respondents sued, charging that the press release, in itself and as coupled with the contemporaneous news reports of senatorial reaction to the plan, defamed them to their injury, and alleging that its publication and terms had been actuated by malice on the part of the petitioner. Petitioner defended, *inter alia*, on the ground that the issuance of the press release was protected by either a qualified or an absolute privilege. The trial court overruled these contentions, and instructed the jury to return a verdict for respondents if it found the release defamatory. The jury found for respondents.

Petitioner appealed, raising only the issue of absolute privilege. The judgment of the trial court was affirmed by the Court of Appeals, which held that "in explaining his decision [to suspend respondents] to the general public [petitioner] . . . went entirely outside his line of duty" and that thus the absolute privilege, assumed otherwise to be available, did not attach. We granted certiorari, vacated the Court of Appeals' judgment, and remanded the case "with directions to pass upon petitioner's claim of a qualified privilege." On remand the Court of Appeals held that the press release was protected by a qualified privilege, but that there was evidence from which a jury could reasonably conclude that petitioner had acted maliciously, or had spoken with lack of reasonable grounds for believing that his statement was true, and that either conclusion would defeat the qualified privilege. Accordingly it remanded the case to the District Court for retrial. At this point petitioner again sought, and we again granted certiorari, to determine whether in the circumstances of this case petitioner's claim of absolute privilege should have stood as a bar to maintenance of the suit despite the allegations of malice made in the complaint.

The law of privilege as a defense by officers of government to civil damage suits for defamation and kindred torts has in large part been of judicial making, although the Constitution itself gives an absolute privilege to members of both Houses of Congress in respect to any speech, debate, vote, report, or action done in session. This Court early held that judges of courts of superior or general authority are absolutely privileged as respects civil suits to recover for actions taken by them in the exercise of their judicial functions, irrespective of the motives with which those acts are alleged to have been performed and that a like immunity extends to other officers of government whose duties are related to the judicial process. Nor has the privilege been confined to officers of the legislative and judicial branches of the Government and executive officers of the kind involved in

Yaselli. In *Spalding v. Vilas*, 161 U.S. 483, 16 S. Ct. 631, 40 L. Ed. 780, petitioner brought suit against the Postmaster General, alleging that the latter had maliciously circulated widely among postmasters, past and present, information which he knew to be false and which was intended to deceive the postmasters to the detriment of the plaintiff. This Court sustained a plea by the Postmaster General of absolute privilege, stating that 161 U.S. at pages 498–499, 16 S. Ct. at page 637:

> In exercising the functions of his office, the head of an executive department, keeping within the limits of his authority, should not be under an apprehension that the motives that control his official conduct may, at any time, become the subject of inquiry in a civil suit for damages. It would seriously cripple the proper and effective administration of public affairs as entrusted to the executive branch of the government, if he were subjected to any such restraint. He may have legal authority to act, but he may have such large discretion in the premises that it will not always be his absolute duty to exercise the authority with which he is invested. But if he acts, having authority, his conduct cannot be made the foundation of a suit against him personally for damages, even if the circumstances show that he is not disagreeably impressed by the fact that his action injuriously affects the claims of particular individuals.

The reasons for the recognition of the privilegé have been often stated. It has been thought important that officials of government should be free to exercise their duties unembarrassed by the fear of damage suits in respect of acts done in the course of those duties — suits which would consume time and energies which would otherwise be devoted to governmental service and the threat of which might appreciably inhibit the fearless, vigorous, and effective administration of policies of government. The matter has been admirably expressed by Judge Learned Hand:

> It does indeed go without saying that an official, who is in fact guilty of using his powers to vent his spleen upon others, or for any other personal motive not connected with the public good, should not escape liability for the injuries he may so cause; and, if it were possible in practice to confine such complaints to the guilty, it would be monstrous to deny recovery. The justification for doing so is that it is impossible to know whether the claim is well founded until the case has been tried, and that to submit all officials, the innocent as well as the guilty, to the burden of a trial and to the inevitable danger of its outcome would dampen the ardor of all but the most resolute, or the most irresponsible, in the unflinching discharge of their duties. Again and again the public interest calls for action which may turn out to be founded on a mistake, in the face of which an official may later find himself hard put to it to satisfy a jury of his good faith. There must indeed be means of punishing public officers who have been truant to their duties; but that is quite another matter from exposing such as have been honestly mistaken to suit by anyone who has suffered from their errors. As is so often the case, the answer must be found in a balance between the evils inevitable in either alternative. In this instance it has been thought in the end better to leave unredressed the wrongs done by dishonest officers than to subject those who try to do their duty to the constant dread of retaliation. . . .

The decisions have, indeed, always imposed as a limitation upon the immunity that the official's act must have been within the scope of his powers; and it can be argued that official powers, since they exist only for the public good, never cover occasions where the public good is not their aim, and hence that to exercise a power dishonestly is necessarily to overstep its bounds. A moment's reflection shows, however, that that cannot be the meaning of the limitation without defeating the whole doctrine. What is meant by saying that the officer must be acting within his power cannot be more than that the occasion must be such as would have justified the act, if he had been using his power for any of the purposes on whose account it was vested in him. . . .

Gregoire v. Biddle, 2 Cir., 177 F.2d 579, 581.

We do not think that the principle announced in *Vilas* can properly be restricted to executive officers of cabinet rank, and in fact it never has been so restricted by the lower federal courts. The privilege is not a badge or emolument of exalted office, but an expression of a policy designed to aid in the effective functioning of government. The complexities and magnitude of governmental activity have become so great that there must of necessity be a delegation and redelegation of authority as to many functions, and we cannot say that these functions become less important simply because they are exercised by officers of lower rank in the executive hierarchy.

To be sure, the occasions upon which the acts of the head of an executive department will be protected by the privilege are doubtless far broader than in the case of an officer with less sweeping functions. But that is because the higher the post, the broader the range of responsibilities and duties, and the wider the scope of discretion, it entails. It is not the title of his office but the duties with which the particular officer sought to be made to respond in damages is entrusted — the relation of the act complained of to "matters committed by law to his control or supervision," — which must provide the guide in delineating the scope of the rule which clothes the official acts of the executive officer with immunity from civil defamation suits.

Judged by these standards, we hold that petitioner's plea of absolute privilege in defense of the alleged libel published at his direction must be sustained. The question is a close one, but we cannot say that it was not an appropriate exercise of the discretion with which an executive officer of petitioner's rank is necessarily clothed to publish the press release here at issue in the circumstances disclosed by this record. Petitioner was the Acting Director of an important agency of government, and was clothed by redelegation with "all powers, duties, and functions conferred on the President by Title II of the Housing and Rent Act of 1947. . . . " The integrity of the internal operations of the agency which he headed, and thus his own integrity in his public capacity, had been directly and severely challenged in charges made on the floor of the Senate and given wide publicity; and without his knowledge correspondence which could reasonably be read as impliedly defending a position very different from that which he had from the beginning taken in the matter had been sent to a Senator over his signature and incorporated in the Congressional Record. The issuance of press releases was standard agency practice, as it has become with many governmental agencies in these times. We think that under these circumstances a publicly expressed statement of the position of the agency head, announcing personnel action which he planned to take in reference to the charges so widely disseminated to the public, was an appropriate exercise of the discretion which an officer of that rank must possess if the public service is to function effectively. It would be an unduly restrictive view of the scope of the duties of a policy-making executive official to hold that a public statement of agency policy in respect to matters of wide public interest and concern is not action in the line of duty. That petitioner was not *required* by law or by direction of his superiors to speak out cannot be controlling in the case of an official of policy-making rank, for the same considerations which underlie the recognition of the privilege as to acts done in connection with a mandatory duty apply with equal force to discretionary acts at those levels of government where the concept of duty encompasses the sound exercise of discretionary authority.

The fact that the action here taken was within the outer perimeter of petitioner's line of duty is enough to render the privilege applicable, despite the allegations of malice in the complaint, for as this Court has said of legislative privilege:

The claim of an unworthy purpose does not destroy the privilege. Legislators are immune from deterrents to the uninhibited discharge of their legislative duty, not for their private indulgence but for the public good. One must not expect uncommon courage even in legislators. The privilege would be of little value if they could be subjected to the cost and inconvenience and distractions of a trial upon a conclusion of the pleader, or to the hazard of a judgment against them based upon a jury's speculation as to motives.

Tenney v. Brandhove, 311 U.S. 367, 377, 71 S. Ct. 783, 788, 95 L. Ed. 1019.

We are told that we should forbear from sanctioning any such rule of absolute privilege lest it open the door to wholesale oppression and abuses on the part of unscrupulous government officials. It is perhaps enough to say that fears of this sort have not been realized within the wide area of government where a judicially formulated absolute privilege of broad scope has long existed. It seems to us wholly chimerical to suggest that what hangs in the balance here is the maintenance of high standards of conduct among those in the public service. To be sure, as with any rule of law which attempts to reconcile fundamentally antagonistic social policies, there may be occasional instances of actual injustice which will go unredressed, but we think that price a necessary one to pay for the greater good. And there are of course other sanctions than civil tort suits available to deter the executive official who may be prone to exercise his functions in an unworthy and irresponsible manner. We think that we should not be deterred from establishing the rule which we announce today by any such remote forebodings.

Reversed

Mr. Justice Black, concurring.

[Omitted]

Mr. Chief Justice Warren, with whom Mr. Justice Douglas joins, dissenting.

[Omitted]

NOTES AND QUESTIONS

(1) Although the authorities split, many courts afford local governmental legislative and executive officials an absolute privilege for statements made within the scope of official proceedings. *See, e.g., Costanzo v. Gaul*, 403 N.E.2d 979 (Ohio 1979). The *Costanzo* court also applied a qualified privilege to local legislators who made defamatory statements pertaining to their public business outside official proceedings. *See also, Nodar v. Galbreath*, 462 So. 2d 803 (Fla. 1985) (parents have a qualified privilege in addressing school boards about the performance of their children's teachers).

Most courts afford an absolute privilege to statements made in the official content of any phase of litigation whether made by litigants, advocates, jurists or witnesses. *See, e.g., McNayr v. Kelly*, 184 So. 2d 428 (Fla. 1966), *Briscoe v. Lahue*, 103 S. Ct. 1109 (1983) and *Dixon v. DeLance*, 579 A.2d 1213 (Md. App. 1990) *cert. denied*, 583 A.2d 275 (Md. 1991) (an attorney's statements in litigation are absolutely privileged "so long as the matter has some reference or relation to the proceeding," and the immunity includes references to persons who are neither parties nor witnesses.)

The foregoing privileges attach to the offices and not to the holders of them while acting in a private capacity. Moreover, the privileges do not attach even to ostensible official acts when the particular act is completely outside the jurisdiction of the official or entity taking the actions. *See, e.g., Marrero v. City of Hialeah*, 625 F.2d 499 (5th Cir. 1980) (state prosecutor loses immunity when acting outside prosecutorial function); *Harris v. Harvey*, 605 F.2d 330 (7th Cir. 1979), *cert. den.* 445 U.S. 938 (judge denied immunity when acting outside jurisdiction); and *Visser v. Magnarelli*, 542 F. Supp. 1331 (N.D.N.Y. 1982) (city councillors denied immunity when operating outside jurisdiction).

(2) Suppose a person transmits unsolicited defamatory information to a legislative body. If the legislative body is actively reviewing the subject which the defamatory information pertains to, will the publisher be entitled to the same absolute privilege that would protect him if he had presented the information directly to the body while in official session? *See Webster v. Sun Co., Inc.*, 731 F.2d 1 (D.C. Cir. 1984).

[D] Qualified Privilege

WATT v. LONGSDON
[1930] 1 K.B. 130 (C.A.)[7]

Scrutton L.J. This case raises, amongst other matters, the extremely difficult question, equally important in its legal and social aspect, as to the circumstances, if any, in which a person will be justified in giving to one partner to a marriage information which that person honestly believes to be correct, but which is in fact untrue, about the matrimonial delinquencies of the other party to the marriage. The question becomes more difficult if the answer in law turns on the existence or

---

[7] [Ed. — King's Bench Division, Law Reports of the principal English Trial Court, appeals therefrom, certain criminal appeals and other cases, decision of the Court of Appeal.]

non-existence of a social or moral duty, a question which the judge is to determine, without any evidence, by the light of his own knowledge of the world, and his own views on social morality, a subject matter on which views vary in different ages, in different countries, and even as between man and man.

The Scottish Petroleum Company, which carried on business, amongst other places, in Morocco, had in Casa Blanca, a port in Morocco, a manager named Browne, and a managing director named Watt. The company had in England a chairman named Singer, who held a very large proportion of shares in the company, and also another director, Longsdon, a young man under thirty years of age. The latter had been in Morocco in business and friendly relations with Watt and Browne, and was a friend of Mrs. Watt, who had nursed him in an illness. The company went into voluntary liquidation in November, 1927, and Longsdon was appointed liquidator. In April, 1928, Mrs. Watt was in England, and her husband in Casa Blanca. It is not clear, and there is no evidence, what the effect of the liquidation had been on the actual employment of Watt and Browne, that is, whether they, or either of them, still received a salary. Watt's directorship was, under the Companies Act, in a state of suspended animation. Under these circumstances Longsdon in England received at the beginning of May from Browne in Casa Blanca a letter stating that Watt had left for Lisbon to look for a job, that he had left a bill for 88 *l.* for whisky unpaid, and that he had been for two months in immoral relations with his housemaid, who was now publicly raising claims against him for money matters. The woman was described as an old woman, stone deaf, almost blind, and with dyed hair. A number of details were given which Browne said Watt's cook had corroborated. The information was mixed up with an allegation that Watt had been scheming to compromise or seduce Mrs. Browne. The letter concluded: "From a letter shown to me by Mr. Watt I know how bitterly disappointed Mrs. Watt is, and how very much troubled she is. It would therefore perhaps be better not to show her this letter as it could only increase most terribly her own feelings in regard to her husband. These awful facts might be the cause of a breakdown to her, and I think she has enough to cope with at present. Mr. Singer, however, should perhaps know." On May 5, Longsdon, without making inquiries, sent Browne's letter on to Singer, the chairman of the board of directors. At the trial Watt's counsel put in Longsdon's [statement] that he believed the statements in the letter to be true. On May 5 Longsdon wrote a long letter to Browne, in which he said that he had long suspected Watt's immorality, but had no proof; that he thought it wicked and cruel that Mrs. Watt, a very old friend of the writer's, should be in the dark when Watt might return to her — did not Browne agree? — that he (Longsdon) would not speak until he had a sworn statement in his possession, "and only with such proof would I speak, for an interferer between husband and wife nearly always comes off the worst." Could Browne get a sworn statement? "It may even be necessary for you to bribe the women to do such, and if only a matter of a few hundred francs I will pay it and of course the legal expenses." Longsdon's letter describes one of the women who was to make this sworn statement as "a prostitute all her life," a description not contained in Browne's letter. Watt returned to England in May. Without waiting for the sworn statement, on May 12, Longsdon sent the letter to Mrs. Watt. Mr. and Mrs. Watt separated, and Mrs. Watt instituted proceedings for divorce, which apparently are still pending.

Mr. Watt then instituted proceedings against Longsdon for libel — namely (1.) the publication of Browne's letter to Singer; (2.) the publication of the same letter to Mrs. Watt; (3.) Longsdon's letter of May 5 to Browne.

. . .

The defendant did not justify, but pleaded privilege. The case was tried before Horridge J. and a jury. The learned judge held that all three publications were privileged, and that there was no evidence of malice fit to be left to the jury. He therefore entered judgment for the defendant. The plaintiff appeals.

The learned judge appears to have taken the view that the authorities justify him in holding that if "there is an obvious interest in the person to whom a communication is made which causes him to be a proper recipient of a statement," even if the party making the communication had no moral or social duty to the party to whom the communication is made, the occasion is privileged. He derives this from the opinions of Tindal C.J. and Erle J. in *Coxhead v. Richards* as approved by Willes J. in *Amann v. Damm*; and by Blackburn J. in *Davies v. Snead*, and especially from the approval of these decisions, and the citation of the judgment of Erle C.J. in *Whiteley v. Adams*', by Lindley L.J. in *Stuart v. Bell*. He has therefore found in the present case that the occasion of each of the three communications, to Singer, to the wife, and to Browne, was privileged, and that there is no evidence of excess of communication or of malice to be left to the jury. "No nice scales should be used," as Lord Dunedin said in *Adam v. Ward*.

By the law of England there are occasions on which a person may make defamatory statements about another which are untrue without incurring any legal liability for his statements. These occasions are called privileged occasions. A reason frequently given for this privilege is that the allegation that the speaker has "unlawfully and maliciously published," is displaced by proof that the speaker had either a duty or an interest to publish, and that this duty or interest confers the privilege. But communications made on these occasions may lose their privilege: (1.) they may exceed the privilege of the occasion by going beyond the limits of the duty or interest, or (2.) they may be published with express malice, so that the occasion is not being legitimately used, but abused. A very careful discussion of the way in which these two grounds of loss of privilege should be considered will be found in Lord Dunedin's judgment in *Adam v. Ward*. The classical definition of "privileged occasions" is that of Parke B. in *Toogood v. Spyring*, a case where the tenant of a farm complained to the agent of the landlord, who had sent a workman to do repairs, that the workman had broken into the tenant's cellar, got drunk on the tenant's cider, and spoilt the work he was sent to do. The workman sued the tenant. Parke B. gave the explanation of privileged occasions in these words: "In general, an action lies for the malicious publication of statements which are false in fact, and injurious to the character of another (within the well-known limits as to verbal slander), and the law considers such publication as malicious, unless it is fairly made by a person in the discharge of some public or private duty, whether legal or moral, or in the conduct of his own affairs, in matters where his interest is concerned. In such cases, the occasion prevents the inference of malice, which the law draws from unauthorized communications, and affords a qualified defence depending upon the absence of actual malice. If fairly warranted by any reasonable occasion or exigency, and honestly made, such communications are protected for the common convenience and welfare of society; and the law has not restricted the right to make them within any narrow limits." It will be seen that the learned judge requires: (1.) a public or private duty to communicate, whether legal or moral; (2.) that the communication should be "fairly warranted by any reasonable occasion or exigency"; (3.) or a statement in the conduct of his own affairs where his interest is concerned. Parke B. had given several other definitions in slightly varying terms. For instance, in *Cockayne v. Hodgkisson* he had directed the jury "Where the writer is acting on any duty, legal or moral, towards the person to whom he writes, or where he has, by his situation, to protect the interests of another, that which he writes under such circumstances is a privileged communication." This adds to the protection of his own interest spoken of in *Toogood v. Spyring* the protection of the interests of another where the situation of the writer requires him to protect those interests. This, I think, involves that his "situation" imposes on him a legal or moral duty. The question whether the occasion was privileged is for the judge, and so far as "duty" is concerned, the question is: Was there a duty, legal, moral, or social, to communicate? As to legal duty, the judge should have no difficulty; the judge should know the law; but as to moral or social duties of imperfect obligation, the task is far more troublesome. The judge has no evidence as to the view the community takes of moral or social duties. All the help the Court of Appeal can give him is contained in the judgment of Lindley L.J. in *Stuart v. Bell:* "The question of moral or social duty being for the judge, each judge must decide it as best he can for himself. I take moral or social duty to mean a duty recognized by English people of ordinary intelligence and moral principle, but at the same time not a duty enforceable by legal proceedings, whether civil or criminal. My own conviction is that all or, at all events, the great mass of right-minded men in the position of the defendant would have considered it their duty, under the circumstances, to inform Stanley of the suspicion which had fallen on the plaintiff." Is the judge merely to give his own view of moral and social duty, though he thinks a considerable portion of the community hold a different opinion? Or is he to endeavour to ascertain what view "the great mass of right-minded men" would take? It is not surprising that with such a standard both judges and text-writers treat the matter as one of great difficulty in which no definite line can be drawn. I refer to the judicial recognition of the difficulty cited in Fraser on Libel, 6th ed., pp. 183 to 186, the late Mr. Blake Odgers' book on Libel, 6th ed., p. 220, and Mr. Gatley's book, 2d ed., p. 252.

A conspicuous instance of the difficulties which arise when judges have to determine the existence of duties, not legal, but moral or social, by the inner light of their own conscience and judgment and knowledge of the world, is to be found in the case of *Coxhead v. Richards.* A correct appreciation of what was the difference of opinion in that case is, in my opinion, of great importance in the decision of the present case. The short facts were that Cass, the mate of a ship, wrote to Richards, an intimate friend of his, a letter stating that on a voyage from the Channel to Wales, which was going to continue to Eastern ports, the captain, Coxhead, had by his drunkenness endangered the safety of the ship, and the lives of the crew; and Cass asked Richards' advice what he should do in view of the risk of repetition of this danger on the voyage to the East. Richards, after consulting "an Elder Brother of the Trinity House, and an eminent shipowner," sent this letter to Ward, the owner of the ship. Richards did not know Ward, and had no interest in the ship. The owner dismissed the captain, who thereupon brought an action against Richards. The judge at the trial directed the jury, if they should think that the communication was strictly honest, and made solely in the execution of what he believed to be a duty, to find for the defendant. They did so, while finding that the plea of justification failed. The plaintiff then moved for a new trial, on which motion the Court after two hearings was equally divided. It is not very clear whether the judges differed on a general principle, or on its application to the facts of the case. I understand Tindal C.J. to have taken the view that if a man has information materially affecting the interests of another, and honestly communicates it to that other, he is protected, though he has no personal interest in the subject matter, and that his protection arises from "the various social duties by which men are bound to each other," and that it was the duty of the defendant to communicate this information to the owner. Erle J. appears to put the matter on "information given to protect damage from misconduct," "the importance of the information to the interest of the receiver," and says that a person having such information is justified in communicating it to the person interested, though the speaker did not stand in any relation to the recipient, and was a volunteer. He does not expressly refer to any social duty. On the other hand, Coltman and Cresswell JJ. both appear to me to hold that in such circumstances there was no moral duty, for that any tendency that way was counterbalanced by the moral duty not to slander your neighbour.

. . .

In 1855, in *Harrison v. Bush*, Lord Campbell C.J. giving the judgment of the Court of Queen's Bench accepted a principle stated thus: "A communication made *bona fide* upon any subject matter in which the party communicating has an interest, or in reference to which he has a duty, is privileged, if made to a person having a corresponding interest or duty, although it contain criminatory matter which, without this privilege, would be slanderous and actionable." This is the first of a series of statements that both parties, the writer and the recipient, must have a corresponding interest or duty. Lord Esher M.R. says in *Pullman v. Hill & Co.:* "An occasion is privileged when the person who makes the communication has a moral duty to make it to the person to whom he does make it, and the person who receives it has an interest in hearing it. Both these conditions must exist in order that the occasion may be privileged."

. . .

Except in the case of common interest justifying intercommunication, the correspondence must be between duty and interest. There may, in the common interest cases, be also a common or reciprocal duty. It is not every interest which will create a duty in a stranger or volunteer.

. . .

In *Stuart v. Bell* there was again a difference of opinion, though not an equal division of the judges, as in *Coxhead v. Richards.* Stanley, the explorer, and his valet, Stuart, were staying with the major of Newcastle, Bell. The Edinburgh police made a very carefully worded communication to the Newcastle police that there had been a robbery in Edinburgh at an hotel where Stuart was staying, and it might be well to make very careful and cautious inquiry into the matter. The Newcastle police showed the letter to the mayor, who after consideration showed it to Stanley, who dismissed Stuart. Stuart sued the mayor. Lindley and Kay L.JJ. held that the mayor had a moral duty to communicate, and Stanley a material interest to receive the communication; Lopes L.J. held that in the circumstances there was no moral duty to communicate, though in some circumstances there might be such a duty in a host towards a guest. I myself should have agreed with the majority, but the difference of opinion between such experienced judges shows the difficulty of the question.

In my opinion Horridge J. went too far in holding that there could be a privileged occasion on the ground of interest in the recipient without any duty to communicate on the part of the person making the communication. But that does not settle the question, for it is necessary to consider, in the present case, whether there was, as to each communication, a duty to communicate, and an interest in the recipient.

First as to the communication between Longsdon and Singer, I think the case must proceed on the admission that at all material times Watt, Longsdon and Browne were in the employment of the same company, and the evidence afforded by the answer to the interrogatory put in by the plaintiff that Longsdon believed the statements in Browne's letter. In my view on these facts there was a duty, both from a moral and a material point of view, on Longsdon to communicate the letter to Singer, the chairman of his company, who, apart from questions of present employment, might be asked by Watt for a testimonial to a future employer. Equally, I think Longsdon receiving the letter from Browne, might discuss the matter with him, and ask for further information, on the ground of a common interest in the affairs of the company, and to obtain further information for the chairman. I should therefore agree with the view of Horridge J. that these two occasions were privileged, though for different reasons. Horridge J. further held that there was no evidence of malice fit to be left to the jury, and, while I think some of Longsdon's action and language in this respect was unfortunate, as the plaintiff has put in the answer that Longsdon believed the truth of the statements in Browne's and his own letter, like Lord Dunedin in *Adam v. Ward*, I should not try excess with too nice scales, and I do not dissent from his view as to malice. As to the communications to Singer and Browne, in my opinion the appeal should fail, but as both my brethren take the view that there was evidence of malice which should be left to the jury, there must, of course, be a new trial as to the claim based on these two publications.

The communication to Mrs. Watt stands on a different footing. I have no intention of writing an exhaustive treatise on the circumstances when a stranger or a friend should communicate to husband or wife information he receives as to the conduct of the other party to the marriage. I am clear that it is impossible to say he is always under a moral or social duty to do so; it is equally impossible to say he is never under such a duty. It must depend on the circumstances of each case, the nature of the information, and the relation of speaker and recipient. It cannot, on the one hand, be the duty even of a friend to communicate all the gossip the friend hears at men's clubs or women's bridge parties to one of the spouses affected. On the other hand, most men would hold that it was the moral duty of a doctor who attended his sister in law, and believed her to be suffering from a miscarriage, for which an absent husband could not be responsible, to communicate that fact to his wife and the husband. Hawkins J. in *Kitson v. Playfair* did not have to rule on this point because of the finding of the jury as to malice, and, I think, postponed ruling as long as he could. If this is so, the decision must turn on the circumstances of each case, the judge being much influenced by the consideration that as a general rule it is not desirable for any one, even a mother in law, to interfere in the affairs of man and wife. Using the best judgment I can in this difficult matter, I have come to the conclusion that there was not a moral or social duty in Longsdon to make this communication to Mrs. Watt such as to make the occasion privileged, and that there must be a new trial so far as it relates to the claim for publication of a libel to Mrs. Watt. The communications to Singer and Browne being made on a privileged occasion, there must be a new trial of the issue as to malice defeating the privilege. There must also be a new trial of the complaint as to publication to Mrs. Watt, the occasion being held not to be privileged. The plaintiff must have the costs of this appeal; the costs of the first trial must abide the result of the second trial, the issues being separated.

NOTES AND QUESTIONS

(1)　Why is the privilege claimed by *Longsdon* referred to as a qualified (or, sometimes, "conditional") privilege? Why does it exist? How does it differ from an absolute privilege? What would you infer from your reading of *Watt v. Longsdon* would it take to eliminate a qualified privilege? *See, e.g., Miller v. Lear Siegler, Inc.,* 525 F. Supp. 46, 60 (D. Kan. 1981), which adds these points:

> The existence of a conditional privilege is a matter of law for the court to decide, unless the circumstances of the publication are in dispute, and then it is a jury question dependent upon findings of fact. . . .

> The defendant has the burden of establishing the existence of a privilege by showing a recognized public or private interest which would justify the making of the communication . . .

Once the existence of the privilege is established, the burden is then on the plaintiff to show abuse of the privilege. A privilege may be abused by excessive publication, use for an improper purpose, or by "actual malice," — that is, ill-will, knowledge of falsity, or reckless disregard as to the truth or falsity of the defamatory matter.

(2)　Which of the following would be entitled to a qualified privilege? A draft complaint sent from one lawyer to another in an attempt to negotiate a settlement prior to filing suit. *See Pledger v. Burnup & Sims, Inc.,* 432 So. 2d 1323 (Fla. App. 1983). A press release stating that a former president had been discharged and that certain accounting irregularities had been corrected in the financial operations of the company. *See Miller v. Lear Siegler, Inc.,* 525 F. Supp. 46 (D. Kan. 1981). A tip given by a wholesale purchaser of gasoline to the wholesaler that one of the wholesaler's supervisory employees was probably implicated in the loss of product being experienced by the wholesaler. *See Dent v. Smith,* 414 So. 2d 77 (Ala. 1982). Statements made by an employer to an unemployment compensation board that a former employee had been discharged because of misconduct. *See Harrison v. Uniroyal, Inc.,* 366 So. 2d 983 (La. App. 1978). A labor grievance letter charging that a management employee was "a known bigot." *See Dunning v. Boyes,* 351 So. 2d 883 (Ala. 1977). A disparaging remark made by a Town Supervisor about a former employee to a news reporter in an interview about why the employee was discharged. *Clark v. McGee,* 49 N.Y.2d 613, 427 N.Y.S.2d 740, 404 N.E.2d 1283 (1980).

(3)　In some jurisdictions a plaintiff must also prove the defamation to be false when a qualified privilege applies. *Rouch v. Enquirer & News of Battle Creek,* 398 N.W.2d 245 (Mich. 1986).

§ 17.06 STATUTORY MODIFICATIONS

Many state legislatures have modified the common law of defamation, particularly in application to publishers of print and broadcast journalism. These statutes may require notice of intent to sue and demands for retraction as condition precedents to suit; may limit damages when a retraction is made; may require negligence in instances of republication of reports and stories produced by other agencies such as news services; and make other modifications to the common law. *See, e.g.*, Chap. 770, Fla. Stat. (1983). You should examine the statutes of a selected jurisdiction to ascertain the policy choices made by a particular legislature. To what extent is legislative intervention required after *Sullivan* and *Gertz*?

In the United Kingdom and New Zealand the law of defamation has been largely codified. Defamation Act 1952 (U.K.) and The Defamation Act 1954 (No. 46, N.Z.). Still, the common law characteristics of defamation remain largely unsullied. The United Kingdom, Australia and New Zealand all extensively examined the law of defamation in the light of the American decisions in *Sullivan* and *Gertz* to determine whether or not public policy required a modification of the common law in the interest of free press. All three rejected the *Sullivan* approach. The United Kingdom committee flatly found that the law of defamation did not "chill" free speech. Comm. of Defamation (U.K.) (The Faulkes Report), Cmd. 5909, § 214(b) (1975). The New Zealand committee reached a different conclusion, mainly on the ground that the publishing environment of a nation of population only slightly more than three million is less robust than in the United Kingdom, but rejected the "American approach" as placing "too much emphasis . . . upon the principle of free speech at the expense of the equally fundamental principle that reputation deserves reasonable protections." Comm. On Defamation (N.Z.), "Recommendations on the Law of Defamation," (Dec. 1977), § 1.16. The New Zealand committee recommended a standard of negligence for publication of matters of "public interest." *Id.*, § 1.25A. Similarly, in a report entitled, "Defamation-Options for Reform," Australian Law Reform Commission Discussion Paper No. 1, p. 9, the Australian Commission recommended the elimination of general damages where the defendant published the defamation "on reasonable grounds and after making all inquiries reasonably open to him" and also printed a timely retraction. Under what circumstances would these authorities be relevant in United States law? What weight should be given them?

---

§ 17.07 INJURIOUS FALSEHOOD

WHILDIN v. KOVACS
Illinois Appellate Court
82 Ill. App. 3d 1018, 38 Ill. Dec. 465, 403 N.E.2d 694 (1980)

McGILLICUDDY, PRESIDING JUSTICE

The Circuit Court of Cook County dismissed the amended counterclaim of Julius Kovacs, Mary Lou Kovacs, Anna Barra and the American National Bank and Trust Company of Chicago, Trustee under Trust No. 77880 (appellants) and denied further amendment thereof. On appeal, the appellants allege that the trial court erred in finding that the amended counterclaim failed to state a cause of action for the tort of slander of title. In addition, they argue that the court abused its discretion when it refused to allow the appellants to file a second amended counterclaim.

The amended counterclaim alleges that Dennis Whildin and Vasilios Melanis (appellees) submitted to appellants an offer to purchase a certain parcel of real estate. The appellants accepted the offer subject to the rescission of an existing contract involving the same parcel of real estate.

Subsequently, the appellees were notified that the first contract had not been cancelled, and the earnest money deposit was returned to them. Nevertheless, the appellees recorded their real estate contract with the Recorder of Deeds of Cook County and filed a notice of lis pendens against the property. The appellants assert that these actions constituted a slander of title which impaired their ability to sell the property.

The trial court granted the appellees' motion to dismiss the counterclaim. The reason for the court's ruling was that the amended counterclaim did not contain an allegation that the appellees had acted with malice. The court also denied appellants' oral request to file a second amended counterclaim.

Slander of title is a false and malicious publication, oral or written, of words which disparage a person's title to property resulting in special damages. (*Midwest Glass Co. v. Stanford Development Co.* (1975), 34 Ill. App. 3d 130, 339 N.E.2d 274; *Home Investments Fund v. Robertson* (1973) 10 Ill. App. 3d 840, 295 N.E.2d 85; Restatement (Second) of Torts § 624 (1977).) The act of maliciously recording a document which casts a cloud upon another's title to real estate is actionable as slander of title. (*Home Investments Fund; see also* Annot., 39 A.L.R.2d 840 (1955).) However, if the party who records the document has reasonable grounds to believe that he has title or a claim to the property, he has not acted with malice. *Midwest Glass Co.*

Although the appellants concede that their counterclaim does not contain the word malice, they point out that it alleges that the appellees filed the contract and lis pendens notice without legal justification. It is the appellants' position that such a filing without legal justification is sufficient to establish malice in a slander of title action. To support this argument they rely on a section of the Restatement of Torts which provides that one who publishes matter disparaging to another's property in land is subject to liability despite the fact that he neither knew nor believed the disparaging matter to be false. Restatement of Torts § 625(b) (1938).

The Restatement Second of Torts, however, has rejected this theory of strict liability. (Restatement (Second) of Torts § 623A (1977); *see also, Annbar Associates v. American Express Co.* (Mo. App. 1978), 565 S.W.2d 701.) The Restatement now provides in section 623A that,

One who publishes a false statement harmful to the interests of another is subject to liability for pecuniary loss resulting to the other if

(a) he intends for publication of the statement to result in harm to interests of the other having a pecuniary value, or either recognizes or should recognize that it is likely to do so, and

(b) he knows that the statement is false or acts in reckless disregard of its truth or falsity.

This provision is consistent with the holding in *Midwest Glass Co.*, that a person has not acted with malice if he possesses reasonable grounds to believe that he has a claim to the property.

Although we have construed the pleading liberally, we agree with the trial court that the amended counterclaim contains no allegation of malice. Such an allegation is essential in order to state a cause of action for slander of title (*Stirs, Inc. v. City of Chicago* (1974), 24 Ill. App. 3d 118, 320 N.E.2d 216; *Allison v. Berry* (1942), 316 Ill. App. 261, 44 N.E.2d 929.) Therefore, the trial court correctly dismissed the amended counterclaim.

. . .

For the foregoing reasons, the judgement of the Circuit Court of Cook County is hereby affirmed.

Affirmed.

NOTES

(1) The cause of action known as injurious falsehood is also referred to as "slander of title," as in *Whildin v. Kovacs.* As to what kind of property interest can be slandered, it has been said, "Any kind of legally protected interest in land, chattels or intangible things may be disparaged if the interest is transferable, and the cause of action will lie not only in the case of true ownership in the classic sense, but also where the property interest consists of a mortgage, lease, easement, reversion or remainder." *Maass v. Christensen,* 414 So. 2d 255, 257 (Fla. App. 1982). *See also,* Restatement, Torts, Second, § 624.

In a sense this tort extends reputational protection to the title of property. Although the quantity of litigation is much smaller than in defamation, the cases tend to apply defamation principles directly. *See, e.g., Sailboat Key, Inc. v. Gardner,* 378 So. 2d 47 (Fla. App. 1980), holding that injurious falsehoods in judicial pleadings are absolutely privileged. According to Prosser:

> In general, it may be said that injurious falsehood, which is a tort that never has been greatly favored by the law, is subject to all the privileges recognized both in cases of personal defamation and in those of other types of interference with economic advantage. The question of absolute privilege to disparage in judicial, legislative, and executive proceedings has seldom arisen, except in connection with pleadings, motions and the like in the course of litigation, where it has been recognized. . . .

Law of Torts, 924 (4th ed. 1971).

In slander of title actions courts acknowledge a qualified privilege arising from the publisher's bona fide claim to the disparaged title. According to Prosser:

> A rival Claimant to the property disparaged, in his capacity as such, is recognized as privileged to assert a bona fide claim by any appropriate means of publication. . . . The privilege is uniformly held, however, to be a

qualified one, and it is defeated if the defendant's motive is shown to be solely a desire to do harm, or if it found that he did not honestly believe his statements to be true, or that the publication of the statement was excessive. A few cases have gone further and have said that he must have reasonable grounds for believing his disparaging words to be the truth; but the better view, which is now more generally accepted, is that a genuine belief in their truth is sufficient, however unfounded or unreasonable it may be. The absence of probable cause for the belief may permit the jury to infer that it does not exist, but it is not necessarily conclusive; and the advice of counsel, while it is evidence in favor of good faith, is likewise not determinative in itself. When it appears that a privilege exists, the burden is upon the plaintiff to establish the existence of the "malice" which will defeat it.

Law of Torts, 974, 975 (5th ed. 1984).

(2) Closely related to slander of title is the tort of commercial disparagement in which a defendant intentionally and falsely disparages the plaintiff's business or products of his business. Under this tort an actionable statement is one "about a competitor's goods [or business] which is untrue or misleading and which is made to influence or tends to influence [others] not to buy." *Edwin L. Wiegand Co. v. Harold E. Trent Co.*, 122 F.2d 920 (3d Cir. 1941). Some courts go so far as to hold a negligent disparagement to be actionable. *Paramount Pictures v. Leader Press*, 106 F.2d 229 (10th Cir. 1939). This is consistent with the position of the original Restatement that held a person accountable for disparagement "under such circumstances as would lead a reasonable man to foresee" the resulting harm to "land, chattels or intangible things." Restatement, Torts, § 624 (1955). The Second Restatement requires more than mere negligence. See § 623A quoted in *Whildin v. Kovacs*. Moreover, mere "puffing" of one's own products is not actionable disparagement, *Aerosonic Corporation v. Trodyne Corporation*, 402 F.2d 223 (5th Cir. 1968), "as long as the comparison attempts primarily to enhance the quality of the advertiser's product without being unduly critical of the other's product," *Smith-Victor Corp. v. Sylvania Electric Products, Inc.*, 242 F. Supp. 302, 308 (N.D. Ill. 1965). *See also* Smith, *Disparagement of Property*, 13 Col. L. Rev. 13 (1913), Note, *The Law of Commercial Disparagement: Business Defamation's Impotent Ally*, 63 Yale L.J. 65 (1953), and Nims, *Unfair Competition by False Statements or Disparagement*, 19 Cornell L. Q. 63 (1933).

§ 17.08   INVASION OF PRIVACY

Consider whether any of these episodes would constitute actionable defamation.

(1) Mrs. X is a beautiful and glamorous woman. John, a voyeur, surreptitiously peeps into the bedroom of the home of Mr. and Mrs. X, hoping to see Mrs. X's nude body. What he saw was even more salacious. Mr. X was engaged in a sex act with Mrs. Y, a neighbor. Unknown to John, a video camera recorded his activities. Do Mr. X and Mrs. Y have a cause of action against him?

(2) Jane came to town five years ago. She started a successful business and is now an important and wealthy member of the community. Jane becomes affianced to Jack, the scion of a wealthy blue blood family of the community. The local newspaper digs into Jane's background and discovers that she was a divorcee of an earlier marriage and had left two children in the sole custody of her former

husband. All of this is true. The newspaper published this information in its "About People" column. Jack broke off the marriage and all Jane's business customers left her. Does Jane have a cause of action against the newspaper?

(3) Bank O held a mortgage on F's farm. When the payment date was near, O refused to renew F's mortgage. O, hoping it would foreclose and gain ownership of F's farm, ran this advertisement in the local newspaper: "F to sell his farm at public auction." Unknown to O, F had successfully negotiated a loan from another lender. Although O's advertisement was untrue, it caused F's new lender to withdraw and F lost his farm to O in foreclosure. Does F have a cause of action against O?[8]

(4) H is a freelance commercial photographer. H spends a day in a crowded public park taking pictures of anything that catches his fancy. Upon reviewing the pictures H discovers that he has captured an unusually happy image of Baby B, an 18 month-old child. H sells the picture to XYZ dairy and XYZ uses it is a highly successfully advertisement that features the picture and this motto: "XYZ milk makes happy children." In fact, Baby B does drink XYZ milk. Does Baby B have a cause of action?

A thoughtful student could readily conclude that none of these episodes gives rise to actionable defamation nor any other tort in regard to invasion of dignity interests. Deeming this state of the law to be unacceptable, Samuel D. Warren and Louis D. Brandeis (later a United States Supreme Court Justice) published, "The Right to Privacy," 4 Harv. L. Rev. 93 (1890). Courts thereafter commenced to provide remedies for non-defamatory invasions of privacy in some contexts. From these decisions Dean Prosser identified four distinct privacy torts in 1960. Prosser, 48 Calif. L. Rev. 383 (1960). The American Law Institute endorsed these torts in the form described in the case below.

FROELICH v. ADAIR
Kansas Supreme Court
213 Kan. 357, 516 P.2d 993

OWSLEY, JUSTICE.

Plaintiff Willaim Froelich appeals from judgment of the trial court denying him recovery for his mental suffering due to an alleged invasion of his privacy by defendant Burneta Adair.

Plaintiff's cause of action for invasion of privacy by intrusion arose sometime in October, 1969, while he was a patient at St. Francis Hospital in Wichita. Burneta Adair's former husband, Tom Hamilton, had previously sued her seeking to recover a million dollars for defamation because she had stated he was homosexual and William Froelich was his lover. Truth is a defense to an action for defamation and Mrs. Adair was interested in obtaining evidence from William Froelich as to the truth of her statements. Syd Werbin, deputy sheriff and a friend of Mrs. Adair, informed her that Froelich had become ill and was at St. Francis Hospital. Mrs. Adair then became alarmed that he might not be able to testify in the defamation action. She had previously obtained hair from her former husband's bed and underclothing and had it analyzed, and she suggested in her conversation with

---

[8] *See* Lovgren v. Citizens First Nat. Bank of Princeton, 534 N.E.2d 987 (Ill. 1989).

Werbin it would be a good idea to get samples of Froelich's hair for analysis and comparison. Werbin paid a hospital orderly who obtained combings from Froelich's hairbrush and a discarded adhesive bandage to which Froelich's hair was attached. Werbin passed these on to Mrs. Adair and she had them analyzed. There was conflicting testimony as to whether she asked Werbin to obtain the hair samples or whether he did so of his own volition after their discussion. During a deposition session with Hamilton's attorneys, she let it be known she had the samples of Froelich's hair obtained from his hospital room. Although he had not been aware of the taking of his hair samples at the time they were taken, when he later learned of the intrusion he claimed he was emotionally upset over the alleged invasion of his privacy and brought suit against both Mrs. Adair and Syd Werbin (*Froelich v. Werbin*, 212 Kan. 119, 509 P.2d 1118) in separate actions.

We have recognized invasion of the right of privacy as a tort upon which a cause of action may be based. (*Kunz v. Allen*, 102 Kan. 883, 172 P. 532; *Johnson v. Boeing Airplane Co.*, 175 Kan. 275, 262 P.2d 808; *Munsell v. Ideal Food Stores*, 208 Kan. 909, 494 P.2d 1063.) Discussion of the right of privacy is found in Prosser, Law of Torts, 4th Ed., Privacy, s 117, p. 802; 62 Am. Jur. 2d, Privacy, s 26, p. 718; American Law Institute, Restatement of the Law Second, Torts, Tentative Draft No. 13, s 652. These authorities point out invasion of the right of privacy comprises four distinct kinds of tort. Prosser points out they are tied together by a common name, but otherwise have almost nothing in common except each protects against interference with the right to be let alone. They are listed in the Restatement as:

§ 652B. INTRUSION UPON SECLUSION

One who intentionally intrudes, physically or otherwise, upon the solitude or seclusion of another, or his private affairs or concerns, is subject to liability to the other for invasion of his privacy, if the intrusion would be highly offensive to a reasonable man.

§ 652C. APPROPRIATION OF NAME OR LIKENESS

One who appropriates to his own use or benefit the name or likeness of another is subject to liability to the other for invasion of his privacy.

§ 652D. PUBLICITY GIVEN TO PRIVATE LIFE

One who gives publicity to matters concerning the private life of another, of a kind highly offensive to a reasonable man, is subject to liability to the other for invasion of his privacy.

§ 652E. PUBLICITY PLACING PERSON IN FALSE LIGHT

One who gives to another publicity which places him before the public in a false light of a kind highly offensive to a reasonable man, is subject to liability to the other for invasion of his privacy.

We are concerned here with an action for invasion of privacy by intrusion upon seclusion. The foregoing authorities recognize such an action and each lists numerous citations of supporting cases. Although Kansas has recognized other actions for invasion of privacy, an action for intrusion upon seclusion is one of first impression in this state. We are impressed by the reasoning of the cases which sanction such a right. Our research discloses the weight of authority is in favor of such a right. We conclude invasion of privacy by intrusion upon seclusion should be recognized in this state.

The rules of civil procedure require that in all actions tried without a jury the judge shall find and, either orally or in writing, state the controlling facts. (K.S.A. 60 252(a); *Duffin v. Patrick*, 212 Kan. 772, 512 P.2d 442.) The law relative to intrusion upon seclusion cannot be applied when the trial court fails to make findings of fact necessary to a determination of the issues. In view of this we must return the case to the trial court for a new trial. We do not believe it advisable to return the case for findings of fact based on the existing record since the judge who heard the case is no longer an active trial judge.

In announcing its judgment, the trial court remarked on the law applicable to this action. Although unnecessary to our ruling herein, we believe it important to review the trial court's conclusions of law in order to avoid initiating a new field of law in this state on questionable foundation. The trial court first stated:

'. . . Gathering evidence to defend one's self from a charge of slander in a substantial action has been excused and has been excepted from the privilege of privacy. . . .'

We construe this statement to mean if a matter is privileged there is no cause of action based on the manner in which the privileged matter was obtained. Conclusions of law based upon the immunities of privileged communications are not relevant to charges of invasion of privacy by intrusion since intrusion does not require publication to be actionable. In *Dietemann v. Time, Inc.*, 449 F.2d 245 (9th Cir. 1971), the First Amendment privilege of news reporters was raised as a defense in an action for intrusion and the court said:

'As we previously observed, publication is not an essential element of plaintiff's cause of action. Moreover, it is not the foundation for the invocation of a privilege. Privilege concepts developed in defamation cases and to some extent in privacy actions in which publication is an essential component are not relevant in determining liability for intrusive conduct antedating publication. . . . ' (pp. 249, 250.)

Invasion of privacy and defamation are separate and distinct torts even though they share some of the same elements and often arise out of the same acts. The first is a cause of action based upon injury to plaintiff's emotions and his mental suffering; the second is a remedy for injury to plaintiff's reputation. Invasion of privacy torts which require publication and defamation torts share the common defense of privileged communications which grant immunity to otherwise actionable publication. Judicial proceedings are absolutely privileged communications, and statements in the course of litigation otherwise constituting an action for slander, libel, or one of the invasion of privacy torts involving publication, are immune from such actions. They are privileged communications because of the overriding public interest in a free and independent court system. This absolute privilege extends immunity to parties to private litigation and to anything published in relation to a matter at issue in court, whether said in pleadings, affidavits, depositions or open court. (*Weil v. Lynds*, 105 Kan. 440, 185 P. 51.)

Since plaintiff's action is not based upon publication, the court's conclusion of excusable conduct based upon gathering privileged communications in connection with a judicial proceeding is not a defense to intrusion in this action.

In its remarks the trial court also stated the evidence did not show any malicious conduct on the part of the defendant toward the plaintiff. This implies that malice is a necessary element of this action. The precise motives for invasion of privacy are unimportant. Defendant's action, rather than precise motives accompanying the act or conduct, is the criterion of liability. (62 Am. Jur. 2d, Privacy, s 15, p. 698; 14 A.L.R.2d 758.) Malice may become material on the issue of damages. (62 Am.Jur.2d, Privacy, s 47, p. 752.) In both instances, we conclude the trial court's statements as to the law applicable to an action for intrusion upon seclusion were erroneous.

In *Kunz, supra,* and *Johnson, supra,* we recognized a cause of action for appropriation without consent of a person's name and likeness for another person's benefit. Since each of the cases involved publication of the material appropriated they cannot be considered as authority for an action for intrusion which requires no publication. It cannot be argued from the language of these cases that a cause of action such as brought in this case is in any way prohibited. In *Munsell, supra,* we stated the right of privacy does not prohibit communication of a matter of a private nature when the publication is made under circumstances which would render it a privileged communication according to the law of libel and slander. We have no criticism of this statement when confined to actions which require publication; but we hasten to point out that the rule in *Munsell* is not applicable to an action when publication is not required as in the action prosecuted in this proceeding. As we have previously stated, in an action for intrusion appropriation of privileged matter is not a defense.

We are reversing this case and granting a new trial on the failure of the trial court to make findings of fact. Whether a cause of action under the law applicable to intrusion upon seclusion has been proven must await the determination of these facts. Our treatment of the law relative to this subject is confined to correcting the trial court's statements.

Reversed and remanded for a new trial.

FROMME, Justice (dissenting).

. . . .

No court has said that every invasion of itself into another person's private quarters constitutes an actionable invasion of privacy. It is only when the invasion is so outrageous that the traditional remedies of trespass, nuisance, intentional infliction of mental distress, etc., will not adequately compensate a plaintiff for the insult to his individual dignity that an invasion of privacy action will lie. The intrusion itself must be patently offensive before an invasion of privacy action will lie. The totality of the intruder's conduct must be extreme, intentional and outrageous; the conduct must be so offensive that it would cause mental harm or anguish in a person of ordinary sensibilities. An invasion of privacy action should not be utilized to avoid the more stringent requirements of other torts designated to compensate an individual for physical or mental injury.

. . . .

Appellant himself asked the question in his brief, ' . . . what kind of intrusion will outrage a man of ordinary sensibilities?' Although appellant correctly notes that malice is not an essential element of an action founded upon intrusion of seclusion, he still premises his cause of action upon appellee's alleged malicious intent to prove his alleged homosexual tendencies. Appellant has misconstrued the issue before this court. It is not whether the appellee's alleged motive is so reprehensible that it brands her actions an intrusion of seclusion; that rather it is whether the act itself (the removal of the hair from the brush and the tape) is so outrageous, regardless of appellee's motives, that it would cause emotional harm to a person of ordinary sensibilities. Every theft of personal property may be upsetting or annoying; but it does not automatically give rise to an invasion of privacy action.

The alleged invasion of the appellant's seclusion was not so callous or indifferent that it would outrage a reasonable man. Actually, the removal of the hair was performed in a very unobtrusive manner. The appellee's activities herein lack the callous and objectionable characteristics which were present in every other case cited by the parties herein which is concerned with an intrusion of seclusion.

Whether or not the appellant may have an action in trespass, defamation, intentional infliction of mental harm, or some other remedy is not the question here. It is the appellant's burden to prove all necessary elements of the theory before he will be granted recovery thereon. The admitted facts herein simply do not support appellant's theory of recovery.

In the present case what was it that was highly offensive to appellant? In appellant's brief the acts are characterized as follows:

> It later became clear how the hair was obtained from Mr. Froelich. It seems that Werbin (a friend of appellee) had tipped the orderly $5.00 to retrieve some hair from a hairbrush which was in the plaintiff's hospital room, and from a bandaid which had apparently held an I.V. secure to his arm and which had ripped out a few hairs upon removal.

Considering the evidence in the light most favorable to the appellant the evidence is insufficient to establish a cause of action for intrusion of seclusion. The evidence was insufficient to establish that such acts were extreme, outrageous or highly offensive to a reasonable person. Accordingly the case should be affirmed.

SCHROEDER, J., joins in the foregoing dissent.

NOTE AND QUESTION

Many courts have adopted one or more of the privacy causes of action as described in *Froelich*. Some have rejected one or more of these torts. For example, the Florida Supreme Court declined to acknowledge the false light tort on the ground that it is indistinguishable from "implied defamation" and "because the benefit of recognizing the tort, which only offers a distinct remedy in relatively few unique situations, is outweighed by the danger of unreasonably impeding constitutionally protected speech." *Jews for Jesus v. Rapp*, 997 So. 2d 1098 (Fla. 2008). Do you agree? The purpose of this book is to introduce the privacy tort. No further development of the many issues raised in the cases is attempted here.

TABLE OF CASES

[References are to pages]

[References are to pages]

[References are to pages]

[References are to pages]

D

[References are to pages]

G

H

[References are to pages]

[References are to pages]

[References are to pages]

[References are to pages]

[References are to pages]

[References are to pages]

[References are to pages]

Y

Z

INDEX

[References are to pages.]

[References are to pages.]

[References are to pages.]

[References are to pages.]

[References are to pages.]